# Marketing

## Second Canadian Edition

Joel R. Evans

Hofstra University

Barry Berman

Hofstra University

William J. Wellington

University of Windsor

Prentice Hall Canada Inc.
Scarborough, Ontario

**Canadian Cataloguing in Publication Data**

Evans, Joel R.
        Marketing

2nd Canadian ed.
ISBN 0-13-011795-1

1. Marketing. I. Berman, Barry. II. Wellington, William Joseph Patrick. III.Title.

HF5415.E92 2000        658.8        C99-932114-5

Prentice-Hall, Inc., Upper Saddle River, New Jersey
Prentice-Hall International (UK) Limited, London
Prentice-Hall of Australia, Pty. Limited, Sydney
Prentice-Hall Hispanoamericana, S.A., Mexico City
Prentice-Hall of India Private Limited, New Delhi
Prentice-Hall of Japan, Inc., Tokyo
Simon & Schuster Southeast Asia Private Limited, Singapore
Editora Prentice-Hall do Brasil, Ltda., Rio de Janeiro

ISBN 0-13-011795-1

Acquisitions Editor: Mike Ryan
Developmental Editor: Sherry Torchinsky
Production Editor: Mary Ann McCutcheon
Copy Editor: Karen Alliston
Production Coordinator: Janette Lush
Cover Design: Julia Hall
Cover Images: Chris McElcheran
Page Layout: Dave McKay

1 2 3 4 5        04 03 02 01 00

Printed and bound in USA

Visit the Prentice Hall Canada Web site! Send us your comments, browse our catalogues, and more at **www.phcanada.com**. Or reach us through e-mail at **phcinfo_pubcanada@prenhall.com**.

**To**
**Linda, Stacey, and Jennifer**
**Linda, Glenna, and Lisa**
**Christine, Roger, and Pamela**

# Brief Contents

# Contents

# Preface

These are very exciting times for all of us. The beginning of the new millennium has been ushered in with massive and exciting Year 2000 celebrations, Y2K problems and the arrival of e-commerce. These events represent more steps in the global movement towards service-driven rather than production-driven economies. Business people have felt the need to acquire a greater understanding and interest in customer service and customer satisfaction, and greater focus on consumer diversity in the marketplace. The power of computers and the database information created with and used by e-commerce firms are helping business people satisfy these needs. Free-market economies are fully emerged in Eastern Europe and the Asian economic crisis appears to have passed. These technological and economic changes have meant that business and government must grapple with such ethical issues as the consumer's right to privacy, the impact of deregulation on society, and many similar events.

The years ahead promise to be even more intriguing as e-commerce becomes a $100 billion dollar industry, the European Union becomes more strongly unified, the North American countries make their markets further accessible to one another with NAFTA, opportunities in developing nations grow, technological advances continue, and we try to cope with slow-growth economies in various parts of the globe. A thorough understanding and appreciation of marketing have always been important and will remain so as the new millennium unfolds.

We believe that a good marketing textbook must do several things in order to provide this critical understanding. It should incorporate both traditional and contemporary aspects of marketing, including the careful consideration of environmental factors; address the roles of marketing and marketing managers; and show the relevance of marketing for those who interact with or who are affected by marketing activities (such as consumers). It must also address the major changes in the marketplace that are being ushered in by the use of information technology. We also believe that presentation is important. A textbook must describe marketing concepts to readers in an interesting, comprehensive, and balanced manner. As we indicate at the beginning of Chapter 1, marketing is truly "an exciting, fast-paced, and contemporary business discipline."

Although the basic, or traditional, components of marketing (such as consumer behaviour, marketing research and information systems, target marketing and product, distribution, promotion, and price planning) form the foundation of any introductory-level marketing textbook, contemporary techniques and topics also need to be covered in depth. Among the contemporary topics examined in full chapter length in the second Canadian edition of *Marketing* are final consumer behaviour; organizational consumers (including manufacturers, wholesalers, retailers, government, and nonprofit institutions); direct and Internet marketing; strategic planning and marketing; and integrating and analyzing the marketing plan. Environmental, ethical, global, and technological effects are noted throughout the book.

The second Canadian edition of *Marketing* explains all major principles, defines key terms, integrates topics, and demonstrates how marketers make everyday and long-run decisions. Examples based on such diverse organizations as Boeing Aircraft, Labatt Breweries, the NHL's Calgary Flames, Mountain Equipment Cooperative in British Columbia, the United Way of Canada, and numerous other firms appear in each chapter. The illustrations build on the conceptual material, reveal the exciting and dynamic nature of marketing, cover a wide variety of firms, and involve students in real-life applications of marketing.

## ORGANIZATION OF THE SECOND CANADIAN EDITION

Based on instructor feedback, the second Canadian edition of *Marketing* has been reorganized from eight to seven parts. Several chapters have been combined for a more focused presentation of material. Discussions considering technology, ethics, global marketing, and the future of marketing have been integrated throughout the text.

- Part 1 presents marketing in a contemporary society, describes the environment within which it operates, and discusses marketing information systems and the marketing research process.
- Part 2 deals with marketing's central thrust: understanding final and organizational consumers in the diverse marketplace. It examines demographics, lifestyle factors, consumer decision making, target marketing strategies, and sales forecasting.
- Part 3 encompasses product planning, the product life cycle, goods versus services marketing, new products, mature products, branding, and packaging.
- Part 4 deals with distribution planning, channel relations, physical distribution, retailing and wholesaling.
- Part 5 examines promotion planning, the channel of communication, personal selling, advertising, public relations, and sales promotion. A new chapter on Internet and direct marketing highlights the growing importance of the Internet as a marketing tool.
- Part 6 covers price planning, price strategies, and applications of pricing.
- Part 7 presents strategic planning from a marketing perspective, integrates marketing planning—including benchmarking and customer satisfaction measurement—and looks to the future.

## NEW AND REVISED FEATURES

The second Canadian edition of *Marketing* includes several new features:

**Chapter 14   Information-Based Marketing: Direct and Internet Marketing** Marketers are fast becoming aware of the power of the Internet as a marketing tool. This new chapter introduces the concept of information-based marketing, including the unique nature of direct marketing and how it relates to the emergence of Internet marketing. Students will learn how to develop a direct marketing plan and will also look specifically at the new world of e-commerce. Internet buyer behaviour, website design, and transacting and distributing on the web are just a few of the topics discussed in this innovative new chapter.

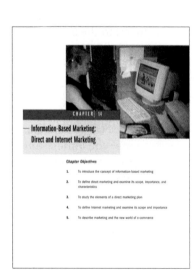

**Merchants of Green Coffee Inc.**

**Marketing Plan: The Merchants of Green Coffee** The Merchants of Green Coffee is a new Canadian company founded by young entrepreneurs who are striving to sell their products to coffee-lovers and convince them of the environmental and ethical benefits of Fair Trade practices. The company's marketing plan will be a special feature of the Companion Website for *Marketing* at **www.prenticehall.ca/ evans**. Each chapter of the website contains questions based on this marketing plan, challenging students to apply their knowledge to a real company's marketing plan as it seeks to find its niche.

The second Canadian edition continues to present these well-received features, revised and updated throughout:

- New and updated cases that deal with real companies or situations.
- Comprehensive coverage of all important marketing concepts, including nine chapters on the marketing mix (product, distribution, promotion, and price planning).
- A balanced treatment of topics (by size of firm, goods- and service-based firms, profit-oriented and nonprofit firms, final and organizational consumers, etc.)
- Service marketing coverage in the section on product planning.
- Part openers that provide integrated overviews of the chapters they contain.
- Part-ending video cases from the prestigious CBC business series *Venture*.
- Margin definitions of marketing terms. All key terms are also printed in bold in the text. The pages on which definitions appear are printed in bold in the Subject Index that so that students may review definitions in context.
- A lively, easy-to-read writing style.
- Numerous endnotes to enable the reader to do further research.
- A full-colour design that includes many attractive new ads, photos, and figures all linked to the text.

Each chapter contains:

- Chapter objectives that outline the major areas to be investigated.
- An opening vignette that introduces the material through a real-world situation.
- An introductory overview to set the tone for the chapter.
- Four types of boxes highlighting key marketing topics, including Technology and Marketing, International Marketing in Action, Ethics and Today's Marketer, and Marketing in the Third Millennium.
- Descriptive margin notes that highlight major concepts.

- Boldface key terms that identify important definitions and are set off in the margins with definitions.
- Flowcharts demonstrating key marketing concepts
- Updated figures and tables that provide the most current information on marketing issues today.
- Exciting and useful Internet sites that appear in the margin and are easily identifiable by the Weblinks icon.
- Chapter summaries keyed to chapter objectives. These summaries are followed by a listing of key terms with text page references.
- End-of-chapter questions divided into separate Review and Discussion categories.

# SUPPLEMENTS

The second Canadian edition of *Marketing* is accompanied by a complete set of supplemental learning and teaching aids.

## For the Instructor

**The Box.** For the second edition we've developed a unique format for providing supplements. The Box contains key instructor support materials for the text in one convenient package.

**Instructor's Resource Manual.** This comprehensive guide contains resource material for each chapter of the text. A detailed lecture outline integrates pictures of transparencies and suggested topics for discussion. Each chapter also includes chapter objectives and summary, a list of key terms, a suggested class exercise, and answers to all text questions. The Instructor's Resource Manual also contains sample syllabi, a list of supplemental sources of information, term paper topics, and a list of trade associations.

**Test Item File.** The Test Item File contains approximately 3000 multiple choice, true/false, and short answer questions and their answers. Questions are labelled according to their difficulty and type (applied or recall).

**Prentice Hall Test Manager.** This powerful computerized testing package uses a state-of-the-art software program that provides fast, simple, and error-free test generation. Tests can be previewed on-screen before printing and can be saved to one of three word processing file formats. Prentice Hall Test Manager can print multiple variations of the same test, scrambling the order of questions and multiple-choice answers.

**Transparency Resource Package.** Over 20 slides per chapter have been created in PowerPoint, complimenting the chapter content and incorporating many figures and tables from the text. These disks allow you to present transparencies to your class electronically and have been integrated into the Instructor's Resource Manual to make class preparation much easier.

**CBC/Prentice Hall Canada Video Library.** Prentice Hall Canada and the CBC have worked together to bring you seven segments from the CBC's *Venture*. Designed specifically to compliment the text, this case collection is an excellent tool for bringing students into contact with the world outside the classroom. These programs have extremely high production quality, present substantial content, and have been chosen to relate directly to the content of each Part. (Please contact your Prentice Hall sales representative for details. These videos are subject to availability and terms negotiated upon adoption of the text.)

## For the Student

**Study Guide.** A comprehensive self-instructional guide, the format of the study guide parallels that of the text. Each chapter contains objectives, an overview, key terms and concepts, true/false questions, completion questions, matching questions, multiple-choice questions, discussion questions, and exercises. A part-ending review quiz tests students' cumulative understanding of all chapters in each part.

**Companion Website.** The Companion Website for the second Canadian edition of *Marketing* includes an online study guide with a variety of practice questions and research tools. This site will also contain a sample marketing plan prepared by The Merchants of Green Coffee. Questions in each chapter encourage students to analyze the marketing plan of this exciting young Canadian company. You'll find valuable opportunities to test and expand your knowledge of marketing at **www.prenticehall.ca/evans**

# ACKNOWLEDGEMENTS

Particular thanks are due to the following people for advising us on content and offering many useful suggestions for this and previous editions of *Marketing* and *Marketing Essentials*:

Dwight Dyson, Centennial College
Gerard Edwards, Douglas College
Scott Follows, Acadia University
Linda Hoffman, NAIT
Marina Jaffey, Camosun College
Marianne Marando, George Brown College
Peter Mitchell, British Columbia Institute of Technology
Diana Serafini, Dawson College
Robert Soroka, Dawson College
Ian Spencer, St. Francis Xavier University
Anne Marie Webb-Hughes, British Columbia Institute of Technology
Wes Balderson, University of Lethbridge

Ken Burns, Cambrian College
Gus Cameron, Fanshawe College
Gloria Darroch, Northern Alberta Institute of Technology
Susan Eck, Seneca College
Paul Garneau, Kwantlen University College
Loreen Gilmour, Alqonquin College
Ted Goddard, Connestoga College
John Lille, Centenniel College
Gerald Stephenson, Okanagan University College
Keith Wright, Mount Royal College
Brian Wrightson, Northern Alberta Institute of Technology
Anthony J. Faria, University of Windsor

We hope the second Canadian edition of *Marketing* will surpass the needs of adopters at Canadian colleges and universities. We would really like to know that we have satisfied the needs of the users and would enjoy receiving feedback. We welcome comments regarding any aspect of *Marketing* or its package and promise to reply to any correspondence we receive.

Joel R. Evans, Barry Berman, and William J. Wellington

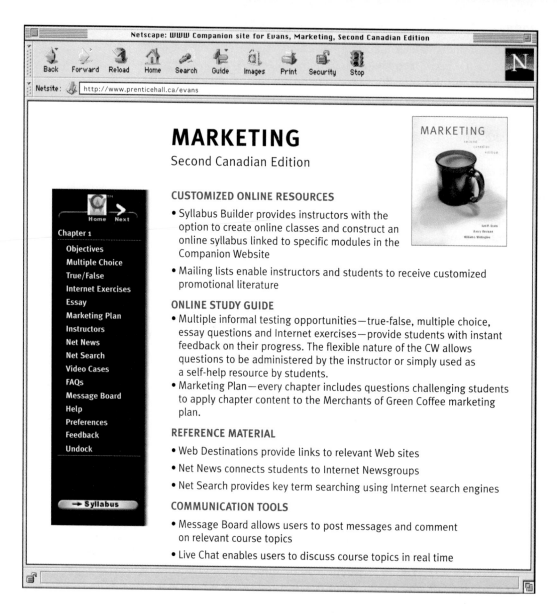

# Introduction to Marketing

In Part 1, we begin our study of marketing and discuss concepts that form the foundation for the rest of the text.

## Marketing in the Third Millennium

Here, we show the dynamic nature of marketing, broadly define the term "marketing," and trace its evolution. We pay special attention to the marketing concept, a marketing philosophy, customer service, and customer satisfaction and relationship marketing. And we examine the importance of marketing, as well as marketing functions and performers.

## The Environments That Affect Marketing

In this chapter, we look at the complex environment within which marketing functions, with an emphasis on both the factors that are controllable and those that are uncontrollable to an organization and its marketers. We demonstrate that without adequate environmental analysis, a firm may function haphazardly or be shortsighted.

## Information for Marketing Decisions

In this chapter, we explain why marketing decisions should be based on sound information. We explain the role and importance of the marketing information system—which coordinates marketing research, continuous monitoring, and data storage and provides the basis for decision making. We also describe marketing research and the process for undertaking it. We show that marketing research may involve surveys, observation, experiments, and/or simulation.

# The Process of Marketing Affects Us All

An organization's marketing philosophy is a key consideration in how it does business.

As we will show throughout *Marketing*, 2nd Canadian Edition, organizations come in all sizes and orientations. The diversity of those engaged in marketing is demonstrated by the examples provided throughout the text and in the descriptions of Canadian organizations found in each of the part-opening vignettes. The marketing philosophies of these firms are important considerations in how they do business. The issues facing these organizations and the forces affecting them are many and varied.

Chapter 1 presents an overview of what marketing is and discusses some of the philosophies behind it. The marketing philosophies of Canadian retailers have been strongly tested since American multinational retailer Wal-Mart invaded Canada in 1994. In a scant five years Wal-Mart became the leading department store retailer in Canada, and in its wake both Eaton's and The Bay have been heavily wounded. Yet in Quebec, the three Les Ailes de la Mode (The Wings of Fashion) department stores located in Ste-Foy, Brossard, and Laval are thriving by making customer service their raison d'être. Customers are treated like royalty in stores that offer a concierge who greets you, a coat check, leather couches to sit on, and even a nursing room for babies with a microwave for warming baby formula. The staff provide elite customer service, including a complimentary facial, and coffee or dessert. And if the item you want is out of stock Les Ailes de la Mode will get it for you, even if it means buying it from the competition.

Chapter 2 presents the uncontrollable environments and forces that affect the marketing strategies firms undertake. Two of the critical forces affecting marketers are competition and government regulation. One of the most intensely competitive and heavily regulated businesses in Canada is the brewing industry, which has undergone a number of changes in the last twenty years. In the early 1980s it was dominated by Molson, Labatt, and Carling-O'Keefe, Canadian-owned and -operated breweries that competed heavily for market share. Molson acquired Carling-O'Keefe in a bid to become the dominant Canadian brewer, then Foster's of Australia acquired Molson in a bid to gain entry into the Canadian market. Foster's then sold a controlling interest to Miller Brewing Company of the U.S. Labatt was the only Canadian-owned major brewery left, until 1995 when it was purchased by the Belgian firm Interbrew S.A. Thus, in the late 1990s the Canadian brewing industry was dominated by foreign firms that controlled over 90 per cent of the market. Selling a beer branded "Canadian" is problematic when your firm is foreign-owned, so in 1998 Molson bought out both Foster's and Miller Brewing Company to make the company 100 per cent Canadian-owned again.

In Chapter 3 we will see that dealing with the environment, developing marketing plans, and making marketing decisions can't be undertaken without good information. Information acquisition can be contracted out to third party market research firms or performed by a business itself, like the way Ron Bremner, President of the NHL's Calgary Flames does it. He's developed a simple, inexpensive, and unique approach to research his customers in a timely fashion so that he can respond quickly. For example, during every game he uses a team of University of Calgary MBA students to survey fans on food selection and cleanliness; fans are asked to fill out comment cards after the game; and groups of season ticket holders are routinely invited to breakfast and asked for their opinions. Bremner analyzes this information as soon as it's acquired, and responds to it immediately.

We hope you enjoy learning about marketing as undertaken by firms operating in Canada, a process that will be introduced in the remaining part-opening vignettes and presented throughout the seventeen chapters of *Marketing*, 2nd Canadian Edition.

## CHAPTER 1

# Marketing in the Third Millennium

## Chapter Objectives

**1.** To illustrate the exciting, dynamic, and influential nature of marketing

**2.** To define marketing and trace its evolution—with emphasis on the marketing concept, a marketing philosophy, customer service, and customer satisfaction and relationship marketing

**3.** To show the importance of marketing as a field of study

**4.** To describe the basic functions of marketing and those who perform these functions

*Reprinted by permission.*

The importance of the role of marketing for businesses in the third millennium will be far greater than ever before. The emergence of e-commerce (electronic commerce through computer networking) via the Internet is creating what *Fortune Magazine* calls the "e-corporation." An e-corp takes a different approach to markets and customers by combining computers, the World Wide Web, and specialized enterprise software into the manner in which the firm operates. The focus of the e-corp is the same as any marketing-oriented conventional firm: customers!

However, in the third millennium advances in information technology will enable businesses to deal one on one with their customers, and vice versa. The information age has provided both the tools and the means by which customers and marketers can interact directly in real time, and in a meaningful way. Prior to this, marketers accepted the notion that in order to sell high-volume consumer products they usually had to sacrifice the ability to know their customers personally. It was difficult to collect customer information cheaply or efficiently, and even if they could, it was hard to use this information in a timely fashion to make really good marketing decisions. Conversely, consumers didn't know much about the makers of their goods, since they bought these products from retail organizations and had little or no contact with the actual producers. Therefore, consumers couldn't effectively communicate their complaints or praise to the makers of the goods they purchased.

In North America and in developed nations throughout the world the lack of communication between consumers and marketers has been overcome by both available technology and a wide infrastructure to deliver it. Linkages are available via telephone line, television cable, and even wireless telecommunication systems. The information transmitted through these linkages can be captured and analyzed by computers made ever more powerful by their large and inexpensive storage capacity. In addition, the software systems used with these computers allow efficient data storage, data manipulation, and data retrieval. The result is that interactions between businesses and their customers are more direct and documented to a greater extent than ever before.

*Fortune* believes that ready access to information about products and competitive markets will give consumers a tremendous advantage. According to *Fortune* the prognosis for the impact of the Net on the future of business is not consumer control by business, but rather business control by consumers: "Indeed, the Internet represents the ultimate triumph of consumerism." The triumph derives from choice and the availability of information, which empowers consumers. An empowered consumer means that only firms that are truly marketing based and marketing oriented will win the day and survive. We can only speculate what impact this will have on business and society.

The challenge of managing effectively and efficiently in this new market landscape will undoubtedly fall most heavily upon you, the readers of this text. Those who are most able to adapt and use this new technology, both to their own and their businesses' advantage, will be the ones who will thrive in the new e-corporations.[1]

In this chapter, we will learn more about the roles of marketing, see how marketing has evolved over the years, and look at its scope.

**FORTUNE MAGAZINE**
www.fortune.com

# Overview

Marketing is an exciting, fast-paced business discipline. We engage in marketing activities or are affected by them on a daily basis, both in our business-related roles and as consumers. Okay, but what exactly does "marketing" mean? Well, it is not just advertising or selling goods and services, although these are aspects of marketing. And it is not just what we do as supermarket shoppers every week, although this too is part of marketing.

As formally defined in the next section, "marketing" encompasses the activities involved in anticipating, managing, and satisfying demand via the exchange process. As such, marketing encompasses all facets of buyer/seller relationships. Specific marketing activities (all discussed later in this chapter) include environmental analysis and marketing research, broadening an organization's scope, consumer analysis, product planning, distribution planning, promotion planning, price planning, and marketing management.

In a less abstract way, here are two examples of real-world marketing—one from a business perspective and one from a consumer perspective.

**BUSINESS PERSPECTIVE** Lynette Jones received her law degree in 1996 and has worked for a large law firm since graduating from university. She is now ready to open her own practice, but must make a number of decisions: Who should her clients be? What legal services should she offer? Where should she open her office? How will she attract her clients? What fee schedule should she set? Is it ethical to try to attract clients that she worked with from her old firm? *Each of these questions entails a business-related marketing decision.*

Let's look at some of Lynette Jones' marketing options:

- *Clients*—Lynette could target small or medium businesses, wealthy, middle income, or poor clients (on legal aid).
- *Legal services*—Lynette could be a full-service lawyer for her clients or specialize in a particular legal task (such as wills and estates or family law).
- *Office location*—Lynette could open an office in a professional building, a small shopping centre, or her home. She could also go on on-site visits to clients, thus making the choice of her office location less important.
- *Attracting clients*—Lynette must determine if she is from the "new" school—where it is acceptable to run ads in local newspapers, send out direct-mail pieces to prospective clients, etc.—or from the "old" school—where most forms of promotion are viewed as being unprofessional.
- *Fee schedule*—Lynette must rely on her own experience with her previous firm and look at what competitors are doing. Then, she could price similar to others or lower/higher than them (depending on her desired image and a realistic reading of the marketplace).
- *Ethics*—Lynette must weigh the personal dilemma of "stealing" clients from her old firm against the difficulty of starting a business from scratch without any client base.

**CONSUMER PERSPECTIVE** At the same time that Lynette Jones is making decisions about her new legal practice, Brian James is reappraising his status as a legal client. He owns a real estate firm and has been a client of a mid-sized law firm for ten years. Yet he is now unhappy with the firm and feels it takes his business for granted. But before switching lawyers, Brian must answer these questions: What kind of firm should he select? What legal services should he seek? Where should the legal firm be located? How will he learn more about possible firms? What fees

*Marketing is a dynamic field, encompassing many activities.*

should he be willing to pay? Is it ethical to show prospective firms samples of the work from his present lawyer? *Each of these questions addresses a consumer-related marketing decision.*

Let's look at some of Brian James' marketing options:

- *Kind of firm*—Brian could select a small, medium, or large legal firm. Given his current dissatisfaction, he would probably avoid medium and large firms.

- *Legal services*—Brian could continue having his law firm perform all legal tasks for him; or he could take on some of the tasks himself (such as printing standard offer sheets and contracts).

- *Office location*—Brian could look for a lawyer that makes on-site visits or seek a firm that has an office near to his residence.

- *Information about prospective firms*—Brian could ask prospective firms for references, check out lawyers' credentials, interview candidates, and/or require firms to perform a sample task.

- *Fee schedule*—Brian knows he must get "fair" quotes, not "low ball" ones. He recognizes that you get what you pay for; and he wants better service.

- *Ethics*—Brian must determine whether he, as the client, has the right to show any old work to prospective firms—or whether there is a client/lawyer relationship that he should not violate.

LINUX
www.linux.com

## TECHNOLOGY AND MARKETING

### How to Beat Microsoft and Windows 98: Give Your Software Away!

You wouldn't think you'd need to know anything about marketing to give something away, but University of Toronto graduate Robert Young, the CEO of Red Hat Software Inc., has found that to be the case. Young wants you to adopt his company's Linux computer operating systems so badly that he's willing to give it to you for nothing. In fact, he's willing to give it to everyone, although he's found that he needs some marketing help to figure out how to do it. It sounds like nonprofit marketing gone mad, but there's a method to this apparent madness. Young knows that the money in operating systems that compete with Microsoft systems (97 per cent of all personal computers operate with one of Windows or DOS) isn't in selling new operating systems, but in selling the services and technical support that they require.

Linus Torvalds of Finland developed Linux, a form of UNIX used for PCs. Torvalds then released this creation to the world, with no conditions. Anyone can improve on Linux and hand it out at will, since Linux comes with the operating system and the software source code. Young and Red Hat Software know that the Linux operating system is difficult for the typical user to install. Therefore, he sees the revenue for Red Hat arising from the support and installation information it can provide, as opposed to the operating systems sales alone. He wants to establish Red Hat Software as *the* supplier of the Linux operating system to the world through the Slackware brand name. Since Linux is in the public domain and anyone—including Microsoft—can make and sell the product, how does Young expect to win out? His reply is simple: "The strength is in the brand." Although anyone can make ketchup, there's only one Heinz, and it's Robert Young's plan to make Red Hat Software the Heinz ketchup of Linux software. Discuss reasons why consumers might ignore Linux, even though it is "free."

Source: Based on Plugged In, "Steal This Software," *Canadian Business* (November 27, 1998), p. 165.

**A MARKETING MATCH** For "marketing" to operate properly, buyers and sellers need to find and satisfy each other (conduct exchanges). Do you think that Lynette Jones and Brian James would make a good marketing match? We do—but only if their strategy (Lynette) and expectations (Brian) are in sync.

As these examples show, goods and service providers ("sellers") make marketing-related decisions like choosing who customers are, what goods and services to offer, where to sell these goods and services, the features to stress in ads, and the prices to charge. They also determine how to be ethical and socially responsible, and whether to sell products internationally (in addition to domestically). Marketing-related activities are not limited to industrial firms, large corporations, or people called "marketers." They are taken on by all types of companies and people.

*In some way, we are all involved with or affected by marketing.*

As consumers ("buyers"), the marketing practices of goods and service providers affect many of the choices made by our parents, spouses, other family members, friends and associates, and/or us. For virtually every good and service we purchase, the marketing process affects whom we patronize, the assortment of models and styles offered in the marketplace, where we shop, the availability of knowledgeable sales personnel, the prices we pay, and other factors. Marketing practices are in play when we are born (which baby formula our parents feed us, the style of baby furniture they buy); while we grow (our parents' purchase of a domestic or foreign family car or mini van, our choice of a college or university); while we conduct our everyday lives (the use of a particular brand of toothpaste, the purchase of status-related items); and when we retire (our consideration of travel options, a change in living accommodations).

The formal study of marketing requires an understanding of its definition, evolution (including the marketing concept, a marketing philosophy, and customer service), importance and scope, and functions. These principles are discussed throughout Chapter 1.

## Marketing Defined

A broad, integrated definition of marketing forms the basis of this text:

> **Marketing** is the anticipation, management, and satisfaction of demand through the exchange process.

*Marketing includes anticipating demand, managing demand, and satisfying demand.*

It involves goods, services, organizations, people, places, and ideas.

Anticipation of demand requires that a firm do consumer research on a regular basis so it can develop and introduce offerings desired by consumers. Management of demand includes stimulation, facilitation, and regulation tasks. Stimulation motivates consumers to want a firm's offerings due to attractive product designs, distinctive promotion, fair prices, and other strategies. Facilitation is the process whereby the firm makes it easy to buy its offering by having convenient locations, accepting credit cards, using well-informed salespeople, and implementing other strategies. Regulation is needed when there are peak demand periods rather than balanced demand throughout the year or when demand is greater than the supply of the offering. Then, the goal is to spread demand throughout the year or to demarket a good or service (reduce overall demand). Satisfaction of demand involves product availability, actual performance upon purchase, safety perceptions, after-sale service, and other factors. For consumers to be satisfied, goods, services, organizations, people, places, and ideas must fulfill their expectations.

Marketing can be aimed at consumers or at publics. **Consumer demand** refers to the attributes and needs of consumers, producers, manufacturers, wholesalers and retailers, government institutions, international markets, and nonprofit organizations. A firm may appeal to one or a combination of these. **Publics' demand** refers

*Demand is affected by both* **consumers** *and* **publics.**

*Exchange completes the process.*

**CANADIAN RED CROSS**
www.redcross.ca/

*Marketing can be traced to the* **barter era**.

to the attributes and needs of employees, unions, shareholders, the general public, government agencies, consumer groups, and other internal and external forces that affect company operations.

The marketing process is not concluded until consumers and publics **exchange** their money, their promise to pay, or their support for the offering of a firm, institution, person, place, or idea. Exchanges must be done in a socially responsible way, with both the buyer and the seller being ethical and honest—and considering the impact on society and the environment.

A proper marketing definition should not be confined to economic goods and services. It should cover organizations (such as the Red Cross), people (for example, politicians), places (Vancouver), and ideas (should our television be required to have a V-chip). A consumer orientation must be central to any definition. And from a societal perspective, a firm needs to ask whether a good or service should be sold, besides whether it can be sold. Figure 1-1 illustrates how a place (Welland, Ontario) can benefit from marketing efforts.

## The Evolution of Marketing

Marketing's evolution in an industry, country, or region of the world may be viewed as a sequence of stages: barter era → production era → sales era → marketing department era → marketing company era. In some industries, nations, and regions, marketing practices have moved through each stage and involve a good consumer orientation and high efficiency; in others, marketing practices are still in their infancy.

Marketing's origins can be traced to people's earliest use of the exchange process: the **barter era**. With barter, people trade one resource for another—like food for animal pelts. To accommodate exchanges, trading posts, travelling salespeople, general stores, and cities evolved, along with a standardized monetary system. In the least developed nations of the world, barter is still widely practised.

**FIGURE 1-1**

**Marketing Welland to Business Firms**

Marketing can be used for the economic development of communities (places).

*Reprinted with permission of Welland Development Commission and Canadian Tire Acceptance Limited.*

The modern system of marketing begins with the industrialization of an industry, country, or region. For the world's most developed nations, this occurred with the Industrial Revolution of the late 1800s. For developing nations, efforts to industrialize are now underway. Why is industrialization so important in marketing's evolution? Unless industrialization takes place, exchanges are limited, since people do not have surplus items to trade. With the onset of mass production, better transportation, and more efficient technology, products can be made in greater volume and sold at lower prices. Improved mobility, densely populated cities, and specialization also let more people share in the exchange process: They can turn from being self-sufficient (for example, making their own clothes) to being consumers of what others produce (such as buying clothes in a store or market). In the initial stages of industrialization, output is limited and marketing is devoted to products' physical distribution. Because demand is high and competition is low, firms typically do not have to conduct consumer research, modify products, or otherwise adapt to consumer needs. The goal is to lift production to meet demand. This is the **production era** of marketing.

*In the **production era**, output increases to meet demand.*

The next stage takes place as companies expand production capabilities to keep up with consumer demand. At this point, many firms hire a sales force and some use advertising to sell their inventory. Yet, since competition is still rather low, when firms develop new products, consumer tastes or needs receive little consideration. The role of the sales force and advertising is to make consumer desires fit the features of the products offered. For example, a shoe manufacturer might make brown wingtip shoes and use ads and personal selling to convince consumers to buy them. That firm would rarely determine consumer tastes before making shoes or adjust output to those tastes. This is the **sales era** of marketing. It still exists where competition is limited, such as in nations in the process of moving to free-market economies.

*In the **sales era,** firms sell products without first determining consumer desires.*

As competition grows, supply begins to exceed demand. Firms cannot prosper without marketing input. They create marketing departments to conduct consumer research and advise management on how to better design, distribute, promote, and price products. Unless firms react to consumer needs, competitors might better satisfy demand and leave the firms with surplus inventory and falling sales. Yet, although marketing departments share in decisions, they may be in a subordinate position to production, engineering, and sales departments. This is the **marketing department era**. It still exists where marketing has been embraced, but not as the driving force in an industry or company.

*The **marketing department era** occurs when research is used to determine consumer needs.*

Over the past forty years, firms in a growing number of industries, nations, and regions have recognized marketing's central role; marketing departments at those firms are now the equal of others. The firms make virtually all key decisions after thorough consumer analysis: Since competition is intense and sophisticated, consumers must be aggressively drawn and kept loyal to a firm's brands. Company efforts are well integrated and regularly reviewed. This is the **marketing company era**. Figure 1-2 indicates the key aspects of each era in marketing's evolution.

*The **marketing company era** integrates consumer research and analysis into all company efforts.*

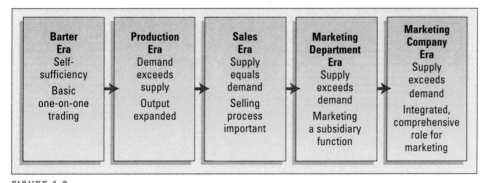

**FIGURE 1-2**
**How Marketing Evolves**

The marketing concept, a marketing philosophy, customer service, customer satisfaction and relationship marketing are the linchpins of the marketing company era. They are examined here.

### The Marketing Concept

*The* **marketing concept** *is consumer-oriented, market-driven, value-based, integrated, and goal-oriented.*

As Figure 1-3 shows, the **marketing concept** is a consumer-oriented, market-driven, value-based, integrated, goal-oriented philosophy for a firm, institution, or person.[2] Here is an illustration of the marketing concept in action:

> Christine Magee, President of Sleep Country Canada, feels that creating excitement and opportunity is the best way to put people to sleep on her company's mattresses. Sleep Country Canada wants to dominate the market with a strong branding approach, and part of the strategy is to let people know that Sleep Country doesn't just sell mattresses. They use a consumer-oriented approach that involves educating customers through salespeople who are "sleep experts." Aside from advice, Sleep Country will also beat the prices of its competitors by 5 per cent. However, consumers are given a lot more than just a good deal and good advice. Sleep Country has a wide selection of mattresses, free delivery, and a 60-day exchange guarantee. It's also in tune with its social responsibilities. Sleep Country will remove the mattresses being replaced (if the customer wishes them removed), refurbish them, and donate them to local charities.
>
> Sleep Country knows that women account for 85 per cent of mattress purchases, and so they target women in their promotion. Consequently, Christine Magee appears in the firm's ads to pitch her products. She believes that women will relate to her much better than they would to a pitch man. This is part of her hands-on approach to running her business. She is so hands-on that it's not unusual for her to return calls to customers who have inquired about the firm's products. This consumer-focused marketing strategy allowed Sleep Country to ring up sales of over $50 million dollars in 1998 while selling over 50 000 mattresses. The firm has 51 stores spread out in Ontario (34 stores and a 20 per cent market share), British Columbia (13 stores and a 30 per cent market share) and Calgary, Alberta (4 stores). Despite her success to date, Christine Magee says, "I don't really sit back and think, Wow! The fact is, there's a lot more to do."[3]

The marketing concept's five elements are crucial to the long-term success of a good, service, organization, person, place, or idea: A *customer orientation* means examining consumer needs, not production capability, and devising a plan to satisfy them. Goods and services are seen as means to accomplish ends, not the ends themselves. A *market-driven approach* means being aware of the structure of the marketplace, especially the attributes and strategies of competing firms. A *value-based philosophy* means offering goods and services that consumers perceive to have superior value relative to their costs and the offerings of competitors. With an *integrated marketing*

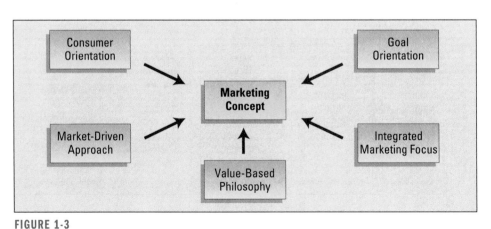

**FIGURE 1-3**

**The Marketing Concept**

*focus*, all the activities relating to goods and services are coordinated, including finance, production, engineering, inventory control, research and development, and marketing. A *goal-oriented firm* employs marketing to achieve both short- and long-term goals—which may be profit, funding to find a cure for a disease, increased tourism, election of a political candidate, a better company image, and so on. Marketing helps attain goals by orienting a firm toward pleasing consumers and offering desired goods, services, or ideas.

These are fifteen things that managers can do to ensure that they adhere to the spirit of the marketing concept:

1. Create customer focus throughout the firm.
2. Listen to the customer.
3. Define and cultivate distinctive competencies.
4. Define marketing as market intelligence.
5. Target customers precisely.
6. Manage for profitability, not sales volume.
7. Make customer value the guiding star.
8. Let the customer define quality.
9. Measure and manage customer expectations.
10. Build customer relationships and loyalty.
11. Define the business as a service business.
12. Commit to continuous improvement and innovation.
13. Manage the company culture along with strategy and structure.
14. Grow with partners and alliances.
15. Destroy marketing bureaucracy.[4]

## Selling Versus Marketing Philosophies

Figure 1-4 highlights the differences between selling and marketing philosophies. The benefits of a marketing, rather than a sales, orientation are many. Marketing stresses consumer analysis and satisfaction, directs the resources of a firm to making

*With a marketing orientation, selling is used to communicate with and understand consumers.*

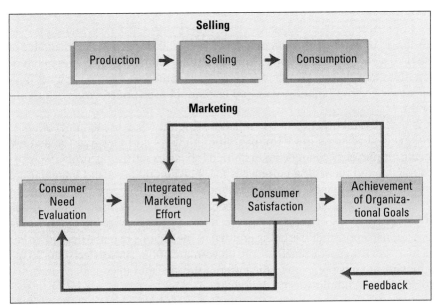

**FIGURE 1-4**

**The Focus of Selling and Marketing Philosophies**

the goods and services consumers want, and adapts to changes in consumer traits and needs. Under a marketing philosophy, selling is used to communicate with and understand consumers; consumer dissatisfaction leads to changes in policy, not a stronger or different sales pitch. Marketing looks for real differences in consumer tastes and devises offerings to satisfy them. Marketing is geared to the long run, and marketing goals reflect overall company goals. Finally, marketing views customer needs broadly rather than narrowly (for example, heating as opposed to fuel oil).

As an example, Randy Powell, CEO of Second Cup Coffee, believes Canada is a nation that drinks crummy coffee. Two-thirds of Canadians average a little more than three cups of coffee a day, so they are not exactly inexperienced consumers. But Powell feels that coffee-drinking Canadians are missing the point of coffee consumption. He sees coffee drinking not just as a caffeine fix, but as an experience. Coffee is "a pleasure, a time-out from a busy day to savour a brew." So the Second Cup is going to go "wherever people live, work, shop, and play" and fulfil the firm's mission, which is "to go out there and educate" consumers.[5]

## Customer Service

*Customer service tends to be intangible, but quite meaningful, to many consumers.*

**Customer service** involves the identifiable, but rather intangible, activities undertaken by a seller in conjunction with the basic goods and/or services it offers.[6] In today's highly competitive marketplace, the level of customer service a firm provides can affect its ability to attract and retain customers more than ever before.

Unless a consumer is happy with *both* the basic good (such as a new auto) or service (such as a car tuneup) offered by a seller *and* the quality of customer service (such as polite, expert sales personnel and punctual appointments), he or she is unlikely to patronize the seller—certainly not in the long run. Imagine your reaction to these situations:

> Stores often tell customers that home deliveries and repairs will be made any time between 8 A.M. and 5 P.M., often effectively killing a workday. Doctors and other health professionals frequently overbook appointments, so patients waste hours waiting to be seen. Federal, provincial, and municipal government agencies are often unreachable on the telephone.[7]
>
> With millions of new buyers, many of them individuals and small businesses, clueless about computers, some manufacturers can't keep up with service complaints and requests for help. The result: hordes of confused and resentful—even outraged—customers.[8]
>
> Yet, firms often have to make customer service tradeoffs. For instance, supermarkets must weigh the potential loss of business if waiting lines are too long versus the cost of opening additional checkout lines.[9]

According to one survey, most people rate the overall level of customer service of businesses as excellent or pretty good, but over 40 per cent rate service as only fair or poor. More than one-third of people say they usually purchase from a business having excellent service but higher prices, rather than a lower-priced competitor with lesser service.[10]

*To offer better customer service, some firms are* **empowering employees**.

This is how several organizations are addressing the issue of customer service: Organizations as diverse as the Winnipeg Blue Bombers and Revenue Canada are **empowering employees**—giving workers broad leeway to satisfy customer requests, and encouraging and rewarding employees for showing initiative and imagination. The Winnipeg Blue Bombers reward their employees with success celebrations to recognize outstanding achievements, whether they are players or other personnel. Revenue Canada has also tried to improve its customer service by empowering employees. More responsibility is being granted to the regions to make decisions. For example, managers are encouraged to consult with the public; make decisions on tax cases by looking at facts rather than the letter of the law; and to consider substance instead of form when administering the Income Tax Act.[11]

Customer service is an important "output" of a marketing system and firms are very conscious of this. McDonald's Restaurants of Canada instituted an incentive pro-

## INTERNATIONAL MARKETING IN ACTION

## Passing the Test: Three Minutes That Could Change Your Life

**N**eeds aside, one of the toughest industries in which to successfully market products is the medical-pharmaceutical industry. This is a key reason why this market is dominated by multinational giants, which can afford the expensive new product development costs associated with all the regulation in this industry. Every nation has different testing standards and requirements for products sold in their home markets, and only the multinational firms can spread product development costs over many markets and develop rigorous research testing standards that can satisfy virtually all nations. Curiously, tiny Mississauga-based Med-Mira Laboratories is trying to establish itself as a player in this market.

The potential for success is great, except that it's not a wonder drug that cures the HIV virus that Med-Mira is offering, but a lab test for HIV that takes only three minutes and costs only $5. The test currently in use costs $20 to administer and takes two to three weeks to provide results. So this new test is a tremendous benefit for medical authorities and testing labs, not to mention the people being tested.

The test has been approved by Health Canada and is simple to administer. A person need only provide a single blood drop, which is processed on an immunoreactive membrane which has a chemical that provides a colour reaction, producing a red dot to indicate a positive reaction. All of this occurs within three minutes. The potential for imme-

diate feedback from an inexpensive and reliable test is tremendous. Of course, because HIV is a life and death proposition, should the outcome not be completely accurate the potential for psychological harm (a false positive), not to mention physical harm to others (a false negative), is great. As such, government medical regulators must act with considerable caution before approving such a product in order to ensure that it lives up to its promise. Med-Mira appears to have provided enough accurate results to receive approval from regulators in Greece, Hong Kong, and from the Commonwealth of Independent States (former Republics of the U.S.S.R.).

If its product is adopted for use around the world, the prognosis for Med-Mira's sales and earnings is mind-boggling. For example, the Commonwealth of Independent States has ordered 1 million test kits already. Since the kits are consumables, the worldwide market potential is limited only by the size of the population and the frequency of blood testing undertaken. Considering the stakes, a price of $5, and a three-minute result, an HIV test with a person's routine physical check-up is bound to become standard—as will astronomical sales and profits for Med-Mira. Although the product is needed, what barriers might hold Med-Mira back from achieving success?

Source: Based on David Berman, "Make It Quick, Doc," *Canadian Business* (July 31/August 14, 1998), p. 106.

gram as early as 1993 to encourage improved customer service by its employees. Employee contests for good service are held and the top performers receive prizes in merchandise or McDonald's food discounts. The contests and their results are publicized in-house using posters, newsletters, payroll stuffers, and bulletin board notices.[12]

The value of customer service is so well recognized as being crucial to success that *Canadian Business* magazine has an award for a Canadian firm that best exemplifies this activity.

For example, Alex Campbell of Thrifty Foods was given a Canadian Business Entrepreneur of the Year Award in 1997 for service excellence by his firm. Thrifty targets family customers who are frequent and heavy purchasers of grocery items. To satisfy this market Thrifty foods offers some unique services like home delivery and undertakes programs such as composting both produce waste and cardboard boxes. The checkout lanes are child-friendly, with displays of fruit, colouring books, and toothpaste as opposed to the traditional chocolate bars and gum. The stores have diaper-changing rooms, seat belts on the shopping carts, and miniature carts that children can push. The store also has a program staffed by volunteers who take orders and deliver groceries to seniors and disabled people who find it difficult to shop in person.[13]

## Customer Satisfaction and Relationship Marketing

*Firms cannot usually prosper without a high level of* **customer satisfaction**.

As previously noted, **customer satisfaction** is a crucial element in successful marketing. It is the degree to which there is a match between a customer's expectations of a good or service and the actual performance of that good or service, including customer service.[14] As one expert says: "Firms that satisfy customers are ones that do their homework. They know a customer satisfaction commitment must be backed up by a complete understanding of the customer, the competition, and the marketplace—and an ability to identify and respond to areas where change is needed."[15] Figure 1-5 shows eleven representative factors that affect overall customer satisfaction.

This is how formidable it can be to keep customers satisfied:

> It would be hard to find an organization more devoted to satisfying customers than the three Les Ailes de la Mode (The Wings of Fashion) department stores, found respectively in Ste-Foy, Brossard, and Laval, Quebec.
>
> When you enter these department stores you're made to feel welcome by the collection of leather couches and newspaper racks that surround a baby grand piano. The stores offer a coat check, a concierge, and a room for mothers who are nursing (which includes a microwave for warming baby formula). It's not only the amenities that indicate the dedication to customer satisfaction in Les Ailes de la Mode, but the way you're treated as well. The staff provide the best service they can, including buying customers coffee or desert from the store's posh food concessions, and providing a complementary facial from one of the store's spa services. The store is out of stock on the item you came shopping for? Voilà, employees will go to almost any length to provide you with what you want, even if they have to go to the competition to buy it!
>
> Customer service like this isn't cheap. Les Ailes de la Mode spends about three times as much on customer service per square foot of sales space as most department store retailers in Canada. However, the reward is almost double the sales per square foot of any other retailer. And since customer service of this type is so exceptional, customers come to these stores from all over North America just for the experience.[16]

Companies with satisfied customers have a good opportunity to convert them into loyal customers who will purchase from them over an extended period. From a consumer perspective, when marketing activities are performed with the conscious intention of developing and managing long-term, trusting customer relations,

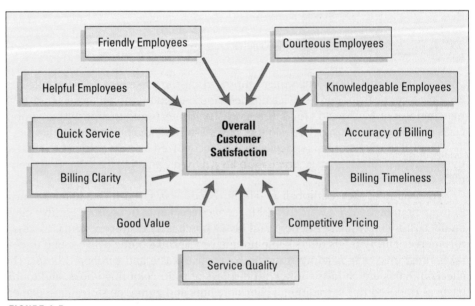

**FIGURE 1-5**

**Factors That Affect Customer Satisfaction**
*Source:* Steven Hokanson, "The Deeper You Analyze, the More You Satisfy Customers," *Marketing News* (January 2, 1995), p. 16. Reprinted by permission of the American Marketing Association.

**relationship marketing** is involved.[17] Why is this so important? According to one observer, "It's far cheaper to hold on to the [customers] you have than to acquire new ones. A happy contingent inside your tent lessens your need to beat the street for business. Loyalists may even drum up fresh prospects for you."[18]

*Through* **relationship** **marketing**, *companies try to increase long-term customer loyalty.*

**COMPAQ**
www.compaq.com

For companies to grow and remain profitable in today's business environment they must establish long-term relationships with their key customers.

William Band describes what he calls "customer-centric thinking," which is a key factor in relationship marketing. He believes that although a lot of companies *think* they are building good customer relationships, they're often not doing this at all. To be truly customer-centric one must do the kind of things that Compaq Computer Corporation has done. Compaq has set up an information system that links its customers and potential customers with the firm's resellers (30 000 worldwide), the firm's call centres, and Compaq's sales force. The system thus contains all customer information—and because it's integrated, when a customer in the Middle East purchases a computer, managers at Compaq's Houston headquarters are aware of the details of the sale. Compaq can then monitor and follow up on sales through direct contact with its customers, without having to depend on its resellers. And customers feel they've bought a computer from Compaq, rather than simply having bought a Compaq computer.

This relationship marketing results in customers who tend to remain brand loyal, as well as more customer referrals. The immediate benefit to profitability is greater than what a firm would gain if it had undertaken product/service innovation or cost-cutting measures.[19]

How's this for getting close to the customer? Great Plains codes every program in a way that blocks its use after 50 transactions. The customer must call the firm for the code that gets the program running again. At this point, the folks who answer the phones ask questions about the customer's business, computer system, and software requirements. Sound annoying? "Customers don't seem to mind a simple phone call," insists CEO Doug Bergum. Today, Great Plains has some 45 000 buyer profiles in its data bank and personally solicits those likely to upgrade. In 1993, the firm persuaded a phenomenal 42 per cent of the owners of Great Plains Accounting Version 6 to buy new Version 7.

**GREAT PLAINS SOFTWARE**
www.gps.com/

These retention skills got dearly tested when Version 7 turned out to contain bugs. Concerned that his reputation for bug-free products would be ruined, Bergum spent $340 000 to mail new disks to every Version 7 buyer. He also wrote all 2700 Great Plains dealers, admitting that he failed to test Version 7 properly and offering cash compensation to anyone whose business suffered from the glitch. Great Plains' goof may have enhanced customer loyalty. More dealers wrote to praise Bergum's response than to claim redress—which amounted to $34 000, less than 0.5 per cent of the sales from Version 7. Accounting Today commended Great Plains for being "a model of how problems should be handled." At "Stampede to Fargo," the firm's annual dealer conference, Bergum won the crowd by standing onstage, explaining his mistakes at length, and smashing three fresh eggs on his head.[20]

# The Importance of Marketing

Because marketing stimulates demand, one of its basic tasks is to generate consumer enthusiasm for goods and services. Worldwide, over $U.S.35 trillion of goods and services are produced annually, with Canada accounting for approximately $CAN866 billion of that sum.

*Marketing stimulates consumers, costs a large part of sales, employs people, supports industries, affects all consumers, and plays a major role in our lives.*

A large amount of each sales dollar goes to cover the costs related to such marketing activities as product development, packaging, distribution, advertising and personal selling, price marking, and administering consumer credit programs. Some estimates place the costs of marketing as high as 50 per cent or more of sales in certain industries. Yet, it should not be assumed that the performance of some marketing tasks by consumers would automatically lead to lower prices. For example, could a small business really save money by having the owner fly to Windsor, Ontario to buy a new minivan directly from the maker rather than from a local dealer? Would a family be willing to buy clothing in bulk to reduce a retailer's transportation and storage costs?

Millions of people work in marketing-related jobs in Canada. They include those employed in the retailing, wholesaling, transportation, warehousing, and communications industries and those involved with marketing jobs for manufacturing, service, agricultural, mining, and other industries. Projections indicate future employment in marketing will remain strong.

Marketing activities also involve entire industries, such as advertising and market research. Total annual worldwide advertising expenditures exceed $480 billion. Many agencies, such as WPP Group and Cordiant of Great Britain, Interpublic Group and Omnicom Group of the United States, and Dentsu of Japan have worldwide billings of several billion dollars each. Around $11 billion worldwide is spent yearly on various types of commercial marketing research. Firms such as A.C. Nielsen, Information Resources Inc., Research International (Great Britain), and GfK (of Germany) generate yearly revenues of more than $130 million each.

**DENTSU (INFORMATION SERVICES INTERNATIONAL-DENTSU, LTD.)**
www.dentsu.co.jp

All people and organizations serve as consumers for various goods and services. By understanding the role of marketing, consumers can become better informed, more selective, and more efficient. Effective channels of communication with sellers can also be established and complaints resolved more easily and favourably. Consumer groups have a major impact on sellers.

Because resources are scarce, marketing programs and systems must function at their peak. Thus, by optimizing customer service, inventory movement, advertising expenditures, product assortments, and other areas of marketing, firms will better use resources. Some industries may even require demarketing (lowering the demand for goods and services). For example, a hydroelectric utility may launch a campaign to encourage consumers to reduce their consumption of electricity.

Marketing strongly affects people's beliefs and lifestyles. In fact, it has been criticized as developing materialistic attitudes, fads, product obsolescence, a reliance on gadgets, status consciousness, and superficial product differences—and for wasting resources. Marketers reply that they merely address the desires of people and make the best goods and services they can at the prices people will pay.

Marketing has a role to play in improving our quality of life. For example, marketing personnel often encourage firms to make safer products, such as child-proof bottle caps. They create public service messages on energy conservation, AIDS prevention, driver safety, alcohol abuse, and other topics. They help new goods, ideas, and services (such as cellular phones, improved nutrition, and ATMs) to be accepted by people and organizations.

A knowledge of marketing is extremely valuable for those not directly involved in a marketing job. For example, marketing decisions must be made by:

*Marketing awareness is invaluable for those in non-marketing jobs.*

- *Doctors*—What hours are most desirable to patients?
- *Lawyers*—How can new clients be attracted?
- *Management consultants*—Should fees be higher, lower, or the same as competitors'?
- *Financial analysts*—What investments should be recommended to clients?
- *Research and development personnel*—Is there consumer demand for a potential "breakthrough" product?
- *Economists*—What impact will the economy have on the way various industries market their offerings?
- *Statisticians*—How should firms react to predicted demographic shifts?
- *Teachers*—How can students become better consumers?
- *City planners*—How can businesses be persuaded to relocate to the city?
- *Nonprofit institutions*—How can donor contributions be raised?

Each of these professions and organizations needs to understand and satisfy patient, client, consumer, student, taxpayer, or contributor needs. And more of them than ever before are now undertaking marketing activities such as research, advertising, and so on.

## Marketing Functions and Performers

There are eight basic **marketing functions**: environmental analysis and marketing research, consumer analysis, target marketing, product planning, distribution planning, promotion planning, price planning, and marketing management.

Here are brief descriptions of the functions:

- *Environmental analysis and marketing research*—Monitoring and adapting to external factors that affect success or failure, such as the economy and competition; and collecting data to resolve specific marketing issues.
- *Consumer analysis*—Examining and evaluating consumer characteristics, needs, and purchasing processes.
- *Target marketing*—Selecting the group(s) of consumers at which to aim marketing efforts.
- *Product planning (including goods, services, organizations, people, places, and ideas)*—Developing and maintaining products, product assortments, product images, brands, packaging, and optional features; and deleting faltering products.
- *Distribution planning*—Forming relations with distribution intermediaries, physical distribution, inventory management, warehousing, transportation, the allocation of goods and services, wholesaling, and retailing.
- *Promotion planning*—Communicating with customers, the general public, and others through some form of advertising, public relations, personal selling, and/or sales promotion.
- *Price planning*—Determining price levels and ranges, pricing techniques, terms of purchase, price adjustments, and the use of price as an active or passive factor.
- *Marketing management*—Planning, implementing, and controlling the marketing program (strategy) and individual marketing functions; appraising the risks and benefits in decision making; and focusing on total quality.

*Basic* **marketing functions** *range from environmental analysis to marketing management.*

Generally, a firm should first study its environment and gather relevant marketing information. The firm should determine how to act in a socially responsible and ethical manner and consider whether to be domestic and/or international. At the same time, the firm should analyze potential customers to learn their needs and select the group(s) on which to focus. It should next plan product offerings, make distribution decisions, choose how to communicate with customers and others, and set proper prices. These four functions (in combination, known as the *marketing mix*) should be performed in a coordinated manner, based on environmental, societal, and consumer analysis. Through marketing management, the firm's overall marketing program would be planned and carried out in an integrated manner, with fine-tuning as necessary.

Although many marketing transactions require the performance of similar tasks, such as being ethical, analyzing consumers, and product, distribution, promotion, and price planning, these tasks can be enacted in many ways (for example, a manufacturer could choose to distribute its product via full-service retailers or self-service ones; or a financial-services firm could choose to rely on either telephone sales or in-office visits by salespeople to potential small-business clients).

*Usually at least one* **market-**
**ing performer** *must*
*undertake each of the basic*
*marketing functions.*

**BOEING**
www.boeing.com

**Marketing performer**s are the organizations or individuals that undertake one or more marketing functions. They include manufacturers and service providers, wholesalers, retailers, marketing specialists, and organizational and final consumers. As Figure 1-6 shows, each performer has a different role. Even though the responsibility for marketing tasks can be shifted and shared in various ways, basic marketing functions usually must be done by one performer or another. They cannot be omitted in many situations.

Sometimes, one marketing performer decides to carry out all—or virtually all—marketing functions (such as Boeing analyzing the marketplace, acting ethically, operating domestically and internationally, seeking various types of customers, developing aerospace and related products, distributing products directly to customers, using its own sales force and placing ads in select media, and setting prices). Yet, for these reasons, one performer often does not undertake all marketing functions:

- Many firms do not have the financial resources to sell products directly to consumers. They need intermediaries to share in the distribution process.

- Marketing directly to customers may require producers of goods and services to offer complementary products or sell the complementary products of other firms so the distribution process is carried out efficiently.

- A performer may be unable or unwilling to complete certain functions and may seek a marketing specialist to fulfil them.

- Many performers are too small to do certain functions efficiently.

- For many goods and services, established distribution methods are in force and it is difficult to set up other methods (such as bypassing independent soda distributors to sell directly to retail stores).

- Some consumers may want to buy in quantity, visit self-service outlets, pay cash, and so on, to save money.

**FIGURE 1-6**
**Who Performs Marketing Functions**

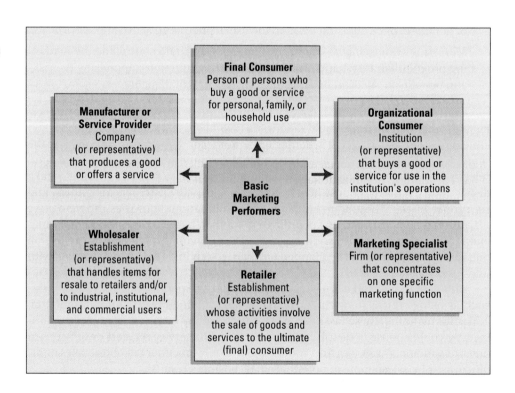

## ETHICS AND TODAY'S MARKETER

## What Practices Do YOU Believe Are Ethical?

Ethical values in marketing can be determined by using a checklist. Here is an opportunity for YOU to assess your level of marketing ethics.

Respond to these statements on a 1 to 9 scale. For items 1–4, let "1" mean that you completely disagree and "9" mean that you completely agree. For items 5–10, use a "1" for complete agreement and a "9" for complete disagreement:

1. Business ethics and social responsibility are critical to the survival of a business enterprise.
2. Business has a social responsibility beyond making a profit.
3. Good ethics is often good business.
4. Social responsibility and profitability can be compatible.
5. If shareholders are unhappy, nothing else matters.
6. The most important concern for a firm is making a profit, even if it means bending or breaking the rules.
7. To remain competitive in a global environment, business firms will have to disregard ethics and social responsibility.
8. Efficiency is much more important to a firm than whether or not the firm is seen as ethical or socially responsible.
9. Although output quality is essential to corporate success, ethics and social responsibility are not.
10. Communication is more important to the overall effectiveness of a firm than whether it is concerned with ethics and social responsibility.

Items 1 to 4 measure a "good ethics is good business" orientation, items 5 to 8 measure a "profits are not paramount" orientation, and items 9 and 10 measure a "quality and communication" orientation. Summarize and describe your ethical nature by determining your total score, as well as your score on the three individual scales.

Source: Based on material in Anusorn Singhapakdi, Kenneth L. Kraft, Scott J. Vitell, and Kumar C. Rallapalli, "The Perceived Importance of Ethics and Social Responsibility on Organizational Effectiveness: A Survey of Marketers," *Journal of the Academy of Marketing Science*, Vol. 23 (Winter 1995), pp. 49–56.

## Format of the Text

This book is divided into seven parts. The balance of Part 1 focuses on the marketing environment; and the information needed for marketing decisions. The discussion in Part 1 sets the foundation for studying the specific components of marketing.

Part 2 deals with marketing's central orientation: understanding consumers. It looks at demographics, social and psychological traits, and the decision process of final consumers; organizational consumer attributes and decision making; and developing a target market and sales forecasting. Parts 3 to 6 discuss the elements of the marketing mix (product, distribution, promotion, and price planning) and the actions needed to carry out a marketing program in depth. Part 7 considers the marketing management implications of the topics raised throughout the text and discusses how to develop marketing plans and how to integrate and analyze an overall marketing plan.

Numerous examples and illustrations of actual marketing practices by a variety of organizations and individuals are woven into our discussions. And although such topics as marketing and society, international marketing, organizational consumers, and goods versus service marketing get separate chapter coverage to highlight certain points, applications in these areas are presented throughout the text.

# MARKETING IN THE THIRD MILLENNIUM

## Welcome to the Net-centric Industrial Order

**G**ary Hamel and Jeff Sampler, writing in *Fortune,* contend that as the third millennium dawns a new "Net-centric industrial order" is developing in the business world. Over 6 million Canadians access the Internet each week, including the 1.5 million Canadian households (13 per cent) who use the Internet from home. In 1997, it was reported that 36 per cent of the Internet users made a purchase online. However, out of concern for security only 22 per cent of these purchases involved a complete online transaction. Nonetheless the rate of growth of e-commerce has been tremendous in recent years, a key sign that the new order should be taken seriously. Data on the U.S. market indicates a doubling of online sales from 1996 to 1997, with 1997 sales being U.S.$7 billion.

Hamel and Sampler believe that businesses will be affected in the following eight ways:

1. *When Push Comes to Suck*—People will prefer being on the Internet rather than passively watching television. Marketers must realize that they won't be able to "push" their messages onto consumers, who will be "sucking" out the information that interests them and avoiding information that doesn't. The Internet is a shopping medium controlled by customers who can seek out the products and services they want.

2. *Just the Plain Truth*—You won't be able to hide mediocrity online. Consumers will be able to compare products' features and prices—and shop the world to do it. And with the ability to chat online, people can ask others how well products have worked for them. Firms like Junglee and C2B Technologies are developing search engines designed to identify bargains and price deals for products on the Net.

3. *As You Like It*—The ultimate in marketing for the consumer is customization. It's also a very good deal for marketers, who are able to "make to order." Marketers won't have to carry inventory, and will have cash in hand before they produce products. Of course, some production efficiency may be lost, and not all products are amenable to customization, although a great many are. In particular, intellectual property in the form of entertainment, literature, advice, or data is easily transmitted on the Internet, and very much a customized purchase.

4. *Everything's an Auction*—For example, Priceline.com is a popular way that air travellers in the U.S. can name their price for airline tickets between cities. Airlines willing to meet their price will issue them a ticket, which travellers are obliged to pay for. The promise of what economists call a "perfectly" competitive market may well be realized on the Web.

5. *The End of Geography*—Consumers will be able to access any business in the world that's online, and vice versa. Electronic goods can be instantly accessed, although since tangible goods and services still have to be shipped some cost-related price advantages may still accrue to their local or domestic suppliers. However, these advantages will be far less than they were in the past.

6. *Search Economies Rule*—People can find exactly what they want on the Web quickly and efficiently rather than travelling around to the local stores (or even phoning around, for that matter). Web seekers will also likely encounter sources that have far more information and expertise to help them with their decision making than they would by talking to the typical retail salesperson at a local store.

7. *My Place, My Time*—Instead of having to go to retailers, customers want retailers to come to them. Weekly grocery delivery, once a relic of the past, may become the wave of the future. Firms that can provide fast, efficient customer delivery will become the leading e-corporations.

8. *Word of Mouse*—The speed at which information can be transmitted and then retransmitted on the Web is incredible—and uncontrollable. For good or ill, marketers and their products can be simultaneously lionized and vilified in real time around the world. The Web is truly a court of public opinion, containing hundreds of millions of judges.[21]

# SUMMARY

In this and every chapter in the text, the summary is linked to the objectives stated at the beginning of the chapter.

**1.** *To illustrate marketing's exciting, dynamic, and influential nature* Marketing may be viewed from both business and consumer perspectives; and it influences us daily. As goods and service providers, we make such marketing-related decisions as choosing who customers are, what goods and services to offer, where to sell them, what to stress in promotion, what prices to charge, how to be ethical and responsible, and whether to operate internationally. As consumers, the marketing process affects whom we patronize, choices in the marketplace, where we shop, the availability of sales personnel, the prices we pay, and other factors.

**2.** *To define marketing and trace its evolution—with emphasis on the marketing concept, a marketing philosophy, customer service, and customer satisfaction and relationship marketing* Marketing involves anticipating, managing, and satisfying demand via the exchange process. It includes goods, services, organizations, people, places, and ideas.

The evolution of marketing can be traced to people's earliest use of barter in the exchange process (the barter era); but it has truly developed since the Industrial Revolution, as mass production and improved transportation have enabled more transactions to occur. For many firms, the evolution of modern marketing can be traced through four stages or "eras": production, sales, marketing department, and marketing company. Yet, in less-developed and developing countries, marketing practices are still in the early stages of development.

The marketing concept requires organizations or individuals to be consumer-oriented, market-driven, value-based, integrated in their efforts, and goal-oriented. A marketing philosophy means assessing and responding to consumer wants, to real differences in consumer tastes, and to long-run opportunities and threats; such a philosophy also requires coordinated decision making.

To prosper today, firms must emphasize customer service: the identifiable, rather intangible, acts performed by a seller in conjunction with the basic goods and/or services being offered. A number of firms now empower employees so as to improve the level of customer service. Customer satisfaction occurs when consumer expectations are met or exceeded; then firms have an opportunity to attract loyal customers by paying attention to relationship marketing.

**3.** *To show the importance of marketing as a field of study* Marketing is a crucial field for several reasons: it stimulates demand; it involves a lot of money and employs a large number of people; it involves entire industries, such as advertising and marketing research; all organizations and people are consumers in some situations; and finally, it has an impact on our beliefs and lifestyles and influences the quality of our lives. Some marketing knowledge is therefore valuable to all of us, regardless of occupation.

**4.** *To describe the basic functions of marketing and those that perform these functions* The major marketing functions are environmental analysis and marketing research; consumer analysis; product, distribution, promotion, and price planning; and marketing management. Responsibility for performing these tasks can be shifted and shared in several ways among manufacturers and service providers, wholesalers, retailers, marketing specialists, and consumers. Due to costs, assortment requirements, specialized abilities, company size, established distribution methods, and consumer interests, one party usually does not perform all functions.

# KEY TERMS

**e-corporation** (p. 4)

**marketing** (p. 7)

**consumer demand** (p. 7)

**publics' demand** (p. 7)

**exchange** (p. 8)

**barter era** (p. 8)

**production era** (p. 9)

**sales era** (p. 9)

**marketing department era** (p. 9)

**marketing company era** (p. 9)

**marketing concept** (p. 10)

**customer service** (p. 12)

**empowering employees** (p. 12)

**customer satisfaction** (p. 14)

**relationship marketing** (p. 15)

**marketing functions** (p. 17)

**marketing performers** (p. 18)

# REVIEW QUESTIONS

1. How does marketing influence us daily both in our business roles and as consumers?

2. Explain the following:
   a. Anticipation of demand.
   b. Management of demand.
   c. Satisfaction of demand.
   d. Exchange process.

3. Distinguish between consumer and public demand.

4. Give an example of a good, service, organization, person, place, and idea that may be marketed.

5. Describe the five eras of marketing.

6. What are the five components of the marketing concept? Give an example of each component.

7. What is customer service? Why is it so important to any firm?

8. What is customer satisfaction? Why is it so important to any firm?

9. What are the basic functions performed by marketing?

10. Why do most consumers not buy products directly from manufacturers?

# DISCUSSION QUESTIONS

1. a. As Lynette Jones, lawyer, what business-related marketing decisions would you make? Why?
   b. As Brian James, legal client, what consumer-related marketing decisions would you make? Why?
   c. Develop a plan for Lynette to attract Brian as a client.

2. Does the presence of a marketing department mean a firm is following the marketing concept? Explain your answer.

3. As the manager of a full-service hotel chain, how would your customer services differ from those offered by a limited-service hotel chain? Why?

4. Develop a seven-item questionnaire to assess the quality of a firm's customer satisfaction efforts.

5. Provide your comments and thoughts on the eight ways that businesses are likely to be affected by the new "Net-centric industrial order."

# Hints for Solving Cases

At the end of each chapter there are one or two short cases, with 33 cases in total. There is also one CBC video case at the end of each part, with seven cases in total. All cases are intended to build on text discussions, improve your reasoning skills, and stimulate class discussions.

The cases in *Marketing,* Second Canadian Edition, describe actual marketing scenarios faced by a variety of organizations and individuals. The facts, situations, and people are all real. The questions following each case are designed to help you pinpoint major issues, foster your analysis, cite alternative courses of future action, and develop appropriate marketing strategies. The information necessary to answer the questions may be drawn from both the case itself and the text chapter(s) to which the case relates.

Each of the part-ending video cases are followed by five or six questions. The material in the text is sufficient to answer the first three or four questions, while the remaining questions pertain to the video.

These hints should be kept in mind when solving a case:

- Read (observe) all material carefully. Underline or take notes on important data and statements.
- List the key issues and company actions detailed in the case.
- Do not make unrealistic or unsupported assumptions.
- Read each question following the case. Be sure you understand the thrust of every question. Do not give similar answers for two distinct questions.
- Write up tentative answers in outline form. Cover as many aspects of each question as possible.
- Review relevant material in the appropriate chapter of the text. In particular, look for information pertaining to the case questions.
- Expand your tentative answers, substantiating them with data from the case and the chapter(s).
- Reread the case and your notes to make sure you haven't omitted any important concepts in your answers.
- Make sure your answers are clear and well written, and that you've considered their ramifications for the organization.
- Reread your solutions at least one day after developing your answers. This ensures a more objective review of your work.
- Make any necessary revisions.
- Be sure your answers are not simply a summary or rehash of the case, and that you've presented concrete analyses and recommendations.

**CASE STUDY**
# Canadian Hospitals Discover Marketing

Although marketing is one of the most pervasive activities in Canadian society, many organizations haven't felt a strong need to embrace it. If an organization is involved in any type of commercial activity all the marketing functions must be performed. Up until now Canadian hospitals hadn't seen their role as commercial in nature, and so hadn't incorporated marketing principles or functions as part of their operations.

But today Canadian hospitals are seeking out and developing marketing expertise as never before. The driving force for change has been the drastic erosion in public funding caused by years of government cutbacks to reduce deficits. These cutbacks have forced hospitals to seek alternative sources of revenue, with commercial ventures being one of their major thrusts. Hospital administrators have to think and act like marketing managers, or to hire marketing managers and consultants to think and act for them.

For example, Toronto's Hospital for Sick Children has developed a "Main Street" retail area in the hospital. This area includes a Shoppers Drug Mart; StarCity Studio, which sells clothing, gifts, and collectibles; and food retailers such as Yogen Fruz, Tim Horton's, and Starbucks. The area is travelled by an estimated 7000 people every day, with the franchise fees and merchandise income generating an estimated $1 million a year for the hospital.

The Foothills Hospital in Calgary offers consumers five retail outlets, including a hair salon, two food vendors, a full-service bank, and an automated teller machine. The Calgary Regional Health Authority has vendors in three of the four hospitals it operates. It earns about $500 000 a year by leasing retail space and taking a percentage of sales from its lessees. It has also sold advertising in an informational booklet provided to maternity patients, and plans to sell more advertising in bedside directories used by patients in all the hospitals. These activities are managed by Susan Black, who is really a marketing manager but whose title is commercial development leader.

The Queen Elizabeth II Health Sciences Centre in Halifax manages five health care facilities, within which it owns and operates five Tim Horton's stores, a Pizza Hut, four gift shops, and three convenience stores. The Centre leases space to four automated teller machines, a kiosk banking service, a hair salon, a home health care store, and a pharmacy. It plans to open some new retail outlets in the near future.

Finally, Sunnybrook & Women's College Health Sciences Centre in Toronto has hired an advertising agency to develop its brand image. The rationale for this is threefold. First, the hospital organization is new—it was created from the amalgamation of the Sunnybrook Health Science Centre, Women's College Hospital, and the Orthopedic & Arthritic Hospital—and this has to be communicated to the public. Second, the image must also be communicated to the current staff of the organizations in order to help them build up morale and to communicate the new image to the patients and constituents they serve. Third, the new organization wants to build brand loyalty among its patrons, since its continued operation and funding depends on patient utilization.

## Questions

1. Discuss the advantages and disadvantages of commercial marketing ventures for hospital organizations. What kinds of marketing issues are likely to crop up in marketing a hospital as compared to marketing a typically commercial service, such as a hotel?

2. Which marketing functions might have less emphasis in marketing a hospital as opposed to marketing a packaged good, such as a chocolate bar?

3. Identify and discuss the kinds of ethical issues that might arise in the marketing of Canadian hospitals and the development of retail space within hospitals.

4. The case mentions a number of retail outlets (gift shops, banks, food retailers, hair salons, pharmacies) that have located in hospitals so far. Identify three other retailer types that weren't mentioned that might be logical and profitable fits for hospitals. Then identify three retailer types that would not be good fits. Explain the reasoning behind your choices.

Sources: The data for this case are drawn from Muriel Draaisma, "Hospitals' Commercial Cures," *Marketing Magazine* (May 17, 1999), pp. 13–14; and Muriel Draaisma, "Hybrid Medical Centres Turn to Branding," *Marketing Magazine* (May 17, 1999), p. 14.

## CHAPTER 2

# The Environments That Affect Marketing

## *Chapter Objectives*

**1.** To examine the environment within which marketing decisions are made and marketing activities are undertaken

**2.** To differentiate between those elements controlled by a firm's top management and those controlled by marketing, and to enumerate the controllable elements of a marketing plan

**3.** To enumerate the uncontrollable environmental elements that can affect a marketing plan and study their potential ramifications

**4.** To explain why feedback about company performance and the uncontrollable aspects of its environment and the subsequent adaptation of the marketing plan are essential for a firm to attain its objectives

*Dairy Farmers of Canada*

**M**any business people believe that competition in business is very much like war—and that marketing supplies a lot of the weaponry. Larry Whetstone's experience bears this out.

Larry Whetsone has been engaged in a fourteen-year battle with Canada's dairy industry. His objective is simple: to sell cheese substitutes to people who either can't (an estimated 10 per cent of the Canadian population is lactose-intolerant, or allergic to milk) or don't want to eat cheese. If the essence of competition is to give people choices, and the essence of marketing is to meet people's needs, then Larry is doing the right thing. Competition from the dairy industry is expected, but when it's linked to government control it takes on another dimension.

Larry Whetsone can't sell his products in most food stores in Ontario and Quebec. It's not that buyers don't want his products, or that they're not safe for consumption. It's that the federal and provincial governments, along with the dairy industry, have regulated and promoted dairy products for many years. Makers of cheese substitutes have been fined, and raided. Makers of imitation cheese in Quebec aren't allowed to make it look like cheese, nor is margarine allowed to look like butter. Makers are prohibited from using the term "imitation" cheese, and from fortifying their products with vitamins. The dairy industry has legal protection in this case, and Whetstone doesn't understand why.

It's not as if Whetstone's product is particularly superior to cheese for the 90 per cent of Canadians who are not lactose-intolerant. The cheese substitutes are cholesterol-free, rennet-free, and 99 per cent lactose-free. They have some natural colouring and flavourings, and a bit of corn oil and soybean oil as additives. As such, the product comes up considerably short of the real thing. Moreover, U.S. data indicates that imitation cheese has about 3 per cent of the market and produces sales of $570 million, a small portion of the total $19 billion in cheese sold there. So what threat is posed to the dairy industry by allowing competition and the meeting of people's needs?

Whetstone first encountered imitation cheese in 1984 in the U.S., where it's legal. He sensed a tremendous opportunity, because he hadn't seen any similar products in the Canadian market. Whetstone was about to find out why. He asked a U.S. supplier of imitation cheese to send him some samples, which he then demonstrated to a Canadian cheese company in the hopes of arranging a distribution deal. The Alberta dairy branch was notified and they called Whetstone to tell him that selling imitation cheese was illegal. So began his crusade against the government and the dairy industry.

The dairy industry contends that it's not against imitation products themselves, but rather the appropriation of such names as cheese, cream, or milk. Dairy production is an important agricultural industry in the Canadian economy, and the federal and provincial governments have intervened to protect and regulate its activity. The industry has worked hard to undertake institutional promotion of its products, and doesn't want any free riders. Moreover, the issue of imitation products is not quite as simple as Larry Whetsone thinks. In his case, imitation is part of aiming at a completely different market. But the problem is that within the dairy industry imitation can take on a different form if unregulated. That is, combination dairy and non-dairy products—which may not fulfil the promise of the real thing but be advertised as such—would mislead people. Still, if safety is not an issue and appropriate labelling and branding laws are followed, shouldn't the market place decide?[1]

The Cowichan First Nations people would agree that business competition can be war. The Cowichans have been selling hand-knit sweaters since the 1880s. They use designs trademarked in Canada: the thunderbird, the whale, the eagle, and the deer. The sweaters were popular with the many Japanese tourists who visited British Columbia every year, and the Cowichans hoped to capitalize on this popularity by selling them in the Japanese market. They were stunned to find Cowichan-brand sweaters already being sold in Japan. These sweaters were imported into the Japanese market from New Zealand. The Kiwi copies are machine-made and much less expensive than the hand-made Cowichan originals. The Cowichans had not ensured international protection for their trademark. The copies have made strong inroads into the Japanese market. Now the Cowichans are fighting back by identifying their sweaters as the genuine article using tags signed by the knitters. The problem is: How do you fight a brand with the same name as yours?[2]

In this chapter, we will study the complex environment in which marketing decisions are made. We will see that an organization's level of success (or failure) is related not only to its marketing efforts, but also to the external environment in which it operates and its ability to adapt to environmental changes.

# Overview

The environment within which marketing decisions are made and enacted is depicted in Figure 2-1. **The marketing environment** consists of five parts:

1. Controllable factors.
2. Uncontrollable factors.
3. The organization's level of success or failure in reaching its objectives.
4. Feedback.
5. Adaptation.

*The* **marketing environment** *consists of* **controllable factors, uncontrollable factors, organizational performance, feedback,** *and* **adaptation**.

**Controllable factors** are those directed by an organization and its marketers. First, several broad, fundamental decisions are made by top management. Then, marketing managers make specific decisions based on these guidelines. In combination, these factors result in an overall strategy or offering (A in Figure 2-1). The major **uncontrollable factors** are beyond the control of an individual organization, but they have an impact on how well an organization does (B in Figure 2-1).

The interaction of controllable factors and uncontrollable factors determines an organization's **performance**, or level of success or failure, in reaching its goals. **Feedback** occurs when a firm makes an effort to monitor uncontrollable factors and assess its strengths and weaknesses. **Adaptation** refers to the changes in a marketing plan that an organization makes to comply with the uncontrollable environment. If a firm is unwilling to consider the entire environment in a systematic manner, it will likely lack direction and may have disappointing results.

When analyzing the environment, an organization should consider it from two perspectives: the macroenvironment and the microenvironment. The **macroenvironment** refers to the broad demographic, societal, economic, political, technological, and other forces that an organization faces. The **microenvironment** refers to the forces close to an organization that have a direct impact on its ability to serve customers, including distribution intermediaries, competitors, consumer markets, and the capabilities of the organization itself.[3]

Throughout this chapter, the various parts of Figure 2-1 are described and drawn together so the complex environment of marketing can be understood. In

*Both the* **macroenvironment** *and the* **microenvironment** *must be understood.*

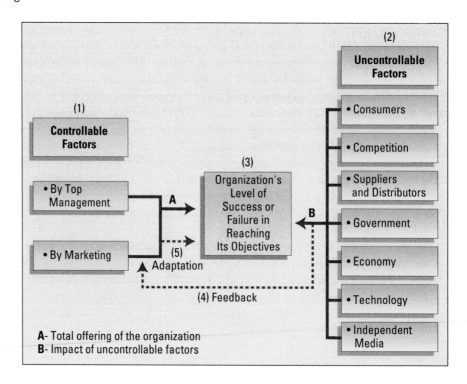

A- Total offering of the organization
B- Impact of uncontrollable factors

Chapter 16, the concept of strategic planning is presented. Such planning establishes a formal process for developing, implementing, and evaluating marketing programs in conjunction with the goals of top management.

## Controllable Factors

*The organization and its marketers can manage* **controllable factors**.

**Controllable factors** are internally directed by an organization and its marketers. Some of these factors are directed by top management; these are not controllable by marketers, who must develop plans to satisfy overall organizational goals. In situations involving small or medium-sized institutions, both broad policy and marketing decisions are often made by one person, usually the owner. Even in those cases, broad policies are typically set first and marketing plans must adjust to them. For example, a person could decide to open an office-supply store selling products to small businesses (broad policy) and stress convenient hours, a good selection of items, quantity discounts, and superior customer service (marketing plan).

### Factors Controlled by Top Management

Although top management is responsible for numerous decisions, five are of extreme importance to marketers: line of business, overall objectives, the role of marketing, the role of other business functions, and corporate culture. They have an impact on all aspects of marketing. Figure 2-2 shows the types of decisions in these areas.

*A firm's* **line of business**

*refers to its business category.*

The **line of business** refers to the general goods/service category, functions, geographic coverage, type of ownership, and specific business of a firm. The general goods/service category is a broad definition of the industry in which a firm seeks to be involved. It may be energy, transportation, computing, or any number of others. The functions of the business outline a firm's position in the marketing system—from supplier to manufacturer to wholesaler to retailer—and the tasks it seeks to do. A firm may want to be in more than one of these positions. Geographic coverage can be a neighbourhood, city, county, or province, or it could be defined as

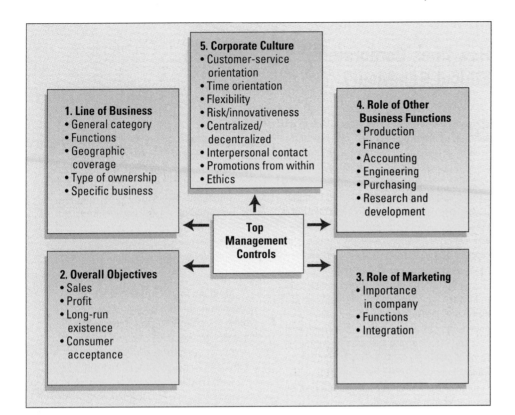

FIGURE 2-2

**Factors Controlled by Top Management**

regional, national, or international. The type of ownership can range from a sole proprietorship, partnership, or franchise to a multi-unit corporation. The specific business is a narrow definition of the firm, its functions, and its operations; for example, a particular dry cleaner might define itself as a local full-service dry cleaner specializing in outerwear.

Overall objectives are the broad, measurable goals set by top management. A firm's success or failure is often determined by comparing these objectives with actual performance. Usually, a combination of sales, profit, and other goals is stated by management for short-run (one year or less) and long-run (several years) periods. Most firms cite customer acceptance as a key goal with a strong effect on sales, profit, and long-run existence.

Top management determines the role of marketing by noting its importance, outlining its activities, and integrating it into a firm's overall operation. Marketing's importance is evident when marketing people have decision-making authority, the rank of the chief marketing officer is equal to that of other areas (usually vice-president), and proper resources are given. It is not considered important by a firm that gives marketing people advisory status, places marketing personnel in a subordinate position (like reporting to the production vice-president), equates marketing with sales, and withholds the funds needed for research, promotion, and other marketing tasks. The larger marketing's role, the greater the likelihood that a firm has an integrated marketing organization. The smaller its role, the greater the possibility that a firm undertakes marketing tasks on a project, crisis, or fragmented basis.

The roles of other business functions and their interrelationships with marketing need to be clearly defined to avoid overlaps, jealousy, and conflict. Production, finance, accounting, engineering, purchasing, and research and development departments each have different perspectives, orientations, and goals.

Top management strongly influences a firm's corporate culture: the shared values, norms, and practices communicated to and followed by those working for the firm. **Corporate culture** may be described in terms of:

*Corporate culture involves shared values, norms, and practices.*

# ETHICS AND TODAY'S MARKETER

## How Does Corporate Culture Influence Ethical Behaviour?

Surveys of recent M.B.A. graduates found that, in many cases, they feel pressure from their companies to engage in unethical and sometimes illegal behaviour. For example, a management trainee at a consumer products company was told to make up the data to support the introduction of a new product. In another situation, a person was asked to overlook a safety defect in a product and to ship items that did not meet published specifications.

According to ethics experts, these new managers are subjected to four commandments: (1) Performance is what really counts, so make your numbers. (2) Be loyal, and show us that you are a team player. (3) Don't break the law. (4) Don't overinvest in ethical behaviour. The first three of these commandments become troublesome when combined with the fourth.

Here is how the managers responded to a series of questions involving ethical and unethical behaviour:

- Only a few believe that "sleazy" behaviour will be a drag on their career.

- Less than a third believe their firms respect or encourage "whistle blowing."
- When asked what offences would result in punishment, they rarely mention unethical behaviour. Instead, such infractions as poor performance, failure at being a team player, stealing, or drinking on the job were noted.
- Many executives fear repercussions from doing what they see as the right thing.

Although many of the managers worked in firms with formal ethics programs, in general, these programs had little effect on their behaviour or attitudes.

As an ethical compliance manager for a bank, how would you help institute a corporate culture that values high moral principles?

Source: Based on material in Joseph L. Badaracco, Jr., and Allen P. Webb, "Business Ethics: A View From the Trenches," *California Management Review*, Vol. 37 (Winter 1995), pp. 8–28.

- *A customer-service orientation*—Is the commitment to customer service clearly transmitted to employees?
- *A time orientation*—Is a firm short- or long-run oriented?
- *The flexibility of the job environment*—Can employees deviate from rules? How formal are relations with subordinates? Is there a dress code?
- *The level of risk/innovation pursued*—Is risk-taking fostered?
- *The use of a centralized/decentralized management structure*—How much input into decisions do middle managers have?
- *The level of interpersonal contact*—Do employees freely communicate with one another?
- *The use of promotions from within*—Are internal personnel given preference as positions open?
- *Ethics applied*—Is the firm's conduct seen as honest and proper?

For example, IBM Canada is trying to change its corporate culture in order to get better in touch with its customers. For starters, the blue suits are out and dressing for the firm's customers is in. The elimination of IBM's dress code was an important symbol of change for both employees and customers alike. Employees are encouraged to speak their minds, and management communicates news to employees directly and provides a forum for comments and suggestions.[4]

The "ten commandments" listed below are what many experts recommend to firms that wish to foster a nurturing corporate culture:

**IBM CANADA**
www.can.ibm.com/

1. Seek consensus—don't bark orders.
2. Set broad visions, then give people the freedom needed to carry them out.
3. Make sure people have the resources and support they need to succeed.
4. Spend more time in the field with employees than in your office.
5. Spend some time with employees off the job, too.
6. Monitor progress on projects—don't micro manage.
7. Be quick to give ambitious employees more responsibilities.
8. Make sure all employees are continuously learning and growing.
9. Reward people for reaching personal, not just financial, goals.
10. Before criticizing someone for "failing," find out why he or she fell short of expectations.[5]

After top management sets company guidelines, the marketing area begins to develop the factors under its control.

## Factors Controlled by Marketing

The major factors controlled by marketing personnel are the selection of a target market, marketing objectives, the marketing organization, the marketing mix, and assessment of the marketing plan. These factors are shown in Figure 2-3.

One crucial marketing-related decision involves selecting a target market. The **target market** is the particular group(s) of customers a firm proposes to serve, or whose needs it proposes to satisfy, with a particular marketing program. When selecting a target market, a company usually engages in some form of **market segmentation**, which involves subdividing a market into clear subsets of customers that act in the same way or that have comparable needs.[6] A company can choose a large target market or concentrate on a small one, or try to appeal to both with separate marketing programs for each. Generally, these questions must be addressed before devising a marketing approach: Who are our customers? What kinds of goods and services do they want? How can we attract them to our company?

At marketing-oriented firms, the choice of a target market has an impact on all other marketing decisions. For example, a book publisher appealing to the high school science market would have a different marketing approach from one appeal-

*A* **target market** *is the customer group to which an organization appeals.*

**Market segmentation** *is often used in choosing a target market.*

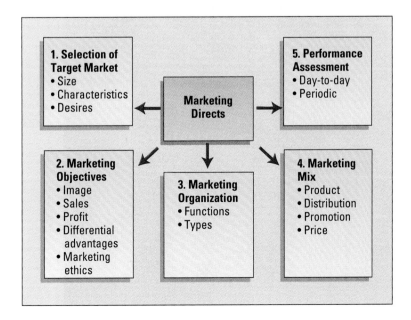

**FIGURE 2-3**

**Factors Controlled by Marketing**

ing to the adult fiction market. The first firm would seek an image as a prestigious, well-established publisher; specialize product offerings; make presentations to high school book-selection committees; sell in large quantities; offer durable books with many photos and line drawings that could be used for several years; and so on. The second firm would capitalize on well-known authors or publish books on hot topics to establish an image; have books on a variety of subjects; use newspaper ads and seek favourable reviews; distribute via bookstores; sell in small quantities (except if large bookstore chains are involved); de-emphasize durability, photos, and line drawings; and produce books as efficiently as possible.

**Differential advantages**

*consist of the firm's unique features that attract consumers.*

Marketing objectives are more customer-oriented than those set by top management. Marketers are quite interested in the image consumers hold of a firm and its products. From a marketing perspective, sales goals will reflect a desire to foster brand loyalty (repeat purchases), encourage growth (through new product introductions), and appeal to unsatisfied market segments. Profit goals may be related to long-term customer loyalty. Most importantly, marketers seek to create **differential advantages**—the unique features in a firm's marketing program that cause consumers to patronize that firm and not its competitors. Without differential advantages, a firm would have a "me-too" philosophy and offer the consumer no reasons to select its offerings over competitors'. Differential advantages can be based on a distinctive image, new products or features, product quality, customer service, low prices, availability, and other factors. For example, Snapple is known for its off-beat beverages, Harvey's restaurants make hamburgers a beautiful thing, and the Toronto Dominion Bank's VISA credit cards are "everywhere you want to be." See Figure 2-4.

**FIGURE 2-4**

**The Marketing of Differential Advantages**
*Courtesy General Motors Canada*

In any marketing situation, **ethical behaviour** based on honest and proper conduct ("what is right" and "what is wrong") should be followed. This applies both to situations involving company actions that affect the general public, employees, channel members (resellers), shareholders and/or competitors, and to situations involving company dealings with consumers. The preeminent organization for marketing in Canada and the United States is the American Marketing Association, which provides information and guidelines for managers who practise marketing. Figure 2-5 shows the code of ethics of the American Marketing Association.

A **marketing organization** is the structural arrangement that directs marketing functions. It outlines authority, responsibilities, and tasks to be accomplished. An organization may be functional, with jobs assigned in terms of buying, selling, promotion, distribution, and other tasks; product-oriented, with product managers for each product category and brand managers for each brand, in addition to functional categories; or market-oriented, with jobs assigned by geographic market and customer type, in addition to functional categories. A single firm may use a combination of these forms.

**Ethical behaviour** *involves honest and proper conduct.*

**AMERICAN MARKETING ASSOCIATION**
www.ama.org/

*A* **marketing organization** *may be functional, product-oriented, or market-oriented.*

---

### CODE OF ETHICS

Members of the American Marketing Association (AMA) are committed to ethical professional conduct. They have joined together in subscribing to this Code of Ethics embracing the following topics:

#### Responsibilities of the Marketer

Marketers must accept responsibility for the consequence of their activities and make every effort to ensure that their decisions, recommendations, and actions function to identify, serve, and satisfy all relevant publics: customers, organizations and society.

Marketers' professional conduct must be guided by:

1. The basic rule of professional ethics: not knowingly to do harm;
2. The adherence to all applicable laws and regulations;
3. The accurate representation of their education, training and experience; and
4. The active support, practice and promotion of this Code of Ethics.

#### Honesty and Fairness

Marketers shall uphold and advance the integrity, honor, and dignity of the marketing profession by:

1. Being honest in serving customers, clients, employees, suppliers, distributors and the public;
2. Not knowingly participating in conflict of interest without prior notice to all parties involved; and
3. Establishing equitable fee schedules including the payment or receipt of usual, customary and/or legal compensation or marketing exchanges.

#### Rights and Duties of Parties in the Marketing Exchange Process

Participants in the marketing exchange process should be able to expect that:

1. Products and services offered are safe and fit for their intended uses;
2. Communications about offered products and services are not deceptive;
3. All parties intend to discharge their obligations, financial and otherwise, in good faith; and
4. Appropriate internal methods exist for equitable adjustment and/or redress of grievances concerning purchases.

It is understood that the above would include, but is not limited to, the following responsiblities of the marketer:

#### In the area of product development and management,

• disclosure of all substantial risks associated with product or service usage;
• identification of any product component substitution that might materially change the product or impact on the buyer's purchase decision;
• identification of extra-cost added features.

#### In the area of promotions,

• avoidance of false and misleading advertising;
• rejection of high pressure manipulation;
• avoidance of sales promotions that use deception or manipulation.

#### In the area of distribution,

• not manipulating the availability of a product for purpose of exploitation;
• not using coercion in the marketing channel;

• not exerting undue influence over the reseller's choice to handle the product.

#### In the area of pricing,

• not engaging in price fixing;
• not practicing predatory pricing;
• disclosing the full price associated with any purchase.

#### In the area of marketing research,

• prohibiting selling or fund raising under the guise of conducting research;
• maintaining research integrity by avoiding misrepresentation and omission of pertinent research data;
• treating outside clients and suppliers fairly.

#### Organizational Relationships

Marketers should be aware of how their behavior may influence or impact on the behavior of others in organizational relationships. They should not demand, encourage or apply coercion to obtain unethical behavior in their relationships with others, such as employees, suppliers or customers:

1. Apply confidentiality and anonymity in professional relationships with regard to privileged information;
2. Meet their obligations and responsibilities in contracts and mutual agreements in a timely manner;
3. Avoid taking the work of others, in whole, or in part, and represent this work as their own or directly benefit from it without compensation or consent of the originator or owner;
4. Avoid manipulation to take advantage of situations to maximize personal welfare in a way that unfairly deprives or damages the organization of others.

Any AMA members found to be in violation of any provision of this Code of Ethics may have his or her Association membership suspended or revoked.

**FIGURE 2-5**

**The American Marketing Association's Code of Ethics**
*Reprinted by permission.*

*The **marketing mix** consists of four elements: product, distribution, promotion, and price.*

A **marketing mix** is the specific combination of marketing elements used to achieve objectives and satisfy the target market. Finding a satisfactory marketing mix requires that managers make decisions regarding four major variables:

- *Product decisions*—What goods, services, organizations, people, places, and/or ideas to market, the number of items to sell and their quality, the degree of innovativeness pursued, packaging, product features, warranties, when to drop existing offerings, and so on.
- *Distribution decisions*—Whether to sell via intermediaries or directly to consumers, how many outlets to sell through, how to interact with other channel members, what terms to negotiate, the functions to assign to others, supplier choice, and so on.
- *Promotion decisions*—The most appropriate combination of promotional tools (ads, public relations, personal selling, sales promotions, etc.), whether to share promotions with others, the image to pursue, the level of personal service, media choice, message content, promotion timing, and so on.
- *Price decisions*—Overall price levels, the range of prices, the relation between price and quality, the emphasis on price, how to react to competitors, when to offer discounts, how prices are computed, what billing terms to use, and so on.

When devising a marketing mix, all of these questions should be considered:

- Is the target market precisely defined?
- Does the total marketing program, as well as each element of the mix, meet the target market's needs?
- Are marketing-mix elements consistent with one another?
- Do the elements add up to form a harmonious, integrated whole?
- Is each marketing-mix element being put to its best use?
- Does the marketing mix build on the firm's cultural and tangible strengths? Does the marketing mix imply a way to correct any weaknesses?
- Does the marketing mix create a distinctive personality in the competitive marketplace?
- Is the company protected from the most obvious competitive threats?[7]

**OLYMPUS**
www.olympus.com/

Olympus, a leading maker of cameras and other products, is an example of a firm applying the marketing-mix concept well. It has distinct marketing mixes for different target markets, such as beginners, serious amateurs, and professional photographers. For beginners, it offers very simple cameras with automatic focus and a built-in flash. The cameras are sold in all types of stores, such as discount and department stores. Ads appear on TV and in general magazines. The cameras retail for well under $100. For serious amateur photographers, Olympus has more advanced cameras with superior features and many attachments. The cameras are sold in camera stores and finer department stores. Ads appear in specialty magazines. The cameras sell for several hundred dollars. For professional photographers, Olympus has even more advanced cameras with top-of-the-line features and attachments. The cameras are quite expensive and are sold through select camera stores, with ads appearing in trade magazines. In sum, Olympus markets the right products in the right stores, promotes them in the right media, and has the right prices for its various target markets. See Figure 2-6.

*Performance assessment involves monitoring and evaluating marketing activities.*

The last factor directed by marketers is extremely important: Performance assessment is the monitoring and evaluation of overall and specific marketing effectiveness. Evaluations need to be done regularly, with both the external environment and internal company data being reviewed. In-depth analysis of performance should be completed at least once or twice each year. Strategy revisions need to be enacted when the external environment changes or the company encounters difficulties.

**FIGURE 2-6**

**Focused Marketing Mixes**

The Olympus Stylus camera is a simple device for beginners, while the Olympus IS-3 is a sophisticated device for advanced camera buffs. A distinct marketing mix is used with each camera.

*Reprinted by permission.*

# Uncontrollable Factors

**Uncontrollable factor**s are the external elements affecting an organization's performance that cannot be fully directed by that organization and its marketers. A marketing plan, no matter how well conceived, may fail if uncontrollable factors have too adverse an impact. Thus, the external environment must be regularly observed and its effects considered in any marketing plan. Contingency plans relating to uncontrollable variables should also be a key part of a marketing plan. Uncontrollable factors that especially bear studying are government, consumers, competition, suppliers and distributors, the economy, technology, and independent media. These factors are shown in Figure 2-7.

**Uncontrollable factors**
*influence an organization and its marketers but are not fully directed by them.*

## Government

Governmental bodies have a great impact on marketing practices by placing (or removing) restrictions on specified activities. In any country, government rulings can be on a national, provincial/state, and/or local level.

In Canada there are myriad federal legislative acts affecting the practice of business and marketing, as shown in Table 2-1.

A key piece of legislation is the Competition Act, Bill C-2, which was passed in 1986. It is administered by the Director of Investigation and Research and the direc-

*Canadian federal legislation involves international and interprovincial commerce. Each province and municipality has its own regulations as well.*

**FIGURE 2-7**

**Uncontrollable Factors**

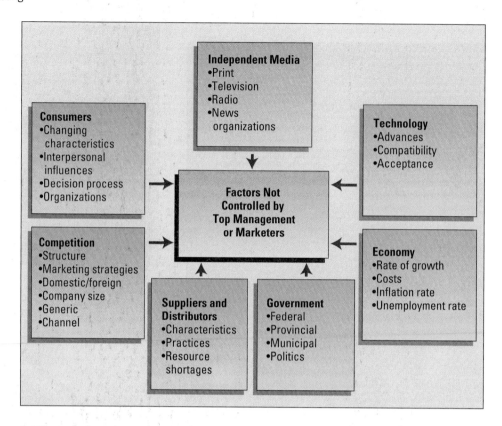

## TABLE 2-1

## Key Canadian Federal Government Legislation Affecting Marketers

Access to Information Act

Bankruptcy Act

Boards of Trade Act

Broadcasting Act

Bulk Sales Act

Canada Agricultural Products Standards Act

Canada Business Corporations Act

Canada Cooperative Association Act

Canada Corporations Act

Canada Dairy Products Act

Canadian Human Rights Act

Competition Act (Bill C–2)

Consumer Packaging and Labelling Act

Copyright Act

Department of Consumer and Corporate
    Affairs Act

Electricity Inspection Act

Fish Inspection Act

Food and Drugs Act

Gas Inspection Act

Gasoline Handling Act

Government Corporations Operations Act

Hazardous Products Act

Income Tax Act

Industrial Design Act

Lobbyists Registration Act

Maple Products Industry Act

Official Languages Act

Patent Act

Pension Fund Societies Act

Precious Metals Marking Act

Public Servants Invention Act

Shipping Conferences Exemption Act

Tax Rebate Discounting Act

Textile Labelling Act

Timber Marking Act

Trade Marks Act

Weights and Measures Act

Winding-Up Act

tor's staff at the Competition Bureau, which is part of Industry Canada. Industry Canada is responsible for administering the federal legislation passed specifically for the purpose of regulating business. Currently, deceptive marketing practices covered in the Competition Act include: misleading advertising, promotional contests, bait-and-switch selling, multi-level marketing, pyramid selling plans, and telemarketing.

The purpose of the act is to ensure healthy competition in the Canadian marketplace by promoting the provision of information about goods and services to both consumers and businesses. Most complaints are made by consumers and handled by the marketing practices branch of the Competition Bureau, but complaints from competitors are made as well and lead to actions more frequently than consumer complaints. Competitor complaints often involve detailed information and if not evaluated, could lead to widespread adoption of the marketing practice in question. Each complaint is considered by an assessment officer and then one of three options is undertaken: the file is closed if the complaint is deemed to not fall under the act or does not fall within the priorities of the marketing practices branch; the subject may be asked to provide more information about the complaint in hopes that this will stop the marketing practice; or an inquiry into the case may be undertaken.

When an inquiry is undertaken, the company whose marketing practice is called into question is contacted for an explanation. The company is able to make its case voluntarily and most companies respond by providing details. The process is designed to create a climate of cooperation and to avoid involving the courts. If it appears that an offence has been committed, then a formal inquiry may be undertaken. The cases that are pursued usually display three characteristics: there is considerable harm done in the marketplace; the case has value in terms of jurisprudence; or the resolution of the case may result in significant deterrence.[8]

In June 1995 the Competition Bureau put forward a discussion paper on issues dealing with competition policy, and this has resulted in the following amendments to the Competition Act. These amendments were designed to deal with issues such as: notifiable merger transactions; the protection of confidential information; mutual assistance with foreign competition law agencies; misleading advertising and deceptive marketing practices; "regular price" claims, price discrimination, and promotional allowances; prohibition orders; deceptive telemarketing solicitations; and finally, access to the Competition Tribunal.

This discussion paper generated some immediate action because Canada and the United States signed a Competition Policy agreement in August 1995 so that the two countries could cooperate to enforce laws on deceptive marketing practices and competition. The Competition Bureau in Canada will cooperate with the U.S. Federal Trade Commission and the Antitrust division of the U.S. Department of Justice. The two countries will notify one another about investigations that involve both jurisdictions and about enforcement proceedings that might affect the interests of the other nation. The agreement also calls for sharing of investigative information and evidence and cooperation in locating witnesses.[9]

In addition to federal regulation and agencies, each province and municipal government in Canada has its own legal environment. Provincial and municipal laws may regulate where a firm is allowed to locate, the business hours, the types of items sold, if prices must be marked on every item sold, how goods must be labelled or dated, and so on. Provincial and municipal governments may also provide incentives, such as small business assistance, for firms to operate there. Examples of key provincial legislation include: the Franchises Act in Alberta, the Environmental Protection Act in Ontario, the Licensing Act in Prince Edward Island, and the Consumer Protection Act in Quebec. The latter is of particular concern for marketers because it contains a ban on all child-directed advertising. As such, marketers of products designed for children are faced with a very difficult task as they are not allowed to advertise directly to the users of their products.

The political environment often affects legislation. Should certain goods and services be prohibited from advertising on TV? Should mail-order sales to out-of-province customers be taxed? Should provincial governments become more active in handling consumer complaints? Marketing issues such as these are typically discussed via the political process before laws are enacted (or not enacted).

Sometimes marketers will act to change a law, and sometimes they won't act even though a law has been changed. For example, on November 24, 1997 Unilever deliberately acted to break Quebec's margarine colouring law by shipping tubs of butter-coloured Country Crock brand margarine into the Consomat grocery store in Alma, Quebec. The law makes it illegal to colour margarine in Quebec, the only jurisdiction on the planet where this is the case. Unilever announced its plans to the government with the express intent to go to court to have this law struck down. The government seized the margarine, but did not lay charges right away. Therefore, Unilever filed a motion on February 5, 1998 to have the colour margarine ban declared unconstitutional, and to have the seizure revoked on the basis that it violated the NAFTA agreement, the Canadian Charter of Rights and Freedoms, and an agreement by the First Ministers of Canada that interprovincial trade barriers be removed.

An example of *not* reacting to a change in a law is the response of Canadian distillers when in 1995 a federal court struck down the ban on television liquor advertising. Very few liquor ads have since been shown on TV. Distillers cite cost, familiarity with promotional approaches that don't involve television, and finally social responsibility as the reasons why they haven't taken advantage of the opportunity.[10]

Both firms and consumer groups may market their positions on such issues to government officials. A strength of Canada's political system is its continuity, which lets organizations and individuals develop strategies for long periods of time.

One of the biggest legal and political challenges facing Canada and other countries is how to privatize organizations that were formerly run by the government. For example, many state-run economies in Eastern Europe had to develop systems to privatize formerly state-run businesses. One method used by Poland's Ministry of Privatization is the Capital Privatization Method. A state-run enterprise is transformed into a joint stock company, whose shares are then sold to potential investors, to employees through a leveraged buy-out, or through a public offering. As of 1995 the Polish government had privatized 138 businesses using this approach. Multinational firms that had purchased formerly government-run enterprises have included PepsiCo (purchased Wedel), Unilever (purchased Pollena Bydgoszcz) and Harnishfeger Industries (purchased Fampa). Barriers to privatization include:

> The lack of a free-market culture; confusion over who owns the enterprises and what they're worth; poor physical infrastructure, which discourages foreign investment; the absence of a legal framework governing the conduct of business; and shortage of investment capital. After privatization, consequences can include higher prices for basic goods and services, large-scale layoffs, loss of national assets to foreign buyers, and the possible closure of vital industries.[10]

> In Canada, privatization of electrical utilities is a key issue for the beginning of the third millennium. Its logic is well established, but the means by which to privatize such large public utilities as Ontario and Quebec Hydro is still an open question. Although a number of the obstacles faced by businesses in state-run economies do not exist in Canada, one key problem for electrical utilities in mixed economies is known as "stranded investment." In Ontario and Quebec, large publicly funded initiatives to operate nuclear power facilities and to generate and transmit hydroelectric power have entailed great investment. The existing debt obligations, as well as the large operating expenses, could not be recovered by a private utility in an openly competitive environment, thus the term "stranded investment." Figuring out ways to overcome this barrier to privatization will be a serious consideration over the next decade.[11]

## Consumers

Although a firm has control over its selection of a target market, it cannot control the changing characteristics of its final or organizational consumers. A firm can react to, but not control, consumer trends related to age, income, marital status, occupation, race, education, place and type of residence, and the size of organizational customers. For example, health insurers who provide drug plans, out-of-province medical benefits, eyeglasses, and other special services must deal with the fact that many of their largest business customers are downsizing; thus, there are fewer employees to be insured there.

Interpersonal influences on consumer behaviour need to be understood. People's purchases are affected by the corporate culture at their jobs as purchasing agents; their family, friends, and other social contacts; and the customs and taboos shaping culture and society. For instance, in some parts of Canada, liquor sales are more regulated (as to outlets, prices, other goods that can be sold, and days open) than in other parts.

People act differently in buying various types of goods and services. In the case of company cars, a purchasing agent carefully searches for information on a number of models, ranks several alternatives, selects a favourite, negotiates terms, and finally completes the purchase. On the other hand, with an inexpensive meal, a person looks at his or her watch, sees it is lunch time, and goes to a nearby fast-food outlet. Because of these differences, the consumer decision process—the steps people go through when buying products—affects the way that products are marketed.

**Consumerism** encompasses "the wide range of activities of government, business, and independent organizations that are designed to protect people from practices that infringe upon their rights as consumers."[12]

Consumerism as practised in Canada is rooted to the consumerism movement in the United States, where it has evolved through four distinct eras, and is now in a fifth. The first era was in the 1900s and focused on the need for a banking system, product purity, postal rates, antitrust, and protection against product shortages. Emphasis was on business protection against unfair practices. The second era lasted from the 1930s to the 1950s. This era's issues were product safety, bank failures, labelling, misrepresentation, stock manipulation, deceptive ads, credit, and consumer refunds. Consumer groups, such as Consumers Union and Consumers' Research, grew, as did the amount of legislation related to consumer issues. Issues were initiated but seldom resolved.

The third era began in the early 1960s and lasted to 1980. Ushering in this era was President Kennedy's **consumer bill of rights**: granting consumers the right to information, to safety, to choice in product selection, and to be heard (see Figure 2-8). These rights apply to people in any nation or economic system.

Following the American example, Canadian consumerism really took wing in this era. In fact, Canada made history when the federal government established Consumer and Corporate Affairs Canada in 1968, thereby becoming the first nation to establish a federal government agency to oversee consumer rights. Canadian consumerism has a strong expression in the electronic media from public affairs shows such as the *Fifth Estate* and *Market Place*. The Consumers' Association of Canada gained a strong following in the 1970s, but this following waned as consumerism moved into its fourth era.

During the 1980s, consumerism entered a mature fourth era, which emphasized business deregulation and self-regulation. Nationally, no major consumer laws were enacted and budgets of federal and provincial agencies concerned with consumer issues were cut. Provincial and local governments remained active, but in general, the federal government believed that most firms took consumer issues into account when devising and applying their marketing plans. Indeed, fewer firms did ignore consumer input or publicly confront consumer groups. Cooperation between business and

*Organizations need to understand consumer trends, interpersonal influences, the decision process, and consumer groups.*

**Consumerism** *protects consumers from practices that infringe upon their rights.*

*U.S. President Kennedy declared a* **consumer bill of rights:** *to information, to safety, to choice, and to be heard.*

**FIGURE 2-8**

**Consumers' Basic Rights**

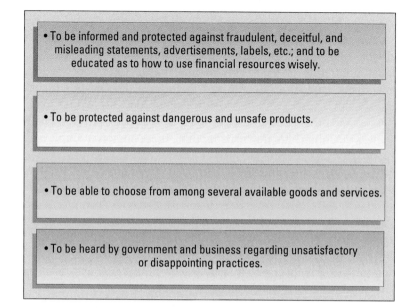

• To be informed and protected against fraudulent, deceitful, and misleading statements, advertisements, labels, etc.; and to be educated as to how to use financial resources wisely.

• To be protected against dangerous and unsafe products.

• To be able to choose from among several available goods and services.

• To be heard by government and business regarding unsatisfactory or disappointing practices.

consumers was better, and confrontations were less likely. It was in this mature phase that what in the 1970s would have been unthinkable, happened in Canada. The Consumers' Association of Canada went broke from a lack of public support and had to be bailed out with federal government money in 1988.

In the 1990s the federal government was still involved with consumer issues through Industry Canada, whose goal was to balance consumer and business rights. Consumer protection from the government mostly derives from the Competition Act, although the enforcement practices in Canada changed in the 1990s. Instead of criminal prosecution the Competition Bureau has adopted a policy of "alternative case resolution," whereby misinformation given to consumers can be offset in one of two ways: A firm can be asked to comply with an "undertaking" or be subject to a "consent prohibition order."

An undertaking is essentially a voluntary action on the part of a business. It involves stopping the business practice in question and making sure the practice does not happen again. The process is usually completed with corrective advertising and sometimes restitution to consumers. A consent prohibition order is a much stronger response to firms that have misrepresented their products or themselves. In this circumstance a written order may be given.

In all cases where firms are involved with alternative case resolution methods, admissions of guilt to offences under the Competition Act are not assumed. Any contraventions of the Competition Act can be prosecuted by Canada's attorney general and cases that are referred for prosecution cannot be resolved under an alternative case resolution approach. Unfair business tactics, product safety, and health issues are the areas of greatest concern.

As the new millennium begins Industry Canada is looking at ways to develop and fund a Canadian Consumer Foundation to protect the rights of consumers. One thought is to have an organization set up and funded in a manner similar to those of the United Way. Yet this may not be necessary, given that Industry Canada's Office of Consumer Affairs lists nearly forty different Consumer Rights Organizations, including: the Association de consommateurs du Québec Inc., Automobile Protection Association, Canadian Consumer Education and Information Forum, Consumers' Association of Canada, Consumers Council of Canada, and the Public Interest Advocacy Centre. These consumer-rights groups speak out on behalf of consumers at public hearings, at shareholder meetings, and before the media. To avoid negative consequences brought on by active consumer groups, a firm must communicate with customers on relevant issues

# INTERNATIONAL MARKETING IN ACTION

## Soft Drinks Explode in India

In 1991 India liberalized its economy and allowed direct foreign investment. This was a key move to help a stagnant economy and bring the country into the global economic environment. Since that time, foreign consumer goods companies have had tremendous sales growth in India. The soft drink industry in particular has experienced an explosion—and we're not talking about what happens when a recently shaken pop can is opened! In the late 1980s about 90 million cases of soft drinks were consumed; in the late 1990s the level reached 150 million cases; and in the new millennium sales are expected to hit the 200 million range.

Not surprisingly, the most popular brands of soft drinks are Pepsi-Cola and Coca-Cola. This is a far cry from the 1977–93 period, when Coca-Cola was banned as an unwanted foreign entity. Pepsi is the market leader but only slightly, having been given permission to market in India in 1991, two years ahead of Coke. The head start came with the provision that the firm brand its product as Pepsi Lehar so that it wouldn't be a completely foreign brand. (This provision has since been removed.) Coca-Cola has wasted little time trying to catch up to Pepsi, and the comparative advertising efforts of both have expressed themselves in India as they have in North America. Their legendary battle for market supremacy in North America led to drastic increases in soft drink consumption here, and this trend is repeating itself in India.

The promotional efforts have been undertaken so well that Indian consumers don't perceive Coke and Pepsi as "alien" brands at all. With such a good reception, the Coca-Cola Company and PepsiCo have made major investments in bottling and distribution facilities, and have undertaken large expenditures in advertising their products and providing sponsorships.

But despite their success to date and prospects for continued soft drink growth in India, Coke and Pepsi are not completely out of the woods. The Indian economy has experienced some instability recently and government policy makers are still unsure about the value and impact of foreign investment. Some policy makers would like to see investment restricted to high technology and important value-added industries, as opposed to consumer packaged-goods firms. The Indian government has also experienced considerable political instability, which means that foreign firms—even ones like PepsiCo and Coca-Cola that have successful track records and have adapted well to the culture—may one day become "unwanted foreign entities."

What kinds of things can Coca-Cola and PepsiCo do to minimize or manage the threat of becoming an "unwanted foreign entity"?

Source: Based on Dilip Subramanian, "India's Reforms Start to See Payoff," *Marketing Magazine* (March 30, 1998), p. 5.

---

(such as a product recall), anticipate problems (such as delays in filling orders), respond to complaints (such as unsatisfactory customer service), and maintain good community relations (such as sponsoring neighbourhood projects).[13]

## Competition

The competitive environment often affects a company's marketing efforts and its success in reaching a target market. Thus, firms need to assess the following characteristics of their competitive environment:

- The industry structure.
- Their competitors' marketing strategies.
- The nationality of their competitors (domestic or foreign).
- The size of their competitors.
- Generic competition.
- Channel competition.

**PEPSICO.**
www.pepsiworld.com/index2.html

**COCA COLA**
www.coke.com/home.html

*Monopoly, oligopoly,*

*monopolistic competition,*

*and* **pure competition** *are*

*the main types of competitive*

*structure.*

**BANK OF MONTREAL**
www.bmo.com/

**MOLSON**
www.molson.com/

**LABATT**
www.labatt.com/

*Foreign competition is*

*intensifying.*

A company may operate under one of four possible competitive structures: monopoly, oligopoly, monopolistic competition, or pure competition. With a **monopoly**, just one firm sells a given good or service and has a lot of control over its marketing plan. This occurs in Canada when a firm has a patent (exclusive rights to sell a product it invented for a fixed number of years, such as new pharmaceutical products), is a public utility (such as local phone or natural gas companies), or is a Crown corporation (such as Canada Post). In an **oligopoly**, a few firms—usually large ones—account for most industry sales and tend to engage in nonprice competition. For example, General Motors, Ford, Chrysler, Honda, and Toyota account for about 95 per cent of Canadian auto sales. In **monopolistic competition**, there are several firms in an industry, each trying to offer a unique marketing mix—based on price or nonprice factors. This is the most common Canadian industry structure, followed by oligopoly. Service stations, beauty salons, stores, garment makers, computer-clone makers, and furniture makers are some firms facing monopolistic competition. In **pure competition**, many firms sell virtually identical goods or services and they are unable to create differential advantages. This rarely occurs in Canada. It is most common for selected food items and commodities (and happens if numerous small firms compete with each other).

After analyzing its industry's competitive structure, a firm needs to study the strategies of competitors. Specifically, it should look at their target markets and marketing mixes, their images, their differential advantages, which markets are saturated and which are unfulfilled, and the extent to which consumers are content with the service and quality provided by competitors.

Both domestic and foreign competition need to be examined. For instance, in Canada, Investors Group competes with the Bank of Montreal, Canada Trust, Canada Life Insurance, and others—besides traditional brokerage firms—for financial-services business. Many Canadian, American, and West European industries are mature; the amount of domestic competition is stable. In some industries, competition is rising due to the popularity of innovations like notebook PCs. In others, domestic competition is intensifying as a result of government deregulation. For instance, witness all the companies offering long-distance telephone services in Canada.[14]

Foreign competitors have played a major role in many industries in North America in the past and will likely continue to do so in the third millennium. For example, in the early 1980s the Canadian brewing industry was owned and dominated by Molson, Labatt, and Carling-O'Keefe, which controlled over 90 per cent of the market. Molson acquired Carling-O'Keefe and was in turn acquired by Foster's of Australia, and then Miller Brewing Company of the U.S. had a controlling interest. In 1995 Labatt was purchased by the Belgian firm Interbrew S.A. So for a time in the late 1990s the Canadian brewing industry was dominated by foreign firms, which controlled 94 per cent of the market. But in 1998 Molson bought out both Foster's and Miller Brewing Company to make the company 100 per cent Canadian-owned. (Prior to this it was difficult for Molson to market its Canadian brand of beer when the firm wasn't really "Canadian.") Still, foreign-based firms have performed well at capturing large market shares in North American industries—50 per cent for steel, 65 per cent for clothing, 75 per cent for shoes, and up to 98 per cent for some consumer electronics.

At the same time, competition in foreign markets is intensifying for Canadian-based firms as rivals stress innovations, cost cutting, good distribution and promotion, and other factors. Many of the industries in which Canadian firms have international dominance are related to the harsh winter climate. For example, Canadian firms excel in the areas of snowmobiles, hockey equipment, and winter boot manufacturing. Of course, the energy and mining industries of Canada are very strong competitors too.

For many industries, there has been a trend toward larger firms because of mergers and acquisitions, as well as company sales growth. Over the last decade, mergers and acquisitions have involved telecommunications firms (AT&T acquiring Unitel, a long distance phone company), food firms (Nestlé acquiring Perrier), pharmaceuticals firms (Bristol-Myers merging with Squibb), transportation firms (Canadian Airlines joining with American Airlines), consumer-products firms (Sony buying CBS Records), retailers (Wal-Mart acquiring Woolco, Zellers acquiring K-Mart Canada), and numerous others. Canadian sales have been growing at a rate of over 50 per cent a year for the last three years for such firms as Potash Corp of Saskatchewan, Philip Environmental, St. Laurent Paperboard, and Westcoast Energy Inc.—each of which were among some of the fastest growing firms in Canada in the late 1990s, with minimum sales of over $500 million.[15]

For small firms, major differential advantages include personal service, a focus on under-served market segments, an entrepreneurial drive, and flexibility; cooperative ventures and franchising allow such firms to buy in quantity and operate more efficiently. Among large firms, widespread distribution, economies of scale, well-known brands, mass-media ads, and low to moderate prices are commonly used competitive tactics.

Every organization should define its competition generically, meaning as broadly as possible. Direct competitors are similar to the firm with regard to their line of business and marketing approach. Indirect competitors are different from the firm, but still compete with it for customers. Both types of competitors should be studied and accounted for in a firm's marketing plan. For instance, a movie theatre not only competes with other theatres (direct competitors), but with video stores, TV and radio shows, video games, sporting events, live music concerts, plays, amusement parks, bookstores, restaurants, and schools (indirect competitors). A theatre owner might ask, "What can I do to compete with this variety of entertainment and recreation forms in terms of movie selection, prices, hours, customer service, refreshments, and parking?"

*Competition should be defined generically—as widely as possible.*

A company also needs to study the competition from its channel members (resellers). Each party in the distribution process has different goals and would like to maximize its control over the marketing mix. Some wholesalers and retailers carry their own brands besides those of manufacturers.

## Suppliers and Distributors

Many firms rely on their suppliers and distributors (wholesalers and retailers) to properly run their businesses. Without their ongoing support, it would be difficult, if not impossible, for a company to succeed.

*Suppliers and distributors can have a dramatic impact on an organization.*

Suppliers provide the goods and services that firms need to operate, as well as those that they resell to their own customers. In general, a firm is most vulnerable when there are relatively few suppliers; specific goods and services are needed to run a business or satisfy customer demand; competitors would gain if the firm had a falling out with a supplier; suppliers are better attuned to the desires of the marketplace; suppliers informally take care of maintenance and repair services; the turnaround time to switch suppliers is lengthy; or suppliers have exclusive access to scarce resources.

Firms that cannot market their products directly to consumers need distributors (wholesalers or retailers). In general, a firm is most vulnerable when there are relatively few distributors in an area; the distributors carry many brands; shelf space is tight; the firm is unknown in the marketplace; particular distributors account for a large portion of the firm's revenues; distributors help finance the firm; distributors are better attuned to the marketplace; or other competitors are waiting in the wings to stock the distributors.

Among the supplier/distributor practices that a firm should regularly study are: delivery time or requests, product availability, prices, flexibility in handling special requests, marketing support, consistency of treatment, returns policies, and other services. Unsatisfactory performance by a supplier or distributor in one or more of these areas could have a lasting impact on the firm's ability to enact its marketing plans.

Regardless of suppliers' good intentions, a firm's ability to carry out its plans can be affected by the scarcity of particular resources. Over the past twenty-five years, sporadic shortages and volatile price changes have occurred for a variety of basic commodities, such as home heating oil, other petroleum-based products, plastics, synthetic fibres, aluminum, chrome, silver, tungsten, nickel, steel, glass, grain, fertilizer, cotton, and wool. And despite efforts at conservation, some raw materials, processed materials, and component parts may remain or become scarce over the next decade.[16]

Resource shortages and/or rapid cost increases require one of three actions. First, substitute materials could be used in constructing products, requiring intensified research and product testing. Second, prices could be raised for products that cannot incorporate substitute materials. Third, firms could abandon products where resources are unavailable and demarket others where demand is greater than it is able to satisfy.

## The Economy

The rate of growth in a nation's or region's economy can have a big impact on a firm's marketing efforts. A high growth rate means the economy is strong and the marketing potential large. Quite important to marketers are consumer perceptions—both in the business and final consumer sectors—regarding the economy. For instance, if people believe the economy will be good, they may spend more; if they believe the economy will be poor, they may cut back. In uncertain times, many organizational consumers are interested in preserving their flexibility.

*Economic growth is measured by the* **Gross Domestic Product.**

A country's economic growth is reflected by changes in its **Gross Domestic Product (GDP)**, which is the total annual value of goods and services produced in a country less net foreign investment. These are the 1996 GDPs (in $U.S. billions) and their percentages in real growth for eight selected OECD countries and then nine big emerging nations in order of GDP size: OECD Countries—United States, $7576, 2.4%; Japan, $2991, 3.7%; Germany, $1670, 1.4%; France, $1267, 1.5%; Italy, $1195, 0.7%; United Kingdom, $1174, 2.1%; Canada, $623, 1.5%; and the Netherlands, $325, 2.7%; Big Emerging Markets—China, $3878, 9.7%; India, $1432, 6.5%; Brazil, $987, 2.9%; Mexico, $694, 5.1%; Turkey, $361, 7.2%; Argentina, $316, 4.4%; Taiwan, $283, 5.7%; Poland, $258, 6.0%; and South Africa, $257, 3.1%.[17] In recent years, the yearly growth in most of the OECD nations has been 3 per cent or less; and when certain industries slow down, such as autos and housing, repercussions are felt in other areas, such as insurance and home furnishings. Canada is expected to have real GDP growth averaging between 2 to 4 per cent annually during the first part of the new millennium.

Several business costs—like raw materials, unionized labour wages, taxes, interest rates, and office (factory) rental—are generally beyond any firm's control. If costs rise by a large amount, marketing flexibility may be limited because a firm often cannot pass along all of the increase; it might have to cut back on marketing activities or accept lower profit margins. If costs are stable, marketers are better able to differentiate products and expand sales because their companies are more apt to invest in marketing activities.

*Real income describes earnings adjusted for inflation. Both inflation and unemployment affect purchases.*

From a marketing perspective, what happens to a consumer's real income is critical. While actual income is the amount earned by a consumer (or his/her family or household) in a given year, **real income** is the amount earned in a year adjusted by the rate of inflation. For example, if a person's actual income goes up by 4 per cent in a year (from $40 000 to $41 600) and the rate of inflation (which measures price changes for the same goods and services over time) is 4 per cent for the year, real income remains constant [($41 600) − ($41 600/1.04) = $40 000]. If actual income increases exceed the inflation rate, real income rises and people can buy more goods and services. If actual income increases are less than the inflation rate, real income falls and people must buy fewer goods and services.

A high rate of unemployment can adversely affect many firms because people who are unemployed are likely to cut back on nonessentials wherever possible. Low unemployment often means substantial sales of large-ticket items, as consumers are better off, more optimistic, and more apt to spend earnings.

## Technology

**Technology** refers to the development and use of machinery, products, and processes. Individual firms, especially smaller ones with limited capital, must usually adapt to technological advances (rather than control them).

Many firms depend on others to develop and perfect new technology, such as computer microchips; only then can they use the new technology in their products, such as automated gas pumps at service stations, talking toys, or electronic sensors in smoke detectors for office buildings. The inventor of new technology often secures patent protection, which excludes competitors from using that technology (unless the inventor licenses rights for a fee).

**Technology** *includes machinery, products, and processes.*

## TECHNOLOGY AND MARKETING

## Should Canadian Marketers Tap the Internet?

In 1995 the Internet became a mainstream medium for marketers. Estimates indicate that there are 4.5 million Canadians with Internet access, and that number is growing daily. Globally, the rate of adoption of Internet usage is growing at 10 to 15 per cent a month!

The attraction of the Internet for both buyers and sellers is its interactive nature. Unlike the traditional media of newsprint, radio, television, magazines and outdoor advertising, which are essentially one-way communications, the Internet allows two-way communication between marketer and customer. Furthermore, the "market" access of the Internet is equal (at least so far) for all marketers. A small firm can compete with a large firm by having a good Web site, a 1-800 number (for transaction security) and a vendor's account with VISA or Mastercard. The Web site is like a store front, so its design and presentation are critical. In this regard large firms may assert an advantage by paying multimedia designers as much as $100 000 for a top-notch site. Still, do-it-your-selfers can save money and satisfy their creative fantasies by designing their own pages using packaged software. It is also pleasing to know that such software will be getting better and cheaper in the future so that updating and changing Web pages will be even easier.

It seems the wheel-of-retailing has come full circle. The new technology promises online catalogue shopping. These catalogues may possess sound and motion and be able to listen to their customers, but in other ways this is just catalogue shopping the way it was over 100 years ago. For the marketer, reaching customers and creating demand interactively on the Internet will present a number of new challenges, but the goods and services will still have to be physically distributed. It seems unlikely that the technology to move goods and services will be able to keep pace with the technology to move information.

How would you design an "electronic store front" for an auto dealer?

Source: Based on Angela Kryhul, "The Internet Makes the Mainstream," *Marketing Magazine* (December 18–25, 1995), p. 11; Jim McElgunn, "Smoke and Mirrors," *Marketing Magazine* (December 18–25, 1995), pp. 11–12; Tony Spencer, "Setting Up a Virtual Store," *Marketing Magazine* (December 18–25, 1995), p. 12; Christopher E. Erickson, "Copyright and New Media Marketing," *Marketing Magazine* (December 18–25, 1995), p. 14; Tony Long, "Telecommunications and New Media Renovate the Old-Style Bazaar," *Marketing Magazine* (December 18–25, 1995), p. 15, and Canadian Media Directors' Council, *Media Digest 1998–99, Marketing Magazine:* Toronto, Ontario (1998), pp. 13–17.

In a number of areas, companies have been unable to achieve practical technological breakthroughs. For example, no firm has been able to develop and market a cure for the common cold, a good-tasting non-tobacco cigarette, a commercially acceptable electric car, or a truly effective and safe diet pill.

When new technology first emerges, it may be expensive and in short supply, both for firms using the technology in their products and for final consumers. The challenge is to mass produce and mass market the technology efficiently. In addition, some technological advances require employee training and consumer education before they can succeed. Thus, an emphasis on user-friendliness can speed up the acceptance of new technology.

Certain advances may not be compatible with goods and services already on the market or may require retooling by firms wanting to use them in products or operations. Every time an auto maker introduces a significantly new car model, it must invest hundreds of millions of dollars to retool facilities. Each time a firm buys new computer equipment to supplement existing hardware, it must see if the new equipment is compatible (Can it run all the computer programs used by the firm and "talk" to the firm's existing machines?).

To flourish, technological advances must be accepted by each firm in the distribution process (manufacturer/service provider, wholesaler, retailer). Should any of the firms not use a new technology, its benefits may be lost. If small retailers do not use electronic scanning equipment, cashiers will still have to ring up prices by hand even though packages are computer-coded by manufacturers.

### Independent Media

*Independent media affect perceptions of products and company image.*

**Independent media** are not controlled by a firm, yet they influence government, consumer, and public perceptions of that firm's products and overall image. Media can provide positive or negative coverage when a firm produces a new product, pollutes the air, mislabels products, contributes to charity, or otherwise performs a newsworthy activity. Coverage may be by print media, TV, radio, or news organizations. To receive good coverage, a firm should willingly offer information to independent media and always try to get its position written or spoken about.

Although the media's coverage of information about a firm is beyond that firm's control, paid advertising is not. Ads may be rejected by the media, but if they are accepted, they must be presented in the time interval and form stipulated by the firm.

## Attainment of Objectives, Feedback, and Adaptation

An organization's success or failure in reaching objectives depends on how well it directs its controllable factors and deals with the impact of uncontrollable factors. As shown in Figure 2-1, the interaction of an organization's total offering and its uncontrollable environment determines how well it does.

*Feedback provides information that lets a firm adapt to its environment.*

To optimize its marketing efforts and secure its long-run existence, a firm must get **feedback**—information about the uncontrollable environment, the organization's performance, and how well the marketing plan is received. Feedback is gained by measuring consumer satisfaction, looking at competitive trends, evaluating relationships with government agencies, studying the economy and potential resource shortages, monitoring the independent media, analyzing sales and profit trends, talking with suppliers and distributors, and utilizing other methods of acquiring and assessing information.

After evaluating feedback, a company—when necessary—needs to engage in adaptation, thereby fine-tuning its marketing plan to be responsive to the surrounding environment, while continuing to capitalize on differential advantages. A firm should look continually for new and attainable opportunities that fit its overall marketing plan and respond to potential threats by revising its marketing policies.

For instance, in what could be called "Wal-Mart Part I," Wal-Mart entered Canada's retail industry by acquiring 122 Woolco stores—and Canadian department store retailers are still adapting to the new competitive environment this has wrought. Now Canadian food retailers are bracing themselves for Wal-Mart Part II, given Wal-Mart's plan to exploit this second niche. Wal-Mart has been in food retailing in the U.S. for a number of years, and is now its third largest food retailer. It recently began offering a wide range of packaged foods and some refrigerated foods in six stores across Canada.

Wal-Mart's promise of low prices has always drawn customers, and so Canadian food retailers are employing a number of strategies to fight this new threat. For example, to renew and maintain their current customer base grocers have undertaken image makeovers and new advertising campaigns. A&P has been promoting its "Fresh Obsessed" slogan; Provigo declares that "All you need is Loeb"; and A&P has developed a store loyalty campaign by signing on with the Air Miles Reward program. Finally, grocery store megamergers (e.g., Sobeys Canada from the Maritimes acquired the Ontario-based Oshawa Group Ltd in 1998, and Toronto-based Loblaws acquired Montreal-based Provigo Inc. in 1998) have made these retailers large enough that they can wield the volume-buying clout necessary to obtain rock-bottom prices from suppliers, and so to better fight the inevitable price war that Wal-Mart will bring.[18]

In preparing for the future, a firm must avoid **marketing myopia**—a shortsighted, narrow-minded view of marketing and its environment. It is a "self-inflicted and avoidable harm caused to an organization due to a lack of attention to and poor implementation of marketing concepts and principles." These are some major warning signs:

**WAL-MART**
www.wal-mart.com/

**Marketing myopia** *is an ineffective marketing approach.*

- *We-know syndrome*—An ongoing assumption that the correct answers to crucial questions are always known.

- *Me-tooism*—Occurs when goods and services are too similar to those of competitors and there is no competitive advantage.

- *Monopricis*—Occurs when a firm's primary (or only) marketing/competitive tool is changing prices.

- *Customerphobia*—The fear of having a close relationship with and really caring about consumers and their wants.

- *Fax-me complex*—Occurs when the firm is completely dominated by tasks that require immediate attention (crises).

- *Hypermentis*—Occurs when executives devote too much of their time to thinking, studying, and planning while they take little action.

- *Global idiosis*—The lack of ability or willingness to compete in the international marketplace.

- *If it works, don't fix it*—Occurs when business is very good, but no one knows why and everyone is hesitant to make changes.

- *Interfunctionalphobia*—A lack of mutual understanding, integration, and cooperation among a firm's various functional areas.

- *Short-run fetish*—Occurs when decisions are too biased toward the short-run, thus sacrificing long-run performance.[19]

## MARKETING IN THE THIRD MILLENNIUM

## Predictions for the Year 2000

**F**uturists try to identify environmental trends that will greatly influence how marketers will have to do business in the world several years into the future. The following predictions for the Year 2000 were made in the mid-1990s. Have they come true? How many do you think are simply general, vague predictions that would likely come true no matter when they were made?

- *Cocooning*—More people at home because they are working there, or they "cashed out," and retired early because of corporate downsizing. They are not going out as much; they are taking delivery of products rather than shopping, spending leisure time at home, focusing on home entertainment (watching videos, playing video games, surfing the Internet), and working out on home exercise equipment. This trend will produce more home renovation business and result in furniture upgrades. The home office will be fully equipped with faxes, cellular phones, computers, modems, and interactive television.

- *Consumer spending*—Recession-weary people will break out and treat themselves. The upper-income earners will buy pricey, upscale products while lower-income earners will look to warehouse stores and non-branded merchandise.

- *Staying alive*—The fitness rage of the eighties is over, but the long term, health, nutrition, fitness, stress man-

agement, meditation, holistic approach to life is here. Wellness programs, new age remedies, organic foods and longevity centres will be in demand.

- *Wildering*—People will go for more outdoor activities. Hiking boots, backpacks, and off-road vehicles should be in demand.

- *One-on-one marketing*—Customized marketing as marketers use advanced technology to get to know their customers intimately and try to establish a long-term relationship by serving as many needs as possible using this knowledge.

- *Globalnomics*—The Canadian economy will become more integrated with the international economy as international trade barriers fall. Tourism, vacationing, and travel will grow.

- *Moving targets*—Marketers will try some new target-market approaches by aiming at women with products not traditionally marketed to them, e.g. cars. Men will also be targeted with non-traditional products such as food and household products. Marketers will rediscover mass marketing by lumping the baby boomers and Generation X segments together.

- *Save our society*—Demand for ethical business practices, lifelong education, and training and environmental conservation will heat up throughout society.[20]

## SUMMARY

**1.** *To examine the environment within which marketing decisions are made and marketing activities are undertaken* The marketing environment consists of controllable factors, uncontrollable factors, the organization's level of success or failure in reaching its objectives, feedback, and adaptation. The macroenvironment includes the broad societal and economic forces that a firm faces, while the microenvironment refers

to the forces that more directly affect a firm's ability to serve its customers. **2.** *To differentiate between those elements controlled by a firm's top management and those controlled by marketing, and to enumerate the controllable elements of a marketing plan* Controllable factors are the internal strategy elements directed by a firm and its marketers. Top management decides on the line of business, overall objectives, the role

of marketing and other business functions, and the corporate culture. These decisions have an impact on all aspects of marketing.

The major factors directed by marketing personnel are the selection of a target market (the group(s) of customers a firm proposes to serve); marketing objectives, which are more customer-oriented than those set by top management; the marketing organization; the marketing mix, which is a specific combination of product, distribution, promotion, and price decisions; and performance assessment, which involves monitoring and evaluating marketing outcomes. It is important for marketing personnel to strive to create differential advantages—the unique features that cause consumers to patronize a firm and not its competitors.

**3.** *To enumerate the uncontrollable environmental elements that can affect a marketing plan and study their potential ramifications* Uncontrollable factors are the external elements affecting a company's performance that cannot be fully directed by the top management and marketers of a firm. Any marketing plan, no matter how well conceived, may fail if uncontrollable factors influence it too much.

Among the key uncontrollable variables are changing consumer traits, interpersonal influences on consumer behaviour, the consumer decision process, and consumer groups; the competitive structure of the industry in which a firm operates (monopoly, oligopoly, monopolistic competition, or pure competition) and such competitor attributes as marketing strategies, country of origin, size, generic competition, and channel competition; suppliers and distributors, their traits and practices, and resource shortages; government legislation and the political environment; the rate of economic growth (as measured by the GDP and real income), the costs of doing business, and other economic factors; technology, which refers to the development and use of machinery, products, and processes; and independent media, the communication vehicles not controlled by the firm.

**4.** *To explain why feedback about company performance and the uncontrollable aspects of its environment and the subsequent adaptation of the marketing plan are essential for a firm to attain its objectives* A firm's level of success or failure in reaching its goals depends on how well it directs and implements its controllable factors and the impact of uncontrollable factors on the marketing plan. When enacting a marketing strategy, a firm should obtain feedback (information about both its overall and marketing performance and the uncontrollable environment) and adapt the strategy to be responsive to the surrounding environment while continuing to exploit its differential advantages. Marketing myopia, a shortsighted view of marketing and its environment, must be avoided.

# KEY TERMS

**marketing environment** (p. 27)

**controllable factors** (p. 27)

**uncontrollable factors** (p. 27)

**organizational performance** (p. 27)

**feedback** (p. 27)

**adaptation** (p. 27)

**macroenvironment** (p. 27)

**microenvironment** (p. 27)

**line of business** (p. 28)

**corporate culture** (p. 29)

**target market** (p. 31)

**market segmentation** (p. 31)

**differential advantages** (p. 32)

**ethical behaviour** (p. 33)

**marketing organization** (p. 33)

**marketing mix** (p. 34)

**consumerism** (p. 39)

**consumer bill of rights** (p. 39)

**monopoly** (p. 42)

**oligopoly** (p. 42)

**monopolistic competition** (p. 42)

**pure competition** (p. 42)

**Gross Domestic Product (GDP)** (p. 44)

**real income** (p. 44)

**technology** (p. 45)

**independent media** (p. 46)

**marketing myopia** (p. 47)

# REVIEW QUESTIONS

**1.** Explain the environment within which marketing operates.

**2.** Differentiate between the "macroenvironment" and the "microenvironment."

**3.** Why are the factors controlled by top management usually considered uncontrollable by marketing personnel?

**4.** What criteria would you use to assess the role of marketing in a company?

5. Why should a firm select a target market before developing a specific marketing mix?

6. What is the most important marketing objective for an organization? Why?

7. Describe the four components of the marketing mix.

8. Why are suppliers an important uncontrollable factor for many companies?

9. What is the intent of the Competition Act, Bill C-2?

10. How do the independent media affect a firm's marketing practices?

# DISCUSSION QUESTIONS

1. How does a firm's corporate culture influence the performance of its personnel? Relate your answer to a small taxi service that caters to corporate accounts.

2. What are the differential advantages for each of these? Explain your answers.
   a. Your college or university.
   b. *People* magazine.
   c. A local printing service.

3. Distinguish between the marketing mixes used by Cadillac and Saturn, two car lines of General Motors.

4. Deregulation represents both opportunities and potential problems for companies. Offer several examples of both for the cable TV industry.

5. Comment on this statement: "By defining competition in generic terms, acquiring information about the uncontrollable environment, and modifying strategy when necessary, an organization will avoid marketing myopia and guarantee its long-term success."

## CASE STUDY

# Herman Miller: An Environmentally Conscious Firm

Herman Miller of Zeeland, Michigan is a leading maker of contemporary-styled furniture and furniture systems for offices and, to a lesser extent, for health-care facilities. It's the second-largest U.S. manufacturer of office furniture (after Steelcase), with annual sales of over U.S.$1.7 billion. One of its best-known products is an office system that consists of an integrated desk and wall unit that's used when office space is both limited and costly. Herman Miller manufactures its products in three nations: the U.S., Mexico, and the United Kingdom. The firm distributes its products through subsidiaries in Canada, Australia, France, Germany, Japan, Mexico, the Netherlands, and the United Kingdom, as well as selling to customers directly over the Internet.

Herman Miller's corporate philosophy is to operate with integrity and take a long-term view of the marketplace. Its blueprint for community states, "We have a responsibility to the environment and to the other people who live in it. We also have a responsibility to those who come after us. Our business decisions are constantly guided by this belief. It helps us decide how we manufacture, what we do with waste, and what kinds of materials we use to make our products."

Herman Miller applies this philosophy in the way it designs and manages its facilities and in the way it uses and conserves energy in these facilities. For example, in 1982—long before most firms were concerned with environmental issues—Herman Miller built a U.S.$11 million waste-to-energy plant that continues to provide a large portion of its power needs. Instead of burning waste products in landfills, the firm uses its trash to supply all the electricity it needs to heat and air-condition its central factory. This plant has reduced the amount of trash the firm discards in landfills by 90 per cent.

Herman Miller's social responsibility extends to employees and customers. It spent U.S.$800 000 for two incinerators to burn 98 per cent of the toxic solvents emitted from its painting and varnishing operations. These furnaces are effective beyond the standards of the U.S. Clean Air Act.

Years in advance, the firm set a goal of sending no trash to landfills as of 1995. It used reduced quantities of packaging and worked with materials that were recyclable. Today, even Herman Miller's scrap fabric is shredded and made into insulation for car-roof linings and dashboards. Not only does this recycling process help the environment, but also it saves the firm annual dumping fees.

Herman Miller uses a "Design for Disassembly" approach in all of its furniture systems so that component parts can be recycled or remanufactured effectively. This design also makes it easier to refurbish these products. Herman Miller believes that making durable products that don't have to be replaced too often is good for the environment. (It's a fine balance to maintain, however, since obsolescence leads of course to replacement sales.)

Herman Miller's Avian chair demonstrates its commitment to designing environmentally friendly products. One of the design criteria for the chair was 100 per cent recyclability. The chair frame is hollow, needs no painting or other finishing materials, and was created with gas-assisted injection moulding. Every type of material in the chair is recyclable. The chair is even shipped partially assembled, in order to save on packaging and shipping volume (and hence, energy).

Environmental impact is strongly considered in the choice of all materials used in Herman Miller's products. For example, when its research manager realized that the firm's use of rosewood and Honduran mahogany in its U.S.$2300 signature-piece chair had contributed to the destruction of tropical rain forests, the company decided to use wood only from sustained-yield forest sources. The chair is now made from walnut and cherry woods.

Yet Herman Miller isn't content with its environmental actions. The company presently recycles only about 15 per cent of its corrugated cardboard, and burns the balance in its energy plant. It also feels that it needs to burn more of the sawdust that accumulates as a by-product of producing wooden furniture.

## Questions

1. Comment on Herman Miller's corporate philosophy. Can any profit-making enterprise live up to these ideals over the long run? What characteristics and sets of circumstances do you think a company must contend with in order to pursue such a philosophy and remain viable?

2. Do you think Herman Miller's environmental activities help it maintain a competitive edge? Explain why or why not.

3. Evaluate Herman Miller's sustained-yield wood selection strategy. What are some of its advantages and disadvantages?

4. Advise Herman Miller on how to promote its environmental policies to its customers.

**HERMAN MILLER**
www.hermanmiller.com

Sources: The data in this case are drawn from Company Capsule, "Herman Miller," Hoovers Infoseek Online; Joseph A. Azzarello, "Long-Time Environmental Leadership Pays Off in Many Ways at Herman Miller," *Total Quality Environmental Management* (Winter 1992/1993), pp. 187–191; Herman Miller, Inc. and Subsidiaries 1994 Annual Report; and Faye Rice, "Who Scores Best on the Environment," *Fortune* (July 26, 1993), pp. 114–122.

## CASE STUDY

# Understanding Japanese Business Philosophy

Competing with Japanese firms either on their home ground or in Canada requires that managers understand how Japanese business philosophies and culture differ from those of Canada. Some insights into these differences have been provided by James Fallows, who lived in Japan and wrote a book about it entitled *Looking at the Sun.*

According to Fallows, the foundation of Western business philosophy is consumer sovereignty, with a focus on individual welfare and the understanding of market forces. This consumer sovereignty and market-driven approach underlies most of the marketing principles and practices used in Canada and the United States. Japan on the other hand relies on state-sponsored capitalism, whose philosophy suggests that production and material economics are the sources of strength and growth for an economy.

The Japanese approach to business is a form of peacetime military structure. In short, business is war. Home markets must be protected, not kept open. Foreign markets are invaded, captured, and held. The producer is seen as the creator of wealth and the source of employment security. Trust is a very important component in business and in war. Your partners or allies must be dependable. Japanese business people prefer to do business with partners and customers with whom they have been properly introduced. And when conducting transactions they want to meet face-to-face.

Part of this peacetime military structure is the notion of "employees for life." Soldiers (employees) are never laid off from their jobs, although they might be fired. The requirement of an employee for life is loyalty to one's company (like soldiers' loyalty to their country). Those who quit their company in Japan will have a much more difficult time getting hired somewhere else because they carry the stigma of disloyalty (soldiers who have committed treason). Getting fired is an even worse situation for an employee (soldiers who have lost battles get relieved).

Japan takes an imperialistic approach to trade. It imports raw materials and exports finished goods. The Japanese mindset views business as part of the country's productive might, with its independence based on the dependence of Asia's industrial structure on Japan. Japan is Canada's second largest trading partner: In 1998 Canada imported $9.7 billion of Japanese goods and exported $9.5 billion in Canadian goods to Japan, giving Canada a modest trade deficit of $200 million.

The United States is also an important trading partner of Japan's, with which it has had consistent trade deficits of $50 billion plus during the 1990s. When he was re-elected in 1996, U.S. President Bill Clinton, like every other American president in the previous twenty-four years, called for open Japanese markets in order to eliminate this trade deficit. James Fallows suggests that dealing with Japan successfully requires the use of protectionist policies, subsidies, and a producer orientation.

On a micro level Japanese consumers as individuals are very much like North Americans. They have the same basic living expectations of employment security, income stability, and the desire for more material possessions. Increased global information and communications via satellite television and the Internet have led to a greater convergence in lifestyles. Yet there are still critical cross-cultural differences. Japanese consumers express one apparent cultural difference in consistently demanding innovative products of the highest quality with less concern for price.

The production orientation of Japanese companies serves them well in their home market, as they produce quality products rapidly. But, the authoritarian approach to business and production orientation used in East Asia is not acceptable to most Westerners. In fact, the most successful Japanese firms and products have developed the ability to tap into Western consumer sovereignty.

Canada's low trade deficit with Japan indicates that the Japanese don't seem to be dominating Canadian markets the way they have Asian markets.

James Fallows thinks Canada's multicultural nature makes us more resilient in our trade relations with Japan.

### Questions

1. Discuss the differences between Japanese and Western business philosophy.
2. Consider the issue of cultural differences and their effect on product and services marketing. Can you think of any obvious examples of products or services commonly available in Canada that might be hard to trade in Japan because of cultural differences? Are there any products or services that would be easy to trade because of cultural similarities? Explain your reasoning.
3. Discuss Fallows' view that protectionism is the way to deal with Japan, or any other nation for that matter.
4. Advise a Canadian company on what things they must consider if they are to market in Japan. Can a Canadian company do business the way the Japanese do?

Sources: Based on Peter Foster, "What Makes Samurai Run?" *Canadian Business* (March 1994), pp. 72–73; Statistics Canada, "Imports and Exports of Goods on a Balance-of-Payments Basis," Canadian Statistics: International Trade, www.statcan.ca; Industry Canada & Department of Foreign Affairs and International Trade, "Business-Related Key Cross-Cultural Differences and Managerial Implications," Strategis Web site, strategis.ic.ca (April 6,1996); and "James Fallows Interview," CBC *Venture* Video 481.

## CHAPTER 3

# Information for Marketing Decisions

## Chapter Objectives

1. To show why marketing information is needed

2. To explain the role and importance of marketing information systems

3. To examine a basic marketing information system, commercial databases, database marketing, and examples of MIS in action

4. To define marketing research and its components and to look at its scope

5. To describe the marketing research process

*Courtesy of Focus Suites*

"Every day in this country, marketers sit in the dark, hoping consumers will show them the light." In the previous chapter you were introduced to the volatile marketplace in which marketing managers must navigate. Since markets are changing very quickly, managers need to make decisions faster and better than ever before—and they need information to do it. One way of collecting information quickly is through a technique called the "focus group."

The "focus group" method is referred to as qualitative research because its results are designed not for statistical analysis but to gain insight into the thoughts and feelings of people. The focus group is often a preliminary step in designing a research study for statistical analysis. (However, in the name of timeliness, researchers are looking very seriously at the notion of undertaking the preliminaries and then jumping to conclusions!) A focus group involves gathering together a small but representative group of people from your market and then sitting down with them to listen to their thoughts and opinions on your topic of research. The group (usually eight to twenty people) is often observed by marketers who sit in the dark behind a one-way mirror while a professional session leader or moderator conducts the discussion. The value of the information provided depends very much on the process by which it's collected. Questions that marketers need to ask themselves include: What are we trying to learn? Do we need to talk to consumers to learn this? If we need to talk to consumers, should we use a focus group or some other approach? If we are going to use focus groups then we have a number of other questions to consider, such as: How many focus groups should be conducted? How large should they be? Who should be selected to participate in them? What questions should be asked? Who should moderate or lead the sessions?

**MARKETING MAGAZINE**
www.marketing.haynet.com/

*Marketing Magazine* recently looked at this approach to research while trying to determine how people felt about advertising as we approach the year 2000. Plunkett Communications Inc. was asked to perform focus group research to determine the attitudes of consumers and the advertising industry toward advertising. It undertook seven two-hour focus group sessions involving groups of consumers and industry professionals. The consumer groups selected were as follows: females aged 13–14 years, males aged 16–17 years, males aged 25–49 years, and females aged 25–49 years. Industry professionals selected for study were advertising agency personnel and clients. Before the session participants were asked to find an example of an advertising campaign they really liked as well as one they thought was effective.

During the focus group sessions the participants were asked for their feelings and thoughts about advertising in general. They were then asked to respond to questions such as: What are the general attitudes toward advertising this year? How have attitudes changed in the past 10–15 years? Is advertising more credible this year, and if so, why? How do advertisers and agencies see themselves? Why? How do consumers see advertising and advertising professionals this year? Why?

The findings of focus research are always presented as being cautionary and for use in developing hypotheses about the market, which are then tested and confirmed by representative follow-up research. Some of the focus group findings for *Marketing Magazine* about general attitudes toward advertising were that consumers are aware of the commercial intentions behind advertising, regard advertising with some cynicism, feel bombarded by the messages but not outraged, and that advertisers should be truthful but accept that they would be self-serving. Industry professionals report that they need to gain a greater understanding of their markets, and realized that consumers were more sophisticated today.

The consumer focus group results indicated that effective advertising respected the intelligence of viewers, was humorous, tapped into human emotions or relationships, expressed simple truths, illustrated recognized dreams, and employed devices (like animals) that effectively conveyed human conditions. Consumers thought advertisers were slick people and part of big business. The advertising professionals, on the other hand, felt the market was cluttered with advertising and that they couldn't break through this clutter. They also felt that with so many alternative media available, and consumer media habits changing so rapidly, they might lose touch. The need for a better understanding of consumers was a key concern that echoed throughout the sessions with advertising professionals.

Making good decisions about advertising strategies is just one of the areas for which marketers need information. It's also necessary for making good decisions on pricing, distribution, product, and other promotional areas such as personal selling, publicity, and sales promotion. In addition, information is required to understand and deal with the uncontrollable environments faced by marketers. To be of use information must be valid, reliable, timely, and affordable.[1]

In this chapter, we will look at the value of marketing information, explain the role of a marketing information system (which gathers, analyzes, disseminates, and stores relevant marketing data), and describe the marketing research process. We will also take another peek at database marketing.

## Overview

It is essential for a firm to have appropriate information before, while, and after making (and enacting) marketing decisions if it wants to accurately assess strengths, weaknesses, opportunities, and threats; tailor its actions to the marketing environment; and maximize its performance. Good information enables marketers to:

*Firms make better marketing decisions when they have good information.*

- Gain a competitive edge.
- Reduce financial and image risks.
- Determine consumer attitudes.
- Monitor the environment.
- Gather competitive intelligence.
- Coordinate strategy.
- Measure performance.
- Improve advertising credibility.
- Gain management support for decisions.
- Verify intuition.
- Improve effectiveness.

Relying on intuition, executive judgment, and past experience is not enough:

In markets that are growing more slowly and are saturated with competition, businesses prosper by following two strategies. First, they learn more and more about the characteristics and location of their customers. Second, they use that knowledge to develop better goods or services and reduce unsuccessful marketing efforts.[2]

Marketing information is collected using the **scientific method**—incorporating objectivity, accuracy, and thoroughness. Objectivity means information is gathered in an open-minded way. Judgments are not reached until all data are collected and analyzed. Accuracy refers to the use of carefully constructed research tools. Each aspect of information gathering, such as the study format, the sample, interviewer training, and tabulation of responses, must be well planned and executed. Thoroughness describes the

*The **scientific method** requires objectivity, accuracy, and thoroughness.*

comprehensive nature of information gathering. Mistaken conclusions may be reached if probing is not intense enough.

In this chapter, two vital aspects of marketing information are covered: marketing information systems and marketing research. A marketing information system guides all of a firm's marketing-related information efforts and stores and disseminates data on a continuous basis. Marketing research involves gathering and analyzing information on specific marketing issues.

# Marketing Information Systems

The collection of marketing information should not be a rare event that occurs only when data are needed about a specific marketing topic. Research done this way exposes the firm to numerous risks:

- Opportunities may be missed.
- There may be a lack of awareness of environmental changes and competitors' actions.
- It may not be possible to analyze data over several periods.
- Marketing plans and decisions may not be properly reviewed.
- Data collection may be disjointed.
- Previous studies may not be stored in an easy-to-use format.
- Time lags may result whenever a new research study is required.
- Actions may be reactionary rather than anticipatory.

*A* **marketing information system** *regularly gathers, analyzes, disseminates, and stores data.*

Thus, it is essential for any firm, regardless of its size or type, to devise and employ some form of marketing information system to aid decision making. A **marketing information system (MIS)** is "a set of procedures and methods designed to generate, analyze, disseminate, and store anticipated marketing decision information on a regular, continuous basis."[3]

To establish an MIS, a firm should:

- Aggressively amass data from internal company documents, existing external documents, and primary studies (when necessary).
- Analyze the data and prepare appropriate reports—in terms of the company mission, strategy, and proposed tactics.
- Disseminate the analyzed data to the right marketing decision makers in the company. They will vary on the basis of the particular topics covered.
- Store data for future use and comparisons.
- Seek out all relevant data that have either current or future marketing ramifications—not just data with specific short-term implications.
- Undertake ongoing data collection, analysis, dissemination, and storage.

Figure 3-1 shows how an information system can be used operationally, managerially, and strategically for several aspects of marketing.

In the following sections, the components of a basic marketing information system, commercial databases, database marketing, and examples of MIS in action are presented.

## A Basic Marketing Information System

Figure 3-2 presents a basic marketing information system. It begins with a statement of company objectives, which provide broad guidelines. These goals are affected by

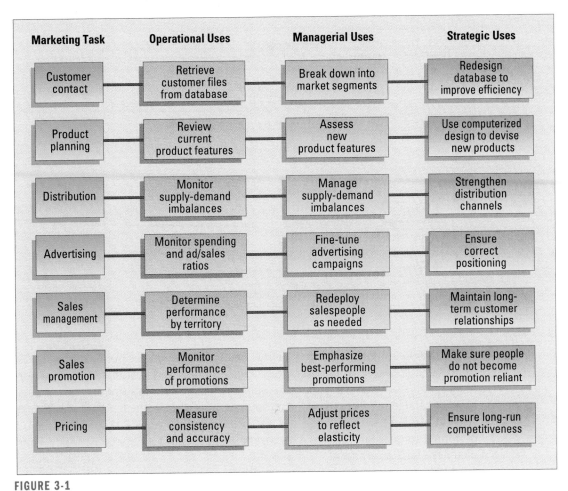

**FIGURE 3-1**

**Uses of a Marketing Information System**

Source: Adapted by the authors from Rajendra S. Sisodia, "Marketing Information and Decision Support Systems for Services," *Journal of Services Marketing*, Vol. 6 (Winter 1992), pp. 51–64.

environmental factors, such as competition, government, and the economy. Marketing plans involve the choice of a target market, marketing goals, the marketing organization, the marketing mix (product, distribution, promotion, and price decisions), and performance measurement.

After marketing plans are outlined, a firm's total marketing information needs can be specified and satisfied with a **marketing intelligence network**, which consists of marketing research, continuous monitoring, and data storage. **Marketing research** is used to obtain information on particular marketing issues (problems). Information may be retrieved from storage (existing company data) or acquired by collecting external secondary data and/or primary data. **Continuous monitoring** is used to regularly study a firm's external and internal environment. It can entail subscribing to trade publications, observing news reports, getting constant feedback from employees and customers, attending industry meetings, watching competitors' actions (competitive intelligence), and compiling periodic company reports. **Data storage** involves retaining all types of relevant company records (such as sales, costs, personnel performance, etc.), as well as information collected through marketing research and continuous monitoring. These data aid decision making and are kept for future reference. Marketing research should be considered as just one part of an ongoing, integrated information system.

Depending on a firm's resources and the complexity of its information needs, a marketing intelligence network may or may not be computerized. Small firms can do

*A* **marketing intelligence network** *includes* **marketing research, continuous monitoring,** *and* **data storage.**

FIGURE 3-2

**A Basic Marketing System**

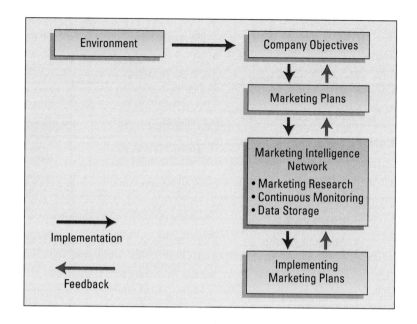

well without computerizing; they merely need to read industry publications, attend trade shows, observe competitors, talk with suppliers and customers, track performance, and store the results of these efforts. In any event, information needs must be stated and regularly reviewed, data sources must be identified, personnel must be given information tasks, storage and retrieval facilities must be set up, and data must be routed to decision makers. The keys to a successful MIS are consistency, completeness, and orderliness.

Marketing plans should be enacted based on information obtained from the intelligence network. For example, by continuous monitoring, a firm could ascertain that a leading competitor intends to cut prices by 7 per cent during the next month. This would give the firm time to explore its own marketing options (e.g., switch to cheaper materials, place larger orders with suppliers to get discounts, or ignore the cuts) and select one. If monitoring is not done, the firm might be caught by surprise and forced to just cut prices, without any other choice.

A basic MIS generally has many advantages: it allows the firm to organize and store data over long time periods; gain a broad perspective on their business; avoid crises; coordinate their marketing plans; make decisions more quickly; and perform cost-benefit analysis. However, forming an information system is not easy. Initial time and labour costs may be high, and setting up a sophisticated system can be complex.

## Commercial Databases

*Commercial databases can provide useful ongoing information.*

Because companies need current, comprehensive, and relatively inexpensive information about the environment in which they operate, many specialized research firms offer ongoing **commercial databases** with information on population traits, the business environment, economic forecasts, industry and company performance, and other items. Databases may include newspaper and magazine articles, business and household addresses culled from Yellow Pages and other sources, industry and company news releases, government reports, conference proceedings, indexes, patent records, and so on. The research firms sell access to their databases to clients, usually for a relatively low fee.

Databases are typically available in printed form; on computer disks, CD-ROMs, or tapes; and online using a computer and a modem. There are commercial database firms that concentrate on tracking and clipping newspaper and magazine articles on an orderly basis; unlike computerized databases, these firms actually look for information on subjects specified by clients. They offer their services for a fee. The *Burwell Directory of Information Brokers* (www.burwellinc.com) cites over 1200 information brokers in the United States, Canada, and about forty-four other nations.

Firms such as Pro CD Inc. and American Business Information (ABI) provide business and household addresses in CD-ROM format. ABI and Pro CD Inc. gather data from phone directories, annual reports, and government agencies; ABI makes 14 million calls per year and sends out more than 700 000 mail surveys to keep its databases current. *Canada Phone*, a $119 CD sold by Pro CD Inc., contains over 12 million Canadian phone listings including households and businesses. The *Canada Phone* CD allows users to conduct a number of database searches. ABI sells a U.S.$39.95 CD which contains data on 70 million U.S. households, while a U.S.$2500 CD has data on 10 million businesses. ABI has over 400 000 customers—from small, single-person firms to giant corporations.[4]

Many companies and libraries subscribe to one or more online computerized databases, whereby users are charged a fee based on the time spent using the database. A few of the well-known computerized database services available to Canadians are America Online, CompuServe, Prodigy, World Linx Telecommunications, WEB, UUNET Canada, and Delphi. A full list of Internet resources can be found in *The 1999 Canadian Internet Directory*. This directory is available from Prentice Hall Canada Inc. and lists thousands of Canadian sources of information on the Internet. With these services, the user can do a search on a particular topic or company, generate the names and abstracts of relevant articles or reports, and then print out the information. Full articles or reports may also be accessed and printed, but doing so could be expensive.

Figure 3-3 highlights the power of information and how cheap and readily available commerical databases are for consumers and business people alike.

**UUNET CANADA**
www.uunet.ca/

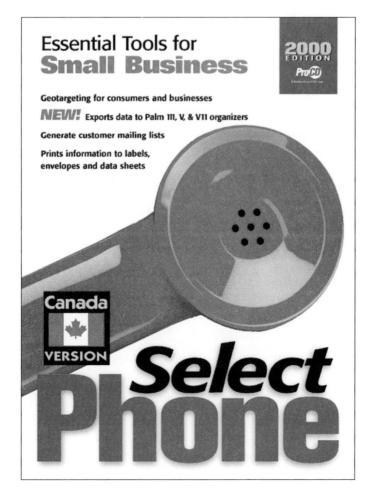

**FIGURE 3-3**
**The Power of Information**
*Courtesy ProCD Canada Phone Book.*

## Database Marketing

In conjunction with their marketing information systems, growing numbers of firms are using database marketing to better identify target markets and more efficiently reach them. **Database marketing** is "an automated system to identify people—both customers and prospects—by name, and to use quantifiable information about them to define the best possible purchasers and prospects for a given offer at a given point in time."[5]

Database marketing creates a bank of information about individual customers (taken from orders, inquiries, external lists), uses it to analyze buying and inquiry patterns, and creates the ability to target goods and services more accurately to specific customers (see Figure 3-4). It may be used to promote the benefits of brand loyalty to customers at risk from competition. It can fuel sales growth by identifying customers most apt to buy new goods and services. It can increase sales effectiveness. It can support low-cost alternatives to traditional sales methods, including telemarketing and direct mail, which can be important in markets where margins are eroding.[6]

Database marketing is especially useful in the relationship marketing process. A company can identify those customers with whom it would most like to have long-term relationships, learn as much as possible about them (such as demographics and purchase behaviour), tailor its marketing efforts toward them, and follow up to learn the level of customer satisfaction. A firm might even compute a "lifetime value" for specific customers, based on their purchase history with the company—and plan its marketing efforts accordingly.[7]

When setting up a database, each actual or potential customer is given an identifying code. Then, contact information (name, address, phone number, fax number, e-mail address, industry code, and demographic data) and marketing information (source and date of contacts with firm, purchase history, product interests, and responses to offers) are entered and updated for each customer. The information should be distributed to marketing decision makers in the firm and kept in the MIS, and company efforts should be coordinated so customers are not bombarded with mailings and there is a consistent image.

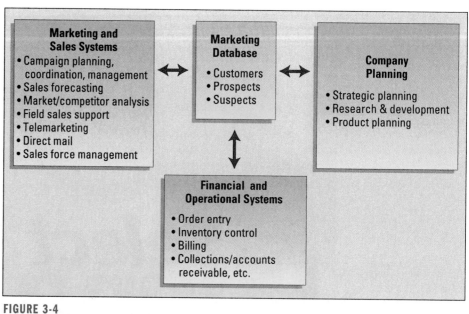

**FIGURE 3-4**

**Fully Integrated Database Marketing**
Source: Robert Shaw and Merlin Stone, *Data-Base Marketing: Strategy & Implementation* (New York, Wiley, 1990). Reprinted by permission of Gower Publishing Company Limited.

## ETHICS AND TODAY'S MARKETER

## Will Legislation Resolve the Privacy Paradox for Direct Marketers?

In the mid-1990s the growth in database-driven information had the Canadian Marketing Association (CMA, formerly CDMA, the Canadian Direct Marketing Association) so worried that it backed away from its longtime stance in favour of industry self-regulation, and took the unusual step of asking the federal government to legislate its discipline. The CMA wanted the industry minister to establish minimum standards of conduct to ensure that anyone collecting or using consumer information did so in a manner that protected privacy. In a letter to the minister the CMA stated: "In an age of information technology, inter-relation of databases and the amassing of transactional data, national legislation appears to be the only practical way of providing comprehensive protection to every Canadian." In 1998 federal legislation on privacy was tabled, but all it does is provide for penalties and recourse for consumers and businesses if their privacy is violated. The legislation really only asks marketers to follow the privacy guidelines that already exist.

For example, the CMA has a privacy code for its member companies, but only 80 per cent of the direct marketers in Canada are members. Canadian direct response sales were approximately $12.2 billion in 1997, but not all sectors of the industry have compulsory privacy codes. The Canadian Association of Internet Providers released an Internet privacy code in 1998 which affects how businesses that use the Internet, many of whom are direct marketers, must behave. These voluntary codes are similar to suggestions provided by the Canadian Standards Association (CSA), and are mainly based on guidelines from the international Organization for Economic Co-operation and Development (OECD). According to these guidelines firms that collect personal information should identify how they plan to use it, as well as get permission from individuals to collect, use, and disclose it. More importantly, the

consumers themselves should be able to gain access to the information that has been collected from them.

The CMA's only recourse to deal with member companies that violate the voluntary code of privacy is to oust them. Chastisement of member organizations isn't a particularly powerful deterrent, and throwing out paying members is harmful to the CMA as well as the offending firm. The CMA saw legislation as the only way the conduct of marketers could be controlled effectively. What's more, non-member direct marketers that often hurt the industry and that weren't previously subject to any codes are now subject to legislative discipline. Still, even with a legislative mechanism, complaints must be filed and then violators must be caught and prosecuted.

Not all firms feel that legislation is necessary; for example, American Express carefully guards its customers' right to privacy. In 1974 it was the first company that offered customers the right not to be on a mailing list. And in 1978 it adopted a series of privacy principles requiring employees to collect only the data absolutely needed. The firm still reviews its data-collection activities each year, and everyone with access to customer information receives customer privacy training. American Express even distributes brochures to consumers explaining how they can refuse to provide the information requested on warranty cards.

Discuss whether legislation will really solve the privacy paradox.

Source: Based on material in Marketing Direct, "Ex-CDMA Enlarges Mandate," *Marketing Magazine* (December 7, 1998) p. 19; Marketing Direct, "Internet Privacy Code Unveiled," *Marketing Magazine* (October 5, 1998) p. 13; James Pollock, "Direct Marketers Want to Regulate How Consumer Data Is Used," *Marketing Magazine* (October 16, 1995), p. 12; Jeffrey Casey, "The Privacy Paradox," *Link* (May 1995), pp. 19–22; and Judith Waldrop, "The Business of Privacy," *American Demographics* (October 1994), pp. 46–54.

In practice, database marketing actually works like this:

1. You may think you're just sending in a coupon, filling out a warranty card, or entering a sweepstakes. But to a marketer, you're also volunteering information about yourself—data that gets fed into a computer, where it's combined with more information from public records.

2. Using sophisticated statistical techniques, the computer merges different sets of data into a coherent, consolidated database. Then, with powerful software, brand managers can "drill down" into the data to any level of detail they require.

3. The computer identifies a model consumer for a chosen product based on the common characteristics of high-volume users. Next, clusters of consumers who share those characteristics—interests, incomes, brand loyalties, for instance—can be identified as targets for marketing efforts.

4. The data can be used in many ways: to determine the values of coupons and who should get them; to develop new products and ensure that the appropriate consumers know about them; to tailor ad messages and aim them at the right audience.

5. Cash-register scanners provide reams of information about exactly what shoppers are buying at specific stores. Merged with the manufacturer's data, this intelligence helps to plan local promotional mailings, fine-tune shelf displays, and design store layouts.

6. The database is continually updated with information collected from product-oriented clubs, responses to coupons, calls to 800 numbers, and sweepstakes entries, as well as with new lists from outside sources.[8]

Although often associated with a computerized MIS, database marketing may also be used by small, non-computerized firms: A company might ask potential and existing customers for their names, addresses, phone and fax numbers, e-mail addresses, and product interests as they contact them, and these data could be entered on large index cards. Consumers could be enticed to provide data by means of a monthly raffle that awards a small prize to the winner. The firm would alphabetize the cards, keep them in a file cabinet, and update the records from sales receipts. Separate mailings could be sent to regular customers and to non-customers from the database.

## MIS in Action

*Information systems are being applied today in various settings.*

Worldwide, millions of organizations now use some form of MIS in their decision making, and the trend is expected to continue. In fact, as a result of computer networking, progressive firms (and divisions within the same firm) around the globe are transmitting and sharing their marketing information with each other—quickly and inexpensively.

One recent study on the use of MIS by large business firms discovered that:

- More than three-quarters have a marketing information system. Of those that do, over 95 per cent are computer-based.

- Nearly 80 per cent use computers to produce reports; and two-thirds store marketing data in their computers.

- All gather customer data, three-quarters are involved with competitive intelligence, and 37 per cent track government actions.

- More than 70 per cent use annual reports, sales call reports, and purchased reports to amass competitive intelligence. Just over one half hire clipping services.[9]

In Sweden, financial institutions have taken the lead in developing MIS:

During the late 1970s, the banking community took an innovative step by organizing a business intelligence (BI) research company called Upplysnigs Centralen (UC Research). It provides fee-based BI services for banks and their major customers, such as database services consisting of public and published information on firms and individuals; proactive intelligence gathering, using participating banks' overseas offices to answer specific and time-urgent requests; and the use of some 3000 business agents around the world who can be tapped for specific expertise or information."[10]

In Japan today, almost all major firms engaged in international business have an internal intelligence unit:

> Typically, it is located in the planning or research departments. Some 10 to 20 employees are assigned responsibilities at company headquarters; but intelligence gathering is company-wide, with virtually every employee participating (from the president to salespeople). Intelligence collection and dissemination are well developed at most Japanese firms. However, it is the ability—almost culturally inherent—for sharing intelligence that makes MIS use in Japanese firms so effective.[11]

**NORTHERN TELECOM**
www.nortelnetworks.com/

Two Canadian firms with superior marketing information systems are Northern Telecom and United Cigar Stores. Each devotes considerable time and resources to its system. Here are examples of how they apply MIS.[12]

Northern Telecom installed its first Enterprise Support System software in 1990 as part of the firm's restructuring toward a more centralized system. Now Northern Telecom has adopted a new support system to enable it to gather and utilize information along product lines and market lines. Importantly, the new system allows managers to cross-reference data along products and markets. The system currently holds information on the company's finances, personnel records, and customer satisfaction surveys. The system is set up so that information is available to hundreds of users instead of just the firm's executives, although only the executives can access all of the information.

United Cigar Stores has installed an enterprise support system that enables senior and middle managers to "log onto the system and check sales at any of its 476 stores." For example, a marketing manager can compare weekly or monthly sales against set targets, and if there is a discrepancy, he or she

> can drill down through the data to find the division, region or district where sales are slackening.... [A manager can] cross-reference by store type or product line to see if, perhaps, its cigarette sales at hotel locations in Ontario that are causing the problem.... [The manager] can even search by promotion, to find out, for example, if a two-pack cigarette discounting program is dragging down revenue instead of boosting it."
>
> One manager has commented "Upper management has had difficulty staying in touch, obtaining accurate, timely data. Now the information is much closer at hand."

## Marketing Research Defined

**Marketing research** involves systematically gathering, recording, and analyzing information about specific issues related to the marketing of goods, services, organizations, people, places, and ideas. It may be done by an outside party or by the firm itself. As indicated earlier, marketing research should be one component of a firm's marketing information efforts.

Marketing research data may be obtained from different sources: the firm itself, an impartial agency (such as the government), or a research specialist working for the firm. The information thus obtained may be applied to any aspect of marketing that requires information to aid decision making. To be effective, however, marketing research must be conducted methodically, following a sequence of tasks: gathering the data, recording it, and analyzing it. Furthermore, the research findings must be communicated to the proper decision maker(s) in the firm.

A firm's decision to use marketing research does not mean it must engage in expensive projects like test marketing and national consumer attitude surveys. It may get enough data by analyzing internal sales reports or from informal meetings with customer-service personnel. Marketing research *does* require an orderly approach and adherence to the scientific method.

*Marketing research involves collecting, tabulating, and analyzing data about specific marketing issues.*

For each marketing issue studied, the amount and cost of research depend upon the kinds of data needed to make informed decisions, the risk involved in making those decisions, the potential consequences of the decisions, the importance of the issue to the firm, the availability of existing data, the complexity of the data-gathering process for the issue, and other factors.

# The Scope of Marketing Research

*Global marketing research expenditures total several billion dollars each year.*

Companies annually spend over U.S.$10 billion worldwide to have data gathered by marketing research firms. The top twenty-five global research firms accounted for more than U.S.$6.1 billion of that amount and collected data in just over ninety countries. The top Canadian-based research firm was Goldfarb Consultants, which ranked twenty-fifth and brought in U.S.$48 million in revenue, of which 46.9 per cent came from outside of Canada.[13] These amounts are in addition to research sponsored by government and other institutions and to internal research efforts of firms themselves—which also run into the billions of dollars each year.

According to an American Marketing Association's Survey of Marketing Research, these are the topical areas in which companies are most apt to engage in or sponsor research efforts: industry/market characteristics and trends, product satisfaction, market-share analyses, segmentation studies, brand awareness and preference, purchase intentions, and concept development and testing. And, on average, the surveyed companies spend 1 per cent of their revenues on marketing research.[14]

Six aspects of marketing research merit special discussion. These involve the rapid rise in customer satisfaction studies, competitive intelligence research, use of state-of-the-art technology, application of single-source data collection, ethical considerations, and complexities of international marketing research.

Companies now participate in more customer satisfaction research than ever before, in keeping with the customer focus noted in Chapter 1. This form of research has more than doubled in recent years, with some firms doing their own studies and others hiring outside specialists. For instance, Whirlpool sends surveys on appliance satisfaction to 180 000 households each year. It also pays hundreds of consumers per year to "fiddle" with computer-simulated products at its Usability Lab. Whirlpool's research also extends to its European marketplace. On the other hand, the Walker Group and Maritz Marketing Research, two U.S.-based research firms, each generate worldwide revenues of several million dollars by doing customer satisfaction studies for clients. As a Maritz executive remarked, the company's success is "due to the quality movement in the country, global competitiveness, and a desire to get back to basics and make the marketing orientation more customer-driven."[15]

**Competitive intelligence**

*focuses on the industry and market environment.*

Once referred to as industrial espionage, collecting information on competitors—or **competitive intelligence**—is one of the hottest kinds of marketing research taking hold in Canada, although only an estimated 5 per cent of Canada's largest firms have the capacity to undertake it. Competitive intelligence differs from traditional market research in that it focuses on what competitors are doing and their capabilities, what's happening in foreign markets, what plans regulators have, and what technologies are evolving that may affect a firm's industry. Focused on the environment rather than on customers, competitive intelligence relies more on researching secondary information sources such as government data, trade papers, trade associations, industry conferences, the Internet, and other public documents and sources. Canadian firms that are known to regularly use competitive intelligence include Labatt, Alcan, and Northern Telecom.[16]

Over the last decade, significant technological innovations have been applied to marketing research, as these examples indicate:

- Toronto-based Internationational Surveys Ltd. (ISL) has developed PC Meter, a system that is loaded onto home computers (by permission of the users) and

TECHNOLOGY AND MARKETING

## Who'll Win the Information Technology Battle?

Electronic data linkages between firms let them reduce their inventory levels and order-processing times. Companies joined by such data linkages can also eliminate duplicate functions that occur in billing and purchasing. According to the author of a book on customer-supplier alliances, 30 to 40 per cent of savings from these alliances come from improving joint processes.

With electronic linkages, firms can gather and study information as products go from raw materials to finished goods to retailer shelves. In many cases, the most influential companies in a value chain are those that have the best knowledge of the marketplace. In particular, managers need to ask three questions: What information drives our business? Who has that information? What is it worth?

MicroAge and W.W. Grainger are two examples of firms that understand the value of information. MicroAge shifted from being a wholesaler that stocked Apple, Compaq, Hewlett-Packard, and IBM computers to a producer of computers tailored to individual consumer needs. Instead of selling systems produced by single companies, MicroAge now assembles computers using parts from over 500 companies. MicroAge relies on its knowledge of customer needs, as well as the costs, features, and compatibilities of different manufacturers' products.

W.W. Grainger, which describes itself as a distributor of maintenance, repair, and operating supplies, has an average order size of U.S.$129. Unlike competitors, the firm is able to tailor its services to customer needs. Based upon the desires of individual customers, Grainger might offer electronic ordering and payment capabilities or even perform a customer's inventory management functions. According to a Grainger vice-president, "On sales calls these days, we're seldom talking about why the motor we sell is better than someone else's motor; we talk about value-added services."

As a W.W. Grainger product manager, describe how a marketing information system can be used to maximize its value-added services.

Source: Based on material in Thomas A. Stewart, "The Information Wars: What You Don't Know Will Hurt You," *Fortune* (June 12, 1995), pp. 119–120.

is designed to monitor the activities of computer users while they "surf" on the Internet.

- Advanced Neurotechnologies has designed MindTrack, to detect emotional responses to ads and other forms of communication. MindTrack detects brainwaves using sensors attached to a headband; people are exposed to an ad campaign or a TV show and quantitative digital results appear.

- More companies are using facsimile machines to get responses to marketing surveys. In general, faxed responses are obtained quicker; response rates are higher due to the ease of return; and answer quality approximates that for other methods of transmission.[17]

Technological advances have facilitated **single-source data collection**—whereby research firms track the activities of individual consumer households from the programs they watch on TV to the products they purchase at stores. For instance, via its BehaviorScan service, Information Resources Inc. (IRI) monitors the viewing habits and shopping behaviour of thousands of households in various markets. Microcomputers are hooked to household TVs and note all programs and ads watched. Consumers shop in supermarkets and drugstores with scanning registers and present cashiers with shoppers cards (resembling credit cards). Cashiers enter each consumer's identification code, which is electronically keyed to every item bought. Via computer analysis, viewing and shopping behaviour are then matched with such information as age and income.

**Single-source data collection** *is a result of high-tech advances.*

**INFORMATION RESOURCES INC.**
www.infores.com/public/prodserv/
AB/bscan.htm/

Due to the unethical practices of some firms, many potential respondents are averse to participating in marketing research projects. To turn the situation around, researchers need to avoid such practices as these:

- Unrealized promises of anonymity.
- False sponsor identification.
- Selling or fundraising under the guise of research.
- Misrepresenting research procedures.
- Observational studies without informed consent.
- Asking overly personal questions.
- Selling consumer demographic information for database use without consent.
- Misportraying research findings in ads and other communications.[18]

With more and more firms striving to expand their foreign endeavours, international marketing research is becoming increasingly important. And this can be quite challenging. The language of the survey, respondent selection, and interviewer training are among the many areas that require special consideration. Consider this example:

Firms deciding how to market to the 350 million consumers in Eastern Europe and Central Asia increasingly do marketing research there. Yet designing and conducting this research is difficult. Often, people have never been surveyed before. Communications systems, especially phone service, may be primitive by Western standards. Secondary data from government agencies and trade associations may be lacking or unavailable. Thus, companies must be adaptable.

When it did research, Kodak could not find relevant consumer data, a photography trade association, or pictures of local cameras for use in a questionnaire. So, to gather data on camera usage and preferences, Kodak took part in a multi-client survey devised by SRG International Ltd., a research firm. The survey was conducted in nine former Soviet republics; since each had its own language, nine questionnaire versions were prepared.[19]

## The Marketing Research Process

*The* **marketing research process** *consists of steps from issue definition to implementation of findings.*

The **marketing research process** consists of a series of activities: defining the issue or problem to be studied; examining secondary (previously collected) data; generating primary (new) data if necessary; analyzing information; making recommendations; and implementing findings.

Figure 3-5 presents the complete process. Each step is completed in order. For example, secondary data are not examined until a firm states the issue or problem to be studied, and primary data are not generated until secondary data are thoroughly reviewed. The dashed line around primary data means these data do not always have to be collected. Many times, a firm can obtain enough information internally or from published sources to make a marketing decision without gathering new data. Only when secondary data are insufficient should a firm generate primary data. The research process is described next.

### Issue (Problem) Definition

*Research efforts are directed by* **issue definition***.*

**Issue (problem) definition** is a statement of the topic to be investigated. Without a focused definition of the issue or problem, irrelevant and expensive data may be gathered. A good problem definition directs the research process to collect and analyze appropriate data for the purpose of decision making.

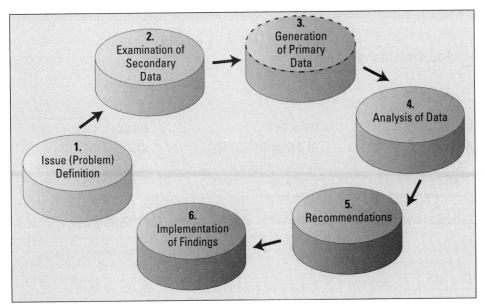

**FIGURE 3-5**
**The Marketing Research Process**

When a firm is uncertain about the precise topic to be investigated or wants to informally study an issue, exploratory research is used. The aim of **exploratory research** is to gain ideas and insights, and to break broad, vague problem statements into smaller, more precise statements.[20] Exploratory research, also called "qualitative research," may involve in-depth probing, small group discussions, and understanding underlying trends.

Once an issue is clarified, conclusive research, also called "quantitative research," is used. **Conclusive research** is the structured collection and analysis of data pertaining to a specific issue or problem. It is more focused than exploratory research, and requires larger samples, and more limited questions in order to provide the quantitative data to make decisions. Table 3-1 contrasts exploratory and conclusive research.

**Exploratory research** *looks at uncertain topics;* **conclusive research** *is better defined.*

## Secondary Data

**Secondary data** consist of information not collected for the issue or problem at hand but for some other purpose; this information is available within a firm or externally. Whether secondary data fully resolve an issue or problem or not, their low cost and availability mean that primary data should not be collected until a thorough secondary data search is done.

**Secondary data** *have been previously gathered for purposes other than the current research.*

**ADVANTAGES AND DISADVANTAGES** Secondary data have these general advantages:

- Many types are inexpensive because primary data collection is not involved.
- Data assembly can be fast, especially for published or company materials.
- There may be several sources and perspectives available.
- A source (such as the government) may obtain data a firm could not get itself.
- There is high credibility for data assembled by independent sources.
- They are helpful when exploratory research is involved.

**TABLE 3-1**

**Examples of Exploratory and Conclusive Research**

| VAGUE RESEARCH TOPIC | EXPLORATORY RESEARCH | PRECISE RESEARCH TOPIC | CONCLUSIVE RESEARCH |
|---|---|---|---|
| 1. Why are sales declining? | 1. Discussions among key personnel to identify major cause | 1. Why is the turnover of sales personnel so high? | 1. Survey sales personnel and interview sales managers |
| 2. Is advertising effective? | 2. Discussions among key advertising personnel to define effectiveness | 2. Do adults recall an advertisement the day after it appears? | 2. Survey customers and non-customers to gauge advertising recall |
| 3. Will a price reduction increase revenues? | 3. Discussions among key personnel to determine the level of a price reduction | 3. Will a 10 per cent price reduction have a significant impact on sales? | 3. Run an in-store experiment to determine effects |

Secondary data also have these general disadvantages:

- Available data may not suit the current research purpose because it is too general or incomplete.
- Information may be dated or obsolete.
- The methodology used in collecting the data (such as the sample size, date of the research, etc.) may be unknown.
- All the findings of a research study may not be made public.
- Conflicting results may exist.
- Because many research projects are not repeated, the reliability of data may not be proven.

**SOURCES OF SECONDARY DATA**   There are two major sources of secondary data. Internal secondary data are available within a firm. External secondary data are available outside a firm. Most companies use both of these sources.

*A firm's records or past studies comprise internal secondary data.*

*Internal Secondary Data*   Before spending time and money searching for external secondary data or collecting primary data, the information contained inside a firm should be reviewed. Internal sources include budgets, sales figures, profit-and-loss statements, customer billings, inventory records, prior research reports, and written reports.

At the beginning of the business year, most firms set detailed budgets for the next twelve months. The budgets, based on sales forecasts, outline planned expenditures for every good and service during the year. By examining the sales of each division, product line, item, geographic area, salesperson, time of day, day of week, and so on and comparing these sales with prior periods, overall performance can be measured. Through profit-and-loss statements, actual achievements can be measured against profit goals by department, salesperson, and product. Customer billings provide information on credit transactions, sales by region, peak selling seasons, sales volume, and sales by customer category. Inventory records show the levels of goods bought, manufactured, stored, shipped, and/or sold throughout the year.

Prior research reports, containing findings of past marketing research efforts, are often stored and retained for future use. When a report is used initially, it is primary data. Later reference to that report is secondary in nature because it is no longer employed for its original purpose. Written reports (ongoing data stored by a firm) may be compiled by top management, marketing executives, sales personnel, and others. Among the information attainable from such reports are typical customer complaints.

**External Secondary Data**   If a research issue or problem is not resolved through internal secondary data, a firm may use external secondary data sources. There are government and nongovernment sources.

All levels of government in Canada distribute various types of economic and business statistics. Statistics Canada is the most important source of external secondary information in Canada. The Statistics Canada catalogue provides a listing of all the facts and figures on Canada's business, economic, and social environment. The catalogue lists sources on trade, income, employment, education, and detailed industry information, all of which have been collected by or for Statistics Canada. Aside from its regular written publications, Statistics Canada disseminates data on CDs, diskettes, computer printouts, microfiche, microfilm, and magnetic tape. Direct online access is available through Statistics Canada's Web site, which gives access to copies of *The Daily*, StatsCan's newsletter, and to CANSIM, Statistics Canada's machine-readable database and retrieval system.

Industry Canada's Strategis (strategis.ic.gc.ca) is billed as Canada's most comprehensive business and consumer Web site. It gives access to a database that provides:

- 2 million electronic documents.
- 3 gigabytes of searchable statistical data.
- 60 000 links to related business sites.
- 2900 outside sites that link back to Strategis.

Users of the site are told that the database can help them "identify new markets, find business partners, form alliances, locate emerging technologies or processes, and assess various risk factors." The Strategis site receives an average of 10 000 visits each day, and in a typical week more than 400 000 documents are accessed.

When using government data, particularly Census statistics, the research date must be noted. There may be a lag before government data are released.

There are three kinds of nongovernment secondary data: regular publications; books, monographs, and other nonregular publications; and commercial research houses. Regular publications contain articles on diverse aspects of marketing and are available in libraries or by subscription. Some are quite broad in scope (such as *Canadian Business*); others are more specialized (*Canadian Advertising Rates and Data*). Periodicals are published by publishing companies, as well as by professional and trade associations.

Books, monographs, and other literature are also published by conventional publishing companies, as well as by professional and trade associations. These materials deal with special topics in depth and are compiled on the basis of interest by the target audience.

Various commercial research houses conduct periodic and ongoing studies and make results available to many clients for a fee. The fee can run as high as the tens of thousands of dollars, depending on the extent of the data. That kind of research is secondary when a firm purchasing the data acts as a subscriber and does not request specific studies pertaining only to itself; in this way, commercial houses provide a number of research services more inexpensively than if data are collected for a firm's sole use. Some examples of research houses are A.C. Nielsen Canada, Canadian Facts, Dun & Bradstreet Canada, Burke International Research, and Goldfarb Consultants, the largest Canadian-owned firm.

*Government and nongovernment sources make available external secondary data.*

**DUN & BRADSTREET CANADA**
www.dnb.com

Lists of commercial research firms and research services available in Canada can be found quickly from two sources: 1) *Marketing Magazine* annually publishes a "Guide to Market Research Services." This guide lists private research organizations in Canada, explains how to contact them, and in many cases gives a brief description of the type of information they trade in; 2) *The International Member & Marketing Services Guide* is an annual publication of the American Marketing Association in Chicago, Illinois. It contains a list of market research firms and services indexed alphabetically and geographically by country. This guide lists private research organizations throughout the world. It also provides details on how to contact these firms, and gives a brief description of the type of services they specialize in.

## Primary Data

**Primary data** *relate to a specific marketing issue.*

**Primary data** consist of information gathered to address a specific issue or problem at hand. Such data are needed when a thorough analysis of secondary data is insufficient for a proper marketing decision to be made.

**ADVANTAGES AND DISADVANTAGES**   Primary data have these general advantages:

- They are collected to fit the precise purpose of the current research topic.
- Information is current.
- The methodology of data collection is controlled and known by the firm.
- All findings are available to the firm, which can maintain their secrecy.
- There are no conflicting data from different sources.
- A study can be replicated (if desired).
- When secondary data do not resolve all questions, collecting and analyzing primary data are the only ways to acquire information.

  Primary data also have these general disadvantages:

- Collection may be time consuming.
- Costs may be high.
- Some types of information cannot be collected (e.g., Census data).
- The company's perspective may be limited.
- The firm may be incapable of collecting primary data.

*The* **research design** *outlines data collection.*

**RESEARCH DESIGN**   If a firm decides primary data are needed, it must devise a **research design**—which outlines the procedures for collecting and analyzing data. A research design includes the following decisions.

*Internal or outside personnel can be used.*

*Who Collects the Data?*   A company can collect data itself or hire an outside research firm for a specific project. The advantages of an internal research department are its knowledge of company operations, total access to company personnel, ongoing assembly and storage of data, and high commitment. The disadvantages of an internal department are the continuous costs, narrow perspective, possible lack of expertise on the latest research techniques, and potentially excessive support for the views of top management. The strengths and weaknesses of an outside research firm are the opposite of those for an inside department.

*What Information Should Be Collected?*   The kinds and amounts of data to be collected should be keyed to the issue (problem) formulated by the firm. Exploratory research requires different data collection from conclusive research.

*Who or What Should Be Studied?*   First, the people or objects to be studied must be stated; they comprise the population. People studies generally involve customers, company personnel, and/or distribution intermediaries. Object studies usually centre on company and/or product performance.

Second, the way in which people or objects are selected must be decided. Large and/or dispersed populations usually are examined by **sampling**, which requires the analysis of selected people or objects in the designated population, rather than all of them. It saves time and money; and when used properly, the accuracy and level of representation of the sample can be measured.

The two approaches to sampling are probability and nonprobability. With a probability (random) sample, every member of the designated population has an equal or known probability of being chosen for analysis. For example, a researcher may select every fiftieth person in a phone directory. With a nonprobability sample, members of the population are chosen on the basis of convenience or judgment. For instance, an interviewer may select the first 100 residence students entering a university cafeteria. A probability sample is more accurate; but, it is more costly and difficult than a nonprobability sample.

Third, the sample size studied must be set. Generally, a large sample will yield greater accuracy and cost more than a small sample. There are methods for assessing sample size in terms of accuracy and costs, but a description of them is beyond the scope of this text.

**What Technique of Data Collection Should Be Used?**   There are four basic primary-data collection methods: survey, observation, experiment, and simulation.

A **survey** gathers information from respondents by communicating with them. It can uncover data about attitudes, purchases, intentions, and consumer traits. However, it is subject to incorrect or biased answers. A questionnaire is used to record survey responses. A survey can be conducted in person, by phone, or by mail.

A personal survey is face-to-face and flexible, can elicit lengthy replies, and reduces ambiguity. It is relatively expensive, however, and bias is possible because the interviewer may affect results by suggesting ideas to respondents or by creating a certain mood during the interview. A phone survey is fast and relatively inexpensive, especially with the growth of discount telephone services. Responses are usually brief, and nonresponse may be a problem. It must be verified that the desired respondent is the one contacted. Some people do not have a phone, or they have unlisted numbers. The latter problem is now overcome through computerized, random digit-dialing devices.

A mail survey reaches dispersed respondents, has no interviewer bias, and is relatively inexpensive. Nonresponse, slowness of returns, and participation by incorrect respondents are the major problems. The technique chosen depends on the goals and needs of the specific research project.

A survey may be nondisguised or disguised. With a nondisguised survey, the respondent is told a study's real purpose; in a disguised survey, the person is not. The latter may be used to indirectly probe attitudes and avoid a person's answering what he or she thinks the interviewer or researcher wants to hear or read. The left side of Figure 3-6 is a nondisguised survey showing the true intent of a study on sports car attitudes and behaviour. The right side of the figure shows how the survey can be disguised: By asking about sports car owners in general, a firm may get more honest answers than with questions geared right at the respondent. The intent of the disguised study is to uncover the respondent's actual reasons for buying a sports car.

A **semantic differential** is a list of bipolar (opposite) adjective scales. It is a survey technique with rating scales instead of, or in addition to, traditional questions. It may be disguised or nondisguised, depending on whether the respondent is told a study's true purpose. Each adjective in a semantic differential is rated on a bipolar scale, and average scores for all respondents are computed. An overall company or product profile is then devised. The profile may be compared with competitors' profiles and consumers' ideal ratings. Figure 3-7 shows a completed semantic differential.

**Sampling** *the population saves time and money.*

*A* **survey** *communicates in person, over the phone, or by mail.*

*A nondisguised survey reveals its purpose, whereas a disguised one does not.*

*A* **semantic differential** *uses bipolar adjectives.*

| Nondisguised | Disguised |
|---|---|
| 1. Why are you buying a sports car? | 1. Why do you think people buy sports cars? |
| 2. What factors are you considering in the purchase of a sports car? | 2. What factors do people consider in the purchase of a sports car? |
| 3. Is status important to you in a sports car?<br>\_ \_ \_ \_ Yes<br>\_ \_ \_ \_ No | 3. Are people who purchase sports cars status-conscious?<br>\_ \_ \_ \_ Yes<br>\_ \_ \_ \_ No |
| 4. On the highway, I will drive my sports car<br>\_ \_ \_ \_ within the speed limit.<br>\_ \_ \_ \_ slightly over the speed limit.<br>\_ \_ \_ \_ well over the speed limit. | 4. On the highway, sports car owners drive<br>\_ \_ \_ \_ within the speed limit.<br>\_ \_ \_ \_ slightly over the speed limit.<br>\_ \_ \_ \_ well over the speed limit. |

**FIGURE 3-6**

**Nondisguised and Disguised Surveys**

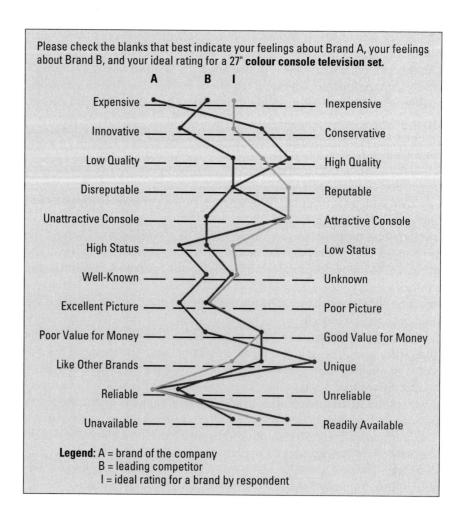

Please check the blanks that best indicate your feelings about Brand A, your feelings about Brand B, and your ideal rating for a 27" **colour console television set.**

| | |
|---|---|
| Expensive | Inexpensive |
| Innovative | Conservative |
| Low Quality | High Quality |
| Disreputable | Reputable |
| Unattractive Console | Attractive Console |
| High Status | Low Status |
| Well-Known | Unknown |
| Excellent Picture | Poor Picture |
| Poor Value for Money | Good Value for Money |
| Like Other Brands | Unique |
| Reliable | Unreliable |
| Unavailable | Readily Available |

**Legend:** A = brand of the company
B = leading competitor
I = ideal rating for a brand by respondent

**FIGURE 3-7**

**A Semantic Differential for a Colour Television**

**Observation** is a research method whereby present behaviour or the results of past behaviour are observed and noted. People are not questioned and cooperation is unnecessary. Interviewer and question bias are minimized. Observation is often used in actual situations. The major disadvantages are that attitudes cannot be determined and observers may misinterpret behaviour.

In disguised observation, a consumer is unaware he or she is being watched. A two-way mirror, hidden camera, or other device may be used. With nondisguised observation, a participant knows he or she is being observed. Human observation is carried out by people; mechanical observation records behaviour through electronic or other means, such as a movie camera filming customer reactions to a sales presentation in a store.

*In **observation**, behaviour is viewed.*

**TELEGLOBE**
www.teleglobe.ca

## INTERNATIONAL MARKETING IN ACTION

### Using Competitive Intelligence to Open Up the Overseas Long-Distance Market

The use of competitive intelligence by business firms isn't really new, but as an organized approach to market research it is relatively recent in Canada. It involves researching uncontrollable factors like competition, government regulation, and technological and economic changes. The effective use of competitive intelligence to open up the overseas long-distance market took Science—as in Adrian Science, CEO, and his wife Emily Aspell-Science, Vice-President of North American Gateway Inc., a Canadian wholesale long-distance carrier. The regulatory environment in Canada for telephone and telecommunications is managed by the Canadian Radio-television and Telecommunications Commission (CRTC). Essentially, the CRTC had granted and was protecting a monopoly position for Teleglobe Canada to be the sole wholesale overseas long-distance carrier for Canada. A wholesale long-distance carrier is a firm that handles the call routing for the telephone companies that serve consumers. Thus, North American Gateway and Teleglobe's customers are other telephone companies rather than consumers.

The first application of competitive intelligence for Gateway came in 1993, when the CRTC granted approval for telephone companies to route some calls to the United Kingdom, Sweden, Finland, Australia, and New Zealand on a limited number of private lines. The volume of Canadian telephone traffic to these destinations was minor and it was not expected that Teleglobe's monopoly would be threatened by opening these markets to some competition. Adrian Science researched the nature of the telephone business in these foreign markets, and then made cooperative partnership arrangements with their carriers. He routed calls into these markets and then rerouted them via his partner's systems to anywhere else in the world. Called "switch-hubbing," this approach meant that Teleglobe's international monopoly from Canada was effectively eliminated, and that competition was created.

The next step for Gateway involved taking Teleglobe and the CRTC to court in order to truly open up the Canadian market. The result was that on October 1, 1998 the CRTC lifted Teleglobe's monopoly on routing all Canadian calls overseas. Now Gateway will really have to employ competitive intelligence, because with the loss of its monopoly Teleglobe will be taking strong actions to defend its turf. Gateway will also be contending with other Canadian firms like Bell Canada and London Telecom, European firms such as British Telecom and Deutsche Telecom AG, and U.S. firms such as MCIWorldcom and Global One, not to mention any other potential competitors. And guess what? These firms are planning to use Science's switch-hubbing technique through Canada to enter the lucrative U.S. market. It seems Gateway isn't the only firm capable of using competitive intelligence!

What kind of competitive intelligence information would you recommend Gateway look for to identify potential competitors in the Canadian market?

Source: Based on Andrew Wahl, "Gate Crashers," *Canadian Business* (December 11, 1998), pp. 84–86.

*An **experiment** varies marketing factors under controlled conditions.*

An **experiment** is a type of research in which one or more factors are manipulated under controlled conditions. A factor may be any element of marketing from package design to advertising media. In an experiment, just the factor under study is varied; all other factors remain constant. For example, to evaluate a new package design for a product, a manufacturer could send new packages to five retail outlets and old packages to five similar outlets; all marketing factors other than packaging remain the same. After one month, sales of the new package at the test outlets are compared with sales of the old package at the similar outlets. A survey or observation is used to determine the reactions to an experiment.

An experiment's key advantage is that it can show cause and effect—such as whether a new package is the cause of increased sales. It is also methodically structured and enacted. Key disadvantages are the rather high costs, frequent use of contrived settings, and inability to control all factors in or affecting a marketing plan.

***Simulation** enables marketing factors to be analyzed using a computer model.*

**Simulation** is a computer-based method to test the potential effects of various marketing factors using a software program rather than real-world applications. A model of the controllable and uncontrollable factors facing the firm is first constructed. Different combinations of the factors are then fed into a computer to determine their possible impact on an overall marketing strategy. Simulation requires no consumer cooperation and can handle many interrelated factors. However, it may be complex and hard to use; does not measure actual attitudes, behaviour, and intentions; and is subject to the accuracy of the assumptions made.

*Research expenses range from personnel time to marketing costs.*

**How Much Will the Study Cost?**    Table 3-2 shows the best uses for each kind of primary data collection.

The overall and specific costs of a study must be clearly outlined. These costs may include executive time, researcher time, support-staff time, pre-testing, computer usage, respondent incentives (if any), interviewers, supplies, printing, postage or phone expenses, special equipment, and marketing expenses (such as advertising).

A study's expected costs should be compared with the expected benefits to be derived. Suppose a consumer survey costing $10 000 would let a firm improve the package design of a new product. With the changes suggested by research, the firm would lift its first-year profit by $30 000. Thus, the net increase due to research is $20 000 ($30 000 profit less $10 000 in costs).

## TABLE 3–2

## The Best Uses of Primary Data-Collection Techniques

| TECHNIQUE | MOST APPROPRIATE USES |
| --- | --- |
| 1. Survey | When determining consumer or distribution intermediary attitudes and motivations toward marketing-mix factors; measuring purchase intentions; relating consumer traits to attitudes |
| 2. Observation | When examining actual responses to marketing factors under realistic conditions; interest in behaviour and not in attitudes |
| 3. Experiment | When controlling the research environment is essential and establishing a cause-and-effect relationship is important |
| 4. Simulation | When deriving and analyzing many interrelationships among variables |

***How Will the Data Be Collected?*** The people needed to collect the data outlined in the research design must be determined and the attributes, skills, and training of the data-collection force specified. Too often, this important phase is improperly planned, and data are collected by unqualified people.

Data collection can be administered by research personnel or can be self-administered. With administered collection, interviewers ask questions or observers note behaviour; they record answers or behaviour and explain questions (if asked) to respondents. With self-administered collection, respondents read questions and write their answers. There is a trade-off between control and interviewer probing (administered) versus privacy and limited interviewer bias (self-administered).

*Interviewers administer surveys or respondents fill them out.*

***How Long Will the Data-Collection Period Be?*** The time frame within which data are collected must be stipulated, or else a study can drag on. Too long a time frame may lead to inconsistent responses and secrecy violations. Short time frames are easy to set for personal and phone surveys. Mail surveys, observation, and experiments often require much more time to implement; nonetheless, time limits must be defined.

***When and Where Should Information Be Collected?*** The day and time of data collection must be set. It must also be decided if a study will be done on or off a firm's premises. The desire for immediacy and convenience have to be weighed against the need to contact hard-to-reach respondents at the proper time.

**DATA COLLECTION** After the research design is thoroughly detailed, data are actually collected. Those engaged in data collection must be properly supervised and follow directions exactly. Responses or observations must be entered correctly.

## Data Analysis

In **data analysis**, the information on questionnaires or answer forms is first coded and tabulated and then analyzed. Coding is the process by which each completed data form is numbered and response categories are labelled. Tabulation is the calculation of summary data for each response category. Analysis is the evaluation of responses, usually by statistical techniques, as they pertain to the specific issue or problem under investigation. The relationship of coding, tabulation, and analysis is shown in Figure 3-8.

**Data analysis** *consists of coding, tabulation, and analysis.*

## Recommendations

Recommendations are suggestions for future actions that are based on marketing research findings. They are typically presented in written (sometimes, oral) form to marketing decision makers. The report must be written for the audience that reads it. Thus, technical terminology must be defined.

After recommendations are passed on to the proper decision makers, the research report should be kept in the data storage part of a firm's marketing intelligence network. It may then be retrieved in the future, as needed.

## Implementation

A research report represents feedback for marketing managers, who are responsible for implementing any changes that may be necessary. If the findings are ignored, the research has little value. If decisions are based on the results, then marketing research has great value and the organization benefits in the short and long run.

Marketing managers are most apt to implement research findings if they have input into the research design, broad control over marketing decisions, and confidence that results are accurate.

FIGURE 3-8

**Data Analysis, Recommendations, and Implementation of Findings for a Study on Coffee**

| | | | |
|---|---|---|---|
| 1. Do you drink coffee? | ☐ Yes | 01 | 300 |
| | ☐ No | 02 | 200 |
| 2. In general, how frequently do you drink coffee? (Check only one answer.) | ☐ Two or more times per day | 03 | 142 |
| | ☐ Once per day | 04 | 84 |
| | ☐ Several times per week | 05 | 42 |
| | ☐ Once or twice per week | 06 | 20 |
| | ☐ One to three times per month | 07 | 12 |
| | ☐ Never | 08 | 200 |
| 3. During what time of day do you drink coffee? (Check all answers that apply.) | ☐ Morning | 09 | 270 |
| | ☐ Lunch time | 10 | 165 |
| | ☐ Afternoon | 11 | 100 |
| | ☐ Dinner time | 12 | 150 |
| | ☐ Evening | 13 | 205 |
| | ☐ None | 14 | 200 |

**Coding:** Questionnaires numbered A001 to A500. Each response is labelled 01 to 14 (e.g., Morning is 09. Evening is 13). Question 3 is a multiple-response question.

**Tabulation:** Total responses are shown above right.

**Analysis:** 60% drink coffee. About 28% drink coffee two or more times daily (representing 47% of all coffee drinkers); almost 25% of coffee drinkers (74 people) consume coffee less than once per day. 90% of coffee drinkers consume coffee in the morning; only one-third consume it in the afternoon.

**Recommendations:** The coffee industry and individual firms need to increase the advertising geared toward noncoffee drinkers, as well as infrequent coffee drinkers. Emphasis should also be placed on lifting coffee consumption during afternoon hours.

**Implementation of findings:** New, more aggressive advertising campaigns will be developed and the annual media budgets devoted to increasing overall coffee consumption will be expanded. One theme will stress coffee's value as an afternoon "pick-me-upper."

## MARKETING IN THE THIRD MILLENNIUM

### Using Qualitative Research to Make Timely Decisions to Get Timely Results

Making timely marketing decisions requires conducting timely analysis on timely results gathered from timely research. This is a necessity for any organization that plans on understanding and responding to customers quickly. Ron Bremner, President of the NHL's Calgary Flames, has recognized that he must respond quickly to meet the inevitable challenge that comes with trying to maintain "product" consistency and provide customer satisfaction for a small professional sports franchise. He has developed a simple, inexpensive, and unique approach to research his customers in a timely fashion so that he can respond quickly.

Bremner believes that nothing is too good for his customers, and he'll put his ear to their mouths to prove it. Well, not literally, but Bremner gets an earful over the phone and in person from Calgary fans on a weekly basis. Since sport franchises cannot guarantee winning teams they must offer fans something besides that.

Bremner is obsessed with customer service, and sees the Calgary Flames as offering a night of entertainment rather than just a hockey game. Responding to customers quickly is how a non-playoff contender can make money in a small market in the NHL.

Researching customers fast and frequently would seem to be an expensive proposition, but Bremner has a method that's quick and basically free. He has a team of University of Calgary MBA students wander through the arena to survey fans on food selection and cleanliness in the arena after each game. Fans are asked to fill out comment cards after each game, along with their contact information. Bremner contributes to their education, the MBA students get into a hockey game free, and Bremner gets the information he needs. The next day he reviews their findings and discusses them with his management team. Bremner then phones or writes the fans to address their concerns or thank them for their compliments. Groups of season ticket holders are routinely invited to breakfast during the season and asked for their opinions. During games Bremner sits in the stands to gauge fan reaction and then inspects the Calgary Saddledome between periods. It's an active inspection that involves checking out lines and service at concessions, talking to fans, and even picking up litter from the floor or in the washrooms. This instills in all employees the belief that customer service and even cleanliness are important. Bremner constantly interacts with his customers by chatting with them, handing out vouchers for free food, and giving away Flame T-shirts and hats.

Bremner says the Calgary Flames organization puts two teams on the ice every night: the hockey team that entertains and the off-ice team that supports the players. For it's not just the players on the ice who need a big game, but the people working the Tim Horton's and Wendy's concessions, the parking attendants, the ticket vendors and ticket takers, the ushers, the washroom attendants, and of course, the management.

Bremner is obsessed with knowing how both teams are doing, and feels that although it's hard to put a winning team on the ice game after game and year after year, the off-ice team can be winners every time. The scoreboard measures the on-ice team, but market research measures the score off the ice.[21]

# SUMMARY

**1.** *To show why marketing information is needed*  Marketing information lets a firm accurately assess its strengths, weaknesses, opportunities, and threats; operate properly in the marketing environment; and maximize performance. Reliance on intuition, judgment, and experience are not sufficient. The scientific method requires objectivity, accuracy, and thoroughness in research projects.

**2.** *To explain the role and importance of marketing information systems*  Collecting marketing information should not be viewed as an infrequent occurrence. Acting in that way can have negative ramifications, especially with regard to misreading the competition and other external factors that can affect a firm's performance.

A marketing information system (MIS) is a set of procedures to generate, analyze, disseminate, and store anticipated marketing decision information on a regular, continuous basis. It can aid a company operationally, managerially, and strategically.

**3.** *To examine a basic marketing information system, commercial databases, database marketing, and examples of MIS in action*  The key aspect of a basic MIS is the marketing intelligence network, which consists of continuous monitoring, marketing research, and data storage. The intelligence network is influenced by the environment, company goals, and marketing plans; and it affects the implementation of marketing plans. Marketing research should be considered as just one part of an ongoing, integrated information system. An MIS can be used by both small and large firms, and does not have to be computerized.

Specialized research firms offer valuable information through commercial databases that contain information on the population, the business environment, the economy, industry and company performance, and other factors. Databases are available in printed form; on computer diskettes, CD-ROMs, or tapes; and via online hookups.

An increasing number of firms are looking to database marketing to improve their interactions with customers. Database marketing involves setting up an automated system to identify and characterize customers and prospects and then using quantifiable information to better reach them.

Marketing information systems are being used by firms of every size and type.

**4.** *To define marketing research and its components and to look at its scope* Marketing research entails systematically gathering, recording, and analyzing data about specific issues related to the marketing of goods, services, organizations, people, places, and ideas. It may be conducted internally or externally.

Globally annual expenditures on marketing research run into the billions. Six key aspects of marketing research are particularly noteworthy: customer satisfaction studies, competitive intelligence, the use of advanced technology, single-source data collection, ethical considerations, and the intricacies of international research.

**5.** *To describe the marketing research process* It has a series of activities: defining the issue or problem to be studied, examining secondary data, generating primary data (when needed), analyzing data, making recommendations, and implementing findings. Many considerations and decisions are needed at each stage of the process.

Exploratory (qualitative) research is used to develop a clear definition of the study topic. Conclusive (quantitative) research looks at a specific issue in a structured manner. Secondary data—not gathered for the study at hand but for some other purpose—are available from internal and external (government, nongovernment, commercial) sources. Primary data—collected specifically for the purpose of the investigation at hand—are available through surveys, observation, experiments, and simulation. Primary data collection requires a research design: the framework for guiding data collection and analysis. Primary data are gathered only if secondary data are inadequate. Costs must be weighed against the benefits of research. The final stages of marketing research are data analysis—consisting of coding, tabulating, and analyzing; recommendations—suggestions for future actions based on research findings; and the implementation of findings by management.

# KEY TERMS

**scientific method** (p. 55)

**marketing information system (MIS)** (p. 56)

**marketing intelligence network** (p. 57)

**continuous monitoring** (p. 57)

**data storage** (p. 57)

**commercial databases** (p. 58)

**database marketing** (p. 60)

**marketing research** (p. 63)

**competitive intelligence** (p. 64)

**single-source data collection** (p. 65)

**marketing research process** (p. 66)

**issue (problem) definition** (p. 66)

**exploratory research** (p. 67)

**conclusive research** (p. 67)

**secondary data** (p. 67)

**primary data** (p. 70)

**research design** (p. 70)

**sampling** (p. 71)

**survey** (p. 71)

**semantic differential** (p. 71)

**observation** (p. 73)

**experiment** (p. 74)

**simulation** (p. 74)

**data analysis** (p. 75)

# REVIEW QUESTIONS

1. Why is marketing information necessary? What may result if managers rely exclusively on intuition?

2. What is the scientific method? Must it be used each time a firm does research? Explain your answer.

3. Describe the elements of a basic marketing information system.

4. Distinguish between commercial databases and database marketing.

5. What is single-source data collection?

6. Differentiate between conclusive and exploratory research. Give an example of each.

7. What are the pros and cons of secondary data?

8. When is primary data collection necessary?

9. Outline the steps in a research design.

10. Under what circumstances should a firm use surveys to collect data? Observation? Explain your answers.

## DISCUSSION QUESTIONS

1. A small jeweller wants to get information on the average amounts that consumers spend on gold jewellery, the incomes and occupations of gold jewellery consumers, the times of year when gold jewellery purchases are heaviest and lightest, sales of the leading competitors, the criteria people use in choosing gold jewellery, and consumer satisfaction. Explain how the firm should set up and implement a marketing intelligence network.

   Include internal and external data sources in your answer.

2. How could a firm use a modified version of the database marketing program as shown in Figure 3-4? Apply your answer to a firm marketing expensive attaché cases to business customers via office-supply stores.

3. Pizza Hut is an internationally oriented fast-food chain. Pierre's Pizza is an independent local European fast-food restaurant. If both wanted to gather data about their respective competitors' marketing practices, how would your research design differ for each?

4. Develop a five-question disguised survey to determine attitudes toward the reputations of colleges and universities in your area. Why use a disguised survey for this topic?

5. Comment on the ethics of disguised surveys. When would you recommend that they not be used?

## CASE STUDY
# Researching the Canadian Market with Scanners

Information on markets and competitors is an absolute must for marketing decision makers. Annual market research billings in Canada range from $110 to $120 million annually. One of the most accurate and important sources of consumer and product information available to packaged goods marketers comes from retail store scanners. Products and packages that have Universal Product Codes (UPC codes) are scanned to record sales, manage inventory, and tabulate bills. The scanner information also includes date of purchase, the brand, and package size; as well as any associated coupon use. All this information can be cross-referenced with demographic information on consumers (such as income, age, dwelling type, house value, occupation, race/ethnicity, and gender), and product marketer's information on selling space devoted to the brand and any related advertising and promotional campaigns, including couponing and in-store promotional campaigns.

This information is critical to the formulation and evaluation of marketing strategies by packaged goods marketers. The ability to understand the marketplace is an absolute necessity for firms that wish to develop effective strategies and tactics to improve their market and profit performance. In the United States and Canada, ACNielsen Incorporated and Information Resources Incorporated (IRI) are two of the leading suppliers of retail sales and market share information gathered by electronic scanners.

"ACNielsen Canada is based in Markham, Ontario and employs over 800 people across the country with regional offices in Vancouver and Montreal. ACNielsen Corporation, offering services in over 90 countries, and with 1997 revenues of U.S.$1.4 billion, is the global leader in delivering market research information and analysis to the consumer products and services industries." Regarded as the first name in market research, ACNielsen has been in business since 1929 performing retail measurement services that "help management gauge product penetration, overall product performance, distribution, promotion effectiveness, and price sensitivity."

Today, using in-store scanning of product codes and store visits by professional auditors, ACNielsen provides information for "long-term strategic planning or tactical decision-making by measuring and tracking sales volume, selling price, observed promotion and merchandising execution, encompassing an organization's own brands as well as competitive brands." The firm offers a complete portfolio of sample and census information across the food, household, health and beauty, durables, confectionery, and beverage product industries. ACNielsen also measures services like advertising, entertainment, media attention, and telecommunications. The firm measures industrial and commercial activities as well.

ACNielsen was virtually in control of research in the consumer packaged goods industry until Information Resources Incorporated burst onto the scene in 1979. IRI was the first firm to commercialize the use of UPC scanner data with its BehaviourScan product for marketing research. ACNielsen implemented a scanner tracking service almost immediately, but not before losing almost 50 per cent of its U.S. customers to IRI. Since then, ACNielsen and IRI have been in a massive battle over the supply of point-of-sale market research information to consumer packaged goods manufacturers. The battle has been fought using pricing and product innovation strategies, with the result that neither firm has been consistently profitable despite having combined sales of about U.S.$2 billion.

For example, in 1987 IRI introduced InfoScan, a national supermarket tracking system. InfoScan is a census of all scanner data from every store IRI monitors and provides information on product sales, market shares, selling prices, distribution availability, and promotional efforts for brands across hundreds of product categories. IRI also has an in-home scanner panel of 55 000 households, which allows it to track purchase behaviour to detailed information on representative sample households. This allows IRI to provide its clients with information on what is being purchased and by whom. IRI can also develop customized marketing strategy models for each of its clients.

IRI has attracted a number of high-profile consumer packaged goods clients with this offering, including Frito-Lay, Procter & Gamble, ConAgra, PepsiCo, Nabisco, Ocean Spray, Reynolds Metals, and Anheuser Busch. Today IRI is "the largest provider of UPC scanner-based business solutions to the consumer packaged goods industry" and has over U.S.$500 million in annual sales and 60 per cent of the supermarket data scanner business. But despite its leadership position in supplying retail scanner information, IRI's operations have been consistently unprofitable.

### Questions

1. Identify and discuss some of the marketing decisions that could be made on the basis of the market research information supplied in the scanner data.
2. What types of information do you think marketing managers would like to have, but don't appear to be available in the scanner data described?
3. Given that competing packaged goods manufacturers can buy exactly the same information from either ACNielsen or IRI, how could the information be used to gain a competitive advantage for either firm?
4. Discuss the strengths and weaknesses of the marketing information offered by scanner technology.

Sources: Based on IRI Web site, www.iri.com; A.C. Nielsen Web site, www.acnielsen.com; Hoovers Online, www.hoovers.com; James Pollock, "IRI Challenges Nielsen's Niche," *Marketing Magazine* (October 16, 1995), p. 13; and James Pollock, "Research Billings Remain Steady," *Marketing Magazine* (January 15, 1996), p. 18.

# CBC

# The World Wrestling Federation Visits Canada

The question has always been, Is professional wrestling for real? And the answers are: It's real entertainment. It can be really dangerous. And it's a really good business—with an annual income of $500 million every year for the professional wrestling industry, comprised of the World Wrestling Federation (WWF), the NWO, and World Championship Wrestling (WCW). The Stamford, Connecticut-based WWF takes in about $200 million a year, and is the step-parent of both the NWO and WCW.

In the WWF, professional wrestling is entertainment, pure and simple. It took the New Jersey Senate to get Vince McMahon Jr., owner of the WWF, to admit this. For if wrestling were to be deemed a sport McMahon would have taken the kind of hit that all his wrestlers put together couldn't deliver: a hit in the pocketbook from taxes and regulation that would be levied by all U.S. state athletic commissions on every WWF event held there.

As an entertainment business the WWF's success and survival are strongly related to its marketing, which begins with its product design. The characters are owned by the WWF, and each wrestler's persona is scripted. The emotional appeal of wrestling is based on the old but popular good versus evil storyline, which takes on new twists every week in the physical soap opera that is wrestling. Take the "Undertaker" who, in front of a sold-out arena, is accused of killing his parents by another wrestler. The Undertaker is a tall, menacing-looking man covered with tattoos, who makes almost any sinister storyline associated with him seem believable. The WWF has a host of other such characters, including Vader, Goldust, the Legion of Doom, Animal and Hawk, and Stone Cold Steve Austin; as well as female characters like Chyna and Sable.

The ring activities of these villains and heroes involve a great deal of ad lib choreography. A wrestling star can earn from $3 to $4 million a year, and is generally on an exclusive contract. The WWF operates what is essentially a studio star system, whose various storylines can make or break the fame of its wrestlers.

When wrestlers become superstars they may decide to go their own way. For example, a number of WWF greats like Hulk Hogan, Randy "The Macho Man" Savage, and Lex Lugar left the WWF and formed the WCW. But although wrestlers can take their talents elsewhere, the script writers usually stay where they are. And unless the actors have tremendous "studio" support for their new "shows," their success may be shortlived.

Sometimes the wrestlers aren't too happy with what's been scripted for them. For example, WWF blonde wrestling diva Sable filed a U.S. $110 million lawsuit against the WWF in June of 1999. Her suit involved a complaint that the WWF wanted her to take part in a lesbian storyline that included her gown being torn off, exposing her breasts on television. She also stated that the WWF wanted her to appear in a series of sexually degrading photographs. She further claimed that since she refused to cooperate the WWF had scripted her demise as a WWF female champion. These charges have been categorically denied by the WWF.

Sable's lawsuit is negative publicity, but publicity—positive or negative—is a powerful tool the WWF uses to market its product. One of its most important forms is the simultaneous TV broadcasts of live WWF events. In Canada TSN reports that the weekly WWF broadcast *RAW Is WAR* draws close to 800 000 Canadian viewers. WWF personalities have also appeared on the show *Off The Record,* hosted by Michael Lansberg, and when they do it almost always results in a tremendous ratings jump. But the WWF doesn't rely solely on TV for publicity. Consider the March 1999 Wrestlemania XV challenge from Canadian WWF superstars Edge, Christian, Test, and Val Venis, who asked Toronto fans to fill a WWF ring with non-perishable food items to be donated to the Daily Bread Food Bank. Fans who donated food were given an autograph by one of these stars.

The danger of professional wrestling can bring it negative publicity, as can its unsuitability for children. A large number of parents have complained to TSN about the 9:00 p.m. Monday night airings of *RAW Is WAR.* The nature of the entertainment, as well as the combatants' liberal expletives, don't make for appropriate children's entertainment, and so TSN recently moved the *RAW Is WAR* live broadcasts onto tape delay at midnight on Mondays.

The bread and butter of the WWF is its travelling road show, which is broadcasted weekly. The WWF holds about forty Canadian events every year, and the fans come out in droves. Carl De Marco, who's the WWF's promoter and manager in Canada, has a demanding task. For example, he knows that showcasing the WWF stars is critical to its success, but at one event in Hamilton, Ahmed Johnson, one of the headliners, came down with food poisoning. De Marco had to find a physician to attend to Johnson so that he could perform. The stars are also important to merchandise sales. There are over 400 different products for sale at any one event. Fans can choose from posters of their favourite wrestlers, championship belt replicas, wrestling action figures, and even Canada's own Bret "The Hitman" Hart sunglasses, which have sold over a million units worldwide.

Carl De Marco leaves as little to chance as possible when he organizes a WWF event. His philosophy is that when the WWF comes to town, they want to own it! De Marco must first make sure that he has sufficient security for both the patrons and wrestlers, since the scripts often call for wrestlers to whip up the crowd, and even to fight each other within it. Local promotion is also critical. For a Calgary event De Marco wanted to get a banner on a tower in the middle of the city, but there just wasn't enough time to pull it off. De Marco's publicity plans included a cross-promotion that had Calgary's own five-time WWF champion Bret "The Hitman" Hart signing autographs at a local Burger King. The President of Burger King Canada was

# The World Wrestling Federation Visits Canada

there to see the 3000 fans brought out by the WWF.

The Calgary event happened to coincide with the Calgary Stampede, so De Marco thought a bit of mayhem might draw some attention from the Stampede to the WWF. He arranged for a couple of the headline wrestlers to come out to the ticket booth and stir up the crowd that was waiting in line for tickets. Of course there were a number of news crews and other media representatives who just happened to be on hand as the wrestlers appeared. De Marco also arranged to have Alberta Premier Ralph Klein attend, an event that wasn't carried off as effectively as it could have been since De Marco didn't greet Klein right away.

The event's TV broadcast brought in an estimated $4 million. The gate in Calgary was $230 000 for an event that featured Bret "The Hitman" Hart and his brother Owen Hart winning a tag team match. The script for the evening called for the ring announcers to banter back and forth about Canada versus the U.S., the intent being to turn patriotism into profit.

The WWF employs a public relations manager and a director of marketing and communications in Canada alone. It also maintains a detailed and colourful Web site. During the 1999 Superbowl the WWF aired a one-minute commercial (estimated cost: U.S.$3.2 million) showing the Stamford WWF headquarters being trashed by the wrestling stars as they fought among themselves while discussing misconceptions about the WWF's image. With an estimated Superbowl audience of 125 million people, the WWF certainly reached a lot of potential viewers.

The WWF's promotional efforts are built around gaining audiences for the real money makers—its twelve annual pay-per-view events. The most important of these is the spring Wrestlemania, which has become the most watched and anticipated event in professional wrestling. In 1998 Wrestlemania XIV was the highest grossing pay-per-view event in the history of the WWF, with $24 000 000 in worldwide

income. The Boston event's gate alone brought in over $1 million.

From the ridiculous to the sublime, the WWF storylines are churned out week after week and take shape in arenas and on TV screens in over 100 countries throughout the world. The basic story is always the same, but people don't seem to tire of it. And like any long-running show, the continuing success of the WWF will depend on the appeal of its scripts as well as its stars.

## Questions

1. As a marketing manager, understanding your customer base is very important. How would you characterize typical wrestling fans? How would you design a market research study to measure their characteristics?

2. How do you think the marketing of professional wrestling would differ if it really was a sport?

3. What do you think is wrestling's major appeal? Is it a fashion or a fad? Do you think it has sufficient staying power to support the WWF, the WCW, and the NWO over the long term? Explain your reasoning.

4. What aspects of the WWF's business did you find surprising? interesting? shocking? Characterize this business considering the following uncontrollable factors in the WWF's marketplace: consumers, competitors, suppliers and distributors, independent media, technology, the government, and the economy.

---

## Video Questions

1. The video gives us a close inside look at the WWF as a business. Promotion management seems to be a critical element in the WWF's marketing mix. Discuss how the WWF uses this element and how it relates to the WWF's pricing, distribution, and product offering strategies.

2. Identify the duties and activities that Carl De Marco has to accomplish in

order to stage a WWF event. Can you suggest ways to help him stage these events more effectively or efficiently? Try to come up with some original ideas for positive publicity for the WWF.

**WORLD WRESTLING FEDERATION**
www.wwf.com

Sources: Based on "WWF Arena Theatre," *Venture* 662 (September 30, 1997); "Wrestlemania XIV: Highest Grossing Wrestling Pay-Per-View in History of World Wrestling Federation Canada Reaps Benefits," Canada NewsWire (April 24, 1998), www.newswire.ca; "Canadian Bret 'Hit Man' Hart New Five-time World Wrestling Federation Champion," Canada NewsWire (August 3, 1998); "Ratings Soar and the World Wrestling Federation Continues to Set Records on TSN," Canada NewsWire (February 12, 1999); "The World Wrestling Federation and Viewers Choice Team Up to Bodyslam Hunger," Canada NewsWire (March 22, 1999); Associated Press, "Sable Sues WWF," *Miami Herald* Web site, www.herald.com/sports/wrestling (Sunday, June 6, 1999); "Where It All Began," *The Wrestling Page*; and Sung-Tae Han, "Wrestling Book Unable to Pin Down Interest," *Slam Sports* (September 19, 1996).

# Consumer Analysis: Understanding and Responding to Diversity in the Marketplace

In Part 2, we see why consumer analysis is so essential and discuss consumer characteristics, needs, profiles, and decision making— and how firms can devise marketing plans responsive to today's diverse global marketplace.

### Final Consumer Behaviour

This chapter discusses final consumer behaviour. We begin with final consumer demographics, the objective and quantifiable characteristics that describe the population. We examine population size, gender, age, location, housing, mobility, income, expenditures, occupations, education, marital status, and ethnicity/race—for Canada, and a number of other countries around the globe. Then, we investigate final consumer lifestyles and decision making, useful concepts in explaining why and how consumers act as they do. Lifestyles encompass various social and psychological factors, many of which we note here. By studying the decision process, we see how consumers move from stimulus to purchase or nonpurchase.

### Organizational Consumers

In this chapter, we focus on the organizational consumers that purchase goods and services for further production, use in operations, or resale to other consumers. We look at how they differ from final consumers and at their individual characteristics, buying objectives, buying structures, constraints on purchases, and decision processes.

### Developing a Target Market Strategy

We are now ready to discuss how to plan a target market strategy. Consumer-demand patterns and segmentation bases are examined; and undifferentiated marketing (mass marketing), concentrated marketing, and differentiated marketing (multiple segmentation) are explained and contrasted. The requirements for successful segmentation and the importance of positioning are also considered. We conclude with a discussion of sales forecasting.

# The Market: The Demands of Satisfying Demand

Marketing is the anticipation, management, and satisfaction of demand through the exchange process. The reasons for and the sources of demand must be understood before undertaking any marketing program. The three chapters in Part 2 are designed to help you understand how to manage demand in Canada.

Chapter 4 introduces the topic of consumer behaviour. Understanding the characteristics that affect consumers' buying behaviour is important to any marketing effort. For example, all too often U.S. multinational firms treat Canada like the fifty-first state and fail to realize that Canadian consumers are different from their American counterparts. For example, Canadians speak English and French, have less household income than Americans, pay more taxes, have universal health care, and have twice as much unemployment to deal with. They don't respond to direct sales pitches as much, and Canadian spokespeople are better received if their honesty and likability takes precedence over the products they sell.

In Chapter 5 we will look at how organizational consumers buy. Selling to government organizations usually involves a very rigid and carefully defined process. Many firms are unaccustomed to the bureaucracy, barriers, political sensitivities, and financial constraints of selling to government consumers. To aid them the federal government agency Contracts Canada has published a guide called "The Basics of Selling to Government." Each federal government unit and division typically has a purchasing department, which is authorized to make direct purchases of goods up to $5000; Public Works and Government Services Canada handles all goods purchases of $5000 or more. Service purchases can be made directly by all federal government units. Suppliers who wish to sell to the federal government need to subscribe to the publication *Government Business Opportunities* (GBO) or suppliers can access MERX, an electronic tendering service.

In Chapter 6 we will discuss how to identify and select target markets. One of the most lucrative target markets in Canada—and the fastest growing—is senior citizens. Yet Canadian marketers have been slow to respond to their needs, partly because marketing practitioners, being much younger than the over-fifty group, have difficulty relating to it. Yet it's well recognized that aging has important implications for marketers, since it produces changes in people's needs and wants and consequently their choices of products and services. Understanding how aging affects consumption behaviour is one factor marketers need to consider when they undertake the development of a marketing mix. Given that seniors represent a market of significant disposable income and absolute size, serving their needs and wants represents a tremendous business opportunity.

**CHAPTER | 4**

# Final Consumer Behaviour

## *Chapter Objectives*

1. To show the importance and scope of consumer analysis

2. To define and enumerate important consumer demographics for the Canadian population and other countries: size, gender, and age; location, housing, and mobility; income and expenditures; occupations and education; marital status; and ethnicity/race

3. To examine trends and projections for these important demographics and study their marketing implications

4. To define and describe consumer lifestyles and their characteristics, examine selected lifestyles, and present marketing implications of lifestyle analysis

5. To define and describe the final consumer's decision process and present marketing implications

Al Harvey / The Slide Farm

**W**e approach the new millennium in a fast-paced, confusing world. Many of today's Canadian consumers are people who have rich, full lives—with everything except the time to enjoy them. Consumers even seem to lack the time to think, so marketers who try to be clever and ask consumers to spend time thinking about anything will likely come up short.

Those who live in Canada's top ten markets are bombarded by marketers. They are exposed to over 5000 corporate messages and symbols every day, including 1000 ads. Canadian consumers live in a world where news is entertainment and entertainment is news. Many of their workplaces are like video games, with new and fast-flowing information coming at them for 60 to 80 hours a week. With fax machines, cellular phones, and Internet-connected home computers there really is no such thing as a day off for a modern working person.

It's ironic that devices touted as being time-saving have turned out instead to be time-enslaving. And because productivity is up, business competition has quickened the pace to the point that the efficiency of the human relative to machines and organizations is in question.

Family life is driven by the working world, so it's hectic too. Parents hurry home from work to deal with child-care providers and feed their children (and maybe themselves) before rushing them off to dance, hockey, scouts, and lessons. If the children don't learn to manage their time they won't be fit to deal with the rigours of the world they're going to inherit. Meanwhile, finding time to do housework, personal finance, and routine medical/dental checkups is a major chore. Heaven help the family that has an unforeseen circumstance, like the car breaking down! After all this, everyone collapses for a few hours' sleep before the whole thing starts again the next day.

When Canadian consumers find the time to read a magazine, listen to the radio, or watch television they're trying to take a break, not apply razor-sharp minds to interpret the witty satire of some marketer's promotional messages. Noted Canadian media thinker Marshall McLuhan explained this phenomenon in his "rear view mirror" theory: Life is travelling so fast that what's happening in front of us is a blur. It is the past that people see clearly (out the rear view mirror); the present is seen as the future; and the future, well it's just not seen at all.

What's a marketer to do? For starters, offering simplicity is key: simple messages, easy-to-use products, and anything that saves time (even if it costs a bit more). In the past a marketer might tell a consumer that the benefit of reliability was saving money. Now a marketer would say that you don't have to waste time getting something fixed! Fast food restaurants aren't new, but they have demonstrated staying power—and still have growth potential because they deliver on the promise that you don't have to wait for your food.

There used to be a saying, "If you can't do the time, don't do the crime." In other words, people and organizations had to accept the consequences of their actions, and this meant acting responsibly. Social responsibility was a critical concern for business people in the 1980s and the 1990s. It's still something marketers must consider, but for the modern marketer a more apt saying would be "You're committing a crime if you don't save them time."[1]

In this chapter, we will focus on a number of important consumer trends in Canada and elsewhere, and consider the marketing implications of these trends. By understanding customers' activities and interests, companies can better pinpoint market needs, reasons for purchases, and changing lifestyles and purchase behaviour patterns. In this chapter, we will also study the way consumers live and spend time and money—as well as how they make purchase decisions.

## Overview

As discussed in Chapters 1 and 2, the consumer is the central focus of marketing. To devise good marketing plans, it is important to study consumer attributes and needs, lifestyles, and purchase processes and then make proper marketing-mix decisions.

*Consumer analysis is crucial in the diverse global marketplace.*

The scope of consumer analysis includes the study of who buys, what they buy, why they buy, how they make decisions to buy, when they buy, where they buy, and how often they buy. For example, a university student (who) purchases textbooks (what) because they are required for various classes (why). The student first looks up the book list at the school store and decides whether to purchase new or used books for each course (how). Then, just before the first week of classes (when), the student goes to the school store to buy the books (where). The student does this three times per year—fall, spring, and summer (how often).

An open-minded, consumer-oriented approach is imperative in today's diverse global marketplace so a firm can identify and serve its target market, minimize consumer dissatisfaction, and stay ahead of competitors. Why is this so important? As Seagate, a leader in computer data-storage products, puts it: "People buy expectations, not just things. Customer satisfaction is dependent not only on our products, but on continuously improving our way of doing business."[2]

In Chapters 4 to 6, the concepts you need to understand consumers in Canada and other nations worldwide, to select target markets, and to relate marketing strategy to consumer behaviour are detailed. Chapter 4 examines final consumer demographics, lifestyles, and decision making. **Final consumers** buy goods and services for personal, family, or household use.

**Final consumers** *buy for personal, family, or household use;* **organizational consumers** *buy for production, operations, or resale.*

Chapter 5 centres on the characteristics and behaviour of **organizational consumers**, those buying goods and services for further production, to be used in operating the organization, or for resale to other consumers. Chapter 6 explains how to devise a **target market strategy** and use sales forecasts.

## Demographics Defined and Enumerated[3]

**Consumer demographics** are objective and quantifiable population characteristics. They are relatively easy to identify, collect, measure, and analyze—and show diversity around the globe. The demographics covered in Chapter 4 are population size, gender, and age; location, housing, and mobility; income and expenditures; occupations and education; marital status; and ethnicity/race.

**Consumer demographics** *are population characteristics that are easy to identify and measure.* **Demographic profiles** *may be formed.*

As shown in Figure 4-1, after separately examining various demographic factors a firm can form a **consumer demographic profile**—a demographic composite of a consumer group. By establishing consumer profiles, a firm can pinpoint both attractive and declining market opportunities. For example, in highly industrialized nations, the population is growing more slowly, people are older, incomes are higher, more people work in white-collar jobs, and there are smaller households than in less-developed and developing countries. Together, these factors have a great impact on the goods and services that are offered and on marketing strategies for these items.

Several secondary sources offer data on consumer demographics. For Canadian demographics, a key source is the *Census of Population* (undertaken by Statistics Canada), a federal government research project. Census information provides a wide

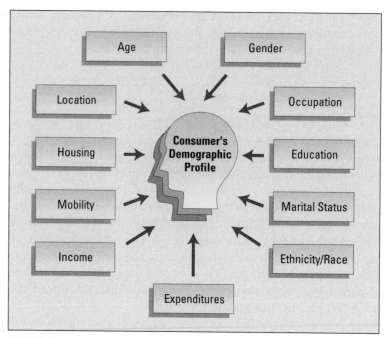

**FIGURE 4-1**

**Factors Determining a Consumer's Demographic Profile**

range of national, provincial, and local data via printed reports, computer tapes, microfiche, CD-ROM diskettes, and online databases. Many marketing research firms and provincial data centres arrange census data by postal code, provide forecasts, and update information.

Since complete census data are gathered only once every five years in Canada, they must be supplemented by Statistics Canada estimates and statistics from chambers of commerce, public utilities, and others. The *Canada Yearbook* and *The Market Research Handbook* (both published by Statistics Canada), along with *Canadian Markets* (published by the *Financial Post*) contain a great deal of useful information. *The Canadian Global Almanac* (published by Macmillan Canada) is also a quick reference source for demographic information.

*American Demographics* is a monthly magazine dealing mostly with U.S. demographic trends. The *Survey of Buying Power* (published annually by *Sales & Marketing Management*) has current Canadian and U.S. data by metropolitan area and state/province, including retail sales by merchandise category, personal disposable income, and five-year estimates. Other secondary sources are *Editor & Publisher Market Guide, Rand McNally Commercial Atlas & Market Guide, Standard Rate & Data Service*, local newspapers, and regional planning boards.

The United Nations (UN), Euromonitor, and the Organization for Economic Cooperation and Development (OECD) are sources of international demographic data. The UN publishes a *Statistical Yearbook* and a *Demographic Yearbook*. Euromonitor publishes *International Marketing Data and Statistics*. OECD issues ongoing demographic and economic reports. In highly industrialized nations, demographic data are fairly accurate because actual data are collected on a regular basis. In less-developed and developing nations, demographic data are often based on estimates rather than actual data. Throughout this chapter, information is provided on Canadian and worldwide demographics. A broad cross-section of country examples is provided to give the reader a good sense of the demographic diversity that exists around the globe.

**ORGANIZATION FOR ECONOMIC CO-OPERATION AND DEVELOPMENT (OECD)**
www.oecd.org/

## TECHNOLOGY AND MARKETING

### Getting and Dealing with Online Demographic Data

**N**eed Canadian demographic data in a hurry? In Canada you can subscribe to Statistics Canada Daily at listproc@statscan.ca. *The Daily* features announcements about products and services, as well as information on new data and releases by Statistics Canada. You can also visit Statistics Canada's Web site (www.statscan.ca), which contains media releases, provides frequently requested statistics, product and service catalogues, and issues of *The Daily*. Of course the real service comes from CANSIM, Statistics Canada's computerized database and information retrieval service. The Canadian Socio-Economic Information Management System (CANSIM) is composed of three basic databases: 1) Census Summary Data Service, 2) Cross-Classified database, and 3) Time Series database. CANSIM is available online for a fee through modem-equipped PCs that can access Stats Canada regional offices or one of the national data transmission networks operating in Canada.

Want more data? Try Industry Canada's Strategis Database at www.strategis.ic.ca. Much of the data found here is based on reports from Statistics Canada, but the access to the information and its form is tailored more to the business person.

You think Canada is the only place to find information about Canada? The U.N. (www.un.org), the OECD (www.oedc.org), and several branches of the U.S. government (e.g., the U.S. Department of Commerce, the CIA, the White House, the Congress of the United States) maintain statistics on Canada too. Much of the foreign data on Canada is originally sourced from Statistics Canada, but foreign databases gather information from private sources as well.

There are a couple of small problems with using foreign databases: any economic data uses U.S. currency to measure the size of the Canadian economy; and you frequently find different values for the same information. For example, population reports for Canada and GDP growth rate percentages can provide different figures for the same year depending on whether the source is *The Daily*, CANSIM, Strategis, the OECD, the CIA factbook, or the U.N.

A market researcher must consider how to reconcile differences, and how important it is to do so. Should the researcher average them, take the median value, report a range of values, or investigate the data collection so as to designate and choose a "most reliable" source? These are just some of the possibilities. How far one goes to validate the information depends on how it is to be used.

For example, a marketing textbook author wishing to make comparisons among markets will have less concern for absolute accuracy, since getting a general picture of the relative size of markets and conveying this notion to others is all that's needed. A marketing manager, on the other hand, who is using the information to establish an accurate sales forecast for production scheduling and marketing expenditures, would want the information to be as accurate as possible. A thorough understanding of the information sources and how they collect and report data is required.

As a marketing researcher, how would you select and report data from different online sources?

Source: Based on material in Jackson Morton, "Census of the Internet," *American Demographics* (March 1995), pp. 52–53 and Jim Carroll and Rick Broadhead, *1999 Canadian Internet Directory and Research Guide* (Scarborough: Prentice Hall Canada).

## Population Size, Gender, and Age

The world population is expected to grow from 6.2 billion in 2000 to 6.5 billion in 2005, an increase of 1.33 per cent annually. Over the same period, Canada's population is expected to grow from 31 million to 32.5 million, an annual increase of 1.0 per cent. Thus, the Canadian population will drop from .508 per cent of the world population in 1995 to .5 per cent of the world population in the year 2000. Figure 4-2 shows world population distribution by region for 1990 and 2000.

*Relatively speaking, the Canadian population is expanding slowly. There are also many firstborns, more women than men, and a rising average age.*

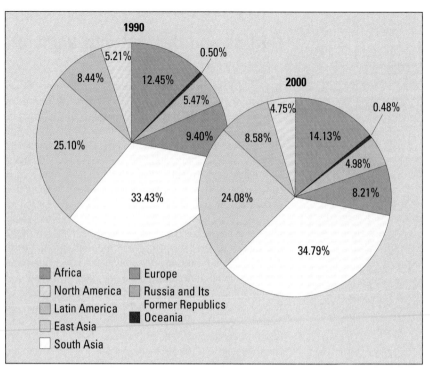

**FIGURE 4-2**

**The World's Population Distribution, 1990 and 2000**
*Source: U.S. Bureau of the Census.*

Newborns account for less than 2 per cent of the population in industrialized nations (1.3 per cent in Canada)—compared to up to 4 per cent or more in nations such as Afghanistan, Syria, and Zaire. For industrialized countries, a large proportion of births are firstborns.

Worldwide, males and females comprise roughly equal percentages of the population (50.5 per cent female in Canada in 1996, 49.5 per cent male). Yet in many industrialized countries, females comprise well over one-half of the population—mostly due to differences in life expectancy. For example, the life expectancy for newborn females is 81 in Canada, 80 years in Italy, 80 in the United States, and 74 in Russia; it is 76 years for newborn males in Canada, 76 in Italy, 73 in the United States, and 64 in Russia.

The populations in industrialized nations are older than those in less-developed and developing nations. Today, the median age of the population is about 35 years in Canada, 37 years in Japan, 36 in Italy and Great Britain, 34 in the United States, 25 in China, 23 in Brazil, 20 in Mexico, and 16 in Nigeria.

**CANSIM**
www.library.ubc.ca/rsrc/cansim.html

## Marketing Implications

Around the world, there are opportunities for marketing all types of goods and services. However, in industrialized countries, the low rate of population growth means that firms there need to focus on specific opportunities, such as firstborns, females, and expanding age groups. There will be heightened battles among firms for market share in industrialized nations.

The number of firstborns is significant because parents have many initial purchases to make, for such items as furniture, clothing, and transportation (stroller, car seat, and so on). On average, parents in industrialized nations spend thousands of dollars (including food, clothing, furniture and bedding, toys, health care, child care, and other items) to raise a first child to just his or her first birthday, far more than on each later child. And today's parents are much more likely to bring their babies with them when they travel.

By the year 2001, there will be 314 800 more females than males in Canada's total population. This has important implications for marketers of clothing, household services, appliances, cars, and other items. Accordingly, more and more companies are gearing their appeals to women. Special interest should be paid to older females, who greatly outnumber their male counterparts.

The shifting age distribution in industrialized countries brings many possibilities. For example, colleges and universities are increasing their recruitment of older, nontraditional students. Sports and recreation companies are becoming more oriented toward the over-45 age group. The over-65 age group represents a growing market for food, medical care, vacation homes, telephone services, travel, entertainment, and restaurants.

On the other hand, the much higher rate of population growth—usually across both genders and all age groups—in less-developed and developing countries means that company opportunities there will be broad-based. There will be openings for companies to substantially increase the overall sales of food, clothing, autos, communications equipment, financial services, and a host of other goods and services—rather than fight over market share or carve up very small market segments. For example, from 1990 to 2000, the total populations in China, Nigeria, and Brazil are expected to rise by 160 million, 42 million, and 28 million people, respectively.

## Location, Housing, and Mobility

During this century, there has been a major move of the world population to large urban areas and their surrounding suburbs. As of 1996, over fifteen cities had at least ten million residents each—led by Tokyo/Yokohama and Mexico City. But, as Figure 4-3 shows, the level of urbanization varies greatly by country.

Today, 77 per cent of the Canadian population resides in urban areas and approximately 80 per cent of the population lives within 160 kilometres of the U.S. border. The population is concentrated in twenty-five **Census Metropolitan Areas** or CMAs (Statistics Canada defines a CMA as a main labour-market area of an urban

*The world is becoming more urban. Canadian urban areas are classed as* **Census Metropolitan Areas** *and* **Census Agglomeration Areas**.

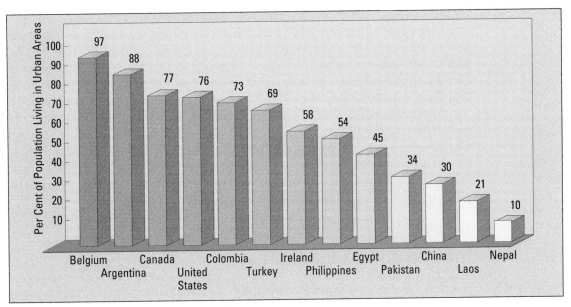

**FIGURE 4-3**

**The Urbanization of Selected Countries**
*Source: United Nations*

area with at least 100 000 people) and 113 **Census Agglomeration Areas** or CAs (Statistics Canada defines a CA as a main labour-market area of an urban area with at least 10 000 people and less than 100 000 people).

*Globally, many people own homes and population mobility is high on a world-wide basis.*

In many parts of the world, the majority of people own the homes in which they reside. Here are some examples: Canada, 64 per cent; Bangladesh, 91 per cent; Paraguay, 81 per cent; New Zealand, 74 per cent; Greece, 73 per cent; Finland, 68 per cent; United States, 65 per cent; and Sri Lanka, 61 per cent.

The worldwide mobility of the population is quite high; annually, millions of people emigrate from one nation to another and hundreds of millions move within their nations. During the last decade more than 2 million people have legally immigrated to Canada, while about 500 000 have left. Among Canadian residents, 15 to 20 per cent change their place of residence annually, with most remaining in the same locality. Still, the number of people who immigrated, emigrated, or moved between provinces in Canada in 1998 was well over 300 000. In Canada the population is generally moving to the west, with virtually all provinces having a net loss due to inter-provincial migration in 1998, with the exceptions of Ontario and Alberta, which had substantial gains. Alberta gained 46 787 people and Ontario 6662, while the provinces with the largest decreases were Quebec (–17 454), Newfoundland (–11 434), Manitoba (–5383), and Nova Scotia (–5040).

### Marketing Implications

When a nation's population is urbanized, marketing programs are more cost efficient, it is easier to offer goods and services to large groups of consumers, and mass distribution and advertising are possible. In some regions of the world, suburban shopping has been growing, leading to branch outlets in suburbs and improved transportation and delivery services.

**HONDA**
www.honda.com/toc/

**SHOPPERS DRUG MART**
www.imasco.com/imasco/e/companies/pharma

**VISA**
www.visa.com

The continuing interest in home ownership offers sales potential for such home-based items as furniture, appliances, carpeting, and insurance. Specially modified products for those occupying small homes and for apartment owners, such as space-efficient washers and dryers, are growing in importance. Because some large-ticket home purchases are greatly affected by the economy, firms need to monitor economic conditions carefully.

Population mobility offers openings for well-advertised global, national, or regional brands; retail chains and franchises; and major credit cards—among others. Their names are well known when consumers relocate and represent an assurance of quality. For example, Crest toothpaste, Heineken beer, British Airways, Honda, McDonald's, and Visa are recognized and successful worldwide, as well as throughout Canada. Shoppers Drug Mart stores do good business in Florida because a number of Canadian "Snowbirds" who winter there or have relocated there patronize them.

Companies often refocus their marketing programs as they anticipate the growth of certain geographic areas and the decline of others. For instance, in Canada, marketing efforts directed at consumers in British Columbia have risen dramatically. Still, firms should be aware of the possibility of oversaturation in these areas. Regions being abandoned by some firms, like Quebec and the Maritimes, should be reviewed by comparing population trends with competition levels.

## Income and Expenditures

*Country-by-country income data are hard to compare.*

Consumer income and expenditure patterns are valuable demographic factors when properly studied. In examining them, these points should be kept in mind:

- Personal income is often stated as GDP per capita—the total value of goods and services produced in a nation divided by its population size. This does not report what people really earn and it inflates per-capita income if a small portion of the population is affluent. A better measure is median income—the income for those at the fiftieth percentile in a nation; it is a true midpoint. Yet median incomes are rarely reported outside Canada and the United States.

- Personal income can be expressed as family, household, and per capita. Because families are larger than households and per-capita income is on an individual basis, these units are not directly comparable. Income can also be stated in pre-tax or after-tax terms, which are not directly comparable.

- Since prices differ by country, a comparison of average incomes that does not take purchasing power into effect will be inaccurate.

- Economic growth is cyclical; at any given time, some countries will be performing well while others are struggling.

- Although the definition of poverty varies greatly by nation, one billion people in the world suffer from malnutrition, illiteracy, and disease.

During the 1960s and early 1970s, real income in Canada rose considerably. Growth then slowed; and from 1981 to 1983, real income fell. Between 1983 and 1990, real income rose moderately—before falling again in 1991. Since then, it has fluctuated slightly each year. Thus, in sum, real Canadian income has gone up rather little over the last twenty-five years.

The most recently released data for Canada indicates that average family income was $54 583 in 1995 for the nation's total of 7.3 million families. This represented a drop of $2756 in 1995 dollars from a 1990 level of $57 339. For the 4.2 million Canadian families that had two working parents the average family income was $67 894. For the other 2.1 million husband and wife families where only the husband earned income the value was $42 200. For the 147 000 families where there was a single male working parent the family income was $45 666, while the 18 000 families headed by a non-working male parent had average incomes of $15 008. In comparison, for the 596 000 single-parent families headed by a working woman the family income was $33 960, while family income was only $12 765 for the 192 000 families where the head was a non-working woman.

The slowdown in real Canadian income growth has occurred because income rises have been virtually offset by higher prices. This has led to a higher **cost of living**, the total amount consumers annually pay for goods and services.

*Changes in the* **cost of living** *are measured by a* **consumer price index**.

Over the last twenty-five years in Canada, the greatest price increases have been for recreation, education, alcohol, and tobacco products; the smallest have been for clothing and food.

Many nations monitor their cost of living by means of a **consumer price index** (CPI), which measures monthly and yearly price changes (the rate of inflation) for a broad range of consumer goods and services. Since 1983, the overall annual rise in the Canadian CPI has been under 5 per cent (except for 1989–1992, when it rose on average by 6 per cent). In 1992, the CPI rose less than 3 per cent in Canada, and less than 5 per cent in the United States, France, Great Britain, and Germany. It went up by 10 per cent or more in many developing and less-developed countries.

Global consumption patterns have been shifting. In industrialized nations, the proportion of income that people spend on food, beverages, and tobacco has been declining. The percentage spent on medical care, personal business, and recreation has been rising. In less-developed and developing nations, the percentage of spending devoted to food remains high. Canadians spend 15.6 per cent of income on food, beverages and tobacco and 1.9 per cent on health care. Americans spend 18 per cent of income on food, beverages, and tobacco and 16 per cent on medical care. In contrast, Argentines spend 40 per cent of income on food, beverages, and tobacco and 4 per cent on medical care, while Pakistanis spend 47 per cent of income on food, beverages, and tobacco and 5 per cent on medical care.

*Consumption reflects* **disposable income** *and* **discretionary income**.

**Disposable income** is a person's, household's, or family's total after-tax income to be used for spending and/or savings. **Discretionary income** is what a person, household, or family has available to spend on luxuries, after necessities are bought. Classifying some product categories as necessities or luxuries depends on a nation's standard of living. In Canada autos and phones are generally considered necessities; in many less-developed countries, they are typically considered luxuries.

## Marketing Implications

Several marketing implications regarding consumer income can be drawn:

- Companies need to be quite careful in drawing conclusions about the income levels in different countries. Terms must be properly defined and purchasing power, as well as income levels, assessed.

- There is great income diversity between countries. Thus, firms' goods, services, and marketing strategies should be consistent with the income levels in the targeted nations.

- There is tremendous income diversity within countries. This means that, even in the same country, some firms can prosper by focusing on lower-income consumers while others succeed by targeting upper-income consumers.

- The cost of living affects the discretionary income that people have available to spend. For goods and services perceived as luxuries, consumers need to have discretionary income available.

U.S.-based Whirlpool is a good example of a firm that understands how to react to consumer income levels. It knows that outside Canada, the United States, and Western Europe, the middle-class consumer is quite different. A consumer has to work 40 to 45 days to afford a washing machine in Poland, 35 days in the Czech Republic, and 30 days in Hungary—versus five days in Western Europe. As a result, Whirlpool arranges for more financing in Eastern Europe.[4]

**WHIRLPOOL**
www.whirlpool.com/

# Occupations and Education

*The trend to white-collar and service occupations is continuing in industrialized countries.*

The labour force in industrialized nations continues to move to white-collar and service occupations. In less-developed and developing nations, many jobs still involve manual work and are more often agriculture-based.

The total Canadian labour force (people over 15 years of age who are eligible to work) is 15.3 million people. The employed labour force in Canada amounts to 13.9 million people. Over the last five years, the percentage of Canadian workers in the service sector has stayed constant at about 73 per cent of all workers, while the goods-producing sector employs the remaining 27 per cent. Employment in service sector areas such as transportation, storage, and communication; trade; finance, insurance, and real estate; and community, business, and personal services has increased over the last five years. The only service sector in which there has been an employment decline in the last five years has been in the area of public administration, where the number of jobs has gone from 902 800 (9.4 per cent of service sector jobs) to 790 900 jobs (7.8 per cent of service sector jobs). Within the goods-producing sector of primary industries there has been a decline in the number and importance of agricultural jobs from 450 500 (13 per cent of goods-producing jobs) to 422 700 (11.2 per cent of goods-producing jobs). In manufacturing, employment has increased in number and importance from 1 893 200 jobs (54.9 percent of goods-producing jobs) to 2 166 800 jobs (57.5 per cent of goods-producing jobs).

*Women are a large and growing percentage of the worldwide labour force; they make up 45 per cent of the Canadian labour force.*

Another change in the labour force throughout the world has been the increase in the number and percentage of working women. For example, in 1971, 3 million women comprised 34 per cent of the total Canadian labour force. Today, 6.9 million women account for 45 per cent of the labour force, and 52 per cent of adult women in Canada are working.

Unemployment rates, which reflect the percentage of adults in the total labour force not working, vary widely by nation. For instance, during 1996, the Canadian unemployment rate was about 9.7 per cent but falling. In comparison, the 1996 unemployment rate in the U.S. was 5.4 per cent, while those in Belgium, Finland, France, Great Britain, and Italy were around 10 per cent; Spain's rate was 22 per cent. Some worldwide unemployment has been temporary, due to weak domestic and international economies. Other times, depending on the nation and industry, many job losses have been permanent. Unemployment is often accompanied by cutbacks in discretionary purchases.

Great strides are being made globally to upgrade educational attainment, but the level of education tends to be much higher in industrialized nations than in less-developed and developing ones. One measure of educational attainment is the literacy rate—the percentage of people in a country who can read and write. Canada's literacy rate is 99 per cent and in industrialized nations the literacy rate exceeds 95 per cent. Here are the rates for some less-developed and developing nations: Bolivia, 78 per cent; Cambodia, 74 per cent; Chad, 30 per cent; China, 78 per cent; Morocco, 50 per cent; and Saudi Arabia, 62 per cent.

*Global education levels are going up.*

Another measure of educational attainment is the number of years of formal schooling expected. According to the United Nations, Canadians can expect to complete 17.5 years of formal schooling, the highest of any nation. Values for some other large industrialized nations include: United Kingdom 16.3 years, U.S. 15.8 years, France 15.4 years, Germany 15.1 years, and Japan 14 years.

The sharp increase in working women and higher educational attainment have generally contributed to the growing number of people in upper-income brackets; the rather high unemployment rates in some nations and industries and slow-growth economies have caused other families to have low incomes.

## Marketing Implications

The occupations and education of the population have marketing implications. A greater number and percentage of the total population are in the labour force than before, and this workforce needs transportation, clothing, restaurants, and personal services; stores have opportunities in commercial centres; and the market for job-oriented goods and services is growing and the shift in jobs means different needs and aspirations in consumer purchases.

Because working women have less time for shopping and operating the home, they tend to be interested in convenience and customer service. They often cannot shop during weekdays and many require evening and weekend store hours, efficient store layouts, and mail-order and phone purchases. Such time-saving devices as microwave ovens and food processors, prepared foods, pre-wrapped goods, and special services (such as automatic teller machines), appeal to working women. Also, child-related services, such as daytime child care, are particularly important for them. Yet, too few firms help employees in this area, leaving a prime opening for specialized firms to market these services.

As the population's education level rises, firms need to respond in terms of better information, better product quality, better customer service, enhanced safety and environmental controls, greater accuracy in learning and meeting consumer expectations, and improved consumer-complaint departments. At the same time, companies marketing in less-developed and developing countries need to keep the literacy rates of those areas in mind and adapt products, packaging, promotion messages, and operating instructions accordingly.

# Marital Status

Marriage and family are powerful institutions worldwide; but in some nations they are now less dominant than they once were. Although 160 000 couples get married each year, only 60 per cent of Canadian adults are married; the percentage of married adults in many other nations is much higher. The average Canadian age at first marriage is 29 years for males and 27 years for females—up from 27.7 and 24.7 in 1960. Thus, the average Canadian family size has gone from 3.9 in 1961 to 3.1 in 1996. The male and female ages at first marriage are much lower in less-developed and developing nations; and the average family is bigger there.

A **family** is a group of two or more persons residing together who are related by blood, marriage, or adoption. A **household** is a person or group of persons occupying a housing unit, whether related or unrelated. In many nations, average household size has been dropping. For example, in 1994 23 per cent of Canadian households were one-person units while 77 per cent were more than one person. In 1996 there were 10.8 million Canadian households, 29 per cent of which were one-person units, with family households accounting for the remaining 71 per cent.

## Marketing Implications

Despite changes over the last thirty or so years, marriage and family are still vital institutions around the world and in Canada. This creates opportunities for industries associated with weddings (such as caterers and travel agents), family life (such as financial services and full-sized cars), and divorce (such as attorneys). When marriages occur later in individuals' lives, those people have better financial resources and two-income families are more prevalent. This presents opportunities for firms involved with clothing, furniture, entertainment, and recreation.

The growth of single-person households provides opportunities for home and home furnishings industries and those that produce specialized products. These implications also apply to divorced and widowed persons. For example, smaller households have a demand for smaller homes, appropriate-sized furnishings and appliances, and single-serving food packages.

# Ethnicity/Race

From a demographics perspective, **ethnicity/race** is studied to determine the existence of diversity among and within nations in terms of language and country of origin or race.

Worldwide, there are over 200 different languages spoken by at least 1 million people each—and twelve of those are spoken by 100+ million people each (including Mandarin, English, Hindi, and Spanish). Thus, there are vast linguistic differences among nations. Even within nations, there is often linguistic diversity. For example, Canada (English and French), Chad (French and Arabic), India (Hindi and English), and Peru (Spanish and Quechua) all have two official languages. One of the issues facing the European Community in its unification drive is the multiplicity of languages spoken in the fifteen member nations.

Most nations consist of people representing different ethnic and racial backgrounds. For instance, among those living in the Philippines are Malays, Chinese, Americans, and Spaniards. Sometimes, the people in various groups continue to speak in the languages of their countries of origin, even though they may have resided in their current nations for one or two generations.

Canada is comprised of people from virtually every ethnic group in the world. Statistics Canada measures ethnic origin, which is defined as the ethnic or cultural group to which the respondent or the respondent's ancestors belonged on first coming to North America. The 1996 Census in Canada was the first time that "ethnicity-race" was measured as a census category. The results of ethnicity reporting from the 1996 Census for the top ten groups were as follows: Canadian 30.8%, English 23.9%, French 19.6%, Scottish 14.9%, Irish 13.2%, German 9.7%, Italian 4.2%, Aboriginal 3.9%, Ukrainian 3.6%, and Chinese 3.2%.

## Marketing Implications

The ethnic/racial diversity of the world's population means firms must be careful not to generalize or stereotype—either in dealing with multiple nations or in marketing to different ethnic/racial groups within the same nation. Companies marketing goods and services in Canada might miss some prime opportunities if they do not research and adapt to the racial/ethnic characteristics of the marketplace:

- Marketers can reach specific ethnic groups in Canada with specialized media. There are 13 television stations and 44 radio stations that air ethnic programming, and 197 magazines and newspapers printed for 43 different ethnic groups. Figure 4-4 shows an ad for one such medium.

- The most recent issue of *Marketing Magazine's* "Guide to Multicultural Marketing Services" lists the following providers that specialize in multicultural marketing services in Canada: ten advertising agencies, three consulting services, two creative services, one direct mail service, one media broker, two market research firms, and five translation services.[5]

- In the 1996 Census of Population 3.2 million people reported themselves as members of visible minorities. This included 860 000 Chinese, 671 000 South Asian, 173 000 Southeast Asian, 68 000 Japanese, and 64 000 Korean. There were 574 000 people who reported their group as Black. Seventy per cent of the visible minorities live in Toronto (1.3 million), Vancouver (564 000), and Montreal (401 000).

- The purchasing power and population growth rate of ethnic markets are expected to be greater than those for the Canadian market as a whole by the year 2000. For example, population growth among Italian, Chinese, East Indian, Portuguese, Greek, and Polish ethnic groups is expected to be 33 per cent, growing from 2.1 million in 1995 to 2.8 million people by the year 2000.[6]

- "For those approaching target marketing correctly, the benefits are there. One of Canada's major banks showed a 400 per cent increase over five years in its Chinese business when it took an aggressive marketing approach. Besides including Chinese people in their mass marketing material, they also developed Chinese-language ads, direct mail and in-branch materials, and took a highly visible role

**FIGURE 4-4**

**Marketing to a Diverse Marketplace**
*Courtesy CFMT-TV*

supporting community events. Another advertiser, an automaker, saw a 25 per cent boost in sales to the Chinese market due to an integrated ethnic-marketing approach." However, media vehicles targeted to ethnic markets have had a tougher time marketing themselves. Maclean Hunter Publications, which launched a Chinese version of *Maclean's* magazine in 1995, suspended its publication in 1998 due to lack of advertiser support and the inability to acquire a paid circulation base among Chinese readers. Competition from Chinese dailies in Toronto, like *Sing Tao*, was another factor that led to the suspension of the Chinese Edition of *Maclean's*.[7]

## Uses of Demographic Data

As we noted at the beginning of the chapter, after studying individual demographics a firm can form consumer demographic profiles to better focus marketing efforts. Here, three examples of demographic profiles are presented.

Profiles of the Canadian, American, and Mexican populations can be contrasted:

|  | CANADA | UNITED STATES | MEXICO |
|---|---|---|---|
| Annual population growth (%) | 1.0 | 0.9 | 1.9 |
| Life expectancy (years) | 78 | 77 | 74 |
| Median age (years) | 35 | 34 | 20 |
| Urban population (%) | 77 | 76 | 71 |
| Income ratio of top fifth of population to bottom fifth | 8.3 | 15 | 14 |
| Working women as part of total labour force (%) | 45 | 46 | 37 |
| Literacy rate (%) | 99 | 96 | 90 |
| Average household size | 2.5 | 2.7 | 5.6 |

One of the best indicators of consumer buying trends and the underlying interplay of needs, tastes, and desires is the rate at which people buy certain household goods and appliances. It comes as no surprise that 98% of households in Canada have a colour television. That figure drops to 86% for microwave ovens and 85% for VCRs. In the not-everyone-has-one category are compact disk players (58%), gas barbecues (54%), and automatic dishwashers (50%). In Canada 4.5 million people have Internet access; 4.2 million households (36%) have a computer, and 1.5 million of these households access the Internet from home. About 19% of Canadian households currently have a cellular phone.[8]

## Limitations of Demographics

*Demographic data may be dated, unavailable, or too general, may require profile analysis, and may not consider reasons for behaviour.*

In applying demographic data, these limitations should be noted:

- Information may be old. In Canada, a full census is done only once every five years and there are time lags before data are released.
- Data on various demographics may be unavailable in some nations, especially less-developed and developing ones.
- Summary data may be too broad and hide opportunities and risks in small markets or specialized product categories.
- Single demographics may not be useful. A demographic profile may be needed.

- The psychological or social factors influencing people are not considered.
- The purchase-making process is not explained.
- Demographics do not provide insights into what motivates people to make purchase decisions. Why do people with similar demographic profiles buy different products or brands?

To overcome these limitations, marketers, in increasing numbers, are going beyond just demographics in studying final consumers. They are using demographic data in conjunction with and as part of consumer lifestyle and decision-making analysis. The latter two topics are the focus of the rest of this chapter.

A **lifestyle** represents the way in which a person lives and spends time and money. It is based on the social and psychological factors that have been internalized by that person—as well as his or her demographic background.[9] These factors overlap and complement each other; they are not independent or exclusive of one another. The consumer's decision process involves the steps a person uses in buying goods and services: stimulus, problem awareness, information search, evaluation of alternatives, purchase, and post-purchase behaviour. Demographics, social factors, and psychological factors all affect the process.

*Consumer **lifestyles** describe how people live. In making purchases, people use a decision process with several stages.*

# Consumer Lifestyles

The social and psychological characteristics that help form final consumer lifestyles are described next.

## Social Characteristics of Consumers

The social profile of a final consumer is based on a combination of culture, social class, social performance, reference groups, opinion leaders, family life cycle, and time expenditures (activities). See Figure 4-5.

A **culture** comprises a group of people who share a distinctive heritage, such as Canadians or Americans. People learn about socially proper behaviour and beliefs

*Each **culture** transmits socially acceptable behaviour and attitudes.*

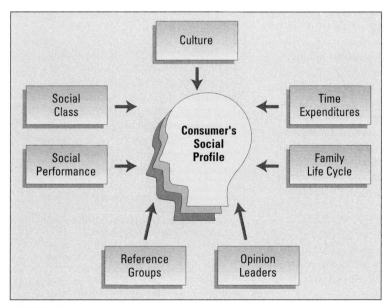

**FIGURE 4-5**

**Factors Determining a Consumer's Social Profile**

through their culture. As a nation, Canada was founded upon the principles of "Law, Order, and Good Government," in contrast to the United States, which enshrined "life, liberty and the pursuit of happiness" in their constitution. Canadians' culture can be characterized as follows: support collective responsibility; have confidence in social institutions such as education, health care, and the police; place importance on consensus; willing to accept difference and diversity; health conscious; pessimistic and skeptical; value driven; frugal; seeking personalization; brand disloyal; informed buyers.[10] When the Canada–U.S. Free Trade Agreement was signed in 1987 there was widespread concern that Canada would lose its cultural sovereignty to the U.S. So far, this concern has not been borne out. Consider the following two views of marketing in Canada, from an American and a Canadian marketer respectively.

Although Americans can feel at home in Canada by attending major league baseball games, eating at McDonald's, and shopping at Wal-Mart, they need to realize that Canada is not a U.S. state. Canadian consumers are different: for example, they are more British and French and less German in their ancestry than are Americans. Canada pursues a multicultural policy, while the U.S. fosters a melting-pot approach. Canada's population is more white and more Asian than that of the U.S., which is more black and Hispanic. Canadians speak English and French, which means packaging must be bilingual. Finally, Canadians have less household income than

## ETHICS AND TODAY'S MARKETER

## What Should Be Done with Unethical Consumers?

Although we often dwell on the unethical practices of business people, consumers can also engage in unethical activities. For example, in a retail setting, there are many opportunities for unethical behaviour by consumers. These include deliberately misrepresenting where an item was bought in order to get an exchange at a local store, returning merchandise beyond a store's posted return period, misrepresenting a price at another store as a bargaining tactic, buying an item (such as a large-screen TV to watch the Grey Cup or Super Bowl) with the intention of returning it, offering to pay a retailer in cash to avoid payment of sales taxes, and shoplifting. In Canada it is estimated that retailers lose about $3 billion in goods to shoplifting and bookkeeping errors (about 1.5 per cent of sales) with about one-half of this amount accounted for by customers, about one-quarter by employees and the other quarter due to bookkeeping errors and other causes.

Many consumers try to rationalize their unethical practices as a way of reducing self-blame or to make the activities appear more socially acceptable. Let's look at how people typically seek to rationalize the act of shoplifting:

- *Denial of responsibility*—"It's not my fault, I had no other choice."

- *Denial of injury*—"What's the big deal? Nobody will miss it."
- *Denial of victim*—"It's their fault; if they had been fair with me, I would not have done it."
- *Condemning the condemners*—"It's a joke they should find fault with me, after the ripoffs they have engineered."
- *Appealing to higher loyalties*—"To some, what I did may appear wrong, but I did it for my family."

These excuses can also be used to rationalize other unethical practices. For instance, denial of injury can be used to suggest that stores plan for consumer shoplifting in setting their original prices.

As vice-president of operations for a retail chain, how would you try to get shoppers to understand that they too have a responsibility to be ethical?

Source: Based on material in David Strutton, Scott J. Vitell, and Lou E. Pelton, "How Consumers May Justify Inappropriate Behaviour in Market Settings: An Application on the Techniques of Neutralization," *Journal of Business Research*, Vol. 30 (July 1994), pp. 253–260; "Retail Council of Canada's Annual Survey," *Globe and Mail*, Metro Edition (April 11, 1995), p. B13 ; "Retailers Get Upper Hand on Five-Finger Discounts," *Globe and Mail*, Metro Edition (April 19, 1994), p. B7.

Americans, pay more taxes, have universal health care, and have twice as much unemployment.[11]

What's the difference between Canadians and Americans? Americans are born salespeople and love hucksters. Americans love to acquire things and love to be told a product is bigger, better, or stronger. The character Joe Isuzu, the lying car salesperson used in a 1980s advertising campaign, was embraced by Americans but not Canadians. Canadians don't seem to respond to direct pitches as much. Canadian spokespeople are well received if they are more interested in their own honesty and likability rather than the products they sell. Americans are proud of conquering and taming their nation, while Canadians preach harmony and survival. John Wayne epitomizes the typical U.S. hero, while Terry Fox typifies a Canadian hero. Canadian heroes are made by deed and not by stature. They are approachable, human, and not too clouded with myths. In fact, Canadians don't really worship heroes in the way that American do; very few Canadians can actually name any Canadian war heroes, while most Americans can name several of their own. "Americans acquire, Canadians use. Americans mythologize, Canadians pragmatize. Americans celebrate hubris, Canadians tenaciousness."[12]

**Social class** systems reflect a "status hierarchy by which groups and individuals are classified on the basis of esteem and prestige."[13] They exist virtually everywhere and separate society into divisions, informally or formally grouping those with similar values and lifestyles. Such systems in industrialized nations have a larger middle class, greater interchange among classes, and less rigidly defined classes than those in less-developed and developing nations. Social classes are based on income, occupation, education, and type of dwelling. Each social class may represent a distinct target market for a firm. Table 4-1 shows an informal social class structure.

**Social class** *separates society into divisions.*

**Social performance** refers to how a person carries out his or her roles as a worker, family member, citizen, and friend. One person may be an executive, have a happy family life, be active in the community, and have many friends. Another may never go higher than assistant manager, be divorced, not partake in community affairs, and have few friends. Many combinations of social performance are possible—such as vice-president and divorced.

**Social performance** *describes how people fulfil roles.*

A **reference group** is one that influences a person's thoughts or actions. For many goods and services, these groups have a large impact on purchases. Face-to-face reference groups, such as family and friends, have the most effect. Yet, other—more general—groups also affect behaviour and may be cited in marketing products. Ads showing goods and services being used by college students, successful professionals, and pet owners often ask viewers to join the "group" and make similar purchases. By pinpointing reference groups that most sway consumers, firms can better aim their strategies.[14]

**Reference groups** *influence thoughts and behaviour.*

Firms want to know which persons in reference groups are **opinion leaders**. These are people to whom other consumers turn for advice and information via face-to-face communication. They tend to be expert about a product category, socially accepted, long-standing members of the community, gregarious, active, and trusted; and they tend to seek approval from others. They normally have an impact over a narrow product range and are perceived as more believable than company-sponsored information.

**Opinion leaders** *affect others through face-to-face contact.*

The **family life cycle** describes how a family evolves through various stages from bachelorhood to solitary retirement. At each stage, needs, experience, income, family composition, and the use of **joint decision making**—the process whereby two or more people have input into purchases—change. The number of people in different life-cycle stages can be obtained from demographic data. Table 4-2 shows the traditional family life cycle and its marketing relevance. The cycle's stages apply to families in all types of nations—both industrialized and less-developed/developing—but the marketing opportunities in Table 4-2 are most applicable for industrialized countries.

*The **family life cycle** describes life stages, which often use **joint decision making**.*

## TABLE 4-1

## The Informal Social Class Structure

| CLASS | SIZE | CHARACTERISTICS |
|---|---|---|
| *Upper Class* | | |
| Upper-upper | 0.3% | Social elite; inherited wealth; exclusive neighbourhoods; summer homes; children attend best schools; money unimportant in purchases; secure in status; spending with good taste |
| Lower-upper | 1.2% | Highest incomes; earned wealth; often business leaders and professionals; college or university educated; educated; seek best for children; active socially; insecure; conspicuous consumption; money unimportant in purchases |
| Upper-middle | 12.5% | Career-oriented; executives and professionals earning well over $50 000 yearly; status tied to occupations and earnings; most educated, but not from prestige schools; demanding of children; quality products purchased; attractive homes; socially involved; gracious living |
| *Middle Class* | | |
| Middle | 32% | Typical Canadians; average-earning white-collar workers and the top group of blue-collar workers; many university educated; respectable; conscientious; try to do the right thing; home ownership sought; do-it-yourselfers; family focus |
| Working | 38% | Remaining white-collar workers and most blue-collar workers; working class lifestyles; some job monotony; job security sought more than advancement; usually high school education; close-knit families; brand loyal and interested in name brands; not status-oriented |
| *Lower Class* | | |
| Upper-lower | 9% | Employed, mostly in unskilled or semiskilled jobs; poorly educated; low incomes; rather difficult to move up the social class ladder; protective against lower-lower class; standard of living at or just above poverty; live in affordable housing |
| Lower-lower | 7% | Unemployed or most menial jobs; poorest income, education, and housing; the bottom layer; present-oriented; impulsive as shoppers; overpay; use credit |

Sources: This information is derived from Richard P. Coleman, "The Continuing Significance of Social Class in Marketing," *Journal of Consumer Research*, Vol. 10 (December 1983), pp. 265–280; James F. Engel, Roger D. Blackwell, and Paul W. Miniard, *Consumer Behaviour*, Seventh Edition (Hinsdale, Ill.: Dryden, 1993), pp. 117–119; and William L. Wilkie, *Consumer Behaviour*, Third Edition (New York: Wiley, 1994), pp. 344–351.

*The* **household life cycle** *includes family and non-family units.*

**Time expenditures** *reflect time allocated to the work week, to family care, and to leisure.*

When using life-cycle analysis, the people who do not follow a traditional pattern because they do not marry, do not have children, become divorced, have families with two working spouses (even if there are very small children), and so on, should be noted. They are not adequately reflected in Table 4-2, but may represent good marketing opportunities. For that reason, the concept of the **household life cycle**—which incorporates the life stages of both family and nonfamily households—is taking on greater significance.[15] Table 4-3 shows the current status of Canadian households.

**Time expenditures** refer to the activities in which a person participates and the time allocated to them. Such activities include work, commuting, personal care, home maintenance, food preparation and consumption, childrearing, social interactions, reading, shopping, self-improvement, recreation, entertainment, vacations, and so on. Although the average work week for an individual's primary job has stabilized at 35 to 40 hours weekly, more people are working at two jobs. Canadians enjoy TV, phone conversations, pleasure driving, swimming, sightseeing, walking, bicycling, attending spectator events, reading, and playing outdoor games and sports.

## TABLE 4-2

## The Traditional Family Life Cycle

| STAGE IN CYCLE | CHARACTERISTICS | MARKETING OPPORTUNITIES |
|---|---|---|
| Bachelor, male or female | Independent; young; early in career; low earnings, low discretionary income | Clothing; auto; stereo; travel; restaurants; entertainment; status appeals |
| Newly married | Two incomes; relative independence; present- and future-oriented | Apartment furnishings; travel; clothing; durables; appeal to enjoyment and togetherness |
| Full nest I | Youngest child under 6; one to one-and-a-half incomes; limited independence; future-oriented | Goods and services for the child, home, and family; durability and safety; pharmaceuticals; day care; appeal to economy |
| Full nest II | Youngest child over 6, but dependent ; one-and-a-half to two incomes; at least one spouse set in career; future-oriented | Savings; home; education; family vacations; child-oriented products; some luxuries; appeal to comfort and long-term enjoyment |
| Full nest III | Youngest child living at home, but independent; highest income level; thoughts of future retirement | Education; expensive durables for children; replacement and improvement of parents' durables; appeal to comfort and luxury |
| Empty nest I | No children at home; independent; good income; thoughts of self and retirement | Vacation home; travel; clothing; entertainment; luxuries; appeal to self-gratification |
| Empty nest II | Retirement; less income and expenses; present-oriented | Travel; recreation; new home; health-related items; less interest in luxuries; appeal to comfort at a low price |
| Sole survivor I | Only one spouse alive; actively employed; oriented; good income | Immersion in job and friends; interest in present-travel, clothing, health, and recreation areas; appeal to productive citizen |
| Sole survivor II | Only one spouse alive; retired; some feeling less income | Travel; recreation; pharmaceuticals; security; of futility; appeal to economy and social activity |

## TABLE 4-3

## The Current Status of Canadian Family and Nonfamily Households

| HOUSEHOLD STATUS | PERCENTAGE OF ALL CANADIAN HOUSEHOLDS |
|---|---|
| Total Husband and Wife Families | 73.7 |
| Married couples, no children | 28.6 |
| Married couples, with children | 45.1 |
| Total Families of Common-law Couples | 11.7 |
| Unmarried couples, no children | 6.2 |
| Unmarried couples, with children | 5.5 |
| Total Lone-Parent Families | 14.5 |
| Female Parent | 12.1 |
| Male parent | 2.4 |

Source: Computed by the authors from Statistics Canada, "The People: Families, Households and Housing," *Canadian Statistics*, www.statscan.ca (January 4, 1999).

## Psychological Characteristics of Consumers

The psychological profile of a final consumer involves his or her personality, attitudes (opinions), class consciousness, motivation, perceived risk, and innovativeness, as well as the importance of the purchase. See Figure 4-6.

*A* **personality** *describes a person's composite internal, enduring, psychological traits.*

A **personality** is the sum total of the enduring internal psychological traits that make a person unique. Self-confidence, dominance, autonomy, sociability, defensiveness, adaptability, and emotional stability are selected personality traits. Personality has a strong impact on an individual's behaviour. For example, a self-confident and sociable person often will not purchase the same goods and services as an inhibited and aloof person. It is necessary to remember that a personality is made up of many traits operating in association with one another.

**Attitudes** *can be positive, negative, or neutral.*

**Attitudes (opinions)** are an individual's positive, neutral, or negative feelings about goods, services, firms, people, issues, and/or institutions. They are shaped by demographics, social factors, and other psychological characteristics. One role of marketing is to generate favourable attitudes; given the intensive competition in many industries, a firm cannot normally succeed without positive consumer attitudes. When studying attitudes, two concepts should often be measured—the attitude itself and the purchase intention toward a firm's brand. For example: (1) Do you like brand A? Would you buy brand A in the future? (2) How does brand A compare with other brands? Would you buy brand A if it were priced higher than other brands?

**Class consciousness** *is low for inner-directed persons and high for outer-directed ones.*

**Class consciousness** is the extent to which a person seeks social status. It helps determine his or her interest in social-class mobility, use of reference groups, and the importance of prestige purchases. Inner-directed people want to please themselves and are generally attracted by products that perform well functionally. They are not concerned with social mobility, rely on their own judgment, and do not value prestige items. Outer-directed people want to please the people around them. Upward social mobility, reference group approval, and ownership of prestige items are sought. These people are generally attracted by products providing social visibility, well-known brands, and uniqueness. Functional performance may be less important.

**Motivation** *is a drive-impelling action; it is caused by* **motives**.

**Motivation** involves the positive or negative needs, goals, and desires that impel a person to or away from certain actions, objects, or situations.[16] By identifying and

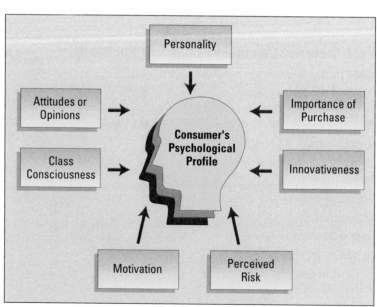

**FIGURE 4-6**

**Factors Determining a Consumer's Psychological Profile**

appealing to people's **motives**—the reasons for behaviour—a firm can produce positive motivation. For example:

| MOTIVES | MARKETING ACTIONS THAT MOTIVATE |
|---|---|
| Hunger reduction | Television and radio ads just before mealtimes |
| Safety | Smoke detector demonstrations in stores |
| Sociability | Perfume ads showing social success due to products |
| Achievement | Use of consumer endorsements in ads specifying how much knowledge can be gained from an encyclopedia |
| Economy | Newspaper coupons advertising sales |
| Social responsibility | Package labels that emphasize how easy it is to recycle products |

Each person has distinct motives for purchases, and these change by situation and over time. Consumers often combine economic (price, durability) and emotional (social acceptance, self-esteem) motives when making purchases.

**Perceived risk** is the level of uncertainty a consumer believes exists as to the outcome of a purchase decision; this belief may or may not be correct. Perceived risk can be divided into six major types:

**Perceived risk** *is the uncertainty felt by the consumer.*

1. *Functional*—risk that a product will not perform adequately.
2. *Physical*—risk that a product will be harmful.
3. *Financial*—risk that a product will not be worth its cost.
4. *Social*—risk that a product will cause embarrassment before others.
5. *Psychological*—risk that one's ego will be bruised.
6. *Time*—risk that the time spent making a purchase will be wasted if the product does not perform as expected.[17]

Because high perceived risk can dampen customer motivation, companies must deal with it even if people have incorrect beliefs. Firms can lower perceived risk by giving more information, having a reputation for superior quality, offering money-back guarantees, avoiding controversial ingredients, and so on.

A person willing to try a new good or service that others perceive as risky exhibits **innovativeness**. An innovator is apt to be young and well educated, and to have above-average income for his or her social class. He or she is also likely to be interested in change, achievement-oriented, open-minded, status-conscious, mobile, and venturesome. Firms need to identify and appeal to innovators when introducing a new good or service.

**Innovativeness** *is trying a new product others see as risky.*

The **importance of a purchase** affects the time and effort a person spends shopping for a product—and the money allotted. An important purchase means careful decision making, high perceived risk, and often a large amount of money. An unimportant purchase means less decision time (an item may be avoided altogether) and low perceived risk, and it is probably inexpensive.

*The* **importance of a purchase** *determines the time, effort, and money spent.*

## Selected Consumer Lifestyles

Many distinct consumer lifestyles are expected to continue, including: family values, voluntary simplicity, getting by, "me" generation, blurring of gender roles, poverty of time, and component lifestyles.

A **family values** lifestyle emphasizes marriage, children, and home life. It encourages people to focus on children and their education; family autos, vacations, and entertainment; and home-oriented products. Yet, as previously noted, the traditional family is becoming less representative of Canadian households. Thus, firms need to be careful in targeting those who say they follow this lifestyle. They should also keep in mind that a family-values lifestyle remains the leading one in many

*In some households,* **family values** *have a great impact.*

nations outside of Canada. For instance, in Italy, less than one-third of women are in the labour force and the divorce rate is about one-sixth that of Canada.

*Voluntary simplicity is based on ecological awareness and self-reliance.*

**Voluntary simplicity** is a lifestyle in which people have an ecological awareness, seek product durability, strive for self-reliance, and buy simple products. People with this lifestyle are cautious, conservative, and thrifty shoppers. They do not buy expensive cars and clothing, hold on to products for long periods, and rarely eat out or go on pre-packaged vacations. They like going to a park or taking a vacation by car, are more concerned with product toughness than appearance, and believe in conservation. They tend to be attracted to rational appeals and no-frills retailing.

*When economic circumstances are tough, people place more emphasis on* **getting by**.

**Getting by** is a frugal lifestyle pursued by people because of economic circumstances. Those who are getting by seek product durability, self-reliance, and simple products. But unlike voluntary simplicity, they do so because they must. In less-developed and developing nations, most people have this lifestyle; a much smaller proportion do in industrialized countries. Getting by consumers are attracted to well-known brands (to reduce perceived risk), do not try new goods and services, rarely go out, and take few vacations. They look for bargains and tend to patronize local stores. They rarely believe they have any significant discretionary income.

*The* **"me"** *generation stresses self-fulfillment.*

A **"me" generation** lifestyle stresses being good to oneself, self-fulfillment, and self-expression. It involves less pressure to conform, as well as greater diversity; there is also less interest in responsibilities and loyalties. Consumers with this lifestyle want to take care of themselves. They stress nutrition, exercise, and grooming. And they buy expensive cars and apparel, and visit full-service stores. These people are more concerned with product appearance than durability, and some place below-average value on conservation if it will have a negative effect on their lifestyle.

*Blurring gender roles involves men and women undertaking nontraditional duties.*

Because many women are working, more men are assuming the once-traditional roles of their wives, and vice versa, thus **blurring gender roles:** "Men are doing more shopping and housework, but only because women are making them change. Knowing how men are changing—and how they aren't—is the key to targeting them. Meanwhile, more women are learning how to buy cars, program VCRs, and use power tools."[18]

*A* **poverty of time** *exists when a quest for financial security means less free time.*

The prevalence of working women, the long distances between home and work, and the large number of people working at second jobs contribute to a **poverty-of-time** lifestyle in many households. For them, the quest for financial security means less free time. This lifestyle leads people to greater use of time-saving goods and services. Included are convenience foods, quick-oil-change services, microwave ovens, fast-food restaurants, mail-order retailers, one-hour film processing, and professional lawn and household care.

*With a* **component lifestyle**, *consumer attitudes and behaviour vary by situation.*

Today, more people are turning to a **component lifestyle**, whereby their attitudes and behaviour depend on particular situations rather than an overall lifestyle philosophy. For example, consumers may take their children with them on vacations (family values), engage in trash recycling programs (voluntary simplicity), look for sales to save money (getting by), take exercise classes ("me" generation), share food-shopping chores (blurring gender roles), and eat out on busy nights (poverty of time). Author Shirley Roberts says the consumer of tomorrow will have the following nine traits:

1. Far less homogeneous.
2. Independent thinkers who seek control over their lives.
3. More educated and sophisticated.
4. Pursuers of a higher quality of life.
5. Extremely demanding.
6. Optimistic, but well grounded in reality.
7. Seekers of new experiences and innovation.

**8.** Pursuers of wellness and environmentalism.

**9.** Aging, but more active.[19]

## Marketing Implications of Lifestyle Analysis

Over the years, analysis of the social and psychological characteristics of final consumers has increased dramatically. In this section, we present both general and specific applications of lifestyle analysis in marketing.

Several organizations are involved with defining and measuring consumer lifestyles. They sell this information to client firms, who use it to improve their marketing efforts. Here are some well-known North American services:

- *VALS (Values and Lifestyles)* is a research program sponsored by SRI International. SRI's VALS 2 classification categorizes consumers into eight basic lifestyle groups: actualizers, fulfilleds, believers, achievers, strivers, experiencers, makers, and strugglers.

- *PRIZM (Potential Rating Index by Zip Market)* is a program that relies on census data and examines consumer lifestyles by postal code. It uses about sixty different neighbourhood designations, such as blue blood ("old money"), to describe lifestyles.

These services have been used by companies marketing financial instruments, cars, health-care products, appliances, women's girdles, liquor, food, and other items. Studies of consumer lifestyles around Canada have been conducted.

**VIRTUAL MEDIA RESOURCES**
www.vmr.com/

- *The Bureau of Broadcast Measurement* (BBM) conducts a Radio Product Measurement study of several thousand respondents on a regular basis in Vancouver, Toronto, and Montreal, with occasional measurements in Winnipeg, Edmonton, and Calgary. The surveys measure lifestyles and shopping behaviour. Lifestyles are categorized as: active, traditional, insecure, and career-driven while shopping behaviour is categorized as: impulse, pro-advertising, early adopter, and uninvolved.[20]

**BBM BUREAU OF MEASUREMENT**
www.bbm.ca/

- *Target Mail* of Toronto has a database of more than 200 000 consumers from across Canada, entitled Target Lifestyle Changes. The consumers are surveyed and asked to report whether they or a family member have undergone a major lifestyle change in the past six months or will be undergoing one in the upcoming year.[21]

- Since 1996 the Angus Reid Group has had an Internet panel composed of over 6000 representative households throughout Canada. These panel members have agreed to respond by e-mail to surveys by Angus Reid on just about any topic. After a survey of their shopping behaviours and attitudes with respect to the Net, Angus Reid reported that 7 per cent of panel members had made fully online transactional purchases in 1996, but by 1998 32 per cent had made fully online purchases. The reason for the growth in usage: increased confidence that the Canadian banking industry can ensure the security and privacy of their online transactions.[22]

**ANGUS REID GROUP**
www.angusreid.com/

Apparel marketers who must stay on top of fashion tastes would be interested in the following research findings on consumer attitudes and behaviour with respect to fashion.

- Canadians spend about 6.7 per cent of their income on clothing. Consumption is related to seasons, but also to pride, status, and social approval. Yet consumers are worried about the future, and are economizing. They're more interested in buying apparel that reflects how they live instead of the latest designer trend. Also, the population is aging and mature consumers value "becomingness" over the latest fashions. Sixty per cent of males and 40 per cent of females think shopping for clothes is a hassle. A survey of Canadian shoppers found that 66 per cent visit an average of 3.3 stores before making a purchase. Working women want seasonless apparel so that they don't have to shop as often. Consumers spent an average of 4.3 hours a month shopping for clothing in 1993, but only 3 hours a month in 1996.[23]

### Limitations of Lifestyle Analysis

*Social and psychological factors can be difficult to measure.*

Unlike demographics, many of the social and psychological aspects of final consumer lifestyles are difficult to measure, somewhat subjective, usually based on the self-reports of consumers, and sometimes hidden from view (to avoid embarrassment, protect privacy, convey an image, and other reasons). In addition, there are still some ongoing disputes over terminology, misuse of data, and reliability.

## The Final Consumer's Decision Process

*The* **final consumer's decision process** *has many stages and various factors affect it.*

The **final consumer's decision process** is the way in which people gather and assess information and choose among alternative goods, services, organizations, people, places, and ideas. It consists of the process itself and factors affecting it. The process has six stages: stimulus, problem awareness, information search, evaluation of alternatives, purchase, and post-purchase behaviour. Demographic, social, and psychological factors affect the process. Figure 4-7 shows the total consumer decision-making process.

When a consumer buys a good or service, decides to vote for a political candidate or donate to a charity, and so on, he or she goes through a decision process. Sometimes, all six stages in the process are used; other times, only a few steps are necessary. For example, the purchase of an expensive stereo requires more decision making than the purchase of a new music video.

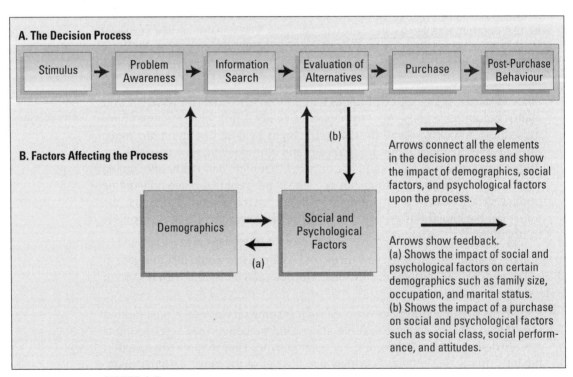

**FIGURE 4-7**

**The Final Consumer's Decision Process**

## INTERNATIONAL MARKETING IN ACTION

### A Moving Target: Understanding Consumer Behaviour in Eastern Europe

**A** North American pet food producer presented a new cat food to former communist Eastern Europeans in an ad showing a Persian cat with a jewelled collar eating cat food off of fine china. The reaction was strong and negative: Western pets eat better than Eastern Europeans. Understanding consumer behaviour in international markets is difficult enough due to cultural and social differences, but when cultural and social change is occurring rapidly it becomes nearly impossible. When formerly communist Eastern European markets first opened up in the early 1990s marketers merely had to translate their product packaging and get the products on the retail shelf to enjoy record sales.

A market that had lots of demand and few products to satisfy it was a new experience to Western marketers—as new as having products to fill demand was to Eastern European consumers. Now formerly communist Eastern Europeans have a wide variety of products to fill their demand and are faced with something they have not experienced before: choice.

The nature of consumer behaviour and the approach to influencing consumers used in the West is much different from what is required in Eastern Europe. Western consumers have been inundated with product choice and variety and have come to accept these as a natural condition. Promotional efforts in Western markets feature puffery and persuasive advertising efforts to convince people to try new products. Formerly communist Eastern European consumers are not used to choice but are used to receiving persuasive messages about making choices, the choices the government wanted them to make! Consequently, the approach to promotion employed by Western marketers needs to be adjusted.

Interestingly, the old approach is what appears to work for these new consumers. Eastern Europeans are responding to a consumer education approach to product marketing, not the usual propaganda approach, which is reminiscent of the former communist government. Post-communist European society bears some similarity to post-World War II North American society: couples marry at young ages, divorce rates are low, women work at home and raise families, and children live with their parents until they marry. And a simple, honest approach to promoting products (reminiscent of North American advertising in the 1950s) seems to work.

As for research on consumer behaviour, it has its own unique problems. Because of past conditioning, consumers tell researchers in Poland what they (the consumers) believe the researchers want to hear, as opposed to what they really feel. Therefore, researchers have to adjust their approach to questioning so they get honest responses and not socially-expected responses.

One thing marketers discovered early on was that Eastern Europeans were very responsive to sales promotions that involved giveaways. However, response rates have been falling as Eastern Europeans, like their North American brethren, have discovered that you generally get what you pay for.

As a marketing manager for a Canadian firm considering marketing a packaged-good product in Slovenia, what approach would you take to keep up with the changes in consumer behaviour?

Source: Based on material in Normandy Madden, "Former Eastern Bloc Consumers Now Savvy to Marketing Wiles," *Marketing Magazine* (May 29, 1995), p. 6.

At any point in the decision process, a person may decide not to buy, vote, or donate—and, thereby, end the process. A good or service may turn out to be unneeded, unsatisfactory, or too expensive.

## Stimulus

A **stimulus** is a cue (social, commercial, or noncommercial) or a drive (physical) meant to motivate a person to act.

*A **stimulus** is a cue or drive intended to motivate a consumer.*

**FIGURE 4-8**

**A Manufacturer-Sponsored Commercial Stimulus**
*Reprinted by permission of Wm. Wrigley Jr. Company.*

A *social cue* occurs when someone talks with friends, family members, co-workers, or another interpersonal source not affiliated with a seller. A *commercial cue* is a message sponsored by a seller—such as that shown in Figure 4-8—to interest a person in a particular good, service, organization, person, place, or idea. Ads, personal selling, and sales promotions are commercial cues. They are less regarded than social cues because people know they are seller-controlled. A *noncommercial cue* is a message from an impartial source, such as Consumer Reports or the government. It has high believability because it is not affiliated with the seller. A *physical drive* occurs when a person's physical senses are affected. Thirst, hunger, and fear cause physical drives.

A person may be exposed to any or all of these stimuli. If sufficiently stimulated, he or she will go to the next step in the decision process. If not, the person will ignore the cue and delay or terminate the decision process for the given good, service, organization, person, place, or idea.

### Problem Awareness

**Problem awareness** *entails recognition of a shortage or an unfulfilled desire.*

At the **problem awareness** stage, a consumer recognizes that the good, service, organization, person, place, or idea under consideration may solve a problem of shortage or unfulfilled desire.

Recognition of shortage occurs when a consumer realizes a repurchase is needed. A suit may wear out. A man or woman may run out of razor blades. An eye examination may be needed. A popular political candidate may be up for re-election. It may be time for a charity's annual fundraising campaign. In each case, the consumer recognizes a need to repurchase.

Recognition of unfulfilled desire occurs when a consumer becomes aware of a good, service, organization, person, place, or idea that has not been patronized before. Such an item may improve status, appearance, living conditions, or knowledge in a manner not tried before (luxury auto, cosmetic surgery, proposed zoning law, encyclopedia), or it may offer new performance features not previously available (laser surgery, tobacco-free cigarettes). Either way, a consumer is aroused by a desire to try something new.

Many consumers hesitate to act on unfulfilled desires due to the greater risk entailed. It is easier to replace a known product. Whether a consumer becomes aware of a problem of shortage or of unfulfilled desire, he or she will act only if the problem is perceived as worth solving.

## Information Search

Next, an **information search** requires listing the alternatives that will solve the problem at hand and determining their characteristics.

*An **information search** determines alternatives and their characteristics.*

A list of alternatives does not have to be written. It can be a group of items a consumer thinks about. With an internal search, a person has experience in the area being considered and uses a memory search to list choices. A person with minimal experience will do an external search to list alternatives; this can involve commercial sources, noncommercial sources, and/or social sources. Often, once there is a list of choices, items (brands, companies, and so on) not on it do not receive further consideration.

The second phase of information search deals with the attributes of each alternative. This information can also be generated internally or externally, depending on the expertise of the consumer and the level of perceived risk. As risk increases, the information sought increases.

Once an information search is completed, the consumer must determine whether the shortage or unfulfilled desire can be satisfied by any alternative. If one or more choices are satisfactory, the consumer moves to the next decision. The process is delayed or discontinued when no alternative provides satisfaction.

## Evaluation of Alternatives

There is now enough information for a consumer to select one alternative from the list of choices. This is easy when one option is clearly the best across all attributes: A product with excellent quality and a low price will be a sure choice over an average-quality, expensive one. The choice is usually not that simple, and a consumer must carefully engage in an **evaluation of alternatives** before making a decision. If two or more alternatives seem attractive, the individual needs to determine which criteria to evaluate and their relative importance. Alternatives are then ranked and a choice made.

*Evaluating alternatives consists of weighing features and selecting the most desired product.*

Decision criteria are the features a person deems relevant—such as price, style, quality, safety, durability, status, and warranty. A consumer sets standards for various features and forms an attitude toward each alternative according to its ability to meet the standards. In addition, each criterion's importance is set because the multiple attributes of a given product are usually of varying weight. For example, a consumer may consider shoe prices to be more important than style and select inexpensive, nondistinctive shoes.

A consumer now ranks alternatives from most to least desirable and selects one. Ranking is sometimes hard because alternatives may have technical differences or be poorly labelled, new, or intangible (as is the case when evaluating two political candidates). On these occasions, options may be ranked on the basis of brand name or price, which is used to indicate overall quality.

In situations where no alternative is satisfactory, a decision to delay or not make a purchase is made.

## Purchase

*The* **purchase act** *includes deciding where to buy, agreeing to terms, and seeing if the item is available.*

After choosing the best alternative, a person is ready for the **purchase act**: an exchange of money, a promise to pay or support in return for ownership of a specific good, the performance of a specific service, and so on. Three considerations remain: place of purchase, terms, and availability.

Although most items are bought at stores, some are bought at school, work, and home. The place of purchase is picked in the same way as a product. Choices are noted, attributes detailed, and a ranking done. The best locale is chosen.

Purchase terms involve the price and method of payment. Generally, a price is the amount (including interest, tax, and other fees) a person pays to gain the ownership or use of a good or service. It may also be a person's vote, time investment, and so on. The payment method is the way a price is paid (cash, short-term credit, or long-term credit).

Availability refers to the timeliness with which a consumer receives a product that he or she buys. It depends on stock on hand (or service capacity) and delivery. Stock on hand relates to a seller's ability to provide a good or service when requested. For items requiring delivery, the period from when an order is placed by a consumer until it is received and the ease with which an item is transported to its place of use are crucial.

A consumer will make a purchase if these elements are acceptable. However, dissatisfaction with any one may cause a consumer to delay or not buy, even though there is no problem with the good or service itself.

## Post-Purchase Behaviour

**Post-purchase behaviour** *often embodies further buying and/or re-evaluation.* **Cognitive dissonance** *can be reduced by proper consumer after-care.*

Once a purchase is made, a person may engage in **post-purchase behaviour**, in the form of further purchases and/or re-evaluation of the original purchase. Many times, one purchase leads to others: A house purchase leads to the acquisition of fire insurance, a PC purchase leads to the acquisition of computer software.

A person may also re-evaluate a purchase after making it: Does performance match expectations? Satisfaction usually leads to a repurchase when a good or service wears out, another contribution when a charity holds a fundraising campaign, and so on, and leads to positive communication with other people interested in the same item. Dissatisfaction can lead to brand switching and negative communication.

Dissatisfaction is often due to **cognitive dissonance**—doubt that a correct decision has been made. A person may regret a purchase or wish another choice was made. To overcome dissonance, a firm must realize the process does not end with the purchase. Follow-up calls, extended warranties, and ads aimed at purchasers can reassure people.

## Factors Affecting the Final Consumer's Decision Process

*The decision process is affected by demographic, social, and psychological factors.*

Demographic, social, and psychological factors affect the way final consumers make choices and can help a firm understand how people use the decision process. For example, an affluent consumer would move through the process more quickly than a middle-income one because he or she faces less financial risk. An insecure consumer would spend more time making a decision than a secure one.

By knowing how these factors influence decisions, a firm can fine-tune its marketing strategies to cater to the target market and its purchase behaviour, and answer these questions: Why do two or more people use the decision process in the same way? Why do two or more people use it differently?

## Types of Decision Processes

Each time a person buys a good or service, donates to a charity, and so on, he or she uses the decision process. This may be done subconsciously, without the person being aware of it. Some situations allow a person to move through the process quickly and de-emphasize or skip certain steps; others may require a thorough use of each step. A consumer may use extended, limited, or routine decision making—based on the degree of search, level of experience, frequency of purchase, amount of perceived risk, and time pressure. See Figure 4-9.

**Extended consumer decision making** occurs when a person fully uses the decision process. Much effort is spent on information search and evaluation of alternatives for expensive, complex items with which a person has little or no experience. Purchases are made infrequently. Perceived risk is high, and the purchase is important. A person has time available to make a choice. Purchase delays often occur. Demographic, social, and psychological factors have their greatest impact. Extended decision making is often involved in picking a college, a house, a first car, or a location for a wedding.

**Limited consumer decision making** occurs when a person uses every step in the purchase process but does not spend a great deal of time on some of them. The person has previously bought a given good or service, but makes a fresh decision when it comes under current purchase consideration—due to the relative infrequency of purchase, the introduction of new models, or an interest in variety. Perceived risk is moderate, and a person is willing to spend some time shopping. The thoroughness with which the process is used depends on the amount of prior experience, the importance of the purchase, and the time pressure facing the consumer. Emphasis is on evaluating a list of known choices, although an information search may be done. Factors affecting the decision process have some impact. A second car, clothing, gifts, home furnishings, and an annual vacation typically need limited decision making.

**Routine consumer decision making** occurs when a person buys out of habit and skips steps in the process. He or she spends little time shopping and often rebuys the same brands (or brands bought before). In this category are items with which a person has much experience. They are bought regularly, have little or no perceived

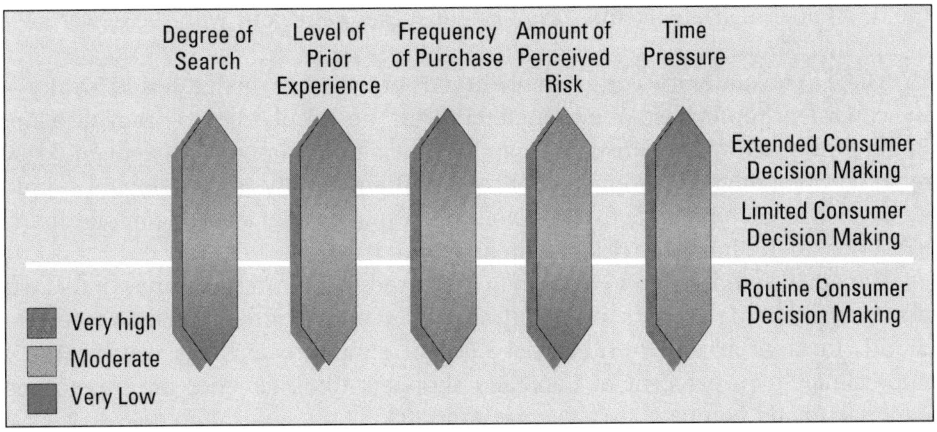

*Final consumer decision making can be categorized as* **extended**, **limited**, *or* **routine**.

| | Degree of Search | Level of Prior Experience | Frequency of Purchase | Amount of Perceived Risk | Time Pressure | |
|---|---|---|---|---|---|---|
| | | | | | | Extended Consumer Decision Making |
| | | | | | | Limited Consumer Decision Making |
| | | | | | | Routine Consumer Decision Making |

Very high
Moderate
Very Low

**FIGURE 4-9**

**The Three Types of Final Consumer Decision Processes**

risk, and are relatively low in price. Once a person realizes a good or service is depleted, a repurchase is made. The time pressure to buy is high. Information search, evaluation of alternatives, and post-purchase behaviour are normally omitted, as long as a person is satisfied. Factors affecting the process have little impact because problem awareness typically leads to a purchase. Examples of items routinely purchased are the daily newspaper, a haircut by a regular stylist, and weekly grocery items.

*The way the decision process is used varies by country.*

There are several differences between consumers in industrialized nations and those in less-developed and developing ones. In general, consumers in less-developed and developing countries:

- Are exposed to fewer commercial and noncommercial cues.
- Have access to less information.
- Have fewer goods and services from which to choose.
- Are more apt to buy a second choice if the first one is not available.
- Have fewer places of purchase and may have to wait in long lines.
- Are more apt to find that stores are out of stock.
- Have less purchase experience for many kinds of goods and services.
- Are less educated and have lower incomes.
- Are more apt to rebuy items with which they are only moderately satisfied (due to the lack of choices).

Because many consumers—in both industrialized nations and less-developed nations—want to reduce shopping time, the use of complex decision making, and risk, most purchases are made using routine or limited decision making. Thus, consumers often rely on low-involvement purchasing and/or brand loyalty.

*Low-involvement purchasing is often used when buying unimportant products.*

With **low-involvement purchasing**, a consumer minimizes the time and effort expended in both making decisions about and shopping for those goods and services he or she views as unimportant. Included are "those situations where the consumer simply does not care and is not concerned about brands or choices and makes the decision in the most cognitively miserly manner possible. Most likely, low involvement is situation-based and the degree of importance and involvement may vary with the individual and with the situation."[24] In these situations, consumers feel little perceived risk, are passive about getting information, act fast, and may assess products after (rather than before) buying.

Firms can adapt to low-involvement purchasing by using repetitive ads to create awareness and familiarity, stressing the practical nature of goods and services, having informed salespeople, setting low prices, using attractive in-store displays, selling in all types of outlets, and offering coupons and free samples. Table 4-4 compares the traditional high-involvement view of consumer behaviour with the newer low-involvement view.[25]

*Brand loyalty involves consistent repurchases of and preference for specific brands.*

Once a consumer tries one or more brands of a good or service, **brand loyalty**—the consistent repurchase of and preference for a particular brand—may develop. Brand loyalty allows the consumer to reduce the amount of time, thought, and risk required when buying a given good or service. Brand loyalty can develop for simple items such as gasoline (due to low-involvement purchasing) and for complex items like autos (to minimize the risk of switching brands).

Canadians are less brand loyal than they used to be. A recent survey indicated that 57 per cent of shoppers would buy a product on sale rather than their favourite brand. In comparison, only 45 per cent of shoppers felt this way in 1989. Approximately 56 per cent of Canadian shoppers think generics are as good as national brands, compared to 52 per cent in 1989.[26]

How can companies generate and sustain customer loyalty? Here is the way Zellers and the Royal Bank of Canada have tackled this issue:

## TABLE 4-4

## High-Involvement View of Active Consumers Versus
## Low-Involvement View of Passive Consumers

| TRADITIONAL HIGH-INVOLVEMENT VIEW OF ACTIVE CONSUMERS | NEWER LOW-INVOLVEMENT VIEW OF PASSIVE CONSUMERS |
|---|---|
| 1. Consumers are information processors. | 1. Consumers learn information at random. |
| 2. Consumers are information seekers. | 2. Consumers are information gatherers. |
| 3. Consumers are an active audience for ads and the effect of ads on them is weak. | 3. Consumers are a passive audience for ads and the effect of ads on them is strong. |
| 4. Consumers evaluate brands before buying. | 4. Consumers buy first. If they do evaluate brands, it is done after the purchase. |
| 5. Consumers seek to maximize satisfaction. They compare brands to see which provide the most *benefits* and buy based on detailed comparisons. | 5. Consumers seek an acceptable level of satisfaction. They choose the brand least apt to have problems and buy based on few factors. Familiarity is key. |
| 6. Lifestyle characteristics are related to consumer behaviour because the product is closely tied to a consumer's identity and belief system. | 6. Lifestyle characteristics are not related to consumer behaviour because the product is not closely tied to a consumer's identity and belief system. |
| 7. Reference groups influence behaviour because of the product's importance to group norms. | 7. Reference groups have little effect on behaviour because the product is unlikely to be related to group norms. |

Source: Henry Assael, *Consumer Behaviour and Marketing Action*, Fourth Edition (Boston: PWS-Kent, 1992), p. 104. Reprinted by permission of Wadsworth, Inc.

Zellers offers all its customers a Club Z card, which entitles them to build up points on all Zellers purchases. These points can be redeemed in merchandise selected from the retailers' Club Z catalogue. Part of the secret to success of Club Z is that merchandise purchases are credited no matter how they are paid for (cash, Zellers Card, VISA, Master Card, etc.). The Club Z approach rewards store loyalty without constraining purchase behaviour. Zellers has expanded the program to children by launching Gen Z. When parents shop at Zellers and use their Club Z card to earn points their children (ages 17 and under) can earn the same number of points. The children can redeem these points just like their parents. Zellers is also working on a scheme to allow points to be used to contribute to a Registered Education Savings Plan (RESP).

Another example is the Royal Bank's VISA Classic II card. Launched in the spring of 1996, the card targets value-conscious consumers, such as young families and students. The idea is for participating retailers to give customers savings discounts of up to 25 per cent and other bonuses when they use the card to make purchases. Participating retailers include Radio Shack, Music World, Cotton Ginny, and Domino's Pizza, among others. Of course, the VISA card is good at non-participating retailers as well, and any card usage allows customers to build up points that can be exchanged for gift certificates on merchandise purchased from Radio Shack or Eaton's.[27]

**RADIO SHACK**
www.tandy.com/

**ROYAL BANK**
www.royalbank.com/

## Marketing Implications of the Final Consumer's Decision Process

Over the years, the marketing implications of the final consumer's decision process have been studied in many settings, as these present-day illustrations indicate:

- The Angus Reid Group researched how consumers make online purchases, and discovered that 36 per cent of purchases are software products, while 16 per cent are books and magazines. The number one reason (54 per cent) why people buy on the Web is convenience. An overwhelming 90 per cent agreed that the ordering process was simple and that the products were delivered in a timely fashion.

The process was aided by the fact that 63 per cent used online order forms, and 72 per cent of the purchases were planned in advance.

- For several reasons, "substantial time often elapses between the time people recognize the need for a product and the time they actually purchase it." People may believe they do not have enough time to devote to the decision. They may feel shopping is an unpleasant experience. They may experience perceived risk. They may need advice from others that is not readily available. They may not know how to gather adequate information about products and their attributes. They may expect prices to fall or improved products to be introduced later.
- Satisfied consumers discuss their experiences with far fewer people than dissatisfied ones. Yet, according to one auto-industry consultant, "It costs you five times as much to get a new customer as to keep an old one."[28]

### Limitations of the Final Consumer's Decision Process

The limitations of the final consumer's decision process for marketers lie in the hidden (unexpressed) nature of many elements of the process; the consumer's subconscious performance of the process or a number of its components; the impact of demographic, social, and psychological factors on the process; and the differences in decision making among consumers in different countries.

Many noted business and marketing thinkers have recently suggested that human beings may act more irrationally when making decisions than previously believed. Some authors support this notion by pointing to discoveries by researchers

## MARKETING IN THE THIRD MILLENNIUM

### The Emergence of New Consumers

Shirley Roberts believes that the arrival of the new millennium will also bring a new consumer, who will have more purchasing alternatives, lower prices, and will be armed with fast and easy access to more information than ever before. Marketers will no longer be able to offer mass marketing approaches, and will have to contend with smaller market segments and offer more customized products. In order to maintain the same levels of sales and profits, Roberts feels that marketers will have to adopt some or all of the following market profitability strategies to deal with tomorrow's powerful consumers.

1. *Restructure organizations with a consumer-driven orientation*—Roberts believes that most businesses are still structured to meet internal considerations, using the decades-old departmentalized approach with specialties like finance, marketing, sales, accounting, production, and human resources. Even firms that have been marketing-oriented have only gone as far as brand management structures. Firms will have to take a further step

and restructure around their customer segments.

2. *Select and focus on the highest priority consumer segments*—The simple segmentation approach based on demographics is too broad; for example, targeting a product at women aged 18–49 is just not descriptive enough. The other extreme being popularized is one-to-one marketing, which does have some validity given advances in communication technology. However, Roberts feels that it just isn't feasible to communicate in this manner for frequently used consumer goods. Clustering consumers into segments according to meaningful consumer behaviour variables will be the most profitable approach to targeting.

3. *Develop standardized customization approaches*—By targeting high priority segments firms can develop products that are customized to these groups but made up of standardized components. The best example of a product that fits this approach is house paint. Paint vendors carry

# MARKETING IN THE THIRD MILLENNIUM

essentially white paint, which comes in many different finishes and quality of coverage and durability; and since colour can be mixed in the customer can choose thousands of different colours and shades. Hence the ultimate combination of standardization and customization.

4. *Leverage global trends and market intelligence*—Marketers need to search out innovative ideas, new trends, technologies, products, sources of competition, and competitive patents throughout the world to stay in the vanguard. Marketers must be wary of using a cookie-cutter approach to their markets when they discover leading-edge initiatives. The customer-driven approach means that each market must still be examined and understood on its own, with initiatives adapted to the segments in each country and not merely imported.

5. *Increase the priority on innovation*—Many firms have been investing in re-engineering themselves for global competition, and although necessary, it must not come at the expense of innovative new products and marketing efforts. Product life cycles are shorter and competitive positions aren't as strong these days, so new product development and service innovation are necessary. New product development must occur very rapidly; Roberts suggests six months as a standard maximum development time.

6. *Increase the priority on value*—Roberts notes that Value used to be defined as Price $\times$ Quality, but in the 1990s the equation changed to Value = Worth − Price. The equation for the third millennium will likely be Value = Consumer Alignment + Relevant Quality + Convenience + Added Benefits (vs. Other Options) + Fair Price. Consumer alignment means that customers need to feel that the product fits with their own psyche before they will adopt it. Clearly, the brand must deliver good quality, and time-stressed consumers will put more value on convenience than ever before. Added benefits are delight features that go above and beyond the basic promises of the product (e.g., contributions to social causes, loyalty programs, and customization). Finally, all of these characteristics are offered at a price that isn't way out of line compared to competing products.

7. *Choose more narrowly targeted and two-way communications vehicles*—Media costs are rising while audience sizes are shrinking—but the trade-off isn't as disastrous as it sounds. The number of narrow-cast media vehicles available today means that waste circulation (the number of prospects who won't be interested in a communication message) will be reduced. In other words, the quality of prospects will be high even as the quantity becomes low. Online marketing offers the best potential for direct interaction with prospective customers. For example, magazines targeted to current customers promise a strong communications link. In 1997 Chrysler Canada launched *Chrysler* magazine, which is sent to all Chrysler purchasers, and thus offers personal attention and communication between Chrysler and its customers.

8. *Align communications strategies with the spirit of tomorrow's consumers*—Tomorrow's consumers will be increasingly sophisticated and independent, desire individual attention, have greater knowledge needs, want improved quality of life, and will seek simplicity. Consumers will want simple and uncomplicated messages that stir their emotions, and to deal with firms that support social causes.

9. *Adopt new marketing research approaches to understand tomorrow's consumers*—The new consumers will be ever-changing, and this means staying in touch with these changes. Marketing research approaches will have to be adjusted to reflect the fact that markets will be more narrowly defined than ever before. Undertaking and understanding ethnic and lifestyle profiles of consumers will be critical in the new millennium. Better projections of changes in family life cycles, household sizes, changes in family structure, and changes in buying behaviour will be critical to understanding and keeping pace with tomorrow's consumers.[29]

on how the human brain works. And so when decision making is based on emotion and rationalized later, researchers may be fooled into thinking that the decision was rational when it was not. The implications of these findings are important, in that approaches used to measure and determine consumer behaviour must be challenged and questioned. Although marketers still need some kind of model of consumer decision making in order to design marketing mixes, they must recognize that the way consumer behaviour is modelled is strictly a guideline that may have to be adjusted to fit the particular market situation.[30]

# SUMMARY

**1.** *To show the importance and scope of consumer analysis* By analyzing consumers, a firm is better able to determine the most appropriate audience to which to appeal and the combination of marketing factors that will satisfy this audience. This is a critical task given the diversity in today's global marketplace. The scope of consumer analysis includes who, what, why, how, when, where, and how often.

**2.** *To define and enumerate important consumer demographics for the Canadian population and other countries* Consumer demographics are objective and quantifiable population statistics. They include size, gender, and age; location, housing, and mobility; income and expenditures; occupations and education; marital status; and ethnicity/race.

**3.** *To examine trends and projections for these important demographics and study their marketing implications* The world population is 6.2 billion people and rising by 1.33 per cent annually. Canada's population is 31 million people and increasing by 1.0 per cent each year. In many nations, a large proportion of births are firstborns. Worldwide, the number of men and women is roughly equal. However, women generally live longer than men; and the average age of populations in industrialized nations is higher than in less-developed and developing countries.

There has been a significant movement of the world population to large urban areas. The level of urbanization does vary by country, with 77 per cent of Canadians living in urban areas. In many countries, the majority of people own the home in which they live, with almost two-thirds of the Canadian population residing in homes they own. Each year, millions of people emigrate from one country to another and hundreds of millions move within their countries. About 240 000 people move to Canada from abroad every year; and about 15 to 20 per cent of the Canadian population moves annually.

For several reasons, comparing countries' personal income data can be rather difficult. The most recently released data for Canada indicates that average family income was $54 583 in 1995 for the nation's total of 7.3 million Canadian families. Many nations measure their cost of living and rate of inflation using a consumer price index. There are differences in consumption patterns between people in industrialized nations and in less-developed and developing countries. When assessing consumption patterns, the distinction between disposable-income spending and discretionary-income expenditures should be kept in mind.

In industrialized nations, the labour force is continuing its movement to white-collar and service occupations; many more jobs in less-developed and developing nations still entail manual work and are agriculture-based. The total employed Canadian civilian labour force is 13.9 million people. Throughout the world, women comprise a significant portion of the labour force (45 per cent in Canada). Unemployment rates vary widely among nations, based on economic conditions and industry shifts. Globally, educational attainment has gone up—though there are great variations among countries. In Canada, a much larger percentage of the population is now graduating from high school and attending college or university than did thirty years ago.

Marriage and family are powerful institutions, although less dominant than in the past for some nations. Three-fifths of Canadian adults are married, with couples waiting until they are older for marriage and having fewer children than in prior decades. A family consists of relatives living together. A household consists of a person or persons occupying a housing unit, related or not. In many nations, both family and household size have declined, due to the growth in single-person households and other factors.

Demographically, ethnicity/race is important as it pertains to the diversity of people among and within nations. Globally, over 200 languages are spoken by at least 1 million people; and some nations have two or more official languages. Most countries have populations representing different ethnic and racial groups. Statistics Canada measures ethnic origin, which is defined as the ethnic or cultural group to which the respondent or the respondent's ancestors belonged on first coming to North America. The results of ethnicity reporting from the 1996 Census for the top ten groups were as follows: Canadian 30.8%, English 23.9%, French 19.6%, Scottish 14.9%, Irish 13.2%, German 9.7%, Italian 4.2%, Aboriginal 3.9%, Ukrainian 3.6%, and Chinese 3.2%.

Each of these demographics has marketing implications, which are discussed in the chapter.

**4.** *To define and describe consumer lifestyles and their characteristics, examine selected lifestyles, and present marketing implications of lifestyle analysis* A final consumer's lifestyle is the way in which a person lives and spends time and money. It is a function of the social and psychological factors internalized by that person, along with his or her demographic background. Consumer social profiles are made up of several elements, including culture, social class, social performance, reference groups, opinion leaders, the family life cycle, and time expenditures. Psychological profiles are based on a combination of personality, attitudes

(opinions), the level of class consciousness, motivation, perceived risk, innovativeness, and purchase importance.

These seven lifestyle types are expected to continue, with their popularity often differing by country. A family-values lifestyle emphasizes marriage, children, and home life. With voluntary simplicity, people have an ecological awareness, seek material simplicity, strive for self-reliance, and buy inexpensive product versions. Getting by is a frugal lifestyle brought on because of economic circumstances. The "me" generation stresses being good to oneself, self-expression, and the acceptance of diversity. With blurring gender roles, more husbands are assuming the once traditional roles of their wives, and vice versa. A poverty of time occurs for some consumers because the quest for financial security means less free time as the alternatives competing for time expand. In a component lifestyle, consumer attitudes and behaviour depend on particular situations, rather than on an overall lifestyle philosophy. The various marketing implications of these consumer lifestyles are discussed further in the text.

**5.** *To define and describe the final consumer's decision process and present marketing implications* The final consumer's decision process is the procedure by which those consumers collect and analyze information and make choices among alternatives. It consists of the process itself and the factors affecting it (demographic, social, and psychological). It can be delayed or terminated by the consumer at any point.

The process has six steps: stimulus, problem awareness, information search, evaluation of alternatives, purchase, and post-purchase behaviour. There are three types of process: extended, limited, and routine. The way people make decisions varies widely between industrialized nations and less-developed and developing nations. Consumers often reduce shopping time, thought, and risk through low-involvement purchasing (for goods and services viewed as unimportant) and brand loyalty (the consistent repurchase of and preference toward a brand).

The marketing implications of the final consumer's decision process have been detailed for years. Several current applications are discussed in the text.

# KEY TERMS

**final consumers** (p. 87)

**organizational consumers** (p. 87)

**consumer demographics** (p. 87)

**consumer demographic profile** (p. 87)

**Census Metropolitan Area (CMA)** (p. 91)

**Census Agglomeration Area (CA)** (p. 92)

**cost of living** (p. 93)

**consumer price index (CPI)** (p. 93)

**disposable income** (p. 94)

**discretionary income** (p. 94)

**family** (p. 96)

**household** (p. 96)

**ethnicity/race** (p. 96)

**lifestyle** (p. 99)

**culture** (p. 99)

**social class** (p. 101)

**social performance** (p. 101)

**reference group** (p. 101)

**opinion leaders** (p. 101)

**family life cycle** (p. 101)

**joint decision making** (p. 101)

**household life cycle** (p. 102)

**time expenditures** (p. 102)

**personality** (p. 104)

**attitudes (opinions)** (p. 104)

**class consciousness** (p. 104)

**motivation** (p. 104)

**motives** (p. 105)

**perceived risk** (p. 105)

**innovativeness** (p. 105)

**importance of a purchase** (p. 105)

**family values** (p. 105)

**voluntary simplicity** (p. 106)

**getting by** (p. 106)

**"me" generation** (p. 106)

**blurring gender roles** (p. 106)

**poverty of time** (p. 106)

**component lifestyle** (p. 106)

**final consumer's decision process** (p. 108)

**stimulus** (p. 109)

**problem awareness** (p. 110)

**information search** (p. 111)

**evaluation of alternatives** (p. 111)

**purchase act** (p. 112)

**post-purchase behaviour** (p. 112)

**cognitive dissonance** (p. 112)

**extended consumer decision making** (p. 113)

**limited consumer decision making** (p. 113)

**routine consumer decision making** (p. 113)

**low-involvement purchasing** (p. 114)

**brand loyalty** (p. 114)

# REVIEW QUESTIONS

1. How does the use of consumer demographics aid marketing decision making?

2. In Canada, how does a Census Metropolitan Area (CMA) differ from a Census Agglomeration Area (CA)?

3. Distinguish between the terms "cost of living" and "consumer price index."

4. Describe the major limitations of demographics.

5. Distinguish between the traditional family life cycle and the household life cycle.

6. How does class consciousness differ for inner-directed and outer-directed people? What does this signify for marketers?

7. Differentiate among social, commercial, and noncommercial stimuli. Provide specific examples of each.

8. What causes cognitive dissonance? How can it be reduced?

9. Draw a flowchart showing the steps in routine purchase behaviour.

10. Define low-involvement purchasing and explain its use by consumers. Give an example.

# DISCUSSION QUESTIONS

1. The biggest CMA in Canada is Toronto, with 4.3 million people. What are the pros and cons of marketing products there? Recommend a marketing approach for a local bank.

2. Using the *Census of Population*, develop a demographic profile of the people residing in the CA or CMA nearest to where you live. What are the marketing overtones of this profile?

3. As the owner-operator of a prospective camera store in Canada, what demographic factors would you study? Describe the demographic profile of your ideal consumer.

4. Canadian culture emphasizes collective responsibility, confidence in social institutions such as education, health care, and the police, consensus, willingness to accept difference and diversity, health consciousness, pessimism, and skepticism; Canadian consumers are value-driven, frugal, seeking personalization, brand disloyal, and informed buyers. What are the implications of this for firms marketing the following goods and services?

   a. Motorcycles.
   b. Tanning salons.
   c. Adult education.

   d. Vacation travel.

5. A large cereal manufacturer has hired you as a marketing consultant. It is particularly interested in learning more about the concept of a component lifestyle and developing an appropriate strategy.

   a. Explain the relevance of the component lifestyle concept for the cereal industry.

   b. Suggest various ways in which the cereal manufacturer can appeal to component lifestyles.

## CASE STUDY

# Levi's: When a Firm Loses Touch with Consumers

You wouldn't think that a large and powerful company would allow itself to lose touch with its markets, especially when it's in a fashion-related business. But that's exactly what happened to Levi Strauss—and it's put the firm in the midst of a major corporate crisis. One of the largest apparel companies in the world (with sales of U.S.$6 billion in 1998), Levi's has seen its sales decline almost $1 billion during the 1990s and its U.S. market share in jeans fall from 48.2 to 25 per cent. A survey of teenage boys showed that only 7 per cent thought Levi's was a cool brand in 1998, down from 21 per cent in 1994. The Levi's brand is still well known, but unless the firm regains touch with its consumer base the downward spiral will continue.

Levi's makes a number of well-known brands, like Levi's Jeans and Levi's Dockers for men. Levi's Dockers has been a particularly successful brand, with almost 75 per cent of American men owning at least one pair of these pants. Launched in 1986, Dockers were a tremendous success, since the trend to casual attire had begun and khaki pants were all the rage. But in 1993 the market was looking for wrinkle-resistant pants; Levi's missed this trend and lost customers.

It also lost customers in the jeans market. Whereas Levi's 501 Blues were the cool jeans in the late 1980s and early 1990s, in 1993 kids were complaining that the legs were too narrow. Baggy pants and deep pockets were the rage and flared jeans were in demand. American retailers like J.C. Penney and Sears started making jeans with flared legs and boot cuts. Designer Tommy Hilfiger entered the market with Tommy Jeans featuring wide legs and deep pockets. Jeans with wide legs from 23 to 40 inches and pockets as deep as 17 inches were cool, while Levi's continued to make jeans with 16-inch wide legs and 6-inch deep pockets. There was a change in store shopping behaviour as well. Young people were going to specialty stores and avoiding the department stores where their parents shopped—which were the main distributors of Levi's products.

Howard Gross, CEO of the 220-store chain Millers Outpost, tried to let Levi's know what was going on. Millers Outpost sells Levi's products and likes to cooperate with its suppliers. The chain conducts a lot of market research to stay in touch with its customers and was willing to share some of its findings. Gross commented, "We told Levi's about extreme fits. We showed them our numbers. We told them what kids were asking for. They even attended some of our focus groups. But they didn't want to believe."

Levi's now believes—and knows that it must get back in touch with its market. The firm realizes that kids don't want to wear the same clothing brands as their parents. And retailers that cater to these kids don't want to stock the same brands as the traditional department stores. Levi's has thus created a new brand called Red Line jeans, which is being insulated as much as possible from Levi's image so that it will be perceived as cool. The brand has its own headquarters and isn't included in any of Levi's promotional materials, nor on its Web site.

Levi's has also launched a new, hip line of Dockers called K-1. One of the ads features a group of attractive male and female dancers wearing the K-1 Dockers and doing a number of acrobatic dance moves. Large firms like Levi's can become convinced of their own infallibility when they are very successful. Many times the reasons for success are poorly understood or if they were once understood, they become forgotten as upper management personnel change. It is because of this problem that previously successful firms begin to struggle and lose direction when environmental changes occur. The only recourse in these kinds of situations is to start over. Levi's seems to have recognized this and so the apparel giant has rediscovered the need and the means to stay in touch with its customers.

## Questions

1. Is there any hope for Levi's Jeans? What do you think Levi's will have to do to resurrect this brand and maintain it?
2. What forms of perceived risk accompany the purchase of Red Line Jeans by a first-time purchaser? A loyal customer?
3. What does Levi's have to do to make sure this kind of situation doesn't happen again?
4. What type of decision process would be used in the purchase of pants like K-1 Dockers or Red Line Jeans? Explain your answer.

**LEVI'S**
www.levi.com

Source: The data in this case are drawn from Nina Munk, "How Levi's Trashed a Great American Brand," *Fortune* (April 12, 1999), pp. 82–90; Cyndee Miller, "A Casual Affair," *Marketing News* (March 13, 1995), pp. 1–2; and Kevin Whitelaw, "Gobbling Up the Gen-X Market," *U.S. News & World Report* (October 9, 1995), p. 68.

## CASE STUDY

# Do Consumers Have Too Much Choice, or Not Enough Real Choice?

Marketers are often heard to say that one of the inalienable rights of consumers is the freedom to choose. (Of course, marketers would prefer that these choices be made from among an assortment of their firm's products alone.) Consumers and consumer groups also advocate freedom of choice, and marketers have responded vigorously. So vigorously in fact that consumers are raising a new complaint: too much to choose from.

These days big box stores are popping up all over the place: Chapters, Home Depot, Toys Я Us, Virgin Records, and many others offer huge assortments of products in large quantities at generally low prices. E-tailers, like Amazon.com, boast of having over 4 million titles. Even smaller specialty stores, like Toronto's Athlete's World, offer over 250 pairs of running shoes. The list goes on: hundreds of satellite TV channels, forty different kinds of coffee at Second Cup Coffee, and Baskin and Robbins' thirty-one flavours and more ("more" meaning a total inventory of 600 to 700 flavours rotated in and out of the stores throughout the year).

Reports of consumers being "irritated and bewildered" by choice have been made in the United Kingdom, France, Germany, and Italy. Interestingly, the issue here is not choice alone, but the number of me-too products. Multiple brands and products on store shelves turn out to have essentially the same ingredients. Since the failure rate of new products is about 90 per cent, in order to avoid risk, new products tend to be minor variations of existing products with established track records. This contributes to brand and product proliferation without adding meaningfully to consumer choice. In short, consumers long for the days when soap was soap and shampoo was shampoo.

Retailers say that even with hundreds of choices some people still aren't satisfied—and that they can't compete successfully unless they offer all the brand names. And when marketers are criticized for not really understanding their market they counter by noting that it's not for lack of trying. Consumers are very fickle. Out of 300 shoe choices only about 150 will really sell—but the retailer doesn't know which 150 it will be.

Maybe the solution is to allow consumers to custom-make their products so that they have to select only one brand. Dell Computers uses this approach. It allows consumers to build their computer to order over the Internet (www.dell.ca). The problem becomes: what do you put into your computer? How big should the hard drive be? 8 gigabytes, 9.6, 13.6? What processor should you choose? A Pentium III at 450 megahertz, 500, or 550? Maybe a less expensive Pentium II or even Celeron chip would be okay. What kind of sound card should the computer have, and what kind of video card? Should you get a CD-ROM drive or a digital video disk? What size of monitor should you purchase and what about a printer? Maybe a package offer might be a good place to start. What kind of software should you consider? Consumers are still bewildered.

One way for marketers to help consumers make choices is to offer a helpful and knowledgeable salesperson— someone who can interpret the needs of a consumer and suggest an appropriate solution. However, many stores that offer a large array of goods seem to be short on helpful salespeople. Internet retailers don't have any salespeople you can consult right away either, and back and forth interaction can't often be undertaken in a timely fashion.

So how can marketers help consumers choose in a marketplace that appears to be a mecca of choice? The only way is to understand the purchasing process of consumers and to market offerings in a way that's helpful to them. Providing sufficient information through advertising and promotional efforts so that consumers are presold is one way a firm can overcome the shortage of salespeople. Still, consumers are likely better off with more choice than less!

## Questions

1. Given your reading so far on marketing, what advice would you give marketers so that they don't offer too much choice?

2. When it comes to consumer goods, are you pro-choice or not? Discuss your views and support them with marketing theory.

3. There are consumers who seem to like all the choices, and those who are confused by them. In light of theory on the consumer's decision process, how might these two groups differ?

4. Information is often considered to be a consumer's best weapon. But even a knowledgeable consumer can be confused by the array of product choices available. Using some of the consumer behaviour principles presented in this chapter, what advice would you give a marketer in helping consumers decide on a computer purchase?

**VIRGIN RECORDS**
www.virgin.com

Sources: Based on material in Dell Canada Web site, www.dell.ca; Virginia Matthews, "Too Much Choice on Store Shelves Leaves Euro Consumers Crabby," *Marketing Magazine* (April 22, 1996), p. 6; and "Too Much Choice," CBC *Venture* Video 488.

**CHAPTER | 5**

# Organizational Consumers

## Chapter Objectives

1. To introduce the concept of industrial marketing

2. To differentiate between organizational consumers and final consumers and look at organizational consumers from an international perspective

3. To describe the different types of organizational consumers and their buying objectives, buying structure, and purchase constraints

4. To explain the organizational consumer's decision process

5. To consider the marketing implications of appealing to organizational consumers

*Courtesy Xwave Solutions*

When most people think of a software company the first name that comes to mind is Microsoft. But being a successful software developer and marketer doesn't have to mean designing products for use in personal computers everywhere in the world (although this certainly isn't a bad idea). Successful marketers identify needs and then fill them. However, not all needs are consumer needs. Take the case of Ottawa-based Software Kinetics, which developed the RAPS (Reconstruction, Analysis and Playback System) computer software designed to recover data from the flight recorder boxes of aircraft that have crashed. The software makes corrections for the errors created by the accident, and then turns the recovered data into a video recreation of the crash.

Canada's Transportation Safety Board used the software to understand what happened in a mid-air collision between two aircraft near Sioux Lookout, Ontario in 1995. The two aircraft collided in daylight, with no other aircraft congestion, no particular viewer obstructions for the pilots involved, and no radio signals from the pilots containing warnings or concerns of imminent collision. The voice cockpit recorders from both aircraft were recovered, but they were silent as well. The investigators had no idea how the collision could have happened. Using the flight recorder data of the two planes RAPS investigators were able to recreate the collision. The software indicated that the global positioning systems of both aircraft malfunctioned, and showed how the pilots banked to avoid the collision but just could not react quickly enough. In effect, the last moments of the aircraft had been recreated.

Software Kinetics developed RAPS on contract for Canada's Transportation Safety Board, and the software has become one of the most important ways that aircraft accident investigators throughout the world recreate and understand air accidents and crashes. The Transportation Safety Board used to give away RAPS to other agencies as a service, but since the software has many non-accident-related applications the Board decided to commercialize it. Because it's neither mandated nor positioned to undertake such sales, it gave Software Kinetics the licence to sell RAPS. Software Kinetics plans to sell a basic version of the software to such organizational consumers as airlines, aircraft manufacturers, and anyone else who might perform crash analysis. RAPS also has applications for training, quality control, aircraft maintenance, and aircraft design.

Software Kinetics was focused on solving difficult customized engineering problems for a few large customers. For example, they developed an electronic system for Canada's navy frigates that would detect approaching planes, missiles, and ships; and an electronic warfare simulation exercise for use by the Department of National Defence. They also developed an Internet link for defence workers in the late 1980s, but chose not to develop Internet hardware devices because they lacked the capital and wanted to remain a service firm. However, with the licensing of RAPS, Software Kinetics has been brought into a new era—and must now develop a new sales and marketing orientation with a good understanding of organizational buying behaviour.[1]

In this chapter we will study the characteristics and behaviour of the organizational consumers that Software Kinetics must come to understand. We will also discuss the different types of organizational customers, their buying objectives, buying structure, and purchasing constraints.

# Overview

As defined in Chapter 4, organizational consumers purchase goods and services for further production, use in operations, or resale to others. In contrast, final consumers buy for personal, family, or household use. Organizational consumers are manufacturers, wholesalers, retailers, and government and other nonprofit institutions. When firms deal with organizational consumers, they engage in **industrial marketing**, as shown in these examples.

Purchasing executives around the world spend trillions of dollars annually for the goods and services their companies require. According to one estimate, "On average, manufacturers shell out 55 cents of each dollar of revenues on goods and services, from raw materials to overnight mail. By contrast, labour seldom exceeds 6 per cent of sales, overhead 3 per cent."[2]

Although purchasing executives at large corporations often deal with major suppliers, in North America over 100 000 small businesses sell goods and services to these big companies. As one purchasing director noted, "We've discovered that smallness just equates with quality. A tiny company just tends to pay more attention. After all, it's risking everything on a small output. Sloppiness can be ruinous." One-third of the largest North American companies use formal programs for seeking out small suppliers. Why then do only a little over 100 000 of the millions of small North American firms sell to big corporations? Many feel there is a "nightmare of paperwork, pre-qualifying inspections, mazes to find the right contact, and the time involved before the contract is signed."[3]

For a long time, Polaroid Corporation earned its reputation (and considerable profits) by making and marketing self-developing cameras for final consumers. But in recent years, due to the popularity of inexpensive 35-mm cameras and the growth of one-hour photo developing labs, Polaroid has reduced its focus on final consumers. Today, Polaroid places greater emphasis on products for organizational consumers, including digital scanners, digital cameras, medical imaging systems, photo ID systems, and security systems.[4] And as Figure 5-1 shows, Polaroid now advertises some of its cameras to such organizational consumers as real-estate brokers.

Bombardier Inc. of Montreal "is an international powerhouse in transportation equipment" and had sales of about $8.5 billion in 1998. Most Canadians think of Bombardier as making snowmobiles and Sea-Doo water craft. However, Bombardier also designs and manufactures mass-transit vehicles, rail cars, and just happens to be the leading executive jet manufacturer in the world. Bombardier owns Canadair, Learjet Inc., Short Brothers PLC and de Havilland Inc. The market for the products of these jet and turboprop manufacturers is small passenger commuter airlines, business jet operators, national heads of state, and a handful of entrepreneurs. In the age of the Internet, which allows executives to communicate online, why is Bombardier expecting to make any sales at all? Because in the increasingly global economy, people will still have to travel on business, especially if it is big business. And big businesses are more likely to need the travelling flexibility and the office in the sky facilities of computers, fax machines, and satellite communication links afforded by corporate jets.[5] See Figure 5-2.

Andersen Consulting has annual revenues of U.S.$6.7 billion, with nearly 59 000 consultants in forty-six countries. It feels it's building the consulting firm of the future, and has established a "Business Integration Client Service Model" that it calls the industry standard. Andersen Consulting helps its clients with all their organizational components, focusing on aligning technology, processes, and human resources to support the organization's strategy.[6]

In this chapter, organizational consumers are distinguished from final consumers and an international perspective is provided. The various types of organizational consumers are described. Key factors in organizational consumer behaviour

*Firms involved with organizational consumers use* **industrial marketing**.

**POLAROID**
www.polaroid.com/

**BOMBARDIER**
www.bombardier.com/

**ANDERSEN CONSULTING**
www.ac.com/

**FIGURE 5-1**

**At Polaroid: A Heightened Emphasis on Industrial Marketing**
As Polaroid's core consumer photography business has stagnated, it has turned to imaginative approaches to industrial marketing.

*Reprinted by permission.*

are presented. The organizational consumer's decision process is outlined, and marketing implications are offered.

# The Characteristics of Organizational Consumers

Organizational consumers differ from final consumers in several key ways. As shown in Table 5-1, these differences are due to the nature of their purchases and the nature of the market. Organizational consumer characteristics also vary by nation.

## The Nature of Organizational Consumer Purchases

Organizational and final consumers vary in the way they use goods and services and in the items they buy. Organizational consumers purchase capital equipment, raw materials, semifinished goods, and other products for use in further production or operations or for resale to others. Final consumers, by contrast, usually acquire finished items (and are not involved with million-dollar purchases of plant and equipment) for personal, family, or household use. As a result, organizational consumers

**FIGURE 5-2**

**Industrial Marketing for Corporate Jets**
*Reprinted with permission of Bombardier Aerospace.*

---

**TABLE 5-1**

**Major Differences Between Organizational and Final Consumers**

**DIFFERENCES IN PURCHASES**

*Organizational consumers*

1. Buy for further production, use in operations, or resale to others. Final consumers buy only for personal, family, or household use.
2. Commonly purchase installations, raw materials, and semifinished materials. Final consumers rarely purchase these goods.
3. Often buy on the basis of specifications and technical data. Final consumers frequently buy based on description, fashion, and style.
4. Utilize multiple-buying and team-based decisions more often than final consumers.
5. Are more apt to apply formal value and vendor analysis.
6. More commonly lease equipment.
7. More frequently employ competitive bidding and negotiation.

**DIFFERENCES IN THE MARKET**

*Organizational consumers*

1. Derive their demand from that of final consumers.
2. Have demand states that are more subject to cyclical fluctuations than final consumer demand.
3. Are fewer in number and more geographically concentrated than final consumers.
4. Often employ buying specialists.
5. Require a shorter distribution channel than do final consumers.
6. May require special relationships with sellers.
7. Are more likely than final consumers to be able to make goods and undertake services as alternatives to purchasing them.

are more apt to use specifications, multiple-buying decisions, value and vendor analysis, leased equipment, and competitive bidding and negotiation than are final consumers.

Many organizational consumers rely on product specifications in purchase decisions and do not consider alternatives unless they meet minimum standards, such as engineering and architectural guidelines, purity, horsepower, voltage, type of construction, and construction materials. Final consumers more often purchase on the basis of description, style, and colour.

**Multiple-buying responsibility** *may be shared by two or more employees.*

Organizational consumers often use **multiple-buying responsibility**, whereby two or more employees formally participate in complex or expensive purchase decisions. For example, a decision to buy computerized cash registers may involve input from computer personnel, marketing personnel, the operations manager, a systems consultant, and the controller. The firm's president might make the final choice about the system's characteristics and the supplier. Though final consumers use multiple-buying responsibility (joint decision-making), they employ it less frequently and less formally.

**Value analysis** *reduces costs;* **vendor analysis** *rates suppliers.*

A lot of organizational consumers use value analysis and vendor analysis. In **value analysis**, organizational consumers thoroughly compare the costs and benefits of alternative materials, components, designs, or processes so as to reduce the cost/benefit ratio of purchases.[7] They seek to answer such questions as: What is the purpose of each good or service under purchase consideration? What are the short-run and long-run costs of each alternative? Is this purchase necessary? Are there substitute goods or services that could perform more efficiently? How long will a good or service last before it must be replaced? Can uniform standards be set to ease reordering?

In **vendor analysis**, organizational consumers thoroughly assess the strengths and weaknesses of current or new suppliers in terms of quality, customer service, reliability, and price.[8] Satisfaction with current vendors often means customer loyalty. Figures 5-3 and 5-4 illustrate value analysis and vendor analysis.

Organizational consumers of all sizes frequently lease major equipment. Each year, Canadian firms spend between $60–70 billion in leasing equipment (measured by the original cost of the equipment). Commonly leased equipment include aircraft, computers, office machinery, and trucks and trailers. The worldwide use of commercial leasing is rising rapidly. Final consumers are less involved with leasing; it is most common in apartment and auto leasing.

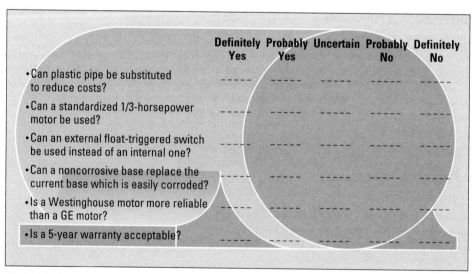

**FIGURE 5-3**

**Value Analysis by a Purchaser of an Electrical Pump**

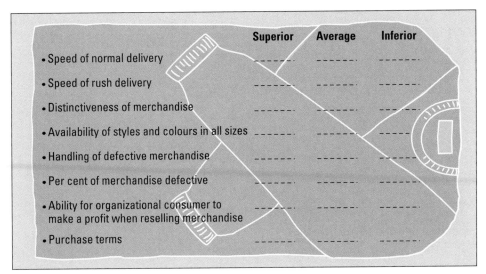

**FIGURE 5–4**
**Vendor Analysis of a Sweater Supplier by a Purchaser**

Organizational consumers often use competitive bidding and negotiation. In **competitive bidding**, two or more sellers submit independent price quotes for specific goods and/or services to a buyer, who chooses the best offer. In **negotiation**, a buyer uses bargaining ability and order size to get sellers' best possible prices. Bidding and negotiation are mostly used for complex, custom-made goods and services.

*In **competitive bidding**, sellers submit price bids; in **negotiation**, the buyer bargains to set prices.*

## The Nature of the Organizational Consumer Market

**Derived demand** occurs for organizational consumers because the quantity of the items they purchase is often based on the anticipated level of demand by their subsequent customers for specific goods and services. For example, the demand for the precision rivets used in cruise ships is derived from the demand for new cruise ships, which ultimately is derived from the demand for cruises. Firms know that unless demand is generated at the end-user level, distribution pipelines become clogged and resellers will not buy fresh goods and services. Organizational consumers' price sensitivity depends on end-user demand. If end users are willing to pay higher prices, organizational consumers will not object to increases. However, if end-user demand is low, organizational consumers will reduce purchases, even if suppliers lower their prices. Figure 5-5 illustrates derived demand for major household appliances.

*Organizational consumers **derive demand** from their own customers. With the **accelerator principle**, final consumer demand impacts on many organizational consumers.*

Organizational consumers' demand tends to be more volatile than final consumers'. A small change in the final demand for highly processed goods and services can yield a large change in organizational consumers' demand. This is due to the **accelerator principle**, whereby final consumer demand affects many layers of organizational consumers. For example, a drop in auto demand by final consumers reduces dealer demand for cars, auto maker demand for steel, and steel maker demand for iron ore. In addition, capital purchases by organizational consumers are highly influenced by the economy.

Organizational consumers are fewer in number than final consumers. In Canada, there are about 36 000 manufacturing establishments, 60 000 wholesaling establishments (including manufacturer-owned facilities), and 200 000 retailing establishments, as compared with 10 million final consumer households. In some industries, large organizational consumers dominate, and their size and importance give them bargaining power in dealing with sellers.

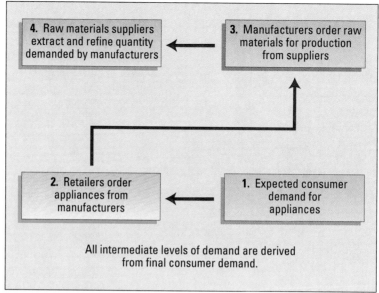

**FIGURE 5-5**

**Derived Demand for Major Appliances**

*Organizational consumers tend to be large and geographically concentrated.*

Over the last several years a number of global firms have exercised this bargaining power. For example, Xerox has gone from dealing with 5000 suppliers to 500, Motorola from 10 000 to 3000, Ford from 10 000 to 2300, and Texas Instruments from 22 000 to 14 000. And Allied Signal has gone from buying valves, pipes, and fittings from more than 400 suppliers to just one. This practice has severely affected those dropped, causing some to go out of business and others to invest considerable amounts to upgrade their facilities and products. Furthermore, the suppliers that are kept are expected to meet the highest levels of quality and customer service—while holding prices down.[9]

Organizational consumers tend to be geographically concentrated. For instance, two provinces (Ontario and Quebec) contain 70 per cent of the nation's manufacturing plants. Some industries (such as steel, wood, petroleum, rubber, auto, and tobacco) are even more geographically concentrated.

Because of their size and the types of purchases they make, many organizational consumers use buying specialists. These people often have technical backgrounds and are trained in supplier analysis and negotiating. Their full-time jobs are to purchase goods and services and analyze purchases. Expertise is high.

Inasmuch as many organizational consumers are large and geographically concentrated, purchase complex and custom-made goods and services, and use buying specialists, distribution channels tend to be shorter than those for final consumers. For example, a laser-printer maker would deal directly with a firm buying 100 printers; a salesperson from the manufacturer would call on the firm's purchasing agent. A company marketing printers to final consumers would distribute them through retail stores and expect final consumers to visit those stores.

Organizational consumers may require special relationships. They may expect to be consulted while new products are developed; want extra customer services, such as extended warranties, liberal returns, and free credit; and want close communications with vendors. Systems selling and reciprocity are two specific tactics used in industrial marketing. In **systems selling**, a combination of goods and services is provided to a buyer by one vendor. This gives a buyer one firm with which to negotiate and an assurance of consistency among various parts and components. For example, Hewlett-Packard uses systems selling for its laser printers, personal computers, and servicing.

**Systems selling** *offers single-source accountability.*

**Reciprocity** is a procedure by which organizational consumers select suppliers that agree to purchase goods and services, as well as sell them. In Canada, the Competition Bureau monitors reciprocity because of its potential lessening of competition. However, in international marketing efforts, sellers may sometimes have to enter into reciprocal agreements (in this case, known as countertrade). For instance, in 1973, because of currency restrictions in the then Soviet Union, PepsiCo began trading soft-drink syrup concentrate for Stolichnaya vodka. Since then, it has exchanged syrup concentrate for more than a million cases of vodka and two Russian-built ships. Its countertrade in today's Russia remains high.[10]

Finally, organizational consumers may produce goods and services themselves, if they find purchase terms, the way they are treated, or available choices unacceptable. They may sometimes suggest to suppliers that they will make their own goods or perform services as a way of improving their bargaining positions.

*In reciprocity, suppliers purchase as well as sell.*

**PEPSICO**
www.pepsi.com/

## An International Perspective

As with final consumers, many dissimilarities exist among organizational consumers around the world, and sellers must understand and respond to them. In this section, several topics are discussed: attitudes toward foreign firms as suppliers, the effects of culture on negotiating styles and decision making, the impact of a nation's stage of economic development, the need for an adaptation strategy, and the opportunities available due to new technology.

Firms doing business in foreign markets need to know how organizational consumers in those markets perceive the goods and services of firms from different countries. The attitudes of purchasing agents in foreign nations to Canadian products are often quite positive, especially with regard to high-technology items, professional services, raw materials, and industrial machinery. Likewise, many Canadian firms believe the product quality and/or prices for some foreign goods and services are better than those of Canadian suppliers. That is why Bombardier's Canadair subsidiary is having Sextant Avionique of France supply the flight-control systems for its new Global Express Airplane.

National culture has a large impact on the way organizational consumers negotiate and reach decisions. Here is an illustration:

*Foreign organizational consumers must be carefully studied.*

> The Chinese believe that one should build the relationship and, if successful, transactions will follow. Westerners build transactions and, if they are successful, a relationship will follow. This difference underlies many negotiating failures.
>
> In China, negotiating responses may be riddled with contradictions. Westerners will see illogical behaviour, evasion, deviousness perhaps, where none may be intended. Disentangling these communications supplies much of the challenge that is China. The deadline-driven, transcontinental executive may find it hard to slow down to the pace required to share "a loaf of bread, a jug of wine, and Tao," but marketing in China requires the patient building of relationships. Not that China is slow. The pace can simultaneously be fast and slow. Those involved in negotiations know how long they can drag when the Chinese side is consulting internally or has other reasons for delay, and yet how swiftly they move on other occasions.[11]

The stage of economic development in foreign countries affects the types of goods and services purchased by organizational consumers there. Many less-developed and developing nations do not yet have the infrastructure (electricity, roads, transportation systems, skilled workers) to properly use state-of-the-art machinery and equipment. In addition, such machinery and equipment may be too expensive for customers in those markets to afford. On the other hand, there is substantial long-term growth potential in those nations due to the scarcity of industrial goods and services. Firms marketing to less-developed and developing nations need to be patient and flexible in dealing with organizational consumers.

## INTERNATIONAL MARKETING IN ACTION

## Does Country of Origin Affect Industrial Buyers?

In the past, most country-of-origin studies looked at the impact of where a product was made on industrial buyers' quality perceptions. But a more recent study assessed country-of-origin effects by distinguishing between where a good was designed and where it was assembled. That study investigated the perceptions of members of the Canadian Association of Purchasing Managers.

The study suggests that, in general, products designed and assembled in industrialized countries have higher evaluations than those designed and assembled in developing and less-developed nations. Among seven industrialized nations, Japan, Germany, the United States, and Canada rank highest as countries of origin for design and assembly. France, Italy, and Belgium have lower ratings on these two criteria. South Korea, a rapidly industrializing nation, rates almost as highly as France and Italy as a country of assembly and was slightly higher than Belgium.

Country of design is a more important cue to purchasing managers than country of assembly for all three product categories

evaluated: computer systems, fax machines, and ballpoint pens. It appears that purchasing managers perceive a large difference in design and assembly capabilities based on a country's stage of economic development. And this perceived difference is greater in design than assembly capabilities.

Although brand name has a significant impact in terms of perceived quality and perceived value for both computer systems and fax machines, it has much less impact than both country-of-origin cues. Brand name has no impact on the evaluation of ballpoint pens. In summary, according to this study, brand name plays a limited role as a predictor of quality or purchase value.

As a consultant to a South Korean-based maker of electronic components, how would you incorporate the results of this study into your recommended marketing plan?

Source: Based on material in Sadrudin A. Ahmed, Alain d'Astous, and Mostafa El Adraoui, "Country-of-Origin Effects on Purchasing Managers' Product Perceptions," *Industrial Marketing Management*, Vol. 23 (October 1994), pp. 323–332.

When marketing goods and services to organizational consumers in foreign markets, firms have to consider how much to adapt their strategies to address the unique characteristics and needs of those customers. Because large organizational consumers can account for a significant part of any firm's overall revenues, selling firms are often quite willing to be responsive to customers' desires—by employing personnel who fluently speak the language of the foreign markets, utilizing the most appropriate negotiating styles, and adapting product features and customer service as requested. In general, it is more likely that selling firms will engage in meaningful adaptation of their marketing efforts if a potential customer order is big, the good or service being marketed is complex, and the business cultures and stage of economic development in their domestic and foreign markets are dissimilar.

With the new technology now available, there are more opportunities to market to international organizational consumers than ever before. For example, the Internet, e-mail, fax machines, satellite TV, and video conferencing all facilitate buyer-seller communications—and tear down the barriers caused by weak transportation infrastructures, differences in time zones, and the inability for both parties to see each other in regular phone calls. See Figure 5-6.

## Types of Organizational Consumers

In devising a marketing plan aimed at organizational consumers, it is necessary to research their attributes: areas of specialization, size and resources, location, and

**FIGURE 5-6**

**All the World's a Stage—for Business**
*From Canadian Business 1996 Performance 500, p. 176. Reprinted by permission of ADCOM Inc.*

goods and services purchased. As shown in Figure 5-7, marketers place organizational consumers into five major categories: manufacturers, wholesalers, retailers, government, and nonprofit institutions.

The Canadian, U.S., and Mexican governments also categorize organizations using the **North American Industry Classification System (NAICS)**, a form of Standard Industrial Classification (SIC) coding. The NAICS is a relatively new classification system (it began in 1997) for organizing economic data. It replaced separate Standard Industrial Classification (SIC codes) systems used by Canada, the U.S., and Mexico. The NAICS provides a standard framework for the collection of economic and financial data for all three nations. NAICS Canada 1997, the Canadian version of the classification, groups economic activity into twenty sectors and 921 industries and replaces the 1980 Canadian Standard Industrial Classification (SIC-E), which had eighteen divisions and 860 industries. The NAICS is designed to classify organizations according to the types of products or services they make available. The system was developed to enable governments and industry to collect, tabulate, and analyze data that was comparable between nations and over time, and to allow for business directories and directory databases to use classification codes for companies.

*The* **North American Industry Classification (NAICS)** *provides information on Canadian, American, and Mexican organizational consumers.*

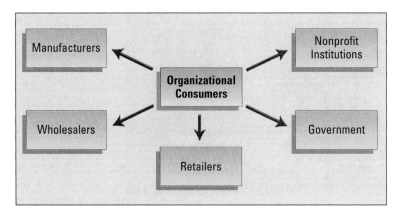

**FIGURE 5-7**
**Types of Organizational Consumers**

Statistics Canada uses the NAICS to collect census data on manufacturers, retailers, and wholesalers. In applying the NAICS, organizations engaged in the same activities are assigned the same NAICS code regardless of their size or form of ownership. The code assigns organizations to one of the following twenty sector classifications:

**CLASSIFICATION**

| Number | Sector Description |
|--------|--------------------|
| 11 | Agriculture, Forestry, Fishing and Hunting |
| 21 | Mining and Oil and Gas Extraction |
| 22 | Utilities |
| 23 | Construction |
| 31-33 | Manufacturing |
| 41 | Wholesale Trade |
| 44–45 | Retail Trade |
| 48–49 | Transportation and Warehousing |
| 51 | Information and Cultural Industries |
| 52 | Finance and Insurance |
| 53 | Real Estate and Rental and Leasing |
| 54 | Professional, Scientific and Technical Services |
| 55 | Management of Companies and Enterprises |
| 56 | Administrative and Support, Waste Management and Remediation Services |
| 61 | Educational Services |
| 62 | Health Care and Social Assistance |
| 71 | Arts, Entertainment, and Recreation |
| 72 | Accommodation and Food Services |
| 81 | Other Services (except Public Administration) |
| 91 | Public Administration |

The sectoral classification numbers represent the first two numbers of a six-digit code that allows for newer industries, compared to the four-digit code of previous SIC systems. The new classification scheme also reorganizes the categories on a production/process-oriented basis. This will enable businesses to classify customers and allow users to identify target markets. For example, if a firm that sells valve stems to tire dealers wants a list of all tire dealers in Canada, it could look up the NAICS (or SIC) code specific to tire dealers in a database that uses these codes. Business databases (like CanadaPhone) provide a listing of all companies that are based on the code.[12]

The use of classification codes is worldwide. Considerable data on industrial activity and companies in other nations are also available in the context of SIC codes like the NAICS Dun & Bradstreet's yearly *Principal International Businesses* directory, which lists 50 000 firms in 140 different nations. *Predicasts F&S Index Europe* annually cites articles with industry and company data by nation for Western and Eastern Europe, and Russia and the former Soviet republics. *Dun's Latin America's Top 25 000* annually provides data on companies in thirty-five countries. The U.S. Department of Commerce's *Global Trade and Economic Outlook* has information on a number of international industries.

**End-use analysis,** by which a seller determines the proportion of sales made to organizational consumers in different industries, is one way in which NAICS data can be employed. Table 5-2 shows end-use analysis for a glue manufacturer (in this example, the seller). First, the firm ascertains the current relative importance of various categories of its customers—5-2(A). It then applies end-use analysis to make an overall sales forecast by estimating the expected growth of each customer category in its geographic area—5-2(B).

*With **end-use analysis**, a seller studies sales made in different industries.*

Next, several characteristics of manufacturers, wholesalers, retailers, government, and nonprofit organizations as consumers are described.

## TABLE 5-2

## End-Use Analysis for a Regional Glue Manufacturer

### (A) SIMPLE END-USE ANALYSIS

| NAICS Code | Industry Classification of Customers | Current Total Sales (in Per Cent)[a] |
|---|---|:---:|
| 3152 | Cut and Sew Apparel Manufacturing | 10 |
| 32121 | Veneer, Plywood, and Engineered | 25 |
| 32221 | Paperboard Container Manufacturing | 13 |
| 3252 | Resin, Synthetic Rubber, and Plastics | 15 |
| 33712 | Household and Institutional Furniture | 20 |
| 51113 | Book Publishers | 17 |
| | Total | 100 |

### (B) APPLYING END-USE ANALYSIS TO SALES FORECASTING

| NAICS Code | Industry Classification of Customers | Per Cent of Current Total Sales | Estimated Annual Percentage Growth Rate of Industry[b] | Overall Sales Percentage for Glue Manufacturer[c] |
|---|---|:---:|:---:|:---:|
| 3152 | Cut and Sew Apparel Manufacturing | 10 | −2.0 | −0.20 |
| 32121 | Veneer, Plywood, and Engineered | 25 | +1.8 | +0.45 |
| 32221 | Paperboard Container Manufacturing | 13 | +2.0 | +0.26 |
| 3252 | Resin, Synthetic Rubber, and Plastics | 15 | +3.0 | +0.45 |
| 33712 | Household and Institutional Furniture | 20 | +3.2 | +0.64 |
| 51113 | Book Publishers | 17 | +1.9 | +0.32 |
| | Total Estimated Sales Increase | | | +1.92 |

[a] Firm examines its sales receipts and categorizes them by NAICS code.
[b] Firm estimates the growth rate of each category of customer (in its geographic area) on the basis of trade association and government data.
[c] Firm multiplies the percentage of current sales in each NAICS group by expected growth rate in each industry to derive its own expected sales for the coming year. It expects sales to increase by 1.92 per cent during the next year.

## Manufacturers as Consumers

**Manufacturers** *make items for resale to others.*

The North American Industry Classification System Manual lists twenty-four two-digit industry segments. Each segment can be divided into three-digit groups and then four-, five-, and six-digit subgroupings. For example, NAICS 31 includes Manufactured Products; 313 Textile Mills; 3131 Fiber, Yarn and Thread Mills; 313111 Yarn Spinning Mills; 313112 Yarn Texturizing, Throwing, and Winding Mills; 313113 Thread Mills.

In Canada, 60 per cent of manufacturers have twenty or more workers. The annual costs of their materials are $309 billion. Their expenditures for plant and equipment (from trucks to generator sets) are billions of dollars each year. They annually use billions of BTUs of energy and their annual net sales (including shipments between firms in the same industry category) exceed $489 billion.

By knowing where different industries are located, a firm can concentrate its efforts and not worry about covering geographically dispersed markets. Because manufacturers' purchasing decisions tend to be made centrally at headquarters or at divisional offices, the seller must identify the location of the proper decision makers.

As consumers, manufacturers buy a variety of goods and services, including land, capital equipment, machinery, raw materials, component parts, trade publications, accounting services, supplies, insurance, advertising, and delivery services. For example, U.S.-based aircraft manufacturer Boeing spends about U.S.$12 billion each year purchasing parts, equipment, and services from more than 34 000 U.S. companies. Outside the U.S., Boeing spent $1.7 billion on supplies and services purchased from approximately 900 companies in more than sixty nations.[13]

## Wholesalers as Consumers

**Wholesalers** *buy or handle merchandise and its resale to nonfinal consumers.*

**Wholesalers** buy or handle merchandise and its subsequent resale to organizational users, retailers, and other wholesalers. They do not sell significant volume to final users but are involved when services are marketed to organizational consumers. Chapter 10 has a broad discussion of wholesaling.

Canadian wholesalers are most prominent in Ontario and Quebec. Annual wholesaling and related sales (excluding manufacturer wholesaling) exceed $326 billion. Sales are largest for motor vehicles and accessories ($58 billion); food products ($53 billion); industrial machinery and equipment ($48 billion); computers, packaged software, and other electronic machinery ($33 billion); lumber and building materials ($24 billion); metals, hardware, plumbing, and heating equipment and supplies ($23 billion); and beverage, drug, and tobacco products ($23 billion).

As consumers, wholesalers buy or handle many goods and services, including warehouse facilities, trucks, finished products, insurance, refrigeration and other equipment, trade publications, accounting services, supplies, and spare parts. A major task in dealing with wholesalers is getting them to carry the selling firm's product line for further resale, thereby placing items into the distribution system. For new sellers or those with new products, gaining cooperation may be difficult. Even well-established manufacturers may have problems with their wholesalers because of the competitive nature of the marketplace, wholesalers' perceptions that they are not being serviced properly, or wholesalers' lack of faith in the manufacturers' products.

## Retailers as Consumers

**Retailers** *sell to the final consumer.*

**Retailers** buy or handle goods and services for sale (resale) to the final (ultimate) consumer. They usually obtain goods and services from both manufacturers and wholesalers. Chapter 11 has a broad discussion of retailing.

Annual Canadian retail sales exceed $238 billion. Chains operate about 20 per cent of all retail stores, accounting for about 40 per cent of total retail sales. A large amount of retailing involves auto dealers, food stores, general merchandise stores, eating and drinking places, gas stations, furniture and home furnishings stores, and apparel stores.

As consumers, retailers buy or handle a variety of goods and services, including store locations, facilities, interior design, advertising, resale items, insurance, and trucks. Unlike wholesalers, they are usually concerned about both product resale and the composition of their physical facilities (stores). This is because final consumers usually shop at stores, whereas wholesalers frequently call on customers. Thus, retailers often buy fixtures, displays, and services to decorate and redecorate stores.

Getting retailers to stock new items or continue handling current ones can be difficult because store and catalogue space is limited and retailers have their own goals. Many retail chains have evolved into large and powerful customers, not just "shelf stockers." Some are so powerful that they may even charge *slotting fees* just to carry manufacturers' products in their stores. For instance:

> Nowadays, most supermarket-savvy manufacturers chalk them up as a cost of doing business. But if fees for shelf-space had been around in the 1980s, products like granola, herbal tea, and yogurt might never have made it into stores and kitchens. These so-called slotting fees [charged by retailers for providing shelf-space] can often exceed $40 000 per retail chain per item, which adds up to millions of dollars for national distribution.[14]

Retailers (and wholesalers) sometimes insist that suppliers make items under the retailers' (or wholesalers') names. For private-label manufacturers, the continued orders of these customers are essential. If a large retailer or wholesaler stops doing business with a private-label manufacturer, then that firm has to establish its own identity with consumers—and it may even go out of business due to its lack of marketplace recognition.

## Government as Consumer

**Government** consumes goods and services in performing its duties and responsibilities. The federal (1), provincial (10), territorial (3), and municipal (6000) governmental units comprise the public sector. The public sector employs 2.7 million people and accounts for the greatest volume of purchases of any consumer group in Canada. For example, the Canadian federal government spent $163 billion in 1997, which netted out to $98.7 billion on goods and services after transfer payments and debt payments were subtracted. The combined provincial governments spent $177 billion in 1997, of which $148.7 was spent on goods and services after transfer payments and debt payments were subtracted. The biggest budget shares (including employee wages) go for operations, capital outlays, military service, postal services, education, highways, public welfare, health care, police, fire protection, sanitation, and natural resources.[15]

Governmental consumers buy a wide range of goods and services, including food, military equipment, office buildings, subway cars, office supplies, clothing, and vehicles. Some purchases involve standard products offered to traditional consumers; others, such as highways, are specially made for a government customer. Bombardier is one of the large Canadian firms that has its own marketing specialists dedicated to making government sales.

Some firms are unaccustomed to the bureaucracy, barriers, political sensitivities, and financial constraints of selling to government consumers. To aid them, the federal government agency Contracts Canada has published a guide called "The Basics of Selling to Government." According to this guide, government purchasing of goods and services from outside suppliers is about $14 billion every year. Public Works and Government Services Canada makes $8 billion of these purchases, but there are over 100 departments, agencies, Crown corporations, and Special Operating Agencies that will make service purchases on their own. Each federal government unit and

**Government** *purchases and uses a variety of routine and complex products.*

division typically has a purchasing department that is authorized to make direct purchases of goods up to $5000, while Public Works and Government Services Canada handles all goods purchases of $5000 or more. Service purchases can be made directly by all federal government units.

Suppliers who wish to sell to the federal government need to subscribe to the publication *Government Business Opportunities* (GBO), or suppliers can access MERX™, an electronic tendering service. Provincial and municipal governments have purchasing departments whose policies are very similar to the one the federal government uses. Every one of these purchasing departments will gladly divulge their procurement policies to anyone who wishes to supply goods and services.

The size of the government market in Canada is further enlarged by the fact that the federal, provincial, and local governments own some of the nation's largest corporations. For example, eighteen of the top 250 Canadian corporations are government-owned. These eighteen corporations had combined sales of $58 billion in 1997, combined net income of $13.2 billion, and used $510 billion in assets and employed 156 103 people. The heavy asset base is due to the fact that six of these companies are public utilities (power companies or telephone companies). These Crown corporations include Petro Canada, Canada Post Corporation, Canadian Broadcasting Corporation, Bank of Canada, Canada Mortgage and Housing Corporation (all owned by the federal government); Hydro-Québec, Caisse du depot et placement du Québec, Sociétés des loteries du Québec, Société des alcools du Québec (all owned by the province of Quebec); Ontario Hydro, Ontario Lottery Corporation, Liquor Control Board of Ontario (all owned by the province of Ontario); Insurance Corporation of B.C., B.C. Hydro and Power, B.C. Liquor Distribution (all owned by the province of British Columbia); New Brunswick Power Corporation, Manitoba Hydro-Electric Board, and EPCOR Utility (owned by the city of Edmonton).[16]

The buying behaviour of these corporations is very much like that of privately owned corporations; however, large contracts are awarded in a fashion very similar to government bid purchasing. Further, political considerations affect the decision-making behaviour of these organizations more often than for privately owned corporations.

## Nonprofit Institutions as Consumers

*Nonprofit institutions function in the public interest.*

**Nonprofit institutions** act in the public interest or to foster a cause and do not seek financial profits. Hospitals, charitable organizations, museums, universities, political parties, civic organizations, and parks are nonprofit institutions. Nonprofits buy goods and services in order to run their organizations and may buy items for resale to generate additional revenues to offset costs. The nonprofit sector consists of approximately 76 000 registered charities and about 100 000 other nonprofit organizations. In 1994 registered charities received over $90.5 billion in revenue (about 12 per cent of GDP), and nonprofits employed approximately 9 per cent of the labour force.[17]

There are many national and international nonprofit institutions, such as the Canadian Cancer Society, the Liberal, Progressive Conservative, New Democratic, Bloc Québécois and Reform parties, the Boy Scouts and Girl Guides, Chambers of Commerce, and the Red Cross. Hospitals, museums, and universities, due to their fixed sites, tend to be local nonprofit institutions.

**CHARITY VILLAGE**
www.charityvillage.com

# Key Factors in Organizational Consumer Behaviour

Organizational consumer behaviour depends on buying objectives, buying structure, and purchase constraints.

## Buying Objectives

Organizational consumers have several distinct goals in purchasing goods and services. Generally, these organizational buying objectives are important: availability of items, reliability of sellers, consistency of quality, delivery, price, and customer service. See Figure 5-8.

Availability means a buyer can obtain items when needed. An organizational consumer's production or resales may be inhibited if products are unavailable at the proper times. Seller reliability is based on its fairness in allotting items in high demand, nonadversarial relationships, honesty in reporting bills and shipping orders, and reputation. Consistency of quality refers to buyers' interest in purchasing items of appropriate quality on a regular basis. For example, drill bits should have the same degree of hardness each time they are bought. Delivery goals include minimizing the length of time from order placement to the receipt of items, minimizing the order size required by the supplier, having the seller responsible for shipments, minimizing costs, and adhering to an agreed-on schedule. Price considerations involve purchase prices and the flexibility of payment terms. Customer service entails the seller's ability or willingness to satisfy special requests, to have staff ready to field questions when needed, to promptly address problems, and to have an ongoing dialogue with customers.

Industrial marketers must recognize that price is only one of several considerations for organizational consumers; and it may be lower in importance than availability, quality, service, and other factors:

> Cutting purchasing costs has surprisingly little to do with browbeating suppliers. Purchasers at companies like Moore Business forms and Chrysler aim to reduce the total cost—not just the price—of each part or service they buy. They form enduring partnerships with suppliers that let them chip away at key costs year after year. Purchasing companies are also packing once-fragmented purchases of goods and services into companywide contracts for each.[18]

With regard to more specific goals, manufacturers are concerned about quality standards for raw materials, component parts, and equipment. Some like dealing with many suppliers to protect against shortages, foster price and service competition, and be exposed to new products. Others have been reducing the number of suppliers from which they buy, to foster better relationships, cut ordering inefficiencies, and have more clout with each supplier.[19]

Wholesalers and retailers consider further salability (their customers' demand) to be the highest priority. If possible, they seek buying arrangements whereby the number of distribution intermediaries that can carry goods and services in a geographic area is limited. They also seek manufacturers' advertising, transportation, and warehousing support.

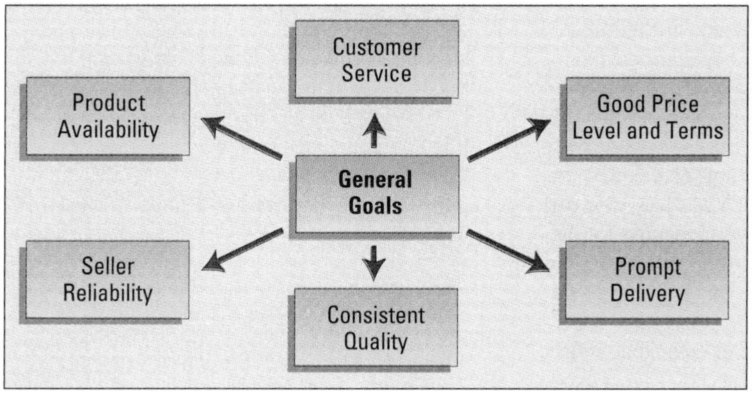

*Organizational buying objectives relate to availability, reliability, consistency, delivery, price, and service.*

*Salability and exclusivity are keys for wholesalers and retailers.*

**FIGURE 5-8**

**Goals of Organizational Consumers**

Government consumers frequently set exact specifications for some products they buy; as large-volume buyers, they can secure them. Government consumers may sometimes consider the economic conditions in the geographic areas of potential sellers. Contracts may be awarded to the firms with the higher unemployment in their surrounding communities.

# TECHNOLOGY AND MARKETING

## Y2K: Market Boom and Market Bust

**M**ention the Y2K problem to anyone in the late 1990s and you might have got a number of comments. The typical consumer would say, "What's the big deal? So what if a few computers crash? I don't see how it will affect me." Doomsayers, on the other hand, were advising people to avoid elevators, hospitals, and airplanes when the clock changed on January 1, 2000.

Although Y2K didn't seem to be perceived by consumers as a major concern, it was definitely a problem for organizational computer system operators and buyers, and thus an opportunity for sellers of Y2K solutions. Manufacturing firms are filled with literally millions of computerized devices such as measuring instruments, valves, and a host of controllers that go with them. Many of the controlling devices were operated by software that would not be able to recognize the Year 2000. In 1999 the "fix" for the Y2K problem was estimated to cost somewhere between $500 billion and a trillion dollars. The solution included a mixture of fixing existing software, replacing existing software with new software, and simply installing new hardware with accompanying new software.

Strangely though, one of the first victims of Y2K wasn't a firm whose network crashed, but a company that sold Y2K fixits. Formal Systems Inc. specialized in repairing Y2K bugs found in Natural software, a product used by many governments and large institutions in the 1980s. In July 1998 Formal's sales revenue dried up, forcing the firm to seek bankruptcy protection: a situation that represented the tip of the iceberg for Y2K firms. The combined revenue stream measured for the thirty-four Y2K firms that were traded on world stock markets showed a massive decline in late 1998.

The market decline stemmed from a couple of sources. The first was unexpected competition from new software suppliers. Some organizations chose to replace their bug-prone software rather than fix it, since by purchasing new software organizations were guaranteed that the problem wouldn't occur. Even though Y2K fixers offered the same guarantee, buyers still had doubts that these claims would be realized. Second, many organizations underestimated the magnitude of the Y2K problem and procrastinated in responding to it. Then, rather than save money by hiring firms like Formal to fix the problem, the procrastinators opted to replace systems entirely since it could be done more quickly.

When approached by firms like Formal some organizational buyers admitted that they were aware of Y2K but had chosen to ignore the problem, and moreover couldn't afford to fix or replace their systems. Other buyers said they weren't sure what the implications would be for their systems, and didn't want to rock the boat in their organizations by raising an alarm. For the boat-rocking worrying folks Formal might have pointed out what happened in 1997. Many computer programmers forgot that 1996 was a leap year, and so at the beginning of 1997 a number of production lines simply quit, resulting in millions of dollars in damages. Formal might have also pointed out that several Year 2000 date change simulations, conducted with robots and controllers using software that was not Y2K-compliant, revealed that they just shut down. (Formal might have wound up by saying that it's nearly impossible to rock a boat once it starts sinking.)

How should a Y2K fixit firm have identified potential buyers of Y2K fixit services, and what kind of sales pitches might it have used to convince these firms to use its services?

Source: Based on David North, "Forget Y2K, It's the No-Can-Pay Problem," *Canadian Business* (December 24, 1998/January 8, 1999), p. 122; Stanley Bing, "I'm OK. You're OK. R U Y2K?" *Fortune* (September 7, 1998), pp. 55–56; Gene Bylinksky, "Industry Wakes Up to the Year 2000 Menace," *Fortune* (April 27, 1998), pp. 163–180.

Nonprofit consumers stress price, availability, and reliability. They may seek special terms in recognition of their nonprofit status.

## Buying Structure

The buying structure of an organization refers to the formality and specialization used in the purchase process. It depends on the organization's size, resources, diversity, and format. The structure is apt to be formal (i.e., separate department) for a large, corporate, resourceful, diversified, and departmentalized organization. It will be less formal for a small, independently owned, financially limited, focused, and non-departmentalized organization.

*The organization's buying structure depends on its attributes.*

Large manufacturers normally have specialized purchasing agents who work with the firms' engineers or production department. Large wholesalers tend to have a single purchasing department or a general manager in charge of operations. Large retailers tend to be quite specialized and have buyers for each narrow product category. Small manufacturers, wholesalers, and retailers often have their buying functions completed by the owner-operator.

As mentioned previously, each government unit (federal, provincial, and municipal) and division typically has a purchasing department. Public Works and Government Services Canada is the federal office responsible for centralized procurement and coordination of purchases. In a nonprofit organization, there is usually one purchasing department, or a member of the operations staff performs buying functions.

## Constraints on Purchases

For manufacturers, wholesalers, and retailers, derived demand is the major constraint on purchase behaviour. Without the demand of consumers, production halts and sales drop as the backward chain of demand comes into play (final consumers $\rightarrow$ retailers $\rightarrow$ wholesalers $\rightarrow$ manufacturers).

*Derived demand is the key constraint on organizational purchases.*

Manufacturers also are constrained by the availability of raw materials and their ability to pay for large-ticket items. Wholesalers and retailers are limited by the finances available to make purchases, as well as by the level of risk they are willing to take. In this case, risk refers to the probability that wholesalers or retailers will be able to sell the products they buy in a reasonable time and at a satisfactory profit. Products like fashion clothing have higher risks than such staple items as vitamins and disposable diapers.

Government consumers are constrained by the budgeting process. Approval for categories of purchases must normally be secured well in advance, and deviations must be explained. Budgets must be certified by legislative bodies. For many nonprofit consumers, cash flow (the timing of the money they have coming in versus the money they spend) is the major concern.

# The Organizational Consumer's Decision Process

Organizational consumers use a decision-making procedure in much the same way as final consumers. Figure 5-9 shows the **organizational consumer's decision process**, with its four components: expectations, buying process, conflict resolution, and situational factors.[20]

*An **organizational consumer's decision process** is like a final consumer's.*

## Expectations

Purchasing agents, engineers, and users bring a set of organizational consumer expectations to any buying situation: "These expectations refer to the perceived

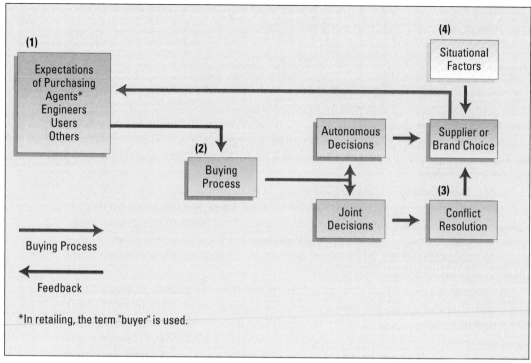

**FIGURE 5-9**

**The Organizational Consumer's Decision Process**
Source: Adapted from Jagdish N. Sheth, "A Model of Industrial Buyer Behaviour," *Journal of Marketing*, Vol. 37 (October 1973), pp. 50–56.

*Expectations are based on buyers' backgrounds, information, perceptions, and experience.*

potential of alternative suppliers and brands to satisfy a number of explicit and implicit objectives."[21]

For purchases to be made, buyers must have positive expectations of such supplier attributes as product availability and quality, vendor reliability, delivery time, price, and customer service. Expectations are based on the backgrounds of those participating in the buying process, the information received, perceptions, and satisfaction with past purchases.

## Buying Process

*Autonomous or joint decision making is based on product and company buying factors.*

During the buying process, a decision as to whether to consider making a purchase is initiated, information gathered, alternative suppliers evaluated, and conflicts among the different representatives of the buyer resolved. The process itself is similar to the final consumer buying process in Figure 4-7.

The buying process may involve autonomous (independent) or joint decisions based on product-specific and company-specific factors. *Product-specific buying factors* include perceived risk, purchase frequency, and time pressure. Autonomous decisions most often occur with low perceived risk, routine products, and high time pressure. Joint ones are more apt to be undertaken when dealing with high perceived risk, seldom-bought products, and low time pressure. *Company-specific buying factors* are an organization's basic orientation, size, and level of decision-making centralization. Autonomous decisions most often occur when the buyer has a high technology or production orientation, is small, or is highly centralized. Joint ones are more likely with a low technology or production orientation, large organization, and little centralization in decision making.

As noted earlier in the chapter, competitive bidding is often used with organizational consumers: Potential sellers specify in writing all terms and conditions of a purchase in addition to the product attributes they offer; the buyer then selects the best bid. With *open bidding*, proposals can be seen by competing sellers. With *closed bidding*, contract terms are kept secret and sellers are asked to make their best presentation in their first bids. Bidding is used in government purchases to avoid charges of bias or unfair negotiations, and bids for government purchases tend to be closed.

## Conflict Resolution

Joint decision making may lead to conflicts due to the diverse backgrounds and perspectives of purchasing agents, engineers, and users. **Conflict resolution** is then needed to make a decision. Four methods of resolution are possible: problem solving, persuasion, bargaining, and politicking.

*Problem solving, persuasion, bargaining, and politicking lead to* **conflict resolution**.

Problem solving occurs when members of a purchasing team decide to acquire further information before making a decision. This is the best procedure. Persuasion takes place when each member of a team presents his or her reasons why a particular supplier or brand should be selected. In theory, the most logical presentation should be chosen. However, the most dynamic (or powerful) person may persuade others to follow his or her lead.

Under bargaining, team members agree to support each other in different situations, with less attention paid to the merits of a purchase. One member may select the supplier of the current item; in return, another member would choose a vendor the next time. The last, and least desired, method of conflict resolution is politicking. With it, team members try to persuade outside parties and superiors to back their positions, and seek to win at power plays.

## Situational Factors

A number of **situational factors** can interrupt the decision process and the actual selection of a supplier or brand. These include "temporary economic conditions such as price controls, recession, or foreign trade; internal strikes, walkouts, machine breakdowns, and other production-related events; organizational changes such as merger or acquisition; and *ad hoc* changes in the marketplace, such as promotional efforts, new-product introduction, price changes, and so on, in the supplier industries."[22]

**Situational factors** *affect organizational consumer decisions.*

## Purchase and Feedback

After the decision process is completed and situational factors are taken into account, a purchase is made (or the process terminated) and a product is used or experienced. The level of satisfaction with a purchase is then fed back to a purchasing agent or team, and the data are stored for future use.

To maintain customer satisfaction and ensure continued purchases, regular service and follow-up calls by sellers are essential. As one study concluded: "Industrial salespeople today are generally younger, better educated, and more professional in their handling of business activities than in the past. That higher level of education is something that both purchasers and sales professionals benefit from. Both sides appear to be more sensitive to the other's responsibilities. Among purchasers and suppliers interested in developing partnerships, it's not unusual to see sales professionals attending purchasing courses, purchasing agents attending sales courses, and even purchasers and suppliers attending seminars together."[23]

## Types of Purchases

A **new-task purchase process** is needed for expensive products an organizational consumer has not bought before. A lot of decision making is undertaken, and per-

*Organizational buyers use a* **new-task purchase process** *for unique items, modified rebuys for infrequent purchases, and* **straight rebuys** *for regular purchases.*

ceived risk is high. This is similar to extended decision making for a final consumer. A **modified-rebuy purchase process** is employed for medium-priced products an organizational consumer has bought infrequently before. Moderate decision making is needed. This type of purchase is similar to limited decision making for a final consumer. A **straight-rebuy purchase process** is used for inexpensive items bought regularly. Reordering, not decision making, is applied because perceived risk is very low. This process is like a routine purchase for a final consumer.

### Research on the Organizational Consumer's Decision Process

Throughout the world, the organizational consumer's decision process has been heavily researched. Here is a sampling of the findings:

- There are significant differences in the way that decisions are made by Russian purchasing managers who are 40 years of age or less and those who are over 40. The younger managers see entrepreneurs, flexibility, and autonomy rising; their older counterparts do not.[24]

- Nigerian purchasers of capital equipment rely mostly on salesperson visits and manufacturers' catalogues for information; joint decision making is used during all stages of the decision process; and dissatisfaction with existing suppliers is a key reason a detailed decision process is triggered.[25]

- Some Eastern European purchasing agents, due to their lack of experience in a free-market economy, are having a tough time adjusting to situations in which they have more autonomy and a greater voice in decisions.[26]

## Marketing Implications

*There are many similarities, as well as differences, between organizational and final consumers.*

Although organizational and final consumers have substantial differences (as mentioned earlier), they also have similarities. Both can be described demographically; statistical and descriptive data can be gathered and analyzed. Both have different categories of buyers, each with separate needs and requirements. Both can be defined by using social and psychological factors, such as operating style, buying structure, purchase use, expectations, perceived risk, and conflict resolution. Both use a decision process, employ joint decision making, and face various kinds of purchase situations.

Industrial marketers must develop plans that reflect the similarities, as well as the differences, between organizational and final consumers. In their roles as sellers, manufacturers and wholesalers may also need two marketing plans—one for intermediate buyers and another for final consumers.

Finally, it must be recognized that purchasing agents or buyers have personal goals, as well as organizational goals. They seek status, approval, promotions, bonuses, and other rewards. And as noted in Figure 5-9, they bring distinct expectations to each buying situation, just as final consumers do.

*Industrial marketing strategies should be insightful.*

One leading consultant offers these suggestions for industrial marketers:

- Understand how your customers run their business.

- Show how your good or service fits into your customer's business.

- Make sure the benefits you sell stay current.

- Know how customers buy and fit your selling to their buying process.

- When selling, reach everyone on the customer's side involved in the buying decision.

**ETHICS AND TODAY'S MARKETER**

### Is Environmental Impact an Issue for Purchasing Agents?

How important is social responsibility—a concern for the environmental impact associated with an industrial good or service—to purchasing managers? According to one study, organizations can be placed into four categories:

- *Type I (Founder's Ideals)*—Social responsibility is an extension of the founder's ideals and values. A social mission for such firms is clearly articulated. This mission often acts as a second "bottom line" by which the firm would be evaluated. For example, "What we're trying to do is to suspend the standard rules in purchasing, which are to get the job done as quickly as possible and as cheaply as possible."
- *Type II (Symbolism)*—Socially responsible buying is indirectly tied to company success. Firms in this group want to discourage further government regulation. For example, "Now that we buy socially responsible products, people perceive us as green. This is important in getting the company name to where we want it to be."
- *Type III (Opportune)*—Socially responsible purchasing is seen as a way to lower costs or to increase sales. In one such firm, the purchase of a socially responsible product reduced costs by 70 per cent. Thus, "We do not buy socially irresponsible products, but it isn't as you say for a moral reason. It's for hassle avoidance more than anything else."
- *Type IV (Restraint)*—There is no deliberate plan as to socially responsible purchasing. And there are negligible "bottom-line" benefits to buying socially responsible products. For example, "If a supplier that we've worked with for twenty years before all the environmental concerns came up didn't share our views, it was hard. I feel much more like an extension of the supplier."

As a product manager for recycled paper, how would you use the preceding typology in marketing to book publishers?

Source: Based on material in Minette E. Drumwight, "Socially Responsible Organizational Buying: Environmental Concern as a Noneconomic Buying Criterion," *Journal of Marketing*, Vol. 58 (July 1994), pp. 1–9.

- Communicate to each decider the message that will address his or her chief concerns.
- Be the person or firm with whom your customers prefer to have a relationship.
- Be sure everything you do is consistent with your chosen level of quality, service, price, and performance.
- Understand your competitors' strengths and weaknesses.
- Strive to dominate your niche.
- Train your people in each aspect of your business and your customers'.
- Have a distribution system that meets your needs and your customers'.
- Seek new markets and new applications for your existing products.
- Enhance your products with customer service.
- Have your goals clearly in mind.[27]

## MARKETING IN THE THIRD MILLENNIUM

### What Happens to the Computer Industry When Big Companies Become Fully Automated?[28]

**C**omputer industry sales grew at dizzying rates throughout the 1980s and 1990s. The industry collects hundreds of billions in annual revenue, 60 per cent of which comes from organizations that employ 100 people or more. It's clear that the economic engine of the computer industry is driven by organizational customers, but in the new millennium it may be facing a crisis brought on by its own success. *Fortune* columnist Stewart Alsop raised the issue of what might happen to the computer industry when entire organizations become automated.

The notion of complete automation isn't far-fetched, given that the Internet and the World Wide Web have meant that any computer can now link and talk to any other computer in the world. We already live in an age when networked computing allows customers to talk directly to the business firms they're interacting with, so complete automation may not be far

behind. Employees of organizations can more easily undertake cross-functional activities by accessing and using networked information. With distributed computing people can do job-related activities from their homes, hotel rooms, cars, airplanes—or from their desks if they want to interact with fellow employees once in a while. "Companies give customers access to their own records, give employees control over their own benefits, let financial departments control purchases of office supplies in innovative ways, and let marketing departments open the development of ad campaigns to others in the company."

In essence, the need for new computing equipment and systems in the future may well level off when computing power exceeds computing requirements. For organizational buyers and the organizational market, this day may be approaching much faster than anyone thought.

## SUMMARY

**1.** *To introduce the concept of industrial marketing* When firms market goods and services to manufacturers, wholesalers, retailers, and government and other nonprofit institutions, industrial marketing is used.

**2.** *To differentiate between organizational consumers and final consumers and look at organizational consumers from an international perspective* Organizational consumers buy goods and services for further production, use in operations, or resale to others; they buy installations, raw materials, and semifinished materials. They often buy on the basis of specifications, use joint decision making, apply formal value and vendor analysis, lease equipment, and use bidding and negotiation. Their demand is gener-

ally derived from that of their consumers and can be cyclical. They are fewer in number and more geographically concentrated. They may employ buying specialists, expect sellers to visit them, require special relationships, and make goods and undertake services rather than buy them.

There are distinctions among organizational consumers around the globe.

**3.** *To describe the different types of organizational consumers and their buying objectives, buying structure, and purchase constraints* Organizational consumers may be classified by area of specialization, size and resources, location, and goods and services purchased. The major types of organizational con-

sumers are manufacturers, wholesalers, retailers, government, and nonprofit organizations. The NAICS can be used to get information on organizational consumers in Canada, the U.S., and Mexico. SIC systems can be used to acquire information on organizational consumers in the rest of the world.

These consumers have general buying goals, such as product availability, seller reliability, consistent quality, prompt delivery, good prices, and superior customer service. They may also have more specific goals, depending on the type of firm involved. An organization's buying structure refers to its level of formality and specialization in the purchase process. Derived demand, availability, further salability, and resources are the leading purchase constraints.

**4.** *To explain the organizational consumer's decision process* The process involves buyer expectations, the buying process, conflict resolution, and situational factors. Of prime importance is whether an organization uses joint decision making and, if so, how. Some form of bidding may be used with organizational consumers (most often with government).

If conflicts arise in joint decisions, firms may use problem solv-ing, persuasion, bargaining, or poli-ticking to arrive at a resolution. Situational factors can intervene between a decision to buy and an actual purchase. Such factors include strikes, economic condi-tions, and organizational changes.

New task, modified rebuy, and straight rebuy are the different pur-chase situations facing organiza-tional consumers.

**5.** *To consider the marketing impli-cations of appealing to organiza-tional consumers* Organizational consumers and final consumers have many similarities and differ-ences. Industrial marketers must understand them and adapt mar-keting plans accordingly. Dual marketing campaigns may be nec-essary for manufacturers and wholesalers that sell to intermedi-ate buyers and have their products resold to final consumers.

Purchasing agents and buyers have personal goals, such as status, promotions, and bonuses; these may have a large impact on deci-sion making.

## KEY TERMS

**industrial marketing** (p. 125)

**multiple-buying responsibility** (p. 128)

**value analysis** (p. 128)

**vendor analysis** (p. 128)

**competitive bidding** (p. 129)

**negotiation** (p. 129)

**derived demand** (p. 129)

**accelerator principle** (p. 129)

**systems selling** (p. 130)

**reciprocity** (p. 131)

**North American Industry Classification System (NAICS)** (p. 133)

**end-use analysis** (p. 135)

**manufacturers** (p. 136)

**wholesalers** (p. 136)

**retailers** (p. 136)

**government** (p. 137)

**nonprofit institutions** (p. 138)

**organizational consumer's deci-sion process** (p. 141)

**conflict resolution** (p. 143)

**situational factors** (p. 143)

**new-task purchase process** (p. 143)

**modified-rebuy purchase process** (p. 144)

**straight-rebuy purchase process** (p. 144)

## REVIEW QUESTIONS

**1.** Describe five of the most important differences between organizational and final consumers.

**2.** Distinguish between vendor analysis and value analysis.

**3.** What is the relationship between derived demand and the accelerator principle?

**4.** How is the North American Industry Classification System a useful marketing tool?

**5.** What are the most important general organizational con-sumer buying objectives?

**6.** For manufacturers, wholesalers, and retailers, what is the major constraint on their purchase behaviour? Why?

**7.** On what basis are organization-al consumer expectations formed?

**8.** How do product-specific and company-specific buying fac-tors affect the use of autonomous or joint decision making?

**9.** Which is the worst form of con-flict resolution? The best? Explain your answers.

**10.** Cite several suggestions that industrial marketers should keep in mind when developing and enacting their strategies.

# DISCUSSION QUESTIONS

1. As a university's purchasing agent, what would you have to do to get useful competitive bids from suppliers of new dormitory furniture?

2. As a chemical manufacturer's liaison to China, how would you handle the cultural relationships that would be necessary to win over prospective Chinese business clients?

3. A packaging firm knows its current sales are allocated as follows: 15 per cent to wine manufacturers (NAICS code 31213), 20 per cent to sugar and chocolate confectionery manufacturing (NAICS code 3113), 30 per cent to soft drink manufacturers (NAICS code 312111), 25 per cent to tea and coffee processors (NAICS code 31192), and 10 per cent to seafood preparation and processing (NAICS code 3117). The firm expects next year's industry sales in these categories to rise as follows: wine manufacturing, 5 per cent; sugar and chocolate confectionery manufacturing, 2 per cent; soft drinks, 3 per cent; tea and coffee, 0 per cent; and seafood preparation and processing, –5 per cent. According to end-use analysis, by how much should the packaging firm's sales increase next year? Explain your answer.

4. Describe a floral arranger's decision process in choosing a transportation firm to ship its products to retailers. Does this process entail a new task, modified rebuy, or straight rebuy? Explain your answer.

5. "It must be understood that organizational purchasing agents or buyers have personal as well as company goals." Comment on this statement.

## CASE STUDY
# Boeing Versus Airbus: The "Plane" Truth

Many consumers remain blissfully unaware of the size and power of many business-to-business marketers. Consider, for example, that the Boeing Company of Seattle, Washington and Airbus Industries of Europe (a consortium company composed of British Aerospace, DaimlerChrysler Aerospace, France's Aerospatiale, and Spain's Casa) sell passenger airplanes whose typical price tags are well over U.S.$100 million.

In 1998 Boeing earned U.S.$63 million on sales of $35.5 billion for its commercial aircraft division, while Airbus Industries lost $204 million on sales of $13.2 billion. Boeing handled about 650 new aircraft orders in 1998; Airbus filled about 550. The late 1990s have been good years for aircraft makers, with orders of 1000 commercial aircraft or more every year, and are expected to remain in the 600 to 800 range for the next decade. (In the early 1990s orders were at about 500 units per year.)

In 1999 Airbus leaped ahead of Boeing and garnered about 60 per cent of the new airplane orders.The competition between the two firms is fierce, since there are only a few airline customers. If an airline switches companies for its new planes it represents a major loss for its supplier. The profits from selling an aircraft only just begin with its sale; the supply of parts and maintenance equipment for an aircraft is an important source of revenue as well. Financing deals, low prices, and performance guarantees are all parts of deals to get airlines to buy new aircraft. The useful life of older aircraft depends on their maintenance and operating expenses. Sometimes replacing older aircraft with new ones can actually reduce the operating and maintenance expenses enough to recoup the financing costs of the new airplane.

Boeing has been trying to reduce its costs so that it can be more price competitive. Each aircraft it currently manufactures is almost a custom-built airplane. Boeing has offered 100 different shades of white paint as a customer option; there are about 100 different cockpit designs, and air carriers can choose from among almost 20 000 different galley and washroom arrange-

ments in the Boeing 777 aircraft. Boeing management wants to reduce these choices to a reasonable number using a modular manufacturing approach, so that aircraft can be turned out in 10 months instead of the usual 12 to 16 months. The firm plans to outsource some of its operations so that it can concentrate more on designing and marketing aircraft and less on manufacturing.

Boeing has dozens of contracts to manufacture aircraft, but three of the key ones are with American, Delta, and Continental Airlines. Airbus Industries recently stole three of Boeing's most important customers, British Airways, United Airlines, and TWA. One of the marketing tools Airbus used was to park a new A319 airplane nose-to-nose with a newly purchased British Airways Boeing 737 at London's Heathrow Airport. Airbus invited British Air Chair Boy Ayling and his staffers to tour the two aircraft and comparison shop. British Airways responded by ordering 188 A319s—the first time British Airways had made a purchase from Airbus.

Airbus would like at least half the commercial airline market, but it may be able to get more. The firm recently announced plans to build a double decker SuperJumbo Jet, which could seat from 555 to 750 passengers. These planes would be priced at about U.S.$213 million, while the development cost alone is pegged at $11 billion. Since Airbus is a consortium of four companies (from four European countries) that each produce specific components, the pooling of capital and risk among these firms was as much a political decision as a business one.

The choice of aircraft manufacturer is simple: Airbus or Boeing. Stephen Wolf, US Airways Chair, chose Airbus for a recent order because "Airbus aircraft offer greater flexibility for wider seats, more overhead bin space, and more aisle space—all important in a consumer-conscious business." These planes are economical to operate. Airbus has always marketed its aircraft as a smart choice, not as cheap imitations of Boeing. (Boeing, moreover, has had some bad publicity with a couple of air crashes of planes that were being investigated for production failures.)

Airbus has also been using modular design for its aircraft cockpits. Because the designs from one plane to another are so similar pilots can be trained more quickly to adapt to flying different aircraft. Crews can be transferred from one model to another far more easily.

The buying process for aircraft is a long and complicated one, involving many critical considerations. Decision making usually involves the CEOs of the airlines in conference with the CEOs of the aircraft makers. This means that the people at the helm of both Airbus and Boeing have to be good salespeople as well as good managers. Airline customers, for their part, are conscious of the need to spread their business around a little bit. After all, when the choice is one of two, they'd be left with little choice in the future if they were to favour one firm to the extent that the other is at risk of going out of business. And in such a capital-intensive and fiercely competitive industry there appears to be little room for any additional players.

### Questions

1. Relationship marketing is commonly considered as the way to conduct business-to-business dealings. Discuss how relationship marketing principles could be applied to the marketing of new aircraft to airline companies.

2. Map out a model of the aircraft purchase decision process on the part of an airline. What kind of buying situation do you think it is? Use the information from the chapter to assist you in designing the model.

3. Identify the main kinds of attributes that airlines would most likely take into consideration when buying an aircraft.

4. As a Boeing executive, what actions would you take to try to recover business from customers such as British Airways?

Based on Kenneth Labich, "Boeing Finally Hatches a Plan," *Fortune* (March 1, 1999), pp. 101–106; and Alex Taylor III, "Blue Skies for Airbus," *Fortune* (August 2, 1999), pp. 102–108.

## CASE STUDY
# Dealing with Computer Obsolescence

Manufacturers of computer systems have been performing incredible feats of magic year after year. Computers are becoming smaller, cheaper, and yet more powerful. According to Moore's law, computing power is doubling every eighteen months. New technological marvels seem to be announced on a daily basis. All this means, of course, that business people considering the purchase of a computer system are faced with a difficult and complex decision. Which system should they recommend to their CEOs to ensure that their firm remains productive and competitive? The rate of technological change is so fast and bewildering that a computer system ordered today seems to be rendered obsolete and inadequate tomorrow.

Manufacturers, consultants, and distributors are confused too. The current business climate requires managers to make good decisions and to do it faster than ever before. Decision makers need high-quality, up-to-the-minute information—and the ability to access and assess this information is directly related to the computer hardware and software at the manager's command. But what's a firm to do when any computer system it buys becomes obsolete in a mere eighteen months? Purchasers need to determine what kinds of decisions they must routinely make and what they need to know to make these decisions. Then they'll be better able to determine whether their firm needs state-of-the-art or state-of-need systems.

Once an investment is sunk into a computer system that's becoming obsolete the costs can't be recovered. Add hardware and software costs and employee training costs, and the decision becomes even graver. Leasing seems like a good way out of the problem, but what about manufacturers and distributors who grant these leases? How can they determine a residual value for equipment that will not only be obsolete but have a potentially higher price tag as used equipment than new equipment?

Purchasers can salve their conscience with a lease, but not their firm's pocketbook. Computer obsolescence is not just a marketing ploy either. Consider that a well cared for automobile can continue to do what it was made to do for a decade or more. The highways are full of ten- and fifteen-year-old vehicles that motor along just fine. Many people own "vehicles" for reasons beyond the need for a transportation tool. But a ten-year-old computer is a different story. The highways that computers employ are best travelled by the most up-to-date systems. Why can old cars work but not old computers? The reason is quite simple: speed limits on highways and the highways themselves have not changed very much in the last 50 years. It makes no sense to build a powerful automobile that can cruise at 300 kilometres an hour and hold 20 people when the law will not allow you to exceed 100 kilometres per hour and puts weight, height and length restrictions on vehicles.

The information highway has no speed limits and virtually no weight, height or length restrictions. Consequently, it has been changing rapidly. Government regulators have looked at this issue to determine how to stabilize this industry but this slowdown would hold up progress to much. The "computer vehicles" that operate on these highways are in a continual state of upgrade and the "limits" have yet to be reached. At some point in the future there are bound to be limits but they do not appear to be in sight at the moment. Until then, obsolescence will remain a problem. It looks as if computer obsolescence is an inescapable trap.

### Questions
1. Present a vendor analysis checklist whereby a purchasing agent could evaluate competing computer systems.
2. Take a computer supplier's point of view. How would you sell your systems knowing that they're likely to soon become obsolete?
3. Discuss how you're dealing with the reality that the computer system you use as a marketing student is either currently obsolete or will be in about eighteen months!
4. What kinds of actions might you recommend to computer systems buyers to help them escape the obsolescence trap?

Source: Based on "Computer Downsizing," CBC *Venture* Video 465.

## CHAPTER | 6

# Developing a Target Market Strategy

### *Chapter Objectives*

**1.** To describe the process of planning a target market strategy

**2.** To examine alternative demand patterns and segmentation bases for both final and organizational consumers

**3.** To explain and contrast undifferentiated marketing (mass marketing), concentrated marketing, and differentiated marketing (multiple segmentation)

**4.** To show the importance of positioning in developing a marketing strategy

**5.** To discuss sales forecasting and its role in target marketing

Al Harvey / The Slide Farm

The fastest growing and most dominant market available to marketers in the early years of the new millennium will be the seniors market (people 50 years of age and over). In the year 2001 the over-50s will represent 28.6 per cent of Canada's population, and 31.3 per cent by the year 2006. This is a generation in better health than ever before, and active in their communities as volunteers, political activists, and educators. Canada's seniors have tremendous amounts of free time on their hands, and spend more of it on sports, hobbies, reading, watching TV, and shopping than any other age group. The over-50s have 75–80 per cent of the discretionary income in the country, and spend 28 per cent of it. Most seniors have paid their mortgages, have no school-aged children, and have saved like crazy because of the scarcity psychology they developed as a result of living through economic recessions and facing high levels of taxation. The net wealth of the country is concentrated in the hands of people over 50. Marketers need to gear up for the time when one in three Canadians will be 50 years of age and older.

A major marketing opportunity involving seniors that is available to firms is retirement housing. For example, Reid's Heritage Homes in Guelph, Ontario has been developing a 115-acre residential development called Village by the Arboretum. The development, which is placed on land leased from the University of Guelph, is what is called an "adult lifestyle community." Aimed at the 65-plus set—and sometimes at pre-retirement, empty-nesters in their 50s—adult lifestyle communities, some of which come close to resembling full-blown resorts, are gaining popularity because they sell exactly what their name implies: a way of life. This development is adjacent to a 500-acre arboretum which has woods and hiking trails. The community itself has a state of the art, 43 000 square foot recreation clubhouse that includes an auditorium with 650 seats and an indoor pool. The community is like a small village, with a gated entrance and such special services as maintenance and medical care. And since the community is right beside the University of Guelph it has a strong upscale, progressive image.

The lifestyle is not cheap in developments like this. Having top-notch recreational facilities to go with nearby fishing, golfing, and hiking means home prices starting at $200 000, but most are more than double this amount. Take the well-established example of Briar Hill, adjacent to the Nottawasaga Inn in Alliston, Ontario. The occupants have access to the 70 000 square foot recreational facility and the nice restaurants of the Nottawasaga Inn, as well as to three nine-hole, executive-length golf courses surrounding the Inn and bordering on the homes. In Ontario in 1998, projected sales of homes in these lifestyle communities was estimated at 10 000 units, with a minimum price of $150 000. Ontario is the largest market for lifestyle communities, but developers in Calgary, Edmonton, and Kamloops plan to rival these.

Understanding the customers and their needs is critical to the success of marketing lifestyle developments. Marketers need to realize that seniors have a younger self-image, so advertising and promotional portrayals must present this. Marketing to people 75–80 years old is better accepted using a person who is 60. Appealing to the psychology and social maturity of this market is more important than appeals related to their demographic make-up. Senior buyers tend to be more brand-loyal than younger buyers and value integrity, so promotion should contain a lot of factual information. Emotional appeals are quite effective, but should not be patronizing or shallow. Seniors seem to use coupons more, watch newscasts, read heavily, and enjoy TV. They also tend to respond more favourably to direct-response promotions. Seniors are a group that marketers can build a relationship with and this means doing lots of research on this market.

Leisure life marketers have realized that seniors do not purchase on glitz alone. Therefore, promotional materials are usually straightforward and packed with information. Successful promotions emphasize good service and present the product offerings in great detail. (For example, good service means offering to water the plants of snowbird occupants who are wintering in Florida.) These seniors aren't declining, they're still building! Homes should have basements and two-car garages. However, the carpeting shouldn't be too thick so that moving a chair is difficult, and too many stairs is a definite no no.

As of 1998, a good understanding of seniors as a target market had allowed Reid's Heritage Homes to sell over 250 homes in a planned 600-home development. This illustrates that, although some people may argue that it doesn't pay to get old, it definitely pays to market to the old![1]

# Overview

After gathering data on consumer traits, desires, and decision making; company and industry attributes; and environmental factors, a firm is ready to select the target market(s) to which it will appeal and for which it will develop a suitable strategy. The total **market** for a particular good or service consists of all the people and/or organizations who desire (or potentially desire) that good or service, have sufficient resources to make purchases, and are willing and able to buy. Firms often use **market segmentation**—dividing the market into distinct subsets of customers that behave in the same way or have similar needs. Each subset could possibly be a target market.

Developing a **target market strategy** consists of three general phases: analyzing consumer demand, targeting the market, and developing the marketing strategy. These phases break down into the seven specific steps shown in Figure 6-1 and described throughout this chapter. First, a firm determines the demand patterns for a given good or service, establishes bases of segmentation, and identifies potential

*A **market** is all possible consumers for a good or service.*

*Through **market segmentation**, it can be subdivided.*

*In a **target market strategy**, a firm first studies demand.*

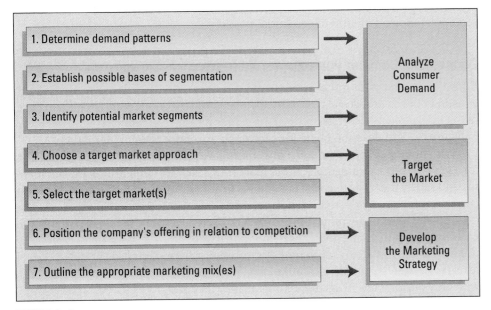

**FIGURE 6-1**

**The Steps in Planning a Target Market Strategy**

market segments. For example, do prospective consumers have similar or dissimilar needs and desires? What consumer characteristics, desires, and behaviour types can be best used to describe market segments?

Second, a firm chooses its approach and selects its target market(s). It can use **undifferentiated marketing** (mass marketing)—targeting the whole market with a single basic marketing strategy intended to have mass appeal; **concentrated marketing**—targeting one well-defined market segment with one tailored marketing strategy; or **differentiated marketing** (multiple segmentation)—targeting two or more well-defined market segments with a marketing strategy tailored to each segment.[2]

*Targeting approaches are* **undifferentiated, concentrated,** *and* **differentiated marketing**.

*The marketing strategy is then actually developed, with emphasis on* **product differentiation**.

Third, a firm positions its offering relative to competitors and outlines the proper marketing mix(es). Of particular importance here is attaining **product differentiation**, whereby "a product offering is perceived by the consumer to differ from its competition on any physical or nonphysical product characteristic, including price." When differentiation is favourable, it yields a differential advantage. A firm may be able to achieve a key differential advantage by simply emphasizing how its offering satisfies existing consumer desires and needs better than do competitors' products. However, sometimes demand patterns may have to be modified for consumers to perceive a firm's product differentiation as worthwhile. Thus, Tylenol is promoted as an alternative to aspirin for persons who cannot take aspirin (appealing to existing consumer needs), whereas Dove is marketed as a nonsoap bar cleanser with moisturizing qualities (modifying consumer perceptions of soap's role). If targeted consumers do not believe that moisturizing is a meaningful product attribute, then they will probably not buy Dove—no matter how much better a job of moisturizing it does compared to competing soaps. Given the fact that Dove is the industry leader, moisturizing is clearly a desirable attribute.[3]

In this chapter, the steps in a target market strategy are detailed—as they pertain to both final and organizational consumers. Sales forecasting and its role in developing a target market strategy are also examined.

## Analyzing Consumer Demand

The initial phase in planning a target market strategy (analyzing consumer demand) consists of three steps: determining demand patterns, establishing possible bases of segmentation, and identifying potential market segments.

### Determining Demand Patterns

**Demand patterns** *show if consumer desires are similar for a good or service. People may demonstrate* **homogeneous, clustered,** *or* **diffused demand**.

A firm must first determine the **demand patterns**—the uniformity or diversity of consumer needs and desires for particular categories of goods and services—it faces in the marketplace. A firm faces one of the three alternative demand patterns shown in Figure 6-2 and described here for each good or service category it markets.

With **homogeneous demand**, consumers have rather uniform needs and desires for a good or service category. A firm's marketing tasks are straightforward—to identify and satisfy the basic needs of consumers in a superior way. For instance, business customers in the express mail-delivery market are most interested in rapid, reliable delivery and reasonable prices. A firm such as United Parcel Service (UPS) appeals to customers by convincing them it is better than competitors in these areas. As competition picks up, firms may try to modify consumer demand patterns so new-product features become desirable and homogeneous demand turns to clustered demand, with only one or a few firms marketing the new features.

With **clustered demand**, consumer needs and desires for a good or service category can be divided into two or more clusters (segments), each having distinct purchase criteria. A firm's marketing efforts must be geared toward identifying and

**UPS**
www.ups.com/about/story.html

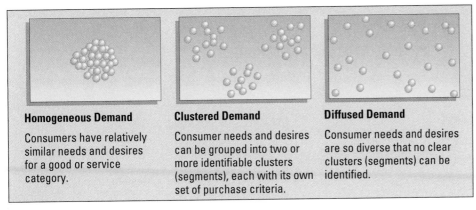

**Homogeneous Demand**

Consumers have relatively similar needs and desires for a good or service category.

**Clustered Demand**

Consumer needs and desires can be grouped into two or more identifiable clusters (segments), each with its own set of purchase criteria.

**Diffused Demand**

Consumer needs and desires are so diverse that no clear clusters (segments) can be identified.

**FIGURE 6-2**

**Alternative Consumer Demand Patterns for a Good or Service Category**

satisfying the needs and desires of a particular cluster (or clusters) in a superior way. For example, in the auto market, people can be grouped by their interest in price, car size, performance, styling, handling, sportiness, and other factors. Thus, auto makers offer luxury cars, economy cars, full-sized family cars, high-performance vehicles, and sports cars—each appealing to a particular cluster of consumer needs and desires. Clustered demand is the most prevalent demand pattern.

With **diffused demand**, consumer needs and desires for a good or service category are so diverse that clear clusters (segments) cannot be identified. A firm's marketing efforts are complex because product features are harder to communicate and more product versions may be offered. For example, consumers have diverse preferences for lipstick colours; even the same person may desire several colours, to use on different occasions or just for variety. Thus, cosmetics firms offer an array of lipstick colours. It would be nearly impossible for a firm to succeed with one colour or a handful of colours. To make marketing strategies more efficient, firms generally try to modify diffused consumer demand so clusters of at least moderate size appear.

Firms today often try to perform a balancing act with regard to consumer demand patterns. Just as the world marketplace is now getting closer due to more open borders and enhanced communications, there is also more information available on the diversity of the marketplace through customer databases, point-of-sale scanning in supermarkets, and other emerging data-collection techniques. On the one hand, some firms are looking for demand patterns that let them standardize (perhaps even globalize) their marketing mixes as much as possible—to maximize efficiency, generate a well-known image, and use mass media. On the other hand, some companies are searching for demand patterns that let them pinpoint more specific market segments—to better address the consumer needs in those segments.

## Establishing Possible Bases of Segmentation

Next, a company studies possible bases for segmenting the market for each of its products or product lines. Some of these are shown in Table 6-1. The firm must decide which of these segmentation bases are most relevant for its particular situation.

**GEOGRAPHIC DEMOGRAPHICS** **Geographic demographics** are basic identifiable characteristics of towns, cities, provinces or states, regions, and countries. A company may use one or a combination of the geographic demographics cited in Table 6-1 to describe its final or organizational consumers.

A segmentation strategy could be geared to geographic differences. Among the top three major metropolitan areas of each of Canada's provinces, annual per-household expenditures on food are highest in Toronto ($6550) and lowest in

**Geographic demographics** *describe towns, cities, provinces, regions, and countries.*

## TABLE 6–1

## Possible Bases of Segmentation

| BASES | EXAMPLES OF POSSIBLE SEGMENTS |
|---|---|
| *Geographic Demographics* | |
| Population (people or organizations) | |
| Location | Maritimes, Quebec, Ontario, Western Canada; domestic, international |
| Size | Small, medium, large |
| Density | Urban, suburban, rural |
| Transportation network | Mass transit, vehicular, pedestrian |
| Climate | Warm, cold |
| Type of commerce | Tourist, local worker, resident; SIC codes |
| Retail establishments | Downtown shopping district, shopping mall |
| Media | Local, regional, national |
| Competition | Underdeveloped, saturated |
| Growth pattern | Stable, negative, positive |
| Legislation | Stringent, lax |
| Cost of living/operations | Low, moderate, high |

**PERSONAL DEMOGRAPHICS**

| *A. Final Consumers* | |
|---|---|
| Age | Child, young adult, adult, older adult |
| Gender | Male, female |
| Education | Less than high school, high school, college, university |
| Mobility | Same residence for 2 years, moved in last 2 years |
| Marital status | Single, married, divorced, widowed |
| Household size | 1, 2, 3, 4, 5, 6, or more |
| Ethnicity | Anglophone, Francophone, European, Asian |

| *B. Organizational Consumers* | |
|---|---|
| Industry designation | SIC codes; end-use analysis |
| Product use | Further production, use in operations, resale to others |
| Institutional designation | Manufacturer, wholesaler, retailer, government, nonprofit |
| Company size | Small, medium, large |
| Industry growth pattern | Slow, moderate, high |
| Company growth pattern | Slow, moderate, high |
| Age of company | New, 5 years old, 10 years old or more |
| Language used | English, French, Chinese |

Charlottetown-Summerside, Prince Edward Island ($5270); annual household expenditures on furnishings are highest in St. John's, Newfoundland at $1601 compared to only $1049 in Montreal; the best-dressed Canadians appear to be in Toronto, where annual household expenditures on clothing were $2484, while the people in Saint John, New Brunswick were most likely to make the worst-dressed list with expenditures of only $1796; the most voracious readers are in Ottawa and spend $359 on reading material, while people in Halifax tend to do other things,

## TABLE 6-1

## Possible Bases of Segmentation (cont.)

### CONSUMER LIFESTYLES

| | |
|---|---|
| Social class (final consumers) | Lower-lower to upper-upper |
| Family life cycle (final consumers) | Bachelor to solitary survivor |
| Buying structure | Informal to formal, autonomous to joint |
| Usage rate | Light, medium, heavy |
| Usage experience | None, some, extensive |
| Brand loyalty | None, some, total |
| Personality | Introverted-extroverted persuasible-nonpersuasible |
| Attitudes | Neutral, positive, negative |
| Class consciousness | Inner-directed, outer-directed |
| Motives | Benefit segmentation |
| Perceived risk | Low, moderate, high |
| Innovativeness | Innovator, laggard |
| Opinion leadership | None, some, a lot |
| Importance of purchase | Little, a great deal |

spending an average of $249 on reading; and annual expenditures on tobacco and alcohol are highest in St. John's ($1498) while the people of Ottawa spend the least with only $963 annual household expenditures on these products. Figure 6-3 shows a demographic map of Canada.[4]

**PERSONAL DEMOGRAPHICS**   **Personal demographics** are basic identifiable characteristics of individual final consumers and organizational consumers and of groups of final consumers and organizational consumers. They are often used as a segmentation base because groups of people or organizations with similar demographics may have similar needs and desires that are distinct from those with different backgrounds. Personal demographics may be viewed singly or in combinations.

*Final Consumers*   As noted in Table 6-1, several personal demographics for final consumers may be used in planning a segmentation strategy.

Applications of personal demographic segmentation are plentiful. In China the dominant market is composed of consumers in the 18–35 age group. The younger portion of this group is forming what is called the "S Generation," so called because the children who were born when China's single child policy was enacted have begun to turn eighteen years old. These only children have been the recipients of a great deal of their parents' attention. One survey of urban Chinese parents indicated that 66 per cent of monthly family expenditures were dedicated to their child. This generation of Chinese consumers has learned to develop a taste for high consumption levels.[5]

In Canada, the United States, and other Western nations, Clairol and many other companies are now placing greater emphasis on wooing consumers in the early stages of middle age. This group is quite large and particularly interested in slowing the aging process. See Figure 6-4.

Procter & Gamble marketed specially designed Luvs Deluxe Diapers for Boys and Luvs Deluxe Diapers for Girls. Radio Station EZ Rock FM 97.3 in Toronto, Ontario, is

**Personal demographics**

*describe people and organizations. They should be used in studying final and organizational consumers.*

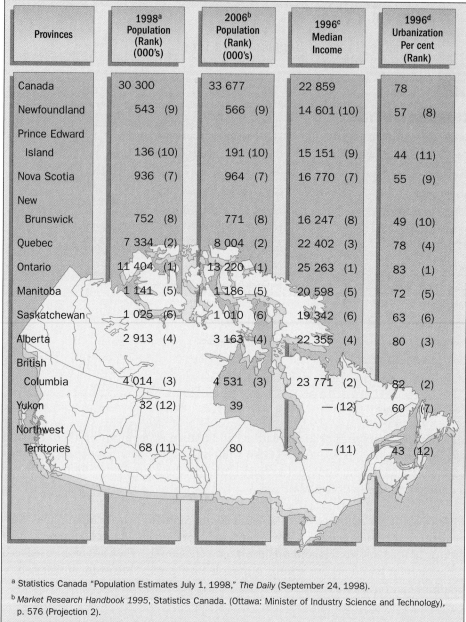

| Provinces | 1998[a] Population (Rank) (000's) | 2006[b] Population (Rank) (000's) | 1996[c] Median Income | 1996[d] Urbanization Per cent (Rank) |
|---|---|---|---|---|
| Canada | 30 300 | 33 677 | 22 859 | 78 |
| Newfoundland | 543 (9) | 566 (9) | 14 601 (10) | 57 (8) |
| Prince Edward Island | 136 (10) | 191 (10) | 15 151 (9) | 44 (11) |
| Nova Scotia | 936 (7) | 964 (7) | 16 770 (7) | 55 (9) |
| New Brunswick | 752 (8) | 771 (8) | 16 247 (8) | 49 (10) |
| Quebec | 7 334 (2) | 8 004 (2) | 22 402 (3) | 78 (4) |
| Ontario | 11 404 (1) | 13 220 (1) | 25 263 (1) | 83 (1) |
| Manitoba | 1 141 (5) | 1 186 (5) | 20 598 (5) | 72 (5) |
| Saskatchewan | 1 025 (6) | 1 010 (6) | 19 342 (6) | 63 (6) |
| Alberta | 2 913 (4) | 3 163 (4) | 22 355 (4) | 80 (3) |
| British Columbia | 4 014 (3) | 4 531 (3) | 23 771 (2) | 82 (2) |
| Yukon | 32 (12) | 39 | — (12) | 60 (7) |
| Northwest Territories | 68 (11) | 80 | — (11) | 43 (12) |

[a] Statistics Canada "Population Estimates July 1, 1998," *The Daily* (September 24, 1998).

[b] *Market Research Handbook 1995*, Statistics Canada. (Ottawa: Minister of Industry Science and Technology), p. 576 (Projection 2).

[c] Canadian Statistics, www.statcan.ca (January 15, 1999).

[d] Transport Canada, "T-Facts—Demography," www.gdsourcing.com/works/transport.html (January 15, 1999).

**FIGURE 6-3**

**Demographic Map of Canada**

targeting the 329 000 women ages 35–44 (8.5 per cent of the population) who live in the area.

At "A Buck or Two," a discount store chain, value-conscious consumers are attracted by low prices: many items are $5 or less. The firm locates in mall locations, sells many irregulars and factory overruns, and has few employees in each store.

Canada's Wonderland has sponsored "Gay Days" in recent years, drawing a number of corporate sponsors, including American Express Travel. According to Amex Canada, "gays and lesbians tend to travel a lot: 60 per cent take one or two pleasure trips a year, and more than 25 per cent take three or four." Gays have a lot

## TECHNOLOGY AND MARKETING

## Targeting Shoppers with Online Grocery Services

**M**ost people take the simple act of grocery shopping for granted, and may even see it as a social event. But for other people grocery shopping can be a pain, literally. Brandi Jasmine of Toronto would take six long hours to grocery shop because she had to use public transit and taxis. Brandi suffers from fibromyalgia, a condition that causes severe and chronic pain. Sheryl Todd suffers from arthritis, which is so severe that she has become wheelchair-bound. Never mind the handicap parking and automatic doors many retailers offer. Once inside the store the accommodations for disabled people disappear: groceries are often located on high shelves that are challenging for a person of average height to reach, let alone a person in a wheelchair. Checkout lanes are often jammed together and too narrow for a person in a wheelchair to fit through. Throw in some Canadian winter, and grocery shopping becomes a nightmare if you are disabled or physically infirm in any respect.

How does a person who is disabled or infirm shop while maintaining some dignity and independence? Why, online, of course. The PeachTree (www.peachtree.ca) is a Quebec-based Web site that accepts grocery orders which are then home-delivered. Home delivery of groceries is actually a very old idea. It was common when grocery stores were small and located close to customers in local neighbourhoods. Most local stores were essentially eliminated by supermarkets, and as they disappeared so did grocery delivery. There are still pockets of local stores that will deliver, but they are few and far between. The allure of PeachTree is the manner in which groceries are ordered and then delivered.

The target market for PeachTree is elderly people, disabled people, urban dwellers who lack cars, and people too busy to shop, such as young mothers or workaholic professional types. PeachTree acts as a "commission broker," in that it receives a small commission on each order placed through them. PeachTree has been setting up arrangements with local grocery firms that will deliver in a number of Canadian markets. So far these include Foodfare in Winnipeg, Food For You in Toronto, Quality Foods on Vancouver Island, and Strong's Market in Vancouver. They're just getting started, however, and it will be a while before the nation is as blanketed as fully with service as it is with Internet providers.

The service works as follows: customers access PeachTree through a password they're given when they register for the service. The site lists the service areas, which will be a key factor in the future growth of PeachTree. The system is based on postal codes so that shoppers are automatically linked to a grocer in their area. The PeachTree site has a number of product category banners, e.g., dairy, produce, meat, bakery, condiments, and packaged foods, that people can click on. Shoppers can then browse through a virtual grocery aisle and fill out a grocery list of the products they want. The items and their prices are listed for the customers, and even totalled so that they can determine their total grocery bill before actually deciding to purchase (very convenient, if you've ever gone through a grocery checkout only to discover that you don't have enough money!).

PeachTree has registered about 4000 shoppers, with 500 of them using the service regularly (every ten to fourteen days). The site also offers recipes and health news, and plans to offer online manufacturer's coupons and nutrition advice in the future. As for customer satisfaction, Sheryl Todd and Brandi Jasmine are very pleased. They've found the quality of the food, especially of the produce, to be much higher than expected. The convenience of home delivery is the key benefit; grocery orders are about $10–$20 more expensive, so price-sensitive shoppers will certainly not fit into the mix.

Discuss the benefits that PeachTree offers consumers and how they fit with the various potential target markets that are available.

Source: Based on Stephanie Whittaker, "On Special in Web Aisle Nine," *Marketing Magazine* (June 15, 1998), p. 27.

of spending power because they tend to be well-educated, have high-paying jobs, and usually do not have children.[6]

New Conditioning Creme Formula

Loving Care now gives you risk-free gray coverage like never before with its new conditioning creme. Your natural color lasts for 6 to 12 shampoos. And Lasting Color provides even longer lasting coverage, up to 24 shampoos.

Loving Care

*Dear Gray,*
*Good-bye. I will never see you again. I'm going back to my Natural color.*
*And if you come within a hair's distance, I'll get you. With Loving Care.*
*xoxo*

CLAIROL

**FIGURE 6-4**

**Wooing Consumers in Early Middle Age**
*Courtesy Bristol-Myers Squibb Canada Inc.*

In Ontario there are 361 000 people who speak Chinese, 274 000 of whom speak only Chinese when in their homes. (In contrast, Ontario has 427 000 people who speak Italian, only 136 000 of whom speak it at home.) The Chinese-speaking segment is significantly large and might well require a Chinese language marketing strategy. Recognizing this fact, *The Toronto Star* spent $20 million to acquire a 55 per cent controlling equity interest in *Sing Tao Daily*, Canada's largest Chinese-language daily newspaper. *The Toronto Star* is confident that it can profit by providing marketers with a medium to reach the Chinese market. Research indicates that the *Sing Tao Daily* is read by 45–50 per cent of all households in Toronto and Vancouver who read Chinese newspapers.[7]

***Organizational Consumers***
Table 6-1 also shows several personal demographics for organizational consumers that may be used in planning a segmentation strategy.

The easiest way to segment organizational consumers is by their industry designation. As an illustration, if you look at the Canadian information technologies and telecommunications industry, you would find that this sector has over 17 427 enterprises with combined revenues of $69.6 billion in 1996. The sector employs about 418 000 Canadians. Manufacturing exports for Canadian firms in this sector amounted to some $20.7 billion in 1996. However, the global market in this industry amounts to $1.9 trillion and has a growth rate of 15 per cent. As such, Canadian firms have a very small 1.75 per cent of this business. North America represents 47 per cent of this market (fully dominated by the U.S.), Europe 32 per cent, and Asia 18 per cent. This sector includes computer hardware, computer software, computer services, telecommunications equipment, telecommunications services, multimedia, geomatics, and training and learning services.[8]

To access potential organizational consumers by institutional type, some sellers rely on trade directories—such as the Canadian Trade Index with 15 000 Canadian manufacturers, Hoover's Masterlist of Major Latin American Companies with 1250 businesses, ABC Europ Production with 100 000 European manufacturers, and Scott's Directories with 53 800 Canadian manufacturers. Mailing lists of organizational consumers are also available. *Canadian Business Information* lists 1.1 million Canadian businesses, such as 27 854 big businesses (more than fifty employees), 1 021 265 small business locations (less than fifty employees), 162 131 professionals, and 74 801 executives. And American Business Lists' U.S. lists cite hundreds of thousands of manufacturers and wholesalers, over one million retailers, one million professional service businesses, and 450 000 membership organizations.

Organizational consumers may be divided into small, medium, and large categories. Some companies prosper by marketing goods and services to smaller customers, while others focus on medium and/or large accounts. For example, Panasonic has a line of inexpensive fax machines for small customers that cost a few hundred dollars, while Pitney Bowes markets fax machines that cost up to $5000, can handle 1200 pages of text, and store 1000 phone numbers. In Canada 97.3 per cent of business locations have under fifty employees, 2.6 per cent have fifty to 499 employees, and 0.1 per cent have 500 or more employees. Fifty per cent of Canadian business locations have annual revenues of less than $500 000, 18 per cent have annual revenues between $500 000 and $999 999, 22 per cent have annual revenues of $1 million or more, and the revenues for the remaining 10 per cent are unknown.[9]

Growth patterns in various industries may give an indication of a firm's future success in marketing to businesses in those industries and provide a good segmentation base. According to the International Trade Administration of the U.S. Department of Commerce, which makes forecasts for North American industries, electronic information services, health services, pre-recorded music, semiconductors, and surgical and medical instruments are fast-growing industries. Aircraft, paper industries machinery, personal leather goods, farm machinery, and newspapers are slow-growing industries.

**CONSUMER LIFESTYLES** Lifestyles are the ways in which people live and spend time and money; and many lifestyle factors can be applied to both final and organizational consumers. Table 6-1 listed a number of lifestyle segmentation bases; except where indicated, these factors are relevant when segmenting either final or organizational consumer markets.

*Final consumer and organizational consumer segments each can be described on the basis of lifestyle factors.*

Marketers have honed in on the importance of family and family activities as part of lifestyle. For example, Hasbro Games Group Canada has observed a trend in increased playing of non-video games. Hasbro observed that games such as Monopoly, Scrabble, and Yahtzee have had 10 per cent annual increases in the 1990s. They have launched a promotional campaign to encourage parents and kids to "play a family game tonight." In line with this trend, Procter and Gamble is encouraging the television medium to develop family-oriented programming by offering an awards program to recognize achievements in this type of programming.[10]

Final and organizational consumer market segments may be based on their usage rate—the amount of a product they consume. People or organizations can use very little, some, or a great deal. A **heavy-usage segment** (at times known as the **heavy half**) is a consumer group that accounts for a large proportion of a good's or service's sales relative to the size of the market. For instance, women buy 85 per cent of all greeting cards. Heavy yogurt consumers eat nearly double the amount consumed by average yogurt consumers. Manufacturers, wholesalers, and retailers account for over 90 per cent of all equipment leasing, while government and non-profit organizations make less than 10 per cent of equipment leases.[11] Sometimes, a heavy-usage segment may be attractive because of the volume it consumes; other times, the competition for consumers in that segment may make other opportunities more attractive.

*A **heavy-usage segment** has a rather large share of sales.*

Consumer motives may be used to establish benefit segments. **Benefit segmentation** groups people into segments on the basis of the different benefits they seek from a product. It was first popularized in the late 1960s when Russell Haley divided the toothpaste market into four segments: sensory—people wanting flavour and product appearance; sociable—people wanting bright teeth; worrier—people wanting decay prevention; and independent—people wanting low prices. Since then, benefit segmentation has been applied in many final and organizational consumer settings.[12] Figure 6-5 shows how benefit segmentation is used to market office furniture.

**Benefit segmentation** *groups consumers based on their reasons for using products.*

**BLENDING DEMOGRAPHIC AND LIFESTYLE FACTORS** It is generally advisable to use a mix of demographic and lifestyle factors to set up possible bases of segmentation. A better analysis then takes place. Two broad classification systems are the

**FIGURE 6-5**

**Applying Benefit Segmentation to Office Furniture**

The ad on the left targets people who are interested in comfort, while the one on the right targets people who are attracted to environmentally friendly products.

*Reprinted by permission.*

**VALS** *and the* **Social Styles model** *describe market segments in terms of a broad range of factors.*

**SRI CONSULTING**
http://future.sri.com/vals/valsindex.html

**VALS (Values and Lifestyles) program**, which divides final consumers into lifestyle categories; and the **Social Styles model**, which divides the personnel representing organizational consumers into lifestyle categories.

In North America, the current VALS 2 typology, shown in Figure 6-6, seeks to explain why and how people make purchase decisions, and places them into segments based on self-orientation and resources. Principle-oriented people are guided by their beliefs; status-oriented people are influenced by others; and action-oriented people are guided by a desire for activity, variety, and risk taking. People's resources include their education, income, self-confidence, health, eagerness to buy, intelligence, and energy level; and resources rise from youth to middle age and fall with old age. Here are descriptions of the basic VALS 2 segments (in terms of adult characteristics):

- *Actualizers*—Highest resources. Successful, sophisticated. Can indulge in any self-orientations. Have a taste for the finer things in life. Comprise 8 per cent of population. Ninety-five per cent have at least some university education. Median age of 43.

- *Fulfilleds*—Principle-oriented, abundant resources. Mature, satisfied, comfortable, and reflective. Mostly professional and well educated. As consumers, concerned with functionality, value, and durability. Comprise 11 per cent of population. Eighty-one per cent have at least some university education. Median age of 48.

- *Believers*—Principle-oriented, lower resources. Follow routines organized around homes, families, and social or religious organizations. Want domestic products and known brands. Resources sufficient for needs. Comprise 16 per cent of population. Six per cent have at least some university education. Median age of 58.

- *Achievers*—Status-oriented, second-highest resources. Committed to jobs and families, and satisfied with them. Like to be in control. Favour established products that demonstrate their success to peers. Comprise 13 per cent of population. Seventy-seven per cent have at least some university education. Median age of 36.

- *Strivers*—Status-oriented, lower resources. Values similar to achievers but fewer resources. Unsure of themselves. Concerned about approval from others. Most-

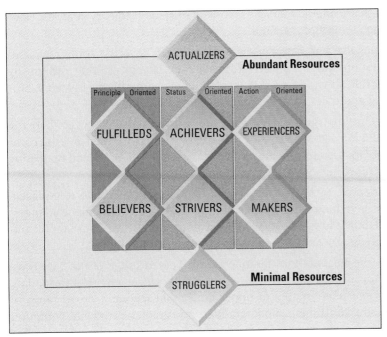

**FIGURE 6-6**

**The VALS 2 Network**
*Reprinted by permission of SRI International, Menlo Park, California.*

desired goods and services generally beyond reach. Comprise 13 per cent of population. Twenty-three per cent have at least some university education. Median age of 34.

- *Experiencers*—Action-oriented, acquiring resources. Young, enthusiastic, and rebellious. Seek variety and excitement. Spend much of income on clothing, fast food, music, movies, and videos. Comprise 12 per cent of population. Forty-one per cent have at least some university education. Median age of 26.

- *Makers*—Action-oriented, lower resources. Live in a traditional context of family, work, and physical recreation. Unimpressed by possessions. Like do-it-yourself projects. Comprise 13 per cent of population. Twenty-four per cent have at least some university education. Median age of 30.

- *Strugglers*—Lowest resources (too few to include in any self-orientation). Chronically poor, ill-educated, older, and low in skills. Concerned about health, safety, and security. Brand loyal and cautious. Comprise 14 per cent of population. Three per cent have at least some university education. Median age of 61.[13]

In conjunction with SRI International (VALS' developer), Market Statistics has devised a high-tech way to use the VALS 2 model—called GeoVALS. Through GeoVALS, the eight VALS 2 market segments can be broken down by metropolitan area, city, and postal code.[14]

The VALS system is so popular that it has been applied in Japan, and tailored to people there. For example, ryoshiki ("socially intelligent") innovators are career-oriented, middle-aged innovators; ryoshiki adapters are shy and look to ryoshiki innovators; tradition adapters are young and affluent; and low pragmatics are attitudinally negative and oriented to inexpensive products.[15]

In addition, SRI is developing an **iVALS** segment profile to describe Internet users. There are currently ten iVALS segments, including:

- *Wizards*—The most active and skilled Internet users. Computers are a key aspect of their lifestyles, and mastery of technology figures prominently in their identities. Wizards are nearly all males, median age under 30. Many are computer tech-

*The **iVALS** segment profile describes ten different types of Internet users.*

nicians, professors, middle managers, consultants, and industry analysts. Have medium to high household income.

- *Pioneers*—A positive and active user segment. They have the strongest recreational orientation and are immersed heavily in cyberspace. They are mostly males with a wide spread of ages. Pioneers include computer technicians, professionals, and graduate students. Have low household incomes.

- *Upstreamers*—Internet generalists. They are mostly males, younger than the Internet population as a whole. They're not experts on computers but are comfortable users. Upstreamers include scientists, consultants, sales and marketing people, and a more business-oriented group.

- *Socialites*—Oriented to the social aspects of the Internet. Have role-played, flirted, flamed, and done other kinds of playing on the Net. They are the youngest segment, well under 30 years of age. Above average number of computer technicians and students. Low income and a strong entertainment focus.

- *Workers*—See the Internet in utilitarian terms. Lowest usage of the Net. Have excellent technical skills and use the Net for mainly career-related information. Heavily male and have middle to upper household incomes. Broad range of careers, including consultants, undergraduate and graduate students, computer technicians, professors, and teachers.

- *Surfers*—A technically modest segment, very active and leisure-oriented group. This segment is the oldest and also has the highest household income. Surfers include retired professionals, middle managers, consultants, professionals, and scientists.

- *Mainstreamers*—Use the Internet to fit their work and personal requirements online, and nothing more. Often connect to the Internet from work. Are one of the most intellectually capable iVALS segments. Have above average household incomes and are highly educated. Occupations include scientists, professionals, senior managers, and graduate students.

- *Sociables*—Oriented to the social activity on the Internet. They are like socialites but they go for chat rooms instead of conferencing. They like to role-play on the Net and treat men and women differently online. They like the entertainment on the Net. They go for movies, cable TV, and own a lot of computer games and multimedia. They don't have a lot of technical ability, but feel comfortable online. The sociables reflect the basic Internet gender split (currently 70 per cent male, 30 per cent female). They are young, with a wide range of household incomes. They are teachers, lawyers, managers, undergraduate students, and secretaries.

- *Seekers*—A very work-focused group who use computers for productivity. Online time is for specific work tasks, such as information searches, communications, and document sharing. Do not really use the Internet recreationally. One of the oldest groups in terms of age, their education level is much higher than most Net users. They are professors, teachers, senior and middle managers, and sales and marketing staff. They are generally learning new computer skills long after becoming adults.

- *Immigrants*—Recent arrivals to cyberspace and have limited familiarity. They are subsidized in their Internet usage via their work or schooling, and wouldn't pay for the Internet on their own. They spend little time on the Net and do not use it for recreational purposes. This group has a 50/50 gender split. There is a wide range of age and occupations, including elementary and secondary school students, undergraduate students, midlife senior executives, and some professionals.[16]

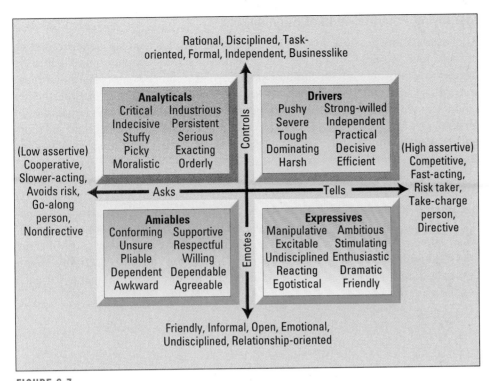

**FIGURE 6-7**

**The Social Styles Model for Organizational Consumers**

Sources: Wilson Learning Corporation and Tracom Corporation, Reprinted by permission of Crain Communications Inc., from Tom Eisenhart, "How to Really Excite Your Prospects," *Business Marketing* (July 1988).

According to the Social Styles model, highlighted in Figure 6-7, social styles affect how people react to various stimuli on and off the job. This model looks at two traits—assertiveness and responsiveness—and divides organizational personnel into "analyticals," "drivers," "amiables," and "expressives." Assertiveness is the degree to which a person states views with assurance, confidence, and force, and the extent to which he or she tries to direct others' actions. Responsiveness is the extent to which a person is affected by appeals, influence, or stimulation and how his or her feelings, emotions, or impressions are shown to others:

- *Analyticals*—Low in both assertiveness and responsiveness. Like facts and details. Money- and numbers-oriented. Work well alone. Stay under control. Interested in processes. Risk avoiders.

- *Expressives*—High in both assertiveness and responsiveness. Personality opposites of analyticals. Use hunches to make decisions. Need to be with people. Focus on generalities. Thrive on freedom from outside control. Risk takers, but seek approval for themselves and their firms.

- *Drivers*—Low in responsiveness and high in assertiveness. Get right to the point. Limited time. "Hard chargers." Self-motivated and impatient. Work well alone. Risk takers. Success-oriented.

- *Amiables*—Low in assertiveness and high in responsiveness. Team players. Like to build relationships. Friendly and loyal. Need support from others. Careful. Less time-oriented. Can be indecisive. Risk avoiders.[17]

The Social Styles model has been used to classify personnel within industries—including banking, computers and precision instruments, chemicals, pharmaceuticals, telecommunications, aerospace, utilities, and industrial and farm equipment. In all cases, the analyticals segment is the largest.

### Identifying Potential Market Segments

*Consumer profiles are used in identifying market segments.*

After establishing possible bases of segmentation, a firm is ready to construct specific consumer profiles—which identify potential market segments for that firm by aggregating consumers with similar characteristics and needs and separating them from those with different characteristics and needs. For example, a supermarket could segment female and male shoppers in terms of their in-store behaviour. In general, on each visit, women spend more time shopping, buy more items, are more apt to bring children, and more often use a shopping list than men; and they are equally apt to shop in the evening.

A photocopier manufacturer could group the office-copier market into benefit segments, such as: basic copying (satisfied with simple, inexpensive machines that make up to 99 black-and-white copies of a single page at a time); extensive copying (satisfied with mid-priced machines that make up to 100 or more one- or two-sided copies of multiple pages and then collate them); and desktop publishing (satisfied with expensive, sophisticated machines that make high-quality colour copies in large quantities). Both domestic and international prospects for each segment are bright.

## INTERNATIONAL MARKETING IN ACTION

## Targeting Japanese Women to Increase Tourism

Japanese women are being targeted with an advertising campaign showing picturesque ads of Canadian landscapes and Canadian attractions. The Canadian Tourism Commission, which is the source of the advertising, wants to maintain Canada's share of outbound Japanese tourists. The Canadian tourism industry has great growth potential because it's virtually unregulated, thus allowing for price competition that can lead to greater demand. The most recent data available indicate that about 25 000 Japanese tourists visited Canada in 1996. Asian tourism increased rapidly in the 1990s, with Japanese visitors accounting for about 40 per cent of the Asian visitors that came to Canada.

Canada's share of Japanese tourism has been slipping in recent years due to the economic turmoil that gripped the Asian economy in the late 1990s. (However, Canada's modest 4 per cent share compares favourably to the fact that Canada's total share of world tourism is only 3.43 per cent.) Japanese tourists are particularly desirable because, as tourists go, they are big spenders. For example, in 1996 a typical Japanese tourist stayed half as long as a visitor from the United Kingdom, yet spent twice as much money.

The Canadian Tourism Commission is targeting its ads at young working women and women over 45 years of age, because research indicates that these are the people who make the decisions on travel in Japanese households. The advertisements show scenes of Niagara Falls, the Notre Dame Basilica in Montreal, and birds flying over the Rockies. The ads are placed in consumer magazines, newspapers and travel publications, as well as some transit ads in Tokyo. The hope is that the offer of the natural beauty and wide open spaces of Canada will have a strong emotional appeal to the influential female decision makers.

Discuss how you might employ VALS Japan to help you design a promotional campaign to draw Japanese tourists to Canada.

Source: Based on Chris Daniels, "Canada Shows Japan Its Colors," *Marketing Magazine* (October 26, 1998), p. 6; Micro-Economic Policy Analysis Branch, "The Asia Pacific Region in the Global Economy: A Canadian Perspective," (General Editor: Richard G. Harris), University of Calgary Press, 1997, Strategis Web site, strategis.ic.gc.ca (January 18, 1999); and Statistics Canada, "Travel Between Canada and Other Countries, January 1997," *The Daily* (Monday, March 17, 1997).

# Targeting the Market

The second phase in planning a target market strategy consists of choosing the proper approach and selecting the target market(s).

## Choosing a Target Market Approach

A firm now decides upon undifferentiated marketing (mass marketing), concentrated marketing, or differentiated marketing (multiple segmentation). These options are shown in Table 6-2, and are discussed next.

**UNDIFFERENTIATED MARKETING (MASS MARKETING)**   An undifferentiated marketing (mass marketing) approach aims at a large, broad consumer market using one basic marketing plan. With this approach, a firm believes consumers have very similar desires regarding product attributes or opts to ignore differences among segments. An early practitioner of mass marketing was Henry Ford, who sold one standard car at a reasonable price to many people. The original Model T had no options and came only in black.

Mass marketing was popular when large-scale production started, but the number of firms using a pure undifferentiated marketing approach has declined in recent years. Competition has grown, and firms need to stimulate consumer demand by appealing to specific segments. In addition, improved marketing research can better pinpoint different segments' desires, and total production and marketing costs can be reduced by segmentation.

Before engaging in undifferentiated marketing, a firm must weigh several factors. Large total resources are needed to mass produce, mass distribute, and mass advertise. At the same time, per-unit production and marketing costs may be lower, because a limited product line is offered and different brand names are not employed. These savings may allow low competitive prices.

## TABLE 6-2

## Contrasting Target Market Approaches

| STRATEGIC FACTORS | APPROACHES | | |
|---|---|---|---|
| | *Undifferentiated Marketing* | *Concentrated Marketing* | *Differentiated Marketing* |
| Target market | Broad range of consumers | One well-defined consumers group | Two or more well-defined consumer groups |
| Product | Limited number of products under one brand for many types of consumers | One brand tailored to one consumer group | Distinct brand or version for each consumer group |
| Distribution | All possible outlets | All suitable outlets | All suitable outlets—differs by segment |
| Promotion | Mass media | All suitable media | All suitable media—differs by segment |
| Price | One "popular" price range | One price range tailored to the consumer group | Distinct price range for each consumer group |
| Strategy emphasis | Appeal to a large number of consumers with a uniform, broad-based marketing program | Appeal to one specific consumer group with a highly specialized but uniform marketing program | Appeal to two or more distinct market segments with different marketing plans catering to each segment |

A major goal of undifferentiated marketing is to maximize sales—that is, a firm tries to sell as many units of an item as possible. Regional, national, and/or international goals are set. Diversification is not undertaken.

For pure mass marketing to succeed, a large group of consumers must have a desire for the same product attributes (homogeneous demand), so a firm can use one basic marketing program. Or, demand must be so diffused that it is not worthwhile for a firm to aim marketing plans at specific segments; the firm would try to make demand more homogeneous. Under undifferentiated marketing, different consumer groups are not identified and sought. For example, if all consumers buy Windsor salt for its freshness, quality, storability, availability, and fair price, a pure mass-marketing strategy is then proper. However, if various consumers want attractive decanters, low-sodium content, larger crystals, and smaller-sized packages (as they now do), Windsor would be unable to appeal to all consumers using one basic marketing mix.

With undifferentiated marketing, a firm sells through all possible outlets. Some resellers may be displeased if a brand is sold at nearby locations and insist on carrying additional brands to fill out their product lines. It may be hard to persuade them not to carry competing brands. The shelf space a firm gets is based on its brand's popularity and the promotion support it provides.

An undifferentiated marketing strategy should take both total and long-run profits into account. Firms sometimes become too involved with revenues and lose sight of profits. For example, for several years, A&P's sales rose as it competed with Safeway for leadership in North American supermarket sales. A&P incurred large losses during that period. Only when it began to close some unprofitable stores and stop pursuing sales at any cost did it regain profitability.

A firm and/or its products can ensure a consistent, well-known image with a mass marketing approach. Consumers have only one image when thinking of a firm (or a brand), and it is retained for a number of years.

*With concentrated marketing, a firm appeals to one segment using a tailored marketing plan.*

**CONCENTRATED MARKETING**    By means of a concentrated-marketing approach, a firm aims at a narrow, specific consumer segment with one specialized marketing plan catering to the needs of that segment. Concentrated marketing is often appropriate if demand is clustered or if diffused demand can be clustered by offering a unique marketing mix.

Concentrated marketing has become more popular, especially for smaller firms, because the firm does not have to mass produce, mass distribute, or mass advertise. It can succeed with limited resources and abilities by focusing efforts. This method does not usually maximize sales; the goal is efficiency—attracting a large portion of one segment at controlled costs. The firm wants recognition as a specialist and does not diversify.

A firm using concentrated marketing must do better than its competitors in tailoring a strategy for its segment. Areas of competitor strength should be avoided and weaknesses exploited. For instance, a new vendor selling standard office stationery would have a harder time distinguishing itself from competitors than a new vendor that provides customers with free recycling services for the office stationery it sells.

When there are two or more attractive market segments from which a firm may choose, it should select the one with the greatest opportunity—while being alert to these two factors:

*To avoid the **majority fallacy**, a company can enter a smaller, but untapped, market segment.*

1. The largest segment may not be the best option, due to heavy competition or high consumer satisfaction with competitor offerings. A firm entering this segment may regret it due to the **majority fallacy**, which causes some firms to fail if they go after the largest market segment because competition is intense (see Figure 6-8).

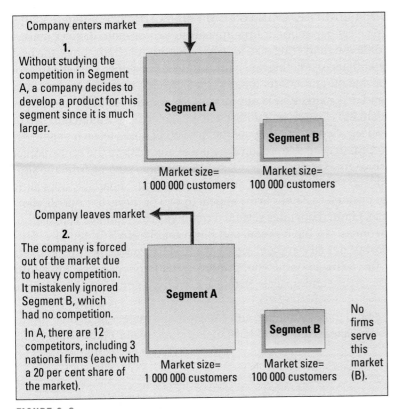

**FIGURE 6-8**

**How the Majority Fallacy Occurs**

**2.** A potentially profitable segment may be one ignored by other firms. As an example, in Canada, Harvey's restaurants have gone after a unique segment in the fast food hamburger market. McDonald's, Burger King, and Wendy's have tended to sell their hamburgers with garnishes and condiments as part of a package using branded offerings, such as Big Macs, Whoppers, and Wendy's Singles. Meals are also packaged with certain sizes of drinks and french fries. In contrast, Harvey's offers customization by allowing customers to "build" their own hamburgers with garnishes and condiments. Meal packages are also customized by offering combos in which customers can choose to forgo drinks or fries in favour of soup and onion rings. Harvey's larger competitors offer some customization, but their food preparation and delivery systems are not designed for this and they tend to be less efficient and accurate at filling these orders.

Concentrated marketing can enable a firm to maximize per-unit profits, but not total profits, because only one segment is sought. It also allows a firm with low resources to vie effectively for specialized markets. There are many local and regional firms that do not have the finances to compete nationally or internationally but that profitably compete in their own markets with national and international companies. However, minor shifts in population or consumer tastes can sharply affect a firm engaging in concentrated marketing.

By carving out a distinct niche through concentrated marketing, a firm may foster a high degree of brand loyalty for a current offering and also be able to develop a product line under a popular name. As long as the firm stays within its perceived area of expertise, the image of one product will rub off on another: Even though it makes several car models, Porsche aims only at the upscale segment of the market—people interested in styling, handling, acceleration, and, of course, status.

*In differentiated marketing, two or more marketing plans are tailored to two or more consumer segments.*

**DIFFERENTIATED MARKETING (MULTIPLE SEGMENTATION)** In differentiated marketing (multiple segmentation), a firm appeals to two or more distinct market segments, with a different marketing plan for each. This approach combines the best aspects of undifferentiated marketing and concentrated marketing: A broad range of consumers can be sought and efforts focused on satisfying identifiable consumer segments. Differentiated marketing is appropriate to consider if there are two or more significant demand clusters, or if diffused demand can be clustered into two or more segments and satisfied by offering unique marketing mixes to each one.

Some firms appeal to each segment in the market and achieve the same market coverage as with mass marketing. Mita markets photocopiers ranging from the simple and inexpensive to the sophisticated and expensive, thus separately appealing to small and large businesses. Other firms appeal to two or more, but not all, market segments. Dylex Limited operates several different apparel outlets: Fairweather and Braemar for women, Tip Top for men, and Biway and Thrifty's for families, thus aiming at several—but not all—apparel segments. And Switzerland's SMH markets Swatch watches for teenagers and young adults, Hamilton watches for adults attracted by classic styles, and upscale Blancpain, Omega, and Tissot brands. See Figure 6-9.

Firms may use both mass marketing and concentrated marketing in their multiple segmentation strategies. They could have one or more major brands aimed at a

**FIGURE 6-9**

**Differentiated Marketing in Action: Targeting Final Consumers**
These two watch brands are both marketed by SMH, but they are targeted at different market segments.

*Reprinted by permission.*

wide range of consumers (the mass market) and secondary brands for specific segments. Maclean Hunter publishes *Maclean's* magazine for general audiences, *Chatelaine* for women, and *Pharmacist News* and *Marketing Magazine* for more specialized segments.

Multiple segmentation requires thorough analysis. The company must have the resources and abilities to produce and market two or more different sizes, brands, or product lines. This can be costly, especially with high-technology products. However, if a firm sells similar products under its own and retailer brands, added costs are small.

Differentiated marketing lets a firm reach many goals. For one thing, it can maximize sales: Procter & Gamble is the world leader in laundry products—with such brands as Tide, Bold, Dash, Cheer, Gain, Oxydol, Era, Ivory Snow, and Ariel; and Boeing leads in the global commercial aircraft business, offering planes with different sizes and configurations (including the 737, 747, 757, 767, and 777). Recognition as a specialist can continue if the firm has separate brands for items aimed at separate segments or has a narrow product line: Whirlpool has a clear image under its own label; few people know it also makes products for Sears under the latter's Kenmore brand. Multiple segmentation lets a firm diversify and minimize risks because all emphasis is not placed on one segment: Honda's motorcycles and small engines (for lawn mowers and outboard motors) provide an excellent hedge against a drop in the sales of its cars.

Differentiated marketing does not mean a firm has to enter segments where competitors are strongest and be subjected to the majority fallacy. Its goals, strengths, and weaknesses must be measured against its competitors. A firm should target only those segments it can handle. And the majority fallacy can work in reverse. If a firm enters a segment before a competitor, it may prevent the latter from successfully entering that segment in the future.

Differentiated marketing requires the existence of at least two consumer segments (with distinct desires by each), and the more potential segments that exist, the better the opportunity for multiple segmentation. Firms that start with concentrated marketing often turn to multiple segmentation and pursue other segments after they become established in one segment.

Wholesalers and retailers usually find differentiated marketing by their suppliers to be attractive. It lets them reach multiple segments, offers some brand exclusivity, allows orders to be placed with fewer suppliers, and may enable them to carry their own private brands. For the selling firm, several distribution benefits exist. Items can be placed with competing resellers under different brands; shelf space is given to display various sizes, packages, and/or brands; price differentials among brands can be maintained; and competitors may be discouraged from entering a distribution channel. Overall, differentiated marketing places the seller in a good bargaining position.

Multiple segmentation can be profitable because total profits should rise as a firm increases the number of segments it services. Per-unit profits should also be high if a firm does a good job of creating a unique marketing plan for each segment. Consumers in each segment would then be willing to pay a premium price for the tailor-made offering.

Even though serving diverse segments lessens the risks from a decline in any one segment, extra costs may be incurred by making product variations, selling in more channels, and promoting more brands. The firm must weigh the revenues gained from selling to multiple segments against the costs.

A company must be careful to maintain product distinctiveness for each market segment and guard its overall image. Many consumers still perceive various General Motors' divisions as having "look-alike" cars, and IBM's image has been affected by its past weak performance in the home PC segment.

## Selecting the Target Market(s)

*A company now chooses which and how many segments to target.*

At this point, a firm must decide which segment(s) offer the best opportunities and how many segments it should pursue. In evaluating market segments, a firm must review its goals and strengths, competition, segment size and growth potential, distribution requirements, necessary expenditures, profit potential, company image, and ability to create and sustain differential advantages, as well as any other factors that are relevant.

Based on the target market approach chosen, the firm then decides whether to pursue one or more segments (or the mass market). For example, due to the high costs of entering the office PC market and the existence of several well-defined demand clusters, it is most likely that a firm new to that industry would start with a concentrated marketing effort. On the other hand, a new sweater maker could easily use differentiated marketing to target boys, girls, men, and women with its products.

*Effectiveness requires segments that are distinct, homogeneous, measurable, large enough, and reachable.*

**REQUIREMENTS FOR SUCCESSFUL SEGMENTATION**  For concentrated marketing or differentiated marketing plans to succeed, the selected market segment(s) have to meet five criteria:

1. There must be *differences* among consumers, or mass marketing would be the appropriate strategy.
2. Within each segment, there must be enough consumer *similarities* to develop an appropriate marketing plan for that segment.
3. A firm must be able to *measure* consumer attributes and needs in order to form groups. This may be hard for some lifestyle attributes.
4. A segment must be *large enough* to produce sales and cover costs.
5. The members of a segment must be *reachable* in an efficient way. For example, young women can be reached via *Teen* magazine. It is efficient because males and older women do not read the magazine.

*The shortcomings of segmentation need to be considered.*

**LIMITATIONS OF SEGMENTATION**  Although segmentation is often a consumer-oriented, efficient, and profitable marketing technique, it should not be abused. Firms could fall into one or more traps. For example, companies may:

- Appeal to segments that are too small.
- Misread consumer similarities and differences.
- Become cost inefficient.
- Spin off too many imitations of their original products or brands.
- Become short-run instead of long-run oriented.
- Be unable to use certain media (due to the small size of individual segments).
- Compete in too many segments.
- Confuse people.
- Get locked into a declining segment.
- Be too slow to seek innovative possibilities for new products.

# Developing the Marketing Strategy

The third phase in planning a target market strategy includes two steps: positioning the company's offering relative to competitors and outlining the appropriate marketing mix(es).

## Positioning the Company's Offering

Positioning is a critical decision because it represents the strategic link between the target market(s) selection, the firm's competitors, and the development of the marketing mix(es). Positioning involves developing a desired image in the minds of customers. In essence, positioning means developing a reputation for a firm and its brands. It is very important for marketers to realize that, for good or ill, once established in the minds of customers a firm's or a brand's position is hard to change. Therefore, the development of a positioning strategy must be seen as a long-term consideration.

Marketers must be fully aware that offerings are positioned to appeal to specific segments. If those segments undergo changes or decline in importance then the firm will find it necessary to develop new offerings with new positioning approaches, or drop an existing offering. Some firms may choose to reposition an existing offering, but this is difficult to do because it involves changing a reputation. Repositioning usually only works if the new position can be related in some fashion to the old. For example, Lysol brand cleaner was originally marketed as a general purpose cleaning agent with disinfectant properties. However, Lysol has always had a very strong and distinct smell associated with it, and when disinfectant cleaners with far less odour became popular Lysol brand was faced with losing business. Lysol was then repositioned as a bathroom cleaner, since in this position having a strong odour was highly desirable because it signified cleanliness and disinfectant properties.

*A good or service must be carefully positioned against competitors.*

## ETHICS AND TODAY'S MARKETER

### Wheelchair Advertising: Targeting Your Market with Billboard Bob's

**B**ob Gerrie offers marketers a unique specific targeting vehicle—vehicle as in wheelchair with a billboard on it. Disabled in a car crash, Bob has turned his handicap into a business opportunity. Based in Toronto, Bob has a 50 cm by 75 cm weatherproof sign board on the back of his wheelchair. He rents this space at a rate of $295 for seven days of exposure. He goes further than simply displaying an ad, however. Bob will hand out coupons and flyers and talk up his client's business too. This unique personal selling touch is certainly a rare commodity in advertising. As for targeting, although Bob may not be ambulatory, he is certainly very mobile. He takes his wheelchair to where the crowds are to provide maximum exposure for his client's message. Local businesses have been the ones who have utilized his services so far. However, Bob is looking for other people in wheelchairs to join his company and expand his business. He has also given some thought to having wheelchairs with corporate logos to supplement the advertising business.

One concern that Bob has had to deal with is the notion that people are responding to his promotional efforts out of sympathy. His position is very professional: he is selling advertising, period. In addition, Bob gets a lot of exposure for his clients but not in a typical fashion. Although it is not considered polite, it is human nature to stare at people in wheelchairs, and Bob is capitalizing on this.

Despite these issues, the advertisers who have hired Bob report that feedback has been very positive and effective. Representatives of organizations for people with disabilities also feel Bob's business is an excellent idea. It shows the public that a wheelchair is a useful tool and shows the person in the wheelchair engaged in meaningful and useful work. Certainly advertisers feel good about supporting Bob while targeting their message to the people living in the areas where they do business. It seems like a winning approach for everyone concerned.

As the marketing manager for a local food store, discuss how you might use Bob Gerrie's services and discuss the possible concerns associated with their use.

Source: Based on material in Peter Kenter, "How Bob Gerrie Used His Wheelchair to Create a Vehicle for Advertising," *Marketing Magazine* (March 11, 1996), p. 6.

Once a firm selects its target markets(s), it must identify the attributes and images of each competitor and select a position for its own offering. For example, a firm considering entry into the office PC market could describe the key strengths of some of the major competitors as follows:

- *IBM*—Reliability, service, range of software applications, product variety.
- *Apple*—Ease of use, graphics, desktop publishing, innovativeness.
- *Compaq*—Innovativeness, construction, monitor quality, competitive pricing.
- *Dell* —Low prices, customized accessories, direct marketing experience.

In positioning itself against these competitors, the firm would need to present a combination of customer benefits that are not being offered elsewhere and that are desired by a target market. Customers must be persuaded that there are clear reasons for buying the new firm's computers. It is not a good idea for the firm to go head-on against big, well-known competitors.

As one alternative, the firm could focus on small businesses that have not yet bought a computer and that need a personal touch during both the purchase process and the initial use of the product. It could thus market fully configured PC systems, featuring IBM clones that are installed by the seller (complete with software libraries and customized programs), in-office training of employees, and a single price for a total system. The positioning emphasis would be "to provide the best ongoing, personalized customer service possible to an underdeveloped market segment, small-business owners."

A fuller discussion of product positioning appears in Chapter 7.

### Outlining the Appropriate Marketing Mix(es)

*The marketing mix must be attractive to the target market.*

The last step in the target marketing process is for a firm to outline a marketing-mix plan for each customer group it is targeting. Marketing decisions relate to product, distribution, promotion, and price factors.

Here is a logical marketing-mix plan for a firm entering the office PC market and concentrating on small-business owners:

- *Product*—Good-quality, Pentium-based PC clone with expansion capability; very user friendly, with a simple keyboard layout; high resolution colour monitor; stereo speakers; sound and video cards; high speed modem; DVD player-drive; 12 gigabyte hard drive; built-in 500 megabyte zip drive; 128 megabytes of RAM; basic software library; Internet ready; customized software; and more.
- *Distribution*—Direct calls and installations at customers' places of business; follow-up service calls.
- *Promotion*—Emphasis on personal selling and direct mail; hands-on, on-site training programs; customer referrals.
- *Price*—Average to above-average; customers presented with nonprice reasons for purchase; positioning linked to high value for the price relationship; price of computer, software, and service bundled together.

## Sales Forecasting

*A **sales forecast** predicts company sales over a specified period.*

As a firm plans a target market strategy, it should forecast its short-run and long-run sales to that market. A **sales forecast** outlines expected company sales for a specific good or service to a specific consumer group over a specific period of time under a specific marketing program. By accurately projecting sales, a firm can better set a marketing budget, allot resources, measure success, analyze sales productivity, monitor the environment and competition, and modify marketing efforts.[18]

A firm should first study industry forecasts; they can strongly affect any company's sales. Next, analysis of the sales potential for the product outlines the upper limit for the firm, based on its marketing and production capacity. A sales forecast then enumerates a firm's realistic sales. The forecast is also based on the expected environment and company performance. Figure 6-10 shows this sales-forecasting process.

A sales forecast should take into account demographics (such as per-capita income), the economy (such as the inflation rate), the competitive environment (such as promotion levels), current and prior sales, and other factors. When devising a forecast, precision is required. A forecast should break sales down by good or service (model 1, 2, 3, etc.), consumer group (for example, adult female), time period (July through September), and type of marketing plan (intensive advertising).

## Data Sources

Several external secondary sources may be consulted to obtain some of the data needed for a sales forecast. Government agencies provide data on global, national, regional, and local demographic trends; past sales by industry and product; and the economy. Trade associations publish various statistics and often have libraries for member firms. General and specialized media, such as *The Financial Post* and *Ward's Automotive Reports*, do regular forecasts.

A firm can also obtain data from present and future customers, executives, salespeople, research studies and market tests, and internal records. These data will usually centre on company rather than industry predictions.

## Methods of Sales Forecasting

Sales forecasting methods range from simple to sophisticated. Among the simple ones are trend analysis, market-share analysis, jury of executive or expert opinion, sales-force surveys, and consumer surveys. Among the more complex ones are the chain-ratio technique, market buildup method, and statistical analyses. Table 6-3 illustrates each. By combining two or more techniques, a firm can have a better forecast and minimize the weaknesses in any one method.

With simple trend analysis, a firm forecasts sales on the basis of recent or current performance. For example, if sales have risen an average of 10 per cent annually over the last five years, it will forecast next year's sales to be 10 per cent higher than the present year's. Although the technique is easy to use, the problems are that sales fluctuations, changing consumer tastes, changing competition, the economy, and market saturation are not considered. A firm's growth may be affected by these factors.

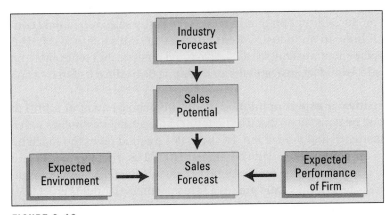

**FIGURE 6-10**

**Developing a Sales Forecast**

## TABLE 6-3

## Applying Sales Forecasting Techniques

| TECHNIQUE | ILLUSTRATION | SELECTED POTENTIAL SHORTCOMINGS |
|---|---|---|
| Simple trend analysis | This year's sales = $2 million; company trend is 5% growth per year; sales forecast = $2 100 000. | Industry decline not considered. |
| Market-share analysis | Current market share = 18%; company seeks stable market share; industry forecast = $10 000 000; company sales forecast = $1 800 000. | New competitors and greater marketing by current ones not considered. |
| Jury of executive opinion | Three executives see strong growth and three see limited growth; they agree on a 6% rise in this year's sales of $11 million; sales forecast = $11 680 000. | Change in consumer attitudes not uncovered. |
| Jury of expert opinion | Groups of wholesalers, retailers, and suppliers meet. Each group makes a forecast; top management utilizes each forecast in forming one projection. | Different beliefs by group about industry growth. |
| Sales-force survey | Sales personnel report a competitor's price drop of 10% will cause company sales to decline 3% from this year's $7 million; sales forecast = $6 790 000. | Sales force unaware a competitor's price cut will be temporary. |
| Consumer survey | 85% of current customers indicate they will repurchase next year and spend an average of $1000 with the firm; 3% of competitors' customers indicate they will buy from the firm next year and spend an average of $800; sales forecast = $460 000. | Consumer intentions possibly not reflecting real behaviour. |
| Chain-ratio method | Unit sales forecast for introductory marketing text = (number of students) × (% annually enrolled in marketing) × (% buying a new book) × (expected market share) = (500 000) × (0.07) × (0.87) × (0.11) = 3350. | |
| Market buildup method | Total sales forecast = region 1 forecast + region 2 forecast + region 3 forecast = $2 000 000 + $7 000 000 + $13 000 000 = $22 000 000. | Incorrect assumption that areas will behave similarly in future. |
| Test marketing | Total sales forecast = (sales in test market A + sales in test market B) × (25) = ($1 000 000 + $1 200 000) × (25) = $55 000 000. | Test areas not representative of all locations. |
| Detailed statistical analyses | Simulation, complex trend analysis, regression, and correlation. | Lack of understanding by management; all factors not quantifiable. |

Market-share analysis is similar to simple trend analysis, except that a company bases its forecast on the assumption that its share of industry sales will remain constant. However, all firms in an industry do not progress at the same rate. Market-share analysis has the same weaknesses as simple trend analysis, but relies more on industry data—and it would let an aggressive or declining firm adjust its forecast and marketing efforts.

*A **jury of executive opinion** has informed people estimate sales.*

A **jury of executive or expert opinion** is used if the management of a firm or other well-informed persons meet, discuss the future, and set sales estimates based on the group's experience and interaction. By itself, this method relies too much on informal analysis. In conjunction with other methods, it is effective because it enables experts to directly interpret and respond to concrete data. Because management lays out goals, sets priorities, and guides a firm's destiny, its input is crucial.

The employees most in touch with consumers and the environment are sales personnel. A sales-force survey allows a firm to obtain input in a structured way. Salespeople are often able to pinpoint trends, strengths and weaknesses in a firm's offering, competitive strategies, customer resistance, and the traits of heavy users. They can break sales forecasts down by product, customer type, and area. However, they can have a limited perspective, offer biased replies, and misinterpret consumer desires.

Many marketers feel the best indicators of future sales are consumer attitudes. By conducting a consumer survey, a firm can obtain information on purchase intentions, future expectations, consumption rates, brand switching, time between purchases, and reasons for purchases. However, consumers may not reply to surveys and may act differently from what they say.

In the **chain-ratio method**, a firm starts with general market information and then computes a series of more specific information. These combined data yield a sales forecast. For instance, a maker of women's casual shoes could first look at a trade association report to learn the industry sales estimate for shoes, the percentage of sales from women's shoes, and the percentage of women's shoe sales from casual shoes. It would then project its own sales of casual women's shoes to its target market. This method is only as accurate as the data plugged in for each market factor. It is useful, since it gets management to think through a forecast and obtain different information.

*With the **chain-ratio** method, general data are broken down. The **market buildup method** adds segment data.*

Opposite to the chain-ratio method is the **market buildup method,** by which a firm gathers data from small, separate market segments and aggregates them. For example, the market buildup method lets a company operating in four urban areas develop a forecast by first estimating sales in each area and then adding the areas. With this method, a firm must note that consumer tastes, competition, population growth, and media differ by geographic area. Segments of equal size may present dissimilar sales opportunities; they should not be lumped together without careful study.

Test marketing is a form of market buildup analysis in which a firm projects a new product's sales based on short-run, geographically limited tests. The company usually introduces a new product into one or a few markets for a short time and carries out a full marketing campaign there. Overall sales are then forecast from test-market sales. However, test areas may not be representative of all locales; and test-market enthusiasm may not carry into national distribution. Test marketing is discussed further in Chapter 8.

There are a number of detailed statistical methods for sales forecasting. Simulation allows a firm to enter market data into a computer-based model and forecast under varying conditions and marketing plans. With complex trend analysis, the firm includes past sales fluctuations, cyclical factors (such as economic conditions), and other factors when looking at sales trends. Regression and correlation techniques explore mathematical links between future sales and market factors, such as annual family income or derived demand. These methods depend on reliable data and the ability to use them correctly. A deeper discussion is beyond the scope of this text.

## Additional Considerations

The method and accuracy of sales forecasting depend on the newness of a firm's offering. A forecast for a continuing good or service could be based on trend analysis, market-share analysis, executive and expert opinion, and sales-force surveys. Barring major alterations in the economy, industry, competition, or consumer tastes, the forecast should be relatively accurate.

*A forecast for a product that has been in the market for a while is usually quite accurate.*

A forecast for an item new to the firm but that already has a track record in the industry could be based on trade data, executive or expert opinion, sales-force and consumer surveys, and test marketing. The first year's forecast should be somewhat accurate, the ensuing years more so. It is hard to project first-year sales precisely, since consumer interest and competition may be tough to gauge.

A forecast for a good or service new to both the firm and the industry should rely on sales-force and consumer surveys, test marketing, executive and expert opinion, and simulation. The forecast for the early years may be highly inaccurate, since the speed of consumer acceptance cannot be closely determined in advance. Later forecasts will be more accurate. While an initial forecast may be imprecise, it is still needed for setting marketing plans, budgeting, monitoring the environment and competition, and measuring success.

*Sales penetration shows whether a firm has reached its potential. Diminishing returns may result if it seeks nonconsumers.*

A company must consider **sales penetration**—the degree to which a firm is meeting its sales potential—in forecasting sales. It is expressed as:

Sales penetration = Actual sales/Sales potential

A firm with high sales penetration needs to realize that **diminishing returns** may occur if it seeks to convert remaining nonconsumers because the costs of attracting them may outweigh revenues. Other products or segments may offer better potential.

A company must always keep in mind that factors such as economic conditions, industry conditions, company performance, competition, and consumer tastes may change and lead to an inaccurate forecast unless the forecast is revised.

# MARKETING IN THE THIRD MILLENNIUM

## Targeting the Interactive Marketplace[19]

As companies look ahead to further advances in interactive technology—and the new marketing opportunities that will accompany such advances—they also need to think about the alternative target market approaches they could pursue. After all, just like other consumer markets, the interactive marketplace will encompass all sorts of potential segments.

Before iVAL was developed (as presented earlier in the chapter), Arbitron's NewMedia Pathfinder Study was one of the first to examine the U.S. interactive marketplace. Arbitron surveyed thousands of American adults, including 612 variables related to demographics, lifestyles, current media experiences, and expectations. Arbitron identified the following segments: fast laners (14 per cent of all respondents), diverse strivers (5 per cent), savvy sophisticates (11 per cent), family-focused (15 per cent), bystanders (16 per cent), sports fanatics (11 per cent), moral Americans (11 percent), and the settled set (17 per cent).

Let's highlight a few of these segments:

- *Fast laners* are mostly Generation Xers and teens. They are more open to new technology.
- *Savvy sophisticates* are high-income, well-educated baby boomers. They are confident and innovative. More own and use PCs than any other group.
- *Family-focused* consumers are mostly price-oriented women with average income and below-average involvement with PCs and technology.
- *Bystanders* are lowest in confidence and innovativeness. They tend to be baby boomers with an above-average number of children living at home.

As summarized in the *Marketing News*, "Home shopping channels appeal most to fast laners, diverse strivers, family-focused, and bystanders. Infomercials have only average appeal among family-focused and well below average appeal among bystanders. Savvy sophisticates show the heaviest involvement with online and print catalogues. They do not see TV as a purchasing medium." Furthermore, "Internet shoppers are pioneers more in the way they shop than in what they buy."

As we move into the third millennium, the descriptions of these segments and the manner in which they behave will evolve and change. Marketers must be aware that segments are not static, but rather in a state of dynamic and sometimes rapid change. As such, constant research on the firm's target markets and regular reviews of the firm's target market strategy need to be undertaken to respond to these changes.

# SUMMARY

**1.** *To describe the process of planning a target market strategy* After collecting information on consumers and environmental factors, a firm is ready to select the target market(s) to which it will appeal. A potential market contains people with similar needs, adequate resources, and a willingness and ability to buy.

Developing a target market strategy consists of three general phases, comprising seven specific steps: analyzing consumer demand—determining demand patterns (1), establishing bases of segmentation (2), and identifying potential market segments (3); targeting the market—choosing a target market approach (4) and selecting the target market(s) (5); and developing the marketing strategy—positioning the company's offering relative to competitors (6) and outlining the appropriate marketing mix(es) (7). Of particular importance is product differentiation, whereby a product offering is perceived by the consumer to differ from its competition on any physical or nonphysical product characteristic, including price.

**2.** *To examine alternative demand patterns and segmentation bases for both final and organizational consumers* Demand patterns indicate the uniformity or diversity of consumer needs and desires for particular categories of goods and services. With homogeneous demand, consumers have relatively uniform needs and desires. With clustered demand, consumer needs and desires can be classified into two or more identifiable clusters (segments), with each having distinct purchase requirements. With diffused demand, consumer needs and desires are so diverse that clear clusters (segments) cannot be identified.

The possible bases for segmenting the market fall into three categories: geographic demographics—basic identifiable characteristics of towns, cities, provinces, regions, and countries; personal demographics—basic identifiable characteristics of individual final consumers and organizational consumers and groups of final consumers and organizational consumers; and lifestyles—patterns by which people (final consumers and those representing organizational consumers) live and spend time and money. It is generally advisable to use a combination of demographic and lifestyle factors to form possible segmentation bases. Although the distinctions between final and organizational consumers should be kept in mind, the three broad segmentation bases could be used in both cases.

After establishing possible segmentation bases, a firm is ready to develop consumer profiles. Such profiles identify potential market segments by aggregating consumers with similar characteristics and needs.

**3.** *To explain and contrast undifferentiated marketing (mass marketing), concentrated marketing, and differentiated marketing (multiple segmentation)* Undifferentiated marketing aims at a large, broad consumer market using one basic marketing plan. In concentrated marketing, a firm aims at a narrow, specific consumer group with one specialized marketing plan catering to the needs of that segment. With differentiated marketing, a firm appeals to two or more distinct market segments, with a different marketing plan for each. When segmenting, a firm must understand the majority fallacy: The largest consumer segment may not offer the best opportunity since it often has the greatest number of competitors.

In selecting its target market(s), a firm should consider its goals and strengths, competition, segment size and growth potential, distribution needs, required expenditures, profit potential, company image, and ability to develop and sustain a differential advantage.

Successful segmentation requires differences among and similarities within segments, measurable consumer traits and needs, large enough segments, and efficiency in reaching segments. It should not be abused by appealing to overly small groups, using marketing inefficiently, placing too much emphasis on imitations of original company products or brands, confusing consumers, and so on.

**4.** *To show the importance of positioning in developing a marketing strategy* In positioning its offering against competitors, a firm needs to present a combination of customer benefits that are not being provided by others and that are desirable by a target market. Customers must be persuaded that there are clear reasons for buying the firm's products rather than those of its competitors.

The last step in the target marketing process is for a firm to develop a marketing mix for each customer group to which it wants to appeal.

**5.** *To discuss sales forecasting and its role in target marketing* Short- and long-run sales should be forecast in developing a target market strategy. This helps a firm compute budgets, allocate resources, measure success, analyze productivity, monitor the environment and competition, and adjust marketing plans. A sales forecast describes the expected company sales of a specific good or service to a specific consumer group over a specific time period under a specific marketing program.

A firm can obtain sales-forecasting data from a variety of internal and external sources. Forecasting methods range from simple trend analysis to detailed statistical analyses. The best results are obtained when methods and forecasts are combined. A sales forecast should consider the newness of a firm's offering, sales penetration, diminishing returns, and the changing nature of many factors.

## KEY TERMS

market (p. 153)

market segmentation (p. 153)

target market strategy (p. 153)

undifferentiated marketing (mass marketing) (p. 154)

concentrated marketing (p. 154)

differentiated marketing (multiple segmentation) (p. 154)

product differentiation (p. 154)

demand patterns (p. 154)

homogeneous demand (p. 154)

clustered demand (p. 154)

diffused demand (p. 155)

geographic demographics (p. 155)

personal demographics (p. 157)

heavy-usage segment (heavy half) (p. 161)

benefit segmentation (p. 161)

VALS (Values and Lifestyles) program (p. 162)

Social Styles model (p. 162)

iVALS (Internet Values and Lifestyles) (p. 163)

majority fallacy (p. 168)

sales forecast (p. 174)

jury of executive or expert opinion (p. 176)

chain-ratio method (p. 177)

market buildup method (p. 177)

sales penetration (p. 178)

diminishing returns (p. 178)

## REVIEW QUESTIONS

1. Distinguish between the terms "market" and "market segmentation."

2. What are the three general phases in planning a target market strategy?

3. Explain this comment: "Sometimes a firm can achieve a key differential advantage by simply emphasizing how its offering satisfies existing consumer desires and needs better than its competitors' products do. Sometimes demand patterns must be modified for consumers to perceive a firm's product differentiation as worthwhile."

4. Differentiate among homogeneous, clustered, and diffused consumer demand. What are the marketing implications?

5. Describe five personal demographics pertaining to organizational consumers.

6. What is the majority fallacy? How can a firm avoid it?

7. Cite the five key requirements for successful segmentation.

8. Why is sales forecasting important when developing a target market strategy?

9. Contrast the jury of executive opinion and the chain-ratio methods of sales forecasting.

10. Why are long-run sales forecasts for new products more accurate than short-run forecasts?

## DISCUSSION QUESTIONS

1. How could an international manufacturer of personal beepers apply geographic-demographic segmentation?

2. Develop a personal-demographic profile of the students in your marketing class. For what goods and services would the class be a good market segment? A poor segment?

3. Describe several potential benefit segments for a firm marketing maintenance services to business clients.

4. Develop a marketing strategy for a utility-vehicle manufacturer that wants to appeal to experiencers (as described in VALS 2). How should the strategy differ if the target market is strivers?

5. If a firm has a sales potential of $4 000 000 and attains actual sales of $2 400 000, what does this signify? What should the firm do next?

## CASE STUDY
# Global Consumers: Welcome to "McWorld"

According to Erla Zwingle, writing in *National Geographic,* globalization is not a new phenomenon. She quotes from Karl Marx and Friedrich Engels' 150-year-old *Communist Manifesto:* "Modern industry has established the world market.... All old-established national industries ... are dislodged by new industries whose ... products are consumed, not only at home, but in every quarter of the globe. In place of the old wants ... we find new wants, requiring for their satisfaction the products of distant lands and climes."

In many nations globalization is viewed as a cultural invasion by mainly Western or American products and values. Sometimes referred to as McWorld, in honour of the global success of McDonald's restaurants, 20 per cent of the world's population now speaks English. The McWorld invasion is spurred on by the power of communications via satellite television and the Internet, which are dominated by American-based, English-language programming.

The offerings of Western culture are seductive. They're disseminated via MTV, CNN World news, ESPN sports, American films from the Disney Studios, the Star Wars movies, and the massive proliferation of Internet Web sites. These communications aren't depicting the "Lifestyles of the Rich and Famous" but rather the lifestyles of the typical and ordinary. The typical and ordinary person in the Western world engages in conspicuous consumption and has a refrigerator, a television, a stereo, a CD player, and an automobile. In the global environment, everyone can participate in these lifestyles by viewing the communications and then using consumer products like Coca-Cola, eating at McDonald's, wearing Nike shoes, and speaking English.

The world has seen a number of culturally transforming innovations in recent history. Agriculture allowed for the development of cities, industry allowed for the development of mass production, and greater agricultural productivity allowed for even more urban development. Finally, the information age appears to be leading to globalization.

The people who are most susceptible to globalization are teens and pre-teens. The worldwide teen (and pre-teen) market is huge. In Europe, Latin America, and the Pacific Rim there are over 200 million teens. Mexico, Brazil, and Argentina together have 57 million 10- to 19-year-olds. Canada has 3.9 million and the U.S. has 35 million youngsters aged 10-19. A global study by Darsey Masius Benton & Bowles (DMB&B) of more than 6500 teens in twenty-six countries concluded that "teens around the world are living very parallel lives." Similarities can be seen in dress (baggy Levi's or Diesel jeans, Doc Martens or Nike shoes, T-shirt, and leather jacket), dining habits (Coca-Cola and Big Macs), and rock groups.

The DMB&B study also revealed that teens throughout the world cited the United States as having the greatest influence in fashion and culture. When asked to state which nation had the most impact on their fashion and culture, 80 per cent of European teens, 80 per cent of teens from the Far East, and 87 per cent of Latin American teens said the United States. Still, "Americanization is not complete. For example, Canadian teens only watch an average of 16.9 hours of television per week compared to an average of 21.6 hours of viewing by American teens."

Some experts implore marketers to be aware of the importance of regional or country-based differences. For example, in Canada there are important differences in consumption habits between anglophone teenagers and francophone teenagers in Quebec, and anglophone teenagers in the other provinces of Canada. Consider that among teens 12–17 years of age, 32 per cent of francophones report consuming beer compared to 21 per cent for Quebec anglophones and 15 per cent of anglophones outside Quebec. Among all Quebec teenagers 12-17 years of age, 16 per cent report consuming fast food once a week while 27 per cent of teenagers in the rest of Canada report having fast food at least once a week.

The fast food visits must not be good for the stomach, because 27 per cent of non-Quebec resident teens also report consumption of upset stomach tablets, while for Quebec residents, 13 per cent of francophone teens and 12 per cent of anglophone teens report consumption of upset stomach tablets. Clearly, there are differences in consumption habits among teens from different regions and cultural backgrounds in Canada.

### Questions

1. Identify the forces driving globalization in this case. Are there any counter forces that may limit globalization? Explain how they might work.
2. Discuss the impact of the information age and how the spread of English as a global language may affect cultures. What do you think the implications are for global marketers?
3. How do you think the need to reflect cultural differences would affect the selection of a basis for segmentation? Consider the differential findings on Canadian teens' consumption behaviour in formulating your answer.
4. Why do you think teens are more susceptible to globalization than any other group?

Sources: The data in this case are drawn from Erla Zwingle, "Goods move. People move. Ideas move. And cultures change." *National Geographic* (August 1999), pp. 12–33. "Teen Interests Appear to Be Universal," *Advertising Age* (July 17, 1995), p. A3; Shawn Tully, "Teens: The Most Global Market of All," *Fortune* (May 16, 1994), pp. 90–97; Cyndee Miller, "Teens Seen as the First Truly Global Consumers," *Marketing News* (March 27, 1995), p. 9; Francois Vary, "Getting Down to Details with PMB '94," *Marketing Magazine* (February 20, 1995) p. 14; "Freeze Frame: A Marketing-Nielsen Update on Television," *Marketing Magazine* (April 3, 1995), p. 18; and Pierre Audet, "The Realistic Generation," *Marketing Magazine* (February 20, 1995) p. 13.

## CASE STUDY
# Targeting the Adult Movie Market

Canada has a very large adult market. The median age for Canadians is in the mid-thirties right now. In the year 2001 the over 50s will represent 28.6 per cent of Canada's population and by the year 2006 this proportion will rise to 31.3 per cent of the population. These older adults have tremendous amounts of free time and they spend more of it on sports, hobbies, reading, watching TV and shopping than any other age group. The over 50s have 75-80 per cent of the discretionary income in the country and they spend 28 per cent of their discretionary income. Most seniors have paid their mortgages, have no school-aged children and have saved like crazy because of the scarcity psychology that they developed as a result of living through economic recessions and facing high levels of taxation. The net wealth of the country is concentrated in the hands of people over 50. The previous chapter mentioned that marketers need to gear up for the time when one in three Canadians will be 50 years of age and older!!

One firm that is gearing up to serve the adult market is Toronto-based Alliance Atlantis Communications, which is the largest distributor and producer of television shows and films in Canada. Some of the more notable television series produced by the firm include "Due South," "Gene Roddenbery's Earth: Final Conflict," and "Sins of the City." The firm has also produced films like David Cronenberg's sex-drama *Crash* and his thriller *Existenz*. Alliance Atlantis has controlling interests in a number of Canada's cable channels, including Showcase Television, History Television, the Life Network, and Home and Garden Television Canada. The firm had sales of U.S.$271 million in 1998 and plans to extend its delivery of films beyond television by operating some high-profile theatres.

The theatres will be called Alliance Atlantis Cinemas, and the plan is to target an adult movie audience. The approach isn't built around offering adult movies, but rather adult theatres. Alliance Atlantis has opened two such theatres in Canada already (in Toronto and Vancouver), and there are more on the way in Ottawa, Edmonton, and Calgary.

An adult theatre is one that's constructed and geared to serve adults. Victor Loewry, Chair of the Motion Picture group of Alliance Atlantis, describes the intended target market as "a high-end art clientele" aged 23–45. "We are not looking for children or families." The demographic is different and so is the offering and the pricing. The movies will be more expensive and will tend to appeal to adults, with the Restricted ratings that many art films and action films carry because they have some adult content that is not suitable for children.

The concessions will also be geared to the adult market. In addition to pop and popcorn they will offer beer, wine, liquor, and non-traditional movie food. (The Toronto cinema has an indoor/outdoor cafe that offers gourmet pizza and sushi. It also has a mini-book store inside.) The lobbies of these theatres are European style (with music, and soft decors), but the cinemas are more typical of North America. Since Alliance Atlantis is new to the business of displaying films it has partnered with Famous Players Cinemas to help with the physical development and operations.

Because Alliance Atlantis is targeting a specific market, it plans to arrange promotional tie-ins with firms that don't traditionally go after movie audiences. Brewers and distillers are at the top of the list. Roots is being sought to sponsor popcorn bags and a national promotional campaign. The hope is that by offering a complete package of films and a venue geared solely to adults people will choose to make a whole evening of it, allowing marketers an opportunity to reach a specific demographic group in a captive setting.

## Questions

1. What are the main risks being taken by Alliance Atlantis and Famous Players in targeting an adult market with these new theatres? Evaluate this concept. Will they make it in the big markets like Toronto, Vancouver, Ottawa, Calgary, and Edmonton? Would it work in smaller Canadian markets like Charlottetown, Halifax, London, Regina, and Winnipeg? Why or why not?

2. What other kinds of offerings could be combined with these theatres, given their intended target audiences?

3. Discuss the following proposition: do people go to the theatre for the films or for the venue? Compare and contrast the relative importance of these two attributes.

4. What are the advantages for Alliance Atlantis in being involved in film production from creation right through to distribution? What are the disadvantages?

**ALLIANCE ATLANTIS COMMUNICATION**
www.alliance.ca
www.atlantis.ca

Sources: Based on Astrid Van Den Broek, "Adult-style Theatre Alliance Aims High," *Marketing Magazine* (July 5, 1998), p. 3; Hoovers Company Capsule, "Alliance Atlantis," Hoovers Online, www.hoovers.com; and Alliance Atlantis Web site, www.alliance.ca and www.atlantis.ca.

# Identifying and Capitalizing on Consumer Trends

Understanding consumer behaviour is critical to the marketing success of virtually every product or service. But when demand is fashion- or trend-based it becomes extremely important to identify trends and fashions as soon as possible.

The music business, for example, is always in a state of change. Hot artists and musical styles have short life cycles. Musical artists who want long careers must remake themselves many times over to stay on top. Madonna is one artist who's remade herself and her musical style a number of times. BMG Music wants to stay on top of these trends when it promotes its artists in Canada, and to this end it's hired trend spotter Molly Brennan. Molly describes trend spotting as finding the leading edge. The idea is to find out what's cool before it hits the mass market and then capitalize on it when it does. This is known as "riding the cool wave."

Most cool trends are generated by young people, who of course want not to conform with the style of the older generation but want very much to conform with their own peer group. The non-conforming trends are what market watchers seek and then hope to capitalize on when the masses of young people follow their trend-setting peers. Cultural anthropologist Grant McCracken describes the cycle: It begins with early adopters, who are the first to accept a new look, sound, activity, or product, which is then adopted by the mainstream and simultaneously abandoned by the early adopters. (Then there are the hopelessly unfashionable types, who watch the trend come and go with no response at all.)

Firms that try to create trends or ride the cool wave have to be willing to accept significant risks, and try very hard to manage them. Chris Jordan of Coca-Cola marketing and Steve Hancock of TBWA Chiat/Day advertising discuss how Fruitopia Ice Tea was developed and launched. A lot of research was undertaken using video cameras, focus groups, and phone interviews to try to identify what people would buy. The plan that emerged was to sell Fruitopia as a "fruit drink with a conscience."

Young people easily see through marketing appeals, and so it's understood that 45-year-old business executives just can't be with it (unless of course they're marketing to other 45-year-olds). Enter firms like Decode, which specializes in researching and targeting young people between the ages of 16 and 25. It uses street scouts and conducts frequent focus groups to search out trends. Decode's Robert Barnard says it can help interpret youth culture for corporate Canada. Clients have included Colgate Palmolive, Molson, Chrysler Canada, and the Royal Bank.

Trends and fashions are often thought of as cyclical. In the 1970s Adidas was *the* sneaker brand; Nike took that position in the 1980s and 1990s, but now Adidas is cool again. It looks like the 70s are reemerging (perhaps to appeal to the remembered youth of all those uncool 45-year-olds). Current advertising is filled with music from the 70s; the Fox Network even features a program called "That 70s Show." Doug Hayes, Director of Marketing for Adidas, recognizes that the brand is cool again, and handles the fact coolly. He notes that skateboarders are adopting the products but that Adidas won't try to tell anyone they're cool: that would be the kiss of death. In order to stay cool Adidas turns out four new product lines every year, hoping to find one that will catch on.

TBWA Chiat/Day's Steve Hancock says that in the game of cool the smartest marketer wins. You've got to know what's going on, and that's why BMG has Molly Brennan discovering a new street sound that's fully woman-driven by a group called the Tastes of Honey. BMG would like to see this sound cross over from the fashion-conscious to the mainstream. In the game of cool, you have to get to youth sooner, not later.

## Questions

1. Why are marketers are trying to discover trends as opposed to setting them?

2. Evaluate the trend-uncovering methods presented in the case. Can you think of any other ways to discover trends that weren't mentioned?

3. What kinds of products or services not mentioned in the case do you think would be most affected by trends? What kinds would be least affected?

4. Sometimes a trend has so much staying power that it becomes a tradition. Can you think of any products or services that fall into this category? What do you think gives them their staying power and why?

## Video Questions

1. What characteristics would you look for in a trend spotter, and how important do you think they are?

2. Trend spotting is innovation but trend exploiting doesn't occur until it hits the mass market. Discuss innovation versus imitation as a trend exploitation strategy. Which do you think might be more effective?

**BMG MUSIC**
www.bmg.com

**ADIDAS**
www.adidas.com

Source: Based on CBC *Venture* #563 (October 22, 1995); and Justin Smallbridge, "Play That Funky Music," *Marketing Magazine* (July 5, 1999), p. 10.

# Product Planning

To adhere to the marketing concept, a firm needs to devise, enact, and monitor a systematic marketing plan. This plan centres on the four elements of the marketing mix: product, distribution, promotion, and price. We present these elements in Parts 3 to 6, with Part 3 concentrating on product planning.

## Basic Concepts in Product Planning

Here we define tangible, augmented, and generic products and distinguish among different types of consumer and industrial products (both goods and services). We look at product mix strategies and product management organizations in detail. We also study product positioning and the product life cycle in depth. The chapter concludes with a look at the international dimensions of product planning.

## Goods Versus Services Planning

Now we look at the scope of goods and services and introduce a goods/services continuum. We review goods and services classification systems. Then we study the special considerations in the marketing of services. We also see that service marketing has lagged behind goods marketing and why this is changing. At this point, we turn to nonprofit marketing and how it is distinct from profit-oriented marketing. We examine how nonprofit organizations can be classified, as well as the role of nonprofit marketing in the economy.

## Conceiving, Developing, and Managing Products

In this chapter, we look at products from their inception to their deletion. We discuss the types of new products, reasons for new-product failures, and the new-product planning process. We look at the branding decisions that centre on corporate symbols, the branding philosophy, the choice of brand names, and the use of trademarks. We also consider the six basic functions of packaging: containment, usage, communication, market segmentation, channel cooperation, and new-product planning. We explain the growth of products in terms of the adoption and diffusion processes, and note several methods for extending the lives of mature products. We also offer product deletion strategies.

# Product and Service Offerings: Satisfying Customer Needs and Wants

Product planning for potential offerings to satisfy customers' demands is the focus of Chapter 7. It's very important to understand that demand is the driving force for product development. For example, Statistics Canada data suggested that at the start of the year 2000 there will be 2.5 million Canadian children between the ages of six and eleven years. Toronto-based Nabisco recognized the opportunity to reach out to this group, and is positioning all of its single-serving packages of snack food brands under the name "Planet Snak." This position will include new product sizes for brands such a Chips Ahoy!, Mini Oreo, Crispers, Bits and Bites, Teddy Grahams, Ritz Bitz Sandwiches, Animal Crackers, and Dino Bites.

In Chapter 8 we will look at some of the unique characteristics of service and nonprofit offerings and how they can be marketed. The importance of the service sector is often underestimated by typical consumers, since it is the business sector that accounts for three-quarters of the spending on services in Canada (including transportation and storage; communications; wholesale trade; retail trade; finance, insurance, and real estate; and business services). the non-business sector accounts for the remaining quarter of service expenditures in categories such as government services; community and personal services; and other services. Among the leading Canadian service industries are finance, insurance, and real estate; business services; and transportation and storage. More than 74 per cent of the private-sector Canadian labour force is in service jobs.

In Chapter 9 we introduce branding, one of the most powerful concepts of modern product marketing. Branding allows customers to purchase goods holistically and efficiently, since without it every purchase transaction would require intensive product inspection. Chapter 9 also presents the process of new product development. The digital camera, for example, is a major innovation because it promises to eliminate the need for film and film developing, providing instant pictures with no developing costs. Digital cameras used to be so expensive that they made economic sense only if you were a professional photographer. But these days high demand for digital cameras is driving down their prices, which in turn creates even more demand. A key factor here is the media convergence associated with the personal computer. People are embracing new technology that can now combine all forms of media and entertainment into one (TV, radio, magazines, newsprint, compact disks, video discs, and data storage).

Marketers offer products and services to satisfy customer needs and wants in exchange for money or the customer's products and services.

Serious Machines.
Serious Commitment.

From the compact 933 to the updated 963B and rugged 973,
today's Cat Track Loader line is the most complete in the industry.
Cat Track Loaders are serious machines, because Caterpillar is committed
to building the most versatile, productive track loaders you can get.

Whether you're replacing a machine or adding to your fleet,
Cat Track Loaders give you all the quality, flexibility,
maneuverability and power you need.

CATERPILLAR 939

CHAPTER | 7

# Basic Concepts in Product Planning

## *Chapter Objectives*

**1.** To define product planning and differentiate among tangible, augmented, and generic products

**2.** To examine the various types of products, product mixes, and product management organization forms from which a firm may select

**3.** To discuss product positioning and its usefulness for marketers

**4.** To study the different types of product life cycles that a firm may encounter and the stages of the traditional product life cycle (introduction, growth, maturity, and decline)

**CATERPILLAR**
www.cat.com

Courtesy Caterpillar Inc.

Caterpillar Incorporated has always been identified with heavy earth-moving construction equipment. However, it approaches the new millennium as a high-technology, global firm with a diversification strategy of developing new products for new markets.

Headquartered in Peoria, Illinois, Caterpillar is a massive multinational company with sales branches in 160 countries. In 1998 it had revenues of U.S.$20.98 billion (half of which were from outside North America), an 11 per cent sales increase over 1997, and profits of U.S.$1.51 billion. In the 1990s Caterpillar decided to become a high technology global growth company, and to this end it spent $1.8 billion on modernization projects to develop faster, more cost-effective, and more flexible production processes.

Caterpillar has factories in Brazil, Belgium, and Japan, as well as in thirty-eight factories in the U.S., twelve of which are in Illinois. Although well known for making such earth-moving equipment as excavators, loaders, graders, and backhoes, Caterpillar boasts more than 300 different machines, 220 of which were introduced in the last five years. However, equipment represents only one of the firm's product lines. Caterpillar contracts to the U.S. military and to other free-world military organizations to make specialized vehicles and equipment for military use. It also sells components to other equipment manufacturing firms. Caterpillar manufactures engines rated from 54 to 13 600 horsepower; they can be incorporated into machines or electrical generation devices. The firm has sold 10 500 solar turbines which are used in more than ninety countries. Its parts and service division supports the maintenance and repair requirements of all of its products. Caterpillar also takes trade-ins of used Caterpillar equipment, which are then refurbished and resold. Finally, it has its own financial services organization, which provides incremental revenue associated with the sales of its products—and enables it to offer flexible terms of purchase to its customers.

Caterpillar is committed to marketplace excellence, and cites the following achievements in 1998 as evidence that it's fulfilling this commitment:

- It was named to *Fortune*'s second list of the "World's Most Admired Companies."
- It received the Alexander Hamilton Award for excellence in treasury management.
- Its Solar Turbines Division won the Malcolm Baldridge National Quality Award.
- The Consumers for World Trade gave Caterpillar its annual award for dedicated service to the cause of open and competitive world trade.

Achieving these goals has involved massive changes in the way Caterpillar designs and produces its products. Whereas it used to take up to ten years to develop and market new machines, the firm has reduced its development time to twenty-seven months. Caterpillar is now more customer-focused; its engineers look at how customers use products so that they can redesign them accordingly, or even develop new products that will better serve customer needs. Caterpillar's customer focus is exemplified by the fact that it serves the following industries: aggregates, agriculture, building construction, forestry, general and road construction, mining, scrap and demolition services, and waste handling.

As Caterpillar enters the new millennium it plans to achieve over $30 billion in sales. The firm expects sales of electric power generation systems to triple in the next few years. It hopes to increase its presence in the agricultural market through a joint venture with Claas, a German combine/harvester manufacturer. Caterpillar has invested in a new facility dedicated solely to the manufacturing of forest products that are environmentally friendly but highly productive. It's looking at developing a wider line of compact machines that can be used in tight spots found in urban areas that are undergoing redevelopment. Finally, it sees markets in emerging nations as a tremendous growth opportunity, since the need for water access, transportation routes, and electrical power are greatest in those areas and only 23 per cent of its sales are currently made there. Caterpillar's strategy of diversification into new markets with new products will require it to engage in management of the complete marketing mix, with particular emphasis on product planning.[1]

In this chapter, we will look at the basic product-planning decisions that firms must make, including the types of product management organizations and the positioning of products.

## Overview

**Product planning** is systematic decision making relating to all aspects of the development and management of a firm's products, including branding and packaging. Each **product** consists of a bundle of attributes (features, functions, benefits, and uses) capable of exchange or use, usually in a mix of tangible and intangible forms. Thus, a product may be an idea, a physical entity (a good), a service, or any combination of the three. It exists for the purpose of exchange in the satisfaction of individual and organizational objectives.[2]

A well-structured product plan lets a company pinpoint opportunities, develop appropriate marketing programs, coordinate a mix of products, maintain successful products as long as possible, reappraise faltering products, and delete undesirable products.

A firm should define its products in three distinct ways: tangible, augmented, and generic. By considering all three definitions, the company is better able to identify consumer needs, competitive offerings, and distinctive product attributes. This is illustrated in Figure 7-1.

A **tangible product** is a basic physical entity, service, or idea; it has precise specifications and is offered under a given description or model number. Windows 98 soft-

*Product planning means devising and managing products that satisfy consumers.*

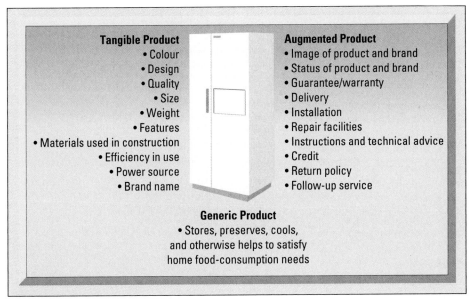

**FIGURE 7-1**

**Illustrating the Three Product Definitions**

*A **tangible product** has precise specifications, while an **augmented product** includes image and service features.*

ware, a Caterpillar diesel engine, *Canadian Business* magazine, a seven-day Caribbean cruise on the QE2 (Queen Elizabeth 2), and a proposal to cut provincial income taxes by 15 per cent are examples of tangible products. Colour, style, size, weight, durability, quality of construction, price, and efficiency in use are some tangible product features.

An **augmented product** includes not only the tangible elements of a product, but also the accompanying cluster of image and service features. For example, one political candidate may receive more votes than another because of charisma (augmented product), despite identical party platform issues (tangible product). Rolex watches are popular chiefly due to the image of luxury and status they convey. One of Caterpillar's augmented products is its "Equipment Protection Plan II," a used equipment warranty. Available only to customers in Canada and the United States, this warranty provides "protection against unexpected warrantable powertrain repair costs for used Caterpillar equipment sold by your Caterpillar dealer."[3]

*A **generic product** centres on consumer benefits.*

A **generic product** focuses on what a product means to the customer, not the seller. It is the broadest definition and is consistent with the marketing concept:

- "In the factory we make cosmetics, and in the drugstore we sell hope." (Charles Revson, founder of Revlon)
- "We know our customers come to us to buy more than bearings and steel. They come to us looking for solutions." (Timken Company)

When applying the generic product concept, several points should be kept in mind. First, because a generic product is a consumer view of what a product represents, a firm should learn what the product means to the consumer before further

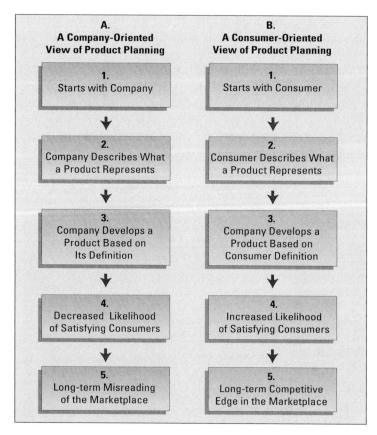

**FIGURE 7-2**

**Applying the Generic Product Concept**

In A, the firm is not properly employing the generic product concept and does not understand its customers' needs. In B, the firm is properly using the generic product concept and is successful with its customers.

Source: Adapted by the authors from Leon G. Schiffman and Elaine Sherman, "Value Orientations of New-Age Elderly: The Coming of an Ageless Market," *Journal of Business Research*, Vol. 22 (March 1991), p. 193.

product planning—as shown in Figure 7-2. Second, inasmuch as people in various nations may perceive the same product (such as a car) in different generic terms (such as basic transportation versus comfortable driving), a firm should consider the impact of this on a possible global strategy.

This chapter provides an overview of product planning. It examines the basic areas in which a firm must make decisions: product type(s), product mix, product management organization, and product positioning. It also covers the product life cycle and its marketing relevance, and presents considerations for international marketers. Chapter 8 covers the planning involved with goods versus services. Chapter 9 presents an in-depth discussion of how to manage products over their lives, from finding new product ideas to deleting faltering products. Chapter 9 concludes with a presentation of two specialized aspects of product planning: branding and packaging.

# Types of Products

The initial product-planning decision is choosing the type(s) of products to offer. Products can be categorized as goods or services and as consumer or industrial. Categorization is important because it highlights the differences in the characteristics of products and the resulting marketing implications.

## Fundamental Distinctions Between Goods and Services

**Goods marketing** entails the sale of physical products. **Durable goods** are physical products that are used over an extended period of time, such as furniture and heavy machinery. **Nondurable goods** are physical products made from materials other than metals, hard plastics, and wood; they are more quickly consumed or worn out; or they become dated, unfashionable, or otherwise unpopular. Examples are food and office supplies.

*Goods marketing involves the sale of durable and nondurable goods.*

**Service marketing** includes the rental of goods, the alteration, maintenance, or repair of goods owned by consumers, and personal services. **Rented-goods services** involve the leasing of goods for a specified period of time—such as auto, hotel-room, office-building, and tuxedo rentals. **Owned-goods services** involve alterations to, or maintenance or repair of, goods owned by consumers, such as house painting, clothing alterations, lawn care, equipment maintenance, and machinery repair. **Nongoods services** involve personal service on the part of the seller, such as accounting, legal, consulting, and tutoring services; they do not involve goods.

*Service marketing covers rented-goods, owned-goods, and nongoods services.*

Four attributes generally distinguish services from goods: intangibility, perishability, inseparability from the service provider, and variability in quality. Their impact is greatest for personal services, which are usually more intangible, more perishable, more dependent on the skills of the service provider (inseparability), and have more quality variations than rented- or owned-goods services.

The sales of goods and services are frequently connected. For instance, a tractor manufacturer may provide—for an extra fee—extended warranties, customer training, insurance, and financing. In goods marketing, goods dominate the overall offering and services augment them. In service marketing, services dominate the overall offering and goods augment them. A full discussion of services marketing will be undertaken in Chapter 8.

## Consumer Products

**Consumer products** are goods and services destined for the final consumer for personal, family, or household use. The use of a good or service designates it as a con-

*Consumer products are final consumer goods and services.*

sumer product. For example, a calculator, dinner at a restaurant, phone service, and an electric pencil sharpener are consumer products only if purchased for personal, family, or household use.

Consumer products may be classed as convenience, shopping, or specialty products, based on shoppers' awareness of alternative products and their characteristics prior to a shopping trip and how extensively people will search for the product. Thus, which class a product belongs in depends on shopper behaviour. See Table 7-1.

**Convenience products** are those bought with a minimum of effort because a consumer has knowledge of product attributes prior to shopping and/or is pressed for time. The person does not want to search for much information and will accept a substitute (Hostess potato chips instead of Humpty Dumpty) rather than visit more than one store. Marketing tasks centre on distribution at all available outlets, convenient store locations and hours, the use of mass advertising and in-store displays, well-designed store layouts, and self-service to minimize purchase time. Resellers often carry many brands.

*Convenience products are purchased with minimum effort and are categorized as staples, impulse products, and emergency products.*

Convenience products can be subdivided into staples, impulse products, and emergency products. Staples are low-priced and routinely purchased on a regular basis, such as detergent, mass transit, and cereal. Impulse products are items or brands a person does not plan to buy on a specific store trip, such as candy, magazines, or lottery tickets. According to the Point-of-Purchase Advertising Institute (POPAI), up to 70 per cent of all purchase decisions are made in the store.[4] Emergency products are bought out of urgent need—such as an umbrella in a rainstorm and aspirin for a headache.

*Shopping products require an information search.*

**Shopping products** are those for which consumers feel they lack sufficient information about product alternatives and their attributes (or prices), and therefore must acquire further knowledge in order to make a purchase decision. People will exert effort searching for information because shopping products are bought infrequently, have large purchase prices, or require comparisons. The marketing emphasis is on full assortments (such as many colours, sizes, and options), the availability

## TABLE 7-1

## Characteristics of Consumer Products

| CONSUMER CHARACTERISTICS | TYPE OF PRODUCT | | |
| --- | --- | --- | --- |
| | Convenience | Shopping | Specialty |
| Knowledge prior to purchase | High | Low | High |
| Effort expended to acquire product | Minimal | Moderate to high | As much as needed |
| Willingness to accept substitutes | High | Moderate | None |
| Frequency of purchase | High | Moderate or low | Varies |
| Information search | Low | High | Low |
| Major desire | Availability without effort | Comparison shopping to determine best choice | Brand loyalty regardless of price and availability |
| Examples | (a) Staple: cereal | (a) Attribute-based: name-brand clothes | Hellmann's mayonnaise |
| | (b) Impulse: candy | (b) Price-based: budget hotel | |
| | (c) Emergency: tire repair | | |

of sales personnel, the communication of competitive advantages, informative ads, well-known brands (or stores), distributor enthusiasm, and customer warranties and follow-up service to reduce perceived risk. Shopping centres and downtown business districts ease shopping behaviour by having many adjacent stores.

Shopping products may be attribute- or price-based. With attribute-based shopping products, consumers get information on product features, performance, and other factors. Items with the best combination of attributes are bought. Sony electronics and Calvin Klein clothes are marketed as attribute-based shopping products. With price-based shopping products, people feel the choices are relatively similar and shop for the best prices. Budget hotels and low-end electronics are marketed as price-based shopping products.

**Specialty products** are particular brands, stores, and persons to which consumers are loyal. People are fully aware of these products and their attributes prior to making a purchase decision. They will make a significant effort to acquire the brand desired and will pay an above-average price. They will not buy if their choice is unavailable: Substitutes are unacceptable. The marketing emphasis is on maintaining the attributes that make the products so unique to loyal consumers, reminder ads, proper distribution (Hellmann's mayonnaise and *Canadian Business* require different distribution to loyal customers: supermarkets versus home subscriptions), brand extension to related products (such as Hellmann's tartar sauce), product improvements, ongoing customer contact (such as *Nintendo Power* magazine for owners of Nintendo game consoles), and monitoring reseller performance.

Because many people may view the same products differently, the preceding classification is excellent for segmentation. For example, Tylenol pain reliever may be a convenience product for some people (who will buy another brand if Tylenol is unavailable), a shopping product for others (who read ingredient labels), and a specialty product for still others (who insist on Tylenol). Johnson & Johnson, maker of Tylenol, must understand how Tylenol fits into the various categories and plan its marketing strategy accordingly.

## Industrial Products

**Industrial products** are goods and services purchased for use in the production of other goods or services, in the operation of a business, or for resale to other consumers. A customer may be a manufacturer, wholesaler, retailer, or government or other nonprofit organization.

Industrial products may be categorized by the degree of decision making involved in a purchase, costs, consumption rapidity, the role in production, and the change in form. Since industrial-product sellers tend to visit customers, store shopping behaviour is often not a factor. Installations, accessory equipment, raw materials, component materials, fabricated parts, business supplies, and business services are types of industrial products—as shown in Table 7-2.

**Installations** and **accessory equipment** are capital goods. They are used in the production process and do not become part of the final product. Installations are nonportable, involve considerable consumer decision making (usually by upper-level executives), are very expensive, last many years, and do not change form. The key marketing tasks are direct selling from producer to purchaser, lengthy negotiations on features and terms, having complementary services such as maintenance and repair, tailoring products to buyers' desires, and offering technical expertise and team selling (in which various salespeople have different areas of expertise). Examples are buildings, assembly lines, major equipment, large machine tools, and printing presses.

Accessory equipment consists of movable goods that require moderate consumer decision making, are less costly than installations, last many years, and do not become part of the final product or change form. The key marketing tasks are tying sales to those of installations; providing various choices in price, size, and capacity;

**SONY CANADA**
www.sony.com

*Consumers are loyal to **specialty products**.*

**JOHNSON & JOHNSON**
www.jnj.com

**Industrial products** *are organizational consumer goods and services.*

**Installations and accessory equipment** *are expensive and do not become part of the final product.*

## What Do You Do When the Pace of Technology Slows the Pace of Technology?

Anyone who's bought a computer in recent years has done so knowing that it would be obsolete the moment it left the store. The pace of technological advance is so rapid that it can be paralyzing.

Early in 1999 Sky Digital, a satellite-based, 200-channel digital TV service, was launched in the U.K. in the hopes of matching the success of Direct TV in the U.S. Sky Digital is expecting competition from ONdigital, a terrestrial-based service, and some large cable-based service operators in the U.K. However, competition is only one of Sky Digital's concerns. The fact is, some 60 per cent of the U.K.'s consumers are totally unaware of digital television services, their three different platforms (satellite, terrestrial, and cable), and the benefits they offer. A massive promotional campaign is needed in order to outline the features and benefits of the new services, and to explain the hardware necessary to deliver them via the different platforms. And as for the 40 per cent of

consumers who *are* aware of the services and the hardware required to deliver them, this group has indicated that they plan to wait and see which service platform takes hold.

In essence, people are reacting to the rapid pace of change by becoming slower in adopting new technologies, which means that producers face even greater risks when they introduce new products. Managers in technology-based firms were usually advised to innovate or die, but there's a growing recognition that the key isn't necessarily being the first to develop new technology, but rather the first to gain acceptance of it.

What advice would you give to Sky Digital's marketing managers to help them respond to consumer fears about adopting the wrong platform for digital TV?

Source: Based on Virginia Matthews, "U.K. Consumers Blissfully Unaware of Digital TV Revolution," *Marketing Magazine* (February 8, 1999), p. 6.

---

**TABLE 7-2**

**Characteristics of Industrial Products**

| | TYPE OF PRODUCT | | | | | | |
|---|---|---|---|---|---|---|---|
| **CHARACTERISTICS** | *Installations* | *Accessory Equipment* | *Raw Materials* | *Component Materials* | *Fabricated Parts* | *Supplies* | *Services* |
| Degree of consumer decision making | High | Moderate | Low | Low | Low | Very low | Low to high |
| Per-unit costs | High | Moderate | Low | Low | Low | Very low | Low to moderate |
| Rapidity of consumption | Very low | Low | High | High | High | High | Low to high |
| Item becomes part of final product | No | No | Sometimes | Yes | Yes | No | Sometimes |
| Item undergoes changes in form | No | No | Yes | Yes | No | No | Sometimes |
| Major consumer desire | Long-term facilities | Modern equipment | Continuous, low-cost, graded materials | Continuous, low-cost, specified materials | Continuous, low-cost, fabricated materials | Continuous, low-cost, efficient supplies | Efficient, expert services |
| Examples | Production plant | Forklift truck | Coal | Steel | Thermostat | Light bulb | Machinery repair, accounting |

having a strong distribution channel or sales force; stressing durability and efficiency; and having maintenance and technical support. Examples are drill presses, trucks, vans, and lathes.

**Raw materials**, **component materials**, and **fabricated parts** are used up in production or become part of final products. They are expense rather than capital items. They require limited consumer decision making, are low cost on a per-unit basis, and are rapidly consumed. Raw materials are unprocessed primary materials from extractive and agricultural industries—minerals, coal, and crops, for example. Component materials are semimanufactured goods that undergo further changes in form—steel, textiles, and basic chemicals, for example. Fabricated parts are placed in products without changes in form—electric motors, thermostats, and microprocessors, for example. The major marketing tasks for materials and parts are to ensure consistent quality, continuity in shipments, and prompt delivery; pursue reorders; have competitive prices; seek long-term contracts; use assertive distributors or sales personnel; and meet buyer specifications.

**Industrial supplies** are convenience goods used in a firm's daily operations. They can be maintenance supplies, such as light bulbs, cleaning materials, and paint; repair supplies, such as rivets, nuts, and bolts; or operating supplies, such as stationery, pens, and business cards. They require little consumer decision making, are very low cost on a per-unit basis, are rapidly consumed, and do not become part of the finished product. Marketing emphasis is on availability, promptness, and ease of ordering.

**Industrial services** involve maintenance and repair services, and business advisory services. Maintenance and repair services (such as janitorial services and machinery repair) usually involve little consumer decision making, are rather inexpensive, and are consumed quickly. They may become part of a final product (for example, keeping for-sale equipment in good working condition) or involve a change in form (for example, janitorial services converting a dirty office into a clean one). The key marketing thrust is on consistent, efficient service at a reasonable price. Business advisory services (such as accounting and legal services) may involve a moderate to high level of consumer decision making when these services are first purchased. Ongoing costs tend to be low to moderate, while benefits may be long-lasting. These services do not become part of the final product. The major marketing task is to present an image of expertise and convey the reasons for a client to use the service.

**Raw materials, component materials,** *and* **fabricated parts** *are consumed in production.*

**Industrial supplies** *are used daily, and* **industrial services** *are classified as maintenance and repair, and business advisory.*

## Elements of a Product Mix

After determining the type(s) of products to offer, a firm needs to outline the variety and assortment of those products. A **product item** is a specific model, brand, or size of a product that a company sells, such as a college course on the principles of marketing, a General Motors truck, or Sony digital video disk drives for PCs. Usually a firm sells a group of closely related product items as part of a **product line**. In each product line, the items have some common characteristics, customers, and/or uses; they may also share technologies, distribution channels, prices, related services, and so on.[5] As an example, Revlon markets lipstick, eye makeup, and other cosmetics. Caterpillar makes several different tractor models. Prentice Hall Canada publishes a number of college and university textbooks on marketing. Many local lawn-service firms offer lawn mowing, landscaping, and tree-trimming services.

The **product mix** consists of all the different product lines a firm offers. For instance, Heinz markets ketchup, tuna fish, low-calorie foods, frozen french fries, soup, pet food, and various other food products in over 200 countries around the globe. Kaufman Footwear markets Sorel, the best-selling brand of winter boots in

**A product item** *is a specific model; a* **product line** *has related items; a* **product mix** *is all a firm's lines.*

**PRENTICE HALL CANADA**
www.phcanada.com

*A product mix has levels of width, depth, and consistency.*

North America, as well as Black Diamond industrial safety footwear and Foamtread brand slippers. Kaufman recently decided to extend the Sorel product line to include rugged outdoor footwear for spring and fall use. It also plans to sell accessories and apparel under this brand name. The firm hopes to round out its product lines so that its sales are not so seasonally based.[6]

A product mix can be described in terms of its width, depth, and consistency. The width of a product mix is based on the number of different product lines a company offers. A wide mix lets a firm diversify products, appeal to different consumer needs, and encourage one-stop shopping. A narrow mix requires lower resource investments and does not call for expertise in different product categories.

The depth of a product mix is based on the number of product items within each product line. A deep mix can satisfy the needs of several consumer segments for the same product, maximize shelf space, discourage competitors, cover a range of prices, and sustain dealer support. A shallow mix imposes lower costs for inventory, product alterations, and order processing; and there are no overlapping product items.

The consistency of a product mix is based on the relationship among product lines in terms of their sharing a common end-use, distribution outlets, consumer group(s), and price range. A consistent mix is generally easier to manage than an inconsistent one. It allows a firm to concentrate on marketing and production expertise, create a strong image, and generate solid distribution relations. However, excessive consistency may leave the firm vulnerable to environmental threats, sales fluctuations, or decreased growth potential, since emphasis is on a limited product assortment. Figure 7-3 shows product mix alternatives in terms of width and depth. Figure 7-4 displays Jergens' deep product line of hand soaps.

Product-mix decisions can have both positive and negative effects on companies,[7] as these examples demonstrate:

- Bombardier Corporation is booming as a result of its product mix diversification strategy. The firm, which began in the 1960s as the maker of Ski-Doo snowmobiles, now also manufactures aircraft for commuter airlines and corporate air fleets, railroad and subway cars, Traxter all-terrain vehicles, and Sea-Doo personal watercraft. Its annual revenues have gone from $11 million in 1964 to $8.5 billion today.[8]

- H.J. Heinz Co. of Pittsburgh, Pennsylvania recently decided to restructure its businesses and invest in brand marketing. (Since Heinz was operating in mature markets it was experiencing slow growth and lower profitability.) Heinz decided to

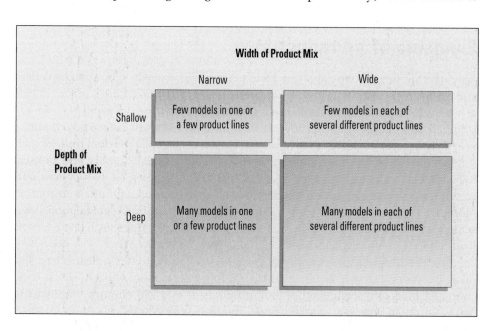

**FIGURE 7-3**

**Product Mix Alternatives**

**FIGURE 7-4**

**Jergens' Deep Product Line**
By offering a wide variety of hand soaps Jergens has become Canada's leader in the liquid hand soap market.

*Courtesy Jergens*

launch a program called "Operation Excel" to cut costs by $300 million. The firm plans to invest the savings into its main brands, which are Heinz ketchup, Star Kist tuna, and Kibbles and Bits dog food. Heinz is going to focus on six product categories: ketchup and other condiments; frozen foods; canned tuna; soups, beans, and pasta meals; infant foods; and pet products. It's also going to concentrate its marketing efforts in six countries: the United States, Canada, the United Kingdom, Australia, New Zealand, and Italy. Heinz manages a number of operating companies, including: Heinz U.S.A., Starkist Seafood, Heinz Pet Products, Weight Watchers International, Ore-Ida Frozen Foods, and Heinz Canada.[9]

**H.J. HEINZ CO.**
www.heinz.com/js/frames.html

## Product Management Organizations

A firm may select from among several organizational forms of product management, including: marketing manager, product manager, product planning committee, new-product manager, and venture team.[10]

*One person is directly in charge of a host of marketing tasks, including product planning, with a* **marketing manager system**.

Under a **marketing manager system**, an executive is responsible for overseeing a wide range of marketing functions (such as research, target marketing, planning for existing and new products, distribution, promotion, pricing, and customer service) and for coordinating with other departments that perform marketing-related activities (such as warehousing, order filling, shipping, credit, and purchasing). It works well for firms with a line of similar products or one dominant product line, and for smaller firms that want centralized control of marketing tasks. It may be less successful if there are several product lines and they require different marketing mixes—unless there are category marketing managers, with each responsible for a broad product line.

The Ontario Lottery Corporation, Lever-Ponds, and Nabisco Ltd. (maker of Oreo cookies and Ritz crackers, among others) have used some form of marketing manager system.[11]

*Middle managers handle new and existing products in a category in the* **product manager system**.

With a **product (brand) manager system**, there is a level of middle managers, each of whom is responsible for planning, coordinating, and monitoring the performance of a single product (brand) or a small group of products (brands). The managers handle both new and existing products and are involved with all the marketing activities related to their product or group of products. The system lets all products or brands get adequate attention. It works well when there are many distinct products or brands, each needing special marketing attention. But, it has two potential shortcomings: lack of authority for the product manager and inadequate attention to new products. Labatt Breweries, Procter & Gamble, and Black & Decker have used product managers.[12]

*A* **product planning committee** *has top executives involved part time.*

A **product planning committee** is staffed by high-level executives from various functional areas in a firm, such as marketing, production, engineering, finance, and research and development. It handles product approval, evaluation, and development on a part-time basis. Once a product is introduced, the committee usually turns to other opportunities and completely gives that product over to a product manager. This system lets management have strong input into product decisions; but, because the committee meets irregularly and must pass projects on to line managers, this method functions best as a supplement to other methods. It is utilized by many large and small firms.

*A* **new-product manager system** *has separate middle managers for new and existing products.*

A **new-product manager system** has product managers to supervise existing products and new-product managers to develop new ones. It ensures enough time, resources, enthusiasm, and expertise for new-product planning. Once a product is introduced, it is given to a product manager who oversees the existing products in that line (or brand). The system can be costly, incur conflicts, and cause discontinuity when an item is introduced. Kraft Canada, General Electric, and Johnson & Johnson have used new-product managers.

*A* **venture team** *is an autonomous new-product department.*

A **venture team** is a small, independent department comprised of a broad range of specialists, drawn from the marketing, finance, engineering, and other functional departments, who are involved with a specific new product's entire development process. Team members work on the team full time and act in a relatively autonomous manner. The team disbands when its new product is introduced, and the product is then managed within the firm's regular management structure. A venture team ensures there are proper resources, a flexible environment, expertise, and continuity in new-product planning. It is valuable if a firm wants to be more far-sighted, reach out for truly new ideas, and foster creativity. It is also expensive to establish and operate. Xerox, Ault Foods, Campbell Soup, and 3M have used venture teams.

The correct organization for a particular firm depends on the diversity of its offerings, the number of new products it introduces, its level of innovativeness, company resources, management expertise, and other factors. A combination organization may be highly desirable; among larger firms, this is particularly common.

# Product Positioning

Critical to a firm's product-planning efforts is how the items in its product mix are perceived in the marketplace. The firm must work hard to make sure that each of its products is perceived as providing some combination of unique features (product differentiation) and that these features are desired by the target market (thereby converting product differentiation to a differential advantage).

When a product is new, a company must clearly communicate its attributes: What is it? What does it do? How is it better than the competition? Who should buy it? The goal is to have consumers perceive product attributes as the firm intends. When a product has an established niche in the market, a company must regularly reinforce its image and communicate the reasons for its success. Once consumer perceptions are formed, they may be hard to alter. And it may also be tough later to change a product's niche in the market (for instance, from low price, low quality, to high price, high quality).

Through **product positioning**, a firm can map each of its products in terms of consumer perceptions and desires, competition, other company products, and environmental changes. Consumer perceptions are the images of products, both a firm's and competitors', in people's minds. Consumer desires refer to the attributes that people would most like products to have—their **ideal points**. If a group of people has a distinctive "ideal" for a product category, that group is a potential market segment. A firm will do well if its products' attributes are perceived by consumers as being close to their ideal.

*Competitive product positioning* refers to people's perceptions of a firm relative to competitors. The goal is for the firm's products to be perceived as "more ideal" than competitors'. *Company product positioning* shows a firm how consumers perceive that firm's different brands (items) within the same product line and the relationship of those brands (items) to each other. The goal is for each of the firm's brands to be positioned near an ideal point, yet not too close to one another in the consumer's mind—the brands should appeal to different ideal points (market segments).

A firm must monitor the environmental changes that may alter the way its products are perceived. Such changes could include new technology, shifts in consumer lifestyles, new offerings by competitors, and negative publicity.

Product positioning is illustrated in Figure 7-5, which depicts the ice cream marketplace in terms of the consumer desires regarding two key ice cream attributes:

*Distinctive and desirable product features must be communicated to the marketplace.*

**Product positioning** *maps out consumer perceptions of product attributes.* **Ideal points** *show the most preferred attributes.*

*Both competitive and company product positioning are important.*

**FIGURE 7-5**

**The Product Positioning of Ice Cream**

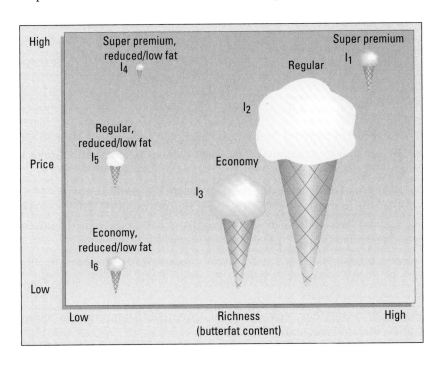

# ETHICS AND TODAY'S MARKETER

## What Can You Do When a Marketer's Product Comes Out of Your Own Backyard and Stinks It Up?

When you think of marketers and the products they sell you usually imagine the products being produced in a factory some distance away. You definitely don't expect a business to come into your own backyard and set up a production facility. However, farmers in Alberta are faced with exactly that prospect. The Alberta Oil and Gas Patch is the economic engine of the province, with its $26 billion revenues representing 20 per cent of Alberta's GDP. It's also a primary source of oil and natural gas for the rest of Canadians, not to mention the substantial quantity of natural gas that's exported to the United States.

The problem for farmers is that the Alberta government owns the mineral rights for their lands. The government leases the rights to oil and gas developers, who are given permission to trespass on privately owned farmland to explore and then develop oil and natural gas wells. It's a messy—and flammable—undertaking. When a well is developed a pipeline is laid; a pump jack installed to pump the oil or natural gas; and then flare stacks are installed to burn off uneconomical gas.

The critical issue is the fact that the air pollution and ground contamination that result from oil and natural gas wells has not been well studied. The more cynical among the farmers believe this is because the findings would be obvious—and the solutions so expensive that the costs would put Alberta at a competitive disadvantage in an industry that's highly cost competitive. Farmers currently have virtually no rights or protections with respect to the number and types of wells that can be

developed on their properties (one farmer has 133 pump jacks on his 500-acre farm). Farmers usually receive a $5000 rental stipend from the oil and natural gas developer, but this income can become unworthy very quickly if oil and natural gas pollution cause illness for the farmers and their families, as well as livestock losses and crop damage.

Indeed, many farmers report adverse health effects among their families and their livestock. Responsible oil and natural gas producers try to minimize the intrusiveness of their production facilities, but even the best of them face problems from time to time when mechanical failures of their equipment result in air or water pollution. The Canadian Association of Petroleum Producers (CAPP) has taken the position that there is very little objective evidence of negative effects of oil and gas emissions on livestock. Still, the industry recognizes that there are some practices they can undertake to minimize the intrusiveness of their activities and the potential for pollution, including: reducing flaring by transporting gas to micro-generators; using angled directional drilling, which disturbs less land and allows access to more oil and natural gas with fewer wells; and setting up a trust fund dedicated to clean up operations when spills or contamination occurs.

As a consultant, advise CAPP on what you think it should do to produce its products in a manner that is both ethical and competitive.

Source: Based on Andrew Nikiforuk, "It Makes Them Sick," *Canadian Business* (February 12, 1999), pp. 47–51.

price and richness (level of butterfat content). In this figure, there are six ideal points (target markets)—I1–I6, each associated with a specific type of ice cream. Here is a brief description of the six categories:

- *I1—super premium.* The creamiest, richest ice cream (butterfat content of 15 to 18 per cent) with the highest price. Häagen-Dazs, Mövenpick's, Richard D's, Laura Secord, and Ben & Jerry's are in this grouping. This segment is the fastest growing and represents about 3 per cent of Canadian ice cream sales.

- *I2—regular.* A creamy, rich ice cream (butterfat content of 10 to 12 per cent) with an average to slightly above-average price. Sealtest, Breyers, Natrel, and Baskin Robbins are positioned here.

- *I3—economy.* An average ice cream (butterfat content of 10 per cent) at a below-average price. Private-label brands fit here.

- *I4—super premium, reduced or low fat.* A flavourful ice cream with a high price for moderately health-conscious consumers (butterfat content of 5 to 10 per cent). The reduced-fat versions of the leading super premiums go here.

- *I5—regular, reduced or low fat.* A good-quality ice cream for more health-conscious consumers (butterfat content of less than 8 per cent) at an average price. Weight Watcher's, Light n' Lively, and Sealtest Parlour 1% are positioned here.

- *I6—economy, reduced or low fat.* An average ice cream for more health-conscious consumers (butterfat content of 4 to 8 per cent) at a below-average price. Private-label brands fit here.

An examination of competitive product positioning reveals that there are competing products in each market niche. In some instances, the marketplace is saturated. Nonetheless, the companies in the industry have done a good job in addressing the needs of the various consumer segments and in differentiating the products offered to each segment.

Breyers, Sealtest, and Light n' Lively are all marketed by Unilever. From an analysis of company product positioning, it is clear that Unilever serves the customers in its markets well. However, it must continue to differentiate carefully between Breyers (the "all natural" ice cream) and Sealtest (the "ice cream parlor" ice cream).

By undertaking product-positioning analysis, a company can learn a great deal and plan its marketing efforts accordingly, as these examples show:

- Statistics Canada data suggest there will be 2.5 million Canadian children between six and eleven years old at the start of the year 2000. Recognizing the opportunity to reach out to this group, Toronto-based Nabisco is positioning all of its single-serving packages of snack food brands under the name "Planet Snak." The Planet Snak position will include new product sizes for brands such as: Chips Ahoy!, Mini Oreo, Crispers, Bits and Bites, Teddy Grahams, Ritz Bitz Sandwiches, Animal Crackers, and Dino Bites (a line extension of Animal Crackers).[13]

- Air Canada believes numerous travellers perceive airlines as indifferent and impersonal. To remedy this, it is emphasizing the quality of its service—depicted in ads by the worldwide symbol for outstanding service, the red carpet.

# The Product Life Cycle

The **product life cycle** is a concept that attempts to describe a product's sales, competitors, profits, customers, and marketing emphasis from its inception until it is removed from the market.

*The **product life cycle** describes each stage in a product's life.*

From a product-planning perspective, there is interest in the product life cycle for several reasons.

1. Some product lives are shorter than before.
2. New products often require high marketing and other investments.
3. An understanding of the concept lets a firm anticipate changes in consumer tastes, competition, and support from resellers and adjust its marketing plan accordingly.
4. The concept enables a firm to consider the product mix it should offer; many firms seek a **balanced product portfolio**, whereby a combination of new, growing, and mature products is maintained.

*Companies often desire a **balanced product portfolio**.*

The life-cycle concept can be applied to a product class (watches), a product form (quartz watches), or a brand (Seiko quartz watches). Product forms generally follow the traditional life cycle more faithfully than product classes or brands.

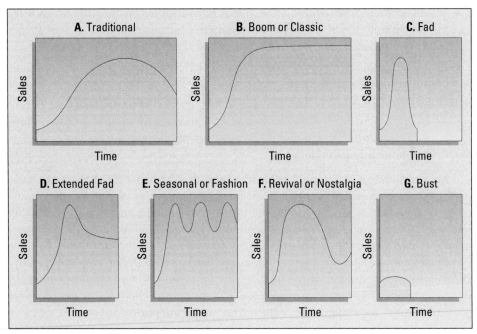

**FIGURE 7-6**

**Selected Product Life-Cycle Patterns**

*Product life cycles may be traditional, boom, fad, extended fad, seasonal, revival, or bust.*

As Figure 7-6 shows, product life cycles vary greatly, in both duration and shape. A *traditional cycle* has distinct periods of introduction, growth, maturity, and decline. A *boom* or *classic cycle* describes a very popular product that sells well for a long time. A *fad* cycle represents a product with quick popularity and a sudden decline. An *extended fad* is like a fad, but residual sales continue at a lower level than earlier sales. A *seasonal* or *fashion cycle* results if a product sells well in nonconsecutive periods. With a *revival* or *nostalgia cycle*, a seemingly obsolete product achieves new popularity. A *bust cycle* occurs for a product that fails.

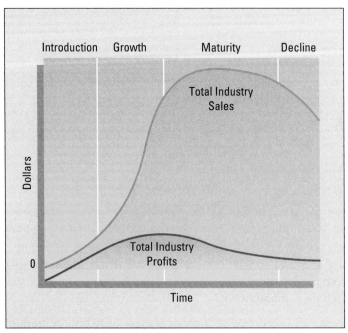

**FIGURE 7-7**

**The Traditional Product Life Cycle**

**TABLE 7-3**

## The Characteristics of the Traditional Product Life Cycle

| | STAGE IN LIFE CYCLE | | | |
|---|---|---|---|---|
| **CHARACTERISTICS** | *Introduction* | *Growth* | *Maturity* | *Decline* |
| Marketing goal | Attract innovators and opinion leaders to new product | Expand distribution and product line | Maintain differential advantage as long as possible | (a) Cut back, (b) revive, or (c) terminate |
| Industry sales | Increasing | Rapidly increasing | Stable | Decreasing |
| Competition | None or small | Some | Substantial | Limited |
| Industry profits | Negative | Increasing | Decreasing | Decreasing |
| Customers | Innovators | Resourceful mass market | Mass market | Laggards |
| Product mix | One or a few basic models | Expanding line | Full product line | Best-sellers |
| Distribution | Depends on product | Rising number of outlets/distributors | Greatest number of outlets/distributors | Decreasing number of outlets/distributors |
| Promotion | Informative | Persuasive | Competitive | Informative |
| Pricing | Depends on product | Greater range of prices | Full line of prices | Selected prices |

## Stages of the Traditional Product Life Cycle

The stages and characteristics of the traditional product life cycle are shown in Figure 7-7 and Table 7-3, which both refer to total industry performance during the cycle. The performance of an individual firm may vary from that of the industry, depending on its specific goals, resources, marketing plans, location, competitive environment, level of success, and stage of entry.

During the **introduction stage of the product life cycle**, a new product is introduced to the marketplace and the goal is to generate customer interest. The rate of sales growth depends on a product's newness, as well as its desirability. Generally, a product modification gains sales faster than a major innovation. Only one or two firms have entered the market, and competition is minimal. There are losses due to high production and marketing costs; and cash flow is poor. Initial customers are innovators who are willing to take risks, can afford to take them, and like the status of buying first. Because one or two firms dominate and costs are high, only one or a few basic product models are sold. For a routine item like a new cereal, distribution is extensive. For a luxury item like a new boat, distribution is limited. Promotion must be informative, and free samples may be desirable. Depending on the product and choice of consumer market, a firm may start with a high-status price or low mass-market price.

*In the* **introduction stage**, *the goal is to establish a consumer market.*

Over the **growth stage of the product life cycle**, a new product gains wider consumer acceptance, and the marketing goal is to expand distribution and the range of available product alternatives. Industry sales increase rapidly as a few more firms enter a highly profitable market that has substantial potential. Total and unit profits are high because an affluent (resourceful) mass market buys distinctive products from a limited group of firms and is willing to pay for them. To accommodate the growing market, modified versions of basic models are offered, distribution is expanded, persuasive mass advertising is utilized, and a range of prices is available.

*During the* **growth stage**, *firms enlarge the market and offer alternatives.*

During the **maturity stage of the product life cycle**, a product's sales growth levels off and firms try to maintain a differential advantage (such as a lower price,

*In the* **maturity stage**, *companies work hard to sustain a differential advantage.*

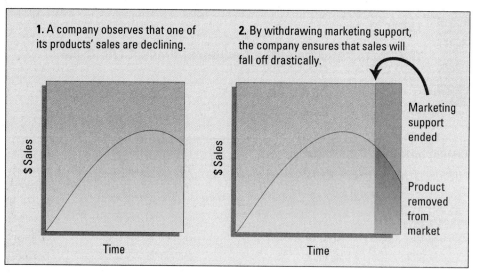

FIGURE 7–8

**A Self-Fulfilling Prophecy**

improved features, or extended warranty) for as long as possible. Industry sales stabilize as the market becomes saturated and many firms enter to capitalize on the still sizable demand. Competition is at its highest. Thus, total industry and unit profits drop because discounting is popular. The average-income mass market makes purchases. A full product line is made available at many outlets (or through many distributors) and many prices. Promotion becomes very competitive.

*In the* **decline stage**, *firms reduce marketing, revive a product, or end it.*

In the **decline stage of the product life cycle**, a product's sales fall as substitutes enter the market or consumers lose interest. Firms have three options. They can cut back on marketing, thus reducing the number of product items they make, the outlets they sell through, and the promotion used; they can revive a product by repositioning, repackaging, or otherwise remarketing it; or they can drop the product. As industry sales decline, many firms exit the market since customers are fewer and they have less money to spend. The product mix focuses on best-sellers, selected outlets (distributors) and prices, and promotion that stresses—informatively—availability and price.

The vinyl record turntable is a good example of a product form that moved through the life cycle. It went from an exclusive, expensive item (RCA Victrola) to a widespread, moderately priced item, then a mass-marketed, inexpensive item, and finally to complete obsolescence. Throughout its lifetime it served only one function: sound reproduction by spinning an encoded vinyl disk impacted by a needle that vibrated to reproduce sound. Today the turntable has been replaced by multi-function reproduction devices in the form of compact disk players and digital video disk players that can reproduce sound, motion pictures, still pictures, and data. The disks still spin, but the information is digitally stored and then read by a laser beam before it's translated into sound and pictures.

## Evaluating the Product Life-Cycle Concept

The product life cycle provides a good framework for product planning; but, it has not proven very useful in forecasting. In using the product life-cycle concept, these key points should be kept in mind:

1. The stages, the time span, and the shape of the cycle (such as flat, erratic, or sharply inclined) vary by product.

# INTERNATIONAL MARKETING IN ACTION

## Does the Best Beer Come from Belch-ium, We Mean Belgium?

The last twenty years has seen an explosion of choice in the beer market for Canadians. It's not just that Labatt and Molson's Breweries, Canada's dominant brewers, have been marketing more brands, or that micro-brewers have been growing at a tremendous rate, but also that international brewers have been making their way into the Canadian market. Some of the best of these international brews come from Belgium. Brewing is a relatively simple process, involving the combining of four main ingredients: malt, hops, yeast, and water. But the selection of these ingredients and the manner in which they're combined can lead to a whole host of different flavours and styles—and this is where Belgian brewers excel.

The Belgians originally entered Canada on a narrow front, with a few specialty brands such as Chimay Grand Reserve, a dark ale brewed by Trappist monks. (If you consider the very few pleasures monks must enjoy, then you'd expect this beer to be very good.) Then there's Duvel (meaning "devil" in Flemish), which has an 8.5 per cent alcohol content; heavy users must no doubt come to appreciate the irony of the name. Another key brand is McChouffe, an 8.5 per cent alcohol ale that's brewed in the Ardennes. This area, probably most famous to North Americans as the location of World War II's Battle of the Bulge, is now achieving new fame as the source of this World Beer Championship Gold Medal winning beer. The La Chouffe brand was the Platinum Medal winning beer at the same championship.

Belgium is described as a mecca for beer drinkers (most people think it's Germany or England) because there are "more beer styles in that one country than anywhere else in the world." Belgian beer drinkers can choose from among ales, lagers, or fermented lambics—a brewing style unfamiliar to many Canadians. Lambics are generally not bitter and have a number of tastes, such as sour and hazy, dry and sweet, or fizzy and fruity. (The fizzy and fruity tastes seem to have achieved the most popularity in Canada.)

The Belgian invasion hasn't been restricted to importing some specialty brews for sale in local pubs. In 1995 Interbrew S.A., one of Belgium's largest commercial brewers, purchased Labatt Breweries of Canada. Since Interbrew S.A. promises to bring some of its Belgian style into new products from Labatt, it looks like Canadian consumers will be able to enjoy the products of the brewers from the "mecca" of beer for a long time.

Using the theoretical information on positioning in this chapter, discuss the various kinds of dimensions by which beer can be positioned. Suggest ways in which the Belgian specialty brewers might position their beers for the Canadian market.

Source: Based on Ruby Andrew, "Brussels Stout," *Canadian Business* (July 31/August 14 1998), p. 110.

2. Such external factors as the economy, inflation, and consumer lifestyles may shorten or lengthen a product's life cycle.

3. A firm may do better or worse than the industry "average" at any stage in the cycle. Just because an industry is in the growth stage for a product does not mean every firm that enters the market will succeed, nor does the decline stage mean lower sales for every firm.

4. A firm may not only be able to manage a product life cycle, it may also be able to extend it or reverse a decline. Effective marketing may lure a new market segment, find a new product use, or foster better reseller support.

5. As Figure 7-8 illustrates, firms may engage in a **self-fulfilling prophecy**, whereby they predict falling sales and then ensure this by reducing or removing marketing support. With proper marketing, some products might not fail.

*A **self-fulfilling prophecy** may occur when a firm anticipates declining sales and reduces marketing efforts.*

## MARKETING IN THE THIRD MILLENNIUM

### Trends in the High Technology Industry

According to *Fortune*, the following ten trends are likely to occur in the high technology industry in the new millennium.[14]

- *The exchange economy*—E-commerce will be dominated by business-to-business rather than consumer transactions; by 2003 about 90 per cent of all business on the Internet will involve business-to-business exchanges. The growth of "infomediaries," firms that specialize in providing detailed purchasing information that can link buyers and sellers, will fuel this trend.
- *Phones get swallowed*—Digital long-distance networks and the Internet allow users to make long-distance phone calls that are basically free. Since networks that are designed to carry data can easily carry voice messages, the "telephone" line is about to be replaced—and cable television and telephone companies are finding themselves in the same business, competing for the same customers.
- *America Online rising*—American Online enables its customers to access Internet services through telephone, cable television, satellite services, and stand-alone set-up boxes. With AOL currently the leading Internet service provider, competing firms like AT&T, WorldNet, MSN, and Earthlink—and potential competitors such as Disney,

Time Warner, and NBC—will be trying to capture a large share of the market.
- *Storage, storage, storage*—The amount of data being generated and exchanged by businesses in the information age is astronomical, and requires sufficient and safe data storage facilities and software. The ability to store, retrieve, access, and analyze corporate data has always been critical in the computer age, and will become even more important in the new millennium.
- *PC-free devices*—Scanners that operate without being hooked up to a PC, printers that print pictures taken with digital cameras without a PC interface—every electrical device will be a "smart" device, operated and controlled by computer chips that can be networked to computer control systems. People will be able to control devices at home or at work through their networked computers. You can preheat your oven or turn up the air conditioning while you're on your way home from work, rather than using a preprogrammed timer that doesn't allow for the fact that you had to work late or decided to come home early!
- *Supersmart cellular*—Cell phones, pagers, and palms are being mated into single devices so that data as well as voice transmissions can be

## The International Dimensions of Product Planning

When an international product plan is being devised, the following points should be kept in mind:

- Although a firm may offer the same products in countries around the globe, these products can have distinct generic meanings in different countries.
- In developing and less-developed countries, product "frills" are often less important than in industrialized countries.
- Due to their intangibility, perishability, inseparability, and variability, international marketing efforts for services are often more complex than those for goods.
- The concept of convenience, shopping, and specialty products is less valid in markets where distribution is limited or consumers have few choices.
- Installations and accessory equipment may be hard to ship overseas.
- Marketing all of the items in a wide and/or deep product mix may not be appropriate, or economically feasible, on an international basis.

conveniently wireless. (Essentially, PCs on the go.) The only problems? Weak human eyes for seeing the small displays, and fingers too large to handle the small key pads.

- *The Y2K play*—Businesses that prepared for the Y2K bug developed new relationships with some suppliers, and these relationships may well continue. Budgets that were expanded to deal with Y2K may remain expanded, thus funding more innovation and use of high technology. Companies selling enterprise software may see a boom in the new millennium, as firms that might have purchased sat on the sidelines, waiting to see what happened with the Y2K bug.

- *Freebies galore*—Internet service providers are providing free access and free Web sites to many users already. Just as cell phone service providers are giving away phones to people who subscribe to the service, it won't be long before Internet service providers give away free PCs to subscribers. The cost of a PC isn't much greater than a cellular phone these days anyway.

- *The morphing of Intel*—Intel has provided the chips that have driven the computer industry. Clone chip manufacturers have taken over a lot of the low-end market, but Intel plans to fight back by offering cheaper chips while still holding onto the high end. Embedding software into chips will bring Intel into direct conflict with Microsoft, since voice recognition software is considered a key future innovation. The increase in PC-free devices will also threaten Intel's position as the number one supplier of the "brain" of the computer.

- *Microsoft waning*—Microsoft is now an old-timer in the computer software game. Although it's the dominant supplier of operating software for PCs, a position that the U.S. Department of Justice is threatening to reduce with its anti-trust activities, it's not the operating supplier of many of the PC-free devices. Palm organizers, the new Apple IMac, and the Java language are three of the top-selling devices that don't depend on Windows operating software. Operating system freeware like the Linux are generating enthusiasm and users. Microsoft's fight against the U.S. Department of Justice will take some of its attention away from its business and competition for a while—and in the fast-changing world of high technology, this may be all it takes for it to topple.

Regardless of whether these ten trends stay the course and play themselves out entirely, the fact is that the industry has always faced rapid change. Market opportunities will abound, and with them product opportunities to meet the needs of these markets.

- The diversity of international markets may necessitate a decentralized product management organization, with some executives permanently assigned to foreign countries.

- For many products, there are differences in product positioning and consumer ideal points by country or region. Simple positioning messages travel better than more complicated ones.

- Some products are in different stages of their life cycles in developing and less-developed countries than in industrialized countries.

- Expectations regarding goods/services combinations may differ by country.

- A product modification or minor innovation in a home market may be a major innovation internationally, necessitating different marketing approaches.

- The characteristics of the market segments—innovators, early adopters, early majority, late majority, and laggards—in the diffusion process (covered in Chapter 8) often differ by country.

- Even though global branding and packaging may be desirable, various nations may have special needs or requirements.

# SUMMARY

**1.** *To define product planning and differentiate among tangible, augmented, and generic products* Product planning systematically allows a firm to pinpoint opportunities, develop marketing programs, coordinate a product mix, maintain successful products, reappraise faltering ones, and delete undesirable products.

Products should be defined in a combination of ways. A tangible product is a basic physical entity, service, or idea with precise specifications; it is offered under a given description or model number. An augmented product includes not only tangible elements, but also the accompanying cluster of image and service features. A generic product focuses on the benefits a buyer desires; this concept looks at what a product means to the consumer rather than the seller.

**2.** *To examine the various types of products, product mixes, and product management organization forms from which a firm may select* Goods marketing entails the sale of physical products. Service marketing includes goods rental, servicing goods owned by consumers, and personal services. Goods and services often differ in terms of intangibility, perishability, inseparability from the service provider, and variability in quality.

Consumer products are goods and services for the final consumer.

They can be classified as convenience, shopping, and specialty items. These products are differentiated on the basis of consumer awareness of alternatives prior to the shopping trip and the degree of search and time spent shopping. Industrial products are goods and services used in the production of other goods or services, in the operation of a business, or for resale. They include installations, accessory equipment, raw materials, component materials, fabricated parts, business supplies, and business services. They are distinguished on the basis of decision making, costs, consumption, the role in production, and the change in form.

A product item is a specific model, brand, or size of a product sold by a firm. A product line is a group of closely related items sold by a firm. A product mix consists of all the different product lines a firm offers. The width, depth, and consistency of the product mix are important.

A firm may choose from or combine several product management structures, including: marketing manager system, product (brand) manager, product planning committee, new-product manager system, and venture team. Each has particular strengths and best uses.

**3.** *To discuss product positioning and its usefulness for marketers* A

firm must ensure that each of its products is perceived as providing some combination of unique features and that they are desired by the target market. Through product positioning, a firm can map its offerings with regard to consumer perceptions, consumer desires, competition, its own products in the same line, and the changing environment. Competitive positioning, company positioning, and consumers' ideal points are key concepts.

**4.** *To study the different types of product life cycles that a firm may encounter and the stages of the traditional product life cycle* The product life cycle seeks to describe a product's sales, competitors, profits, customers, and marketing emphasis from its inception until its removal from the market. Many firms desire a balanced product portfolio, with products in various stages of the life cycle. The product life cycle has several derivations, ranging from traditional to fad to bust. The traditional cycle consists of four stages: introduction, growth, maturity, and decline. During each stage, the marketing objective, industry sales, competition, industry profits, customers, and the marketing mix change. While the life cycle is useful in planning, it should not be used as a forecasting tool.

# KEY TERMS

**product planning** (p. 189)

**product** (p. 189)

**tangible product** (p. 189)

**augmented product** (p. 190)

**generic product** (p. 190)

**goods marketing** (p. 191)

**durable goods** (p. 191)

**nondurable goods** (p. 191)

**service marketing** (p. 191)

**rented-goods services** (p. 191)

**owned-goods services** (p. 191)

**nongoods services** (p. 191)

**consumer products** (p. 191)

**convenience products** (p. 192)

**shopping products** (p. 192)

**specialty products** (p. 193)

**industrial products** (p. 193)

**installations** (p. 193)

accessory equipment (p. 193)

raw materials (p. 195)

component materials (p. 195)

fabricated parts (p. 195)

industrial supplies (p. 195)

industrial services (p. 195)

product item (p. 195)

product line (p. 195)

product mix (p. 195)

marketing manager system (p. 198)

product (brand) manager system (p. 198)

product planning committee (p. 198)

new-product manager system (p. 198)

venture team (p. 198)

product positioning (p. 199)

ideal points (p. 199)

product life cycle (p. 201)

balanced product portfolio (p. 201)

introduction stage of the product life cycle (p. 203)

growth stage of the product life cycle (p. 203)

maturity stage of the product life cycle (p. 203)

decline stage of the product life cycle (p. 204)

self-fulfilling prophecy (p. 205)

---

# REVIEW QUESTIONS

1. Why is it so important to understand the concept of a generic product?

2. Distinguish between a consumer product and an industrial product.

3. How can the same product be a convenience, shopping, and a specialty product? What does this mean to marketers?

4. What are the similarities and differences between raw materials and component parts?

5. What is a wide/shallow product mix? State the advantages and disadvantages of such a mix.

6. Under what circumstances is a product manager system appropriate? A new-product manager system?

7. What is the role of product positioning for a new product? A continuing product?

8. How do competitive positioning and company positioning differ? Give an example of each.

9. Explain the basic premise of the product life cycle. What is the value of this concept?

10. What is the key marketing objective during the growth stage of the product life cycle? Why?

---

# DISCUSSION QUESTIONS

1. For each of the following, describe the tangible, augmented, and generic product:
   a. A review course for the Graduate Management Aptitude Test (GMAT).
   b. A computer mouse.
   c. A Britney Spears CD.
   d. Highway paving materials.

2. Identify, describe, and differentiate between two product lines offered by the Pepsi-Cola company. Refer to the definition of "product line" offered in the chapter to support your answer.

3. Evaluate the product mix for Heinz, a company discussed in the chapter on p. 196.

4. What product management organization would you recommend for a large firm that makes, installs, and services home security systems? The firm is thinking about getting involved with auto alarms, fire detectors, and/or television satellite dishes. Explain your answer.

5. How has the positioning of the cellular telephone changed since the product has been on the market? Why?

## CASE STUDY
# E-ZEEWRAP 1000

Jim Scharf is an entrepreneur with a capital E—E as in E-ZEEWRAP 1000, a plastic wrap dispenser that is the firm's main product. (The 1000 refers to the number of feet of plastic wrap in a roll.) Jim Scharf Holdings Ltd. has been operating since 1986 and markets a wide variety of products and services, including "Nona's Instant Lentils" and "Heavenly Fresh Odor Absorber," the firm's latest products; a grain hoe for cleaning the corners of grain trucks called the "Safety Hoe"; "Canada's Loony Nest" for storing the $1 coin; "Loony Thoughts," a line of shirts and mugs licensed to a Minnesota company; "CRe-ATE Gift," a line of wooden crates used for packaging; and a marketing services division that sells other firms' products, such as "The Lettuce Knife," "Bakeware Buddy," and "Grocery Grip."

The unique E-ZEEWRAP plastic food wrap dispenser and the plastic wrap refills are the bread-and-butter sellers for Jim Scharf Holdings. E-ZEEWRAP 1000 came on the market in 1986. The product has a broad appeal since plastic wrap is used worldwide. "We've solved the problem of dispensing it," says Jim Scharf. He promotes E-ZEEWRAP as being environmentally friendly because it uses 1000-foot rolls of plastic (about ten times the length of conventional rolls) in a permanent dispenser. The system eliminates the need for cardboard boxes and plastic or metal cutter blades.

The main benefits of E-ZEEWRAP are its ease of use and the convenience and economy of buying in bulk. A promotional statement states: "E-ZEEWRAP 1000 wraps up convenience and savings with an indispensable plastic wrap dispenser. The dispenser offers a patented space saving design, allows easy grasping of wrap with precise cutting—users will never have to search for the end again. The dispenser has a universal mounting system, a lifetime warranty, reduces waste, and has a 1000 feet of premium quality wrap starter roll included. Put the professional quality of E-ZEEWRAP to work for you in your home. The Beautiful and Practical Gift! Save our forests ... 90% less packaging used on refills."

Jim has no misconceptions about his product whatsoever: he says he's marketing plastic food wrap. The E-ZEEWRAP dispenser is the means by which he gets the wrap into his customers' hands and obtains some customer loyalty on repurchases, where the real money is made. Jim Scharf has a very clear understanding of what his product represents to people. It's also important to note that his customers seem to perceive the product concept in the same fashion, and this is driving his success. E-ZEEWRAP has over $2.5 million in sales in Canada; Jim Scharf is now marketing this product throughout the world.

Scharf began marketing E-ZEEWRAP via direct response marketing using TV ads to demonstrate its advantages. Because Jim couldn't afford the out-of-pocket expenses for the TV air time in Canada he made a unique arrangement. He cut the TV stations in on the profits and sales of the product created by the advertising. Many of the stations took him up on his offer and were rewarded with more revenue than if they'd charged directly for the air time. The product first retailed for $50 in 1986, but more recent versions have been priced in the $20–$30 range. Physical distribution was accomplished via mail delivery. The success in Canada made it possible for Jim to bridge from direct response marketing to retail distribution through outlets such as Canadian Tire and Wal-Mart.

Jim pursued the same strategy to penetrate the United States. That is, he developed demand with direct response promotion and then distributed through conventional retailers. He set up a barter deal with Turner Broadcasting System (TBS Superstation and CNN), trading product for some advertising air time. The company has also exported to Mexico, South Africa, Spain, Poland, and the United Kingdom. The packaging carries a number of languages, including English, French, Spanish, Dutch, German, and Italian. In his latest bid for international expansion, Scharf exhibited E-ZEEWRAP at a Chicago Trade show for international business with new packaging designed for the Southeast Asian market. The Southeast Asian packaging will include languages such as English, Chinese, Indonesian, and Malaysian.

Scharf "believes in his product and is tireless in promoting it." The measure of his success has been the six industry awards that his company has won. These awards were for "Best New Canadian Housewares Product; Best in Retail Packaging; Abex Award for Marketing Achievement in Business Excellence; Entrepreneur of the Year; finalist for Wholesale Distributor; and making the list of *Profit Magazine*'s Top 100 companies, ranking forty-sixth on the list of fastest growing companies. It may be E-ZEEWRAP for Jim's customers, but the success of the product and the company comes entirely from JIM'S HARDWORK.

## Questions

1. Describe E-ZEEWRAP's product-planning strategy from the perspective of the generic product concept.
2. How would you characterize Jim Scharf Holdings' product mix? Explain your answer.
3. List the features and benefits of E-ZEEWRAP for consumers. What do you consider to be its most and least important attributes?
4. Discuss what you think is the main source of Jim Scharf's success. Can this source be transferred easily from product to product or firm to firm? Why or why not?

Sources: The material in this case is based on E-ZEEWRAP Web site, www.ezeewrap.ca (July 1999); "E-ZEEWRAP," CBC *Venture* Video 565; and "The Enterprising Entrepreneur (E-ZEEWRAP Plastic Wrap Dispenser)," *Saskatchewan Business* (April, 1992), p. 12.

**CASE STUDY**

# Arm & Hammer Baking Soda: Getting the Most Out of Your Product

Church & Dwight, based in Princeton, New Jersey, is the world's largest producer of sodium bicarbonate (also known as baking soda), with annual sales of U.S.$684 million. The firm sells baking soda products under the Arm & Hammer name brand. Consumer products account for 80 per cent of the firm's sales and include laundry detergent, cat litter, carpet deodorizer, air fresheners, dishwashing detergent, toothpaste, and antiperspirants.

Baking soda was originally formulated for use in kitchens in the 1830s by Dr. Austin Church. In the 1840s Dr. Church's brother-in-law, John Dwight, marketed baking soda as a time-saver for homemakers who made yeast-based breads and biscuits. When the product was combined with vinegar or buttermilk it released carbon dioxide—which created an instant leavening agent. Early in its history, baking soda was also used to neutralize stomach acids. Then, over time, other household uses were discovered. These include refrigerator freshener, garage floor cleaner, toothpaste ingredient to deter the formation of plaque, and fire extinguisher for grease-based fires. Many of these applications were discovered by consumers, who communicated them to Dwight & Church, the parent company of Arm & Hammer.

Marketing research studies show that 90 per cent of North American households have at least one box of baking soda on hand. Each year, 450 million kilograms of baking soda are sold in North America alone. Arm & Hammer brand has the lion's share of sales for this product category in the U.S. and in Canada. However, Church & Dwight is constantly seeking new growth opportunities for this versatile but singular product.

For example, it's strongly promoting its newest products: Super Scoop, The Baking Soda Clumping Cat Litter; and Cat Litter Deodorizer. The firm has developed a Web site for these products alone, which provides generous amounts of information and details on what the products are for, how to use them, and how to acquire them.

Church & Dwight believes it has "created the most effective cat litter you can buy." The product is presented as meeting a "cat lovers' #1 unmet need: litter box odour control!" The cat litter is promoted as having an advanced formula that locks feces and urine odours on contact and prevents them from escaping into the air. Church & Dwight is trying to capitalize on its knowledge and experience as the world's largest odour control company. Aside from its superior deodorizing properties, Super Scoop is also promoted as having "an advanced clumping system that not only clumps faster than ordinary litters, it also clumps harder. Our hard clumps don't crumble as you clean the litter box. Hard clumps mean that you can easily remove the entire 'odour clump' in one scoop, thereby eliminating the odour source."

Church & Dwight recognized the need to provide some assurance as to the safety of the product on its packaging. Therefore, Super Scoop carries the "Veterinarian Recommended" seal, which lets you know that it's been evaluated by veterinary professionals. Super Scoop is offered with a fresh scented or an unscented formula and comes in either a 7 or 14 lb. package size.

Church & Dwight also recognized that people might purchase a competitor's cat litter while still being interested in controlling litter odour. Therefore, the firm created the Cat Litter Deodorizer, "a unique product that effectively destroys litter box odour with the power of genuine ARM & HAMMER Baking Soda and a fresh, clean, moisture-activated fragrance that's released every time the box is used." The product also keeps "soiled litter from sticking to the bottom of the box" and therefore makes litter box cleaning easier. It's sold in a 20 oz. carton that states the product is safe for both people and felines.

Both products are distributed through grocery stores, mass merchandise chains, and pet superstores. The Web site provides UPC number codes and specific instructions on how consumers can get retailers to order and stock the product if they can't find it at their favourite stores. Clearly, Church & Dwight is informing consumers while encouraging product distribution.

## Questions

1. Describe Arm & Hammer's product mix based on its width, depth, and consistency.
2. What product management organization do you think would be most appropriate for Church & Dwight? Explain your answer.
3. Describe the features and benefits that Church & Dwight has used to promote its newest baking soda-based products: ARM & HAMMER Super Scoop, The Baking Soda Clumping Cat Litter, and Cat Litter Deodorizer. In what ways are these products superior to competitive products? In your answer discuss the advantages that Arm & Hammer might have over competitive products in promoting odour control.
4. Church & Dwight has been selling baking soda for about 170 years. Discuss how it has dealt with the product life cycle for baking soda during this time.

**ARM & HAMMER**
www.armandhammer.com

Sources: The data in this case are drawn from Hoovers, "Church & Dwight," Hoover's Company Capsule, www.hoovers.com (July 1999); ARM & HAMMER Super Scoop and ARM & HAMMER Cat Litter Deodorizer Web site (July 1999); Judge Rules Sifto Must Alter Packaging," *Globe and Mail*, Metro Edition (September 28, 1994), p. B7; and "Arm & Hammer Muscles In on Maud: Namesake Is Downplayed in New Marketing of Baking Soda," *Marketing Magazine* (October 12, 1992), p.3.

**CHAPTER** | **8**

# Goods Versus Services Planning

## *Chapter Objectives*

1. To examine the scope of goods and services, and explain how goods and services may be categorized

2. To discuss special considerations in the marketing of services

3. To look at the use of marketing by goods versus services firms and provide illustrations of service marketing

4. To distinguish between profit-oriented and nonprofit marketing

5. To describe nonprofit marketing organizations, the role of nonprofit marketing in society, and applications of nonprofit marketing

*Courtesy of ING Direct*

**ING DIRECT**
www.ingdirect.ca/home.html

**E**ven the most casual observers have noted major changes in the kinds of services offered by the Canadian banking industry in recent years. However, no one expected "coffee shop banking."

But that's exactly what ING Direct, a formerly branchless Canadian bank, has decided to do. ING Direct is owned by International Nederlanden Groep NV, a large multinational Dutch financial services firm. ING Groep NV operates in sixty countries worldwide and has $350 billion in assets. ING Direct Bank of Canada was set up as part of a test market for ING Groep NV's first offering of virtual banking services.

ING Direct began as a bank that didn't have branches and offered only a few financial services. For example, it had one savings product, an investment savings account that paid 4.25 per cent annual interest on any balance without any service charges or monthly fees. This savings account attracted a lot of customers because, aside from no fees or service charges, the annual interest rate was higher than GIC rates offered by competing banks and trust companies. ING also offered consumers a line of credit with an interest rate charge of 7.25 per cent, and a line of RRSPs for retirement investments.

At the outset ING delivered these services to its customers by phone, fax, or mail twenty-four hours a day, seven days a week. Deposits were made by mail or electronically. Now ING has launched a transactional Web site with a full set of banking services, including mortgages and mutual funds. From 25 000 customers at its Canadian inception in 1997 ING has expanded to 150 000 customers in early 1999, with Canadian assets of about $1.5 billion. And considering that it had only 140 employees in Canada in 1998, the firm has done very well.

To become an ING Direct customer you can access its Express Online Enrolment site, which states that it uses the Secure Sockets Layer (SSL) Protocol and 128-bit encryption to protect client information.

All this business has been done without any actual physical branches. So when ING Direct decided to serve customers who insisted on having a physical place to engage in transactions, it was still playing by a different set of rules; hence, coffee shop banking. ING calls them "client cafés," but they're actually marketing centres that just happen to include a Starbucks coffee shop.[1]

In this chapter, we will study key concepts pertaining to the marketing of services. We will also focus on the differences and similarities between goods and services marketing.

## Overview

When devising and enacting product plans, a firm must fully comprehend the distinctions between goods and services—beyond the brief coverage in Chapter 7. Although the planning process is the same for goods and services, their differences need to be reflected in the decisions made during planning.

Chapter 8 covers the scope of goods and services, a goods/services continuum, goods and services classifications, special considerations in service marketing, and the use of marketing by goods and services firms. Also included is information on nonprofit marketing because most nonprofits (such as universities, health facilities, and libraries) are involved with services.

# The Scope of Goods and Services

**Goods marketing** entails the sale of physical products. **Durable goods** are physical products that are used over an extended period of time, such as furniture and heavy machinery. **Nondurable goods** are physical products made from materials other than metals, hard plastics, and wood; they are more quickly consumed or worn out; or they become dated, unfashionable, or otherwise unpopular. Examples are food and office supplies.

**Service marketing** includes the rental of goods, the alteration, maintenance, or repair of goods owned by consumers, and personal services. **Rented-goods services** involve the leasing of goods for a specified period of time—such as auto, hotel-room, office-building, and tuxedo rentals. **Owned-goods services** involve alterations to, or maintenance or repair of, goods owned by consumers, such as house painting, clothing alterations, lawn care, equipment maintenance, and machinery repair. **Nongoods services** involve personal service on the part of the seller, such as accounting, legal, consulting, and tutoring services; they do not involve goods.

Overall, the value of manufacturers' shipments of Canadian-made nondurable goods slightly exceeds that of durable goods. The leading durable products are transportation equipment, electronic and electrical equipment, machinery, and fabricated metal products. Among Canadian final consumers, 54 per cent of expenditures are on services, 24 per cent on nondurables led by food products, 13 per cent are on durables, and 9 per cent are on semi-durable goods. Because nondurables are bought more often and consumed more quickly, sales are more influenced by ads and sales promotions.

In industrialized nations, services account for well over one-half of the GDP. In developing and less-developed nations, services account for a lower share of GDP; goods production (including agricultural items and extracted resources) is more dominant. Yet even there the role of services is growing rapidly. In Canada, services-producing industries account for 67 per cent of the total output of the economy, with $490 billion.

Three-quarters of the spending on services in Canada is by the business sector, which includes services such as transportation and storage; communications; wholesale trade; retail trade; finance, insurance, and real estate; and business services. In contrast, the non-business sector accounts for the remaining quarter of service expenditures in categories such as government services; community and personal services; and other services. Among the leading Canadian service industries are finance, insurance, and real estate; business services; and transportation and storage services. More than 74 per cent of the private-sector Canadian labour force is in service jobs. Among the other nations with at least 50 per cent of their labour forces in service jobs are Australia, Great Britain, France, Japan, Germany, and the United States.[2]

These reasons have been cited for the worldwide growth of final consumer services: the rising living standard of the population; the complex goods that require specialized installation and repair; the lack of consumers' technical skills; the high purchase prices of items that can be rented rather than bought; and the greater need for health care, child care, and educational services. In the industrial sector, some of the services experiencing the greatest growth are computer repair and training, management consulting, engineering, and equipment leasing. There are 798 600 people in Canada working in business services, and these services are worth $43 billion to the nation's economy.[3]

The scope of services is sometimes underestimated because they may be lumped together with goods in assigning revenues. The **hidden service sector** encompasses the delivery, installation, maintenance, training, repair, and other services provided by firms that emphasize goods sales. For instance, although IBM is a

**Goods marketing** *involves the sale of* **durable** *and* **nondurable goods**.

**Service marketing** *covers* **rented-goods, owned-goods,** *and* **nongoods services**.

*Service marketing is huge in industrialized nations, and accounts for two-thirds of the total output of the Canadian economy.*

*The* **hidden service sector** *refers to services offered by goods-oriented firms.*

manufacturer, its Integrated Systems Solutions division now generates billions of dollars in revenues. Through outsourcing, IBM takes back a company's data-processing operations and then sells back computing service or simply runs the operation for a fixed annual fee. In 1994 Air Canada signed an agreement for $800 million in contracts over a seven-year period with Advantis Canada. Advantis is a subsidiary of IBM Canada and operates in conjunction with ISM (Information Systems Management), IBM's outsourcing company. Advantis will also outsource. For example, it signed a three-year, $5.9 million contract with Wang Canada Ltd. to provide computer systems and support for Air Canada's maintenance operations located at Dorval International Airport in Montreal.[4]

## Categorizing Goods and Services

Goods and services can be categorized in two ways. They can be located on a goods/services continuum; and they can be placed into separate classification systems.

### A Goods/Services Continuum

*With a **goods/services continuum**, products are positioned from pure goods to pure services.*

A **goods/services continuum** categorizes products along a scale from pure goods to pure services. With pure goods, the seller offers the consumer only physical goods without any accompanying services. With pure services, the seller offers the consumer only nongoods services without any accompanying physical goods. Between the two extremes, the seller would offer a combination of goods and services to the consumer.

Figure 8-1 shows a goods/services continuum with four different examples. In each one, a pure good is depicted on the far left and a pure service is depicted on the far right. Moving from left to right within each example, the combined

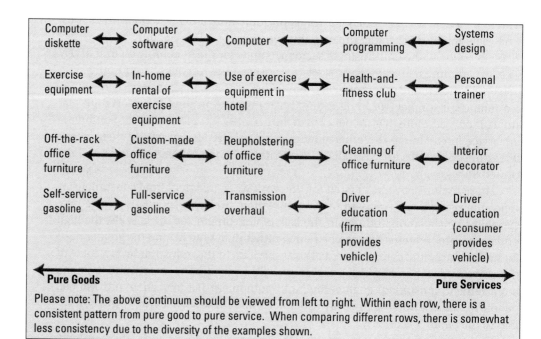

**FIGURE 8-1**

**Illustrating the Goods/Services Continuum**

good/service offerings become more service-oriented. For example, a computer diskette is usually marketed as a pure good—a product free from defects. With most computer software, there is a telephone hotline to answer questions. A PC is typically set up (configured) by the seller, pre-loaded with software, and accompanied by on-site servicing. Computer programming involves labour-intensive service on a physical good. Systems design entails professional consultation regarding a client's information system needs; the seller provides a pure service and does not sell or service goods.

Several things can be learned from a goods/services continuum. First, it applies to both final-consumer and organizational-consumer products. Second, most products embody goods/services combinations; the selling firm must keep this in mind. Third, each position along the continuum represents a marketing opportunity. Fourth, the bond between a goods provider and its customers becomes closer as the firm moves away from marketing pure goods. Fifth, a firm must decide if it is to be perceived as goods- or services-oriented.[5]

Whether it is goods- or services-oriented, a company needs to specify which are its core services and which are peripheral—and then decide what level of peripheral services to offer. **Core services** are the basic services that firms must provide to their customers to be competitive. At Casio, core services include prompt delivery, credit, advertising support, and returns handling for the retailers that carry its watches in 150 nations around the globe. At Federal Express, core services involve taking phone orders, picking up packages, tracking them, shipping them overnight, and delivering them the next morning or afternoon.

**Peripheral services** are supplementary (extra) services that firms provide to customers. Casio's peripheral services are extended credit terms and advice on how to set up displays for its retailers, and a toll-free phone number for consumer inquiries. Federal Express' peripheral services include giving shipping advice to customers, making address labels and special packaging materials available, and tracing packages in transit. Although these services may increase a firm's costs, require added employee and management skills, and be time-consuming, they may also help a company create and sustain a competitive advantage.[6]

## Goods and Services Classification Systems

In selecting a market segment, a goods seller should remember that final and organizational consumers have similarities and differences. The same good may be offered to each segment. The major distinctions between the segments are the reasons for purchases, the amount bought, and the features desired.

Durable-goods marketers have a particular challenge. On the one hand, they want to emphasize the defect-free, long-running nature of their products. On the other hand, inasmuch as they need to generate repeat business from current customers, they must continually strive to add unique features and enhance the performance of new models—and then convince people to buy again while the durable goods they own are still functional. For nondurable goods marketers, the key task is to engender brand loyalty, so consumers rebuy the same brands.

High value-added goods are those where manufacturers convert raw materials or components into distinctive products. The more value firms add to the goods they sell, the better the chance for a goods-based differential advantage. Low value-added goods are those where manufacturers do little to enhance the raw materials or components they extract or buy. These firms often must compete on price, since their goods may be seen as commodities. Superior customer service can be a major differential advantage and enable marketers of low value-added goods to avoid commodity status.

*By adding* **peripheral services** *to their core services, firms can create a competitive advantage.*

**FEDERAL EXPRESS**
www.fedex.com/

*Goods may be classified as to market, durability, value added, goals, regulation, distribution channel, and customer contact.*

For the most part, goods-oriented firms are profit-oriented. Sometimes goods are marketed by nonprofit organizations—usually as a way of generating revenues to support their activities. Nonprofit marketing is discussed in depth later in this chapter.

Goods may be grouped by the extent of government regulation. Some items, such as those related to the health and safety of people and the environment, are highly regulated. Others, generally those not requiring special health and safety rules, are subject to less regulation.

Distribution channel length refers to the number of intermediaries between goods producers and consumers. Final-consumer goods tend to have more intermediaries than organizational-consumer goods due to the size and importance of the latter. Furthermore, goods that are complex, expensive, bulky, and perishable are more apt to have shorter channels.

Goods may be classified by the degree of customer contact between sellers and buyers. Contact is greater for sophisticated equipment, items requiring some training, and custom-made goods. In these instances, proper employee training is needed. Low customer contact is required for goods that consumers are able to buy and use with little assistance from sellers.

A good would normally be classified on a combination of the factors. *Chatelaine* magazine appeals to final consumers, is nondurable, has a high added value, is profit-oriented, is subject to few regulations, is sold through newsstands (long channel) and home delivery (short channel), and has low customer contact.

Figure 8-2 displays a detailed, seven-way classification system for services. It is helpful in showing the diversity of service marketing.

As with goods, final and organizational consumers have similarities and differences in their use of services. Both groups can counter high prices or poor service by doing some tasks themselves. The major differences between the segments are the reasons for the service, the quantity of service required, and the complexity of the service performed.

In general, the less tangible a service, the less services marketing resembles goods marketing. For nongoods services, performance can only be judged after the service is completed. Rentals and owned-goods services involve physical goods and may be marketed in a manner somewhat similar to goods.

*Services may be classified as to market, tangibility, skill, goals, regulation, labour intensity, and customer contact.*

Services may be provided by persons of greatly varying skills. For services requiring high skill levels, customers are quite selective in picking a provider. That is why professionals often achieve customer loyalty. For services requiring low levels of skill, the range of acceptable substitutes is usually much greater.

Service firms may be profit- or nonprofit-oriented. Nonprofit service marketing may be undertaken by government or private organizations. The major distinctions between profit- and nonprofit-oriented marketing are noted later in this chapter.

Services may be classed by the extent of government regulation. Some firms, such as insurance companies, are highly regulated. Others, such as caterers and house painters, are subject to limited regulation.

The traditional view of services has been that they are performed by one person for another. However, this view is too narrow. Services do differ in labour intensity—for example, automated versus teller-oriented bank services. Labour intensity rises if highly skilled personnel are involved or services must be provided at the customer's home or business. Some labour-intensive services may be done by do-it-yourself consumers—for example, home repair.

Services may be grouped by their degree of customer contact. If contact is high, training personnel in interpersonal skills is essential, in addition to the technical schooling needed to perform a service properly. An appliance repair person or a car mechanic may be the only contact a person has with a firm. If contact is low, technical skills are most essential.

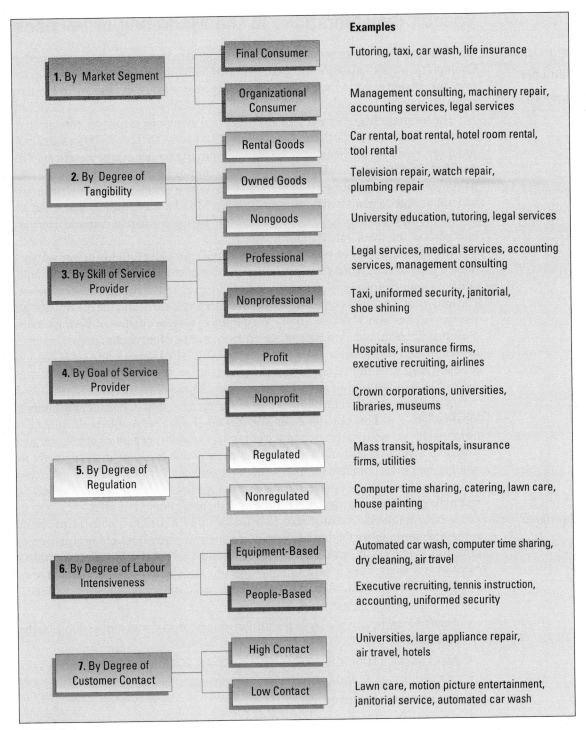

**Examples**

**1. By Market Segment**
- Final Consumer — Tutoring, taxi, car wash, life insurance
- Organizational Consumer — Management consulting, machinery repair, accounting services, legal services

**2. By Degree of Tangibility**
- Rental Goods — Car rental, boat rental, hotel room rental, tool rental
- Owned Goods — Television repair, watch repair, plumbing repair
- Nongoods — University education, tutoring, legal services

**3. By Skill of Service Provider**
- Professional — Legal services, medical services, accounting services, management consulting
- Nonprofessional — Taxi, uniformed security, janitorial, shoe shining

**4. By Goal of Service Provider**
- Profit — Hospitals, insurance firms, executive recruiting, airlines
- Nonprofit — Crown corporations, universities, libraries, museums

**5. By Degree of Regulation**
- Regulated — Mass transit, hospitals, insurance firms, utilities
- Nonregulated — Computer time sharing, catering, lawn care, house painting

**6. By Degree of Labour Intensiveness**
- Equipment-Based — Automated car wash, computer time sharing, dry cleaning, air travel
- People-Based — Executive recruiting, tennis instruction, accounting, uniformed security

**7. By Degree of Customer Contact**
- High Contact — Universities, large appliance repair, air travel, hotels
- Low Contact — Lawn care, motion picture entertainment, janitorial service, automated car wash

**FIGURE 8-2**

**A Classification System for Services**

A service would typically be classified using a combination of the factors in Figure 8-2. A firm tutoring students for graduate school entrance examinations appeals to final consumers, has an intangible service, requires skill by the service provider, is profit-oriented, is not regulated, has many trainers, and has high customer contact. A company may also operate in more than one part of a category (this also applies to goods marketers): A CA (Chartered Accountant) may have both final and organizational consumer clients.

# Special Considerations in the Marketing of Services

*Services differ from goods in terms of* **intangibility, perishability, inseparability,** *and* **variability**.

Services have four attributes that typically distinguish them from goods (as noted in Chapter 7): higher intangibility, greater perishability, inseparability of the service from the service provider, and greater variability in quality. Their effect is greatest for personal services.

The **intangibility** of services means they often cannot be displayed, transported, stored, packaged, or inspected before buying. This occurs for repair services and personal services; only the benefits to be derived from the service can be described. The **perishability** of services means many of them cannot be stored for future sale. If a painter who needs eight hours to paint a single house is idle on Monday, he or she will not be able to paint two houses on Tuesday; Monday's idle time is lost. A service supplier must try to manage consumer usage so there is consistent demand over various parts of the week, month, and/or year.

The **inseparability** of services means a service provider and his or her services may be inseparable. When this occurs, the service provider is virtually indispensable, and customer contact is often considered an integral part of the service experience. The quality of machinery repair depends on a mechanic's skill and the quality of legal services depends on a lawyer's ability. **Variability** in service quality—differing service performance from one purchase occasion to another—often occurs even if services are completed by the same person. This may be due to a service firm's difficulty in problem diagnosis (for repairs), customer inability to verbalize service needs, and the lack of standardization and mass production for many services.

In planning its marketing strategy, a service firm needs to consider how intangible its offering is, how perishable its services are, how inseparable performance is from specific service providers, and the potential variability of service quality. Its goal would be to prepare and enact a marketing strategy that lets consumers perceive its offering in a more tangible manner, makes its services less perishable, encourages consumers to seek it out but enables multiple employees to be viewed as competent, and makes service performance as efficient and consistent as possible.

*Service intangibility makes positioning decisions more complex.*

Service intangibility can make positioning harder. Unlike goods positioning, which stresses tangible factors and consumer analysis (such as touching and tasting) prior to a purchase, much service positioning must rely on performance promises (such as how well a truck handles after a tune-up), which can only be measured once a purchase is made. But, there are ways to use positioning to help consumers perceive a service more tangibly. A firm can:

- Associate an intangible service with tangible objects better understood by the customer.

- Focus on the relationship between the company and its customers. It can sell the competence, skill, and concern of its employees.

- Popularize the company name.

- Offer tangible benefits, such as BDO Dunwoody Limited promoting specific reasons for small businesses to use their accounting services. (See Figure 8-3.)

- Establish a unique product position, such as 24-hour, on-site service for the repair of office equipment.[7]

*Services often cannot be stored for later sale, so demand must be carefully matched with supply.*

Service intangibility may be magnified if only a small portion of the provided service is visible to the consumer. For example, in-shop repairs are normally not seen by consumers. Although a repair person may spend two hours repairing a camcorder and insert one part priced at $60, when the consumer sees a bill for $190 he or she may not appreciate the service time required. Thus, a firm must explain how much time is needed to render each aspect of service—and the tasks performed—to make that service more tangible to customers.

# TECHNOLOGY AND MARKETING

## Buying Insurance or Any Other Intangible? Go Online!

The home, auto, and travel insurance industry is one of the most efficient and purely competitive service industries in North America these days. These kinds of insurance products are essentially commodities, since coverages are virtually the same from company to company. And because people make purchase decisions on the basis of price, these products are just right for Internet selling.

A recent survey of 1000 Internet users indicated that about one-third of them would be willing to purchase home, auto, or travel insurance online. A real test of this proportion is being undertaken in the U.S. by Intuit Inc., which has set up a Web site (www.insuremarket.com) that offers users quotes, information, and agent contact, and allows people to make actual policy purchases from leading U.S. insurance firms. Intuit offers the service in eighteen U.S. states. Sales rose 300 per cent in 1998; in January 1999, Intuit provided users with over 1.6 million quotes.

As a shopping medium (shopping, as in acquiring information prior to making a purchase), the Internet is a very powerful tool. It can help marketers reduce some of the drawbacks associated with the unique characteristics of services: intangibility, perishability, inseparability, and variability.

For example, consider intangibility: Insurance is really a conditional promise or guarantee that you pay for. A contract is made between the insurance provider and the customer, and this contract can be transmitted electronically, as can the money to pay for it. The customer can complete the contract online, download it immediately, and print off a hard copy. Hence the offering becomes tangible. Further examples of intangible services that can be readily exchanged on the Internet include intellectual property (e.g., information, expert advice, software tools), entertainment services (music and video transmissions), and communications (e-mail, telephone, and even TV calls).

The Internet can reduce some of the risks of perishabilty for some service providers as well. Services can be made available twenty-four hours a day to people the world over. A person can access some expert advice, which is downloaded for viewing later. Entertainment sites can be accessed by a number of people in real time and on their own time. They can download music or videos for viewing later, or view them online at their leisure. Users aren't restricted to the times the provider wants to offer, but have complete control over when they want to access and use the service.

The issue of inseparability between the service and the service provider can also be overcome with the technology of the computer and the Internet. By virtue of experience, service providers can and do anticipate almost every possible service requirement. As such, sites with good search programs can allow users to explain their needs or problems and thus access the information or assistance they're likely to need. The service providers can essentially duplicate themselves simultaneously for a large number of users.

The latter feature also helps service providers overcome some of the problems associated with variability of services. Do people receive the same service treatment each time? On the Internet, they are more likely to find a very consistent response and handling of their queries by the machines and software they interact with.

The ability to overcome some or all of the four differentiating characteristics of services through the use of computer technology and the Internet promises to create a lot of new online service opportunities, and to revolutionize many of the existing service opportunities for intangible products.

Think of some examples of services that we typically use. Discuss whether they could be offered efficiently over the Internet, and the reasons why they do or don't lend themselves well to this technology.

Source: Based on Brett Matthews, "Insuring an Online Future," *Marketing Magazine* (April 12, 1999), p. 49

Because of service perishability, a service firm needs to match demand and supply patterns as well as it can. Thus, it might have to alter the timing of consumer demand and/or exert better control over the supply of its service offering. It should try to avoid situations in which excess demand goes unsatisfied and cases in which excess capacity causes an unproductive use of resources. To better match demand with supply, a firm can:

- Market similar services to segments having different demand patterns.
- Market new services with different demand patterns from existing services.
- Market new services that complement existing ones.
- Market service "extras" during nonpeak periods.
- Market new services not affected by existing capacity constraints.
- Train personnel to perform multiple tasks.
- Hire part-time employees during peak periods.
- Educate consumers to use services during nonpeak periods.
- Offer incentives and price reductions in nonpeak periods.[8]

*Interpersonal skills are cru-cial for service businesses.*

The existence of a close relationship between service provider and consumer makes employee interpersonal skills important. The workforce must be trained to

**FIGURE 8-3**

**BDO Dunwoody: Offering Tangible Benefits**
*Courtesy BDO Dunwoody LLP.*

The professionals at BDO know and understand the business issues smaller and medium-sized enterprises face - growth strategies, managing change, securing financing and expanding their markets.

BDO predominately serves the needs of entrepreneurial and owner-managed businesses. Clients come from virtually every industry sector and business service imaginable across Canada. And, we want to serve more of them.

In fact, BDO is committed to being the leading firm advising entrepreneurial businesses and the people behind them – through a team of accessible, experienced professionals.

We can provide you with a broad range of financial, tax and business advisory services – all tailored to meet the particular needs of today's entrepreneurs.

Call us at 1-800-805-9544 for the BDO office nearest you. We'll get the job done for you.

Call BDO.

BDO Dunwoody LLP
Chartered Accountants
and Consultants

*Helping Canadian Business Succeed...*
*through over 80 offices nationwide.*

For more information on BDO Dunwoody, see our home page at http://www.bdo.ca

interact well with people in such diverse situations as selling and performing services, handling payments, and delivering repaired goods. Generally, more personal involvement, personal contact, and customer input are needed to market services than to market goods. Thus, employee empowerment can be quite beneficial. Those who participate in the marketing of complex services often act as *relationship managers*. As such, the quality of the relationship between a firm's employees and its customers "determines the probability of continued interchange between those parties in the future." Greyhound Courier Express, the courier division of Greyhound Lines of Canada, wanted to build customer loyalty through a one-to-one relationship with shippers and decision makers. Greyhound had the names of the companies they have dealt with in their database, but not the names of the shippers or decision makers of these firms. Using a $3.6 million Sweepstakes promotion Greyhound encouraged shippers to register their names to build a database so these individuals could be contacted personally along with their companies.[9]

Many customers of personal service firms become loyal to a particular employee rather than the company. If that person leaves the firm, he or she may take some customers too. That is why it is important for a firm to show its customers that multiple employees are equally capable of providing excellent service.

By their nature, many services have the potential for great variability in their quality. It is hard for lawn care firms to mow lawns in exactly the same way each week, for marketing consultants to make sales forecasts for clients that are always accurate, and for each airline flight to arrive on time. But what service firms can do is strive to make their performance as efficient and consistent as possible. One solution to the issue of high costs (inefficiency) and low reliability (performance variability) is the **industrialization of services** by using hard, soft, and hybrid technologies.[10] Service reliability can also be improved by setting high-level standards and by tying employee pay and promotions to performance levels.

*Hard technologies* substitute machinery for people. An example is the implementation of an electronic credit authorization system to replace manual credit checks. Hard technologies cannot be as readily applied to services requiring extensive personal skill and contact, such as medical, legal, and hairstyling services. *Soft technologies* substitute pre-planned systems for individual services. For example, travel agents sell pre-packaged vacation tours to standardize transportation, accommodations, food, and sightseeing. *Hybrid technologies* combine both hard and soft technologies. Examples include muffler repair and quick oil-change shops.

This is how the Bank of Nova Scotia industrialized its services to improve the Customer Service Centre that supports its VISA card and banking services for customers and branches. In 1990 the Centre began receiving so many customer inquiries by mail and telephone that the paper-based system of responding was overwhelmed. The bank decided to use technology to help solve the problem, so a computer system using IBM's ImagePlus imaging technology, running on an AS/400 minicomputer linked to fifty networked PCs, was put in place. The bank set up a pilot team of eight people doing day-to-day work in the VISA centre to enable a hands-on system development approach. The system evolved and was customized as a result of this development approach, resulting in improvements in: customer service, operating efficiency, employee morale, and productivity. Other imaging applications for Scotiabank include: VISA sales draft processing, mortgage discharging, automated draft retrievals, and processing of chargebacks.[11]

To industrialize their services better, many firms use a **service blueprint**, which is a visual portrayal of the service process: "It displays each subprocess (or step) in the service system, linking the various steps in the sequence in which they appear. A service blueprint is essentially a detailed map or flowchart of the service process."[12] Figure 8-4 shows how a service blueprint can be used in administering an X-ray to a patient.

**GREYHOUND COURIER EXPRESS**
www.greyhound.ca/courier.html

*The* **industrialization of services** *can lower inefficiency and excessive variability using hard technologies, soft technologies, or hybrid technologies.*

**BANK OF NOVA SCOTIA**
www.scotiabank.ca/

*A* **service blueprint** *enhances productivity.* **Service gaps** *must be reduced.*

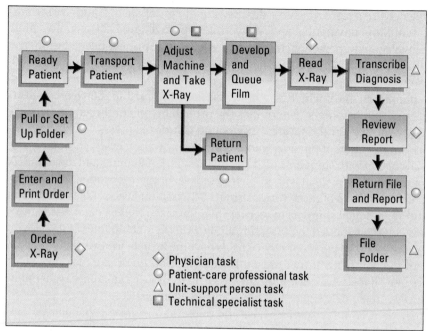

**FIGURE 8–4**

**A Service Blueprint for an X-Ray**

This service blueprint depicts the thirteen steps involved in a typical hospital's X-ray process. The steps can be completed in under one hour and they require multiple employees. Without such a blueprint, the X-ray process would probably be less systematic, more time-consuming, and less efficient.

*Source: Stephen H. Baum, "Making Your Service Blueprint Pay Off!" Journal of Services Marketing, Vol. 4 (Summer 1990), p. 49. Reprinted by permission.*

While planning their marketing strategies, it is also important for firms to understand service quality from the perspective of their customers. They must try to minimize any possible **service gaps**—the difference between customer expectations and actual service performance. Consumer expectations regarding service companies cover these ten areas:

1. *Tangibles*—facilities, equipment, personnel, communication materials.
2. *Reliability*—ability to perform a desired service dependably and accurately.
3. *Responsiveness*—willingness to provide prompt service and assist customers.
4. *Competence*—possession of the necessary skills and knowledge.
5. *Courtesy*—respect, politeness, and friendliness of personnel.
6. *Credibility*—honesty, trustworthiness, and believability of service performers.
7. *Security*—freedom from risk, doubt, or danger.
8. *Access*—ease of contact.
9. *Communication*—keeping customers informed and listening to comments.
10. *Understanding the customer*—knowing the customer's needs.[13]

*The low use of marketing for services has been due to small firm size, an emphasis on technical expertise, limited competition, negative attitudes, and other factors.*

## The Use of Marketing by Goods and Services Firms

Goods and services firms have differed in their use of marketing, but service firms are now better adapting to their special circumstances than in the past.

## A Transition in the Marketing of Services

Service firms have tended to lag behind manufacturers in the use of marketing for several reasons.

1. Many service firms are so small that marketing specialists cannot be afforded.

2. Because manufacturers often have a larger geographic market, they can more efficiently advertise.

3. A lot of service firms are staffed by people with technical expertise in their fields but limited marketing experience.

**INTERNATIONAL MARKETING IN ACTION**

## Service Exports: One of Canada's Fastest Growing Markets

**C**anadian service industries account for about $490 billion of Canada's GDP, which represents 67 per cent of the total output of the economy. Despite the fact that services dominate the domestic economy, the majority of the nation's exports are made up of goods. Many Canadians believe that goods exports consist primarily of commodity items (timber, potash, minerals, wheat, and other cash crops), but the fact is that commodity items represented only 30 per cent of the $320 billion in Canadian export goods sold in 1998. Service exports represent about $42 billion of that amount, and commercial services exports (such as finance, research, high technology, and engineering) account for half of the exports, or $21 billion each year. However, the annual growth rate of commercial service exports has been much higher than travel and transportation service exports, which are the two largest service export sectors in terms of dollars.

A breakdown of the figures for the approximately $21 billion in Canadian commercial service exports is: 25 per cent in financial services; 13 per cent in architectural, engineering, and technical services; 12 per cent in research and development services; and 9 per cent in computer and software services. The U.S. is the prime market for these services, handling about 66 per cent of the total, but the European market receives about 14 per cent of commercial service exports, the Asian market 9.5 per cent, and Central America and the Caribbean around 6 per cent.

Canada has a long way to go before our service exports match the same proportion of the export market as service offerings represent in the domestic market (67 per cent). A critical issue for Canadian firms in the near future will be how the World Trade Organization establishes new rules for trade in services. Such rules already exist for trading in goods, and it's likely that the rules for services will be developed in a similar fashion. But it will be considerably more difficult to establish the new rules, given the inseparability, variability, intangibility, and perishability of services.

The sale of goods need not involve the transfer of people between nations at all, whereas the inseparability of services requires that providers be able to travel between countries relatively freely. Since in most cases services involve expertise and intellectual properties, the valuation of the offerings will vary. The intangibility of services, combined with the potential need for language translation between Canadian providers and the nation of export, mean that Canadian firms have to pay even more attention to communicating the benefits of what they have to offer, which is another factor affecting valuation. The perishable nature of services means that providers who run into delays or red tape as a result of restrictions on freedom of movement, trade restrictions, or adapting to a foreign culture could find their profitable opportunities turn unprofitable very quickly. And, since trade relations are often bilateral and thus closely tied to foreign relations between governments, there is greater risk of market losses because of perishability if such relations sour. Whereas goods can be inventoried by either party, services offerings would be suspended until relations improved.

Negotiations will be much more complicated given the fact that trade in services requires greater freedom of movement for people and goods, and thus entails a greater threat to the integrity of national boundaries and national economies. The fact that people can move of their own accord makes trade in services much easier than in goods, and carries the prospect for much greater competition in most service industries. Commercial service industries in particular represent both high earning opportunities and strong competition for Canadian firms. For these reasons, Canadian service providers must be very attentive and get strong input into any World Trade Organization rulings on service offerings.

Identify what you consider to be some of the risks, and some of the opportunities, for international commercial service providers. Discuss ways in which firms might reduce these risks and seize these opportunities.

Source: Based on Statistics Canada, *The Daily* (April 9, 1999); and Jayson Myers, "Trends: Serving Up Sales," *Canadian Business* (March 26, 1999), p. 88.

4. Strict licensing provisions sometimes limit competition among service firms and therefore the need for marketing; in most industries, manufacturers have faced intense competition for years.

5. Consumers have held some service professionals, such as doctors and lawyers, in such high esteem that marketing has not been needed.

6. In the past, some professional associations banned advertising by members; this was changed by various court rulings that now permit it.

7. There are still service professionals who dislike marketing, do not understand it, or question the use of marketing practices, such as advertising, in their fields.

8. Many manufacturers have only recently set up services as profit centres.

*Service providers' use of marketing practices is expected to continue increasing in the future.*

Over the next few years, the use of marketing for services will continue to rise, due to a better understanding of the role of customer service in gaining and retaining consumers; worldwide service opportunities; deregulation in the banking, transportation, and communication industries; competition among service providers; consumer interest in renting/leasing rather than buying, the aggressive marketing of services by firms that once focused on manufacturing (such as IBM), the advent of high-technology services (such as computer-based video conferencing), the growing number of do-it-yourselfers because of high service costs, and the number of service professionals with formal business training.

## Nonprofit Marketing

*Nonprofit marketing serves the public interest and does not seek financial profits.*

**Nonprofit marketing** is conducted by organizations and individuals that operate in the public interest or that foster a cause and do not seek financial profits. It may involve organizations (Crown corporations, charities, unions, trade associations), people (political candidates), places (resorts, convention centres, industrial sites), and ideas ("stop smoking"), as well as goods and services. See Figure 8-5.

Although nonprofit organizations conduct exchanges, they do not have to be in the form of dollars for goods and services. Politicians request votes in exchange for promises of better government services. Canada Post wants greater use of postal

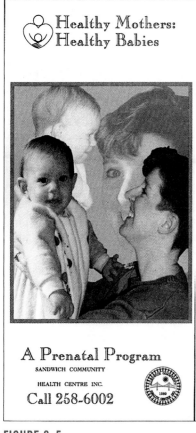

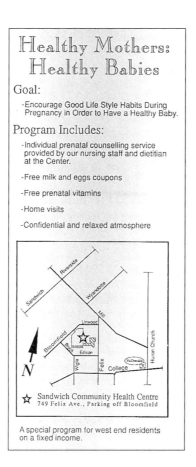

**FIGURE 8-5**

**Nonprofit Marketing in Action**

Nonprofit marketing is very broad in scope and growing in stature. In this leaflet, the Sandwich Community Health Centre in Windsor, Ontario, promotes its "Healthy Mothers: Healthy Babies" prenatal program.

*Reprinted with permission of Sandwich Community Health Centre Inc.*

codes in exchange for improved service and lower rate hikes. The Canadian Red Cross seeks funds to help victims of all kinds of disasters.

Prices charged by nonprofit organizations often have no relation to the cost or value of their services. The Brownies and Girl Guides of Canada sell cookies to raise funds; only part of the price goes to pay for the cookies. In contrast, the price of a chest X-ray at an overseas health clinic may be below cost or free.

Due to its unique attributes, marketing by nonprofit organizations rates a thorough discussion from a product-planning perspective. In the following sections, nonprofit marketing is compared with profit-oriented marketing, a classification system is given for nonprofit marketing, and the extent of nonprofit marketing in the economy is examined along with some examples of nonprofit marketing.

## Nonprofit Versus Profit-Oriented Marketing

There are a number of marketing similarities between nonprofit and profit-oriented firms. In today's uncertain and competitive arena, nonprofit organizations must apply appropriate marketing concepts and strategies if they are to generate adequate support, financial or otherwise.

With both nonprofit and profit-oriented organizations, people usually can choose among competing entities; the benefits provided by competitors differ; con-

*Nonprofit marketing has both similarities with and distinctions from profit-oriented marketing.*

sumer segments may have distinct reasons for their choices; people are lured by the most desirable product positioning; and they are either satisfied or dissatisfied with performance.

A number of years ago, a well-known Calgary company was faced with a 30 per cent decline in demand in spite of offering a high quality product. The firm hired a marketing director who carefully studied Calgary's demographics. He recommended targeting higher income, fewer-children families, and improving customer service with the installation of a dedicated telephone line for regular customers. In addition, a direct-mail and telemarketing campaign of current and past customers was undertaken including a follow-up telephone call to 50 000 individuals who were targeted with a specially designed brochure. What kind of organization was this, a luxury car dealership? No, the nonprofit Calgary Philharmonic Orchestra. The result of the marketing efforts was sales of 11 000 tickets, a sell-out of three-quarters of the orchestra's regular fifty-five concerts, as well as all of the Saturday Night Pop's concerts; and there was a retention rate of 90 per cent of the previous season's ticket subscribers for the next season.[14]

There are also some basic differences in marketing between nonprofit and profit oriented organizations. They are highlighted in Table 8-1 and described in the following paragraphs.

Nonprofit marketing includes organizations, people, places, and ideas, as well as goods and services. It is much more apt to be involved with social programs and ideas than is profit-oriented marketing. Examples include AIDS prevention, recycling, highway safety, family planning, gun control, and energy conservation. The use of marketing to increase the acceptability of social ideas is referred to as **social marketing**.[15]

*Nonprofit marketing is broad in scope and frequently involved with* **social marketing**.

The nonprofit exchange process can include nonmonetary and monetary transactions. Nonmonetary transactions can be votes, volunteers' time, blood donations, and so forth. Monetary transactions can be donations, magazine subscriptions, tuition, and so on. Sometimes, nonprofit marketing does not generate revenues in

---

### TABLE 8-1

### The Basic Differences Between Nonprofit and Profit-Oriented Marketing

| NONPROFIT MARKETING | PROFIT-ORIENTED MARKETING |
|---|---|
| 1. Nonprofit marketing is concerned with organizations, people, places, and ideas, as well as goods and services. | 1. Profit-oriented marketing is largely concerned with goods and services. |
| 2. Exchanges may be nonmonetary or monetary. | 2. Exchanges are generally monetary. |
| 3. Objectives are more complex because success or failure cannot be measured strictly in financial terms. | 3. Objectives are typically stated in terms of sales, profits, and recovery of cash. |
| 4. The benefits of nonprofit services are often not related to consumer payments. | 4. The benefits of profit-oriented marketing are usually related to consumer payments. |
| 5. Nonprofit organizations may be expected or required to serve economically unfeasible market segments. | 5. Profit-oriented organizations seek to serve only those market segments that are profitable. |
| 6. Nonprofit organizations typically have two key target markets: clients and donors. | 6. Profit-oriented organizations typically have one key target market: clients. |

day-to-day exchanges; instead, it may rely on infrequent fundraising efforts. In addition, a successful marketing campaign may actually lose money if services or goods are provided at less than cost. Thus, operating budgets must be large enough to serve the number of anticipated clients, so none are poorly treated or turned away.

Goals may be complex because success or failure cannot be measured in purely financial terms. A nonprofit organization might have this combination of goals: raise $250 000 from government grants, increase client usage, find a cure for a disease, change public attitudes, and raise $750 000 from private donors. Goals must include the number of clients to be served, the amount of service to be rendered, and the quality of service to be provided.

The benefits of nonprofit organizations may not be allotted on the basis of consumer payments. Only a small portion of the population contracts a disease, requires humanitarian services, visits a museum, uses a public library, or goes to a health clinic in a given year; yet the general public pays to find cures, support fellow citizens, or otherwise assist nonprofit organizations. Many times, the people who would benefit most from a nonprofit organization's activities may be the ones least apt to seek or use them. This occurs for libraries, health clinics, remedial programs, and others. With profit-oriented organizations, benefits are usually distributed equitably, based on consumers' direct payments in exchange for goods or services.

*Consumer benefits may not be related to their payments.*

Crown corporations fall generally within the terms of reference of nonprofit organizations. They are owned and operated by the government in the public interest and they are often expected, or required, to serve markets that profit-oriented firms find uneconomical. For example, Canada Post must have rural post offices. Crown corporations are given the same tax treatment as profit organizations but because they serve in the public interest they are usually only marginally profitable at best. This usually gives profit-oriented, privately-owned firms an edge; they can concentrate on the most lucrative market segments.

Profit-oriented firms have one major target market—clients (customers)—to whom they offer goods and services and from whom they receive payment; a typical nonprofit organization has two: **clients**, to whom it offers membership, elected officials, locations, ideas, goods, and services, and **donors**, from whom it receives resources (which may be time from volunteers or money from foundations and individuals). There may be little overlap between clients and donors.

*Nonprofit organizations must satisfy* **clients** *and* **donors**.

Private nonprofit organizations have been granted many legal advantages. These include tax-deductible contributions, exemptions from most sales and real-estate taxes, and reduced postal rates. Profit-oriented firms often feel they are harmed competitively by these legal provisions.[16]

## Classifying Nonprofit Marketing

As shown in Figure 8-6, nonprofit organizations may be classified in terms of tangibility, structure, goals, and constituency. An organization would be classed by a combination of factors. For example, postage stamps for collectors are tangible, distributed by Canada Post (a Crown corporation), intended to reduce Canada Post's usual operating losses, and aimed at the general public.

*The classification of non-profit marketing may be based on tangibility, structure, goal, and constituency.*

As already noted, nonprofit marketing may involve organizations, people, places, ideas, goods, and services. Organizations include foundations, universities, religious institutions, and government; people include politicians and volunteers; places include resorts and industrial centres; ideas include family planning and multiculturalism; goods include postage stamps and professional journals; and services include medical care and education.

Nonprofit organizations may have a government-affiliated, private, or cooperative structure. The federal government markets military service to recruits, and owns and operates Crown corporations (such as the Canadian Broadcasting Corporation,

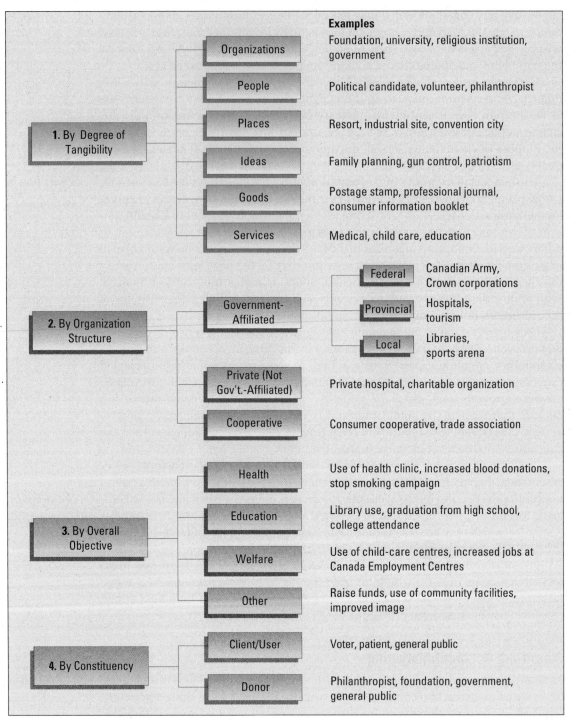

**Examples**

| | |
|---|---|
| Organizations | Foundation, university, religious institution, government |
| People | Political candidate, volunteer, philanthropist |
| Places | Resort, industrial site, convention city |
| Ideas | Family planning, gun control, patriotism |
| Goods | Postage stamp, professional journal, consumer information booklet |
| Services | Medical, child care, education |

**FIGURE 8-6**

**A Classification System for Nonprofit Marketing**

Canada Post, and Atomic Energy of Canada), and other goods and services; provincial governments market tourism and hospitals; local governments market libraries and sports arenas. Government marketing is also used to secure support for tax increases, programs, and legislative initiatives. Private organizations market religions, charities, social services, and other goods and services. They also use marketing to increase membership and donations. Cooperative organizations (such as the Better Business Bureau) aid consumers and businesses; their success depends on securing a large membership base and performing their function efficiently.

Overall nonprofit marketing goals may be divided into health (increase the number of nonsmokers), education (increase usage of the local library), welfare (list more job openings at the Canada Employment Centre office), and other (finding leaders for Scouts Canada) components.

Nonprofit organizations usually require the support of both clients/users and donors. Clients/users are interested in the direct benefits they get by participating in an organization, such as their improved health, education, or welfare. Donors are concerned about the efficiency of operations, success rates, the availability of goods and services, and the recognition of their contributions. For each constituency, an organization must pinpoint its target market. For example, the Easter Seal Society would focus on households with direct mail during the Easter campaign season and seek funds from corporate donors during the rest of the year. Figure 8-7 shows some of the differing interests of clients and donors.

## The Extent of Nonprofit Marketing in the Economy

Millions of organizations and hundreds of millions of people worldwide engage in nonprofit marketing. A survey of Canadians undertaken in 1997 indicated that eight out of every ten individuals aged fifteen and over made direct financial contributions to at least one charitable organization. The most recent data available from Revenue Canada shows that in 1997 individual Canadian tax filers claimed $4.3 billion in charitable donations, representing a 6 per cent increase in donations over 1996. A total of 5.3 million tax filers reported charitable donations, down 3.1 per cent from 1996 donations. These changes are believed to be related to two changes in Revenue Canada's taxation rules, whereby people are now allowed to give a higher percentage of their income to charity, and for married couples the person with the higher income is now allowed to claim all deductions.

The median charitable donation in Canada was $170 in 1997. The most generous donors lived in Newfoundland, which reported the highest median donation ($270), despite having the lowest median total income of $27 900. Canadians who are over 65 years of age are also very generous, with 37 per cent reporting charitable donations in 1997 compared to only 18.8 per cent for 25–34-year-olds. And older people don't merely donate more often, they donate more money too. Tax filers aged 65 and over gave more than $1.4 billion, compared with $310.1 million donated by 25–34-year-olds. Canadians also provided $1.3 billion in indirect support to charitable and nonprofit organizations by buying charity-sponsored raffle or lottery tickets, participating in charity-sponsored bingos and casinos, and

*There are millions of nonprofit organizations in the world and their use of marketing is increasing.*

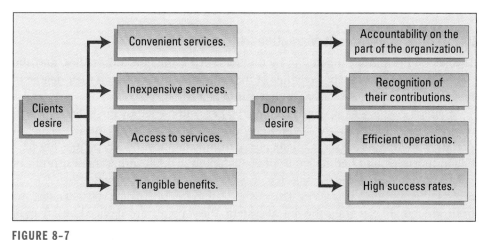

**FIGURE 8-7**

**Clients Versus Donors**

by purchasing goods offered for sale by nonprofits. According to Revenue Canada's definition, charitable donations can be claimed only if they are made to nonprofit organizations.

The Canadian nonprofit sector is substantial—and important with respect to marketing. For example, in 1997 7.5 million Canadians aged fifteen and older (30 per cent) volunteered an average of 149 hours of their time and skills to nonprofit organizations. This proportion could well increase, because in 1999 the Ontario Ministry of Education and Training decided to include a mandatory forty hours of volunteer work as part of the new provincial educational curriculum for Ontario secondary school students.[17]

Nonprofit organizations often use direct-mail solicitation for donations and the Canadian Marketing Association reports that nearly one-third of all revenues reported by direct marketers go to the fundraising efforts of nonprofit organizations.

Employment in Canadian nonprofit sectors such as health and social services, education, and public administration was 2.8 million people in 1995, which represented 25 per cent of industrial employees.

These examples further demonstrate the scope of nonprofit marketing:

- Scouts Canada is just one of a number of Canadian nonprofit organizations that operates an Internet site. It contains a summary of the history of scouting in Canada, a directory of regional council offices, and general information on scouting activities.

- After a survey showed that 92 per cent of the world's population was unaware of its social and humanitarian activities, the United Nations enacted its first major advertising campaign. Ninety advertising agencies in thirty nations donated their time, and they sought U.S.$53 million in free media space.

- The Canadian Council on Smoking and Health annually sponsors National Non-Smoking Week, a key part of a national public education campaign that has these five objectives: to educate Canadians about the dangers of tobacco use; to prevent people from becoming addicted to tobacco; to help smokers quit; to ensure a smoke-free environment for non-smokers; and to help Canada become a smoke-free society.

- An exhibit of dresses worn by the late Princess Diana of England entitled "Dresses for Humanity" raised $140 000 for four Toronto charities. The exhibition, hosted by The Bay department store, involved a showing of twenty dresses once worn by the Princess. The money raised was divided equally among the Casey House Hospice, the Corrine Boyer Fund for Ovarian Cancer Treatment and Research, the Marvelle Koffler Breast Clinic at Mount Sinai Hospital, and Operation Herbie at the Hospital for Sick Children.[18]

## Illustrations of Nonprofit Marketing

This section examines marketing by Canada Post, Canadian universities, and the United Way of Canada. The activities of these organizations differ in their degree of tangibility, structure, objectives, and constituencies.

Canada Post is a Crown corporation 100 per cent owned by the federal government. It was created by the federal government in 1981, when the Canada Post Corporation Act was passed. Canada Post currently employs 63 529 people, has $2.7 billion in assets, and had revenues of $5.08 billion in 1998 with a modest profit of $112.5 million. It handled 9.2 billion pieces of mail in 1998 and provided 20 000 retail outlets to access postal services. The postal system in Canada has 900 000 locations from which mail can enter the postal system; these points are serviced by a fleet of over 6000 vehicles.

Canada Post's Business Mission is stated as follows:

We are in business to serve all Canadians, businesses and organizations, through the secure delivery of messages, information and packages to any address in Canada or the world, at a level of quality and value that makes customers want to repeat the experience.

Canada Post faces intense competition in the most lucrative parts of the market from alternative document and information transfer services (such as private couriers, fax machines, and direct funds transfer), and from telecommunications firms (many of which provide e-mail services).

Canada Post is constrained because as a Crown corporation it must deliver all mail, no matter how uneconomical. Consequently, Canada Post is at greater risk of losing money on its operations than are private corporations. The firm's operations are also subject to intense government scrutiny. A recent report on Canada Post's mandate stated, "Canada Post was created as a Crown corporation with a certain view of the balance it should strike between public policy responsibilities and commercial orientation."

Canada Post competes against private sector firms in order to gain revenues to fund its core operations. The firm is diversifying to reduce the impact of reduced mail volume, which is likely to occur as a result of such alternative communications vehicles as e-mail and cheaper telephone usage. It has enacted several new approaches to marketing its services, comprising a mix of continuing and new offerings, extensive advertising, and different ways of pricing. For example, one of Canada Post's new ventures involves a pilot project with UBI for interactive TV service in Quebec. Canada Post offers services (Lettermail, electronic, and hybrid services) in the communications market, and advertising services such as addressed and unaddressed Admail. It also offers physical distribution services through its Regular Parcel, Xpresspost, and Priority Courier offerings.

Canada Post's subsidiary, Purolator Courier, competes head-to-head with FedEx and UPS and operates as an autonomous unit that can select its service areas so that it can operate profitably. Canada Post has invested a lot of money into technology to operate Purolator, which in 1998 increased its shipment volumes by 10.7 per cent and made $849 million in sales revenue.

In order to operate more effectively on the international scene Canada Post has a subsidiary called Canada Post Systems Management Limited, which has completed over eighty projects in thirty-eight countries. This international consulting firm markets business solutions to postal administrations around the world. For example, the firm signed a $4.3 million contract with Guatemala to provide postal operations advisory services in 1998.

Canada Post has become very customer-service conscious. It can be reached through a 1-800 number, on the Internet (www.canpost.ca/), and of course, by mail. The comments, complaints, and suggestions that arise from these contacts are analyzed via enquiry management systems. The goal of the corporation is to respond as quickly as possible, since the feedback is considered important in improving its services. In this regard, Canada Post strives to achieve its objective of being a customer-driven organization.[19]

Colleges and universities realize that the population trends (such as smaller households and a relatively low birth rate) in many industrialized nations have been affecting their enrolment pools, especially with the numbers of 18–24-year-olds falling in some areas. Government funding of post-secondary education has also been severely cut in recent years, and while new initiatives have been promised for the future, these aren't expected to reach former levels of funding. The result is that universities must get more of their operating funds from students through tuition increases and from private donors. In 1981/82 tuition fees accounted for about 8 per cent of the total operating revenue of Canadian universities, but by 1997/98 tuition fees accounted for 14.5 per cent.

# ETHICS AND TODAY'S MARKETER

## How Can Cause Marketers Avoid Crass Commercialism?

Being a good corporate citizen involves giving something back to the community. But a business that donates money may be viewed cynically by consumers if they perceive its sole motivation to be enhancement of its own image. While the motivation of donors usually doesn't affect how far their donated dollars go, organizations that benefit from the donations don't want to be viewed as the puppets or dupes of profit-making enterprises. Still, what's the use of being a good corporate citizen if the general public doesn't know about it? Clearly, it's a double-edged sword.

According to Jacqueline Foley of *Marketing Magazine*, charity organizations and nonprofits need to avoid the following pitfalls when seeking a corporate partner:

- Compromising their mission or values.
- Not setting clear objectives and expectations for what the partnership will accomplish.
- Not looking at the partnership as an integrated element of a larger marketing strategy.
- Setting up a bad match that undermines the organization's credibility.
- Lack of attention to the return on investment that a partnership will bring (partnerships always have a human resource cost to them that many charities don't measure).

Kids Help seems to have avoided these pitfalls, and so has its corporate partner, Bell Canada. Since 1990 it's operated the national "Kids Help Phone," a service that's readily available for kids who are lost, in trouble, or have run away; with one phone call they can find out how to get the help they need. In 1996 Kids Help established a Web site to give children one more communication vehicle to use.

This project has involved an investment of $1.5 million for Bell Canada over the last three years. It does have its logo displayed (but not overtly) on all printed materials associated with Kids Help Phone. Bell Canada also donates Bell QuickChange Cards as prizes at fundraising events. However, the firm doesn't feel that its involvement manifests "crass commercialism," but rather that this kind of project fits into its line of business very well. And as for Kids Help, where could it find a better partner to offer a phone service than the phone company itself?

Go out and find two or three cause-related marketing examples, and identify the commercial partner and the nonprofit or charity partner. Consider the pitfalls mentioned by Jacqueline Foley, and discuss the degree to which the organizations involved have managed to avoid these.

Sources: Based on Astrid Van Den Broek, "Benevolent Dictators," *Marketing Magazine* (September 7, 1998), pp. 14–16; and Jacqueline Foley, "Picking a Philanthropic Partner," *Marketing Magazine* (September 7, 1998), p. 16.

**KIDS HELP**
www.kidshelp.sympatico.ca

As a result, Canadian post-secondary institutions have found themselves in competition with one another more than ever before—and have realized that they need to undertake marketing strategies to increase demand for their services. Some have even made high-profile programs totally self-funding. For example, for the 1997/98 year students enrolled in the two-year Executive MBA program at Queen's University were being charged $52 000!

The number of university students enrolled in full-time undergraduate studies in Canada in the fall of 1998 was 507 195. Full-time undergraduate enrolment has been relatively steady at between 500 000 and 504 000 during the last half of the 1990s, but part-time enrolment fell for the sixth straight year with a total of 200 050 students in the fall of 1998. Graduate student enrolment was 76 596 full-time students and 38 573 part-time students.

Universities have been forced to hike tuition fees as a result of cutbacks in government funding. During the 1997/98 academic year tuition fees at Canadian universities rose an average of 8.7 per cent, from $2867 to $3117 for a typical arts student. In Ontario, Canada's most populous province, fees rose an average of 10.1 per cent, from $2936 to $3234, whereas Quebec was the most affordable with tuition fees of $1726, a negligible $1 increase from the previous year. This price is available only to Quebec residents; out-of-province students pay an additional fee of $40 per credit. Out-of-province fees haven't been a feature of post-secondary education in Canada prior to this, although in the U.S. it's common practice to charge out-of-state premiums. When one considers all the cuts in federal funding to education and the fact that a large portion of the cost burden is borne by provincial taxpayers, it's a wonder that provinces haven't levied such fees before. Still, the actions in Quebec do take market forces into consideration; the out-of-province fees bring its educational costs in line with other provinces, so that out-of-province students aren't dissuaded from studying in Quebec because of tuition differentials. On the other hand, in-province students are encouraged to remain in Quebec to study.

Canadian universities are actively seeking foreign students, especially those from the U.S. The University of Guelph used a direct mail campaign involving 50 000 brochures mailed to American students in the northeastern U.S near the Canadian border. The brochure was entitled "So you think you know Canada, eh?" and was designed to dispel myths about Canada and encourage the students to come here to study, in particular at the University of Guelph. The response rate of inquiries from the brochure was 10 per cent, but enrolment response has not yet been identified. In 1998 the University of Windsor also targeted southeastern Michigan with a direct mail campaign to attract American students. Advertising that the University of Windsor was just across the border and that the tuition fee was being lowered from U.S.$8000 to $3500, the university was able to acquire thirty more U.S. applicants than in previous years. The ability to selectively lower fees for foreign students is a recent occurrence for Ontario universities, and follows the 1997 deregulation of tuition fees by the provincial government. This fee deregulation activity is expected to generate a great deal of competitive activity all across the nation. Quebec also offers international students a good deal: it has reciprocal agreements with forty-nine countries whereby students from Quebec and these nations pay the same fees for tuition.

Many universities are actively seeking nontraditional students. Today, 32 per cent of Canadian university students attend part-time; many of them over twenty-five years old. This market demands convenient sites and classes not infringing on work hours. The Division of Continuing Education at the University of Windsor is specifically designed to provide academic advice and support to part-time and non-traditional students. This division funds and coordinates the course offerings at campuses in Chatham and Sarnia, Ontario as well as locations in Windsor that are off the main campus. The university also has a distance education program through which students may obtain a Bachelor of Commerce degree as well as take credit courses toward other degrees.

Traditional students are also being vigorously sought. Schools are no longer relying on the usual recruitment tools of high school visits, open houses, calendars, posters, and brochures, but are pursuing mass media campaigns. For example, the University of Western Ontario distributed an eight-page glossy colour tabloid in *The Globe and Mail* to attract students. The tabloid discussed Western's 118-year history as a leading Canadian university and presented its educational disciplines as continuing its leading-edge tradition. Virtually every university maintains a Web site, and several distribute to high schools recruiting films or videocassettes that cost tens of thousands of dollars (and up) to produce.

This heightened use of marketing isn't limited to recruiting undergraduate students. Universities are seeking to retain their student populations longer by encouraging growth of their graduate programs. *Canadian Business Magazine* routinely carries advertising for Executive MBA programs offered by Queen's University and the University of Western Ontario. The University of Windsor has a co-op MBA program targeted specifically at students with non-business degrees and no work experience, and has produced posters, ads, and brochures based on the theme "Earn As You Learn."[20] See Figure 8-8.

The United Way is a global nonprofit organization, with Centraides in over thirty countries in the world. The Canadian national headquarters of the United Way in Ottawa is affiliated with 126 local United Way Centraides whose annual fundraising efforts yielded $266 million in 1997. Most donations come from deductions made from workers' pay cheques. (In contrast, such organizations as the Salvation Army generate most of their donations from non-workplace sources.) These 126 local organizations used the money they raised to directly fund 4300 different agencies. They also provided funding to another 10 000 organizations via donor direct giving.

The United Way of America, headquartered in Alexandria, Virginia, supports 1400 United Ways across the U.S. These organizations raised U.S.$3.4 billion in 1997, which was allocated to community agencies. Outside of North America, United Way International fundraising organizations raised and allocated over U.S.$525 million in 1997.

The agencies that the United Way-Centraides fund provide the following:

- Services to families.
- Services to youth and children.
- Services to senior citizens.
- Services for the disabled.

**FIGURE 8-8**

**The Marketing of Higher Education**

*Reprinted with permission of University of Windsor, graphic design by Steve Daigle.*

## MARKETING IN THE THIRD MILLENNIUM

### Becoming a Global Destination for Financial Information[21]

**C**anada's service economy is expected to continue to grow in the third millennium, and one of the potential high-growth offerings will be online information services. Entrepreneurs who are first to develop quality services that people will purchase stand to make a lot of money. Scott Blue is one of these entrepreneurs. He hopes to earn his fortune by operating a cheap, Internet-based financial services firm that provides investor information to people around the world. At the moment, Blue is the CEO in charge of Stox.com Inc., a Vancouver-based firm that provides real-time stock quotes to people via the Internet. The firm used to deliver its quotes directly to customers' computers through cables, telephone lines, and radio signals, but this technology limited the firm's business to customers in the Vancouver area. Now it will deliver its services through the universal medium of the Internet.

Earning money hasn't been easy for Stox.com; it hasn't been profitable in the last five years. In fact, the prospects for future profits must be considered questionable, since even a "cheap" Internet-based financial information provider will struggle in a market where stock quotes and financial information are abundantly available for free. So how does one compete with free? Blue feels that depth and detail of information is what investors will pay for. For example, most free stock quotes provide only the highest and lowest bids for a particular equity, whereas Stox.com plans to provide five quotes to investors along with order size information. (Order size is of particular value to investors trading in low-activity stocks.) Stox.com has secured permission to broadcast live quotes from every major North American stock exchange, and is seeking to carry quotes from every stock

exchange in the world, including London, Hong Kong, and even Istanbul. Aside from stock quotes in depth, and coverage of every exchange, Stox.com also plans to offer analysts' reports, historical data for the previous ten years, news releases, insider trading reports, other regulatory filings, and live video news. Subscribers will be able to flag price moves on selected stocks, and to be contacted via telephone, fax, pager, or e-mail when a stock hits a certain prearranged price. Subscribers will enjoy all these services for the low price of $50 per month.

Stox.com is planning on targeting individual rather than professional investors, but also hopes to license its service to brokerage houses that want to offer online services on their Web sites. The key behavioural factor that Stox.com is banking on is the desire by individual investors to manage their own portfolios. The estimated break-even for the service at $50 a month is 50 000 users worldwide ($2.5 million). But the prospect of achieving this number quickly is very uncertain. For example, January, 1999 performance information on Data Broadcasting Corporation (DBC), a competing Internet stock information service provider in the U.S., indicated that in less than a year it had acquired 8000 Internet subscribers. If this level represents the tip of the iceberg Stox.com may well be in for a great future, but if these subscribers represent the cream of the crop, it may find itself offering a service that few people want.

Finally, even if people want the service, with so many potential competitors available Stox.com will have to find a way to cut through the clutter on the Internet. It isn't enough to have the best service—marketers must still put together the rest of the marketing mix!

- Help for the disadvantaged.
- Social and community planning.

The burden on the services funded by United Way Centraides promises to grow larger as the federal and provincial governments in Canada continue to restrain or download such social programs as welfare, unemployment insurance, old age security, the Canada Pension Plan, and medical care. Fortunately, the United Way Centraides are finding some unique sources of support.

**UNITED WAY**
www.uwc-cc.ca

For years, the United Way has had an outstanding marketing orientation. In the U.S. it's well known for its long-held association with the National Football League (NFL) and the touching ads that appear during NFL games. In Canada, the United Way has conducted cross-promotions with The Bay stores to raise funds. The Bay has donated a percentage of sales made on certain days (called "Bay Day X") to the United Way. A Web site has also been established to inform the public as well as the various United Way Centraides as to what the United Way of Canada is doing.

Employees in affiliated chapters are trained in marketing; yearly marketing and advertising conferences are held. Affiliated chapters present United Way home videos, films, and slide-show programs to potential contributors and volunteers. The United Way of America published a book, *Competitive Marketing*, so that all United Way chapters and other charitable groups could learn from it. The United Way's present situation can be summed up thusly: "Keen competition and urgent need cry out for creativity. For an organization that has thrived on automatic generosity, that is a challenge."[22]

# SUMMARY

**1.** *To examine the scope of goods and services, and explain how goods and services may be categorized* Goods marketing encompasses the sales of durable and nondurable physical products; service marketing involves goods rental, goods alteration, maintenance, or repair, and personal services. In Canada, consumer expenditures on nondurable goods are slightly higher than those for durable goods. Services account for a very large share of the GDP in industrialized nations, 67 per cent of Canada's GDP, and a smaller share in developing and less-developed nations. Both final-consumer and business services have seen significant growth in recent years. The scope of services is sometimes underestimated due to the hidden service sector.

With a goods/services continuum, products can be positioned on a scale from pure goods to goods/services combinations to pure services. Much can be learned by studying this continuum, including its use for final and organizational consumer products, the presence of unique marketing opportunities, and the changing relationship between sellers and buyers as pure goods become goods/services combinations. Both goods- and services-oriented firms need to identify core and peripheral services.

Goods can be classed by market, product durability, value added, company goal, degree of regulation, distribution channel length, and extent of customer contact. Services can be classed by market, level of tangibility, service provider skill, service provider goals, degree of regulation, labour intensiveness, and amount of customer contact. A firm would be categorized on the basis of a combination of these factors.

**2.** *To discuss the special considerations in the marketing of services* Services are generally less tangible, more perishable, less separable from their provider, and more variable in quality than goods that are sold. The effect of these factors is greatest for personal services. Service firms need to enact strategies that enable consumers to perceive their offerings more tangibly, make their offerings less perishable, encourage consumers to seek them out but enable multiple employees to be viewed as competent, and make performance as efficient and consistent as possible. Such approaches as the industrialization of services, the service blueprint, and gap analysis enable service firms to better devise and implement marketing plans by improving their performance.

**3.** *To look at the use of marketing by goods versus services firms and provide illustrations of service marketing* Many service firms have lagged behind manufacturers in the use of marketing because of their small size, the larger geographic coverage of goods-oriented companies, their technical emphasis, less competition and the lack of need for marketing, the high esteem of consumers for certain service providers, past bans on advertising, a dislike of marketing by some service professionals, and the reluctance of some manufacturers to view services as profit centres. Yet, for a number of reasons, this has been changing and the marketing of services is now expanding greatly.

**4.** *To distinguish between nonprofit and profit-oriented marketing* Nonprofit marketing is conducted by organizations and people that operate for the public good or to foster a cause and not for financial profits. It is both similar to and different from profit-oriented marketing. These are some of the differences: Nonprofit marketing is more apt to involve organizations, people, places, and ideas. Nonprofit firms' exchanges do not have to involve money, and goals can be hard to formulate. The benefits of nonprofit firms may be distributed unequally, and economically unfeasible market segments may have to be served. Two target markets must be satisfied by nonprofit organizations: clients and donors.

**5.** *To describe a classification system for nonprofit marketing, the role of nonprofit marketing in the economy, and applications of nonprofit marketing* Nonprofit organizations can be classed on the basis of tangibility, organization structure, objectives, and constituency. A nonprofit organization would be categorized by a combination of these factors. Worldwide, there are millions of organizations and people engaged in nonprofit marketing. Nonprofit organizations play a key role in the Canadian economy. Seven and a half million Canadians 15 years of age and older volunteered an average of 149 hours of their time to nonprofits in 1997. Funding for nonprofits comes from corporations, government, and individuals. In 1997 5.3 million individual Canadian tax filers claimed $4.3 billion in charitable donations on their taxes. The marketing practices of Canada Post, Canadian universities, and the United Way of Canada are highlighted.

## KEY TERMS

**goods marketing** (p. 215)

**durable goods** (p. 215)

**nondurable goods** (p. 215)

**service marketing** (p. 215)

**rented-goods services** (p. 215)

**owned-goods services** (p. 215)

**nongoods services** (p. 215)

**hidden service sector** (p. 215)

**goods/services continuum** (p. 216)

**core services** (p. 217)

**peripheral services** (p. 217)

**intangibility of services** (p. 220)

**perishability of services** (p. 220)

**inseparability of services** (p. 220)

**variability in service quality** (p. 220)

**industrialization of services** (p. 223)

**service blueprint** (p. 223)

**service gap** (p. 223)

**nonprofit marketing** (p. 226)

**social marketing** (p. 228)

**clients** (p. 229)

**donors** (p. 229)

## REVIEW QUESTIONS

**1.** Differentiate among rented-goods services, owned-goods services, and nongoods services.

**2.** What is a goods/services continuum? Why should firms be aware of this concept?

**3.** Distinguish between core and peripheral services. What is the marketing role of each?

**4.** How can a service be positioned more tangibly?

**5.** Describe how hard, soft, and hybrid technologies may be used to industrialize services.

**6.** Why have service firms lagged behind manufacturers in the development and use of marketing strategies?

**7.** What are some of the similarities and differences in the marketing efforts of nonprofit and profit-oriented organizations?

**8.** When is an organization engaged in social marketing?

**9.** Discuss the factors that may be used to classify nonprofit marketing.

**10.** How do the goals of clients and donors differ?

# DISCUSSION QUESTIONS

1. Present a goods/services continuum related to entertainment. Discuss the implications of this continuum for a firm interested in developing a marketing plan in the entertainment field.

2. Give several ways that a car rental agency can match demand and supply on days following holidays.

3. Draw and discuss a service blueprint for an insurance broker dealing with small-business clients.

4. Present five objectives that could be used to evaluate the effectiveness of cause-related marketing.

5. Discuss several innovative fundraising programs for the Canadian Heart and Stroke Foundation.

## CASE STUDY

# H&R Block: Helping Consumers Be Less Fearful of Taxes

One of the most frequently used services in Canada and the U.S. is tax preparation—and no firm's name is more widely known for this than H&R Block. It earned U.S.$1.9 billion in revenue in 1998, with profits of $392 million.

H&R Block has other interests, including a mortgage unit and a financial services unit, which offer such services as annuities and mutual funds. H&R Block offers essentially a seasonal service, but it needs to maintain year-round premises in a number of locations in order to store records and maintain its presence. As such, the firm has been developing other services and offerings to cover some of its costs and exploit its customer relationships.

One such initiative involved owning an 80 per cent stake in the Internet service provider American Online. H&R Block recently sold off this interest, however, because American Online's business was too unrelated to its main thrust. A more promising initiative has been undertaken in Canada, where H&R Block has more than 1100 offices operating under the names H&R Block and Financial Stop.

Financial Stop is a new service with offices in every Canadian province except Quebec. Designed to overcome the seasonal cycle that characterizes so much of H&R Block's business, Financial Stop offices provide cheque cashing services, factoring services, and other cash convenience services such as money orders, money transfers, foreign exchange, faxes, and phone cards.

Still, the bread and butter of H&R Block is its tax preparation services. The firm has 125 full-time employees in Canada, but at tax time more than 8000 tax associates are employed to assist people in preparing their taxes. It offers regular tax preparation for all types of tax returns, including business, corporate, farm, personal, U.S., and estate/trust tax filing; cash-back tax refund discounting; electronic filing of income tax returns directly with Revenue Canada; and affordable, on-site tax preparation for groups. H&R Block will prepare your tax return at your home or office; and provide home or office pick-up and delivery of tax returns. It also provides professional monthly bookkeeping and small business accounting; and assistance with the guidelines for clients who pay or receive child support.

H&R Block thinks of its service in much broader terms than just simple tax preparation. The firm really understands its customers when it comes to taxes, and undertakes research to maintain this understanding. Its advertising agency Young and Rubicam recently researched some of the attitudes of Canadian taxpayers. They found the following: "Some people hate filling out forms. Some hate getting things wrong. Some hate the government. Some hate taxes. And an awful lot of them are just totally intimidated by the whole bureaucratic/arithmetic pile of indecipherable goo sitting in front of them every April." The conclusion drawn was pretty obvious: the majority of people feel intimidated by the tax preparation process.

Consequently, Young and Rubicam developed a promotional campaign to make people more aware of H&R Block and to encourage them to use its services at tax time. The campaign theme was "H&R Block Take the Fear Out of Taxes." The primary way in which H&R Block fulfils this campaign promise is by offering the following guarantee:

> If your income tax return is audited, H&R Block will appear with you at that audit at no extra cost and explain how your return was prepared, even though we cannot act as your legal representative.
>
> Our employee training and system of safeguards are carefully designed to ensure the accuracy of your return. If we make any error in the preparation of your tax return that costs you any interest or penalty on additional taxes due, although we do not assume the liability for the additional taxes, we will reimburse you for the interest and penalty.

## Questions

1. Explain why service perishability is a particularly acute problem for a firm like H&R Block. Discuss some of the steps it has taken to reduce the perishability of its offerings. Can you suggest any other related steps that H&R Block could take?

2. What is the core service that H&R Block offers its customers? What are some of its peripheral services? In your answer discuss how H&R Block's guarantee makes its service more tangible for customers.

3. Explain what industrialization of services means. Do the services of H&R Block lend themselves to this? Why or why not?

4. Identify the customer segments that H&R Block serves and identify their likely needs and wants with respect to H&R Block's services. Are there any unserved segments or needs that the firm could satisfy?

**H&R BLOCK**
www.hrblock.ca

Sources Based on Fortune 1000 Ranked Within Industries, "H&R Block," *Fortune* (April 26, 1999), p. F-73; John Farquhar, "Sweaty Palms at Tax Time," *Marketing Magazine* (June 21, 1999), p. 26; Hoovers, "H&R Block Company Capsule," Hoovers Online, www.hoovers.com; and H&R Block Canada Web site, www.hrblock.ca (July 1999).

## CASE STUDY

# A Service Firm and a Nonprofit Firm Come Together: CIBC and Girl Guide Cookies

Nonprofit organizations often have difficulty finding successful fundraising and marketing tools to support their operations. However, Canada's Girl Guides has developed one winning approach with its annual cookie sales. There are very few Canadians who haven't at least once bought or eaten Girl Guide cookies. The Canadian Imperial Bank of Commerce (CIBC) recently agreed to sponsor the Girl Guides and their cookie operations.

How does an organization like the CIBC get hooked up with the Girl Guides or undertake any other sponsorship? In an article in *Marketing Magazine* Tricia Barry, general manager of the youth/emerging customer segment at CIBC Wealth Management in Toronto, explained how the relationship came about. According to Barry, the CIBC considered the following factors in selecting the Girl Guides:

- Strategic fit with CIBC's overall goals and objectives
- Ability to achieve youth customer segment marketing objectives
- Tangible and intangible benefits of the proposal, such as goodwill, reputation, and cost/potential revenue
- Organizational impact
- Business risks (if any)

The CIBC feels that a consistent process should be followed at all times in selecting potential nonprofit sponsorship partners. Many large firms receive continual sponsorship requests and it's important that these be handled through some type of logical process so that the firm can evaluate them. The CIBC goes through a series of steps where it asks questions about the potential partner. The first step considers whether the organization's objectives fit with those of the CIBC. The CIBC asks the following related questions: Is there a logical link between the organizations? Is there a strong likelihood of future opportunities by virtue of the linkage?

The second step involves looking at the nonprofit organization's proposal. Does it complement CIBC's core strate-

gies? Does it move CIBC closer to its goals? Is the proposal relevant, exciting, and/or groundbreaking? Does it offer something exclusive?

The third step considers the economic viability of the opportunity. What are the costs versus the benefits? How do various proposals compare on costs versus potential revenues? Are there better uses for the investment?

The final step looks at the potential impact on CIBC's operations. Will the proposal require any employee training or retraining? Will new operational processes be required?

CIBC looked at the Girl Guides' request for sponsorship and then considered its key questions. The deliberations revealed that the sponsorship was a good fit for the following reasons: The Girl Guides sell about 7 million boxes of cookies on an annual basis. These boxes are sold to about 3 million Canadian households (about 30 per cent of all households). CIBC could put its logo on these boxes for both the year 2000 and 2001 and thus reach these Canadian households at less cost than six three-quarter page ads in a typical magazine.

The Girl Guides are a youth organization and the CIBC was seeking to develop a relationship with young people. Further, the Girl Guides is a well-respected organization with a long history and strong traditions. A direct sales estimate from the efforts couldn't be made, but this isn't unusual for any goodwill or image campaign. The CIBC didn't see any major impact on its operations. There was some concern that the CIBC might be called a "cookie monster" and possibly face a backlash from conservative elements among its customers and Girl Guide members who might not view sponsorships favourably. However, CIBC saw the whole relationship as being win-win for itself and the Girl Guides.

### Questions

1. The case discusses CIBC's process of choosing a nonprofit partner for sponsorship. Outline the process that the Girl Guides or any other nonprofit organizations could undertake to select a business partner for sponsorship.

2. Two service organizations came together to help with fundraising by selling a tangible product. Discuss how their thinking might have to change in order to make this offering.

3. The CIBC demonstrates an interesting process for selecting sponsorships. Should the same criteria be applied to both for-profit and nonprofit partners? Why or why not? Outline a separate process for each based on the process provided in the case.

4. Discuss the ethical concerns that might arise for the CIBC and the Girl Guides as a result of accepting sponsorships. In your view, how serious are these concerns and at what level do you feel they would necessitate a break in a partnership?

**CANADIAN IMPERIAL BANK OF COMMERCE**
www.cibc.com/index.html

**GIRL GUIDES OF CANADA**
www.girlguides.ca

Source: Based on Tricia Barry, "Smart Cookies," *Marketing Magazine* (May 31, 1999), pp. 11, 14.

Smile!

*Fido's got a treat for you.*

## CHAPTER 9

# — Conceiving, Developing, and Managing Products

## Chapter Objectives

1. To detail the importance of new products and describe why new products fail

2. To present the stages in the new-product planning process

3. To define and distinguish among branding terms, to examine the importance of branding, and to study the key branding decisions that must be made

4. To define and distinguish among packaging terms and to examine the importance of packaging

5. To analyze the growth and maturity of products, including the adoption process, the diffusion process, and extension strategies, and to examine product deletion decisions and strategies

*Courtesy of Fido*

**FIDO**
www.fido.ca

**P**eople often say that talk is cheap, but that doesn't seem to be the case when you look at your phone bill. Still, no matter where you are these days it seems everyone is talking on wireless phones. People are talking in their cars, in the malls, while watching the ball game, cruising under Niagara Falls, and even during university lectures! And for most business people today, it's difficult to remember what life was like before cellular telephones made it possible to stay in touch with their offices and customers no matter where they are. While Statistics Canada reports that only about one-fifth of Canadian households have a cellular phone, Clearnet of Toronto wants to make talk so cheap that everyone will go completely wireless.

Since Clearnet is targeting people who have yet to embrace the new technology it's presenting the product as user-friendly, and this includes offering its phones and service without a contract. Clearnet wants to convince people that its PCS service can replace wire line telephone service completely. It's offering unlimited weekend and evening calling for $45 per month. The market potential for Clearnet is certainly large, since virtually every household in Canada has at least one telephone, with 37 per cent having three or more. The use of cellular phones varies from province to province; 26 per cent of the households in Alberta have wireless communication, while only 8 per cent do in Newfoundland.

Because the business market for cellular phones is well tapped, new adoptions will be related to price decreases and a focus on home use. The 1998 sales of cellular phones were estimated at 2.2 million units, most of which were expected to be for household use. The market is competitive, with Cantel AT&T, Bell, Microcell Fido, and Clearnet being the main service competitors. And while cell phones appeal to the business market for their productivity, a different appeal must be used for the home market. Initially, cell phones were sold for home use as peace-of-mind, emergency devices. Both Bell Mobility and Cantel have used "emergency" appeals to encourage users to adopt their products. However, now that the market is well developed, Clearnet is taking the approach that cell phones are a commodity and will serve in place of the traditional wired telephone.

That the cellular telephone is an evolved market is also well illustrated by the development of the phones themselves. Motorola, Nokia, and Ericsson are the hardware manufacturers that sell through service providers like Bell, Cantel, Clearnet, and Fido. Motorola is offering phones with smaller and lighter batteries that provide more talk time; and Nokia even plans to offer cell phones with replaceable, colour-coordinated covers. Built-in alarm clocks, AM-FM radios, and video games are other popular additions. As well as being reliable, light, and easy to carry, the cell phone is becoming an all-purpose utility device and fashion accessory. In the last sixty years the realm of fiction and TV gave us the Dick Tracy wrist radio, Agent 86 Maxwell Smart's shoe phone, and the Star Trek communicator. Extremely expensive cell phones equivalent to the wrist radio exist today, but are novelties. An inexpensive version for the masses is still a product for the future.[1]

In this chapter, we will study how new products are developed, the factors causing rapid or slow growth for new products, how to manage mature products, and what to do when existing products falter. In addition, the various types of brand designations, key branding decisions, the basic functions of packaging, key packaging decisions, and selected criticisms of packaging are discussed. As our cell phone discussion illustrates, it takes a lot of work—and persistence—to stay ahead.

## Overview

While any product combines tangible and intangible features to satisfy consumer needs, a **new product** involves a modification of an existing product or an innovation the consumer perceives as meaningful. To succeed, a new product must have desirable attributes, be unique, and have its features communicated to consumers. Marketing support is therefore necessary.[2]

**Modifications** are alterations in or extensions of a firm's existing products and include new models, styles, colours, features, and brands. **Minor innovations** are items not previously marketed by a firm that have been marketed by others. For example, many financial institutions are offering credit card holders "affinity credit cards," which are allied with a particular business, a nonprofit institution, or worthy cause, such as the Royal Bank's World Wildlife Fund Visa Card. The credit card company agrees to donate a small percentage (0.1-0.25) of purchases made with such cards to the cause they endorse. Since different customers will endorse different causes, institutions can segment their customers according to different affinities and thus offer a variety of cards.[3]

**Major innovations** are items not previously sold by any firm (like the first cellular telephone). If a firm works with major innovations, the costs, risks, and time required for profitability all rise. Overall, most new products are modifications; few are major innovations.

New products may be conceived of and developed by a company itself or purchased from another firm. A company may buy a firm, buy a specific product, or sign a licensing agreement (whereby it pays an inventor a royalty fee based on sales). Acquisitions may reduce risks and time demands, but they rely on outsiders for innovations and may require large investments.

Early in a product's life, there is usually strong sales growth, as more people purchase and repurchase. This is an exciting time; and if a product is popular, it can last for quite a while. Later, the market becomes more saturated and competition intensifies. At that point, a firm can maintain high sales by adding features that provide convenience and durability, using new materials in construction, offering a range of models, stressing new packaging, and/or adding customer services. It can also reposition a product, enter untapped geographic markets, demonstrate new uses, offer new brands, set lower prices, use new media, and/or appeal to new segments. At some point, however, firms must decide whether these items have outlived their usefulness and should be dropped.

When conceiving, developing, and managing its products, a firm needs to make and enact a variety of decisions regarding the brand and package used with each item. A **brand** is a name, term, design, symbol, or any other feature that distinguishes the goods and services of one seller from those of other sellers. A **package** is a container used to protect, promote, transport, and/or identify a product.[4] It may consist of a product's physical container, an outer label, and/or inserts.

*Product planning involves* **new products** *and existing products.*

*New products may be* **modifications**, **minor innovations**, *or* **major innovations**.

*Brands identify a firm's products;* **packages** *are product containers that serve many functions.*

## The Importance of New Products

A firm's product policy should be future-oriented and recognize that products, no matter how successful, tend to be mortal—they usually cannot sustain a peak level of sales and profits indefinitely. "Innovation can give a company a competitive advantage and

*New products offer differential advantages.*

*New products lead to sales growth or stability.*

**POWERBAR**
www.powerbar.com

**BLACK & DECKER**
www.blackanddecker.com/

*New products can take time.*

*New products can increase profits and control.*

*Risk may be lessened through diversity.*

*New products may improve distribution.*

profits, but nothing lasts forever. Success brings on imitators, who respond with superior features, lower prices, or some other new way to draw customers. Time ultimately renders nearly all advantages obsolete."[5] So, replacements should be constantly planned and a balanced product portfolio pursued—by both small and large firms.

Introducing new products is important for several reasons. Desirable differential advantages can be attained. For example, the Seiko Kinetic Quartz watch is the first quartz watch that does not require a battery or have to be wound. It is advertised as "No more batteries. No more winding. No more hassles." Goodyear's "smart tire" for trucks is embedded with a computer chip allowing drivers to easily see the wear and air pressure of tires; this improves tire life and fuel efficiency.

New products may be needed for continued growth, which is why Sony Mobilecomm America has launched a new line of car amplifiers and speakers called XPlod. This new sound system puts out 164 dB of sound, and is targeted at 16- to 35-year-old single males. The targeting and product positioning is illustrated by the promotional line, "My girlfriend's father hates my music. I like that."[6]

For firms with cyclical or seasonal sales, new products can stabilize revenues and costs. Union Carbide manufactures medical-testing equipment, to reduce its dependence on cyclical chemicals. Black & Decker has cut back on lawn mowers and looks for new opportunities in less seasonal products (such as power tools for the home).

Planning for growth must allow for the time it takes for a new product to move from idea stage to commercialization. For instance, in 1983 Canadian Brian Maxwell came up with the idea for a food bar for exercise enthusiasts, which would let them fuel for long workouts while circumventing the stomach problems that often accompany eating while exercising. He immediately began experimenting with various recipes, but it took three years and 800 recipes to find one that worked: "For three years, people would say the texture wasn't right, the bar was upsetting their stomachs, or there was something wrong with the taste." At that point, Maxwell and his partner, Jennifer Biddulph, invested their life savings to contract for a 50 000-bar production run and start a mail-order business. In 1989, they opened their first plant.

Since then, PowerBar has become the number one brand among energy bar marketers, with $100 million in sales. It's sold in eight flavours through supermarkets, health-food stores, sports stores, and the Powerbar Web site in Canada, the U.S., and thirty other countries.[7] See Figure 9-1.

New products can lead to larger profits and give companies better control over their marketing strategies. For example, the new Lincoln Navigator and Ford Expedition lines of sport utility vehicles are quite popular. These vehicles have been selling at close to the sticker price (U.S.$46 900 for the Navigator) and have been estimated to produce almost 31 per cent of all profits of the Ford Motor Company. Because there are fewer sport utility offerings relative to lower-priced cars, sport utility dealers don't use much price discounting and have firm command over their marketing efforts.[8]

To limit risk, many firms seek to reduce dependence on one product or product line. That is why many movie theatres converted to multiplexes; their revenues are not tied to any one film's performance. Hewlett-Packard makes electronic components and test equipment, medical electronic equipment, and analytical instrumentation—in addition to its core computing and printing products; and it regularly adds new products. Turtle Wax, the world's leader in car care products, now makes shoe polish, household cleaners, and fabric protectors.

Firms may try to improve the efficiency of their established distribution systems by placing new products in them. They can then spread advertising, sales, and distribution costs among several products, gain dealer support, and discourage other companies from entering the market. Manufacturers like Neilsen-Cadbury's, Unilever, and Revlon can place new products in many outlets quickly. Service firms, such as banks, also can efficiently add new products (financial services) into their distribution networks.

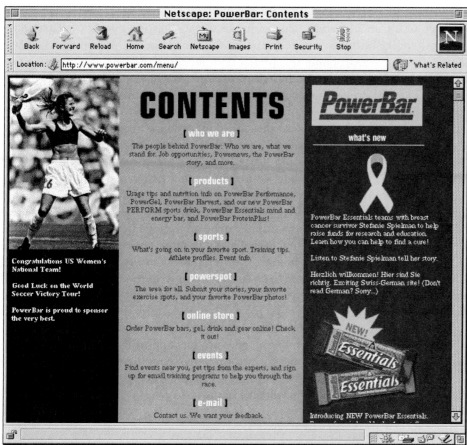

**FIGURE 9-1**

**PowerBar Web Site**
*Used by permission of PowerBar.*

Firms often seek technological breakthroughs. For instance, it's only a matter of time before the demise of traditional film-based cameras—and the core of Kodak's business. To remain viable Kodak has chosen to embrace digital technology, as it did with the VCRs and camcorders that replaced film-based movie cameras in the 1980s. Kodak is now revolutionizing the photo developing business with its line of digital cameras that create electronic images.

Offering specialty or novelty versions of new products is also a way to expand sales. For example, when *The Phantom Menace*, the fourth Stars Wars film, was launched in May 1999 a hardcover book version of the movie was put on the market with four different illustrated covers. The idea was that collectors would purchase all four books in order to have a version with each of the covers, even though the story was the same. Hence, multiple sales were made to the same customer. A few years earlier *TV Guide* similarly capitalized on the last episode of "Star Trek: The Next Generation" by producing its *Guide* with four different Star Trek covers.

Sometimes, firms want to find uses for waste materials from existing products—to aid productivity or be responsive to environmental concerns. Just over a decade ago, the chicken industry found that "we have four billion broilers, and the consumer generally doesn't want the necks and backs. What do we do? We grind them into baloney and hot dogs."[9] The sales of these products have skyrocketed since then. For environmental and cost reasons, Johnson Controls makes auto batteries from recycled lead and plastic; Reynolds Metals uses recycled paperboard in foil and wax paper packaging; and Scotch-Brite steel wool pads are made from recycled bottles and packaged in recycled paper.

*Technology can be exploited.*

**KODAK**
www.kodak.com/

*Waste materials can be used.*

**JOHNSON CONTROLS**
www.johnsoncontrols.com/

*New products respond to consumer needs.*

Companies may bring out new products to respond to changing consumer demographics and lifestyles. For example, Royal Plastics markets a basic 500-square-foot plastic house targeted at underdeveloped nations. At a cost of U.S.$30 a square foot for construction, it is priced right for these markets. Added to the fact that many of the homes are built in tropical climates where termites and dampness are very hard on wood-frame construction, it is a product well positioned to meet people's needs.[10]

*Government mandates are addressed.*

New products may have to be developed in response to government mandates. One of the most recent products mandated by the Canadian Radio-television Telecommunications Commission (CRTC) was the V-chip rating system for use by television broadcasters in Canada. Ratings of a whole program or parts of it appear on-screen at the beginning and during television programming. Notices that the scenes are 18+, 14+, or PG let viewers know if the content is appropriate for their viewing. More importantly, these ratings can be interpreted by the V-chip, a computer chip embedded in the TV tuner that allows parents to choose which programs are acceptable to come into their homes. The V-chip decodes broadcasters' ratings and blocks the signals if programmed to do so. For example, the V-chip can be set to block out an entire broadcast, or just parts of a broadcast that contain too much violence or sex.[11]

Good long-run new-product planning requires systematic research and development, matching the requirements of new-product opportunities against company abilities, emphasizing consumer desires, properly spending time and money, and defensive—as well as offensive—planning. A firm must accept that some new products may fail; a progressive firm will take risks:

> Innovation is a risky business, and failure is commonplace. Rewarding success is easy, but rewarding intelligent failure is more important. Don't judge people strictly by results; try to judge them by the quality of their efforts. People should take intelligent business risks without also risking their compensation or their careers.[12]

And there has been some criticism of the negative effects of many Canadian firms' short-run, bottom-line orientation on their level of innovativeness (and willingness to take risks).

## Why New Products Fail

Despite better product-planning practices today than ever before, the failure rate for new products is quite high. According to the consulting firm of Booz, Allen, & Hamilton, an average of 35 per cent of new industrial and consumer products fail. Others say the rate may be as high as 94 per cent![13]

*With **absolute product failure**, costs are not regained. With **relative product failure**, goals are not met.*

Product failure can be defined in both absolute and relative terms. **Absolute product failure** occurs if a firm is unable to regain its production and marketing costs. It incurs a financial loss. **Relative product failure** occurs if a firm makes a profit on an item but that product does not reach profit goals and/or adversely affects a firm's image. In computing profits and losses, the impact of the new product on the sales of other company items must be measured.

Even firms with good new-product records have had failures along the way. These includes "light" pizza (Pizza Hut), Crystal Pepsi (PepsiCo), Bic perfume, Arch Deluxe and McLean Deluxe (McDonald's), "new" Coke (Coca-Cola), and Premier smokeless cigarettes (R.J. Reynolds).

*Leading to failure are lack of an advantage, poor planning and timing, and excess enthusiasm.*

Numerous factors may cause new-product failure. The key ones are lack of a differential advantage, poor planning, poor timing, and excessive enthusiasm by the sponsor. Illustrations of poor performance due to those factors follow.

Vancouver's Harvard Capital Corporation thought they had a sure winner with the "Spud Stop," a french fry vending machine, till they filed for bankruptcy in October 1994. The concept of bringing french fries to the masses in every location where there are vending machines is very alluring. The differential advantage of delivering a desired product with the convenience of a vending machine was very appealing to investors. The problem is that fast food outlets are easy to access too and very good at making french fries.

The "Spud Stop" machines were designed to deliver fries in 50 seconds by mixing dehydrated potato powder with water, producing thirty-two potato strands, dipping the strands in oil and then putting them in a box. But the machines could not deliver on their potential. For example, a "Spud Stop" machine was tested in Sedgewick Hall at the University of British Columbia. The students found that the machine would often begin smoking, the quality of the fries dispensed was often less than acceptable, and there were sanitation problems as well. In one instance the fire department was called and this resulted in the removal of the machine. Despite investments of over $10 million, Harvard Capital was unable to make a product that was able to deliver on its promise.[14]

Thermalux was the only North American maker of aerogels, "special substances that look like glass, feel like styrofoam, and are as light as a feather. They are great insulators." Despite the apparent potential of the product, after two years of poor planning, Thermalux had no customers; its aerogels remained "a solution looking for a problem." At first, it thought refrigerator makers would be the best market since they were under pressure to avoid using insulation materials made from certain fluorocarbons and to cut energy use. But the company underestimated competition from other insulation-materials firms. It also had a tough time setting the prices of its aerogels; and when aerogel insulation was tested in refrigerators, it did not show the benefits expected. Finally, Thermalux could not produce aerogels in sufficient quantity.[15]

Poor timing led to the failure of Zap Mail by Federal Express. When it was introduced, Federal Express expected its Zap Mail (which was essentially a facsimile machine service) to change the way business customers sent documents. With it, a customer could send a copy of a document almost anywhere in Canada or the United States in under two hours. The sender called a Federal Express operator, who had a courier pick up a document and take it to a Zap Mail office, which forwarded a copy to a receiving site. The copy was delivered by courier. Yet, within three years, Zap Mail was off the market. Although Federal Express felt Zap Mail would be successful, it failed for three reasons: computer modems let customers communicate instantly and without a delivery firm; many clients did not believe two-hour service (at a high price) was better than overnight service; and as Zap Mail started, inexpensive fax machines began to flood the market.[16]

Excessive enthusiasm caused RCA to overinvest in its videodisc player, causing a loss of nearly $600 million before the product was dropped. RCA felt the player's superior picture quality and low price would lead to success with the mass market. It underestimated consumer interest in recording programs (which the videodisc player could not do, but a VCR could).[17]

# New-Product Planning

The **new-product planning process** involves a series of steps from idea generation to commercialization. See Figure 9-2. During the process, a firm generates ideas, evaluates them, weeds out poor ones, obtains consumer feedback, develops the product, tests it, and brings it to market. An idea can be terminated at any time, and costs rise

*The **new-product planning process** moves goods and services from ideas to commercialization.*

FIGURE 9-2

**The New-Product Planning Process**

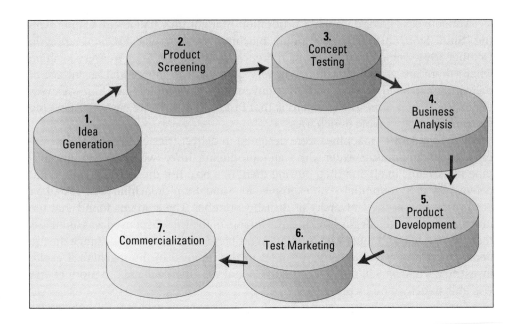

as the process goes on. The process could be used by firms of any size or type, and applies to goods and services.

Booz, Allen, & Hamilton says it generally takes a firm an average of seven well-defined ideas to yield one commercially successful new product. But this number can be much higher. A study of new-product managers found that it took nearly seventy-five ideas to yield one successful new product. In the pharmaceuticals industry, it may take up to 10 000 compounds to come up with one drug that is approved by government regulators.[18]

During the new-product planning process, a firm tries to balance such competing goals as these:

- A systematic process should be followed; however, there must be flexibility to adapt to each unique new-product opportunity.
- The process should be thorough, yet not unduly slow down introductions.
- True innovations should be pursued, yet fiscal constraints must be considered.
- An early reading of consumer acceptance should be sought, but the firm must not give away too much information to potential competitors.
- There should be an interest in short-run profitability, but not at the expense of long-run growth.[19]

Figure 9-3 highlights 3M's perspective on new-product planning: The "unique 3M culture, passed on from generation to generation, has resulted in more than 60 000 small miracles that make our lives safer, easier, better."

### Idea Generation

**Idea generation** *is the search for opportunities.*

**Idea generation** is a continuous, systematic search for new product opportunities. It involves new-idea sources and ways to generate ideas.

Sources of ideas may be employees, channel members, competitors, outside inventors, customers, government, and others. *Market-oriented sources* identify opportunities based on consumer needs and wants; laboratory research is used to satisfy them. Light beer, many ice cream flavours, and easy-to-open soda cans have evolved from market-oriented sources. *Laboratory-oriented sources* identify opportunities based on pure research (which seeks to gain knowledge and indirectly leads to specific new-product ideas) or applied research (which uses existing scientific

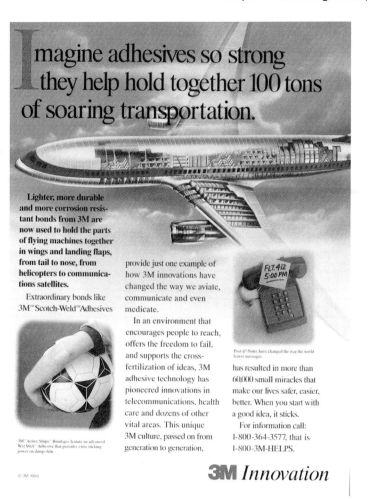

techniques to develop new-product ideas). Penicillin, antifreeze, and synthetic fibres have evolved from laboratory sources.

The key to idea generation is to stimulate creativity in an organization and then allow the creativity to surface. Bringing together a team of people in a firm to generate ideas in a creative session is one way to start the new-product process. The following are some guidelines that can result in creative stimulation while allowing ideas to surface.

- *Explore the ridiculous*—The idea of a time traveller who collected coins became a campaign for the Royal Canadian Mint.
- *Seek quantity, not quality*—A good session involving six to ten people could produce 300 ideas in about two hours!
- *Build and combine ideas with others in the session to take advantage of synergy.*
- *Challenge conventional wisdom*—Consider or tackle something that has never been done before. The idea of windowing in computer programs was developed by Apple Computer's Steven Jobs, who saw a demonstration that involved windowing. What he didn't know was that the demonstration was animated, not computer technology. He figured out a windows system to match what he thought already existed—and ended up inventing a new technology.
- *Question assumptions*—Ask why things are the way they are.
- *Think positively*—Don't judge ideas or criticize them until the ideation session is over. Always keep idea generation and evaluation separate, because combining them can kill creativity.[20]

FIGURE 9-4

**A New-Product Screening Checklist**

| General Characteristics of New Products | Rating |
|---|---|
| Profit potential | _ _ _ _ _ _ |
| Existing competition | _ _ _ _ _ _ |
| Potential competition | _ _ _ _ _ _ |
| Size of market | _ _ _ _ _ _ |
| Level of investment | _ _ _ _ _ _ |
| Patentability | _ _ _ _ _ _ |
| Level of risk | _ _ _ _ _ _ |
| **Marketing Characteristics of New Products** | |
| Fit with marketing capabilities | _ _ _ _ _ _ |
| Effect on existing products (brands) | _ _ _ _ _ _ |
| Appeal to current consumer markets | _ _ _ _ _ _ |
| Potential length of product life cycle | _ _ _ _ _ _ |
| Existence of differential advantage | _ _ _ _ _ _ |
| Impact on image | _ _ _ _ _ _ |
| Resistance to seasonal factors | _ _ _ _ _ _ |
| **Production Characteristics of New Products** | |
| Fit with production capabilities | _ _ _ _ _ _ |
| Length of time to commercialization | _ _ _ _ _ _ |
| Ease of production | _ _ _ _ _ _ |
| Availability of labour and material resources | _ _ _ _ _ _ |
| Ability to produce at competitive prices | _ _ _ _ _ _ |

## Product Screening

**Product screening** *weeds out undesirable ideas.*

Once a firm spots potential products, it must screen them. In **product screening**, poor, unsuitable, or otherwise unattractive ideas are weeded out. Today, many firms use a new-product screening checklist for preliminary analysis. In it, they list the attributes deemed most important and rate each idea on those attributes. The checklist is standardized and allows ideas to be compared.

Figure 9-4 shows a new-product screening checklist with three major categories: general characteristics, marketing characteristics, and production characteristics (which can be applied to both goods and services). In each category, there are several product attributes to assess. They are scored from 1 (outstanding) to 10 (very poor) for each product idea. In addition, the attributes would be weighted because they vary in their impact on new product success. The checklist yields an overall score for every idea. Here is an example of how a firm could develop overall ratings for two product ideas. Remember, in this example, the best rating is 1 (so, 3 is worse than 2):

1. Product idea A gets an average rating of 2.5 on general characteristics, 2.9 on marketing characteristics, and 1.4 on production characteristics. Product idea B gets ratings of 2.8, 1.4, and 1.8, respectively.

2. The firm assigns an importance weight of 4 to general characteristics, 5 to marketing characteristics, and 3 to production characteristics. The best overall rating is 12 $[(1 \times 4) + (1 \times 5) + (1 \times 3)]$. The poorest possible overall average rating is 120 $[(10 \times 4) + (10 \times 5) + (10 \times 3)]$.

3. Idea A gets an overall rating of 28.7 $[(2.5 \times 4) + (2.9 \times 5) + (1.4 \times 3)]$. B gets an overall rating of 23.6 $[(2.8 \times 4) + (1.4 \times 5) + (1.8 \times 3)]$.

4. Idea B's overall rating is better than A's because of its better marketing evaluation (the characteristics judged most important by the firm).

*A* **patent** *gives exclusive selling rights to an inventor.*

In screening, patentability must often be determined. A **patent** grants an inventor of a useful product or process exclusive selling rights for a fixed period. An invention may be patented if it is a "useful, novel, and nonobvious process, machine, manufacture, or composition of matter" and not patented by anyone else. Separate applications are needed for protection in foreign markets. Many nations have simplified matters by signing patent cooperation treaties; however, some do not honour such treaties. Today, Canada and the other members of the World Trade Organization grant patents that last for twenty years from the date that applications are filed. In 1996, 49 254 patent applications were filed in Canada, 7145 of which were granted. While only 6.7 per cent of the patent applications were filed by Canadians, 9.9 per cent of those that were granted went to Canadians. The remaining 93.3 per cent of applications and 90.1 per cent of patents granted involved foreign nationals (mainly U.S., European, and Japanese), of which over 50 per cent were from the U.S.[21]

A company should answer several questions regarding patents during the screening stage. For example:

- Can the proposed new product be patented by the firm?
- Are competitive items patented?
- When do competitors' patents expire?
- Are patents on competing items available under a licensing agreement?
- Would the firm be free of patent liability (infringement) if it introduced the proposed new product?

## Concept Testing

Next, a firm needs consumer feedback about the new-product ideas that pass through screening. **Concept testing** presents the consumer with a proposed product and measures attitudes and intentions at an early stage of the new-product planning process.

Concept testing is a quick, inexpensive way to assess consumer enthusiasm. It asks potential consumers to react to a picture, written statement, or oral product description. This lets a firm learn initial attitudes prior to undertaking costly, time-consuming product development. Heinz, Kodak, Sony, and Sunbeam are among those using concept testing.

Concept testing generally asks consumers these types of questions:

- Is the idea easy to understand?
- Would this product meet a real need?
- Do you see distinct benefits for this product over those on the market?
- Do you find the claims about this product believable?
- Would you buy the product?
- How much would you pay for it?
- Would you replace your current brand with this new product?
- What improvements can you suggest in various attributes of the concept?
- How frequently would you buy the product?
- Who would use the product?[22]

*Concept testing determines customer attitudes before product development.*

## Business Analysis

At this point, a firm does business analysis for the new-product concepts that have thus far been deemed attractive. **Business analysis** involves the detailed review, projection, and evaluation of such factors as consumer demand, production costs, marketing costs, break-even points, competition, capital investments, and profitability for each proposed new product. It is much more detailed than product screening.

Here are some of the considerations at this planning stage:

*Business analysis looks at demand, costs, competition, etc.*

| CRITERIA | SELECTED CONSIDERATIONS |
|---|---|
| Demand projections | Short- and long-run sales potential; speed of sales growth; price/sales relationship; seasonality; rate of repurchases |
| Production cost projections | Total and per-unit costs; startup vs. continuing costs; estimates of raw materials and other costs; economies of scale; break-even points |
| Marketing cost projections | Product planning (patent search, product development, testing); promotion; distribution; marketing research; break-even points |
| Competitive projections | Short-run and long-run market shares of company and competitors; competitors' strengths and weaknesses; potential competitors; likely strategies by competitors in response to firm |
| Capital investment projections | Need for new equipment and facilities vs. use of existing facilities and resources |
| Profitability projections | Time to recoup initial costs; short- and long-run total and per-unit profits; reseller needs; control over price; return on investment; risk |

Because the next step is expensive and time-consuming, critical use of business analysis is essential to eliminate marginal items.

## Product Development

**Product development**

*focuses on devising an actual product and a broad marketing strategy.*

During **product development**, an idea for a new product is converted into a tangible form and a basic marketing strategy is identified. Depending on the product involved, this stage in the planning process encompasses product construction, packaging, branding, positioning, and consumer attitude and usage testing.

Product construction decisions include the type and quality of materials comprising the product, the method of production, production time, production capacity, the assortment to be offered, and the time needed to move from development to commercialization. Packaging decisions include the materials used, the functions performed, and alternative sizes and colours. Branding decisions include the choice of a name, trademark protection, and the image sought. Product positioning involves selecting a target market and positioning the new good or service against competitors and other company offerings. Consumer testing studies perceptions of and satisfaction with the new product.

If a modification is involved, product-development costs may be relatively low. However, an innovation may be costly (up to several million dollars or more) and time-consuming (up to four years for a new car). And this is true of services, as well as goods.

Digital video disk (DVD) players are the most versatile multimedia tool there is. They're able to reproduce movies and their soundtracks to near perfection, play music from compact disks, and are an excellent computer software medium. But it's their video capability that's most impressive, and manufacturers and distributors of these machines were expecting 1999 to be a big take-off year. So what's been holding the DVD back from sweeping the market? The ability to rent a DVD for the same price as a video at the local video rental store. For example, at Blockbuster Video's 230 Canadian stores people could purchase DVDs in 1999 but not rent them. This is a classic new-offering dilemma: people won't buy DVD players unless they can rent DVD disks, and retailers won't offer DVD movies to rent until there's a large enough market to make it worthwhile! A large market is needed because video stores already have large investments and a strong customer base in VHS video cassettes. Adding DVD movie rental services could potentially double their inventory of movies, but won't likely double their customers. Offering DVD movies on a sell-through basis to start is a good in-between strategy.[23]

Besides being costly and time consuming, product development can be complicated. For example:

**BLOCKBUSTER**
www.blockbuster.com

Boeing's traditional method for designing new aircraft has three phases. First, engineers design a plane's shape and components. Then, they hand blueprints to manufacturing experts, who plan the production of components and final assembly. Finally, the manufacturing plan goes to tooling specialists who design specialized production machinery. Since the phases are completed in sequence, they take a long time and the system forces each group to turn out reams of corrections, consuming millions of hours a year in engineering time.

Once final drawings are ready, carpenters and artisans go to work. They build a full-scale mock-up of the plane incorporating replicas of every part. Converted for the first time from drawings to three-dimensional reality, parts don't necessarily fit. Electricians stringing mock instrument wires through the model, for instance, may discover that a structural beam gets in the way. Result: more expensive changes, as engineers redesign the beam so it has a hole in the centre and tool makers reconfigure machines to accommodate the fix. Similar mistakes inevitably plague construction of the first few planes. And since subsequent planes must be tailored to the customer, Boeing goes through a minor version of the same tortuous process with each order.[24]

## Test Marketing

**Test marketing** involves placing a fully developed new product (a good or service) in one or more selected areas and observing its actual performance under a proposed marketing plan. The purpose is to evaluate the product and pre-test marketing efforts in a real setting prior to a full-scale introduction. Rather than just study intentions, test marketing lets a firm monitor actual consumer behaviour, competitor reactions, and reseller interest. After testing, the firm could decide to go ahead, modify the product and then go ahead, modify the marketing plan and then go ahead, or drop the product.

Many companies routinely use test marketing to help introduce new products and refine their marketing strategies. In selected U.S. cities the Campbell Soup Co. recently tested a new line of ready-to-serve Supper Soups aimed at consumers with busy lifestyles who want a convenience product. These soups are designed to be consumed as a full meal, come packaged in glass jars, and take about two and half minutes to prepare. The soups are low in fat and are offered in four varieties, including pasta primavera with chicken and pot roast with vegetables.[25] Consumer products firms are much more apt to engage in test marketing than industrial products firms:

> In consumer products, test marketing is a science dominated by marketing consultants, database collection firms, and electronic test marketing services. The business is so sophisticated that Information Resources Inc. of Chicago, which runs several electronic test markets, not only measures what every member of its participating households buys but also identifies exactly which television ads propelled them into stores.
>
> By contrast, the test marketing of business-to-business products has only recently become a widespread practice. In the past, a manufacturer created a product, ran it by a few executives, and hoped customers would buy it. Thus, manufacturers often spent huge sums on parts and labour to fix any problems that cropped up after installation. Now, a growing number of manufacturers in such diverse industries as computers, electronics, industrial chemicals, cleaning equipment, maintenance products, and insurance have begun intensive on-site tests of new products. In most cases, these tests are conducted with anywhere from five to fifty clients and last from two to six months.[26]

The test-marketing process requires several decisions: when to test, where to test, how long to test, what test information to acquire, and how to apply test results. Figure 9-5 shows the criteria to weigh in making the choices.

Although test marketing has been beneficial in many cases, some firms now question its effectiveness and downplay or skip this stage in new-product planning. Their dissatisfaction arises from test marketing's cost, the time delay required before full introduction, the fact that it may provide information to competitors, the inability to predict national (global) results based on limited test-market areas, and the

*Test marketing occurs in selected areas and observes real performance.*

**FIGURE 9-5**
**Test-Marketing Decisions**

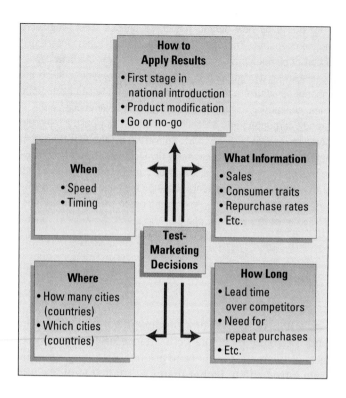

impact of such external factors as the economy and competition on test results. Test marketing can even allow nontesting competitors to catch up with an innovative firm by the time a product is ready for a full rollout.

## Commercialization

*Commercialization involves a major marketing commitment.*

When testing goes well, a firm is ready to introduce a new product to its full target market. This involves **commercialization** and corresponds to the introductory stage of the product life cycle. During commercialization, the firm enacts a total marketing plan and works toward production capacity. Among the factors to be considered are the speed of acceptance by consumers and distribution intermediaries, the intensity of distribution (how many outlets), production capabilities, the promotion mix, prices, competition, the time until profitability, and commercialization costs.

Commercialization may require large outlays and a long-term commitment. For example, manufacturers may spend an average of $5 million for a national rollout in both Canadian and U.S. supermarkets—nearly half on consumer promotion and the rest on product costs, market research costs, and promotions for supermarkets. Yet, commercialization costs can go much higher. When Coca-Cola Canada launched PowerAde, a new sports drink, in Canada, it paid $1 million for its promotional campaign alone (which included TV and print ads, coupons, and in-store promotions).[27]

The commercialization of a new product sometimes must overcome consumer and reseller reluctance because of ineffective prior company offerings. Diet Coke's test marketing of new sweeteners in Canada encountered consumer resistance because of the failure of New Coke.[28] The same thing happened to Texas Instruments, which encountered resistance in the business computer market after it bowed out of the home computer market.

**COCA-COLA CANADA**
www.cocacola.com/

# Branding

An important part of product planning is *branding,* the procedure a firm follows in researching, developing, and implementing its brand(s). As noted at the beginning of the chapter, a brand is a name, term, design, or symbol (or combination of these) that identifies the products of a seller or group of sellers. By establishing well-known brands, firms gain acceptance, distributor cooperation, and above-average prices.

There are four types of brand designation:

1. A **brand name** is a word, letter (number), group of words, or letters (numbers) that can be spoken. Examples are Labatt's Blue, Windows 98, and Lipton Cup-a-Soup.

2. A **brand mark** is a symbol, design, or distinctive colouring or lettering that cannot be spoken. Examples are Lexus' stylized L crest, the Nike swoosh, and Prudential's rock.

3. A **trade character** is a brand mark that is personified. Examples are Qantas Airlines' koala bear, McDonald's Ronald McDonald, and the Pillsbury Doughboy.

4. A **trademark** is a brand name, brand mark, or trade character or combination thereof that is given legal protection. When it is used, a registered trademark is followed by ®. Examples are Scotch Brand® tape and MasterCard®.

Brand names, brand marks, and trade characters do not offer legal protection against use by competitors, unless registered as trademarks. Trademarks ensure exclusivity for trademark owners or those securing their permission and provide legal remedies against firms using "confusingly similar" names, designs, or symbols. With the exception of Labatt's Blue, all of the previous examples are registered trademarks. Trademarks are discussed more fully later in the chapter.

Branding started during the Middle Ages, when craft and merchant guilds required producers to mark goods so output could be restricted and inferior goods traced to their producer. The marks also served as standards for quality when items were sold outside the local markets in which the guilds operated. The earliest and most aggressive promoters of brands in North America were patent medicine manufacturers. Examples of current well-known brands that started more than 100 years ago are Vaseline Petroleum Jelly and Pillsbury's Best Flour. The best known Canadian brand names in the world are Molson's and Seagram's.[29]

Worldwide, there are now millions of brand names in circulation; and Canadian advertisers spend over $13.3 billion advertising their brands each year.[30] Permanent media expenditures (such as company logos, stationery, brochures, business forms and cards, and vehicular and building signs) for brands are another large marketing cost. For instance, when Allied-Signal decided to remove its hyphen and become AlliedSignal, it cost U.S.$500 000 for new stationery, signs, and so forth.

A key goal of firms is to develop brand loyalty, which allows them to maximize sales and maintain a strong brand image. One firm that's trying to quantify consumer brand loyalty and image is the WPP Group, which has developed a loyalty measurement approach called "Brandz." For example, using Brandz, WPP has determined that New Balance has more loyal customers then Reebok, despite the fact that Reebok spends $154 million a year to build its image. Brandz produces bonding score measures ranging from 0–60 per cent to indicate consumer loyalty. WPP considers these to be superior to awareness measures for determining brand strength and potential market shares. For example, in the U.S. the bonding scores for well-known brands were Gerber, 56 per cent; Nike, 53 per cent; Marlboro cigarettes, 30 per cent; McDonald's, 25 per cent; and Disney, 20 per cent—but well-known brands like Canon and Fuji received bonding scores of only 1 per cent! A low bonding score

*Branding involves* **brand names**, **brand marks**, **trade characters**, *and* **trademarks**.

**MASTERCARD**
www.canadatrust.com/credit/index.html

Trade Marks

**FIGURE 9-6**

**The Most Popular and Powerful
Brand in the World**

*"Coca-Cola" trademarks appear courtesy of Coca-
Cola Ltd.*

**ADIDAS**
www.adidas.com/

**KELLOGG**
www.kelloggs.com/

implies that consumers are loyal not to the brand but to the pricing and distribution initiatives that the firm marketing it has employed.[31]

Sometimes brands do so well that they gain "power" status, meaning that they're both well known and highly esteemed. At present, according to a survey of 25 300 people in sixteen nations, the world's ten most powerful brands are (in order): Coca-Cola, Kodak, Sony, Mercedes-Benz, Pepsi-Cola, Nestlé, Gillette, Colgate, Adidas, and Volkswagen. The ten brands with the greatest "vitality"—global growth potential—are: Coca-Cola, Nike, Adidas, Sony, Ferrari, Reebok, Disney, Porsche, Pepsi-Cola, and Mercedes-Benz.[32] See Figure 9-6.

Brand rankings do differ by region. In China, six of the top ten brands are from Japan, led by Hitachi; three are from the United States—Coca-Cola, Mickey Mouse, and Marlboro; and one is from China—Tsing Tao (beer).[33] Europeans favour such brands as BMW, Porsche, and Rolls-Royce. Sony is the most powerful brand for Japanese consumers. In North America the top brands include Coca-Cola, Campbell, Disney, Pepsi-Cola, Kodak, NBC, Black & Decker, Kellogg, McDonald's, and Hershey.

The use of popular brands can also speed up public acceptance and gain reseller cooperation for new products. For instance, the Gillette Company is know worldwide for its razors and blades, which are its principal line of business. In mid-1998 the Gillette Company unveiled its newest razor, the MACH3 triple-blade shaving system. It was initially introduced in North America, Western Europe, the former Soviet Union, and selected markets in Eastern Europe and the Far East. Gillette described this as the most successful new system introduction in the history of the firm. See Figure 9-7.

This is impressive, given that Gillette's history is long and storied. Among its well-known brands of razor is the Sensor family of shaving systems; first introduced in the 1990s, this razor system accounts for over $1 billion in sales. Gillette also markets the Atra and Trac II shaving systems, major brands for more than twenty years; and the Gillette twin blade disposable razors. The firm also produces and markets disposable brands such as CustomPlus, Good News, and Agility brands.

Razors are only part of Gillette's business; it also manufactures and distributes a lot of consumer products. For example, in the get-ready-in-the-morning market

**FIGURE 9-7**

**The Gillette MACH3 Razor Blade: Gillette's newest shaving system brand.**

*Courtesy of the Gillette Company.*

Gillette sells shaving cream under the Gillette Series name. After you've shaved you can apply one of the firm's deodorant brands such as Right Guard, Soft & Dri, or Dry Idea. Then you can brush your teeth with an Oral-B CrossAction toothbrush or an Oral-B Advantage Control Grip toothbrush. Children can choose from among leading children's toothbrushes, including Nickelodeon, Rugrats, and Sesame Street models. For people who don't want to use a wet shaving system, Gillette markets the Braun Flex Integral family of pivoting head electric shavers. The Braun name is co-branded with Oral-B to sell Braun Oral-B powered plaque removers, and Braun also markets ThermoScan infrared ear thermometers. Gillette helps most of the world power up with Duracell Ultra alkaline batteries and regular Duracell alkaline batteries. Finally, Gillette markets the Parker, Paper Mate, and Waterman brands of writing instruments. And for those who make mistakes, Gillette offers the Liquid Paper line of correction fluids, correction pens, and DryLine correction films.[34]

Gaining and maintaining brand recognition is often a top priority for all kinds of firms. For example, the national TV networks in Canada (CBC and CTV) and the U.S. (ABC, CBS, Fox, and NBC) "are facing increasing competition and are very conscious of the need to get their brands out there. As more choices are given to consumers, networks have to make sure their viewers understand who they are and what they offer. That can mean anything from a logo subtly popping up in the corner of the viewer's TV screen to a major cross-promotion with some big-name packaged goods marketers."[35]

Branding is one of the most important marketing concepts there is, but it's an abstract concept nonetheless. Marketers recognize that brands exist in the minds of customers, but that this existence isn't independent of marketers' actions. Marketers can consider their relationships with customers using the concept of the "brand trinity." The first part of the brand trinity is the product itself, what customers know about it, and the experiences they've had with it. The second part of the trinity is the reputation of the firm that makes and sells the brand. The firm's name, its logo, and its other trademarks all provide a basis for confidence (or lack thereof) in a brand. The third part of the trinity relates to the values and beliefs of the customers about using the product and the product category. Each part of the trinity is crucial, and unless all three parts are brought together a firm doesn't really have a brand, but merely an identifying mark.

Marketers believe strongly that "the brand strength is the ultimate determinant of profit margins. By extension, brand strength is an important determinant of the long-term profit potential of the company, and in this capacity becomes a valuable (if intangible) component of the balance sheet."[36] The worth of brands is known as **brand equity** and measures the "financial impact associated with an increase in a product's value accounted for by its brand name above and beyond the level justified by its quality (as determined by its configuration of brand attributes, product features, or physical characteristics)."[37] As one expert noted:

> In a general sense, brand equity is defined in terms of the marketing effects uniquely attributable to the brand—for example, when certain outcomes result from the marketing of a good or service because of its brand name that would not occur if the same good or service did not have that name. A brand is said to have positive (negative) customer-based brand equity if consumers react more (less) favourably to the product, price, promotion, or distribution of the brand than they do to the same marketing-mix element when it is attributed to a fictitiously named or unnamed version of the good or service.[38]

According to *Financial World*, the fifteen most valuable brands in the world—based on sales, profitability, and growth potential—are Coca-Cola, Marlboro, IBM, Motorola, Hewlett-Packard, Microsoft, Kodak, Budweiser, Kellogg, Nescafé, Intel, Gillette, Pepsi-Cola, GE, and Levi's.[39]

Here is an example of how the brand equity concept can be applied. When Cadbury Schweppes acquired the Hires and Crush soda lines from Procter & Gamble, it paid U.S.$220 million. Twenty million dollars of that amount was for physical assets and the balance was for "brand value."[40] Brand equity is even higher when licensing royalties can be generated from other firms' use of the brand, such as occurs with trade characters like Walt Disney's Mickey Mouse. Nonetheless, there are no widely approved techniques for assessing overall brand equity.

These reasons summarize why branding is important:

- Product identification is eased. A customer can order a product by name instead of description.

- Customers are assured that a good or service has a certain level of quality and that they will obtain comparable quality if the same brand is reordered.

- The firm responsible for the product is known. The producer of unbranded items cannot be as directly identified.

- Price comparisons are reduced when customers perceive distinct brands. This is most likely if special attributes are linked to different brands.

- A firm can advertise (position) its products and associate each brand and its characteristics in the buyer's mind. This aids the consumer in forming a **brand image**, which is the perception a person has of a particular brand. It is "a mirror reflection (though perhaps inaccurate) of the brand personality or product being. It is what people believe about a brand—their thoughts, feelings, expectations."[41]

- Branding helps segment markets by creating tailored images. Multiple market segments can be attracted by using two or more brands.

- For socially visible goods and services, a product's prestige is enhanced by a strong brand name.

- People feel less risk when buying a brand with which they are familiar and toward which they have a favourable attitude. This is why brand loyalty occurs.

*Brand equity represents a product's worth.*

*Branding creates identities, assures quality, and performs other functions.*

**Brand images** *are the perceptions that consumers have of particular brands.*

- Cooperation from resellers is greater for well-known brands. A strong brand also may let its producer exert more control in the distribution channel.
- A brand may help sell an entire line of products, as with Kellogg cereals.
- A brand may help a company enter a new product category, like Reese's peanut butter.
- "A product is something made in a factory [or offered by a service firm]; a brand is something bought by a customer. A product can be copied by a competitor; a brand is unique. A product can be quickly outdated; a successful brand is timeless."[42]

There are four basic branding decisions firms must make: choosing their corporate symbols, creating their branding philosophy, selecting a brand name, and deciding whether or not to use trademarks.

## Corporate Symbols

**Corporate symbols** are a firm's name (and/or divisional names), logo(s), and trade characters. They are significant parts of an overall company image. If a firm begins a business; merges with another company; reduces or expands product lines; seeks new geographic markets; or finds its name to be unwieldy, nondistinctive, or confusing, it needs to evaluate and possibly change its corporate symbols. Here are examples of each situation.

About twenty years ago a new PC maker hired a consultant to devise a company name. It wanted a name that "would be memorable and at the same time take command of the idea of portableness; something that would distinguish it from all other IBM PC compatibles." The consultant recommended a name combining two syllables representing "communications" and "small but important." Today, Compaq is the twenty-eighth largest firm in North America.[43]

In the fall of 1998 Daimler-Benz AGH of Stuttgart, Germany and Chrysler Corporation of Auburn Hills, Michigan merged to become Daimler Chrysler. The merger hasn't been strongly noticeable in the Canadian marketplace, since the Chrysler and Mercedes-Benz brands have been kept separate. The former Chrysler Canada no longer exists and the company is now Daimler Chrysler Canada. Mercedes-Benz Canada still exists and does have a dotted line to Daimler Chrysler Canada. The marketing and distribution systems of the two Canadian firms are also separate. (It makes sense to keep the firms separate in Canada, since they tend to appeal to very different markets.) The immediate value of the merger for Daimler Chrysler will be the potential cost savings in its amalgamation of such operating units as supplies purchasing, media purchasing, and financial administration. Regardless, every corporate name and symbol on every piece of stationery and on every installation had to be changed, and as of this writing, the cost estimates for this have yet to be made.[44] See Figure 9-8.

In April 1999 Maple Leaf Foods changed its logo. It still features the familiar red, white, and blue colours, but now has a brighter and more prominent maple leaf. Maple Leaf believes customers will perceive that the change in the logo "will stand for innovation, will stand for risk taking, and will stand for leadership."[45]

Federal Express now promotes the FedEx name, since it's easier to say. United Telecommunications converted its nondistinctive name to Sprint, in recognition of its leading brand. And when Corel software of Ottawa acquired the rights to WordPerfect, a leading word processing product from Novell of Orem, Utah in January 1996, it wanted to link its corporate name with this new brand. WordPerfect has been marketed for years as Corel WordPerfect, thereby linking the product and its producer.[46]

**Corporate symbols** *help establish a companywide image.*

COREL
www.corel.com/

Mika Hakkinen
*McLaren-Mercedes Formula One Driver*
Even at 300 km per hour,
he stays as laid-back as life
in his native Finland.

Robert J. Eaton
*Chrysler Corporation Chairman*
His weekends seem to fly by.
Especially when he's behind the
wheel of a Neon race car.

*Courage meets Courage*

Can you imagine two companies, synonymous with bold thinking, taking the most daring step of all as a team? We can. Because the courageous people who led the development of a navigational system that guides drivers as if by magic are now together with the people who designed a proving ground where vehicles can be tested on roads too extreme for even the toughest human driver. The extraordinary minds that conceived of these ideas are now one at DaimlerChrysler. It's the place where the transportation industry's most fearless thinkers are working to shape the future.

**FIGURE 9-8**

**Daimler Chrysler's new team.**
*Used with permission from Daimler Chrysler.*

## Branding Philosophy

While developing a brand strategy, a firm needs to determine its branding philosophy. This philosophy outlines the use of manufacturer, private, and/or generic brands, as well as the use of family and/or individual branding.

**Manufacturer brands** *are well known and heavily promoted.*

**MANUFACTURER, PRIVATE, AND GENERIC BRANDS**[47] **Manufacturer brands** use the names of their makers. They generate the vast majority of North American revenues for most product categories: over 85 per cent of food, all autos, 75 per cent of major appliances, and over 80 per cent of gasoline. They appeal to a wide range of people who desire low risk of poor product performance, good quality, routine purchases, status, and convenience shopping. The brands are often well known and trusted because quality control is strictly maintained. They are identifiable and present distinctive images. Producers may have a number of product alternatives under their brands.

Manufacturers have better channel control over their own brands, which may be sold through many competing intermediaries. Yet individual resellers can have lower investments if the brands' pre-sold nature makes turnover high—and if manufacturers spend large sums promoting their brands and sponsor cooperative ads with resellers (so costs are shared). Prices are the highest of the three brands, with the bulk going to the manufacturer (which also has the greatest profit). The marketing goal is to attract and retain loyal consumers for these brands, and for their makers to direct the marketing effort for the brands.

**Private brands** *enable channel members to gain loyal customers.*

**Private (dealer) brands** use names designated by their resellers, usually wholesalers or retailers—including service providers. They account for sizable North American revenues in many categories: 50 per cent of shoes, one-third of tires, 14 per cent of food items, and one-quarter of major appliances. And unit market shares are

## TECHNOLOGY AND MARKETING

### Firm Names KO'd by Y2K: The Risk of Linking Your Name with the Times

Naming your firm with the times is one way of appearing contemporary. But the advent of the year 2000 has entailed not only a problem for firms with computers that are technologically obsolete, but also for those businesses whose names are linked to the century. For example, 20th Century Fox studios might have to change its name to 21st Century Fox, or maybe just Fox Studios. The artificial insemination firm 20th Century Breeders, and hairstyling firm 20th Century Hair, are also faced with the prospect of changing their names. The computer firm Gateway 2000 changed its name to Gateway; Twentieth Century, a large U.S.-based mutual fund company, changed its name to American Century; and a think tank called 20-Century Foundation changed its name to the Century Foundation.

A name change can be extremely expensive. For example, an autobody firm in New Windsor, New York changed its name from 20th Century Towing and Autobody to 21st Century Collision at a cost of U.S.$2500—and this is just a small local firm. A large firm is bound to

spend a lot more. When Wal-Mart entered Canada in the early 1990s it was threatened by a lawsuit from Wool-Mart, who wanted Wal-Mart not to use the name and to pay Wool-Mart damages. Wal-Mart decided it was worth fighting because it wanted to keep its name—and because it would cost it an estimated $2 million in signage and stationery costs alone to make a change.

The problem of names tied to an obsolete date is, of course, bound to happen again. For example, Century 21 Real Estate will be fine for the next 100 years, but what about after that?

It seems as though choosing a firm name that's linked to a date has nothing but drawbacks. Are there any advantages? What advice would you give to managers who are thinking about date-related firm or brand names?

*Sources: "The Y2K Tragedy," Fortune (August 17, 1998), p. 44; Brian Banks and David North, "Ticked-off: Wal-Mart's Infuriating Ways, Canadian Business (January 1996), pp. 23–24; and Eric Swetsky, "Wool-Mart Versus Wal-Mart," Marketing Magazine (June 24, 1996), p. 20.*

even higher. Some firms, such as Bata Shoes and McDonald's, derive most revenues from their own brands. Private brands account for 26 per cent of unit food sales in Canadian supermarkets. In the Canadian grocery store soft drink market (worth about $3 billion per year), private brands now hold about 18 per cent of the market, down from a high of 25 per cent in the mid-1990s. The dominant private label manufacturer is Canada's Cott Corporation, which makes 90 per cent of the private label sodas in the world and is the fourth largest soft drink manufacturer. Cott Corporation has agreements with Wal-Mart, Safeway, and many other retail chains to supply private label soft drinks. Private-brand foods are currently more popular in Canada and Europe than in the United States. For example, private labels typically generate a quarter of retail sales in Canadian and European stores, while in the U.S. private label sales generate only 20 per cent of sales.[48]

Private brands appeal to price-conscious people who buy them if they feel the brands offer good quality at a lower price. In the past Canadians used to accept some risk as to quality, but brands like President's Choice from Loblaws, Master Choice from A&P, Our Best from Sobey's, and Life Brands from Shopper's Drug Mart have made people consider the private brands as comparable to national brands. In some cases, like President's Choice Decadent Chocolate Chip Cookies, private brands are even considered superior. Private brands are usually presented as having similar quality to manufacturer brands but with less emphasis on packaging, and are often made to dealer specifications. In the past, brand assortments were smaller and the brands were unknown to people not shopping with a given reseller. However, the President's Choice brand has transcended this. In 1998 Loblaw launched President's

**LOBLAWS**
www.loblaw.com

**TABLE 9-1**

**Manufacturer, Private, and Generic Brands**

| CHARACTERISTIC | MANUFACTURER BRAND | PRIVATE BRAND | GENERIC BRAND |
|---|---|---|---|
| Target market | Risk avoider, quality conscious, brand loyal, status conscious, quick shopper | Price conscious, comparison shopper, quality conscious, moderate risk taker, dealer loyal | Price conscious, careful shopper, willing to accept lower quality, large family or organization |
| Product | Well known, trusted, best quality control, clearly identifiable, deep product line | Same overall quality as manufacturer, less emphasis on packaging, less assortment, not known to nonshoppers of the dealer | Usually less overall quality than manufacturer, little emphasis on packaging, very limited assortment, not well known |
| Distribution | Often sold at many competing dealers | Usually only available from a particular dealer in the area | Varies |
| Promotion | Manufacturer-sponsored ads, cooperative ads | Dealer-sponsored ads | Few ads, secondary shelf space |
| Price | Highest, usually suggested by manufacturer | Moderate, usually controlled by dealer | Lowest, usually controlled by dealer |
| Marketing | To generate brand loyalty and manufacturer control | To generate dealer loyalty and control | To offer a low-priced, lesser-quality item to those desiring it |

Choice Financial, an in-store bank with literally no service fees, along with a President's Choice bank card. Loblaw simultaneously launched *President's Choice Magazine,* a lifestyle magazine that contains cooking tips, recipes, food information, and other lifestyle features and is only available at Loblaw and its affiliated stores.

Resellers have more exclusive rights for these brands, and are more responsible for distribution and larger purchases. Inventory turnover may be lower than for manufacturer brands, and promotion and pricing are the reseller's job. Due to lower per-unit packaging and promotion costs, resellers can sell private brands at lower prices and still have better per-unit profits (due to their higher share of the selling price). The marketing goal is to attract people who become loyal to the reseller and for that firm to exert control over marketing. Large resellers advertise their brands widely; essentially every major Canadian retailer sells some type of private brand. Loblaw's President's Choice brand is even more popular than some manufacturer brands; and in Loblaw's stores, private label products represented 33 per cent of the products purchased by customers.[49]

*Generic brands are low-priced items with little advertising.*

**Generic brands** emphasize the names of the products and not that of the manufacturer or reseller. They started in the drug industry as low-cost alternatives to expensive manufacturer brands. Today, generics have expanded into cigarettes, batteries, motor oil, and other products. The pharmaceutical industry in Canada is worth $6 billion, and the generic manufacturers have about 10 per cent of this market. (The prescription volume for generic drugs is closer to 40 per cent, but the low prices of the drugs result in significantly lower dollar volume.) Virtually all of

Canada's supermarkets stock some generic products, which account for only about 1 per cent of supermarket revenues. Generics appeal to price-conscious, careful shoppers, who perceive them as a very good value, are sometimes willing to accept lower quality, and often purchase for large families or large organizations.[50]

Generics are seldom advertised and receive poor shelf locations; consumers must search them out. Prices are lower than those of other brands by anywhere from 10 to 50 per cent, due to quality, packaging, assortment, distribution, and promotion economies. The major marketing goal is to offer low-priced, lower-quality items to consumers interested in price savings. Table 9-1 compares the three types of brands.

Many companies—including service firms—use a **mixed-brand strategy**. This strategy involves producing products that are sold under both manufacturer and private brands (and maybe generic brands). For example, apple juice producers often put many different brand labels on their juice cans. Mixed branding benefits manufacturers and resellers: it gives the firm associated with the brand name a chance to gain a customer franchise. Multiple segments may be targeted. Loyalty to manufacturers and loyalty to dealers can be fostered separately. In addition, mixed branding means a producer firm is given more shelf space (under different brand names), gets more cooperation in the distribution channel (when they supply products branded in the reseller's cheaper juice), and allows producers to offer a wider assortment (sweeter apple juice, cheaper juice). Selling more means producing more, which stabilizes production and uses excess capacity. As such, sales are maximized for manufacturing firms and profits are shared more equitably between producers and resellers. Planning is better too. For example, in Japan, Kodak markets its own brand of film and COOP private-brand film (for the 2500-store Japanese Consumer Cooperative Union). By doing this, it hopes to make a dent in Fuji's 75 per cent share of the Japanese market.

Manufacturer, private, and generic brands also repeatedly engage in a **battle of the brands**, in which each strives to gain a greater share of the consumer's dollar, control over marketing strategy, consumer loyalty, product distinctiveness, maximum shelf space and locations, and a large share of profits. In recent years, this battle has been intensifying:

> You know the old joke: Just because you're paranoid doesn't mean that they're not out to get you. In a nutshell, that describes how manufacturers of brand-name products react to competition from private labels. On one hand, manufacturers have the right to be concerned: There are more private labels on the market than ever before. Collectively, private labels in North America command higher unit shares than the strongest national brands in 77 of 250 supermarket product categories. But on the other hand, many manufacturers have overreacted to the threat posed by private labels without fully recognizing two essential points. First, private-label strength generally varies with economic conditions. Second, through their actions, manufacturers of brand-name products can temper the challenge posed by private labels.[51]

**FAMILY AND MULTIPLE BRANDING** In **family (blanket) branding**, one name is used for two or more individual products. Many firms selling industrial goods and services (such as Boeing and IBM), as well as those selling consumer services (such as Bell Canada), and consumer products (such as Kraft and Heinz) use some form of family branding for all or most of their products. Other companies employ a family brand for each category of products. For example, Sears has Kenmore appliances and Craftsman tools and Canadian Tire Corporation has Mastercraft tools and parts. Family branding can be applied to both manufacturer and private brands, and to both domestic and international (global) brands.

Family branding is best for specialized firms or those with narrow product lines. Companies capitalize on a uniform, well-known image and promote the same name regularly—keeping promotion costs down. The major disadvantages to family

*A **mixed-brand strategy** combines brand types.*

*In a **battle of the brands**, the three brand types compete.*

**Family branding** *uses a single name for many products.*

**CANADIAN TIRE CORPORATION**
www.canadiantire.com

**FIGURE 9-9**

**How Highliner Foods is applying brand extension to its seafood products line.**

*Photograph by Clint Adam Smyth.*

**Brand extension** *gains quick*

*acceptance.*

branding are that differentiated marketing opportunities may be low (if only one brand is used to target all of a firm's customers), company image may be adversely affected if vastly different products (such as men's and women's cologne) carry one name, and innovativeness may not be projected to consumers.

**Brand extension**, whereby an established name is applied to new products, is an effective use of family branding. It is a way of gaining quick customer acceptance, since people are familiar with existing products having the same name. Figure 9-9 shows how High Liner Foods is applying brand extension to its seafood products line. Keep in mind that brand extension may have a negative effect if people do not see some link between the original product and a new one. Most new products now use some form of brand extension.

These are seven situations in which brand extension could be effective:

1. The same product is produced in a different form—for example, Jell-O Pudding Pops.

2. A distinctive taste/ingredient/component is presented in a new item—for example, Arm & Hammer detergent.

3. A new companion product is introduced—for example, Colgate Plus toothbrush.

4. A different product is offered to the same target market—for example, Visa travellers cheques aimed at Visa credit card customers.

5. A brand's perceived expertise is conferred on a new product—for example, Canon bubble-jet printers.

6. An existing benefit/attribute/feature is conferred on a new product—for example, Ivory shampoo (which connotes mildness).

7. A designer image/status is conveyed to a new product—for example, Pierre Cardin sunglasses.[52]

**HIGHLINER FOODS**
www.highlinerfoods.com

With **individual (multiple) branding**, separate brands are used for different items or product lines sold by a firm.

**Individual branding** *uses distinct brands.*

Through individual branding, a firm can create multiple product positions (separate brand images), attract various market segments, increase sales and marketing control, and offer both premium and low-priced brands. Individual branding also lets manufacturers secure greater shelf space in retail stores.

However, each brand incurs its own promotion costs and there is no positive brand-image rub-off. Economies from mass production may be lessened and new products may not benefit from an established identity. And there may be some cannibalization among company brands. Consumer products firms are more likely than industrial products firms to engage in individual branding.

To gain the benefits of family and individual branding, many firms combine the approaches, perhaps by having a flagship brand and other secondary brands. For example, one-third of Heinz's products have the Heinz name; the rest have names like StarKist, 9-Lives, Ore-Ida, and Weight Watchers. Or, a family brand could be used together with individual brands: Honda markets the upscale Acura and mainstream Honda auto lines. The Honda line includes the Honda Accord, Honda Civic, Honda Del Sol, Honda Odyssey, and Honda Prelude. It has an overall image and targets a specific market. New models gain from the Honda name, and there is a relationship among models. Individual brands are used with each model so differences can be highlighted.

## Choosing a Brand Name

A firm may choose a brand name from several potential sources. Under brand extension, an existing name is employed with a new product. (Zellers' Truly brand is selling health and beauty aids, household cleaning products, and fashion under such names as Truly Beauty, Truly Clean, and Truly Casual.)[53] For a private brand, the reseller specifies the name (BayCrest—a traditional clothing and soft goods brand name of The Bay).

**ZELLERS**
www.hbc.com/zellers/

If a new name is sought, these alternatives are available:

- Initials (YTV, A&W).
- Invented name (Kleenex, Compaq).
- Numbers (Boeing 777, Century 21).
- Mythological character (Atlas tires, Samsonite luggage).
- Personal name (Labatt, Ford).

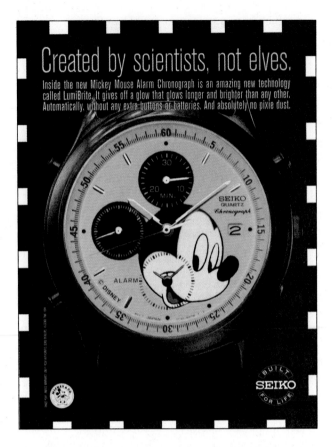

**FIGURE 9-10**

**Co-Branding: The Seiko Mickey Mouse Alarm Chronograph**

*Reprinted by permission.*

- Geographical name (Texas Instruments, Air Canada).
- Dictionary word (Close-Up toothpaste, Airlift water-based release agents—Air Products and Chemicals, Inc.'s way for its industrial customers to reduce or eliminate solvent emissions).
- Foreign word (Nestlé, Lux).
- Combination of words, initials, numbers, etc. (General Foods International Coffee, Head & Shoulders shampoo).

*Brand sources range from existing names to **licensing agreements**, and **co-branding**.*

Under a **licensing agreement**, a company pays a fee to use a name or logo whose trademark rights are held by another firm. Due to the high consumer recognition of many popular trademarks, sales for a product may be increased by paying a royalty fee to use one. Examples of names used in licensing are Coca-Cola, Anne of Green Gables, and the NHL. Beginning with the 1999-2000 season Roots Canada began a three-year licensing agreement with the NHL which saw them rolling out programs with all the Canadian NHL teams to sell Roots apparel that features the NHL logo and NHL team logos.[54]

In **co-branding**, two or more brand names are used with the same product to gain from the brand images of each. Typically, a company uses one of its own brand names in conjunction with another firm's—often under a licensing agreement. For instance, credit card companies have embraced this idea, and there are now Canadian Tire MasterCards and GM-Visa cards; and Zeller's and the Canadian Imperial Bank of Commerce have launched a Club Z Visa Card. Other examples of co-branding include the Pillsbury Deluxe Bar with M&M's, and the Seiko Mickey Mouse Alarm Chronograph. See Figure 9-10.

*Brand names should be suggestive, easy to remember, and flexible.*

A good brand name has several attributes, depending on the situation. It suggests something about a product's use or attributes (Sleep-Eze, Wash 'n Dry); is easy to spell and remember and is pronounceable in only one way (Bic, Tang); can be applied to a whole line of products (Deere tractors, Calvin Klein clothing); is capable

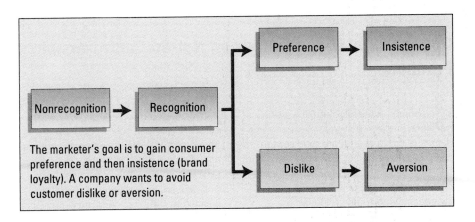

The marketer's goal is to gain consumer preference and then insistence (brand loyalty). A company wants to avoid customer dislike or aversion.

**FIGURE 9-11**

**The Consumer's Brand Decision Process**

of legal protection from use by others (Perrier, Equal artificial sweetener); has a pleasant or at least neutral meaning internationally (Esso, Kodak); and conveys a differential advantage (Pert Plus, Acutrim).

As firms expand globally, branding takes on special significance. Regardless of whether brands are "global" or tailored to particular markets, their meanings must not have negative connotations or violate cultural taboos. To avoid this, specialized firms such as NameLab (which can devise names that are acceptable around the world) can be hired. But brands must also reflect cultural and societal differences. This example illustrates why:

> The Lewis Woolf Griptight company makes infant and toddler products such as pacifiers. These products are sold in Great Britain, and the United States. When it talked to parents in Great Britain about the Griptight brand name being used before a new line was launched, the company discovered that it was 'the most un-user-friendly name.' People thought it was a carpet glue, a denture fixative, a kind of tire. The brand name became Kiddiwinks, a British word for children. In the United States, however, recognition of the name Binky was high, with some consumers using it as a generic term for pacifiers— hence, the name Binkykids.[55]

*The **consumer's brand decision process** moves from nonrecognition to insistence (or aversion).*

When branding, a firm should plan for the stages in the **consumer's brand decision process**, as displayed in Figure 9-11. For a new brand, a consumer begins with nonrecognition of the name, and the seller must make the person aware of it. He or she then moves to recognition, wherein the brand and its attributes are known, and the seller stresses persuasion. Next, the person develops a preference (or dislike) for a brand and buys it (or opts not to buy); the seller's task is to gain brand loyalty. Last, some people show a brand insistence (or aversion) and become loyal (or never buy); the seller's role is to maintain loyalty. Often people form preferences toward several brands but do not buy or insist upon one brand exclusively.

Using brand extension, a new product begins at the recognition, preference, or insistence stage of the brand decision process because of the carryover effect of the established name. However, consumers who dislike the existing product line would be unlikely to try a new product under the same name; but they might try another company product under a different brand.

## The Use of Trademarks

Finally, a firm must decide whether to seek trademark protection.[56] In Canada, the Canadian Trademarks Act is administered by Industry Canada through the Competition Bureau. Trademarking gives a firm the exclusive use of a word, name, symbol, combination of letters or numbers, or other devices—such as distinctive packaging—to identify the goods and services of that firm and distinguish them from others for as long as they are marketed. Both trademarks (for goods) and service marks (for services) are covered by trademark law.

*Trademark protection grants exclusive use of a brand or mark for as long as it is marketed.*

# ETHICS AND TODAY'S MARKETER

## Controversial Brand Names on Not-So-Controversial Products

Sometimes it seems that the marketplace is plagued by controversial brand names of products that are themselves non-controversial. Beer, perfume, and soda pop can certainly be consumed in front of children, but having to explain the meanings behind names like Nude Beer, Lakeport Truly Naked Beer, Opium perfume, and Sexual perfume presents more difficulty. And you'd have to know a bit of history to explain how Revolution Soda's name and image is associated with communist revolutionary Che Guevara, along with its flavours of Brainwash Cola, Guerrilla Punch, and Swamp Water. Although many people feel that these brand names are in questionable taste, most would agree that a name alone doesn't make a product. The fact is, many of these brands sell very well.

Lakeport brewing company is having success with Truly Naked beer; the beer's name ostensibly comes from the fact that it's a filtered beer, and thus pure, or "naked." The beer, which has nothing to hide, is pioneering a new category of beers. (One has to wonder though, if it's merely a coincidence that the brand has a sexy name and is being targeted at 18- to 25-year-old males). And when "Sexual," a new high-end perfume developed in Canada by Parfums Michel Germain of Toronto, was introduced it was expected to produce sales of $1 million, which is very strong for the Canadian market.

Firms usually choose a name in relation to a brand's target market and positioning strategy. They will choose a sexy or risqué type of name with the express intent of appealing to a certain type of customer. (Consumers of controversial brands tend to use them because of their shock value. But once this wears off, the brands usually fade away.) Contrary to popular belief, offending people is not necessarily something marketers wish to avoid. Market experience with controversial brands clearly proves this.

When a brand presents an unwholesome image—like "Death Cigarettes" (shocking name, but it clearly reflects the actual nature of the product), "Nude Beer" (which featured women on its containers who became nude when the containers became wet with condensation), and Opium perfume (which would be addictive to your lover)—then it's clear that some segments will be offended. Have marketers crossed the line of decency in these cases? It's not simply a matter of selling "smut" (a product in itself) or being shocking (which falls under freedom of speech), but of using smut or shock to sell a product that is itself not particularly smutty or shocking.

Beer, perfumes, pop, and cigarettes can be branded and promoted on the basis of their own inherent benefits and characteristics. But a large number of sexual appeals are associated with these products, even if the brand names themselves are not "sexy." For example, advertising for Molson's Canadian beer, Alfred Sung's Sung perfume, Pepsi, and Virginia Slims cigarettes have featured sexual appeals. Perhaps the overt appeals presented by brand names like Sexual Perfume, Truly Naked Beer, Revolution Soda, and Death Cigarettes are simply more honest.

Research and identify some "controversial" brand names associated with non-controversial products, and try to determine how long these brands have lasted. Discuss the advantages and disadvantages of controversial branding for a firm's product strategy.

*Sources*: Based on material in Eve Lazarus, "Daring Creative for B.C. Soda Makers," *Marketing Magazine* (September 14, 1998), p. 3; News Line, "The Naked and the Dinosaur in Brewing," *Marketing Magazine* (September 4, 1995), p. 3; and Gail Chiasson, "Canadian Sexual Goes National," *Marketing Magazine* (May 22, 1995), p. 4.

Trademarks are voluntary and require registration and implementation procedures that can be time-consuming and expensive (challenging a competitor may mean high legal fees and many years in court). A multinational firm must register trademarks in every nation in which it operates; even then, trademark rights may not be enforceable. For a trademark to be legally protected in Canada, it must have a distinct meaning that does not describe an entire product category, be used in interprovincial commerce (for federal protection), not be confusingly similar to other trademarks, and not imply attributes a product does not possess. A surname by itself cannot be registered because any person can generally do business under his or her name; it can be registered if used to describe a specific business (for example, McDonald's restaurants).

**KRAFT**
www.kraft.ca

The distinct meaning of a trademark can even apply to the unique shape of a product. Kraft Canada has the exclusive rights to import and distribute the Toblerone chocolate bar in Canada. Toblerone chocolate bars have been sold in Canada since 1910. The triangular-shaped chocolate with its sectioned peaks, as well as the triangular-shaped packaging with its off-yellow colouring and distinctive lettering, are all part of the uniqueness of the Toblerone brand. In 1997 Hagemayer Canada Inc. brought out Alperhorn brand chocolate bars in exactly the same size and shape as a Toblerone bar. The ingredients were the same and the packaging was similar in colour, shape, and lettering design. The major distinction was the difference in brand name.

Kraft asked Hagemeyer to stop selling Alperhorn because of the trademark infringement, but Hagemeyer refused and the dispute went to court. The court ruled that the packaging and product design approach used by Hagemeyer was confusing to the public such that they would think the product was sold by the same manufacturer. Even though the brand names were distinctly different, the court felt that Hagemeyer was passing its chocolate bar off as a Toblerone. An injunction was granted prohibiting Hagemeyer from selling any kind of chocolate bar with a peaked design or in triangular packaging. In addition, Hagemeyer had to deliver its on-hand product inventory to Kraft and then destroy all its advertising and packaging material. All inventory in the marketplace had to be recalled.[57]

When brands become too popular or descriptive of a product category, they run the risk of becoming public property. A firm then loses its trademark position. Brands fighting to remain exclusive trademarks include L'eggs, Rollerblade, Xerox, Levi's, Plexiglas, Formica, Kleenex, and Teflon. Former trademarks that are now considered generic—and, thus, public property—are cellophane, aspirin, shredded wheat, cola, linoleum, monopoly, and lite beer.

Trademark rulings can have wide implications. For example, a ruling in Ontario on a trademark infringement case involving Orkin pest control affected a ruling in India on a trademark case involving Calvin Klein. In the Ontario situation, Orkin of America tried to force an Ontario company named Orkin to change its name. Orkin was an unregistered foreign trademark in Canada. If the trademark is unregistered, a firm needs a local reputation acquired through doing business locally to gain protection. The problem was that Orkin of America had no history of doing business in Canada under the name Orkin. The court ruled, however, that Orkin of America did have a local reputation acquired by virtue of "spillover" advertising and by the fact that millions of Canadians were exposed to the brand in the Southern U.S. when they travelled there. Consequently, the Ontario Court ruled in favour of Orkin of America.

A similar situation cropped up in India where International Apparel Syndicate (IAS) sought to market "Calvin Klein" brand jeans in India. The real Calvin Klein company did not have a distribution relationship with IAS, had not registered its trademark in India, and was not selling any jeans there at the time. However, Calvin Klein sought trademark protection from IAS. The justice of the High Court of Calcutta looked for legal precedents for the case in jurisdictions throughout the British Commonwealth and came upon the Orkin decision in Ontario. As a result, a ruling was made in favour of Calvin Klein and trademark protection in India was granted.

# Packaging

**Packaging** has sometimes been described as the fifth element of the marketing mix (with product, distribution, promotion, and pricing being the other four). Whether it merits being a fifth element or not, its role in the marketing mix has been expanding. With the current proliferation of brands (a large retail store may hold as many as 80 000 items), standing out on the shelf is extremely important. Shelf clutter is a critical issue for marketers these days and unique packaging is about the only answer. The role of packaging in overcoming shelf clutter can be best illustrated by the following comments made by a number of Canadian packaged goods marketers:

- "If you're not seen, tough luck."
- "It's got to say pick me up and take me home."
- "Package design has to 'seduce' the consumer from the shelf."
- "It really has to have standout packaging just to get interest."
- "With impulse products package design plays an important part in the purchase decision."
- "Canadians and Americans are picking up what are called 'the extrinsic cues' about a product's quality from its package design."
- "No matter how much you advertise, when consumers get into the store they're faced with this [huge] selection, so the process really begins again when they make decisions based on packaging."[58]

Packaging is the part of product planning wherein a firm researches, designs, and produces package(s). As noted in the beginning of the chapter, a package consists of a product's physical container, label, and/or inserts.

The physical container may be a cardboard, metal, plastic, or wooden box; a cellophane, waxpaper, or cloth wrapper; a glass, aluminium, or plastic jar or can; a paper bag; styrofoam; some other material; or a combination of these. Products may have more than one container: Cereal is individually packaged in small cardboard boxes, with inner waxpaper wrapping, and shipped in large corrugated boxes; and watches are usually covered with cloth linings and shipped in plastic boxes. The label indicates a product's brand name, the company logo, ingredients, promotional messages, inventory codes, and/or instructions for use. Inserts are (1) instructions and safety information placed in drug, toy, and other packages or (2) coupons, prizes, or recipe booklets. They are used as appropriate.

Prior to the advent of the modern supermarket and department store, manufacturers commonly shipped merchandise in bulk containers such as: cracker barrels, sugar sacks, and butter tubs. Retail merchants repackaged the contents into smaller, more convenient units to meet customer needs. With the growth of mass merchants and self-service, manufacturers came to realize the value of packaging as a marketing tool. Today, it is a vital part of a firm's product development strategy; a package may even be the product itself (such as the drawstring tea bag shown in Figure 9-12) or an integral part of the product (such as the aerosol can for shaving cream).

Packaging plays a key role in helping consumers form perceptions about a product (brand). As one packaging expert noted, "Our experience, supported by research, indicates that the consumer does not conceptually strip away the packaging and consider the actual product when making a buying decision. For instance, in the case of food and beverages, the package communicates a promise of quality, taste, and enjoyment, and the consumer expects the product inside to measure up. If it does not, or if the package fails to deliver on the product's promise, another product failure is the likely result."[59]

About 10 per cent of a typical product's final selling price goes for its packaging. The amount is higher for such products as cosmetics (up to 40 per cent and more). The complete package redesign of a major product might cost millions of dollars for machinery and production. Packaging decisions must serve both resellers and consumers. Plans are often made in conjunction with production, logistics, and legal personnel. Errors in packaging can be costly.

Package redesign may occur when a firm's current packaging receives a poor response from channel members and customers or becomes too expensive; the firm seeks a new market segment, reformulates a product, or changes or updates its product positioning; or new technology becomes available.

Glynne Jones is President of Tetley Canada, which controls 25 per cent of the Canadian tea market—and he wants more. Innovation and taking risks is one way he plans to expand Tetley's market share and maintain the firm's edge in its battle with rival Lipton tea. Innovation in this case comes in the form of the "no drip, no mess" drawstring tea bag. Jones recently demonstrated this new packaging for tea by "dangling a freshly steeped tea bag over the flawless white of his shirt sleeve. After a few tense moments it was clear that the Tetley Drawstring tea bag's pitch delivers." The new tea bags are designed so that users can squeeze all the liquid out by pulling the drawstrings. Tetley has certainly developed a needed innovation for all the tea drinkers who have ever struggled to squeeze the excess liquid of a tea bag, or wondered what to do with a drippy tea bag.[60]

The basic functions of packaging, factors considered when making packaging decisions, and criticisms of packaging are described next.

**TETLEY CANADA**
www.tetley.ca

## Basic Packaging Functions

The basic **packaging functions** are containment and protection, usage, communication, segmentation, channel cooperation, and new-product planning:

*Packaging functions range from containment and protection to product planning.*

- *Containment and protection*—Packaging enables liquid, granular, and other divisible products to be contained in a given quantity and form. It also protects a product while it is shipped, stored, and handled.
- *Usage*—Packaging lets a product be easily used and re-stored. It may even be reusable after a product is depleted. Packaging must also be safe to all who use it, from the youngest child to the oldest senior.
- *Communication*—Packaging communicates a brand image, provides ingredients and directions, and displays the product. It is a major promotion tool.
- *Segmentation*—Packaging can be tailor-made for a specific market group. If a firm offers two or more package shapes, sizes, colours, or designs, it may employ differentiated marketing.
- *Channel cooperation*—Packaging can address wholesaler and retailer needs with regard to shipping, storing, promotion, and so on.
- *New-product planning*—New packaging can be a meaningful innovation for a firm and stimulate its sales.

## Factors Considered in Packaging Decisions

*What image is sought?*

Several factors must be weighed in making packaging decisions. Colour, shape, and material all influence consumer perceptions. For example:

> It used to be so predictable. A carton of milk sat in the fridge, a symbol of health and nutrition in the all-too-familiar square white packaging. Nearby stood the colourful pop cans and juice bottles. Now Canada's four major dairies have launched a variety of portable milkshakes and flavoured milks to capture the taste buds of the younger set. Jazzy new packaging, with plastic resealable bottles and eye-catching labels, are revealing milk's cool, on-the-go potential, while downplaying health and nutritional benefits.[61]

The changes are working; portable bottles are now the fastest growing segment of the market, with about 1 per cent share of Canada's total sales of $3 billion. Sales are expected to reach $60 million in the new millennium. See Figure 9-13.

*Should family packaging be used?*

In family packaging, a firm uses a common element on each package in a product line. This approach parallels family branding. Campbell has virtually identical packages for its traditional soups, distinguished only by flavour or content identification. Procter & Gamble, the maker of Head & Shoulders and Pert Shampoo, does not use family packaging with the two brands; they have distinct packages to attract different segments.

*Should standard packages be used worldwide?*

An international firm must determine if a standardized package can be used worldwide (with only a language change on the label). Standardization boosts global recognition. Thus, Coke and Pepsi have standard packages when possible. Yet some colours, symbols, and shapes have negative meanings in some nations. For example, white can mean purity or mourning, two vastly different images.

*What should costs be?*

Package costs must be considered on both a total and per-unit basis. As noted earlier, total costs can run into the millions of dollars; and per-unit costs can go as high as 40 per cent of a product's selling price—depending on the purpose and extent of the packaging.

*What materials and innovations are right?*

A firm has many packaging materials from which to select, such as paperboard, plastic, metal, glass, styrofoam, and cellophane. In making the choice, trade-offs are often needed: cellophane allows products to be attractively displayed, but it is highly susceptible to tearing; paperboard is relatively inexpensive, but it is hard to open. A firm must also decide how innovative it wants its packaging to be.

*What features should the packaging incorporate?*

There is a wide range of package features from which to choose, depending on the product. These features include pour spouts, hinged lids, screw-on tops, pop-tops, see-through bags, tuck- or seal-end cartons, carry handles, product testers (for

**FIGURE 9-13**

**Plastic resealable bottles and eye-catching labels reveal cool, on-the-go potential.**

*Courtesy Neilson Dairy.*

items like batteries), and freshness dating. They may provide a firm with a differential advantage.

A firm has to select the specific size(s), colour(s), and shape(s) of its packages. In picking a package size, shelf life (how long a product stays fresh), convenience, tradition, and competition must be considered. In the food industry, new and larger sizes have captured high sales. The choice of package colour depends on the image sought. In 1999 Tetley Tea repackaged its iced tea line with "Tetley Blue" packaging in order to focus on the refreshment aspect of the tea. The packaging had previously used the colour of the flavour that it contained.[62] Package shape also affects a product's image. Hanes created a mystique for L'eggs pantyhose via the egg-shaped package. The number of packages used with any one product depends on competition and the firm's use of differentiated marketing. By selling small, medium, and large sizes, a firm may ensure maximum shelf space, appeal to different consumers, and make it difficult and expensive for a new company to gain channel access.

*What size(s), colour(s), and shape(s) are used?*

The placement, content, size, and prominence of the label must be determined. Both company and brand names (if appropriate) need to appear on the label. The existence of package inserts and other useful information (some of which may be required by law) should be noted on the label. Sometimes, a redesigned label may be confusing to customers and hurt a product's sales. As one analyst noted, "Marketers are always trying to improve things, and they may end up causing problems for themselves."[63]

*How should the label and inserts appear?*

Multiple packaging couples two or more product items in one container. It may involve the same product (such as razor blades) or combine different ones (such as a comb and a brush or a first-aid kit). The goal is to increase usage (hoarding may be a problem), get people to buy an assortment of items, or have people try a new item (such as a new toothpaste packaged with an established toothbrush brand). Many multiple packs, like cereal, are versatile—they can be sold as shipped or broken into single units.

*Should multiple packaging be used?*

Individually wrapping portions of a divisible product may offer a competitive advantage, but this must be weighed against the fact that it's often costly and contributes to environmental waste. Kraft has done well with its individually wrapped

*Should items be individually wrapped?*

cheese slices. Alka-Seltzer sells tablets in individually wrapped tin-foil containers, as well as in a bottle without wrapping. Nabisco Ltd. of Toronto is trying to reach children under fifteen by offering single-serve packages and mini-sizes of its Chips Ahoy, Oreo, Crispers, and Bits and Bites brands under its Planet Snak positioning.

*Should a package have a pre-printed price and use the* **Universal Product Code***?*

For certain items (such as shirts, magazines, watches, and candy), some resellers want pre-printed prices. They then have the option of charging those prices or adhering their own labels. Some resellers prefer only a space for the price on the package and insert their own price labels automatically. Because of the growing use of computer technology by resellers in monitoring their inventory levels, more of them are insisting on pre-marked inventory codes on packages. The **Universal Product Code (UPC)**, is a voluntary marking standard used by retailers and manufacturers in Canada and the United States. Using the UPC, manufacturers pre-mark items with a series of thick and thin vertical lines. Price and inventory data codes are represented by these lines, which appear on outer package labels—but are not readable by employees and customers. The lines are "read" by computerized optical scanning equipment at the checkout counter. The cashier does not have to ring up a transaction manually and inventory data are instantly transmitted to the main computer of the retailer (or the manufacturer). In the UPC system, human-readable prices must still be marked on items, either by the manufacturer or the reseller.[64]

The Product Code Council of Canada, located at 885 Don Mills Rd., Ste. #301, Don Mills, Ontario, M3C 1V9, is responsible for assigning and administering Universal Product Codes in Canada.

*How does the package interrelate with other marketing variables?*

Last, a firm must be sure the package design fits in with the rest of its marketing mix. A well-known perfume brand may be extravagantly packaged, distributed in select stores, advertised in upscale magazines, and sold at a high price. In contrast, a firm making perfumes that imitate leading brands has more basic packaging, distributes in discount stores, does not advertise, and uses low prices. The two perfume brands may cost an identical amount to make, but the imitator would spend only a fraction as much on packaging.

### Criticisms of Packaging

*Packaging is faulted for waste, misleading labels, etc.*

The packaging practices of some industries and firms have been heavily criticized and regulated in recent years due to their impact (or potential impact) on the environment and scarce resources, the high expenditures on packaging, questions about the honesty of labels and the confusion caused by inconsistent designations of package sizes (such as large, family, super), and critics' perceptions of inadequate package safety.

Yet, consumers—as well as business—must bear part of the responsibility for the negative results of packaging. Throwaway bottles (highly preferred by consumers) use almost three times the energy of returnable ones. Shoplifting annually adds to packaging costs because firms must add security tags and otherwise alter packages.

In planning their packaging programs, firms need to weigh the short-term and long-term benefits and costs of providing environmentally safer ("green"), less confusing, and more tamper-resistant packages. Generally, firms are responding quite positively to the criticisms raised here.

## Growing Products

Once a new product is commercialized, the goal is for consumer acceptance and company sales to rise rapidly. This occurs in some cases; in others, it may take a long while. The growth rate and total sales level of new products rely heavily on two related consumer behaviour concepts: the adoption process and the diffusion process. In managing growing products, a firm must understand these concepts and plan its marketing efforts accordingly.

The **adoption process** is the mental and behavioural procedure an individual consumer goes through when learning about and purchasing a new product. It consists of these stages:

1. *Knowledge*—A person (organization) learns of a product's existence and gains some understanding of how it functions.
2. *Persuasion*—A person (organization) forms a favourable or unfavourable attitude about a product.
3. *Decision*—A person (organization) engages in actions that lead to a choice to adopt or reject a product.
4. *Implementation*—A person (organization) uses a product.
5. *Confirmation*—A person (organization) seeks reinforcement and may reverse a decision if exposed to conflicting messages.[65]

The rate (speed) of adoption depends on consumer traits, the product, and the firm's marketing effort. Adoption is faster if consumers have high discretionary income and are willing to try new offerings; the product has low perceived risk; the product has an advantage over other items on the market; the product is a modification and not an innovation; the product is compatible with current consumer lifestyles or ways of operating a business; product attributes can be easily communicated; product importance is low; the product can be tested before a purchase; the product is consumed quickly; the product is easy to use; mass advertising and distribution are used; and the marketing mix adjusts as the person (organization) moves through the adoption process.

The **diffusion process** describes the manner in which different members of the target market often accept and purchase a product. It spans the time from product introduction through market saturation and affects the total sales level of a product as it moves through the life cycle:

1. Innovators are the first to try a new product. They are venturesome, willing to accept risk, socially aggressive, communicative, and worldly. It must be determined which innovators are opinion leaders—those who influence others. This group is about 2.5 per cent of the market.
2. Early adopters are the next to buy a new product. They enjoy the prestige, leadership, and respect that early purchases bring—and tend to be opinion leaders. They adopt new ideas but use discretion. This group is about 13.5 per cent of the market.
3. The early majority is the initial part of the mass market to buy a product. They have status among peers and are outgoing, communicative, and attentive to information. This group is about 34 per cent of the market.
4. The late majority is the second part of the mass market to buy. They are less cosmopolitan and responsive to change, and include people (firms) with lower economic and social status, those past middle age (or set in their jobs), and skeptics. This group is about 34 per cent of the market.
5. Laggards purchase last, if at all. They are price-conscious, suspicious of change, low in income and status, tradition bound, and conservative. They do not adopt a product until it reaches maturity. Some sellers ignore them because it can be hard to market a product to laggards. Thus, concentrated marketing may do well by focusing on products for laggards. This group is about 16 per cent of the market.[66]

*The **adoption process** explains the new-product purchase behaviour of individual consumers.*

*The **diffusion process** describes when different segments are likely to purchase.*

**FIGURE 9-14**

**The SensorExcel™ for Women: a minor innovation**

*Courtesy of the Gillette Company.*

Growth for a major innovation often starts slowly, because there's an extended adoption process and the early majority may be hesitant to buy. Sales may then rise quickly. The digital camera, for example, is a major innovation because it promises to eliminate the need for film and film developing. It provides instant pictures and no developing costs, and photographers can immediately view the pictures they've taken and instantly determine if they want to take another shot. Of course, the benefit isn't relevant for candid or action shots, but one does receive immediate gratification with a digital camera. Digital cameras have been used by professional photographers for well over ten years, but there has recently been a tremendous increase in purchases by consumers. Since digital cameras currently require a personal computer to download and store pictures, the size of the market is tied to personal computer usage.

Still, in Canada digital camera sales were $26 million in 1997 and around $39 million in 1998 (a 50 per cent increase). The expectations for this market are for continued strong growth spurred on by a couple of factors: retail prices have been falling steadily, from a high of $2000 for some models to the $500 range for some name brand cameras; and the design and technology of the cameras has become more sophisticated, which also appeals to buyers.[67]

For minor innovations or product modifications, growth is usually much faster. Therefore, marketers often prefer to launch these kinds of products as opposed to developing "innovations." As an example, in the spring of 1996, Gillette introduced SensorExcel™ for women with a $2.5 million multi-media rollout. The SensorExcel is a premium adaptation from the Sensor line of razors for men.[68] See Figure 9-14.

The following products are among those currently in the growth stage of the product life cycle, and represent good opportunities for firms: DVD players and software, audio-visual products like data projection systems and flat wall-mounted monitor screens, digital cameras, Internet service providers and services offered via the Internet, specialty TV channels, specialized skin care products, nutraceuticals, solar-powered products, high definition TVs, international financial services, rechargeable batteries, subnotebook PCs, and Internet video conferencing.

# Mature Products

Products are in the maturity stage of the life cycle when they reach the late majority and laggard markets. Goals turn from growth to maintenance. Because new products are so costly and risky, more firms are placing marketing emphasis on mature products with steady sales and profits, and minimal risk.

*Proper marketing can let mature products maintain high sales.*

In managing mature products, a firm should examine the size, attributes, and needs of the current market; untapped market segments; competition; the potential for product modifications; the likelihood of new company products replacing mature ones; profit margins; the marketing effort required for each sale; reseller attitudes; the promotion mix; the impact of specific products on the overall product line; each product's effect on company image; the number of years remaining for the products; and the management effort needed.

Having a popular brand in a mature product category has many benefits. First, the life cycle may be extended almost indefinitely. Budweiser beer, Coke Classic soft drink, Goodyear tires, Ivory soap, Lipton tea, Maxwell House coffee, Life Savers mints, Sherwin-Williams paints, and Quaker Oats oatmeal are among the leaders in their product categories; each is well over seventy-five years old. Second, the brand attracts a loyal customer group and has a stable, profitable position in the market. Third, the likelihood of future low demand is greatly reduced; this is a real risk for new products. Fourth, a firm's overall image is enhanced, allowing the firm to extend a popular name to other products. Fifth, it allows for more control over marketing efforts and more precision in sales forecasting. Sixth, mature products can be used as cash cows to support spending on new products. However, some marketing support must be continued if a mature product is to remain popular.

*Popular mature brands offer several benefits for companies.*

Successful industries and companies market products that stay in maturity for long periods, as the following illustrate:

- The paper clip was invented in 1899 by Norwegian Johan Vaaler. Since then, "several hundred inventors have patented paper clips in every conceivable shape—square, round, oval, triangular, teardrop, and arrowhead." Today, it is more popular than ever due to its ease of use, flexible applications, and large customer following. It seems that after nearly 100 years, there is still nothing to match a paper clip. Twenty billion are sold yearly.[69]

- "Whether clothes are lean or loose, short or long, there's a common thread running through much of today's fashion: Lycra—DuPont's trademark for spandex fibre that started out in the 1950s as a substitute for rubber in girdles." After sales stagnated for a while, the fibre gained attention in the 1980s with the advent of cycling pants and leggings, and technological advances that let Lycra fibres be used in sheer hosiery. Lycra is now "in everything from long, willowy cotton and

### TABLE 9-2

### Selected Strategies for Extending the Mature Stage of the Product Life Cycle

| STRATEGY | EXAMPLES |
|---|---|
| **1.** Develop new uses for products | Jell-O used in garden salads<br>WD-40 used in the maintenance of kitchen appliances |
| **2.** Develop new product features and refinements | Disposable 35mm cameras<br>Battery-powered televisions |
| **3.** Increase the market | Bell Canada's 1-800 & 1-888 phone services for small businesses<br>International editions of major magazines |
| **4.** Find new classes of consumers for present products | Nylon carpeting for institutional markets<br>Johnson & Johnson's baby shampoo used by adults |
| **5.** Find new classes of consumers for modified products | 5 in 1 Fax, scanner, copier, printer, and telephone machines for home offices |
| **6.** Increase product usage among current users | Multiple packages for soda and milk<br>Discounts given for making more long distance phone calls |
| **7.** Change marketing strategy | Greeting cards sold in supermarkets<br>Office furniture promoted in mail-order catalogues |

linen sheaths by Liz Claiborne's Lizsport to crewneck bodysuits from Anne Klein II and tank dresses from designer Donna Karan's DKNY division." In certain parts of Europe, the Lycra name has a consumer recognition rate of 98 per cent; and expansion in Latin America and the Far East are under way.[70]

There are many options available for extending the mature stage of the product life cycle. Table 9-2 shows seven strategies and gives examples of each.

Not all mature products can be revived or extended. Consumer needs may disappear, as when frozen juice replaced juice squeezers. Lifestyle changes may lead to less interest in products, such as teller services in banks. Better and more convenient products may be devised, such as digital disk players which replaced vinyl record turntables. The market may be saturated and further marketing efforts may be unable to garner enough sales to justify time and costs, which is why Electrohome of Canada withdrew from consumer electronics.

## Product Deletion

*Products need to be deleted if they have consistently poor sales, tie up resources, and cannot be revived.*

Products should be deleted from a firm's offerings if they offer limited sales and profit potential, reflect poorly on the firm, tie up resources that could be used for other opportunities, involve large amounts of management time, create reseller dissatisfaction due to low inventory turnover, and divert attention from long-term goals.

However, there are many points to weigh before deleting a product: As a product matures, it blends in with existing items and becomes part of the total product line (mix). Customers and distribution intermediaries may be hurt if an item is dropped. A firm may not want competitors to have the only product for customers. Poor sales and profits may be only temporary. Or the marketing strategy, not the product, may be the cause of poor results. Thus, a systematic procedure should be used to handle faltering products.

## INTERNATIONAL MARKETING IN ACTION

### Building NHL Fans in Japan

If the name weren't already taken, the National Hockey League might want to be renamed the "International" Hockey League. The league is filled with Canadians, Americans, Russians, Swedes, Finns, Czechs, Slovaks, Germans, Belarussians, and many other nationalities (although most players are from North America and Europe). Because the NHL wants hockey to become a truly global game, just like soccer, building up interest in the sport in Asia is one of its current objectives. In the long run it's hoped that Asia may develop hockey players who will be good enough to play in the league, and bring with them fan support as well.

The NHL believes that the best way to showcase hockey is to have people see it live and not just on television. So in 1997–1998 the Anaheim Mighty Ducks and the Vancouver Canucks opened their regular season in Tokyo, and the next year the Calgary Flames and San Jose Sharks did the same. In conjunction with the games the NHL sponsored a HockeyFest, which involved an inline hockey tournament, autograph signings by players, and hockey clinics run by coaches.

You might question the selection of these teams to showcase the game in Japan, since aside from the Calgary Flames none of the other franchises has ever won a Stanley Cup. Even at that, Calgary doesn't bring as rich or storied a hockey history as would a couple of the original six franchises, such as Toronto or Montreal. On the surface a better plan might have involved having the New York Rangers play in either of these contests, offering Japanese fans a look at a pre-retired Wayne Gretzky, one of the best known athletes in the world and the most prolific scorer in NHL history!

But the teams were chosen because it was believed that Japanese fans would already have a link with them. Banff, Alberta is a well-known destination for Japanese tourists; Vancouver is also a major tourist and business destination. San Jose sits in the middle of California's Silicon Valley, a world-class business destination; and Anaheim is home to Disneyland, one of the major tourist destinations on the U.S. West Coast. Japan was chosen as the place to showcase hockey because Nagano, as host to the 1998 Winter Olympic games, placed a team in both the men's and women's Olympic ice hockey tournaments. It was felt that hockey interest would be at its highest as a result of these links.

The hopes of developing both a fan and a player base for hockey in Japan go hand-in-hand. But hockey is a game that requires not only interest, but infrastructure. Ice rinks aren't common in Japan, and given the intensity of land use there, are bound to be relatively expensive. On the other hand, inline hockey doesn't require ice, and the skating, puck handling, and shooting skills it develops are transferable to the ice-based game, as would be the interest created. One immediate benefit for the NHL has been an increase in merchandise sales in Japan, along with the establishment of official NHL shops selling licensed merchandise.

Discuss the selection of Japan as a market for hockey development. What other nations or areas might the NHL consider as being ripe for hockey? If you could advise NHL Commissioner Gary Bettman on hockey development, what advice would you give him?

*Source:* Based on Norma Reveller, "The NHL Takes a Well-Aimed Shot at Building Fans in Japan," *Marketing Magazine* (May 11, 1998), p. 6.

As these examples show, low-profit or rapidly declining products are often dropped or de-emphasized:

- After seven years on the market, the Cadillac Allante, a U.S.$62 000 General Motors' two-seat luxury roadster, was discontinued due to weak sales. Although the car was profitable, only 2000 units were sold during its last year. And the Allante was very complicated to build, with undercarriages made in Detroit and bodies and interiors made in Italy.

# MARKETING IN THE THIRD MILLENNIUM

## Building Brand Longevity with Branded Buildings[73]

The task of building up a firm's brand name image is often thought of as monumental. But a number of firms have chosen to make their brand names literally monumental, by sponsoring buildings. This might not seem like a particularly new idea, since most large companies do have a corporate headquarters named after the company, and university benefactors have been getting their names on buildings for years in response to generous donations.

However, the new trend emerging in Canada and the United States is to brand public sports and entertainment venues in response to major donations by corporations. Examples include the recently opened Air Canada Centre in Toronto, Vancouver's GM Place, the Canadian Airlines Saddle Dome in Calgary, the United Centre in Chicago (United Airlines is the sponsor), the Corel Centre in Ottawa (formerly the Palladium), and the Molson's Centre in Montreal. The hockey teams located in the Corel Centre and the Molson's Centre are owned by their corporate sponsors, although they are not the main businesses of their owners. And corporations haven't restricted their sponsorships to sports centres; for example, Ford has its name on performing arts centres in both Toronto and Vancouver.

What possible advantages accrue to these companies by virtue of "branding" these buildings? For starters, the level of publicity exposure is extremely high and should continue as long as the building stands. Since the firm's name is linked with the entertainment taking place at the venue, the exposure starts with the 17 000 to 22 000 fans who pack the various arenas and concert halls, and expands to the millions who watch on TV and the millions more who see the sports highlights later or read about the event in the newspaper the next day. In comparison, only thousands may use your university building or visit your corporate headquarters. And this "free" publicity goes on game after game, and if the building was built to last, year after year.

There are a couple of potential problems with branding a building. The teams using the venue may be losers, and as the building ages over time it may begin to look run down. Both instances could reflect negatively on the sponsor. Because Molson and Corel own teams, disaffection for the teams' performance may spill over to their products. But it's doubtful that anyone would blame Canadian Airlines for an early playoff exit by the Calgary Flames. As for decay of the building, one can remove sponsorship from the run-down building, make sponsorship conditional on the structure being maintained, or even ante up to renovate or rebuild, thus garnering more positive public relations!

- The Scott Paper Company decided to drop the White Swan brand of facial tissues and paper towels in Atlantic Canada and Quebec because they could not see significant product differentiation in the facial tissue and paper towel markets. The reduction in the number of products would allow Scott Paper to focus its efforts on building national and international brands, like Scotties facial tissues and Scott towels.[71]

- Although it's part of the most successful fast food chain in the world, McDonald's of Canada has seen its share of products that have had to be discontinued. Because of a poor sales response, McDonald's no longer serves pizza in its western Canadian stores. It also seems that adding "Deluxe" to the name is the kiss of death for a new McDonald's hamburger. Recently the Arch Deluxe was quietly discontinued because it didn't have the sustained impact that McDonald's was hoping for. It's been replaced by the Big Xtra meal. About five years prior to this, McDonald's "McLean Deluxe," which was an attempt to offer a healthier burger, was also discontinued because of a poor sales response.[72]

In discontinuing a product, a firm must take replacement parts, the notification time for customers and resellers, and the honouring of warranties/guarantees into account. For example, a company planning to delete its line of office telephones must resolve these questions: Who will make replacement parts? How long will they be made? How soon before the actual deletion will an announcement be made? Will distributors be alerted early enough so they can line up other suppliers? How will warranties be honoured? After they expire, how will repairs be handled?

*During deletion, customer and distributor needs must be considered.*

# SUMMARY

**1.** *To detail the importance of new products and describe why new products fail* New products are important because they may foster differential advantages, sustain sales growth, require a lot of time for development, generate large profits, enable a firm to diversify, make distribution more efficient, lead to technological breakthroughs, allow waste products to be used, respond to changing consumers, and address government mandates.

When a firm suffers a financial loss, a product is an absolute failure. When it makes a profit but does not attain its goals, a product is a relative failure. Failures occur because of such factors as a lack of a significant differential advantage, poor planning, poor timing, and excessive enthusiasm by the product sponsor.

**2.** *To study the stages in the new-product planning process* New-product planning involves a comprehensive, seven-step process. During idea generation, new opportunities are sought. In product screening, unattractive ideas are weeded out using a new-product screening checklist. At concept testing, the consumer reacts to a proposed idea. Business analysis requires a detailed evaluation of demand, costs, competition, investments, and profits. Product development converts an idea into a tangible form and outlines a marketing strategy. Test marketing, a much-debated technique, involves placing a product for sale in selected areas and observing performance under actual conditions. Commercialization is the sale of a product to the full target market.

A new product can be terminated or modified at any point in the process.

**3.** *To define and distinguish among branding terms, to examine the importance of branding, and to study the key branding decisions that must be made* Branding is the procedure a firm follows in planning and marketing its brand(s). A brand is a name, term, design, or symbol (or combination) that identifies a good or service. A brand name is a word, letter (number), or group of words or letters (numbers) that can be spoken. A brand mark is a symbol, design, or distinctive colouring or lettering. A trade character is a personified brand mark. A trademark is a brand name, brand mark, or trade character given legal protection.

There are millions of brand names in circulation worldwide. Ad spending on them is many billions of dollars annually. Through strong brands, brand loyalty can be secured. Popular brands also speed up the acceptance of new products. Gaining and keeping brand recognition is a top priority, as are the development of brand equity and a brand image. Branding benefits all parties: manufacturers, distribution intermediaries, and consumers.

Four fundamental decisions are necessary in branding. First, corporate symbols are determined and, if applicable, revised. The company's name (and/or divisional names), logo(s), and trade characters set its overall image. Second, a branding philosophy is set, which includes the proper use of manufacturer, private, and/or generic brands, as well as

family and/or individual branding. At this stage, a mixed-brand strategy, the battle of the brands, and brand extension (a popular approach) are also assessed.

Third, a brand name is chosen from one of several sources, including brand extension from existing names, private brands, licensing a name from another firm, and co-branding. With a new brand, the consumer's brand decision process moves from nonrecognition to recognition to preference (or dislike) to insistence (or aversion). With a continuing name applied to a new product, the brand decision process would begin at recognition, preference (or dislike), or insistence (or aversion). Fourth, the use of trademarks is evaluated and planned.

**4.** *To define and distinguish among packaging terms and to examine the importance of packaging* Packaging is the procedure a firm follows in planning and marketing their product package(s). A package consists of a physical container, label, and/or inserts. Today, packaging is an integral part of a firm's new-product planning strategy.

Ten per cent of a typical product's final selling price goes for packaging. Package redesign can be quite expensive. Both channel member and final consumer needs must be taken into consideration. Errors can be quite costly.

**5.** *To analyze the growth and maturity of products, including the adoption process, the diffusion process, and extension strategies, and to examine product deletion decisions* *and strategies* Once a new product is commercialized, the firm's goal is consumer acceptance and for company sales to rise as rapidly as possible. However, the growth rate and sales level for a new product are dependent on the adoption process—which describes how a single consumer learns about and purchases a product—and the diffusion process—which describes how different members of the target market learn about and purchase a product. These processes are faster for certain consumers, products, and marketing strategies.

When products mature, company goals turn from growth to maintenance. Mature products can provide stable sales and profits and loyal consumers. They do not require the risks and costs of new products. There are several factors to consider and alternative strategies from which to choose when planning to sustain mature products. It may not be possible to retain aging products if consumer needs disappear, lifestyles change, new products make them obsolete, or the market becomes too saturated.

At some point, a firm may have to determine whether to continue a faltering product. Product deletion may be difficult because of the interrelation of products, the impact on customers and resellers, and other factors. It should be done in a structured manner; and replacement parts, notification time, and warranties should all be considered in a deletion plan.

## KEY TERMS

**new product** (p. 245)

**modifications** (p. 245)

**minor innovations** (p. 245)

**major innovations** (p. 245)

**brand** (p. 245)

**package** (p. 245)

**absolute product failure** (p. 248)

**relative product failure** (p. 248)

**new-product planning process** (p. 249)

**idea generation** (p. 250)

**product screening** (p. 252)

**patent** (p. 252)

**concept testing** (p. 253)

**business analysis** (p. 253)

**product development** (p. 254)

**test marketing** (p. 255)

**commercialization** (p. 256)

**brand name** (p. 257)

**brand mark** (p. 257)

**trade character** (p. 257)

**trademark** (p. 257)

**brand equity** (p. 260)

**brand image** (p. 260)

**corporate symbols** (p. 261)

**manufacturer brands** (p. 262)

**private (dealer) brands** (p. 263)

**generic brands** (p. 264)

**mixed-brand strategy** (p. 265)

**battle of the brands** (p. 265)

**family (blanket) branding** (p. 265)

**brand extension** (p. 266)

**individual (multiple) branding** (p. 267)

**licensing agreement** (p. 268)

**co-branding** (p. 268)

**consumer's brand decision process** (p. 269)

**packaging** (p. 272)

**packaging functions** (p. 273)

**Universal Product Code (UPC)** (p. 276)

**adoption process** (p. 277)

**diffusion process** (p. 277)

## REVIEW QUESTIONS

1. Distinguish among a product modification, a minor innovation, and a major innovation. Present an example of each for a hospital.

2. Give four reasons why new products are important to a company.

3. What are the pros and cons of test marketing?

4. Differentiate among these terms: brand, brand mark, trade character, brand name, and trademark.

5. Why do manufacturer brands have such a large percentage of sales in so many product categories? Will private brands and generic brands eventually displace manufacturer brands? Explain your answer.

6. In which circumstances is brand extension most effective? Least effective?

7. Describe the six major functions of packaging. Give an example of each.
8. How does the Universal Product Code (UPC) assist channel members, such as wholesalers and retailers?
9. Cite five ways in which a firm could extend the mature stage of the product life cycle. Provide an example of each.
10. Why is a product deletion decision so difficult?

# DISCUSSION QUESTIONS

1. Comment on the following statement: "We never worry about relative product failures because we make a profit on them. We only worry about absolute product failures."
2. Differentiate between the commercialization strategies for a product modification and a major innovation. Relate your answers to the adoption process and the diffusion process.
3. An office-supply company, Horizon Paper Corporation, recently changed its name to Horizon Products Corporation. Why do you think this name change was necessary? Do you think this is a good name? Explain your answer.
4. Comment on this statement: "In planning packaging programs, firms need to weigh the short-term and long-term benefits and costs of environmentally safer, less confusing, and more tamper-resistant packages."
5. Select a product that has been in existence for twenty or more years and explain why it has been successful for so long.

## CASE STUDY

# A Marketer's Nightmare: New Product Flops

There's an old saying, "Success has many parents, but failure is an orphan." Since 80 to 90 per cent of all new products fail, unfortunately orphans are the rule in marketing new products, not the exception. This means that a marketer needs a tough-minded approach and a poker player's instinct for when to call and when to fold.

In Ithaca, New York, the New Product Showcase and Learning Center (better known as the Museum of Flops) represents a monument to folly and a set of object lessons for marketers. "Those who forget the past are doomed to repeat it" is the raison d'etre of this institution. The museum contains 80 000 "odd" items—and the law of averages says there will be more to come. A guided tour of the learning centre reveals a number of fascinating products and product concepts, some of which don't seem all that bad (like Campbell's no-salt tomato soup and Short and Sassy shampoo). The need seems apparent, but the timing was off. People just didn't buy them when they were put on the market. Timing is also a factor in such products as Republican Choice Coffee, with former U.S. President George Bush's face on the label. Its popularity fell as fast as his did.

One also finds products that made it onto the market for reasons that are hard for even a casual observer to fathom, let alone an experienced marketer. Aerosol ketchup? Toaster chicken patties? Toaster eggs? Canada's Cold Buster Bar? Richard Simmon's Salad Spray? Spray-U-Thin, a weight loss product? The aerosol ketchup cans exploded after awhile as the corrosive ketchup placed under pressure ate through the metal can. The toaster chicken would drip fat into the toaster and set it on fire. As for Cold Buster Bars, toaster eggs, salad spray, and Spray-U-Thin, it's not hard to understand why they failed.

The museum contains a host of products for which the need is apparent but the brand name decisions seem hard to relate to. For example, Warheads candy and Harley Davidson Heavy Beer certainly tap into commonly satisfied needs. The candy and beer markets are large so the products concepts are viable, but "Warhead" certainly doesn't evoke the image of candy, and a beer named after a motorcycle seems to be stretching things too far.

Sometimes a firm has a great product concept but just can't get it to work. This was the case for R.J. Reynolds, which spent $325 million in trying to develop and market Premier, a smokeless cigarette. Great idea— no second-hand smoke to bother other people, and you might even be able to use the product in all those no smoking areas. After all, how can you be smoking if your cigarette is smokeless? What a tremendous competitive advantage! The problem was that the cigarettes were too smokeless, as in they wouldn't stay lit. And the user had to have the sucking power of an industrial vacuum just to get a drag.

Robert McMath, the museum's curator, spent a great deal of time as a market researcher before assuming his role as the custodian of this ominous supermarket. McMath is available to tell you what went wrong with all the products in the museum and to provide a history lesson on what not to do. But he's the first to tell you that knowing how to avoid repeating mistakes doesn't guarantee that you'll make marketing history, like Bill Gates did with Microsoft. Success is a lot more elusive than that. McMath even admits that he advised Campbell's Soup not to launch Prego Spaghetti Sauce. He just didn't think people needed it. Campbell's ignored him and launched it anyway; Prego has had sales in the hundreds of millions of dollars and continues to sell well.

### Questions

1. Had common sense prevailed, perhaps many of the products in the Museum of Flops would never have made it to the market in the first place. Discuss some of the reasons why marketers can't simply rely on common sense.

2. Identify all the products referred to in this case that failed by virtue of bad timing. Identify at least one other product that you either know of or can find in the business press that probably failed for the same reason. Describe the details of this product failure and explain why timing was the problem.

3. As a future marketing manager of new product development, discuss the lessons you've learned from this case that will better enable you to perform in this capacity.

4. Consider Premier cigarettes, toaster eggs, Harley Davidson beer, and Short and Sassy shampoo in light of the various stages of new product development presented in this chapter. If this process were applied to these products, at which stages might some warning signs have become evident to a marketing manager, and what might those warning signs have been?

**CAMPBELL'S SOUP**
www.campbellsoup.com

Source: Based on "Flops," CBC *Venture* Video 476.

## CASE STUDY

# Microsoft: Going for America's Most Admired Company

According to the most recent surveys of 10 000 executives, directors, and security analysts, the top three Most Admired Companies in America in 1999 were General Electric, Coca-Cola (the world's number one brand), and Microsoft. Bill Gates, Microsoft's controlling owner, has unabashedly stated that it's his goal to make Microsoft the number one known company on the planet.

In 1998 and through 1999 Microsoft was embroiled in defending itself against a U.S. Department of Justice anti-trust suit (the American equivalent of Canada's Competition Bureau). Although government prosecution isn't usually a cause for admiration, it is a tremendous source of publicity. The impact of the lawsuit, combined with Bill Gates' desire to make Microsoft number one, has spurred the firm to shift from a product focus to a customer focus. Microsoft plans to split into five groups designed to serve the needs of the following five customer groups: corporate systems customers; programmers; knowledge workers; ordinary Windows customers; and consumers who want shopping, entertainment, and digitized content.

The main profit makers are expected to remain the Windows operating system and the Office desktop-applications software. The key brand relationship lies in the linking of the Microsoft name with specific brands or products. For example, Microsoft Network has 44 per cent of the Internet browser market, Windows CE has 25 per cent of the handheld organizer market, Windows has 88 per cent of the PC operating systems market, Microsoft Office has 90 per cent of the PC office applications market, Windows NT has 36 per cent of the server operating system market, and Microsoft has only 5 per cent of the server database market.

Microsoft believes that if it can establish itself in relation to its customers rather than its products alone it will have a better opportunity to introduce new products, and even more importantly, new services. But a firm that seeks to serve different customer groups with many different products usually finds it less expensive to promote a single corporate image. At the moment, Microsoft's image is linked to its Windows operating software for the PC. And the PC is clearly going to be the tool of the twenty-first century.

Scientist, hacker, and author of the book *Silicon Snake Oil,* Clifford Stoll is critical of the social impact of Microsoft and computers in general. He says he's not against computers themselves (he has six in his house), but their cult, i.e., the notion that if you're not a computer user, life and progress are passing you by. Other commentators have criticized computer firms, and Microsoft in particular, for associating computers with a certain righteousness. People are made to feel guilty about not owning and operating a computer. Of course, from Microsoft's point of view, the ease of operation associated with the latest Windows operating system is a good reason to make anyone feel guilty about not owning and operating a computer. If you can read, point, and click, you can operate a computer!

Rex Murphy commented in a CBC report that computers are the indispensable product of the 90s; the invention of our time that's shaping the global economy. He also notes that information technology is the business of our time. Clearly, Microsoft's success is driven by its ability to fulfil powerful and important needs. One can't help but wonder how many people are sipping away on a Coke, under lighting supplied by General Electric light bulbs, while they surf the Net on their computers using Microsoft Explorer.

### Questions

1. What do you think accounts for the popularity of brands like Coca-Cola and Microsoft? Review the branding theory outlined in this chapter and use it to support your answer.
2. Do you think Microsoft will become America's Most Admired Company? Why or why not? In branding terminology, what kind of a brand is Microsoft? Windows? Windows NT? Evaluate Windows according to this chapter's criteria for what makes a good brand name.
3. Consider the branding strategies employed by various computer firms. Identify and present examples of manufacturer's brands, private label brands, and generic brands. Consider the product life cycle of computers and discuss the relationship between these and branding strategies.
4. Clifford Stoll once said that people are becoming so focused on computing and computing technologies that they won't be able to cope when change occurs in the future. It's hard to imagine change being more rapid than it already is in the computing industry. A lot of people keep from buying computers out of fear that they'll be stuck with obsolete equipment. Discuss how branding plays a role in dealing with these fears.

**MICROSOFT**
www.microsoft.com

Sources: The data in this case are drawn from Eryn Brown, "America's Most Admired Companies," *Fortune* (March 1, 1999), pp. 68–73; Eric Nee, "Microsoft Gets Ready to Play a New Game," *Fortune* (April 26, 1999), pp. 107–112; Jo Marney, "Top of Mind, Top of Market," *Marketing Magazine* (November 27, 1995), p. 13; and "Software-Hardsell," CBC Video—Host: Allison Smith, Reporter: Rex Murphy, Producer: Robin Christmas, *The National Magazine* (November 7, 1995).

# McDonald's: Competing in a Maturing Market

McDonald's Corporation is one of the best known firms in the world. At one time it was rapidly expanding as it pioneered the fast food industry. But now the fast food industry is mature and McDonald's has found itself slumping. According to *Fortune*'s most recent American Customer Satisfaction Index (the largest ongoing research project on customer satisfaction in the world), McDonald's scored 60 out of a maximum of 100, down 4.8 per cent from its previous year's score. The firm ranked 189th of out 190 firms, coming in just ahead of the Internal Revenue Service but ranking behind the police, who scored 63! McDonald's key competitors did much better. Burger King had a score of 67 and ranked 171st, while Wendy's International was the best of the burger chains with a ranking of 144th and a score of 71. KFC was the only other major fast food competitor evaluated, and it ranked 156th with a score of 69. The average score for all companies was 72.

*Fortune* commented, "Rarely has a dominant brand gone so wrong." The low ranking was believed to be due to "confused pricing and a tired menu." Financial consultant Dean Haskell observes that McDonald's has slumped on both its product quality and its image. Restaurant consultant Douglas Fisher says that McDonald's is "trying but missing the mark." The sales per store have been falling, and in Canada McDonald's market share has gone from 53 to 51 per cent. (Burger King, Harvey's, and Wendy's hold about 27 per cent of the Canadian market between them, up from 24 per cent.)

Douglas Fisher says the problem for McDonald's is one faced by many dominant firms: "How do you hold a big piece of the pie forever?" Dean Haskell notes that McDonald's went along for almost thirty years without any problems. A company begins to believe that everything it does will work after that. McDonald's occupied itself with international expansion and forgot to protect its home markets. As the market matured and competition intensified, McDonald's didn't realize soon enough that it needed to reinvent itself in order to maintain its position and continue to grow.

McDonald's is in trouble, but is still in a good position; there is no strong number two challenger for it yet. At one time it set a standard that none of the competitors could match. But they've learned, caught up to McDonald's, and are now threatening to pass it by if McDonald's fails to respond. Brian Grube of Wendy's comments how the acquisition of Tim Horton's is allowing it to share customers and operate under one roof. Wendy's is also offering healthier choices for customers to keep them coming back. Harvey's restaurants developed a healthy alternative by offering a chicken breast sandwich that doesn't have any breading.

According to Dean Haskell, the last successful new product introduction for McDonald's was the Big Mac, launched in the 1970s. Recently McDonald's has had a series of new product flops, including the McLean Deluxe, the Arch Deluxe, and Pizza. McDonald's is still opening new restaurants around the world, but it needs to respond to its competitors, which have been very aggressive in the U.S. and Canada. McDonald's is faced with the prospect of emulating its competitors instead of the other way around, and will have to change its operating system so that it can serve fresher food that doesn't sit in bins. Douglas Fisher predicts that McDonald's will remain a leader, but that it will be reduced in size as it loses market share.

## Questions

1. Identify some of the factors that contributed to McDonald's success in the past. Have any of these factors changed in the current environment, and if so, how?
2. Evaluate the reasons why McDonald's is struggling at the moment. Suggest some courses of action that might help it overcome some of its difficulties. It took McDonald's awhile to get into trouble—how long do you think it will take to get out of it?
3. Invent a product concept that you think might lead to success for McDonald's. Describe this concept and explain why you think it will lead the firm out of the doldrums it's in now.
4. Ranked just ahead of the IRS and just behind the police in customer satisfaction: if you were McDonald's CEO how would you explain this to your shareholders? What goal would you set for customer satisfaction in the near future at McDonald's, and how would you go about achieving it?

## Video Questions

1. Identify as many activities as you can that McDonald's competitors have undertaken in order to challenge the market leader.
2. The video focused on McDonald's food offerings but there is more to many McDonald's restaurants than just food. What other "offerings" have you observed in McDonald's restaurants?

**MCDONALD'S**
www.mcdonalds.com

Sources: Based on "McDonald's," *Venture* #676 (January 27, 1998); and Ronald B. Lieber, "Now Are You Satisfied: The 1998 American Customer Satisfaction Index," *Fortune* (February 16, 1998), pp. 161–168.

# PART 4

# Distribution Planning

## Considerations in Distribution Planning and Physical Distribution

Here, we broadly study distribution planning, which involves the physical movement and transfer of ownership of a product from producer to consumer. We explore the functions of distribution, types of channels, supplier/distribution intermediary contracts, channel cooperation and conflict, the industrial channel, and international distribution. We also look at physical distribution, in particular at transportation and inventory management issues.

## Retailing and Wholesaling

Here, we present retailing, which consists of those business activities involved with the sale of goods and services to the final consumer. We show the impact of retailing on the economy, its functions in distribution, and its relationship with suppliers. We categorize retailers by ownership, store strategy mix, and nonstore operations. We also describe several retail planning considerations and note recent trends in retailing.

Next, we examine wholesaling, which entails buying and/or handling goods and services and their subsequent resale to organizational users, retailers, and/or other wholesalers. We show the impact of wholesaling on the economy, its functions, and its relationships with suppliers and customers. We describe the major types of company-owned and independent wholesalers and note recent trends in wholesaling.

# Goods and Service Distribution

The exchange process of marketing involves a physical transfer from producer to consumer of both goods and services. It also involves the associated transaction requirements; that is, the title to goods or rights to services. Chapters 10 and 11 describe goods and service distribution in Canada.

In Chapter 10 we introduce the terms distribution planning, supply chain management, and logistical management. All three mean the same thing: the systematic decision making regarding the physical movement of goods and services from producer to consumer, as well as the related transfer of ownership (or rental) of them. Physical distribution of goods is an important issue for Canadian firms, since Canada is such a large country and has a relatively small and widely dispersed population. The linear distribution of its population makes traffic and trade activity linear too, i.e., goods movement basically goes east or west. According to an Industry Canada study, physical distribution costs amount to 7.5 per cent of the Canadian GDP. The physical distribution system in Canada includes warehousing, couriers, freight forwarders, customs brokers, and transportation.

Chapter 11 presents the retailing and wholesaling institutions used by marketers to reach their customers. The Canadian retail landscape has been undergoing a number of fundamental shifts. The major, and continuing, story has been the entry of Wal-Mart into Canada as part of a modern retail revolution. The impact is still reverberating, with Eaton's going bankrupt, The Bay in deep trouble, and Canada's grocery retailers preparing to meet Wal-Mart's anticipated invasion of the grocery market. Wal-Mart sees itself as the leader in the channel of distribution, since it works backwards through the channel to the producers. This constant interaction with suppliers helps Wal-Mart build relationships, raise quality, and lower costs—to the detriment of its competitors and the satisfaction of its customers.

In Chapter 11 we will also be looking at the role of wholesaling in distribution channels and how these channels are in a continuous state of change. For example, one of Canada's most important drug wholesalers has decided to evolve into one of Canada's most important drug retailers. Drug Trading Company plans to integrate 1500 pharmacies—the largest number of retail pharmacies in Canada—as part of a plan to reinvent itself. The firm hopes to develop significant market power with its PharmAssist program that links the firm's dispensary services, technology, and consumer programs. The idea is to take Drug Trading's loose assortment of stores operating under the I.D.A., Guardian, $R_X$ Central, and Community Drug Banners and integrate them under the PharmAssist umbrella. With this unified offering Drug Trading is hoping to take on Shoppers Drug Mart and the grocery store competitors more effectively.

Distribution is part of the exchange process of marketing and involves the physical transfer of goods and services from producer to consumer.

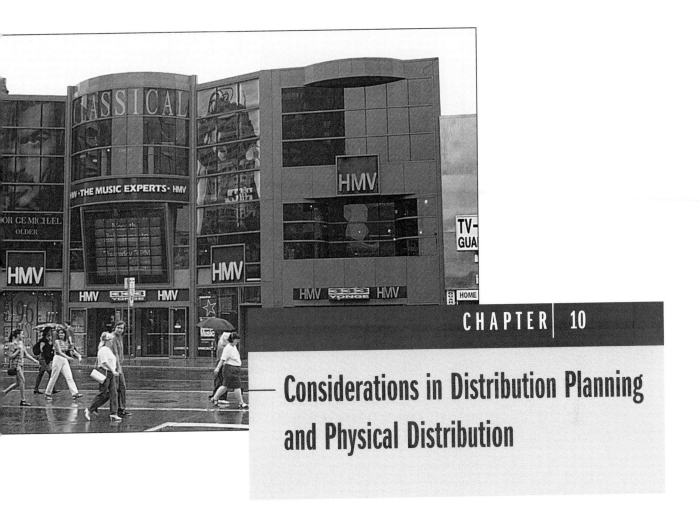

## CHAPTER 10

# Considerations in Distribution Planning and Physical Distribution

## *Chapter Objectives*

1. To define distribution planning and to examine its importance, distribution functions, the factors used in selecting a distribution channel, and the different types of distribution channels

2. To describe the nature of supplier/distribution intermediary contracts, and cooperation and conflict in a channel of distribution

3. To examine the special aspects relating to a distribution channel for industrial products and to international distribution

4. To define physical distribution and to demonstrate its importance

5. To discuss transportation alternatives and inventory management issues

Photo by Bob Carroll

**HMV**
www.hmv.ca

It would not be over-dramatic to say there is a war over the distribution of recorded music taking place in Canada. This war is being fuelled by changes in technology and demographics. The following statement sums up the situation: "Nowhere in the world is music retailing more brutally competitive than Canada." And this is happening in a market that represents only about 2.29 per cent of the world market, with sales of $1.24 billion on 81.9 million units!

Traditional music retailers like Music World, HMV Records (ninety stores across Canada) and Sam the Record Man (120 stores across Canada) are in a life-and-death struggle with superstore retailers like Tower Records and Virgin Records, and the record clubs BMG and Columbia House, which sell ten CDs for a penny. If this isn't enough, retailers of stereos and computers, like Future Shop and A&B Sound, are in the market selling music too. There are also regional chains like Archambault Music in Quebec, Total Sound in western Canada, and Sunrise Records and CD Plus in southern Ontario that are trying to compete.

The distribution channels for recorded music are undergoing a rapid change and the promise is for more of the same. Currently, the major Canadian music retailers are: HMV Canada (19 per cent market share), Music World (17 per cent), Sam the Record Man (12 per cent), BMG and Columbia House music clubs (25 per cent), with the remainder of the market going to an assortment of: independent record retailers, department stores (like The Bay, Eaton's, Sears, Zellers, and Wal-Mart), and sound equipment outlets like the Future Shop and A&B Sound. However, these players are facing new competition wrought by technology.

The dominant medium for music these days is the compact disk (CD). People can carry personal CD players and play them in their cars, in multi-CD players in a home stereo, and in CD-equipped home computers. Technology for "recordable" CDs has arrived: it's expensive, but it's only a matter of time before the costs fall dramatically. The existence of copyright piracy has always been a thorn in the side of the recording industry, and the thorn is getting sharper. The CD's utility as a storage medium, combined with its marriage to the computer, has opened up the potential for another channel of distribution: direct from producer to consumer, with the producer being the musician who recorded the music.

John Parry Barlow, a co-founder of the Electronic Frontier Foundation, believes that in the future copyright and intellectual property will not exist. Recordings, technology designs, video games, books, and videos will be "free." He claims that the interchange of information and technology brought about by the computer's ability to copy and transfer digital images will mean that enforcing copyright and intellectual property rights will be impossible, and hence collecting royalties and fees will be impossible too. Barlow can point to an already existing world where people browse through online catalogues (Columbia House Canada offers one now), and then download the music or entertainment they see to their computers. From there they can permanently record the entertainment (music, video, game, computer software, etc.) on a recordable CD or on their mega-megabyte hard drives. This phenomenon is known as convergence, where radio and music retailing are becoming intertwined.

The new technology is dual-edged; it's both a threat and an opportunity. To seize the opportunity, firms like EMI Music Canada (www.emimusic.ca) have developed enhanced CDs, or ECDs. The benefit is that purchasers can put an ECD in their computers to listen to music and then log onto the EMI Web site. The enhanced CD allows listeners to have an interactive experience with the CD. Still, the physical distribution of these ECDs is an issue.

CDnow! is a commercial service with an online catalogue (look out, music clubs) that allows browsers to sample the products from their computers, place a mail order, and even download items for a fee. Cerberus Sound + Vision in Britain has a licence to sell music online. Meanwhile, Cyberspace Promotions in Los Altos, California offers "Virtual Radio." Bands can pay to have their demo music played on virtual radio, which is accessed through the Internet. Listeners can download the music free of charge. According to Barlow, it's only a matter of time before the artists will be selling music directly to the listeners, bypassing the record companies and their distributors. At the moment, Internet music products are only half-CD quality. However, this is merely a technological issue that will likely be resolved in the future. From the marketing standpoint, reaching out directly to customers is the key. If customers want "full CD" quality now, they will order actual CDs through their computers and get them in the mail.

Will there be a growth in Internet purchases and a fall-off in music store buying? The demographics and the early results say yes. Apparently the older crowd, people in their late twenties up through the forties (a crowd that's getting older and represents the largest market potential), aren't buying as much music as they once did. The most likely reason is that they've been mostly ignored by the music industry in favour of the younger crowd. They don't feel at home in music stores, which play "alternative" music and prominently display and feature-price the artists targeted at the teenage group. This older 20- to 40-year-old segment also represents the Internet types who are more likely to respond to mail order and Internet appeals and shun music stores. The evolving distribution in the music industry will be interesting to watch. As for predicting the winners and losers, one winner has already emerged: the consumers.[1]

In this chapter, we will learn more about the decisions made in distribution planning and the activities involved in physical distribution, including quick response inventory systems.

# Overview

**Distribution planning, supply chain management, and logistical management** are all terms used to refer to the systematic decision making regarding the physical movement of goods and services from producer to consumer, as well as the related transfer of ownership (or rental) of them. Distribution planning will be the preferred term in this chapter; it encompasses such diverse functions as transportation, inventory management, and customer transactions.

Functions are carried out via a **channel of distribution**, which is comprised of all the organizations or people involved in the distribution process. Those organizations or people are known as **channel members** and may include manufacturers, service providers, wholesalers, retailers, marketing specialists, and/or consumers. When the term **distribution intermediaries** is used, it refers to wholesalers, retailers, and marketing specialists (such as transportation firms) that act as facilitators (links) between manufacturers/service providers and consumers.

This chapter presents an in-depth look at distribution planning and looks at the role of physical distribution. Chapter 11 covers retailing's and wholesaling's role in the distribution process.

**Distribution planning**
*involves movement and ownership in a* **channel of distribution**. *It consists of* **channel members**.

**Distribution intermediaries**
*often have a channel role.*

# Distribution Planning

*Distribution arrangements vary widely.*

A channel of distribution can be simple or complex. It can be based on a handshake agreement between a small manufacturer and a local reseller or require detailed written contracts among numerous manufacturers, wholesalers, and retailers. Some firms seek widespread distribution and need independent wholesalers and/or retailers to carry their merchandise and improve cash flow. Others want direct customer contact and do not use independent resellers. Industrial channels usually have more direct contact between manufacturers/service providers and customers than final consumer channels. International channels also have special needs.

The importance of distribution planning, the range of tasks performed in the distribution process, the criteria to consider in picking a distribution channel, supplier/distribution intermediary contracts, channel cooperation and conflict, the industrial channel of distribution, and international distribution are discussed next.

## The Importance of Distribution Planning

The distribution decisions of firms, industries, and indeed nations are critical to their ability to compete locally, nationally, and globally. Recently Industry Canada made an assessment of the distribution systems of Canadian firms in comparison with U.S. firms. The purpose was to identify issues that might put Canadian firms at a disadvantage with our largest trading partner, and to raise awareness of the importance of distribution management for Canadian firms. The assessment identified the following six issues.

1. Most Canadian firms did not perform distribution functions as well as American firms. Canadian firms did not have as effective strategies and tactics in developing programs for customer and supplier interfaces, warehousing, transportation, and materials management.

2. Canadian distribution channels were far less efficient than American channels. There were more intermediaries used in the channel, which were about half the size of comparable American firms.

3. Canadian firms lagged behind American firms in the use of electronic commerce; the small- and medium-size Canadian firms in particular had failed to computerize their order processing.

4. Both industry and government in Canada have failed to develop any comprehensive distribution management indicators to help Canadian firms develop and improve their supply chain strategies.

5. Canadian traffic and trade densities are less efficient than U.S. ones. A lot of this has to do with the fact that Canada is a linear country in terms of population density, which makes traffic and trade activity linear too. Goods movement basically goes east or west within the country, while north and south movements usually mean goods coming from or going to the U.S. The U.S., meanwhile, has a population spread out in all directions. Efficient hub and spoke distribution configurations are therefore possible.

6. Canadian firms have tended to be less aware of the importance of the role of transportation and logistics in helping their competitiveness. Some Canadian firms do not even include distribution planning in their marketing plans![2]

It's very clear from the foregoing that distribution decisions can have a great impact on a company's marketing efforts and must therefore be included in the firm's marketing planning. Because intermediaries can perform a host of functions, a firm's marketing plan will differ if it sells direct rather than via intermediaries; a decision to sell in stores rather than through the mail or the World Wide Web requires a different marketing orientation and the accomplishment of different tasks.

The choice of a distribution channel is one of the most critical decisions a firm will make. Close ties with intermediaries and/or customers may take time to develop; if there are existing bonds among channel members, it may be hard for a new firm to enter. Once channel alliances are achieved, suitable new products can be put into distribution more easily. Channel members need to act in a coordinated way. Strong resellers enhance manufacturers' marketing abilities. Consumers like to buy products the same way over time.

Today, more companies recognize the value of having good relationships throughout the distribution channel. As a result, many firms now engage in relationship marketing, whereby they seek to develop and maintain continuous long-term ties with suppliers, distribution intermediaries, and customers. By doing so, these firms ensure a more consistent flow of goods and services from suppliers, encourage intermediaries to act more as partners than adversaries, and increase the likelihood of having loyal customers. They improve employee morale by empowering them to respond positively to reasonable requests—in the employees' judgment—from suppliers, intermediaries, and/or customers. They get earlier and better data on prospective new products and the best strategies for continuing ones. They also lower operating and marketing costs, thus improving efficiency. As one expert noted, with relationship marketing, it is "traumatic to leave someone who you believe is responsive to your personal needs. We don't change doctors, lawyers, or accountants at the drop of a hat. Firms want to build the same relationships with suppliers, distribution intermediaries, and customers so they won't leave every time they get a better offer."[3] See Figure 10-1.

*Through relationship marketing, companies strive for ongoing ties with suppliers, intermediaries, and customers.*

These are several recommendations as to how effective relationship marketing in a distribution channel may be achieved:

- Relationship marketing should be conducted as a continuous and systematic process that incorporates both buyer and seller needs.
- Relationship marketing needs top management support; and its principles should permeate a firm's corporate culture.
- At a minimum, relationship marketing means understanding consumer expectations, building service partnerships, empowering employees, and total quality management (from buyer and seller perspectives).
- Suppliers, intermediaries, and customers should be surveyed—by category—to determine the aspects of relationship marketing to be emphasized for them.
- Although increased profitability is a desirable result from relationship marketing, other important measures of success are customer satisfaction, customer loyalty, and product quality.
- Both positive and negative feedback (going far beyond just passively receiving customer complaints) can provide meaningful information.
- Sellers need to communicate to their customers that relationship marketing involves responsibilities, as well as benefits, for both parties.
- Mutually agreeable (by buyers and sellers) contingency plans should be devised in case anything goes awry.[4]

Costs, as well as profits, are affected by the selection of a particular type of distribution channel. A firm doing all functions must pay for them itself; in return, it reaps all profits. A firm using intermediaries reduces per-unit distribution costs; it also reduces per-unit profits because those resellers receive their share. With intermediaries, a firm's total profits would rise if there are far higher sales than the firm could attain itself.

Distribution formats are long-standing in some industries. For example, in the beverage and food industry, manufacturers often sell through wholesalers that then deal with retailers. Auto makers sell through franchised dealers. Mail-order firms line

**Relationship Marketing and Digital Equipment**

To illustrate its commitment to relationship marketing, Digital Equipment Corporation discusses its partnerships and willingness to cooperate. Firms are encouraged to phone or visit Digital's Web site.

*Reprinted with permission of Digital Equipment Corporation.*

up suppliers, print catalogues, and sell to consumers. So, firms must frequently conform to the channel patterns in their industries.

A firm's market coverage is often influenced by the location and number, market penetration, image, product selection, services, and marketing plans of the wholesalers, retailers, and/or marketing specialists with which it deals. In weighing options, a firm should note that the more intermediaries it uses, the less customer contact it has and the lower its control over marketing.

These examples show the scope of distribution planning:

- Shoppers Drug Mart is Canada's largest drugstore chain with 850 stores and $4 billion in annual sales. Shoppers doesn't just distribute and sell prescription and over-the-counter drugs (as well as numerous other items). It also distributes customized health management information through the "Health Watch" system. Each prescription customer is given a detailed fact sheet on their prescription medications, which provides warnings to both pharmacists and customers about the dangers of drug interactions with other drugs, food, beverages, and even types of activities. The information is produced by linking the customer information database with a large drug information database and then having a computer print out the details on the medicines, the customer, and their physicians.[5]

- Chapters Internet hopes to match some of the success of Amazon.com by offering Canadian buyers Canadian titles in Canadian dollars. Sales of Canadian books online were estimated at $50 million for 1999 and Chapters wanted to have a piece of this market. In addition, Chapters was estimating that in the near future 15 per cent of the firm's sales would derive from online orders. Despite this, Chapters is still opening large comfortable stores, akin to libraries, with huge selections of books and plenty of places to sit and glance them over. Chapters Internet is seen as a complement to its physical retail premises, not a replacement.[6]

- Krave's Candy Company relies on its distributors for success. It has to because Krave's does not spend money on radio, TV, or print advertising. The firm sells a 300-gram box of candy composed of white chocolate, cashews, and graham crackers under the brand name of Clodhoppers. The product is sold through Wal-Mart, Overwaitea, The Bay, Safeway's western Canada stores, some Shoppers Drug Marts, and a number of independent grocers. The firm made $650 000 in sales in 1998. The key to success? Krave's targeted its product at distributors in the first place. It sent samples to distributors, and went to trade shows to find more distributors. Krave's developed unique shelf packaging so that the product would promote itself. Finally, Krave's hired an in-store demonstration firm to go into stores to sample the products. One of Krave's real successes was a series of on-site, pre-Christmas product sampling demonstrations in Wal-Mart that secured them a product placement.[7]

## Channel Functions and the Role of Distribution Intermediaries

For most goods and services, the **channel functions** shown in Figure 10-2 and described here must be undertaken somewhere in the distribution channel and responsibility for them assigned.

Distribution intermediaries can play a vital role in marketing research. Due to their closeness to the market, they generally have good insights into the characteristics and needs of customers.

In buying products, intermediaries sometimes pay as items are received; other times, they accept items on consignment and do not pay until after sales are made. Purchase terms for intermediaries may range from net cash (payment due at once) to net sixty days (payment not due for sixty days) or longer. If intermediaries do not pay until after resale, manufacturers risk poor cash flow, high product returns, obsolescence and spoilage, multiple transactions with the intermediaries, and potentially low sales to customers.

*Intermediaries can perform* **channel functions** *and reduce costs, provide expertise, open markets, and lower risks.*

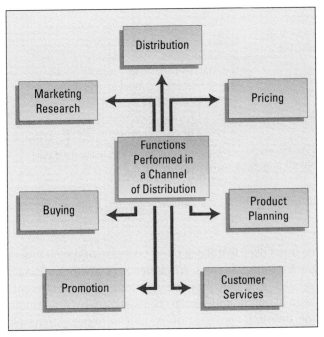

**FIGURE 10-2**

**Channel Functions**

# ETHICS AND TODAY'S MARKETER

## Managing Conflict in Distribution Channels

Some people may find this statement surprising, but conflict among members of the same distribution channel is a normal state of affairs. Given the existence of different objectives among the channel members, combined with different levels of power, it's only to be expected that conflicts will arise. However, although a normal occurrence, it's also an undesirable situation that must be resolved for a channel to function.

Some of the common conflicts that occur in channels involve such issues as customers demanding price concessions or longer payment periods; purchasing agents demanding special services and faster delivery; retailers demanding more frequent delivery in smaller quantities so that they have less inventory; and suppliers demanding longer lead times and large order quantities.

Therefore, since conflict is both a normal occurrence and something that must be resolved, marketers must develop methods and approaches to managing conflict in distribution channels. Channel conflicts usually have rational, business-based sources, but they may produce feelings of anger and resentment that can make it difficult to come a resolution. They may also lead to emotionally based decisions, and this raises ethical concerns. Is the manager making a decision that is in the best interests of the firm, and all the other stakeholders, or is it based on a desire to "save face," "get even," or "punish" the source of the conflict?

1. *Know thyself*—You begin by realizing that you probably can't change the other party. This means you must know how you feel and what your firm's views are.
2. *Build bridges, not walls*—You must interact with the firm or individual with which you have the conflict. If you know yourself, you can explain feelings and views of the other party. Reaching an understanding is the goal of this exercise. Since it won't be possible without trust between the parties, try to re-establish trust in an existing relationship and establish it in a new relationship.
3. *Reach a resolution*—Take a "problem solving" approach. Look at the conflict as a problem that needs to be solved, not a war that must be won.
4. *Try to avoid allowing conflict to become a group sport in your organization*—Members of cross-functional teams are often involved in distribution decision making, and they bring different points of view with them. Just as building bridges between the firm and its channel members involves interaction, so does unifying a team. Ask the team members to evaluate their positions and why they've taken them. Have them consider other positions, and ask themselves "why not?" The group should come up with options to solve the problem, and then develop fair and objective criteria for evaluating these options. It's very important to encourage everyone to think of the problem, and the individuals involved, as two separate things.

Find a specific example of marketing channel conflict. Try to look at the issue from both sides, and come to a resolution that you think would be mutually beneficial. Document the process and then explain your resolution.

Source: Based on Maria Goldstone, "Conflict: Making Your Point Without 'Losing It,'" *Modern Purchasing* (October, 1998), Maclean Hunter Bizlink, www.bizlink.com.

Manufacturers and service firms like H&R Block often take care of national (and international) ads when assigning promotion roles. Wholesalers may help coordinate regional promotions among retailers and may motivate and train retail salespeople. Most retailers use local ads, personal selling, and special events as forms of promotion.

Customer services include delivery, credit, in-office and in-home purchases, training programs, warranties, and return privileges. Again, these services can be provided by one channel member or a combination of them.

Distribution intermediaries can contribute to product planning in several ways. They often provide advice on new and existing products; test marketing requires their cooperation; and intermediaries can be helpful in positioning products against competitors and suggesting which products to drop.

Wholesalers and retailers often have strong input into pricing decisions. They state their required markups and then price-mark products or specify how they should be marked. Court rulings limit manufacturers' control over final prices. Intermediaries thus have great flexibility in setting prices.

Distribution incorporates three major factors: transportation, inventory management, and customer contact. Goods must be shipped from a manufacturer to consumers; intermediaries often provide this service. Because production capabilities and customer demand frequently differ, inventory levels must be properly managed (and items may require storage in a warehouse before being sold). Consumer transactions may require a store or other selling location, long hours of operation, and store fixtures (such as dressing rooms).

Manufacturers typically like to make a limited variety of items in large quantities and have as few transactions as possible to sell their entire output. On the other hand, consumers tend to want a variety of brands, colours, sizes, and qualities from which to select—and opt to buy a small amount at a time. Manufacturers might also prefer to sell products from the factory, have nine to five hours and spartan fixtures, and use a limited sales force. Yet organizational consumers may want salespeople to come to their offices and final consumers may want to shop at nearby locations and visit attractive, well-staffed stores on weekends and evenings.

To resolve these differences, intermediaries can be used in the **sorting process**, which consists of four distribution functions: accumulation, allocation, sorting, and assorting. Accumulation is collecting small shipments from several firms so shipping costs are lower. Allocation is apportioning items to various consumer markets. Sorting is separating products into grades, colours, and so forth. Assorting is offering a broad range of products so the consumer has many choices.

*The* **sorting process** *coordinates manufacturer and consumer goals.*

## Selecting a Channel of Distribution

In choosing a distribution channel, several key factors must be considered:

- *The consumer.*

  Characteristics—number, concentration, average purchase size.

  Needs—shopping locations and hours, assortment, sales help, credit.

  Segments—size, purchase behaviour.

- *The company.*

  Goals—control, sales, profit, timing.

  Resources—level, flexibility, service needs.

  Expertise—functions, specialization, efficiency.

  Experience—distribution methods, channel relationships.

- *The product.*

  Value—price per unit.

  Complexity—technical nature.

  Perishability—shelf life, frequency of shipments.

  Bulk—weight per unit, divisibility.

- *The competition.*

  Characteristics—number, concentration, assortment, customers.

  Tactics—distribution methods, channel relationships.

*Channel choice depends on consumers, the company, the product, competition, existing channels, and legalities.*

- *Distribution channels.*

  Alternatives—direct, indirect.

  Characteristics—number of intermediaries, functions performed, tradition.

  Availability—exclusive arrangements, territorial restrictions.

- *Legalities*—current laws, pending laws.

*In a* **direct channel** *one firm performs all tasks. An* **indirect channel** *has multiple firms.*

While assessing the preceding factors, a firm would make decisions about the type of channel used, contractual arrangements or administered channels, channel length and width, channel intensity, and whether to use dual channels.

There are two basic types of channels: direct and indirect. A **direct channel of distribution** involves the movement of goods and services from producer to consumers without the use of independent intermediaries. An **indirect channel of distribution** involves the movement of goods and services from producer to independent intermediaries to consumers. Figure 10-3 shows the transactions necessary for the sale of 200 000 men's umbrellas under direct and indirect channels. Figure 10-4 shows the most common indirect channels for final consumer and organizational consumer products.

If a manufacturer or service provider sells to consumers via company-owned outlets (for example, Imperial Oil's Esso gas stations), this is a direct channel. In an indirect channel, a manufacturer may employ several layers of independent whole-

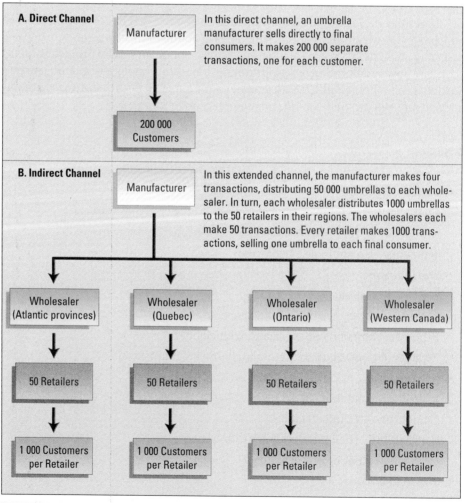

**FIGURE 10-3**

**Transactions in a Direct Versus an Indirect Channel**

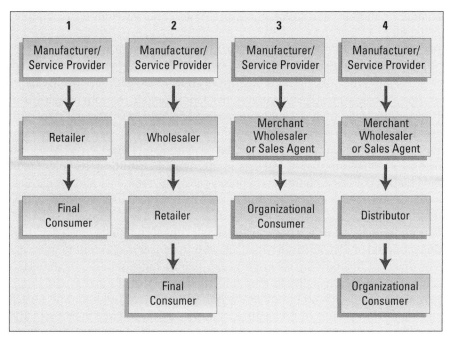

**FIGURE 10-4**

**Typical Indirect Channels of Distribution**

salers (for example, regional, provincial, and local) and sell through different kinds of retailers (such as discount, department, and specialty stores). A direct channel is most used by firms that want control over their entire marketing programs, desire close customer contact, and have limited markets. An indirect channel is most used by firms that want to enlarge their markets, raise sales volume, and give up distribution functions and costs, and that are willing to surrender some channel control and customer contact.

Because an indirect channel has independent members, marketing responsibilities may be assigned in different ways. With a *contractual channel arrangement*, all the terms regarding distribution tasks, prices, and other factors are stated in writing for each member. A manufacturer and a retailer could sign an agreement citing promotion support, delivery and payment dates, and product handling, marking, and displays. In an *administered channel arrangement*, the dominant firm in the distribution process plans the marketing program and itemizes and coordinates each member's duties. Depending on their relative strength, a manufacturer/service provider, wholesaler, or retailer could be a channel leader. Accordingly, a manufacturer with a strong brand could set its image, price range, and selling method.

**Channel length** refers to the levels of independent members along a distribution channel. In Figure 10-3, *A* is a short channel and *B* is a long channel. Sometimes, a firm shortens its channel by acquiring a company at another stage, as when a manufacturer merges with a wholesaler. Doing so allows the firm to be more self-sufficient, ensure supply, control channel members, lower distribution costs, and coordinate timing throughout the channel. However, it may also limit competition and foster inefficiency, and may not result in lower consumer prices.

**Channel width** refers to the number of independent members at any stage of distribution. In a narrow channel, a manufacturer or service provider sells through few wholesalers or retailers; in a wide channel, it sells through many. If a firm wants to enhance its position at its stage of the channel, it may buy other companies like itself, such as one janitorial-services firm buying another. This lets a firm increase its size and share of the market, improve bargaining power with other channel mem-

**Channel length** *describes the number of levels of independent members.*

**Channel width** *refers to the independent members at one level.*

bers, enlarge its market, and utilize mass promotion and distribution techniques more efficiently.

In selecting a distribution channel, a firm must decide on the intensity of its coverage. Under **exclusive distribution**, a firm severely limits the number of resellers utilized in a geographic area, perhaps having only one or two within a specific shopping location. It seeks a prestige image, channel control, and high profit margins, and accepts lower total sales than it would attain using another type of distribution. With **selective distribution**, a firm employs a moderate number of resellers. It tries to combine some channel control and a solid image with good sales volume and profits. A firm uses a large number of resellers in **intensive distribution**. Its goals are to have wide market coverage, channel acceptance, and high total sales and profits. Per-unit profits are low. It is a strategy aimed at the greatest number of consumers. See Table 10-1.

Some additional factors are noteworthy in selecting a channel. First, a firm may use a **dual channel of distribution**, which allows it to appeal to different market segments or diversify business by selling through two or more separate channels. A company could use selective distribution for a prestige brand of watches and intensive distribution for a discount brand, or use both direct and indirect channels (such as an insurance firm selling group health insurance directly to large businesses and individual life insurance indirectly to final consumers via independent agents). Kodak uses a three-tiered distribution approach for microfilm, supplies, and imaging systems and software: (1) Kodak's own sales representatives concentrate on complex document-imaging systems. (2) Well-trained brokers market such Kodak equipment

*Exclusive, selective, and* **intensive distribution** *depend on goals, sellers, customers, and marketing.*

*A* **dual channel** *lets a company reach different segments or diversify.*

## TABLE 10-1

## Intensity of Channel Coverage

| ATTRIBUTES | EXCLUSIVE DISTRIBUTION | SELECTIVE DISTRIBUTION | INTENSIVE DISTRIBUTION |
|---|---|---|---|
| Objectives | Prestige image, channel control and loyalty, price stability and high profit margins | Moderate market coverage, solid image, some channel control and loyalty, good sales and profits | Widespread market coverage, channel acceptance, volume sales and profits |
| Resellers | Few in number, well-established, reputable firms (outlets) | Moderate in number, well-established, better firms (outlets) | Many in number, all types of firms (outlets) |
| Customers | Final consumers: fewer in number, trend setters, willing to travel to store, brand loyal. Organizational consumers: focus on major accounts, service expected from manufacturer | Final consumers: moderate in number, brand conscious, somewhat willing to travel to store. Organizational consumers: focus on many types of accounts, service expected from manufacturer or intermediary | Final consumers: many in number, convenience-oriented. Organizational consumers: focus on all types of accounts, service expected from intermediary |
| Marketing | Final consumers: personal selling, pleasant shopping conditions, good service. Organizational consumers: availability, regular communications, superior service | Final consumers: promotional mix, pleasant shopping conditions, good service. Organizational consumers: availability, regular communications, superior service | Final consumers: mass advertising nearby location, items in stock. Organizational consumers: availability, regular communications, superior service |
| Major weakness | Limited sales potential | May be difficult to carve out a niche | Limited channel control |
| Examples | Autos, designer clothes, capital equipment, complex services | Furniture, clothing, mechanics' tools, industrialized services | Household products, groceries, office supplies, routine services |

as reader-printers and other stand-alone components; they must be certified to sell and service each product line carried. (3) Other intermediaries handle film sales, film processing, and delivery to all business clients in their territories.

Second, a firm may go from exclusive to selective to intensive distribution as a product passes through its life cycle. However, it would be hard to go in the opposite direction, from intensive to selective to exclusive distribution. For example, designer jeans rapidly moved from prestige stores to better stores to all types of outlets. This process would not have worked in reverse. Third, a firm may distribute products in a new way and achieve great success. The sale of women's hosiery was revolutionized when L'eggs products were placed in supermarkets.

## Supplier/Distribution Intermediary Contracts

Supplier/distribution intermediary contracts focus on price policies, conditions of sale, territorial rights, the services/responsibility mix, and contract length and conditions of termination. The highlights of a basic contract follow.

Price policies largely deal with the discounts given to intermediaries for their functions, quantity purchases, and cash payments, and with commission rates. Functional discounts are deductions from list prices given to intermediaries for performing storage, shipping, and other jobs. Quantity discounts are deductions for volume purchases. Cash discounts are deductions for early payment. Some intermediaries are paid commissions for their tasks.

Conditions of sale cover price and quality guarantees, payment and shipping terms, reimbursement for unsold items, and return allowances. A guarantee against a price decline protects one intermediary from paying a high price for an item that is then offered to others at a lower price; if prices are reduced, the original buyer receives a rebate so its product costs are like competitors'. Otherwise, it could not meet the prices that competitors charge customers. Suppliers sometimes employ full-line forcing, whereby intermediaries are required to carry an entire line of products. This is legal if they are not prevented from also buying items from other suppliers.

Territorial rights outline the geographic areas (such as greater Vancouver) in which resellers may operate and/or the target markets (such as small-business accounts) they may contact. In some cases, they have exclusive territories, as with McDonald's franchisees; in others, many firms are granted territorial rights for the same areas, as with retailers selling Sharp calculators.

The services/responsibility mix describes the role of each channel member. It outlines such factors as who delivers products, stores inventory, trains salespeople, writes ad copy, and sets up displays; and it sets performance standards. If included, a hold-harmless clause specifies that manufacturers or service providers—and not resellers—are accountable for lawsuits arising from poor product design or negligence in production.

Contract length and conditions of termination protect an intermediary against a manufacturer or service provider prematurely bypassing it after a territory has been built up. The manufacturer or service provider is shielded by limiting contract duration and stating the factors that may lead to termination.

Not all relationships among channel members are so formal. Some firms rely on handshake agreements. However, without a contract, the danger exists that there will be misunderstandings regarding goals, compensation, tasks to be performed, and the length of the agreement. The one constraint of a written contract may be its inflexibility under changing market conditions.

## Channel Cooperation and Conflict

All firms in a distribution channel have similar general goals: profitability, access to goods and services, efficient distribution, and customer loyalty. Yet, the way these

*Supplier/distribution intermediary contracts cover prices, sale conditions, territories, commitments, timing, and termination.*

*Channel member goals need to be balanced.*

and other goals are achieved often leads to differing views, even if the parties engage in relationship marketing. For example, how are profits allocated along a channel? How can manufacturers sell products through many competing resellers and expect the resellers not to carry other brands? Which party coordinates channel decisions? To whom are consumers loyal—manufacturers/service providers, wholesalers, or retailers?

There are natural differences among the firms in a distribution channel by virtue of their channel positions, the tasks performed, and the desire of each firm to raise its profits and control its strategy. A successful channel will maximize cooperation and minimize conflict. Table 10-2 cites causes of channel conflict. Table 10-3 shows how channel cooperation can reduce these conflicts.

In the past, manufacturers dominated channels because they had the best market coverage and recognition; resellers were small and localized. Now, with the growth of large national (and international) wholesalers and retailers, the volume accounted for by them, and the popularity of private brands, the balance of power has shifted more to resellers. As one expert said:

## TABLE 10-2

## Potential Causes of Channel Conflict

| FACTOR | MANUFACTURER'S/SERVICE PROVIDER'S GOAL | DISTRIBUTION INTERMEDIARY'S GOAL |
|---|---|---|
| Pricing | To establish final price consistent with product image | To establish final price consistent with the intermediary's image |
| Purchase terms | To ensure prompt, accurate payments and minimize discounts | To defer payments as long as possible and secure discounts |
| Shelf space | To obtain plentiful shelf space with good visibility so as to maximize brand sales | To allocate shelf space among multiple brands so as to maximize total product sales |
| Exclusivity | To hold down the number of competing brands each intermediary stocks while selling through many intermediaries | To hold down the number of competing intermediaries carrying the same brands while selling different brands itself |
| Delivery | To receive adequate notice before deliveries are required | To obtain quick service |
| Advertising support | To secure ad support from intermediaries | To secure ad support from manufacturers/service providers |
| Profitability | To have adequate profit margins | To have adequate profit margins |
| Continuity | To receive orders on a regular basis | To receive shipments on a regular basis |
| Order size | To maximize order size | To have order size conform with consumer demand to minimize inventory investment |
| Assortment | To offer a limited variety | To secure a full variety |
| Risk | To have intermediaries assume risks | To have manufacturers/service providers assume risks |
| Branding | To sell products under the manufacturer's/service provider's name | To sell products under private brands as well as manufacturers'/service providers' brands |
| Channel access | To distribute products wherever desired by the manufacturer/service provider | To carry only those items desired by intermediaries |
| Importance of account | To not allow any one intermediary to dominate | To not allow any one manufacturer/service provider to dominate |
| Consumer | To have consumers loyal to the manufacturer/service provider | To have consumers loyal to the intermediary |
| Channel control | To make key channel decisions | To make key channel decisions |

## TABLE 10-3

## Methods of Channel Cooperation

| FACTOR | MANUFACTURER'S/SERVICE PROVIDER'S ACTIONS | DISTRIBUTION INTERMEDIARY'S ACTIONS |
|---|---|---|
| New-product introduction | Thorough testing, adequate promotional support | Good shelf location and space, enthusiasm for product, assistance in test marketing |
| Delivery | Prompt filling of orders, adherence to scheduled dates | Proper time allowed for delivery, shipments immediately checked for accuracy |
| Marketing research | Data provided to resellers | Data provided to manufacturers/service providers |
| Pricing | Prices to intermediaries let them gain reasonable profits, intermediary flexibility encouraged | Infrequent sales from regular prices, maintaining proper image |
| Promotion | Training reseller's salespeople, sales force incentives, developing appropriate ad campaign, cooperative ad programs | Attractive store displays, knowledgeable salespeople, participation in cooperative programs |
| Financing | Liberal financial terms | Adherence to financial terms |
| Product quality | Product guarantees | Proper installation and servicing of products for customers |
| Channel control | Shared and specified decision making | Shared and specified decision making |

In highly competitive markets, with so many manufacturers competing for the same customers, distributors and dealers can afford to be choosy about which firms' products they will push. Getting them to push your products is what motivation in marketing channels is all about. With so many [North American] manufacturers interested in marketing products overseas, and needing foreign dealers and distributors to do so, the motivation of channel partners needs to be addressed from an international perspective, as well as a domestic one.[8]

If conflicts are not resolved cooperatively, confrontations may occur. A manufacturer or service provider may then ship late, refuse to deal with certain resellers, limit financing, withdraw promotional support, or use other tactics. Similarly, a reseller may make late payments, give poor shelf space, refuse to carry items, return many products, and apply other tactics. A channel cannot function well in a confrontational framework. Here is an example of channel conflict:

Warner Music Canada and its affiliates refused to supply music club marketer BMG Music with products in 1997, literally forcing BMG to stop advertising in Canada, which is tantamount to extinction when you're a direct marketer. The problem arose because Warner Music is a 50 per cent stakeholder in BMG's largest direct competitor, Columbia House music club. BMG's response was to file a formal complaint with the Competition Bureau in Ottawa to force Warner to supply BMG with products. Warner Music argued that if they were forced to sell music through BMG it would amount to a case of compulsory licensing on copyrighted works. The case went to the Competition Tribunal and Warner's position was upheld: they could refuse to supply BMG. The Competition Tribunal did not have the jurisdiction to force Warner to license its intellectual property. After all this BMG began advertising again in 1998, and the firm is even offering Warner labels in their catalogue! When asked to comment on this after the legal battling, BMG simply said, "product supply issues have been resolved."[9]

**WARNER MUSIC CANADA**
www.warnermusic.ca

A thriving existing manufacturer or service provider can often secure reseller support and enthusiasm when introducing new products and continuing popular ones. This occurs because resellers know the manufacturer's or service provider's past track record, the promotion support that will be provided, and the manufac-

*In a **pushing strategy**, there is cooperation among channel members. With **pulling**, a firm generates demand before receiving channel support.*

turer's or service provider's reliability in future deliveries. Thus, a **pushing strategy** is used, whereby the various firms in a distribution channel cooperate in marketing a product. With this approach, a manufacturer or service provider uses relationship marketing.

As a rule, it is harder for a new manufacturer or service provider to break into an existing channel. Resellers are unfamiliar with the firm, not able to gauge its sales potential, and wonder about its support and future deliveries. So, a new firm would need a **pulling strategy**, whereby it first stimulates consumer demand and then gains dealer support. This means heavy promotion expenses, fully paid by the manufacturer or service provider; it must often offer guarantees of minimum sales or profits to resellers, and make up shortfalls. Figure 10-5 contrasts pushing and pulling strategies.

In today's competitive environment, with so many new domestic and foreign products being introduced each year, even market-leading firms must sometimes use pulling strategies. They have to convince resellers that consumer demand exists for their products, before the resellers agree to tie up shelf space.

## The Industrial Channel of Distribution

*An industrial channel has unique characteristics.*

The distribution channel for industrial products differs from that for consumer products in the following key ways:

1. Retailers are typically not utilized.
2. Direct channels are more readily employed.
3. Transactions are fewer and orders are larger.
4. Specification selling is more prevalent.
5. Intermediaries are more knowledgeable.
6. Team selling (two or more salespeople) may be necessary.
7. Distinct intermediaries specialize in industrial products.[10]
8. Leasing, rather than selling, is more likely.
9. Customer information needs are more technical.
10. Activities like shipping and warehousing may be shared.

## International Distribution Planning

*International distribution requires particular planning.*

When devising an international distribution plan, a number of factors should be kept in mind. Here are several of them.

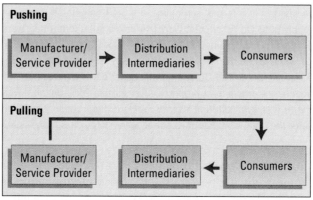

**FIGURE 10-5**

**Pushing Versus Pulling Strategies**

Channel length often depends on a nation's stage of economic development and consumer behaviour patterns. Less-developed and developing nations tend to use shorter, more direct channels than industrialized ones. They have many small firms marketing goods and services to nearby consumers; and the more limited transportation and communications networks encourage local shopping. At the same time, cultural norms in nations—both developing and industrialized—affect the expected interactions between sellers and consumers. For instance, in Japan, people treasure personal attention when making purchases, especially of expensive products. Unlike North American shoppers, Japanese consumers are not used to making purchases by telephone.

Distribution practices and formats vary by nation, as these examples show:

- The Treaty of Rome, under which the European Union was created, banned exclusive distribution agreements because they were considered anti-competitive. Therefore, a supplier cannot appoint a reseller as an exclusive distributor, nor can a distributor agree to source products from a single supplier. Exemptions have been granted in a few cases, such as supplying beer to bars and taverns and automobile dealerships. Acquiring an exemption involves a lot of bureaucratic red tape, however, because firms must draw up an agreement with terms that are acceptable to the European Commission, the body that enforces the Treaty of Rome.[11]

- Some Mexican supermarkets shut off their electricity overnight to hold down costs. Thus, items such as dairy products have a much shorter shelf life and must be more frequently delivered than in Canada.

- Large Japanese firms often set up *keiretsus*. A vertical keiretsu is an integrated network of suppliers, manufacturers, and resellers. A horizontal keiretsu typically consists of a money-centre bank, an insurance company, a trust banking company, a trading company, and several major manufacturers. North American firms have some channels that resemble vertical keiretsus, but they do not have networks that emulate horizontal keiretsus.[12]

- Although it has about three times as many people as both Canada and the United States, India has roughly the same number of retail establishments; just one-quarter of them are in metropolitan areas. "Pan-bidi" are the popular neighbourhood grocery and general stores that offer very low prices.[13]

If a firm enters a foreign market for the first time, it must resolve various questions, including: Should products be made domestically and shipped to the foreign market or be made in the foreign market? If products are made domestically, what form of transportation is best? What kind of distribution intermediaries should be used? Which specific intermediaries should be used?

Industry Canada and the Department of Foreign Affairs and International Trade are only too willing to help Canadian businesses that wish to distribute products internationally.

Industry Canada, along with over twenty different partners, have set up a network of Canada Business Service Centres in each major urban centre of every province in Canada. Each centre can be currently contacted by a toll-free number, fax, or e-mail (strategis.ic.gc.ca). The purpose of these centres is to provide small businesses with one-stop shopping convenience for information on provincial and federal government programs and services, as well as private programs and services. Canada Business Service Centres offer their users The Business Information Service (a database of information on programs and services offered by federal, provincial, and private sector organizations), faxables (a condensed version of the Business Information service which can be accessed through an automated FaxBack system), pathfinders (which describe services and programs by topic), toll-free telephone information and referral services, and leading-edge business products (such as interactive videos, how-to manuals, CD-ROM products, and external database access).

**CANADIAN BUSINESS SERVICE CENTRES**
http://cbsc.org/main.html

# INTERNATIONAL MARKETING IN ACTION

## Getting Distribution for Coca-Cola in China

In order to build brand awareness and develop product distribution in China, Coca-Cola had to get the ruling party's eyes and ears working for them. In the residential areas of every Chinese city are senior citizens wearing red arm bands and keeping an eye on what's happening in their neighbourhoods. These people are the Communist Party's watchers. Coca-Cola decided to use these neighbourhood watch organizations to help market its product in Shanghai.

In 1996 Coca-Cola approached fourteen neighbourhood committees with a modest proposal. Basically, Coke thought these people had time to do more things, and that they wouldn't be averse to raising some cash. The deal was that the committees would stock some Coke products to sell to people in the neighbourhood.

By 1998 the head of Coke's Shanghai division reported that the neighbourhood committees were a good sales force. While sales weren't really overwhelming, they had created considerable brand awareness. Considering that Communist societies aren't oriented toward free enterprise, the use of a grassroots system to grow both a distribution system and brand awareness was an innovative approach.

Both Coca-Cola and its main competitor, Pepsi, have met with a lot more resistance on the parliamentary level. For example, one member sponsored a motion to restrict the sale of both Cola products in China. When you're going after a potential market of more than a billion people it's important to keep your objectives in sight, and understand that you must adapt. Working from the grassroots level and getting the support of the people is a key factor in getting the support of the government.

Distribution channels usually evolve over time. What kind of evolution might you expect to occur for Coca-Cola in China? What kinds of problems might arise as a result of a shift from dependence on neighbourhood committees to alternative distribution channels? Recommend a plan of action for Coca-Cola to manage this change.

Source: Based on Richard Tomlinson, "The China Card," *Fortune* (May 25, 1998), p. 82.

Through these centres, or through your own computer with an Internet feed, you can access Strategis, the online database and information system for Industry Canada and the Department of Foreign Affairs and International Trade. Strategis has computerized market data on industries in many foreign nations, and has included the names of contacts in many of these industries.[14] Legal requirements regarding distribution differ by country, and some have strict laws as to hours, methods of operation, and sites. For example, France has severe limits on Sunday retail hours, and Germany has strict limits on both size and Sunday hours. And many nations have complex procedures for foreign firms to distribute products there. Thus, firms interested in standardized (global) distribution may be stymied in their efforts.

What is likely to cause a company to be more or less satisfied with its international distribution channel? According to one study:

- The better a firm's domestic channel performs relative to its international channel, the lower its satisfaction with the international channel.
- The more experience a firm has in foreign markets, the greater its satisfaction with its existing international channel.
- A firm is more satisfied with an existing international channel if it believes it has the ability to change channels.
- A firm has less satisfaction with its existing international channel if environmental uncertainty is high.
- A firm is less satisfied with its existing international channel if it is difficult to monitor the behaviour of channel members.[15]

# Physical Distribution

**Physical distribution** (also known as **logistics**) encompasses the broad range of activities concerned with efficiently delivering raw materials, parts, semifinished items, and finished products to designated places, at designated times, and in proper condition. It may be undertaken by any member of a channel, from producer to consumer.

**Physical distribution** *involves the location, timing, and condition of deliveries. An* **order cycle** *covers many activities.*

Physical distribution involves such functions as customer service; shipping; warehousing; inventory control; private trucking-fleet operations; packaging; receiving; materials handling; and plant, warehouse, and store location planning. The physical distribution activities involved in a typical **order cycle**—the period of time from when the customer places an order to its receipt—are illustrated in Figure 10-6.

## The Importance of Physical Distribution

Physical distribution is important for a number of reasons: its costs, the value of customer service, and its relationship with other functional areas.

**COSTS**  According to an Industry Canada study, physical distribution costs amount to 7.5 per cent of the Canadian GDP. The physical distribution system in Canada includes warehousing, couriers, freight forwarders, customs brokers, and transportation.[16] To contain costs, firms have been working hard to improve efficiency. Today, physical distribution tasks are completed faster, more accurately, and with fewer people than twenty years ago. Due to computerization and improved transportation, firms have reduced their inventory levels by hundreds of millions of dollars, thus saving on warehousing and interest expenses.

*Cost control is a major goal.*

Distribution costs vary widely by industry and company type. At individual firms, total physical distribution costs depend on such factors as the nature of the business, the geographic area covered, the tasks done by other channel members, and the weight/value ratio of the items involved. For example, while many retailers spend 2 to 3 per cent of their revenues on transportation from vendors and receiving, marking, storing, and distributing goods, petroleum refiners spend almost one-quarter of their sales just on inbound and outbound transportation. And whenever Canada Post raises parcel rates, shipping costs are dramatically affected for all kinds of firms.

Firms must identify the symptoms of poor distribution systems and strive to be more efficient. Up to one-fifth of the perishable items carried by Canadian grocers, like fish and dairy items, are lost to spoilage due to breakdowns in shipping or too much time on store shelves. To reduce losses, many grocers now insist on smaller, more frequent deliveries and have upgraded their storage facilities. Table 10-4 shows several cost ramifications of poor distribution.

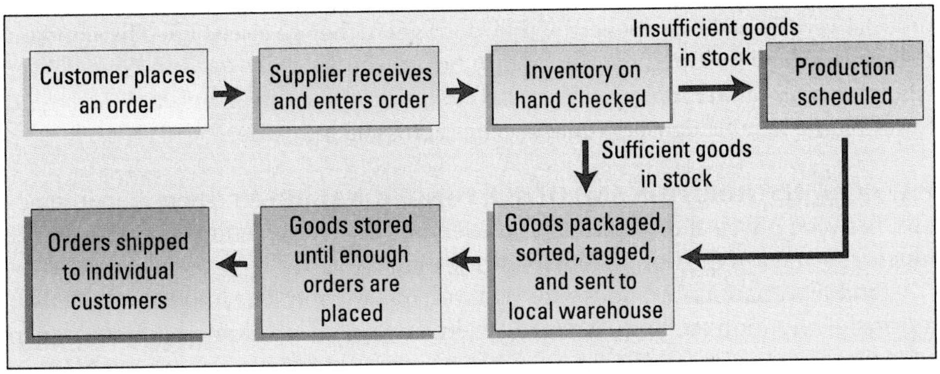

**FIGURE 10-6**

**Selected Physical Distribution Activities Involved in a Typical Order Cycle**

## TABLE 10-4

## Selected Symptoms of a Poor Physical Distribution System

| SYMPTOM | COST RAMIFICATIONS |
| --- | --- |
| **1.** Slow-turning and/or too-high inventory | Excessive capital is tied up in inventory. The firm has high insurance costs, interest expenses, and high risks of pilferage and product obsolescence. Merchandise may be stale. |
| **2.** Inefficient customer service | Costs are high relative to the value of shipments; warehouses are poorly situated; inventory levels are not tied to customer demand. |
| **3.** A large number of interwarehouse shipments | Merchandise transfers raise physical distribution cost because items must be handled and verified at each warehouse. |
| **4.** Frequent use of emergency shipments | Extra charges add significantly to physical distribution costs. |
| **5.** Peripheral hauls and/or limited backhauling | The firm uses its own trucking facilities; but many hauls are too spread out and trucks may only be full one way. |
| **6.** A large number of small orders | Small orders often are unprofitable. Many distribution costs are fixed. |

**CUSTOMER SERVICE** A major concern in planning a firm's physical distribution program is the level of customer service it should provide. Decisions involve delivery frequency, speed, and consistency; emergency shipments; whether to accept small orders; warehousing; coordinating assortments; whether to provide order progress reports; and other factors. Weak performance may lose customers.

Accordingly, distribution standards—clear and measurable goals as to service levels in physical distribution—must be devised. Examples are filling 90 per cent of orders from existing inventory, responding to customer requests for order information within two hours, filling orders with 99 per cent accuracy, and limiting goods damaged in transit to 2 per cent or less.

*The **total-cost approach** considers both costs and opportunities.*

One way to set the proper customer service level is the **total-cost approach**, whereby the distribution service level with the lowest total costs—including freight (shipping), warehousing, and lost business—is the best service level. An ideal system seeks a balance between low expenditures on distribution and high opportunities for sales. Seldom will that be at the lowest level of distribution spending; lost sales will be too great. Figure 10-7 illustrates the total-cost approach.

By offering superior customer service, a firm may establish a significant competitive advantage. The opposite is also true: "Customers increasingly demand on-time delivery from their suppliers. If they don't get it, they go elsewhere. The standard delivery window in supermarkets used to be four hours. Now, top suppliers deliver within an hour of their promised times, sometimes within fifteen minutes. The trend toward more reliable delivery times reaches across all industries."[17]

*Physical distribution must be coordinated with other areas.*

**PHYSICAL DISTRIBUTION AND OTHER FUNCTIONAL AREAS** There is an interaction between physical distribution and every aspect of marketing, as well as other functional areas in the firm, as the following indicate.

Product variations in colour, size, features, quality, and style impose a burden on a firm's distribution facilities. Greater variety means lower volume per item, which

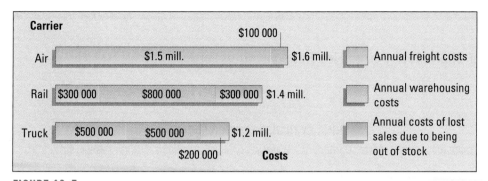

**FIGURE 10-7**

**An Illustration of the Total-Cost Approach in Distribution**

increases unit shipping and warehousing costs. Stocking a broader range of replacement parts also becomes necessary.

Physical distribution is related to an overall channel strategy. A firm seeking extensive distribution needs dispersed warehouses. One involved with perishables needs to be sure that most of a product's selling life is not spent in transit.

Because promotion campaigns are often planned well in advance, it is essential that distribution to resellers be done at the proper times to ensure ample stocks of goods. Resellers may get consumer complaints for not having sufficient quantities of the items they advertise, even if the manufacturer is at fault. Some new products fail due to poor initial distribution.

Physical distribution also plays a key part in pricing. A firm with fast, reliable delivery and an ample supply of replacement parts—that ships small orders and provides emergency shipments—may be able to charge higher prices than one providing less service.

A distribution strategy has a link with production and finance functions. High freight costs inspire firms to put plants closer to markets. Low average inventories in stock allow firms to reduce finance charges. Warehouse receipts may be used as collateral for loans.

Overall, there are many decisions to be made and coordinated in planning a physical distribution strategy: the transportation form(s) used, inventory levels and warehouse form(s), and the number and sites of plants, warehouses, and shopping facilities. A strategy can be simple: A firm can have one plant, focus on one geographic market, and ship to resellers or customers without the use of decentralized warehouses. On the other hand, a strategy can include multiple plants, assembly and/or warehouse locations in each market, thousands of customer locations, and several transportation forms.

The rest of this chapter looks at two central aspects of a physical distribution strategy: transportation and inventory management.

## Transportation

According to the World Economic Forum's 1997 *Global Competitiveness Report*, Canada has the best transportation infrastructure among the G-7 countries. There are five basic transportation forms: railroads, motor carriers, waterways, pipelines, and airways. Table 10-5 ranks them on seven operating characteristics. Because the range of products that can be shipped by pipeline is so restricted, business firms typically ship products using one or a combination of railroads, motor carriers, waterways, and airways. Table 10-6 shows the share of Canadian cargo tonnage and revenue for these four most commonly employed forms of transportation. Each transportation form and three transport services will now be presented.

*Transportation is rated on speed, availability, dependability, capability, frequency, losses, and cost.*

## TABLE 10-5

## The Relative Operating Characteristics of Five Transportation Forms

| OPERATING CHARACTERISTICS | RANKING BY TRANSPORTATION FORM[a] | | | | |
|---|---|---|---|---|---|
| | *Railroads* | *Motor Carriers* | *Waterways* | *Pipelines* | *Airways* |
| Delivery speed | 3 | 2 | 5 | 4 | 1 |
| Number of locations served | 2 | 1 | 4 | 5 | 3 |
| On-time dependability[b] | 3 | 2 | 4 | 1 | 5 |
| Range of products carried | 1 | 2 | 3 | 5 | 4 |
| Frequency of shipments | 4 | 2 | 5 | 1 | 3 |
| Losses and damages | 5 | 4 | 2 | 1 | 3 |
| Cost per tonne-mile | 3 | 4 | 1 | 2 | 5 |

[a]1 = highest ranking.

[b]Relative variation from anticipated delivery time.

Sources: Adapted by the authors from Donald J. Bowersox and David J. Closs, *Logistical Management: The Integrated Supply Chain Process* (New York: McGraw-Hill, 1996); Ronald H. Ballou, *Business Logistics Management: Planning and Control*, Third Edition (Englewood Cliffs, N.J.: Prentice Hall, 1992); and James C. Johnson and Donald F. Wood, *Contemporary Logistics*, Fourth Edition (New York: Macmillan, 1990).

**Railroads** *ship mostly heavy items over long distances.*

**CANADIAN PACIFIC RAILWAYS**
www.cprailway.com/

**CANADIAN NATIONAL RAILWAYS**
www.cn.ca

**RAILROADS  Railroads**  usually carry heavy, bulky items that are low in value (relative to weight) over long distances. They ship items too heavy for trucks. Canada has 77 387 km of operational railway track connecting the nation from coast to coast. Because Canada's economy is commodity-based, railways will always have a unique position as a transportation mode. Canada's railway companies have had many ups and downs in profitability performance in the past decade, although the two main railroads, Canadian Pacific and Canadian National, have recently been performing fairly well. For example, in 1997 Canadian Pacific earned $1.25 billion in profits on sales of $9.5 billion, and Canadian National earned $403 million in profits on sales of $4.3 billion. Nonetheless, railway operations are risky because fixed costs are high due to investments in facilities. Shippers face rail car shortages in high-demand months for agricultural goods. Some tracks and rail cars are in serious need of repair. Trucks are faster, more flexible, and are more easily packed. In response to these problems, railroads are relying on new shipping techniques and operating flexibility to improve efficiency.[18]

## TABLE 10-6

## The Relative Share of Canadian Cargo Tonnage and Revenue by Transportation Form

| TRANSPORTATION FORM | % SHARE OF TONNAGE SHIPPED | SHIPPING REVENUE |
|---|---|---|
| Railroads | 34 | 29.6 |
| Motor carriers | 28 | 54.0 |
| Waterways | 38 | 12.4 |
| Airways | .09 | 3.86 |

Sources: Adapted by the authors from Transport Canada, "Canada's Transportation System," Transport Canada Web site, www.tc.gc.ca (May, 1999).

**MOTOR CARRIERS** **Motor carriers** predominantly transport small shipments over short distances. They handle about 80 per cent of Canadian shipments weighing less than 500 kg and operate on Canada's 900 000 km of roadway. Seventy per cent of all motor carriers are used for local deliveries and two-thirds of total truck miles are local. For these reasons, motor carriers account for the largest share of shipping revenue. They're more flexible than rail because they can pick up packages at a factory or warehouse and deliver them to the customer's door. They're often used to supplement rail, air, and other forms that can't deliver directly to customers. Trucks are also faster than rail for short distances.

*Motor carriers handle small shipments for short distances.*

Statistics on for-hire motor carriers are reported by Statistics Canada and Transport Canada, but a great deal of truck freight is hauled by private carriers (business firms have their own truck fleets, which carry their own goods and raw materials). The Private Motor Truck Council of Canada reported in 1998 that private motor carriers had an economic value of $18.8 billion per year, for-hire carriers took in about $18.1 billion in revenues, and couriers about $2.1 billion. For-hire carriers hauled 229 million metric tons, which represents an estimated 40 per cent of all haulage. Therefore, private carriers hauled an estimated 344 million metric tons of merchandise in 1998. In the for-hire carrier motor transport segment carriers had an operating ratio of .95 in 1997 (the ratio of operating expenses divided by revenues), which is considered a sign of a healthy industry. Ratios near 1 indicate problems, while ratios over 1 mean the industry is losing money.[19]

**WATERWAYS** In Canada, **waterways** involve the movement of goods on barges via inland rivers and on tankers and general-merchandise freighters through the Great Lakes, intercoastal shipping, and the St. Lawrence Seaway. They are used primarily for transporting low-value, high-bulk freight (such as coal, iron ore, gravel, grain, and cement). Waterways are slow, and may be closed by ice in winter, but rates are quite low. Various improvements in vessel design have occurred over the last several years. For example, many "supervessels" now operate on the Great Lakes and other waterways. Their conveyor systems are twice as efficient as the ones on older boats. Navigation is computer-controlled.

*Waterways specialize in low-value, high-bulk items.*

In 1997 Canada's 200 ports handled a total of 375.5 million metric tons of goods (282.3 million tons of foreign goods and 93.2 million tons of domestic goods), the most tonnage on record. Canada's ports employ 30 000 Canadians; the busiest port is Vancouver, which handled about 20 per cent of all of Canada's tonnage.[20]

**PIPELINES** Within **pipelines**, there is continuous movement and there are no interruptions, inventories (except those held by a carrier), and intermediate storage sites. Handling and labour costs are minimized. Although pipelines are very reliable, only certain commodities can be moved through them. In the past, emphasis was on gas and petroleum-based products. Pipelines have now been modified to accept coal and wood chips, which are sent as semiliquids. Still, the lack of flexibility limits their potential. Some pipelines carry enormous volumes of products. For example, in Canada natural gas is transported through a system of pipelines that have an accumulated length of 335 000 kilometres. The main interprovincial natural gas pipeline is operated by TransCanada Pipelines, which is a leading transporter of natural gas in North America.[21]

*Pipelines centre on liquids, gases, and semiliquids.*

**TRANS CANADA PIPELINES**
www.transcanada.com

**AIRWAYS** **Airways** are the fastest, most expensive transportation form. High-value, perishable, and emergency goods dominate air shipments. For example, flowers from the Caribbean can be flown north to Canada during the winter; electronics parts and emergency repair items or high-fashion clothing items might also be shipped airfreight. Although air transit is costly, it may lower other costs, such as the need for outlying or even regional warehouses. The costs of packing, unpacking, and preparing goods for shipment are lower than for other transportation forms.

*Airways handle valuable, perishable, and emergency items.*

*These transportation service
companies ship packages:
government parcel post,
private parcel, and express.*

Modern communications and sorting equipment have also been added to airfreight operations to improve their efficiency. Firms specializing in air shipments have done well by stressing speedy, guaranteed service at acceptable prices. In 1996 Canadian Airlines received $959 million to ship 760 000 metric tons of goods. In terms of volume, air freight represents a minuscule amount of goods shipped.[22]

**TRANSPORTATION SERVICES** Transportation service companies are marketing specialists that chiefly handle the shipments of small and moderate-sized packages. Some pick up at the sender's office and deliver direct to the addressee. Others require packages to be brought to a service company outlet. The major kinds of transportation service firms are parcel post (Canada Post's service), private parcel, and express.

Canada Post's parcel post service operates out of post offices and has rates based on shipping weight and distance shipped. Parcel post can be insured or sent COD (collect on delivery). Regular service is completed in a few days, and special handling is available to expedite shipments. Priority Post mail is available for next-day service from a post office to an addressee.

Private parcel services specialize in small-package delivery, usually less than 50-pound shipments. Most shipments go from businesses to their customers; these services are expected to operate domestically and internationally and deliver on time. Regular service usually takes two to three days, while more expensive next-day service is also available from many carriers. Some of the firms that compete in this industry include: TNT Express Worldwide, Roberts Express, DHL Worldwide Express, RPS Limited, Purolator Courier, and United Parcel Service (UPS). UPS is a multibillion-dollar international company and the largest firm worldwide. See Figure 10-8.

Specialized express companies, such as Federal Express and Purolator (majority-owned by Canada Post), typically provide guaranteed nationwide delivery of small packages for the morning after pickup. The average express delivery is under 4 kilograms.[23]

# TECHNOLOGY AND MARKETING

## How Are Carriers Weblike in Tracking Shipments?

According to experts, the role of the Internet has gone from being a library of data (phase one) to a provider of important customer services (phase two). In its third phase, the Internet will enable customers to better handle financial transactions. Evidence of the transition from phase one to phase two is the use of the Internet's World Wide Web by business customers to track packages shipped by Federal Express and United Parcel Service (UPS).

Since November 1994, all Federal Express customers have been able to log on to the FedEx home page on the World Wide Web and enter their bill-tracking numbers into online package-tracking forms. Within minutes, the Internet server connects with Federal Express' main computer and returns reports to customers on the locations of their packages. As packages move through the FedEx distribution system, the data passed on to clients are constantly updated by Federal Express personnel.

Although Federal Express had to design special software and contract with an Internet provider, the overall costs of implementing its system have been very low. In addition, the FedEx site—which receives over 4500 inquiries per day—saves money by reducing the need for customer service personnel. All customers have access to this Internet-based service, but larger ones can also access the firm's private network. According to a Federal Express spokesperson, 60 per cent of all package tracking is now done through automated procedures.

Likewise, UPS has begun to offer package tracking on the Internet. As with Federal Express, UPS's site was not started to save money for the firm, but is less costly than other package tracking methods.

As a customer service supervisor for Federal Express, outline the pros and cons of using the World Wide Web to automate package tracking.

Source: Based on material in Laurie Flynn, "Companies Use Web Hoping to Save Millions," *New York Times* (July 17, 1995), p. D5.

**FIGURE 10-8**

**Purolator Courier offers guaranteed overnight delivery to most of Canada.**
*Courtesy of Purolator*

**PUROLATOR COURIER LTD.**
www.purolator.com/

**COORDINATING TRANSPORTATION** Because a single shipment may involve a combination of transportation forms—a practice known as *intermodal shipping*—coordination is needed. A firm can enhance its ability to coordinate shipments by using containerization and freight forwarding.

With **containerization**, goods are placed in sturdy containers that can be loaded on trains, trucks, ships, or planes. The marked containers are sealed until delivered, thereby reducing damage and pilferage. Their progress and destination are monitored. The containers are mobile warehouses that can be moved from manufacturing plants to receiving docks, where they remain until the contents are needed. Containers are a key part of intermodal transportation. In Canada, 1 715 000 containers were loaded and unloaded in 1996. About 7 per cent of all international tonnage shipped was via container. In comparison, only 1 per cent of Canada's total domestic tonnage involved container shipments.[24]

In **freight forwarding**, specialized firms (freight forwarders) collect small shipments (usually less than 200 kilograms each) from several companies. They pick up merchandise at each shipper's place of business and arrange for delivery at buyers' doors. Freight forwarders prosper because less-than-carload (lcl) shipping rates are sharply higher than carload (cl) rates. They also provide traffic management services, such as selecting the best transportation form at the most reasonable rate.

*Containerization and*
*freight forwarding simplify*
*intermodal shipping.*

## Inventory Management

The intent of **inventory management** is to provide a continuous flow of goods and to match the quantity of goods kept in inventory as closely as possible with customer demand. When production or consumption is seasonal or erratic, this can be particularly difficult.

Inventory management has broad implications: A manufacturer or service firm cannot afford to run out of a crucial part that could put a halt to its business. Yet inventory on hand should not be too large because the costs of storing raw materials, parts, and/or finished products can be substantial. If models change yearly, as with autos, large inventories can adversely affect new-product sales or rentals. Excessive stock may also lead to stale goods, cause a firm to mark down prices, and tie up funds.

To improve their inventory management, a lot of companies are now applying either or both of two complementary concepts: a just-in-time inventory system and electronic data interchange. With a **just-in-time (JIT) inventory system**, a purchasing firm reduces the amount of inventory it keeps on hand by ordering more often

**Inventory management**
*deals with the flow and*
*allocation of products.*

**JIT** *and* **QR inventory**
**systems** *closely monitor*
*inventory levels.*

and in lower quantity. This requires better planning and information on the part of the purchaser, geographically closer sellers, improved buyer–seller relationships, and better production and distribution facilities. To retailers, a JIT system is known as a **quick response (QR) inventory system**—a cooperative effort between retailers and suppliers to reduce retail inventory while providing a merchandise supply that more closely addresses the actual buying patterns of consumers.[25]

In Canada, JIT and QR systems are being used by essentially all of the auto makers, as well as Midas Canada Inc., Hewlett-Packard, Canon, DuPont, Ryder, Wal-Mart, Motorola, General Electric, Deere, Black & Decker, and many other large and small firms. For example, Raymond Industrial Equipment, a forklift truck manufacturer in Brantford, Ontario, implemented a JIT system to replace its batch production system. It benefited by reducing its inventory by 60 per cent, releasing warehouse space, and reducing the manufacturing time to make a fork lift truck from fifteen days to only four![26]

*With **EDI**, computers are used to exchange information between suppliers and their customers.*

Through **electronic data interchange (EDI)**, suppliers and their manufacturers/ service providers, wholesalers, and/or retailers exchange data through computer linkups. This lets firms maximize revenues, reduce markdowns, and lower inventory carrying costs by speeding the flow of data and products. For EDI to work well, each firm in a distribution channel must use the Universal Product Code (UPC) and electronically exchange data. Although all major food makers use the UPC, many makers of general merchandise do not. However, the number of general merchandise manufacturers using the UPC on their products has been rising; and more will begin using the UPC in the near future.

Four specific aspects of inventory management are examined next: stock turnover, when to reorder, how much to reorder, and warehousing.

*Stock turnover shows the ratio between sales and average inventory.*

**STOCK TURNOVER**   Stock turnover—the number of times during a stated period (usually one year) that average inventory on hand is sold—shows the relationship between a firm's sales and the inventory level it maintains. It is calculated in units or dollars (in selling price or at cost):

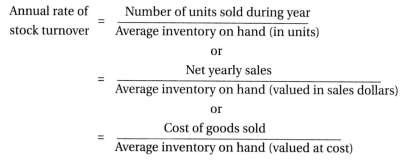

$$\text{Annual rate of stock turnover} = \frac{\text{Number of units sold during year}}{\text{Average inventory on hand (in units)}}$$

or

$$= \frac{\text{Net yearly sales}}{\text{Average inventory on hand (valued in sales dollars)}}$$

or

$$= \frac{\text{Cost of goods sold}}{\text{Average inventory on hand (valued at cost)}}$$

For example, in retailing, average annual stock turnover ranges from less than three in jewellery stores to more than thirty in gasoline service stations.

A high stock turnover rate has many advantages: inventory investments are productive, items are fresh, losses from style changes are reduced, and inventory costs (such as insurance, breakage, warehousing, and credit) are lower. Turnover can be improved by reducing assortments, dropping slow-selling items, keeping only small amounts of some items, and buying from suppliers that deliver on time. On the other hand, too high a turnover rate may have adverse effects: small purchases may cause a loss of volume discounts, low product assortment may reduce sales volume if consumers do not have enough choice or related items are not carried, discounts may be needed to lift sales volume, and chances of running out of stock go up when average inventory size is low. Figure 10-9 shows how people can act should a firm run out of stock.

Knowing when to reorder merchandise helps protect against stockouts while minimizing inventory investments.

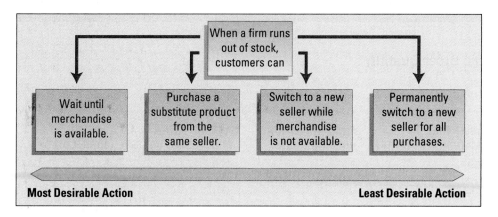

**FIGURE 10-9**

**What Happens When a Firm Has
Stock Shortages**

**WHEN TO REORDER INVENTORY**  By having a clear reorder point for each of its products (or raw materials or parts), a firm sets the inventory levels for new orders. A **reorder point** depends on order lead time, the usage rate, and safety stock. Order lead time is the period from the date an order is placed until the date items are ready to sell or use (received, checked, and altered, if needed). Usage rate is the average unit sales (for a reseller) or the rate at which a product is used in production (for a manufacturer). Safety stock is extra inventory kept to guard against being out of stock due to unexpectedly high demand or production and delivery delays.

*The **reorder point** is based on lead time, usage, and safety stock.*

The reorder point formula is:

Reorder point = (Order lead time $\times$ Usage rate) + (Safety stock).

For instance, a wholesaler that needs four days for its purchase orders to be placed and received, sells ten items per day, and wants to have ten extra items on hand in case of a supplier's delivery delay of one day, has a reorder point of fifty [(4 $\times$ 10) + (10)]. Without safety stock, the firm would lose ten sales if it orders when inventory is forty items and the items are received in five days.

**HOW MUCH TO REORDER**  A firm must decide its order size—the right amount of products, parts, and so on, to buy at one time. Order size depends on volume discounts, the firm's resources, the stock turnover rate, the costs of processing each order, and the costs of holding goods in inventory. If a firm places large orders, quantity discounts are usually available, a large part of its finances are tied up in inventory, its stock turnover rate is relatively low, per-order processing costs are low, and inventory costs are generally high. The firm is also less apt to run out of goods. The opposite is true for small orders.

Many companies seek to balance their order-processing costs (filling out forms, computer time, and product handling) and their inventory-holding costs (warehouse expenses, interest charges, insurance, deterioration, and theft). Processing costs per unit fall as orders get bigger, but inventory costs rise. The **economic order quantity (EOQ)** is the order volume corresponding to the lowest sum of order-processing and inventory-holding costs.

*EOQ balances ordering and inventory costs.*

Table 10-7 demonstrates three ways to compute EOQ. In this illustration, a firm has an annual demand of 3000 units for a product; the cost of each unit is $1; order-processing costs are $3 per order; and inventory-holding costs equal 20 per cent of each item's cost. As shown in the table, the economic order quantity is 300 units. Thus, the firm should place orders of 300 units and have 10 orders per year.

**WAREHOUSING**  **Warehousing** involves the physical facilities used to store, identify, and sort goods in expectation of their sale and transfer within a distribution channel. Warehouses can be used to store goods, prepare goods for shipment, coordinate shipments, send orders, and aid in product recalls.

**Warehousing** *involves storing and dispatching goods.*

## TABLE 10-7

## Computing an Economic Order Quantity

**A.**

| AVERAGE ORDER QUANTITY (UNITS) | INVENTORY MAINTAINED (UNITS)[a] | ANNUAL INVENTORY-HOLDING COSTS[b] | ANNUAL ORDER-PROCESSING COSTS[c] | ANNUAL TOTAL COSTS |
|---|---|---|---|---|
| 100 | 50 | $10 | $90 | $100 |
| 200 | 100 | 20 | 45 | 65 |
| EO → 300 | 150 | 30 | 30 | 60 |
| 400 | 200 | 40 | 24 | 64 |
| 500 | 250 | 50 | 18 | 68 |

**B.**

**C.**

$$EOQ = \sqrt{\frac{2DS}{IC}} = \sqrt{\frac{2\,(3,000)\,(\$3)}{0.20\,(\$1)}} = 300$$

where EOQ = Order quantity (units)    I = Annual holding costs (as a % of unit costs)
      D = Annual demand (units)      C = Unit cost of an item ($)
      S = Costs to place an order ($)

[a] The average inventory on hand = $\frac{1}{2}$ × Order quantity.

[b] Inventory-holding costs = Annual holding costs as a per cent of unit cost × Unit cost × Average inventory.

[c] Order-processing costs = Number of annual orders × Costs to place an order. Number of orders = Annual demand/Order quantity.

Private warehouses are owned and operated by firms that store and distribute their own products. They are most likely to be used by those with stable inventory levels and long-run plans to serve the same geographic areas.

Public warehouses provide storage and related distribution services to any interested firm or individual on a rental basis. They are used by small firms that do not have the resources or desire to have their own facilities, larger firms that need more storage space (because their own warehouses are full), or any size of firm entering new geographic areas. Public warehouses offer shipping economies for users by receiving carload shipments from factories or distribution centres; and then allowing short-distance, smaller shipments to be made from these warehouses to customers. Firms can also reduce their investments in facilities and maximize flexibility by using public warehouses. If products must be recalled, these warehouses can be used as collection points, where items are separated, disposed of, and/or salvaged. There are hundreds of public warehouses in Canada.

Public warehouses can accommodate both bonded warehousing and field warehousing. In bonded warehousing, imported or taxable goods are stored and can be released for sale only after applicable taxes are paid. This enables firms to postpone tax payments until they are ready to make deliveries to customers. Cigarettes and liquor are often stored in bonded warehouses. In field warehousing, a receipt is issued by a public warehouse for goods stored in a private warehouse or in transit to consumers. The goods are put in a special area, and the field warehouser is responsible for them. A firm may use field warehousing because a warehouse receipt serves as collateral for a loan.

## MARKETING IN THE THIRD MILLENNIUM

### Using Logistics to Gain Competitive Advantage in the Twenty-first Century[27]

How will the managers of distribution channels have to respond to maintain or improve the competitive advantage of their organizations in the twenty-first century? This question was posed to a number of experienced supply chain managers to gain some insight into what they believe the future will bring. What follows is a sample of some of their opinions.

Michel Leenders, a Professor of Purchasing Management at the Ivey School of Business, agrees that it will be very important for firms to make their supply chain a source of competitive advantage in the twenty-first century. He feels that to be successful firms must use logistics in a strategic role more effectively. A key input would be finding capable people who want to pursue a career in logistics management.

Martin Williams, Vice-President of Logistics and Supply at Hiram Walker & Sons Ltd., feels that logistics is a key factor in the sale of distilled spirits. He suggests that managers will need to view the supply chain as a web that's critical to the success of the organization. He cites the experience of Hiram Walker, which charges high retail prices for distilled spirits as a result of taxes. The high prices mean profitability in this industry must come from cost-containment efforts and improved efficiency, which logistical systems can provide. Using logistics to gain competitive advantage will require firms to develop more responsive supply bases, use relationship management, model costs, and measure performance.

Richard Giesbrecht, President of Shared Healthcare Supply Services, emphasizes that supply managers must realize they are involved in sales and that quality products and services must be delivered on time. When managers recognize that customers are the focus of the organization, and that logistical services can add value, they'll be on the road to making logistics a strategic marketing tool.

Ken Bradley, Vice-President of Nortel Supply Management, states that "fast new product introduction, short product life cycles, leveraged supply chains, Web commerce, and more global activity" will be the key trends of the new millennium. He predicts that staffing and skill management in supply chains will be critical in dealing with these trends. Managers in the supply chain will have to develop new skills to deal with these changes, since the current sets of skills will not be adequate.

Bob Gallant of Strategies Plus Associates Inc. believes that supply management executives will be faced with the challenge of convincing upper managers to accept the need to focus more attention on this area of the business. Supply management professionals must think more as general managers and be prepared to integrate all the processes of the supply chain so that they can relate the impact of what they do directly to the firm's net income and earnings per share. Only when they do this will upper managers clearly see the strategic value of an effective logistics system.

Finally, Daniel Olsen, General Manager of Logistics Transformation at Bell Canada, believes that electronic commerce is creating change in the role of supply chain managers. He notes that product life cycles are getting shorter and firms must get products to market much faster. Firms will have to source products and services to support these initiatives much more effectively. The competitive landscape is changing very rapidly, as is technology, and this requires supply chain managers to change as well.

## SUMMARY

**1.** *To define distribution planning and to examine its importance, distribution functions, the factors used in selecting a distribution channel, and the different types of distribution channels* Distribution planning is systematic decision making as to the physical movement of goods and services from producer to consumer, as well as the related transfer of ownership (or rental). A channel of distribution consists of the organizations or people—known as channel members or distribution intermediaries—involved in the distribution process.

Distribution decisions often affect a firm's marketing plans. For many firms, the choice of a distribution channel is one of the most important decisions they make. More companies now realize the value of relationship marketing and work for long-term relations with suppliers, intermediaries, and customers. Both costs and profits are affected by the channel chosen. Firms may have to conform to existing channel patterns; and their markets' size and nature are also influenced by the channel employed.

No matter who does them, channel functions include research, buying, promotion, customer services, product planning, pricing, and distribution. Intermediaries can play a key role by doing various tasks and resolving differences in manufacturer and consumer goals through the sorting process.

In selecting a method of distribution, these factors must be considered: the consumer, the company, the product, the competition, the distribution channels themselves, and legal requirements.

A direct channel requires that one party do all distribution tasks; in an indirect channel, tasks are done by multiple parties. In comparing methods, a firm must weigh its costs and abilities against control and total sales. An indirect channel may use a contractual or an administered agreement. A long channel has many levels of independent firms; a wide one has many firms at any stage. A channel may be exclusive, selective, or intensive, based on company goals, resellers, customers, and marketing. A dual channel lets a company use two or more distribution methods.

**2.** *To describe the nature of supplier/distribution intermediary contracts, and cooperation and conflict in a channel of distribution* In contracts between suppliers and distribution intermediaries, price policies, sale conditions, territorial rights, the services/responsibility mix, and contract length and termination conditions are specified.

Cooperation and conflict may both occur in a distribution channel. Conflicts must be settled fairly because confrontation can cause hostility and negative acts by all parties. Frequently, a pushing strategy— based on channel cooperation—can be employed by established firms. But a pulling strategy—based on proving that consumer demand exists prior to gaining intermediary support or acceptance—must be used by many new companies.

**3.** *To examine the special aspects relating to a distribution channel for industrial products and to international distribution* An industrial channel normally does not use retailers; it is more direct, entails fewer transactions and larger orders, requires specification selling and knowing resellers, uses team selling and special intermediaries, includes more leasing, provides more technical data, and embraces shared activities.

Channel length depends on a nation's stage of economic development and consumer behaviour. Distribution practices and structures differ by nation. International decisions must be made as to shipping and intermediaries. Each country has distinct legal provisions pertaining to distribution.

**4.** *To define physical distribution and to demonstrate its importance* Physical distribution (logistics) involves efficiently delivering products to designated places, at designated times, and in proper condition. It may be undertaken by any member of a channel, from producer to consumer.

There are various reasons for studying physical distribution: its costs, the value of customer service,

and its relationship with other functional areas in a firm. With the total-cost approach, the service level with the lowest total cost (including freight, warehousing, and lost business) is the best one. In a physical distribution strategy, decisions are made as to transportation, inventory levels, warehousing, and facility locations.

**5.** *To discuss transportation alternatives and inventory management issues* Railroads typically carry bulky goods for long distances. Motor carriers dominate small shipments over short distances. Waterways primarily ship low-value freight. Pipelines provide ongoing movement of liquid, gaseous, and semiliquid products. Airways offer fast, expensive movement of perishables and high-value items. Transportation service firms are specialists that mostly handle small and medium-sized packages. Coordination can be improved through containerization and freight forwarding.

Inventory management is needed to provide a continuous flow of goods and to match the stock kept in inventory as closely as possible with demand. In a JIT or QR system, the purchasing firm reduces the stock it keeps on hand by ordering more often and in lower quantity. With electronic data interchange, channel members exchange information via computer linkages.

The interplay between a firm's sales and the inventory level it keeps is expressed by its stock turnover. A reorder point shows the inventory level when goods must be reordered. The economic order quantity is the optimal amount of goods to order based on order-processing and inventory-holding costs. Warehousing decisions include selecting a private or public warehouse and examining the availability of public warehouse services.

# KEY TERMS

# REVIEW QUESTIONS

1. What is relationship marketing?

2. Explain the sorting process. Provide an example in your answer.

3. Which factors influence the selection of a distribution channel?

4. Under what circumstances should a company engage in direct distribution? Indirect distribution?

5. What is meant by a short, narrow channel of distribution?

6. Explain how a product could move from exclusive to selective to intensive distribution.

7. Compare motor carrier and waterway deliveries on the basis of the total-cost approach.

8. The average stock turnover rate in jewellery stores is less than three. What does this mean? How could a jewellery store raise its turnover rate?

9. Two wholesalers sell identical merchandise. Yet, one plans a safety stock equal to 20 per cent of expected sales, while the other plans no safety stock. Comment on this difference.

10. Why would a firm use both private and public warehouses?

# DISCUSSION QUESTIONS

1. What distribution decisions would a new firm that rents vans to small, seasonal businesses have to make?

2. Devise distribution channels for the sale of a daily newspaper, pianos, and cellular phones. Explain your choices.

3. Present a checklist that a firm could use in making international distribution decisions on a country-by-country basis.

4. Develop a list of distribution standards for a firm delivering fresh fruit to supermarkets.

5. Are there any disadvantages to a JIT or QR system? Explain your answer.

## CASE STUDY

# Physical Distribution at Vancouver's Port

Efficient physical distribution of goods and services is one of the keys to success in international trade. This must be combined with some type of comparative or absolute advantage in production of goods to enable a nation to trade effectively and not run a trade deficit. Canada had a merchandise trade surplus of $18.8 billion in 1998. The declining trade with European nations and the tremendous growth in international trade with Pacific Rim nations have meant that the majority of the natural resources exported from Canada now go through the port of Vancouver.

In 1997 Canada's 200 ports handled a total of 375.5 million metric tons of goods (282.3 million tons of foreign goods and 93.2 million tons of domestic goods), the most tonnage on record. Canada's ports employ 30 000 Canadians, of whom 9000 are employed with the port of Vancouver. Vancouver is Canada's busiest port, handling about 20 per cent of its tonnage. The port recently opened a second harbour terminal, giving it more capacity than the ports of Halifax, Montreal, St. John, and Quebec City combined. The port of Vancouver is a virtual hub of intermodal transportation activity.

The logistical demands associated with visiting ships give a perspective on the activities that go on in Vancouver's port. Consider the Saga Spray, a Norwegian-owned vessel that was constructed at a cost of U.S.$70 million in Japan and is operated by a crew from India. This ship was built for one task: to load lumber from B.C., ship it to Japan, and then return from Japan for more lumber. A round trip takes about thirty days for this ship. The vessel is self-loading and unloading with its own roofed, double gantry system. Because the operating/depreciation costs for this vessel are approximately U.S.$30 000/day, the owners don't like it to stand awaiting either loading or unloading for very long. The labour agreement associated with the port of Vancouver requires that only teamster workers be involved in the loading and unloading work. This can present

some problems if a crew of teamsters fails to show up for work, something the Saga Spray experienced during one trip to Vancouver.

In contrast, the Golden Empire is a much older general freight vessel taking on a cargo of grain for Mexico. The standing cost for this vessel is about $10 000/day. The crew of this ship is from Greece and, like the Saga Spray, the Captain is anxious to have as fast a loading and unloading process as possible. But the Golden Empire isn't a self-loading vessel and must depend on the facilities of Vancouver's port. Rainy weather (a very common occurrence in Vancouver) can present a major problem for grain loading. Moisture can cause germination of the grain in the hold of a ship, which could ruin the entire cargo. Therefore, during loading the hold must be covered to keep moisture out of the grain. This requires rigging up tarpaulins and creates delays in ship loading, which of course costs the ship owners more money.

A second logistical matter for the ships involves acquiring provisions for the vessel and crew. On the high seas a ship can't stop for food and fuel as trucks do on the highway. Arya Marine is a $15 million/year ship stocking company that sells provisions to ships in Vancouver. Ship schedules are constantly changing and this means that Arya Marine must handle the provisions quickly and carefully to see that they don't spoil before being loaded onto a ship. Furthermore, the provisions must arrive in time to be loaded before a ship has to depart from the port. For example, the Saga Spray requested bread and chicken burgers as part of their provision order. Ship chandler Nick Jacic was able to fill the bread order but the chicken burger order arrived after the vessel had sailed. Although changing schedules and hurried deadlines are a problem for Arya Marine, its customers do pay in cash. This is a tremendous business advantage because Arya Marine's suppliers likely wait for their payments. For example,

Arya Marine was paid U.S.$10 000 by the Saga Spray, even without the chicken burgers.

### Questions

1. Define the term multi-modal and discuss it with respect to the operations of Vancouver's port.

2. The case gives us some figures for the operating costs, frequency of visits, and building costs of the Saga Spray. If you were the owner of this ship, estimate the total shipping fees you'd have to charge per trip to make owning this ship reasonably profitable on an annual basis. (Remember that there is competition in this market.)

3. Compare the advantages and disadvantages of owning a specialized ship like the Saga Spray versus a general freighter like the Golden Empire.

4. Identify as many logistical problems as you can that were presented in this case. Categorize these problems into two types: facility related and non-facility related. Suggest some potential solutions for one facility related problem and one non-facility related problem.

Sources: Based on Statistics Canada, "Imports and Exports of Goods on a Balance-of-Payments Basis," Canadian Statistics: International Trade, www.statcan.ca; Statistics Canada, "Port Activity 1997," The Daily (May 21, 1998); and "Vancouver's Port" CBC Venture Video 552.

## CASE STUDY

# PEI's Confederation Bridge: Road to Prosperity or Road to Ruin?

The most versatile mode of transportation is the motor carrier, since it can pick up packages at a factory or warehouse and deliver them to the customer's door. Motor carriers handle about 80 per cent of Canadian shipments weighing less than 500 kilograms. The ability to ship door-to-door for firms serving Prince Edward Island was merely a dream until June 1, 1997. It was on that day that the 12.9 kilometre-long Confederation Bridge linking Borden-Carleton, Prince Edward Island to Cape Jourimain, New Brunswick was opened to traffic.

It was also on that day that the Marine Atlantic ferry and the 650 people employed in its operation were thrown out of work. No longer needed to move goods, cars, and people from the mainland to the Island, about 80 per cent of the workers were still unemployed after nearly a year. Many people were lamenting the loss of some of the Island's charm, as it was perceived by tourists who arrived by ferry for summer visits in the past. The Island has found itself cluttered with tourists who were afraid to travel by ferry before but were more than happy to drive onto the Island, even after paying tolls to Strait Crossing Bridge Limited, the bridge's operator.

Strait Crossing Bridge Limited is a private company that was involved in constructing the bridge for an estimated $1 billion. The firm is to be paid $42 million a year in inflation-adjusted dollars for a period of thirty-five years. The firm is authorized to collect tolls, and to use the money to maintain the bridge and of course to turn some profits as well. The bridge alone represents a tremendous attraction for PEI; people will drive over it just to say that they did. And because it's a toll bridge it also represents a commercial venture on its own.

The Bank of Montreal forecasted that PEI would see an economic boom, given that the bridge would result in lower transportation costs and increased demand fuelled by tourism. Jeannette Arsenault is indeed expecting a booming business for her company, Cavendish Figurines, which will be located at the foot of the bridge. She has set up a seven-foot statue of Anne of Green Gables in hopes of drawing in tourists. In one short year tourism on the Island jumped from 750 000 in 1996 to 1.2 million in 1997. The 1997 economy also saw tourist expenditures increase to $246 million from $86 million the year before. Clearly the bridge brought in big spenders, because although the number of tourist visits only went up by 60 per cent the dollars they spent went up 186 per cent.

Although truck traffic can now carry products to and from the Island faster and far more cheaply than the ferry service, the reliability of the service is still not equal to that of the mainland. In its first year of operation the bridge was closed sixteen times to trucks between November and March because of high winds off the ocean. Cars are able to proceed on the bridge regardless of winds. (Since in the past ferry service was also interrupted by foul weather, Islanders aren't flustered by these events.) One solution to the problem would be to allow trucks to convoy across the bridge when winds are high.

The major benefit of the bridge in terms of physical distribution capabilities is that trucks can travel door-to-door with no need for trans-shipment on a ferry and along with greatly reduced travel time. There is no need to worry about the ferry schedule and the time to traverse a 12.9 kilometre bridge is only about 15 minutes at 50 km/hour. A ferry travels at a far slower rate of speed and must load and unload to make the journey. In addition, the need to ship cargo or limit the size and shape of trucks is a major limitation of ferry service. Canadian consumers can now expect to get their PEI potatoes much sooner than ever before at greatly reduced prices because of the savings in transportation.

## Questions

1. Compare and contrast the effectiveness of trucking as a mode of transportation versus water-borne transportation. Do you think there are any products on PEI that would be transported by water or any mode of transportation other than motor carrier now that the Confederation Bridge is open? Why or why not?

2. Discuss the benefits of improved physical distribution that will accrue to PEI's potato farmers. Refer to the chapter to help you identify as many as possible.

3. The Confederation Bridge cost $1 billion. How would you determine its cost/benefit to the Islanders and the people of Canada whose taxes are being paid to Strait Crossing Bridge Ltd. at $42 million a year for thirty-five years? Evaluate whether you think the bridge is worth its cost.

4. Retail spending in PEI is reported as increasing. Explain how the Confederation Bridge has helped PEI retailers. Can you think of a situation where the Confederation Bridge could end up hurting PEI retailers? Discuss.

Sources: Based on Graeme Hamilton, "Bridge Brings Good Times, Bad," The Windsor Star (May 19, 1998) p. C11; Private Motor Truck Council of Canada, "Profile of Private Trucking in Canada 1998," Strategis Web site, strategis.ic.gc.ca; and Industry Canada, "Trucking Services," Strategis Web site.

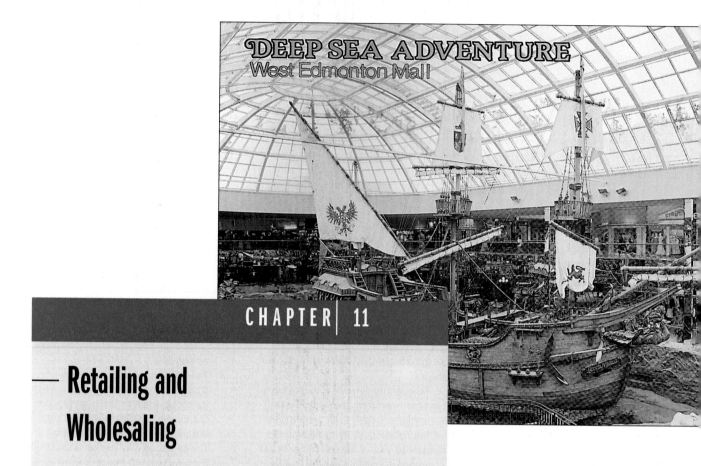

**DEEP SEA ADVENTURE**
West Edmonton Mall

## CHAPTER | 11

# Retailing and Wholesaling

### Chapter Objectives

1. To define retailing and show its importance

2. To discuss the different types of retailers, in terms of ownership, store strategy mix, and nonstore operations

3. To explore five major aspects of retail planning: store location, atmosphere, scrambled merchandising, the wheel of retailing, and technological advances

4. To define wholesaling and show its importance, and to describe the three broad categories of wholesaling (manufacturer/service provider wholesaling, merchant wholesaling, and agents and brokers)

5. To examine recent trends in retailing and wholesaling

Photo courtesy of West Edmonton Mall

**T**he department stores' response to losing business to specialty retailers was quite simple: they cut prices to regain customers, causing profit margins to fall, leading to staff reductions in order to maintain profitability. The result? Less customer service from stores that built their reputations on customer service! Eaton's failed and The Bay may follow it, because the level of mall competition itself is also expected to see major changes. Mega-malls (those with 1 million-plus square feet of retailing space) like the West Edmonton Mall and the Mall of America are being presented as both retailing environments and tourist destinations. Cambridge Shopping Centres and U.S.-based Mills Corporation of Arlington, Virginia are looking for retailers to fill mega-malls planned for Canada's three major urban centres: Montreal, Toronto, and Vancouver. The first centre, a 1.4 million square foot facility, is under development just north of Toronto and is expected to open in the fall of 2001. The plan is to draw customers from as far away as 200 kilometres, who will make shopping a planned destination trip rather than a convenience trip.

**THE MILLS CORPORATION**
www.millscorp.com

A mega-mall will offer a lot of fun and entertainment to accompany the available shopping. For example, fishing ponds, televised football games, and virtual reality games will be available. These mega-malls pose a major threat to department store retailers that operate as "departments." Every innovative retail approach, along with tried-and-true approaches, will be found in these mega-malls. Factory outlets from Florsheim shoes, Brooks Brothers, and Guess? will compete with big-box "category killer" stores like the Sports Authority and Books-A-Million.

The experience of Mills Malls with seven previously operating locations is that mega-mall shoppers spend about three hours of time shopping versus one hour in a typical mall, and spend about U.S.$167 per shopping trip compared to U.S.$64 per trip in a standard mall. If these results are produced here the impact on the Canadian retail market will be huge.

Mills Malls' CEO Larry Siegel is very enthusiastic about the market potential in Canada. It may seem strange to feel encouraged at a time when real income levels and standard of living have levelled off, and maybe even deteriorated. But the success of Wal-Mart in Canada points to the fact that providing low prices and good service (always desirable features) is particularly appealing under the current Canadian market conditions. And this is something that Mills Malls is planning to provide.

How can The Bay survive in this new retail environment? Alan Gee recommends that The Bay reinvents itself. Specifically, it can take advantage of one of the main consumer issues in the competitive retail market: too much choice and not enough time. If a retailer can make choices for a consumer and assist in his or her purchasing, that consumer will become a loyal customer of the store. Gee calls this building a "brand-style." Offering a brand-style means thinking about selling lifestyles, not just products. For example, a brand-style approach might involve packaging up a whole weekend. Put together a set of offerings such as clothes to wear for a weekend barbecue party, throw in the food to be barbecued, the barbecue itself, the outdoor furniture that goes with the barbecue, the matching plates, napkins, and tablecloths to go with the furniture, and on and on. A specialty store can't bring all of this together, but a "department" store can! The question is, are there enough customers looking to buy a brand-style?[1]

In this chapter, we will examine various aspects of retailing—including trends affecting shopping centres—and consider their ramifications. We will study wholesalers and their relationships with their suppliers and customers. We will also examine the different types of firms that perform wholesaling activities and the strategies they use to compete in the marketplace.

## Overview

*Retailing, the last channel stage, entails selling to final consumers.*

**Retailing** encompasses those business activities involved with the sale of goods and services to the final consumer for personal, family, or household use. It is the final stage in a channel of distribution. Manufacturers, importers, and wholesalers act as retailers when they sell products directly to the final consumer.

Surveys undertaken for the Grocery Products Manufacturers of Canada and the Canadian Council of Grocery Distributors indicated the following about Canadian shoppers: The average spending on groceries was about $85 per week. The shoppers were mostly female (83 per cent) and 80 per cent of the shoppers bought brands with which they were familiar. Methods of payment were cash (55 per cent), debit card (29 per cent), and cheque (13 per cent). In Canada, grocery shoppers accounted for 28 per cent of all Canadian interactive direct payment transactions. Studies of shopping behaviour in North America indicate that the average retail sale per shopping trip is small, about $40 for department stores and $50 for specialty stores. Convenience stores, such as 7-Eleven, have average sales of just a few dollars (not including gasoline).

Chain supermarkets average $25.31 per customer transaction. Accordingly retailers try to increase their sales volume by using one-stop shopping appeals, broadening merchandise and service assortments, increasing customer shopping frequency, and encouraging more family members to go shopping. Inventory controls, automated merchandise handling, and electronic cash registers enable retailers to reduce their transaction costs.[2]

Despite the low average size of customer transactions, about one-half of sales for such retailers as department stores involve some form of customer credit. This means these retailers must pay a percentage of each transaction to a bank or other credit card service company or absorb the costs of their own credit programs—in return for increased sales.[3] For example, The Bay and Sears each have millions of holders of their own credit cards; these people buy hundreds of millions of dollars in goods and services every year.

Whereas salespeople regularly visit organizational consumers to initiate and conclude transactions, most final consumers patronize stores. This makes the location of the store, product assortment, store hours, store fixtures, sales personnel, delivery, customer service, and other factors critical tools in drawing customers.

Final consumers make many unplanned purchases. In contrast, those that buy for resale or use in production (or operating a business) are more systematic in their purchasing. Therefore, retailers need to place impulse items in high-traffic locations, organize store layout, train sales personnel in suggestion selling, place related items next to each other, and sponsor special events to stimulate consumers.

In the first part of this chapter, the importance of retailing, the various types of retailers, considerations in retail planning, and recent trends in retailing are all discussed.

*Wholesaling is the buying/handling of products and their resale to organizational buyers.*

**Wholesaling** encompasses the buying and/or handling of goods and services and their subsequent resale to organizational users, retailers, and/or other wholesalers—but not the sale of significant volume to final consumers. Wholesaling undertakes many vital functions in a channel of distribution, particularly those in the sorting process.

Manufacturers and service providers sometimes are their own wholesalers; other times, independent firms are employed. Independents may or may not take title to or possession of products, depending on the type of wholesaling. Some independents have limited tasks; others perform a wide range of functions.

Industrial, commercial, and government institutions are wholesalers' leading customers, followed closely by retailers. Sales from one wholesaler to another also represent a significant proportion of wholesaling activity.

In the second part of this chapter, the importance of wholesaling, the different types of wholesaling, and recent trends in wholesaling are all discussed.

# The Importance of Retailing

Retailing is a significant aspect of distribution because of its impact on the economy, its functions in the distribution channel, and its relationships with suppliers.

## Retailing's Impact on the Economy

Retail sales and employment account for substantial amounts of sales and employment. In 1998 Canadian retail store sales volume was approximately $241 billion. This figure does not include non-store retail activities such as house parties, mail order, and door-to-door selling. In 1998, Canada's ten largest retail organizations included: George Weston Ltd. ($13.9 billion in sales), Loblaw Cos. Ltd. ($11 billion), Oshawa Group Ltd. ($6.8 billion), Hudson's Bay Co. ($6.4 billion), Provigo Inc. ($5.9 billion), Canada Safeway Ltd. ($4.7 billion), Sears Canada Inc. ($4.6 billion), Canadian Tire Corporation Ltd. ($4.1 billion), Shoppers Drug Mart Ltd. ($4.0 billion) and Westfair Foods Ltd. ($3.8 billion). The world's top 100 retailers generate over U.S.$1.3 trillion in total annual revenues and include firms from fourteen different nations. The largest retailer on the planet, by far, is U.S.-based Wal-Mart—with annual sales of U.S.$139 billion, approximately 3000 stores, and multiple store formats (such as Wal-Mart and Sam's Clubs).[4]

The retailing sector employed 1 731 300 Canadians in 1997, about 12 per cent of all working Canadians. Within the Canadian market and around the globe a wide range of retailing career opportunities are available, including store management, merchandising, and owning one's own retail business.[5]

From a cost perspective, retailing is a significant field in North America. For example, on average, 38 to 40 cents of every dollar a consumer spends in a department or specialty store goes to it as compensation for the functions it performs. (The corresponding figure is 21 cents for a supermarket.) This compensation—known as gross margin—is for rent, taxes, fuel, advertising, management, personnel, and other retail costs, as well as profits. One of the reasons Wal-Mart is the world's leading retailer is that its operating costs are so low (16 per cent of sales) compared to its close competitors like Sears Roebuck, whose operating costs are 22 per cent. Despite this, actual profit margins after expenses are very low for retail enterprises, typically around 2 per cent![6]

## Retailing Functions in Distribution

Retailers generally perform four distinct functions. They:

- Engage in the sorting process by assembling an assortment of goods and services from a variety of suppliers and offering them for sale. The width and depth of assortment depend on the individual retailer's strategy.
- Provide information to consumers via ads, displays and signs, and sales personnel. And marketing research support (feedback) is given to other channel members.

*Retailing embodies high annual sales, employment, and costs.*

**LOBLAWS**
www.loblaw.com

**SEARS CANADA INC.**
www.sears.ca

*Retailers undertake four key functions.*

- Store products, mark prices, place items on the selling floor, and otherwise handle products. Retailers usually pay for items before selling them to final consumers.
- Facilitate and complete transactions by having appropriate locations and hours, credit policies, and other services (like delivery).

## The Relationship of Retailers and Suppliers

Retailers deal with two broad supplier categories: those selling goods or services for use by the retailers and those selling goods or services that are resold by the retailers. Examples of goods and services purchased by retailers for their use are store fixtures, computer equipment, management consulting, and insurance. Resale purchases depend on the lines sold by the retailer.

Suppliers must have knowledge of their retailers' goals, strategies, and methods of business operation to sell and service accounts effectively. Retailers and their suppliers may have divergent viewpoints, which must be reconciled. For example:

> Kentucky Fried Chicken sued its largest franchisee in the world, Scott's Restaurants of Markham, Ontario, over a breach of their franchise agreement and won. With this, KFC won the right to strip Scott's of its 370 franchises and grant them to someone else. The heart of the dispute was the royalties that KFC would receive from Scott's in their franchise agreement. Scott's was paying 2.8 per cent of its sales in royalties, compared to U.S. restaurants which pay 6 per cent of sales. KFC wanted to renegotiate with Scott's to have them pay 6 per cent, but the only way to do this was to have Scott's accept a new agreement. Therefore, KFC used a legal technicality to break their franchise agreement with Scott's and thus force the firm to make a new agreement that would be more favourable to KFC. This isn't the first time KFC has played hardball with its retailers. In the U.S. it battled for eight years with 60 per cent of its retailers so that it could grant more franchises and not be held as closely to exclusive territorial agreements that had been granted in the past  but were keeping the firm from expanding to meet the competition of other fast food distributors.[7]

# Types of Retailers[8]

Retailers can be categorized by ownership, store strategy mix, and nonstore operations. See Figure 11-1. The categories overlap; that is, a firm can be correctly placed in more than one grouping. For example, 7-Eleven is a chain, a franchise, and a convenience store. The study of retailers by group provides data on their traits and orientation, and the impact of environmental factors.

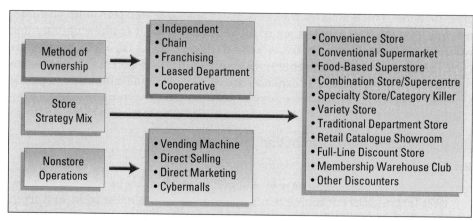

**FIGURE 11-1**

**Categorizing Retailers**

**ETHICS AND TODAY'S MARKETER**

## "Bleep" the "Bleeping" Angels Sing: The Obscene Singing Santa

Retailer Canadian Tire acted quickly in response to a customer complaint about an obscene Santa that was found inside one of its stores. The obscene Santa came unexpectedly in the form of a toy made in China and supplied by Gemmy Industries Corporation. Designed as a novelty product to be sold to adults, this Santa would sing obscene Christmas songs with profane lyrics. The customer who complained wasn't particularly offended, but concerned that some Canadian Tire patrons might unknowingly purchase the Santa as a gift for their children. Canadian Tire officials seemed unaware that the singing Santa on their shelves would sing songs such as "Rudolph the Red Nosed (bleep) head" and other unsavoury tunes in the same kind of voice as the famous deceased folk singer, Burl Ives.

After listening to the singing Santas Canadian Tire officials ordered their immediate removal from all stores, and offered full refunds to customers who wish to return them. Charles Zarb made the complaint, but is keeping the Santa, which is now part of his Santa collection. He commented, "This is the first time I ever got one that talks like this." Assistant store manager Frank Ehrhardt described the lyrics as "pretty explicit." The store also sent out a news release to newspapers across Canada so that customers would be made aware and could return the Santa if they so wished. As for how the Santas came to appear on Canadian Tire's shelves, Ehrhardt said he wasn't sure but believes it was a supplier glitch.

From a supplier standpoint, one might ask why Gemmy toys would manufacture and market such a product in the first place. One can imagine that sales of Santas singing Christmas carols as they were meant to be sung would be potentially quite lucrative. Is there really a need in the marketplace for a product that's so clearly in questionable taste? It seems the ethics of Gemmy Industries Corporation are due for some consideration.

Comment: Did Canadian Tire act properly? What would you have done differently, if anything? As a paid consulting advisor to Gemmy Industries Corporation, what would you recommend they do about the obscene Singing Santa line, and why?

*Source:* Canadian Press Release from Welland, Ontario, "Obscene Singing St. Nick Pulled from Store Shelves," *The Windsor Star* (December 17, 1998), p. A2.

## Ownership

An **independent retailer** operates only one outlet and offers personal service, a convenient location, and close customer contact. Nearly 80 per cent of North American retail establishments (including those staffed solely by the owners and their families)—and an even higher percentage in some foreign nations—are operated by independents, including many dry cleaners, beauty salons, furniture stores, gas stations, and neighbourhood stores. This large number is due to the ease of entry because various kinds of retailing require low investments and little technical knowledge. Therefore, competition is plentiful. Numerous retailers do not succeed because of the ease of entry, poor management skills, and inadequate resources. About one-third of new retailers do not last one full year and two-thirds do not make it past the first three years.

A **retail chain** involves common ownership of multiple outlets. It usually has central purchasing and decision making. Although independents have simple organizations, chains tend to rely on specialization, standardization, and elaborate control systems. Chains can serve a large, dispersed target market and have a well-known company name. There are approximately 1200 chains in Canada operating about 38 000 stores. They represent 17 per cent of Canadian retail establishments and account for 40 per cent of all retail store sales. Chains are common for depart-

*An **independent retailer** has one store, while a **retail chain** has multiple outlets.*

ment stores, supermarkets, and fast-food outlets, among others. Examples of chains are The Bay, Loblaws, Wal-Mart, and Foot Locker.

**Retail franchising** *uses an established name and operates under certain rules.*

**Retail franchising** is a contractual arrangement between a franchiser (a manufacturer, wholesaler, or service sponsor) and a retail franchisee, which allows the latter to run a certain form of business under an established name and according to specific rules. It is a form of chain retailing that lets a small-business person benefit from the experience, buying abilities, and name of a large multi-unit retailer. Many times, the franchisee gets management training and engages in cooperative buying and advertising. The franchiser benefits by obtaining franchise fees and royalties, faster payments, strict operating controls, consistency among outlets, and motivated owner-operators. There are an estimated 25 000 franchise outlets in Canada. The total sales statistics for Canadian franchises are not accurately known but estimates range from a low of $13 billion[9] up to $90 billion.[10] Franchising is popular for auto and truck dealers, gasoline stations, doughnut shops, fast-food outlets, hotels and motels, service firms, and convenience-foods stores. Examples of retail franchises include: Chevrolet dealers, Petro-Canada Service Stations, Tim Horton's Donuts, Pizza Hut, and H&R Block. See Figure 11-2.

*A* **leased department** *is one rented to an outside party.*

A **leased department** is a section of a retail store rented to an outside party. The lessee operates a department—under the store's rules—and pays a percentage of sales as rent. Lessors gain from the reduced risk and inventory investment, expertise of lessees, lucrative lease terms, increased store traffic, and appeal to one-stop shop-

**FIGURE 11-2**

**Tim Horton's Donuts**
A well-known Canadian franchise.

*photo by A.M. McNeill.*

ping. Lessees gain from the location in established stores, lessor name awareness, overall store traffic, one-stop customers attracted to stores, and whatever services (such as ads) lessors provide. Leased departments are popular for beauty salons, jewellery, photo studios, shoes and shoe repairs, cosmetics and food service. Radio Shack and AT&T Canada have set up AT&T stores inside of Radio Shack's 450 Canadian outlets. The idea of this alliance is to provide one-stop shopping for telecommunications services and products.[11]

With a **retail cooperative**, independent retailers share purchases, storage and shipping facilities, advertising, planning, and other tasks. Individual stores remain independent—but agree on broad, common policies. Cooperatives are growing due to chains' domination of independents. They are popular for pharmacies, hardware stores, and grocery stores. An example of a well-known retail cooperative is IDA Pharmacies (Independent Druggists Association). *Retail cooperative* and *retailer-owned wholesale cooperative* are synonymous terms.

Table 11-1 compares the various forms of retail ownership.

## Store Strategy Mix

Firms can be classed by the store strategy mix they choose. A typical **retail store strategy mix** consists of an integrated combination of hours, location, assortment, service, advertising, prices, and other factors retailers employ. Store strategy mixes vary widely, as the following indicate.

A **convenience store** is usually a well-situated, food-oriented store with long hours and a limited number of items. In Canada, chain convenience stores have annual sales of $3.3 billion, including gasoline, and account for about 6.3 per cent of total grocery sales. The average store has yearly sales of about $515 000, compared to $16 200 000 for a typical supermarket chain grocery store. Consumers use a convenience store for fill-in merchandise, often at off-hours. Gasoline, milk, groceries, newspapers, pop, cigarettes, beer, and fast food are popular items. 7-Eleven and Becker's operate convenience stores.

A **conventional supermarket** is a departmentalized food store with minimum annual sales of $2 million; it emphasizes a wide range of food and related products—general merchandise sales are limited. It originated in the 1930s, when food retailers realized a large-scale operation would let them combine volume sales, self-service, low prices, impulse buying, and one-stop grocery shopping. The car and refrigerator aided the supermarket's success by lowering travel costs and adding to perishables' life spans. Loblaws, A&P, Provigo, Sobey's and Safeway are among the large chains operating conventional supermarkets.

A **food-based superstore** is a diversified supermarket that sells a broad range of food and nonfood items. A food-based superstore typically has greeting cards, floral products, VCR tapes, garden supplies, some apparel, film developing, and small household appliances—besides a full line of supermarket items. A food-based superstore typically has about twice the floor space of a conventional supermarket and generates about $16 million in average sales. Several factors have caused many conventional supermarkets to switch to superstores: consumer interest in one-stop shopping, the levelling of food sales due to population stability and competition from fast-food stores and restaurants, and higher margins on general merchandise (double those of food items). For large food chains, the superstore is now the preferred supermarket format.

A **combination store** unites food/grocery and general merchandise sales in one facility, with general merchandise providing 25 to 40 per cent or more of sales. It goes further than a food-based superstore in appealing to one-stop shoppers and

*With a* **retail cooperative***, stores organize to share costs.*

*A* **retail store strategy mix** *combines the hours and products, etc. offered.*

*A* **convenience store** *stresses fill-in items.*

*A* **conventional supermarket** *is a large, self-service food store.*

*A* **food-based superstore** *stocks food and other products for one-stop shoppers.*

*A* **combination store** *offers a large assortment of general merchandise, as well as food. One type is a* **supercentre***.*

**TABLE 11-1**

**Key Characteristics of Retail Ownership Forms**

| OWNERSHIP FORM | CHARACTERISTICS | | |
| --- | --- | --- | --- |
| | *Distinguishing Features* | *Major Advantages* | *Major Disadvantages* |
| Independent | Operates one outlet, easy entry | Personal service, convenient location, customer contact | Much competition, poor management skills, limited resources |
| Retail chain | Common ownership of multiple units | Central purchasing, strong management, specialization of tasks, larger market | Inflexibility, high investment costs, less entrepreneurial |
| Retail franchising | Contractual arrangement between central management (franchiser) and independent business persons (franchisees) to operate a specified form of business | To franchiser: investments from franchisees, faster growth, entrepreneurial spirit of franchisees. To franchisee: established name, training, experience of franchiser, cooperative ads | To franchiser: some loss of control, franchisees not employees, harder to maintain uniformity. To franchisee: strict rules, limited decision-making ability, payments to franchisers |
| Leased department | Space in a store leased to an outside operator | To lessor: expertise of lessee, little risk, diversification. To lessee: lower investment in store fixtures, customer traffic, store image | To lessor: some loss of control, poor performance reflects on store. To lessee: strict rules, limited decision-making ability, payments to store |
| Retail cooperative | Purchases, advertising, planning, and other functions shared by independent retailers | Independence maintained, efficiency improved, enhances competitiveness with chains | Different goals of participants, hard to control members, some autonomy lost |

occupies 30 000 to 100 000 square feet or more. It lets a retailer operate efficiently, expand the number of people drawn to a store, raise impulse purchases and the size of the average transaction, sell both high-turnover/low-profit food items and lower-turnover/high-profit general merchandise, and offer fair prices. A **super-centre** is a combination store that integrates an economy supermarket with a discount department store, with at least 40 per cent of sales from nonfood items. It is 75 000 to 150 000 square feet in size, and carries 50 000 or more items. Among the firms with combination stores are Loblaws Superstore Atlantic, Real Canadian Superstore, Price/Costco warehouse, and France's Carrefour.

A **specialty store** concentrates on one product line, such as stereo equipment or hair-care services. Consumers like these stores since they are not faced with racks of unrelated products, do not have to search through several departments, are apt to find informed salespeople, can select from tailored assortments, and may avoid

*A **specialty store** emphasizes one kind of product, with a **category killer** store being a large version.*

crowding. Specialty stores are quite successful with apparel, appliances, toys, electronics, furniture, personal care products, and personal services. Specialty stores include Tip Top Tailors, LensCrafters, and The Body Shop. See Figure 11-3.

A rather new type of specialty store—the category killer—is now gaining strength. The **category killer** is an especially large specialty store. It features an enormous selection in its product category and relatively low prices; and consumers are drawn from wide geographic areas. Toys 'Я' Us and Staples/Business Depot are among the many specialty store chains that are opening new category killer stores to complement their existing stores. Blockbuster Video, the Sports Authority, and The Home Depot are among the chains fully based on the category killer store concept.

A **variety store** sells a wide assortment of inexpensive and popularly priced merchandise. It features stationery, gift items, women's accessories, toiletries, light hardware, toys, housewares, and confectionery items. With the growth of other retail store strategy mixes, variety stores have lost a lot of ground in recent years. Bi-Way stores and Army and Navy stores are examples of this type of store.

*A **variety store** sells an assortment of lower-priced items.*

A department store employs at least fifty people and usually sells a general line of apparel for the family, household linens and textile products, and some mix of furniture, home furnishings, appliances, and consumer electronics. It is organized into separate departments for purposes of buying, promotion, service, and control. The Canadian department store market had sales of $15.95 billion in 1997. There are two types of department stores: the traditional department store and the full-line discount store.

A **traditional department store** has a great assortment of goods and services, provides many customer services, is a fashion leader, and often serves as an anchor store in a shopping district or shopping centre. Prices are average to above average. It has high name recognition and uses all forms of advertising media. In recent years traditional department stores have set up more boutiques, theme displays, and designer departments to compete with other firms. They face intense competition from specialty stores and discounters. Canada essentially has two traditional department store chains operating nationally: Sears and The Bay with 1997 market shares of 18.5% and 15.9% on estimated department store sales of $2.95 billion and $2.4 billion respectively.

*A **traditional department store** is a fashion leader with many customer services.*

A **full-line discount store** is a department store with lower prices, a broad product assortment, a lower-rent location, more emphasis on self-service, brand-name merchandise, wide aisles, shopping carts, and more goods displayed on the sales floor. In 1997 Canadian full-line discounters annually sold $9.1 billion in goods and services. They are among the largest retailers of apparel, housewares, electronics, health and beauty aids, auto supplies, toys, sporting goods, photographic products, and jewellery. Wal-Mart (27.6 per cent market share and sales of $4.4 billion) and Zellers (22.6 per cent market share and sales of $3.6 billion) are examples of these kinds of retail operations.[12]

*A **full-line discount store** has self-service and popular brands.*

With a **membership warehouse club**, final consumers and businesses pay small yearly dues for the right to

*A **membership warehouse club** offers deep discounts to its member customers.*

**FIGURE 11-3**

**The Body Shop: A Focused Specialty Store Chain**
Around the world, The Body Shop offers a deep selection of goods and services—all related to its natural cosmetics and personal-care products. Shown here is Anita Roddick, the founder and managing director.

*Reprinted by permission.*

shop in a huge, austere warehouse. Products are often displayed in their original boxes, large sizes are stocked, and some product lines vary by time period (since clubs purchase overruns and one-of-a-kind items that cannot always be replaced). Consumers buy items at deep discounts. Canada's most significant retailer using the club format is currently Price/Costco, with estimated annual sales of $2.6 billion.[13]

In recent years, other forms of low-price retailing have also grown. Among them are warehouse-style food stores, off-price specialty chains, discount drugstore chains, and factory outlet stores. These retailers all hold their prices down by maximizing inventory turnover, using plain store fixtures, locating at inexpensive sites, running few ads, and offering less customer service. They appeal to price-sensitive consumers. Examples of these retailers include Loblaws-owned No Frills (a warehouse-style food store) and A Buck or Two (an off-price specialty chain).

### Nonstore Operations

**Nonstore retailing** *is nontraditional.*

With **nonstore retailing**, a firm uses a strategy mix that is not store-based to reach consumers and complete transactions. It does not involve conventional store facilities.

**Vending machines** *allow 24-hour self-service sales.*

A **vending machine** uses coin- or card-operated machinery to dispense goods (such as beverages) or services (such as video rentals). It eliminates the need for salespeople, allows 24-hour sales, and can be placed outside rather than inside a store. Its sales are concentrated in a few products—beverages, food items, and cigarettes yield 99 per cent of the Canadian total. Machines may need intensive servicing due to breakdowns, stock-outs, and vandalism. Improved technology lets vending machines make change for bills, "talk" to consumers, use video screens to show products, brew coffee, and so on. Canadian sales through vending machines were $391.4 million in 1995, a rise from $376.8 million in 1994. Coffee accounted for 34 per cent of the total sales, soft drinks accounted for another 29 per cent of the total sales, and confectionaries comprised a further 17 per cent of the total.[14]

**Direct selling** *encompasses personal contacts with consumers in nonstore settings.*

**Direct selling** involves personal contact with consumers in their homes (and other nonstore locations) and phone solicitations initiated by the retailer. Cosmetics, vacuum cleaners, household services (like carpet cleaning), dairy products, and newspapers are sometimes marketed via direct selling. In a cold canvass, a salesperson calls people or knocks on doors to find customers. With referrals, past buyers recommend friends to the salesperson. In the party method, one consumer acts as host and invites people to a sales demonstration in his or her home (or other nonstore site). To some consumers, direct selling has a poor image. In addition, sales force turnover is high and many people are not home during the day. To increase business, salespeople for firms such as Avon now target working women using office presentations during breaks and lunch hours. Direct selling has yearly revenues of $3.4 billion. Avon, Tupperware, and Kids Only Clothing are direct selling organizations.[15]

*In* **direct marketing,** *a seller first communicates with consumers via nonpersonal media.*

**Direct marketing** occurs when a consumer is first exposed to a good or service by a nonpersonal medium (such as direct mail, TV, radio, magazine, newspaper, or PC) and then orders by mail, phone, or PC. Many people find it a convenient way to shop because they don't have to leave their homes, but this is slightly offset by having to wait to receive their goods. However, express transportation services have reduced some of the delay in delivery and made this form of retailing even more attractive. A detailed discussion of direct marketing will be undertaken in Chapter 14.

# Considerations in Retail Planning

There are many factors for retailers to weigh in devising marketing plans—and for manufacturers, service providers, and wholesalers to keep in mind. Five key factors are store location, atmosphere, scrambled merchandising, the wheel of retailing, and technological advances.

## Store Location

Store location is meaningful because it helps determine the customer mix and competition faced. Once selected, it is also inflexible. The basic forms of store location are the isolated store, the unplanned business district, and the planned shopping centre.

An **isolated store** is a freestanding retail outlet located on a highway or street. There are no adjacent stores with which the firm competes; but, there are also no stores to help draw shoppers. Customers may hesitate to travel to an isolated store unless it has a good product assortment and an established image. This site may be used by discount stores due to low rent and to accommodate suppliers who prefer them to be far enough away from stores selling goods and services at full prices. Some Canadian Tire and 7-Eleven stores are isolated.

*An **isolated store** is a freestanding outlet on a highway or side street.*

An **unplanned business district** exists where multiple stores are located close to one another without prior planning as to the number and composition of stores. The four unplanned sites are central business district, secondary business district, neighbourhood business district, and string.

*In an **unplanned business district**, stores locate together with no prior planning.*

A central business district (CBD) is the hub of retailing in a city and is sometimes called "downtown." It has the most commercial, employment, cultural, entertainment, and shopping facilities in a city—with at least one major department store and a broad grouping of specialty and convenience stores.

A secondary business district (SBD) is a shopping area bounded by the intersection of two major streets. Cities tend to have several SBDs, each with at least one branch department store, a variety store, and/or some larger specialty stores, as well as several smaller shops.

A neighbourhood business district (NBD) satisfies the convenience-shopping and service needs of a neighbourhood. It has a number of small stores, with the major retailer being a supermarket, a large drugstore, or a variety store.

A string is ordinarily composed of a group of stores with similar or compatible product lines that situate along a street or highway. Because this location is unplanned, various store combinations are possible. Car dealers, antique stores, and clothing stores often locate in strings.

A **planned shopping centre** has centrally owned or managed facilities; it is planned and operated as an entity, ringed by parking, and based on balanced tenancy. With balanced tenancy, the number and composition of stores are related to overall shopper needs—stores complement each other in the variety and quality of their offerings. To ensure balance, a centre may limit the products a store carries.

*A **planned shopping centre** is centrally planned and has balanced tenancy.*

## Atmosphere

**Atmosphere** is the sum total of the physical attributes of a retail store or group of stores that are used to develop an image and draw customers. It affects the target market attracted, the customer's shopping mood and time spent in the store, impulse purchases, and store positioning; and is related to the strategy chosen. For example, a discount store would have simple fixtures, linoleum floors, and crowded displays. A full-service store would have elaborate fixtures, carpeted floors, and attractive displays.

**Atmosphere** *consists of a store's exterior, general interior, layout, and displays.*

There are four basic components of a store's atmosphere:

- *Exterior*—elements such as the storefront, the marquee, entrances, display windows, store visibility, store design, the surrounding area, and traffic congestion.

- *General interior*—elements such as flooring, colours, scents, lighting, fixtures, wall textures, temperature, aisle width, vertical transportation, personnel, cash register placement, and overall cleanliness.

- *Store layout*—elements such as the floor space allotted for customers, selling, and storage; product groupings; and department locations.
- *Interior (point-of-sale) displays*—elements such as merchandise cases and racks, mobiles, in-store ads, posters, and mannequins.

Canada's West Edmonton Mall—the world's largest planned shopping centre—uses an innovative atmosphere to draw 20 million people annually, some from 750 miles away and farther. It has eleven department stores, 800+ other shops, a mile-long concourse, and fifty-eight entrances. Its size equals 115 football fields. The mall contains an amusement park, an ice-skating rink, a miniature golf course, and other attractions such as Planet Hollywood, the Hard Rock Café, Hooters Restaurant, the Palace Casino, and Red's, a 110 000 square-foot club. The mall has parking for 20 000 vehicles. Total investment in the mall is over $1.1 billion, and it brings in $1.2 billion to Alberta each year.[16] See Figure 11-4.

## Scrambled Merchandising

*In* **scrambled merchandising**, *a retailer adds items to obtain one-stop shopping, higher margins, and impulse purchases.*

**Scrambled merchandising** occurs when a retailer adds goods and services that are unrelated to each other and to the firm's original business. Examples are supermarkets adding videocassette rentals, department stores offering theatre ticket services, restaurants carrying newspapers, and car washes stocking postcards.

There are limits to how far a firm should go with scrambled merchandising, especially if adding unrelated items would reduce buying, selling, and service effectiveness. Furthermore, stock turnover might be low for certain product lines should a retailer enter too many diverse product categories. Finally, scrambled merchandising may make a firm's image fuzzy to consumers.

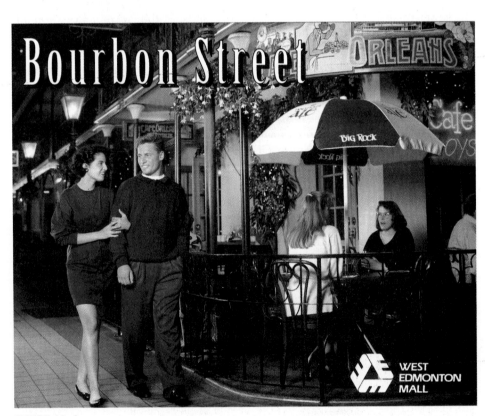

**FIGURE 11-4**

**The World's Largest Mall**
Canada's West Edmonton Mall is the world's largest planned shopping centre.

*Photo courtesy of West Edmonton Mall.*

## The Wheel of Retailing

The **wheel of retailing** describes how low-end (discount) strategies can evolve into high-end (full-service, high-price) strategies and thus provide opportunities for new firms to enter as discounters. Retail innovators often first appear as low-price operators with low profit-margin requirements and low costs. As time passes, the innovators look to increase their sales and customer base. They upgrade product offerings, facilities, and services and turn into more traditional retailers. They may expand the sales force, move to better sites, and usher in delivery, credit, and alterations. The improvements lead to higher costs, which in turn cause higher prices. This creates openings for a new generation of retailers to emerge by appealing to the price-conscious shoppers who are left behind as existing firms move along the wheel. Figure 11-5 shows the wheel in action.

*The* **wheel of retailing** *shows how strategies change, leaving opportunities for new firms.*

There are some limitations in applying the wheel-of-retailing theory too literally. In particular, many retailers do not follow the pattern suggested; and trying to move along the wheel may cause a firm to lose its loyal customers. The best use of the wheel is in understanding that retailers can pursue distinct low-end, medium, and high-end strategies.

## Technological Advances

Over the last several years, a number of technological advances related to retailing have emerged. The most dramatic are the computerized checkout system, video shopping services, data warehousing, computer-aided site selection, electronic banking, and operating efficiency.

*Technological advances range from computerized checkout systems to enhanced operating efficiency.*

In a computerized checkout (electronic point-of-sale) system, a cashier manually rings up a sale or passes an item over or past an optical scanner; a computerized register instantly records and displays a sale. The customer gets a receipt, and inventory data are stored in the computer's memory bank. Such a system reduces checkout time, employee training, misrings, and the need for price marking on all products. It also generates a current listing of the merchandise in stock without taking a physical inventory, improves inventory control, reduces spoilage, and aids ordering.

Video shopping services let retailers efficiently, conveniently, and promptly present information, receive orders, and process transactions. These services can be divided into two basic categories: merchandise catalogues, and in-store and in-home ordering systems.

**FIGURE 11-5**

**The Wheel of Retailing in Action**

Video catalogues (shown on special monitors or via disk players/VCRs using conventional TV sets) allow consumers to view pre-recorded product and sales presentations in store and nonstore settings without the seller having to set up costly displays. With such catalogues (sometimes called kiosks), supermarkets can market appliances, airports can market watches, department stores can market gourmet foods, and mail-order firms can make their offerings come to life.

With an in-store video-ordering system, a consumer orders products by entering data into a self-prompting computer, which processes the order. After placing the order, the consumer usually goes to a checkout area where the item can be picked up and an invoice received. The consumer then pays a cashier.

The availability of inexpensive computerized site-selection software is so prevalent that retailers of any size and type can now use it. For as little as U.S.$500, a retailer can buy geographic information systems (GIS) software that graphically depicts population characteristics, location attributes, roadways, and so on for numerous potential or existing store sites. Canadian retail firms interested in locating in the U.S. can buy a CD-ROM diskette that lists 400 000 retail tenants in 34 000 U.S. shopping centres for U.S.$1795.[17]

Electronic banking involves the use of automatic teller machines (ATMs) and the instant processing of purchases. It provides central record keeping and lets customers conduct transactions twenty-four hours a day, seven days a week at many locations (such as banks and supermarkets). Deposits, withdrawals, and other banking and retailing tasks can be completed. ATMs are widely available in Canadian banks and trust companies, shopping centres, stores, airports, and other sites. To allow customers to make financial transactions over wider geographic areas, many banks have formed ATM networks. In North America there are hundreds of local and regional networks and half a dozen national (international) systems. Some retailers are even setting up their own electronic banking systems. For example, Loblaw has partnered with the Canadian Imperial Bank of Commerce to open in-store bank branches called "President's Choice Financial" outlets.[18]

---

# TECHNOLOGY AND MARKETING

## In-Store Bank Machines: Integrated Shopping and Financial Services

Canadian Tire and ING Direct recently teamed up as part of one of the latest trends in integrated shopping and financial services. While not new, the availability of financial services in retail outlets has accelerated to the point where it's almost a necessity. Loblaw and the Canadian Imperial Bank of Commerce formed one of the first alliances to offer in-store kiosks, providing savings and credit card accounts, as well as mortgages and cooperative promotion programs that would lead to free groceries. Wal-Mart and Toronto Dominion have a similar arrangement, and Southland Corporation through its 7-Eleven convenience stores has also teamed up with the CIBC.

These integrated, value-added, low-cost banking services are part of the trend called "branchless" banking. Clearly this is a misnomer, since ATMs are in fact automated branches, and these relationships extend the reach of financial institutions farther than ever before. It's the "exclusive" nature of a cooperative effort with key retailers that's most notable in this case. The financial institution and the retailer team up to accept transactions from the retailer's and the bank's own credit cards.

The advantages for the retailer are greater potential sales and value added in credit card interest charges, whereas the advantages for the financial institution are more deposits and more customers who link their banking directly with their shopping. Discuss the threat of "home" banking via the Internet to further expansion of in-store bank machines.

*Source*: Based on Canadian Press, "Canadian Tire Gets ATMs," *The Windsor Star* (Saturday, May 9, 1998), p. D2.

As electronic banking has spread more firms are participating in **debit transactions**. In this arrangement, when a purchase is made the amount is immediately charged against a buyer's account; there is no delayed billing without an interest charge. A debit-card system is different from current credit-card policy, whereby consumers are sent bills and then remit payment. Debit cards have received wide acceptance as a substitute for both cheques and cash.

In 1997 Canadians used debit cards to purchase goods and services a record one billion times. Indeed, Canadians are among the heaviest users of debit payment in the world. Shoppers purchased $14.6 billion worth of goods in supermarkets with their bank cards, which represents 33 per cent of total IDP volume in Canada. Interac is one of the most used brands of debit cards in Canada. By year's end, 7793 supermarkets across Canada offered Interac direct payment; these locations accounted for 28 per cent of all Canadian transactions.[19]

Technological advances are also leading to greater retailer efficiency by:

- Increasing the use of self-service operations by firms marketing gasoline, airline tickets, and rental cars, and for hotel registrations and payment.
- Linking manufacturers, warehouses, and transportation firms.
- Introducing anti-shoplifting tags that set off an alarm if not properly removed by employees.
- Automating energy-control systems to monitor store temperature carefully and reduce fuel costs.
- Computerizing order entry in restaurants.

Furthermore, "The good news is that small retailers can also use technology as a tool in achieving greater efficiency. And the technology that's used doesn't have to be the highly complicated or expensive *Star Wars* variety."[20] It is essentially the same technology found in the home computers owned by millions of Canadians.

*With **debit transactions**, payments are immediately deducted from customers' accounts.*

## Recent Trends in Retailing

Retailing is in a great state of flux, particularly in Canada, as firms strive to defend or expand their positions in the marketplace. Many consumers no longer want to spend as much time shopping as they once did, various retail sectors have become saturated, a number of large retailers are operating under high levels of debt (typically caused by leveraged buyouts or overexpansion), and some retailers—after running frequent sales—have found it difficult to maintain regular prices. Here's what has been happening:

*This is a tough period for many retailers, due to changing consumer lifestyles, competition, and other factors.*

> The new rules of retailing include coping with nonstore competition, technology, and consolidation, as well as entertaining customers. Traditional jewellers are increasingly threatened by TV home shopping and catalogues. Hosiery manufacturers may sell pantyhose and socks on the Internet; perfumers are already doing so with scents. Small family nurseries are giving way to conglomerates in the bulb-and-seed business. Shoppers will soon see entertainment-retail destinations at which they can play tennis before buying a racquet or see a show about Julius Caesar's coronation. Virtually every retail business is involved with at least one of these issues.[21]

To succeed in the long run, Canadian retailers must respond properly to the trends they are facing. Among the most prominent are those relating to consumer demographics and lifestyles, database marketing, competitive forces, operating costs, the labour force, and opportunities in foreign markets. Here's how various retailers are dealing with them.

Demographic changes in the form of a boom in the youth population, the increasing size of ethnic markets, and the saturation of many prime markets have resulted in various innovative retailing strategies. For example, Club Monaco, a youth-oriented clothier owned by Dylex of Toronto, has chosen to expand by opening outlets in Japan, Korea, and Thailand, where the youth markets are larger and growing much faster than in Canada. However, Nancy Dennis chose to target tweener girls (aged 5-13) with her Ch!ckaboom store, which is designed to let young girls come in and literally shop on their own. Leon's Furniture of Toronto has targeted the multicultural population of Toronto with specially designed ads for the Chinese, Italian, and Portuguese communities. Finally, underserved locations are being targeted; Price/Costco opened up a store in Moncton, a relatively small population centre, in hopes of drawing customers from throughout New Brunswick and the neighbouring Atlantic provinces.[22]

Lifestyle changes have caused retailers to adapt to the shopping needs and time constraints of working women and dual-earner households, an increased consumer interest in quality and customer service, and a shift to more casual attire in the workplace. Retailers are stocking such labour-saving products as ready-to-eat foods and pre-loaded PCs; lengthening store hours and opening additional days; expanding catalogue and phone sales efforts; re-emphasizing personal selling; pre-wrapping gift items to eliminate waiting lines; setting up comprehensive specialty boutiques to minimize the number of departments a consumer must visit; adding special services, such as fashion coordinators; marketing high-quality private brands; and putting up more attractive displays. One of the innovative approaches is lifestyle merchandising. Retailers such as Chateauworks, Club Monaco, Roots, and Urban Outfitters are selling housewares, stationery, clothing, candy, and make-up as complete fashion offerings that will meet more needs and save consumers time and effort in shopping. Clothing specialty retailers are surprised to find themselves facing tremendous competition from discount stores in the apparel market. It's not that the discount stores have gone upscale, it's that consumers have gone downscale! Clothing retailers must also deal with an aging market, where more people want to dress casually; as well, the workplace trend of dressing casually on Fridays has evolved into dressing casually everyday.[23]

More and more, retailers have come to realize that they must develop a direct relationship with their customers to maintain loyalty. Developing database information on customers and then promoting to or rewarding them directly is a common approach these days. Zellers launched its Gen Z loyalty program in 1998 to reward children with Club Z points when their parents shopped at Zellers. The loyalty program was on target to have 1 million members in the new millennium, with the added benefit of providing Zellers with a database on its youngest customers. Not to be outdone, the aforementioned Ch!ckaboom store has a relationship marketing program that contains the names of 2000 of the 5- to 13-year-old girls who have shopped there. The girls are encouraged to join a birthday club and receive a card and gift certificate to Ch!ckaboom on their birthdays. There are also parties on Valentine's Day and Halloween for members of the database.[24]

Building customer loyalty is also the philosophy of Co-op Atlantic stores. Co-op Atlantic operates member-only stores that have two approaches to building customer loyalty. Some stores charge weekly fees of $3-$5 no matter how much a member spends. After paying their fee, members make their purchases at essentially no markup. A second approach allows both members and non-members to shop at the store; at the end of the year members receive a dividend cheque. Developing a loyal customer franchise ensures the stores operating profits and efficiency, and the consumers benefit from low prices.[25]

Retailing's intense competition has led to a wide spectrum of company responses. Here are some examples: In 1999 market analysts predicted that Wal-Mart would begin to offer grocery items in many of their department stores. Wal-Mart entered Canada in 1994 and by 1999 it was the largest department store retailer in Canada, with estimated sales of $5.3 billion. The prediction was that with grocery offerings, the firm could reach $16 billion in sales in short order. To counter this

**FIGURE 11-6**

**Zellers is attracting new customers with its Truly Canadian line of goods**
*Courtesy Zellers*

threat a number of Canadian grocery retailers put together merger plans. Loblaw decided to merge with Provigo and produce an organization with $17 billion in sales in Canada. To counter the Loblaw-Provigo merger and to fend off Wal-Mart, The Oshawa Group and Sobey's planned to merge to create a $10 billion in sales grocery chain. The reasons for the mergers? To get big enough to extract the same kind of supplier concessions that Wal-Mart receives so that these new organizations can compete with it on price. Meanwhile A&P-Dominion has implemented a new positioning campaign under the "We're Fresh Obsessed" banner to maintain customer loyalty. On the department store front, Zellers merged with K-Mart Canada in 1998 to acquire some larger facilities and better locations. The firm then decided to develop some brands exclusive to its stores. Zellers took on the Martha Stewart line of bath and home fashions and developed the Truly Canadian private label to go on health and beauty products, household cleaning products, and fashion items to be marketed under the Truly Beauty, Truly Clean, and Truly Casual brand lines.[26]

Because of the level of competition in many sectors of retailing, the price sensitivity of a large segment of consumers, and their general interest in improving efficiency (and profit margins), retailers are more concerned with cost control than ever before. For instance, several fast-food companies now use a format whereby different outlets occupy the same building (as food courts have done for years in shopping malls). This format allows common costs, and some employees, to be shared. Most small hardware stores participate in buying cooperatives that enable them to secure quantity discounts and to "buy smarter." Many supermarkets have increased their use of bulk selling, by which consumers select exact quantities of items such as candy and dried fruit from open displays. A number of mail-order firms are better targeting customers and containing their catalogue costs.

Some Canadian retailers are having trouble attracting and retaining a quality labour force. According to surveys, retailers rank the labour shortage as one of the most crucial issues for them to address. Among the reasons why the shortage exists are that the number of available young people has declined; full-time career opportunities in other industries have attracted a number of part-time retail workers; many retail workers are inexperienced and have overly high job expectations, leading to employee dissatisfaction and turnover; hours can be long and irregular; some people do not like the pressure of interacting with customers on a regular basis; and the pay in other industries has been relatively higher.

A few of the actions retailers are taking to resolve the labour shortage are to recruit more at high schools, community colleges and universities, hire retired persons, offer child-care services for working mothers, raise starting salaries (sometimes to double the minimum wage or more), rotate employees among tasks to reduce boredom, reward good performance with bonuses, and encourage the best employees to pursue full-time career paths in retailing.

# The Importance of Wholesaling

Wholesaling is an important aspect of distribution because of its impact on the economy, its functions in the distribution channel, and its relationships with suppliers and customers.

## Wholesaling's Impact on the Economy

*Wholesale sales are high; and wholesalers greatly affect final prices.*

In 1997 Canadian wholesalers employed 654 600 people and made sales of $325.5 billion. These revenues are higher than 1997 retail revenues of $237 billion, even though wholesale prices are lower than retail prices and there are approximately three times as many retailers as there are wholesalers.[27] Wholesale revenues are higher because wholesaling involves any purchases made by organizational consumers, not just purchases that are resold. Some products also move through multiple levels of wholesalers (e.g., regional, then local); an item can be sold twice or more at the wholesale level. There are more retailers because they serve individual, geographically dispersed final consumers, and they handle fewer, larger, and more concentrated customers.

From a cost perspective, wholesalers have a great impact on prices. Table 11-2 shows the per cent of wholesale selling prices that go to selected wholesalers to cover

## TABLE 11-2

### Selected Performance Data for Wholesalers by Product Category[a]

| PRODUCT CATEGORY OF WHOLESALER | GROSS PROFIT (AS PER CENT OF SALES)[b] | OPERATING EXPENSES (AS PER CENT OF SALES) | ALL OTHER EXPENSES (AS PER CENT OF SALES) | PROFIT BEFORE TAXES (AS PER CENT OF SALES) |
|---|---|---|---|---|
| Building materials | 25.3 | 22.5 | 0.4 | 2.3 |
| Chemicals and allied products | 28.8 | 25.7 | 0.3 | 2.8 |
| Coffee, tea, and spices | 29.0 | 25.4 | 1.1 | 2.5 |
| Drugs, drug proprietaries, and druggists' supplies | 29.3 | 25.0 | 0.5 | 3.8 |
| Electronic parts and equipment | 29.7 | 26.5 | 0.5 | 2.6 |
| Fish and seafoods | 15.2 | 12.9 | 0.4 | 1.8 |
| Flowers, nursery stock, and florists' supplies | 33.7 | 30.3 | 0.9 | 2.4 |
| General groceries | 18.2 | 16.4 | 0.4 | 1.5 |
| General merchandise | 31.3 | 28.4 | 0.7 | 2.2 |
| Hardware and paints | 29.9 | 26.8 | 0.6 | 2.4 |
| Jewellery | 28.2 | 24.6 | 0.9 | 2.7 |
| Motor vehicle supplies and new parts | 30.9 | 27.3 | 0.7 | 2.9 |
| Petroleum bulk stations and terminals | 14.8 | 13.7 | 0.0 | 1.2 |
| Wine, liquor, and beer | 23.7 | 20 | 0.4 | 2.4 |

[a] In interpreting these data, RMA cautions that the Studies be regarded only as a general guideline and not as an absolute industry norm. This is due to limited samples within categories, the categorization of firms by their primary Standard Industrial Classification (SIC) number only, and different methods of operations by firms within the same industry. For these reasons, RMA recommends that the figures be used only as general guidelines in addition to other methods of financial analysis.

[b] Total costs of wholesaling, which include expenses and profit. There are some rounding errors.

Source: Adapted from *RMA Annual Statement Studies 1995* (Philadelphia: Robert Morris Associates, 1995). Copyright © 1995, Robert Morris Associates; reprinted by permission.

their operating expenses and pre-tax profits. For example, 31 per cent of the price that a general merchandise wholesaler charges its retailers covers that wholesaler's operating and other expenses (29 per cent) and pre-tax profit (2 per cent). Operating costs include inventory charges, sales force salaries, advertising, and rent.

Wholesaler costs and profits depend on inventory turnover, the dollar value of products, the functions performed, efficiency, and competition.

## The Functions of Wholesalers

With regard to functions performed, wholesalers can:

*Wholesalers perform tasks ranging from distribution to risk taking.*

- Enable manufacturers and service providers to distribute locally without making customer contacts.
- Provide a trained sales force.
- Provide marketing and research assistance for manufacturers, service providers, and retail or institutional consumers.
- Gather assortments for customers and let them make fewer transactions.
- Purchase large quantities, thus reducing total physical distribution costs.
- Provide warehousing and delivery facilities.
- Offer financing for manufacturers and service providers (by paying for products when they are shipped, not when they are sold) and retail or institutional consumers (by granting credit).
- Handle financial records.
- Process returns and make adjustments for defective merchandise.
- Take risks by being responsible for theft, deterioration, and obsolescence of inventory.[28]

Wholesalers that take title to and possession of products usually perform several or all of these tasks. Agents and brokers that facilitate sales, but do not take title or possession, tend to concentrate on more limited duties.

The use of independent wholesalers varies by industry. Most consumer products, food items, replacement parts, and office supplies are sold through independent wholesalers. In other industries, including heavy equipment, mainframe computers, gasoline, and temporary employment, manufacturers and service providers may bypass independent resellers.

Without independent wholesalers, organizational consumers would have to develop supplier contacts, deal with a number of suppliers and coordinate shipments, do more distribution functions, stock greater quantities, and place more emphasis on an internal purchasing agent or department. Many small retailers and other firms might be avoided as customers because they might not be profitably reached by a manufacturer or service provider; and they might not be able to buy necessary items elsewhere.

An illustration of the value of wholesaling is found in the North American auto parts industry, in which there used to be thousands of firms making a wide range of products and marketing them through a multitude of sales organizations. At that time, customers (mostly specialty stores and service stations) faced constant interruptions by salespeople; and manufacturers' sales costs were high. A better system exists today, with the organized use of a moderate number of independent distributors.

## Wholesalers' Relationships with Suppliers and Customers

Independent wholesalers are often very much "in the middle," unsure whether their allegiance should be to manufacturers/service providers or their own customers. These comments show the dilemma many wholesalers face:

*Wholesalers have obligations to both suppliers and customers.*

It used to be a simple equation that worked for everyone. Distributor takes magazine from publisher, hands it over to wholesaler, who delivers to retail outlets. Of every dollar worth of magazines sold in the store, the magazine kept 50 cents, while 10 cents went to the distributor and 40 cents went to the wholesaler, who split its gains 50-50 with the retailer. The magazine paid shipping fees and other extra costs, such as special displays, out of its 50 cents. No more: Wholesalers, after being squeezed for the last 18 months by a changing industry in which retailers have wrung themselves an extra 4–8 per cent out of that old 50-50 split, are asking—some would say demanding—a larger slice of the pie from publishers.[29]

Many wholesalers feel they get scant support from manufacturers/service providers. They desire training, technical assistance, product literature, and advertising. They dislike it when vendors alter territory assignments, shrink territory size, add new distributors to cover an existing geographic area, or decide to change to a direct channel and perform wholesale tasks themselves. Wholesalers want manufacturers/service providers to sell to them and not through them. Selling to the wholesaler means a distributor is viewed as a customer to be researched and satisfied. Selling through the wholesaler means retailers or final consumers are objects of manufacturers'/service providers' interest and wholesaler needs are less important. See Figure 11-7.

To remedy the situation, this is how many wholesalers are reacting:

Wholesalers have traditionally viewed themselves as extensions of either their suppliers or customers. Wholesalers that saw themselves as extensions of suppliers adopted the mind set of their suppliers, structured operations to best assist suppliers, and viewed customers as "outside" this relationship. And wholesalers that saw their role as extensions of their customers adopted that mind set and business structure and viewed the supplier as "outside." In short, wholesalers have typically viewed themselves as "distributors."

Today, more wholesalers feel they are in the "marketing support business." They view themselves as marketing *with* their suppliers and customers, not just being distributors. They recognize their primary role is to help both suppliers and customers devise better marketing programs. The marketing-support oriented wholesaler is willing to perform any task,

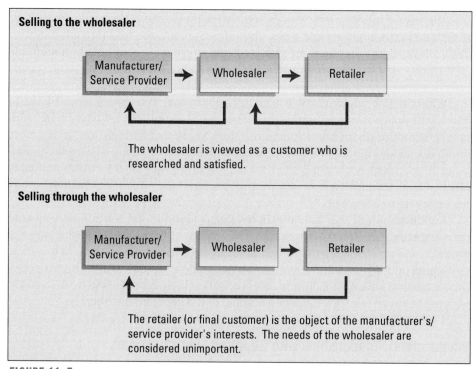

**FIGURE 11-7**

**Selling to Versus Selling Through the Wholesaler**

activity, or function for either suppliers or customers that will result in more effective and efficient marketing for the entire channel.[30]

# Types of Wholesaling

The three broad categories of wholesaling are outlined in Figure 11-8: manufacturer/service provider wholesaling, merchant wholesaling, and agents and brokers. Table 11-3 contains detailed descriptions of every type of independent wholesaler and shows their functions and special features.

## Manufacturer/Service Provider Wholesaling

In **manufacturer/service provider wholesaling**, a producer does all the wholesaling functions itself. This occurs if a firm feels it's best able to reach retailers or other organizational customers by being responsible for the wholesaling. Manufacturer/service provider wholesalers include General Motors, IBM, Frito-Lay, Pitney Bowes, Intercontinental Packers of Saskatchewan, and public utilities.

*In **manufacturer/service provider wholesaling**, a firm acts via its own sales or branch offices.*

Wholesale activities by a manufacturer or service provider may be carried out via sales offices and/or branch offices. A sales office is located at a firm's production facilities or a site close to the market. No inventory is carried there. In contrast, a branch office has facilities for warehousing products, as well as for selling them.

Manufacturer/service provider wholesaling is most likely if independent intermediaries are unavailable, existing intermediaries are unacceptable to the manufacturer or service provider, the manufacturer or service provider wants control over marketing, customers are relatively few in number and each is a key account, cus-

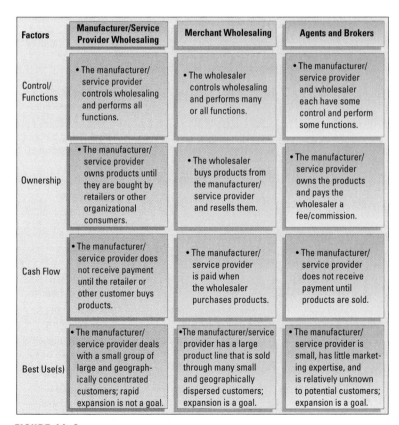

| Factors | Manufacturer/Service Provider Wholesaling | Merchant Wholesaling | Agents and Brokers |
|---|---|---|---|
| Control/ Functions | • The manufacturer/ service provider controls wholesaling and performs all functions. | • The wholesaler controls wholesaling and performs many or all functions. | • The manufacturer/ service provider and wholesaler each have some control and perform some functions. |
| Ownership | • The manufacturer/ service provider owns products until they are bought by retailers or other organizational consumers. | • The wholesaler buys products from the manufacturer/ service provider and resells them. | • The manufacturer/ service provider owns the products and pays the wholesaler a fee/commission. |
| Cash Flow | • The manufacturer/ service provider does not receive payment until the retailer or other customer buys products. | • The manufacturer/ service provider is paid when the wholesaler purchases products. | • The manufacturer/ service provider does not receive payment until products are sold. |
| Best Use(s) | • The manufacturer/ service provider deals with a small group of large and geographically concentrated customers; rapid expansion is not a goal. | •The manufacturer/service provider has a large product line that is sold through many small and geographically dispersed customers; expansion is a goal. | • The manufacturer/ service provider is small, has little marketing expertise, and is relatively unknown to potential customers; expansion is a goal. |

**FIGURE 11-8**

**The Broad Categories of Wholesaling**

## TABLE 11-3

## Characteristics of Independent Wholesalers

| WHOLESALER TYPE | Provides Credit | Stores and Delivers | Takes Title | Provides Merchandising and Promotion Assistance | Provides Personal Sales Force | Performs Research and Planning | SPECIAL FEATURES |
|---|---|---|---|---|---|---|---|
| | | | | MAJOR FUNCTIONS | | | |
| **I. Merchant wholesaler** | | | | | | | |
| **A.** *Full service* | | | | | | | |
| **1.** General merchandise | Yes | Yes | Yes | Yes | Yes | Yes | Carries nearly all items a customer normally needs. |
| **2.** Specialty | Yes | Yes | Yes | Yes | Yes | Yes | Specializes in a narrow product range |
| **3.** Rack jobber | Yes | Yes | Yes | Yes | Yes | Yes | Furnishes racks and shelves, consignment sales |
| **4.** Franchise | Yes | Yes | Yes | Yes | Yes | Yes | Use of common business format, extensive management services |
| **5.** Cooperative | | | | | | | |
| **a.** Producer-owned | Yes | Yes | Yes | Yes | Yes | Yes | Farmer controlled, profits divided among members |
| **b.** Retailer-owned | Yes | Yes | Yes | Yes | Yes | Yes | Wholesaler owned by several retailers |
| **B.** *Limited service* | | | | | | | |
| **1.** Cash and carry | No | Stores, | Yes | No | No | No | No outside sales force, no wholesale store for delivery business needs |
| **2.** Drop shipper | Yes | Delivers, no storage | Yes | No | Yes | Sometimes | Ships items without physically handling them |
| **3.** Truck/wagon | Rarely | Yes | Yes | Yes | Yes | Sometimes | Sales and delivery on same call |
| **4.** Mail order | Sometimes | Yes | Yes | No | No | Sometimes | Catalogues used as sole promotion tool |
| **II. Agents and brokers** | | | | | | | |
| **A.** *Agents* | | | | | | | |
| **1.** Manufacturers' (service providers') | No | Sometimes | No | Yes | Yes | Sometimes | Sells selected items for several firms |
| **2.** Selling | Sometimes | Yes | No | Yes | Yes | Yes | Markets all the items of a firm |
| **3.** Commission (factor) merchants | Sometimes | Yes | No | No | Yes | Yes | Handles items on a consignment basis |
| **B.** *Brokers* | | | | | | | |
| **1.** Food | No | Sometimes | No | Yes | Yes | Yes | Brings together buyers and sellers |
| **2.** Stock | Sometimes | Sometimes | No | Yes | Yes | Yes | Brings together buyers and sellers |

tomers desire personal service from the producer, customers are near to the firm or clustered, a computerized order system links a firm with customers, and/or laws (particularly in foreign markets) limit arrangements with independent resellers.

For instance, because Boeing makes multimillion dollar aircraft and individual customer orders can be in the billions of dollars, manufacturer wholesaling is a must. When Boeing sold $3 billion in jets to General Electric, the complex negotiations took over a year.[31] And at Chrysler, manufacturer wholesaling means closer relationships with its auto dealers. Chrysler distributes its Mopar brand replacement parts directly to the retailers and works with them to market the parts.

**BOEING**
www.boeing.com/

## Wholesale Merchants

**Wholesale merchants** buy, take title, and take possession of products for further resale. At over $286 billion per year in Canada, this is the largest wholesale category in sales. As an example, Sysco is a merchant wholesaler that buys and handles 150 000 products from 3000 producers of food and related products from around the world. It resells these products and offers many customer services to its 250 000 clients—restaurants, hotels, schools, hospitals, fast-food chains, and other organizations in both Canada and the United States.[32]

**Full-service merchant wholesalers** perform a full range of distribution tasks. They provide credit, store and deliver products, offer merchandising and promotion assistance, have a personal sales force, offer research and planning support, pass along information to suppliers and customers, and provide installation and repair services. They are frequently used for grocery products, pharmaceuticals, hardware, plumbing equipment, tobacco, alcoholic beverages, and television program syndication.

**Limited-service merchant wholesalers** do not perform all the functions of full-service merchant wholesalers. For instance, they may not provide credit, merchandising assistance, or marketing research data. They are popular for construction materials, coal, lumber, perishables, equipment rentals, and specialty foods.

On average, full-service merchant wholesalers require more compensation than limited-service ones because they perform more functions.

**FULL-SERVICE MERCHANT WHOLESALERS** Full-service merchant wholesalers can be divided into general merchandise, specialty merchandise, rack jobber, franchise, and cooperative types.

**General-merchandise (full-line) wholesalers** carry a wide product assortment—nearly all the items needed by their customers. Thus, some general-merchandise hardware, drug, and clothing wholesalers stock many products, but not much depth in any one line. They seek to sell their retailers or other organizational customers all or most of their products and develop strong loyalty and exclusivity with them.

**Specialty-merchandise (limited-line) wholesalers** concentrate on a rather narrow product range and have an extensive selection in that range. They offer many sizes, colours, and models—and provide functions similar to other full-service merchant wholesalers. They are popular for health foods, seafood, retail store displays, frozen foods, and video rentals.

**Rack jobbers** furnish the racks or shelves on which products are displayed. They own the products on the racks, selling them on a consignment basis—so their clients pay after goods are resold. Unsold items are taken back. Jobbers set up displays, refill shelves, price-mark goods, maintain inventory records, and compute the amount due from their customers. Rack jobbers usually handle heavily advertised, branded merchandise that is sold on a self-service basis. Included are magazines, health and beauty aids, cosmetics, drugs, hand tools, toys, housewares, and stationery.

In **franchise wholesaling**, independent retailers affiliate with an existing whole-

**Wholesale merchants** *buy products and may offer* **full** *or* **limited service**.

**General-merchandise wholesalers** *sell a range of items.*

**Specialty-merchandise wholesalers** *sell a narrow line of products.*

**Rack jobbers** *set up displays and are paid after sales.*

*With **franchise wholesaling**, retailers join with a wholesaler.*

**INDEPENDENT GROCERS ALLIANCE (IGA) INC.**
www.igainc.com/

**HOME HARDWARE**
www.pagemaker.com/~home/overview.html

*Producers or retailers can set up **wholesale cooperatives**.*

*In **cash-and-carry wholesaling**, the customer drives to a wholesaler.*

**Drop shippers** *buy goods, but do not take possession.*

**Truck/wagon wholesalers** *offer products on a sales route.*

**Mail-order wholesalers** *sell through catalogues.*

**Agents** *and* **brokers** *do not take title to products.*

saler to use a standardized storefront design, business format, name, and purchase system. Many times, suppliers produce goods and services according to specifications set by the franchise wholesaler. This form of wholesaling is utilized for hardware, auto parts, and groceries. Franchise wholesalers include Independent Grocers Alliance (IGA), Independent Druggists Association (IDA), Western Auto, and Home Hardware Stores. At IGA, affiliated retailers are supplied with such services as site selection, store engineering, interior design, and merchandising assistance.

**Wholesale cooperatives** are owned by member firms to economize functions and provide broad support. Producer-owned cooperatives are popular in farming. They market, transport, and process farm products—as well as make and distribute farm supplies. These cooperatives often sell to stores under their own names, such as Blue Diamond, Ocean Spray, Sunkist, and Welch's. With retailer-owned cooperatives, independent retailers form associations that purchase, lease, or build wholesale facilities. The cooperatives take title to merchandise, handle cooperative advertising, and negotiate with suppliers. They are used by hardware and grocery stores.

**LIMITED-SERVICE MERCHANT WHOLESALERS** Limited-service merchant wholesalers can be divided into cash-and-carry, drop shipper, truck/wagon, and mail-order types.

In **cash-and-carry wholesaling**, people from small businesses drive to wholesalers, order products, and take them back to a store or business. These wholesalers offer no credit or delivery, no merchandising and promotion help, no outside sales force, and no research or planning assistance. They are good for fill-in items, have low prices, and allow immediate product use. They are common for construction materials, electrical supplies, office supplies, auto supplies, hardware products, and groceries.

**Drop shippers (desk jobbers)** buy goods from manufacturers or suppliers and arrange for their shipment to retailers or industrial users. They have legal ownership, but do not take physical possession of products and have no storage facilities. They purchase items, leave them at manufacturers' plants, contact customers by phone, set up and coordinate carload shipments from manufacturers directly to customers, and are responsible for items that cannot be sold. Trade credit, a personal sales force, and some research and planning are provided; merchandising and promotion support are not. Drop shippers are often used for coal, coke, and building materials. These goods have high freight costs, in relation to their value, because of their weight. Thus, direct shipments from suppliers to customers are needed.

**Truck/wagon wholesalers** generally have a regular sales route, offer items from a truck or wagon, and deliver goods at the same time as they sell them. They do provide merchandising and promotion support; however, they are considered limited service because they usually do not extend credit and offer little research and planning help. Operating costs are high due to the services performed and low average sales. These wholesalers often deal with goods requiring special handling or with perishables—such as bakery products, tobacco, meat, candy, potato chips, and dairy products.

**Mail-order wholesalers** use catalogues, instead of a personal sales force, to promote products and communicate with customers. They may provide credit but do not generally give merchandising and promotion support. They store and deliver goods, and offer some research and planning assistance. These wholesalers are found with jewellery, cosmetics, auto parts, specialty food product lines, business supplies, and small office equipment.

## Agents and Brokers

**Agents** and **brokers** perform various wholesale tasks, but do not take title to products. Unlike merchant wholesalers, which make profits on the sales of products they own, agents and brokers work for commissions or fees as payment for their services.

## INTERNATIONAL MARKETING IN ACTION

### Grey Markets: Retailers Versus Wholesalers

There are many potential sources of conflict between retailers, wholesalers, and manufacturers. However, one of the most difficult issues for all of them to overcome is that of "grey markets." Grey markets are generally legal but unauthorized parallel channels of distribution that usually involve goods crossing an international border. An authorized channel means that a manufacturer or distributor has a formal, established relationship with certain intermediaries to handle, distribute, and service its products in certain countries or markets.

Grey markets usually arise because an unauthorized parallel channel of distribution is in some manner more efficient. This efficiency is usually price-based, but it can also arise as a result of better customer service from the parallel channel. The existence of grey markets can become a major source of channel conflict. Sometimes large retailers exploit these markets purposely to put pressure on the authorized channels of distribution for lower prices. For example, in Great Britain, supermarket retailers Tesco and Asda are buying grey market goods in order to break supplier strangleholds on resale prices. It seems a strange situation because, just as in Canada, resale price maintenance isn't legal in Great Britain. However, retailers who don't engage in price maintenance often find it difficult to acquire products for resale.

The grey market is particularly popular for sports apparel manufacturers like Nike, Reebok, and Adidas. British retailers acquire these products from American dealers who have surplus supplies. For example, even after shipping, grey market Nikes can be sold at a profit at prices 25–50 per cent below the manufacturer's suggested retail price.

Footwear isn't the only product that British retailers have been importing via grey markets. Levi's and Calvin Klein clothing and even World Cup soccer shirts have been imported through grey markets and sold at prices 25 per cent below the suggested price that authorized distributors require. Although bookselling and over-the-counter pharmaceuticals were exempt from the law on resale price maintenance, British retailers have been successful at pressuring these industries to lower prices through grey market activities.

Discuss some of the issues associated with grey market goods, and in particular consider how the practice affects manufacturers. Identify some of the actions that manufacturers and distributors can take to deal with this practice.

*Source:* Based on Samuel Tulip, "Grey Markets Used to Break Minimum Pricing Rules," *Modern Purchasing* (July/August 1998), www.mhbizlink.com.

---

Agents and brokers let a manufacturer or service provider expand sales volume despite limited resources. Their selling costs are a predetermined per cent of sales; and they have trained salespeople. There are manufacturers'/service providers' agents, selling agents, and commission (factor) merchants.

**Manufacturers'/service providers' agents** work for several manufacturers or service providers and carry noncompetitive, complementary products in exclusive territories. By selling noncompetitive items, the agents eliminate conflict-of-interest situations. By selling complementary products, they stock a fairly complete line of products for their market areas. They do not offer credit but may store and deliver products and give limited research and planning aid. Merchandising and promotional support are provided. These agents may supplement the sales efforts of their clients, help introduce new products, enter dispersed markets, and handle items with low average sales. They may carry only some of a firm's products; a manufacturer or service provider may hire many agents; larger firms may hire a separate one for every product line. Agents have little say on marketing and pricing. They earn commissions of 5 to 10 per cent of sales, and are popular for auto products, iron, steel, footwear, textiles, and commercial real estate and insurance.

**Manufacturers'/service providers' agents** *work for many firms and carry non-competing items.*

**Selling agents** *market all the products of a manufacturer or service provider.*

**Selling agents** are responsible for marketing the entire output of a manufacturer/service provider under a contractual agreement. They become the marketing departments for their clients and can negotiate price and other conditions of sale, such as credit and delivery. They perform all wholesale tasks except taking title. While a firm may use several manufacturers'/service providers' agents, it may employ only one sales agent. These agents are more apt to work for small firms than large ones. They are common for textile manufacturing, canned foods, metals, home furnishings, apparel, lumber, and metal products. Because they perform more tasks, they often get higher commissions than manufacturers'/service providers' representatives.

**Commission merchants** *assemble goods from local markets.*

**Commission (factor) merchants** receive goods on consignment, accumulate them from local markets, and arrange for their sale in a central location. They may offer credit; they do store and deliver goods, provide a sales force, and offer research and planning help. They normally do not assist in merchandising and promotion; but, they can negotiate prices with buyers, provided the prices are not below sellers' stated minimums. They may act in an auction setting; commissions vary. These wholesalers are used for agricultural and seafood products, furniture, and art.

Brokers are common for food and financial services. They are well informed about market conditions, terms of sale, sources of credit, price setting, potential buyers and sellers, and the art of negotiating. They do not take title and usually are not allowed to complete a transaction without approval.

**Food brokers** *and* **commercial stock brokers** *unite buyers and sellers to conclude sales.*

**Food brokers** introduce buyers and sellers of food and related general-merchandise items to one another and bring them together to complete a sale. They operate in specific locales and work for a limited number of food producers. Their sales forces call on chain-store buyers, store managers, and purchasing agents. Food brokers work closely with ad agencies. They generally represent the seller, who pays the commission; they do not actually provide credit but may store and deliver. Commissions are 3 to 5 per cent of sales.

**Commercial stock brokers** are licensed sales representatives who advise business clients, take orders, and then acquire stocks and/or bonds for the clients. They may aid the firms selling the stocks or bonds, represent either buyers or sellers (with both buyers and sellers paying commissions), and offer some credit. Although operating in particular areas, they typically sell the stocks and bonds of firms from throughout Canada, the United States, and around the world. They deal a lot over the phone and may help publicize new stock or bond offerings. The average commission for commercial stock brokers is 1 to 10 per cent of sales, depending on volume and stock prices.

## Recent Trends in Wholesaling

*Firms are becoming larger and more productive.*

During the last fifteen years, wholesaling has changed dramatically, with independent wholesalers striving to protect their place in the channel. Among the key trends are those related to the evolving wholesaler mix, productivity, customer service, international opportunities, and target markets.

Distribution channels and the role of wholesaling in these channels are in a continuous state of change. As the new millennium approaches one of Canada's most important drug wholesalers has decided to evolve into one of its most important drug retailers. Drug Trading Company plans to integrate 1500 pharmacies, the largest number of retail pharmacies in Canada. There are an estimated 5700 drug stores in Canada, with the 800 stores operated by Shoppers Drug Mart controlling 32 per cent of the sales, even though they represent only 14 per cent of the outlets. To counter the presence of Shoppers Drug Mart and the power of pharmacy outlets in grocery stores, Drug Trading is planning to launch a new "Pharmacy 2000 Program" as part of a plan to reinvent itself. The firm hopes to develop significant market power by developing a PharmAssist program that links the firm's dispensary services, technology, and consumer programs. The idea is to take Drug Trading's loose assortment of stores operating under the I.D.A., Guardian, RxCentral, and Community Drug Banners and integrate them under the PharmAssist umbrella. With a unified offering, Drug Trading is hoping to take on Shoppers Drug Mart and the grocery store competitors more effectively.[33]

Since wholesalers' profit margins are small (1.5 per cent of sales for food wholesalers and less than 3 per cent of sales for general merchandise wholesalers), they are constantly seeking gains in productivity. For example, VWD Distributors, a Western Canadian pharmaceutical wholesaler, installed a $400 000 electronic carousel order-filling system, the first of its kind in Canada, in their Burnaby, B.C. facility. The new system allows one person to fill fourteen orders simultaneously. The system holds almost 80 per cent of VWD's inventory and the company hopes the new system will reduce handling and shipping errors, provide better inventory control, and reduce labour expenses.[34]

Wholesalers have learned that customer service is extremely important in securing a competitive advantage, developing client loyalty, and attaining acceptable profit margins. For example, W.W. Grainger, a wholesaler of maintenance, repair, and operating supplies, offers a "value package" that includes electronic ordering and payment, cost-reduction consulting services, and so forth. As a Grainger vice-president says, "On sales calls these days, we seldom talk about why the motor we sell is better than someone else's motor; we talk about value-added services."[35]

Intercontinental Packers of Saskatchewan, known as Mitchell's, is Canada's third-largest pork processor with sales of $329 million in 1998. Mitchell's is trying to take on Maple Leaf Foods of Toronto and J.M. Schneider of Kitchener. One of its main strategies has been to reach out to consumers by offering a money-back guarantee on all its product packages (something unique for meat products) and to allow consumers to sample products in the store. The firm also attentively reads and answers all the mail sent in by customers. (A few complaints, but mostly compliments.)

Mitchell's used to be a me-too packing company that was faced with bankruptcy. Its response was to modernize its packing facilities, and to reposition itself as a quality meat packer by launching a new brand line called Mitchell's Gourmet Food. Mitchell's has also leveraged its third-place position to become the top private-label supplier of meats in Canada. Grocery chains were more willing to deal with Mitchell's to supply private labels because there was less potential for channel conflict than with the two market leaders. Mitchell's modernization program gave them a cost advantage as well, which was particularly important to the success of lower-priced, private-label products. Mitchell's markets products under the Mayfair brand name, has 290 products in its Olympic Fine Foods line, fifty-one products in the Mitchell's Gourmet Foods line, and produces 287 private-label products marketed under the President's Choice, No Name, Seven Farms, and Master's Choice Gourmet Bacon brands, as well as other labels associated with grocery chains.[36]

More wholesalers are turning to foreign markets for growth. As an example, Finning Ltd., a B.C.-based wholesaler of Caterpillar and allied equipment, is concentrating on international expansion. Finning sells, finances, and provides customer service for the equipment it sells. The company serves geographic markets in western Canada, Britain, and Chile. It has over 5400 employees in its worldwide operations, and sells heavy equipment to industry market segments such as mining, agricultural, petroleum, construction, and forestry. To service this equipment Finning has a hydraulic rebuild company and a component remanufacturing centre, both located in Edmonton. In order to be accepted more readily by international customers, Finning has sought and received certification under International Quality Standard ISO-9002.

*Wholesalers are emphasizing customer service and looking to international markets.*

**WW GRAINGER**
www.grainger.com/

**MITCHELL'S**
www.mitchellsgourmetfoods.com

**FINNING LTD.**
www.finning.ca/

Its efforts at expanding international sales have paid off: Finning's international business accounted for 57 per cent of its 1998 sales of $2.5 billion. British sales represented 30.5 per cent of this, Chilean sales represented 19.5 per cent, and other international sales 5.9 per cent. In contrast, in 1997 Canadian sales represented 49.2 per cent of the total $2.3 billion in sales while British sales accounted for 24.3 per cent, Chilean sales 22 per cent, and other international sales for 4.3 per cent. However, British operations were very unprofitable in 1998 and the firm had to depend on Canadian performance to yield a meagre profit of $3.19 million, or .13 per cent profit margin on sales. An important factor to consider is that British profit margins were -4 per cent of sales in 1998 and only 3.6 per cent in 1997. In contrast, Canadian profit margins were higher, at 3.0 per cent in 1998 and 5.4 per cent in 1997. Chilean sales suffered a 2.2 per cent decrease, and the associated profit margins were lower than in Canada, with 1998 profit margins falling to .68 per cent from a 1997 profit margin of 3.8 per cent. Still, international sales increased at a rate of 22.8 per cent while Canadian sales actually decreased by 1 per cent, indicating that the best growth potential for Finning is in international markets.[37]

*Target market strategies are more complex.*

Wholesalers in large numbers are diversifying the markets they serve or the products they carry: farm and garden machinery wholesalers now sell to florists, hardware dealers, and garden supply stores. Plumbing wholesalers have added industrial accounts, contractors, and builders. Grocery wholesalers deal with hotels, airlines, hospitals, schools, and restaurants. Some food wholesalers have moved into apparel retailing and opened auto-parts stores.

Yet some wholesalers are taking the opposite approach, and are seeking to appeal to one customer niche or need. Vancouver-based Mountain Equipment Co-operative is manufacturer, wholesaler, retailer, and customer all rolled into one. Yet despite its organizational diversity, Mountain Equipment Co-operative has a singular purpose: "To support people in achieving the benefit of wilderness-oriented recreation."

**MOUNTAIN EQUIPMENT CO-OP**
www.mec.ca

The firm is a retail consumer cooperative, and as such has no profit and doesn't pay income tax. Mountain Equipment Co-operative has over a million members and in 1997 had sales of over $115 million. The firm sells high-tech outerwear and equipment for mountaineering, rock climbing, ski mountaineering and touring, hiking, paddling, and bicycle touring. Only members are allowed to purchase merchandise and they can only buy from mail order or store locations in Vancouver, Calgary, Edmonton, Toronto, and Ottawa. The firm doesn't advertise, and sales are made through catalogues issued twice a year.[38]

## Grocery Retail Forecasts for the Year 2005[39]

A number of predictions for Canadian grocery retailing in the third millennium were made by Elaine Pollack, director of Management Horizons of Columbus, Ohio. Elaine's predictions are based on the expectation that consumers will be the main driving force for supermarket retailing. Consumers are expecting to be far more demanding in the new millennium.

They will want more consistency in product lines, service, product selection, quality, and convenience; and will want to spend less time, money, effort, and risk.

Here are some of Elaine Pollack's predictions for the Canadian grocery industry:

- Supercentres (a combination of full-scale discount department stores with full-size supermarkets occupying

# MARKETING IN THE THIRD MILLENNIUM

160 000 to 180 000 square feet of retail space) will grab 10 per cent of the food business and 40 per cent of the discount department store business. This will force the supermarket industry to consolidate, which will have the greatest impact on independent and small chain supermarkets and on smaller discount department stores. Supercentres tend to underprice their competition, so inefficient practices or competitors will be forced out.

- Sales growth will be slow at best—and possibly even absent or negative for most food, drug, and mass retail sectors—because more retail shelf space will be chasing the same level of customer expenditures.

- Market shares will consolidate among fewer, bigger, and better competitors. The result will be more acquisitions and a continued shakeout of weaker retailers. Success in retailing will require competitors to become leaner and meaner, to operate on lower gross margins, to carry less inventory, and turn it around faster. Retailers will build fewer stores to handle higher traffic with less overhead.

- The retail business will become more customer-driven, resulting in suppliers, retailers, and consumers becoming tightly integrated.

- Wholesalers as we now know them will become obsolete. The days of wholesalers acting as buyers, resellers, and low-tech expediters are over. Wholesalers will reinvent themselves to add value to the supply chain by providing third-party service, logistics, information, marketing, merchandising, and advertising programs.

- Category-killer stores will attack traditional supermarkets on an "aisle-by-aisle" basis. Retailers such as Petsmart and Baby's R Us represent this new trend in food retailing. These category killers may well raise consumer attention and spending to a point where supermarkets can benefit just by going along for the ride. Supermarkets that rethink and revitalize the hot growth categories to get their own share of these growing markets will be the real winners.

- Electronic retailing will likely represent a 5–10 per cent share of the grocery market. The major growth spurt in electronic retailing will probably occur between the years 2000 and 2005.

- Private label retailing will double in growth. Supermarkets will concentrate on their private labels as a way to differentiate themselves and to gain greater pricing flexibility.

- Fear of violence will spur a resurgence in neighbourhood shopping development and home shopping.

- Targeting customers will be more challenging because of the growing diversity of consumer demographics and lifestyles. Marketers will meet the challenge by using more micro-marketing and micro-merchandising approaches and fewer "cookie-cutter" approaches.

- Pull strategies will dominate over push strategies as the conventional way manufacturers go to the market. Manufacturers will adopt pay-on-scan or pay-on-ship practices in their distribution channels.

- Retailers and suppliers will pursue a relentless drive to know the sources of their costs and get them paid for by these sources. Activity-based costing will be the tool that firms use to identify their real profit drivers. Retailers will use activity-based costing to scrutinize their costs to source; and manufacturers will use it to scrutinize their costs to serve, and to identify which customers, products, and vendors are really profitable.

- Manufacturers will find it harder to get products on retailers' shelves. However, getting shelf space may become less important as more shoppers make purchases using alternative formats, and seek alternative meal solutions.

- There will be major and ongoing transformations in the supermarket industry. Leading supermarkets will focus on adding value to the shopping experience, and will act not just as ingredient providers, but as meal and shopping problem solution providers. Many supermarkets will shift their shelf space away from commodities and toward a larger selection of fresh, just-prepared, takeout and eat-in options.

# SUMMARY

**1.** *To define retailing and show its importance* Retailing encompasses those business activities involved with the sale of goods and services to the final consumer for personal, family, or household use. It is the final stage in a distribution channel. Average retail sales are small, yet the use of credit is widespread. Final consumers generally visit a retail store to make a purchase and they also make many unplanned purchases.

Retailing has an impact on the economy because of its total sales and the number of people employed. Retailers provide a variety of functions, including gathering a product assortment, providing information, handling merchandise, and completing transactions. Retailers deal with suppliers that sell products the retailers use in operating their businesses as well as suppliers selling items the retailers will resell.

**2.** *To discuss the different types of retailers, in terms of ownership, store strategy mix, and nonstore operations* Retailers may be categorized in several ways. The basic ownership formats are independent—a retailer operating only one outlet; chain—a retailer operating two or more outlets; franchise—a contractual arrangement between a franchiser and a franchisee to conduct a certain business; leased department—a department in a store that is leased to an outside party; and retail cooperative—an enterprise shared by retail owners. The ease of entry into retailing fosters competition and results in many new firms failing.

Different strategy mixes are used by convenience stores—well-situated, food-oriented retailers; conventional supermarkets—departmentalized food stores with minimum annual sales of $2 million; food-based superstores—diversified supermarkets that sell a broad range of food and nonfood items; combination stores (including super-

centres)—outlets that go further than food-based superstores in carrying both food and general merchandise; specialty stores (including category killers)—outlets that concentrate on one merchandise or service line; variety stores—outlets selling a wide assortment of inexpensive and popularly priced merchandise; traditional department stores—outlets that have a great assortment, provide customer services, are fashion leaders, often dominate surrounding stores, and have average to above-average prices; full-line discount stores—department stores with a low-price, moderate-service orientation; membership warehouse clubs—stores that offer very low prices in austere settings; and other discounters—including limited-line stores and off-price chains.

Nonstore retailing occurs when a firm uses a strategy mix that is not store-based. Vending machines use coin- or card-operated machinery to dispense goods and services. Direct selling involves both personal contact with consumers in their homes (or other places) and phone solicitations initiated by retailers. Direct marketing occurs when consumers are exposed to goods and services through nonpersonal media and then order by mail, phone, or computer. Cybermalls and sales through Web sites are among the newest approaches to direct marketing. Nonstore retailing is now a large part of retailing.

**3.** *To explore five aspects of retail planning: store location, atmosphere, scrambled merchandising, the wheel of retailing, and technological advances* A firm may select from among three forms of store location: an isolated store—a freestanding outlet located on a highway or street; an unplanned business district—in which two or more stores locate close to one another without

prior planning as to the number and composition of stores; and a planned shopping centre—which is centrally managed, as well as planned and operated as an entity. Only planned shopping centres utilize balanced tenancy, thus relating the store mix to consumer needs.

Atmosphere is the sum total of a store's physical characteristics that help develop an image and attract customers. It depends on the store's exterior, general interior, layout, and interior displays.

Scrambled merchandising occurs when a retailer adds products unrelated to its original business. The goals of scrambled merchandising are to encourage customer one-stop shopping, increase sales of high-profit items and impulse purchases, attract different target markets, and balance sales throughout the year.

The wheel of retailing explains low-end and high-end retail strategies and how they emerge. As low-cost, low-price innovators move along the wheel, they leave opportunities for newer, more cost-conscious firms to enter the market.

A number of technological advances have emerged over the past several years. These include computerized checkouts, video shopping services, data warehousing, computerized site selection, electronic banking, and techniques to improve operating efficiency.

**4.** *To define wholesaling and show its importance, and to describe the three broad categories of wholesaling (manufacturer/service provider wholesaling, merchant wholesaling, and agents and brokers)* Wholesaling involves the buying and/or handling of goods and services and their resale to organizational users, retailers, and/or other wholesalers but not the sale of significant volume to final consumers. In Canada, about 65 000 wholesale establishments distribute over $325 billion in goods and services annually.

Wholesale functions encompass distribution, personal selling, marketing and research assistance, gathering assortments, cost reductions, warehousing, financing, returns, and risk taking. These functions may be assumed by manufacturers/service providers or shared with independent wholesalers. The latter are sometimes in a precarious position because they are located between manufacturers/service providers and customers and must determine their responsibilities to each.

In manufacturer/service provider wholesaling, a producer undertakes all wholesaling functions itself. This form of wholesaling can be conducted through sales or branch offices. The sales office carries no inventory.

Merchant wholesalers buy, take title, and possess products for further resale. Full-service merchant wholesalers gather assortments of products, provide trade credit, store and deliver products, offer merchandising and promotion assistance, provide a personal sales force, offer research and planning support, and complete other functions as well. Limited-service merchant wholesalers take title to products but do not provide all wholesale functions.

Agents and brokers provide various wholesale tasks, such as negotiating purchases and expediting sales; but, they do not take title. They are paid commissions or fees. Agents are used on a more permanent basis than brokers.

**5.** *To examine recent trends in retailing and wholesaling* The nature of retailing has changed dramatically in recent years. Among the key trends retailers are adapting to are those relating to consumer demographics and lifestyles, competitive forces, operating costs, the labour force, and international opportunities. The nature of wholesaling has changed over the last several years. Trends involve the evolving wholesaler mix, productivity, customer service, international openings, and target markets.

## KEY TERMS

**retailing** (p. 326)

**wholesaling** (p. 326)

**independent retailer** (p. 329)

**retail chain** (p. 329)

**retail franchising** (p. 330)

**leased department** (p. 330)

**retail cooperative** (p. 331)

**retail store strategy mix** (p. 331)

**convenience store** (p. 331)

**conventional supermarket** (p. 331)

**food-based superstore** (p. 331)

**combination store** (p. 331)

**supercentre** (p. 332)

**specialty store** (p. 332)

**category killer** (p. 333)

**variety store** (p. 333)

**traditional department store** (p. 333)

**full-line discount store** (p. 333)

**membership warehouse club** (p. 333)

**nonstore retailing** (p. 334)

**vending machine** (p. 334)

**direct selling** (p. 334)

**direct marketing** (p. 334)

**isolated store** (p. 335)

**unplanned business district** (p. 336)

**planned shopping centre** (p. 335)

**atmosphere** (p. 335)

**scrambled merchandising** (p. 336)

**wheel of retailing** (p. 337)

**debit transactions** (p. 339)

**manufacturer/service provider wholesaling** (p. 345)

**wholesale merchants** (p. 347)

**full-service merchant wholesalers** (p. 347)

**limited-service merchant wholesalers** (p. 347)

**general-merchandise (full-line) wholesalers** (p. 347)

**specialty-merchandise (limited-line) wholesalers** (p. 347)

**rack jobbers** (p. 347)

**franchise wholesaling** (p. 348)

**wholesale cooperatives** (p. 348)

**cash-and-carry wholesaling** (p. 348)

**drop shippers (desk jobbers)** (p. 348)

**truck/wagon wholesalers** (p. 348)

**mail-order wholesalers** (p. 348)

**agents** (p. 348)

**brokers** (p. 348)

**manufacturers'/service providers' agents** (p. 349)

**selling agents** (p. 350)

**commission (factor) merchants** (p. 350)

**food brokers** (p. 350)

**commercial stock brokers** (p. 350)

# REVIEW QUESTIONS

1. Describe the four basic functions performed by retailers.

2. Differentiate between selling to a wholesaler and selling through a wholesaler.

3. What are the benefits of retail franchising to the franchisee? To the franchiser?

4. Why would a store want to have leased shoe departments rather than operate these departments itself?

5. Under what circumstances should a manufacturer or service provider undertake wholesaling?

6. Distinguish between direct marketing and direct selling. Which has greater sales? Why?

7. Distinguish between limited-service merchant wholesalers and full-service merchant wholesalers.

8. Explain the wheel of retailing from the perspective of the battle between traditional department stores and full-line discount stores for market share.

9. How do manufacturers'/service providers' agents and selling agents differ?

10. Why is attracting and retaining a quality labour force so difficult for many Canadian retailers?

# DISCUSSION QUESTIONS

1. The typical retailer earns a profit of 2 per cent or less on its sales revenues. How can this amount be so low if 38 to 40 cents of every customer dollar spent in department stores and specialty stores go to the retailers?

2. As a prospective franchisee for a Robin's Donuts outlet, what criteria would you use in deciding whether Robin's Donuts is right for you? What criteria do you think Robin's Donuts should use in assessing potential franchisees? Explain the differences in your answers to these two questions.

3. "Wholesalers are very much in the middle, often not fully knowing whether their first allegiance should be to the manufacturer/service provider or the customer." Comment on this statement. Can wholesalers rectify this situation? Why or why not?

4. Develop a short checklist that Mitchell Foods Inc. could use in determining whether to use merchant wholesalers or agents/brokers in different countries around the world to distribute its meat products intended for retail sale.

5. Select a planned shopping centre near your college or university and evaluate it with respect to its size and the size of its trading area. (Note that the term "size" can have several definitions—take as many of them into account as possible when answering this question.)

# Wal-Mart: Transforming Canada's Retail Landscape

Wal-Mart, often described as a consumer's dream, is a competing retailer's nightmare. Expanding its retail market by opening new stores is how Wal-Mart has become the fastest firm to double sales from $50 billion to $100 billion in the history of the U.S. Fortune 500. With U.S.$139 billion in sales from approximately 3000 stores, it's the third largest company in the United States and the fourth largest company in the world. Globally, Wal-Mart has 3.5 times as many sales as Sears Roebuck, its next largest competitor, and 4.5 times as many sales as K-Mart, the world's third largest general merchandise retailer.

The success of the company is based on two main concepts: 1) big-city discounting offered to small-town America, and 2) low-price positioning supported by a fanatical dedication to retail efficiency and a large buying power conferred by its large size. Wal-Mart's efficiency is based on how it has embraced computer technology and developed software to keep its "merchandisers in sync with its stores, its stores in sync with its distribution centres, and its distribution centres in sync with its suppliers." Wal-Mart has the second largest computer system in the United States, second only to the U.S. Department of Defence. The system links Wal-Mart's head office to its 3000 stores via satellite. All merchandise sold is laser scanned; the computer system records sales and inventory levels, which are communicated to head office and suppliers' factories. Head office can then order from a central location from its suppliers and get the maximum quantity discounts possible.

Bargaining hard with suppliers to get lower prices is a natural way for Wal-Mart to hold its price position and to maintain profits. Wal-Mart re-engineers its suppliers by investigating the manufacturing costs of their products and asking them to justify the prices they charge. This constant interaction with suppliers helps Wal-Mart build relationships and lower costs, to the detriment of its competitors.

When the Canada–U.S. free trade agreement was signed in 1987 it provided American firms more access to the Canadian market. Wal-Mart was looking for international opportunities at the time, and the agreement reinforced its choice of Canada as the first major site for international expansion. Canada was considered an attractive market for Wal-Mart because of its geographic proximity and the fact that English Canada and the U.S. are as similar in culture as two independent countries can be.

In 1994 Wal-Mart entered the Canadian market by buying 122 Woolco stores from Woolworth—and Canadian retailers began to worry about how they'd compete. They did have some advantages over their U.S. counterparts. While similar to the States, Canada is still a different country, with different laws and a different political system. And with the acquisition of the Woolco chain Canadian competitors knew where Wal-Mart was going to physically locate. Since the Woolco stores were going concerns, the market wasn't really absorbing another competitor, just a newer one—albeit a much leaner and meaner one.

In a scant five years Wal-Mart has become the market leader among Canadian department stores. In 1998 total department store sales were an estimated $17.2 billion, up from $16.2 billion in 1997. Wal-Mart had a 29.3 per cent share of the market in 1998, up from 26 per cent the year before. In comparison, Zellers had a 26.1 per cent share, up from 23.5 per cent the previous year, and Sears had a 19.2 per cent market share, up from 17.6 per cent the year before. The losers in this time were The Bay, with a 14.4 per cent market share, down from 15.6 per cent the year before, and Eaton's with a 9.3 per cent share, down from 10.4 per cent. Finally, the K-Mart Canada chain, which held a 6.8 per cent market share in 1997, had been acquired by Zellers—and its market share fell to 1.7 per cent as Zellers closed and converted the stores. The true picture? Zellers' gain was only half of K-Mart's business, so only Wal-Mart and Sears had real market share gains in 1998.

In 1999 market analysts predicted that Wal-Mart would begin to offer grocery items in many of its department stores. The prediction was that with grocery offerings, the firm could reach $16 billion in sales in short order. To counter this threat a number of Canadian grocery retailers put together merger plans. Loblaw decided to merge with Provigo and produce an organization with $17 billion in sales in Canada. To counter the Loblaw-Provigo merger and to fend off Wal-Mart, The Oshawa Group and Sobey's planned to merge to create a $10 billion in sales grocery chain. The mergers were carried out, of course, to become large enough to exact the same kind of supplier concessions that Wal-Mart receives so that the new organizations could compete on price. Meanwhile A&P-Dominion has implemented a new positioning campaign under the "We're Fresh Obsessed" banner to maintain customer loyalty.

It looks like it's too late for the department stores, but Canadian food retailers could get advice on dealing with Wal-Mart by looking at its U.S. history and by hiring Wal-Mart's nemesis, Dr. Ken

## CASE STUDY continued

# Wal-Mart: Transforming Canada's Retail Landscape

Stone, an economics professor from the University of Iowa. Ken Stone is a consultant who has advised retailers for years on how to challenge Wal-Mart. The two keystones of Ken Stone's advice are "Know Thy Competitor" and "Change the Way You Do Business to Respond to Wal-Mart." Ken Stone's pet peeve is retailers saying "It's worked for the last twenty years, so why should I change?" "Know Thy Competitor" means knowing that a typical Wal-Mart carries 75 000 to 80 000 different items in fifty different departments. It also means knowing that Wal-Mart is heavily price competitive on only 500 to 600 of these items, and this is how it has built its image.

So how can you compete against Wal-Mart? The key is finding a niche that Wal-Mart isn't filling, and being price competitive on the 500 to 600 items about which consumers are price conscious. Failing price competition, abandoning some products and concentrating on others is important. For example, a hardware store can't compete against Wal-Mart in small appliances and commonly used cleaning items. However, Wal-Mart has very little in the way of plumbing supplies or specialty items. The local hardware retailer can position itself as an advisor to its customers. Wal-Mart salespeople, as helpful as they are, are unlikely to be trained to fulfil this function. Finally, competing retailers must give cash refunds, as does Wal-Mart.

## Questions

1. Briefly discuss Wal-Mart's new store location strategy in the U.S. How did Wal-Mart's store location and market entry strategy in Canada differ from its typical U.S. approach? What implications might these differences have had for its Canadian competitors?

2. Evaluate the pros and cons of Wal-Mart's low price marketing strategy, then discuss the validity of this statement: Wal-Mart's success is built on logistics, pure and simple.

3. Some Canadian retailers, like Canadian Tire, have survived just fine against Wal-Mart. What do you think the reasons are for the difficulties of the department store retailers like Sears, The Bay, Eaton's, and Zellers? Consider yourself as a Canadian counterpart of Dr. Ken Stone. What suggestions do you have for these retailers to help them compete?

4. Wal-Mart is competing heavily with department store retailers in Canada, and now plans to take on grocery store retailers. What do you think the next target(s) might be? Advise Wal-Mart on where it should expand next and how.

Sources: Based on Performance 2000, *Canadian Business* (June 26/July 10, 1998), pp. 138–141; Fortune 500 Largest U.S. Corporations, *Fortune* (April 26, 1999), p. F1; Report on Market Shares, "Department Stores," *Marketing Magazine* (June 7, 1999), p. 24; Eryn Brown, "America's Most Admired Companies," *Fortune* (March 1, 1999), pp. 68–73; Fawzia Sheikh, "Grocers Get Ready for Wal-Mart Threat," *Marketing Magazine* (November 9, 1998), p. 3; Editorial, "The Wal-Mart Threat," *Marketing Magazine* (December 7, 1998), p. 35; Sean Silcoff, "Pay Now, Buy Later," *Canadian Business Canadian Economic Outlook* (February 12, 1999) pp. 36–37; Fawzia Sheikh, "Zellers Unveils Plan to Fight Wal-Mart," *Marketing Magazine* (June 8, 1998), p. 2; Mark Stevenson, "The Store to End All Stores," *Canadian Business* (May 1994), pp. 20–29; James Pollock, "Retreaded," *Marketing Magazine* (July 31/August 7, 1995), pp. 1, 11; Michael Treacy, "Success Through Cannibalism," *Marketing Magazine* (September 4, 1995), p. 17; James Pollock, "Retailers in Scramble to Reposition Stores," *Marketing Magazine* (November 20, 1995), p. 4; "Wal-Mart Wizard," CBC *Venture* Video 465; and "Wal-Mart Update," CBC *Venture* Video 471.

# Retail Winners

The Canadian retail market is extremely competitive, and the 1990s have been one of the toughest periods in recent memory. Eaton's fight for survival is over, and catalogue store retailer Consumer's Distributing went out of business as well. In Canada retailing is an entrepreneurial business and a very tough one at that. Still, Canadians are good at retail, despite the success of American invaders like Wal-Mart and Home Depot.

In western Canada Revy Home and Garden is trying to take on Home Depot. Revy owner Carl Grittner notes that it's "not that hard to do." Grittner is just one example of a growing number of gutsy Canadian retailers. A former truck driver, Carl Grittner owned a few lumber and hardware outlets in western Canada. When Home Depot came on the scene and began to hurt his business, Grittner decided that he had to either get into the game or get out. He studied American big box stores, got to know his competition, and decided to copy what they did that worked. He knew his stores had to have clout with suppliers in order to get the kind of low price discounts he needed to compete, and so Grittner formed a buying group in order to get this clout.

The result? Grittner beat Home Depot into Winnipeg, where he opened a 150 000 square foot Revy hardware superstore. He doesn't just copy Home Depot, mind you; he also orders things that Home Depot doesn't. For example, at Revy they cater to women customers with larger displays of home improvements and by offering more home decorating products. Grittner reports success at drawing women into his store. Retail analyst Ian Thomas noted that Revy was doing well, but that big box retailing is a brutally competitive business that can change very quickly.

Colleen Fleming, President of Laura Secord, is expanding and reinventing a well-known retail operation. Laura Secord is moving from its candy retailer niche to the broader gift retailing market. Fleming is overseeing the refurbishing of old stores and the opening of new

ones featuring a new line of Hallmark Cards. She notes that focus groups and market research information told her that customers are anxious to save time, hence the gift cards from Hallmark and the gift-wrapped items. She believes that good retailers must be innovative and that this stems from good instincts and market research. Laura Secord has developed a detailed feedback system for customers and employees, which even measures what she's doing as the firm's president!

According to retail commentator Joan Pajunen, "Retailers must have passion to be successful." She believes that whatever motivating force got them into the business is what they need to keep them going. She notes that retailers face a constantly changing environment, and that focusing on failures is the wrong thing to do. Retail stores often make many changes over time so that they're never the same store twice. Aldo's shoe chain has turned this equation around, concentrating instead on being predictable. Canadian Tire has also been consistent in offering the "world's best loyalty program," Canadian Tire money. A couple of Canadian retailers have developed unique strategies and have been acquired by U.S. firms to capitalize on this. Winners (a good name in this regard), offers high quality fashion at discount prices, as does Moore's the Suit People.

Tony Chanine, owner of the sixty-store Battery Plus chain, has this advice: In retail, you never relax. Battery Plus tries its hardest so that its customers have no reason to shop anywhere else. It has the battery you need or can get it for you, even if it has to make it. Chanine sees his retail store as a solution provider for customers. He says that his firm is constantly questioning everything it does, and is willing to change its plans to adapt to customers and competitive market changes. Chanine's experience has told him that individual products have a short life. Retailers must reinvent themselves or their lives will be as short as the products they sell.

## Questions

1. Based on the case, what do you believe are the main factors in successful retail operations? Comment on these factors.
2. Discuss the importance of attitude and motivation as key characteristics for successful retailers. Are they the only keys to success? What other characteristics would a good retail person possess?
3. In retailing it's not what you sell, it's how you sell it. Debate this statement by drawing on the case as well as the chapter material on distribution, wholesaling, and retailing.
4. Identify and discuss the strategies used by the retailers described in this case. How are they similar? How are they different? Is there a generic strategy for success as a retailer? Why or why not?

## Video Questions

1. Discuss Carl Grittner's observation that taking on Home Depot is not that hard to do. Evaluate the strategy he has employed with his Revy stores.
2. Consider Colleen Fleming's new concept for Laura Secord. What kind of risk is she taking with remaking these stores?

Source: Based on "Retail Winners," Venture #640 (May 4, 1997).

# PART 5

# Promotion Planning

## Promotion Planning and Personal Selling

Here, we broadly discuss promotion planning, which involves all communication used to inform, persuade, and/or remind people about an organization's or individual's goods, services, image, ideas, community involvement, or impact on society. We describe the basic types of promotion and the stages in a channel of communication. Next, we present the steps in developing an overall promotion plan, international promotion considerations, the legal environment, and criticisms of promotion. We also focus on personal selling, one of the four types of promotion. We define personal selling as oral communication with one or more prospective buyers by paid representatives for the purpose of making sales. We describe the scope, characteristics, and stages of planning for personal selling.

## Advertising, Public Relations, and Sales Promotion

In this chapter, we examine three of the four types of promotion: advertising, public relations, and sales promotion. We define advertising as paid, nonpersonal communication by an identified sponsor; public relations as any form of image-directed communication by an identified sponsor or the independent media; and sales promotion as the paid marketing communication activities (other than advertising, publicity, or personal selling) that stimulate consumer purchases and dealer effectiveness. We detail the scope of advertising, public relations, and sales promotion and their attributes. We discuss the development of advertising, public relations, and sales promotion plans in depth.

## Information-Based Marketing: Direct and Internet Marketing

Here we define information-based marketing, direct marketing and internet marketing. We present the scope and importance of direct marketing as well as the characteristics of direct marketing. We discuss how to develop a direct marketing plan by setting objectives, designing offers, developing prospect lists, creating the advertising, selecting the media, implementing the campaign, and then evaluating response. We present the scope and importance of internet marketing and its role as part of the new world of e-commerce. Internet buyer behaviour is discussed as is how to target on the internet. We offer website design recommendations and discuss how to promote on the internet. We conclude by discussing how to transact and distribute on the web and then evaluate internet marketing efforts. We conclude the chapter with 30 suggested direct marketing principles.

# Promotion: Stimulating Marketplace Demand with Information

Communicating information to help create and support marketing transactions is what promotion is all about.

Promotion involves communicating information to help people find goods and marketers find customers. It establishes and reinforces the product positioning image that has been selected for a good or service. Chapters 12 and 13 introduce promotional concepts and the four basic types of promotion: personal selling, advertising, public relations, and sales promotion. Chapter 14 discusses the special circumstances around direct and Internet marketing.

Chapter 12 deals with the topic of promotion theory, such as the use of promotion in image positioning. The chapter also discusses personal selling, which is one of the most important communication elements in business. Personal selling goes far beyond the people in identified sales positions, since every contact between a company representative and a customer entails some personal interaction. The Canadian Professional Sales Association (CPSA), which has 30 000 individual members who work in every industry sector in Canada, can help marketers with personal selling. This organization provides assistance in sales and marketing; regularly offers seminars in major Canadian cities; offers courses toward Sales Certification; provides online publications; distributes *Contact* magazine (published five times a year); and maintains the most comprehensive library resource centre in Canada dedicated to sales and marketing professionals.

Chapter 13 presents the other three promotional elements: advertising, public relations, and sales promotion. For example, the Insurance Corporation of B.C. (ICBC) wanted to convey a new, non-authoritative brand personality to its customers while focusing on getting drivers to change poor driving behaviours that lead to accidents. The campaign theme was "What would happen if people retained their driver personality in everyday life?" To discourage tailgating, for example, an ad was produced showing someone walking down the street with another person right behind them, breathing down their neck and saying "Move it, move it." The voiceover asks, "You'd never walk like this, so why would you drive like this?"

Chapter 14 introduces direct and Internet marketing. Direct marketing uses one or more advertising media to effect a measurable response and/or transaction at any location. The activity is usually stored on a database. The Internet is a medium that allows marketers to engage in direct marketing via e-commerce, i.e., the buying and selling of information, products, and services via computer networks.

Direct marketing may be the only recourse when a marketer is denied access to distribution through conventional retailers. Firms may conduct a direct marketing program whose ultimate purpose is to establish a customer franchise and brand image that can pull the product into conventional retail channels. Saskatchewan-based E-zee Wrap first used direct marketing to introduce plastic wrap dispensers and refills to consumers. After E-zee Wrap developed a brand image and a customer franchise, retailers like Zellers, Wal-Mart, and Home Hardware stores were happy to resell the firm's dispensers and refills.

Direct marketing via the Internet is becoming an extremely viable alternative for all business organizations. In Canada, consumer acceptance and use of the Internet for e-commerce has been increasing dramatically every year. According to the Angus Reid Group, only 22 per cent of its Internet panel members completed an online purchase in 1997, whereas 32 per cent of the members did so in 1998.

**CHAPTER** | 12

# Promotion Planning and Personal Selling

## *Chapter Objectives*

**1.** To define promotion planning and show its importance

**2.** To describe the general characteristics of advertising, public relations, personal selling, and sales promotion

**3.** To explain the channel of communication and how it functions

**4.** To examine the components of a promotion plan, international promotion considerations, the legal environment, and criticisms and defences of promotion

**5.** To examine the scope, importance, and characteristics of personal selling

**6.** To study the elements in a personal selling plan

Joseph Marranca Photography

"**G**ross is good. When you're targeting male teens with snack food TV pitches, old-fashioned is definitely toast." Getting attention and setting your products apart from those of the competitors' has always been an important ingredient to the success of any promotional campaign. In the past, marketers have tried "beauty shots" to reach young teenage males. You know, attractive guys eye attractive girls, they get together, and then consume the marketer's product while they socialize. Then comes the classic happy ending, with the product as the wholesome hero. These days, marketers are trying a new approach: the product is gross, and maybe even the villain!

Pillsbury Pizza is trying to get the attention of young teenage males for its product by "splatting scalding microwaved Pillsbury Pizza Pops at the wall and letting the gunk drip down." The spots seem to work, because Pillsbury had a 51 per cent share of Canada's $69 million pizza snack market in 1998.

McCain's Pizza Pockets decided it wanted to challenge Pillsbury's lead in this market. The firm used to appeal to moms with the typical "beauty shot" approach, but now it's decided to take what has been called the "edgy" approach.

The edgy approach came about from research that McCain's undertook to design its promotional campaign. When McCain's interviewed teenage males it found that they wanted to see portrayals of teenagers that showed them talking fast, wearing fast clothes, looking like "real" teens, and definitely no moms! Looking real meant that ads should show teens as they really appear, with unkempt hair and baggy clothes. One part of looking real was making sure that the language the teens spoke was right too. So in McCain's new spots, one sees body-pierced, chain-laden teenage males leaning on some parked cars and eating Pizza Pockets while talking down "ad company geniuses." The product is not featured in a close-up shot and it appears the way it is, not "made-up."

Pillsbury's marketing manager Bryan Nykoliation says unabashedly, "Gross is good ... We could have done a voiceover saying they're jampacked with tomatoes and vegetables and used a nice beauty shot to showcase all that on a nice plate. But this [ads that show Pizza Pops going splat on the wall, splat in the face, splat everywhere] is what we call 'gut fill.' Teens can never be full."

Other snack food marketers are also trying the edgy approach to reach teens. Hostess-Frito Lay has developed a series of ads that show how opening a bag of Doritos will let you rebel from the ordinary. For example, one ad shows a teen eating Doritos in the library. There's a flavour explosion when the bag is opened: the hot flavour of the Doritos sets off the fire alarm while the teen disrupts everyone by eating the chips and making a loud crunch, crunch sound.

The power of designing promotions for a specific target market is the main issue with the edgy approach. Certainly, sales of pizza snacks and other snack foods have responded quite well. Now, if carpet cleaning, wall washing, stain removing, and dry cleaning sales also start to rise, marketers may encounter an edgy response from the families of these teens![1]

In this chapter, we will study many dimensions of promotion planning, including the usefulness of celebrities (human or animated) as sources in the channel of communication. Our discussion will also cover how the channel of communication works and the roles of the source, encoding, the message, the media, decoding, the audience, and feedback. Finally, we will study personal selling, which is one of the four basic types of promotion marketers can employ.

## Overview

**Promotion** is any communication used to inform, persuade, and/or remind people about an organization's or individual's goods, services, image, ideas, community involvement, or impact on society. **Promotion planning** is systematic decision making relating to all aspects of an organization's or individual's communications efforts.

Communication occurs through brand names, packaging, company marquees and displays, personal selling, customer service, trade shows, sweepstakes, and messages in mass media (such as newspapers, TV, radio, billboards, magazines, transit, direct mail, e-mail, and Web sites). It can be company-sponsored or controlled by independent media. Messages may emphasize information, persuasion, fear, sociability, product performance, humour, and/or comparisons with competitors.

In this chapter, the context of promotion planning is provided. Included are discussions on promotion's importance, the basic promotion types, the channel of communication, promotion planning, international considerations, the legal environment, and general criticisms and defences of promotion. This chapter also looks at one of the major promotion forms: personal selling. Personal selling involves oral communication with one or more prospective buyers by paid representatives for the purpose of making sales. It relies on personal contact, unlike advertising and the publicity aspect of public relations. Its goals are similar to other promotion forms: informing, persuading, and/or reminding. Chapter 13 covers advertising, public relations, and sales promotion, and Chapter 14 covers direct and Internet marketing.

*Promotion planning focuses on a total promotion effort—informing, persuading, and reminding.*

*Personal selling is one-on-one with buyers. Sales promotion includes paid supplemental efforts.*

## The Importance of Promotion

Promotion is a key element of the marketing mix. For new products, people must be informed about items and their features before they can develop favourable attitudes toward them. For products with some consumer awareness, the focus is on persuasion: converting knowledge to preference. For very popular products, the focus is on reminding: reinforcing existing consumer beliefs.

The people and/or organizations to whom a firm's promotional efforts are aimed may fall into various categories: consumers, shareholders, consumer advocacy groups, government, channel members, employees, competitors, and the general public. Firms often communicate with each of these audiences, not just with consumers. In addition, communication with each may be different because each category has distinct goals, knowledge, and needs.

Within an audience category (like consumers), a firm needs to identify and appeal to opinion leaders—those who influence others' decisions. It also should understand **word-of-mouth communication**, the process by which people express opinions and product-related experiences to one another. Unless a product or service has a sustained positive word-of-mouth reputation, it is hard to succeed.[2]

A company's promotion plan usually stresses individual goods and services, with the intent of moving people from awareness to purchase. Yet the firm may also convey its overall image (industry innovator), views on ideas (nuclear energy), community service (funding a new hospital), or impact on society (the size of its workforce). Table 12-1 shows many valuable promotion functions.

A good promotion plan complements the product, distribution, and price aspects of the marketing mix. For example, Waterman—a maker of pens—distributes

**Word-of-mouth communication** *occurs as people state opinions to others.*

**TABLE 12-1**

**The Value of Promotion**

**PROMOTION**

- Establishes an image for a company and its goods and services.
- Communicates features of goods and services.
- Creates awareness for new goods and services.
- Keeps existing goods and services popular.
- Can reposition the images or uses of faltering goods and services.
- Generates enthusiasm from channel members.
- Notes where goods and services can be purchased.
- Can persuade consumers to trade up from one product to a more expensive one.
- Alerts consumers to sales.
- Justifies (rationalizes) the prices of goods and services.
- Answers consumer questions.
- Closes transactions.
- Provides service for consumers after transactions are completed.
- Reinforces loyal consumers.
- Places the firm and its goods and services in a favourable light, relative to competitors.

its products to finer stores and sets premium prices. It advertises in magazines such as *Canadian Business,* and expects retailers to provide first-rate personal selling. Ads are in colour and refer to product features, not prices. See Figure 12-1.

Well-conceived promotion plans are feasible even if companies have limited resources. Almost every community is served by some type of media which is interested in what is happening in the marketplace. Therefore, one of the best ways to begin a promotion strategy involves securing media coverage. The two fundamental things that marketers must do are develop a media mindset and cultivate effective media relations. Developing a media mindset involves overcoming fear of reporters and the press. Marketers must realize that the media represents the public at large, and for the most part employs people who are professionals. The second step is the most important and difficult. Cultivating media relationships takes time and involves making contact with the reporters and media people in your community. Here are some suggested steps for cultivating the media:

- Submit press release incessantly. Only some will be read or even noted, but it's the repetition that will establish awareness of your company or product in the mind of the reader.
- Set up a database of media representatives as your mailing list and make sure they receive relevant and newsworthy releases monthly. Be sure to include company information, new products, significant sales, major new clients, and key appointments. Always date the release and provide contact name information.
- Take the press people to dinner, lunch, or breakfast. Arrange a simple meeting at their office or yours. Don't be afraid to pester them; call politely until you get a time and a date to meet. Do it annually.
- Be available when a reporter calls, or return the call as soon as possible (within the hour). Don't let an opportunity for media coverage be lost because the call was trapped in voice mail and you weren't able to return it until the deadline had passed.
- Keep in contact. Call your media contacts on a regular basis with genuine industry news. Drop them a note from time to time complimenting or critiquing stories, articles, and features they've written or produced.

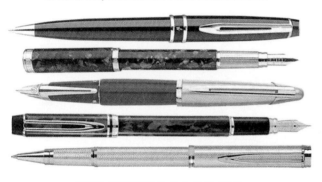

ALTHOUGH THE McCOOEY BROTHERS AND THEIR SISTER HAVE
ALWAYS BEEN REMINDED OF THEIR STRIKING SIMILARITIES, IT IS THEIR
DIFFERENCES THEY HAVE ALWAYS INSISTED ON. IT IS NO WONDER
THEN, THAT EACH OWNS A DIFFERENT WATERMAN PEN. FOR WHILE
STYLE IS KEY, INDIVIDUALITY IS STILL EVERYTHING.

**WATERMAN** (W) PARIS

Introducing Rhapsody, shown above in Mineral Red. One of over 100 styles and finishes to choose from,
each with a lifetime guarantee. For the store nearest you, call 1-800-668-6385.

**FIGURE 12-1**

**The Consistent, High-Quality Promotional Emphasis of Waterman Pens**

*Reprinted by permission of Waterman.*

- Everyone loves new products. New product stories always stand a better chance of being featured. In fact, most trade publications feature a regular new product section.

- Resist the urge to exaggerate, or worse still, lie. And don't become offended or irate if they get the story wrong or don't tell it your way. Be cool and be prepared to go back for another round. Cultivating media relationships is never a game for the thin-skinned or faint of heart.[3]

Promotion's importance is also evident from the expenditures and jobs in this area. The world's fifty largest advertising agencies have overall annual billings of U.S.$29 billion. The International Advertising Association's thousands of members are from 116 nations. In Canada alone, each year business firms spend nearly $9 billion on media advertising; 3.6 million people work in sales and service occupations; 17.1 billion coupons are given out; and Canadian firms participate in the 4000 North American trade shows.[4]

**INTERNATIONAL ADVERTISING ASSOCIATION**
www.iaaglobal.org

# Types of Promotion

In their communications programs, organizations use one or more of four basic types of promotion:

**Advertising, public relations (publicity), personal selling,** *and* **sales promotion** *are the four key promotion types.*

- **Advertising** is paid, nonpersonal communication regarding goods, services, organizations, people, places, and ideas that is transmitted through various media by business firms, government, and other nonprofit organizations, and individuals who are identified in the advertising message as the sponsor. The message is generally controlled by the sponsor.

- **Public relations** includes any communication to foster a favourable image for goods, services, organizations, people, places, and ideas among their publics—such as consumers, investors, government, channel members, employees, and the general public. It may be nonpersonal or personal, paid or nonpaid, and sponsor controlled or not controlled. **Publicity** is the form of public relations that entails nonpersonal communication passed on through various media but not paid for by an identified sponsor. Wording and placement of publicity messages are generally media controlled.

- **Personal selling** involves oral communication with one or more prospective buyers by paid representatives for the purpose of making sales.

## TABLE 12-2

## Characteristics of Promotional Types

| FACTOR | ADVERTISING | PUBLICITY FORM OF PUBLIC RELATIONS[a] | PERSONAL SELLING | SALES PROMOTION |
|---|---|---|---|---|
| Audience | Mass | Mass | Small (one-to-one) | Varies |
| Message | Uniform | Uniform | Specific | Varies |
| Cost | Low per viewer or reader | None for media space and time; can be some costs for media releases and publicity materials | High per customer | Moderate per customer |
| Sponsor | Company are not paid | No formal sponsor in that media | Company | Company |
| Flexibility | Low | Low | High | Moderate |
| Control over content and placement | High | None (controlled by media) | High | High |
| Credibility | Moderate | High | Moderate | Moderate |
| Major goal | To appeal to a mass audience at a reasonable cost, and to create awareness and favourable attitudes | To reach a mass audience with an independently reported message | To deal with individual consumers, to resolve questions, to close sales | To stimulate short-run sales, to increase impulse purchases |
| Example | Television ad for a Sony CD player for use in cars | Magazine article describing the unique features of a Sony CD player for cars | Retail sales personnel explaining how a Sony CD player for cars works | A Sony CD player for cars exhibited at trade shows |

[a] When public relations embodies advertising (an image-related message), personal selling (a salesperson describing the firm's public service efforts to college students), and/or sales promotion (distributing special discount coupons to low-income consumers), it takes on the characteristics of those promotional types. However, the goal would be more image-related than sales-related.

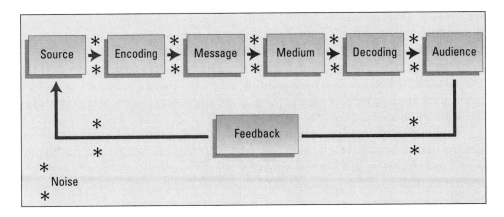

**FIGURE 12-2**

**A Channel of Communication**

- **Sales promotion** involves paid marketing communication activities (other than advertising, publicity, or personal selling) that are intended to stimulate consumer purchases and dealer effectiveness. Included are trade shows, premiums, incentives, giveaways, demonstrations, and various other efforts not in the ordinary promotion routine.[5]

The general characteristics of each type of promotion are shown in Table 12-2. As discussed later in the chapter, many firms in some way combine them into an integrated promotional blend. This lets them reach their entire target market, present both persuasive and believable messages, have personal contact with customers, sponsor special events, and balance the promotional budget.

## The Channel of Communication

To develop a proper promotion mix and interact effectively with a target audience, the **channel of communication (communication process)** shown in Figure 12-2 must be understood. Through such a channel, a source develops a message, transmits it to an audience by some medium, and gets feedback from the audience. The components of a communication channel are discussed next.

*A message is sent to an audience through a* **channel of communication.**

## The Source

The **source** of communication is usually a company, an independent institution, or an opinion leader seeking to present a message to an audience. A firm communicates through a spokesperson, celebrity, actor playing a role, representative consumer, and/or salesperson.

*A* **source** *presents a message.*

A company spokesperson is typically a long time employee who represents the firm in communications. The spokesperson has an aura of sincerity, commitment, and expertise. Sometimes the spokesperson is a top executive, such as Wendy's Dave Thomas, who pitches virtually all the firm's fast food products. Front-line employees are also used, such as a Shoppers Drug Mart pharmacist or a sales clerk from the Subway Sandwich shop. In general, this source has been quite effective.

A celebrity is used when the goal is to gain the audience's attention and improve product awareness. Popular celebrities include hockey player Wayne Gretzky for McDonald's, The Bay, Post Cereals, CIBC, Coca-Cola, Zurich Financial, and Campbell Soup Company; basketball player Michael Jordan for Nike; Candace Bergen for Sprint Canada; and Snoopy and other Peanuts characters for Metropolitan Life Insurance. Problems can arise if the celebrity is perceived as insincere, unknowledgeable, or if the celebrity's reputation becomes damaged or faded. The recent

**NIKE**
www.nike.com

retirements of Wayne Gretzky and Michael Jordan are of considerable concern to the firms which they endorse. For example, Michael Jordan's Chicago Restaurant saw a considerable drop in sales during his first retirement stint.[6]

Many ads have actors playing roles rather than celebrity spokespeople. In these commercials, the emphasis is on presenting a message about a good, service, or idea rather than on the consumer recognizing a celebrity. The hope is that the consumer will learn more about product attributes.

A representative consumer is one who likes a product and recommends it in an ad. The person is shown with his or her name and hometown. The intent is to present a real consumer in an actual situation. A hidden camera or blind taste test is often used with this source. Today, viewers are more skeptical about how representative the endorser is.

Finally, a firm may use a salesperson to communicate with consumers. Many salespeople are knowledgeable, assertive, and persuasive. However, consumers may doubt their objectivity and tactics. Auto salespeople rate particularly low in consumer surveys.

An independent institution is not controlled by the firms on which it reports. It presents information in a professional, nonpaid (by the firms) manner. The Canadian Automobile Association and the local newspaper restaurant critic are examples of independent sources. They have great credibility for their readers because they discuss both good and bad points, but some segments of the population may not be exposed to these sources. The information presented may differ from that contained in a firm's commercials or sales-force presentations.

An opinion leader is a person who has face-to-face contact with and influences other potential consumers. Because he or she deals on a personal level, an opinion leader often has strong persuasive impact and believability; and he or she can offer social acceptance for followers. Thus, firms often address initial messages to opinion leaders, who then provide word-of-mouth communication to others. Many marketers believe opinion leaders not only influence, but also are influenced by, others (opinion receivers); even opinion leaders need approval for their choices.

In assessing a source, these questions are critical:

- Is the source believable?
- Is the source convincing?
- Does the source present an image consistent with the firm?
- Do consumers value the message of the source?
- Is the source seen as knowledgeable?
- Does the source complement the product he/she communicates about—or overwhelm it?
- Do significant parts of the market dislike the source?

**CANADIAN AUTOMOBILE ASSOCIATION**
www.caa.ca

## Encoding

*In **encoding,** a source translates a thought into a message.*

**Encoding** is the process whereby a thought or idea is translated into a message by the source. At this stage, preliminary decisions are made as to message content, such as the use of symbolism and wording. It is vital that the thought or idea be translated exactly as the source intends. For example, a firm wanting to stress its product's prestige would include the concepts of status, exclusive ownership, and special features in a message. It would not emphasize a price lower than competitors, availability in discount stores, or the millions of people who have already purchased.

**FIGURE 12-3**

**A Humorous Ad**

*The Brain Storm Group*

## The Message

A **message** is a combination of words and symbols transmitted to an audience. Its thrust depends on whether a firm's goal is to inform, persuade, or remind its audience. Almost all messages include some information on the company name, the product name, the desired image, differential advantages, and product attributes. A firm would also give information about availability and price at some point during the consumer's decision process.

Most communication involves one-sided messages, in which only the benefits of a good, service, or idea are cited. Fewer firms use two-sided messages, in which both benefits and limitations are noted. Firms are not anxious to point out their short-comings, although consumer perceptions of honesty may be improved by two-sided messages. For example, in June 1996, Standard Life ran an ad in *Canadian Business* admitting they were headquartered in Scotland and had not been listed as one of the top insurance companies in Canada. However, the ad pointed out that the rankings of Canadian firms included worldwide assets, while foreign firms were ranked only by their Canadian assets. Standard Life's ad stated they had $90 billion in assets and that Canadian policyholders were fully protected.[7]

Many messages use symbolism and try to relate safety, social acceptance, or sexual appeal to a purchase. In symbolic messages, a firm stresses psychological benefits rather than tangible product performance. Clothing ads may offer acceptance by peers; and toothpaste may brighten teeth and make a person more sexually attractive. One type of symbolism, the use of fear appeals, has had mixed results. Although people respond to moderate fear appeals, strong messages may not be as well received.

*A **message** combines words and symbols.*

**FIGURE 12-4**

**A Humorous Dutch Ad: Feel Human Again, Eat Vegetarian**

*Reprinted by permission.*

Fear appeals can be useful. Ads alerting people to potential natural resource depletion, the danger of forest fires, ramifications of drunk driving, and the potential health hazards of permissive sexual behaviour are examples. The public good and advertisers' self-interest are compatible. In addition, these ads have an educational value that may prove useful over an extended period. However, marketers must avoid creating too much anxiety or discomfort among recipients, or the message may backfire.[8]

Humour is sometimes used to gain audience attention and retain it. Two popular examples are the Leon's Furniture "Ho, Ho, Hold the Payments" commercials and the Sunlight Detergent "Go ahead. Get dirty." ads. However, a firm needs to be careful to get across the intended message when using humour, which should not make fun of the company, its goods, or its services. Also, humour should not dominate a message so that the brand name or product's attributes go unnoticed. Figure 12-3 shows a Mike's Hard Lemonade ad, and Figure 12-4 shows a Netherlands Vegetarian Council ad. Because humour has cultural underpinnings, the Dutch ad would probably not work well in North America.

**Comparative messages**

*position a firm in relation to its competitors.*

**Comparative messages** implicitly or explicitly contrast a firm's offerings with those of competitors. Implicit comparisons use an indirect brand X or leading brand approach ("Our industrial glues are more effective than other leading brands"). Explicit comparisons use a direct approach (such as the Nissan print ad, "We can see by your face that you've priced the new Camry from Toyota"). Comparative messages, in one form or another, are used in various TV and radio commercials, print ads, and other media. In addition, salespeople often compare their products' attributes with competitors'. When using comparative messages, a

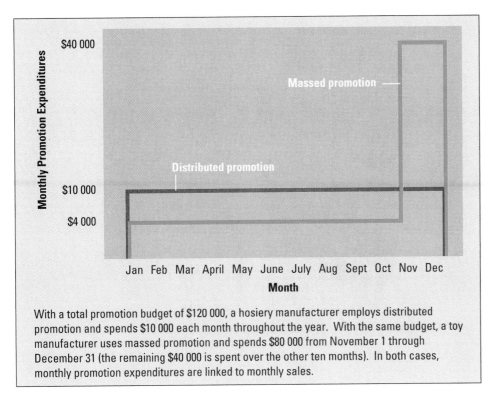

With a total promotion budget of $120 000, a hosiery manufacturer employs distributed promotion and spends $10 000 each month throughout the year. With the same budget, a toy manufacturer uses massed promotion and spends $80 000 from November 1 through December 31 (the remaining $40 000 is spent over the other ten months). In both cases, monthly promotion expenditures are linked to monthly sales.

**FIGURE 12-5**
**Massed Versus Distributed Promotion**

firm has to be quite careful not to turn off consumers, place too much emphasis on a competitor's brand, or lose sight of its own differential advantages that should be promoted.

A message must be presented in a desirable, exclusive, and believable way. The good, service, or idea must be perceived as something worth buying or accepting. It also must be seen as unique to the seller—that is, it cannot be gotten elsewhere. Finally, the message must make believable claims.

Message timing must also be carefully planned. First, during what times of the year should a firm advertise, seek publicity, add salespeople, or run sales promotions? In **massed promotion**, communication efforts are concentrated in peak periods, like holidays. In **distributed promotion**, communication efforts are spread throughout the year. Figure 12-5 compares massed and distributed promotion.

Second, the **wearout rate**—the time it takes for a message to lose its effectiveness—must be determined. Some messages wear out quickly; others last for years. The wearout rate depends on the frequency of communications, message quality, the number of different messages used by a firm, and other factors. Ford has done such a good job with its "Quality is Job 1" message that it is still strong after many years.

*Massed or distributed promotion and the wearout rate must be carefully planned.*

## The Medium

The **medium** is the personal or nonpersonal means used to send a message. Personal media are company salespeople and other representatives, as well as opinion leaders. Nonpersonal (mass) media include newspapers, television, radio, direct mail, billboards, magazines, and transit.

Personal media offer one-to-one audience contact. They are flexible, can adapt messages to individual needs, and can answer questions. They appeal to a small audience and are best with a concentrated market. Nonpersonal media have a large audience and low per-customer costs. They are not as flexible and dynamic as one-to-one contacts. They work best with a dispersed target market.

*A **medium** is a personal or nonpersonal channel for a message.*

TAKE TWO AND CALL US IN THE MORNING. Healthcare professionals take Polaroid photos with healthy results. Our GridFilm is used to measure and enhance written descriptions of wounds. Our MicroCam instantly records microscopic specimens. We've even created an imaging system that's revolutionizing radiology departments. If your business needs to document information stat, call 1-800-348-5287, ext 793 for a free brochure. Until you know what we can do for your business, you haven't seen the whole picture. **Polaroid**

**FIGURE 12-6**

**Is This Business-to-Business Ad Easily Decoded?**

*Reprinted by permission.*

In deciding between personal and nonpersonal media, a firm should consider both total and per-unit costs, product complexity, audience attributes, and communication goals. The two kinds of media go well together since nonpersonal media generate consumer interest and personal media help close sales.

## Decoding

*In **decoding,** the audience translates the message sent by the source.*

**Decoding** is the process by which a message sent by a source is interpreted by an audience. The interpretation is based on the audience's background, and on the clarity and complexity of the message. For example, a woman who works in the home and a woman who works in an office might have different interpretations of a message on the value of child-care centres. Usually, as symbolism and complexity increase, clarity decreases. "National Geographic: Connect. Convince." is not as understandable a message as "Yellow Pages. It Pays. We'll Prove It." As noted earlier, it is essential that a message be decoded in the manner intended by the source (encoding = decoding). Is the business-to-business ad depicted in Figure 12-6 too provocative or merely attention grabbing? Is the serious message buried in the imagery or quite clear to the targeted audience?

**Subliminal advertising**

*aims at a consumer's subconscious.*

**Subliminal advertising** is a highly controversial kind of promotion because it does not enable the audience to consciously decode a message. Instead, visual or verbal messages are presented so quickly that people do not see, hear, or remember them. Yet, the assumption is that they will buy goods and services because of subconscious impulses stimulated by these messages. The overwhelming evidence shows that subliminal ads cannot get people to buy things they do not want. In addition, subliminal ads are often misinterpreted; clear, well-labelled ads are much more effective. In Canada subliminal advertising is illegal.[9]

## The Audience

An **audience** is the object of a source's message. In most marketing situations, it is the target market. However, a source may also want to communicate an idea, build an image, or give information to shareholders, independent media, the public, government officials, and others.

*The **audience** is usually the target market; but it can also include others.*

The way a communication channel is used by a firm depends on the size and dispersion of the audience, demographic and lifestyle audience traits, and the availability of appropriate media. Because the communication process should be keyed to the audience, AIDS prevention groups have had a tough time getting their message across to teens and young adults:

> Past AIDS-related public service announcements have defined the problem as one of HIV/AIDS awareness, the assumption being that once young people are aware of AIDS, they will be motivated to practice APBs (AIDS preventive behaviours). However, this definition is outdated. It is now evident that AIDS awareness has been accomplished among teens and young adults. They are already aware that sexual intercourse and IV drug use represent the major modes of AIDS transmission. The challenge facing communicators is how to convert AIDS awareness into APBs. Although there is some need to keep generic AIDS messages before the public, rudimentary information/awareness-based appeals are of little use to a market that knows the elementary facts or when there is little evidence that basic knowledge leads to adoption of APBs.[10]

And to make matters still tougher for marketers, one global consumer survey found that people are rather down on promotion messages:

- 72 per cent believe marketers exaggerate health benefits.
- 70 per cent do not believe marketers respect consumers' intelligence.
- 70 per cent believe marketers brainwash children.
- 62 per cent do not believe marketers give accurate information.
- 55 per cent do not believe marketers sponsor worthwhile events.
- 40 per cent do not believe ads are creative and entertaining.[11]

## Feedback

**Feedback** is the response an audience has to a message. It may be a purchase, an attitude change, or a nonpurchase. A firm must understand that each of these responses is possible and devise a way of monitoring them.

***Feedback** consists of purchase, attitude, or nonpurchase responses to a message.*

The most desirable kind of feedback occurs if a consumer buys a good or service (or accepts an idea) after communication with or from the firm. This means a message is effective enough to stimulate a transaction.

A second type of feedback takes place if a firm finds its promotion efforts elicit a favourable audience attitude toward it or its offerings. For new goods or services, positive attitudes must usually be formed before purchases (awareness→favourable attitude→purchase). With existing products, people may have bought another brand just before receiving a message or be temporarily out of funds; generating their favourable attitudes may lead to future purchases.

The least desirable feedback is if the audience neither makes a purchase nor develops a favourable attitude. This may happen for one of several reasons: The audience does not recall the message; the audience is content with another brand; the audience did not believe the message; or no differential advantage is perceived.

## Noise

**Noise** *may interfere with the communication process at any stage.*

**Noise** is interference at any point along a channel of communication. Because of it, messages are sometimes encoded or decoded incorrectly or weak audience responses are made. Examples of noise are:

- A phone call interrupting a company's marketing manager while he or she is developing a promotional theme.
- A salesperson misidentifying a product and giving incorrect information.
- An impatient customer interrupting a sales presentation.
- A conversation between two consumers during a TV commercial.
- A direct-mail ad being opened by the wrong person.
- A consumer seeing a sale on a competitor's item while waiting at an office-supply store's checkout counter.

# Promotion Planning

After a firm gains an understanding of the communication process, it is ready to develop an overall promotion plan. Such a plan consists of three parts: objectives, budgeting, and the promotion mix.

## Objectives

Promotion objectives can be divided into two main categories: stimulating demand and enhancing company image.

*The* **hierarchy-of-effects model** *outlines demand goals.*

In setting demand goals, the **hierarchy-of-effects model** should be used. It outlines the sequential short-term, intermediate, and long-term promotion goals for a firm to pursue—and works in conjunction with the consumer's decision process that was discussed in Chapter 4:

1. *Provide information*—Obtain consumer product recognition, then gain consumer knowledge of product attributes.
2. *Develop positive attitudes and feelings*—Obtain favourable attitudes, then gain preference for the company's brand(s) over those of competitors.
3. *Stimulate purchases and retain desires*—Obtain strong consumer preference, gain purchase of good or service, encourage continued purchases (brand loyalty).

**Primary demand** *is for a product category;* **selective demand** *is for a brand.*

By applying the hierarchy-of-effects model, a company can move from informing to persuading and then to reminding consumers about its offerings. At the early stages of the model, when a good or service is little known, **primary demand** should be sought. This is consumer demand for a product category. At later stages, with preference the goal, **selective demand** should be sought. This is consumer demand for a particular brand. Sometimes, organizations may try to sustain or revitalize interest in mature products and revert to a primary demand orientation. If promotion goals are image-oriented, a firm engages in public relations efforts—using suitable advertising, publicity, personal selling, and/or sales promotion (as noted in Table 12-2). **Institutional advertising** is used when the advertising goal is to enhance company image—and not to sell goods or services. This is illustrated in Figure 12-7, an ad for CanWest Global. Many of the leading advertisers in Canada run institutional ads.

**Institutional advertising** *is involved with image goals.*

## Budgeting

There are five basic ways to set a total promotion budget: all you can afford, incremental, competitive parity, percentage of sales, and objective and task. The choice depends on the requirements of the individual firm. Budgets can range from 1 to 5

**FIGURE 12-7**

**Institutional Advertising by CanWest Global Communications**

*Reprinted with permission of CanWest Global Communications Corp.*

per cent of sales for industrial-products firms to up to 20 to 30 per cent of sales for consumer-products firms.[12]

In the **all-you-can-afford method**, a firm first allots funds for other elements of marketing; any remaining marketing funds then go to the promotion budget. It is the weakest technique and used most often by small, production-oriented firms. It gives little importance to promotion, spending is not linked to goals, and there is a risk of having no promotion budget if finances are low.

With the **incremental method**, a company bases its new promotion budget on the previous one. A percentage is added to or subtracted from this year's budget to determine next year's. The technique is also used by small firms. It has these advantages: it gives the firm a reference point, it bases the budget on a firm's feelings about past performance and future trends, and it is easy to calculate. Important disadvantages do exist: budget size is rarely tied to goals, "gut feelings" are overemphasized, and it is hard to evaluate success or failure.

In the **competitive parity method**, a firm's promotion budget is raised or lowered according to competitors' actions. It is useful to both large and small firms. The benefits are that it is keyed to a reference point, market-oriented, and conservative. The shortcomings are that it is a follower and not a leadership approach, it is difficult

*Budgeting methods are* **all you can afford, incremental, competitive parity, percentage of sales,** *and* **objective and task.**

## INTERNATIONAL MARKETING IN ACTION

## Global Marketing and Promotion for Seagram's Spirits

Montreal-based Seagram Co. Limited reorganized its senior marketing organizations so that the firm could become a more effective global competitor. Seagram is without a doubt a global firm, since only 3 per cent of its sales are made in Canada. In fact, according to the U.N. Conference on Trade and Development, Seagram is the most global of all the firms in the world! The reorganization plan was designed for Seagram to become a leaner organization, without boundaries, and to be both consumer- and customer-focused.

Seagram plans to move from a regional and brand group structure to a centralized senior team-management structure based in New York. The marketing communications group will also be based in New York, but will be supported by functional teams in other nations. Seagram plans to maintain four brand groups, consisting of the Chivas Regal Group, focusing on Scotch whisky; the Martell Group, focusing on cognac, wines, port, and champagne (both based in London, England); the Crown Royal group, focusing on Canadian whiskies and bourbon; and the Captain Morgan Group, focusing on rum, gin, and tequila (both based in New York). Seagram's Absolut Vodka brand is being handled separately from this reorganization.

By restructuring itself for global competition Seagram can present consistent products, in consistent packages, with consistent positioning. The reorganization is very clear though: Seagram has become a New York-based firm. Given the fact that New York is the centre for the United Nations, it seems natural for a global firm to located its main operations there.

Still, when one considers the extreme variety of distribution and consumption practices associated with alcohol marketing (and that's just in Canada), it does raise the question: Can a spirits firm really implement a global marketing and promotion strategy?

Discuss Seagram's reorganization approach with respect to the preceding question. Identify a number of the barriers to implementing a global marketing strategy for spirits, and discuss some possible means for overcoming them.

*Sources*: Based on Lara Mills, "Seagram Revamp Will Delay and Centralize Marketing," *Marketing Magazine* (November 23, 1998), p. 8; and Editorial, "Thinking Too Globally," *Marketing Magazine* (November 23, 1998), p. 31.

**THE SEAGRAM CO. LTD.**
www.seagram.com

*The **marginal return** is the sales generated by incremental promotional spending.*

to get competitors' promotion data, and it assumes a similarity between the firm and its competitors (as to years in business, goods or services, image, prices, and so on) that may not exist.

With the **percentage-of-sales method**, a firm ties its promotion budget to sales revenue. In the first year, a promotion-to-sales ratio is set. During succeeding years, the ratio of promotion to sales dollars is constant. The benefits of this method are that it uses sales as a base, it is adaptable, and it links revenues and promotion. However, it bears no relation to promotion goals; promotion is a sales follower, not a sales leader; and promotion cuts occur in poor sales periods (when increases could help). The technique yields too large a budget in high sales periods and too small a budget in low sales periods.

Under the **objective-and-task method**, a firm sets promotion goals, determines the activities needed to satisfy them, and then establishes the proper budget. This is the best method. The advantages are that goals are clearly stated, spending is related to goal-oriented tasks, adaptability is offered, and it is easy to evaluate performance. The major weakness of objective and task is the complexity of setting goals and specific tasks, especially for small firms. Most large companies use some form of objective-and-task technique.

During promotional budgeting, a firm should keep the concept of **marginal return** in mind. The marginal return is the amount of sales each increment of promotion spending will generate. When a product is new, the marginal return is high because the market is expanding. When a product is established, the marginal return is lower because each additional increment of promotion has less of an impact on sales (due to a saturated target market).

## The Promotion Mix

After establishing a total promotion budget, a company must determine its **promotion mix**. This is the firm's overall and specific communication program, including its involvement with advertising, public relations (publicity), personal selling, and/or sales promotion. Seldom does a company use just one type of promotion—such as a mail-order firm relying on ads, a hospital on publicity, or a flea-market vendor on selling. Typically, a promotion mix is used.

When a well-coordinated promotion mix is involved, a firm is undertaking **integrated marketing communications (IMC)**. An IMC program would be defined as one that "recognizes the value of a comprehensive plan that evaluates the strategic roles of a variety of communication disciplines—advertising, public relations, personal selling, and sales promotion—and combines them to provide clarity, consistency, and maximum communication impact."[13] For example, Frito-Lay has a sales force that visits every store stocking its products, advertises in papers and magazines and on TV, and distributes cents-off coupons. Hitachi has a large technical sales force, advertises in business and trade publications, and sends representatives to trade shows.

Each type of promotion has a distinct function and complements the other types. Ads appeal to big audiences and create awareness; without them, selling is more difficult, time-consuming, and costly. The publicity aspect of public relations provides credible information to a wide audience, but content and timing cannot be controlled. Selling has one-to-one contact, flexibility, and the ability to close sales; without it, the interest caused by ads might be wasted. Sales promotion spurs short-run sales and supplements ads and selling.

*A **promotion mix** somehow combines advertising, public relations, personal selling, and/or sales promotion. When done well, **integrated marketing communications** results.*

**FIGURE 12-8**

**Contrasting Promotion Mixes**

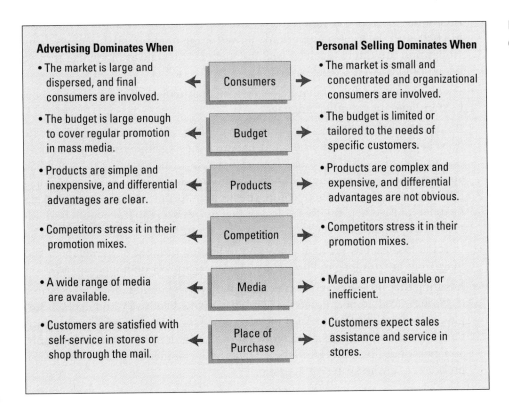

The selection of a promotion mix depends on company attributes, the product life cycle, media access, and channel members. A small firm is limited in the kinds of ads it can afford or use efficiently; it may have to stress personal selling and a few sales promotions. A large firm covering a sizable geographic area could combine many ads, personal selling, and frequent sales promotions. As products move through the life cycle, promotion emphasis goes from information to persuasion to reinforcement; different media and messages are needed at each stage. Some media may not be accessible (no cigarette ads on TV) or require lengthy lead time (Yellow Pages). In addition, channel members may demand special promotions, sales support, and/or cooperative advertising allowances.

It is the job of a firm's marketing director (or vice-president) to set up a promotion budget and a promotion mix, as well as to allocate resources to each aspect of promotion. In large firms, there may be separate managers for advertising, public relations, personal selling, and sales promotion. They report to, and have their efforts coordinated by, the marketing director.

Figure 12-8 contrasts promotion mixes in which advertising and personal selling would dominate.

## International Promotion Considerations

*International promotion decisions should not be made until each market is carefully studied.*

**SPRINT CANADA**
www.sprint.ca

While preparing a promotion strategy for foreign nations, the channel of communication, promotion goals, budgeting, and the promotion mix should be carefully reviewed as they pertain to each market.

With regard to the channel of communication, a firm should recognize that:

- Source recognition and credibility vary by nation or region. In Canada, celebrities who are popular in English Canada may not be popular in Quebec. For example, Sprint Canada was using Candace Bergen as their advertising spokesperson in both languages. Candace Bergen was married to the late French film director Louis Malle and is fluently bilingual in both of Canada's official languages. Yet she was not well received in Quebec so Sprint replaced her with three spokespersons who are well known in Quebec: Jean-Luc Brassard, an Olympic gold medal-winning aerial skier; actor Dominique Michel; and Jacques Languirand, a well-known radio host. Actors from Hollywood are rarely received well in Quebec: "they always look like they've been dubbed, even if they haven't."[14]

- Encoding messages can be quite challenging, particularly if the messages must be translated into another language.

- Because the effects of message symbolism depend on the nation or region, care must be taken if fear, humorous, and/or sexual messages are used. Themes have to correspond to local customs. For example, for firms targeting the Canadian youth market it is important that approaches to advertising recognize regional differences. "In Toronto there's more stress on uniformity. A key to teens is 'Let's be different together,' but there's less of that in Quebec. You'll see more flexibility in terms of being unique."[15]

- In some locales, few residents have TVs, a limited number of newspapers and magazines are printed, and programs (channels) limit or do not accept ads.

- Ensuring that messages are decoded properly can be demanding: "To promote its Wash & Go shampoo, Procter & Gamble blanketed Polish TV and mailed samples. Poles found the dubbed ad culturally out of touch: It showed a woman popping out of a swimming pool and into a shower. 'We don't have swimming pools, and most of us don't have showers. We have baths,' sniffed Eugeniusz Smilowski, president of a Warsaw research group."[16]

- Making assumptions about audience traits in foreign markets without adequate research may lead to wrong assumptions: Western marketers entered the Indian market believing well-known brands would be accepted in India just like they had been accepted elsewhere. What they found out was that in India, "the consumer does not buy a global brand just because it is global. . . International brands have to be relevant in terms of perceived image, performance, and value if they are to succeed locally."[17]

- Global techniques for measuring promotion effectiveness are emerging.

In terms of promotion goals, budgeting, and the promotion mix, these points should be considered:

- For nations where a firm and its brands are unknown, a firm should have a series of promotion goals to lead people through the hierarchy-of-effects model. For nations in which a product category is new, primary demand must be created before selective demand is gained. To show goodwill, image ads may be even more important in foreign than in domestic markets.

- The promotion budgets in foreign countries must be keyed to the size of the markets and the activities required to succeed there. The objective-and-task method is highly recommended in setting international promotion budgets.

- Due to cultural, socioeconomic, infrastructure, and other differences, promotion mixes must be consistent with the countries served. In Western Europe, Germans listen to the radio most; the Dutch and British watch the most TV. And when Procter & Gamble mailed free samples (a form of sales promotion) of Wash & Go shampoo to people's homes in Poland, thieves broke into mailboxes to get the samples—which they resold. As a Procter & Gamble manager said, "The tools we were using were new to that area."[18]

# The Legal Environment of Promotion

Federal, provincial, and local governmental bodies in Canada—and similar bodies in other nations around the globe—have laws and rules regarding promotion practices. These regulations range from banning billboards in some locales to requiring celebrity endorsers to use products if they say they do. The Canadian federal agencies most involved with promotion are Industry Canada's Competition Bureau and the Canadian Radio-television and Telecommunications Commission (CRTC). Table 12-3 shows selected promotional practices that are subject to regulation.

The CRTC regulates all broadcast advertising in Canada. In 1999, the CRTC considered its role and whether it should also directly regulate the Internet (the decision was made that it should not). It remains to be seen whether any other government agency will step forward with direct regulation, but as of this writing it seems unlikely. The CRTC delegates some of its regulatory authority to other governmental bodies responsible for specific products. For example, Health Canada's Protection Branch regulates promotion for the Canadian pharmaceutical and cosmetic industry. There are five regulatory tools available to protect consumers and competing firms from undesirable promotion practices: full disclosure, substantiation, cease-and-desist orders, corrective advertising, and fines.

**Full disclosure** requires that all data necessary for a consumer to make a safe and informed decision be provided in a promotion message. That is why Alka-Seltzer must mention that its regular version contains aspirin, and diet products must note how many calories they contain. In this way, consumers can assess the overall benefits and risks of a purchase.

**CRTC**
www.crtc.gc.ca/

**Full disclosure, substantiation, cease-and-desist orders, corrective advertising,** *and* **fines** *are major governmental limits on promotion activities.*

## TABLE 12-3

## Selected Canadian Regulations (Federal & Provincial) Affecting Promotion

| MARKETING PRACTICE | LEGAL CONSIDERATIONS |
| --- | --- |
| Access to media | Cigarette, liquor, and drug manufacturers have restricted access. |
| Deception | It is illegal to make false statements or use messages that would mislead reasonable consumers and potentially harm them. |
| Bait-and-switch | It is illegal to lure a customer with an ad for a low-priced item and then, once the customer talks to a salesperson, to use a strong sales pitch intended to switch the shopper to a more expensive item. |
| Door-to-door selling | Many locales restrict door-to-door sales practices. A cooling-off period allows a person to cancel an in-home sale up to seven days after an agreement is reached. |
| Promotional allowances | Such allowances must be available to channel members in a fair and equitable manner. |
| Comparative advertisements | Claims must be substantiated. Federal and provincial regulators favour naming competitors in ads (not citing a competitor as brand X). |
| Testimonials or endorsements | A celebrity or expert endorser must actually use a product if he or she makes such a claim. |
| Contests | Advertisers must disclose the chances of winning and the manner in which prizes are to be distributed. |

Source: Ed Ratushny, Q.C., "Report of the Consultative Panel on Amendments to the Competition Act," Strategis, Industry Canada, http://strategis.ic.gc.ca. Ottawa: Competition Bureau (April 15, 1996); and Keith J. Tuckwell, *Canadian Advertising in Action*, Third Edition, Prentice Hall: Scarborough, Ontario (1995), pp. 20, 635–654.

**Substantiation** requires that a firm be able to prove all the claims it makes in promotion messages. This means thorough testing and evidence of performance are needed before making claims. In a recent Ontario court case, Unilever, maker of Dove soap, sued Procter & Gamble, maker of Oil of Olay, for an injunction against their comparative ads. Procter & Gamble ran an ad claiming Oil of Olay helped retain more skin moisture than Dove soap. The case hinged on the ability of Procter & Gamble to prove their claim with verifiable test results. Because they were able to do so, Unilever was denied an injunction.[19]

Under a **cease-and-desist order**, a firm must discontinue a promotion practice that is deemed deceptive and modify a message accordingly. The firm is usually not forced to admit guilt or pay fines, as long as it obeys the order.

**Corrective advertising** requires a firm to run new ads to correct the false impressions left by previous ones. Several years ago, Listerine was told to spend U.S.$10.2 million on ads in Canada and the U.S. to correct prior messages claiming it was a cold remedy. Listerine decided to run the ads (with the phrase "Listerine will not help prevent colds or sore throats or lessen their severity") after learning it would not otherwise be permitted to continue any advertising.

The last major remedy is **fines**, which are dollar penalties for deceptive promotion. A company may have to pay a sum to the government, as when the Click Modelling and Talent Agency of Canada, operating as the International Model and Talent Agencies, pleaded guilty to a total of fifteen counts of misleading advertising

# ETHICS AND TODAY'S MARKETER

## Euthanasia and the Media

Euthanasia is a very controversial topic; it's been one of the most covered social issues in North America in recent times. The prominent Canadian cases of Sue Rodriguez of Vancouver, who fought in court to be euthanized, and Saskatchewan farmer James Latimer, who was jailed for euthanizing his daughter, are still fresh in the minds of most Canadians. In the U.S., Dr. Jack Kevorkian of Michigan is both famous and infamous (it depends on one's point of view on euthanasia) for his activities as the "Suicide Doctor." Dr. Kevorkian's numerous assisted suicides have generated massive publicity for the issue. The publicity culminated in a top-rated "60 Minutes" TV broadcast in which Dr. Kevorkian was filmed euthanizing a person—an action for which he was subsequently tried and jailed on a charge of murder.

This issue is not confined to North America, and media coverage is not confined to publicity. Recently a shock ad campaign was run in Australia by the Voluntary Euthanasia Society of New South Wales. The campaign featured June Burns, a real-life cancer patient, in a TV commercial in which she begs physicians to end her agony in a tearful plea. Burns says things like, "If I was a dog my husband would have me put down straight away. I don't want to have to kill myself, but if nobody can help me, I'm going to have to." Burns

talks of being in tremendous pain and having to take twenty pills each day, plus morphine. The Voluntary Euthanasia Society is putting together a whole campaign of ads that will follow June Burns as her health declines.

Clearly, with such a powerful message, there has been a great deal of controversy over these ads. An Australian right-to-life group wants the ads pulled from the airways. They argue that it sends a message that suicide can be the answer to life's problems, and that this will affect depressed young teens. A voluntary euthanasia supporter, Dr. Phillip Nitschke, believes that these ads demonstrate to the public that there's a need to change the law because voluntary euthanasia is currently illegal in Australia. Without a doubt, these ads are a form of public advocacy on a controversial topic about which everyone feels uncomfortable.

As an advertising agency manager, would you have accepted the assignment from the Voluntary Euthanasia Society of New South Wales? Why or why not? Discuss the risks involved in accepting controversial advertising, and then discuss your ethical position on this issue to support your answer.

Source: Based on Chris Pritchard, "Australian Ad Ignites Euthanasia Debate," *Marketing Magazine* (April 12, 1999), p. 6.

under the Competition Act. The International Model and Talent Agencies ran approximately 1000 display and classified advertisements in daily newspapers and weekly tabloids in Toronto stating that specific modelling and acting opportunities were available through their agencies. An investigation of the firm revealed that they weren't securing modelling or acting jobs for their customers, but were instead selling modelling courses and photographs. The firm was fined $200 000, which was used to reimburse victims named in the case. A prohibition order was also imposed, requiring that the International Model and Talent Agencies comply with the Competition Act and not misrepresent the nature of the modelling and acting opportunities available through the firm.[20]

In addition to government legislation, marketers must recognize that trade associations and professional associations often have rules or guidelines governing the use of promotion by their members. The International Advertising Association sets guidelines for the self-regulation of promotion throughout the world. Within Canada, marketers are asked to voluntarily abide by The Canadian Code of Advertising Standards and the Gender Portrayal Guidelines, which are administered nationally by Advertising Standards Canada (ASC). Both of these documents, as well as other industry codes and guidelines, can be viewed on the ASC website.

**ADVERTISING STANDARDS COUNCIL**
www.canad.com

**BETTER BUSINESS BUREAU**
www.bbb.org

Some cities have their own advertising councils to handle complaints. For example, the Windsor Media Council (Windsor, Ontario) places ads in the local media informing the community where they can register complaints and seek resolution concerning local advertising and media programming. Another important local body involved in self-regulation is the Better Business Bureau. The Better Business Bureau usually deals with more product and service complaints but complaints about promotional practices are handled as well.

## Criticisms and Defences of Promotion

For many years, various industry trade groups have campaigned to improve the overall image of promotion. According to the general director of the International Advertising Association, "There's been enough talk about the bad—the clutter, the obtrusiveness, the stuffed mailboxes. It's time that people know about the good."[22]

Nonetheless, promotion is the most heavily criticized area of marketing. Here are a number of criticisms and the defences of marketers to them:

*Promotion controversies centre on materialism, honesty, prices, symbolism, and consumer expectations.*

| DETRACTORS FEEL THAT PROMOTION: | MARKETING PROFESSIONALS ANSWER THAT PROMOTION: |
|---|---|
| Creates an obsession with material possessions. | Responds to consumer desires for material possessions. In affluent societies, these items are plentiful and paid for with discretionary earnings. |
| Is basically dishonest. | Is basically honest. The great majority of companies abide by all laws and set strict self-regulations. A few dishonest firms give a bad name to all. |
| Raises the prices of consumer goods and services. | Holds down prices. By increasing demand, promotion enables firms to use mass production and mass distribution and reduce per-unit costs. Employment is higher when demand is stimulated. |
| Overemphasizes symbolism and status. | Differentiates goods and services through symbolic and status appeals. Consumers desire distinctiveness and product benefits. |
| Causes excessively high expectations. | Keeps expectations high; it thereby sustains consumer motivation and worker productivity in order to satisfy expectations. |

## The Scope and Importance of Personal Selling

In Canada, 3.6 million people work in sales and service positions; millions more in other nations are also employed in sales jobs. Professional salespeople generate new customer accounts, ascertain needs, interact with consumers, emphasize knowledge and persuasion, and offer substantial service. They include stockbrokers, insurance agents, manufacturer sales representatives, and real estate brokers. Top salespeople can earn $100 000+ per year. Clerical salespeople answer simple queries, retrieve stock from inventory, recommend the best brand in a product category, and complete transactions by receiving payments and packing products. They include retail, wholesale, and manufacturer sales clerks.

Personal selling goes far beyond the people in identified sales positions, since every contact between a company representative and a customer entails some personal interaction. Lawyers, plumbers, hairdressers, and cashiers aren't defined as salespeople, yet each engages in a lot of customer contact. One organization that can help marketers with personal selling is The Canadian Professional Sales Association

(CPSA), which has 30 000 individual members who work in every industry sector in Canada. This organization provides assistance in sales and marketing; regularly conducts seminars in major Canadian cities; offers courses toward "Sales Certification"; provides online publications; distributes *Contact* magazine (published five times a year); and maintains the most comprehensive library resource centre in Canada dedicated to sales and marketing professionals.[23]

In some situations, a strong personal-selling emphasis may be needed. Large-volume customers require special attention. Geographically concentrated consumers may be more efficiently served by a sales force than by ads in mass media. Custom-made, expensive, and complex goods or services require in-depth consumer information, demonstrations, and follow-up calls. Tangential sales services—like gift wrapping and delivery—may be requested. If ads are not informative enough, questions can be resolved only by personal selling. New products may need personal selling to gain reseller acceptance. Entering a foreign market may best be achieved by personal contact with prospective resellers and/or consumers. Finally, many organizational customers expect a lot of personal contact. Generally, a decision to stress personal selling depends on such factors as cost, audience and needs, and a desire for flexibility.

*Selling is stressed when orders are large, consumers are concentrated, items are expensive, and service is required.*

**FIGURE 12-9**

**The Canadian Professional Sales Association**
Promoting excellence in sales.

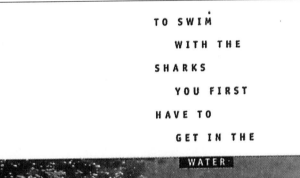

Personal selling costs are often greater than advertising costs. For example, Fuller Brush sales commissions range up to 50 per cent of sales and auto parts firms, office and equipment firms, and appliance makers all spend far more on selling than on ads. The average cost of a single business-to-business field sales call is several hundred dollars; and it may take several visits to make a sale.[24]

A number of strategies have been devised to keep selling costs down and improve the efficiency of the sales force, as these examples show:

- Many firms are routing salespeople more effectively to minimize travel time and expenses. Some firms are bypassing smaller customers in their personal selling efforts and specifying minimum order sizes for personalized service. This means opportunities for sellers willing to serve small accounts.

*High selling costs have led to a concern for efficiency. In* **telemarketing,** *phone calls initiate sales or set up sales appointments.*

- With **telemarketing**, telephone communications are used to sell or solicit business or to set up an appointment for a salesperson to sell or solicit business. By using it, salespeople can talk to several consumers per hour, centralize operations and lower expenses, screen prospects, process orders and arrange shipments, provide customer service, assist the field sales staff, speed communications, and increase repeat business. A lot of companies rely on telephone personnel to contact customers; outside sales personnel (who actually call on customers) are then more involved with customer service and technical assistance. A broad range of both small and large firms use some form of telemarketing.

- Computerization is improving sales efficiency by providing salespeople with detailed—and speedy—data, making ordering easier, coordinating orders by various salespeople, and identifying the best prospects and their desires (such as preferred brands) based on prior purchases. Thousands of Canadian salespeople now have notebook PCs: "Anything that allows reps to squeeze a couple more hours out of their day has great benefits."[25]

- A lot of firms now view computerized customer databases as among their most valuable sales resources. These databases enable the firms to focus their efforts better, make sure their key accounts are regularly serviced, and use direct mailings to complement telephone calls and salesperson visits.

## The Characteristics of Personal Selling

On the positive side, personal selling provides individual attention for each consumer and passes on a lot of information. There is a dynamic interplay between buyer and seller. This lets a firm use a **buyer-seller dyad**, the two-way flow of communication between both parties (see Figure 12-10). That is not possible with advertising. Thus, personal selling can be flexible and adapted to specific consumer needs. For example, a real estate broker can use one sales presentation with a first-time buyer and another with a person who has already bought a home. A salesperson can also apply as much persuasion as needed and balance it against the need for information. Furthermore, through the buyer-seller dyad, a "relationship selling" approach is possible, whereby customer friendships may be developed.[26]

*Selling uses a* **buyer-seller dyad** *and is flexible and efficient, closes sales, and provides feedback.*

Personal selling targets a more defined and concentrated audience, which means less waste than with advertising. In addition, people who enter a store or who are contacted by a salesperson are more apt to buy a product than those watching an ad on TV. Because ads stimulate interest, those who make it to the personal selling stage are often key members of the target market. When unsolicited, direct selling has the most waste in personal selling.

Personal selling often clinches a sale and is usually conducted during the purchase stage of the consumer's decision process, taking place after an information

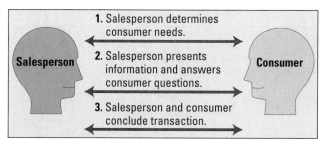

**FIGURE 12-10**
**The Buyer-Seller Dyad**

search and exposure to ads. It holds repeat customers and those already convinced by advertising—and resolves any concerns of undecided consumers by answering questions about price, warranty, and other factors. It settles service issues, like delivery and installation. Feedback is immediate and clear-cut: Consumers may be asked their feelings about product features or they may complain; and salespeople may unearth a marketing program's strengths and weaknesses.

On the negative side, selling is ineffective for generating awareness because salespeople can handle only a limited number of consumers. A retail furniture salesperson may be able to talk to fewer than twenty people per day if the average length of a customer contact is fifteen minutes to a half hour. Sales personnel who call on customers can handle even fewer accounts, due to travel time. In addition, many consumers drawn by advertising may want self-service. This is discouraged by some aggressive salespeople.

Personal selling costs per customer can be very high due to the one-on-one nature of selling. An in-store furniture salesperson who talks to twenty customers daily might cost a firm $7 per presentation ($140/day compensation divided by 20), an amount much higher than an ad's cost per customer contact. For outside salespeople, hotel stays, meals, and transportation can amount to $250 or more daily per salesperson, and compensation must be added to these costs.

*Selling has a limited audience, high costs per customer, and a poor image.*

Finally, personal selling, especially among final consumers, has a poor image. It is criticized for a lack of honesty and pressure tactics:

> The public's consistent interpretation of the term salesperson has provided fodder for many dramatic works, anecdotes, and jokes that reflect the widely held negative stereotype of salespeople. As a result, people may avoid them deliberately. The consumer practice of visiting car dealerships after business hours [indicates the common distrust] of salespeople. This practice may be due to beliefs that consumers can evaluate alternative cars better in the absence of the "dreaded" salesperson. Sometimes, salespeople may even inhibit, rather than facilitate, mutually satisfying exchanges.[27]

The situation can be improved by better sales-force training, the use of consumer-oriented rather than seller-oriented practices, and by adherence to a code of ethics like the one developed by the Canadian Professional Sales Association, presented below:

1. Maintain honesty and integrity in all relationships with customers, prospective customers, and colleagues, and continually work to earn their trust and respect.

2. Accurately represent products or services to the best of his/her ability in a manner that places the customer or prospective customer and the company in a position that benefits both.

3. Respect and protect the proprietary and confidential information entrusted to them by their company and their customers and not engage in activities which may conflict with the best interests of their customers or company.

4. Continually upgrade their knowledge of their products/services, skills, and industry.

**FIGURE 12-11**

**Developing a Promotion Plan for
Personal Selling**

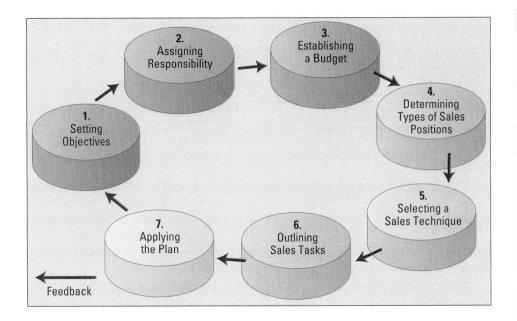

5. Use the time and resources available to them only for legitimate business purposes, and only participate in activities that are ethical and legal, and when in doubt, shall seek counsel.

6. Respect competitors and their products and services in a manner that is honest, truthful, and based on accurate information that has been substantiated.

7. Endeavour to engage in business and selling practices which contribute to a positive relationship with the community.

8. Assist and counsel fellow sales professionals where possible in the performance of their duties.

9. Abide by and encourage others to adhere to this Code of Ethics.[28]

# Developing a Promotion Plan for Personal Selling

A personal selling plan can be divided into the seven steps shown in Figure 12-11 and highlighted here.

## Setting Objectives

Selling goals can be demand- and/or image-oriented. When image-oriented, they involve public relations. Although many firms have some interest in information, reminder, and image goals, the major goal usually is persuasion: converting consumer interest into a sale. Examples appear in Table 12-6.

## Assigning Responsibility

The personal selling function may be assigned to a marketing or sales manager who oversees all areas of selling, from planning to sales-force management. A small or specialized firm is likely to have its marketing manager oversee selling or use one general sales manager. A large or diversified firm may have multiple sales managers—assigned by product line, customer type, and/or region.

*A manager must oversee
selling functions.*

These are the basic responsibilities of a sales manager:

• To understand the firm's goals, strategies, market position, and basic marketing plan and to convey them to the sales force.

**TABLE 12-6**

**Specific Personal Selling Objectives**

| TYPE OF OBJECTIVE | ILLUSTRATIONS |
|---|---|
| *Demand-Oriented* | |
| Information | To fully explain all attributes of goods and services |
| | To answer any questions |
| | To probe for any further questions |
| Persuasion | To distinguish attributes of goods or services from those of competitors |
| | To maximize the number of purchases relative to the presentations made |
| | To convert undecided consumers into buyers |
| | To sell complementary items—e.g., a telephoto lens with a camera |
| | To placate dissatisfied customers |
| Reminding | To ensure delivery, installation, etc. |
| | To follow-up after a good or service has been purchased |
| | To follow-up when a repurchase is near |
| | To reassure previous customers as they make a new purchase |
| *Image-Oriented* | |
| Industry and company | To have a good appearance for all personnel having customer contact |
| | To follow acceptable (ethical) sales practices |
| | To be respected by customers, employees, and other publics |

- To determine and outline a sales philosophy, sales-force characteristics, selling tasks, a sales organization, and methods of customer contact.
- To prepare and update sales forecasts.
- To allocate selling resources based on sales forecasts and customer needs.
- To select, train, assign, compensate, and supervise sales personnel.
- To synchronize selling tasks with advertising, product planning, distribution, marketing research, production, and other activities.
- To assess sales performance by salesperson, product, product line, customer, customer group, and geographic area.
- To continuously monitor competitors' actions.
- To make sure the sales force acts in an ethical manner.
- To convey the image sought by the company.

## Establishing a Budget

A **sales-expense budget** allots selling costs among salespeople, products, customers, and geographic areas for a given period. It is usually tied to a sales forecast and relates selling tasks to sales goals. It should be somewhat flexible in case expected sales are not reached or are exceeded.

These items should be covered in a budget: sales forecasts, overhead (manager's compensation, office costs), sales-force compensation, sales expenses (travel, lodging, meals, entertainment), sales meetings, selling aids (including computer equipment), and sales management (employee selection and training) costs. Table 12-7 shows a budget for a small maker of business machinery.

The budget will be larger if customers are geographically dispersed and a lot of travel is required. Complex products need costly, time-consuming sales presenta-

*A* **sales-expense budget** *assigns spending for a specific time.*

**TABLE 12-7**

**A Sales-Expense Budget for a Small Manufacturer Specializing in Business Machinery, 1997**

| ITEM | ESTIMATED ANNUAL COSTS (REVENUES) |
|---|---|
| Sales forecast | $1 950 000 |
| Overhead (1 sales manager, 1 office) | $   100 000 |
| Sales-force compensation (2 salespeople) | 90 000 |
| Sales expenses | 40 000 |
| Sales meetings | 5 000 |
| Selling aids | 15 000 |
| Sales management costs | 10 000 |
| Total personal selling budget | $   260 000 |
| Personal selling costs as a percentage of sales forecast | 13.3 |

tions and result in fewer calls per salesperson. An expanding sales force needs expenditures for recruiting and training salespeople.

## Determining the Type(s) of Sales Positions

Salespeople can be broadly classed as order takers, order getters, or support personnel. Some firms employ one type of salesperson, others a combination.

*An **order taker** handles routine orders and sells items that are pre-sold.*

An **order taker** processes routine orders and reorders. This person is involved more with clerical than creative selling, typically for pre-sold goods or services. He or she arranges displays, restocks items, answers simple questions, writes up orders, and completes transactions. He or she may work in a warehouse (manufacturer clerk) or store (retail clerk) or call on customers (a field salesperson). An order taker has these advantages: compensation is rather low, little training is required, both selling and nonselling tasks are performed, and a sales force can be expanded or contracted quickly. However, an order taker is improper for goods and services that need creative selling, or where extensive information must be available for customers. Personnel turnover is high and enthusiasm may be limited due to the low salary and routine tasks.

*An **order getter** obtains leads, provides information, persuades customers, and closes sales.*

An **order getter** generates customer leads, provides information, persuades customers, and closes sales. He or she is the creative salesperson used for high-priced, complex, and/or new products. There is less emphasis on clerical work. The person may be inside (jewellery store salesperson) or outside (photocopier salesperson).[29] He or she is expert and enthusiastic, expands sales, and can convince undecided customers to buy or decided customers to add peripheral items—such as carpeting and appliances along with a newly built house. Yet, for many people, the order getter has a high-pressure image. He or she may also need expensive training. Such nonsales tasks as writing reports may be avoided because they take away from a seller's time with customers and are seldom rewarded. Compensation can be very high for salespersons who are effective order getters. Figure 12-12 contrasts order takers and order getters.

**Missionary salespersons, sales engineers, *and* service salespersons *are support personnel.***

Support personnel supplement a sales force. A **missionary salesperson** gives out information on new goods or services. He or she does not close sales but describes items' attributes, answers questions, and leaves written matter. This paves the way for later sales and is commonly used with prescription drugs. A **sales engineer**

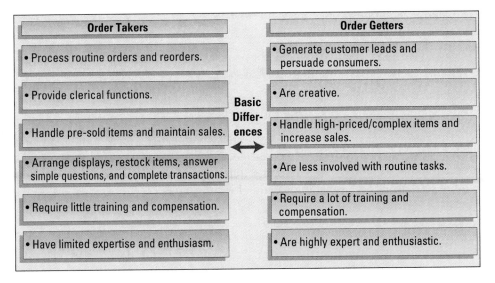

| Order Takers | Basic Differences | Order Getters |
|---|---|---|
| • Process routine orders and reorders. | | • Generate customer leads and persuade consumers. |
| • Provide clerical functions. | ⟷ | • Are creative. |
| • Handle pre-sold items and maintain sales. | | • Handle high-priced/complex items and increase sales. |
| • Arrange displays, restock items, answer simple questions, and complete transactions. | | • Are less involved with routine tasks. |
| • Require little training and compensation. | | • Require a lot of training and compensation. |
| • Have limited expertise and enthusiasm. | | • Are highly expert and enthusiastic. |

**FIGURE 12-12**

**Contrasting Order Takers and Order Getters**

accompanies an order getter if a very technical or complex item is involved. He or she discusses specifications and long-range uses, while the order getter makes customer contacts and closes sales. A **service salesperson** ordinarily deals with customers after sales. Delivery, installation, and other follow-up tasks are done.

## Selecting a Sales Technique

The two basic techniques for selling are the canned sales presentation and the need-satisfaction approach. The **canned sales presentation** is a memorized, repetitive presentation given to all customers interested in a given item. It does not adapt to customer needs or traits but presumes a general presentation will appeal to everyone. Although criticized for its inflexibility and nonmarketing orientation, it does have some value:

> Inexperienced salespeople who are lacking in selling instinct and confidence will benefit from the professionalism, anticipation of questions and objections, and other fail-safe mechanisms often inherent in a company-prepared, memorized, audiovisual or flip-chart presentation. Consequently, this method should be considered when qualified new salespeople are scarce and when brevity of training is essential.[30]

The **need-satisfaction approach** is a high-level selling method based on the principle that each customer has different attributes and wants, and therefore the sales presentation should be adapted to the individual consumer. With this technique, a salesperson first asks such questions of the consumer as: What type of product are you looking for? Have you ever purchased this product before? What price range are you considering? Then the sales presentation is more responsive to the particular person; and a new shopper is treated quite differently from an experienced one. The need-satisfaction approach is more popular and customer-oriented; however, it requires better training and skilled sales personnel. This approach includes:

- Using the buyer-seller dyad to generate two-way respect.
- Listening well.
- Making presentations based on a good grasp of the facts.
- Spending time on pre-sales research ("homework").
- Being punctual for appointments (and willing to leave when the allotted time is over).
- Allowing the customer to talk.

*The* **canned sales presentation** *is memorized and nonadaptive.*

*The* **need-satisfaction approach** *adapts to individual consumers.*

- Offering "solutions," not goods and services.
- Showing competence.
- Acknowledging if a question cannot be answered, but getting back to the customer immediately with the correct answer.
- Not wasting a prospect's time.
- Providing superior service after the sale.[31]

The canned sales presentation works best with inexpensive, routine items that are heavily advertised and relatively pre-sold. The need-satisfaction approach works best with more expensive, more complex items that have moderate advertising and require substantial additional information for consumers.

## Outlining Sales Tasks

*The* **selling process** *consists of seven steps.*

The tasks to be performed by the personal sales force need to be outlined. The **selling process** consists of prospecting for leads, approaching customers, determining consumer wants, giving a sales presentation, handling objections, closing the sale, and following up. See Figure 12-13.

**Prospecting** *creates customer leads.*

Outside selling requires a procedure, known as **prospecting**, to generate a list of customer leads. Blind prospecting uses phone directories and other general listings of potential customers; a small percentage of those contacted will be interested in a firm's offering. Lead prospecting depends on past customers and others for referrals; thus, a greater percentage of people will be interested because of the referral from someone they know. Inside selling does not involve prospecting because customers have already been drawn to a store or office through ads or prior purchase experience.

*The pre-approach and greeting are part of* **approaching customers.**

**Approaching customers** is a two-stage procedure: pre-approach and greeting. During pre-approach, a salesperson tries to get information about the customer from the firm's database, census materials, and/or other secondary data—as well as from referrals. The salesperson is then better equipped to interact with that customer. Inside retail salespeople may be unable to use a pre-approach; they often know nothing about a consumer until he or she enters the store. During the greeting, a salesperson begins a conversation. The intention is to put the customer at ease and build rapport.

The next step is to ascertain customer wants by asking the person a variety of questions regarding past experience, price, product features, intended uses, and the kinds of information still needed.

*The* **sales presentation** *converts an uncertain consumer.*

The **sales presentation** includes a verbal description of a product, its benefits, options and models, price, associated services like delivery and warranty, and a demonstration (if needed). A canned sales presentation or need-satisfaction method may be used. The purpose of a sales presentation is to convert an undecided consumer into a purchaser.

After a presentation, the salesperson usually must handle objections from the consumer. Objections are of two kinds: the first kind request more information; the second kind raise issues that must be settled before a sale is made.

**FIGURE 12-13**
**The Selling Process**

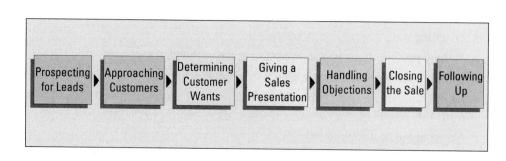

Once any objections have been settled, a salesperson is ready for **closing the sale**. This means getting a person to agree to a purchase. The salesperson must be sure no major objections remain before trying to close a sale. In addition, a salesperson must not argue with a consumer.

*The **closing** clinches a sale.*

The Canadian Professional Sales Association suggests the four following closing techniques:

- **Direct approach**—Asking directly for the order is most effective where a strong presentation has generated positive prospect response. Some sales representatives find it valuable to soften the wording: "Can I write that up now, Joan?"

- **Assumption method**—This indirect closing method requires a confident assumption that the prospect will buy: "As soon as we get the paperwork out of the way, your truck will be on its way from the factory."

- **Alternative-choice closing**—This works well where a prospect can be given two purchase alternatives: "Would you like the compact or the family size order?"

- **Personal recommendation**—Nothing is as powerful as the personal recommendation from someone the prospect trusts. This points out the importance of creating the closest possible rapport with the prospect so that he or she values your recommendation.[32]

For a large purchase, the salesperson should follow up after the sale to make sure the customer is pleased. Doing so achieves three goals: the customer is better satisfied; referrals are stimulated; and, repurchases are more likely. "Relationship selling is not about getting an order; it is about convincing customers that you will be there after an order, no matter what. Relationships are based on doing what is right, not doing what you can get away with."[33]

Besides the tasks in the selling process, a firm must clearly enumerate the nonselling tasks it wants sales personnel to perform. Among the nonselling tasks that may be assigned are setting up displays, writing up information sheets, marking prices on products, checking competitors' strategies, doing test-marketing analysis and consumer surveys, and training new employees.

## Applying the Plan

**Sales management**—planning, implementing, and controlling the personal sales function—should be used in applying a personal selling plan. Sales management covers employee selection, training, territory allocation, compensation, and supervision.

*Sales management tasks range from employee selection to supervision.*

In selecting sales personnel, a combination of personal attributes should be assessed: mental (intelligence, ability to plan), physical (appearance, speaking ability), experiential (education, sales/business background), environmental (group memberships, social influences), personality (ambition, enthusiasm, tact, resourcefulness, stability), and willingness to be trained and to follow instructions.[34] Contrary to earlier beliefs, it is now pretty much accepted that good salespeople are not necessarily born; they are carefully selected and trained: "How would you describe the ideal salesperson? Extroverted, aggressive? Quick to develop a rapport? A good sense of humour, a competitive spirit, charisma? This has been a popular stereotype, to be sure, and no doubt there are some excellent sales professionals out there who actually do possess these qualities. On the other hand, it's also a popular misconception. The truth is, these factors aren't always the most important ones to consider when selecting and training top salespeople."[35]

The traits of potential salespeople must be compatible with the customers with whom they will interact and the requirements of the good or service being sold. The buyer-seller dyad operates better when there are some similarities in salesperson and customer characteristics. And certain product categories require much different education, technical training, and sales activities than others (such as jewellery versus computer sales).

Once these factors are studied, the firm would develop a formal selection procedure that specifies the personal attributes sought, sources of employees (such as colleges and employment agencies), and methods for selection (such as interviews and testing). It would be based on the firm's overall selling plan.

Salesperson training may take one or a combination of forms. A formal program uses a trainer, a classroom setting, lectures, and printed materials. It may also include role playing (in which trainees act out parts) and case analysis. Field trips take trainees out on actual calls so they can observe skilled salespeople in action. On-the-job training places trainees in their own selling situations under the close supervision of the trainer or a senior salesperson. Training often covers a range of topics; it should teach selling skills and include information on the firm and its offerings, the industry, and employee duties. At Caterpillar (the industrial and farm equipment manufacturer), "We train our sales force to understand why our customers buy our products, what their needs are, the importance of follow-up, the need to let a customer vent his/her anger, and how to help a customer resolve problems without passing the responsibility on to someone else in the company."[36] Besides initial training, continuous training or retraining of sales personnel may teach new techniques, explain new products, or improve performance.

*A **sales territory** contains the area, customers, and/or products assigned to a salesperson.*

Territory size and salesperson allocation are decided next. A **sales territory** consists of the geographic area, customers, and/or product lines assigned to a salesperson. If territories are assigned by customer type or product category, two or more salespeople may cover the same geographic area. Territory size depends on customer locations, order size, travel time and expenses, the time per sales call, the yearly visits for each account, and the amount of hours per year each salesperson has for selling tasks. The mix of established versus new customer accounts must also be considered. Allocating salespeople to specific territories depends on their ability, the buyer-seller dyad, the mix of selling and nonselling functions (such as one salesperson training new employees), and seniority. Proper territory size and allocation provide adequate coverage of customers, minimize territory overlap, recognize geographic boundaries, minimize travel expenses, encourage solicitation of new accounts, provide enough sales potential for good salespeople to be well rewarded, and are fair to the whole sales force.

*Sales compensation may be **straight salary**, **straight commission**, or a **combination** of the two.*

Salespeople can be compensated by straight salary, straight commission, or a combination of salary and commission or bonus. With a **straight salary plan**, a salesperson is paid a flat amount per time period. Earnings are not tied to sales. The advantages are that both selling and nonselling tasks can be specified and controlled, salespeople have security, and expenses are known in advance. The disadvantages are the low incentive to increase sales, expenses not being tied to productivity, and the continuing costs even if there are low sales. Order takers are usually paid straight salaries.

With a **straight commission plan**, a salesperson's earnings are directly related to sales, profits, customer satisfaction, or some other type of performance. The commission rate is often keyed to a quota, which is a productivity standard. The advantages of this plan are the motivated salespeople, the elimination of fixed sales compensation costs, and the fact that expenses are tied to productivity. The disadvantages are the firm's lack of control over nonselling tasks, the instability of a firm's expenses, and salesperson risks due to variable pay. Insurance, real estate, and direct-selling order getters often earn straight commissions. Typically, Canadian real estate salespersons receive a 6 per cent commission of $9000 for selling a $150 000 house.

To gain the advantages of both salary- and commission-oriented methods, many firms use elements of each in a **combination compensation plan**. Such plans balance company control, flexibility, and employee incentives; and some award bonuses for

## TECHNOLOGY AND MARKETING

### Technology and the Sales Force: Replacing People with People

Since the industrial revolution in the mid-1800s workers have had a constant fear that technology in the form of new machines would replace people in their jobs. Technology is still replacing people with machines but, in a related phenomenon, it's also replacing people with other people.

Employment for salespeople whose duties involve primarily order taking is virtually at an end as a result of technology. Just ask any former representative of Gerber baby food in the U.S. In January 1998, Gerber dismissed its entire U.S. sales force of 389 people, replacing them with food brokers who handle a lot of their ordering via electronic data interchange. Since the cost of having a field sales force is very high, unless their functions specifically require personal selling interchanges they can be replaced with intermediaries and electronic interaction.

As for technology replacing people with people, new technology is causing a battle of the generations in the business world. Younger people are more attuned to and more prepared to embrace new technology. They're also more experienced with the need to adapt to rapid change. As a result, a large number of firms have recently been replacing older people with younger people. (Younger people also work for less money.) So it's no surprise that personal selling is a prime area where marketers want people who are young, have lots of energy, and a gift for handling technology.

Today's travelling salesperson has to be a technological wizard—and virtually all these wizards are under forty years old. A modern salesperson comes equipped with a cellular phone and a notebook computer, which is loaded with software designed for sales territory management, has electronic data interchange capabilities, and can be linked to a network through any available phone jack or with cellular service (less reliable). A modern salesperson, in short, is the epitome of efficiency; there's no downtime during travelling. Phone calls are made from cars, trains, and aircrafts. Reports and presentations are composed on a notebook computer while travelling via public transit; and orders and customer information are transmitted to head office. Meanwhile support from sales management is instantaneous, with updates on the market sent to the salesperson daily, if not several times a day.

Sales managers have found that convincing older salespeople to adapt is a lot more difficult than hiring younger salespeople. It may well be said that being a salesperson is a game for the young, but the truth is that it's a game for the energetic, for the progressive learner, and for the person who really understands people.

Develop a list of characteristics and skills that a good salesperson must possess. Discuss whether these are likely to be age-related, and if so, whether they're related to younger or older people.

Source: Based on Nina Munk, "Finished at Forty," *Fortune* (February 1, 1999), pp. 50–66.

---

superior individual or company performance. All types of order getters work on a combination basis. According to various studies, about two-thirds of North American firms compensate sales personnel via some form of combination plan, one-fifth use a straight salary plan, and the rest use straight commissions. Smaller firms are more apt to use a straight salary plan and less apt to use a combination plan.

Supervision encompasses four aspects of sales management:

1. Sales personnel must be motivated. Their motivation depends on such factors as the clarity of the job (what tasks must be performed), the salesperson's desire to achieve, the variety of tasks performed, the incentives for undertaking each task, the style of the sales manager, flexibility, and recognition.

*Supervision involves motivation, performance measures, nonselling tasks, and behaviour modification.*

# MARKETING IN THE THIRD MILLENNIUM

## Preparing for the Future of Personal Selling

Salespeople have to adapt to a volatile business environment that seems to change on a daily basis. Maintaining an edge on competition is much more difficult than ever before, and this means keeping an eye on what the future may bring. Dr. Matthew Kiernan, Chairman of Innovest Group International, recently spoke at the Canadian Professional Sales Association's annual conference. Here's the advice he gave on how to prepare for the future in personal selling:

- Don't play by the dominant competitive rules of your industry; invent your own and make others follow you.
- Get innovative, or get dead. If you don't innovate constantly, one of your competitors will.
- Re-examine your company for hidden strategic assets, then leverage the hell out of them.
- Create a bias for speed and action in your company.
- Be entrepreneurial, pro-active, and experimental. These days, the riskiest approach of all is to do nothing.
- Break barriers, both inside and outside your company.
- Use all of your people, all of their skills, all of the time.
- Globalize your perspective and knowledge base.
- Understand and leverage the power of the eco-industrial revolution. Environmental considerations are rapidly becoming key competitive factors.
- Turn organizational learning into a corporate religion.
- Develop strategic performance measurement tools. There's no point in trying to measure progress in your twenty-first century company using archaic nineteenth century tools.[42]

2. Performance must be measured. To do this, achievements must be gauged against such goals as sales and calls per day. The analysis should take into account territory size, travel time, and experience. The failure of a salesperson is often related to poor listening skills, a lack of concentration on priorities, a lack of effort, the inability to determine customer needs, a lack of planning for presentations, overpromising on product performance, and inadequate knowledge.

3. The sales manager must ensure that all nonselling tasks are completed, even if sales personnel are not rewarded for them.

4. If a salesperson's performance does not meet expectations, then some action may be needed to modify behaviour.[37]

In sales management, these key factors should also be taken into account: the evolving role of women in selling and the special nature of selling in foreign markets.

One of the major changes in industrial sales forces over the last twenty years is "the accelerated recruitment of women into traditionally male-dominated sales positions."[38] According to Statistics Canada,[39] women hold 46 per cent of the sales positions in Canada and industry observers expect that even more women will be recruited into sales forces in the future. Two researchers have noted:

> Sales managers do not have to provide special considerations or training programs for female salespersons to facilitate their socialization into the industrial sales force. Consequently, sales managers should not be concerned with incurring additional training expenses for females, nor do they need to behave more solicitously in their management practices toward women than men. To do otherwise will probably result in the demotivation of male salespersons, and will probably handicap females by intimating that they are deficient in some way and require additional assistance. Instead, sales managers should include women equally in all sales training, motivation, and socialization activities, just as these opportunities are extended to men.[40]

When firms go international, "they are faced with the task of establishing and managing sales forces in foreign markets. Once in place, they must decide how much home-office influence to exert on subsidiary sales policies. When faced with the diversity of the international marketplace, top marketing management is often uncertain about how much it should influence its overseas sales forces. Management benefits from knowing which sales decisions are suited to home-office input and, just as important, which are not."[41] In particular, the attributes of salespeople; salesperson training, compensation, and supervision; the dynamics of the buyer-seller dyad; and the selling process may need to be tailored to different foreign markets. For example, in many Arab countries, negotiations—particularly bargaining—are viewed as an enjoyable activity or even as a social event. Foreign salespeople need to respect the religious traditions of their Arab customers and recognize that Arab personnel may not be available at all times. In addition, they are known to refrain from saying "no" and to engage in contract renegotiations if the need arises. Arabs end negotiations by orally committing themselves, rather than doing so in writing.

# SUMMARY

**1.** *To define promotion planning and show its importance* Promotion involves any communication that informs, persuades, and/or reminds people about an organization's or individual's goods, services, ideas, community involvement, or impact on society. Promotion planning is systematic and relates to all aspects of communication.

Promotion efforts are needed for both new products and existing ones. The audience for promotion may be consumers, shareholders, consumer advocacy groups, government, channel members, employees, competitors, and the public. With word-of-mouth communication, people express opinions and product-related experiences to one another. A firm may communicate its image, views on ideas, community involvement, or impact on society—as well as persuade people to buy. Good promotion enhances the other elements of the marketing mix. Promotion is a major activity around the world.

**2.** *To describe the general characteristics of advertising, public relations, personal selling, and sales promotion* Advertising is paid, nonpersonal communication transmitted through various media by organiza-

tions and individuals who are in some way identified as the sponsor. Public relations includes any communication (paid or nonpaid, nonpersonal or personal, sponsored by a firm or reported by an independent medium) designed to foster a favourable image. Publicity is the nonpaid, nonpersonal, nonsponsored form of public relations. Personal selling involves oral communication with one or more prospective buyers by paid representatives for the purpose of making sales. Sales promotion involves paid marketing activities to stimulate consumer purchases and dealers.

**3.** *To explain the channel of communication and how it functions* A source sends a message to its audience through a channel of communication. A channel consists of a source, encoding, the message, the medium, decoding, the audience, feedback, and noise.

A source is a company, an independent institution, or an opinion leader that seeks to present a message to an audience. Encoding is the process by which a thought or an idea is translated into a message by the source. A message is a combination of words and symbols transmitted to the audience. A

medium is a personal or nonpersonal channel used to convey a message. Decoding is the process by which a message sent by a source is translated by the audience. The audience is the object of a source's message. Feedback is the response the audience makes to a message: purchase, attitude change, or nonpurchase. Noise is interference at any stage.

**4.** *To examine the components of a promotion plan, international promotion considerations, the legal environment, and criticisms and defences of promotion* Promotion goals may be demand- or image-oriented. Demand goals should correspond to the hierarchy-of-effects model, moving a consumer from awareness to purchase. Primary demand is total consumer demand for a product category; selective demand refers to consumer interest in a particular brand. Institutional advertising is used to enhance company image.

Five ways to set a promotion budget are: all you can afford (the weakest method), incremental, competitive parity, percentage of sales, and objective and task (the best method). Marginal return should be considered when budgeting.

A promotion mix is the overall and specific communication program of a firm, including its use of advertising, public relations (publicity), personal selling, and/or sales promotion. The mix can be well-rounded through integrated marketing communications. Many factors need to be considered in developing a promotion mix.

When devising an international promotion plan, the channel of communication, promotion goals, budgeting, and promotion mix should be studied for and applied to each market.

There are many laws and rules affecting promotion. The major ways to guard against undesirable promotion are full disclosure, substantiation, cease-and-desist orders, corrective advertising, and fines.

Critics are strong in their complaints about promotion practices and their effects. Marketers are equally firm in their defences.

**5.** *To examine the scope, importance, and characteristics of personal selling* Personal selling involves oral communication with one or more prospective buyers by paid representatives for the purpose of making sales. About 3.6 million Canadians work in sales and service jobs; millions more work in sales jobs throughout the world. Yet these numbers understate the value of personal selling because every contact between a company employee and a customer involves some degree of selling.

Selling is emphasized with high-volume clients, geographically concentrated customers, expensive and/or complex products, customers wanting sales services, and entries into foreign markets. Selling also handles objections and addresses other issues. Selling costs are higher than advertising costs at many firms. An average business-to-business sales call costs several hundred dollars. Thus, efficiency is important.

Selling fosters a buyer-seller dyad (a two-way communication flow), offers flexibility and adaptability, adds to relationships with customers, results in less audience waste, clinches sales, and provides immediate feedback. Yet, personal selling can handle only a limited number of customers, is rather ineffective for creating consumer awareness, has high costs per customer, and has a poor image for some consumers.

**6.** *To study the elements in a personal selling plan* A selling plan has seven steps: setting goals—demand- and/or image-related; assigning responsibility—to one manager or to several managers; setting a budget; choosing the type(s) of sales positions—order takers, order getters, and/or support salespeople; selecting a sales technique—the canned sales presentation or the need-satisfaction approach; outlining tasks—including each of the relevant steps in the selling process and nonselling tasks; and applying the plan—which centres on sales management.

# KEY TERMS

promotion (p. 365)

promotion planning (p. 365)

word-of-mouth communication (p. 365)

advertising (p. 368)

public relations (p. 368)

publicity (p. 368)

personal selling (p. 368)

sales promotion (p. 369)

channel of communication (communication process) (p. 369)

source (p. 369)

encoding (p. 370)

message (p. 371)

comparative messages (p. 372)

massed promotion (p. 373)

distributed promotion (p. 373)

wearout rate (p. 373)

medium (p. 373)

decoding (p. 374)

subliminal advertising (p. 374)

audience (p. 375)

feedback (p. 375)

noise (p. 376)

hierarchy-of-effects model (p. 376)

primary demand (p. 376)

selective demand (p. 376)

institutional advertising (p. 376)

all-you-can-afford method (p. 377)

incremental method (p. 377)

competitive parity method (p. 377)

percentage-of-sales method (p. 378)

objective-and-task method (p. 378)

marginal return (p. 378)

promotion mix (p. 379)

integrated marketing communications (IMC) (p. 379)

full disclosure (p. 381)

substantiation (p. 382)

cease-and-desist order (p. 382)

corrective advertising (p. 382)

fines (p. 382)

telemarketing (p. 386)

**buyer-seller dyad** (p. 386)

**sales-expense budget** (p. 389)

**order taker** (p. 390)

**order getter** (p. 390)

**missionary salesperson** (p. 390)

**sales engineer** (p. 390)

**service salesperson** (p. 391)

**canned sales presentation** (p. 391)

**need-satisfaction approach** (p. 391)

**selling process** (p. 392)

**prospecting** (p. 392)

**approaching customers** (p. 392)

**sales presentation** (p. 392)

**closing the sale** (p. 393)

**sales management** (p. 393)

**sales territory** (p. 394)

**straight salary plan** (p. 394)

**straight commission plan** (p. 394)

**combination compensation plan** (p. 394)

## REVIEW QUESTIONS

1. Why is promotion planning important?
2. Distinguish among advertising, public relations, personal selling, and sales promotion.
3. What is the role of an opinion leader in a channel of communication?
4. Explain the hierarchy-of-effects model. How is it related to demand objectives?
5. Describe each of the methods of promotional budgeting.
6. State the basic criticisms and defences of promotion.
7. Statistics Canada lists 3.6 million people in sales and service positions in Canada. Why does this figure understate the importance of personal selling?
8. Under what circumstances should personal selling be emphasized? Why?
9. Distinguish among order-taker, order-getter, and support sales personnel.
10. When is a canned sales presentation appropriate? When is it inappropriate?

## DISCUSSION QUESTIONS

1. What are the advantages and disadvantages of changing messages (themes) infrequently?
2. As the marketing manager for a small Canadian-based Portuguese book publisher that is entering the Brazilian market for the first time, devise a promotion budget relying on the objective-and-task method.
3. Develop a promotion mix for:
   a. A global restaurant chain.
   b. A small janitorial service.
   c. A four-person dental practice.
   d. A medium-sized sporting-goods manufacturer.
4. Comment on this statement: "Although its role may differ, telemarketing may be successfully used during the selling process for any type of good or service."
5. How would you handle these objections raised at the end of a sales presentation?
   a. "I saw the price of the same item at a competing store for 10 per cent less than what you are asking."
   b. "Your warranty period is much too short."
   c. "None of the alternatives you showed me is satisfactory."

## CASE STUDY
# Super Selling

Craig Procter is an agent who sells housing for the RE/MAX real estate firm in Newmarket, a city of 50 000 people in the suburbs of Toronto. He represents an excellent example of what it takes to be a top-performing salesperson. In a typical year Craig is responsible for the sale of 200 homes, while most real estate agents average about ten. It's been said that a great salesperson is someone "who could sell ice cubes in the Arctic." This refers of course to the power of persuasion, but within the larger context of marketing, a great salesperson is also someone who helps customers buy. Craig Procter does both.

Real estate agents require an all-out marketing effort in order to make sales. Their task is twofold, in that they must create both ends of a transaction by finding both sellers and buyers and bringing them together. Finding people who wish to sell their homes is called getting a "listing." Sellers agree to pay their agent a commission, customarily about 6 per cent of the selling price, although it can be negotiated (it's usually no less than 3 per cent). Once the agent has acquired a listing he or she markets the home and needs to find buyers. There's an informal agreement in the real estate industry whereby an agent who finds a buyer for a home listed by another agent will normally split the commission with that agent. The customers' needs are served, since the agent is encouraged to help them find a home that's suited to them, and not necessarily one that the agent has listed. Still, an inherent conflict of interest exists in that the agent is ultimately paid by the seller from the proceeds of a sale. In this regard the listing agent ultimately acts in his or her own interest and the interests of the seller, not the buyer.

The task of finding sellers and buyers and bringing them together means that Craig Procter must get his name in the public eye in Newmarket. He spends about $250 000 a year to promote himself using billboards, bus shelters, bus stop benches, and special promotional materials like key chains, pens, pencils, business cards, and even plastic milk jugs! Craig has introduced the idea of a toll-free line so that people in Newmarket can call people in Toronto for free—after listening to his sales pitch. It costs Craig about $40 000 a year, but the line has handled millions of calls.

These techniques create awareness for Craig's name and link him with real estate, which helps when his own team of cold callers go out knocking on doors or phoning people in Newmarket to see if they want to sell their homes—and to do it through Craig.

Craig realizes that word-of-mouth is important to his image. He's got to do a good job for his customers, who will then tell other customers. So he does everything he can to help the customers sell their home. For starters, he has customer service agents who contact sellers and let them know how their homes are being perceived by potential buyers. In this way the sellers can make changes by sprucing up their home a little bit so that it will show better. Craig has a team of people on his payroll (including associate agents) who do the basic tasks, freeing Craig's time to sign up new listings and to present offers. Essentially, Craig closes the sales. His reward: $1.2 million in commissions earned; after expenses, he takes home $150 000.

Craig also knows he has to stay ahead of his competition. His success isn't easy to hide, especially since his promotion brags about how good a salesperson he is! So Craig is parlaying competitive interest into cash by taking a fee of $1000 a week from other real estate agents who travel with him to study his operation. Craig offers these guidelines to these and other aspiring salespeople: 1) Don't waste your time. Be organized. Understand your prospects. Customers may be unrealistic in what they want. If you can't help them, move on. 2) Stay in touch with customers. Send them letters. Make phone calls. Maintain your relationship before, during, and after a sale. 3) Practise self marketing. Get your name out.

## Questions

1. Craig Procter demonstrates that advertising and personal selling aren't the only promotional elements used in real estate sales. Discuss the roles of the other elements of a promotion mix. Calculate a "cost per thousand" for Craig's free phone line, based on the information in the case and the assumption that the line has been running for one year. Research the reach, frequency, and advertising costs for some local newspapers, television, and magazines. How would you rate Craig's phone line as an advertising medium in comparison to these?

2. Successful real estate agents will often make two sales for every house sold. Discuss this statement within the context of the stages of the personal selling process and the nature of real estate transactions.

3. Identify the stage in the selling process that you think would be most difficult for a new real estate agent to manage. Identify what the difficulties would be and then suggest some approaches you think would help a new agent deal with them.

4. Develop two sales presentations that Craig Procter could use to acquire new listings of resale homes for his real estate firm.

**RE/MAX**
www.remax.ca/

Sources: The data in this case are drawn from George Vasic, "Today's Millstones, Tomorrow's Castles," *Canadian Business* (August 1995), p. 87; Andrea Haman, "RE/MAX Ads Aim to Lure First-Time Buyers," *Marketing Magazine* (July 24, 1995), p. 4; and "Top Seller," CBC *Venture* Video 492.

## CASE STUDY

# Intuit and Intel: Dealing with Negative Publicity

When a California sculptor found a serious error in MacIn-Tax, the version of TurboTax software for Apple Macintosh users, he complained to Intuit (the software's developer). After the firm brushed off the complaint, the sculptor took his story to the *San Francisco Chronicle*.

Right after the newspaper story appeared Scott D. Cook, Intuit's chairman, admitted the firm's tax software had a number of errors that could produce inaccurate calculations. Intuit offered to replace the diskettes of all 1.7 million MacIn-Tax customers, even though the calculation errors affected less than one per cent of them. Those consumers desiring to quickly correct their software were given the opportunity to download the corrected version from commercial online services. Along with the replacement software, Cook sent an apology letter to registered users. Intuit also complied with consumer requests for refunds.

According to experts, errors in tax packages are inevitable due to the short time a firm has to adapt its software to the latest changes in tax legislation. In total, only 75 000 of Intuit's 1.4 million registered users requested the new diskette, and only about 3000 consumers downloaded the corrected program from online services.

Intuit's reaction is directly attributable to the business philosophy of Scott D. Cook, the firm's chairperson. Clearly, Cook looks at the business for Intuit from a long-term perspective. Cook believes that Intuit needs to maintain a long-term relationship with its customers, especially in relation to the sales of tax packages that must be updated almost every year. Any other reaction on the part of Intuit to the negative publicity might have permanently damaged its relationship with its existing customers and this would have had far greater consequences in the long term than the costs involved in the immediate recall.

Intuit's handling of its problem was in sharp contrast to Intel's reaction to the flawed Pentium chip, which generated division errors in complex mathematical calculations. The flaw was discovered in November 1994, and only after weeks of pressure from final and intermediate customers (including IBM and Gateway 2000) did Intel offered to replace the flawed chips. At first it asked customers to prove they were affected by the flaw. The firm also took the position that errors would occur in only one of 9 billion calculations. Furthermore, Intel knowingly sent defective chips to customers prior to correcting the problem, instead of immediately stopping production.

Intel was berated in an almost endless stream of negative TV, newspaper, and Internet reports. Then, on December 12, 1994, IBM announced it was temporarily stopping the sale of Pentium-based computers (based on IBM's estimate that errors could occur as frequently as once every twenty-four days for heavy users). IBM also pledged to replace defective Pentium chips free of charge. Soon thereafter, other PC manufacturers agreed to "no questions asked" free replacements.

Eventually Intel capitulated. As Andrew Grove, Intel's chief executive officer said then, "We got caught between our mindset, which is a fact-based, analysis-based engineer's mindset, and the customers' mindset, which is not so much emotional but accustomed to making their own choice. I think the kernel of the issue we missed was that we presumed to tell somebody what they should or shouldn't worry about, or should or shouldn't do."

Although Intel will not disclose actual numbers, analysts estimate the total Pentium chip return rate was less than 10 per cent, compared with initial estimates of about 25 per cent. Market analysts estimated that half of corporate users and 10 per cent of final consumers would ask for replacement chips, whereas the actual replacement rate was 25 per cent for corporate users and between 1 and 3 per cent for final consumers.

Some marketing experts say the high initial customer outcry, followed by such a low return rate, was a sign that people were more concerned with Intel's attitude than with the actual defect.

## Questions

1. Develop appropriate public relations objectives for both Intuit and Intel in handling their product recalls.
2. Why do you think Intuit acted so much more quickly than Intel to recall its defective product?
3. Do you think the barrage of media criticism that Intel faced was fair? Explain your answer.
4. How can Intel ensure that a similar situation of negative publicity doesn't happen again? Recommend a process for the firm to follow to handle negative publicity.

**INTEL**
www.intel.com/

**INTUIT**
www.intuit.com

Sources: The data in this case are drawn from Jim Carlton and Stephen Kreider Yoder, "Humble Pie: Intel to Replace Its Pentium Chips," *Wall Street Journal* (December 21, 1994), pp. B1, B6; Dean Foust, "Good Instincts and Intuit," *Business Week* (March 27, 1995), p. 46; and G. Christian Hill, "Despite Furor, Most Keep Their Pentium Chips," *Wall Street Journal* (April 13, 1995), pp. B1–B2.

# CHAPTER | 13

# Advertising, Public Relations, and Sales Promotion

*Chapter Objectives*

1. To examine the scope, importance, and characteristics of advertising

2. To study the elements in an advertising plan

3. To examine the scope, importance, and characteristics of public relations

4. To study the elements in a public relations plan

5. To examine the scope, importance, and characteristics of sales promotion

6. To study the elements in a sales promotion plan

*Dick Hemingway*

**OLIVER JEWELLERY**
www.keithn.com/oliver/

The fundamental purpose of promotion is to remind, inform, and persuade people. And if it takes outrageous, wacky, cheesy ads to do it, so be it. No matter where you live these days it seems you can't avoid advertising from local retailers that is, to put it bluntly, terrible. Are these retailers as crazy as they appear? Yes—crazy like a fox, that is.

Consider the advertising by Russell Oliver of Oliver Jewellery in Toronto. He dresses up in blue tights and a red cape and presents himself as "Cashman." Cashman he may be, but with his portly frame, balding head, and spectacles, any attempt to emulate Superman is quickly put aside. His television spots are basically all the same. Oliver stands in front of the camera and waves wads of $20 and $50 bills while he says as loudly and emphatically as possible, "I'm Russell Oliver, and I buy your old, used jewellery for my cash! I pay big bucks for your Rolex, Cartier, and Patek watches!" Oliver then ends the commercial message the way he ends all his commercials, with the tag line "Ohhh, yeahhh!"

"Ohhh, yeahhh!" is what Oliver says now that his store's sales have quadrupled to $4 million a year. Before "Cashman" the firm's marketing mix consisted of a Yellow Pages ad, some small newspaper ads, and transit-bench signs. Oliver decided to try commercials on low-cost, late-night TV. Even in Toronto, thirty-second TV spots during late-night hours generally cost only $200 to $300. Oliver started out with a straightforward approach and simply explained the logic of exchanging old jewellery for cash. The commercial ran a minimum of five times a night on three local stations—and customer traffic held steady, a clear indication that Oliver was wasting his money.

The media sales representatives at the TV stations, not wanting to lose a client, suggested he present something a little more memorable. Russell decided to take it from the top—or rather, over the top—and Cashman was born. Viewers generally indicate one of two feelings for the advertising: hate and contempt. But you've got to remember an ad in order to have an emotion about it. Soon after airing these commercials Oliver found himself with more customers, and they weren't just selling their jewellery, but also seeking his autograph. Oliver's response was to launch even wackier ads. For example, with a rooster perched on his shoulder, he tossed $20 bills to a flock of chickens as he shouted, "While other guys hand out chicken feed, I give cash! Ohhh, yeahhh!"

Oliver spends almost $700 000 a year on his TV advertising campaign, but according to Alan Middleton, a marketing professor at Toronto's York University, the secret of his success is paradoxical. The "primary role of any advertising is to gain awareness. And these ads really do stand out, because they're so bad they're actually great."[1]

In this chapter, we will study the advertising, public relations, and sales promotion aspects of promotion.

## Overview

*Advertising and public
relations are two of the
major forms of promotion.*

This chapter covers three promotion forms: advertising, public relations, and sales promotions. As defined in Chapter 11, advertising is paid, nonpersonal communication regarding goods, services, organizations, people, places, and ideas; it may be used by businesses, government, and other nonprofit organizations, and individuals. Its distinguishing features are that a sponsor pays for its message, a set format is sent to an entire audience through mass media, the sponsor's name is clearly presented, and the sponsor controls the message.

In contrast, public relations involves communication that fosters a favourable image for goods, services, organizations, people, places, and ideas among their various publics. Its unique features are that it is more image- than sales-oriented; it includes image-oriented advertising, personal selling, and sales promotion; and it often seeks favourable publicity for a firm. As an aspect of public relations, publicity entails nonpersonal communication that is transmitted via mass media but not paid for by an identified sponsor. The media usually control the wording and placement of publicity messages.

The distinctions between advertising and publicity are in part revealed by this statement: "Advertising is paid for, publicity is prayed for."

Sales promotion involves paid marketing communication activities (other than advertising, publicity, or personal selling) that stimulate consumers and dealers. Among the kinds of promotions classed as sales promotions are coupons, trade shows, contests and sweepstakes, and point-of-purchase displays.

The scope and importance, characteristics, and planning considerations for advertising, public relations, and sales promotions are examined in this chapter.

## The Scope and Importance of Advertising

In 1999 an estimated U.S.$235.7 billion was spent on advertising in the world's top ten advertising nations, with half that amount spent in the U.S. alone. In Canada the amount was U.S.$5.4 billion (CAN$8.3 billion).[2] Table 13-1 provides an advertising profile of Canada, the U.S., Germany, Japan, and Australia. The U.S., Germany, and Japan are profiled because they represent the largest advertising nations of the world, and are on different continents. Australia was selected because its culture, history as a British colony, and population are similar to those of Canada. The advertising profile shows the percentage of expenditures by media for TV, newspaper, magazines, radio, outdoor, and cinema. (The profiles aren't complete because they don't report the level of direct mail.) The profile provides information on specialty media infrastructure for cable TV, satellite TV, and Internet use. Finally, the profile compares the total advertising expenditures and the advertising expenditures per capita.

Some of the notable differences found in Table 13-1 are that the dominant media expenditure in Germany, Australia, and Canada is on newspapers while in the U.S. and Japan it's on TV. Newspapers rank second in Japan and the U.S. but in Germany magazines rank second, with TV a close third. Radio represents a higher proportion of media expenditure in Canada than any of the other nations, while magazines are the second highest proportion compared to the other nations. In terms of media infrastructure Canada is generally very well developed, with the highest proportion of homes wired for cable TV. It makes sense to combine the cable TV and satellite numbers to get a picture of the total TV spectrum. In this regard Germany comes out on top with 87.6 per cent of its dwellings wired; Canada is second at 81 per cent. Canada is tops in Internet availability, with the U.S. and Australia close behind.

The huge population differences among the nations make it difficult to compare expenditures on advertising, but the per capita numbers are very interesting.

## TABLE 13-1

## An Advertising Profile of Canada and Selected Nations

| MEDIA | PER CENT OF TOTAL EXPENDITURES | | | | |
|---|---|---|---|---|---|
| | *Canada* | *U.S.* | *Japan* | *Germany* | *Australia* |
| Newspapers | 39.1 | 35.8 | 27.2 | 45.5 | 42.2 |
| Television | 37.6 | 39.2 | 44.3 | 23.1 | 34.2 |
| Magazines | 17.1 | 13.0 | 9.8 | 24.2 | 11.2 |
| Radio | 12.9 | 10.2 | 5.0 | 3.3 | 7.9 |
| Outdoor | 3.1 | 1.8 | 13.7 | 3.1 | 3.7 |
| Cinema | 0.1 | — | — | 0.9 | 0.8 |

| MEDIA INFRASTRUCTURE | PER CENT OF DWELLINGS WIRED | | | | |
|---|---|---|---|---|---|
| | *Canada* | *U.S.* | *Japan* | *Germany* | *Australia* |
| Cable TV | 77.0 | 66.6 | 28.2 | 55.8 | 14.0 |
| Satellite TV | 4.0 | 8.3 | 30.1 | 315.8 | — |
| Internet | 37.0 | 33.0 | 15.7 | 8.4 | 33.0 |

**TOTAL EXPENDITURES (Billions $U.S.)**

| *Canada* | *U.S.* | *Japan* | *Germany* | *Australia* |
|---|---|---|---|---|
| 5.4 | 117.0 | 35.7 | 20.3 | 5.5 |

**AD SPENDING PER CAPITA ($US)**

| *Canada* | *U.S.* | *Japan* | *Germany* | *Australia* |
|---|---|---|---|---|
| 157 | 399 | 297 | 230 | 264 |

Source: Ad Age Database, "Top Global Markets," Advertising Age Web site, adage.com (May 1999).

Americans are the most exposed to advertising messages, while Canadians are the least (although few Canadians would likely complain about this disparity). However, Canadians are the recipients of large amounts of spillover advertising from U.S. sources, and this partially offsets the low total expenditures per capita.

The percentage of sales devoted to advertising varies by industry and firm; company advertising as a percentage of sales is very low. Typically, expenditures are less than 2 per cent of sales in 40 per cent of North American industries; 2 to 3.9 per cent of sales in 35 per cent of North American industries; and at least 4 per cent of sales in 25 per cent of North American industries. Among the leading advertisers in the world, such as Procter & Gamble which spends about U.S.$5.1 billion annually, the percentages often far exceed industry averages.[3]

An advertising emphasis is most likely if products are standardized, have easily communicated features, appeal to a large market, have low prices, are marketed through independent resellers, and/or are new. Leading brands often get large ad budgets to hold their positions. For example, Zurich Canada, a large insurance company, runs ads positioning itself with two themes: customer-focused and responsive. Zurich believes people see insurance companies as cold and impersonal and wants to change this perception for its firm. To fulfil this positioning change the firm has set up Zurich-Assist, a 24-hour help line to deliver advice and guidance to Zurich policy holders, and is advertising this fact. Zurich uses an external advertis-

*Three-quarters of North American firms spend less than 4 per cent of sales on advertising. Ads are most important for standardized products aimed at large markets.*

**ZURICH CANADA**
www.zurcan.com/

**J. WALTER THOMPSON COMPANY**
www.jwtworld.com/

ing agency and its ads are placed on television and in magazines; in addition, Zurich has paid to have its logo displayed at Maple Leaf Gardens in Toronto. Through advertising, Zurich wants to be seen as a different kind of insurance company that is there to help.[4]

As a senior executive at the J. Walter Thompson advertising agency once noted, "Advertising works on television and it works in print. What's more, it especially pays to advertise during recessions. All too often, by focusing on the bottom line, firms sacrifice the long-term, brand-building gains advertising makes possible. In our view, this is a serious mistake."[5]

Due to low-involvement purchases, consumer behaviour may be easier to change than attitudes. One ad can have a strong effect on brand awareness. By advertising, it is easier to raise people's opinions of a little-known product than a well-known one. Ad effectiveness often rises over long-term campaigns.

## The Characteristics of Advertising

On the positive side, advertising reaches a large, geographically dispersed market; in print media, circulation is supplemented by the passing of a copy from one reader to another. The costs per viewer or listener are low. For example, a single-page, four-colour magazine ad in the English edition of *Readers Digest* may cost $20 000 and reach about 1 million people—a cost of $0.02 per person (for media circulation). A broad range of media is available from national (international) television to local newspapers and even the Internet. Thus, a firm's goals and resources may be matched with the most appropriate medium.

*Advertising attracts an audience, has low per-customer costs, offers varied media, is surrounded by information, and aids selling.*

A sponsor has control over message content, graphics, timing, and size or length, as well as the audience targeted. A uniform message is sent to the whole audience. With print media, people can study and restudy messages. Editorial content (a news story or segment of a broadcast show) often borders an ad. This can raise readership or viewing/listening, enhance an image, and create the proper mood for an ad. A firm may even seek specialized media or sections of media (like a paper's sports section for a sports equipment ad).

Ads ease the way for personal selling by creating audience awareness and liking for brands. They also enable self-service wholesalers and retailers to operate, and they sustain the mail order industry. With a pulling strategy, advertising enables a firm to show its resellers that consumer demand exists.

On the negative side, because messages are standardized, they are rather inflexible and not responsive to consumer questions. This makes it hard to satisfy the needs of a diverse audience. And since many media appeal to broad audiences, a large portion of viewers or readers may be wasted for a sponsor. For instance, a single-unit health spa or a local roofing-materials firm might find that only one-fifth of a newspaper's readers live in its shopping area.

*Advertising is inflexible and can be wasteful, costly, and limit information and feedback.*

Although costs per viewer or reader are low, advertising sometimes requires high total expenditures and this may keep smaller firms from using some media. As noted earlier, a TV ad might cost only $0.02 per viewer, while one four-colour magazine page alone could cost $20 000. Also, because high costs lead to brief messages, most ads don't provide much information. TV commercials average thirty seconds or less; few are as long as one minute. And because ads are impersonal, feedback is harder to get and it may not be immediately available.

Mass media are used by many people who do not view or listen to ads. They watch TV, read print media, and so on, but ignore ads and discard direct mail. Of concern to television advertisers is "zapping," whereby a viewer uses a remote-control device to switch programs when an ad comes on.

## Media Buying in Asia: Accounting for Your Expenditures

Canadian advertisers are spoiled, and don't even know it. When they arrange to purchase advertising media they pretty much know what they are paying for. So when these advertisers go to an Asian nation like Japan they expect the same treatment; however, media development here, and in many Asian nations for that matter, lags behind that of Canada and the United States.

As recently as 1997 a scandal broke out in the Japanese advertising industry when it was discovered that a large number of TV and radio stations were billing advertisers for advertising spots that hadn't even been transmitted. In January, 1999 three executives of the Hong Kong Standard were convicted and sentenced to jail for fraud. They had been artificially inflating the circulation of their newspaper by setting up fraudulent shell organizations that would buy up any copies that weren't sold. These excess copies were counted as circulation, but were never read and ended up being recycled. Paul Broeren, managing director of Media Discovery, bluntly states, "In general, nine out of ten companies in Asia do not get the optimum return for their advertising dollar."

So how do you ensure that you get what you pay for? Ultimately, advertisers want what they get in Canada: acceptable standards of audience measurement for their advertisements. But this is just not widely available in Asian nations. For example, some advertisers would pay people to sit in front of TV sets to log the commercials that are supposed to be aired. To deal with this issue WPP and PricewaterhouseCoopers decided to launch Media Discovery, a new service firm that will offer media process auditing, media planning reviews, media buying reviews, and monitor process reviews in Taiwan, Japan, Singapore, Thailand, and India. This service promises to bring some of the same organization and detail to the Asian media buying process as we have in North America.

Discuss why it's so important for advertisers to have detailed information on the audience of the media they buy. Consider the issue of what it costs to get this information versus what it might be worth to advertisers.

Sources: Based on David Kilburn, "Asian Media Sellers Face Accountability," *Marketing Magazine* (February 15, 1999), p. 6; and David Kilburn, "Japan's Ad Agencies Move Toward Global Standards," *Marketing Magazine* (January 25, 1999), p. 6.

# Developing a Promotional Plan for Advertising

The process of developing a promotional plan for advertising consists of the nine steps shown in Figure 13-1 and discussed below.

## Setting Objectives

An organization's advertising goals relate either to the demand for its product or service or to its image, with image-oriented ads being part of the firm's public relations effort. Table 13-2 cites several possible goals. Usually, a number of them are pursued in an advertising plan.

As an example, the Insurance Corporation of B.C. wanted to convey a new brand personality to its customers while focusing on getting drivers to change poor driving behaviours. The firm wanted to be perceived as honest and open with its customers, and as one that listened and responded to them. The firm's previous advertising had been focused on getting people to stop speeding, and had an authoritative tone that was critical of drivers. The ads generally talked at drivers, and not with them.

FIGURE 13-1

**Developing a Promotional Plan for Advertising**

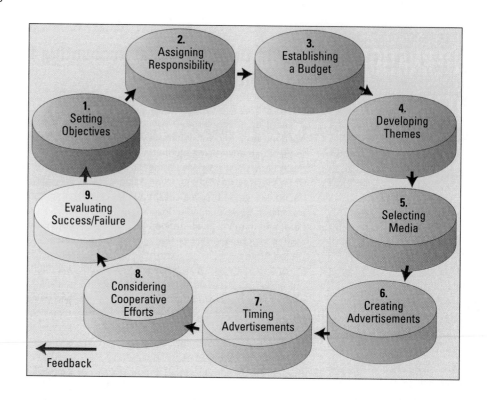

## TABLE 13-2

## Illustrations of Specific Advertising Objectives

| TYPE OF OBJECTIVE | ILLUSTRATIONS |
|---|---|
| *Demand-Oriented* | |
| Information | To create target market awareness for a new brand |
| | To acquaint consumers with new business or store hours |
| | To reduce the time salespeople take to answer basic questions |
| Persuasion | To gain brand preference |
| | To increase store traffic |
| | To achieve brand loyalty |
| Reminding (retention) | To stabilize sales |
| | To maintain brand loyalty |
| | To sustain brand recognition and image |
| *Image-Oriented* | |
| Industry | To develop and maintain a favourable industry image |
| | To generate primary demand |
| Company | To develop and maintain a favourable company image |
| | To generate selective demand |

The Insurance Corporation of B.C. worked with its advertising agency, Palmer Jarvis DDB of Vancouver, to change its image and the tone of its advertising. It decided to focus on getting people to change four unsafe driving behaviours: tailgating, unsafe lane changes, reckless driving at intersections, and distracted driving. To fit these ads into their broader goal of image change, the Insurance Corporation of B.C. and its agency decided that they needed to get drivers to think about their driving behaviour, which would hopefully lead to change.

The campaign theme was "What would happen if people retained their driver personality in everyday life?" To discourage tailgating an ad was produced showing someone walking down the street with another person right behind, breathing down their neck and saying "Move it, move it." A voiceover asks, "You'd never walk like this, so why would you drive like this?" An ad about unsafe land changes showed a swimmer diving over a lane marker and cutting off another swimmer; one about reckless driving at intersections had a shopper roaring down an aisle at the local supermarket and crashing into someone else's shopping cart; and the one about distracted drivers showed a cyclist pedalling along while reading a paper and drinking a coffee.[6]

## Assigning Responsibility

In assigning advertising responsibility, a firm can rely on its internal personnel involved with marketing functions, use an in-house advertising department, or hire an outside advertising agency. Although many firms use internal personnel or in-house departments, most involved with advertising on a regular or sizable basis employ outside agencies (some in addition to their own personnel or departments). Diversified firms may hire a different agency for each product line. A firm's decision to use an outside agency depends on its own expertise and resources and on the role of advertising for the firm.

An **advertising agency** is an organization that provides a variety of advertising-related services to client firms. It often works with clients in devising their advertising plans—including themes, media choice, copywriting, and other tasks. A large agency may also offer market research, product planning, consumer research, public relations, and other services.

*An **advertising agency** may work with a firm to develop its ad plan, conduct research, or provide other services.*

## Establishing a Budget

After figuring its overall advertising spending by the all-you-can-afford, incremental, competitive parity, percentage-of-sales, or objective-and-task method, a firm sets a detailed ad budget—to specify the funds for each type of advertising (such as product and institutional messages) and each medium (such as newspapers and radio). Because demand-oriented ads generate revenues, firms should be cautious about reducing these budgets. A better campaign, not a lower budget, may be the answer if performance does not reach goals.

These points should be addressed: What do various alternatives cost for time or space (a thirty-second TV spot versus a full-page magazine ad)? How many placements are needed for an ad to be effective? (If it takes four telecasts of a single ad to make an impact, a budget must allow four placements.) Have media prices risen recently? How should a firm react during an industry sales slump? What channel members are assigned to which promotion tasks? Do channel members require contributions toward advertising? What does it cost to produce an ad? How should a budget be allocated for domestic versus international ads?

According to a recent survey of international advertising executives, 28 per cent of firms allow personnel in each pan-geographic region to determine their own needs and then petition headquarters for a budget; 28 per cent allow each individual market to have its own advertising strategy and budget; and 20 per cent control budgeting decisions from their world headquarters. Airlines are most likely to use the pan-geographic approach. Consumer products and high-tech companies are most apt to have individual market budgeting.[7]

## Developing Themes

A firm next develops **advertising themes**, the overall appeals for its campaign. A good or service appeal centres on the item and its attributes. A consumer appeal

*Basic **advertising themes** are product, consumer, and/or institutional appeals.*

## TABLE 13-3

## Advertising Themes

| THEME | EXAMPLE |
|---|---|
| *Good- or Service-Related* | |
| Dominant features described | Maytag washers emphasize dependability and durability. |
| Competitive advantages cited | Aiwa stresses the superior quality of its portable stereos. |
| Price used as dominant feature | Suave beauty products advertise low prices. |
| News or information domination | New-model laser printers point out enhancements in colour and fonts. |
| Size of market detailed | Chrysler emphasizes its leading position as a mini-van maker. |
| Primary demand sought | The Dairy Bureau, Canadian Dairy Product symbol. |
| *Consumer-Related* | |
| Good or service uses explained | Pillsbury ads have cake recipes. |
| Cost benefits of good or service shown | Owens-Corning states how consumers reduce heating bills with Fiberglas insulation. |
| Emphasis on how good or service helps consumer | Canadian Pacific Hotels mentions how its rooms are set to accommodate all the needs of business travellers with new work centres. |
| Threatening situation | Ombrelle sunscreen talks about the threat of skin cancer and how the product can help reduce the risk. |
| Incentives given to encourage purchases | An ad mentions $1 off the purchase as an introductory offer for a new brand of coffee. |
| *Institutional-Related* | |
| Favourable image sought | The Canadian Society of Management Accountants talks about Certified Management Accountants: "A CMA on your team strengthens your leadership."[8] |
| Growth, profits, and potential described to attract investors | Companies regularly take out full-page ads in business sections of major newspapers. |

describes a product in terms of consumer benefits rather than features. An institutional appeal deals with a firm's image. Table 13-3 presents a full range of advertising themes from which a firm may select. Figure 13-2 shows a thematic ad from The Canadian Dairy Bureau.

### Selecting Media

There are many media available, as noted in Table 13-4. In selecting them, costs, reach, waste, narrowcasting, frequency, message permanence, persuasive impact, clutter, lead time, and media innovations should be reviewed.

**Advertising media costs** *are total and per person.*

**Advertising media costs** are outlays for media time or space. They are related to ad length or size, as well as media attributes. First, the total cost to place an ad in a given medium should be computed—for example, $30 000 for a full-page colour ad in a magazine. Second, per-reader or -viewer costs should be derived (stated on a per-thousand basis). If a $30 000 ad goes in a magazine with a 500 000 circulation, the cost per thousand is $60.

**Reach** *includes circulation and passalongs.*

**Reach** refers to the number of viewers, readers, or listeners in a medium's audience. For TV and radio, it is the total number of people who watch or listen to an ad. For print media, it has two aspects: circulation and passalong rate. Circulation is the number of copies sold or distributed to people. The passalong rate is the number of

**FIGURE 13-2**

**The Canadian Dairy Bureau: Seeking Primary Demand**

*Reprinted with permission of Dairy Farmers of Canada.*

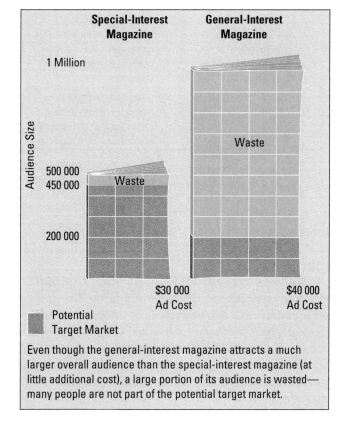

**FIGURE 13-3**

**Waste in Advertising**

## TABLE 13-4

## Advertising Media

| MEDIUM | MARKET COVERAGE | BEST USES | SELECTED ADVANTAGES | SELECTED DISADVANTAGES |
|---|---|---|---|---|
| Daily newspaper | Entire metropolitan area; local editions used sometimes | Medium and large firms | Short lead time, concentrated market, flexible, high frequency, passalongs, surrounded by content | General audience, heavy ad competition, limited colour, limited creativity |
| Weekly newspaper | One community | Local firms | Same as daily | Heavy ad competition, very limited colour, limited creativity, small market |
| Commercial television | Regional, national, or international | Regional manufacturers and large retailers; national, large manufacturers and largest retailers | Reach, low cost per viewer, persuasive impact, creative options, flexible, high frequency, surrounded by programs | High minimum total costs, general audience, lead time for popular shows, short messages, limited availability |
| Cable television | Local, regional, national, or international | Local, regional, and national manufacturers and retailers | More precise audience and more creative than commercial television | Not all consumers hooked up; ads not yet fully accepted on programs |
| Direct mail | Advertiser selects market | New products, book clubs, financial services, catalogue sales | Precise audience, flexible, personal approach, less clutter from other messages | High throwaway rate, receipt by wrong person, low credibility |
| Magazines | Local, national, or international (with regional issues) | Local service retailers and mail-order firms; major manufacturers and retailers | Colour, creative options, affluent audience, permanence of messages, passalongs, flexible, surrounded by content | Long lead time, poor frequency (if monthly), ad clutter, geographically dispersed audience |
| Radio | Entire metropolitan area | Local or regional firms | Low costs, selective market, high frequency, immediacy of messages surrounded by content | No visual impact, commercial clutter, channel switching, consumer distractions |

**Waste** *is the audience segment not in the target market.*

times each copy is read by another reader. For instance, each copy of *Maclean's* is read by several people. The magazine passalong rate is much higher than that for daily papers.

**Waste** is the part of a medium's audience not in a firm's target market. Because media appeal to mass audiences, it can be a big factor. This can be shown by continuing the magazine example noted in media costs. If the magazine is a special-interest one for amateur photographers, a film producer would know that 450 000 readers might have an interest in a new fast-speed film; 50 000 would have no interest. The latter represents the wasted audience for its ad. So, the real cost is $66.67 ($30 000/450 000 × 1000 = $66.67) per thousand circulation. The firm also knows a general-interest magazine runs ads for film. That magazine sells one million copies and a full-page ad costs $40 000—$40 per thousand. Yet,

## TABLE 13-4 (CONT'D)

| MEDIUM | MARKET COVERAGE | BEST USES | SELECTED ADVANTAGES | SELECTED DISADVANTAGES |
|---|---|---|---|---|
| Business publications | National, regional, or international | Corporate advertising, industrial firms | Selective market, high readability, surrounded by content, message permanence, passalongs | Restricted product applications, may not be read by proper decision maker, not final-consumer oriented |
| Outdoor | Entire metropolitan area or one location | Brand-name products, nearby retailers, reminder ads | Large size, colour, creative options, repetition, less clutter, message permanence | Legal restrictions, consumer distractions, general audience, inflexible, limited content, long lead time |
| Transit | Urban community with a transit system | Firms located along transit route | Concentrated market, message permanence, repetition, action-oriented messages, colour, creative options | Clutter of ads, consumer distractions, geographically limited audience |
| Telephone directories | Entire metropolitan area (with local supplements) | All types of retailers, professionals, service companies | Low costs, permanence of messages, repetition, coverage of market, specialized listings, action-oriented messages | Clutter of ads, limited creativity, very long lead time, low appeal to passive consumers |
| Internet | Local, national, or international | All types and sizes of firms | Low costs, huge potential audience, vast geographic coverage and amount of information conveyed, interactivity | Clutter of ads, viewed as a novelty by some, goals unclear (advertising vs. entertainment and education), no set rate structure |
| Flyers | Single neighbourhood | Local firms | Low costs, market coverage, little waste, flexible | High throwaway rate, poor image |

the firm expects only 200 000 people to have an interest in photography. Thus, the real cost is $200 ($40 000/ 200 000 × 1000 = $200) per thousand circulation. See Figure 13-3.

**Narrowcasting**, which presents advertising messages to rather limited and well-defined audiences, is a way to reduce the audience waste with mass media. It may be achieved using direct mail, local cable TV, specialty magazines, and other targeted media. In narrowcasting, a firm gets less waste in return for a smaller reach. Given that 77 per cent of Canadian homes get cable TV programs, this medium has great potential for local narrowcasting. See Table 13-4.

*In* **narrowcasting,** *advertisers seek to reduce waste.*

**Frequency** is how often a medium can be used. It is greatest for papers, radio, and TV. Different ads may appear daily and a strategy may be easily changed. Phone

**Frequency** *is highest for daily media.*

**TECHNOLOGY AND MARKETING**

## Welcome, Sports Fans, to Virtual Television

Just about any sports fan who's ever watched a Superbowl or Rose Bowl football game has seen shots of, and from, the "blimp." The shots from the blimp will continue as usual, but those of the blimp are about to change, thanks to live virtual advertising. This uses the same technology that allows fans at home to see a first-down line superimposed on the football field. Since it's a "virtual" line, the viewers can see the line on their TV screens, but the fans, players, and officials on the football field can't.

The technology will now provide viewers with more advertising. During sporting events, company logos can be electronically painted on raceway surfaces, the boards of hockey arenas, the tennis court, the golf green, you name it. Princeton Video Image (PVI) has developed a Live Video Insertion System for TV broadcasting. The system can work for live or taped broadcasts. The idea is for advertisers to keep their names in the minds of consumers during the sports action. They don't have to wait for station breaks, and more viewers will see their messages since they're unlikely to leave during the sports action. However, these insertions are limited to static logos that must blend into the action, since if the messages were moving about they would distract viewers from the sport.

Even virtual blimps can be inserted into any sporting event; viewers at home won't know they aren't real. For example, Global Television put some virtual blimps into the 1999 Superbowl for General Motors, National Car and Truck Rentals, and Ben Gay. Of course, the fans at the Superbowl only saw the real blimps.

Identify and discuss some of the ethical issues that might arise with the use of virtual advertising. As a broadcaster, how would you handle the concerns of advertisers who were putting up real blimps?

Source: Based on David Carr, "TV Advertising Goes Virtual," *Marketing Magazine* (March 22, 1999), p. 20.

---

directories, outdoor ads, and magazines have the poorest frequency. A Yellow Pages ad may be placed only once per year.

**Message permanence** *refers to exposures per ad.*

**Message permanence** refers to the number of exposures one ad generates (repetition) and how long it remains available to the audience. Outdoor ads, transit ads, and phone directories yield many exposures per message; and many magazines are retained by consumers for long periods. On the other hand, radio and TV ads last only 5 to 60 seconds.

**Persuasive impact** *is highest for TV.*

**Persuasive impact** is the ability of a medium to stimulate consumers. Television often has the highest persuasive impact because it is able to combine audio, video, colour, and animation. Magazines also have high persuasive impact. Many newspapers are improving their technology in order to feature colour ads and increase their persuasive impact.

**Clutter** *occurs when there are many ads.*

**Clutter** involves the number of ads found in a single program, issue, and so forth of a medium. It is low when few ads are presented, such as Hallmark placing only scattered commercials on the TV specials for which it is the exclusive sponsor. It is high when there are many ads, such as the large amount of supermarket ads in a newspaper's Wednesday issue. Overall, magazines have the highest clutter. And TV is criticized for allowing too much clutter, particularly for assigning more time per hour to commercials and for letting firms show very brief messages (e.g., 15 seconds or shorter). About one-third of all television ads are 15-second spots.[9]

**Lead time** *is needed for placing an ad.*

**Lead time** is the period required by a medium for placing an ad. It is shortest for newspapers and longest for magazines and phone directories. Popular TV shows may also require a lengthy lead time since the number of ads they can carry is limited. With a long lead time, because a firm must place ads well in advance, it risks improper themes in a changing environment.

**FIGURE 13-4**

**Sony's Use of a Long-Time Advertising Message**

*Sony of Canada Ltd.*

There have been many media innovations in advertising in recent years. These include commercial online computer services such as Compuserve, America Online Canada, and the other fast-emerging services that let people "surf the Web"; regional editions and special one-sponsor issues ("advertorials") to revitalize magazines; specialized Yellow Pages; televised ads in supermarkets, movie theatres, and aircraft; more radio stations handling ads in stereo; better quality in outdoor signs; full-length televised advertising programs (infomercials); and direct-mail ads with CD-ROM diskettes.

**AMERICA ONLINE**
www.aol.com/

**COMPUSERVE**
www.compuserve.com/

## Creating Advertisements

There are four fundamental decisions that the advertiser must make when creating advertisements:

*Ad creation involves content, scheduling, media placement, and variations.*

1. Determining the message content and devising the ads. Each ad needs a headline or opening to create consumer interest and copy that presents the message. Content decisions also involve the use of colour and illustrations, ad size or length, the source, the use of symbolism, and the adaptations needed for foreign markets. The role of these factors depends on a firm's goals and resources.

2. Outlining a promotion schedule. This should allow for all copy and artwork and be based on the lead time needed for the chosen media.

3. Specifying each ad's location in a broadcast program or print medium. As costs have risen, more firms have become concerned about ad placement.

4. Choosing how many variations of a basic message to use. This depends on the frequency of presentations and the ad quality. Sony has been able to run its "There's Nothing Like a Real Trinitron" message for years (see Figure 13-4).

## Timing Advertisements

*Timing refers to how often an ad is shown and when to advertise during the year.*

Potential advertisers must make two major decisions about the timing of advertisements: how often a given ad will be shown and when to advertise during the year. First, a firm must balance audience awareness and knowledge with the danger of irritating the audience if it places an ad a number of times in a short period. Thus, McDonald's runs its ads repeatedly, but changes them often. Second, a firm must choose whether to advertise throughout the year or in concentrated periods. Distributed ads maintain brand recognition and increase sales in nonpeak periods. They are used by most manufacturers and general-merchandise retailers. Massed ads are concentrated in peak periods to generate short-run consumer enthusiasm; they ignore sales in nonpeak periods. Specialty manufacturers and retailers use this method.

Other timing considerations include when to advertise new products, when to stop advertising existing products, how to coordinate advertising and other promotional tools, when to change basic themes, and how to space messages during the hierarchy-of-effects process.

## Considering Cooperative Efforts

*In **cooperative advertising**, costs are shared by multiple parties.*

To stimulate advertising by channel members and/or to hold down its own ad budget, a firm may consider cooperative efforts. With **cooperative advertising**, two or more firms share some advertising costs. In a vertical cooperative-advertising agreement, firms at different stages in a distribution channel (such as a manufacturer and a wholesaler) share costs. In a horizontal cooperative-advertising agreement, two or more independent firms at the same stage in a distribution channel share costs (such as retailers in a mall).

Good cooperative agreements state the share of costs paid by each party, the functions and responsibilities of each party, the advertisements to be covered, and the basis for termination. They also benefit each participant.

Each year, manufacturers offer millions of dollars in vertical cooperative-advertising support in Canada. Yet distribution intermediaries typically use only about two-thirds of the money offered. The nonuse by so many resellers is due to their perceptions of manufacturer inflexibility involving messages and media, the costs of cooperative advertising to the resellers, restrictive provisions (such as high minimum purchases to be eligible), and the emphasis on the manufacturer's name in ads. To remedy this, more manufacturers are now flexible as to the messages and media they will support, pay a larger share of advertising costs, have eased restrictive provisions, and feature reseller names more prominently in ads.

## Evaluating Success or Failure

Advertising's success or failure depends on how well it helps an organization to achieve promotion goals. Creating customer awareness and increasing sales are distinct goals; success or failure in reaching them must be measured differently. In addition, advertising can be quite difficult to isolate as the single factor leading to a certain image or sales level.

Here are various examples dealing with the evaluation of advertising's success or failure:

- The typical consumer is bombarded with 300 advertising messages each day—about 110 000 per year. According to one major research study, two-thirds of people believe a nationally advertised brand creates the perception that it is of better quality than brands that are not heavily advertised; and in choosing among two unfamiliar brands, two-thirds of people will select the one that is advertised most.[10]

- A survey of consumers in twenty-two nations found that advertising is favourably regarded, although opinions differ by country: "Individuals in former Communist nations are among the most enthusiastic supporters of advertising, apparently reflecting their current desire to embrace consumer-oriented Western capitalism. Egypt was the only market where respondents were consistently anti-advertising."[11]
- Young adults (those 18 to 34) account for one-third of all Yellow Pages use. They are more apt than older adults to rely on information in display ads and less likely to have a specific company name in mind when consulting the Yellow Pages.[12]

# The Scope and Importance of Public Relations

Each firm would like to foster the best possible relations with its publics and to receive favourable publicity about its offerings or the firm itself. Sometimes, as with restaurant or theatre reviews, publicity can greatly increase sales or virtually put a firm out of business. For example, Tout Sweet Chocolates went bankrupt when letters were sent to some of the retailers carrying its products claiming they had been poisoned. Retailers pulled all of the products off their shelves and consumers balked at buying any newly produced chocolates even though no tampering was discovered in any of the recalled products. The negative publicity associated with this incident undermined Tout Sweet with its creditors and they put the firm into receivership despite the fact that Tout Sweet chocolate products were of the highest quality.[13]

The Canadian Public Relations Society has 1700 members, and many of the larger business firms and trade associations have their own public relations departments. *Marketing Magazine* lists eighty-eight different public relations firms located in major cities all across Canada. The International Public Relations Association has thousands of members from seventy-two nations, although the role of public rela-

*Public relations efforts can have a major impact.*

**CANADIAN PUBLIC RELATIONS SOCIETY**
www.cprs.ca/

**TABLE 13-5**

**Public Relations-Related Situations and How a Firm Could Respond to Them**

| SITUATION | POOR RESPONSE | GOOD RESPONSE |
|---|---|---|
| Fire breaks out in a company plant | Requests for information by media are ignored. | Company spokesperson explains the fire's causes and the precautions to avoid it and answers questions. |
| New product introduced | Advertising is used without publicity. | Pre-introduction news releases, product samples, and testimonials are used. |
| News story about product defects | Media requests for information are ignored, blanket denials are issued, and there is hostility to reporters. | Company spokesperson says tests are being done, describes the procedure for handling defects, and takes questions. |
| Competitor introduces new product | A demand-oriented advertising campaign is stepped up. | Extensive news releases, statistics, and spokespeople are made available to media to present firm's competitive features. |
| High profits reported | Profits are justified and positive effects on the economy are cited. | Profits are explained, comparative data are provided, and profit uses are noted: research and community development. |
| Overall view of public relations | There is an infrequent need for public relations; crisis fighting is used when bad reports are circulated. | There is an ongoing need for public relations, strong planning, and plans to counter bad reports. |

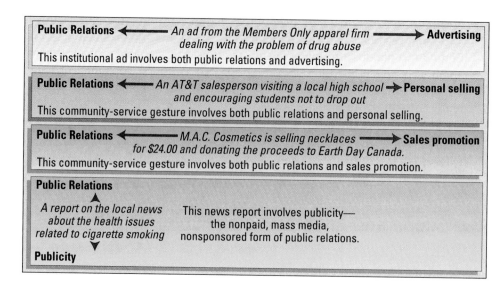

**FIGURE 13-5**

**The Relationship Between Public Relations and the Other Elements of the Promotion Mix**

tions varies greatly by nation: "In many foreign areas, the term public relations really means press relations. Working with the press abroad is not easy; there may be a language barrier, and many times, government controls the media."[14]

The competition to gain media attention for publicity is intense. After all, in Canada, TV broadcasting is done on three national networks (two English and one French), with seventeen regional commercial networks and thirty cable specialty networks available as well. In comparison there are only eleven consumer magazines with circulations of 500 000 or more. Nonetheless, there are many opportunities for publicity, with 346 AM radio stations, 564 FM radio stations, 131 originating commercial TV stations covering 43 markets, 108 daily newspapers, and 1050 community newspapers.[15]

**FIGURE 13-6**

**A Socially Responsible Public Relations Campaign**

*Reprinted by permission.*

Some firms have poor policies to deal with their publics and the media, and fail to develop a sustained public relations effort. Table 13-5 shows several public relations-related situations and how a firm could deal with them. Since unfavourable publicity can occur, a firm must be ready to deal with it in the best way possible. Negative publicity can happen to any firm; a successful one will have a plan to handle it. A firm may get the media on its side by being candid and acting promptly; media may be used to help explain complex issues; and by cooperating with reporters, preconceived notions may be dispelled.

The interrelationship of public relations and other promotion forms must be understood. If advertising, personal selling, and sales promotion are image-oriented, public relations is involved. If they are demand-oriented, it is not. Figure 13-5 shows the interface between public relations and other promotion tools. Figure 13-6 shows an effective institutional ad.

*Public relations encompasses image-directed ads, selling, and sales promotion—as well as publicity.*

Public relations has consistently demanded a more central role in the life of an organization. It has argued for recognition as a management function with the right to participate in key decision making. Public relations has increasingly gained entrance to executive committees and boardrooms with the opportunity to directly contribute to the formation of strategy. With growing frequency public relations is being elevated to stand as a peer with marketing, strategic planning, and operations.[16]

## The Characteristics of Public Relations

Public relations offers several benefits. Since it is image-oriented, good feelings toward a firm by its external publics can be fostered. In addition, employee morale (pride) is enhanced if the firm is community and civic minded.

When publicity is involved, there are no costs for message time or space. A prime-time television ad may cost $44 000 to $90 000 or more per minute of media time; a five-minute report on a network newscast does not cost anything for media time. However, there are costs for news releases, a public relations department, and so on. As with advertising, publicity reaches a mass audience. In a short time, new products or company policies are well known.

Message believability is higher with publicity because stories appear in independent media. A newspaper's movie review is more credible than an ad in the same paper—the reader links independence with objectivity. Similarly, people may pay more attention to news than to ads. *Canadian Living* has both cooking advice and food ads; people read the stories, but flip through ads. There are a dozen or more ads in a half-hour TV show and hundreds of them in a typical magazine; feature stories are fewer in number and stand out more.

Public relations also has limitations, compared to other promotion forms. Some firms question the value of image-oriented communications and are disinterested in activities not directly tied to sales and profits. They may give the poor responses that were indicated in Table 13-5.

With publicity, a firm has less control over messages and their timing, placement, and coverage by the media. It may issue detailed press releases and find only parts cited in the media; and media may be more critical than a firm would like. Media tend to find disasters, scandals, and product recalls more newsworthy than press releases. And the accessibility of the Internet for disgruntled consumers provides another outlet for bad publicity.

Bad publicity can quickly affect how a firm does business. For example, in 1989 the Holiday Inn opened a hotel in Lhasa, Tibet in conjunction with the CYTS, the Chinese government's tourist agency. Holiday Inn decided to make the hotel one of the most luxurious in the region by putting in reliable phone lines, satellite TV, and a glitzy disco. It was described as the best available hotel property in Lhasa, but

*Public relations engenders good feelings; publicity has no time costs, a large audience, high credibility, and attentiveness.*

*Public relations may be downplayed by some firms; publicity cannot be controlled or timed accurately by a company.*

problems began a mere two months after the hotel opened. Chinese troops battled with Tibetan nationalists in an uprising, tourism dropped off dramatically, and the Holiday Inn's business came to depend on its role as the place to rest for Communist Party members who were visiting Tibet. In commemoration of the tenth anniversary of the 1989 uprising, a London-based group called the Free Tibet Society led a worldwide boycott against Holiday Inn. They accused the firm of cooperating with the Chinese government to oppress Tibet. As a result Holiday Inn relinquished the hotel, which is now operated solely by the CYTS under the name Lhasa Hotel. Although the sign says "Lhasa Hotel," an accompanying sign reads "Formerly Holiday Inn."[17]

Sometimes bad publicity can be good for a firm. For example, Micron Electronics was surprised to discover that it had strong brand recognition when it began selling personal computers in Japan in 1995. The recognition was somewhat negative, however, because its parent firm, Micron Technology, had publicly accused Japanese manufacturers of dumping memory chips into the U.S. market during the 1980s. Micron was heavily attacked in the Japanese press in the 1980s for these accusations. The result? Micron Electronics has an established brand name as a large American manufacturer in Japan and has been able to build a U.S.$60 million a year business there with no advertising.[18]

A firm may want publicity during certain periods, such as when a new product is introduced or a new store opened, but the media may not provide coverage until much later. Similarly, the media determine a story's placement; it may follow a crime or sports report. Finally, the media choose whether to cover a story at all and the amount of coverage devoted to it. A firm-sponsored jobs program might go unreported or get three-sentence coverage in a local paper.

Publicity may be hard to plan in advance because newsworthy events occur quickly and unexpectedly. Thus, short-run and long-run public relations plans should differ in approach. Publicity must complement advertising and not be a substitute. The assets of each (credibility and low costs for publicity, control and coverage for ads) are needed for a good communications program.

To optimize their public relations efforts, at many companies:

- Public relations personnel have regular access to senior executives.
- The publicity value of annual reports is recognized.
- Public relations messages are professionally prepared (with the same care used in writing ad copy) and continuously given to media.
- Internal personnel and media personnel interaction is fostered.
- Public-service events are planned to obtain maximum media coverage.
- Part of the promotion budget goes to publicity-generating tasks.
- There is a better understanding of the kinds of stories the media are apt to cover and how to present stories to the media.

# Developing a Promotion Plan for Public Relations

Developing a public relations plan is much like devising an advertising plan. It involves the seven steps shown in Figure 13-7, and which are described next.

## Setting Objectives

Public relations goals are image-oriented (firm and/or industry). The choice of goals guides the entire public relations plan.

These are some goals that could be set:

# ETHICS AND TODAY'S MARKETER

## Applying Professional Standards to Public Relations Practice

The members of the Canadian Public Relations Society are asked to adhere to the following Code of Professional Standards:

1. A member shall practise public relations according to the highest professional standards.
2. A member shall deal fairly and honestly with the communications media and the public.
3. A member shall practise the highest standards of honesty, accuracy, integrity, and truth, and shall not knowingly disseminate false or misleading information.
4. A member shall deal fairly with past or present employers/clients, with fellow practitioners, and with members of other professions.
5. A member shall be prepared to disclose the name of their employer or client for whom public communications are made and refrain from associating themselves with anyone who would not respect such policy.
6. A member shall protect the confidences of present, former, and prospective employers/clients.
7. A member shall not represent conflicting or competing interests without the express consent of those concerned, given after a full disclosure of the facts.
8. A member shall not guarantee specified results beyond the member's capacity to achieve.
9. Members shall personally accept no fees, commissions, gifts, or any other considerations for professional services from anyone except employers or clients for whom the services were specifically performed.

On the condition of anonymity, the president of a Manhattan-based promotions company discussed in *Phos 4* magazine a public relations campaign that made his firm one of the hottest around. He described how his firm managed a new product launch for a drug company. The drug firm had come up with a way to package an existing product in a new form at half the price. The firm wanted to launch the new product with considerable impact. Rather than conduct a typical "new and improved" campaign, the promotions firm invented a strategy that would let the firm make the switch and appear heroic at the same time. The promotion firm staged a news event where a person tampered with the old drug and somebody died. The firm stepped forward to recall the old drug and replace it overnight with the new design. Despite the recall expenses, the firm gained tremendous publicity, launched the new and cheaper drug, made lots of money, and looked socially responsible as well. Since then the promotion firm claims to have received considerable client interest.

How many of the nine codes of professional standards set out by the Canadian Public Relations Society were broken in the *Phos 4* story, and how were they broken? Was it ethical of *Phos 4* to publish such a story? Why or why not? Research *Phos 4* itself. Would you expect this kind of publication to have any credibility or responsibility for this story?

Sources: Based on Canadian Public Relations Society, Code of Professional Standards, www.cprs.ca; and Jon Armstrong, "Bad Publicity Is Good Publicity," *Phos 4* (1995), www.phos4.com.

- To gain placement for news releases and coverage of company spokespersons with a variety of media.
- To have the media report on the accomplishments of the company.
- To have the company's position presented when controversy arises.
- To coordinate publicity with advertising.
- To gain more media coverage than competitors.
- To sustain favourable publicity as long as possible.

FIGURE 13-7

**Developing a Promotion Plan for Public Relations**

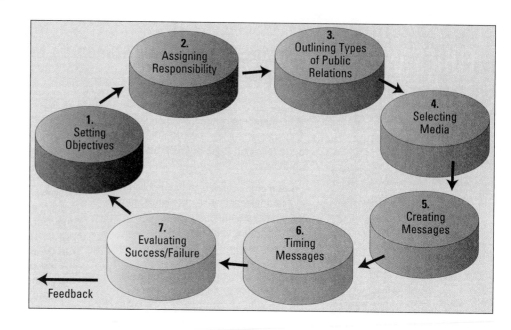

- To reach out to community groups.
- To have publics view the firm and its industry favourably.

While setting goals, this truism should be kept in mind: "PR involves both *performance* and *recognition*. It is possible to boast excellent performance without being properly recognized, but it is not possible to earn recognition that is not based on solid performance. Woe to the firm that tries to get the R (recognition) without the P (performance)."[19]

## Assigning Responsibility

*A firm can use an in-house department, hire an outside ad agency, or hire a specialist.*

A firm has three options in assigning public relations responsibility: it may use its existing marketing personnel, an in-house public relations department, or an in-house publicity department; it may have an outside advertising agency handle public relations; or it may hire a specialized public relations firm. Internal personnel or an in-house department ensure more control and secrecy. An outside firm often has better contacts and expertise. Each approach is popular; and they may be combined.[20]

Procter & Gamble has an in-house publicity department and several outside public relations agencies. In contrast, some smaller firms rely on the services of specialists, which may charge retainer fees of $25 000 to $50 000 per year. Computer software, such as PRpower, can also let smaller firms easily set up media mailing lists.

## Outlining the Types of Public Relations to Be Used

In this step, a firm first chooses the mix of institutional advertising, image-oriented personal selling, image-oriented sales promotion, and publicity to incorporate into an overall promotion plan. Next, public relations efforts must be coordinated with the demand-oriented promotion activities of the firm.

**Publicity types** *involve news, features, releases, background material, and emergency information.*

Finally, the general **publicity types** must be understood and envisioned. Each can play a role in an integrated public relations program:

- *News publicity* deals with international, national, regional, or local events. Planned releases can be prepared and regularly given out by a firm.
- *Business feature articles* are detailed stories about a company or its offerings that are given to business media.

- *Service feature articles* are lighter stories focusing on personal care, household items, and similar topics, and are sent to newspapers, cable TV stations, and magazines.
- *Finance releases* are stories aimed at the business sections of newspapers, TV news shows, and magazines.
- *Product releases* deal with new products and product improvements; they aim at all media forms.
- *Pictorial releases* are illustrations or pictures sent to the media.
- *Video news releases* are videotaped segments supplied to the media.
- *Background editorial material* is extra information given to media writers and editors; it enhances standard releases and provides filler for stories (like the biography of the chief executive of a company).
- *Emergency publicity* consists of special spontaneous news releases keyed to unexpected events.[21]

## Selecting the Media for Public Relations Efforts

For institutional ads, personal selling, and sales promotion, traditional nonpersonal and/or personal media would be used. For publicity, a firm would typically focus on newspapers, television, magazines, radio, and business publications. Due to the infrequent publication schedule of many magazines and some business publications, publicity-seeking efforts may be aimed at daily or weekly media.

Public relations executives rank newspapers and business publications the highest. *The Globe and Mail, The Toronto Star, The Vancouver Sun,* and *Le Journal de Montreal* are preferred newspapers. *Canadian Business, The Financial Post,* and *En Route* are preferred business publications. *Maclean's* and *Time* magazine are preferred general news magazines.

**FINANCIAL POST**
www.canoe.ca/FP/

## Creating Messages

The creation of public relations messages involves the same factors as other promotion forms—deciding on content and variations, and drawing up a production schedule. Messages can be conveyed in one or a combination of forms, such as news conferences, media releases, phone calls or personal contacts, media kits (a combination of materials on a story), special events (the Molson Grand Prix in Toronto), or videos.

Because it is essential that the media find a firm's publicity messages to be useful, these points need to be kept in mind:

1. Messages should be newsworthy.
2. Reporter deadlines should be respected.
3. Appropriate company representatives should be accessible to reporters.
4. "Mind-fogging" jargon should be avoided.
5. The phrase "no comment" should not be used.
6. Attribution rules (making the source and the content of a story "on" or "off" the record) should be set in advance.
7. A reporter should not be asked to kill a story.
8. Releases should be both easy to read (or view or hear), and easy to use.
9. There should be no hesitancy to volunteer a "bad" story (it will probably get out anyway).
10. Attention should be paid to the needs of each type of medium.[22]

### Timing Messages

Public relations efforts should precede new-product introductions and generate excitement for them. For emergencies, media releases and spokespeople should be made available immediately. For ongoing public relations, messages should be properly spaced through the year. As already noted, a firm may find it hard to anticipate media coverage for both unexpected and planned publicity because the media control the timing.

### Evaluating Success or Failure

Nowadays research is used to evaluate public relations campaigns. Firms measure the input, output, and outcomes of their public relations to determine their effectiveness. Input means that a firm must know what its starting point is. What are the attitudes of the firm's stakeholders and the public? What would those individuals like to hear and through what media would they prefer to hear it? Just as in a paid advertising campaign, a public relations campaign begins with an understanding of consumers.

The results of a public relations campaign can be measured in two ways: how widely the information was picked up by the media (the output of the campaign) and what impact the coverage had on consumers (the impact of the campaign). A firm can measure its output by counting the stories about it, analyzing coverage length and placement, comparing the desired with the actual timing of stories, and computing the cost of comparable advertising. The impact of a campaign might involve looking at institutional ads, image-oriented personal selling, and image-oriented sales promotion, and then conducting simple surveys to see how well these communications were received and their impact on the firm's image with the specific target (group(s).[23]

Here are some measures of public relations' success:

- Are more people aware of the product or issue? Have attitudes toward the product, company, or issue changed? Have calls to a sales centre or visits to a Web site increased? Have sales increased? Overall, has the message changed the attitude or behaviour of the target group?[24]

- Labatt ran a print campaign offering its thoughts on beer and asking readers to share some of theirs. Respondents were offered a free bottle opener for responding. In a two-week period almost 100 000 letters and phone calls came in. The information from these letters and calls provided Labatt with insights on its customers and their perception of beer marketing.[25]

- Wal-Mart now tracks the quality as well as the quantity of its media coverage. It classifies items as news stories, letters to the editor, editorials, or opinion articles for each market area.[26]

# The Scope and Importance of Sales Promotion

Due to intense competition in their industries, numerous firms are aggressively seeking every marketing edge possible. Thus, sales promotion activities worldwide are at their highest level. In the Canadian food and beverage industry, sales promotion expenditures are estimated to be $6.7 for every $1 spent on advertising. In comparison, in the United States the ratio is $2.57 for every $1 spent on advertising.[27]

The extent of sales promotion activities are illustrated in the following examples:

*Sales promotion efforts are now quite extensive.*

- In Canada, households receive about 400 coupons every year—a drop in the bucket compared to the U.S., where each household receives an average of 5000 coupons per year! Virtually all coupons have an expiry date to encourage faster redemption and to allow marketers to evaluate their effectiveness. In a typical year, most Canadian households use coupons, half on a regular basis. Yet, all told, people redeem only 2 per cent of distributed coupons.[28]

- Business-to-business firms spend about 13 per cent of their marketing budgets on trade shows and exhibits. Fifty per cent of industrial trade show attendees report signing a purchase order as a result of a trade show visit.[29]

- Point-of-purchase displays (POPs) are categorized as in-store media and are estimated to represent about $150 million in spending each year in Canada.[30] These displays stimulate impulse purchases and provide information. Besides traditional cardboard, metal, and plastic displays, more stores are now using digital electronic signs and video displays.

- For over ten years Zellers has been operating a frequent shopper program called Club Z. It allows customers to build up points that can be redeemed for merchandise from a special catalogue, and in some cases merchandise in the Zellers stores themselves. Customers get rewarded with special discounts, and Zellers is able to build its customer database. There are currently over 10.5 million members, of which about 1.5 million redeem rewards on an annual basis. Recently Zellers expanded the program to include children from one month to seventeen years of age. Called Generation Z, the program is expected to have over one million members in the year 2000.[31]

- According to International Events Group, North American firms spend U.S.$5.4 billion annually to sponsor special events, two-thirds of which are sports-related. And this number promises to reach new heights in the year 2000 as firms rush to take part in the turn of the millennium. That's why telephone company MT&T of Halifax contributed $50 000 cash, telecom services including a Web site, and the services of a number of its employees to Tall Ships 2000. Tall Ships 2000 is a trans-Atlantic ship race that promised to be one of the largest international millennium events in the world. Halifax organizers expect a million people to be on the waterfront from July 19 to July 25 of the year 2000 to see the 150 sailing ships crewed by nearly 5000 people. The host ports include Halifax; Southampton, England; Genoa, Italy; Cadiz, Spain; Bermuda; Amsterdam; and Boston.[32]

**COLGATE-PALMOLIVE**
www.colgate.com/

Several factors account for the strength of sales promotion as a marketing tool. As noted at the beginning of this section, firms are looking for any competitive edge they can get and this often involves some kind of sales promotion; sales promotions are more acceptable to firms and consumers than in the past; many firms want to improve short-run profits, and promotions allow for quick returns; more consumers look for promotions before buying (especially in economic downturns) and resellers put pressure on manufacturers to provide them; advertising and personal selling have become more expensive relative to sales promotion; and technology advances make aspects of sales promotion, like coupon redemption, easier to administer.

## The Characteristics of Sales Promotion

Sales promotion has many advantages. It helps attract customer traffic, for example, with new-product samples and trial offers, and it helps keep brand or company loyalty. A manufacturer can retain brand loyalty by giving gifts to regular customers and coupons for its brands. A reseller can retain loyal customers by offering incentives to frequent shoppers and using store coupons.

Rapid results can be gained from some promotions. Calendars, matchbooks, T-shirts, pens, and posters with the firm's name provide consumer value and are

*Sales promotion lures customers, maintains loyalty, creates excitement, is often keyed to patronage, and appeals to channel members.*

retained; thus, they remind the consumer of the company name every time they are used. Impulse purchases can be stimulated by in-store displays. For example, an attractive supermarket display for batteries can dramatically raise sales. In addition, a good display may lead a shopper to a bigger purchase than originally intended.

Excitement can be created by short-run promotions involving gifts, contests, or sweepstakes; and high-value items or high payoffs encourage consumers to participate. Contests offer the further benefit of customer involvement (through the completion of some skill-oriented activity). Many promotions are keyed to customer patronage—with the awarding of coupons, frequent shopper gifts, and referral gifts directly related to purchases. In these cases, promotions can be a fixed percentage of sales and their costs not incurred until transactions are completed. And resellers may be stimulated if sales promotion support is provided in the form of displays, manufacturer coupons, manufacturer rebates, and trade allowances.

*Sales promotion may hurt image, cause consumers to wait for special offers, and shift the focus from the product.*

Sales promotion also has limitations. A firm's image may be tarnished if it always runs promotions. People may view discounts as representing a decline in product quality and believe a firm could not sell its offerings without them. Profit margins are often lower for a firm if sales promotion is used. When coupons, rebates, or other special deals are employed frequently, people may not buy when products are offered at regular prices; they will stock up each time there is a promotion. Some consumers may even interpret a regular price as an increase for items that are heavily promoted.

Some promotions shift the marketing focus away from the product itself to secondary factors. People may be lured by calendars and sweepstakes instead of product quality and features. In the short run, this generates consumer enthusiasm. In the long run, it may adversely affect a brand's image and sales because a product-related advantage has not been communicated. Sales promotion can enhance—not replace—advertising, personal selling, and public relations.

## Developing a Promotion Plan for Sales Promotion

A sales promotion plan consists of the steps shown in Figure 13-8 and explained next.

### Setting Objectives

Sales promotion goals are usually demand-oriented. They may be related to channel members and to consumers.

Objectives associated with channel-member sales promotions include gaining distribution, receiving adequate shelf space, increasing dealer enthusiasm, raising sales, and getting cooperation in sales promotion expenditures. Objectives pertaining to consumer sales promotions include boosting brand awareness, increasing product trials, hiking average purchases, encouraging repurchases, obtaining impulse sales, emphasizing novelty, and supplementing other promotional tools.

### Assigning Responsibility

Sales promotion duties are often shared by advertising and sales managers, with each directing the promotions in his or her area. Thus, an advertising manager would work on coupons, customer contests, calendars, and other mass promotions. A sales manager would work on trade shows, cooperative promotions, special events, demonstrations, and other efforts involving individualized attention directed at channel members or consumers.

Some companies have their own specialized sales promotion departments or hire outside promotion firms. Outside sales promotion firms tend to operate in narrow areas—such as coupons, contests, or gifts—and generally can develop a sales

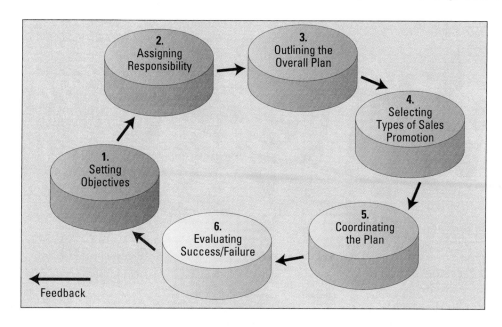

**FIGURE 13-8**

**Developing a Promotion Plan for Sales Promotion**

promotion campaign at less expense than the user company could. These firms offer expertise, swift service, flexibility, and, when requested, distribution.

## Outlining the Overall Plan

Next, a sales promotion plan should be outlined and include a budget, an orientation, conditions, media, duration and timing, and cooperative efforts. In setting a sales promotion budget, it is important to include all costs. For example, the average face value of a grocery coupon is over 65 cents; supermarkets receive a handling fee for each coupon they redeem; and there are costs for printing, mailing, and advertising coupons.

**Sales promotion orientation** refers to the focus of the promotion—channel members or consumers—and its theme. Promotions for channel members should raise their product knowledge, provide sales support, offer rewards for selling a promoted product, and seek better cooperation and efficiency. Promotions for consumers should induce impulse and larger-volume sales, sustain brand-name recognition, and gain participation. A promotion theme refers to its underlying channel-member or consumer message—such as a special sale, store opening, new-product introduction, holiday celebration, or customer recruitment.

**Sales promotion conditions** are requirements channel members or consumers must meet to be eligible for a specific sales promotion. These may include minimum purchases, performance provisions, and/or minimum age. A channel member may have to stock a certain amount of merchandise to receive a free display case from a manufacturer. A consumer may have to send in proofs of purchase to get a refund or gift. In some cases, strict time limits are set as to the closing dates for participation in a sales promotion.

The media are the vehicles through which sales promotions reach channel members or consumers. They include direct mail, newspapers, magazines, television, the personal sales force, trade shows, and group meetings.

A promotion's duration may be short or long, depending on its goals. Coupons usually have quick closing dates because they are used to increase store traffic. Frequent shopper points often can be redeemed for at least one year; their goal is to maintain loyalty. As noted earlier, if promotions are lengthy or offered frequently, consumers may come to expect them as part of a purchase. Some promotions are seasonal, and for these timing is crucial. They must be tied to such events as fall school openings or model or style changes. See Figure 13-9.

**Sales promotion orientation** *may be toward channel members and/or final consumers.*

**Sales promotion conditions** *are eligibility requirements.*

**FIGURE 13-9**

**Tying into the hockey playoffs: Labatt Blue's Stanley Cup replica promotion.**

*Courtesy Labatt.*

Finally, the use of shared promotions should be decided. In cooperative efforts each party pays some costs and gets benefits. These promotions can be sponsored by industry trade associations, manufacturers and/or service firms, wholesalers, and retailers. For example, in 1998 Dairy Queen teamed up with Betty Crocker's Fruit by the Foot to offer a "buy one sundae, get one sundae free" coupon on each Fruit by the Foot package sold in Canada. Dairy Queen is an ice cream retailer, while Betty Crocker is a packaged goods manufacturer that sells through grocery retailers. Betty Crocker uses the Dairy Queen offer as an incentive to buy a Fruit by the Foot while Dairy Queen gets advertising exposure on every package. The promotion works well because the firms are trying to reach the same target market (kids), and have a similar offering (snack food).[33]

### Selecting the Types of Sales Promotion

There is a wide range of sales promotion tools available. The attributes of several promotion tools oriented to channel members are shown in Table 13-6. The attributes of several consumer-oriented sales promotion tools are noted in Table 13-7. Examples for each tool are also provided in these tables.

The selection of sales promotions should be based on such factors as company image, company goals, costs, participation requirements, and the enthusiasm of channel members or customers.

### Coordinating the Plan

*Advertising and sales promotion should be integrated.*

It is essential that sales promotion activities be well coordinated with other elements of the promotion mix. In particular:

- Advertising and sales promotion plans should be integrated.

**TABLE 13-6**

**Selected Types of Sales Promotion Directed at Channel Members**

| TYPE | CHARACTERISTICS | ILLUSTRATION |
|---|---|---|
| Trade shows or meetings | One or a group of manufacturers invites channel members to attend sessions where products are displayed and explained. | The annual National Home Centre Show attracts more than 1000 exhibitors and tens of thousands of attendees. |
| Training | The manufacturer provides training for personnel of channel members. | Compaq trains retail salespeople in how to operate and use its computers. |
| Trade allowances or special offers | Channel members are given discounts or rebates for performing specified functions or purchasing during certain time periods. | A local distributor receives a discount for running its own promotion for GE light bulbs. |
| Point-of-purchase displays | The manufacturer or wholesaler gives channel members fully equipped displays for its products and sets them up. | Coca-Cola provides refrigerators with its name on them to retailers carrying minimum quantities of Coca-Cola products. |
| Push money | Channel members' salespeople are given bonuses for pushing the brand of a certain manufacturer. Channel members may not like this if their salespeople shift loyalty to the manufacturer. | A salesperson in an office-equipment store is paid an extra $50 for every desk of a particular brand that is sold. |
| Sales contests | Prizes or bonuses are distributed if certain performance levels are met. | A wholesaler receives $2500 for selling 1000 microchips in a month. |
| Free merchandise | Discounts or allowances are provided in the form of merchandise. | A retailer gets one case of ballpoint pens free for every 10 cases purchased. |
| Demonstration | Free items are given to channel members for demonstration purposes. | A hospital-bed manufacturer offers demonstrator models to its distributors. |
| Gifts | Channel members are given gifts for carrying items or performing functions. | During one three-month period, a book publisher gives computerized cash registers to bookstores that agree to purchase a specified quantity of its books. |
| Cooperative | Two or more channel members share the cost of a promotion. | A manufacturer and retailer each pay part of the cost for T-shirts with the manufacturer's and retailer's names embossed. |

- The sales force should be notified of all promotions well in advance and trained to implement them.
- Publicity should be generated for special events, such as the appearance of a major celebrity.
- Sales promotions should be consistent with channel members' activities.

## Evaluating Success or Failure

Measuring the success or failure of many types of sales promotions is straightforward, since the promotions are so closely linked to performance or sales. By analyzing before-and-after data, the impact of these promotions is clear. Trade show effectiveness can be gauged by counting the number of leads generated from a show, examining the sales from those leads and the cost per lead, getting customer feedback about a show from the sales force, and determining the amount of literature given out at a show. Companies can verify changes in sales as a result of dealer-training programs. Firms using coupons can review sales and compare redemption rates with industry

*The success or failure of some sales promotions is simple to measure.*

## TABLE 13-7

## Selected Types of Sales Promotion Directed at Consumers

| TYPE | CHARACTERISTICS | ILLUSTRATION |
|---|---|---|
| Coupons | Manufacturers or channel members advertise special discounts for customers who redeem coupons. | P&G mails consumers a 50-cents-off coupon for Sure deodorant, which can be redeemed at any supermarket. |
| Refunds or rebates | Consumers submit proofs of purchase (usually to the manufacturer) and receive extra discount. | First Alert provides rebates to consumers submitting proofs of purchase for its fire alarms. |
| Samples | Free merchandise or services are given to consumers, generally for new items. | Health clubs offer a free one-month trial. |
| Contests or sweepstakes | Consumers compete for prizes by answering questions (contests) or filling out forms for random drawings of prizes (sweepstakes). | Publishers Clearing House sponsors annual sweepstakes and awards cash and other prizes. |
| Bonus packs or multipacks | Consumers receive discounts for purchasing in quantity. | An office-supply store runs a "buy one, get one free" sale on desk lamps. |
| Shows or exhibits | Many firms co-sponsor exhibitions for consumers. | The Canadian National Exhibition is annually scheduled for the public in Toronto. |
| Point-of-purchase displays | In-store displays remind customers and generate impulse purchases. | *TV Guide* sales in supermarkets are high because displays are placed at checkout counters. |
| Special events | Firms sponsor the Olympics, fashion shows, and other activities. | Air Canada is a worldwide sponsor of the Olympics. |
| Product placements | Branded goods and services depicted in movies and TV shows. | Nike sneakers appear in the movie *Forrest Gump*. |
| Gifts | Consumers get gifts for making a purchase or opening a new account. | Banks offer a range of gifts for consumers opening new accounts or expanding existing ones. |
| Frequent shopper | Consumers get gifts or special discounts, based on cumulative purchases. Points are amassed and exchanged for gifts or money. | Airline travellers can accumulate gifts and receive free trips or mileage gifts when enough miles have been earned. |
| Referral gifts | Existing customers are given gifts for referring their friends to the company. | Tupperware awards gifts to the hosts of their Tupperware parties. |
| Demonstrations | Goods or services are shown in action. | Different models of Apple computers are demonstrated in a complimentary lesson. |

averages. Surveys of channel members and consumers can indicate satisfaction with promotions, suggestions for improvements, and the effect of promotions on image.

Some sales promotions—such as event sponsorships and T-shirt giveaways—are more difficult to evaluate. Objectives are less definitive.

Here are three examples relating to the effectiveness of sales promotion:

- About two-thirds of supermarket shoppers say that end-aisle displays and circular coupons "frequently" catch their attention.[34]
- A study by the Canadian Congress of Advertising indicated that for nonpersonal sources of purchase information 42 per cent of Canadians rely on flyers and cir-

# MARKETING IN THE THIRD MILLENNIUM

## Marketing the Third Millennium[37]

The third millennium is itself one of the great marketing opportunities (after all, it's a once-in-a-thousand-years event), so it's no surprise that a number of Canadian cities and organizations are capitalizing on the turn of the century to attract tourists and supporters.

As noted earlier, the telephone company MT&T of Halifax is taking part in the Tall Ships 2000 trans-Atlantic ship race. MT&T has also contributed $250 000 to the funds of Halifax-Dartmouth 2000, a large project commemorating the year 2000 in the Maritimes. It's a hefty price tag, but as Phil Hartling of MT&T observes, "It's a big sponsorship, but the long-term potential is much greater than a one-time marketing opportunity." Other cities are trying to draw tourists to commemorate a new age. Millennium Vancouver 2000 is promoting the theme "explore the horizon in a better city, in a better world, in a better future." There's also Calgary 2000, and not to be outdone by any city, Ottawa 2000 as well.

A number of organizations like MT&T are involved in Year 2000 events. The most significant is Canada's federal government, which has created the millennium bureau to administer the $145 million set aside to fund millennium projects. It's seeking private partners with the theme "Sharing the Memory, Shaping the Dream." The $145 million is designated to fund one-third of the cost of non-commercial national and local projects, with the other two-thirds from the private sector. The limitations on the funding are fairly strict: a lasting legacy must be created, but the funds can't be used for construction or buildings; nor can they be used for parties or fireworks.

One beneficiary of the fund that fits the tight restrictions is Natural Legacy 2000, which has received $10 million for an environmental preservation and protection project. Partnered with the World Wildlife Fund of Canada, the Nature Conservancy of Canada, and the Canadian Nature Federation, it is hoped that these partners can find private donors that will provide the additional $20 million needed to secure the government's $10 million.

The Trans Canada Trail 2000 also fits the criteria for federal millennium dollars. The plan is to build 15 000 km of recreational trails along Canada's three coasts at a cost of $15 million. The fund has $10 million so far, with $5 million in federal dollars and $5 million from Chrysler Canada, Canada Trust, and Cable Specialty networks TSN/RDS. The Trans Canada Trail is still looking for partners to put up the other $5 million. Meanwhile, it's planning an event in April 2000 where water will be drawn from Canada's three coastlines and then passed down the entire trail via a relay team made up of local community members. With 15 000 km of trail to cover, it's bound to be the relay of the millennium.

---

culars. This rating was barely behind newspapers, which were mentioned by 44 per cent of the respondents, and way ahead of TV, the third-ranked source at 35 per cent.[35]

- Labatt Breweries linked up with the NHL in 1999 to sponsor a "Stanley Cup Replica" giveaway in specially marked boxes of its Labatt's Blue beer. The firm was targeting the May 24 holiday weekend, which occurs in the midst of the Stanley Cup Playoffs. The giveaway was so popular that Labatt sold out its Stanley Cup Replica Blue inventory before the weekend and picked up two market-share points that were directly traceable to the promotion. Labatt also received tremendous publicity coverage associated with the giveaway.[36] See Figure 13-9.

# SUMMARY

**1.** *To examine the scope, importance, and characteristics of advertising* Advertising is paid, nonpersonal communication sent through various media by identified sponsors. Canadian ad spending is $8.3 billion annually, and non-Canadian spending among the top ten international advertisers is an estimated U.S.$235 billion per year in such media as newspapers, television, magazines, radio, outdoor ads, and cinema. In many industries, advertising is under 2 per cent of sales.

It is most apt with standardized products and when features are easy to communicate, the market is large, prices are low, resellers are used in distribution, and/or products are new. In general, behaviour is easier to change than attitudes; one ad can have an impact; ads do well with little-known products; and effectiveness rises during extended campaigns.

Among advertising's advantages are its appeal to a geographically dispersed audience, low per-customer costs, the availability of a broad variety of media, the firm's control over all aspects of a message, the surrounding editorial content, and how it complements personal selling. Disadvantages include message inflexibility, the fact that some viewers or readers are not in the target audience, high media costs, limited information provided, difficulty in getting audience feedback, and low audience involvement.

**2.** *To study the elements in an advertising plan* An advertising plan has nine steps: setting goals—demand and image types; assigning duties—internal and/or external; setting a budget; developing themes—good/service, consumer, and institutional; selecting media—based on costs, reach, waste, narrowcasting,

frequency, message permanence, persuasive impact, clutter, lead time, and media innovations; creating ads—including content, placement, and variations; timing ads; considering cooperative efforts—both vertical and horizontal; and evaluating success or failure.

**3.** *To examine the scope, importance, and characteristics of public relations* Public relations includes any communication that fosters a favourable image among a firm's various publics. It is more image- than sales-oriented; embodies image-oriented ads, personal selling, and sales promotion; and seeks favourable publicity—the nonpersonal communication sent via various media but not paid for by identified sponsors. There are thousands of companies with their own public relations departments and many specialized public relations firms. Companies try to get positive publicity and to avoid negative publicity. Competition is intense for placing publicity releases. Some firms have ineffective policies to deal with independent media or develop a sustained publicity campaign.

Among its advantages are its image orientation, its positive effects on employee morale, and—for publicity—its lack of cost for message time, its high credibility, and audience attentiveness. The disadvantages of public relations—compared with other promotion forms—include the lack of interest by some firms in image-oriented communications and the lack of control over publicity placements by the firm, the media's interest in negative events, and the difficulty in planning publicity in advance.

**4.** *To study the elements in a public relations plan* A public relations plan has seven steps: setting

goals—company and/or industry; assigning duties—internal and/or external; outlining types of public relations—the mix of image-oriented promotion forms and the categories of publicity (news publicity, business and service feature articles, finance releases, product and pictorial releases, video news releases, background editorial releases, and emergency publicity); choosing media; creating messages; timing messages; and weighing success or failure.

**5.** *To examine the scope, importance, and characteristics of sales promotion* Sales promotion encompasses paid marketing communication activities (other than advertising, publicity, or personal selling) that stimulate consumer purchases and dealer effectiveness. In the Canadian food and beverage industry, sales promotion expenditures are estimated to be $6.7 for every $1 spent on advertising.

The rapid growth of sales promotion is due to firms aggressively looking for a competitive edge, the greater acceptance of sales promotion tools by both firms and consumers, quick returns, the pressure by consumers and channel members for promotions and their popularity during economic downturns, the high costs of other promotional forms, and technological advances that make them easier to administer.

A sales promotion helps attract customer traffic and loyalty, provides value and may be retained by consumers, increases impulse purchases, creates excitement, is keyed to patronage, and improves reseller cooperation. However, sales promotions may also hurt a firm's image, encourage consumers to wait for promotions before making purchases, and shift the focus away from product attributes. Sales promotion cannot replace other forms of promotion.

**6.** *To study the elements in a sales promotion plan* A promotion plan has six steps: setting goals—ordinarily demand-oriented; assigning responsibility—to advertising and sales managers, company departments, and/or outside specialists; outlining the overall plan—including orientation, conditions, and other factors; selecting the types of sales promotion; coordinating the plan with the other elements of the promotion mix; and evaluating its success or failure.

## KEY TERMS

**advertising agency** (p. 409)

**advertising themes** (p. 409)

**advertising media costs** (p. 410)

**reach** (p. 410)

**waste** (p. 412)

**narrowcasting** (p. 413)

**frequency** (p. 413)

**message permanence** (p. 414)

**persuasive impact** (p. 414)

**clutter** (p. 414)

**lead time** (p. 414)

**cooperative advertising** (p. 416)

**publicity types** (p. 422)

**sales promotion orientation** (p. 427)

**sales promotion conditions** (p. 427)

## REVIEW QUESTIONS

1. Explain the statement "Advertising is paid for, publicity is prayed for."

2. List five objectives of advertising and give an example of how each may be accomplished.

3. A small firm has an overall annual budget of $50 000 for advertising. What specific decisions must it make in allocating the budget?

4. Differentiate among these advertising concepts: reach, narrowcasting, waste, clutter, and frequency.

5. What are the pros and cons of cooperative advertising?

6. Explain several ways that public relations as practised in both Canada and the U.S. may differ from public relations in other countries.

7. According to public relations executives, which are the two most preferred media for receiving publicity?

8. State three ways for a firm to evaluate the success or failure of its public relations efforts.

9. What are the limitations associated with sales promotion?

10. Why is the success or failure of many types of sales promotion relatively easy to measure?

## DISCUSSION QUESTIONS

1. Devise an advertising plan for generating primary demand for domestically made TVs.

2. A hotel chain knows a full-page ad in a general-interest magazine like *Maclean's* would cost $30 000; the magazine's total audience is 500 000, 200 000 of whom are part of the chain's target market. A full-page ad in *Ski Canada* magazine would cost $5400; its total audience is 42 000, 40 000 of whom are part of the chain's target market. Which magazine should the chain choose? Why?

3. Present and evaluate current examples of companies using institutional advertising, image-oriented personal selling, image-oriented sales promotion, and publicity.

4. Why do you think so many firms handle public relations-related situations poorly?

5. List several sales promotion techniques that would be appropriate for a university. List several that would be appropriate for a minor league baseball team. Explain the differences in your two lists.

## CASE STUDY
# Effective Long-term Sales Promotions

Most sales promotion efforts are short-lived, a fact that can be summed up by Julius Caesar's famous quote, "sic transit gloria" (all glory is fleeting). But some promotions have so much allure that they could seemingly continue forever. Not many people know who said "sic transit gloria," but ask about "Roll Up the Rim to Win" and they'll likely know it's from Tim Horton's.

The "Roll Up the Rim to Win" promotion is over thirteen years old, but Canadians still seem to love turning up the rim of a paper coffee cup to see if they've won a prize. The Royal Canadian Air Farce has spoofed the promotion on one of its shows, and do regular comedy bits involving ordinary people talking down at the doughnut and coffee shop (ostensibly Tim Horton's). In fact, the promotion is so good that Country Style Donuts has copied it with their own "Turn Up a Winner" program.

Another long-running promotion is McDonald's Monopoly game, which is almost twelve years old. Customers purchase certain McDonald's products and receive monopoly board game pieces. If they collect sets of these pieces that match the monopoly board property sets they can win prizes. The grand prize has always been $1 million.

One of the longest running promotional vehicles is Canadian Tire money. The money, which acts as a discount on future purchases, is given to customers who pay cash for their goods, and is accepted at Canadian Tire stores throughout Canada. Normally a 2 per cent discount, Canadian Tire may offer double discounts for certain products (e.g., on gasoline purchases).

The power of these promotions derives from rewarding loyal customers while encouraging them to buy certain kinds of products. For example, only medium and large coffee cups are included in the "Roll Up the Rim to Win" contest. Similarly, the purchase of only certain McDonalds combo meals or sizes of drinks and fries allows you to participate in the Monopoly game. At Canadian Tire you're encouraged to pay cash for your goods, but if you use a Canadian Tire credit card you're rewarded with loyalty points that can be spent in the same fashion as Canadian Tire money.

The success of these promotions is predicated on a number of things. Firstly, they need to follow the KISAS theory (Keep It Simple and Silly). Promotions that are easy to understand and easy to play are the best. You roll up the rim and you get the prize that's listed there. You collect the McDonald's Monopoly pieces and put them on a Monopoly board. You give them cash, they give you Canadian Tire money back with your change. The other key requirement is that the games be fun. Think of the anticipation as you drink your coffee (you shouldn't roll up the rim until you finish it, what with hot coffee burns and messy spilled-coffee stains). And your McDonald's french fries may have the $1 million Monopoly game piece attached to them right now!

Games that have many small prizes, like a free coffee or a dozen doughnuts at Tim Horton's, or free french fries or a sandwich at McDonald's, are the most appealing. It's better to have a lot of small winners in order to spread the promotion's impact around and encourage people to continue to play. When there are only a few large prizes people don't get as excited, since the odds of winning are too remote.

Promotions like these can run for many years, but are most effective if they're limited to a month or two within a given year. Any more than this risks overexposure. The interesting thing about these promotions is that they require their own advertising campaigns, with little or no time devoted to products themselves. The long-term nature of advertising is sacrificed for a short-term focus. In most instances, special promotions are financial failures. They're expensive to deliver and administer and they only work by giving up some of the regular gross margin of a product. As such, long-term loyalty promotions work well because they reward longstanding customers and bring them in more often. And more frequent visits translates into greater sales.

## Questions

1. Based on this case, the chapter material, and your own experiences, sketch out a list of attributes that you think would be associated with successful promotions.
2. Try to find some examples of unsuccessful promotions that you're either aware of or can research. What were the attributes of these promotions that kept them from working?
3. Discuss the ways in which you can measure the success of a promotional effort. What measures would you recommend for each of Tim Horton's "Roll Up the Rim to Win," McDonald's Monopoly, and Canadian Tire money?
4. Try to identify at least ten different promotions that you've been exposed to in the last month. Make a list. Then come up with an original idea of your own for a promotion that meets the success criteria you sketched out in question 1 and avoids the unsuccessful attributes of the promotions you identified in question 2.

**TIM HORTON'S**
www.timhortons.com/

**CANADIAN TIRE**
www.canadiantire.ca/

Source: Based on Liza Finlay, "Perpetual Promos," *Marketing Magazine* (May 31, 1999), pp. 11–12.

**CASE STUDY**

# Auto Dealer Advertising: Searching for Truth

Automobile dealers have notorious reputations for running misleading advertising. They promise the best trades and the lowest prices, and promote themselves as award winners or sales leaders. One underlying factor is that the market for automobiles is intensely competitive, which can lead to excessive claims in advertising. In addition, although local automobile dealers are part of one of the world's largest industries, they themselves are relatively small players in this industry. Most are independent organizations and thus the advertising management function for their businesses is not in the hands of a promotion specialist. As such, promotional ads may be developed and implemented by a person who is not fully aware of the regulations and implications related to misleading advertising. Consequently, some of the questionable activities are due more to ignorance and inexperience as opposed to willful attempts to mislead.

Price advertising can be particularly confusing for consumers. Take the example of lease rates quoted in any daily paper. The array of prices is mind-boggling. Consumers see ads that promote a $299 month lease. The problem is that it doesn't matter what price the car is, you can advertise any lease rate you want. The headline promises a $299 a month lease, while the facts are disclosed in the fine print. A $299 month, zero down payment lease would be a good deal. But what about $299 a month with $1500 down, $2500 down, or $4500 down? It can be argued that any lease ad headline should be for a zero down, since if the fine print mentions large down payments it's difficult to compare lease payments among competitors. Another misleading promotional tactic is to advertise a weekly lease or payment. Customers see "$80 payments" and might overlook the fact that it's a weekly estimate.

These practices are common, but there's some hope for people who live in Ontario. The Ontario Motor Vehicle Industry Council (OMVIC) is available to handle all complaints associated with automobile retailing, including complaints about advertising. In October 1998 the OMVIC brought in strict standards to ensure that dealers could prove the claims they make in their advertising. Ontario has 9000 licensed new and used car dealers, and they're all subject to OMVIC. When the new standards were brought in OMVIC issued warnings to 237 of these dealers, indicating that their advertising—and their fine print— was misleading.

The response of the dealers was positive. They were looking for guidelines to help them, and wanted to be able to compete with one another fairly and to provide their customers with what they need. OMVIC hopes that the new standards will prompt dealers to put more vital information in their ads and remove the outrageous claims. The idea is to allow consumers to make meaningful comparisons among dealers based on their advertising.

The new standards are intended to "guard against any form of misleading advertising or innuendo in marketing products and services." Claiming that a dealer has the best prices in town is no longer adequate. The dealer must be able to prove that it monitors competitors' prices and follows up by beating them. Another casualty of the new standards is one of the most powerful words in advertising: free. The guidelines state that since nothing is free, you can't state that it is. A dealer can make an incentive offer if it mentions that it's included in the price of the car. Ads must also indicate what charges aren't included in the price. Items such as freight, pre-delivery inspections, and dealer administration fees are often extra charges. The guidelines stop short of insisting that dealers advertise zero down lease rates, but they do state that "full leasing details have to be provided, including the size of the down payment, the length of the lease, the allowable mileage, and any residual obligations." Finally, ads must reveal the material history of a used car, e.g., its mileage, and whether the car was a rental, leased, or personal vehicle.

## Questions

1. What is it about automobile advertising that seems to lead to so many complaints about its integrity?

2. Discuss the role of advertising as a promotional element in selling an automobile. Look at what's happening in the marketplace these days. Is advertising becoming more or less important as a promotional tool? Explain.

3. Take a look at ten to twenty different automobile dealer ads in a couple of different editions of your local papers. Rate the ads according to the OMVIC standards discussed in this case (e.g., exceed standards, meet standards, marginal, doesn't meet standards), and then rank-order the ads according to your rating. Evaluate the distribution.

4. Search out some automobile ads that don't live up to the OMVIC standards mentioned in this case. Explain why they don't meet the standards, and rewrite the ads so that they do.

Sources: Based on Iris Winston, "Honesty's the Policy," *The Windsor Star* (March 23, 1999), pp. B1, B3; and Bob Meyer, "New Rules Lauded by Vehicle Sellers," *The Windsor Star* (March 23, 1999), pp. B1, B3.

# CHAPTER | 14

# Information-Based Marketing:
# Direct and Internet Marketing

## Chapter Objectives

1. To introduce the concept of information-based marketing

2. To define direct marketing and examine its scope, importance, and characteristics

3. To study the elements of a direct marketing plan

4. To define Internet marketing and examine its scope and importance

5. To describe marketing and the new world of e-commerce

Dick Hemingway

**A**s the twentieth century comes to a close, marketers, consumers, and governments are being challenged to manage a technological marvel, an incredible social force, and probably the most unique communications medium ever created: the Internet. For marketers, the Internet holds some of the greatest commercial potential ever imagined. (Although a number of skeptics believe that much of this potential will turn out to be, indeed, imagined.) Still, in 1998 an estimated U.S.$8–10 billion in consumer goods were bought on the Internet, compared to U.S.$43 billion in business-to-business goods. It is predicted that by 2003 Internet commerce will account for U.S.$1.4 trillion, 90 per cent of which will be business-to-business transactions, leaving $140 billion in consumer sales.

In the next decade personal computers, stereo music systems, and TVs will be merged into a single device that connects to everything via coaxial cable, optical fibre, satellite dish, or a combination of these. People will use these new devices (most likely a form of personal computer) for entertainment, information, education, and commerce. The Internet will fade from our consciousness as both a term and a concept, in the same way that people no longer mention whether their TVs are colour or black and white.

In the future people will spend a huge portion of their time in a world where they can make limitless connections with ease. Marketers need to realize that people will seek brands that stand out in an extremely cluttered environment, and in an over-communicated world. Therefore, branding—which represents the content of what firms have to offer and is communicated using advertising principles—will be just as important in electronic commerce as it is in the non-electronic world.

A marketing transaction normally involves the exchange of a title to goods and of rights to services, an exchange of value (usually money), an exchange of information, an assumption of risk in the exchange, and physical distribution of the goods or services. Virtually all the aspects of marketing transactions can be accomplished via the Internet, with the exception of physical distribution. Packaged goods, foodstuffs, toys, automobiles, computers, cosmetics, clothing, and all other tangible goods can be transacted for online, but must then be physically transported. However, for products and services that can be transmitted electronically (e.g., software, audio-video recordings, transmissions of performances, pictorial representations, and text materials) the Internet can also be used as a vehicle for distribution.

Firms will have to develop marketing strategies based on the fact that the Internet is both a content and a distribution medium—and one of the most powerful tools for information-based and direct response marketing ever created.[1]

## Overview

**Information-based marketing** depends on the use and creation of informational databases as part of the total marketing effort, which includes direct and Internet marketing.

The Canadian Marketing Association defines **direct marketing** as "an interactive system of marketing that uses one or more advertising media to effect a measurable response and/or transaction at any location, with this activity stored on a database."[2]

*Marketers depend on the use and creation of informational databases in* **information-based marketing**.

**Direct marketing** *uses one or more advertising media to effect a measurable response..*

**Direct response advertising** *is marketing through a nonpersonal medium.*

The goods and services exchanged are usually distributed directly to the consumer from the marketer. Direct marketing depends heavily on nonpersonal media. It occurs when a consumer is first exposed to a good or service via **direct response advertising** through a nonpersonal medium (such as direct mail, television, radio, magazine, catalogue, newspaper, telephone, fax machine, personal computer, free-standing inserts inside products or product shipments, and bounce-back circulars, or inserts in bills) and places an order by mail, phone, fax, or personal computer. Many people find it a convenient way to shop because they don't have to leave their homes. This is slightly offset by having to wait to receive their goods; however, express transportation services have reduced some of the delay in delivery and made this form of retailing even more attractive.

**Internet marketing** *involves using the Internet system as a medium for marketing.*

**Internet marketing** is used particularly for direct marketing. But since the Net combines virtually all the other media (magazines, newspapers, catalogues, billboards, direct mail, television, radio, telephone, fax machines) and is interactive (like the telephone, or a personal sales call), it's unlike any tool marketers have used before.

Indeed, the Internet is a marketer's dream. It allows a marketer to accomplish every single marketing function identified in Chapter 1 without leaving the office and without consumers leaving their homes. It also allows a marketer to be the primary performer in creating an exchange, since it functions as a tool for research, customer communication, promotion, distribution (for certain products and services), product development, and sales. For customers the Internet is an entertainment medium, a distribution channel, and a tool for information research, shopping, and communication.

In this chapter, the unique nature of direct marketing will be discussed and then related to the emergence of Internet marketing. The discussion will relate to the concepts covered in the previous chapters on product planning, distribution planning, and retailing, wholesaling, and promotion planning.

## The Scope and Importance of Direct Marketing

Direct marketing is best understood as a combination of promotion and distribution. It is one of the fastest-growing forms of marketing and retailing activities in Canada. The Canadian Marketing Association (CMA, formerly the Canadian Direct Marketing Association, or CDMA), is the main representative of direct marketers in Canada. See Figure 14-1.

The CMA describes the industry as involving "information-based marketers, those who reach consumers through media such as the Internet, television, telephone, radio, and addressed advertising mail." The CMA currently represents over 750 member organizations, which account for over 80 per cent of the annual $13.5 billion in information-based sales that are made in Canada. Member organizations include, but are not limited to, Canada's major financial institutions, insurance companies, publishers, cataloguers, charitable organizations, relationship marketers, and those engaged in electronic commerce and multimedia marketing.[3]

Statistics Canada reports that in 1997 consumers purchased $3.4 billion in merchandise from direct sellers operating in Canada. The discrepancy between the Statistics Canada estimate and that reported by the Canadian Marketing Association is most likely due to the wider definition of direct marketing employed by the CMA. Statistics Canada reports its estimates based on activities such as personal selling via group demonstrations at house parties, sales by mail or telephone, sales from manufacturing premises, home delivery sales, newspaper sales, consumer purchases of cosmetics, books, and encyclopedias, and sales of audio tapes, compact disks, and equipment.[4]

**FIGURE 14-1**

**The Canadian Marketing Association**
The CMA is the main representative of direct marketers in Canada.

*Reprinted with permission of The Canadian Marketing Association*

# CANADIAN MARKETING ASSOCIATION

According to the most recent data, more than one-half of U.S. households make a direct marketing purchase each year. The Canadian market is less responsive, with one report indicating that Canadians spend 50 per cent less per capita on home shopping than do Americans. One source indicated that only 15 per cent of Canadians order every year; however, statistics on Internet shopping behaviour indicate that about 36 per cent of Internet users have ordered over the Internet. So it seems likely that the percentage of Canadians ordering via direct marketing is probably much higher. In any case, sales growth in direct marketing is 7–10 per cent each year in Canada, making it one of the fastest-growing sectors of Canadian retailing.[5]

The market is being driven by both consumer- and marketer-related forces. The consumer forces include popularity of both the manufacturer and private brands of many direct marketing firms (and consumer confidence in them), mass availability and use of credit cards, poverty of time, convenience of ordering directly, the large number of working women, traffic congestion, wider use of telecommunications via computers hooked into the Internet, fax machines and computer faxes, falling long-distance rates, and the belief that direct marketing is a good way to shop. The marketer-related forces include the wider availability and ease of manipulation of databases due to the growth in computer power via hardware and software development, expanded TV channels with cable and satellite TV, the growing use of the Internet by businesses, wider availability and less expensive access to toll-free numbers, and the growth in efficient and less expensive expedited carriers like Purolator, UPS, Federal Express, and Priority Post from Canada Post.[6]

FIGURE 14-2

**Popular Direct Marketing Product**

*Webpage by Dell Home*

## The Characteristics of Direct Marketing

Direct marketing involves the use of nonpersonal media to reach potential customers in order to make a complete sales presentation offer that could lead to a sales transaction. A key decision that must be made before undertaking a campaign is whether a good or service can be successfully sold with a direct marketing approach.

Five considerations need to be addressed if a firm is going to offer a product as a direct marketing item. First, the product should have more than one basic appeal. Second, the product should have some kind of exclusivity. Third, the marketer must be able to reach the intended market efficiently. Fourth, the product should lend itself to strong advertising copy and a favourable art treatment. Finally, the product should have enough profit margin and sales volume potential to make the direct marketing activity worthwhile. Among the most popular direct-marketing items are: audiotapes; books; CDs; clothing; collectibles; computers, computer equipment, and software; cosmetics, beauty aids, and health products; credit cards; film and film developing equipment; hobby, craft equipment, and related supplies; home accessories; housewares; insurance; jewellery; magazines; packaged foods; seeds, plants, and garden supplies; sports equipment; and videocassettes.[7] See Dell's Website in Figure 14-2.

Direct marketing involves the use of promotional offers that are targeted to an audience through a carefully selected, nonpersonal medium. Marketers target television and radio audiences by selecting the program and time slot in which it airs. Direct marketing through magazines and newsprint may involve ads placed in the body of the publication, or free-standing inserts. The latter gives marketers greater flexibility in targeting particular geographic areas for newsprint, and may even allow the targeting of certain prospects for magazines. Marketers use readership information in order to choose the particular type of magazine or newspaper for these inserts or ads. And when using telemarketing, fax marketing, addressed mail, catalogue retailing, or the Internet, they depend on a detailed database.

Direct marketing through media such as television, radio, magazines, and newsprint often results in a large amount of waste circulation (see Chapter 13), and firms will see far lower response rates. Free-standing inserts in newsprint and magazines can help reduce waste circulation, but this can be offset by the fact that readers find it a nuisance when items fall out of their magazines or newspapers.

Direct marketing that involves database development is often referred to as **database marketing**.

> Database marketing is the process of extracting all relevant information from a customer purchase for use in future marketing programs and customer contacts. Basic information includes what customers purchase, how much (in units, dollars, or both), and how often they purchase. At more sophisticated levels, it can include demographic information (age, income, etc.) as well as psychographic information (e.g., buying preferences, likes and dislikes).[8]

Database marketing involves keeping records on customers, and over time adding new information about their behaviour to their files. It's the most powerful tool available for direct marketers, for the following three reasons: 1) their decisions are based on actual customer behaviour as opposed to market research; 2) the database allows personalized communication with customers, as opposed to treating them as part of a nameless mass of people; and 3) database marketers have insights into the people who comprise their databases and so can find products to suit the markets they know, rather than knowing their products but having to search for markets.[9]

The power of database marketing is being fully realized these days because of the wide availability of inexpensive but powerful personal computers containing excellent relational database management software that allows marketers to make open queries about the data.[10] In addition, the ability to collect data for use in database systems has been greatly expanded by the use of online data gathering systems. Market research firms and independent marketers have been collecting proprietary databases for years, but have had to code and input the database information themselves. Online systems enable customers to input information according to a format provided by a marketer's Web site.

Database marketing is a continuous learning process that involves collecting data on customers and refining it over time as the marketer and the customer undergo continuous contact. As the results of these contacts are recorded in the database the marketer can assess the quality of the customer relationship. From the viewpoint of a marketer, a good relationship involves frequent and sizable purchases. See Figure 14-3.

However, despite its tremendous power and potential, database marketing is not always feasible. It may not work if the business doesn't depend on repeat purchases from the same buyer. For example, unless tourist attractions are popping up daily, a vendor selling tourist guide maps of downtown Vancouver would likely sell only one map to each buyer. Database marketing isn't worth the expense if unit values and the quantities sold to any one buyer are small. The tourist guide maps wouldn't justify the use of database marketing, since a single map doesn't command a high price. Finally, database marketing isn't feasible unless the marketer is both inclined and able to capture information around the purchase. The guide map seller is likely taking cash for the maps, and the buyer is probably making a hurried, impulse purchase. The situation is just not conducive to information collection on the part of the map seller.[11]

Marketers also need to be aware of the pitfalls that can cause database marketing to fail:

*Database marketing is a process of extracting all relevant information from a customer purchase for use in future marketing programs.*

*Marketers need to be aware of pitfalls that can cause database marketing to fail.*

**FIGURE 14-3**

**The Continuous Process of Database Marketing**

*Source: Jack Schmid and Alan Weber, Desktop Database Marketing (1998). NTC Business Books: Lincolnwood, Illinois.*

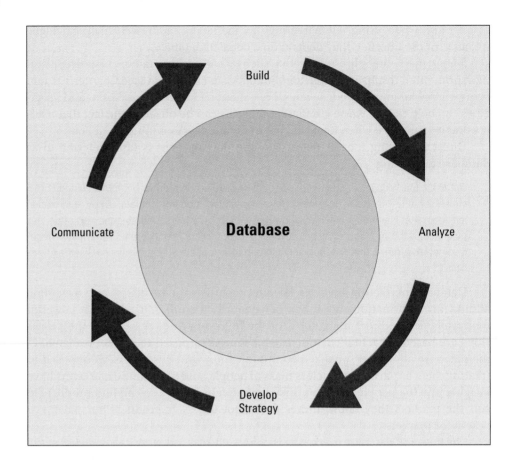

1. Senior managers don't buy into the strategy.

2. Firms develop databases, but don't develop supporting marketing strategies.

3. Organizations don't commit to using database marketing.

4. Data is mistaken for information. Data must be analyzed and made meaningful.

5. Marketers don't involve their companies' management information people and finance people in strategic decision making.

6. Marketers may believe that database marketing is the solution to all problems.

7. Marketers may believe that direct mail is database marketing.

8. Marketers may expect immediate results from database marketing.

9. Marketers build databases before deciding what they want to do with them.

10. Database marketing needs an organizational champion.[12]

Finally, there are two ethical issues—marketing to children and privacy rights — associated with direct marketing.

The Canadian Marketing Association amended its code of ethics on April 1, 1999 to provide guidance to direct marketers who target children. In the guidelines a child is any person under the age of thirteen. Direct marketing techniques for adults are not necessarily appropriate for children, and information collected on children must be done with the permission of the child's guardian. Marketing programs to children must be clear and simple, and not exploit their inexperience. Marketers should not accept any orders from children unless they are authorized by the parents.[13]

**TABLE 14-1**

## The Canadian Marketing Association's Seven Principles of Privacy

1. **Giving Consumers Control of How Information About Them Is Used**

   Consumers must be given an opportunity to decline from having their name and any other information used for marketing purposes by a third party before any information is transferred. This opportunity must be repeated once every three years.

2. **Providing Consumers with the Right of Access to Information**

   The consumer has the right to know the source of his/her name used in any information-based marketing program. Consumers have the right to know what is in their customer files and they have the right to question the information and request correction of any errors.

3. **Consumers Should Be Enabled to Reduce the Amount of Mail They Receive**

   All CMA members must make available the Do Not Mail/Do Not Call service of the Association when conducting a campaign to give non-current consumers (those who haven't made a purchase within the last six months) an opportunity to delete their names from mail and telemarketing lists.

4. **Controlling the Use of Information by Third Parties**

   At the time at which the information is collected, the purposes for which it is collected shall be identified. The personal information collected shall be limited to that which is necessary for the purposes identified.

5. **Information About Consumers Shall Be Safely Stored**

   Anyone involved in the transfer, rental, sale, or exchange of mailing lists must protect the list data from access, alteration, or dissemination unless these actions are authorized.

6. **Confidential and Sensitive Information Will Be Respected**

   All list owners and users must be protective of the consumer's right to privacy and sensitive to the information collected in lists and subsequently considered for use, transfer, rental, or sale. Private personal data such as medical, financial, and credit data must be protected by sectoral regulatory codes.

7. **Enforcement**

   Complaints concerning violations of the privacy code will initiate a process of review and hearings by the CMA. Members found to be in violation of the Code will have the opportunity to correct their practices; if further complaints are proven justified, members will be expelled from the Association.

   The provisions of the Canadian Marketing Association's Privacy Code were developed in accordance with the privacy principles of the Organization for Economic Co-operation and Development (OECD).

Source: Canadian Marketing Association, "Privacy Code," Canadian Marketing Association Web site, www.cdma.org (1999).

A person's right to privacy is a primary ethical issue that consistently arises with respect to the acquisition and use of database information for direct marketing. Since the strength of database marketing is often in the level of detail of the information, a key question is: How much detail do marketers really need to implement their direct marketing campaigns? What kinds of information should marketers be allowed to collect, and how should its use be restricted in order to respect people's privacy? The Canadian Marketing Association has developed a **privacy code** to guide its members and anyone else who uses databases for direct marketing. See Table 14-1.

*The CMA's **privacy code** guides those who use databases for direct marketing.*

FIGURE 14-4

**Developing a Direct Marketing Plan**

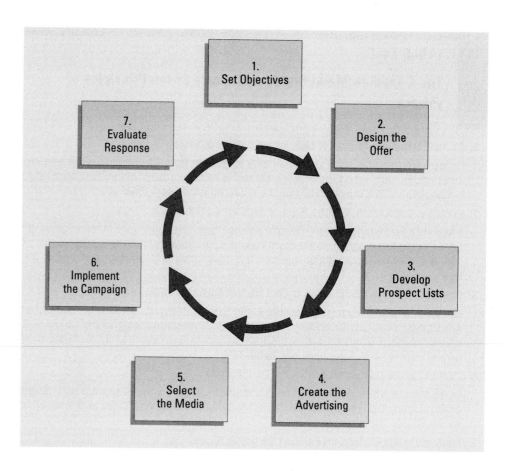

## Developing a Direct Marketing Plan

It is important to note that target market selection and tangible product or basic service development have usually been completed before direct marketing programs are developed. The process of developing a direct marketing plan consists of the seven steps shown in Figure 14-4.

### Set Objectives[14]

*Direct marketing objectives are focused on achieving an immediate and specific behavioural response.*

Direct marketing objectives are almost always focused on achieving an immediate and specific behavioural response from customers. The nature of the objective(s) set may depend on whether the marketer is seeking to sell to final consumers or to organizational consumers.

Typical objectives that might be set when selling to final consumers include:

- Attract new customers
- Obtain repeat business
- Product sales
- Profitability
- Acquire fundraising donations
- Develop customer relationships
- Test elements of the direct marketing program

Objectives that might be set when selling to organizational consumers include:

- Product sales
- Profitability

- Generate salesperson leads
- Qualify salesperson leads
- Develop customer relationships
- Test elements of the direct marketing program

One of the objectives of direct marketing that distinguishes it from other marketing activities is the frequent application of controlled field testing. Testing the elements of a direct marketing program involves a combination of both practical and academic knowledge. Practically, marketers want to get the best return on investment. They also want to learn which kinds of programs work and which don't. Academically, marketers are interested in knowing how the programs are working, and why they work or don't work.

Direct marketing allows testing of both products and offers. But tests come at a cost, and (as mentioned in Chapter 3) there must be a potential benefit of the research that exceeds its cost. For example, producing completely different infomercials can be very expensive. If a marketer wanted to test out different infomercial hosts and different infomercial products the production costs would be very high. Conversely, one might be able to change voiceovers, price displays, screen graphics, and tag-along commercials relatively easily.

Testing is usually done with a smaller sample of the total market and using print materials, which aren't as expensive to produce or distribute as are TV offers. But no matter how it's done, testing does cost more and will delay the implementation of a full marketing program. Direct marketers must be vigilant about over-testing, and recognize that although tests make for a more scientific approach, direct marketing is still a business and there will always be some risks.

One other objective of direct marketing is its role in larger initiatives. For example, it may be used as a lever to get new products into conventional distribution channels. Marketers often encounter considerable resistance from established retailers who are unwilling to stock new and unproven products or add new brands of proven products to their shelves. Retail shelf space is not unlimited, retailers want to sell what people are sure to buy, and retailers are asked to stock thousands of new products every year and can't take them all.

When marketers are denied access to distribution through conventional retailers, they are forced to operate a direct marketing program whose ultimate purpose is to establish a customer franchise and brand image that can pull the product into conventional retail channels. Saskatchewan-based E-zee Wrap first used direct marketing to introduce its plastic wrap dispensers and refills to consumers. After E-zee Wrap developed a brand image and a customer franchise, retailers like Zellers, Wal-Mart, and Home Hardware stores were happy to resell the firm's dispensers and refills.

More commonly, though, direct marketing functions as a lead-in for a personal selling call. This is often the case for organizational marketing. It's sometimes used for such high-priced consumer goods as vacuum cleaners and home repair and improvement items; or for offerings that require a lot of interpersonal interaction, such as life insurance and financial planning. In both cases, direct marketing initiatives are planned as a support to the personal selling program.

The reasons for using a direct marketing approach as a lead-in are quite simple: Personal selling time is a limited resource, personal sales calls are very expensive, and marketers don't want to waste their salespeople's time on poor prospects. A direct marketing effort allows them to identify customers with the highest purchasing potential, which is then realized through a personal selling effort. Used in this fashion, direct marketing may be part of a two-step, or even a multi-step process.

In a **two-step process** the response to the first contact is designed to trigger an immediate personal sales call. For example, a telemarketer contacts a potential cus-

*Direct marketing programs are often field tested.*

*Direct marketing may be used as a lever to get new product distribution.*

*Direct marketing can be used to get sales leads.*

*A response to the first contact is designed to trigger a sales call in a* **two-step process**.

tomer on the phone with the express purpose of arranging a personal sales call. The telemarketer gets an immediate yes/no response and should be acting to gauge the relative buying potential.

*A relationship is built up before a sales call is made in a* **multiple-step process***.*

A **multiple-step process** builds up a relationship through a series of contacts before a sales call is made. For example, a potential customer makes an inquiry in response to an advertisement. The inquiry is followed up by a detailed information package sent through the mail, fax, or even e-mail. The information package is followed up by a personal telephone call to make contact and to set up an appointment for a personal sales call. The marketer is able to hone in on potential customers, and to develop an information basis upon which to develop a sales presentation more fully customized to the needs and wants of the particular customer.

Before being handed on to salespeople, leads generated by direct marketing initiatives should be evaluated and categorized according to how likely they are to buy. The marketing organization must also be careful about the quality of the salespeople who receive the leads; a good lead deserves a good salesperson. A firm will not maximize its sales if it wastes its best salespeople on marginal leads and its good leads on marginal salespeople. The outcome in both cases is underperformance. Finally, the salespeople who are given the leads should be informed of their quality so that they can prioritize their time and efforts in following them up.

## Design the Offer[15]

An offer should be developed before any creative advertising or promotion is designed. An offer can be defined as "the complete proposition made by the direct marketer to the prospect." It must contain the following elements: a product offering, the price of the offering, and details of the terms of sale, such as the length of commitment the buyer is making, the terms of payment for the offer, and terms to reduce risk of purchase. Offers may also contain incentives to buy, other offers, and specific customer obligations.

*The* **offer design** *begins with the product itself.*

The **offer design** begins with the product itself. It must be the kind of product that people will feel both comfortable and confident about purchasing without a direct inspection. It's all the better if a means can be found to let them inspect the product at a distance. Brand familiarity, TV demonstrations, computer-based demonstrations, and even software downloads can allow for inspection. Still, the brand name and the image of the product are critical to success.

When designing an offer direct marketers must realize that in some cases people feel more comfortable buying a product at a distance. This happens when people feel embarrassed about buying the product in a store, or if they don't want friends or family to know they have made such a purchase. Books, videotapes, or personal items related to sex often fall into this category. Marketers who sell such products need to consider whether anonymity is a key purchasing factor. If buyers want to be anonymous, marketers are advised against using a name like "Erotica Industries" in their offers and on their packaging and labels, and instead to use a less descriptive brand name, like "Vitality Incorporated."

*The* **offer design** *begins with the product itself.*

**Package offers** *can work better than single product offers.*

Direct marketers can also package a couple of products together in an offer. On their own they may not sell well, but have greater impact when put together. Canadian cable companies have been doing this for some time. By offering five channels as part of a **package offer** the cable company may be able to get more subscribers per channel than they would if the channels were offered separately. See Table 14-2.

**Pricing policies** will be discussed in detail in Chapter 15, but some points are warranted here. Pricing is one of the key parts of an offer. People generally feel that since they are dealing direct they should be receiving the most economical price. They also expect some compensation for the fact that they have to wait for their

## TABLE 14-2

## How a Packaged Offer Works

A cable company is trying to determine whether to offer five new channels as a package or to offer them separately.

The suggested retail price of each channel by their originators is $5 per month. The cable company pays a $20 000 fixed fee per month for each channel to its originator, plus a 10 per cent royalty on sales to each subscriber every month. This amounts to $0.50 per subscriber (10 per cent of the $5 suggested retail price). Even if the cable company charges less than $5 per channel it must still pay a minimum of $0.50 per subscriber to the originator.

The cable company tests two offers: a separate offer listing each channel at $5 per month and a package offer of five channels for $10 per month. The package offer is presented with the benefit of an average price of only $2 per channel. That's a $3 saving per channel, or 60 per cent off. The response rates to the testing indicate the following subscription and revenue patterns.

### FUNCTIONAL ACCOUNTS

| | Separate Household Subscribers | Revenue | Package Household Subscribers | Revenue |
|---|---|---|---|---|
| Action Channel | 10 000 × $5 | $50 000 | 25 000 × $2 | $50 000 |
| Auto Channel | 5000 × $5 | $25 000 | 25 000 × $2 | $50 000 |
| Variety Channel | 7000 × $5 | $35 000 | 25 000 × $2 | $50 000 |
| Classic Movie Channel | 8000 × $5 | $40 000 | 25 000 × $2 | $50 000 |
| Lifestyle Channel | 4000 × $5 | $20 000 | 25 000 × $2 | $50 000 |
| | | | | |
| Totals (less costs) | 34 000 | $170 000 | 125 000* | $250 000 |
| Fixed fees | | $100 000 | | $100 000 |
| *Subscriber Royalty | ($0.50 × 34 000) $17 000 | | ($0.50 × 125 000) $62 500 | |
| Cable Company Margin | | $53 000 | | $87 500 |

*This row is added to determine royalty payments, but the total number of individual household subscribers is just 25 000.

Even though 34 000 households would subscribe to individual channels and only 25 000 households would take the package, the cable company makes more money from the package. The company decides to sell only the package offer.

goods. Direct marketers often do have a cost advantage, which they can include in their pricing by virtue of having neither intermediaries who need income nor a lot of fixed facility costs. Market evidence for this comes from the competitive price-matching policies of a number of fixed retailers. For example, Future Shop offers a price-matching guarantee that excludes direct marketers.

*Direct marketers can have a cost advantage by not having intermediaries.*

Another issue is the value of goods that direct marketers sell. Considering that shipping and handling costs can easily be $3–$5 per package, the direct marketer must recover these costs in the selling price. These costs tend to be highly visible, and they complicate the offer.

Another pricing issue occurs when customers are asked to do a lot of computing to figure out how much they have to pay. Shipping and handling, goods and services tax, provincial sales tax, harmonized sales tax, and possibly even customs duties may all be added to the price. A $75 advertised item can quickly jump to $100 when shipping and handling costs of $10 are tacked on, along with associated sales taxes and custom duties. People want to know what amount to write on their cheques or look for on their credit cards! The easier the direct marketer makes this, the better it is for the customer. However, with different tax rates and tax jurisdictions, it's difficult to present a nationwide offer with a uniform price. Further, shipping and handling charges differ depending on how far away the customer is. Many firms charge an average fee or a per-

*Sales taxes, custom duties, plus shipping and handling are often added onto the advertised price.*

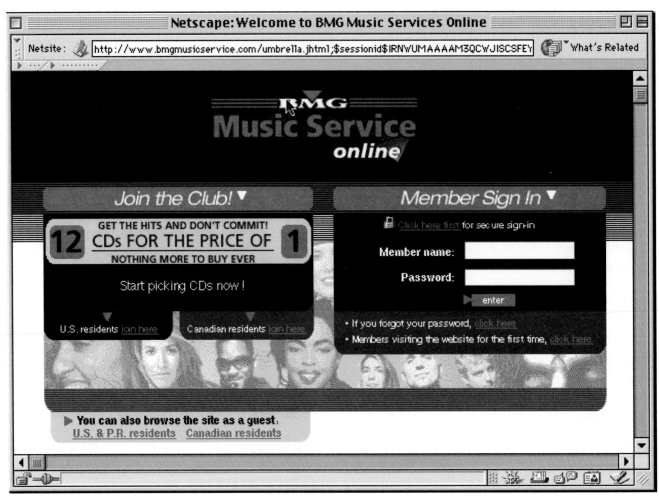

**FIGURE 14-5**

**Offers Explain Any Long-Term Commitment**

*Courtesy BMG Music*

centage of order value to reflect this cost. Finally, the issue of designing appropriate package prices may arise. See Table 14-2 for an example of package pricing.

*Offers should inform buyers of any* **long-term commitments**.

Offers need to explain if the buyer is making any kind of **long-term commitment**. Because direct marketers want a long-term relationship with their customers, many offers are presented to encourage repeat transactions. This is accomplished through "continuity" offers, which include fixed term offers, automatic shipment plans, and club plans. See BMG's Website in Figure 14-5.

A fixed offer may simply involve buying a number of months or years of service in advance. The best example is a magazine subscription: you don't just send away for the June 1 issue of *Marketing Magazine;* you take a year's worth of issues.

Automatic shipment plans mean that a person subscribes to an entire series and receives regular shipments and then regular bills. The shipments keep coming until the buyer cancels, or all the items in the series are shipped. Consumers are wary of these plans because it seems like the series of items never ends!

Club plans are extremely popular; for example, they're used by record companies like Columbia House and BMG, which are well-known direct marketers in Canada. Customers take on an obligation to purchase so many compact disks over a period of time. Every month they are sent a selection of items and asked to make a purchase. If a customer fails to respond, a club selection is sent automatically and the person is billed. Customers may cancel anytime after they fulfil their purchase obligation.

*Offer must include the* **terms of payment**.

The **terms of payment** must be provided in all offers. Credit card terms are the most popular, since the marketer receives the money immediately and the buyer experiences a delay between the time of purchase and payment. As well, the delay between receipt of the ordered goods and actual payment is less apparent. Debit cards offer the same convenience for a marketer, although in this case the customer's payment is not delayed. Instalment payments by cheque or credit card and delayed billing options are all possibilities. Since the level of risk increases for marketers when they ship before receiving payment, billing later is best for continuity offers.

Because direct marketing success depends heavily on consumer confidence, marketers must **offer terms that reduce the risk of purchase**. This can include offering warranties, money-back guarantees, satisfaction promises to pay return shipping, and free trial offers. As mentioned above, customers often have a need and desire to inspect the products they are buying. The degree to which a direct marketer can help a customer fulfil this need will make the sale much easier.

*Direct marketing can gain consumer confidence by* **offering terms that reduce the risk of purchase**.

The need to inspect or test out products can become an ethical issue if the direct marketer suggests that customers go to a local conventional retailer to inspect brands that will then be ordered direct. For example, customers might be told to test-drive a new automobile, examine a computer, or match colours on furniture even though they have no intention to buy from the local retailer. This situation can create channel conflict for a marketer, and is one reason why it can be difficult for a product to make the transition from a direct marketing channel to one that uses intermediaries.

Offers can sometimes be enhanced in some way that increases the urgency to buy and adds value to an offer. Marketers can use **incentives** like free gifts, free information, samples, discounts, sweepstakes, etc. Publishers Clearing House is a famous example of a firm that has run a consistent sweepstakes contest to encourage magazine subscriptions.

**Incentives** *include sweepstakes, free gifts, free information, samples, and discounts.*

**Multiple offers** is another possible enhancement. A customer might receive a deck of offer cards for a wide variety of different products. This works best if the offers are complementary. For example, a person with a home business might receive a set of offer cards that includes offers for products like computers, computer peripheral devices, computer software, stationery supplies, printing services, photocopy machines, long-distance telephone services, fax machines, tax accountants, financial advisers, credit cards, business directories, convention information on their industry, travel agencies, and even mailing list services.

*Marketers can enhance a transaction with* **multiple offers**.

Finally, offers may contain **customer obligations**, which aren't a consumer enhancement so much as a direct marketer enhancement. A customer may be receiving a cellular phone for free, but has to agree to sign on for two or three years of monthly cellular phone service with the provider at a set price rate.

*Offers may contain* **customer obligations**.

## Develop Prospect Lists

It's important to note that the selection and development of **prospect lists** occurs after a firm has designed its target market strategy. (The target market strategy may be refined later.)

**Prospect lists** *are selected and developed after the firm has designed its target market strategy.*

Many elements go into the development of a successful direct marketing campaign: the product and the associated offer, the timing of the offer, the quality and placement of the advertising used to promote the product, and the customer list/database. According to most experienced direct marketers, the customer list/database is the most important. See Figure 14-6.

Lists are often categorized in three ways: response, compiled, or house. **Response lists** are lists of customers who have bought via direct response before and have an associated product interest, but haven't bought from the firm before. **Compiled lists** are composed of people who are not identified as direct mail responders, but are grouped according to one or more common characteristics, e.g., members of a certain profession or interest group. **House lists** are made up of people who have transacted with or contacted the firm before, and for whom it has more detailed records.

**Response lists** *are of customers who have bought before,* **compiled lists** *of people are grouped according to their common characteristics, and* **house lists** *are made up of customers known to the firm.*

**FIGURE 14-6**

**The Importance of the Customer List/Database**

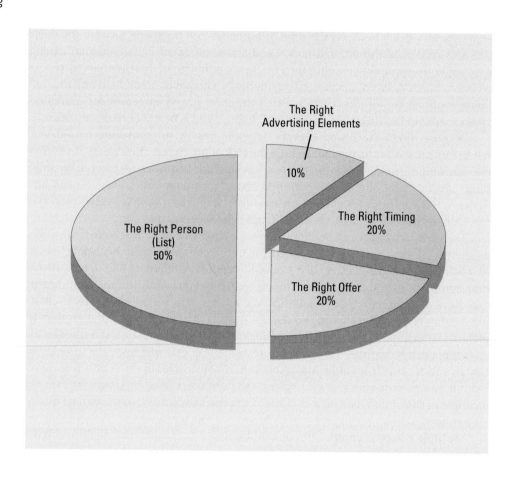

*A direct marketer may rent a list that has been compiled by someone else.*

InfoCanada has lists of 1.1 million Canadian businesses and 11 million Canadian consumers.

List/database development involves the use of database marketing and its tools for developing a house list. However, a direct marketer may simply rent a list that has been compiled by somebody else. Lists can be acquired as part of an exchange of house lists with another firm, or from a list broker who arranges for list exchanges. Lists may also come from a list compiler, a firm that specializes in developing customer lists.[16] For example, *Info*Canada of Mississauga, Ontario has lists of 1.1 million Canadian businesses that can be broken down by type of business, city, postal code, province, and number of employees. These lists also contain names of at least one key executive. The firm also has a list of 11 million Canadian consumers who can be selected by age, gender, income, lifestyle, median home value, ethnicity, and most importantly, by mail order response history.[17] See Figure 14-7.

Regardless of where the customer list originates, direct marketers should begin by applying their selected market segmentation and target market plans. This may be difficult if the list information does not match up exactly with the characteristics that the firm has identified as being critical to expected purchase behaviour. In this instance, marketers can apply the segmentation and targeting techniques to the list in accordance with the approach they took to segment and target the market originally. They can choose from a number of the bases for segmentation presented in Table 6-1, including geographic demographics, personal demographics, and consumer lifestyles.

*Customers may be classified according to a hierarchy of response.*

Experienced direct marketers have found that a good basis for selecting customers is their potential response behaviour. This is estimated from their direct marketing response history, and is one of the most reliable forms of segmentation for determining the likely response to any future offer. Customers may be classified according to the following hierarchy of response behaviour:

Suspect → Prospect → One-Time Buyer → Two-Time Buyer → Advocate

**FIGURE 14-7**

***Info*Canada**
Lists for 1.1 million businesses and 11 million consumers.

*Courtesy Info Canada*

A **suspect** is someone who fits the profile of existing customers for a particular firm, has usually made a direct marketing purchase before, but who has not purchased from the firm before.

**Prospects** are customers who have not purchased from the firm but have responded or interacted with it in some fashion. They may have called for information, visited the firm's Web site, visited its store, sent it an inquiry, etc.

**One-time buyers** have tried the firm's service but cannot be considered loyal buyers. One-time buyers tend to have a low order value. Only about half will ever make another purchase, and they tend to have a low response percentage to offers.

When a first-time buyer becomes a two-time buyer, a firm is in a good position to build a strong relationship. **Two-time buyers** have higher response rates to offers, higher average order values, and a lot more buying confidence.

The ultimate customer for a direct marketing firm is an advocate. **Advocates** go beyond simply giving a firm business; they actually recommend the firm to other customers. Considered to be a firm's most loyal customers, they tend to have the highest response rates to offers and the highest average order values.[18]

## Create the Advertising

Direct marketing's approach to advertising and promotion is to generate an immediate response to an offer in order to accomplish the objective(s) set down by the firm. Regardless of whether the intended response is a purchase, inquiry, donation, phone call, yes or no answer, or anything else, the key consideration is its immediacy.

A framework for a creative approach to direct marketing advertising begins with the understanding that the advertising must tell a complete story, with a beginning, middle, and end. A good way to tell a straightforward story is to use the **PAPA**

*Direct response ads should have a **PAPA**: **P**romise of Benefit, **A**mplification, **P**roof of Claim, and **A**ction to Take.*

## TECHNOLOGY AND MARKETING

## A Customer Loyalty Program for College and University Students

If you're a college or university student, iVision wants you to use its Camplus loyalty card. This card was distributed to 250 000 students in Quebec in the fall of 1998, and iVision planned to roll the program into Ontario in 1999. The firm's partners include Mont Tremblant skiing, Lunetterie New Look, TV cable company Group Videotron, Banque Nationale's MasterCard, and the federal health department. The advantage for the students is discounts at theatres and museums, rebates for skiing, restaurant discounts, and discounts with other retailers. With 250 000 student members, iVision expects a lot more firms to participate in honouring the card. Its market is large, considering that Quebec has 417 000 college and university students and Ontario has 429 000. The incomes of college students are modest—$11 972 in Quebec and $16 855 in Ontario—but they tend to contain more disposable income. Students, who can basically spend their money on themselves, are heavy consumers of movies, sports activities, beverages, audio-visual equipment, clothing, restaurants, and cars.

Students are issued the Camplus cards during frosh week on campuses. They are encouraged to log onto the Camplus Web site (www.camplus.com) to get information on issues and products that relate to them. The log-in procedure requires students to provide information profiles on themselves, which marketers can use to target them later. The products and services are marketed to the individual and customized to the profile that is provided.

Camplus is excited about its offering for both students and marketers. According to Philippe Racine, iVisions's President and CEO, "We've created a virtual community. We've created a technological infrastructure that allows us to put into a powerful database all the services, products, and information this community wants." The idea is for marketers to establish a relationship with these students that continues for a lifetime. And iVision isn't hung up on university students: they're planning to market similar kinds of cards for older consumers too.

Discuss some of the advantages and disadvantages of the Camplus discount card for marketers who join the program. If you were the decision maker for your marketing firm, what kinds of things would you want from iVision before agreeing to join the program? What kinds of things might iVision want from your firm?

Source: Based on Stephanie Whittaker, "The Gen Next Card," *Marketing Magazine* (May 31, 1999), p. 14.

---

approach.[19] PAPA is an acronym for the basic creative elements that every direct response advertisement should present: **P**romise of Benefit, **A**mplification, **P**roof of Claim, and **A**ction to Take. See Table 14-3.

*Direct marketers can advertise using the Internet; catalogues; television; radio; direct mail; magazines, newspapers, telemarketing and fax machines, free-standing inserts inside products or product shipments, and bills.*

Making sure that a direct marketing ad and promotional materials have a PAPA approach does not guarantee that they'll work, but if they lack any of these elements they are very unlikely to perform.

### Select the Media

Direct marketers have a wide variety of media to select from in order to implement a campaign: the Internet, catalogues, television, radio, direct mail, magazines, newspapers, telemarketing and fax machines, free-standing inserts inside products or product shipments, and bills. The newest, most unique, and one of the most interesting of these media is the Internet. It will be covered later in this chapter, but bears on the present discussion.

**TABLE 14-3**

**Creating Direct Marketing Advertising with PAPA**

**PROMISE OF BENEFIT**

People buy benefits. The main headline in any advertisement should present the main benefit to be derived from using the product. A good headline should have some or all of the following characteristics. It will:

- present a new benefit
- promise existing benefits
- be curiosity invoking
- be selective of the target market

**AMPLIFICATION**

This is essentially the story of the advertising. It will support the benefits expressed and may present some new benefits. It will reach out to the target market and provide them with the key information they need in order to make a purchasing decision. It must be personal, emotion evoking, interesting, and compelling. If it does not reach out to its audience quickly and effectively, the ad will fail.

**PROOF OF CLAIM**

Every direct response ad requires some kind of proof or support for the promised benefits and the amplified story. Confidence in the marketer and its products must be higher for direct marketers than ordinary retailers, because customers can't use personal contact to redress grievances or concerns about product failures. Therefore, direct marketing advertising must provide strong proof to support any claims by offering one or all of the following:

- warranties and guarantees
- special offers
- a seal of approval
- a meaningful testimonial
- a clear and compelling demonstration of product use

**ACTION TO TAKE**

By definition, a direct response ad asks for a specific and immediate response. A person is asked to phone now, stick some stickers on an order form and drop it in the mail now, log on to the Web site now, fax the order now, select eleven CDs for a penny and join the music club now, and maybe even come to the store now.

Source: Based on Otto Kleppner, Thomas Russell, Glen Verril, and Byron Collins, *Otto Kleppner's Advertising Procedure*, Canadian Eighth Edition, (Scarborough: Prentice Hall Canada, 1984).

Before discussing the media individually, it's important to note that media selection is all about reaching a target market. The target market guides list selection and should guide media selection too. But mailing lists will miss a lot of people, since (as noted in Chapter 4) 15–20 per cent of the Canadian population moves each year. Therefore, using secondary media to reach the target market can make a lot of sense. While mobile people are hard to reach through any mail- or telephone-based approach, broadcast, magazines, newspapers, and to a fair extent the Internet are relatively unaffected by this. The Shopping Channel, for example, launched a catalogue that was shipped out to all the customers on its house list as well as "poly-

*Retailers market direct with* **catalogue selling**.

**SEARS**
www.sears.ca

*American catalogue marketers operate in Canada.*

bagged" with the March 1999 issue of Flare magazine. This initiative was followed up by a Web site launched in March, 1999.[20]

One of the most popular forms of direct marketing by retailers involves the use of **catalogue selling**. According to the CMA, of the yearly Canadian direct marketing retail sales of $13.5 billion, about $2.2 billion is in catalogue sales. Catalogue ordering has recently been a growth business in Canada, although not all retailers have experienced it. The dominant Canadian catalogue direct marketer is Sears Canada, which has almost half of Canadian catalogue sales. In 1998 alone, Sears mailed out nineteen catalogues, ranging from seventy-two pages to the 1000-page Christmas Wish Book. Regal Greetings & Gifts, Canadian Geographic Enterprises, Hampstead House Books of Thornhill, the Winnipeg Fur Exchange, and Golfinn International are just some of the Canadian catalogue retailers trying to take advantage of the Canadian market.

Hoping to expand their sales, a large number of American catalogue direct marketers have been operating in the Canadian market, including Land's End, L.L. Bean, Victoria's Secret, Walt Disney, and the most recent entrant, Spiegel Catalogue. But American catalogue retailers have been plagued by low sales, caused by the weak Canadian dollar combined with the hassles of cross-border shipping through customs. Consequently, after Spiegel Catalogue entered the Canadian market with a lot of fanfare in early 1996 it found the market conditions much tougher than it expected—and announced it was pulling out in January 1999.[21]

The United States, Europe, and Japan account for 95 per cent of the world's mail order business. The U.S. alone is responsible for 47 per cent of the total. These global markets represent excellent opportunities for sales growth of Canadian direct marketers. Despite its size and a favourable exchange rate, Canadian catalogue retailers haven't focused on the the U.S. market, believing it to be overexposed and too competitive. Many Canadian catalogue marketers are instead looking to Japan, which is an underexposed market with a favourable exchange rate.[22]

Television commercials for direct response products have been around for many years. They tend to be very short—thirty to sixty seconds—and occupy the fringe time slots or appear on specialty cable TV channels which have lower advertising rates. Of course, the The Shopping Channel is a TV station devoted solely to direct response marketing. One of the key kinds of programs on The Shopping Channel, and on many other commercial stations, are **infomercials**.

*An* **infomercial** *is a full-length TV program.*

An infomercial is a full-length (typically thirty minutes) advertising program that airs on cable television or broadcast media at a fringe time. While watching infomercials, consumers call in orders and items are then delivered directly to their homes or offices. Infomercials are successful at promoting a variety of goods and services, including food preparation devices (such as juice machines and pasta makers), cosmetics, exercise equipment, instructional videos on computer software, and car waxes.

There are several factors behind a good infomercial, including the use of testimonials, program length, two-step offers, production considerations, and in particular, product pricing. According to one industry expert, the price of a product appearing on an infomercial should exceed $40–$50, due to the high production costs and media expenditures. If an appropriate item is priced at a lower amount, sponsors may sell the product as a package of three for $49.95 or as part of a "Buy two for $49.95, get one free" promotion.

Infomercials can be very effective: Royal Diamond Cookware used a French-language infomercial running twice a day on Infopub, an infomercial channel which is part of Le Groupe Videotron Ltée of Montreal. Royal Diamond Cookware received 2000 calls and generated $200 000 in sales in less than three weeks.[23]

**Radio direct marketing** has a number of similarities to television direct marketing. Since it's a less involving medium than television, people can listen to it while engaging in a wide variety of activities. There are no national radio networks in Canada that accept advertising, so radio time for direct response offers has to be purchased on a station-by-station basis. Some of radio's advantages as a direct response medium are that its formats have select audiences, its relative costs to other media are fairly low, ad production costs are very low, access to the medium is fast, audiences tend to be fairly loyal to particular stations, and the ads can be quickly changed.

Radio formats that are not suited to direct response products are the ones whose music is soft and mellow and whose volume is kept low for background music, and formats where the audience is so engaged with the show that they won't make the phone call right away or write down the contact information to call later.

A good radio direct response ad is sixty seconds long (about 200 words) and, like all direct response ads, has a PAPA approach. It's critical that the contact information be presented at least four times and in a highly memorable fashion. Radio is an auditory medium, and one minute isn't a lot of time. People usually need to hear a message at least twice before they have any chance of remembering it. The more compelling the message, the less it needs to be heard. However, providing memorable contact information can be difficult. The best responses will involve easy-to-remember phone numbers or e-mail addresses. For example, a florist who advertises "Call 1-800-356-9377" won't get much of a response. However, ask someone to phone 1-800-Flowers (the same phone number) and see what happens. The same is true of e-mail addresses. How likely is it that someone will remember www.JoanGirards_FlowerEmporium.ca versus www.flowers.ca? Getting exclusive rights to some of these easy-to-remember numbers and addresses can be challenging, but savvy direct marketers do figure out ways.

**Direct mail** response rates typically make up 0.7–5 per cent of the mailing list,[24] making it a relatively expensive medium in terms of cost per contact. Some estimates are that it's fifteen to twenty times more expensive to reach a prospect via direct mail as it is through television. However, direct mail has a number of advantages that offset this expense differential.

- It's very selective, allowing a marketer to choose and evaluate the individuals who will be contacted.
- Direct mail offers a wide variety of formats. A marketer doesn't have to just send a letter. A firm can send a video tape, audio tape, DVD software, pop-ups, fold-outs, 3-D displays, scratch and sniff, samples—just about anything you can think of.
- Direct mail is personalized. (Of course, this can backfire if names are spelled incorrectly, or when someone receives personalized mail for the previous tenant or owner.)
- Direct mail is not an adjunct to some other vehicle, as with most advertising. There is no competing programming as with television and radio; no other content as with magazines and newsprint. It's presented on its own, to be viewed at the leisure of the receiver.
- Well-designed direct mail can be highly involving if it can engage readers in some activity. For example, the Publishers Clearing House offers always ask recipients to place some stickers or stamps on an offer sheet, so that even if you send back a "no" response you're still able to engage in the dream of winning $10 million! See the Publisher's Clearing House website in Figure 14-8 for an illustration.

*Radio direct marketing is similar to television.*

*A good radio ad is sixty seconds long, has a PAPA, and presents memorable contact information at least four times.*

*Direct mail response rates typically range from 0.5-5 per cent.*

*Direct mail is personalized.*

**FIGURE 14-8**

**Well-Designed Direct Mail**

*Courtesy of Publisher's Clearing House.*

---

*Direct mail is the most controlled medium for testing offers.*

*The **mailing package** contains an envelope, a personalized letter, an informational brochure, an order form, and a reply envelope.*

- The highly selective and targeted nature of direct mail makes it the most controlled medium for testing offers. Marketers can know when the letters were sent, reliably estimate when they were likely received, measure how quickly responses have come back, and who has and hasn't yet responded. Theoretically, one could provide a custom offer to every recipient.

A key decision in direct mail is what to put in the **mailing package**. A typical package contains five elements: an outer envelope, a personalized letter, an informational brochure or insert, an order form, and a reply envelope.

The sole purpose of the outer envelope is to get itself opened. This can be done by promising important benefits, offering a free gift inside the envelope, disguising it to look like a cheque or a bill, making it very plain so that it arouses curiosity, or making it look so unusual that the recipient has to see what's inside.

The personalized letter and the accompanying brochure or insert are the selling tools. They must accomplish the four basic AIDA sales ingredients: get Attention, arouse Interest, create Desire, and request immediate Action.

A brochure or a **free-standing insert** may be included in the package. Letters are designed to be personal and get the interest of the potential buyer, but the additional details that the insert provides may be required to make the sale. (The inserts also represent extra items that can be passed over; a person is more willing to pass over an insert than a personally addressed letter.) The term "preprint" or "freefall" is used to describe these inserts. They're basically an ad unto themselves, although they're often used for coupon or special offer distribution. One guideline for the successful use of a free-standing insert is that the headline must state the item that's being offered. Inserts usually ask that a person transmit an order electronically (by phone, fax, or e-mail) as opposed to a mail-in.[25]

*Free standing inserts state what is being offered in the headline and ask for an electronically transmitted order.*

The order form and reply envelope are critical to making it easy to respond to the offer. Even when the respondent is ready to take action, if the order form is too complicated to be filled out easily the action will be blunted and not carried through. Likewise, a reply envelope makes it easy to respond. It might be too much to ask people to fill out an address on their own envelope, which might not even conform to the size of the order form.

A critical consideration for any direct mail package is the cost of the mailing. The larger and heavier the mail pieces, the more expensive the mailing. The choice of mail classification is important too. Considerable research on the topic of direct mail has indicated that **third class mail**, known as **junk mail**, is generally more efficient than first class mail. People may evaluate the postal classification of their mail before opening it, but if they're going to be that discriminating the odds of fooling them with a first class stamp on a direct mail solicitation are pretty low.[26]

*Third class mail (junk mail) is more efficient than first class mail.*

**Bill inserts and bounce-back circulars** are additional offers that are shipped with products or placed in bills that are sent to customers. They are basically tag-alongs and have many of the characteristics of free-standing inserts. They're used because wise direct marketers are always selling, even when they've already sold. Every customer contact should be viewed as a selling opportunity, and when marketers have a chance to convert a first-time buyer into a second-time buyer, they should take it. Since products are being shipped, adding a few offers in with the product won't affect the shipping costs much and may create another sale. The same is true of billing. If you can send an offer along with the bill for the same postage, why not do it?

*Bill inserts and bounce-back circulars are offers that are shipped with produces or placed in bills.*

**Newspaper direct marketing** involves purchasing space in newspapers as well as using them as a distribution medium for free-standing inserts. Newsprint is often described as a shopping medium—and at least one weekly paper, the PennySaver, is nothing but a shopping medium. People expect to find advertising in newspapers, and in the case of classified advertising, are actually looking for it. Although newspapers have fallen behind the electronic media as the main sources of news, they still provide greater local and in-depth coverage than do the electronic media. Consequently, newspaper circulation and market coverage is generally very high in most places in Canada (see Chapter 13).

*Newspaper direct marketing can be a distribution medium for free-standing inserts.*

Purchasing space in the newspaper provides a great deal of flexibility. Advertisers can choose from a wide variety of presentations, including full-page ads, classified ads, supplements, and free-standing inserts. But with the exception of the latter, the quality of reproduction, especially for colour, is relatively poor. Daily newspapers have very short lives (the *PennySaver* has seven days), so responses to advertising need to be almost immediate. Still, advertising rates are often quoted over three- to seven-day runs.

Placing a free-standing insert in a newspaper is far less expensive than sending the same piece through the mail. Moreover, one reported study indicated that newspaper inserts had higher readership than the same inserts used in direct mail. But although distribution costs are far lower, the ability to target is also substantially reduced.[27]

**Magazine direct marketing** generally has a lower cost per contact than direct mail.[28] When choosing a magazine for direct marketing the key considerations are its

*Magazine direct marketing has a lower cost per contact than direct mail.*

content, its circulation, the special services it offers, and its audience's receptivity to direct response offers.[29]

Content refers to the fact that magazines are generally highly targeted with respect to interest, which is the main difference between them and newspapers. When designing their promotions direct marketers must therefore consider the **vehicle source effect**, which means that while you might place an ad to sell a house-painting system in almost any newspaper, you can't do that with magazines. A house-painting ad wouldn't fit with the content of *Ski* or *Brides* magazine very well. Conversely, if you were selling ski equipment then you'd expect readers of *Ski* magazine to be far more responsive to your ad than would newspaper readers.

*Direct marketers should consider* **vehicle source effect** *when designing promotions.*

The size of the circulation of the magazine and the characteristics of the audience are of critical concern. Is there a large enough circulation with sufficient interest in your product to generate a large enough response to make advertising worthwhile? Magazines have paid subscriptions, newsstand sales, and pass-along circulation as part of their readership. The problem is that it's virtually impossible to know the characteristics of the individuals who make newsstand purchases or represent pass-along circulation. (***Canadian Advertising Rates and Data*** (CARD) is the source to consult to confirm the audience characteristics.) An advantage of magazines for direct mailing lies in the fact that a significant number of mailing lists are derived from magazine subscriptions. Placing a magazine ad and supporting it by a direct mailing campaign to the magazine's mailing list can have a synergistic effect in increasing responses to both media.

***Canadian Advertising Rates and Data*** **(CARD)** *is a source for audience characteristics.*

Special services are very important when it comes to testing your advertising efforts and customizing them to increase responses. Being able to buy preferred positions or into special issues can enhance response rates for a firm, but these come at a cost. Magazines frequently have a direct marketing area similar to the classified ads in newspapers. These areas often have special rates, but there's clutter to be considered if your ad is placed here. Magazines that offer split-run privileges allow you to test offers in the field; there may also be regional and demographic editions. For example, you might want to place a direct response ad for an electronic thermometer in the physician edition of a magazine. It's not that you want to sell to physicians—no, you want to sell to the people with a high fever who are in the waiting room reading the magazine! Will the magazine accept inserts, either free-standing or bound-in, and will it **polybag** a catalogue or even another magazine? With free-standing inserts you can test out your advertising more easily, as well as save money by using the same pieces as you would in newspapers and direct mail. With polybagging, a catalogue or even another magazine can be distributed with a magazine.

*Magazines may accept free-standing or bound-in inserts, and will even* **polybag** *a catalogue or another magazine.*

Yet, no matter how well a magazine may seem to fit with your intended target market, and how well your product might seem to fit with the format and content of the magazine, if the readers aren't receptive to direct marketing appeals, there is little point in advertising.

**Telemarketing** is one of the most powerful direct marketing tools there is. While it's often perceived as involving only unsolicited inbound calls, it also involves outbound calls to 1-800, 1-888, and 1-900 numbers, and both inbound and outbound fax transmissions. For business-to-business marketing it's a highly desirable selling tool. Customers in the business-to-business market are fairly receptive to telemarketing calls and inbound faxes, and are also very willing to send outbound faxes and to call marketers.

**Telemarketing** *is not just unsolicited inbound calls; it also includes 1-800, 1-888, and 1-900 numbers plus inbound and outbound faxes.*

In the consumer market the use of the telephone for outbound calls in response to an offer made through another medium is very positive. However, the reaction to telemarketing as an inbound initial contact and solicitation medium is very different, with only 13 per cent of people indicating a willingness to accept a telemarketing call. Still, research on telemarketing indicates that 15 per cent of call receivers have made telemarketing purchases.[30]

Telemarketing is one of the most expensive direct response media there is. As such, it may not be wise to use this medium as the primary first contact to qualify buyers in consumer markets. This isn't true of organizational markets, where buying and selling are designated duties and professions for many people. Almost any marketer will be given a chance to make a first contact as part of an organizational sale, but a second chance may not be forthcoming if the first contact isn't handled well. Usually a telemarketing contact for an organizational market falls into one of three categories: it's done to generate leads and arrange a sales call, it's part of a sales call follow-up, or it's part of an established relationship involving a routine sales contact.

Inbound consumer telemarketing is probably one of the most difficult activities a marketer can undertake. Modern telephone technology has provided both barriers and solutions for telemarketers. Barriers include answering machine devices, call display features that allow call screening, busy signals, and unavailable prospects.[31] To overcome the first three barriers, telemarketers have computer devices loaded with software that will automatically dial numbers of people identified on a prospect list and then check for busy signals, voice mail, or answering machine devices. A live salesperson won't come on the line unless a live person has answered the telephone.

*Barriers to telemarketing include answering machines, call display, busy signals, and unavailable prospects.*

The issue of unavailable prospects is more difficult to handle. The prospect may be genuinely unavailable or simply does not want to talk. A call back can be arranged with the person at a more convenient time. When a person doesn't want to talk it may be a sign that he or she isn't interested, and should be evaluated as a poor prospect and perhaps removed from the call list.

The real power in telemarketing lies in its support of other marketing initiatives and its use when a "relationship" has already been established.

## Implement the Campaign

The key issue in implementing a direct marketing campaign is timing. When should you run your campaign and how often should it be repeated? A direct marketing campaign that's properly timed can increase market response without increasing costs.

*Timing is a key issue in implementing a direct marketing campaign.*

When should you run a campaign? This depends to some extent on the product. If it's seasonally related, such as clothing, paint, Christmas music, outdoor furniture, outdoor sporting goods, etc., then offers should be sent out or presented prior to and during the season. Post-season sales can also offer some potential, but only the most avid of customers are likely to respond. For example, Suit Yourself Sunwear in Richmond, B.C. specializes in clothing that is resistant to the sun. People with fair skin or who have suffered from skin cancer need to avoid overexposure to the sun and will readily seek the firm's products. But concern about sun exposure is seasonal, and so Suit Yourself Sunwear does not actively solicit orders during the winter. Come spring, they send out special offers to past customers and advertise them on their Web site.

Some of the media experience seasonally related changes in audience. It's well established that TV viewership tends to decline during the summer months and increase during winter. Conversely, radio listenership increases a bit in the summer as people listen to the radio while they sit or work outdoors. In general, January is a good time for direct response in magazines because they're not as cluttered by other advertisers. Summer doesn't seem to be a strong season for magazine readership. Certain magazine issues may be more popular than others as well. The readership of *Sports Illustrated*'s swimsuit issues and the college and pro football reviews tend to be the highest for this magazine.

The Christmas retail season tends to evoke the most frenzied level of selling competition there is, but it also involves the highest level of purchasing activity. This is a very important selling season for all direct marketers.

The time of day a solicitation is made is critical for broadcast media and tele-marketers. Viewership, listenership, and availability to take phone calls are all synchronous activities, i.e., the offer must be viewed or heard when it's presented. (Print media and the Internet don't suffer from this problem because they can be accessed at the customer's leisure.) Morning drive time is best for radio listenership and evening prime-time is best for TV viewing. But since media costs tend to be highest when audiences are highest, direct marketing in broadcast media tends to occur during fringe times in order to keep costs low. The wider availability of multiple specialty cable channels has helped reduce some of the absolute media costs of TV advertising, with the added benefit of offering very specialized audiences—which of course represents the very core of success for direct marketers.

Inbound consumer telemarketers tend to call people in the evenings during the dinner hour because this is when people are likely to be home. Earlier in the day people may be working, or resting if they work nights, and later in the evening people may have gone out or even gone to bed. Still, it's hard for telemarketers to win, since the nature of the activity is intrusive, and hence annoying. When a cold-calling tele-marketer calls between 5:00 and 7:00 p.m.—which for many households is dinner time, family time, or personal time—well, a telemarketer's skin has to be pretty thick. If the telemarketer is involved in organizational marketing, the best time to contact the person is at their place of employment between 9:00 a.m. and 5:00 p.m.

Newspaper ads work best in Sunday papers because they are highly read. If the market doesn't have a Sunday paper, the Saturday paper is the next most highly read, and the Monday paper will be much more important.

Direct marketers have examined seasonal response patterns and time-of-day response patterns of almost every kind of media there is. The Canadian Marketing Association and the Direct Marketing Association sell reports that contain information on these patterns.

The issue of how often to repeat a campaign is usually not independent of response evaluation, but it should nonethelesss be considered in an initial planning stage. For example, advertising research has indicated that most people need three to four exposures to a typical ad before it makes a strong enough impression that they remember it with aided recall. The conclusion is simple: direct marketers need to consider making three to four contacts with their customers before assuming there will likely be no response.

## Evaluate Response

The term "direct marketing" derives from the nature of its transactions and customer contact. But it could just as well derive from the fact that virtually all the costs and expenses associated with the marketing effort can be traced to their source and analyzed.

*Evaluating direct marketing involves looking at **response rates**, profitability, and the value of customers.*

Evaluating response is undertaken on three basic levels: One can look at the **response rate** of a number of people exposed to the promotional offer; the profitability of direct marketing operations; and the value of the customer.

Many different measures can be used to evaluate response rates. For example, if 1000 people were sent a mailing asking for a donation and twenty-five of them sent one in, we could say the response rate was 2.5 per cent. On the other hand, if the mailing asked for a yes/no response and 100 letters were returned with seventy-five no's and twenty-five donations, the response rate is 10 per cent and the donation rate is 25 per cent of response and 2.5 per cent of mailing. Response rates to direct marketing campaigns have been researched in great detail. It's beyond the scope of this text to report all of them, but here are some general findings:

- The success or failure of direct marketing efforts in general is based 40 per cent on selecting the right market segment, 40 per cent on the image of your firm and products, and 20 per cent on the creative efforts, format, and postal/delivery activity.[32]
- If January is rated as the best month on a 100-point scale for a direct mailing, a general rating of the other months is as follows: February 95; March, April, and May 70; June 65; July 70; August 85; September 80; October 90; November 85; and December 75.[33]
- Direct mail response rates average about 2 per cent of the mailing list.[34]
- About 6 per cent of cable TV shoppers purchase from home shopping services.[35]
- One study of business-to-business marketing found a 2 per cent response rate to mail, a 7.5 per cent response rate to telemarketing, and a 13 per cent response rate if the two approaches were combined.[36]
- The response pattern from any one issue of a monthly magazine will be 3–7 per cent after the first week, 50–55 per cent after the first month, 75–80 per cent after the second month, and 92–95 per cent after four months.[37]
- Olan Mills Portrait Studios reported a 3 per cent response rate with its telemarketing campaign.[38]
- Free-standing insert coupons return about 71 per cent of their cost within the first twelve weeks after the coupon drop.[39]
- Magazine direct response rates range from .05–.2 per cent of circulation.[40]
- Fifteen percent of call receivers have made telemarketing purchases.[41]

Profitability measures—another way to measure the effectiveness of direct response advertising—depend on analyzing the response rates. A marginal analysis of the situation is the most basic approach to take.[42] If it costs $30 000 to mail 20 000 direct mail packages and you have enough margin in the product you're selling to spend $20 to get an order (e.g., selling price is $50 and the item costs your firm $30 after shipping) then the breakeven is:

$30 000/$20 = 1500 orders per 20 000 mail packages.
1500/20 000 = 7.5 per cent response rate.

The value of a customer is often measured with a formula called the **lifetime value**. It is:

> the value today of future profits from customers. It measures the value of making an investment in gaining new customers, based on what future sales (and profits) from those customers are likely to be. In all, lifetime value involves four basic assumptions:
>
> 1. Marketing to repeat buyers is more profitable than marketing to prospects.
> 2. An investment (advertising, mailings, etc.) is made to acquire the customer.
> 3. There is a return on the investment.
> 4. The return occurs every time.[43]

*The **lifetime value** formula measures future profits from customers.*

Lifetime value is calculated by looking at the amount the customer has spent, the cost of goods the customer bought (to determine margin), and the cost of marketing to reach the customer.

Responses and non-responses must be traced back to the firm's house list and updated into the firm's list/database. Direct marketing is all about creating relationships with customers and maintaining them. This means updating and clean-

*Responses and non-responses must be updated into the firm's house list.*

ing direct marketing lists on a daily basis. After all, the onus is often on the marketer to call or write to maintain the relationship. On the other hand, it's well known that many consumers wait anxiously to see the newest version of their favourite catalogue and are not above giving a marketer a call to find out where it is or when it's coming.

Finally, it is a lonely person indeed who does not even get mail or telephone calls from direct marketers. And even if the person prefers loneliness and has the Canadian Marketing Association remove their name from CMA member lists, they have only informed the most ethical 80 per cent of direct marketers about their decision!

## The Scope and Importance of Internet Marketing

E-commerce is not only changing the way business is conducted, it is changing the fundamental economic assumptions on which business is based. Canadian executives must take action now to survive and succeed during this shift from an industrial economy to an electronic economy.[44]

One definition for **e-commerce** is:

The buying and selling of information, products, and services via computer networks as well as support for any kind of business transactions over a digital infrastructure.[45]

*E-commerce includes the buying and selling of information, products, and services via computer networks.*

As noted at the beginning of this chapter, in 1998 an estimated U.S.$8–$10 billion in consumer goods were bought on the Internet (less than 1 per cent of the value of the total U.S. retail market). This was dwarfed by the estimated U.S.$43 billion in business-to-business goods that were purchased. It is predicted that by 2003 e-commerce will account for U.S.$1.4 trillion, with 90 per cent of that involving business-to-business transactions, leaving $140 billion in consumer sales.[46]

*Six and a half million Canadians access the Internet each week and will be spending $6.9 billion online by the year 2002.*

Total Canadian Internet sales were estimated at $255 million in 1997 and projected to be $6.9 billion by the year 2002. Fifty-one per cent of Canadian adults have access to the Internet, with 6.49 million Canadians going online on a weekly basis. Canada currently ranks fifth in the world in Internet use; however, this ranking will fall as the populations of other nations go online. About 13 per cent of Canadians purchased online in 1997, up 2 per cent from 1996.[47] See Figure 14-9 for an example.

According to the *Computer Industry Almanac*, at the end of 1998 there were over 150 million people in the world who used the Internet on a weekly basis. Approximately 76 million of these users live in the U.S. The number of users in the top fifteen nations in the world account for 87 per cent of the users worldwide. It is predicted that the number of total users will more than double to 320 million by the end of the year 2000, and that this number will more than double again to 720 million users by the end of 2005.[48]

Use of the the World Wide Web for advertising in Canada is growing rapidly, but lags behind the U.S. For example, advertising expenditures are predicted to be about $38 million for 1999, while in 1998 they were about $20.7 million and in 1997 they were $9.5 million. In contrast, U.S. expenditures were predicted to be U.S.$2 billion for 1999.[49]

Given these levels and the expected volume of e-commerce, it's clear that the Internet is emerging as a unique and important medium as well as a tremendous global business opportunity.

## Marketing and the New World of E-commerce

The expansion of both organizational and consumer retail markets on the Internet is astounding. The growth rate of retail e-commerce is outstripping almost every other retail innovation before it.

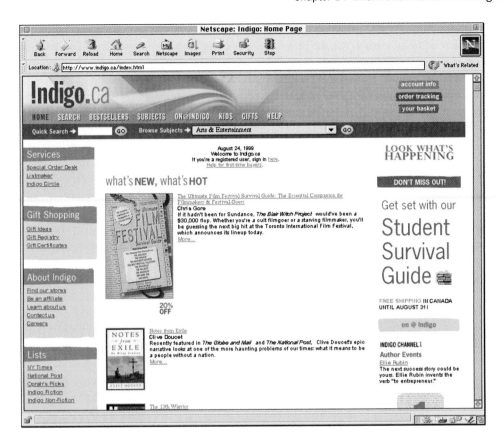

**FIGURE 14-9**

**E-commerce**
Reaching out to the 6.5 million Canadians who are online.

*Courtesy of Indigo Online, www.indigo.ca.*

It has caught on far more quickly than shopping centres in the 1950s, discount stores in the 1960s, and big-box category killers like Toys 'R' Us and Home Depot in the 1980s. . . . Bricks-and-mortar retailers such as Brooks Brothers and Toys 'R' Us reluctantly turned cyber—overcoming their "cannibalization inertia," or fear of pulling customers away from their stores. Any merchant that wasn't on the Web lost customers.[50]

Internet use is driven by a number of forces. One of the most important of these is the economic strength of a country, since unless a nation is "wired" with the most up-to-date communications system it's hard to access the Internet. This wiring must include firms that offer Internet services (Internet Provider Organizations, or IPOs). Not surprisingly, wealthier nations have tended to have higher Internet use; and those that are geographically isolated, like Australia and New Zealand, have embraced the Internet on a higher per capita basis than even the U.S. In these countries the Internet is used as a tool to help firms conduct their import-export business more efficiently, since it's cheaper and easier to use than telephones and fax machines, and far faster than the mail.[51]

A second factor is even more fundamental: ownership of a modern personal computer. At the end of 1998 there were an estimated 364 million PCs in use around the world, with 129 million of them in the U.S. and about 11.75 million in Canada. At the end of the year 2000 there will be an estimated 500 million personal computers in use, and by the end of the year 2005 over 990 million personal computers and computer-like devices![52]

In 1998 $5.2 billion in personal computers were sold in Canada. This was an increase in sales of 21 per cent over the previous year, which is all the more significant when you consider that personal computer prices have been steadily dropping. Internet service providers have seen a huge increase in subscribers, with an estimated 3 million Canadian subscribers in 1998, up from 2 million in 1997—a 50 per cent increase![53]

*Canada's e-commerce is driven by our economic strength, up-to-date communications systems, and ownership of modern personal computers.*

*The Internet is a **convergent medium** because it combines the characteristics of all other media.*

The Internet has been described as a **convergent medium** because it combines the characteristics of virtually all the other media while simultaneously acting as a distribution channel. Andersen Consulting conducted their first survey on e-commerce in 1999 to track and measure its evolution among Canadian business organizations. The study sampled the opinions of 293 business leaders and decision makers from Canadian firms in the financial, resources, communications and high technology, and manufacturing and retailing sectors. The findings ran contrary to what might be expected: more than 70 per cent of the respondents did not consider e-commerce to be a high priority, although 84 per cent indicated that their firms would be more dependent on e-commerce in the next five years.

Instead, the respondents in the study listed the following five items as top priorities: improving customer service (78 per cent); Y2K readiness (76 per cent); increasing customer loyalty (68 per cent); attracting new customers (65 per cent) and cost reduction (62 per cent). E-commerce was identified by only 29 per cent of the respondents as a business priority.[54]

Yet, it's a foregone conclusion that firms that have not yet embraced the Internet will soon be compelled to do so. A Web site is already becoming a customary and expected communications device by both consumers and organizational customers and suppliers. Businesses will need Web sites in the same fashion as they need telephone service. Think of the Internet as becoming the equivalent of a global, electronic Yellow Pages. Businesses have found that when they weren't listed in these "Yellow Pages" they had trouble getting customers, and worse, existing customers who were aware of the firms concluded that they had gone out of business.

Many firms are using the Internet as their exclusive approach for doing business, even though there are well-established alternative communication and distribution channels. Firms in this category include virtual retailers like eToys and bookseller Amazon.com, a firm that had $610 million in sales in 1998, up from $15.7 million in 1997;[55] Internet-based financial news and information services like Stox.com; and the online auction house eBay.

Other firms have opted to use the Internet as an alternative channel of distribution and communication. For example, Canada Trust, The Shopping Channel, *The Globe and Mail*, and Chapters bookstore all have Web sites through which customers can carry on transactions. These firms have also maintained their previous distribution channels and methods of serving customers.

Firms using the Internet as primarily a communications medium to support their current business include: Labatt Breweries, Caterpillar, and the Canadian Broadcasting Corporation. Each of these firms maintains an information base as well as a communications centre for customer contact and feedback, but is not seeking to create an immediate "retail" transaction with people who visit its site.

A number of firms that started out using the Internet solely as a communications medium are now revamping their Web sites in order to function as an alternative distribution channel. For example, Ford, General Motors, and Daimler-Chrysler are redesigning their Web sites so that customers can get quotes for automobiles, and possibly even custom-order vehicles. At this writing, none of these firms had taken the full e-commerce step; the potential for channel conflict with their dealer networks is a key issue for these companies.[56]

The following comment addresses the issue of adapting to the new world of e-commerce:

> Winning in the e-economy requires more than creating Web sites and virtual channels, or automating customer service and building new skills. Organizations must continuously evaluate their entire business in the context of the e-economy.[57]

Finally, educators are keenly aware of the power and importance that e-commerce is likely to have in the future of the Canadian economy. In 1999 Toronto's Centennial

## INTERNATIONAL MARKETING IN ACTION

### Australian Advertisers and the Internet

The most recent information indicates that 15 per cent of Australian households are connected to the Internet, 33 per cent of Australians use it regularly, and use is growing at an estimated 10 per cent per month. Australian advertisers were slow to embrace the marketing potential of Web sites until they noticed a heavy volume of offshore Web shopping. Australians were in particular buying books (www.amazon.com) and compact disks, products that were not locally available.

Just as in Canada, Australian businesses are seeing the Web as both an advertising and shopping medium to support their businesses. McGills, a bookstore with a 120-year history, developed a new Web site geared to purchasing (www.mcgills.com.au) to replace an older, informational Web site. Advertising expenditures on the Web went from A$3.6 million in 1997 to A$11.5 million in 1998, and were expected to top A$34 million in 1999. The advertising expenditures are tripling each year so far, but in a nation with total ad spending of U.S.$5.5 billion these figures have a way to go before Internet advertising becomes a major force.

Nancy Pageau, the marketing director for Yahoo! in Australia, says that market development involves educating both advertising agencies and advertisers on the effectiveness of the Web as an advertising and marketing medium.

Web marketing was pioneered in Australia by the banks, which offer online banking services, and the travel agencies, which present vacation options and allow people to buy discounted travel and accommodation packages. The Web is expected to be a major source of direct purchasing for Australians, who have been described as less likely to purchase from catalogues as are North Americans and Europeans. Australians generally like to test out products, to see them and feel them before purchasing. Only when they've had a positive experience of buying a product by direct marketing are they likely to buy more often. The level of Australians' resistance to direct marketing purchases seems to have been reduced by the interactive and detailed nature of the offerings on the Web.

Another key factor in Australian Web marketing development is the use of other media to advertise new sites. Although Web sites are a medium unto themselves, it's a well-established practice to advertise one medium through another (e.g., TV stations using radio ads, and vice versa). These days it's common practice to supply a Web site address in virtually all of a firm's advertising.

It seems natural to expect that the whole world will be swept into Internet use, and therefore Internet marketing. Identify some of the physical, psychological, and social barriers that may slow down or even prevent the successful use of Internet marketing. Discuss how Internet marketers can overcome these barriers.

Sources: Based on Chris Pritchard, "Australian Marketers Wake Up to Internet Potential," *Marketing Magazine* (February 1, 1999), p. 6; and Ad Age database, "Top Global Markets—Australia," *Advertising Age* Web site, adage.com (May 1999).

College teamed up with IBM Canada, SAP Canada, Cisco Systems Canada, Bell Canada, and Teknion Furniture Systems to open an e-commerce institute in Toronto. The idea is for Centennial College to offer a post-diploma program for students with a marketing or business degree. Later, Centennial plans to offer a three-year program in e-commerce to high school graduates.[58]

## Internet Buyer Behaviour

How do people and organizations use the Internet, and how are online purchases made? The general theories on consumer behaviour presented earlier in the text

**FIGURE 14-10**

**Electronic Commerce Model**

*Source: Mark Nissen, "Commerce Model and the Intelligence Hub," in Michael Bloch, Yves Pigneur and Arie Segev, "On the Road of Electronic Commerce — a Business Value Framework, Gaining Competitive Advantage and Some Research Issues," Strategis (May 4, 1999).*

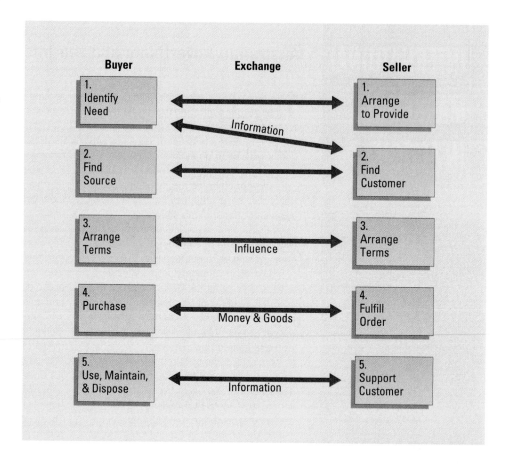

don't change just because people use the Internet to make purchases. However, actual consumer buying behaviour does seem a little different for Internet purchases than for typical retail purchases. A model of how e-commerce works is presented in Figure 14-10.

Here are some facts on consumers' Internet use as of May 1999:

- Fifty-nine per cent of Internet users access the Internet from home.
- Office users surf the Net for an average of fourteen minutes per day.
- The number one search term used on the Internet is "sex."
- Clothing was the top-selling product in the 1998 Christmas season.[59]

*Online shoppers are concerned about the security of their transactions and using their credit cards and debit cards on the Net.*

Consumer use of the Internet for e-commerce has been increasing steadily in Canada over the last few years. According to the Angus Reid Group Internet panel, 32 per cent of the members had completed a fully transactional online purchase in 1998, making an average of 4.7 online purchases, which were planned 82 per cent of the time. In comparison, the 1997 panel data indicated only 22 per cent had completed an online purchase, and the purchase was planned in only 72 per cent of the cases. In 1996 only 7 per cent of the panel members reported making any purchases at all. Panel members who shopped online said they did so because it was very convenient. The panel members liked Web sites that made the ordering process simple, and noted that most product deliveries were fast. A large number of the panel members indicated that they would shop online even more, except that they're concerned about the security of their transactions and using their credit cards numbers online.[60]

To deal with their security concerns many customers will shop on a Web site and then place orders by phoning a toll-free number, where they feel secure about using their credit card numbers. Suit Yourself Swimwear in Richmond, B.C., for example,

**ETHICS AND TODAY'S MARKETER**

## Will Marketers Respect the Privacy of Web Site Visitors?

Asking someone if they'd like a cookie is normally a polite thing to do, and an offer that many people find hard to refuse. But getting a cookie on the Internet isn't the same thing at all! On the World Wide Web a "cookie" refers to a tracking file, which are essentially electronic identification tags that are sent from a Web server to the user's browser. These ID tags are used to monitor site traffic, identify the site visitors, and allow the site to see what other sites the user visited.

Cookies may carry such information as the name of the Web site that issued them, where on the site the user visited, passwords, and possibly user names and credit card numbers. Cookies are supposedly retrievable only by the site that issued them. They link the information gathered to a unique ID number assigned to the particular cookie, which means the information may be available from one session to another. They were designed to offer a time-saving benefit to users so that repeat visitors to Web sites wouldn't have to register on each visit. Online search engines (e.g., Infoseek) use cookies to identify users and offer them news and services based on their prior use.

But online advertisers can also use the information in cookies to target customers without their knowledge and consent. "Since cookies can be matched to the profile of a user's interests and browsing habits, they are a natural tool for the 'targeting' of advertisements to individual users. Marketing consultants such as DoubleClick Inc. and MatchLogic . . . utilize cookies to increase the efficiency of the placing of advertisements on Web sites." This raises the major ethical issue associated with cookie use: violation of privacy.

Will Web site managers gather and sell the consumer profiles they've developed to other organizations? And what information will these profiles contain? The kinds of Web sites a person visits may say a great deal about him or her. For example, a person may not want to be too forthcoming about the Web sites he or she visits if they carry a social stigma or there's something controversial about them (e.g., going to the *Playboy* site to read the articles, or researching communism). The why isn't clear, but the cookies will tell the when and where, and maybe even who. And the who question puts the value of the information for the purchasers into question. After all, do you really know who's at the keyboard? What good is a profile that doesn't clarify the unit of analysis? What if the Internet activity of a particular account actually reflects Mom's interests, Dad's interests, and the interests of a couple of teens and a couple of tweens?

Some other ethical issues associated with cookies include the fact that it's not always clear where the cookie is coming from. You can't be sure if it's from the Web site you're on or from an advertiser that's operating on the site. And personal information stored on a user's hard drive may be accessible to outsiders using cookies to search for such information. Although this is a possibility, most industry observers believe the risk is very low.

Look at the code of ethics for direct marketers, as well as Table 12-4: Excerpts of the Canadian Code of Advertising Standards, and evaluate the ethical considerations surrounding the use of cookies by Web marketers and advertisers.

Sources: Based on Deborah Stokes, "Are Cookies Bad for You?" *Marketing Magazine* (May 4, 1998), p. 18; and Lori Eichelberger, "The Cookie Controversy," Cookie Central, www.cookiecentral.com.

---

has set up its Web site so that orders are made online but credit card information is taken later on a toll-free number.

Another factor affecting consumer acceptance of online shopping is that many of the retailers are new and unfamiliar to consumers, who feel they are taking more risk when they shop online. Conversely, if consumers know the vendor, there is far less hesitation in using its service. For example, when Eaton's went online (www.eatons.com) customers were willing to give their Eaton's account number on its Web site, in part because of Eaton's well-established reputation, and also because people believe that Eaton's would protect its credit cards on its own site.[61]

The online buying behaviour of organizational consumers is vastly different from that of individuals. Here are some facts on organizational buying behaviour on the Internet:

- It is expected that the top five industry sectors that will engage in business-to-business e-commerce will be: computing and electronics; automotive; petrochemicals; utilities; and paper and office products. By the year 2004 business marketers will spend as much as 10 per cent of their marketing budgets on the Web. This may represent as much as $8.7 billion in business-to-business advertising.[62]

- A survey of 1000 small businesses in Canada revealed that 17 per cent of them were planning to engage in business-to-business marketing in the future using the Internet.[63]

*Organizational marketers use the Internet far more than do consumer markets.*

Organizational marketers use the Internet far more than consumer marketers. Report after report indicates that very few e-tailers are currently making any money. Business-to-business marketers, on the other hand, are reporting a different story. The level of infrastructure business alone is mindboggling: hardware and software sales; development of Internet provider services; the online advertising business; the Web page development business—all are part of the business-to-business market of the Internet.

For example, Dell Computers does 80 per cent of its business with corporations, and as shocking as it sounds, it actually uses real live salespeople and executives to cater to these customers. Dell supports its corporate computer sales with an online presence that includes a special business product for organizations with 400 employees or more. The Premier Web page provides access to technical support and Dell sales representatives almost immediately. Aside from providing valuable communications for customers, these pages also allow for online ordering for employees of the 5000 U.S. companies currently supported by the Premier page—which produces about $5 million a day in business for Dell.[64]

Organizational buyers will send purchase orders to their suppliers—and even identify and approve vendors—over the Web. Communication via Web sites is one of the basic approaches to staying in touch with customers as well. For example, FedEx lets customers keep track of the packages they've shipped via the Internet. Fedex.com has over 8000 pages on its Web site, through which customers can track their one of the 315 000 packages in the 209 countries that Fedex services.[65]

**DELL COMPUTERS**
www.dell.ca/index.htm

## Targeting on the Internet

How can Canadian marketers target the 6.49 million Canadians online as well as the 150 million people online in the rest of the world? As with all target market strategies, marketers need to develop a logical way to segment their markets. Internet users can be segmented using the **iVals** scheme presented in Chapter 6, which categorizes people into one of nine categories (Wizards, Pioneers, Upstreamers, Socialites, Workers, Surfers, Mainstreamers, Sociables, Seekers, and Immigrants) according to their usage behaviour, lifestyles, and demographics.

The hierarchy of response behaviour presented earlier in this chapter is another approach that could be employed. It would be most useful for examining customers who have already purchased on the Internet.

Most of the widely available information on the Internet provides demographic information that can be used for segmentation. For example, one recent article provides this profile of consumers who buy online:

Online shoppers are primarily male heads of household (49 per cent), forty years or older (68 per cent), better educated (94 per cent, some college), and wealthier (46 per cent generating more than $50 000 in annual income).[66]

Targeting on the Web is very similar to the approach to list development discussed earlier with direct response marketing. The use of keywords to allow users to find a Web site is a self-selection targeting approach. The marketer lets users reveal themselves as potential customers when they visit the firm's Web site. The next step is to get visitors to identify themselves and provide some information for targeting. A lot of Web sites do this by simply asking you to register on the site and provide some information about yourself. The process is usually included as part of an exchange in which you get access to information or entertainment after you've registered.

A particularly good process for targeting is called **personalization**, meaning that a Web site allows visitors to create their own "on-site" home page that will allow them to alter the content of the site to view the things that interest them. A personalized site allows people to have their own e-mail account, news, weather, sports, and financial information. Such sites offer "the ultimate in targeted marketing." Pointcast, Hotmail, My Yahoo!, Netcenter, and Microsoft Home are all examples of personalized Web sites.[67]

The use of **cookies** is another way for marketers to gather information on Web site visitors, but there are ethical issues associated with this (see the Ethics and Today's Marketing box). A cookie is a tracking file made up of electronic identification tags that are sent from a Web server to the user's browser. These ID tags are used to monitor site traffic, identify the site visitors, and identify other sites the user has visited.

The information gathered by online marketers for segmentation purposes is usually put into a database and then analyzed. The speed at which information can be analyzed and processed is quite amazing. In fact, during their searches many people find themselves staring at banner ads for products or services they're searching for as soon as they type in their search terms. This kind of instantaneous targeting is only possible online, and is one of the most powerful features for Internet marketers.

*Internet users can be segmented with **iVals**, the hierarchy of response behaviour, demographic information, **personalization**, and **cookies**.*

## Web Site Design for Marketing

**Web site design** is the equivalent of creating an advertisement, an interactive communications system, an information system, a searchable database, and an online ordering system. There are numerous books on how to design Web sites, and the technology for design and implementation is changing so rapidly that it's nearly impossible to do justice to this topic. There are two fundamental objectives of Web site development: getting people to visit your site for the first time, and getting them to come back.

A commercial Web site should possess a number of characteristics. HotWired recommends the following:

*Web site design should get people to visit and then revisit.*

**HOTWIRED**
www.hotwired.com

- *The most important decision*—A company must be clear about why it wants to be on the Web. Is its goal brand-building, publicity, selling products, providing information, customer service, or order tracking?

- *The only valid measure is response*—An actual customer has much more value than an anonymous impression.

- *Bandwidth is still limited*—Because so many people are joining the Web, the average access speed is slowing. Thus, a company should keep its image, video, and text files small—and not waste customers' time.

**FIGURE 14-11**

**Web Site Characteristics Affecting Revisitation**

*Source: "What Makes Users Revisit a Web Site?"*
*Dr. Marshall Rice, Survey Site (www.surveysite.com).*

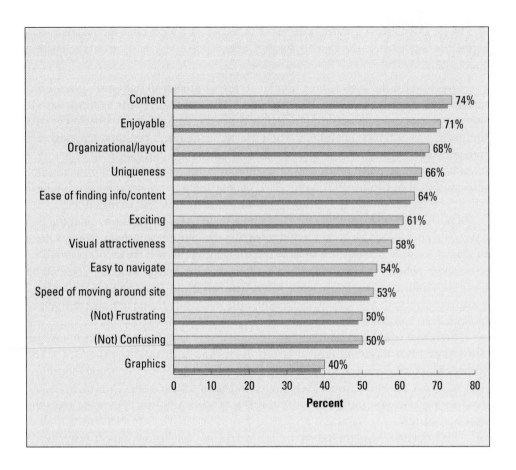

- *Bigger is not always better*—A 1000-page site may not be better than a one-page site. The best sites are quick, personalized, and user-friendly.
- *Static sites are toxic*—The easiest way to lose traffic is to set up a site and not change its look often enough.
- *It's more than advertising*—"Marketing on the Web is about providing information and entertainment, and about fostering community. Many companies have also discovered that Web-based customer service functions are improving customer relations and saving money."
- *If it's not part of your media mix, you lose*—To succeed, a company must commit itself to the Web as an integral part of its media mix.
- *Don't ignore demographics or lifestyles*—"All sites are not equal, any more than all magazines or TV shows are equal."
- *No "Under Construction" signs*—"Vaporware is not appreciated. Don't open your site until it's ready."
- *No shovelware*—"TV isn't just radio with pictures, and the Net isn't just a brochure with buttons. It's a whole new medium, with a whole new dynamic."[68]

Most of the foregoing discussion has dealt with getting people to visit your site for the first time—but you have to get people to come back if you want to have a commercial success. What characteristics are people looking for that would make them want to revisit a Web site? According to SurveySite, the top three things people look for are content, enjoyment, and a well-organized and well laid-out site. See Figure 14-11.[69]

According to Jill and Matthew Ellsworth in their book *Marketing on the Internet*, you need to supply activity and interactivity to get people to revisit. Here's what they recommend Web designers do to keep people coming back:

- *Curiosity*—Large sites with lots of things to see and do can keep people coming back. But don't confuse people; they should feel that there's more to explore and find.

- *Item turnover*—Make sure that at least one or more items on your site changes often, maybe even each time a person visits, e.g., a "what's new" feature, a daily piece of advice, or a new audio file.

- *Indispensable tool or resource*—Link your page to existing databases, or Internet Web guides or tools. Try to relate them to your business. Make them as comprehensive as possible so that people will link through you.

- *Personalization*—Let visitors make the site their own by allowing them to develop their own home page on your site.

- *Unique event or resource*—Provide contests, giveaways, and other promotions to keep visitors coming. Feature an "ask an expert" information section that gives people information nobody else has.[70]

*Web sites with activity and interactivity get people to revisit.*

Once a Web site is operating, it needs to be taken care of. Here's some advice for marketers whose Web sites are up and running:

- *Respond to e-mails*—Review them every day and try to answer them within forty-eight hours. Delegate responsibility for reviewing and prioritizing mail to an assistant if necessary.

- *Provide updates*—Business information ages quickly, so review and update this information at least four times a year.

- *Register with all the active search engines*—A site alone isn't sufficient—you've got to be part of the electronic highway. Make sure your Web designer handles the registration of your site with the major players, like Yahoo!, InfoSeek, Excite, AltaVista, Lycos, and AOL's NetFind.

- *Update links to other sites*—You must continue to generate traffic, and this means keeping current with the "hot links." Hot links are meant literally. Be sure to have the links that people are interested in now, not the ones they were interested in last week, last month, or last year. Links should be relevant to your site (similar products, partnerships, or strategic alliances).

- *Get listed in all the online directories possible*—These directories are like the Internet Yellow Pages. They list sites by category and geography, and many of them will currently list your organization for free.

- *Advertise your site*—It should at least be on all your business literature (business cards, stationery, brochures), as well as giveaways, marked company vehicles, and on every other type of advertising you do.

- *Measure response*—Count the number of times your site has been accessed, using a hit counter that gives an up-to-the-minute count. Access any domain lists to measure your hits per day and get a breakdown of the country and region from where these hits are originating.[71]

# Internet Promotion

Canadian advertisers have not embraced the Internet for advertising as much as American firms have. As noted earlier, while Canadian advertising expenditures were predicted to be about $38 million for 1999, U.S. expenditures were predicted at U.S.$2 billion. Unfamiliarity with this new medium, and the fact that advertising agencies tend to steer clients toward existing, commisionable media, are two reasons why advertising has lagged. The basic process of online promotion is no different from that outlined in Chapters 12 and 13. Nonetheless, here are some of the important considerations for using the Internet:

- The Web isn't really a mass market; rather it favours one-on-one promotion. It's more of a "pull" than a "push" channel of information distribution.
- Markets are both vertical and horizontal on the Internet. You can market direct to consumers (horizontal) or to other organizations through a distribution system (vertical).
- People who are scanning the Web for environmental information are taking very narrow looks when they search for competitive, technological, or cultural information.
- Market segmentation and demographic research are still relatively new on the Internet. The ways to assess markets and promotional effectiveness are mainly based on experience with other media. Reliable and valid surveys are becoming more common.[72]
- "The intimacy and expanding reach of this medium offers marketers a synthesis of direct response, print, outdoor, radio, and television all rolled into one, with the added component of transactional capability."[73]

*The Internet is an intimate synthesis of all the other media with the addition of transactional capability.*

Effective use of the Internet for promotion involves understanding the promotional vehicles available on the Internet and their characteristics. It's important to keep in mind that promoting or advertising on the Net isn't the same thing as having a Web site. In fact, a firm doesn't even need a site to promote online, although as discussed earlier Web sites have become an expected communications device.

*Promoting on the Internet is not the same thing as having a Web site.*

Just as with other advertising media, promoting on the Net involves exposing your firm and its products to people who are online for other reasons. It's important therefore to use such online vehicles as banners, sponsorships, permission-based e-mail communications and e-flyers, and Web-based contests and promotions.[74]

**FIGURE 14-12**

**Banner Advertising**

*Courtesy Canada.com*

**Banners** are graphic buttons or images that invite users to click through them to get more information. The most recent survey of Internet advertising in Canada included these findings:

- Banner advertising is the largest revenue-generating Internet advertising product, accounting for about 59 per cent of total industry advertising revenues.
- Advertisers paid an average of $34.86 CPM (cost per thousand) in 1997.
- Twenty per cent of the reporting sites had over 10 million impressions (page views) every month, but the click-through percentage on these sites was only 1.95 per cent.[75]

**Sponsorships**, found on Web pages and discussion lists, are simply displays of a firm's logo and/or name. The prices charged for sponsorships usually depend on the site traffic. While sponsorships aren't as intrusive as banner ads, they don't impart very much information either. They act as electronic billboards to support a firm's other media advertising, keep its name in the minds of customers, and reinforce its image.

**Permission-based e-mail** communications can take many forms, including: sending direct response e-mail solicitations (which people can perceive as being a bit offensive), sending e-flyers (more accepted), and sending requested information, responding to direct inquiries, or providing updates to information that was accessed. The key to these e-mails is the understanding under which people give "permission" to the Web site manager for future contacts and for the use of their e-mail addresses. Permissions are usually granted when people register on a site, and can range from allowing the site manager to develop and sell the address as part of a mailing list, to the more restricted "please just send me relevant information and updates."

Customized **e-flyers** are a very popular permission-based e-mail. Canadian Tire has implemented an e-flyer campaign:

> This is how the e-flyer works: A consumer registers for it at the company's Web site (www.canadiantire.ca) and specifies merchandise preferences. For example, a handyman requesting information on power tools may receive a customized e-flyer featuring drills, jigsaws, and routers, complete with product descriptions, photos, and prices. A customer can print a shopping list of product choices that may make him or her eligible for double Canadian Tire money or double options points, depending on the payment method.[76]

The Internet is an excellent medium for conducting contests and promotions. TV and radio stations are very adept at supporting their main broadcasting functions with supplementary information and cross-promotions linked to their Web sites. For example, in 1999 YTV ran a "Pokemon" contest whereby child viewers were encouraged to answer questions about the TV show and then log onto the Specialty Channels site with the answers. The children could then win Pokemon-related merchandise.

Web promotions are also very popular. One of the most notable examples involved using the Internet as part of an event. When Victoria's Secret advertised a Web broadcast during the 1999 Superbowl, the impact was significant: "Victoria's Secret Webcast topped all online events, with 1.5 million viewers."[77]

# Transacting and Distributing on the Web

The key difference between the Internet and other media is its transactional capability and the speed with which transactions can be effected. New tools are developed every day, and marketers must keep pace. As noted earlier, barriers to

---

*Marginal notes:*

**Banners** *invite users to click through them to get more information.*

**Sponsorships** *act as electronic billboards.*

*Consumers allow marketers to send them e-mail solicitations with* **permission-based e-mail**.

**E-flyers** *are customized based on a customer's merchandise preferences.*

full-blown Web marketing still exist, with consumers wary of shopping online for security reasons.

Marketers who wish to transact and to distribute products on the Web must address this concern. Promotion and a well-designed site may get people to visit and even revisit, but it's all for naught unless they are willing to complete a transaction. The key issue for marketers in securing online transactions involves authenticating data, people, products, and actual transactions. As with any direct marketing transaction, perfect safety cannot be assured, but risks can be reduced to acceptable levels.

Security concerns can be addressed in the following ways:

*Internet marketers facilitate transactions with* **offline accounts, purchase order systems, virtual bucks, encrypted e-mail, cyber credit cards,** *and* **e-commerce providers**.

- *Create an* **offline account**—Billing is done by phone, fax, or mail payment in response to an order made online.
- *Use a* **purchase order system**—Business-to-business marketers use this approach all the time. Providing a P.O. number online would be very simple.
- *Develop your own money, or* **virtual bucks**—People can purchase virtual money or tokens from a secure provider and then use these to buy merchandise from online stores. There's still a security issue when the virtual bucks are purchased by consumers, and marketers will still have to verify the existence of the virtual bucks.
- **Encrypted e-mail** *and page entry*—Credit card and debit card numbers are sent via electronically secured means such as Secure HTTP.
- *Offer* **cyber credit cards** *or cheques*—These electronic versions of cash, credit cards, and cheques can be used to make purchases.[78]

*IBM is a well-known* **e-commerce provider**.

- *Engage the services of an* **e-commerce provider**—IBM offers an IBM Home Page Creator for e-business, which acts both as a provider to set up and service the Web page and as an intermediary that engages an online transactions specialist firm, such as Automated Transactions Services (www.atsbank.com). The fee for these services is about $50–$100 per month.[79]

The Direct Marketing Association reports the following facts about Internet transactions:

- Ninety-five per cent of direct marketers report using the Web for sales or marketing applications; 39 per cent of these use e-commerce technology in marketing their products and services.
- About 90 per cent of direct marketers report having Web sites, whose primary purposes are marketing/information (88 per cent); lead generation (60 per cent); and e-commerce or sales (51 per cent).

*Internet marketing efforts do not always involve online transactions*.

- Forty-three percent of direct marketers indicate that transactions are conducted electronically at their Web sites. About half of these firms (49 per cent) report that their online transactions are profitable.
- Slightly more than half (52 per cent) report that their Web sites and capabilities are maintained by using both in-house and outside resources. A bit over one-third (38 per cent) maintain their sites using only in-house resources, and the remaining 10 per cent rely completely on outsourcing for maintenance and operations.[80]

## Evaluating Internet Marketing

How can firms evaluate the success of their Internet marketing efforts? At the most basic level are the results of transactions, i.e., sales and profitability. A survey of direct marketers by the Direct Marketing Association revealed the following measurement approaches: of the 73 per cent that attempted to measure the effectiveness of the medium, 69 per cent measured the sales generated, 60 per cent measured the number of "hits" (connections) to their home page, and 39 per cent tried to estimate their return on investment.[81] Direct marketers engaged in e-commerce can use the response measures discussed in this section (lifetime customer value, response rates, and profitability).

However, Internet marketing efforts aren't always tied to the direct creation of an online transaction. The purpose may be to create a transaction at a "bricks and mortar" location, use the Internet as a supporting advertising medium, generate sales leads, respond to inquiries, or support a retail or business-to-business transaction. For example, Canadian Tire issues e-flyers to create transactions at their retail stores. They report that the transaction value of customers who use e-flyers is at least twice the value of typical customers.[82]

When the Internet is used as sales support medium, marketers try to examine sales lead generation tied to their sites. Counting the number of e-mail inquiries submitted and then responded to is another way to measure the effectiveness of handling inquiries. As far as providing informational and sales support, the firm could look at the use of technical or informational pages on the site that were designed for this purpose. Inquiries from customers with specific questions and concerns can also be examined.

Measuring the effectiveness of the Internet as an advertising medium is an area that has probably generated some of the most development activity. The Internet Advertising Bureau of Canada (IAB Canada) was formed in 1997 to provide Web publishers, advertisers, advertising agencies, and service providers with a forum in which to voice opinions on such issues as audience measurement, advertising standards, and market size estimates.[83]

**IAB CANADA**
www.iabcanada.com

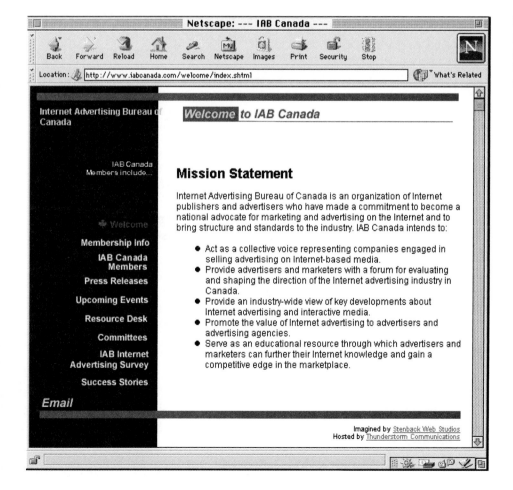

**FIGURE 14-13**

**Measuring Effectiveness of Web Sites Through a Reliable Auditing Procedure**

*Courtesy Internet Advertising Bureau of Canada.*

# MARKETING IN THE THIRD MILLENNIUM

*There are some direct marketing success principles that are timeless.*

## The Thirty Timeless Direct Marketing Principles[84]

Although the Internet and other technologies are revolutionizing many of the approaches to marketing, Bob Stone nonetheless believes that there are timeless principles for success in direct marketing. Based on his research he's developed what he calls "The Thirty Timeless Direct Marketing Principles." These have emerged out of the experiences of direct marketers, and are expected to hold true for the Internet and for any other media that are likely to evolve in the new millennium. Here are Bob Stone's thirty timeless principles that will lead to direct marketing success:

1. All customers are not created equal. Eighty per cent of repeat business for goods and services will come from 20 per cent of the customer base.
2. The most important order you'll ever get from a customer is the second one. A two-time buyer is twice as likely to buy again as a one-time buyer.
3. Maximizing direct mail success depends first upon the lists you use, second upon the offers you make, and third upon the copy and graphics you create.
4. If the hot prospects on a given list don't work out, the other names on the list will offer little opportunity for success.

5. Merge/purge names. Those names that appear on two or more lists will outpull any single list from which these names have been extracted.
6. Direct response lists will usually outpull compiled lists.
7. Enhancements on lists, like lifestyle characteristics, income, education, age, marital status, and propensity to respond, will always improve response.
8. A follow-up to the same list within thirty days will pull 40–50 per cent of the first mailing.
9. Yes/No offers consistently produce more orders than offers that don't request a No response.
10. The take rate for negative option offers will always outpull positive option offers by at least two to one.
11. Credit card privileges will outperform cash with an order by at least two to one.
12. Credit card privileges will increase the size of the average catalogue order by 20 per cent or more.
13. Time limit offers, particularly those that give a specific date, outpull offers with no time limit practically every time.
14. Free-gift offers, particularly where the

---

*Advertisers pay on a* **CPM (cost per thousand)** *basis.*

The Bureau of Broadcast Measurement in Toronto measures the effectiveness of Web sites through a reliable auditing procedure so that advertisers will know if they're getting what they pay for. The accepted standard is that advertisers will pay on a **CPM (cost per thousand)** basis. The issue is: cost per thousand of what? Presented below, in rough order of least to most involving, is a list of the "whats" measured by the Bureau of Broadcast Measurement and the U.S.-based Audit Bureau of Circulation:[85]

*Internet advertising effectiveness can be measured with* **hits**, **visits**, **page requests**, **visit duration**, **click-through**, *and* **ad impressions**.

- *Hits*—Connections to Internet sites.
- *Visits*—Distinct and separate requests for pages on a site. A visit make take an extended period of time, and if a visitor leaves a site for more than thirty minutes and then returns, it's considered a separate visit.
- *Page requests*—A request to view, and the successful transfer for viewing, of one or more document pages.
- *Visit duration*—The time between the first and last request during a visit. This does not include the amount of time spent on the last page requested.
- *Click-through*—The result of clicking on an ad that links to the advertiser's site or to a page designated by the advertiser within the site where the ad was viewed.
- *Ad impressions*—An ad that was delivered successfully to a qualified visitor.

gift appeals to self-interest, outpull discount offers consistently.

15. Sweepstakes, particularly in conjunction with impulse purchases, will increase order volume by 35 per cent or more.

16. You'll collect far more money in a fundraising effort if you ask for a specific amount. You'll also collect more money if the appeal is tied to a specific project.

17. People buy benefits, not features.

18. The longer you can keep someone reading your copy, the better your chances of success.

19. The timing and frequency of renewal letters is vital. The quality of copy on renewals doesn't seem to matter; rather it's the product that's the factor in renewal.

20. Self-mailers are cheaper to produce, but they practically never outpull envelope-enclosed letter mailings.

21. A preprint of a forthcoming ad, accompanied by a letter and response form, will outpull a postprint mailing package by 50 per cent or more.

22. It's easier to increase the average dollar amount of an order than it is to increase the percentage of response.

23. You'll get far more new catalogue customers if you put your proven winners in the front pages of your catalogue.

24. Assuming items of similar appeal, you'll always get a higher response rate from a 32-page catalogue than a 24-page catalogue.

25. A new catalogue to a catalogue customer base will outpull cold lists by 400 to 800 per cent.

26. A print ad with a bind-in card will outpull the same ad without a bind-in up to 600 per cent.

27. A direct response, direct sale TV commercial of 120 seconds will outpull a 60-second direct response commercial better than two to one.

28. A TV support commercial will increase response from a newspaper insert by up to 50 per cent.

29. The closure rate from qualified sales leads can be from two to four times as effective as cold calls.

30. Telephone-generated leads are four to six times more likely to close than are mail-generated leads.

# SUMMARY

**1.** *To introduce the concept of information-based marketing* This type of marketing depends on the use and creation of informational databases as part of the total marketing effort. Direct marketing is an interactive system that uses one or more advertising media to effect a measurable response and/or transaction at any location, with this activity stored on a database. Direct marketing is a form of retailing that heavily depends on the use of nonpersonal media. Internet marketing uses the Net as a medium for marketing through personal computers, and in particular, for direct marketing. The Internet can allow a marketer to accomplish every single marketing function.

**2.** *To define direct marketing and examine its scope, importance, and characteristics* Direct marketing is best understood as a combination of promotion and distribution. The 750-member Canadian Marketing Association is the key industry organization. With sales growth of 7–10 per cent each year, direct marketing is one of the fastest-growing forms of marketing and retailing activities in Canada. Annual sales are about $13.5 billion, although Canadians spend 50 per cent less per capita on home shopping than do Americans.

The consumer forces driving this market include popularity of manufacturer brands, mass availability and use of credit cards, poverty of time for consumers, convenience and ease of ordering, large number of working women, traffic congestion, electronic communications via the Internet and fax machines, increased telephone use, and a belief that direct marketing is a good way to shop. Marketer forces include increased computing power allowing greater availability and ease of manipulation of databases, expanded television channels, growth in Internet use, less expensive access to toll-free numbers, and growth in expedited carriers.

Direct marketing items should have more than one basic appeal, have some kind of exclusivity, be able to reach the intended market efficiently, lend themselves to strong advertising copy, and have sufficient sales and profit margin potential.

Database marketing is a continuous learning process that involves collecting data on customers which is then refined over time as the marketer and the customer undergo continuous contact.

There are ethical issues associated with direct marketing surrounding marketing to children and rights to privacy.

**3.** *To study the elements of a direct marketing plan* The first element of a direct marketing plan involves setting objectives, which are almost always focused on achieving an immediate and specific behavioural response from customers. The nature of the objective(s) set may depend on whether the marketer is seeking to sell to final or organizational consumers. Direct marketing may involve a two-step process, where the response to the first contact is designed to trigger a sales call; or a multiple-step process, where a relationship is built up through a series of contacts leading to a sales call.

The second element of a plan is designing offers. An offer is the complete proposition made by the direct marketer to the prospect. It must contain the following elements: a product offering, the price of the offering, and details on the terms of sale, such as the length of commitment the buyer is making, the terms of payment for the offer, and terms to reduce risk of purchase. Offers may also contain incentives to buy, other offers, and specific customer obligations.

The third element is the selection and development of prospect lists. Response lists identify people who have bought before; compiled lists group customers according to common characteristics; and house lists are made up of customers known to the firm. Direct marketers may rent a list that has been compiled by someone else, such as InfoCanada which has lists of 1.1 million Canadian businesses and 11 million Canadian consumers.

The fourth element is to create the advertising. A good creative approach for direct marketing is PAPA, an acronym for **P**romise of Benefit, **A**mplification, **P**roof of Claim, and **A**ction to Take. The fifth element is to select direct marketing media, such as direct mail, television, radio, magazines, catalogues, newspapers, telephone, fax machines, the Internet, free-standing inserts inside products or product shipments, and bounce-back circulars. Media selection should take into account target market(s), costs, customer mobility, and vehicle source effects. The sixth element is to implement the campaign. A direct marketing campaign should be timed with both product and media seasonality in mind. Time of day may also affect viewership of television, listenership of radio, and availability to make or receive telephone calls. Direct marketers need to consider making three to four contacts with their customers to get a response.

Finally, direct marketers must evaluate responses. This involves looking at response rates, profitability, and the value of customers. Firms need to update both responses and non-responses in their house lists. Direct marketing is all about creating and maintaining customer relationships.

**4.** *To define Internet marketing and examine its scope and importance* In 1998 an estimated U.S.$8–$10 billion in consumer goods and U.S.$43 billion in business-to-business goods were purchased on the Internet. Canadian Internet sales were $255 million in 1997 and projected to be $6.9 billion by the year 2002. The Internet is accessed by 6.49 million Canadians on a weekly basis, and about 13 per cent of Canadians purchase online. The Internet is emerging as a unique and important medium—and a tremendous global business opportunity.

**5.** *To describe marketing and the new world of e-commerce* The growth rate of retail e-commerce is outstripping almost every other retail innovation before it. The forces driving e-commerce in Canada include our economic strength, up-to-date communications systems, and the level of ownership of modern personal computers. The Internet is a "convergent" medium because it combines the characteristics of all other media along with transactional capabilities. Consumer behaviour on the Internet involves accessing it mainly from home, with more and more Canadians completing online transactions every year. The biggest hold-back to consumer use is security concerns around providing credit and debit card numbers on the Net, whereas organizational buyers send purchase orders to their suppliers, and even identify and approve vendors over the Web. Marketers can segment Internet users with iVals, the hierarchy of response behaviour, demographic information, personalization, and cookies. In designing Web sites marketers should focus on getting people to visit and then revisit. The most successful sites are those that feature both activity and interactivity. Good Web sites arouse curiosity, change often, make themselves an indispensable tool, allow for personalization, and offer unique events or resources.

Promoting on the Internet is not the same thing as having a Web site. Canadian advertising expenditures were predicted to be about $38 million for 1999. Marketers can promote by using banners, which invite users to click through them to get more information; sponsorships, which act as electronic billboards; and permission-based e-mail. Successfully transacting on the Web involves overcoming the security concerns of consumers. Internet marketers can facilitate transactions with offline accounts, purchase order systems, virtual bucks, encrypted e-mail, cyber credit cards, and e-commerce providers like IBM. Firms can evaluate the success of their Internet marketing efforts using sales, profitability, and response rates. Internet advertising effectiveness can be measured with hits, visits, page requests, visit duration, click-through, and ad impressions. But no matter what medium is used, there are some direct marketing success principles that are timeless.

## KEY TERMS

**information-based marketing** (p. 437)

**direct marketing** (p. 438)

**direct response advertising** (p. 438)

**Internet marketing** (p. 438)

**database marketing** (p. 441)

**privacy code** (p. 443)

**two-step process** (p. 445)

**multiple-step process** (p. 446)

**offer design** (p. 446)

**package offer** (p. 446)

**long-term commitment** (p. 448)

**terms of payment** (p. 448)

**offering terms that reduce the risk of purchase** (p. 449)

**incentives** (p. 449)

**multiple offers** (p. 449)

**customer obligations** (p. 449)

**prospect lists** (p. 449)

**response lists** (p. 449)

**compiled lists** (p. 449)

**house lists** (p. 449)

**suspect** (p. 451)

**prospect** (p. 451)

**one-time buyer** (p. 451)

**two-time buyer** (p. 451)

**advocate** (p. 451)

**PAPA approach** (p. 451)

**Promise of Benefit** (p. 453)

**Amplification** (p. 453)

**Proof of Claim** (p. 453)

**Action** (p. 453)

**catalogue selling** (p. 454)

**infomercial** (p. 454)

**radio direct marketing** (p. 455)

**direct mail** (p. 455)

**mailing package** (p. 456)

**free-standing inserts** (p. 456)

**third class mail (junk mail)** (p. 457)

**bill inserts and bounce-back circulars** (p. 457)

**newspaper direct marketing** (p. 458)

**magazine direct marketing** (p. 458)

**vehicle source effect** (p. 458)

**Canadian Advertising Rates and Data (CARD)** (p. 458)

**polybag** (p. 458)

**telemarketing** (p. 458)

**response rates** (p. 460)

**lifetime value** (p. 461)

**e-commerce** (p. 462)

**convergent medium** (p. 464)

**iVals** (p. 468)

**personalization** (p. 469)

**cookies** (p. 469)

**Web site design** (p. 469)

**banners** (p. 473)

**sponsorships** (p. 473)

**permission-based e-mail** (p. 473)

**e-flyers** (p. 473)

**offline accounts** (p. 474)

**purchase order systems** (p. 474)

**virtual bucks** (p. 474)

**encrypted e-mail** (p. 474)

**cyber credit cards** (p. 474)

**e-commerce provider** (p. 474)

**CPM (cost per thousand)** (p. 476)

**hits** (p. 476)

**visits** (p. 476)

**page requests** (p. 476)

**visit duration** (p. 476)

**click-through** (p. 476)

**ad impressions** (p. 476)

# REVIEW QUESTIONS

1. Describe what is unique about direct marketing. Compare and contrast it with marketing through the use of intermediaries.

2. How is direct response marketing different from direct response advertising? How is direct response marketing different from Internet marketing? What are the similarities?

3. Identify the customer-based forces and marketer-based forces that are driving the use of direct response marketing.

4. What characteristics should a direct response type product or service have and why?

5. Database marketing often raises the issue of privacy. What are the seven principles of privacy recommended by the Canadian Marketing Association? Can you think of any other privacy principles you might want to add to them?

6. What are the ingredients of a good direct response offer? One of them is packaging. Review Table 14-2. Would the package deal work as well if it had to be priced at $7.50 instead of $10 to produce 25 000 subscribers? Using this new price, work through Table 14-2 and see if it's feasible. What would happen if a sixth channel (the 60s channel) with 10 000 viewers were added with the same individual price and the same package price? Would this be feasible?

7. Identify all the media you can readily think of that are available for advertising. (Don't include promotional specialties like matches, pens, key chains, etc.) Rank them according to the ones that are best for direct response and the ones that are not as good. Justify your rankings.

8. Describe Internet buying behaviour. What are some of the barriers to increasing Internet use and online purchasing? How can marketers overcome them?

9. Describe the Internet advertising vehicles that are available. Compare and contrast them. Which ones do you think are most effective, most ineffective, and why?

10. Measuring response is very important in any direct Internet marketing initiative. Identify the response measures presented in the chapter and evaluate them.

# DISCUSSION QUESTIONS

1. Describe database marketing and its importance as part of direct response marketing. Discuss the strengths of database marketing. What kinds of things might cause database marketing to fail, and why?

2. Using the information in Table 14-2, analyze Figure 14-8 to see if it has a PAPA approach. Gather a few other direct response ads and see if they fit the PAPA style. Look at some regular image ads. Do they fit the PAPA creative style? Why or why not? Should every ad use the PAPA approach? Why or why not?

3. For both direct response and Internet marketing the prospect list is key. Compare and contrast how lists are developed and used for traditional direct response and Internet marketing. How should target marketing considerations be related to list development?

4. Getting people to visit a firm's Web site for the first time, and then to revisit it, are critical to success in online marketing. Discuss what characteristics make a good Web site and how marketers can accomplish their goal of visitation and revisitation.

5. Bob Stone's timeless principles of marketing were written before e-commerce and Internet marketing really developed. Examine these principles to see if the advent of the Internet has caused them to outlive their time. Identify the ones you think may have become outdated and explain why. Rewrite these and any of the other principles to make them relevant to the world of e-commerce.

## CASE STUDY

# Telemarketing: The Key to Business-to-Business Selling

Telemarketing and telemarketers have a bad public image. Telemarketers always seem to call during dinner or some other inopportune time. After intruding on your privacy they try to sell you something you absolutely do not want or need. And many telemarketers put our good manners to the test. Take the case of one man who was unable to get a word in edgewise as a telemarketer, anxious to sell pet food and pet supplies, went on and on for nearly three minutes before ascertaining that the man did not have a pet. Even then the conversation didn't end. The enterprising telemarketer asked whether the man was interested in acquiring a pet so that he'd need the pet food and supplies. But as bad as this is for the receiver, it's even worse for the telemarketer's firm when its salespeople waste time calling the wrong prospects.

Almost everyone has a telemarketing story to tell. Consider telemarketing scams, which are rampant these days and damage telemarketing's effectiveness as a selling tool. One favourite scam is to call you up and congratulate you on winning something like a free trip, but for a few incidentals that have to paid for by credit card before the prize is collected. You provide the number and whammy, you've licensed some pirates to go on a shopping spree. If you're lucky you actually get a trip, but those incidentals end up costing more than if the trip were booked through a regular agency.

It's for these kinds of things that business-to-business telemarketer suppliers sometimes get rebuffed by potential clients. Given the image of consumer telemarketing, some people find it hard to understand that business-to-business transactions are the perfect place for telemarketing activities. One estimate indicates that business-to-business telemarketing employs nearly 3 million people throughout the world and produces $800 billion in business transactions. Businesses often rely on their salespeople to undertake the firm's telemarketing activities, but this can be difficult when the salesperson is on the go and trying to engage customers in face-to-face sales presentations.

A firm's salesforce can be more productive if it has a telemarketing support team. Business-to-business telemarketers can generate sales leads, set appointments for salespeople, perform research, and even do direct selling to secondary customers. Business-to-business telemarketers aren't unwanted callers to the degree that consumer telemarketers are. They make their calls to professional buyers and purchasing agents, whose job it is to receive calls from people who want to sell.

The quality of phone lists for business-to-business marketers is far superior to those of consumer marketers. Professional firms like Dun & Bradstreet and Micromedia make their living producing viable business-to-business customer lists. However, the decision-making process in business-to-business situations is often far more complex than in consumer markets. As such, telemarketing contacts are often lead-ins to personal sales calls or follow-ups to sales calls that have already been made. If the buying and selling organizations have an established relationship, the telemarketing call may be all that's needed to trigger an order.

To be effective, business-to-business telemarketing must involve detailed and discreet planning for its use as a marketing tool. Which roles will it concentrate on? It can be used for lead generation, appointment setting, research, selling, and sales call follow-ups. How will it be coordinated with the firm's other promotional and marketing activities? It could be used to follow up the leads generated from trade show exhibits. It could also be the firm's main thrust in reaching customers to generate sales leads. Who will undertake the business-to-business marketing? It could be the firm itself or an outsourced specialist telemarketing company. In the business-to-business world, personal and employee-to-employee calls aside, virtually every inbound telephone communication involves some form of telemarketing.

## Questions

1. Explain the main differences between business-to-business and business-to-consumer telemarketing.
2. Identify the tasks of the business-to-business telemarketers mentioned in this case. Discuss the relative importance of each of these tasks to a marketing organization.
3. What factors would a firm have to consider in deciding whether to operate its own telemarketing operation or outsource it?
4. Customer lists are the key to all direct marketing operations. Discuss why customer lists for business-to-business marketers seem to be more widely available and more accurate than consumer lists. What are some of the difficulties associated with using business-to-business lists? How can an organization overcome some of these difficulties?

**DUN & BRADSTREET**
www.bdeuro/eu_abou.htm

Source: Based on Louise Parkes, "Like Apples and Bananas," *Marketing Magazine* (May 3, 1999), p. MD4.

## CASE STUDY
# The Power of Interactive Web Sites

E-commerce, e-tailing, Web marketing, Internet marketing—call it what you will, the fundamental problems are the same. If you want people to engage with your firm on the Internet you need them to first find your Web site, and then you need them to come back.

In order for people to find your site you must do the following. Make sure you're properly registered with all the active search engines, like Yahoo!, InfoSeek, Excite, AltaVista, Lycos, and AOL's NetFind. Update links to other sites to generate traffic. Select links that people are interested in now, not the ones they were interested in last week or last month. Get listed in all the online directories possible. When you advertise your products, advertise your Web site along with them.

In order to get people to revisit your site you need to supply both activity and interactivity. According to Ellsworth and Ellsworth in their book *Marketing on the Internet,* a Web site should invoke curiosity, since large sites that have lots of things to do will encourage people to return later to see more. A site should have constant item turnover so that there's something new on the site every day. Make your site an indispensable tool or resource and offer people links to other information they may want. Also offer people the ability to build their own custom Web page on your site. Finally, offer such unique events as contests, giveaways, or other promotions.

Sony New Media Group in Toronto has taken a lot of this advice to heart. They've even taken the idea of a unique event to the next level: interactive online video gaming. Sony's New Media Group has created a virtual Canadian pop band called Prozzak. It's composed of Simon and Milo, two animated characters with their own album entitled *Hot Show.* Simon and Milo's music is actually composed and performed by members of the real live band the Philosopher Kings.

People can visit Prozzak at www.prozzak.com. Visitors report that the Simon and Milo characters seem real—you'll get Simon's life story and you can

go along as he searches for love inside the video game "Hot Show, Hot Rod." Modelled after Pac Man, you drive along with Simon from Moscow to Paris collecting hearts along the way, arriving in a new city as you reach each new level. The icing on the cake is that if you're the top scorer for the week, you'll get a congratulatory phone call from Simon or Milo (actually one of the Philosopher Kings).

The www.prozzak.com site is part of Sony's promotional push for the Philosopher Kings, but almost any product or service can be linked to interactive game play. For example, Toronto's Splashworks.com, the Internet games designer that came up with "Hot Show, Hot Rod," has developed Internet games for clients such as The Bay, Clearnet, and PepsiCo's 7-Up brand. These companies have Splashworks.com design custom games for particular brands or offerings. For example, Clearnet included a pinball game on its Web site that was tied to a particular promotion. The Bay's site has offered a virtual space flight tour and a game called Zeddy's Cookie Crunch, which is based on Zellers mascot Zeddy Bear.

Splashworks.com believes that the next step in online gaming will involve synchronous real-time interactive games, where visitors can chat with each other and then go toe-to-toe. The key to getting people to play is to offer some type of reward: either a contest entry, promotional giveaways, or a phone call from one of the Philosopher Kings.

Marketers must not forget that the purpose behind getting people to visit, and return, to their Web sites is to conduct business. If people have to register to play the games, it can help firms collect market research and develop contact lists. If the Web site's purpose is for online sales then the use of games has to be managed a bit more carefully, because you want visitors to buy as well as play. This can be accomplished by tying game play into product promotions. Finally, the effectiveness of these activities has to be measured. Marketers need to measure hits, the

length of time visitors spent on the Web site, and the activities they undertook while on the site.

### Questions

1. Discuss the advantages and disadvantages of interactive Web sites for marketers.
2. Although the case doesn't discuss them directly, there are a number of technical requirements and issues associated with Internet game play that can be barriers to using these games. Identify as many of these barriers as you can, and discuss how signficant they are and what marketers can do to overcome them.
3. Based on the related chapter material, the case material, and your own experience, discuss the kinds of things people are really looking for when they visit a Web site designed for e-commerce. Evaluate the role of game playing in meeting the needs of these people.
4. Evaluate Sony's New Media approach for an interactive Web site to promote the Philosopher Kings. In your answer, identify which criteria for getting people to revisit a Web site it meets. (If you can, check out the www.prozzak.com Web site yourself.)

Sources: Based on Raju Mudhar, "Play Power," *Marketing Magazine* (May 24, 1999), pp. 19–20; Alf Nucifora, "Shoestring Marketing: What to Do With a Web Site," *American City Business Journals* (November 24, 1997), Atlanta, Georgia; and Jill H. Ellsworth and Matthew V. Ellsworth, *Marketing on the Internet,* Second Edition (New York: John Wiley and Sons), pp. 63–64.

# Marketing with Infomercials

Infomercials are full-length TV advertising programs (typically 30 minutes) that air on cable television or broadcast media at a fringe time. With annual sales of an estimated U.S.$9 billion, they're an attractive way to promote and sell products. Infomercials are direct-response vehicles that are successful at promoting a variety of goods and services, including food preparation devices (such as juice preparation machines and pasta makers), cosmetics, exercise equipment, instructional videos on computer software, and car waxes. Good infomercials use attributes such as testimonials, program length, product pricing, two-step offers, and production considerations.

Testimonials are particularly important in two types of infomercials—those that sell a product replacing an "earlier generation" item, and the "I made a ton of money and so can you" type of program. Testimonials don't have to come from a celebrity; they can come from satisfied customers. Some celebrity testimonials can be very effective, although celebrities can potentially double an infomercial's production cost.

Even though the usual infomercial is 30 minutes long, most viewers watch only part of a show. Therefore, infomercial sponsors often divide their programs into self-sustaining parts (such as three 10-minute segments) and give people a chance to order merchandise during each portion of the program.

According to one industry expert, the price of a product appearing on an infomercial should exceed $40 to $50, due to the high production costs and media expenditures. If an appropriate item is priced at a lower amount, sponsors may sell the product as a package of three for $49.95 or as part of a "Buy two for $49.95, get one free" promotion.

Some products require a two-step offer, in which a sponsor first generates a list of prospects from an infomercial and then makes separate calls to try to close sales. Two-step offers are useful for screening prospects, in that they acquire additional information about their needs, product use, or company size. The drawback is that the sponsor needs to sell the potential consumer twice, on both the initial inquiry and the close.

Producers need to consider the following when planning and implementing infomercials: The offer should be listed as available for a limited time only to increase sales responses. A toll-free number should be clearly listed. Humour can be used in establishing rapport with the customer, but infomercial experts warn against using humour when promoting a product. And the qualifications of an "expert host" should be mentioned in the infomercial in order to enhance credibility.

Many ordinary entrepreneurs would like to get in on the action by producing their own infomercials. There are a number of ways they can go about this. For example, Joseph Diaz of Fattache will produce an infomercial for anyone for $150 000. It takes Fattache about eight days to properly shoot an infomercial. After that, you have an infomercial you can air anywhere, but the rest is up to you. Diaz notes that the failure rate of infomercials is high: only one out of five brings a successful return to its product. Rob Woodriffe, Chair of Interwood Marketing, will take on products at factory cost. The firm will produce an infomercial and market a product if it thinks it can sell. The supplier gets a royalty equal to between 5 and 10 per cent of sales.

Direct marketer Northern Response provides broadcast time for marketers, who must supply their own infomercials and products. Northern Response buys the products wholesale and then markets them. According to Don Cameron of Northern Response, successful infomercial products appeal to either strongly felt needs, greed, or vanity.

Finally, Shaw Cable will let you do your own in-studio infomercial for a mere $1000. Shaw wants to sell air time so it will air these infomercials on their own cable information system and also on shoppers teleguide, a cable programming information service.

At the moment the infomercial industry is in a state of transition. While they've traditionally peddled housewares and fitness products with price tags of $50 and up, their boundaries need to be expanded if they're to remain an important promotional/selling tool.

## Questions

1. Watch a couple of infomercials and evaluate them according to the criteria set out in the case. Do you think they were effective? Why or why not?
2. What would be the advantages of producing your own infomercial versus having someone else do it for you?
3. Do you think infomercials are really here to stay, or are they a promotional fad that's on the way out? Discuss this issue and then support your answer.
4. Assess why people watch infomercials. Try to develop two or three barrier-breaking infomercial products that are neither housewares, exercise, nor get-rich-quick products. Justify your selections.

## Video Questions

1. Based on the video, which approach to infomercial development did you find most appealing? Justify your answer.
2. Joseph Diaz of Fattache commented that the failure rate of infomercials is fairly high. Identify as many causes as you can and support your choices with reasons.

Sources: Based on CBC *Venture* #712 (February 9, 1999), Infomercials; Andrea Haman, "Powerful Pitches," *Marketing Magazine* (December 4, 1995), p. 14; Kim Cleland, "Infomercial Audience Crosses Over Cultures," *Advertising Age* (January 15, 1996), p. I-8; Hershell Gordon Lewis, "Information on Infomercials," *Direct Marketing* (March 1995), pp. 30–32; and Zachary Schiller and Ron Grover, "And Now, a Show from Your Sponsor," *Business Week* (May 22, 1995), pp. 100–104.

# PART 6

# Price Planning

## Price Planning and Strategy

In this chapter, we study the role of price, its importance in transactions, and its interrelationship with other marketing variables. We contrast price-based and nonprice-based approaches. We also look at each of the factors affecting price decisions in depth: consumers, costs, government, channel members, and competition. Next, we explain how to construct and enact a pricing strategy. First, we distinguish among sales, profit, and status quo objectives. We discuss the role of a broad price policy. Then, we introduce three approaches to pricing (cost-, demand-, and competition-based) and show how they may be applied. We also explain why these three pricing methods should be integrated. We examine a number of pricing tactics, such as customary and odd pricing. We conclude the chapter by noting methods for adjusting prices.

# Pricing for Competition

Price planning means ensuring that the marketplace values a firm's offerings at a price that is greater than the costs of providing them.

For marketers, the value of goods and services is created by the choice of target market combined with the product, promotion, and distribution decisions. Capturing the value created and recovering the costs incurred from being in business is an objective of the pricing strategy. Marketers must ensure that the marketplace confers greater value to their offerings than it costs to provide them. Chapter 15 will look at the issues associated with pricing decisions.

Price can be one of the toughest ways to compete for customers, especially when your competitors undersell you. So why would any organization choose this approach? Businesses compete on price because it is the easiest way to differentiate products in the marketplace.

WestJet is a relatively new Canadian airline, having launched its service in 1996. It's doing something that no other Canadian airline has done before or since: making it in the airline business using price competition. The trick in this business is to offer lower fares than the competition while remaining profitable. It's a difficult feat, since very few of the world's airlines are profitable, even without using discount pricing. The one exception has been Southwest Airlines in the United States. Southwest has been able to combine a low cost structure with high capacity utilization of its aircraft. WestJet's strategy has been to duplicate Southwest's formula, and it seems to have done so quite successfully. It will remain profitable as long as it continues to achieve the capacity utilization necessary when using a low price position.

Price is the most visible and obvious weapon marketers have, especially when it's advertised. However, marketers who advertise their prices must be careful not to violate Canada's Competition Act. Inspired by Canada's retailers, recent amendments to the Act's definition of ordinary prices make it less likely that marketers will violate the Act unwittingly.

It used to be that an ordinary price was the price for which 50 per cent or more of a retailer's goods were sold in a prescribed period (normally a year). But because retailers often put goods on sale, and because sales volumes tended to be high, sale prices could end up being defined as ordinary prices. Since retailers could not control sales volumes, they could easily end up in violation of the Competition Act. Retailers can, however, control the amount of time for which a price is offered. Therefore, under the new provisions an ordinary price has two components: the price at which goods are normally offered for sale for over 50 per cent of the time, and/or the price for which 50 per cent or more of a retailer's goods are sold in a prescribed period of time (normally a year).

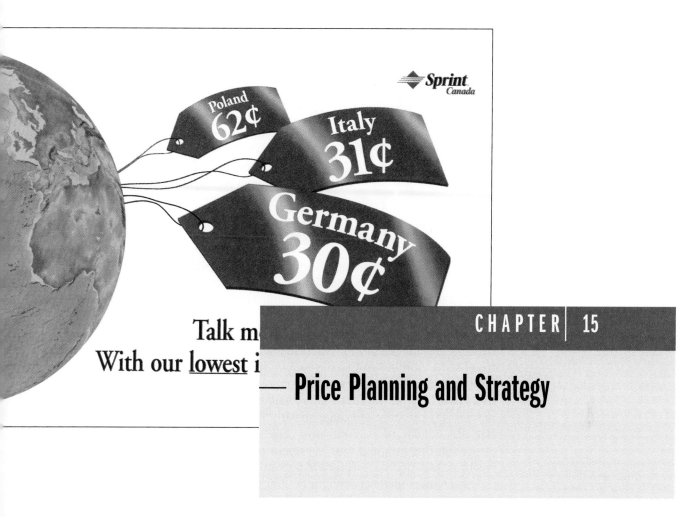

Poland
62¢

Italy
31¢

Germany
30¢

◆Sprint
Canada

Talk m
With our lowest i

CHAPTER | 15

Price Planning and Strategy

## Chapter Objectives

1. To define the terms price and price planning

2. To demonstrate the importance of price and study its relationship with other marketing variables

3. To differentiate between price-based and nonprice-based approaches

4. To present an overall framework for developing and applying a pricing strategy

5. To analyze sales-based, profit-based, and status quo-based pricing objectives, and to describe the role of a broad price policy

6. To discuss several specific decisions that must be made in implementing a pricing strategy

*Courtesy of Sprint Canada Inc.*

In the never-ending battle for customers, the most obvious basis for comparison among brands—and the weapon of choice for most marketers—is price. Engaging in a price war is the easiest thing to do, but among the most fearsome of all marketing activities for business people. It's the strongest sign of the adversarial nature of business, yet it usually brings great joy to consumers. In the short term, when unit sales and market shares are climbing, it can bring great joy to marketers as well. But in the long term, as unit sales level off and profitability falls in response to low profit margins, upper managers and stakeholders throughout the affected industry begin to question the wisdom of continuing to fight a price war.

And so it is in Canada as the telephone companies prepare to enter the new millennium. In 1998 Canadian telephone companies went to the mat with their pricing strategies: that summer Sprint Canada launched a major offensive by offering unlimited long-distance calling anywhere in Canada on weekends and weeknights for a flat fee of $20 a month. Bell Canada counterattacked with a 10 cent per minute rate on evenings and weekends and a $20 per month maximum, meaning that less frequent users paid only for the calls they actually made. MTT in Halifax studied the battleground very carefully and came up with "Freedom Time" for its customers: residential and cellular users were given unlimited long-distance calling anywhere in Canada during evenings and weekends, plus 200 minutes of long distance during weekday peak periods—all for $25 a month.

Some users made an astounding 100 hours worth of phone calls in one month. Well, even phone companies can't afford to give consumers long-distance time at 20 cents an hour, so in October 1998 Sprint Canada capped its offer at $20 for 800 minutes (13.3 hours) or $1.50 per hour. In the end the price wars (described as "madness") resulted in an almost 5 per cent fall in long-distance revenues, from a high of $9.64 billion in 1997 to $9.17 billion in 1998.

So what do you do for an encore? After all, the customers aren't happy to see a price war end. If they've been calling at 20 cents an hour, how do you convince them overnight, and without getting them really angry, that the service is now worth $1.50 per hour?

The way out of a price war is to offer some type of bundled services, for example Internet service packaged with e-mail, fax service, long-distance, cellular, and local calling services. Offer customers a communications package at a different price structure. In other words, take their minds off long distance and the price war, at a price that's fair to both consumer and marketer.

But what about when competitors inevitably match your bundle of services with their bundle of the same services at (guess what) a lower price? If only it weren't such an easy thing to do—and such a source of joy for consumers.[1]

## Overview

*Through* **price planning**, *each* **price** *places a value on a good or service.*

A **price** represents the value of a good or service for both the seller and the buyer. **Price planning** is systematic decision making by an organization regarding all aspects of pricing.

The value of a good or service can involve both tangible and intangible factors. An example of a tangible factor is the cost saving to a soda distributor from buying a

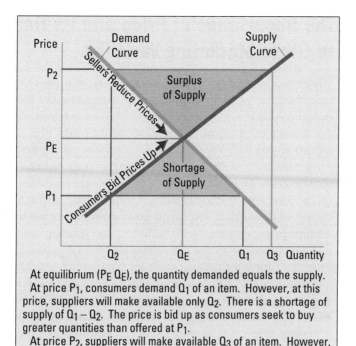

FIGURE 15-1

**The Role of Price in Balancing
Supply and Demand**

At equilibrium ($P_E$ $Q_E$), the quantity demanded equals the supply.
At price $P_1$, consumers demand $Q_1$ of an item. However, at this
price, suppliers will make available only $Q_2$. There is a shortage of
supply of $Q_1 - Q_2$. The price is bid up as consumers seek to buy
greater quantities than offered at $P_1$.
    At price $P_2$, suppliers will make available $Q_3$ of an item. However,
at this price, consumers demand only $Q_2$. There is a surplus of
supply of $Q_3 - Q_2$. The price is reduced by sellers in order to
attract greater demand by consumers.

new bottling machine; and an example of an intangible factor is a consumer's pride
in owning a Corvette rather than another brand of car.

From an exchange to take place, both buyer and seller must feel that the price of a
good or service provides an equitable ("fair") value. To the buyer, the payment of a
price reduces the purchasing power available for other items. To the seller, the receipt
of a price is a source of revenue and a key determinant of sales and profit levels.

Many words are substitutes for the term *price*, including admission fee, membership fee, rate, tuition, service charge, donation, rent, salary, interest, retainer, and
assessment. No matter what it is called, a price refers to all the terms of purchase:
monetary and nonmonetary charges, discounts, handling and shipping fees, credit
charges and other forms of interest, and late-payment penalties.

A nonmonetary exchange would be a department store awarding a gift to a person who gets a friend to shop at that store, or an airline offering tickets as payment
for advertising space and time. Monetary and nonmonetary exchanges may be combined. This is common with autos, where the buyer gives the seller money plus a
trade-in. That combination leads to a lower monetary price.

From a broader perspective, price is the mechanism for allocating goods and services among potential buyers and for ensuring competition among sellers in an open
marketplace. If demand exceeds supply, prices are usually bid up by consumers. If
supply exceeds demand, prices are usually reduced by sellers. See Figure 15-1.

In this chapter, the importance of price and its relationship to other marketing
variables, price-based and nonprice-based approaches, and the factors affecting
price decisions are studied. Next, we will look at the overall process of developing
and applying a pricing strategy—including the setting of pricing objectives, the use
of various pricing approaches, how a pricing strategy is implemented, and how
prices can be adjusted.

# The Importance of Price and Its Relationship to Other Marketing Variables

*The stature of price decisions has risen because more firms recognize their far-reaching impact.*

The importance of price decisions has risen considerably over the last thirty years. First, because price in a monetary or nonmonetary form is a component of the exchange process, it appears in every marketing transaction. More firms now realize the impact of price on image, sales, and profits. Second, deregulation in several industries has led to more price competition among firms. Third, in the 1970s and early 1980s, Canadian costs and prices rose rapidly—leading both firms and consumers to be price-conscious. In some other nations, costs and prices continue to escalate very quickly. Fourth, in the 1970s through the mid-1980s, a strong Canadian dollar with respect to other currencies gave foreign competitors a price advantage in Canadian markets. Today, the Canadian dollar is much weaker relative to such currencies as the U.S. dollar and the Japanese yen; and a larger number of firms monitor international currency fluctuations and adapt their marketing strategies accordingly. Fifth, the rapid pace of technological advances has caused intense price competition for such products as PCs, DVD players, and VCRs. Sixth, service-based firms are placing more emphasis on how they set prices. Seventh, in slow economic times, it is hard for firms to raise prices.

Many marketers share this view:

> Pricing is a manager's biggest marketing headache. It's where they feel the most pressure to perform and the least certain that they are doing a good job. The pressure is intensified because, for the most part, managers believe they don't have control over price: It is dictated by the market. Moreover, pricing is often seen as a difficult area in which to set goals and measure results. Ask managers to define the firm's manufacturing function, and they will cite a concrete goal, such as output and cost. Ask for a measure of productivity, and they will refer to cycle times. But pricing is hard to pin down. High unit sales and increased market share sound promising, but they may in fact mean a price is too low. And foregone profits do not appear on any scorecard.[2]

Inasmuch as a price places a value on the overall marketing mix offered to consumers (such as product features, product image, store location, and customer service), pricing decisions must be made in conjunction with product, distribution, and promotion plans. For instance, Parfums de Coeur makes imitations of expensive perfumes from Chanel, Estée Lauder, and Giorgio and sells them for one-third to one-fifth the price of those perfumes. It uses similar ingredients, but saves on packaging, advertising, and personal selling costs, and then distributes through mass merchandisers.

These are some basic ways in which pricing is related to other marketing and company variables:

- Prices ordinarily vary over the life of a product category, from high prices to gain status-conscious innovators to lower prices to lure the mass market.
- Customer service is affected since low prices are often associated with less customer service.
- From a distribution perspective, the prices charged to resellers must adequately compensate them for their functions, yet be low enough to compete with other brands at the wholesale or retail level.
- There may be conflict in a distribution channel if a manufacturer tries to control or suggest final prices.
- Product lines with different features—and different prices—can attract different market segments.

- A sales force may need some flexibility in negotiating prices and terms, particularly with large business accounts.

- The roles of marketing and finance personnel must be coordinated. Marketers often begin with the prices that people are willing to pay and work backward to ascertain acceptable company costs. Finance people typically start with costs and add desired profits to set prices.

- As costs change, the firm must decide whether to pass these changes on to consumers, absorb them, or modify product features.

For firms marketing products in foreign countries, "One of the most significant and perplexing of decisions has to do with pricing. Determining what prices to charge and when to change those prices are almost always tough decisions, but they become even more complicated when a company begins offering products to customers in several international markets." The greater complexity is typically due to the divergent company goals in different markets, the varying attributes of each market, and other factors. Furthermore, the ability to set prices in foreign markets may be affected by variations in government rules, competition, currency exchange rates, anti-dumping laws, operating costs, the rate of inflation, the standard of living, and so on.[3]

*Pricing internationally can be quite complicated.*

## Price-Based and Nonprice-Based Approaches

With a **price-based approach**, sellers influence consumer demand primarily through changes in price levels. With a **nonprice-based approach**, sellers downplay price as a factor in consumer demand by creating a distinctive good or service by means of promotion, packaging, delivery, customer service, availability, and other marketing factors. The more unique a product offering is perceived to be by consumers, the greater a firm's freedom to set prices above competitors'. See Figure 15-2.

In a price-based approach, sellers move along a demand curve by raising or lowering prices. This is a flexible marketing technique because prices can be adjusted quickly and easily to reflect demand, cost, or competitive factors. Yet, of all the controllable marketing variables, price is the easiest for a competitor to copy. This may result in "me-too" strategies or even in price wars. Furthermore, the government may monitor anti-competitive aspects of price-based strategies.

In a nonprice-based approach, sellers shift consumer demand curves by stressing the distinctive attributes of their products. This lets firms increase unit sales at a given price or sell their original supply at a higher price. The risk with a nonprice

*A **price-based approach** occurs when sellers stress low prices; a **nonprice-based** approach emphasizes factors other than price.*

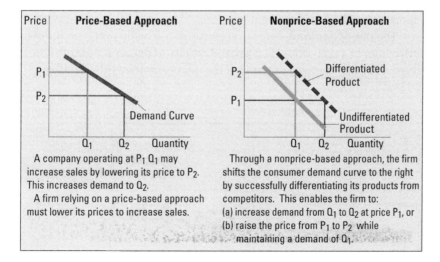

**FIGURE 15-2**

**Price-Based and Nonprice-Based Approaches**

Price-Based Approach

A company operating at $P_1 Q_1$ may increase sales by lowering its price to $P_2$. This increases demand to $Q_2$.

A firm relying on a price-based approach must lower its prices to increase sales.

Nonprice-Based Approach

Through a nonprice-based approach, the firm shifts the consumer demand curve to the right by successfully differentiating its products from competitors. This enables the firm to:
(a) increase demand from $Q_1$ to $Q_2$ at price $P_1$, or
(b) raise the price from $P_1$ to $P_2$ while maintaining a demand of $Q_1$.

strategy is that consumers may not perceive a seller's product as better than a competitor's. People would then buy the lower-priced item.

These are examples of price- and nonprice-oriented strategies:

- In recent years Labatt and Molson breweries have engaged in temporary price wars in the regulated Ontario market. Price reductions are legal, but they have to be approved by the Liquor Control Board of Ontario. During the summer of 1997 Labatt announced a $2 price reduction on cases of twenty-four beers just prior to each long weekend. Molson countered with a $3 reduction of its own.

But because price reductions have to be approved—a process that takes about two weeks—it's difficult to react immediately. Labatt surprised Molson with a $3 reduction on its Double Blue offering (twelve Labatt Blue beers and twelve Blue Light beers) just before Christmas in 1998. Molson was caught a bit flat, since it couldn't get approval for its own price reduction until December 28—too late for Christmas, but at least in time for New Year's![4]

- Shiseido, a giant Japanese cosmetics firm, operates a Beauty Gallery in Berlin, Germany. Visitors to the Gallery notice that it looks like a regular beauty shop, even to the point that prices aren't displayed on any of the merchandise. For it's not price that's emphasized in the Gallery's operation, but rather personalized service from the store's beauty consultants. Customers are encouraged to test out fragrances and cosmetic colours with the assistance of the beauty consultants, and then to make their purchase decisions based on how they look and feel, not on what they cost.[5]

## Factors Affecting Pricing Decisions

Before a firm develops a pricing strategy it should analyze the outside factors affecting decisions. Like distribution planning, pricing depends heavily on elements external to the firm. This contrasts with product and promotion decisions, which, with the exception of publicity, are more controlled by a firm. Sometimes, outside elements greatly influence the firm's ability to set prices; in other cases, they have little impact. Figure 15-3 outlines the major factors, which are discussed next.

### Consumers

Company personnel involved with pricing decisions must understand the relationship between price and consumer purchases and perceptions. This relationship is explained by two economic principles—the law of demand and the price elasticity of demand—and by market segmentation.

*According to the* **law of demand**, *more is bought at low prices; price* **elasticity** *explains reactions to changes.*

The **law of demand** states that consumers usually purchase more units at a low price than at a high price. The **price elasticity of demand** indicates the sensitivity of buyers to price changes in terms of the quantities they will purchase.[6]

**FIGURE 15-3**

**Factors Affecting Price Decisions**

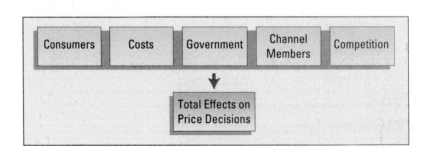

Price elasticity represents the percentage change in the quantity demanded relative to a specific percentage change in the price charged. This formula shows the percentage change in demand for each one per cent change in price:

$$\text{Price elasticity} = \frac{\dfrac{\text{Quantity 1} - \text{Quantity 2}}{\text{Quantity 1} + \text{Quantity 2}}}{\dfrac{\text{Price 1} - \text{Price 2}}{\text{Price 1} + \text{Price 2}}}$$

Because the quantity demanded usually falls as price rises, elasticity is a negative number. However, for purposes of simplicity, elasticity calculations are usually expressed as positive numbers.

**Elastic demand** occurs if relatively small changes in price result in large changes in quantity demanded. Numerically, price elasticity is greater than 1. With elastic demand, total revenue goes up when prices are decreased and goes down when prices rise. **Inelastic demand** takes place if price changes have little impact on the quantity demanded. Price elasticity is less than 1. With inelastic demand, total revenue goes up when prices are raised and goes down when prices decline. **Unitary demand** exists if price changes are exactly offset by changes in the quantity demanded, so total sales revenue remains constant. Price elasticity is 1.

*Demand may be* **elastic, inelastic,** *or* **unitary** *depending on the availability of substitutes and urgency of need.*

Demand elasticity is based mostly on two criteria: availability of substitutes and urgency of need. If people *believe* there are many similar goods or services from which to choose or have no urgency to buy, demand is elastic and greatly influenced by price changes: Price increases lead to purchases of substitutes or delayed purchases, and decreases expand sales as people are drawn from competitors or move up the date of their purchases. For some people, the airfare for a vacation is highly elastic. If prices go up, they may travel to a nearer location by car or postpone a trip.

If consumers believe a firm's offering is unique or there is an urgency to buy, demand is inelastic and little influenced by price changes: neither price increases nor declines will have much impact on demand. In most locales, when heating oil prices go up or down, demand remains relatively constant because there is often no feasible substitute—and homes and offices must be properly heated. Brand loyalty also generates inelastic demand; consumers feel their brands are distinctive and do not accept substitutes. Finally, emergency conditions increase demand inelasticity. A truck driver with a flat tire would pay more for a replacement than a driver with time to shop around.

It should be noted that demand elasticity usually varies over a wide range of prices for the same good or service. At very high prices, even revenues for essential goods and services may fall (mass-transit ridership would drop a lot if fares rose from $1.50 to $3; driving would become a more reasonable substitute). At very low prices, demand cannot be stimulated further; market saturation is reached and consumers may begin to perceive quality as inferior.

Price sensitivity varies by market segment because all people are not equally price-conscious. Consumers can be divided into such segments as these:

*Consumers can be segmented in terms of their price orientation.*

- *Price shoppers*—They are interested in the "best deal" for a product.
- *Brand-loyal customers*—They believe their current brands are better than others and will pay "fair" prices for those products.
- *Status seekers*—They buy prestigious brands and product categories and will pay whatever prices are set; higher prices signify greater status.
- *Service/features shoppers*—They place a great value on customer service and/or product features and will pay for them.
- *Convenience shoppers*—They value ease of shopping, nearby locations, long hours by sellers, and other approaches that make shopping simple; they will pay above-average prices.

A firm must determine which segment or segments are represented by its target market and plan accordingly.

The consumer's (market segment's) perception of the price of a good or service as being high, fair, or low—its **subjective price**—may be more important than its actual price. For example, a consumer may feel a low price represents a good buy or inferior quality—or a high price represents status or poor value.

*A consumer's perception of a price level is the* **subjective price**.

The following factors affect a consumer's (market segment's) subjective price:

- *Purchase experience with a particular good or service*—"How much have I paid in the past?"
- *Purchase experience with other, similar goods or services*—"What's a fair price for an item in the same or adjacent product category that I bought before?"
- *Self-image*—"How much should a person like me pay for something like this?"
- *Social situation*—"How much do the people around me expect me to pay for something like this?"
- *Context of the purchase*—"What should this cost in these circumstances?"[7]

## Costs

The costs of raw materials, supplies, labour, transportation, and other items are commonly beyond a firm's control. Yet, they have a great impact on prices.

In Canada, from the early 1970s into the 1980s, many costs rose rapidly and pushed prices to high levels, before levelling off. For example:

- Provincial minimum wages in Canada have risen from $2 per hour in 1972 to $5-$6 per hour. (Alberta is lowest at $5 an hour, and at $7.15 B.C. is highest.) Minimum wage rates have their greatest impact on fast-food retailers and other firms relying on semiskilled and unskilled labour.[8]
- Mortgage interest rates more than doubled between 1977 and 1981, severely dampening the housing market, before starting to decline in 1983. Since 1993, they have been at twenty-five-year lows.
- The cost of prime-time TV ads has gone up dramatically. For example, the most expensive commercial broadcast time on earth is an ad on the NFL's championship, the Super Bowl. A 30-second ad on the 1972 Super Bowl cost U.S.$100 000—and in 1999, U.S.$1.6 million!

Over the past fifteen years overall Canadian cost increases have been rather low. While the 1980 inflation rate was 15 per cent, the 1999 rate was under 2 per cent. This means better cost control and more stable prices for most firms. Yet, unexpected events can still strike specific industries. For example, a few years ago the price of rhodium, a precious metal used to make catalytic converters for cars, rapidly rose from U.S.$1750 to U.S.$7000 per ounce due to problems at a refinery. Rhodium's cost per car went from U.S.$15 to U.S.$60.[9]

*When costs rise, companies pass along increases, alter products, or delete some items.*

During periods of rapidly rising costs, firms can react in one or more ways: They can leave products unchanged and pass along all their cost increases to consumers; leave products unchanged and pass along only part of their increases and absorb part of them; modify products to hold down costs and maintain prices (by reducing size, using lesser-quality materials, or offering fewer options); modify products to gain consumer support for higher prices (by increasing size, using better-quality materials, offering some options, or upgrading customer service); and/or abandon unprofitable products. For instance, in response to a 50–60 per cent increase in the cost of pulp paper, Scott decided to reduce the number of sheets in the smallest roll of Scott Clean paper towels from 96 to 60—and *lower* the price by 10 per cent.[10]

Despite a firm's or an industry's best intentions it may sometimes take years to get runaway costs (and prices) under control. A good illustration is the very important North American auto industry, where costs and prices have risen substantially since 1970. The average new car had a retail price of under U.S.$3500 then; the average price is now over U.S.$22 000. Among the costs that auto executives have had to deal with are the billions of dollars required to retool from large to small cars; high fixed costs for plant, equipment, and unionized labour; hundreds of millions of dollars for anti-pollution and safety devices; and investments of up to U.S.$1 billion or more to develop each major new model. As a result pricing decisions have to be made far in advance, and flexibility is limited.

If costs decline firms can drop selling prices or raise profit margins. For example, the use of microchips has reduced PC costs by requiring less wiring and assembly time in production, improving durability, and enlarging information-processing capability. PC prices have gone down steadily, thus expanding the market. On the other hand, low sugar prices let candy makers increase package size (and profits) without raising prices.

*Cost decreases have mostly positive benefits for marketing strategies.*

Sometimes low costs can actually have a negative long-run impact. For example, since oil prices collapsed in 1986 energy prices have remained relatively cheap (averaging about U.S.$19.27 a barrel in 1996 dollars), which has taken away the impetus for greater energy efficiency. This has resulted in greater social costs as well as long-term economic costs associated with excessive energy use, i.e., increased dependence on foreign oil, air pollution, and environmental damage, including carbon dioxide emissions, which could result in catastrophic global warning.

Researchers at the U.S. Department of National Energy have studied the impact of carbon-based fuels on the production of carbon dioxide in the U.S. They determined that if the price of carbon were set at U.S.$50 per ton consumption of carbon-based fuels would decrease enough to bring carbon dioxide levels back to their 1990 levels. A $50 per ton price for carbon would increase oil prices from their long-term average of $19.27 to the $25.50 range, a 30 per cent price increase.[11]

## Government[12]

As set out in the Competition Act, federal government actions related to pricing fall into two major areas: criminal and non-criminal provisions (see Figure 15-4). The Competition Act became law in June 1986, replacing the former Combines Investigation Act. Criminal provisions related to pricing include: conspiracy to price-fix, bid-rigging, price maintenance, discriminatory and predatory pricing, and double ticketing of prices. Non-criminal matters include: misleading advertising, sale above advertised price, bait-and-switch selling, abuse of dominant position, refusal to deal, consignment selling, tied selling, and delivered pricing. Practices that fall under criminal provisions are normally dealt with through the court system, whereas non-criminal matters go before the Competition Tribunal, which is empowered to issue injunctions. Finally, individuals or firms can file civil suits if they have suffered damage due to anti-competitive behaviour in the marketplace.

*Canada's Competition Act regulates pricing behaviour with criminal and non-criminal provisions.*

## Criminal Provisions

**CONSPIRACY TO PRICE FIX**   There are restrictions on price fixing among competitors. Often referred to as horizontal price fixing, it results from agreements among manufacturers, among wholesalers, or among retailers to set prices at a given stage in a channel of distribution. Such agreements are illegal according to the Competition Act, regardless of how "reasonable" prices are.

Violations may result in severe federal penalties. For example, in 1999 a fine of $11 million—the largest fine ever imposed under section 46 of the Competition Act—

**Conspiracy to price fix** *results from agreements among companies at the same stage in a channel to control resale prices.*

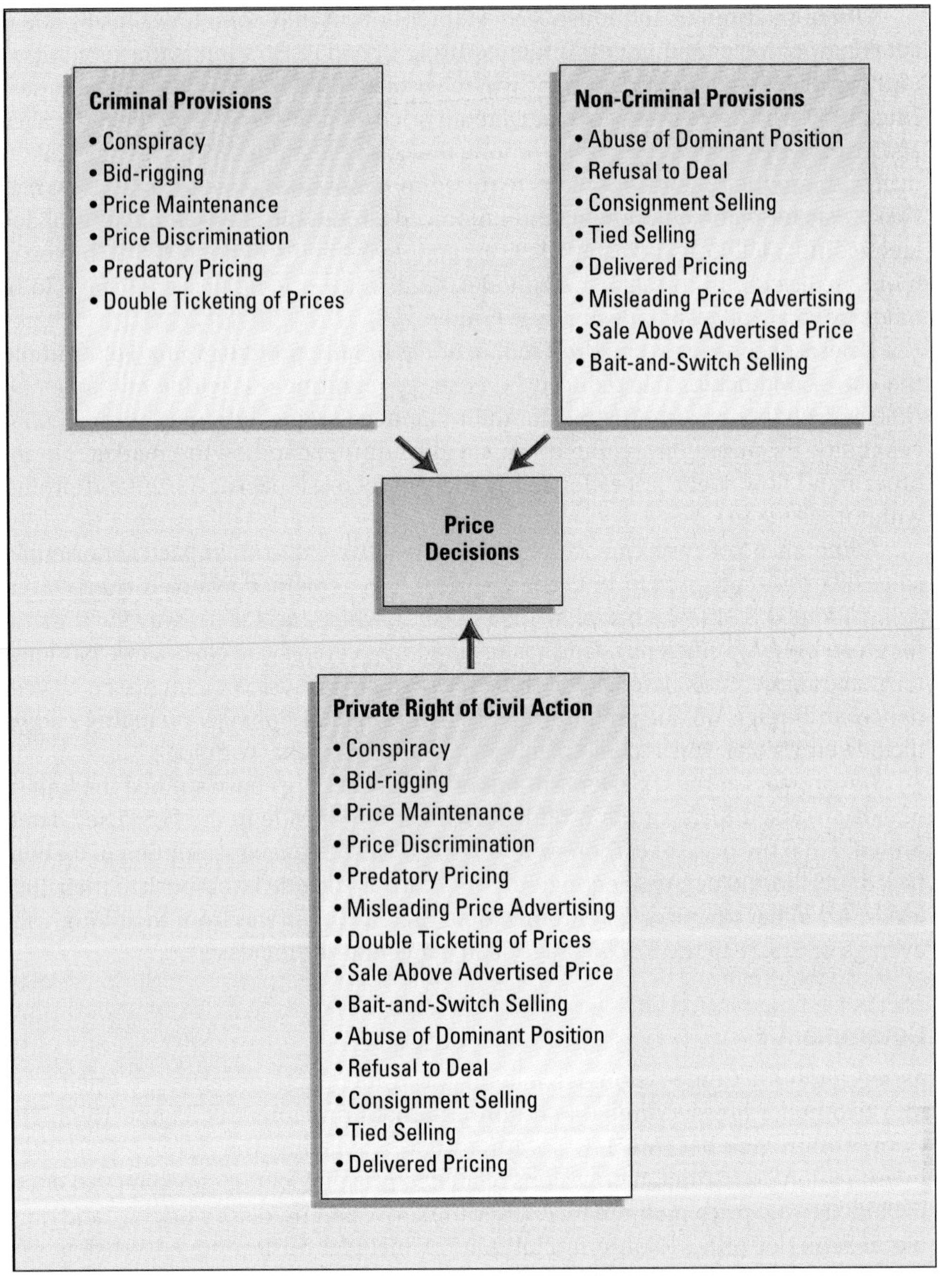

**Criminal Provisions**
- Conspiracy
- Bid-rigging
- Price Maintenance
- Price Discrimination
- Predatory Pricing
- Double Ticketing of Prices

**Non-Criminal Provisions**
- Abuse of Dominant Position
- Refusal to Deal
- Consignment Selling
- Tied Selling
- Delivered Pricing
- Misleading Price Advertising
- Sale Above Advertised Price
- Bait-and-Switch Selling

**Price Decisions**

**Private Right of Civil Action**
- Conspiracy
- Bid-rigging
- Price Maintenance
- Price Discrimination
- Predatory Pricing
- Misleading Price Advertising
- Double Ticketing of Prices
- Sale Above Advertised Price
- Bait-and-Switch Selling
- Abuse of Dominant Position
- Refusal to Deal
- Consignment Selling
- Tied Selling
- Delivered Pricing

**FIGURE 15-4**

**Canadian Legislative Regulations Affecting Price Decisions**

was levied against UCAR, an American-based steelmaker. UCAR also had to agree to pay restitution of approximately $19 million to Canadian steel companies.[13]

To avoid price fixing charges, a firm must be careful not to:

- Coordinate discounts, credit terms, or conditions of sale with competitors.
- Talk about price levels, markups, and costs at trade association meetings.
- Plan with competitors to issue new price lists on the same date.
- Plan with competitors to rotate low bids on contracts.
- Agree with competitors to limit production to keep high prices.
- Exchange information with competitors, even informally.

*With **bid-rigging**, bidders collude with tendering parties to inflate bids.*

**Bid-rigging** is very much akin to conspiracy. Bidders collude together or collude with the party offering the bid tender to restrain competition or to inflate bids. It may result in some competitors not submitting bids or in one competitor being given preferential bid treatment.

**Price maintenance** occurs when manufacturers or wholesalers seek to control the final selling prices of their goods or services. Price maintenance is also known as fair trade, resale price maintenance, and vertical price fixing. It originated out of a desire by manufacturers and wholesalers to protect small resellers and maintain brand images by forcing all resellers within a given area to charge the same price for affected products. Price maintenance was criticized by consumer groups and many resellers and manufacturers as being noncompetitive, keeping prices too high, and rewarding reseller inefficiency.

The use of price maintenance has been illegal in Canada since 1951. Under the Competition Act, resellers cannot be forced to adhere to manufacturer or wholesaler list prices.

Manufacturers or wholesalers may only control final prices by one of these methods:

- Manufacturer or wholesaler ownership of sales facilities.
- Consignment selling. The manufacturer or wholesaler owns items until they are sold and assumes costs normally associated with the reseller, such as advertising and selling.
- Careful screening of the channel members that sell goods or services. A supplier can bypass or drop distributors if they are not living up to the supplier's performance standards, as long as there is no collusion between the supplier and other distributors. (A firm must be careful not to threaten channel members that do not adhere to suggested prices).
- Suggesting realistic selling prices.
- Pre-printing prices on products.
- Establishing customary prices (such as $1.25 for a newspaper) that are accepted by consumers.

**PRICE DISCRIMINATION** The Competition Act prohibits manufacturers and wholesalers from **price discrimination** when dealing with different channel-member purchasers. It is illegal to charge different prices for products with "like quality" if the effect of such discrimination is to injure competition. Price practices that can fall under the price discrimination portion of the Act include: differential prices, discounts, rebates, premiums, coupons, guarantees, delivery, warehousing, and credit rates. Terms and conditions of sale must be made available to all competing channel-member customers on a proportionately equal basis.

The price discrimination prohibitions of the Competition Act were originally intended to protect small retailers from unfair price competition by large chains. It was feared that small firms would be driven out of business due to the superior bargaining power (and the resultant lower selling prices) of chains. However, the price discrimination prohibitions of the Competition Act are applicable at all levels of the channel of distribution—including the retail level. Under the Competition Act price differences charged to competing purchasers (whether resellers or consumers) are limited to quantity or volume discounts or when products are of different quality. There are no other bases upon which a price differential can be legally granted and this includes so-called "functional discounts," which are legal in the United States.

**Predatory pricing** is of two types. The first involves selling products in different regions at different prices (not due to transportation costs) for the express purpose of eliminating existing competitors or lessening competition—such as preventing market entry of competitors. The second involves selling products at unreasonably low prices (essentially at cost or below cost) with the same purpose.

Complaints about pricing are normally made to the Competition Bureau, whose commissioner determines whether a suspected violation of the Competition Act has occurred. The commissioner then decides whether it involves criminal or non-criminal provisions.[14] Violations of any of the previously discussed criminal provisions are referred to the Attorney General of Canada for prosecution under the Act. Prosecution of firms and individuals under criminal provisions require that strict rules of evidence be applied and cases proved beyond reasonable doubt. Alternatively, the suspected violation may be considered under one of the non-criminal provisions, as discussed in the following section.

*Regulations on* **double ticketing** *ensure that when a product has two different prices, consumers pay the lowest price.*

**DOUBLE PRICE TICKETING**  The **double ticketing** provision states that when two prices are marked on an item (as often occurs with sale products) it is illegal to charge the higher price.

## Non-Criminal Provisions

In recent amendments to the Competition Act, enforcements for misleading advertising and deceptive marketing practices were moved from criminal to non-criminal provisions. As such, the Competition Bureau will have a choice of approaches to deal with violations.

Non-criminal matters go before the Competition Tribunal, which is empowered to issue injunctions to stop the practices. The normal rules of evidence that apply in court cases do not apply in proceedings undertaken by the Competition Tribunal, although firms do have recourse through the court system if they so desire. Let's look at some of the pricing practices subject to the non-criminal provisions of the Competition Act.

*Regulation of* **misleading price advertising** *is one of the most frequently enforced provisions of the Competition Act.*

**MISLEADING PRICE ADVERTISING**  The Competition Act has its most visible impact on consumers through **misleading price advertising**. In particular, the Act seeks to regulate advertising with respect to regular prices or ordinary price claims.

The Competition Bureau offers a Program of Advisory Opinions from which marketers can receive advice on their approach to pricing and price advertising. Price advertising guidelines have also been developed by such trade associations as the Better Business Bureau. Here are some of the most recent ordinary price claim guidelines that a firm can follow in order to avoid contravening the Competition Act.[15]

An advertiser can make a price comparison about a product if the higher price reflects the price at which sellers in the market area have either:

- sold a substantial volume (more than 50 per cent of sales) of the product within a reasonable period of time before making the representation, or
- offered the product for sale in good faith for a substantial period of time (more than 50 per cent of the time) recently before or immediately after making the representation.

These two provisions are the key tests of whether a firm can fairly make a price comparison; and lead to the following:

- Where the comparison is made to the advertiser's own prices, the above two tests will apply to those prices.
- The nature of the market and of the product will be considered in determining whether a violation under the section has occurred. For example, a market may be able to correct itself through competition, especially where the products are frequently purchased, low-priced items. Similarly, a seasonal product may be sold or offered for sale for a shorter period of time than other products.
- Where price comparisons are made to like products, the above tests will apply with reference to the prices of those like products.
- Price comparison representations that fail these tests may not raise an issue if the advertiser can prove that they weren't otherwise misleading in a material

respect. For example, a clearance sale may fail both tests, but an advertiser promoting the sale will likely be able to show that the price comparison representations were not otherwise misleading if it can be demonstrated that the sale was clearly marked as a clearance sale; that the representation referred to the original price and any subsequent interim prices; and that the original price was offered in good faith.

**SALE ABOVE ADVERTISED PRICE**   When an item is advertised in the media at a special price (assuming the price was not a misprint), the marketer is obliged to honour that price according to the terms of the advertising. Charging higher prices to individuals who have not heard of the sale or refusing to honour the price for individuals who have heard of the sale is a violation of the Competition Act.

*Marketers are not allowed to make **sales above advertised prices**.*

**Bait-and-switch selling** is the intended practice of advertising a bargain price on a sale item and then not carrying a sufficient supply to satisfy the created demand. The intention is to "switch" customers to other, higher priced items. Signs of bait-and-switch are a refusal to demonstrate sale items, the belittling of sale items, inadequate quantities of sale items on hand, a refusal to take orders, demonstrations of defective items, and the use of compensation plans encouraging salespeople to use the tactic. However, advertisers can avoid violating this regulation by stating the quantity available, offering rain cheques during the sale, or making a reasonable attempt to obtain a large enough quantity.

*Under **bait-and-switch selling**, sellers illegally draw customers by deceptive pricing.*

**ABUSE OF DOMINANT POSITION**   The competitive actions of firms that have a dominant position in sectors of the Canadian marketplace can adversely affect their competitors and lessen competition in the marketplace. Pricing considerations that involve **abuse of dominant position** include purchasing products to prevent the reduction of existing price levels and selling articles at a price lower than the acquisition cost to discipline or eliminate a competitor. When this practice involves a sale to a foreign market, it is referred to as product dumping. Before this provision can be enacted, it must be established that an individual or a firm does have substantial control of a class of business in Canada.

*Large firms who sell products below cost to eliminate competition are guilty of **abuse of dominant position**.*

The Competition Tribunal can recommend almost any remedy that can restore the level of competition to the marketplace, including prohibiting any actions that have been lessening competition and divesting a firm of its assets to reduce its market power.

**REFUSAL TO DEAL**   Retailers or wholesalers might encounter a situation where a supplier will refuse to supply a product to them even though they are willing to deal under the supplier's usual trade terms and the supplier has an ample amount of products. If this refusal to deal is related to a dispute between the supplier and the retailer or wholesaler over price maintenance it is a violation of the Competition Act. In this case, the Competition Tribunal can order the supplier to accept the customer under the usual trade terms.

**Refusal to deal** *is an illegal practice that may be used to force channel members to maintain prices.*

**Consignment selling** occurs when a dealer is supplied products and only pays for what is sold, when it is sold. The dealer can return unsold goods to the supplier without any penalty. If the practice is undertaken so the supplier is able to price discriminate between consignees and other dealers or to ensure price maintenance, then it is a violation of the Competition Act. The Competition Tribunal can make an order to force the supplier to discontinue the practice.

**Consignment selling** *is a way of ensuring price maintenance and can be used to practise price discrimination.*

**Tied sales** occur when a supplier will only provide a product wanted by a customer on the condition that the customer agrees to purchase another type of product or refrain from purchasing a second product from another firm—in effect, tying one transaction to a second. If the tying results in less competition the Competition Tribunal can issue a prohibition order to stop the practice. Tied selling is a common

**Tied sales** *are a problem when the "tied" product is unwanted.*

approach in marketing and usually only becomes a problem when the tie is "unwanted." In this case, a firm may want only one product and find their supplier refuses to deal unless the firm accepts or rejects a second product too.

Tied selling is very hard to prove. For example, a recent investigation of tied selling in Canada occurred in the auto glass industry. The Competition Tribunal was concerned that insurance companies were tying claims services to the purchase of auto glass for auto glass replacement companies that were "nominated" by the insurance firms. In order to determine if tied selling was occurring the commissioner of competition had to:

- be satisfied that tied selling had occurred
- be satisfied that it was being engaged in by a major supplier of auto insurance, or that it was widespread in the auto insurance market
- be satisfied that it was likely to impede entry into or expansion of a firm in the auto glass repair market.

An investigation of the situation established that insurance companies directing people to auto glass repair shops was indeed a widespread practice. However, the Competition Tribunal determined that entry into the auto glass market was not impaired and that consumers were not required to go to designated repair shops. The Tribunal found that there were actually savings occurring because of the practice, and that these savings were passed onto consumers. As such, no further action was taken with respect to the auto glass industry.[16]

*Delivered pricing means that customers in the same geographic area should be charged the same price.*

**DELIVERED PRICING** The practice of refusing a customer delivery on the same trade terms as similar customers in essentially the same location is a violation of **delivered pricing**. This regulation applies only if the customers have a comparable ability to receive delivery. For example, if a supplier had to make major capital investments or other accommodations to serve a customer, they could legitimately demand different trade terms. Another situation might involve products that are customarily supplied in bulk quantities on skids and off-loaded with a forklift truck to save labour. If a customer required that the product be broken down from the skids and handled manually, differential trade terms could be applied. Once again, the Competition Tribunal would make an order prohibiting the practice.

## Channel Members

Each channel member seeks to play a significant role in setting prices so as to generate sales volume, obtain adequate profit margins, create a suitable image, ensure repeat purchases, and meet specific goals.

A manufacturer can gain greater control over prices by using an exclusive distribution system or avoiding price-oriented resellers; pre-marking prices on products; owning sales outlets; offering products on consignment; providing adequate margins to resellers; and, most importantly, by having strong brands to which people are brand loyal and for which they will pay premium prices.

A wholesaler or retailer can gain better control over prices by stressing its importance as a customer to the supplier, linking resale support to the profit margins allowed by the supplier, refusing to carry unprofitable items, stocking competing items, having strong private brands so people are loyal to the seller and not the supplier, and purchasing outside traditional channels.

*To increase private-brand sales, some channel members* **sell against the brand.**

Wholesalers and retailers may engage in **selling against the brand**, whereby they stock well-known brands at high prices, and then sell other brands for lower prices to increase sales of their private brands. This practice is disliked by manufacturers since sales of their brands decline.

**Grey market goods** *bypass authorized channels.*

Sometimes, wholesalers and retailers go outside traditional distribution channels and buy **grey market goods**—foreign-made products imported by distributors (suppliers) that are not authorized by the products' manufacturers. Personal stereos, VCRs, car stereos, watches, and cameras are just some of the items handled in this way.

If wholesalers and retailers buy grey market goods, their purchase prices are less than they would be otherwise and they have greater control over their own selling prices. The result is often discounted prices for consumers, which may be upsetting to manufacturers and authorized dealers.[17]

To maximize channel-member cooperation on pricing decisions, these factors should be considered: channel-member profit margins, price guarantees, special deals, and the impact of price increases. Wholesalers and retailers require appropriate profit margins to cover their costs (such as shipping, storage, credit, and advertising) and earn reasonable profits. Thus, the prices that are charged to them must take these profit margins into account. An attempt to reduce traditional margins for channel members may lose their cooperation and perhaps make them unwilling to carry a product. Pricing through a distribution channel is discussed later in the chapter.

Channel members may seek price guarantees to maintain inventory values and profit. **Price guarantees** assure resellers that the prices they pay are the lowest available. Any discount given to competitors will also be given to the original purchasers. Guarantees are most frequently requested for new firms or new products that want to gain entry into an established channel.

*Price guarantees reassure channel members.*

Special deals—consisting of limited-time discounts and/or free products—are often used to stimulate purchases by resellers. The deals may require channel members to share their savings with final consumers to increase the latter's demand. For example, soda bottlers normally give retailers large price discounts on new products to encourage them to make purchases and then offer low introductory prices to consumers.

The effects of price increases on channel members' behaviour must also be assessed. When firms raise prices to resellers, these increases tend to be passed along to consumers. This practice is more difficult for items with customary prices, such as candy, where small cost rises may be absorbed by the resellers. In any event, cooperation depends on an equitable distribution of costs and profit within the channel.

## Competition

Another factor contributing to the degree of control a firm has over prices is the competitive environment within which it operates.

A **market-controlled price environment** is characterized by a high level of competition, similar goods and services, and little control over prices by individual firms. Those trying to charge much more than the going price would attract few customers because demand for any single firm is weak enough that customers would switch to competitors. There would similarly be little gained by selling for less because competitors would match price cuts.

*A firm may face a **market-controlled, company-controlled, or government-controlled price environment**.*

A **company-controlled price environment** is characterized by moderate competition, well-differentiated goods and services, and strong control over prices by individual firms. Companies can succeed with above-average prices because people view their offerings as unique. Differentiation may be based on brand image, features, associated services, assortment, or other elements. Discounters also can carve out a niche in this environment by attracting consumers interested in low prices.

A **government-controlled price environment** is characterized by prices being set or strongly influenced by some level of government. Examples are public utilities, mass transit, insurance, and publicly funded colleges and universities. In each case, government bodies determine or affect prices after obtaining input from the relevant companies, institutions, and/or trade associations, as well as other interested parties (such as consumer groups).

Companies may have to adapt to a changing competitive environment in their industries. Firms in the transportation, telecommunications, and financial industries have seen their price environment shift from government- to market-controlled—although some strong firms in these industries have managed to develop a company-controlled price environment.

Price strategies are easy and quick to copy, so marketers must view price from both short- and long-run perspectives. Excessive price competition may lead to lengthy and costly **price wars**, in which various firms continually try to undercut each other's prices to draw customers. These wars often result in low profits or even losses for the participants, and in some companies being forced out of business.

In recent years, there have been price wars among some car-rental firms, airlines, blank videocassette tape manufacturers, PC makers, semiconductor manufacturers, supermarkets, insurance companies, and others. Although price wars have been more common in Canada and the United States (due to fierce competition in some industries), they are now spreading overseas—particularly to Europe and, to a lesser extent, Japan.

**Price wars** *occur when competitors constantly lower prices.*

**FIGURE 15-5**

**A Framework for Developing and Applying a Pricing Strategy**

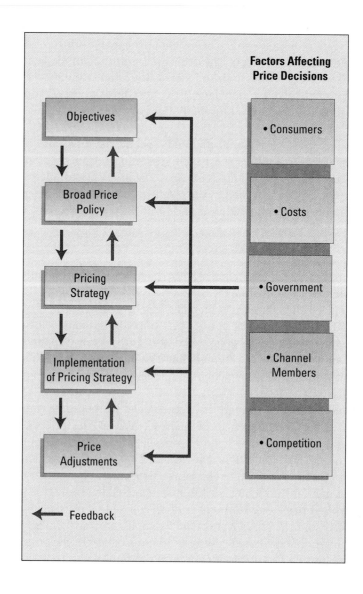

# Developing and Applying a Pricing Strategy

As Figure 15-5 shows, a pricing strategy has five steps: objectives, broad policy, strategy, implementation, and adjustments. All of them are affected by the outside factors noted earlier in the chapter. Like any planning activity, a pricing strategy begins with a clear statement of goals and ends with an adaptive or corrective mechanism. Pricing decisions are integrated with the firm's overall marketing program during the broad price-policy step.

The development of a pricing strategy is not a one-time occurrence. It needs to be reviewed when a new product is introduced, an existing product is revised, the competitive environment changes, a product moves through its life cycle, a competitor initiates a price change, costs rise or fall, the firm's prices come under government scrutiny, and other events take place.

These are some indications a pricing strategy may be performing poorly:

- Prices are changed too frequently.
- Pricing policy is difficult to explain to consumers.
- Channel members complain that profit margins are inadequate.
- Price decisions are made without adequate marketing-research information.
- Too many different price options are available.
- Too much sales personnel time is spent in bargaining.
- Prices are inconsistent with the target market.
- A high percentage of goods is marked down or discounted late in the selling season to clear out surplus inventory.
- Too high a proportion of customers is price-sensitive and attracted by competitors' discounts. Demand is elastic.
- The firm has problems conforming with pricing legislation.

The rest of this chapter describes in detail the pricing framework outlined in Figure 15-5.

# Pricing Objectives

A pricing strategy should be consistent with and reflect overall company goals. It is possible for different firms in the same industry to have dissimilar objectives and, therefore, distinct pricing strategies.

There are three general pricing objectives from which a firm may select: sales-based, profit-based, and status quo-based. With sales-based goals, a firm is interested in sales growth and/or maximizing market share. With profit-based goals, it is interested in maximizing profit, earning a satisfactory profit, optimizing the return on investment, and/or securing an early recovery of cash. With status quo-based goals, it seeks to avoid unfavourable government actions, minimize the effects of competitor actions, maintain good channel relations, discourage the entry of competitors, reduce demands from suppliers, and/or stabilize prices.

A company may pursue more than one pricing goal at the same time, such as increasing sales by 5 to 10 per cent each year, achieving a 15 per cent return on capital investments, and keeping prices near those of competitors. It may also set distinct short- and long-run goals. In the short run, it may seek high profit margins on new products; in the long run, these profit margins would drop to discourage potential competitors.

## Sales-Based Objectives

**Sales-based objectives** *seek high volume or market share.*

A firm with **sales-based pricing objectives** is oriented toward high sales volume and/or expanding its share of sales relative to competitors. The company focuses on sales-based goals for either (or all) of three reasons: It sees market saturation or sales growth as a major step leading to market control and sustained profits. It wants to maximize unit sales and will trade low per-unit profits for larger total profits. It assumes greater sales will enable it to have lower per-unit costs.

**Penetration pricing** *aims at the mass market.*

To gain high sales volume, **penetration pricing** is often employed—whereby low prices are used to capture the mass market for a good or service. It is a proper approach if customers are highly sensitive to price, low prices discourage actual and potential competitors, there are economies of scale (per-unit production and distribution costs fall as sales rise), and a large consumer market exists. Penetration pricing also recognizes that a high price may leave a product vulnerable to competition.

**WAL-MART**
www.wal-mart.com/

Penetration pricing is used by Wal-Mart and Kia Motors. Wal-Mart's slogan is "Watch for Falling Prices," and it concentrates on "everyday low pricing" instead of running frequent sales. Korean automaker Kia Motors recently planned to enter the Canadian market with a penetration pricing strategy. Its positioning approach was "Japanese quality at a Korean price." The firm planned to sell a 4x4 sport utility vehicle for $20 995 and a compact sedan for $12 995, prices that are well under those of comparable vehicles in the Canadian market.[18]

Penetration pricing may even tap markets not originally anticipated. For example, few people forecasted that cordless phones would reach the sales volume attained during their peak. The market expanded rapidly after prices fell below $100. It grew again as new models were introduced for $60 and less.

## Profit-Based Objectives

**Profit-based objectives** *range from maximization to recovery of cash. Goals can be per unit or total.*

A company with **profit-based pricing objectives** orients its strategy toward some type of profit goals. With profit-maximization goals, high dollar profits are sought. With satisfactory-profit goals, stability over time is desired; rather than maximize profits in a given year (which could result in declines in nonpeak years), steady profits for a number of years are sought. With return-on-investment goals, profits are related to investment costs; these goals are often pursued by regulated utilities as a way of justifying rate increases. With early-recovery-of-cash goals, high initial profits are sought because firms are short of funds or uncertain about their future.

Profit may be expressed in per-unit or total terms. Per-unit profit equals the revenue a seller receives for one unit sold minus its costs. A product like custom-made furniture has a high unit profit. Total profit equals the revenue a seller receives for all items sold minus total costs. It is computed by multiplying per-unit profit times the number of units sold. A product like mass-marketed furniture has a low unit profit; success is based on the number of units sold (turnover). Products with high per-unit profits may have lower total profits than ones with low per-unit profits if the discount prices of the latter generate a much greater level of consumer demand. However, this depends on the elasticity of demand.

**Skimming pricing** *is aimed at the segment interested in quality or status.*

**Skimming pricing** uses high prices to attract the market segment more concerned with product quality, uniqueness, or status than price. It is proper if competition can be minimized (by means of patent protection, brand loyalty, raw material control, or high capital requirements), funds are needed for early cash recovery or further expansion, consumers are insensitive to price or willing to pay a high initial price, and unit costs remain equal or rise as sales increase (economies of scale are absent).

Skimming prices are used by such firms as Genentech, Canondale, and Tequila Herradura S.A. Genentech is the maker of Activase, a patented brand of TPA (tissue

## INTERNATIONAL MARKETING IN ACTION

### Sunday Is a Good Time and Place for Your Phone Business

Beginning its operations in 1997 (the year of the Hong Kong handover to China), Mandarin Communications of Hong Kong entered the mobile phone market well behind its major competitors. In order to attract customers the firm had to think of a way to get into the market and make a strong impression fast. It settled on a two-pronged approach: a memorable brand image, and a competitive marketing strategy to support this image. The firm decided to call itself Sunday, develop some innovative and memorable advertising to go with the name, and use a low pricing approach. The latter was designed to target first-time mobile phone buyers, since at the time cell phone numbers weren't portable in Hong Kong and it was difficult to get existing users to switch.

Sunday promoted its unique name in its advertising to show how people spent their Sundays relaxing. Then it offered a six-month introductory price that was equivalent to CAN$17 per month for unlimited airtime service. This offer was extremely competitive, given that other firms were charging about $69 a month for 100 min-

utes. The response was overwhelming: the firm received 10 000 calls per day and signed up 80 000 subscribers.

At the end of the six-month introductory period the price rose to CAN$17 a month for 100 minutes and 19 cents a minute after that. Of course, Sunday's competitors did not sit idly by. At first they aired counter-advertising aimed at Sunday's main weakness, a limited calling area. One competitor, Orange, has guaranteed to match the rates of any competitors. And because cell phone numbers in Hong Kong have become portable, competitors can now steal customers from Sunday during Monday to Saturday!

Evaluate Sunday's penetration pricing market entry strategy. With what price would you have entered the market? How do you think Sunday determined its price, and why was it so low? Now that the competitors are matching it, where does Sunday go today?

Source: Based on material in Susan Mulley, "Sunday Really Is a Special Day," *Marketing Magazine* (May 10, 1999), p. 33.

plasminogen activator), a product that quickly clears the blood clots associated with heart attacks and effectively treats certain kinds of strokes. It sells Activase for about $1500 per dose. Canondale's Super V bikes retail for $3500 each. They have rear shock absorbers to boost comfort, rear frames that pivot vertically to keep the back wheels in constant contact with bumpy roads, light aluminum frames to maximize pedalling efficiency, and front suspensions that ease steering and ensure smoother rides. Finally, although bottles of tequila cost about 10 cents a litre in materials and are made by labourers earning about U.S.$3 a day, it's not unusual to find a bottle priced in the hundreds of dollars—with some as high as $1450. Tequila Herradura S.A. of Mexico packages the beverage in elegant, tapered bottles and promotes the product with an exclusive upscale image.[19]

Firms sometimes first employ skimming pricing and then penetration pricing, or they market both a premium brand and a value brand. High prices may be charged when competition is limited, or when a product is new. The first group of customers to buy a new product is usually less price sensitive than later groups. High initial prices may also be used to portray a high-quality image. Another advantage of starting a product off with high prices is the fact that it is always easier to lower prices than it is to raise them. After the initial market segment is saturated, penetration pricing can be used to appeal to the mass market and expand total sales volume. Thus, multiple segments can be reached with one product simply by altering pricing strategy.

**TABLE 15-1**

**Key Cost Concepts and their Application to Big-Screen Television Sets**

| COST CONCEPT | DEFINITION | EXAMPLES[a] | SOURCES OF INFORMATION | METHOD OF COMPUTATION |
|---|---|---|---|---|
| Total fixed costs | Ongoing costs not related to volume. They are usually constant over a given range of output for a specified time. | Rent, salaries, electricity, real estate taxes, and plant and equipment. | Accounting data, bills, cost estimates. | Addition of all fixed cost components. |
| Total variable costs | Costs that change with increases or decreases in output (volume). | Parts (such as tuners and speakers), hourly employees who assemble sets, and sales commissions. | Cost data from suppliers, estimates of labour productivity, sales estimates. | Addition of all variable cost components. |
| Total costs | Sum of total fixed and total variable costs. | See above. | See above. | Addition of all fixed and variable cost components. |
| Average fixed costs | Average fixed costs per unit. | See above under total fixed costs. | Total fixed costs and production estimates. | Total fixed costs/ Quantity produced in units. |
| Average variable costs | Average variable costs per unit. | See above under total variable costs. | Total variable costs and production estimates. | Total variable costs/ Quantity produced in units. |
| Average total costs | Sum of average fixed costs and average variable costs. | See above under total fixed and total variable costs. | Total costs and production estimates. | Average fixed costs + Average variable costs or Total costs/Quantity produced in units. |
| Marginal costs | Costs of making an additional unit. | See above under total fixed and total variable costs. | Accounting data, bills, cost estimates of labour and materials. | (Total costs of producing current quantity + one unit) - (Total costs of producing current quantity). |

[a]Such marketing costs as advertising and distribution are often broken down into both fixed and variable components.

## Status Quo-Based Objectives

**Status quo-based objectives**

*seek good business*

*conditions and stability.*

**Status quo-based pricing objectives** are sought by a firm interested in continuing a favourable or stable business climate for its operations.

The pricing strategy is used to minimize the impact of such outside parties as government, competitors, and channel members—and to avoid sales declines.

One should not infer that status quo goals require no effort. A firm must instruct salespeople not to offer different terms to competing channel members or else the government may accuse it of a Competition Act violation. It may have to match competitors' price cuts to keep customers—while striving to avoid price wars. It may have to accept lower profit margins in the face of rising costs to hold channel cooperation. It may have to charge penetration prices to discourage competitors from also marketing certain product lines.

# Broad Price Policy

A **broad price policy** sets the overall direction (and tone) for a firm's pricing efforts and makes sure pricing decisions are coordinated with the firm's choices as to a target market, an image, and other marketing-mix factors. It incorporates short- and long-term pricing goals, as well as the role of pricing. Pricing can play a passive role—with customer purchases based on superior service, convenience, and quality—or it can play an active role—with purchases based on discount prices. Thus, a high-income segment buying status brands at upscale stores would expect premium prices. A moderate-income segment buying private brands at flea markets would expect low prices.

A firm outlines a broad price policy by placing individual decisions into an integrated format. It then decides on the interrelationship of prices for items within a product line, how often special discounts are used, how prices compare to competition, the frequency of price changes, and the method for setting new-product prices. As such, "marketing strategies attempt to define where the firm wants to be in the marketplace, and how it plans to get there. They provide the larger framework within which pricing and other programs are developed. Correspondingly, there should be a clear link between strategies and individual programs."[20]

*A **broad price policy** links prices with the target market, image, and other marketing elements.*

# Pricing Strategy

A pricing strategy may be cost-, demand-, and/or competition-based. When the three approaches are integrated, combination pricing is involved. See Figure 15-6.

## Cost-Based Pricing

In **cost-based pricing**, a firm sets prices by computing merchandise, service, and overhead costs and then adding an amount to cover its profit goal. Table 15-1 defines the key concepts in cost-based pricing and how they may be applied to big-screen television sets.

Cost-based prices are rather easy to derive because there is no need to estimate elasticity of demand or competitive reactions to price changes. There is also greater certainty about costs than demand or competitor responses to prices. Finally, cost-based pricing seeks reasonable profits since it is geared to covering all types of costs. It is often used by firms whose goals are stated in terms of profit or return on investment. A **price floor** is the lowest acceptable price a firm can charge and attain its profit goal.

When used by itself, cost-based pricing does have some significant limitations. It does not consider market conditions, the full effects of excess plant capacity, competitive prices, the product's phase in its life cycle, market share goals, consumers' ability to pay, and other factors.

Sometimes, it is hard to figure how such overhead costs as rent, lighting, personnel, and other general expenses should be allocated to each product. These costs are often assigned on the basis of product sales or the personnel time associated with each item. For instance, if product A accounts for 10 per cent of sales, it might be allotted 10 per cent of overhead costs. If product B receives 20 per cent of personnel time, it might be allotted 20 per cent of overhead costs. Yet, problems may arise since different methods for assigning costs may yield different results: How would costs be allocated if product A yields 10 per cent of sales and requires 20 per cent of personnel time?

In the following subsections, five cost-based pricing techniques are covered: cost-plus, markup, target, price-floor, and traditional break-even analysis. Figure 15-7 gives a synopsis of each technique. And Table 15-2 contains numerical examples of each.

*Under **cost-based pricing**, expenses are computed, profit is projected, and a **price floor** set.*

FIGURE 15-6

**Ways of Developing a Pricing Strategy**

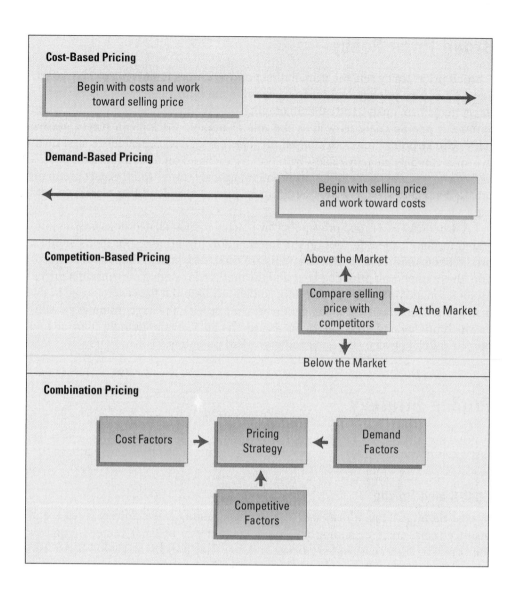

FIGURE 15-7

**Cost-Based Pricing Techniques**

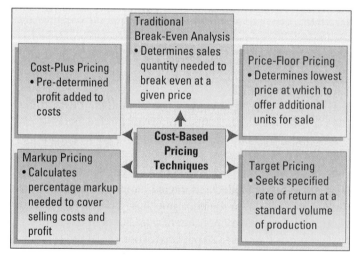

## TABLE 15-2

## Examples of Cost-Based Pricing Techniques

**Cost-Plus Pricing**—A custom-sofa maker has total fixed costs of $50 000, variable costs of $500 per sofa, desires $10 000 in profits, and plans to produce 100 couches. What is the selling price per couch?

$$\text{Price} = \frac{\text{Total fixed costs} + \text{Total variable costs} + \text{Projected profit}}{\text{Units produced}}$$

$$= \frac{\$50\ 000 + \$500(100) + \$10\ 000}{100} = \$1100$$

**Markup Pricing**—A retailer pays $30 for touch-tone phones and wants a markup on selling price of 40 per cent (30 per cent for selling costs and 10 per cent for profit). What is the final selling price?

$$\text{Price} = \frac{\text{Merchandise costs}}{(100 - \text{Markup per cent})/100} = \frac{\$30}{(100 - 40)/100} = \$50$$

**Target Pricing**—A specialty auto maker has spent $160 million for a new plant. It has a 25 per cent target return on investment. Standard production volume for the year is 5000 units. Average total costs, excluding the new plant, are $14 000 for each car (at a production level of 5000 cars). What is the selling price to the firm's retail dealers?

$$\text{Price} = \frac{\text{Investment costs} \times \text{Target return on investment (\%)}}{\text{Standard volume}}$$
$$+ \text{Average total costs (at standard volume)}$$

$$= \frac{\$160\ 000\ 000 \times .25}{5000} + \$14\ 000 = \$22\ 000$$

**Price-Floor Pricing**—A big-screen TV manufacturer's plant capacity is 1000 units. Its total fixed costs are $500 000 and variable costs are $375 per unit. At full production, average fixed costs are $500 per unit. The firm sets a price of $1100 to retailers and gets orders for 800 TVs at that price. It must operate at 80 per cent of capacity, unless it re-evaluates its pricing strategy. With price-floor pricing, it can sell the 200 additional sets to retailers. How?

The firm could let resellers buy one TV at $425 for every four they buy at $1100. Then, it earns a profit of $90 000 [revenues of ($1100 × 800) + ($425 × 200) less costs of ($875 × 1000)]. If it just makes and sells 800 TVs at full price, it earns $80 000 [revenues of ($1100 × 800) less variable costs of ($375 × 800) and fixed costs of $500 000]. The higher profits are due to the fact that marginal revenue > marginal cost.

**Traditional Break-Even Analysis**—A small candy maker has total fixed costs of $150 000 and variable costs per unit of $0.25. It sells to retailers for $0.40 per bar. What is the break-even point in units? In sales dollars?

$$\frac{\text{Break-even point}}{\text{(units)}} = \frac{\text{Total fixed costs}}{\text{Price} - \text{Variable costs (per unit)}} = \frac{\$150\ 000}{\$0.40 - \$0.25} = \underline{\underline{1\ 000\ 000}}$$

$$\frac{\text{Break-even point}}{\text{(sales dollars)}} = \frac{\text{Total fixed costs}}{1 - \dfrac{\text{Variable costs (per unit)}}{\text{Price}}} = \frac{\$150\ 000}{1 - \dfrac{\$0.25}{\$0.40}} = \underline{\underline{\$250\ 000}}$$

**Cost-plus pricing** *is the easiest form of pricing, based on units produced, total costs, and profit.*

**COST-PLUS PRICING** For **cost-plus pricing**, prices are set by adding a predetermined profit to costs. It is the simplest form of cost-based pricing.

Generally, the steps for computing cost-plus prices are to estimate the number of units to be produced, calculate fixed and variable costs, and add a desired profit to costs. The formula for cost-plus pricing is:

$$\text{Price} = \frac{\text{Total fixed costs} + \text{Total variable costs} + \text{Projected profit}}{\text{Units produced}}$$

This method is easy to compute; yet, it has shortcomings. Profit is not expressed in relation to sales but in relation to costs, and price is not tied to consumer demand. Adjustments for rising costs are poorly conceived, and there are no plans for using excess capacity. There is little incentive to improve efficiency to hold down costs, and marginal costs are rarely analyzed.

Cost-plus pricing is most effective when price fluctuations have little influence on sales and when a firm is able to control prices. For example, the prices of custom-made furniture, ships, heavy machinery, and extracted minerals typically depend on the costs incurred in producing these items; thus, companies set prices by computing costs and adding a reasonable profit. Cost-plus pricing often allows firms to get consumer orders, produce items, and then derive prices after total costs are known. This protects sellers.

**Markup pricing** *considers per-unit product costs and the markups required to cover selling costs and profits. Markups should be expressed in terms of price rather than cost.*

**MARKUP PRICING** In **markup pricing**, a firm sets prices by computing the per-unit costs of producing (buying) goods and/or services and then determining the markup percentages needed to cover selling costs and profit. It is most commonly used by wholesalers and retailers, although it is employed by all types of organizations. The formula for markup pricing is:[21]

$$\text{Price} = \frac{\text{Product cost}}{(100 - \text{Markup per cent})/100}$$

There are several reasons why markups are commonly stated in terms of selling price instead of cost. One, since expenses, markdowns, and profits are computed as percentages of sales, citing markups as percentages of sales also aids in profit planning. Two, firms quote their selling prices and trade discounts to channel members as percentage reductions from final list prices. Three, competitive price data are more readily available than cost data. Four, profitability appears smaller if based on price rather than cost. This can be useful in avoiding criticism over high earnings.

Markup size depends on traditional profit margins, company selling and operating expenses, suggested list prices, inventory turnover, competition, the extent to which products must be serviced, and the effort needed to complete transactions. Due to differences in selling costs among products, some firms use a **variable markup policy**, whereby separate categories of goods and services receive different percentage markups. Variable markups recognize that some items require greater personal selling, customer service, alterations, and end-of-season markdowns than others. For example, expensive cosmetics need more personal selling and customer service than paperback books, suits need greater custom alterations than shirts, and fashion items are marked down more than basic clothing late in the selling season.

Markup pricing, while having many of cost-plus pricing's limitations, is popular. It is fairly simple, especially for firms with uniform markups for several items. Channel members get fair profits. Price competition is less if firms have similar markups. Resellers can show their actual prices compared to suggested prices. Adjustments can be made as costs rise. Variable markups are responsive to selling-cost differences among products or channel members.

*A* **variable markup policy** *responds to differences in selling costs among products.*

**Target pricing** *enables a rate of return on investment to be earned for a standard volume of production.*

**TARGET PRICING** In **target pricing**, prices are set to provide a particular rate of return on investment for a standard volume of production—the level of production a firm anticipates achieving. For example, in the paper industry, the standard volume of production is usually set at around 90 to 92 per cent of plant capacity.[22] For target pricing to operate properly, a company must sell its entire standard volume at specified prices.

Target pricing is used by capital-intensive firms (like auto makers) and public utilities (like water companies). The prices charged by utilities are based on fair rates of return on invested assets and must be approved by regulatory commissions. Mathematically, a target price is computed as:

$$\text{Price} = \frac{\text{Investment costs} \times \text{Target return on investment (\%)}}{\text{Standard volume}}$$
$$+ \text{Average total costs (at standard volume)}$$

Target pricing has five major shortcomings. First, it is not useful for firms with low capital investments; it understates selling price. Second, because prices are not keyed to demand, the entire standard volume may not be sold at the target price. Third, production problems may hamper output and standard volume may not be attained. Fourth, price cuts to handle overstocked inventory are not planned under this approach. Fifth, if the standard volume is reduced due to expected poor sales performance, the price would have to be raised under a target-pricing calculation.

**PRICE-FLOOR PRICING** A firm's usual goal is to set prices to cover the sum of average fixed costs, average variable costs, and profit per unit. But, when a firm has excess (unused) capacity, it may use price-floor pricing to determine the lowest price at which it is worthwhile to increase the amount of goods or services it makes available for sale.

*Price-floor pricing may be used if there is excess capacity.*

The general principle in price-floor pricing is that the sale of additional units can be used to increase profits or help pay for fixed costs (which exist whether or not these items are made), as long as marginal revenues are greater than marginal costs. Although a firm cannot survive in the long run unless its average total costs are covered by prices, it may improve performance through price-floor pricing. The formula is:

$$\text{Price-floor price} = \text{Marginal revenue per unit} > \text{Marginal cost per unit}$$

**TRADITIONAL BREAK-EVEN ANALYSIS** Like target pricing, **traditional break-even analysis** looks at the relationship among costs, revenues, and profits. While target pricing yields the price that results in a specified return on investment, traditional break-even analysis finds the sales quantity in units or dollars that is needed for total revenues (price × units sold) to equal total costs (fixed and variable) at a given price. If sales exceed the break-even quantity, a firm earns a profit. If sales are less than the break-even quantity, it loses money. Traditional break-even analysis does not consider return on investment, but can be extended to take profit planning into account. It is used by all kinds of sellers.

*Traditional break-even analysis computes the sales needed to break even at a specific price.*

The break-even point can be computed in terms of units or sales dollars:

$$\frac{\text{Break-even point}}{\text{(units)}} = \frac{\text{Total fixed costs}}{\text{Price} - \text{Variable costs (per unit)}}$$

$$\frac{\text{Break-even point}}{\text{(sales dollars)}} = \frac{\text{Total fixed costs}}{1 - \dfrac{\text{Variable costs (per unit)}}{\text{Price}}}$$

These formulas are derived from the equation: Price × Quantity = Total fixed costs + (Variable costs per unit × Quantity).

Break-even analysis can be adjusted to take into account the profit sought by a firm:

$$\text{Break-even point (units)} = \frac{\text{Total fixed costs} + \text{Projected profit}}{\text{Price} - \text{Variable costs (per unit)}}$$

$$\text{Break-even point (sales dollars)} = \frac{\text{Total fixed costs} + \text{Projected profit}}{1 - \dfrac{\text{Variable costs (per unit)}}{\text{Price}}}$$

There are limitations to traditional break-even analysis. First, as with all forms of cost-based pricing, demand is not considered. The presumption is that wide variations in quantity can be sold at the same price; this is highly unlikely. Second, it is assumed that all costs can be divided into fixed and variable categories. Yet, some, like advertising, are difficult to define; advertising can be fixed or a per cent of sales. Third, it is assumed that variable costs per unit are constant over a range of quantities. However, purchase discounts or overtime wages may alter these costs. Fourth, it is assumed that fixed costs remain constant; but increases in production may lead to higher costs for new equipment, new full-time employees, and other items.

By including demand considerations, each of the cost-based techniques can be improved. Demand-based pricing techniques are discussed next.

## Demand-Based Pricing

*Under* **demand-based pricing,** *consumers are researched and a* **price ceiling** *set.*

With **demand-based pricing,** a firm sets prices after studying consumer desires and ascertaining the range of prices acceptable to the target market. This approach is used by companies that believe price is a key factor in consumer decision making. These companies identify a **price ceiling,** which is the maximum amount consumers will pay for a given good or service. If the ceiling is exceeded, consumers will not make purchases. Its level depends on the elasticity of demand (availability of substitutes and urgency of need) and consumers' subjective price regarding the particular good or service.

Demand-based techniques require that the firm research the quantities that consumers will purchase at various prices, sensitivity to price changes, the existence of market segments, and consumers' ability to pay. Demand estimates tend to be less precise than cost estimates. Also, firms that do inadequate cost analysis and rely on demand data may end up losing money if they make unrealistically low cost assumptions.

Under demand-based pricing, very competitive situations may lead to small markups and lower prices because consumers will purchase substitutes. In these cases, costs must be held down or prices will be too high—as might occur with cost-based pricing. For noncompetitive situations, firms can set large markups and high prices since demand is rather inelastic. There is less emphasis on costs when setting prices in these situations. With cost-based pricing, firms are more apt to set overly low prices in noncompetitive markets.

**FIGURE 15-8**

**Demand-Based Pricing Techniques**

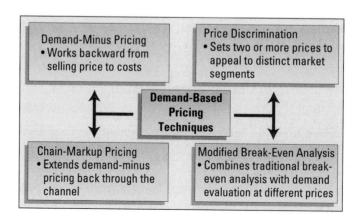

## TABLE 15-3

## Examples of Demand-Based Pricing Techniques

**Demand-Minus Pricing**—A mail-order CD-ROM encyclopedia publisher has done consumer research and found people are willing to spend $60.00 for its brand. Its selling expenses and profits are expected to be 35 per cent of the selling price. What is the maximum it can spend to develop and produce each CD-ROM encyclopedia?

$$\text{Maximum merchandise costs} = \text{Price} \times [(100 - \text{Markup per cent})/100]$$
$$= \$60.00 \times [(100 - 35)/100] = \underline{\$39.00}$$

**Chain-Markup Pricing**—A ladies' shoe maker knows women will pay $50.00 for a pair of its shoes. It sells via wholesalers and retailers. Each requires a markup of 30 per cent; the manufacturer wants a 25 per cent markup. (a) What is the maximum price that retailers and wholesalers will spend for a pair of shoes? (b) What is the maximum the manufacturer can spend to make each pair of shoes?

(a) $\text{Maximum selling price to retailer} = \text{Final selling price} \times [(100 - \text{Retailer's markup})/100]$
$$= \$50.00 \times [(100 - 30)/100] = \underline{\$35.00}$$

$\text{Maximum selling price to wholesaler} = \text{Selling price to retailer} \times [(100 - \text{Wholesaler's markup})/100]$
$$= \$35.00 \times [(100 - 30)/100] = \underline{\$24.50}$$

(b) $\text{Maximum merchandise costs to manufacturer} = \text{Selling price to wholesaler} \times [(100 - \text{Manufacturer's markup})/100]$
$$= \$24.50 \times [(100 - 25)/100] = \underline{\$18.38}$$

**Modified Break-Even Analysis**—An aspirin maker has total fixed costs of $2 000 000 and variable costs of $1.50 per bottle. Research shows the following demand schedule. At what price should the company sell its aspirin?

| Selling Price | Quantity Demanded | Total Revenue | Total Cost | Total Profit (Loss) | |
|---|---|---|---|---|---|
| $ 3.00 | 2 000 000 | $ 6 000 000 | $ 5 000 000 | $ 1 000 000 | Maximum |
| 2.50 | 3 200 000 | 8 000 000 | 6 800 000 | 1 200 000 | profit at |
| 2.00 | 5 000 000 | 10 000 000 | 9 500 000 | 500 000 | ← price of $2.50 |

**Price Discrimination**—A sports team knows people will pay different prices for tickets, based on location. It offers 10 000 tickets at $30 each, 25 000 at $20 each, and 20 000 at $12 each. What are profits if total costs per game are $750 000?

$$\text{Profit} = (\text{Revenues from Segment A} + \text{Segment B} + \text{Segment C}) - \text{Total costs}$$
$$= (\$300\ 000 + \$500\ 000 + \$240\ 000) - \$750\ 000 = \underline{\$290\ 000}$$

Four demand-based pricing techniques are reviewed next: demand-minus, chain-markup, modified break-even, and price discrimination. Figure 15-8 gives a synopsis of each technique, and Table 15-3 contains numerical examples of each.

Two aspects of competition-based pricing are discussed in the following subsections: price leadership and competitive bidding.

**DEMAND-MINUS PRICING** Through **demand-minus (demand-backward) pricing**, a firm finds the proper selling price and works backward to compute costs. This approach stipulates that price decisions revolve around consumer demand rather than company operations. It is used by firms selling directly to consumers.

*In **demand-minus pricing**, selling price, then markup, and finally maximum product costs are computed.*

Demand-minus pricing has three steps: first the selling price is determined by consumer surveys or other research; then the required markup percentage is set, based on selling expenses and desired profits; finally, the maximum acceptable per-unit cost for making or buying a product is computed. This formula is used:

$$\text{Maximum product cost} = \text{Price} \times [(100 - \text{Markup per cent})/100]$$

It shows that product cost is derived after selling price and markup are set.

The difficulty in demand-minus pricing is that marketing research may be time-consuming or complex, particularly if many items are involved. Also, new-product pricing research may be particularly inaccurate.

**CHAIN-MARKUP PRICING** **Chain-markup pricing** extends demand-minus calculations all the way from resellers back to suppliers (manufacturers): the final selling price is determined, markups for each channel member are examined, and the maximum acceptable costs to each member are computed.

In a traditional consumer-goods channel, the markup chain is composed of:

*Chain-markup pricing traces demand-minus calculations from channel members to suppliers.*

**1.** Maximum selling price to retailer $= \text{Final selling price} \times \left[ \dfrac{(100 - \text{retailer's markup})}{100} \right]$

**2.** Maximum selling price to wholesaler $= \text{Selling price to retailer} \times \left[ \dfrac{(100 - \text{wholesaler's markup})}{100} \right]$

**3.** Maximum product cost to manufacturer $= \text{Selling price to wholesaler} \times \left[ \dfrac{(100 - \text{manufacturer's markup})}{100} \right]$

By using chain-markup pricing, price decisions can be related to consumer demand and each reseller is able to see the effects of price changes on the total distribution channel. The interdependence of firms becomes more clear; they cannot set prices independently of one another.

**MODIFIED BREAK-EVEN ANALYSIS** **Modified break-even analysis** combines traditional break-even analysis with an evaluation of demand at various levels of price. Traditional analysis focuses on the sales needed to break even at a given price. It does not indicate the likely level of demand at that price, examine how consumers respond to different levels of price, consider that the break-even point can vary greatly depending on the price the firm happens to select, or calculate the price that maximizes profits.

*Melding traditional break-even analysis with demand evaluation at various prices is* **modified break-even analysis**.

Modified analysis reveals the price-quantity mix that maximizes profits. It shows that profits do not inevitably rise as the quantity sold increases because lower prices may be needed to expand demand. It also verifies that a firm should examine various price levels and select the one with the greatest profits. Finally, it relates demand to price, rather than assuming that the same volume could be sold at any price.

**PRICE DISCRIMINATION** With a **price discrimination** approach, a firm sets two or more distinct prices for a product so as to appeal to different final consumer or organizational consumer segments. Higher prices are offered to inelastic segments and lower prices to elastic ones. Price discrimination can be customer-based, product-based, time-based, or place-based.

*Setting distinct prices to reach different market segments is* **price discrimination**.

In customer-based price discrimination, prices differ by customer category for the same good or service. Price differentials may relate to a consumer's ability to pay (lawyers and accountants partially set prices in this manner), negotiating ability (the price of an office building is usually set by bargaining), or buying power (discounts are given for volume purchases).

Through product-based price discrimination, a firm markets a number of features, styles, qualities, brands, or sizes of a product and sets a different price for each

## ETHICS AND TODAY'S MARKETER

## Gerber Baby Foods: Should You Prevent Dumping by Granting a Monopoly?

In April 1998 Gerber Foods of Canada was "shocked" when the Canadian International Trade Tribunal ruled that it was guilty of "dumping" baby food on the Canadian market and imposed a 148 per cent tariff on Gerber's imported baby food. Gerber was effectively prevented from being the least bit competitive in the Canadian market.

Dumping is essentially predatory pricing applied to a foreign market, and occurs when the normal price of goods in the firm's home market is greater than the price of the goods sold to a foreign importer. It can be very hard to prove, given the difficulty of gathering data on foreign market competitors. Moreover, the practice is hard to distinguish from discount pricing, which many firms use to establish themselves in new markets.

The Canadian International Trade Tribunal was asked by H.J. Heinz, Gerber's only Canadian competitor, to investigate Gerber for dumping. Not surprisingly, a great deal of the evidence and information gathered in the investigation was provided by Heinz. From its investigation the Tribunal concluded that the export prices were on average 40 per cent below the normal values in the United States.

But there's a twist to this particular situation. H.J. Heinz holds an estimated 80 per cent market share of Canada's $100 million baby food market. As the only other competitor, Gerber holds the other 20 per cent. If Gerber is slapped with the huge tariff and thus rendered uncompetitive, the government will be effectively handing a monopoly to H.J. Heinz.

This issue is now being considered by Canada's Competition Bureau, which has filed a submission with the Canadian International Trade Tribunal. It's a fascinating problem. To quote Konrad von Finckenstein, the Commissioner of the Bureau of Competition:

> In the Bureau's view, this will create a monopoly in the Canadian market. This is the first time we have taken such action, but I believe very strongly that my role is to protect and promote competition, and this includes taking action when I believe that anybody, including an agency of government, is acting in a way that will limit or eliminate competition.

The underlying purpose of all anti-dumping legislation is to protect domestic firms from injurious price competition perpetuated by foreign-owned firms. But what do you do when the only two domestic competitors are owned and operated by foreign multinationals?

Assume you have the power to adjudicate the situation with Heinz and Gerber. What would you recommend, and why? Keep in mind that you have to balance many different interests, especially that of the public.

*Sources:* Based on News Line, "Trade Rule Could Double Gerber Prices," *Marketing Magazine* (May 11, 1998), p. 3; Industry Canada—Competition Bureau, "Speaking Notes by Konrad von Finckenstein," Strategis Web site, strategis.ic.gc.ca (September 25, 1998); Minister of National Revenue, "Baby Food," Revenue Canada Initiation, www.rc.gc.ca (October 3, 1997); and "Gerber Shocked by Decision of Trade Tribunal," Canada NewsWire, www.newswire.ca (April 29, 1998).

product version. Price differentials are greater than cost differentials for the various versions. For example, a dishwasher may be priced at $400 in white and $450 in brown, although the brown colour costs the manufacturer only $10 more. There is inelastic demand by customers desiring the special colour, and product versions are priced accordingly.

Under time-based price discrimination, a firm varies prices for day versus evening (movie theatre tickets), peak versus off-peak hours (telephone and utility

**GERBER**
www.gerber.com/home1.html

rates), or season (hotel rates). Consumers who insist on prime-time use pay higher prices than those who are willing to make their purchases at other times.

For place-based price discrimination, prices differ by seat location (sports and entertainment events), floor location (office buildings, hotels), or geographic location (resort cities). The demand for locations near the stage, elevators, or warm climates drives the prices of these locations up. General admission tickets, basement offices, and moderate-temperature resorts are priced lower to attract consumers to otherwise less desirable purchases.

**Yield management pricing** *lets firms optimize price discrimination efforts.*

When a firm engages in price discrimination, it should use **yield management pricing**—whereby it determines the mix of price–quantity combinations that generates the highest level of revenues for a given period. A company wants to make sure that it gives itself every opportunity to sell as many goods and services at full price as possible, while also seeking to sell as many units as it can. It does not want to sell so many low-price items that it jeopardizes full-price sales. Thus, a 1000-seat theatre offering first-run plays must determine how many tickets to sell as orchestra (at $50 each) and how many to sell as general admission (at $25 each). If it tries to sell too many orchestra tickets, there may be empty seats during a performance. If it looks to sell too many general admission tickets, the theatre may be full—but total revenues may be unsatisfactory.[23]

Before using price discrimination, a firm should consider these questions: Are there distinct market segments? Do people communicate with each other about product features and prices? Can product versions be differentiated? Will some consumers choose low-priced models when they might otherwise buy high-priced models if they are the only ones available? How do the marginal costs of adding product alternatives compare with marginal revenues? Will channel members stock all models? How difficult is it to explain product differences to consumers? Under what conditions is price discrimination legal?

## Competition-Based Pricing

**Competition-based pricing** *is setting prices relative to other firms.*

In **competition-based pricing**, a firm uses competitors' prices rather than demand or cost considerations as its primary pricing guideposts. The company may not respond to changes in demand or costs unless they also have an effect on competitors' prices. It can set prices below the market, at the market, or above the market, depending on its customers, image, marketing mix, consumer loyalty, and other factors. This approach is applied by firms contending with others selling similar items (or those perceived as similar).

Competition-based pricing is popular. It is simple, with no reliance on demand curves, price elasticity, or costs per unit. The ongoing market price level is assumed to be fair for both consumers and companies. Pricing at the market level does not disrupt competition, and therefore does not lead to retaliation. However, it may lead to complacency; and different firms may not have the same demand and cost structures.

**Price leadership** *occurs when one or a few firms initiate price changes in an industry; they are effective when others follow.*

**PRICE LEADERSHIP Price leadership** exists in situations where one firm (or a few firms) is usually the first to announce price changes and others in the industry follow. The price leader's role is to set prices that reflect market conditions, without disrupting the marketplace—it must not turn off consumers with price increases perceived as too large or precipitate a price war with competitors by excessive price cuts.

Price leaders are generally firms that have significant market shares, well-established positions, respect from competitors, and the desire to initiate price changes. As an illustration, a frequent price leader in the newsprint industry has been Canada's Abitibi-Price. It is the world's largest newsprint maker, has the largest production capacity, and has the dominant market share. Because over

**TABLE 15-4**

**Selected Issues to Consider When Combining Pricing Techniques**

**COST-BASED**

What profit margin does a price level permit?

Do markups allow for differences in product investments, installation and servicing, and selling effort and merchandising skills?

Are there accurate and timely cost data by good, service, project, process, and/or store?

Are cost changes monitored and prices adjusted accordingly?

Are there specific profit or return-on-investment goals?

What is the price-floor price for each good, service, project, process, and/or store?

What are the break-even points for each good, service, project, process, and/or store?

**DEMAND-BASED**

What type of demand does each good, service, project, process, and/or store face?

Have price elasticities been estimated for various price levels?

Are demand-minus, chain-markup, and modified break-even analyses utilized?

Has price discrimination been considered?

How loyal are customers?

**COMPETITION-BASED**

How do prices compare with those of competitors?

Is price leadership used in the industry? By whom?

How do competitors react to price changes?

How are competitive bids determined?

Is the long-run expected profit concept used in competitive bidding?

one-half of its revenues are in newsprint, the firm has a strong commitment to maintain stable prices.

Over the last several years, the role of price leaders has been greatly reduced in many industries, including steel, chemical, glass container, and newsprint, as many smaller firms have sought to act more independently. Even Abitibi-Price has been affected by this trend. At various times, it has announced higher newsprint prices and then has had to backtrack after competitors decided not to go along.

Announcements of price changes by industry leaders must be communicated through the media. It is illegal for firms in the same industry or in competing ones to confer with one another regarding the setting of prices.

**COMPETITIVE BIDDING** Through competitive bidding (discussed in Chapter 5), two or more firms independently submit prices to a customer for a specific good, project, and/or service. Sealed bids may be requested by some government or organizational consumers; each seller then has one chance to make its best offer.

Various mathematical models have been applied to competitive bidding. All use the expected profit concept, which states that as the bid price increases, the profit to a firm increases but the probability of its winning a contract decreases. Although a firm's potential profit (loss) at a given bid amount can usually be estimated accurately, the probability of getting a contract (underbidding all other qualified competitors) can be hard to determine.

### Combination Pricing

Although cost-, demand-, and competition-based pricing methods have been discussed separately, aspects of the three approaches are usually integrated into a **combination pricing** approach. A cost-based approach sets a price floor and outlines the various costs incurred in doing business. It establishes profit margins, target prices, and/or break-even quantities. A demand-based approach finds out the prices consumers will pay and the ceiling prices for each channel member. It develops the price–quantity mix that maximizes profits and allows a firm to reach different market segments (if it so desires). A competition-based approach examines the proper price level for the firm in relation to competitors.

Unless the approaches are integrated, critical issues may be overlooked. Table 15-4 shows a list of questions a firm should consider in setting prices.

*It is essential that companies integrate cost, demand, and competitive pricing techniques through* **combination pricing**.

## Implementing a Pricing Strategy

Implementing a pricing strategy involves a wide variety of separate but related specific decisions, besides the broader concepts just discussed. The decisions involve whether and how to use customary versus variable pricing, a one-price policy versus flexible pricing, odd pricing, the price–quality association, leader pricing, multiple-unit pricing, price lining, price bundling, geographic pricing, and purchase terms.

### Customary Versus Variable Pricing

*With* **customary pricing***, one price is maintained over an extended period. Under* **variable pricing***, prices reflect costs or differences in demand.*

**Customary pricing** occurs when a firm sets prices and seeks to maintain them for an extended time. Prices are not changed during this period. Customary pricing is used for items like candy, gum, magazines, restaurant food, and mass transit. Rather than modify prices to reflect cost increases, firms may reduce package size, change ingredients, or have a more restrictive transfer policy among bus lines. The assumption is that consumers prefer one of these alternatives to a price hike.

**Variable pricing** allows a firm to intentionally alter prices in response to cost fluctuations or differences in consumer demand. When costs change, prices are lowered or raised accordingly; the fluctuations are not absorbed and product quality is not modified to maintain customary prices. Through price discrimination, a firm can offer distinct prices to appeal to different market segments. In this way, the prices charged to diverse consumers are not based on costs, but on consumer sensitivity to price. Many firms use some form of variable pricing.

It is possible to combine customary and variable pricing. For example, a magazine may be $4 per single copy and $24 per year's subscription ($2 an issue)—two customary prices are charged; and the consumer selects the offer he or she finds most attractive.

### A One-Price Policy Versus Flexible Pricing

*All buying the same product pay the same price under a* **one-price policy***. Different customers may pay different prices with* **flexible pricing***.*

A **one-price policy** lets a firm charge the same price to all customers seeking to purchase a good or service under similar conditions. Prices may differ according to the quantity bought, time of purchase, and services obtained (such as delivery and installation); but all consumers are given the opportunity to pay the same price for the same combinations of goods and services. This builds consumer confidence, is easy to administer, eliminates bargaining, and permits self-service and catalogue sales. Today, throughout Canada, one-price policies are the rule for most retailers. In industrial marketing, a firm with a one-price policy would not allow sales personnel to deviate from a published price list.

With **flexible pricing**, a firm sets prices based on the consumer's ability to negotiate or on the buying power of a large customer. For instance, people who are knowledgeable or are good bargainers would pay lower prices than those who are not knowledgeable or are weaker bargainers. Jewellery stores, car dealers, flea markets, real estate brokers, antique shops, and many types of industrial marketers frequently use flexible pricing. In some cases, salesperson commissions are keyed to the profitability of orders; this encourages salespeople to solicit higher prices. Flexible prices to resellers are subject to the Competition Act restrictions explained earlier. Flexible pricing is much more prevalent outside North America, where this practice (sometimes known as "haggling") may be culturally ingrained.

One result of flexible pricing is the practice whereby consumers gather information from full-service sellers, shop around for the best available price, and then challenge discount sellers to "beat the lowest price." This practice is detrimental to full-service firms and allows discounters to hold down selling costs (and encourage further bargaining).

## Odd Pricing

**Odd pricing** is used when selling prices are set at levels below even dollar values, such as 49 cents, $4.95, and $199. It has proven popular for several reasons. For one thing, people like getting change. Because the cashier must make change, employers ensure that transactions are properly recorded and money is placed in the cash register. Consumers gain the impression that a firm thinks carefully about its prices and sets them as low as possible. They may also believe that odd prices represent price reductions; a price of $8.95 may be viewed as a discount from $10.

*Odd prices are those set below even-dollar values.*

Odd prices one or two cents below the next even price (29 cents, $2.98) are common up to $4 or $5. Beyond that point and up to $50 or so, five-cent reductions from the highest even price ($19.95, $49.95) are more usual. For expensive items, odd endings are in dollars ($499, $5995).

Odd prices may help consumers stay within their price limits and still buy the best items available. A shopper willing to spend "less than $20" for a tie will be attracted to a $19.95 tie and might be as likely to purchase it as a $17 tie because it is within the defined price range. Yet the imposition of sales taxes like the federal Goods and Services Tax, the Harmonized Sales Tax in the Maritimes, and provincial sales taxes result in the raising of odd prices into higher dollar levels, and thus may reduce the impact of odd pricing as a selling tool.

## The Price-Quality Association

According to the **price–quality association**, consumers may believe high prices represent high quality and low prices represent low quality. This association tends to be most valid when quality is difficult to judge on bases other than price, buyers perceive large differences in quality among brands, buyers have little experience or confidence in assessing quality (as with a new product), high prices are used to exclude the mass market, brand names are unknown, or brand names require certain price levels to sustain their images.

*The **price–quality association** deals with perceptions. **Prestige pricing** indicates that consumers may not buy when a price is too low.*

If brand names are well-known and/or people are confident of their ability to compare different brands in terms of nonprice factors, the price–quality association may be less valid. Then, many consumers may be more interested in the perceived value they receive for their money—and not necessarily believe a higher price represents better quality. It is essential that prices properly reflect both the quality and the image a firm seeks for its offerings.

With **prestige pricing**, a theory drawn from the price–quality association, it is assumed that consumers will not buy goods or services at prices they consider to be too low. Most people set their own price floors and will not purchase at prices below those floors—because they feel quality and status would be inferior at extremely low prices. Most people also set ceilings with regard to the prices they consider accept-

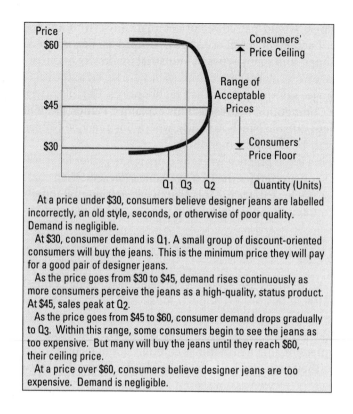

At a price under $30, consumers believe designer jeans are labelled incorrectly, an old style, seconds, or otherwise of poor quality. Demand is negligible.

At $30, consumer demand is $Q_1$. A small group of discount-oriented consumers will buy the jeans. This is the minimum price they will pay for a good pair of designer jeans.

As the price goes from $30 to $45, demand rises continuously as more consumers perceive the jeans as a high-quality, status product. At $45, sales peak at $Q_2$.

As the price goes from $45 to $60, consumer demand drops gradually to $Q_3$. Within this range, some consumers begin to see the jeans as too expensive. But many will buy the jeans until they reach $60, their ceiling price.

At a price over $60, consumers believe designer jeans are too expensive. Demand is negligible.

able for particular goods or services. Above those ceilings, items would be seen as too expensive. For each good or service, a firm should set its prices in the target market's acceptable range between the floor and ceiling. See Figure 15-9 for an example using designer jeans.

## Leader Pricing

*Leader pricing is used to attract customers to low prices.*

With **leader pricing**, a firm advertises and sells key items in its product assortment at less than their usual profit margins. For a wholesaler or retailer, the goal is to increase customer traffic. For a manufacturer, the goal is to gain greater consumer interest in its overall product line. In both cases, it is hoped that consumers will buy regularly priced merchandise in addition to the specially priced items that attract them.

Leader pricing is most used with well-known, high-turnover, frequently bought products. For example, in some drugstores, one of the best-selling items in terms of dollar sales is Kodak film. To stimulate customer traffic into these stores, film may be priced very low; in some cases, it is sold at close to cost. Film is a good item for leader pricing because consumers are able to detect low prices and they are attracted into a store by a discount on the item, which regularly sells for several dollars.

There are two kinds of leader pricing: loss leaders and prices higher than cost but lower than regular prices. The use of loss leaders must be undertaken carefully to avoid violating the Competition Act.

## Multiple-Unit Pricing

*With* **multiple-unit pricing**, *quantity discounts are intended to result in higher sales volume.*

**Multiple-unit pricing** is a practice whereby a firm offers discounts to consumers to encourage them to buy in quantity, so as to increase overall sales volume. By offering items at two for 89 cents or six for $139, a firm attempts to sell more units than at 50 cents or $25 each.

There are four major benefits from multiple-unit pricing: customers may increase their immediate purchases if they feel they get a bargain; they may boost

**FIGURE 15-10**

**Price Lining at MacWarehouse**
By offering products at several different price points, MacWarehouse addresses the needs of all of its customers.

*Used with permission.*

long-term consumption if they make larger purchases, as occurs with soda pop; competitors' customers may be attracted by the discounts; and a firm may be able to clear out slow-moving and end-of-season merchandise.

Multiple-unit pricing will not be successful if consumers merely shift their purchases and do not hike their consumption. For example, multiple-unit pricing for Heinz ketchup may not result in consumers using more ketchup with their meals. Thus, it would not raise total dollar sales; consumers would simply buy ketchup less frequently because it can be stored. However, it does have the benefit of protecting against competitive activity because consumers are carrying an inventory of ketchup and although they are not buying more Heinz ketchup, they are also not in the market for the competitor's ketchup either.

## Price Lining

**Price lining** involves selling products at a range of prices, with each representing a distinct level of quality (or features). Instead of setting one price for a single version of a good or service, a firm sells two or more versions (with different levels of quality or features) at different prices. Price lining involves two decisions: prescribing the price range (floor and ceiling) and setting specific price points in that range.

A price range may be low, intermediate, or high. For example, inexpensive radios may be priced from $8 to $20, moderately priced radios from $22 to $50, and expensive radios from $55 to $120. After the range is chosen, a limited number of price points is set. The price points must be distinct and not too close together. Inexpensive radios could be priced at $8, $12, and $20. They would not be priced at $8, $9, $10, $11, $12, $13, $14, $15, $16, $17, $18, $19, and $20. This would confuse consumers and be inefficient for the firm. Figure 15-10 illustrates how MacWarehouse uses price lining to sell its Apple computers.

When price lining, a firm must consider these factors: Price points must be spaced far enough apart so customers perceive differences among product versions—otherwise, consumers might view the price floor as the price they should pay and believe there is no difference among models. Price points should be spaced farther apart at higher prices because consumer demand becomes more inelastic. Relationships among price points must be kept when costs rise, so clear differences are retained. If radio costs rise 25 per cent, prices should be set at $10, $15, and $25 (up from $8, $12, and $20).

Price lining offers benefits for both sellers and consumers. Sellers can offer a product assortment, attract market segments, trade up shoppers within a price range, control inventory by price point, reduce competition by having versions over a price range, and increase overall sales volume. Consumers gain because choices are greater, confusion is lessened, comparisons are easier, and quality options are available within a given price range.

Price lining does have constraints. Consumers may feel price gaps are too large—a $25 handbag may appear cheap, while the next price point of $100 may be too expensive. Rising costs may squeeze individual prices and make it hard for a firm to keep the proper relationships in its line. And markdowns or special sales may disrupt the balance in a price line, unless all items in the line are proportionately reduced in price.

## Price Bundling

Some form of price bundling can be used in a strategy. With **bundled pricing**, a firm sells a basic product, options, and customer service for one total price. An industrial-equipment manufacturer may have a single price for a drill press, its delivery, its installation, and a service contract. Individual items, such as the drill press, would not be sold separately.

With **unbundled pricing**, a firm breaks down prices by individual components and allows the consumer to decide what to purchase. A discount appliance store may have separate prices for a refrigerator, its delivery, its installation, and a service contract.

Many companies choose to offer consumers both pricing options and allow a slight discount for bundled pricing.

## Geographic Pricing

**Geographic pricing** outlines responsibility for transportation charges. Many times, it is not negotiated but depends on the traditional practices in the industry in which the firm operates; and all companies in the industry normally conform to the same

## TECHNOLOGY AND MARKETING

## The Internet: Bringing Perfection to Pricing

When economists talk about competitive markets a major underlying assumption they make is that people have "perfect" information, meaning that people know the prices of all the suppliers in the marketplace and will choose the supplier with the lowest price. In the past, of course, markets have generally been anything but perfect. But all this is about to change, as the Internet brings perfection to pricing.

Perfection begins with the fact that drastically falling computer prices mean that in the near future almost every household in North America will be online. And as discussed in Chapter 14, people are willing, if not to buy, then at least to shop online. Consider the following examples:

- The automobile, home, and travel insurance industry has evolved into a commodity service business. Aside from prices, there's very little difference between one firm and the next.

- Radio airwaves have recently been awash with commercials featuring William Shatner. Star Trek's Captain

Kirk is plugging www.priceline.com, where you can bid on just about any product there is (including airline flights for $50 and hotel rooms for $19).

William Shatner certainly makes it sound like a perfect world. But how are marketers to cope with it all? One way is to introduce a perfect relationship using a nonprice-based strategy. Marketers wanting a profitable future need to develop customized services, personalized contacts, unique products, and unique brands. In essence, the firms that will prosper in the online world will have both excellent price and nonprice strategies.

Choose a product that you're thinking of buying, for example a book or a new computer. Visit some competing e-tailer Web sites for this product, and compare their pricing and service. Recommend one of the e-tailers for the purchase, and justify your recommendation.

Source: Based on Brett Matthews, "Insuring an Online Future," *Marketing Magazine* (April 12, 1999), p. 49.

geographic pricing format. Geographic pricing often involves industrial marketing situations.

These are the most common methods of geographic pricing:

- *FOB mill (factory) pricing*—The buyer picks a transportation form and pays all freight charges, the seller pays the costs of loading the goods (hence, "free on board"), and the delivered price to the buyer depends on freight charges.
- *Uniform delivered pricing*—All buyers pay the same delivered price for the same quantity of goods, regardless of their location; the seller pays for shipping.
- *Zone pricing*—It provides for a uniform delivered price to all buyers within a geographic zone; through a multiple-zone system, delivered prices vary by zone.
- *Base-point pricing*—Firms in an industry establish basing points from which the costs of shipping are computed; the delivered price to a buyer reflects the cost of transporting goods from the basing point nearest to the buyer, regardless of the actual site of supply.

## Purchase Terms

**Purchase terms** are the provisions of price agreements. They include discounts, the timing of payments, and credit arrangements.

Discounts are the reductions from final selling prices that are available to resellers and consumers for performing certain functions, paying cash, buying large amounts, buying in off-seasons, or enhancing promotions. As an example, a whole-

**Purchase terms** *outline pricing provisions.*

saler may buy goods at 40 per cent off the manufacturer's suggested final list selling price. This 40 per cent covers the wholesaler's expenses, profit, and discount to the retailer. The retailer could buy goods for 25 per cent off list (the wholesaler keeping 15 per cent for its costs and profit). In giving discounts, firms must make them proportionately available to all competing channel members, to avoid violating the Competition Act.

Payment timing must be specified in a purchase agreement. Final consumers may pay immediately or after delivery. In credit transactions, payments are not made until bills are received; they may be made over time. Organizational consumers are also quite interested in the timing of payments and negotiate for the best terms. For example, terms of net 30 mean products do not have to be paid for until 30 days after receipt. They must then be paid for in full. Terms of 2/10, net 30 mean a buyer receives a 2 per cent discount if the full bill is paid within 10 days after merchandise receipt. The buyer must pay the face value of a bill within 30 days after the receipt of products. Various time terms are available.

When marketing internationally, sellers must sometimes be prepared to wait an extended period to receive payments. At one time, it took North American firms an average of 337 days to get paid by Iranian businesses, 129 days to get paid by Kenyan businesses, 123 days to get paid by Argentine businesses, and 119 days to get paid by Brazilian clients.[24]

**Open** *and* **revolving credit accounts** *are possible.*

A firm that allows credit purchases may use open accounts or revolving accounts. With an **open credit account**, the buyer receives a monthly bill for the goods and services bought during the preceding month. The account must be paid in full each month. With a **revolving credit account**, the buyer agrees to make minimum monthly payments during an extended period of time and pays interest on outstanding balances. Today, various types of organizations (from Xerox to some physicians offering laser eye corrective surgery) offer some form of credit plan. Auto makers provide their own cut-rate financing programs to stimulate sales and leasing.

## Price Adjustments

After a price strategy is enacted, it often requires continuous fine-tuning to reflect changes in costs, competitive conditions, and demand. Prices can be adjusted by alterations in list prices, escalator clauses and surcharges, added markups, markdowns, and rebates.

**List prices, escalator clauses, surcharges, additional markups, markdowns,** *and* **rebates** *are key pricing tools.*

**List prices** are the regularly quoted prices provided to customers. They may be pre-printed on price tags, in catalogues, and in dealer purchase orders. Modifications in list prices are necessary if there are sustained changes in labour costs, raw material costs, and market segments and as a product moves through its life cycle. When these events are long term in nature, they enable customary prices to be revised, new catalogues to be printed, and adjustments to be completed in an orderly fashion.

Costs or economic conditions may sometimes be so volatile that revised list prices cannot be printed or distributed efficiently. Escalator clauses or surcharges can then be used. Both allow prices to be adjusted quickly. With **escalator clauses**, a firm is contractually allowed to raise the prices of items to reflect higher costs in those items' essential ingredients without changing printed list prices. It may even be able to set prices at the time of delivery. **Surcharges** are across-the-board published price increases that supplement list prices. These may be used with catalogues because of their simplicity; an insert is distributed with the catalogue.

When list prices are not involved, **additional markups** can be used to raise regular selling prices if demand is unexpectedly high or costs are rising. There is a risk to this. For example, supermarkets get bad publicity for relabelling low-cost existing

# MARKETING IN THE THIRD MILLENNIUM

## Pricing Strategies Are All About Making a Profit[25]

The dawning of a new millennium won't change the fact that marketers will always need to balance many different objectives when they set their prices. Pricing strategy determines whether a firm's efforts at creating value with its product, distribution, and promotion will in fact be realized. This value must be perceived by customers as worth the expenditure of their hard-earned income, and the firm must realize a return on its investment. Pricing strategy is the linchpin that brings these values together.

Paul Hunt of Toronto's Advantage Group notes that "a marketing agency can spend years building value for its services, but if its pricing is inadequate or inappropriate, it can squander profits in a matter of months. On the other hand, when the price is right, the profits follow." He offers the following advice to marketers who want to price profitably:

- Have a 1 per cent pricing mindset. Firms that increase prices by 1 per cent can realize a profit margin increase of 12.5 per cent or even more. (Price decreases of 1 per cent also decrease profit margins by 12.5 per cent.) Know what your customers are willing to pay, and then charge that price. All price changes should involve strategic thinking.

- Deliver more value and do it consistently. If you give people more, they'll be willing to pay more. It's that simple. Concentrate on customer satisfaction and sell on non-price factors.

- Let strategy dictate your pricing, not opportunity. Identify your target market(s) and price for those markets. Altering a pricing strategy to chase price-conscious customers (unless these are your customers) is going to put your core business at risk. Prices reflect the value provided. When you lower price, you lower value. Change your offering if you want to lower price to reflect the value differential.

- Know your competition. Make sure your pricing is driven by what competitors are doing, which means having a system to collect, analyze, and disseminate information on them.

- Pricing decisions should be process-based. Pricing isn't a one-time event, but rather a process that must be constantly tuned and refined to keep up with changing environmental and competitive conditions. The process should be clear, well established, and communicated to everyone in the organization. If salespeople are involved in price negotiations, pay them on profitability margins, not sales.

items at higher prices so they match those of newer merchandise purchased at higher costs.

**Markdowns** are reductions from items' original selling prices. All types of sellers use them to meet the lower prices of competitors, counteract overstocking of merchandise, clear out shopworn merchandise, deplete assortments of odds and ends, and increase customer traffic.

Although manufacturers regularly give discounts to resellers, they may periodically offer cash **rebates** to customers to stimulate the purchase of an item or a group of items. Rebates are flexible, do not alter basic prices, involve direct communication between consumers and manufacturers (since rebates are usually sent to consumers by manufacturers), and do not affect resellers' profits (as regular price reductions do). Price cuts by individual resellers may not generate the same kind of consumer enthusiasm. Rebate popularity can be traced to their usage by the auto industry to help cut down on inventory surpluses. Rebates have also been offered by Canadian Tire, Sega, Gillette, Polaroid, Minolta, and a number of others. The major disadvantage is that so many firms have used rebates that their impact may be lessened.

Whenever adjustments are needed, channel members should cooperatively agree on their individual roles. Price hikes or cuts should not be unilateral.

# SUMMARY

**1.** *To define the terms price and price planning* A price represents the value of a product for both the seller and the buyer. Price planning is systematic decision making relating to all aspects of pricing by a firm; it involves both tangible and intangible factors, purchase terms, and the nonmonetary exchange of goods and services. Exchange does not take place unless the buyer and seller agree a price represents an equitable value. Price also balances supply and demand.

**2.** *To demonstrate the importance of price and study its relationship with other marketing variables* Price (monetary or nonmonetary) is part of every type of exchange. During the last three decades, price decisions have become more important to business executives. This is due to factors such as deregulation, cost increases, currency rates, technological advances, the greater price emphasis by service companies, and periodic economic slowdowns.

Price decisions must be made in conjunction with other marketing-mix elements. And pricing is often related to the product life cycle, customer service levels, and other specific marketing and company variables. Setting prices for international markets can be complex and influenced by factors specific to the country.

**3.** *To differentiate between price-based and nonprice-based approaches* Under a price-based approach, sellers influence demand primarily by means of changes in price levels; they move consumers along a demand curve by raising or lowering prices. With a nonprice-based approach, sellers downplay price and emphasize such marketing attributes as image, packaging, and features; they shift the demand curves of consumers by stressing product distinctiveness.

**4.** *To present an overall framework for developing and applying a pricing strategy* A pricing strategy has five stages: objectives, broad policy, strategy, implementation, and adjustments. The stages are affected by outside factors and must be integrated with a firm's marketing mix.

**5.** *To analyze sales-based, profit-based, and status quo-based pricing objectives, and to describe the role of a broad price policy* Sales goals centre on volume and/or market share. In penetration pricing, a company sets low prices to capture a mass market. Profit goals focus on profit maximization, satisfactory profits, optimum return on investment, and/or early cash recovery. In skimming pricing, a firm seeks to capture the segment less concerned with price than with quality or status. Status quo goals are geared toward minimizing the impact of outside parties and ensuring stability. Two or more pricing objectives may be combined.

A broad price policy sets the overall direction for a firm's pricing efforts. Through it, a firm decides if it is price- or nonprice-oriented.

**6.** *To discuss several specific decisions that must be made in implementing a pricing strategy* Enacting a price strategy involves a variety of interlocking specific decisions. Customary pricing is employed when a firm sets prices for an extended period. With variable pricing, a firm alters prices to coincide with cost or consumer demand fluctuations.

In a one-price policy, all consumers purchasing under similar conditions pay the same price. Flexible pricing allows a firm to vary prices based on a shopper's ability to negotiate or the buying power of a large customer.

Odd-pricing is used if selling prices are set below even-dollar values. According to the price–quality association, consumers may believe there is a correlation between price and quality. With prestige pricing, it is assumed that consumers do not buy products at prices that are considered too low. They set price floors, as well as price ceilings.

Under leader pricing, key items are sold at less than their usual profit margins to increase consumer traffic. Multiple-unit pricing is a practice in which a company offers discounts to consumers for buying in quantity.

Price lining involves the sale of goods and services at a range of prices, with each embodying a distinct level of quality (or features). In bundled pricing, a firm offers a basic product, options, and customer service for one total price; through unbundled pricing, it breaks down prices by individual components and lets consumers decide what to buy.

Geographic pricing outlines the responsibility for transportation. Purchase terms are the provisions of price agreements, including discounts, timing of payments, and credit.

Once a pricing strategy is implemented, it usually needs regular fine-tuning to reflect cost, competition, and demand changes. Prices can be adjusted by changing list prices, including escalator clauses and surcharges in contracts, marking prices up or down, and offering direct rebates.

# KEY TERMS

price (p. 488)

price planning (p. 488)

price-based approach (p. 491)

nonprice-based approach (p. 491)

law of demand (p. 492)

price elasticity of demand (p. 492)

elastic demand (p. 493)

inelastic demand (p. 493)

unitary demand (p. 493)

subjective price (p. 494)

conspiracy to price fix (p. 495)

bid-rigging (p. 496)

price maintenance (p. 497)

price discrimination (p. 497)

predatory pricing (p. 497)

misleading price advertising
(p. 498)

double ticketing (p. 498)

sale above advertised price (p. 499)

bait-and-switch selling (p. 499)

abuse of dominant position (p. 499)

refusal to deal (p. 499)

consignment selling (p. 499)

tied sales (p. 499)

delivered pricing (p. 500)

selling against the brand (p. 500)

grey market goods (p. 500)

price guarantees (p. 501)

market-controlled price environment (p. 501)

company-controlled price environment (p. 501)

government-controlled price environment (p. 501)

price wars (p. 502)

sales-based pricing objectives (p. 504)

penetration pricing (p. 504)

profit-based pricing objectives (p. 504)

skimming pricing (p. 504)

status quo-based pricing objectives (p. 506)

broad price policy (p. 507)

cost-based pricing (p. 507)

price floor (p. 507)

cost-plus pricing (p. 510)

markup pricing (p. 510)

variable markup policy (p. 510)

target pricing (p. 510)

price-floor pricing (p. 511)

traditional break-even analysis (p. 511)

demand-based pricing (p. 512)

price ceiling (p. 512)

demand-minus (demand-backward) pricing (p. 513)

chain-markup pricing (p. 514)

modified break-even analysis (p. 514)

price discrimination (p. 514)

yield management pricing (p. 516)

competition-based pricing (p. 516)

price leadership (p. 516)

combination pricing (p. 518)

customary pricing (p. 518)

variable pricing (p. 518)

one-price policy (p. 518)

flexible pricing (p. 518)

odd pricing (p. 519)

price-quality association (p. 519)

prestige pricing (p. 519)

leader pricing (p. 520)

multiple-unit pricing (p. 520)

price lining (p. 522)

bundled pricing (p. 522)

unbundled pricing (p. 522)

geographic pricing (p. 522)

purchase terms (p. 523)

open credit account (p. 524)

revolving credit account (p. 524)

list prices (p. 524)

escalator clauses (p. 524)

surcharges (p. 524)

additional markups (p. 524)

markdowns (p. 525)

rebates (p. 525)

# REVIEW QUESTIONS

1. Cite at least three reasons why price decisions are so important today.

2. What is the risk of using a non-price-oriented strategy?

3. At a price of $40, a firm could sell 900 units. At a price of $25, it could sell 1200 units. Calculate the elasticity of demand and state what price the firm should charge—and why.

4. Is conspiracy to price fix always illegal? Explain your answer.

5. In what way are loss leaders different from bait-and-switch advertising?

6. When should a firm pursue penetration pricing? Skimming pricing?

7. Why are markups usually computed on the basis of selling price?

8. A firm requires a 14 per cent return on a $700 000 investment in order to produce a new electric garage-door opener. If the standard volume is 50 000 units, fixed costs are $500 000, and variable costs are $48 per unit, what is the target price?

9. A company making office desks has total fixed costs of $2 million per year and variable costs of $450 per desk. It sells the desks to retailers for $750 apiece. Compute the traditional break-even point in both units and dollars.

10. How does price lining benefit manufacturers? Retailers? Consumers?

# DISCUSSION QUESTIONS

1. How could a firm estimate price elasticity for a new industrial product? A mature industrial product?

2. Present five examples of price advertising for a hardware store that would violate the price advertising guidelines mentioned in the chapter.

3. A movie theatre has weekly fixed costs (land, building, and equipment) of $3500. Variable weekly costs (movie rental, electricity, ushers, etc.) are $1800. From a price-floor pricing perspective, how much revenue must a movie generate during a slow week for it to be worthwhile to open the theatre? Explain your answer.

4. A retailer determines that customers are willing to spend $27.95 on a new John Grisham (author of *The Client* and other best-sellers in the legal arena) novel. The publisher charges the retailer $22.50 for each copy. The retailer wants a 30 per cent markup. Comment on this situation.

5. a. A wholesaler of small industrial tools has fixed costs of $350 000, variable costs of $20 per tool, and faces this demand schedule from its hardware-store customers:

| Price | Quantity Demanded |
|-------|-------------------|
| $24   | 100 000 |
| $27   | 85 000 |
| $30   | 65 000 |
| $33   | 40 000 |

At what price is profit maximized?

b. If the company noted in Question 5a decides to sell 40 000 small tools at $33 and 45 000 of these tools at $27, what will its profit be? What are the risks of this approach?

## CASE STUDY

# Price Competition in the Energy Business

The advent of free trade has opened up the U.S. markets for Canadian energy producers, and the northeastern United States is one of their most lucrative markets. For example, New York City alone has 750 000 buildings needing heating and lighting for the 5 billion square feet of floor space they contain. The city also has 3 million housing units to light and heat. Energy costs for U.S. consumers measured in 1982–1984 U.S. dollars are gasoline at $6.32 per million BTUs (British Thermal Units), heating oil at $4.12 per million BTUs, natural gas at $3.86 per million BTUs, and electricity at $16.19 per million BTUs. It's clear that natural gas is the best value, and electricity the least.

The export of natural gas from Canada to the United States has increased more than threefold since the mid-1980s. This increase has been facilitated by the opening of natural gas pipelines, which enable the transmission of natural gas from Alberta to California, New York, and New England.

The increased use of natural gas as a fuel for electric power generation is a major reason for the increase in exports. Independent suppliers of natural gas are able to produce electricity for one-third the price of hydroelectrical producers. The cost advantage of natural gas is conferred by its ease of transmission and inexpensive methods of conversion to electricity.

Natural gas is an easy-to-use source of energy. Since it's transported in its basic form, there's no loss of energy during transmission. Large U.S. customers have built their own Non-Utility Generation plants (NUGs), which has become a chief concern for both Ontario and Quebec Hydro. Large customers have found they can acquire natural gas direct from the pipeline, and build and operate their own electrical generation plants for less money than buying electricity. For example, because the Methodist Hospital in Brooklyn, New York has its own gas-powered electrical generator it saves almost $1.2 million per year in energy costs.

As well, American NUGs and other enterprising producers are able to compete with utilities by selling their excess power. This may soon become an issue in Ontario, since the electrical power industry has been deregulated by the government. Ontario Hydro has accordingly changed its mission statement to read: "To make Ontario Hydro a leader in energy efficient and sustainable development, and to provide its customers with safe and reliable energy services at competitive prices." The fact that pricing is overtly acknowledged here is testament to its importance.

But including competitive pricing in a mission statement is a lot easier than actually achieving it. Competing with gas-generated electricity, which is priced at about 4 cents per kilowatt hour less than electricity, will be difficult; Ontario and Quebec Hydro will have to cut their costs dramatically. Both utilities have high costs due to excessive debt loads (which claim about 30 cents of every dollar Ontario Hydro earns for servicing), expensive facilities, and large workforces. Natural gas operated power plants are relatively cheap, easy to operate, don't require a lot of labour, and can be built and brought on line in less than a year.

Were it not for the monopolies granted to both Ontario and Quebec Hydro many NUGs would have been in operation in Eastern Canada before 1996. Up to now Ontario and Quebec Hydro have argued that since they have excess capacity NUGs aren't needed. But given the huge cost differentials it becomes harder to consider the public interest being served by maintaining a monopoly. Allowing NUGs and private power plants will bring the Ontario and Quebec energy markets into line with other markets in North America—but the price competition may mean the death of Ontario and Quebec Hydro as they now exist.

Two arguments favour maintaining the status quo. Had the Quebec ice storm of 1998 befallen a group of small independent utilities instead of Quebec Hydro, the massive infrastructure damage might not have been repaired so quickly. And hydroelectric power is an environmentally friendly, renewable energy resource, while natural gas, although environmentally friendly, is non-renewable. In the long run, it may make more economic sense to subsidize renewable energy resources.

### Questions

1. Characterize the kind of pricing strategies used by both Quebec and Ontario Hydro. What kind of pricing strategies will they have to use in the future to deal with their competitive situation?

2. Describe the kind of market environment you would envision for electrical power companies under deregulation. What do you think the main bases for competition would be?

3. Fossil fuel energy has always been cheaper than hydroelectric power by a considerable margin. What is it about the current market that seems to be putting so much pressure on big utilities like Ontario and Quebec Hydro? Assess this new situation. Do Ontario and Quebec Hydro really have to change, or do they merely have to ride out a storm? Justify your answer.

4. Evaluate the advantages and disadvantages of dealing with a large power utility supplier like Ontario or Quebec Hydro versus a small NUG supplier. Who is more likely to be price sensitive, large industrial customers or household consumers?

Sources: Based on Randall Litchfield, "The Never-Never Land of a Public Utility," *Canadian Business* (November, 1992) p 19; "Power Failure," *Canadian Business* (November, 1992), pp. 50–58; Ontario Hydro's Web site, www.hydro.on.ca (August 1996); New York City Web site, www.ci.nyc.ny.us (August 1996); United States Department of Energies Web site, www.eia.doe.gov/emeu/mer/mer.html (August 1996); and CBC *Venture* video 479.

# WestJet: Canada's Discount Airline

Throughout the world one of the toughest businesses in which to make money is the airline business. Canada's two major airlines, Air Canada and Canadian Airlines International, both lost money in 1998. Air Canada lost $16 million on sales of $5.9 billion, while Canadian Airlines International lost $136.7 million on sales of $3.2 billion. But there's one Canadian-based airline that's flying high with profits. In 1998 Calgary-based discount airline WestJet reported an after-tax profit margin of 5.1 per cent on total operating revenues of $125.9 million.

WestJet's results are amazing, considering that the prior success rate of discount airlines in Canada was zero. Notable firms that have failed in the discount airline position include Nationair, City Express, Intair, Astoria Airlines, and Greyhound Air, which opened its business the same year as WestJet.

WestJet Chair Clive Beddoe was the driving force behind the airline, which started up on February 29, 1996. Its initial plans were modest, with service to six Western cities, but in 1999 it was flying twelve Boeing 737 aircraft, employing 900 people, and serving eleven western Canadian cities.

WestJet's business strategy is "to find and develop successful niche markets, getting travellers off the roads and into the air." It operates as a regional airline in western Canada, and positions itself as a low-fare carrier. For example, WestJet advertised fares as low as $29 one way between Calgary and Edmonton and $59 from Calgary to Vancouver. A low-price positioning in the airline business isn't difficult to pursue, but making it profitable is something else. WestJet appears to have successfully duplicated the success formula of Southwest Airlines, the seventh largest airline in the U.S. with 1998 sales of U.S.$4.1 billion and a profit margin of 10 per cent on sales, the highest in the industry. This means having a low cost structure and high capacity aircraft utilization. In order to break even typical airlines require an average of 65 per cent capacity, or load

factor, on each plane; in 1998 Westjet's load factor was 71.6 per cent.

WestJet has achieved a low cost structure by owning its aircraft and instituting ticketless travel (almost 35 per cent of a typical airline's employees are involved in ticketing). Another way costs are reduced is by not having connecting baggage handling. There's no inflight meal service, which reduces operating costs and the number of flight attendants required. As a result, since it started up WestJet has been experiencing 50 per cent annual growth rates in seat miles and revenue passenger miles.

When WestJet got off the ground in 1996 it precipitated a price war with both Air Canada and Canadian Airlines International, which matched prices for fares from Calgary to Vancouver. Clive Beddoe insisted at that time that WestJet could handle a price war and that it would be profitable within the first year of operations. He was right, and WestJet has been consistently profitable every year since.

Commenting on operations in 1999, WestJet's President and CEO Stephen Smith said, "We have prudently grown our airline and results show that there continues to be no doubt that additional capacity, in combination with a sensible fare structure, can be absorbed into the marketplace. We have steadily increased revenues, maintained costs and expanded our airline, all while maintaining a strong load factor. These achievements continue to confirm our strategy of offering low fare regional air travel."

## Questions

1. Drawing on the text background on pricing decisions, what are the main bases upon which WestJet selected its pricing strategies? Discuss alternative bases that WestJet could have reasonably used.

2. Identify the competitors against which WestJet has been competing. Are there competitors over which WestJet does not have a price advantage? On what basis will WestJet be able to compete against them?

3. Use the following information to determine the price that a discount airline like WestJet needs to charge in order to break even: An aircraft holds a maximum of 160 passengers, costs $15 million, and has a useful life of twenty years. The airline has ten planes, overhead costs of $300 000 per month, and investors expect an annual before-tax profit of $500 000 per month. Each aircraft can make two return flights a day and is grounded for servicing and inspection at least one day a week. Each flight incurs $6000 in variable costs (e.g., to pay for flight attendants, pilots, and fuel). The airline flies with a load factor of 70 per cent.

4. Evaluate WestJet's strategy/positioning in the case. How is it different from what you might expect from air carriers like Air Canada and Canadian Airlines?

Sources: The data in this case are drawn from WestJet Corporate Web site, www.westjet.com; "Performance 2000," *Canadian Business* (June 25/July 9, 1999), pp. 72–74; "The Fortune 1000 Ranked Within Industries," *Fortune* (April 26, 1999), p. F52; and Terry Bullick, "No-Frills Airline Takes Flight in Western Canada," *Marketing Magazine* (February 19, 1996), p. 2.

# Is Predatory Pricing Unenforceable?

Sometimes paying low prices can be a crime if they have been set as part of a predatory pricing scheme. But sometimes paying low prices *is* a crime when predatory pricing is involved. The immediate victims are usually small business owners who are trying to compete with large businesses. Consumers become the victims later, after the larger firm eliminates the competition and then raises its prices.

Predatory pricing comes in two forms. The first involves selling products in different regions at different prices (not due to transportation costs) for the express purpose of eliminating existing competitors or preventing market entry of new competitors. The second involves selling products at unreasonably low prices (at cost or below cost) with the same purpose.

Predatory pricing is illegal, and falls under the criminal provisions of Canada's Competition Act, which is enforced by Canada's Competition Bureau. The bureau receives complaints about pricing and then investigates them. After an investigation its commissioner determines whether a violation of the act may have occurred. The commissioner then decides whether the suspected violation involves a criminal or non-criminal provision. Violations of criminal provisions are referred to the Attorney General of Canada for prosecution. Prosecution of firms and individuals require that strict rules of evidence be applied and that the cases be proved beyond reasonable doubt.

In one recent year the Competition Bureau received 202 complaints of predatory pricing. Very few of these were even investigated, and fewer still were ever prosecuted. The reason is simple: because the rules of evidence for predatory pricing are so stringent, it's virtually impossible to prosecute. The government has to prove three things for a successful prosecution: that the low prices were unreasonable, that the low pricing strategy was part of a plan, and that the low pricing was intended to eliminate competitors. Hence, the general feeling is that if

a large firm wants to capture the market from a smaller firm, it will just do it. Nonetheless, a number of small Canadian businesses have recently tried to seek help from the Competition Bureau.

In Gander, Newfoundland, independent pharmacist Kevin O'Brien was enraged when both Shoppers Drug Mart and Wal-Mart pharmacies eliminated their prescription dispensing fees. O'Brien, who was charging $7.90 to fill a prescription, called the Competition Bureau to complain. The response was that it certainly looked like an illegal situation; clearly a zero dispensing fee was not a reasonable business practice. However, successfully proving the case in court was considered unlikely, and O'Brien was advised to consider a civil case. He determined that it would far too expensive to be worth his while.

In Belleville, Ontario, Pat Kell was successfully operating the *Real Estate Weekender,* a newsprint publication advertising real estate. The firm took in annual revenues of $600 000 from real estate advertisers and employed six people. One day Pat Kell learned that a competing firm called the *Intelligencer* was going to enter the market and give away ads for free. Although Kell offered to sell his operation, he was rebuffed. The new firm opened up and all his business disappeared. After he went out of business the *Intelligencer* raised its prices to about half of what the *Weekender* had charged. Kell called the Competition Bureau, but to no avail. He was told that they didn't believe they could prove the three tests needed to prosecute.

Fred Wade of Wade's Food stores in Atlantic Canada felt his chain of grocery stores was a victim of a price war between Sobey's and Loblaws. He too felt rebuffed when the Competition Bureau suggested that he sue them on his own.

When asked why the Competition Bureau was apparently so lax with prosecutions of predatory pricing, Federal Minister of Justice John Manley admitted that the Bureau had managed only three convictions in sixteen years. The problem was that the Competition Bureau has a budget

of only $18 000 000 to do all its duties. It chooses either those criminal cases that have a high probability for success, or ones that can represent demonstrations and therefore make case law.

Many people feel that the federal government has let them down. Gerard Boutonier discusses how Quebec's independent gas stations were being hammered by Ultramar during a protracted gas price war. He felt that a long inquiry into the firm's behaviour was needed to protect independent producers. The Competition Bureau refused to get involved. However, the Quebec government undertook an investigation and then acted with provincial legislation to protect gasoline retailers from low cost selling.

## Questions

1. Evaluate the behaviour of Canada's Competition Bureau with respect to predatory pricing complaints.
2. Consult the portion of this chapter that deals with the Competition Act. Do you have any suggestions that might enable the Competition Bureau to better enforce the predatory pricing statutes?
3. What are the advantages and disadvantages of trying to regulate prices? Is it really necessary to have a Competition Act with pricing regulations? Why or why not?
4. Advise Kevin O'Brien, Pat Kell, and Fred Wade. Is there anything else they can do besides simply taking it on the chin?

## Video Questions

1. Do you think consumers care about predatory pricing? Why or why not?
2. Discuss why you think the Quebec government responded to regulate gasoline prices in Quebec when the federal government refused to act.

Sources: Based on "Price Wars," *Venture* #616 (November 10, 1996); and Industry Canada, "Canada's Competition Act: An Overview," Strategis Web site, strategis.ic.gc.ca, Industry Canada: Ottawa.

# PART 7

# Marketing Management

### Strategic Planning: A Marketing Perspective

Here we first distinguish between strategic business plans and strategic marketing plans, and describe the total quality approach to strategic planning. Next, we look at the different kinds of strategic plans and the relationship between marketing and other functional areas. We then present the steps in the strategic planning process in considerable detail. A sample outline of a strategic plan for a business firm is highlighted.

### Integrating and Analyzing the Marketing Plan

We first note the value of developing and analyzing integrated marketing plans. Next, we examine the elements in a well-integrated marketing plan: clear organizational mission, long-term competitive advantages, precisely defined target market, compatible subplans, coordination among SBUs, coordination of the marketing mix, and stability over time. Then, we study five types of marketing plan analysis: benchmarking, customer satisfaction research, marketing cost analysis, sales analysis, and the marketing audit. These are important tools for evaluating the success or failure of marketing plans. We conclude with a look at why and how firms should anticipate and plan for the future.

# Integrated Marketing Plans

Marketers who view the marketing mix as an integrated whole realize that it's seldom beneficial to optimize particular elements.

Marketing involves putting together component parts to produce a result. In short, marketers must try to see the big picture. The marketing concept as shown in Figure 1-3 includes these elements: a consumer orientation, a market-driven approach, a value-based philosophy, a goal orientation, and an integrated marketing focus. Throughout the preceding six parts we have focused on a number of organizations that, to varying degrees, have implemented the marketing concept. Although when we looked at these organizations we focused on a particular element of marketing, in most instances we also looked at the other elements of the marketing mix in relation to the element under discussion. The overall strategy of the organization was considered as well.

In Part 7 we will consider how a firm's strategic marketing planning and its marketing mix are related. Chapter 16 introduces strategic market plans that are made to coordinate marketing activity with other functional activities of business firms. A key part of strategic market planning is performing a situation analysis. Sometimes this analysis reveals weaknesses or threats that can't be overcome, and a company opts to drop or sell a product line or division. When Edgar Bronfman Jr. became CEO of Montreal's Seagram in 1994, the firm consisted of a spirits and wine business, Tropicana juices, and holdings in chemical giant DuPont. He saw that American pop culture seemed to rule everywhere, so he took an opportunity to transform Seagram's into an entertainment company. He sold off his DuPont shares and used the cash to buy a controlling interest in MCA (Universal Studios' parent company) in 1996. In 1998, to purchase Polygram music. He sold off Tropicana. Now Seagram is positioned to be the number two entertainment company in the world behind Disney.

Chapter 17 introduces the importance of developing and evaluating integrated marketing plans. Managing and integrating marketing plans is very important for a firm like Bell Canada and its parent company BCE, which is the second largest firm in Canada with annual sales of over $27 billion. BCE started out as *the* phone company, but is today competing in a host of different but related businesses. For example, while Bell Canada is the leading long-distance telephone, local telephone, and Internet service provider in Canada, the Bell Mobility division of BCE is in third place behind leader AT&T Cantel and Clearnet in PCS (cellular telephone) service provision. BCE is involved in the broadcasting business, with a 90 per cent ownership position in Bell ExpressVu (direct-to-home broadcasting).

BCE has holdings in a number of network companies located in developing nations and publishes a number of telephone directories in these nations. Two other holdings that give BCE a strong international presence include Teleglobe, an international telecommunications carrier, and Nortel Networks, a leading company in the design and building of communications networks.

In March 1999 U.S.-based Ameritech purchased 20 per cent of Bell Canada so that the two firms could share technology and marketing experiences to the benefit of both. In the short term Bell Canada has gained expertise in Web service technology and call-management services.

Managing so many enterprises in a global environment would be next to impossible for BCE without the use of strategic market planning.

## CHAPTER 16

# Strategic Planning: A Marketing Perspective

## Chapter Objectives

**1.** To define strategic planning and consider its importance for marketing

**2.** To describe the total quality approach to strategic planning and show its relevance to marketing

**3.** To look at the different kinds of strategic plans and the relationships between marketing and the other functional areas in an organization

**4.** To describe thoroughly each of the steps in the strategic planning process: defining organizational mission, establishing strategic business units, setting marketing objectives, performing situation analysis, developing marketing strategy, implementing tactics, and monitoring results

**5.** To show how a strategic plan may be devised and applied

*Courtesy of Coca-Cola Company*

**Y**ou'd think that having the number one brand name product on the planet would give Coca-Cola's CEO Douglas Ivester very little to worry about. After all, 50 per cent of the soft drinks consumed worldwide are Coca-Cola products. Coca-Cola has been in business for over 112 years, and financial analysts on New York's Wall Street love the company. But that's just it: having so much gives you a lot to worry about. Douglas Ivester is embracing several new approaches to see that the firm remains number one in its industry; indeed, his objective is to widen the gap.

Ivester is transforming the way Coca-Cola makes plans and then carries them out. Coca-Cola treats planning not as an annual activity but as a continuous process. One key tool involves gathering copious amounts of information and data and then quickly and effectively analyzing and disseminating it to decision makers. Ivester believes that Coca-Cola must become a learning organization, and to this end he's hired a Chief Learning Officer (CLO), who is assigned the task of figuring out a way to share information, ideas, and experiences among the different countries where Coca-Cola operates and the different executives who work for the firm.

Ivester does not believe in a hierarchical approach to managing. He communicates with people in his organization freely and expects his managers to do the same. He wants Coca-Cola people to leave their desks behind. Ivester thinks of them as knowledge workers: "We are trying to make the person command central, so that your office is not a place with a desk and a telephone. Your office is the intellectual capital you carry with you and the technology that supports it."

The Coca-Cola Company is wired globally. Ivester calls and leaves two-minute voice mails to inform and guide his managers around the world. Anywhere and everywhere is just where Ivester wants people to be able to find a cold Coca-Cola, especially when over 80 per cent of the firm's profits come from foreign operations.

Database management is another key tool for Coca-Cola. It used to take two and a half months to collect financial data from Coca-Cola's international markets, which meant that quarterly reports would be on the agenda for forty weeks a year! Ivester forced Coca-Cola to redesign its data collection, and now the process takes only five days. Information gathering and dissemination systems are key to making good decisions at Coca-Cola. For example, it has issued 55 million Coke cards that consumers can use to get discounts, and has set up a tracking system to follow their use. Competitive moves by Pepsi are tracked quickly, and their impacts analyzed and responded to almost immediately. During the 1996 Olympics Coke tracked ratings on the audiences and their characteristics—and in one day was able to produce and air advertising to fit these characteristics.

Getting out of the office and learning what's going on is Douglas Ivester's management style, which helped him become the CEO of Coca-Cola after the untimely passing in 1997 of former CEO Robert Goizueta. Ivester challenged the assumption that the U.S. market was mature and that growth rates in sales would match GDP growth rates. He took a team of managers and walked around Atlanta and other cities to observe places that a person might reasonably expect to buy a Coke, yet were unserved by the company. Ivester saw to it that Coca-Cola put machines and fountains into these places. This is his basic plan for the rest of the world: find places where Coke could be sold, yet isn't, and put outlets there and sell it! And the objective of all these efforts? Coca-Cola has a 2 per cent share of belly for all beverages (e.g., water, tea, coffee, milk, juice, beer, wine, alcohol, etc.) consumed in the world today. Douglas Ivester would like to see that double to 4 per cent.[1]

In this chapter, we will consider strategic planning from a marketing perspective and review in depth each of the steps in the strategic planning process. We will also examine the use of strategic planning by both small and large firms.

**COCA-COLA COMPANY**
www.cocacola.com/home.html

## Overview

As described earlier in Chapter 2, the environment within which marketing operates includes a number of factors directed by top management and others directed by marketing. To coordinate these factors and provide guidance for decision making, it is helpful to employ a formal strategic planning process. To marketers, such a process consists of two main components: a strategic business plan and a strategic marketing plan.

A **strategic business plan** "describes the overall direction an organization will pursue within its chosen environment and guides the allocation of resources and effort. It also provides the logic that integrates the perspectives of functional departments and operating units, and points them all in the same direction." It has (1) an external orientation; (2) a process for formulating strategies; (3) methods for analyzing strategic situations and alternatives; and (4) a commitment to action.[2]

A **strategic marketing plan** outlines the marketing actions to undertake, why those actions are needed, who is responsible for carrying them out, when and where they will be completed, and how they will be coordinated. Thus, a marketing plan is carried out within the context of a firm's broader strategic plan.

There are a number of reasons why marketers need an appreciation of the relationship between strategic planning and marketing. One, strategic planning gives direction to a firm's efforts and better enables it to understand marketing research; consumer analysis; and product, distribution, promotion, and price planning. It is a hierarchical process, moving from company-wide guidelines down to specific marketing decisions. Two, a strategic plan ensures each company division has clear goals that are integrated with the firm's overall goals. Three, different functional areas are encouraged to coordinate efforts. Four, strategic planning forces a firm to assess its strengths and weaknesses and to consider environmental opportunities and threats. Five, the alternative actions or combinations of actions a firm can take are outlined. Six, a basis for allotting resources is set. Seven, the value of having a procedure for assessing performance can be shown.

Marketing's role in strategic planning is indeed a crucial one:

*Strategic planning involves* **both strategic business plans** *and* **strategic marketing plans**.

*Marketing should have a key role in strategic planning.*

> In industry after industry, the opportunity today is clear. It is now possible for companies to focus directly on achieving the full potential of customer relationships. Doing so will require executives to abandon outdated management models. But, as with prior shifts in management thinking, those who act early will reap disproportionate rewards.[3]

> Strategic planning should stress market information, market-segment definition, and market targeting. All company activities should be built around the goal of creating the desired position with a well-defined set of customers. Separate market segments should be the subject of separate plans that focus on developing customer relationships that emphasize the firm's distinctive competence. [Marketing's] contribution to strategic planning and implementation begins with the analysis of market segments and an assessment of a firm's ability to satisfy customer needs. This includes analyzing demand trends, competition, and in industrial markets, competitive conditions. Marketing also plays a key role by working with top management to define business purpose in terms of customer-need satisfaction. In a market-oriented view of the strategic planning process, financial goals are seen as results and rewards, not the fundamental purpose of business.[4]

In Chapter 16 we discuss a total quality approach to strategic planning, various kinds of strategic plans, relationships between marketing and other functional areas, and the strategic planning process—and show how strategic planning may be applied. Chapter 17, which concludes the text, deals with how marketing plans are integrated and analyzed using a total quality framework.

# A Total Quality Approach to Strategic Planning

*All firms should adopt a* **total quality** *approach, thereby becoming more process- and output-oriented in satisfying consumers.*

When devising strategic plans, any firm—small or large, domestic or international, manufacturing or services driven—should adopt a total quality perspective. **Total quality** is a process- and output-related philosophy, whereby a firm strives to fully satisfy customers in an effective and efficient manner. To flourish, a total quality program needs all of the following:

- *A process-related philosophy*—Total quality is based on all the activities undertaken to create, develop, market, and deliver a good or service to the customer. A firm gains a competitive advantage if it can offer the same quality good or service at a lower cost or if it can offer a better-quality good or service than other companies.

- *An output-related philosophy*—Although process-related activities give a good or service its value, usually the consumer can only judge the total quality of the finished product. Many consumers care about what they buy, rather than how it was made.

- *Customer satisfaction*—To the consumer, total quality refers to how well a good or service performs. Thus, customer service is a key element in a person's ultimate satisfaction, which is affected by the gap between that person's expectations of product performance and actual performance.

- *Effectiveness*—To a marketer, this means how well various marketing activities (such as adding new product features) are received by consumers.

- *Efficiency*—To a marketer, this involves the costs of various marketing activities. A firm is efficient when it holds down costs, while offering consumers the appropriate level of quality.

- *Customer focus*—From a total quality perspective, a firm views the consumer as a partner and seeks input from that partner as it creates, develops, markets, and delivers a good or service.

- *Top management commitment*—Because a total quality program must be believed in by everyone who works for and comes into contact with a firm, senior executives must be dedicated to making it work and make sure corners are not cut in an attempt to be more efficient. In the best firms, "total quality" becomes ingrained as part of the corporate culture.

- *Continuous improvement*—In most cases, today's total quality will become tomorrow's sub-optimal quality; so, a firm must continuously improve. A complacent firm will be hurt by the dynamics of the marketplace and fast-paced technological and global trends.

- *Employee support and involvement*—For a total quality program to work, employees must buy into it. Empowering employees not only gets them involved in the total quality process, but it also assures that customer problems are promptly addressed and resolved in the customer's favour.

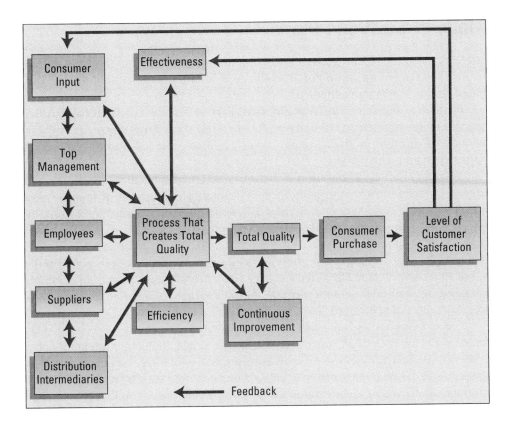

**FIGURE 16-1**

**The Keys to a Successful Total Quality Program**

- *Supplier and distributor support and involvement*—Due to their involvement in creating total quality, both suppliers and resellers can have a dramatic effect on it. They too must buy into a firm's efforts at total quality.

Figure 16-1 shows how a successful total quality program works. At the left are the participants in a total quality program, who together engage in the process of creating total quality. There is an interchange among the parties and between the parties and the process. A good's or service's effectiveness and efficiency both influence and are influenced by the total quality process, and the output of the process is total quality. Both process and outcome are regularly improved.

If consumers feel a good or service has superior quality, they will buy it; when the experience with a good or service is positive, the result is customer satisfaction, which is one measure of effectiveness. Finally, the level of customer satisfaction affects the consumer's future input into the total quality process, as represented by the feedback loop in the figure. The fact that the consumer appears three times in the diagram (consumer input, consumer purchase, and customer satisfaction) is evidence of the importance of the consumer in total quality.

As one expert notes, "To see things truly from the customer's perspective is to stand at the end of a long sequence of events, all of which have to mesh smoothly. Hotel clerks may be charming and attentive, but if the computer system is down, their courtesy isn't going to help much. Within any company, TQM theory holds, is a whole chain of 'internal customers' like the hotel clerk, ending with the person at the cash register, credit card in hand. The trick is to get everyone working together while keeping the ultimate customer in focus." To Siemens (the German-based industrial firm), "Quality is when your customers come back and your products don't."[5]

*For a total quality program to work, every party in the process must participate.*

# Kinds of Strategic Plans

*Short-run plans are precise; long-run plans outline needs.*

**CANON CORPORATION**
www.canon.com/

Strategic plans can be categorized by their duration, scope, and method of development. They range from short-run, specific, and department generated to long-run, broad, and management generated.

Plans may be short-run (typically one year), moderate in length (two to five years), or long-run (five to ten or even fifteen years). Many firms rely on a combination: Short-run and moderate-length plans are more detailed and operational in nature than long-run plans.

At Japan's Canon Corporation (which makes cameras, business machines, and optical products), short-run plans show a "numerical expression of management activities during defined operating periods"; moderate-length plans "develop strategies to achieve the direction and goals defined by long-range plans, to provide guidelines for short-range plans, and to ensure optimum resource procurement and allocation"; and long-run plans are "more a vision or concept rather than plans, in the sense that they provide the direction and goals for a firm to pursue in a rapidly changing environment, and they lead to the achievement of qualitative innovations in every aspect of operations."[6]

*Consumer-products firms often have plans for each line.*

The scope of strategic marketing plans also varies. There may be separate marketing plans for each of a firm's major products; a single, integrated marketing plan encompassing all products; or a broad business plan with a section devoted to marketing. Separate marketing plans by product line are often used by consumer-goods manufacturers; a single, integrated marketing plan is often employed by service firms; and a broad business plan is often utilized by industrial-goods manufacturers. A firm's diversity and the number of distinct market segments it seeks both have a strong influence here.

Last, strategic plans may be developed via a bottom-up, top-down, or combination approach. In bottom-up marketing planning, input from salespeople, product managers, advertising personnel, and other marketing areas is used to set objectives, budgets, forecasts, timetables, and marketing mixes. Bottom-up plans are realistic and good for morale. Yet it may be hard to coordinate each bottom-up plan and to include different assumptions about the same concept when setting an integrated, company-wide marketing plan.

*Bottom-up plans foster employee input; top-down plans are set by top management.*

The shortcomings of bottom-up plans are resolved in the top-down approach, whereby senior managers centrally direct and control planning activities. A top-down plan can use complex assumptions about competition or other external factors and provide a uniform direction for the marketing effort. Yet, if input from lower-level managers is not actively sought, morale may suffer.

The solution may be to use a combination of the two approaches, with senior executives setting overall goals and policy and marketing personnel forming plans for carrying out marketing policies. As the chief executive of one firm remarked:

> You can't have a workable strategy forced down from the top. Empowering middle managers is a necessity. They manage what we as a corporation want to accomplish. To make them think strategically comes from sharing the direction and from having a set of supportive organizational systems. So it's real work, not sermons, that makes us and our middle managers strategic thinkers.[7]

# Strengthening Relationships Between Marketing and Other Functional Areas

An organization's strategic planning must accommodate the distinct needs of marketing and other functional areas. This is not always simple, due to the different orientations of each area. Marketing people may seek tailor-made products, flexible budgets, non-routine transactions, many product versions, frequent purchases, customer-driven new products, employee compensation incentives, and aggressive actions against competitors. These may conflict with the goals of other functional areas to seek mass production (production), well-established budgets (finance), routine transactions (accounting), limited models (engineering), infrequent orders (purchasing), technology-driven new products (research and development), fixed employee compensation (personnel), and passive actions against competitors (legal).

Top management makes sure every functional area sees the need for a balanced view in company decision making and has a say in the decisions that are made. Although some degree of tension among departments is inevitable, conflict can be lessened by encouraging interdepartmental contact; seeking employees with both technical and marketing expertise; forming multifunctional task forces, committees, and management-development programs; and setting goals for each department that take the other departments into account.[8]

*The perspectives of marketing and other functional areas need to be reconciled.*

## The Strategic Planning Process

As Figure 16-2 illustrates, the **strategic planning process** has seven interrelated steps: defining organizational mission, establishing strategic business units, setting marketing objectives, performing situation analysis, developing marketing strategy, implementing tactics, and monitoring results. Because the process encompasses both strategic business planning and strategic marketing planning, it is usually conducted by a combination of senior company executives and marketers.

This process is applicable to small and large firms, consumer-products and industrial-products firms, goods- and services-based firms, domestic and international firms, and profit-oriented and nonprofit-oriented institutions. While planning at each step in the process may differ by type of organization, using a thorough strategic plan is beneficial for any organization.

The steps in strategic planning are discussed in the following sections.

*The **strategic planning process** includes steps from defining a mission to monitoring results.*

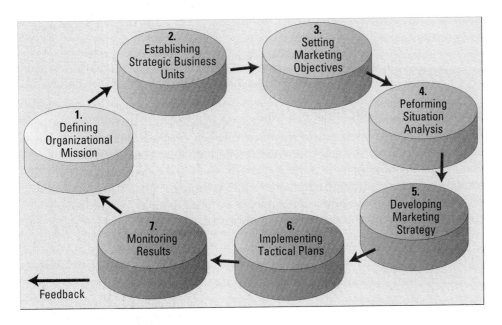

**FIGURE 16-2**

**The Strategic Planning Process**

## Defining Organizational Mission

*A firm sets its direction in an* **organizational mission**.

An **organizational mission** is a long-term commitment to a type of business and a place in the market. It "describes the scope of the firm and its dominant emphasis and values," based on that firm's history, current management preferences, resources, and distinctive competences, and on environmental factors.[9]

An organizational mission can be expressed in terms of the customer group(s) served, the goods and services offered, the functions performed, and/or the technologies utilized. It is more comprehensive than the line-of-business concept noted in Chapter 2. And it is considered implicitly whenever a firm seeks a new customer group or abandons an existing one, introduces a new product (good or service) category or deletes an old one, acquires another company or sells one of its own businesses, engages in more marketing functions (a wholesaler opening retail stores) or in fewer marketing functions (a small innovative toy maker licensing its inventions to an outside company that produces, distributes, and promotes them), or shifts its technological focus (a phone manufacturer placing more emphasis on cellular phones).

Here are two diverse illustrations of clear organizational missions:

> Mountain Equipment Co-operative is a member-owned and -directed retail consumer cooperative. It provides products and services for self-propelled wilderness-oriented recreational activities, such as hiking and mountaineering, at the lowest reasonable price in an informative, helpful, and environmentally responsible manner.[10]

> Canadian Pacific Railway has a rich history dating from 1881, and in that time has developed an extended modern railway system. CPR is a Calgary-based company and is a wholly-owned subsidiary of Canadian Pacific Limited, which also operates Canadian Pacific Hotels, CP Ships, PanCanadian Petroleum, and Fording Coal. Our company mission is to be the preferred business partner in rail-based transportation services. Through teamwork we will create value by delivering superior customer-focused transportation solutions.[11]

Sometimes well-established organizations lose their sense of direction. For example, Levi Strauss and Company was once the largest apparel manufacturer in the world, with one of the best brand names, Levi's Jeans. However, starting in 1990 the Levi's brand name began to lose strength. The firm decided to reengineer itself with the following outcomes:

> Levi's market share among males aged 14 to 19 has since dropped in half, it hasn't had a successful new product in years, its advertising campaigns have been failures, its in-store presentations are embarrassing, and its manufacturing costs are bloated. The reengineering—with an U.S.$850 million budget—was a disaster. J.C. Penney, Levi's biggest customer, reports that last fall (1998) Levi's delivered its all-important back-to-school line—get ready—forty-five days late.... Since 1997 ... Levi Strauss' market value has shrunk from U.S.$14 billion to about U.S. $8 billion. One executive commented, "I don't think we fully accomplished anything, to be honest."[12]

**LEVI STRAUSS AND CO.**
www.levistrauss.com

## Establishing Strategic Business Units

**Strategic business units** *are separate operating units in an organization.*

After defining its mission, a firm may form strategic business units. Each **strategic business unit (SBU)** is a self-contained division, product line, or product department in an organization with a specific market focus and a manager with complete responsibility for integrating all functions into a strategy.[13] An SBU may include all products with the same physical features or products bought for the same use by customers, depending on the mission of the organization. Each SBU has these general attributes:

- A specific target market.
- Control over its resources.
- Clear-cut competitors.

- Its own senior marketing executive.
- Its own marketing strategy.
- Distinct differential advantages.

## TABLE 16-1

## The Strategic Business Units of Canadian Pacific

### CANADIAN PACIFIC RAILWAY

Canadian Pacific Railway provides rail and intermodal freight transportation services over a 15 314-mile network extending from Montreal to Vancouver and into the U.S. midwest and northeast. It serves ports on the east coasts of Canada and the U.S. and the Port of Vancouver, moving large volumes of import and export goods across the continent. More than 80 per cent of its business is west of the Great Lakes and consists primarily of bulk commodities such as grain, coal, sulphur, potash, fertilizers, and petrochemicals. Canadian Pacific Railway is also a leading carrier in the intermodal industry, with twenty-three terminals across Canada and the northern U.S.

### CP SHIPS

CP Ships operates in three key regional markets: the North Atlantic, Latin America, and Australasia. CP Ships comprises six container shipping companies: Canada Maritime, Cast, Lykes Lines, Contship Containerlines, Ivaran Lines, and Australia New Zealand Direct Line. In early 1999 CP Ships and Transportacion Maritima Mexicana (TMM) formed a joint venture to merge the container shipping businesses of TMM, Lykes Lines, and Ivaran. CP Ships also operates CP Ships Logistics and Montreal Terminals.

### PANCANADIAN PETROLEUM

PanCanadian is one of Canada's largest producers and marketers of crude oil, natural gas, and natural gas liquids. Its extensive exploration and production activities stretch from coast to coast in Canada and include a variety of international interests in the Gulf of Mexico, the United Kingdom, Australia, South Africa, and Venezuela. PanCanadian has been among Canada's most active and successful drillers for a number of years.

### FORDING

Fording is Canada's lowest-cost and largest producer of export coal. Its three mines in southeastern British Columbia produce primarily high-quality metallurgical coal for the international steel industry. Its operations in Alberta include two mines supplying thermal coal to electric utilities and an oil sandoverburden removal operation. Fording is also the world's largest producer of the industrial mineral woolastonite.

### CANADIAN PACIFIC HOTELS

Canadian Pacific Hotels is Canada's largest owner-operator of full service hotels, with sixty-five hotels and over 25 000 rooms across Canada, the United States, Mexico, Bermuda, and Barbados. With eighteen resorts, Canadian Pacific Hotels is the fourth largest destination resort operator in North America. It operates under two distinct brands, Canadian Pacific Hotels and Delta Hotels.

The SBU concept lets companies identify those business units with the greatest earnings potential and allocate to them the resources needed for their growth. For instance, at General Electric, every SBU must have a unique purpose, identifiable competitors, and all its major business functions (manufacturing, finance, and marketing) within the control of that SBU's manager. Units not performing up to expectations are constantly reviewed and, if necessary, consolidated with other units, sold, or closed down.[14]

The proper number of SBUs depends on a firm's organizational mission, its resources, and the willingness of top management to delegate authority. A small or specialized firm can have as few as one SBU; a diversified one up to 100 or more. Thus, Canadian Pacific has the five SBUs depicted in Table 16-1; General Electric has

# INTERNATIONAL MARKETING IN ACTION

## Lottery Expertise: It's Not What You Know, But Who You Know

Business opportunities often depend on building relationships with customers and then showing them how a firm's offerings can fill their needs. But is it a good idea to offer to satisfy someone's need when you don't really know anything about the business? Probably not, but Calgary's Applied Gaming Solutions didn't let that stop it from landing a $40 million contract with the Socialist Republic of Vietnam—a contract with a longer-term potential of $200 million in profits!

David Aftergood, President of Applied Gaming Solutions, had made good business contacts with a number of important Vietnamese officials when he was a political advisor to Prime Minister Brian Mulroney and several of his cabinet ministers. So when Aftergood was approached by these officials about setting up equipment, computer software, and training for Lotto 6-36 (a Vietnamese version of Canada's Lotto 6-49) he agreed. Then he went to work figuring out how to keep his word.

For starters, he couldn't find any Canadian companies that had the equipment or expertise to set up this kind of system. Cost estimates were as high as $80 million, and Applied Gaming had no capital to go with its lack of expertise. So Aftergood essentially assumed the role of a broker, and tracked down Delaware-based Automated Wager Incorporated (AWI) to join his firm as part of a consortium. AWI saw the advantages immediately. Aftergood had the contacts and was Canadian, both of which were key to putting together a deal, since AWI was an American firm and might not be welcomed in Vietnam. Applied Gaming and Automated Wager Incorporated then partnered up with Motorola to beat out ten other firms to become the operators of Hanoi's 6-36 lottery in May 1998. Applied Gaming has a seven-year contract that gives 4 per cent of sales during the first five years of operations and 1 per cent of sales after that.

Now that Aftergood knows something about the video lottery business he's pursuing contracts in other Third World countries, such as Honduras, Peru, and Kazakhstan.

Try to put yourself in David Aftergood's shoes when the Vietnamese approached him. Perform a situation analysis (SWOT) of his firm as it was then. What do you think possessed him to pursue this opportunity?

Source: Based on Norma Ramage, "Calgary Firm Bets on Lottery Expertise," *Marketing Magazine* (May 31, 1999), p. 6.

eleven SBUs ranging from aircraft engines to lighting to information services; Dover has forty-five SBUs ranging from elevators to garbage trucks to welding torches; and Johnson & Johnson has 188+ SBUs, related to consumer, pharmaceutical, and professional products.[15]

## Setting Marketing Objectives

*Marketing objectives may include quantitative and qualitative measures.*

A firm needs overall marketing objectives, as well as goals for each SBU. Objectives are often described in both quantitative terms (dollar sales, percentage profit growth, market share, etc.) and qualitative terms (image, level of innovativeness, industry leadership role, etc.).

For example, Canadian Pacific has set the following objectives:

Our future depends on our ability to compete successfully not only at home but also on a global scale. More and more, we are extending our vision beyond our Canadian borders. We are picking our spots carefully to ensure that our businesses are positioned to compete successfully in the global marketplace.

CP Ships has expanded from its traditional stronghold on the North Atlantic to become a leader in the Latin American and Australasian regional trade lanes, while Canadian Pacific Hotels has gained a platform for international growth through its acquisition of the Princess Hotel Chain.[16]

Small firms' goals are often less ambitious, but no less important. For example, Upper Canada Brewing of Toronto is a small regional brewer in an industry dominated by the Labatt and Molson giants. Upper Canada has positioned itself as a Canadian and community brewery. One of its advertising themes is: "Think Globally, Drink Locally." Microbrewery operations by their very nature are small and local and the cost of going to the next level is often not worth the trouble to their owners.[17]

## Performing Situation Analysis

In **situation analysis**, also known as SWOT analysis, an organization identifies its internal strengths (S) and weaknesses (W), as well as external opportunities (O) and threats (T). Situation analysis seeks to answer: Where is a firm now? In what direction is it headed? Answers are derived by recognizing the company's strengths and weaknesses relative to its competitors, studying the environment for opportunities and threats, assessing the firm's ability to capitalize on opportunities and to minimize or avoid threats, and anticipating competitors' responses to company strategies.

Situation analysis can, and should be, conducted at any point in a firm's life. For instance, when Ann Bayley, President of Iceculture Inc., started her business it was to provide ice bowls as a free add-on to her husband's catering business. Ann has been quick to recognize opportunities and Iceculture is now a $100 000 business, going beyond weddings and hospitality events to include winter carnival displays. Iceculture got into the winter carnival business when Ann offered to supply ice carving as a backup to worried Winter Carnival organizers in Grand Bend, Ontario, who had planned a carnival but did not plan on a lack of snow. Winter carnivals have now become a major growth market for Iceculture. Of course, the product does have one important problem, customers complain that it melts. Ann plans to seize this opportunity by launching fake ice.[18]

Sometimes situation analysis reveals weaknesses or threats that can't be overcome, and a company opts to drop or sell a product line or division. When Edgar Bronfman Jr. became CEO of Montreal's Seagram in 1994 the firm consisted of a spirits and wine business, Tropicana juices, and holdings in chemical giant DuPont. Edgar Bronfman Jr. had travelled the world and had seen that American pop culture seemed to rule everywhere. He perceived this as a threat to the way Seagram was currently structured—and hence an opportunity to transform it into an entertainment company. He sold off his DuPont shares, and used the cash to buy a controlling interest in MCA (Universal Studios' parent company) in 1996. In 1998, in order to purchase Polygram music, Bronfman sold off Tropicana to PepsiCo for $3.3 billion. Now Seagram is positioned to be the number two entertainment company in the world behind Disney.[19]

## Developing Marketing Strategy

A **marketing strategy** outlines the way in which the marketing mix is used to attract and satisfy the target market(s) and achieve an organization's goals. Marketing-mix decisions centre on product, distribution, promotion, and price plans. A separate strategy is necessary for each SBU in an organization; these strategies must be coordinated.

A marketing strategy should be explicit to provide proper guidance. It should take into account a firm's mission, resources, abilities, and standing in the marketplace; the status of the firm's industry and the product groups in it (such as light versus ice beer); domestic and international competitive forces; such environmental

**Situation analysis** *investigates a firm's strengths, weaknesses, opportunities, and threats.*

*A good* **marketing strategy** *provides a framework for marketing activities.*

**FIGURE 16-3**

**The Product/Market
Opportunity Matrix**

*Source: Adapted from H. Igor Ansoff, "Strategies for
Diversification," Harvard Business Review, Vol. 35
(September–October 1957), pp. 113–124.*

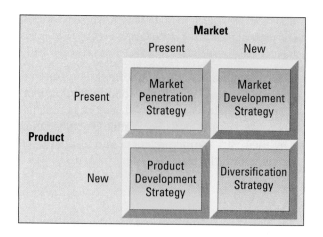

factors as the economy and population growth; and the best opportunities for growth—and the threats that could dampen it.

Four strategic planning approaches are presented next: the product/market opportunity matrix, the Boston Consulting Group matrix, the General Electric business screen, and the Porter generic strategy model.

*The* **product/market opportunity matrix** *involves* **market penetration**, **market development**, **product development**, *and* **diversification** *options.*

**THE PRODUCT/MARKET OPPORTUNITY MATRIX**  The **product/market opportunity matrix** identifies four alternative marketing strategies to maintain and/or increase sales of business units and products: market penetration, market development, product development, and diversification (see Figure 16-3).[20] The choice of an alternative depends on the market saturation of an SBU or product and the firm's ability to introduce new products. Two or more alternatives may be combined.

**Market penetration** is effective when the market is growing or not yet saturated. A firm seeks to expand the sales of its present products in its present markets through more intensive distribution, aggressive promotion, and competitive pricing. Sales are increased by attracting non-users and competitors' customers and raising the usage rate among current customers. United Parcel Service is a good example of a firm that has pursued a market penetration strategy. UPS (see Figure 16-4) is the world's largest package-delivery firm. It advertises extensively on TV and in magazines. Low prices and extensive distribution are centrepieces of its strategy.

**Market development** is effective when a local or regional business looks to widen its market, new market segments are emerging due to changes in consumer lifestyles and demographics, and innovative uses are discovered for a mature product. A firm seeks greater sales of present products from new markets or new product uses. It can enter new geographic markets, appeal to market segments it is not yet satisfying, and reposition existing products. New distribution methods may be tried; promotion efforts are more descriptive. For example, UPS is stepping up efforts around the world, where client use of delivery services tends to be much less frequent than in North America.

**Product development** is effective when an SBU has a core of strong brands and a sizable consumer following. A firm develops new or modified products to appeal to present markets. It stresses new models, better quality, and other minor innovations closely related to entrenched products—and markets them to loyal customers. Traditional distribution methods are used; promotion stresses that the new product is made by a well-established firm. For example, UPS now offers more shipping choices than ever before, including GroundSaver, GroundTrac, 3 Day Select, Next Day Air, 2nd Day Air, and Worldwide Expedited Package services.

**Diversification** is used so a firm does not become too dependent on one SBU or product line. The firm becomes involved with new products aimed at new mar-

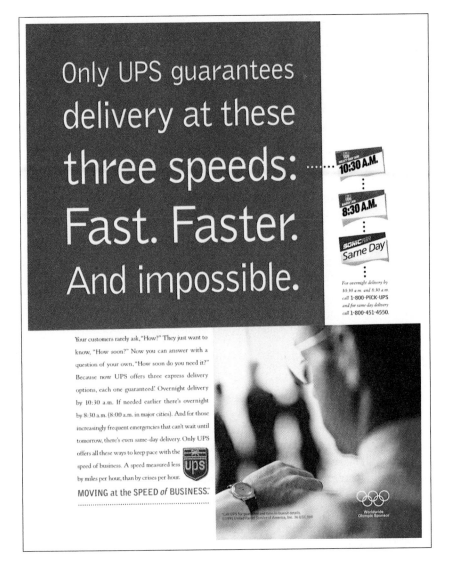

**FIGURE 16-4**
**UPS: The Leader in Package Delivery**
*Reprinted by permission.*

kets. These products may be new to the industry or new only to the company. Distribution and promotion orientations are both different from those usually followed by the firm. UPS has diversified by gaining a 15 per cent stake in Mail Boxes Etc., the leading North American neighbourhood mailing and business service-centre franchiser.[21]

**THE BOSTON CONSULTING GROUP MATRIX** The **Boston Consulting Group matrix** lets a firm classify each SBU in terms of its market share relative to major competitors and annual industry growth (see Figure 16-5). A firm can see which SBUs are dominant—compared to competitors—and whether the industries in which it operates are growing, stable, or declining. The matrix identifies four types of SBUs: star, cash cow, question mark, and dog, and offers strategies for each of them.[22]

The assumption is that the higher an SBU's market share, the better its long-run marketplace position because of rather low per-unit costs and high profitability. This is due to economies of scale (larger firms can automate or standardize production, service tasks, distribution, promotion, and so on), experience (as operations are repeated, a firm becomes more effective), and better bargaining power. At the same time, the industry growth rate indicates a firm's need to invest. A high growth rate means a big investment will be needed to maintain or expand the firm's position in a growing market.

*The* **Boston Consulting Group matrix** *uses market share and industry growth to describe* **stars**, **cash cows**, **question marks**, *and* **dogs**.

**FIGURE 16-5**

**The Boston Consulting Group Matrix**

*Source: Adapted from Bruce D. Henderson, "The Experience Curve Reviewed: 1V. The Growth Share Matrix of the Product Portfolio" (Boston: Boston Consulting Group, 1973). Perspectives No. 135.*

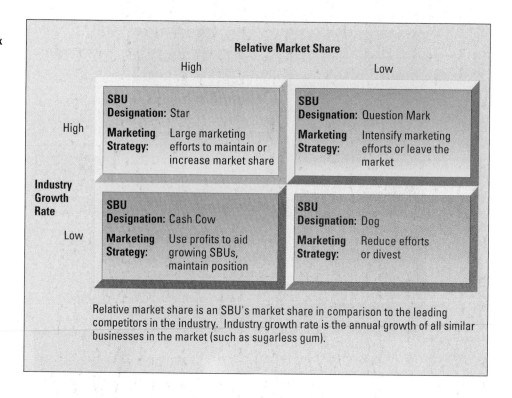

**Relative Market Share**

High — Low

**Industry Growth Rate** — High / Low

| SBU **Designation:** Star | SBU **Designation:** Question Mark |
| **Marketing Strategy:** Large marketing efforts to maintain or increase market share | **Marketing Strategy:** Intensify marketing efforts or leave the market |
| SBU **Designation:** Cash Cow | SBU **Designation:** Dog |
| **Marketing Strategy:** Use profits to aid growing SBUs, maintain position | **Marketing Strategy:** Reduce efforts or divest |

Relative market share is an SBU's market share in comparison to the leading competitors in the industry. Industry growth rate is the annual growth of all similar businesses in the market (such as sugarless gum).

A **star** is a leading SBU (high market share) in an expanding industry (high growth). The main goal is to sustain differential advantages in the face of rising competition. A star can generate substantial profits but requires financing for continued growth. Market share can be kept or increased through intensive advertising, product introductions, greater distribution, and/or price reductions. As industry growth slows, a star becomes a cash cow.

A **cash cow** is a leading SBU (high market share) in a mature or declining industry (low growth). It often has loyal customers, making it hard for competitors to woo them. Since sales are steady, without high costs for product development and the like, a cash cow produces more cash (profit) than needed to keep its market share. Profits support the growth of other company SBUs. Marketing is oriented to reminder ads, periodic price discounts, keeping up distribution channels, and offering new styles or options to encourage repurchases.

A **question mark** is an SBU that has had little impact (low market share) in an expanding industry (high growth). There is low consumer support, differential advantages are weak, and competitors are leaders. To improve, a big marketing investment is needed in the face of strong competition. A firm must decide whether to beef up promotion, add distributors, improve product attributes, and cut prices—or to abandon the market. The choice depends on whether a firm believes the SBU can compete successfully with more support and what that support will cost.

A **dog** is an SBU with limited sales (low market share) in a mature or declining industry (low growth). Despite time in the marketplace, a dog has a small customer following—and lags behind competitors in sales, image, and so on. A dog usually has cost disadvantages and few growth opportunities. A firm with such an SBU can appeal to a specialized market, harvest profits by cutting support services, or exit the market.

Over time, Dylex Ltd. has been the parent firm of the women's fashion clothiers Fairweather and Braemar, men's clothiers Tip Top and Harry Rosen, and Bi-Way and Thrifty's. It also had a holding in Club Monaco. Dylex's most recent strategy has been to build market share for its stores by maintaining customer loyalty and emphasizing store branding.

**DYLEX**
www.dylex.com

TECHNOLOGY AND MARKETING

## Dell Computers: Selling in China

China is the fifth largest market in the world for personal computers, and in five years is expected to be the second largest market ahead of Japan. Dell Computer feels compelled to enter this market, but there's a problem with the way the firm does business. Although personal computer prices have been falling dramatically in North America, they still represent nearly two years worth of life savings for a buyer in China. With such a large relative expenditure on the line, a Chinese consumer wants to be able to try out a machine. This means having a local retail presence, but Dell Computer is a make-to-order direct response retailer. So how does it implement its direct marketing strategy in a country where consumers don't buy direct?

Dell isn't targeting retail buyers in China, since they represent only about 10 per cent of the market. Instead it's targeting institutional buyers with customized computers, topnotch and reliable software, and very low prices (because there are no intermediaries). Its Chinese market share was 1.2 per cent in 1998, triple that of 1997. Dell feels that Chinese organizational buyers are no different from those anywhere else, in that they want speed of ordering, convenience, and service.

According to Dell salesperson Peter Chan, "We don't have to change the formula. It will work in the U.S., China, India, or even in space."

It's unlikely that Dell can reach number one, since its competition is copying its strategy for corporate sales in China. Moreover, some of the local Chinese competitors are selling computers with free software (bootlegged software has meant that copyright protection is virtually absent in the Chinese computer industry).

Although Internet hookups are occurring at an incredible rate and there are plenty of phones to use, Dell's main stumbling block in reaching Chinese consumers is that not many of them have credit cards. And those who do have them don't feel comfortable giving out the numbers over the phone or the Net (much like their North American counterparts).

Comment on Peter Chan's statement about not changing the formula. Look at how Dell sells computers in North America and what underlies its success. Do those same factors currently exist in China, and if not, is there anything that Dell can do to help the situation along?

Source: Based on Neel Chowdhury, "Dell Cracks China," *Fortune* (July 21, 1999), pp. 120–124.

---

Dylex is the kind of firm to which the Boston Consulting Group matrix can be applied. For example, Braemar and Fairweather have been treated as "Cash Cow SBUs." To sustain growth in its retail business Dylex is considering developing products for an aging population and capitalizing on the casual-business attire market. Dylex is planning to go after the upscale men's attire market by repositioning the Tip Top division, thus making it a "Question Mark SBU." The firm is also planning to launch a new low-price clothing and giftware chain of stores (which have 22 000 square feet of retail space) named "Labels" in order to add a "Star SBU" to its portfolio. Dylex divested the "Dog SBUs" of Harry Rosen and Club Monaco, but still has its Bi-Way stores, whose image the firm is planning to change. The focus on growth and market share for Dylex falls right in line with the principles suggested by the Boston Consulting Group matrix. Dylex is seeking growth opportunities to "build on the diversity of the Dylex portfolio."[23]

**THE GENERAL ELECTRIC BUSINESS SCREEN** The **General Electric business screen** categorizes SBUs and products in terms of industry attractiveness and company business strengths. It involves more variables than the product/market opportunity matrix or the Boston Consulting Group matrix. Industry attractiveness factors include market size and growth, competition, technological advances, and the social/legal environment. Company business strength is measured according to dif-

*The **General Electric business screen** measures industry attractiveness and company business strengths.*

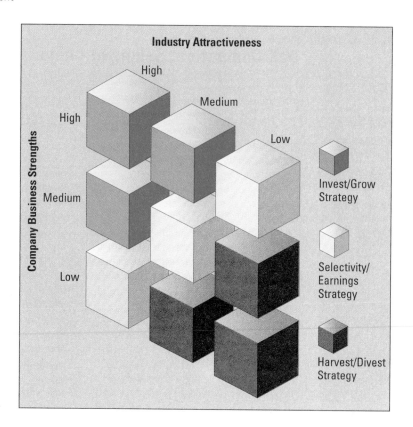

**FIGURE 16-6**

**The General Electric Business Screen**

*Source: Maintaining Strategies for the Future Through Current Crises (Fairfield, Ct.: General Electric, 1975).*

ferential advantages, market share, patent protection, marketing effectiveness, control over prices, and economies of scale. An SBU may have high, medium, or low industry attractiveness, as well as high, medium, or low company business strengths; it would be positioned accordingly on the business screen in Figure 16-6.[24]

SBUs in green are investment/growth areas. They are in strong industries and performing well. They are similar to stars in the Boston Consulting Group matrix. Full marketing resources are proper, and high profits are expected. Innovations, product-line extensions, product and image ads, distribution intensity, and solid price margins are pursued.

SBUs in yellow are selectivity/earnings areas. They are not positioned as well as investment/growth ones. An SBU may be strong in a weak industry (like a cash cow), okay in a somewhat attractive industry, or weak in an attractive industry (like a question mark). A firm wants to hold the earnings and strength of cash cows, and use marketing to maintain customer loyalty and distribution support. For question marks, a firm must decide whether to raise its marketing investment, focus on a specialized market niche, acquire another business in the industry, or trim product lines. The medium/medium SBU is an opportunity to appeal to under-served segments and to selectively invest in marketing.

SBUs in red represent harvest/divest areas. They are similar to dogs in the Boston Consulting Group matrix. A firm can minimize its marketing effort, concentrate on a few products rather than a product line, divest, or close down the SBU. Profits are harvested because investments are minimal.

Bausch & Lomb applies the fundamentals of the business screen: It has "a heritage of technical achievement and product excellence dating to 1853. The company markets personal health, medical, biomedical, and optics products on the basis of quality and differentiated benefits. Its strategic focus is on selected segments of global health care and optical markets where it is advantaged with superior technology, low production costs, and established brand names. Products have earned worldwide consumer recognition and are frequently recommended by health-care professionals."[25]

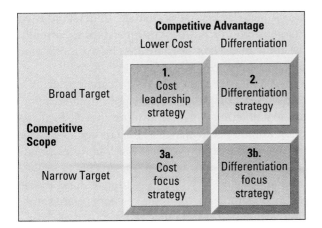

**FIGURE 16-7**

**The Porter Generic Strategy Model**

*Source: Michael E. Porter, Competitive Advantage: Creating and Sustaining Superior Performance (New York: Free Press, 1985), p. 12. Reprinted with the permission of The Free Press, a division of Macmillan Inc. Copyright © 1985 by Michael E. Porter.*

**THE PORTER GENERIC STRATEGY MODEL** The **Porter generic strategy model** identifies two key marketing planning concepts and the options available for each: competitive scope (broad or narrow target) and competitive advantage (lower cost or differentiation). The model, shown in Figure 16-7, pinpoints these basic strategies: cost leadership, differentiation, and focus.[26]

With a cost-leadership strategy, an SBU aims at a broad market and offers goods and services in large quantities. Due to economies of scale, a firm can reduce per-unit costs and offer low prices. This gives it higher profit margins than its competitors, allows it to respond better to cost rises, and/or lures price-conscious consumers. Among those using cost leadership are UPS; Wal-Mart, Canada's largest department store retailer; and WestJet Airlines. WestJet Airlines has been called Canada's most efficient carrier. It began operations in 1996, and is fanatically dedicated to keeping overhead low and revenue and profits high. Its managers speak with pride about how they've borrowed heavily from management approaches developed by the world's most efficient air carrier, U.S.-based Southwest Airlines. Several discount airlines have succeeded in the U.S. and WestJet is copying their strategies. It has purchased its aircraft outright to avoid such operating costs as leases and interest payments, and plans to implement ticketless travel to further reduce costs. CEO Clive Beddoes expects this to produce considerable savings, since nearly 35 per cent of an airline's employees are involved with ticketing.[27]

In a differentiation strategy, an SBU aims at a large market by offering goods or services that are viewed as distinctive. The goods or services have a broad appeal, yet are perceived by consumers as unique by virtue of features, availability, reliability, etc.; price is less important. Among those using differentiation are Federal Express, Seiko, Caterpillar Tractor, and Harry Rosen's menswear stores.[28]

With a focus strategy, an SBU (which could be a small firm) seeks a narrow market segment by offering low prices or a unique product. It can control costs by concentrating on a few key products aimed at specific consumers or by having a specialist reputation and serving a market unsatisfied by competitors. Samsung is a South Korean producer of inexpensive consumer electronics; James Izatt of Vancouver develops turf-growing systems for golf courses and sports fields, which he then licenses.[29]

The Porter model shows that a small firm can profit by concentrating on one competitive niche, even though its total market share may be low. A firm does not have to be large to do well.

**EVALUATION OF STRATEGIC PLANNING APPROACHES** The strategic planning approaches just discussed are widely used—at least informally. Many firms assess alternative market opportunities; know which products are stars, cash cows, ques-

*The* **Porter generic strategy model** *distinguishes among cost leadership, differentiation, and focus strategies.*

*Strategic models have pros and cons, and should be only part of planning.*

tion marks, and dogs; recognize what factors affect performance; understand their industries; and realize they can target broad or narrow customer bases. Formally, strategic planning models are most apt to be used by larger firms; and the models are adapted to the needs of the specific firm employing them.

The major strengths of these approaches are that they let a firm analyze all SBUs and products, study the effects of various strategies, learn the opportunities to pursue and the threats to avoid, compute marketing and other resource needs, focus on meaningful differential advantages, compare performance against designated goals, and discover principles for improving. Competitors' actions and long-term trends can also be followed.

The major weaknesses of these approaches are that they may be hard to use (particularly by a small firm), may be too simplistic and omit key factors, are somewhat arbitrary in defining SBUs and evaluative criteria (like relative market share), may not be applicable to all companies and situations (a dog SBU may actually be profitable and generate cash), do not adequately account for environmental conditions (like the economy), may over-value market share, and are often used by staff planners rather than line managers.

These techniques only aid planning. They do not replace the need for managers to study each situation and base marketing strategies on the unique aspects of their industry, firm, and SBUs.

## Implementing Tactical Plans

*A marketing strategy is enacted using* **tactical plans**.

A **tactical plan** specifies the short-run actions (tactics) that a firm undertakes in implementing a given marketing strategy. A tactical plan has three basic elements: specific tasks, a time frame, and resource allocation.

The specific tasks relate to the marketing mix and may be aimed at creating a variety of combinations, from high quality, high service, low distribution intensity, personal-selling emphasis, and above-average prices to low quality, low service, high distribution intensity, advertising emphasis, and low prices. Each SBU has a distinct marketing mix, based on its target market and strategic emphasis. The individual mix elements must be coordinated for each SBU and conflicts among SBUs minimized.

The time frame may mean being the first to introduce a product, bringing out a product when the market is most receptive, or quickly reacting to a competitor's strategy to catch it off guard. A firm must balance its desire to be an industry leader with clear-cut competitive advantages against its concern for the risks of innovation. Marketing opportunities exist for limited periods of time, and the firm needs to act quickly.

Resource allocation (or marketing investments) can be classed as order processing or order generating. Order-processing costs are associated with recording and handling orders, such as order entry, computer-data handling, and merchandise handling. The goal is to minimize those costs, subject to a given level of service. Order-generating costs, such as advertising and personal selling, produce revenues. Reducing them may have a harmful effect on sales and profits. Thus, a firm should estimate sales at various levels of costs and for various combinations of marketing functions. Maximum profit rarely occurs at the lowest level of expenditure on order-generating costs.

Tactical decisions differ from strategic decisions in several key ways:

- They are less complex and more structured.
- They have a much shorter time horizon.
- They require a considerably lower resource commitment.
- They are enacted and adjusted more often.

# ETHICS AND TODAY'S MARKETER

## When Trying to Build a "Racy" Image Is Too Racy

A key part of implementing any marketing strategy is the positioning and the image building for your target market. The most obvious sign of a firm's positioning strategy should be in its advertising. (Although this isn't always the case.) If a firm positions itself toward a young audience, it likely wants to be seen as cutting edge. The advertising takes on this edge, and can sometimes be, well, too cutting. Indeed, when a firm goes too far in building its image it may receive complaints—and so will Advertising Standards Canada, the industry's watchdog agency.

When Advertising Standards Canada receives a complaint it's investigated and the party about which the complaint is made is informed of its nature and the results of the complaint. If the complaint is frivolous ("I hate advertising"), there is usually nothing done. But if Advertising Standards Canada sees merit in the complaint it asks the advertiser to stop the kind of advertising and then publishes the results of the action. In other words, advertisers that push too far risk a dose of public humiliation.

Labatt breweries has experienced this twice in recent years. Beer commercials are known for sometimes being out of hand, but it's usually over concerns about sexual themes (Miller Lite's Swedish Bikini team) or promoting excess drinking (one brewer actually ran a campaign with the theme: "The beer to have when you are having more than one beer"). Labatt, however, was cited for safety issues regarding activities in its ads.

In 1998 Labatt ran a "Welcome to Your Carlsberg Years" campaign aimed at thirty-somethings. The commercial showed two men setting up for a garage sale and putting out a Stop sign and a Yield sign as items to sell. The idea was to show how the target market had changed: these men had once engaged in some wild youthful activities and were now settling down a bit. The ad was controversial because it suggested that removing traffic signs is just a mischief activity, and okay if you're young. Advertising Standards Canada stated that the ad was a "display of disregard for public safety," and Labatt of course removed the ad.

Labatt was in hot water a year previous to this for a more obvious unsafe activity. Advertising Standards Canada received complaints about an "Out of the Blue" campaign spot that featured young people riding lock-and-pay shopping carts down the streets of Toronto. The young people were racing the carts back to the shopping centres, where they'd lock them up and get the change that was in them. The ad closes with the people buying beer with handfuls of quarters. Advertising Standards Canada feld the ad promoted the unsafe activity of racing shopping carts, and asked Labatt to stop airing it. Labatt removed the ad as soon as it received the request.

As a marketing manager for Labatt who's had to face two embarrassing situations, how would you set guidelines for marketing strategies that would give them the edge you wanted without drawing complaints about the image you presented?

Source: Based on Lara Mills, "ASC Report Names Carlsberg TV Spot," *Marketing Magazine* (April 19, 1999), p. 2.

At Frito-Lay, tactical planning means preparing its delivery people and its retailers for new product introductions, aggressively promoting its products, maintaining its profit margins—while not giving competitors any opportunities to win market share through lower prices, and servicing its retail accounts very well. How do Frito-Lay personnel avoid complacency in light of such a strong position? As its chief executive says, "I wake up every morning thinking, I haven't sold one bag of Fritos yet. We're always raising the bar on ourselves and our future."[30]

## Monitoring Results

**Monitoring results** involves comparing the actual performance of a firm, business unit, or product against planned performance for a specified period. Actual performance data are then fed back into the strategic planning process. Budgets, timetables, sales and profit statistics, cost analyses, and image studies are just some measures that can be used to assess results.

When actual performance lags behind plans, corrective action is taken. For instance, "If implementation problems persist, it is not (in most instances) because employees mean to do the wrong thing. It is because they do not know the right thing to do. The first task in making strategy work, then, is to identify the right behaviour—that is, behaviour that reduces costs, improves quality, pleases customers, and adds to profitability."[31]

Some plans must be revised due to the impact of uncontrollable factors on sales and costs. Many far-sighted firms develop contingency plans to outline their responses in advance, should unfavourable conditions arise. (Techniques for evaluating marketing effectiveness are covered in Chapter 17.)

# Devising a Strategic Plan

Having a written strategic plan encourages executives to carefully think out and coordinate each step in the planning process, pinpoint problem areas, be consistent, tie the plan to goals and resources, measure performance, and send a clear message to employees and others. A sample outline for a written strategic plan and an application of strategic planning by a small firm are presented next.

## Sample Outline for a Written Strategic Plan

What are the ingredients of a good strategic plan? Here is a brief list:

- It should affect the consideration of strategic choices.
- It should force a long-range view.
- It should make the resource allocation system visible.
- It should provide methods to help strategic analysis and decision making.
- It should be a basis for managing a firm or SBU strategically.
- It should provide a communication and coordination system both horizontally (between SBUs and departments) and vertically (from senior executives to front-line employees).
- It should help a firm and its SBUs cope with change.[32]

Table 16-2 presents a sample outline for a written strategic plan from a marketing perspective. This outline may be used by firms of any size or type.

## Labatt Breweries: Dealing with an Evolving Beer Market[33]

Labatt has the reputation in Canada as "the savviest marketer in sudsland." Earning and keeping this reputation hasn't been easy, and won't get any easier. Labatt has been brewing beer in Canada since 1847. It brews and markets a number of well-known national brands of beer, including Labatt Genuine Draft, Labatt Ice, Labatt 50, Labatt Blue, Blue Light, Labatt Extra Dry, Labatt Lite, John Labatt Classic, Labatt Wildcat, Labatt Select, and Labatt 0.5. It also brews and markets Budweiser, Bud Light, Carlsberg, Carlsberg Light, Guinness Extra Stout, and the PC family of beer under licence. In addition, Labatt brews a number of regional brands of beer, including Crystal and Labatt Select in Ontario, Labatt Velvet Cream Porter and Labatt 50 Légère in Quebec, Kokanee in B.C., and Keith's in the Maritimes.

Labatt and Molson, its main competitor, each have about 45 per cent of the Canadian brewing industry. A few years ago they shared 94 per cent of the market, but have since had to deal with changes in their competitive environment caused by the emergence of strong local microbrewers and home brewing. In the face of this competition Labatt's market planning will be very important to its future.

**ORGANIZATIONAL MISSION** In 1995 Interbrew S.A., a Belgian brewing conglomerate, acquired Labatt in a friendly takeover. Interbrew is committed to superior-quality products, industry innovation, and a consumer-driven approach to marketing. It was quite specific in stating that it wanted no part of any of the other businesses Labatt was involved in, and so promptly let it be known that companies in the entertainment division of Labatt were for sale.

**ESTABLISHING STRATEGIC BUSINESS UNITS** When Labatt was acquired by Interbrew it had essentially two SBUs: brewing and entertainment. In 1993 Labatt was a multinational conglomerate with 5700 employees and annual sales of $2.135 billion. Its strong sales base in Canada accounted for 84 per cent of company revenues, while the brewing operation accounted for 84 per cent of its total sales as well. Labatt's entertainment business included ownership of the Toronto Argonauts football team, 90 per cent ownership of the Toronto Blue Jays, and nearly 50 per cent of the SkyDome.

By 1999 Labatt employed 3700 Canadians and was a major part of Interbrew S.A., contributing to combined net sales of over $4 billion. Labatt operates eight breweries and markets sixty brands of beer. As of March 1999 it held a 46 per cent share of the Canadian market worth an estimated $2.2 billion. (Molson held a market share of just about 45 per cent at this time, with sales of $2.1 billion.) Labatt also exports beer to twenty other countries, including the U.S. Interbrew describes itself as an international brewer, with a portfolio of 120 brands of beer served in eighty countries. Its brands have become Labatt's SBUs, the most important of which these days is Labatt Blue, the leading selling beer in Canada.

**SETTING MARKET OBJECTIVES** According to Labatt CEO Hugo Powell, "It is our goal to be the best brewery in the Americas. Our strong business in Canada provides us the platform to realize this objective as we expand into the Americas. By producing the best products and putting in place the best distribution networks wherever we are in the world, Labatt is clearly focused on winning."

One of Labatt's main objectives is to be the leading brewer in Canada, and to this end it has set two secondary objectives: to expand the market share of Labatt's Blue, and to develop international markets in the U.S. and Mexico.

**PERFORMING SITUATION ANALYSIS** Beer distribution in Canada is unique in that each of the ten provinces has independent control over its distribution. The two major markets for beer, Quebec and Ontario, have very diverse distribution channels. In Quebec beer is sold through company-owned and independent beer distributors, while in Ontario all beer is sold through Brewers Warehousing Corporation, which is owned by the brewers themselves. In the remaining provinces beer is distributed through outlets owned and operated by the provincial governments, except in Alberta where distribution has been privatized the way it is in Quebec. In Ontario price competition between brands of beer is regulated. However, it's mainly the non-price factors that are critical to marketing beer in this province.

Brew-your-own-beer operations are becoming a significant threat through their low-price positioning, and several microbreweries have been asserting themselves in

---

**TABLE 16-2**

**A Sample Outline for a Written Strategic Plan—From a Marketing Perspective**

Using as much detail as possible, please address each of these points for your firm:

1. Organizational Mission
   (a) In 50 words or less, describe the current mission of your organization.
   (b) In 50 words or less, describe how you would like your organizational mission to evolve over the next five years, and over the next ten years.
   (c) Is your firm on track regarding the mission statements in (a) and (b)? Explain your answer.
   (d) Discuss the organizational mission in terms of your target market(s), your functions performed, and your overall style of marketing.
   (e) Discuss the organizational mission in terms of company diversification.
   (f) How is the organizational mission communicated to employees?

2. Strategic Business Units
   (a) State the present organizational structure of your firm.
   (b) Assess the present organizational structure.
   (c) How would you expect the organizational structure to evolve over the next five years? The next ten years?
   (d) Does your firm have strategic business units? If yes, describe them. If no, why not?
   (e) Does your firm have a separate marketing plan for each target market, major product, and so on? Explain your answer and relate it to (d).
   (f) Does each product or business unit in your firm have a marketing manager, proper resources, and clear competitors? Explain your answer.

3. Marketing Objectives
   (a) Cite your organization's overall marketing goals for the next one, three, five, and ten years.
   (b) Cite your organization's specific marketing goals by target market and product for the next one, five, and ten years:
      • Sales.
      • Market share.
      • Profit.
      • Image.
      • Customer loyalty.
   (c) What criteria will be used to determine whether goals have been fully, partially, or unsatisfactorily reached?

4. Situation Analysis
   (a) Describe the present overall strengths, weaknesses, opportunities, and threats (SWOT) facing your organization.
   (b) How do you expect the factors noted in your answer (a) to change over the next five to ten years?
   (c) For each of the key products or businesses of your firm, describe the present strengths, weaknesses, opportunities, and threats.

---

**MOOSEHEAD**
www.moosehead.ca/

the large metropolitan markets across Canada. These microbreweries are growing at a tremendous rate. Sleeman's Brewery of Guelph, Ontario merged recently with Okanagan Spring Brewery of Vernon, B.C.; Moosehead Breweries in Dartmouth, Nova Scotia is competing aggressively; and Pacific Western Brewery in Prince George, B.C. has even marketed its products in Japan.

The Canadian beer market has been experiencing no volume growth in consumption, so Labatt has been looking at foreign markets, in particular the U.S. and Mexico. Labatt has also been preparing for an influx of foreign competitors, since Canada has been asked to comply with a GATT (General Agreement on Trade and Tariffs) ruling to eliminate trade barriers to foreign beer.

**TABLE 16-2 (CONTINUED)**

   (d) How do you expect the factors noted in your answer to (c) to change over the next five to ten years?

   (e) How will your firm respond to the factors mentioned in the answers for (a) to (d)?

**5.** Developing Strategy

   (a) Describe the target market, marketing mix, and differential advantages for each of your products or businesses.

   (b) Does your firm have sufficient resources and capabilities to carry out its marketing strategy? Explain your answer.

   (c) Compare your firm's strategy with those of leading competitors.

   (d) Describe your use of these strategic approaches: market penetration, market development, product development, and diversification.

   (e) For each product or business, detail the characteristics of your firm's present customers, as well as those who should be sought in the future.

   (f) Categorize each of your products or businesses as a star, cash cow, question mark, or dog. Explain your reasoning.

   (g) What is the impact of the categorization cited in (f) on your strategy?

   (h) For each product or business, which of these approaches is most apt: invest/grow, selectivity/earnings, or harvest/divest? Explain your reasoning.

   (i) For each of your products or businesses, which of these approaches is most appropriate: cost leadership, differentiation, cost focus, or differentiation focus? Explain your reasoning.

   (j) Describe how the plans for all of your firm's products or businesses are coordinated.

**6.** Implementation

   (a) Describe the procedures to activate your firm's strategy.

   (b) For each product or business, how does your firm ensure that the strategy is implemented as intended with regard to the target market and marketing mix?

   (c) Do marketing personnel have appropriate authority (i.e., are they empowered) and resources to implement plans? Explain your answer.

   (d) Are ongoing marketing budgets sufficient? Does your organization differentiate between order-generating and order-processing costs? Explain your answers.

   (e) How do you expect competitors to react as you implement your strategy?

   (f) Are there contingency plans in case of unexpected results?

**7.** Monitoring Results

   (a) Describe the procedures used by your firm to monitor steps 1 to 6.

   (b) For each company product or business, is planned performance compared with actual performance on a regular basis? Explain your answer.

   (c) Is a SWOT analysis conducted regularly? Explain your answer.

   (d) How are performance results communicated through the organization?

   (e) What procedures do you use to respond to the findings of performance reviews?

---

**DEVELOPING MARKETING STRATEGY** In order to accomplish the objective of attaining and then maintaining the number one in market share in Canada, Hugo Powell is employing a number of approaches. In the past few years Labatt has introduced many new products or line extensions to gain market share, which must then be held. The strategy has been a successful one, as a significant proportion of its current sales are represented by products that have been introduced since 1992.

However, Labatt has recently focused on holding and increasing the number one beer brand position with Labatt's Blue, and to this end it's launched a two-pronged campaign. The first initiative involved seizing an almost unbelievable opportunity: acquiring the rights (relinquished by Molson) to Hockey Night in Canada. When

Labatt Marketing VP David Kincaid first mentioned the possibility of acquiring the rights his management team all laughed. But it was no joke, and Labatt set about injecting tremendous energy into the relationship. The second initiative involved "Out of the Blue," a promotional campaign that ties the NHL sponsorship to its flagship brand. Brand loyalty to beer can be very strong, particularly in the 19- to 29-year-old age group, which is influenced heavily by advertising. The Hockey Night in Canada sponsorship and the Out of the Blue campaign are both designed to build and then maintain the loyalty of this group.

Labatt has a leadership position in Canada, the U.S., and Mexico, the three markets that make up the North American Free Trade Agreement. Because Mexico's beer market is twice the size of Canada's and is growing at about 6 per cent annually, Labatt formed a partnership with Mexico's Formento Económico Mexicano, S.A. de C.V. (FEMSA) and its brewing subsidiary, Cerveceria Cuauhtémoc Moctezuma (CCM). Labatt is counting on using this partnership as a future springboard into Central and South American markets.

In addition, Labatt recently signed an agreement with Anheuser-Busch, the world's largest brewer, to be the exclusive brewer and distributor of Budweiser and Bud Light in Canada as part of a partnership in perpetuity. Receiving the rights to distribute the main brands of the world's largest brewer, forever, goes a long way toward reducing the fear of foreign competition.

**IMPLEMENTING TACTICAL PLANS** Leveraging the new Hockey Night in Canada relationship along with the Out of the Blue campaign has given Labatt a tremendous opportunity. The Out of the Blue campaign was launched during the Nagano Winter Olympics in 1998, while the HNIC sponsorship kicked off with an Out of the Blue commercial whose theme was a hockey version of the movie *Field of Dreams*. Labatt followed this up with a series of commercials showing the Stanley Cup being left in a cab outside a Detroit bar by some Detroit Redwings and falling into the hands of enthusiastic Canadian fans who then shuttle it all across Canada. Labatt also sponsored a successful Stanley Cup replica promotion and a set of hockey highlight tapes packaged with its Labatt Blue brands.

Labatt has also used price as a weapon in Ontario, Canada's largest beer market, by requesting temporary reductions from the Liquor Licensing Board. For example, when Labatt surprised Molson with a Christmas 1998 price reduction, regulatory controls prevented Molson from reacting until after Christmas.

Internationally, Labatt and its Mexican partner, CCM, have combined their U.S. import businesses to form Labatt USA, the second largest specialty beer company in the U.S. It recently launched an "Labatt Blue: Pure Canada" advertising campaign featuring a "guy in a bear suit." The bear travels to New York City from the Rocky Mountains, and while it's ridiculously obvious that it's a guy in a bear suit, nobody seems to notice. The followup advertising shows the bear in a series of adventures, including trying to buy beer without identification, trying to pick up women in a bar, and having a wild party in a sushi bar with Japanese tourists.

**MONITORING RESULTS** David Kincaid reports that since the Out of the Blue campaign was launched in 1998 advertising awareness has gone up 50 per cent from the previous year, volume rose 35 per cent in some key bars and restaurants, and packaged sales went up two market share points. More importantly, the share of consumption among the 19- to 29-year-olds has doubled.

In the U.S. Labatt Blue is sold as a premium beer, and ranks third behind Heineken and Corona as an imported product.

# MARKETING IN THE THIRD MILLENNIUM

## A Guru's View of Management[34]

Management guru Peter Drucker was recently asked for his opinions on the current and future state of business strategy and management in North America. The following is worth noting by marketers:

- Future business growth will occur in medium-size firms, in which managers will have a better opportunity to develop their skills.
- Young managers will for the most part start their careers with large firms. As they learn the business their skills will be in greater demand and they'll migrate to smaller firms, where they'll gain greater appreciation.
- Managers need to talk less and do more. There's a lot of publicity and hype in the market, most of it baseless.
- Managers need to avoid being too fashion-conscious when it comes to management trends. A lot of firms have engaged in downsizing and re-engineering because they were the thing to do. These days cross-functional teams are popular, although managers need to realize that it takes years to build a good team. Many organizations are rushing the process, expecting instant results. Develop a team to handle a specific situation or strategic activity. Teams need to have a structure that identifies the accountability of actions. And teams can't function without some prescribed leadership.
- Managers need to measure performance, but only if it's meaningful. Performance is far more than a firm's stock price, which is often a fallacy anyway, because security analysts foolishly believe that money is real. Companies don't make money, they make products! Stock price is important only to the extent that it affects a firm's ability to raise capital.
- Managing is a balancing act between the long and short term, and between different objectives at different times. Performance concepts and measures should be tied to these different times. Since the stock market is strictly short term it's a severe impediment to long-term planning.
- Mergers have been occurring in the rapidly emerging information technology industry because, in order to remain competitive at this stage, it's more efficient for firms to acquire competitors than to develop their own resources. Conversely, industries that are shrinking use mergers as part of a defensive move. Thus, when you choose a merger partner or make an acquisition you need to understand the business of that firm.
- Managers need to understand what the stock market doesn't: innovation has the power to change everything. In most manufacturing companies 95 per cent of profits come from products that are three or more years old. Innovation is an investment in long-term profitability.

Every quarter Hugo Powell goes before Labatt's board of directors to report where the company is now and where it will be in the next two quarters. One board member has described Powell as a very focused individual who provides specific targets, specific reasoning for the targets, and the specific means of accomplishing them. Given Labatt's commitment to planning, its sound marketing principles, and its reputation as "the savviest marketer in sudsland," it's a good bet that the company will handle any future changes to its industry quite well.

# SUMMARY

**1.** *To define strategic planning and consider its importance for marketing* Strategic planning encompasses both strategic business plans and strategic marketing plans. Strategic business plans describe the overall direction firms will pursue within their chosen environment and guide the allocation of resources and effort. Strategic marketing plans outline what marketing actions to undertake, why those actions are needed, who is responsible for carrying them out, when and where they will be completed, and how they will be coordinated.

Strategic planning provides guidance via a hierarchical process, clarifies goals, encourages cooperation among departments, focuses on strengths and weaknesses (as well as opportunities and threats), examines alternatives, helps allocate resources, and points up the value of monitoring results.

**2.** *To describe the total quality approach to strategic planning and its relevance to marketing* A total quality approach should be used while devising and enacting business and marketing plans. With this approach, a firm adopts a process- and output-related philosophy, by which it strives to fully satisfy consumers in an effective and efficient manner. There is a customer focus; a top management commitment; emphasis on continuous improvement; and support and involvement from employees, suppliers, and channel members.

**3.** *To look at the different kinds of strategic plans and the relationships between marketing and other functional areas in an organization* A firm's strategic plans may be short-run, moderate in length, or long-run. Strategic marketing plans may be for each major product, presented as one company-wide marketing plan, or considered part of an overall business plan. A bottom-up, top-down, or combined management approach may be used.

The interests of marketing and the other key functional areas in a firm need to be accommodated in a strategic plan. Departmental conflict can be reduced by improving communications, employing personnel with broad backgrounds, establishing interdepartmental development programs, and blending departmental goals.

**4.** *To describe thoroughly each of the steps in the strategic planning process* First, a firm defines its organizational mission—the long-term commitment to a type of business and a place in the market. Second, it establishes strategic business units (SBUs), which are self-contained divisions, product lines, or product departments with specific market focuses and separate managers. Third, quantitative and qualitative marketing objectives are set. Fourth, through situation analysis, a firm identifies its internal strengths and weaknesses, as well as external opportunities and threats.

Fifth, a firm develops a marketing strategy—to outline the way in which the marketing mix is used to attract and satisfy the target market(s) and accomplish organizational goals. Every SBU has its own marketing mix. The approaches to strategy planning include the product/market opportunity matrix, the Boston Consulting Group matrix, the General Electric business screen, and the Porter generic strategy model. They should be viewed as planning tools that aid decision making; they do not replace the need for executives to engage in hands-on planning for each situation.

Sixth, a firm uses tactical plans to specify the short-run actions necessary to implement a given marketing strategy. At this stage, specific tasks, a time horizon, and resource allocation are operationalized. Seventh, a firm monitors results by comparing actual performance against planned performance; and this information is fed back into the strategic planning process. Adjustments in strategy are made as needed.

**5.** *To show how a strategic plan may be devised and applied* Strategic planning works best when it is done systematically and comprehensively. This is exemplified by Labatt Brewing Company, one of Canada's finest brewers.

# KEY TERMS

**strategic business plan** (p. 537)

**strategic marketing plan** (p. 537)

**total quality** (p. 538)

**strategic planning process** (p. 541)

**organizational mission** (p. 542)

**strategic business unit (SBU)** (p. 542)

**situation analysis** (p. 545)

**marketing strategy** (p. 545)

**product/market opportunity matrix** (p. 546)

**market penetration** (p. 546)

**market development** (p. 546)

**product development** (p. 546)

**diversification** (p. 546)

**Boston Consulting Group matrix** (p. 547)

**star** (p. 548)

**cash cow** (p. 548)

**question mark** (p. 548)

**dog** (p. 548)

**General Electric business screen** (p. 549)

**Porter generic strategy model** (p. 551)

**tactical plan** (p. 552)

**monitoring results** (p. 554)

# REVIEW QUESTIONS

1. What are the benefits of strategic planning?
2. Explain Figure 16-1, which deals with the total quality approach.
3. Distinguish between bottom-up and top-down strategic plans. What are the pros and cons of each?
4. Why are conflicts between marketing and other functional areas inevitable? How can these conflicts be reduced or avoided?
5. Under what circumstances should a company consider reappraising its organizational mission?
6. What is a strategic business unit? Why is this concept so important for strategic planning?
7. In situation analysis, what is the distinction between strengths and opportunities and between weaknesses and threats? How should a firm react to each of these factors?
8. Compare the BCG matrix, the General Electric business screen, and the Porter generic strategy models.
9. Explain how tactical decisions differ from strategic decisions.
10. What are the ingredients of a good strategic plan?

# DISCUSSION QUESTIONS

1. Do you think your college or university is following a total quality approach? Why or why not? What total quality recommendations would you make for your school?
2. Comment on this statement: "In the market-oriented view of the strategic planning process, financial goals are seen as results and rewards, not the fundamental purpose of business."
3. What issues should a small airline study during situation analysis? How could it react to them?
4. Give a current example of each of these strategic approaches: market development, product development, market penetration, and diversification. Evaluate the strategies.
5. Develop a rating scale to use in analyzing the industry attractiveness and company business strengths of a small stock brokerage firm, a medium-sized management consulting firm, or a large auto supplies manufacturer.

## CASE STUDY

# Softimage: A Portfolio Acquisition and Divestiture

Montreal software company Softimage (Soff Imajh in French), was a world leader in technology. It was purchased by Microsoft in 1994 for $130 million because Bill Gates, CEO of Microsoft, saw Softimage's products as the wave of the future. Softimage had advanced its software technology years ahead of Microsoft's, and Gates realized that Microsoft would never be able to catch up. His solution was simple: he bought Softimage and Microsoft caught up immediately.

Softimage is a computer animation software company. The driving force behind the firm was former owner Daniel Langlois, who developed the software that put Softimage on the leading edge. It has animated advertising spots for soft drink cans, as well as the dinosaurs for the blockbuster film *Jurassic Park*. The customers for Softimage were largely filmmakers and video game firms, which had big budgets and special needs. Bill Gates acquired the company because he felt there was a powerful desire on the part of consumers to go beyond playing games and movies on their computers. He believed that users would want to create their own games and films and to customize existing ones to their own needs—and that Softimage's technology was what they'd need to reach this new level of sophistication.

Microsoft was betting that the young generation of computer savants would get as much fun out of designing games as playing them. Today's players are demanding more and more sophistication and virtual reality from video games— and Softimage has the technology that will allow them to design such games for themselves. Imagine: people designing their own virtual reality, limited solely by their dreams and the amount of RAM they have in their computers. Softimage was well positioned to seize this future, and after the acquisition, so was Microsoft. It drew on Softimage's expertise in 3-D animation and gathered key technology and specifications to create programs such as Direct3D API, Microsoft's 3-D rendering API.

But when the expected mass market of "self-game designers" didn't materialize and Microsoft decided it was too big to worry about the niche markets served by Softimage, it decided to divest it. In June 1998 Microsoft sold Softimage to Avid Technology Inc., a Massachusetts-based provider of digital video, film, and audio solutions. Softimage fit perfectly into Avid's portfolio, since it produced the very products that Avid Technology was seeking to market. Avid gained leading-edge technology, and Softimage was able to return to its primary focus, with access to more customers and markets than ever before. (Avid Technologies has sales offices in Canada, the U.S., Japan, Singapore, the United Kingdom, Germany, Italy, and France.)

With Avid's expertise and customer access, the list of Softimage customers reads like a who's who of the professional content-creation and post-production industries. Nearly every major production company uses Softimage products, including Blue Sky Studios, BUF Compagnie, Casablanca, CBS Television, Centropolis Effects, Colossal Pictures, Cyan, Digital Domain, Dreamworks Interactive, Dreamworks SKG, Electronic Arts Inc., First Edition Editorial, Fox Animation Studios, The Framestore, Industrial Light & Magic, Mainframe Entertainment, The Mill, Modern Video and Film, NBC, Nintendo of America, Pacific Data Images, Psygnosis Inc., R/Greenberg Associates Inc., Sega Enterprises, Sony Music Entertainment, TerraGlyph Interactive Studios, Tippett Studios, Varga Studio Ltd., and Viacom New Media.

As part of Avid Technology, Softimage has the following mission: "Softimage Inc. is a leading developer of high-end software for all areas of professional visual content production, with tools for creating 3-D and 2-D animation, as well as for creating, editing, and finishing video programs. The company's goal is to make the industry's leading tools available to the broadest possible audience of professional digital artists. Softimage is achieving this goal by devel-oping groundbreaking products, inspired by artists and editors, that are transparent to the creative process. The company is also dedicated to forging strong alliances with independent software and hardware developers, offering customers software on a choice of hardware platforms, and conducting ongoing research and development that sets the industry pace for future products."

## Questions

1. Evaluate the reasons why Microsoft first acquired Softimage and then divested it. Which do you think benefited most during the four-year relationship, and why?
2. Evaluate Softimage's mission under Avid Technologies in the context of the organizational missions described in this chapter. Is it a good mission statement? How do you think it's changed since the firm was owned by Microsoft?
3. Comment on Softimage's position in the software industry. How would you classify the firm according to the Boston Consulting Group Matrix and to the Porter Generic Strategy Model? Justify your classifications.
4. Develop some short-term and basic marketing strategy objectives for Softimage to help it accomplish its mission. Consider its customer list and current target-market strategy in developing these objectives.

**SOFTIMAGE**
www.softimage.com

Sources: Based on Softimage Corporate Web site, Merle MacIsaac, "Wizard of Awe," *Canadian Business* (December 1994), p. 29; and "Softimage" CBC *Venture* Video 476.

## CASE STUDY
# Reebok's Seven-Point Turnaround Plan

American Paul Fireman became aware of Reebok (then a small British shoe maker) at a 1979 Chicago trade show, and quickly purchased the exclusive rights to sell Reebok running shoes in North America. Fireman acquired Reebok in 1984 and later renamed it Reebok International.

After Fireman's acquisition Reebok's first major new-product success was its Freestyle line of aerobic shoes. In order to avoid directly competing against Nike, Reebok targeted Freestyle shoes at the female market—and they became one of the best-selling shoes in history. This was instrumental in pushing Reebok's sales from $U.S.3.5 million in 1982 to $U.S.919 million in 1986, and in giving Reebok a sales edge over Nike. Reebok kept this sales advantage until 1990. Since then Nike has surged ahead and Reebok has struggled, although it's still the world's second-largest athletic shoe maker with 1998 sales of $U.S.3.22 billion.

Reebok Unlimited had a very poor year in 1998. To turn the division around Paul Fireman hired Carl Yankowski, formerly of Sony Corporation, to be president and CEO. Together Fireman and Yankowski designed a seven-point plan, a key element of which was to reposition Reebok Unlimited using the concept of "humanity." The idea was to demonstrate Reebok Unlimited as having "the values of creativity, free-spiritedness, and individualism."

Here is Reebok Unlimited's seven-point plan:

1) Reebok is implementing a new SBU organizational structure. The purpose is to increase internal accountability and enable Reebok to get closer to its customers while understanding their needs. Reebok created the following five SBUs: classic footwear; performance footwear and global apparel; kids' products; retail operations; and new business that will extend the Reebok brand beyond the current product mix.
2) The Reebok brand will stand for humanity, fair play, and doing the right thing. Reebok will stand for products that deliver performance. The new marketing platform will be "Are you feeling it?"
3) Reebok will "create three annual prime mover events. These events will be large-scale global events and will be specifically designed to generate retail interest and excitement for the Reebok brand." Reebok is "committed to refocusing our efforts on the 'last three feet' of the sale, assisting retailers and their sales associates in closing sales and moving more product through their stores."
4) Consumers want product personalization and Reebok is going to give it to them with a "new multi-functional personalization team." Reebok "will develop a wider variety of widths, lengths, and fits for many popular Reebok footwear sizes and models."
5) Because many consumers have a hard time distinguishing among shoe products and brands displayed on shoe store walls, Reebok is going to develop a distinctive look so that its brand stands out. Reebok plans to make its "apparel and footwear ... so unique in style, colour, and choice of materials that you would recognize it as Reebok merchandise even if [the] name or logo was not prominent."
6) Sales declines for Reebok brand products were related to a number of global industry factors, such as "changing fashion trends, a lingering shoe glut in the U.S., deteriorating economic conditions in Asia-Pacific, Latin America, and Russia, as well as currency fluctuations." Because Reebok is a global company that wants to be able to identify and react to these trends as soon as possible, it intends to install a new state-of-the-art SAP information system, which "should provide definitive performance benchmarks to guide and improve the accountability of our newly formed strategic business units. They should also enable us to manufacture, market, and fulfill our products to retailers and consumers in new and exciting ways."
7) The R&D group must improve Reebok's efficiency and speed to market. Overall product quality will be improved, while development times and costs will be reduced "through processes such as computer-aided engineering and rapid prototyping." Reebok will "invest in innovative technologies, processes, and controls to improve the speed and efficiency of ... product development, manufacturing, sample generation, and overall distribution and logistics to keep Reebok on the leading edge of change."

### Questions
1. Evaluate the five SBUs listed in point 1 of Reebok's plan according to the attributes for SBUs presented in this chapter. Are the SBUs appropriate according to these criteria? Explain.
2. Examine the seven points of the plan and identify the marketing objectives that Reebok has set. Evaluate their appropriateness.
3. Evaluate Reebok's planned positioning statement. What do you think of it? Does the seven-point plant support this positioning? Why or why not?
4. Reebok is a global competitor. Evaluate its seven-point plan with respect to global competition. Is it adequate or inadequate? Write out a point 8 that deals specifically with global issues mentioned in the case.

Sources: Based on Hoovers, Reebok Company Capsule, Hoovers Online, www.hoovers.com; Reebok 1998 Annual Report, Reebok Corporate Web site, www.reebok.com; Press Release, "Christopher Lee Named Creative Director of the Reebok Brand," *GO News* (July 10, 1999), www.gonews.com; Jeff Jensen, "Better Days Ahead for Planet Reebok," *Advertising Age* (June 26, 1995), p. 4; and Kenneth Labich, "Nike Vs. Reebok: A Battle for Hearts, Minds, and Feet," *Fortune* (September 18, 1995), pp. 90–106.

CHAPTER | 17

# Integrating and Analyzing the Marketing Plan

### Chapter Objectives

**1.** To show the value of an integrated marketing plan

**2.** To discuss the elements of a well-integrated marketing plan

**3.** To present five types of marketing plan analysis: benchmarking, customer satisfaction research, marketing cost analysis, sales analysis, and the marketing audit

**4.** To see the merit of anticipating and planning for the future

Al Harvey: The Slide Farm

**S**imply stated, corporate strategy involves doing the right things—and doing these things right. Management tools are critical if an organization is going to implement strategic changes and then evaluate the results. Management tools that were widely discussed in the late 1990s included: strategic planning, strategic alliances, customer satisfaction measures, mission and vision statements, pay for performance, core competencies, benchmarking, growth strategies, total quality management, and corporate reengineering (also called downsizing).

Management techniques and tools seem to go in and out of style. According to a survey in *Fortune* presented by Darrell K. Rigby of Bain and Company, the most popular management tools at the end of the 1990s were: strategic planning (90 per cent), mission and vision statements (87 per cent), benchmarking (86 per cent), customer satisfaction measurement (79 per cent), and pay for performance (78 per cent).

Most of the managers surveyed by Bain and Company said that the tools promised more than they delivered. In many cases the effectiveness of the tools varied considerably in their ability to improve financial performance, create competitive advantage, or establish a consumer franchise. Rigby states: "Management tools are not silver bullets. They are more like chain saws—potentially powerful when applied to the right problems, but extraordinarily dangerous in the wrong hands."

Executives reported having the greatest difficulty using activity-based costing, knowledge management, and in particular, reengineering. In 1995 78 per cent of managers reported the latter as their favourite tool, but by 1997 its rating was favourable with only 64 per cent of managers. In a comparative measurement subtracting dissatisfied users from satisfied users, reengineering comes out negative with a score of -1; total quality management, also a hot tool in the mid-1990s, comes out with a score of 2. In short, there are some strongly dissatisfied users of these tools.

The hot tools for managers today include those that focus on retaining customers, overcoming competition, speeding up innovation, and motivating employees. The first three usually require organizations to focus a great deal on their marketing activities. Managers are now seeking to achieve earnings performance from sales growth, not cost cutting, and so there's been a corresponding shift to tools that involve strategy rather than operations.[1]

In this chapter, we will study how a firm can integrate and analyze its marketing plan—and see the value of developing and implementing a clear, forward-looking, cohesive, and adaptable strategy.

## Overview

Chapters 1 and 2 introduced basic marketing concepts and described the marketing environment. Chapter 3 focused on the role of marketing information systems and marketing research. Chapters 4 to 13 centred on specific aspects of marketing: describing and selecting target markets, and the marketing mix (product, distribution, promotion, and price planning). Chapter 16 presented the strategic planning process as it applies to marketing.

This chapter ties things together, and describes how a marketing plan can be integrated and evaluated. It builds on the discussion of strategic planning in Chapter 16—particularly, the total quality approach (whereby a firm strives to fully satisfy customers in an effective and efficient manner). With an integrated marketing effort, individual marketing components are synchronized and everyone is "on the same page." And when an organization wants to appraise performance, capitalize on strengths, minimize weaknesses, and plan for the future, marketing analysis (including benchmarking and customer satisfaction) is necessary.

This is the challenge, as one expert sees it:

> Do you know where your marketing plan is? In a world where competitors observe and rapidly imitate each other's advancements in product development, pricing, packaging, and distribution, internal and external communication is more important than ever as a way of differentiating your business from those of competitors. At its most basic level, a marketing plan defines a business niche, summarizes objectives, and presents strategies for getting from point A to point B. But roadmaps need constant updating to reflect the addition of new routes. Likewise, in a decade in which technology, international relations, and the competitive landscape are constantly changing, the concept of a static marketing plan has to be reassessed.
>
> Two of today's hottest buzzwords are "interactive" and "integrated." A successful marketing plan has to be both. "Interactive" means your marketing plan should be a conversation between your business and your customers. It's your chance to tell customers about your business and to listen and act on their responses. "Integrative" means the message in your marketing is consistently reinforced by every department within your company. Marketing is as much a function of the finance and manufacturing areas as it is the advertising and public relations areas.[2]

*Wal-Mart's ten basic rules are applied to a wide range of firms.*

Thus, every organization can learn from the focused management rules of Wal-Mart, the world's leading retailer. These principles were developed by the late Sam Walton, the firm's founder, and are in his words:

1. "Commit to your business. Believe in it more than anybody else."

2. "Share your profits with all your associates [workers] and treat them as partners. In turn, they will treat you as a partner."

3. "Motivate your partners [workers]. Constantly, day by day, think of new and more interesting ways to motivate and challenge. Set high goals, encourage competition, and keep score."

4. "Communicate everything you possibly can to your partners [workers]. The more they know, the more they'll understand. The more they understand, the more they'll care. Once they care, there's no stopping them."

5. "Appreciate everything your associates do for the business. Nothing else can quite substitute for a few well-chosen, well-timed, sincere words of praise. They're absolutely free and worth a fortune."

6. "Celebrate your successes. Find humour in your failures. Don't take yourself so seriously. Loosen up and everybody around you will loosen up."

7. "Listen to everyone in your company. The folks on the front lines—the ones who actually talk to the customer—are the only ones who really know what's going on out there. You'd better find out what they know. This is really what total quality is all about."

8. "Exceed your customers' expectations. If you do, they'll come back over and over. Make good on all your mistakes, and don't make excuses—apologize. The two most important words I ever wrote were on the first Wal-Mart sign: SATISFACTION GUARANTEED."

9. "Control your expenses better than your competition. This is where you can always find the competitive advantage. You can make a lot of different mistakes and still recover if you run an efficient operation. Or you can be brilliant and still go out of business if you're inefficient."

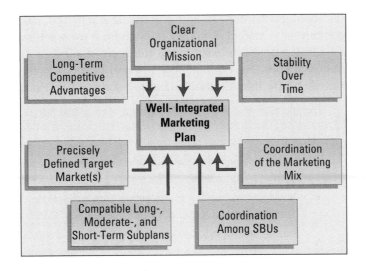

**FIGURE 17-1**

**Elements Leading to a Well-Integrated Marketing Plan**

10. "Swim upstream. Ignore the conventional wisdom. If everybody else is doing it one way, there's a good chance you can find your niche by going in exactly the opposite direction."[3]

# Integrating the Marketing Plan

When a marketing plan is properly integrated, all of its various parts are unified, consistent, and coordinated; and a total quality approach can be followed. Although this appears a simple task, it is important to recall that a firm may have long-run, moderate-length, and short-run plans; the different strategic business units in an organization may require separate marketing plans; and each aspect of the marketing mix requires planning. For example:

*From a total quality perspective, the many parts of a marketing plan should be unified, consistent, and coordinated.*

- An overall plan is poorly integrated if short-run profits are earned at the expense of moderate- or long-run profits. This could occur if marketing research or new-product planning expenditures are reduced to raise profits temporarily. A firm could also encounter difficulties if plans are changed too frequently, leading to a blurred image for consumers and a lack of focus for executives.

- Resources need to be allocated among SBUs, so funds are given to those with high potential. The target markets, product images, price levels, and so on, of each SBU must be distinctive—yet not in conflict with one another. Physical distribution efforts and channel member arrangements need to be timed so the system and its role in a total quality program are not strained by two or more SBUs making costly demands simultaneously.

- Even though a promotion plan primarily deals with one strategic element, it must also be integrated with product, distribution, and pricing plans. It must reflect the proper image for a firm's products, encourage channel cooperation, and demonstrate that products are worth the prices set.

A well-integrated marketing plan incorporates the elements shown in Figure 17-1. These elements are explained next.

## Clear Organizational Mission

A clear organizational mission outlines a firm's commitment to a type of business and a place in the market. It directs the company's total quality efforts. The organizational mission is involved whenever a firm seeks new customer groups or abandons existing ones, adds or deletes product lines, acquires other firms or sells part of its own business, performs different marketing functions, and/or shifts technological focus

*The organizational mission should be clear and directive.*

(as noted in Chapter 16). Both top management and marketing personnel must be committed to an organizational mission for it to be achieved; and the mission must be communicated to customers, company employees, suppliers, and distribution intermediaries. For example, the Internet Advertising Bureau of Canada's mission statement specifies the constituencies it serves and the activities it undertakes:

> The Internet Advertising Bureau of Canada is an organization of Internet publishers and advertisers who have made a commitment to become a national advocate for marketing and advertising on the Internet and to bring structure and standards to the industry. IAB Canada intends to:
>
> - Act as a collective voice representing companies engaged in selling advertising on Internet-based media.
> - Provide advertisers and marketers with a forum for evaluating and shaping the direction of the Internet advertising industry in Canada.
> - Provide an industry-wide view of key developments in Internet advertising and interactive media.
> - Promote the value of Internet advertising to advertisers and advertising agencies.
> - Serve as an educational resource through which advertisers and marketers can further their Internet knowledge and gain a competitive edge in the marketplace.[4]

Many experts believe a firm should reappraise its organizational mission if the company has values that do not fit a changing environment, its industry undergoes rapid changes, its performance is average or worse, it is changing size (from small to large or large to small), or opportunities unrelated to its original mission arise.

## Long-Term Competitive Advantages

*Competitive advantages should centre on company, product, and marketing attributes with long-range distinctiveness.*

Long-term competitive advantages are company, product, and marketing attributes whose distinctiveness and appeal to consumers can be maintained over an extended period of time. A firm must capitalize on the attributes that are most important to consumers and prepare competitive advantages accordingly. For competitive advantages to be sustainable, consumers must perceive a consistent positive difference in key attributes between the company's offerings and those of competitors; that difference must be linked to a capability gap that competitors will have difficulty in closing (due to patents, superior marketing skills, customer loyalty, and other factors); and the company's offerings must appeal to some enduring consumer need. While concentrating on its competitive advantages, a company should not lose sight of the importance of customer service and its role in a total quality program.

As Michael Treacy and Fred Wiersema say in their best-selling book, *The Discipline of Market Leaders*:

> Today's market leaders understand the battle they're in. They know they have to redefine value by raising customer expectations in the one component of value they choose to highlight. Casio, for instance, establishes new affordability levels for familiar products such as calculators; Hertz makes car rental nearly as convenient as taking a cab; Lands' End shows individuals that they're not just a number; and Home Depot proves that old-fashioned, knowledgeable advice hasn't gone the way of trading stamps.
>
> But wait a minute. These companies don't shine in every way. A successful company like Wal-Mart doesn't peddle haute couture; Lands' End doesn't sell clothing for the lowest possible cost; and Starbucks, the Seattle coffee chain, doesn't slide a cup of java under your nose any faster or more conveniently than anyone else. Yet, all of these companies are thriving because they shine in a way their customers care most about. They have honed at least one component of value to a level of excellence that puts all competitors to shame. Our research shows that no company can succeed today by trying to be all things to all people. It must instead find the unique value that it alone can deliver to a chosen market.[5]

Because smaller firms often cannot compete on the basis of low prices, they tend to concentrate on other competitive advantages, such as:

**STARBUCKS**
www.starbucks.com/home.asp

# INTERNATIONAL MARKETING IN ACTION

## Deregulation: Turning a Challenge into an Opportunity

When an industry that used to be a protected monopoly is forced into the world of competition it faces new challenges and is given new opportunities. Here are examples of companies from the United States, the United Kingdom, France, and Australia that were given this challenge, and how they turned it into an opportunity.

When Sempra Energy of California was faced with deregulation it realized that it needed to establish a brand name and an image with consumers. Its unique solution? Sempra spent U.S.$20 million and took out a ten-year sponsorship in the new Staples Centre, home-to-be of the NHL's Los Angeles Kings and the NBA's L.A. Lakers and L.A. Clippers. According to Jerry Florence, senior vice-president of corporate communications, the reason was simple: "Our name recognition is not that high. Associating with a state-of-the-art arena is allowing us to get our name out in a big way with the major, major companies."

Deregulation of the utility sector in the U.K. is allowing both gas and water companies to sell electricity, as well as former electric companies. Of course, the electric companies can also sell gas. The result? A flurry of advertising to get consumers to combine their utility services with one company. So far it's been the commercial customers that have really jumped on the bandwagon, since they're price-sensitive and price-responsive. Consumer markets, however, have been slow to respond. Britons are used to the poor service that came with high prices, and don't want to risk the poorer service that one expects with low prices.

The telecommunications market in France was deregulated in response to the requirements of the European Union. France Telecom now has two competitors in the long-distance national and international market, but it's been well prepared. In the mid-1990s the French government hired the head of Carrefour, a topnotch French retailer, to run the company, which then prepared and implemented an aggressive pricing and marketing strategy. So even before competition arrived France Telecom had been lowering long-distance rates while slowly raising local phone rates, where it wouldn't face competition. As a result French phone customers have been inoculated against competitors' appeals of "lower" long-distance rates.

Finally, deregulation of the telephone industry in Australia brought in two new national competitors and caused the former government-owned Telecom Australia to change its name to Telstra. Telstra has developed into "the largest direct marketer in Australia, as well as one of the biggest advertisers." It's relying on pricing, telemarketing, and advertising to secure a leadership position and promote its long-distance, cellular, and Internet service. Of course, Telstra has the same ace up its sleeve as France Telecom: monopoly control of the local phone market.

Discuss how each of these firms seized the opportunity presented by deregulation.

Sources: Based on Kathy Tyrer, "A Shift in Power," *Marketing Magazine* (April 26, 1999), p. 14; Virginia Matthews, "Will They Stay or Will They Go?" *Marketing Magazine* (April 26, 1999), p. 16; Dilip Subramanian, "France Telecom Holds Its Own," *Marketing Magazine* (April 26, 1999), p. 18; and Chris Pritchard, "Slugging It Out Down Under," *Marketing Magazine* (April 26, 1999), p. 19.

- Targeting underserved market niches, including international ones.
- Having unique offerings through specialization. Firms can be innovative, process customized orders, or otherwise adapt products for particular customers.
- Stressing product quality and reliability. "The more crucial the performance of a product to customer needs, the lower will be the concern with pricing."
- Engaging in extra efforts to gain customer loyalty by making the purchase process easy, giving superior service, and promising the long-term availability of goods and services. As one small-firm manager said, "We know our products are reliable and do not require visits. But when our clients see us physically inspect-

ing machines, sometimes merely dusting them, they have a sense of security and comfort." This is a total quality approach.

- Emphasizing relationship marketing, whereby personal relationships with their suppliers are viewed as important by customers.[6]

When implementing a marketing strategy, a firm should note that its competitive advantages may not apply in all situations. For instance, an advantage can lose its value when transferred to another nation. This can occur because an advantage is not relevant in a different context or because it can easily be countered by local competitors: "Products that are superior in the home market may not offer customer-perceived value in the target country because the price is too high or the degree of sophistication is excessive. The value of well-known brand names and trademarks can be reduced by piracy and imitation. Technological advantages can be neutralized by the weakness of intellectual property law and laxity in enforcing the law. Whether an advantage retains its value depends on the fit between conditions in the target country and the nature of the advantage."[7]

## Precisely Defined Target Market(s)

By precisely defining its target market(s), a firm identifies the specific customers to be addressed in its marketing plans. This guides the firm's current marketing efforts and future direction. For example, as noted in Figure 17-2, IBM is focused on business customers interested in computer networking. IBM has been repositioning its image away from being a company that provides hardware to businesses to being a company that provides expertise to businesses on a global basis. The "Solutions for a small planet" slogan is so critical to this new positioning that IBM has trademarked it. This ad features an IBM e-business, medical consulting, but IBM runs a number of ads with different themes to appeal to different business needs. In one ad the theme is "Secure" and the focus of the ad is how IBM can help protect businesses' system networks from hackers and other people who might break in. Another ad uses the theme "Merge" and talks about how IBM can help a firm's various offices around the world work as a team even if the various offices have different computer platforms such as Windows, UNIX, Mac or OS/2.[8] Whenever a firm such as IBM engages in differentiated marketing (multiple segmentation), it is essential that each segment be described fully.

A firm's target market approach may have to be fine-tuned due to changing demographics and lifestyles—or falling sales. Today, a lot of consumers are more demanding:

> The balance of power between producers and buyers has shifted to the latter. Most industries today are no longer constrained by supply. In fact, an overabundance of suppliers is crowding every part of the market. Customers, who are becoming more astute in their buying practices every day, have tremendous choice in deciding who will get their business. The 1990s have become the "value decade"; buyers carefully examine total offerings to find out which one yields the best overall value compared to alternatives. The challenge is to give customers all of what they want, and none of what they don't want: the best quality *and* the best prices, served quickly *and* with a smile![9]

In this context, a total quality approach is especially crucial in attracting and retaining consumers.

## Compatible Long-, Moderate-, and Short-Term Subplans

The long-, moderate-, and short-term marketing subplans of a firm need to be compatible with one another. Long-term plans are the most general and set a broad framework for moderate-term plans. Short-term plans are the most specific; but they need to be derived from both moderate- and long-term plans. At Motorola, this means "placing farsighted bets on a wide array of technologies while expanding in fast-growing, developing markets. We think we're making balanced investments for the future."[10]

Unfortunately, adequate plans and subplans are not always set—or are not communicated to employees. According to one study of employees at small and midsized firms, 77 per cent say their firms have a clear organizational mission; 55 per cent feel top management actions support the organizational mission; 57 per cent believe all departments, branches, and divisions have specific and measurable goals; 38 per cent feel all employees understand what is expected of them; and 22 per cent say all employees are held accountable for daily performance.[11] For a total quality program to work, these percentages must be considerably higher.

*Long-, moderate-, and short-term subplans must be compatible.*

**MOTOROLA**
www.mot.com/

One important current trend among many companies is the shrinking time frame of marketing plans:

> Because customer priorities are constantly changing, a marketing plan should change with them. For years, conventional wisdom was "prepare a five-year marketing plan and review it every year." But change happens a lot faster than it did twenty or even ten years ago. For that reason, Bob Dawson of The Business Group, a consulting firm, recommends that firms prepare three-year plans and review them every quarter. Frequent reviews enable companies to identify potential problems and opportunities before the competition does. "Preventative maintenance for a company is as important as putting oil in a car," Dawson says. "You don't wait a whole year to do it. You can't change history, but you can anticipate what's going to happen."[12]

## Coordination Among SBUs

*SBUs should be coordinated.*

Coordination among an organization's SBUs is enhanced when the functions, strategies, and resources allocated to each are described in long-term, moderate-term and short-term plans. For instance, at GE (General Electric), the firm from which the SBU concept was first derived, there are now ten SBUs (Aircraft Engines, Capital Services, Lighting, NBC, Power Systems, Appliances, Industrial Systems, Medical Systems, Plastics, and Transportation Systems), down from 350 several years ago: "Only businesses that were number one or number two in their markets could win in the increasingly global arena. Those that were not leaders were fixed, closed, or sold." Today, GE states: "We are a learning company, a company that studies its own successes and failures and those of others—a company that has the self-confidence and the resources to take big swings and pursue numerous opportunities based on winning ideas and insights, regardless of their source. That appetite for learning, and the ability to act quickly on that learning, will provide GE with what we believe is an insurmountable and sustainable competitive advantage as we pursue our three big growth initiatives." General Electric's three big growth initiatives will involve: 1) globalization, 2) a concentration on selling product services to augment the firm's products, and 3) implementation of an operating process efficiency program called Six Sigma quality.[13]

The coordination of SBUs by large multinational firms can be particularly complex. For example, ABB (Asea Brown Boveri) has 175 global managers at its Swiss headquarters. They oversee 200 000 employees and 1000+ companies, which operate in 140 countries around the globe and generate U.S.$31.2 billion in sales. ABB is primarily involved in developing systems for the generation, transmission, and distribution of power. In particular ABB invests in such countries as China, which is developing new projects and infrastructure for power generation. "ABB isn't Japanese, nor is it Swiss or Swedish. It's a global firm without a national identity, though its mailing address is in Zurich. The company's top thirteen managers hold frequent meetings in different countries. Since they share no common first language, they speak only English, a foreign tongue to all but one."[14]

## Coordination of the Marketing Mix

*The marketing mix within each SBU has to be coordinated.*

The components of the marketing mix (product, distribution, promotion, and price) need to be coordinated and consistent with a firm's organizational mission. For example, Intuit Inc. is a computer software maker that was founded in 1984. It specializes in user-friendly, personal-finance programs for PCs. From 1984 to 1986 sales were very low due to a lack of startup capital: "Without money, there were no distribution channels and no customers. What computer store would carry an unknown software product , unsupported by advertising?" The firm then invested $170 000 in advertising—and sales took off. Today Intuit is a U.S.$600 million firm and the leading personal-finance software company. Intuit products are preloaded offerings on many of the personal computer products sold, and are carried by virtually every type of computer software store. Its current marketing mix is outstanding and adheres to a total quality philosophy:

- *Products*—Intuit's Quicken software is the leading personal-finance program on the market. Quicken helps consumers balance their chequebooks, set up budgets, and monitor investments. Intuit also offers TurboTax, a special tax filing application that must be upgraded and sold each year. Consumers can log onto Quicken.com and get help with their personal finances. They can bank online, plus make investments, shop for mortgages and insurance, and get advice on retirements, life events, small businesses, tax planning, and savings and spending.

- *Distribution*—Intuit products are sold by all types of retailers across North America and in a number of other countries, including Wal-Mart, major computer chains, a number of bookstores, and mail-order firms. Some of Intuit's software is even bundled with computer hardware, such as the Quicken program available with PCs sold by Dell Computer. Through www.quicken.com people can also download the software products, and acquire the online banking services direct from Intuit.

- *Promotion*—Although ad expenditures are modest, Intuit runs ads in such magazines as *PC* and *ComputerLife*, and seeks out publicity. Intuit has also developed relationships with Excite, America Online, and CNNfn to promote their Internet offerings to customers. The firm spends about 10 per cent of revenues on customer service personnel, including technical-support people who handle 800-number telephone calls.

- *Price*—Quicken and TurboTax are priced at $59.95 and $44.95 on Intuit's Web site. The "street prices" (the discounted prices offered by resellers) are often even less. Included in purchases are a detailed owner's manual, the right to upgrades at a modest price, and telephone support service. Finally, Quicken's online banking service is based on transactions processed. Of course users must have purchased the Quicken software before they can access the online banking service, which charges $9.95 a month and provides the user with twenty free transactions. After that, the cost is $2.95 for every five transactions.[15]

## Stability Over Time

A marketing plan must have a certain degree of stability over time for it to be implemented and evaluated properly. This does not mean a plan should be inflexible and therefore unable to adjust to a dynamic environment. Rather, it means a broad marketing plan, consistent with a firm's organizational mission and total quality approach, should guide long-term efforts and be fine-tuned regularly; the basic plan should remain in effect for a number of years. Short-run marketing plans can be much more flexible, as long as they conform to long-term goals and the organizational mission. Thus, low prices might be part of a long-term marketing plan, but in any particular year, prices might have to be raised in response to environmental forces.

An example of a firm striving to maintain a stable but flexible approach is Bell Canada. It's been serving Canadians since the 1880s, and up until July 1994 when it faced full competition in the long-distance phone market, it was *the* phone company. Today Bell wages a battle to maintain its long-distance customer base in the face of severe competition, which has seen its market share fall from 100 to 42.5 per cent in five years. Bell Canada is the leading Internet service provider in Canada; its Sympatico.ca service commands 16.8 per cent of the market, which is about four times as much as the next largest competitor. (But although the number of users has been increasing at rates near 50 per cent, Sympatico's market share has been falling.)

*The stability of the basic plan should be maintained over time.*

**BELL CANADA**
www.bell.ca

Bell Canada had revenues of $12.7 billion in 1998, which ranks it with the top twenty businesses in Canada. Bell's parent firm, BCE, was the second largest company in Canada in sales, with $27.4 billion in 1998.

Bell Canada will soon face a new threat. The local calling services for which the firm held a monopoly are being thrown open to competition. There are already twenty local phone companies that have successfully made application to the CRTC.

Bell Canada plans to battle these competitive threats with a series of new retail services and initiatives. For example, high-speed Internet services will allow users to take calls or send and receive faxes while they're online. The service will use Nortel's advanced 1-meg modem that will give users an "always on" direct connection to the Internet. In combination with Bell Mobility, Bell Canada will be offering a messaging service that allows a single voice mailbox for both wireline and wireless phone messages. This "Integrated Message Centre" will be extremely convenient for business and non-business customers. Bell is also offering e-mail services whereby people will be able to send and receive e-mail via "screen phones."

Future threats and opportunities for Bell Canada are likely to come from the international market. Thus, in March 1999 U.S.-based Ameritech bought 20 per cent of Bell Canada so that the two firms could share technology and marketing experiences to the benefit of both. In the short term Bell Canada gained some new caller identification technology, and Ameritech gained expertise in Web service technology and call-management services.[16]

# Analyzing the Marketing Plan

**Marketing plan analysis**

*compares actual and targeted achievements.*

**Marketing plan analysis** involves comparing actual performance with planned or expected performance for a specified period of time. If actual performance is unsatisfactory, corrective action may be needed. Also, plans must sometimes be revised because of the impact of uncontrollable variables.

Five techniques used to analyze marketing plans are discussed in the following sections: benchmarking, customer satisfaction research, marketing cost analysis, sales analysis, and the marketing audit. Though our discussion of these tools is limited to their utility in evaluating marketing plans, they may also be employed when developing and modifying these plans.

## Benchmarking

In **benchmarking,** *specific points of comparison are set so performance can be measured.*

**MARRIOTT INTERNATIONAL**
www.marriott.com/

**ALTAMIRA**
www.altamira.com/

For a firm to properly assess the effectiveness of its marketing plans, it must set performance standards. That is, it must specify exactly what constitutes "success." One way to do this is to utilize **benchmarking**, whereby a firm sets its own marketing performance standards based on the competence of the best companies in its industry, innovative companies in other industries anywhere around the world, the prowess of direct competitors, and/or prior actions by the firm itself. Xerox, a leader in this area, uses benchmarking to measure its goods, services, and practices "against the toughest competitors or those recognized as industry leaders."[17] Among the growing number of other firms now using benchmarking are Bell Canada, DuPont, Ford, IBM, Kodak, Marriott, Motorola, and Altamira Mutual Funds. The benchmark for Altamira Mutual Funds is the "10 largest Canadian equity funds." See Figure 17-3.

Benchmarking may be divided into two main categories:

Strategic benchmarks for business performance are measures which set overall direction, and show managers how others have succeeded in similar circumstances. Process bench-

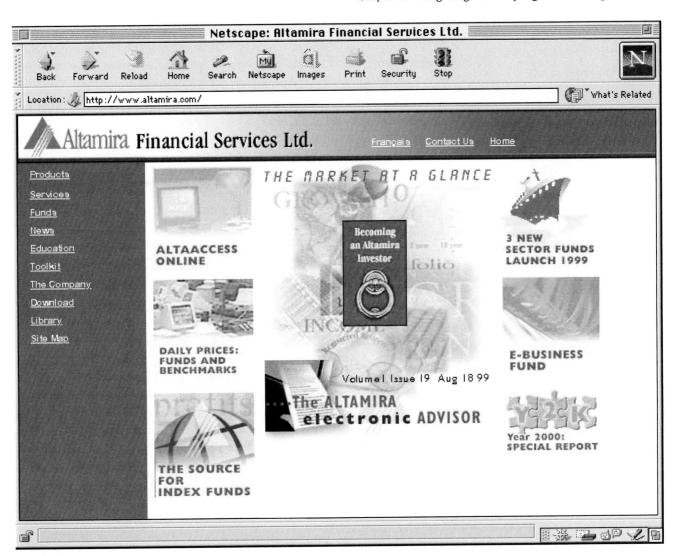

FIGURE 17-3

**Altamira: Benchmarking Versus the Competition**

*Altamira Financial Services*

marks, in contrast, usually indicate standards which should be achievable in day-to-day operations, given the willingness to learn.[18]

A survey of 4137 managers in fifteen different countries indicated that benchmarking was a commonly used tool in their organizations. However, the same survey indicated that only 16 per cent of the respondents were extremely satisfied with the tool while 7 per cent were dissatisfied. According to another worldwide study of over 580 companies in four industries (computer, auto, health care, and banking), a greater percentage of North American firms regularly engage in benchmarking than do their Japanese and German counterparts. Nonetheless, there are some universal truths about total quality that can aid any firm. Those that do best communicate the corporate strategic plan to employees, customers, suppliers, and channel members; upgrade and simplify development and production processes; set up formal practices to certify suppliers and scrutinize and reduce cycle time (how long it takes a firm to get from designing to delivering a good or service).[19]

*There are three steps in the benchmarking ladder: novice, journeyman, and master.*

The sponsors of the just-mentioned study, Ernst & Young and the American Quality Foundation, recommend that a benchmarking program be approached in three stages. Firms can hurt themselves by setting unrealistic goals if they compare themselves to those at a later stage:

- *Novice*—A firm in this category should strive to emulate direct competitors, not world-class companies. It should rely on customers for new-product ideas and choose suppliers mostly on price and reliability criteria. There should be a focus on cost-reduction potential, with a "don't develop it, buy it" thrust. Workers should be rewarded for teamwork and quality. The firm should identify processes that add value, simplify those processes, and move faster in responding to the marketplace.

- *Journeyman*—A firm in this category should encourage workers to find ways to do their jobs better and to simplify operations. It should strive to emulate market leaders and selected world-class companies. Consumer input, formal marketing research, and internal ideas should be used in generating new products. The firm should select suppliers having good quality, and then look at their prices. Compensation for both workers and managers should be linked to teamwork and quality. The firm should refine practices to improve the value added per employee, the time to market, and customer satisfaction.

- *Master*—A firm in this category relies on self-managed, multiskilled teams that emphasize horizontal processes (like product development and logistics). It measures its product development, distribution, and customer service against the world's best. Consumer input, benchmarking, and internal research and development should be used in generating new products. The firm should select suppliers that are technologically advanced and offer superior quality. Strategic partnerships are employed to diversify production. Compensation for senior executives should be linked to teamwork and quality. The firm should continue to refine its practices to improve the value added per employee, the time to market, and customer satisfaction.[20]

Some useful benchmarks for Canadian firms are award achievements like the Canada Export Awards, the Entrepreneur of the Year Award, the Award for Canadian-American Business Achievement, and the Ontario Global Traders Awards. For Canadian firms that do business in the United States, the Malcolm Baldridge National Quality Award criteria and *Fortune's* Corporate Reputations survey criteria are good benchmarks.

Every year the Department of Foreign Affairs and International Trade sponsors a set of Export Awards for Canadian firms that are the leading exporters in their industries in terms of growth. In 1995 the Export Development Corporation and the Canadian Imperial Bank of Commerce also became official sponsors.

The Entrepreneur of the Year Award is sponsored by Air Canada, The Bank of Montreal, Ernst & Young, Nesbitt Burns, McCarthy Tetrault law firm, and *Canadian Business Magazine*. It's granted to firms in five regions: Pacific Canada, the Prairies, Ontario, Quebec, and Atlantic Canada. Within each of these regions an entrepreneur of the year is chosen and then the best entrepreneurs in ten sectors of business are identified. The categories are manufacturing, agriculture and food, retailing, services, emerging entrepreneurs, turnaround entrepreneurs, master entrepreneur, high technology, supporter of entrepreneurship, and socially responsible entrepreneurs.

The award for Canadian–American Business Achievement is sponsored by Nortel (Northern Telecom), FHS International, The Canadian–American Business Council, *Profit Magazine*, and *Canadian Business Magazine*. This award honours cooperative ventures between a Canadian and American firm that "demonstrate business success, innovation, and community contribution."

The Ontario Global Traders Awards began in 1998 and are designed to honour top exporting firms from across Ontario that had sales of less than $25 million and have fewer than 200 employees. The following awards are granted: Partnership Award, Leadership Award, Innovation Award, Market Expansion Award for Products, Market Expansion Award for Services, and an International Business Studies and Achievement Award. The sponsors for these awards include: *Canadian Business Magazine, Profit Magazine,* the government of Ontario, the Bank of Montreal, Deloitte & Touche, Canadian Airlines, the Chartered Accountants of Ontario, and the Export Development Corporation.[21]

A firm does not have to actually participate in any of these competitions to benefit from the benchmarks. Any organization can assess itself and compare its results with others. Canadian firms can benchmark themselves against competitors by applying the cri-teria used for the various awards.

For example, the criteria used for the Baldridge Award involve rating companies in seven areas: leadership; information and analysis (such as competitive comparisons and benchmarks); strategic quality planning; human resource development and management; management of process quality; quality and operational results; and customer focus and satisfaction. Of the maximum 1000 points a company can score, 300 are for customer focus and satisfaction. Fortune's Corporate Reputations survey rates companies in eight areas: quality of management; quality of goods or services; innovativeness; long-term investment value; financial soundness; the ability to attract, develop, and keep talented people; responsibility to the community and the environment; and wise use of corporate resources. Companies are rated within their own industry.

## Customer Satisfaction Research

As defined in Chapter 1, **customer satisfaction** is the degree to which there is a match between a customer's expectations of a good or service and the actual performance of that good or service, including customer service. Today more than ever, companies realize they must measure the level of customer satisfaction through regular research:

> How little we know about these indispensable strangers, our customers. Are they happy? Restless? Was it good for them, too? Will they come back tomorrow? The answers to these questions profoundly affect any business. Indeed, one could say they define a business. They also define the meaning of economic activity, for in the largest sense an economy cannot be described by adding up how many passenger-miles of air travel it logs or how much wood its woodchucks chuck per hour. All these count (and we count them). But in the final analysis, what matters is how well an economy satisfies its customers' needs and wants.[22]

*Research is needed to gauge* **customer satisfaction.** *ACSI is a broad project that is doing so.*

The largest ongoing research project on customer satisfaction in the world is undertaken annually in the United States. The American Customer Satisfaction Index (ACSI) is conducted by the National Quality Research Center and then compiled by statisticians at the University of Michigan. The Research Center contacts over 50 000 U.S. consumers each year and asks them to evaluate 200 different companies and a number of government departments on six different quality indices. The surveys cover "perceptions of service, quality, value, how well the good or service lived up to expectations, how it compared to an ideal, and how willing people were to pay more for it." With a maximum score of 100, these were the highest-rated firms in the 1998 index: Mercedes-Benz (87); H.J. Heinz food processing (86); Colgate-Palmolive, H.J. Heinz pet foods, Mars food processing, Maytag, and Quaker Oats (all at 85); Cadillac, Hershey Foods, Coca-Cola, Toyota, Volvo, and Zenith Electronics (all at 84). The lowest-rated organization in the survey was the United States Internal Revenue Service (54). The average score for all companies was 72.0.[23]

**MERCEDES-BENZ**
www.mercedes.com/

## ETHICS AND TODAY'S MARKETER

### The Car Strip

Launching new products, and especially cars, is a critical strategic move. The first impressions are often lasting ones, so the promotional approaches used to establish a new brand or product need to be carefully thought through. Of course, dull advertising and promotional techniques don't make lasting impressions at all. So French car maker Citroen decided to launch its new Xsara Coupe in the United Kingdom using supermodel Claudia Schiffer in its advertising.

The potential approaches to establishing a high-impact, unique image for the Xsara Coupe ad involving one of the most beautiful women in the world are almost too numerous to mention. Especially when you consider that the car is targeted at young men to begin with. One can imagine a number of possible story lines, including some of the basics:

1. Guy gets car, supermodel likes car, comments on nice features, guy gets supermodel.
2. Supermodel has choice of any car and any guy in the world, supermodel picks ordinary guy in Xsara Coupe.
3. Supermodel is spokesperson for car.

These approaches could exploit Claudia Schiffer's persona and lead to some memorable advertising if they were well done. However, Citroen came up with the following story: Supermodel comes down staircase, supermodel strips completely naked, supermodel drives away in car.

The ad was considered to be in poor taste and drew a large number of complaints from British viewers. Britain's Independent TV Commission upheld the complaints and ruled that the ad was not particularly decent, but they stopped short of banning it. The commission did recommend that the ad not be aired prior to 9:00 p.m.

Citroen's use of the ad is controversial, but it seems to have accomplished its purposes: it had impact and recall and is the most talked-about ad in Britain. Sales of the Xsara Coupe haven't been spectacular, but they are meeting forecasts. The British tabloid press lambasted Claudia Schiffer, but they always do that. Schiffer was paid U.S.\$2.9 million to "bare all," and based on reports she's had very little trouble handling the controversy.

Discuss the risks of building the kind of reputation and image that Citroen is building with advertising like this. See if you can develop an advertising storyline that would carry a lot of impact, reach the intended male target market, and still use Schiffer's supermodel image without being overly sexy.

Source: Based on Virginia Matthews, "Sex That Didn't Sell," *Marketing Magazine* (May 10, 1999), p. 24.

---

Any firm can measure its own customer satisfaction. Here is an eight-step procedure to do so:

1. "Institute a process to tap management, employees, outside consultants, and industry sources for input on the dimensions critical to customer satisfaction. Environmental scanning of trade publications and competitors and a regular program of internal focus groups can accomplish this."

2. "Use this feedback to develop an ongoing program of customer focus groups and personal interviews to identify critical customer satisfaction dimensions."

3. "Work with a professional staff to develop telephone and/or mail survey instruments to reliably and validly incorporate identified dimensions."

4. "Regardless of whether the people developing the survey are internal or external, make sure they understand the theoretical basis of the instruments and are familiar with standard procedures for developing and testing reliable, valid

items. Keep in mind that customer satisfaction survey results that simply describe what was found provide no guidance for developing an action plan to improve satisfaction."

5. "Regularly do surveys and re-evaluate their reliability and validity."

6. "From these data, develop a customer satisfaction metric that not only relates the level of satisfaction of your customers, but also analyzes the importance of the various dimensions of that satisfaction."

7. "Use the dimensional information to develop an action plan for improving each dimension and communicating these improvements to customers. Remember: delivery of customer satisfaction is not a reality if the customer does not notice it."

8. "Tie the performance evaluation and compensation of each employee involved in the action plan to its accomplishment. This will ensure that the customers' goals match employees' goals. Remember: what gets measured gets rewarded, and what gets rewarded gets done."[24]

## Marketing Cost Analysis

**Marketing cost analysis** is used to evaluate the cost efficiency of various marketing factors, such as different total quality configurations, product lines, order sizes, distribution methods, sales territories, channel members, salespersons, advertising media, and customer types. Although a firm may be very profitable, it is highly unlikely that all of its products, distribution methods, and so on are equally cost efficient (or profitable).

*Cost efficiency is measured in* **marketing cost analysis**.

With marketing cost analysis, a firm can determine which factors (classifications) are the most efficient and which are the least efficient, and make appropriate adjustments. It can also generate information that may be needed to substantiate price compliance with the Competition Act.

For this type of analysis to work properly, a firm needs to obtain and to use continuous and accurate cost data. Table 17-1 presents several examples of marketing cost analysis.

Marketing cost analysis consists of three steps: studying natural account expenses, reclassifying natural accounts into functional ones, and allocating functional accounts by marketing classification.

**STUDYING NATURAL ACCOUNT EXPENSES** The first step is to determine the level of expenses for all **natural accounts**, which report costs by the names of the expenses and not by their purposes. Such expense categories include salaries, rent, advertising, supplies, insurance, and interest. These are the names most often entered in accounting records. Table 17-2 shows a natural-account expense classification.

**Natural accounts** *are reported as salaries, rent, and insurance.*

**RECLASSIFYING NATURAL ACCOUNTS INTO FUNCTIONAL ACCOUNTS** Natural accounts are then reclassified into **functional accounts**, which indicate the purposes or activities for which expenditures have been made. Included as functional expenses are marketing administration, personal selling, advertising, transportation, warehousing, marketing research, and general administration. Table 17-3 reclassifies the natural accounts of Table 17-2 into functional accounts.

**Functional accounts** *denote the purpose or activity of expenditures.*

Once functional accounts are established, cost analysis becomes clearer. For instance, if salaries and fringe benefits increase by $25 000 over the prior year, natural account analysis cannot allocate the rise to a functional area. Functional account analysis can pinpoint the areas of marketing that have higher personnel costs.

## TABLE 17-1

## Examples of Marketing Cost Analysis

| MARKETING FACTOR | STRATEGY/TACTICS STUDIED | PROBLEM/OPPORTUNITY DISCOVERED | ACTION APPLIED |
|---|---|---|---|
| Customer type | What are the relative costs of selling X-rays to dentists, doctors, and hospitals? | Per-unit costs of hospital sales are lowest (as are prices); per-unit costs of dentist and doctor sales are highest (as are prices). | Current efforts are maintained. Each customer is serviced. |
| Product | Should a manufacturer accept a retailer's proposal that the firm make 700 000 private-label sneakers? | Substantial excess capacity exists; the private label would require no additional fixed costs. | A contract is signed. Different features for private and manufacturer labels are planned. |
| Distribution | Should a men's suit maker sell directly to consumers, as well as through normal channels? | Startup and personal selling costs would be high. Additional sales would be minimal. | Direct sales are not undertaken. |
| Order size | What is the minimum order size a hardware manufacturer should accept? | Orders below $30 do not have positive profit margins; they are too costly to process. | Small orders are discouraged through surcharges and minimum order size. |
| Advertising media | Which is more effective, TV or magazine advertising? | TV ads cost $0.05 for every potential customer reached; magazine ads cost $0.07. | TV ads are increased. |
| Personal selling | What are the costs of making a sale? | 15 per cent of sales covers compensation and selling expenses, 2 per cent above the industry average. | Sales personnel are encouraged to phone customers before visiting them, to confirm appointments. |

## TABLE 17-2

## A Natural-Account Expense Classification

| | | |
|---|---:|---:|
| Net sales (after returns and discounts) | $ 1 000 000 | |
| Less: Costs of goods sold | 450 000 | |
| Gross profit | | $ 550 000 |
| Less: Operating expenses (natural account expenses) | | |
| Salaries and fringe benefits | 220 000 | |
| Rent | 40 000 | |
| Advertising | 30 000 | |
| Supplies | 6 100 | |
| Insurance | 2 500 | |
| Interest expense | 1 400 | |
| Total operating expenses | | 300 000 |
| Net profit before taxes | | $ 250 000 |

## TABLE 17-3

### Reclassifying Natural Accounts into Functional Accounts

| NATURAL ACCOUNTS | TOTAL | FUNCTIONAL ACCOUNTS | | | | | | |
| | | Marketing Adminis-tration | Personal Selling | Adver-tising | Transpor-tation | Ware-housing | Marketing Research | General Adminis-tration |
| --- | --- | --- | --- | --- | --- | --- | --- | --- |
| Salaries and fringe benefits | $220 000 | $30 000 | $50 000 | $15 000 | $10 000 | $20 000 | $30 000 | $65 000 |
| Rent | 40 000 | 3 000 | 7 000 | 3 000 | 2 000 | 10 000 | 5 000 | 10 000 |
| Advertising | 30 000 | | | 30 000 | | | | |
| Supplies | 6 100 | 500 | 1 000 | 500 | | | 1 100 | 3 000 |
| Insurance | 2 500 | | 1 000 | | | 1 200 | | 300 |
| Interest expense | 1 400 | | | | | | | 1 400 |
| Total | $300 000 | $33 500 | $59 000 | $48 500 | $12 000 | $31 200 | $36 100 | $79 700 |

**ALLOCATING FUNCTIONAL ACCOUNTS BY MARKETING CLASSIFICATION** The third step assigns functional costs by product, distribution method, customer, or another marketing classification. This reports each classification as a profit centre. Table 17-4 shows how costs can be allocated among different products, using the data in Tables 17-2 and 17-3. From Table 17-4, it is clear that product A has the highest sales and highest total profit. However, product C has the greatest profit as a per cent of sales.

*Functional costs are assigned with each marketing classification becoming a profit centre.*

In assigning functional costs, these points should be kept in mind. One, assigning some costs—such as marketing administration—to different products, customers, or other classifications is usually somewhat arbitrary. Two, the elimination of a poorly performing classification would lead to overhead costs—such as general administration—being allotted among the remaining product or customer categories. This may actually result in lower overall total profit. Thus, a firm should distinguish between those separable expenses that are directly associated with a given classification category and can be eliminated if a category is dropped, and those common expenses that are shared by various categories and cannot be eliminated if one is dropped.[25]

A firm must differentiate between order-generating and order-processing costs (described in Chapter 16) before making any strategic changes suggested by marketing cost analysis:

> After a decade of frantic cost-cutting, the downside of downsizing is beginning to take its toll: decimated sales staffs turn in lousy numbers. "Survivor syndrome" takes hold, and overburdened staffers just go through the motions of working. New-product ideas languish. Risk-taking dwindles because the culture of cost-cutting emphasizes the certainties of cutting costs over the uncertainties—and expense—of trying something new."[26]

In making cost cuts, a company must be especially sure to judge the effects of those cuts on the total quality of its goods and services.

## TABLE 17-4

## Allocating Functional Expenses by Product

| | TOTAL | PRODUCT A | PRODUCT B | PRODUCT C |
|---|---|---|---|---|
| Net sales | $1 000 000 | $500 000 | $300 000 | $200 000 |
| Less: Cost of goods sold | 450 000 | 250 000 | 120 000 | 80 000 |
| Gross profit | $550 000 | $250 000 | $180 000 | $120 000 |
| Less: Operating expenses (functional account expenses) | | | | |
| Marketing administration | 33 500 | 16 000 | 10 000 | 7 500 |
| Personal selling | 59 000 | 30 000 | 17 100 | 11 900 |
| Advertising | 48 500 | 20 000 | 18 000 | 10 500 |
| Transportation | 12 000 | 5 000 | 5 000 | 2 000 |
| Warehousing | 31 200 | 20 000 | 7 000 | 4 200 |
| Marketing research | 36 100 | 18 000 | 11 000 | 7 100 |
| General administration | 79 700 | 40 000 | 23 000 | 16 700 |
| Total operating expenses | 300 000 | 149 000 | 91 100 | 59 900 |
| Net profit before taxes | $250 000 | $101 000 | $88 900 | $60 100 |
| Profit as per cent of sales | 25.0 | 20.2 | 29.6 | 30.1 |

## Sales Analysis

**Sales analysis** *looks at sales data to assess the effectiveness of a marketing strategy.*

**Sales analysis** is the detailed study of sales data for the purpose of appraising the appropriateness and effectiveness of a marketing strategy. Without adequate sales analysis, a poor response to the total quality offered by a firm may not be seen early enough, the value of certain market segments and territories may be overlooked, sales effort may be poorly matched with market potential, trends may be missed, or support for sales personnel may not be forthcoming. Sales analysis enables plans to be set in terms of revenues by product, product line, salesperson, region, customer type, time period, price line, method of sale, and so on. It also compares actual sales against planned sales. More firms engage in sales analysis than in marketing cost analysis.

The main source of sales analysis data is the sales invoice, which may be written, typed, or computer generated. An invoice may contain such information as the customer's name and address, the quantity ordered, the price paid, purchase terms, all the different items bought at the same time, the order date, shipping arrangements, and the salesperson. Summary data are generated by adding invoices. The use of computerized marking, cash register, and inventory systems speeds data recording and improves their accuracy.

**Control units** *are an essential aspect of sales analysis.*

In conducting sales analysis, proper control units must be selected. **Control units** are the sales categories for which data are gathered, such as boys', men's, girls', and women's clothing. Although a marketing executive can broaden a control system by adding several sales categories together, wide categories cannot be broken down into components. Thus, a narrow sales category is preferable to one that is too wide. It is also helpful to select control units consistent with other company, trade association, and government data. A stable classification system is necessary to compare data from different time periods.

A key concept in undertaking sales analysis is that summary data, such as overall sales or market share, are usually insufficient to diagnose a firm's areas of strength and weakness. More intensive investigation is needed. Two sales analysis techniques that offer in-depth probing are the 80-20 principle and sales exception reporting.

According to the **80-20 principle**, in many organizations, a large proportion of total sales (profit) is likely to come from a small proportion of customers, products, or territories. Thus, to function as efficiently as possible, firms need to determine sales and profit by customer, product, or territory. Marketing efforts can then be allocated accordingly. Firms that do not isolate and categorize data are acting in error. Through faulty reasoning, they would place equal effort into each sale instead of concentrating on key accounts. These errors are due to a related concept, the **iceberg principle**, which states that superficial data are insufficient to make sound evaluations.

*The **80-20 principle** notes that a large share of sales (profits) often comes from few customers, products, or territories. Analysis errors may be due to the **iceberg principle**.*

This is how one firm is using the 80-20 principle in its sales analysis:

The Pepsi "Get Stuff" promotion has been described as "one of the largest consumer-loyalty programs ever run by a packaged-goods company in Canada." The promotion was designed to bolster youth loyalty and encourage frequent purchasing by young Canadians. The approach of the campaign involved consumers collecting points off specially marked packages of Pepsi, Diet Pepsi, and Pepsi Max. The points could be collected and redeemed for merchandise from a Pepsi Get Stuff catalogue. Described as a consumer "outreach" campaign, the promotion was designed to help Pepsi identify the heaviest product users through point redemption. Furthermore, the product usage of these users could be assessed since the Pepsi points associated with different packages were slightly different too. For example, 7-Eleven had Pepsi points on their Big Gulp cups, which were different in value and shape from the Pepsi points carried on other packages. Pepsi ran the promotion for a six-month period, distributing 460 million points on 175 million packages with $92 million in premiums available.[27]

Analysis can be further enhanced by **sales exception reporting**, which highlights situations where sales goals are not met or sales opportunities are present. A slow-selling item report cites products whose sales are below forecasts. It could suggest such corrective actions as price reductions, promotions, and sales incentives to increase unit sales. A fast-selling item report cites items whose sales exceed forecasts. It points out openings, as well as items that need more inventory on hand to prevent stockouts. Finally, sales exception reporting enables a firm to evaluate the validity of forecasts and make the proper modifications in them. Figure 17-4 presents examples of the 80-20 principle, the iceberg principle, and sales exception reporting.

**Sales exception reporting** *centres on unmet goals or special opportunities.*

Organizations also may use sales analysis to identify and monitor consumer buying patterns by answering such questions as these:

- Who purchases? Organizational vs. final consumer, geographic region, end use, purchase history, customer size, customer demographics.
- What is purchased? Product line, price category, brand, country of origin, package size, options purchased.
- Where are purchases made? Place of customer contact, purchase location, warehouse location.
- How are items purchased? Form of payment, billing terms, delivery form, packaging technique.
- When are purchases heaviest and lightest? Season, day of week, time of day.
- How much is purchased? Unit sales volume, dollar sales volume, profit margin.
- What types of promotion get the best sales results? Advertising, personal selling, sales promotion.
- What prices are paid? List prices vs. discounted prices.

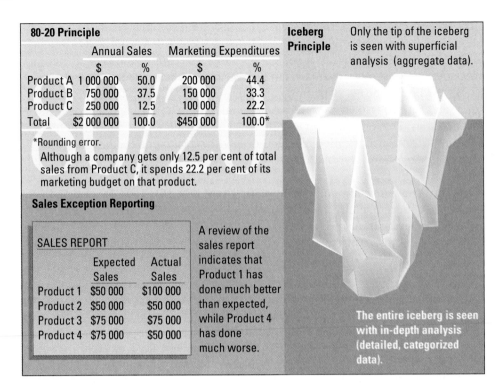

| 80-20 Principle | | | | |
|---|---|---|---|---|
| | Annual Sales | | Marketing Expenditures | |
| | $ | % | $ | % |
| Product A | 1 000 000 | 50.0 | 200 000 | 44.4 |
| Product B | 750 000 | 37.5 | 150 000 | 33.3 |
| Product C | 250 000 | 12.5 | 100 000 | 22.2 |
| Total | $2 000 000 | 100.0 | $450 000 | 100.0* |

*Rounding error.
Although a company gets only 12.5 per cent of total sales from Product C, it spends 22.2 per cent of its marketing budget on that product.

**Iceberg Principle** Only the tip of the iceberg is seen with superficial analysis (aggregate data).

**Sales Exception Reporting**

| SALES REPORT | | |
|---|---|---|
| | Expected Sales | Actual Sales |
| Product 1 | $50 000 | $100 000 |
| Product 2 | $50 000 | $50 000 |
| Product 3 | $75 000 | $75 000 |
| Product 4 | $75 000 | $50 000 |

A review of the sales report indicates that Product 1 has done much better than expected, while Product 4 has done much worse.

The entire iceberg is seen with in-depth analysis (detailed, categorized data).

**FIGURE 17-4**

**Sales Analysis Concepts**

## The Marketing Audit

*A **marketing audit** examines a firm in a systematic, critical, and unbiased manner.*

A **marketing audit** is a systematic, critical, impartial review and appraisal of the basic goals and policies of the marketing function, and of the organization, methods, procedures, and personnel employed to implement the policies and achieve the goals.[28] The purpose of a marketing audit is to determine how well a firm's marketing efforts are being conducted and how they can be improved. Audits should be conducted on a regular basis.

The marketing audit process involves the six steps shown in Figure 17-5:

1. A marketing audit may be conducted by company specialists, by company division or department managers, or by outside specialists. Expertise, access to information, costs, and potential biases are some of the factors to be considered when choosing audit personnel.

2. An audit may be undertaken at the end of a calendar year, at the end of a firm's annual reporting year, or when conducting a physical inventory. An audit should be performed at least annually, although some firms prefer more frequent analysis. It should be completed during the same time period each year to allow comparisons. In some cases, unannounced audits are useful to keep employees alert and to ensure spontaneous answers.

*A **horizontal audit** studies overall marketing performance; a **vertical audit** analyzes one aspect of marketing.*

3. A **horizontal audit** (also known as a marketing-mix audit) studies the overall marketing performance of a firm with particular emphasis on the interrelationship of variables and their relative importance. A **vertical audit** (also known as a functional audit) is an in-depth analysis of one aspect of a firm's marketing strategy, such as product planning. The two audits should be used in conjunction with one another because a horizontal audit often reveals areas needing further study.

4. Audit forms list the topics to be examined and the exact information required to evaluate each topic. Forms usually resemble questionnaires, and they are completed by the auditor. Examples of audit forms are contained in Figures 17-6 and 17-7.

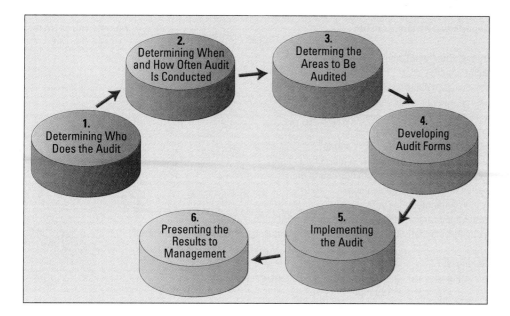

**FIGURE 17-5**

**The Marketing Audit Process**

5. When implementing an audit, decisions need to be made with regard to its duration, whether employees are to be aware of the audit, whether the audit is performed while a firm is open or closed for business, and how the final report is to be prepared.

6. The last step in an audit is to present findings and recommendations to management. However, the auditing process is complete only after suitable responses are taken by management. It is the responsibility of management, not the auditor, to determine these responses.

Despite the merits, many firms still do not use formal marketing audits. Three factors mostly account for this. First, success or failure is difficult to establish in marketing. A firm may have poor performance despite the best planning if environmental factors intervene. On the other hand, good results may be based on a firm being at the right place at the right time. Second, if marketing audits are completed by company personnel, they may not be comprehensive enough to be considered audits. Third, the pressures of other activities often mean that only a small part of a firm's marketing strategy is audited or that audits are done irregularly.

# Anticipating and Planning for the Future

The next decade promises to be a complex one for marketers everywhere, as they try to anticipate trends and plan long-run strategies. On the positive side, this period should see increasing consumer affluence in many countries, improvements in technological capabilities, expanding worldwide markets, greater deregulation of industry, and other opportunities. On the negative side, the period will probably witness greater competition among firms based in different countries, relatively slow to moderate growth in North American and European markets, some resource instability, and an uncertain worldwide economy.

Long-range plans must take into account both the external variables facing a firm and its capacity for change. Specifically, what variables will affect the firm? What trends are forecast that might affect the firm? Is the firm able to respond to these trends (for example, does it have the necessary resources and lead time)? A firm that does not anticipate and respond to future trends has a good possibility of falling into

*Planning efforts for the future must consider external factors and company abilities.*

| Does Your Department, Division, or Firm ... | Answer Yes or No to Each Question |
|---|---|
| **Planning, Organization, and Control** | |
| 1. Have specific objectives? | _____ |
| 2. Devise objectives to meet changing conditions? | _____ |
| 3. Study customer needs, attitudes, and behaviour? | _____ |
| 4. Organize marketing efforts in a systematic way? | _____ |
| 5. Have a market planning process? | _____ |
| 6. Engage in comprehensive sales forecasting? | _____ |
| 7. Integrate buyer behaviour research in market planning? | _____ |
| 8. Have strategy and tactics within the marketing plan? | _____ |
| 9. Have clearly stated contingency plans? | _____ |
| 10. Monitor environmental changes? | _____ |
| 11. Incorporate social responsibility as a criterion for decision making? | _____ |
| 12. Control activities via marketing cost analysis, sales analysis, and the marketing audit? | _____ |
| | |
| **Marketing Research** | |
| 13. Utilize marketing research for planning, as well as problem solving? | _____ |
| 14. Have a marketing information system? | _____ |
| 15. Give enough support to marketing research? | _____ |
| 16. Have adequate communication between marketing research and line executives? | _____ |
| | |
| **Products** | |
| 17. Utilize a systematic product-planning process? | _____ |
| 18. Plan product policy relative to the product life-cycle concept? | _____ |
| 19. Have a procedure for developing new products? | _____ |
| 20. Periodically review all products? | _____ |
| 21. Monitor competitive developments in product planning? | _____ |
| 22. Revise mature products? | _____ |
| 23. Phase out weak products? | _____ |
| | |
| **Distribution** | |
| 24. Motivate channel members? | _____ |
| 25. Have sufficient market coverage? | _____ |
| 26. Periodically evaluate channel members? | _____ |
| 27. Evaluate alternative shipping arrangements? | _____ |
| 28. Study warehouse and facility locations? | _____ |
| 29. Compute economic order quantities? | _____ |
| 30. Modify channel decisions as conditions warrant? | _____ |
| | |
| **Promotion** | |
| 31. Have an overall promotion plan? | _____ |
| 32. Balance promotion components within the plan? | _____ |
| 33. Measure the effectiveness of advertising? | _____ |
| 34. Seek out favourable publicity? | _____ |
| 35. Have a procedure for recruiting and retaining sales personnel? | _____ |
| 36. Analyze the sales-force organization periodically? | _____ |
| 37. Moderate the use of sales promotions? | _____ |
| | |
| **Prices** | |
| 38. Have a pricing strategy that is in compliance with government regulations? | _____ |
| 39. Have a pricing strategy that satisfies channel members? | _____ |
| 40. Estimate demand and cost factors before setting prices? | _____ |
| 41. Plan for competitive developments? | _____ |
| 42. Set prices that are consistent with image? | _____ |
| 43. Seek to maximize total profits? | _____ |

**FIGURE 17-6**

**A Horizontal Marketing Audit Form**

**FIGURE 17-7**

**A Total-Quality Vertical-Audit Form**

*Source: Dick Berry, "How Healthy Is Your Company?"*
Marketing News *(February 15, 1993), p. 2.*
*Reprinted by permission of the American Marketing Association.*

**Total Quality
Health Check-up Questionnaire**

After filling out questionnaire, return to : _____

The purpose of this questionnaire is to provide a means for companies to conduct a study of their employees, to determine the degree of involvement and commitment to the principles and practices of Total Quality Management.

The questionnaire is based on the criteria embodied in the Baldridge Quality Award categories (being employed by many companies as an integrated management system and to conform to requirements in attaining the award).

**INDIVIDUAL INSTRUCTIONS**

Identify your position title and company department in the spaces below, then respond to each of the following ten statements, indicating your personal opinion as to the degree of compliance with the criteria in company operations. When completed, return to the individual identified at the top of the sheet for tabulation and reporting of results.

Your Position: _____     Department: _____

| QUALITY HEALTH CRITERIA (Circle numbers at right to indicate agreement) | HOW ARE WE DOING? Not true / Very true | | | | | |
|---|---|---|---|---|---|---|
| 1. External customer expectations define the quality of our goods and services. | 0 | 1 | 2 | 3 | 4 | 5 |
| 2. Cross-functional and inter-departmental cooperation are encouraged and supported. | 0 | 1 | 2 | 3 | 4 | 5 |
| 3. There is active leadership for quality improvement at all levels of management. | 0 | 1 | 2 | 3 | 4 | 5 |
| 4. Employees have the authority to act on goods and service quality problems. | 0 | 1 | 2 | 3 | 4 | 5 |
| 5. A team approach is used to solve quality problems and to meet customer expectations. | 0 | 1 | 2 | 3 | 4 | 5 |
| 6. Measures of internal and external customer expectations are well understood. | 0 | 1 | 2 | 3 | 4 | 5 |
| 7. Employees are brought into decisions that affect the quality of their work. | 0 | 1 | 2 | 3 | 4 | 5 |
| 8. There is major emphasis on the prevention and solving of quality problems. | 0 | 1 | 2 | 3 | 4 | 5 |
| 9. Individuals and teams are given recognition for contributions to quality improvement. | 0 | 1 | 2 | 3 | 4 | 5 |
| 10. Systems are in place to assess and respond to changing customer expectations and needs. | 0 | 1 | 2 | 3 | 4 | 5 |

does not anticipate and respond to future trends has a good possibility of falling into Levitt's marketing myopia trap and losing ground to more farsighted competitors:

Most managers manage for yesterday's conditions because yesterday is where they got their experiences and had their successes. But management is about tomorrow, not yesterday. Tomorrow concerns what should be done, not what has been done. "Should" is determined by the external environment—what competitors (old, new, and potential) can and might do, the choices this will give customers and those who advise or direct customers, the rules constantly being made by governments and other players, demographic changes, advances in generalized knowledge and technology, changing ecology and public sentiments, and the like.

The most precious thing a manager brings to a job is the wisdom conferred by experience—precisely so that he or she can operate decisively and effectively with limited information, with dispatch and confidence. But when change accelerates, when it comes

## TECHNOLOGY AND MARKETING

## Why Amazon.com Won't Win

Are "bricks and mortar" retailers on the way out, or just branching out? If you read the current business press it seems that everyone is shopping online, and retail organizations that miss this trend won't be around for long. Imagine if you were U.S.-based Barnes and Noble owner Lenny Riggio, who picked up his newspaper in December of 1998 to read that in one day Jeff Bezos, Amazon.com's owner, increased his net worth by nearly $1 billion. The market appears to be sending a clear signal.

How do bricks-and-mortar retailers compete when the manufacturers of products they distribute are also selling them on the Internet for less money, and in some cases distributing them via an immediate online download? Well, if people are shopping to buy, they can't compete; their retail operation has been "Amazoned."

So how do you keep from being Amazoned? The only defence is to realize that not everyone is shopping to buy. Shopping is also a social activity. People shop with their friends and their family; they walk around the stores and look at what's on display; and they look at other shoppers to see who's on display too. A monitor screen just doesn't do it. People want to talk with a friendly and helpful salesperson (hopefully). They want to try on, or try out the products. If they make a purchase, it can be easily returned, exchanged, or repaired at the local store. These days bookstores are for "live" browsers. Smart book retailers are putting coffee shops in their stores and comfy chairs so that people can glance at the books they're interested in. People can play with computer games and computer software. Get people to come to your store because they like to—and finish them off by pricing competitively so that they don't go and order the books from Amazon.com!

Finally, the bricks-and-mortar retailer must press its main advantage, the unrelated checkout impulse buy. It's so hard to resist the gum, chocolate bars, and magazines at the checkout counter. Your basic e-tailer just can't compete with that; they've been "bricked and mortared." No, the smart bricks-and-mortar retailers will always be there as long as there are shoppers. It's the buyers who will be the problem.

Try to develop some alternative marketing strategy approaches that bricks-and-mortar retailers could employ to counter e-tailer competition. It doesn't seem likely that prices could be matched, but how could a bricks-and-mortar retailer match value?

Source: Based on Nina Munk, "Barnes and Noble: Title Fight," *Fortune* (June 21, 1999), pp. 84–94.

unexpectedly from constantly unexpected directions, when new technologies and social and environmental conditions occur so disjunctively, the wisdom conferred by experience needs help. That is one reason professional staffs and consultants proliferate. It is also why, in this age of rapid acceleration, this hazardous new age of fast history, managers must take time to carefully think for themselves.[29]

Many North American middle managers think they've beaten the Japanese. They think they've won. They think they're smarter. But they don't understand the nature of the competition. The Japanese have a proven ability to cope with crisis. Japanese companies are, of necessity, becoming world-class experts at managing through tough times. Today, their customers won't spend enough, their currency won't fall enough, and their government won't—or can't—do enough. So Japanese managers are going back to the drawing board, sometimes literally. They are redesigning products, redeploying workers, reconfiguring distribution systems, and generally retooling some of their most storied management practices—from just-in-time production to consensus decision-making, from flexible manufacturing to continuous improvement.[30]

3M illustrates what a firm can do to prepare for the uncertain future. It recently decided to divest itself of businesses with annual sales of U.S.$3 billion (including

## Forget E-Commerce, Look Out for D-Commerce[34]

In the third millennium Darwin's laws will rule corporate strategy. The most famous of these laws is "survival of the fittest." From a business standpoint the word "fit" is to be taken literally, i.e., those businesses or organizations that fit best with their environments will survive. The volatility of business environments means that managers must constantly adjust the fit of their organizations. The advent of e-commerce represents not only the latest, but also a revolutionary and evolutionary force in these business environments.

Marketers are well advised to consider some of the basic principles of biology and psychology to understand their markets. Michael Schrage offers these insights:

- Consider segmenting by birth order. First-borns are often conservative and authoritarian. Later-borns are more receptive to new ideas and innovation.
- If your product or service will be used by children or youths, target them, even if the product is purchased by the parents. Peer groups are more influential on the personality formation of children than are parents.
- Make your organization tribal. The optimal size of human tribes is approximately 150 people. Don't let your organization grow far beyond that. Smaller groups don't generate the diversity needed for creative effort, and larger groups tend to be less productive.
- Competition and differentiation should be viewed according to Darwin's laws. Target marketing and positioning are the same as biological niche strategies. Two firms can't long co-exist if they try to occupy the same niche in the marketplace. Therefore firms need to differentiate their products and their services.

computer diskettes, videotape, and audiotape). 3M believed its long-term prospects in those businesses were not strong. The firm is expanding its efforts in "microreplication" technologies that can "refract light or transport it, strip adhesive from plastic film or serve as a fastener, reduce water drag on boat hulls or polish golf clubs." 3M is more aggressive in obtaining ideas from business customers; and it is extremely interested in gaining insights into the unarticulated needs of those customers. As 3M's chief executive says, "We're going to do two principal things: be very innovative and satisfy our customers in all respects."[31]

To prepare for the future, companies can do the following:

- *Company vision planning*—This articulates the firm's future mission.
- *Scenario planning*—This identifies the range of events that may occur in the future.
- *Contingency planning*—This prepares alternative strategies, each keyed to a specific scenario (such as a slow-growth economy).
- *Competitive positioning*—This outlines where a firm will be positioned in the future versus competitors.
- *Competitive benchmarking*—This keeps the firm focused on how well it is doing versus its competitors.
- *Ongoing marketing research*—This entails consumer and other relevant research.[32]

As we look ahead, it is clear that the role of marketing will take on greater importance at many companies. Here is why:

Marketing is responsible for more than the sale, and its responsibilities differ depending on the level of organization and strategy. It is the management function responsible for making sure that every aspect of the business is focused on delivering superior value [total quality] to customers in the competitive marketplace. The business is increasingly likely to be a network of strategic partnerships among designers, technology providers, manufacturers, distributors, and information specialists. The business will be defined by its customers, not its products or factories or offices. This is a critical point: in network organizations, it is the ongoing relationship with a set of customers that represents the most important business asset. Marketing as a distinct management function will be responsible for being expert on the customer and keeping the rest of the network organization informed about the customer. At the corporate and business unit levels, marketing may merge with strategic planning or, more generally, the strategy development function, with shared responsibility for information, environmental scanning, and coordination of the network activities.[33]

# SUMMARY

**1.** *To show the value of an integrated marketing plan* Integrated planning builds upon a firm's strategic planning efforts and its use of a total quality approach. In this way, everyone is "on the same page." An integrated marketing plan is one in which all of its various parts are unified, consistent, and coordinated.

**2.** *To discuss the elements of a well-integrated marketing plan* There are several major elements in an integrated marketing plan. A clear organizational mission outlines a firm's commitment to a type of business and a place in the market. Long-term competitive advantages are company, product, and marketing attributes—whose distinctiveness and appeal to consumers can be maintained over an extended period of time. A precisely defined target market enables a firm to identify the specific consumers it addresses in a marketing plan.

The long-, moderate-, and short-term marketing subplans of a firm need to be compatible with one another. Coordination among SBUs is enhanced when the functions, strategies, and resources of each are described and monitored by top management. The components of the marketing mix need to be coordinated within each SBU. The plan must have a certain degree of stability over time.

**3.** *To present five types of marketing plan analysis: benchmarking, cus-*tomer satisfaction research, marketing cost analysis, sales analysis, and the marketing audit* Marketing plan analysis compares a firm's actual performance with its planned or expected performance for a specified period of time. If actual performance is unsatisfactory, corrective action may be needed. Plans may have to be revised because of the impact of uncontrollable variables.

Through benchmarking, a company can set its own marketing performance standards by studying the best firms in its industry, innovative firms in any industry, direct competitors, and/or the company itself. There are strategic benchmarks and process benchmarks. In general, firms progress through three stages: novice, journeyman, and master. Awards such as the Canada Export Awards, Entrepreneur of the Year Award, Award for Canadian–American Business Achievement, and Ontario Global Traders Award are good benchmarks. Surveys using criteria such as those used to award the Malcolm Baldridge National Quality Award and measure *Fortune's* Corporate Reputations are good benchmarking tools.

In customer satisfaction research, a firm determines the degree to which customer expectations regarding a good or service are actually satisfied. The world's largest research project in this area is the American Customer Satisfaction Index (ACSI), which rates hundreds of U.S. companies and thousands of goods and services. In 1998, the average ACSI score for all companies was 72.0 (out of 100).

Marketing cost analysis evaluates the cost efficiency of various marketing factors, such as different total quality configurations, product lines, order sizes, distribution methods, sales territories, channel members, salespersons, advertising media, and customer types. Continuous and accurate cost data are needed. Marketing cost analysis involves studying natural account expenses, reclassifying natural accounts into functional accounts, and allocating accounts by marketing classification.

Sales analysis is the detailed study of sales data for the purpose of appraising the appropriateness and effectiveness of a marketing strategy. Sales analysis enables plans to be set in terms of revenues by product, product line, salesperson, region, customer type, time period, price line, or method of sale. It also monitors actual sales against planned sales. More firms use sales analysis than marketing cost analysis. The main source of sales data is the sales invoice; control units must be specified. Sales analysis should take the 80-20 principle, the iceberg principle, and sales exception reporting into account.

The marketing audit is a systematic, critical, impartial review and appraisal of a firm's marketing objectives, strategy, implementation, and organization. It contains six steps: determining who does the audit, establishing when and how often the audit is conducted, deciding what the audit covers, developing audit forms, implementing the audit, and presenting the results. A horizontal audit studies the overall marketing performance of a firm. A vertical audit is an in-depth analysis of one aspect of marketing strategy.

**4.** *To see the merit of anticipating and planning for the future* Long-range plans must take into account both the external variables facing a firm and its capacity for change. A firm that does not anticipate and respond to future trends has a good chance of falling into Levitt's marketing myopia trap—which should be avoided.

## KEY TERMS

**marketing plan analysis** (p. 574)

**benchmarking** (p. 574)

**customer satisfaction** (p. 577)

**marketing cost analysis** (p. 579)

**natural accounts** (p. 579)

**functional accounts** (p. 579)

**sales analysis** (p. 582)

**control units** (p. 582)

**80-20 principle** (p. 583)

**iceberg principle** (p. 583)

**sales exception reporting** (p. 583)

**marketing audit** (p. 584)

**horizontal audit** (p. 584)

**vertical audit** (p. 584)

## REVIEW QUESTIONS

**1.** State five of Wal-Mart's ten focused management rules.

**2.** Explain Figure 17-1, which deals with a well-integrated marketing plan.

**3.** Why might competitive advantages not travel well internationally?

**4.** What is benchmarking? How should a novice firm use it differently from a master firm?

**5.** Discuss the value of measuring customer satisfaction with studies like the American Customer Satisfaction Index (ACSI).

**6.** Why is functional account cost analysis more useful than natural account analysis?

**7.** Distinguish between marketing cost analysis and sales analysis.

**8.** When conducting sales analysis, why is it necessary that control units not be too wide?

**9.** Differentiate between a vertical and a horizontal marketing audit.

**10.** What are some of the positive and negative trends firms are likely to face over the coming decade?

## DISCUSSION QUESTIONS

**1.** Do you think your college or university is applying an integrated marketing approach? Why or why not? What marketing recommendations would you make for your school?

**2.** Develop a customer satisfaction survey for your local bank. Discuss the kinds of information you are seeking.

**3.** What data could a manufacturer obtain from a monthly analysis of its sales to wholesalers? How could this information improve marketing plans?

**4.** Develop a vertical marketing audit form for Sony to appraise its relationship with the retailers that carry its products.

**5.** As the marketing vice-president for a small book publisher, how would you prepare for the future? What key trends do you foresee over the next decade? How would you address them?

## CASE STUDY

# Makeup Art Cosmetics (M.A.C.) Joins Estée Lauder's Portfolio

M.A.C. President Frank Toskan says he doesn't take makeup seriously. Makeup Art Cosmetics started up as an innovative Canadian company with a simple philosophy: "Make a good product, and people will come to you." M.A.C. makes products for "all races, all sexes, all ages." This sounds heretical in the age of target marketing: something for everyone, and a production orientation to boot. Moreover, in an industry traditionally dominated by a "sell products on fantasy" marketing approach, Frank Toskan says that M.A.C. doesn't dictate what women should wear and look like.

Frank Toskan was a fashion photographer when he approached Frank Angelo to help him develop new products for makeup shoots. They employed makeup artists to help them with product development, and sold the products to other makeup artists at a discount. Through word of mouth the demand for their products began to build, and by 1995 M.A.C. employed about 1000 people and had sales of $150 million.

M.A.C. believes in breaking the rules of cosmetic marketing. Its celebrity spokesmodel is RuPaul, a seven-foot tall transvestite. Frank Toskan sees RuPaul as an excellent representative of M.A.C. because he's "a stunningly beautiful woman and strikingly handsome man [who] represents M.A.C.'s belief that beauty is genderless, [and because] we couldn't find anyone who wore more makeup and had so much fun doing it."

When M.A.C. started up 1984 competitors took it lightly. M.A.C. had no advertising, no promotional giveaways, and its approach was to push products to makeup artists. In fact, Frank Toskan admits that M.A.C. was unaware of its competitors' actions, and that he made decisions based on what felt right.

M.A.C.'s biggest problem was getting access to retail distribution. Rod Ulmer, The Bay's Toronto buyer, saw the product and agreed to give M.A.C. some showcases in his store. Sales exploded, reaching $300 000 in one year. Results like this prompted U.S. retail chains like Saks Fifth Avenue and Henri Bendel to give M.A.C. selling space in their stores too. There was tremendous demand in North America and throughout the world, but M.A.C. didn't have enough distributors to meet it.

M.A.C. approached Estée Lauder, the world's leading cosmetic manufacturer, to see if it would take them on. Estée Lauder initially declined, but M.A.C. became so successful that Estée Lauder had to consider creating a line to compete with it. It purchased M.A.C. instead, acquiring a 51 per cent controlling interest in 1994 and then the remaining shares in 1998. Estée Lauder is a U.S. multinational firm with U.S.$3.6 billion in sales. The firm dominates the world's cosmetic market with a 46 per cent market share of the U.S. prestige cosmetics market, 22 per cent of the European market, and 33 per cent of the Japanese market.

Although Estée Lauder has let founder Frank Toskan control M.A.C.'s creative approach, it handles the business and distribution. CEO Leonard Lauder revealed his view of where M.A.C. fits into Estée Lauder's brand portfolio: "Our product balance offers brands like Estée Lauder, Clinique, and Aramis, the 'rule makers' that set the tone and the direction of the entire prestige industry. But it also includes 'rule breakers'— newer brands like Origins, Tommy Hilfiger, Bobbi Brown Essentials, and M.A.C., which have formed whole new platforms for growth in taking prestige products to new consumers. We have products for those who prefer classic brands, as well as those on the forward edge of fashion. We have brands that appeal for their advanced use of technology, and others that are chosen based on lifestyle."

Leonard Lauder outlines five marketing strategies that will help Estée Lauder grow: 1) Keep the new products coming; 2) Reach more consumers through new concepts like the store within a store, a resource, education, and shop concept created exclusively for professional makeup artists and showcased by the M.A.C. Pro Shop in New York City; 3) Grow fragrance; 4) Expand globally; 5) Pursue unique business opportunities that complement but do not cannibalize Estée Lauder's brands.

### Questions

1. Discuss M.A.C.'s segmentation and positioning strategy in its use of spokesmodel RuPaul versus its competitors' traditional use of female supermodels.

2. So far M.A.C. has been successful. What factors have accounted for this success, and what risk factors might M.A.C. face in the future? Explain your answer.

3. Discuss Estée Lauder's growth strategy plans, and evaluate how well M.A.C. fits into these plans.

4. Discuss the history of M.A.C. as presented in this case. Forecast M.A.C.'s future as part of Estée Lauder's product portfolio. Do you think M.A.C. will lose its marketing edge under Estée Lauder? Why or why not?

**ESTÉE LAUDER**
www.esteelauder.com

Sources: Based on Estée Lauder Annual Report, Estée Lauder Corporate Web site; Lara Mills, "Fantasy's End," *Marketing Magazine* (April 17, 1995), p. 11; Lara Mills, "M.A.C. Finds the Ideal Spokesperson," *Marketing Magazine* (March 20, 1995), p. 9; Lara Mills, "That Old M.A.C. Magic," *Marketing Magazine* (February 5, 1996), p. 1; Doug Forster, "In Your Face," *Canadian Business* (December 1995), p. 54; and "Makeup Art Cosmetics," CBC *Venture* Video 580.

## CASE STUDY

# General Electric: Maximizing Corporate Performance

General Electric was the ninth largest company in the world in 1998 with sales of U.S.$100.5 billion. It was also rated number one on the list of America's Most Admired Companies. Under dynamic CEO Jack Welch, the company has experienced many consecutive years of double digit sales growth and strong profitability.

Jack Welch attributes GE's performance to three fundamental factors: its corporate philosophy; the implementation of growth initiatives such as globalization, product services, and Six Sigma quality; and having the best business leaders implement these initiatives.

The firm views itself as a learning company. It studies its own successes and failures and those of other firms inside and outside the industry. Welch wants the firm to have an appetite for learning and to act quickly upon it. For example, GE learned that American Standard, one of its big accounts, had successfully installed a "Demand Flow Technology" system that doubled inventory turnover rates, and was working toward a goal of zero working capital. GE now uses this technique in its Power Systems, Plastics, and Medical Systems businesses. In another instance, GE observed that Caterpillar reduced its service costs and new-product development time by standardizing parts. Using this system in its Appliances and Power systems businesses GE was able to cut new-product introduction times in half.

The globalization initiative has been responsible for GE's ability to maintain a double digit revenue growth rate. Foreign sales amounted to U.S.$43 billion of GE's 1998 revenues, of which European operations accounted for $24 billion. Welch notes that GE is globalizing not only its sales results but every other activity. It's looking for intellectual capital in particular, and plans to hire the best people in every country in which it operates. "The GE of the next century must provide high-value global products and services, designed by global talent, for global markets."

The product services growth initiative involves thinking of GE as not merely a product provider but as a customer solutions provider. This means redefining its services beyond simply replacing its parts and overhauling and reconditioning its machines. It means employing GE's engineers, R&D people, and managers to upgrade and enhance the performance of the products they've installed, thereby making their customers more competitive.

GE's third growth strategy involves the implementation of a Six Sigma quality program designed to improve its cost structure, inventory management, and overall product quality. These changes are intended to attract new customers and increase the loyalty of existing ones. Six Sigma's new measures of operating efficiency have resulted in an increase of inventory turnover from 5.8 to 9.2 per year. Gross margins improved from 13.6 to 16.7 per cent, and the ratio of plant and equipment expenditures to depreciation fell to 1.2 and is expected to be as low as .7 to .8 in the near future.

Six Sigma has also led to dramatic improvements in product quality, such as the development of the Lightspeed Scanner, which is the first multi-slice CT scanner that can "scan a patient's chest in 17 seconds, in comparison to three minutes for conventional CT scanners."

The implementation of the Six Sigma program has also meant dramatic improvements in customer service. For example, order delivery times have been reduced from an average seventeen days to an average twelve days. GE also plans to remove the variances in customer service.

It will take good managers to implement these initiatives, and Jack Welch is looking for business leaders who have what he calls the four E's: high Energy so that they'll be motivated to stick to their tasks; the ability to Energize or motivate others; an Edge or ability to make tough decisions about what tasks to undertake; and the ability to Execute their tasks by turning their vision into results.

## Questions

1. Discuss GE's corporate philosophy. Is GE really following it, or is it just window dressing? Elaborate.
2. Discuss GE's three growth strategies. Evaluate them in terms of whether they have complementary or conflicting objectives.
3. Describe how GE could make use of marketing cost analysis as part of its Six Sigma program.
4. How would you go about discovering whether a manger has the four E's that Jack Welch believes good managers should have?

**GENERAL ELECTRIC**
www.ge.com

Sources: Based on General Electric 1998 Annual Report; Fortune 500 "Largest U.S. Corporations," *Fortune* (April 26, 1999), p. F1; Fortune 500 "The World's Largest Corporations," *Fortune* (August 2, 1999), p. F1; Eryn Brown, "America's Most Admired Companies," *Fortune* (March 1, 1999), pp. 68–73; and Tim Smart and Zachary Schiller, "Just Imagine If Times Were Good," *Business Week* (April 17, 1995), pp. 78–80.

# Dylex: Managing a Portfolio of Companies

Dylex is a multi-faceted Canadian clothing retailer based in Toronto. It was founded by Wilf Poslans and Jimmy Kaye, two ex-military men who named their firm Dylex because during their military careers they constantly heard the phrase "Damn Your Lousy Excuses." The name was selected to foster a "can do" attitude in their business. Despite a lot of early success, Dylex ran into some major financial difficulties during the mid-1980s. Before then Dylex had $2 billion in sales, 13 000 employees, and operated 2800 stores clothing stores under the Harry Rosen, Braemar, Fairweather, Tip Top, Biway, Ruby's, Suzy Shier, and Town and Country banners.

Retail analyst Richard Talbot commented that Dylex nearly failed when it was hit by a recession in the 1980s. Sales fell by 50 per cent, and Dylex was on the verge of bankruptcy with only two ways to go—up or out of business. Talbot lays the near demise of Dylex at the door of its former management. He notes, for example, that the Fairweather women's clothing store promoted a high class fashion image and offered dresses in the $90 range, but also sold cheap dresses in the $20 range. The merchandise wasn't consistent with the projected image, and this confused customers and turned them off.

To deal with their difficulties, the board of directors fired the founders and chose Elliot Wahle to be their new CEO. Wahle, who once scouted for the Toronto Blue Jays and later brought Toys'R'Us to Canada, was seen as the person best suited to turning around Dylex. But performing a turnaround is a more difficult task than introducing a new retail chain like Toys'R'Us. Wahle was faced with a lot of difficult decisions. He began by letting thousands of employees go in order to cut costs. To raise cash he put the company headquarters building—located on prime land in Toronto—up for sale, and with it the Harry Rosen and Braemar retail chains.

Wahle wasn't planning to simply slash and burn. He realized that the firm needed building, and looked to invest in potential growth retailers like Thrifty's and Club Monaco in order to return some of the lost sales revenue and restore Dylex to profitability. He also wanted to maintain some of the more mainstream retail chains that were the backbone of Dylex, specifically Fairweather, Tip Top Tailors, and Biway.

Wahle hired Steve Summers, a clothing retail veteran, to restore Fairweather to its former position. Summers got right to work by going to New York, the number one trend-setting clothing retail market in the world. Summers likens women's fashion retailing to putting on a Broadway show; that is, a clothing retailer has to offer some sizzle and glitz to bring in customers. Summers also believes that to sell clothing you need quality products supported by the proper image and proper presentation.

Wahle selected Rick Blicksted, a former Wal-Mart executive, to be the new company president for Biway. Biway is an important contributor to Dylex, accounting for 50 per cent of its sales. Blicksted went to work almost immediately with an enthusiastic approach. He's refurbishing the Biway stores, and rearranging the merchandise into power wall displays. (The transformation has been described as making Biway a "Wal-Mart Wannabe," but considering that Wal-Mart is the world's largest retailer, it's hard to criticize Dylex for aiming high.)

Wahle wasn't sure what to do about Tip Top Tailors. The firm had a well-known name, but a dull image to go with it. Young people thought of the store as the place where their dad bought them their first suit. In the end, Wahle chose to try to reposition Tip Top in the upscale men's retail fashion market, a position in Dylex's portfolio left vacant when the Harry Rosen chain was sold off.

In his first year on the job Wahle made Dylex into a firm that was a quarter of its former size, but he also made it profitable (albeit a small profit). As a former Blue Jay scout, Wahle is fully aware of the importance of having talented people working for him. Now that he has some of these people in

place, he must do what CEOs of all firms want to do: build a winning strategy to go with his winning management team.

## Questions

1. Evaluate Wahle's turn-around strategy for Dylex. Can you think of any other alternatives he could have used to keep Dylex afloat? Discuss these alternatives.
2. Clothing retail operations are risky because they function at the whim of fashion trends. What is it about the way Dylex has organized its retail portfolio that has allowed it to stay in business?
3. Before Elliot Wahle took over Dylex, do you think the firm had an integrated marketing plan for its stores? Discuss this situation.
4. Identify some of Dylex's potential competitive advantages. Suggest some actions you think could help Dylex build upon them further.

## Video Questions

1. The video discusses how Dylex got its name. What kind of corporate culture do you think this breeds for an organization? Discuss whether Dylex should rename itself. Explain why and suggest a new name.
2. Elliot Wahle developed a management team to help turn Dylex around. Identify the kinds of managers he has chosen for Bi-Way and Fairweather. What kind of a manager do you think he needs to hire to get Tip-Top back into form? Identify the kinds of hiring criteria you would recommend for such a manager.

Sources: Based on "Dylex," *Venture* #591 (May 19, 1996); News Line, "Dylex Ltd," *Marketing Magazine* (June 7, 1999), p. 2; James Pollock, "At Bat for Dylex," *Marketing Magazine* (November 13, 1995), pp. 1, 12; and "Dylex to Unload Rosen and Braemar Stakes," *Marketing Magazine* (February 19, 1996), p. 1.

# Endnotes

## CHAPTER 1

1. Gary Hamel and Jeff Sampler, "The E-Corporation," *Fortune* (December 7, 1998), pp. 81–92.
2. For a comprehensive analysis of the marketing concept, see Frederick E. Webster, Jr., "Defining the New Marketing Concept," *Marketing Management*, Vol. 2 (Number 2, 1994), pp. 23–31.
3. Diana Luciani, "The Bed Magee Made," *Marketing Magazine* (November 16, 1998), pp. 10–12.
4. Frederick E. Webster, Jr., "Executing the New Marketing Concept," *Marketing Management*, Vol. 3, No. 1 (1994), pp. 9–16.
5. Sean Silcoff, "Black Gold," *Canadian Business* (October 30, 1998), pp. 94–99.
6. Peter D. Bennett (Ed.), *Dictionary of Marketing Terms,* Second Edition (Chicago: American Marketing Association, 1995), p. 73.
7. Theodore D. Kemper, "Good Service Serves the Economy, Too," *New York Times* (January 9, 1994), Section 3, p. 13.
8. Jim Carlton, "Support Lines' Busy Signals Hurt PC Makers," *Wall Street Journal* (July 6, 1995), p. B1.
9. Steve Weinstein, "Rethinking Customer Service," *Progressive Grocer* (May 1995), pp. 63–68.
10. "Many Consumers Expect Better Service—and Say They Are Willing to Pay for It," *Wall Street Journal* (November 12, 1990), pp. B1, B4.
11. "Smart Football," *Manitoba Business*, Vol. 13, No. 2 (March 1991), p. 16; "Revenue Canada Tries to Put on a Happy Face," *Financial Post*, Vol. 5, No. 162 (November 13, 1991), p. 14.
12. "Incentives Help to Improve Service," *Strategy*, Vol. 4, No. 11 (February 8, 1993), pp. 22–24.
13. Joyce Lau, "Reaching for the Top Shelf," *Canadian Business* (December 26, 1997), p. 67.
14. Bennett, *Dictionary of Marketing Terms*, p. 73.
15. Stanley Brown, "You Can Get Satisfaction," *Sales & Marketing Management* (July 1995), p. 106.
16. Sean Silcoff, "Move Over Timothy Eaton," *Canadian Business* (June 26/July 10, 1998), pp. 58–64.
17. Bennett, *Dictionary of Marketing Terms*, p. 242.
18. Patricia Sellers, "Keeping the Buyer You Already Have," *Fortune* (Autumn–Winter 1993), p. 56.
19. William Band, "The Power of Customer-centric Thinking," *Marketing Magazine* (May 11, 1998), p. 34.
20. Gary Hamel and Jeff Sampler, "The E-Corporation," *Fortune* (December 7, 1998), pp. 81–92. *Media Digest,* 1998–99, Canadian Media Directors' Council, pp. 13–16.

## CHAPTER 2

1. David Berman, "Squeezed Out by the Dairy Cartel," *Canadian Business* (May 8, 1998), pp. 81–83.
2. "Woolly Bully," *Canadian Business* (February 1996), p. 22.
3. Peter D. Bennett (Ed.), *Dictionary of Marketing Terms,* Second Edition (Chicago: American Marketing Association, 1995), pp. 159, 177.
4. Tamsen Tillson, "Be It Ever So Humble," *Canadian Business* (June 25, 1995), Special Technology Issue, pp. 26–32.
5. Geoffrey Brewer, "The New Managers," *Performance* (March 1995), p. 32.
6. Bennett, *Dictionary of Marketing Terms*, pp. 165–166.
7. Benson P. Shapiro, "Rejuvenating the Marketing Mix," *Harvard Business Review*, Vol. 63 (September–October 1985), p. 34. See also Walter van Waterschoot and Christophe Van den Bulte, "The 4P Classification of the Marketing Mix Revisited," *Journal of Marketing*, Vol. 56 (October 1992), pp. 83–93.
8. Rachel Larabie-Lesieur, "Ottawa's Competition Act, How It Works," *Marketing Magazine* (May 1, 1995), p. 15; and Industry Canada Web site (strategis.ic.gc.ca) (December, 1998).
9. Tom Messer and James Pollock, "Canada, U.S. Agree to Share Deceptive Marketing Info," *Marketing Magazine* (August 21–28, 1995), p. 3; and Industry Canada Web site (June 1996).
10. Helena Katz, "The Great Margarine Caper," *Marketing Magazine* (May 11, 1998), p. 12; Lara Mills, "The Missing Liquor Ads," *Marketing Magazine* (October 26, 1998), p. 32.
11. Christopher McIntosh, "To Market, to Market," *Futurist* (January–February 1994), p. 24; Industry Canada, "Poland—Textile Company Privatization," Strategis Web site, strategis.ic.gc.ca (December, 1998); George Koch, "You'll Get a Charge Out of This," *Canadian Business* (October 1995), pp. 105–113.
12. Bennett, *Dictionary of Marketing Terms*, p. 62.
13. Office of Consumer Affairs, "Part Two: Assessing the Value of a Canadian Consumer Foundation," Strategis Web site, strategis.ic.gc.ca (December, 1998); and Office of Consumer Affairs, "Directory of Consumer Associations," Strategis Web site, strategis.ic.gc.ca (December, 1998).
14. "Psst, Wanna Buy Some Long-Distance?" p. 98.
15. "Performance 2000," *Canadian Business* (June 1998), pp. 129–233.
16. William B. Wagner, "Establishing Supply Service Strategy for Shortage Situations," *Industrial Marketing Management*, Vol. 23 (1994), pp. 393–401.
17. *CIA World Fact Book,* www.odci.gov/cia/ (December 1998).
18. Fawzia Sheikh, "Grocers Get Ready for Wal-Mart Threat," *Marketing Magazine* (November 9, 1998), p. 3; Editorial, "The Wal-Mart Threat," *Marketing Magazine* (December 7, 1998), p. 35.
19. John H. Antil, "Are You Committing Marketcide?" *Journal of Services Marketing*, Vol. 6 (Spring 1992), pp. 45–53.
20. Marvin J. Cetron, *An American Renaissance in the Year 2000* (New York: St. Martin's Press, 1994); and Jo Marney, "Towards the Next Millennium," *Marketing Magazine* (July 24, 1995), p. 17.

## CHAPTER 3

1. Lesley Daw, "Reflections from Behind the Glass," *Marketing Magazine* (May 18, 1998), pp. 23–24; "Advertising Under the Microscope," *Marketing Magazine* (May 18, 1998), pp. 23–26; "Doing Their Homework," *Marketing Magazine* (May 18, 1998), p. 25; "The Photo Sort," *Marketing Magazine* (May 18, 1998), p. 26; Marion Plunkett, "Fables, Fantasies and Facts," *Marketing Magazine* (May 18, 1998), p. 27.
2. Peter Francese, "Managing Market Information," *American Demographics* (September 1995), p. 59.
3. Adapted by the authors from Robert A. Peterson, *Marketing Research*, Second Edition (Dallas: Business Publications, 1988), p. 31; and Peter D. Bennett (Ed.), *Dictionary of Marketing Terms*, Second Edition (Chicago: American Marketing Association, 1995), p. 167.
4. Jacqueline M. Graves, "Building a Fortune on Free Data," *Fortune* (February 6, 1995); American Business Information brochures;

and *Canada Phone User Guide* (Danvers, Mass: ProCD Incorporated, 1995) pp. 1–5.

5   Susan K. Jones, *Creative Strategy in Direct Marketing* (Lincolnwood, Ill.: NTC Publishing, 1991), p. 5.

6   Robert Shaw and Merlin Stone, Data-Base Marketing: Strategy & Implementation (New York: Wiley, 1990), p. 4. See also Mary Lou Roberts, "Expanding the Role of the Direct Marketing Database," *Journal of Direct Marketing*, Vol. 6 (Spring 1992), pp. 51–60; and Terry G. Vavra, "The Data-Base Marketing Imperative," *Marketing Management*, Vol. 2 (Number 1, 1993), pp. 47–57.

7   See Timothy J. Keane and Paul Wang, "Applications for the Lifetime Value Model in Modern Newspaper Publishing," *Journal of Direct Marketing*, Vol. 9 (Spring 1995), pp. 59–66.

8   Coopers & Lybrand Consulting, "Data-Base Marketing: How It Works," *Business Week* (September 5, 1994), pp. 56–57.

9   Eldon Y. Li, "Marketing Information Systems in the Top U.S. Companies: A Longitudinal Analysis," *Information & Management*, Vol. 28 (January 1995), pp. 13–31.

10  Jan P. Herring, "Business Intelligence in Japan and Sweden: Lessons for the U.S.," *Journal of Business Strategy*, Vol. 13 (March–April 1992), p. 45.

11  Ibid., p. 47.

12  Mark Stevenson, "He Sees All He Knows All," *Canadian Business* (Spring 1994), Special Technology Issue; and *General Host Corporation 1994 Annual Report*.

13  Jack Honomichl, "Top 25 Global Firms Earn $6.1 Billion in Revenue," *Marketing News* (August 18, 1997), Special Section, p. H2.

14  Thomas C. Kinnear and Ann R. Root (Eds.), *1994 Survey of Marketing Research* (Chicago: American Marketing Association, 1995), pp. 38, 49.

15  Sally Solo, "How to Listen to Consumers," *Fortune* (January 11, 1993), pp. 77, 79; Laura Loro, "Customer Is Always Right," *Advertising Age* (February 10, 1992), p. 26; and "1995 Directory of Customer Satisfaction Measurement Firms," *Marketing News* (October 23, 1995), Special Section.

16  Michael McCullough, "The Truth Is Out There," *Marketing Magazine* (September 28, 1998), pp. 10–11.

17  James Pollock, "Measured Growth," *Marketing Magazine* (January 15, 1996), p. 16; Kelly Shermach, "Respondents Get Hooked Up and Show Their Emotions," *Marketing News* (August 28, 1995), p. 35; and John P. Dickson and Douglas L. MacLachlan, "Fax Surveys?" *Marketing Research*, Vol. 4 (September 1992), pp. 26–30.

18  Gene R. Laczniak and Patrick E. Murphy, *Ethical Marketing Decisions: The Higher Road* (Needham Heights, Mass.: Allyn and Bacon, 1993), pp. 53–68.

19  Lourdes Lee Valeriano, "Western Firms Poll Eastern Europeans to Discern Tastes of Nascent Consumers," *Wall Street Journal* (April 27, 1992), pp. B1–B2; Richard W. Stevenson, "Teaching the Hard Sell of Soap to Eastern Europe," *New York Times* (February 18, 1993), pp. D1, D7; and R. Craig Endicott, "European Dream Captivates Researchers," *Advertising Age* (October 18, 1993), p. S-6.

20  Bennett, *Dictionary of Marketing Terms*, p. 103.

21  Peter Verburg, "Ice Guy Finishes First," *Canadian Business* (February 27, 1998), pp. 39–58.

**CHAPTER 4**

1   Peter Weis, "Desperately Seeking Simplicity," *Marketing Magazine* (June 8, 1998), p. 12.

2   *Seagate 1992 Annual Report*, p. 9.

3   Unless otherwise indicated, the data presented in this chapter are all from Statistics Canada (www.statscan.ca); Strategis (strategis.ic.gc.ca); the United Nations (www.un.org); U.S. Bureau of the Census; CIA World Factbook (www.odci.gov/cia); Organization for Economic Cooperation and Development (OECD) (www.oecd.org); and American Demographics (www.demographics.org).

4   Rahul Jacob, "The Big Rise," *Fortune* (May 30, 1994), pp. 74–90.

5   Canadian Media Directors' Council, "Media Digest 1998–99," *Marketing Magazine*: Toronto, Ontario; "1998 Guide to Multicultural Marketing Services," *Marketing Magazine* (September 14, 1998), pp. 26–28.

6   Charles Laughlin, "Speaking in Tongues," *Link* (October 1993), p. 15; "The Economics of Growing Communities," *Marketing Magazine*, (July 3/10, 1995), p. 11.

7   Jennifer Lynn, "Approaching Diversity," *Marketing Magazine* (July 3/10, 1995), p. 11; and David Chilton, "Maclean's Suspends Its Chinese Edition," *Marketing Magazine* (May 11, 1998), p. 4.

8   Statistics Canada, "Household Facilities and Equipment, 1997," *The Daily* (Thursday, November 27, 1997).

9   Peter D. Bennett (Ed.), *Dictionary of Marketing Terms*, Second Edition (Chicago: American Marketing Association, 1994), p. 154.

10  Elliott Ettenberg, "Les blokes Canadiens," *Marketing Magazine* (March 13, 1995), p. 8; Graham Watt, "History and the Canadian Way," *Marketing Magazine* (May 1, 1995), p. 8; Shirley Roberts, "New Consumer Attitudes," *Strategy* (April 14, 1994), p. 4; "A Common Border Does Not Mean Shared Values," *Marketing Magazine,* (January 25, 1993), p 3.

11  Wilson Baker, "O Canada," *American Demographics* (June 1997).

12  Fritz Kuhn, "Across the Border," *Marketing Magazine* (June 29, 1998), pp. 40–43.

13  Bennett, *Dictionary of Marketing Terms*, p. 265. See also Chip Walker, "The Global Middle Class," *American Demographics* (September 1995), pp. 40–46.

14  See Basil G. Englis and Michael R. Solomon, "To Be *and* Not to Be: Lifestyle Imagery, Reference Groups," *Journal of Advertising*, Vol. 24 (Spring 1995), pp. 13–28.

15  Robert E. Wilkes, "Household Life-Cycle Stages, Transitions, and Product Expenditures," *Journal of Consumer Research*, Vol. 22 (June 1995), pp. 27–42.

16  Bennett, *Dictionary of Marketing Terms*, pp. 179–180.

17  Leon G. Schiffman and Leslie Lazar Kanuk, *Consumer Behaviour*, Fifth Edition (Englewood Cliffs, N.J.: Prentice-Hall, 1994), pp. 562–564.

18  Diane Crispell, "The Brave New World of Men," *American Demographics* (January 1992), pp. 38, 43.

19  Shirley Roberts, "The New Consumer," *Marketing Magazine* (April 13, 1998), pp. 12–13.

20  "RPM Adds to Radio's Sales Arsenal," *Marketing Magazine* (May 4, 1992), p. 2.

21  "Harvesting the Power of Synchrographics," *Marketing Magazine* (November 30, 1992), p 10.

22  Bonnie Sherman, "The New Way to Shop," *Marketing Magazine* (November 19, 1998), p. 36.

23  Jo Marney, "Ready-to-Wear Research," *Marketing Magazine* (April 6, 1998), p. 13.

24  Bennett, *Dictionary of Marketing Terms*, p. 157.

25  See also Stephen L. Vargo, "Consumer Involvement: An Historical Perspective and Partial Synthesis," in Barbara B. Stern and George M. Zinkham (Eds.), *1995 AMA Educators' Proceedings* (Chicago: American Marketing Association, 1995), pp. 139–145.

26  "Brand Loyalty Declining, Study Shows," *Marketing Magazine* (April 27, 1992), p 2.

27  Lara Mills, "Royal Bank Rolls Out New Customer Loyalty Card," *Marketing Magazine* (May 13, 1996), p. 4; News Line, "Zellers Creates Kids Loyalty Club," *Marketing Magazine* (October 12, 1998), p. 1.

28  "Eric A. Greenleaf and Donald R. Lehmann, "Reasons for Substantial Delay in Consumer Decision Making," *Journal of Consumer Research*, Vol. 22 (September 1995), pp. 186–199; Bonnie Sherman, "E-Buying Takes Off," *Marketing Magazine* (May 4, 1998), p. 17.

29  Shirley Roberts, "The New Consumer," *Marketing Magazine* (April 13, 1998), pp. 12–13.

30  Dennis Bruce, "Reason Be Damned," *Marketing Magazine* (November 9, 1998), p. 29.

## CHAPTER 5

1  Ian Austen, "Videos from the Dead," *Canadian Business* (February 27, 1998), pp. 72–75.

2  Shawn Tully, "Purchasing's New Muscle," *Fortune* (February 20, 1995), pp. 75–76.

3  Arthur Bragg, "How to Sell in the Big Time," *Sales & Marketing Management* (February 1990), pp. 42–44; and Michael Selz, "Some Suppliers Rethink Their Reliance on Big Business," *Wall Street Journal* (March 29, 1993), p. B2.

4  Polaroid Web site, www.polaroid.com (December 31, 1998).

5  Bombardier Web site, www.bombardier.com (Jan 8, 1999).

6  Andersen Consulting, "1997 Annual Report," www.9c.com (January 4, 1999).

7  Peter D. Bennett (Ed.), *Dictionary of Marketing Terms*, Second Edition (Chicago: American Marketing Association, 1995), pp. 297–298.

8  Ibid., p. 299. See also Stephanie Gruner, "The Smart Vendor-Audit Checklist," *Inc.* (April 1995), pp. 93–95.

9  John R. Emshwiller, "Suppliers Struggle to Improve Quality as Big Firms Slash Their Vendor Rolls," *Wall Street Journal* (August 16, 1991), pp. B1–B2; Kathleen Kerwin and Bill Vlasic, "A Shrinking Supply of Suppliers," *Business Week* (January 8, 1996), p. 83; Tully, "Purchasing's New Muscle," p. 79; and *Market Research Handbook 1995*, Statistics Canada (Ottawa: Minister of Industry, Science, and Technology).

10  Nathaniel Gilbert, "The Case for Countertrade," *Across the Board* (May 1992), p. 44. See also Peter W. Liesch, "Government-Mandated Countertrade in Australia," *Industrial Marketing Management*, Vol. 23 (October 1994), pp. 299–305.

11  Tim Ambler, "Reflections in China: Re-Orienting Images of Marketing," *Marketing Management* (Summer 1995), pp. 24, 25–26.

12  Statistics Canada, NAICS 1997, Statistics Canada Web site, www.statscan.ca/english/standard (January 9, 1999); NAICS Association Web site, www.naics.com (January 9, 1999).

13  Boeing Home News, "Boeing Spends $12 Billion with 34,000 U.S. Companies," Boeing Web site, www.boeing.com (January 9, 1999).

14  Bernice Kanner, "Shelf Control," New York (January 22, 1990), p. 22.

15  Statistics Canada, *The Daily* (Tuesday, December 8, 1998), Statistics Canada Web site, www.statscan.ca.

16  Contracts Canada, "How We Buy," Contracts Canada Web site, contractscanada.gc.ca (December 31, 1998); "Performance 2000," *Canadian Business* (June 26/July 10, 1998), pp. 138–149.

17  Sherry Ferronato, "The Status Quo or Quo Vadis? The Present and Future of the Charitable Sector," *CharityVillage NewsWeek News* (November 9, 1998), www.charityvillage.com (January 9, 1999).

18  Tully, "Purchasing's New Muscle," p. 76; Shona McKay, "A Paper Tiger in the Paperless World," *Canadian Business* (April 1996), pp. 25–29.

19  See Cathy Owens Swift, "Preferences for Single Sourcing and Supplier Selection Criteria," *Journal of Business Research*, Vol. 32 (February 1995), pp. 105–111.

20  The material in this section is drawn from Jagdish N. Sheth, "A Model of Industrial Buyer Behaviour," *Journal of Marketing*, Vol. 37 (October 1973), pp. 50–56.

21  Ibid., p. 52.

22  Ibid., p. 56.

23  Derrick C. Schnebelt, "Turning the Tables," *Sales & Marketing Management* (January 1993), p. 23.

24  John F. Veiga and John N. Yanouzas, "Emerging Cultural Values Among Russian Managers: What Will Tomorrow Bring?" *Business Horizons*, Vol. 38 (July–August 1995), pp. 20–27.

25  E. D. Bamgboye, "Equipment Buying in Nigeria," *Industrial Marketing Management*, Vol. 21 (August 1992), pp. 181–185.

26  Johan Roos, Ellen Veie, and Lawrence S. Welch, "A Case Study of Equipment Purchasing in Czechoslovakia," *Industrial Marketing Management*, Vol. 21 (August 1922), pp. 257–263; and Dale A. Lunsford and Bradley C. Fussell, "Marketing Business Services in Central Europe," *Journal of Services Marketing*, Vol. 7 (Number 1, 1993), pp. 13–21.

27  F. Michael Hruby, "Seventeen Tips (Not Just) for Industrial Marketers," *Sales & Marketing Management* (May 1990), pp. 68–76.

28  The material in this section is based on Stewart Alsop, "Is There Life After ERP? For the Valley, Maybe Not," *Fortune* (August 3, 1998), pp. 231–232.

## CHAPTER 6

1  Anita Lahey, "Marketing the Leisure Life," *Marketing Magazine* (August 24/31, 1998), pp. 20–21; *Today's Seniors* (October 1995); Eric Miller, "A 24-point Guide to Mature Minds," *Marketing Magazine* (May 15, 1995), p. 29; and *Market Research Handbook 1995*, Statistics Canada. (Ottawa: Minister of Industry Science and Technology), p. 579.

2  Peter D. Bennett (Ed.), *Dictionary of Marketing Terms*, Second Edition (Chicago: American Marketing Association, 1995), p. 166.

3  Peter R. Dickson and James L. Ginter, "Market Segmentation, Product Differentiation, and Marketing Strategy," *Journal of Marketing*, Vol. 51 (April 1987), pp. 1–10; and "Superbrands '96: Category Charts," *Superbrands 1996: Brandweek's Marketers of the Year* (October 6, 1995), p. 129.

4  Statistics Canada, "Canadian Statistic—Average Household Expenditures, Canada, the Provinces. and Selected Metropolitan Areas, 1996," Statistics Canada Web site, www.statcan.ca (January, 1999).

5  Recommended Reading: "Setting Sights on China's S Generation," *Marketing Magazine* (April 13, 1998), p. 42.

6  Lesley Daw, "Corporate Gay Marketing Takes Off," *Marketing Magazine* (July 20/27, 1998), p. 2.

7  Sylvia Criger, "Big Enough to Target," *Marketing Magazine* (September 14, 1998), p. 22; and Media Briefs, "Toronto Star Buys into Sing Tao," *Marketing Magazine* (April 13, 1998), p. 4.

8  Industry Canada, "ITT Sector Overview," Strategis Web site, strategis.ic.gc.ca (January 18, 1999).

9  *Statistical Abstract of the United States 1995* (Washington, D.C.: U.S. Department of Commerce, 1995), various pages; Karen Maru File, "Is There a Trillion-Dollar Family Business Market?" *Industrial Marketing Management*, Vol. 24 (August 1995), pp. 247–255; and "A Catalogue of Sales Leads," *Canadian Business Information* (Fall, 1997), p. 280.

10  News Line, "Hasbro Pushes Family Games," *Marketing Magazine* (November 9, 1998), p. 1; and News Line, "P&G to Reward Family Programming," *Marketing Magazine* (November 30, 1998), p. 6.

11  Gerri Hirshey, "Happy [ ] Day to You," *New York Times Magazine* (July 2, 1995), p. 27; Henry Assael and David F. Poltrack, "Can Demographic Profiles of Heavy Users Serve as a Surrogate for Purchase Behavior in Selecting TV Programs?" *Journal of Advertising Research*, Vol. 34 (January–February 1994), pp. 11–17; "Brewing Up a Storm," *Advertising Age* (May 15, 1995), pp. I–3; *Statistical Abstract of the United States 1995*, various pages; and *U.S. Industrial Outlook 1994*, various pages.

12  Russell I. Haley, "Benefit Segmentation: A Decision-Oriented Research Tool," *Journal of Marketing*, Vol. 32 (July 1968), pp. 30–35; Russell I. Haley, "Benefit Segments: Backwards and Forwards," *Journal of Advertising Research*, Vol. 24 (February–March 1984), pp. 19–25; James W. Harvey, "Benefit Segmentation for Fund Raisers," *Journal of the Academy of Marketing Science*, Vol. 18 (Winter 1990), pp. 77–86; P. J. O'Connor and Gary L. Sullivan, "Market Segmentation: A Comparison of Benefits/Attributes Desired and Brand Preference," *Psychology & Marketing*, Vol. 12 (October 1995), pp. 613–635; and Chatrathi P. Rao and Zhengyuan Wang, "Evaluating Alternative Segmentation Strategies in Standard Industrial Markets," *European Journal of Marketing*, Vol. 29 (Number 2, 1995), pp. 58–75.

13  SRI International, Menlo Park, California.

14  "The Best 100 Sources for Marketing Information," *American Demographics* (January 1995), p. 29.

15  Lewis C. Winters, "International Psychographics," *Marketing Research*, Vol. 4 (September 1992), pp. 48–49; VALS Web site, future.sri.com/Vals (January 18, 1999).

16  VALS Web site, future.sri.com/Vals (January 18, 1999).

17  Tom Eisenhart, "How to Really Excite Your Prospects," *Business Marketing* (July 1988), pp. 44–45 ff.; and Raymond E. Taylor, Lorraine A. Krajewksi, and John R. Darling, "Social Style Application to Enhance Direct Mail Response," *Journal of Direct Marketing*, Vol. 7 (Autumn 1993), pp. 42–53.

18  See Paul A. Herbig, John Milewicz, and James E. Golden, "The Do's and Don'ts of Sales Forecasting," *Industrial Marketing Management*, Vol. 22 (February 1993), pp. 49–57; Theodore Modis, "Life Cycles: Forecasting the Rise and Fall of Almost Anything," *Futurist* (September–October 1995), pp. 20–25; and John B. Mahaffie, "Why Forecasts Fail," *American Demographics* (March 1995), pp. 34–40.

19  The material in this section is based on Kelly Shermach, "Study Identifies Types of Interactive Shoppers," *Marketing News* (September 25, 1995), p. 22.

**CHAPTER 7**

1  Caterpillar Web site, www.cat.com (April 9, 1999); "Caterpillar's Comeback," *The Economist* (June 20, 1998); www.economist.com (January 19, 1999).

2  Peter D. Bennett (Ed.), *Dictionary of Marketing Terms*, Second Edition (Chicago: American Marketing Association, 1995), p. 219.

3  Caterpillar Web site, www.cat.com (April 9, 1999).

4  "POPAI's 1995 Study: 'More Purchase Decisions Made In-Store,'" *Promo* (October 1995), p. 15.

5  Bennett, *Dictionary of Marketing Terms*, p. 222.

6  Chris Daniels, "In Your Face," *Marketing Magazine* (March 8, 1999), pp. 15–17.

7  See John A. Quelch and David Kenny, "Extend Profits, Not Product Lines," *Harvard Business Review*, Vol. 72 (September–October 1994), pp. 153–160.

8  Helena Katz, "Bombardier Makes Tracks into ATVs," *Marketing Magazine* (January 25, 1999), p. 2; "Performance 2000," *Canadian Business* (June 26/July 10, 1998), p. 138; and Patrick J. Spain and James R. Talbot (Eds.), *Hoover's Handbook of World Business 1995–1996* (Austin, Texas: Reference Press, 1995), pp. 138–139.

9  World Line, "Heinz to Invest More in Brand Marketing," *Marketing Magazine* (March 1, 1999), p. 6; World Line, "H. J. Heinz," *Marketing Magazine* (November 1, 1998), p. 8.

10  The definitions in this section are drawn from Bennett, *Dictionary of Marketing Terms*, various pages.

11  "Interview with Tom Dawley, Marketing Director of Online Products Ontario Lottery Corp," *Strategy* (June 27, 1994), p. 9; Chris Daniels, "Planet Snak Orbits Singles Scene," *Marketing Magazine* (March 22, 1999), p. 2; and Eve Lazarus, "Finesse Brand Aims to Be No. 1 Again," *Marketing Magazine* (March 22, 1999), p. 3.

12  "Career Labatt Man Set to Fill New VP Slot," *Marketing Magazine* (December 21–28, 1992), p. 2.

13  Chris Daniels, "Planet Snak Orbits Singles Scene," *Marketing Magazine* (March 22, 1999), p. 2.

14  Based on Nelson D. Schwartz, "The Tech Boom Will Keep on Rocking: Ten Trends to Bet On," *Fortune* (February 15, 1999), pp. 65–80.

**CHAPTER 8**

1  Katrina Onstad and Tamsen Tillson, "Get 'Em While They're Hot," *Canadian Business* (April 1996), pp. 37–55; "Service Sector Jobs Double in 30 Years," *Globe & Mail*, Metro edition (June 9, 1993), p. B3; and "Modern Technology Fails to Bring About Productivity Boom," *Financial Post* (April 24–26, 1993), p.18.

2  Bureau of Economic Analysis, U.S. Commerce Department; and *Statistical Abstract of the United States 1995* (Washington, D.C.: U.S. Department of Commerce, 1995), various pages. See also Fanglan Du, Paula Mergenhagen, and Marlene Lee, "The Future of Services," *American Demographics* (November 1995), pp. 30–47; Statistics Canada, *The Daily* (April 30, 1996); and Statistics Canada, *The Daily* (January 29, 1996).

3  Statistics Canada, *The Daily* (January 29, 1996).

4  "Advantis Takes Over Air Canada IS," *Computing Canada* (September 1, 1994), pp. 1,4; and Ira Sager, "The View from IBM," *Business Week* (October 30, 1995), p. 145.

5  See Ralph W. Jackson, Lester A. Neidell, and Dale Lunsford, "An Empirical Investigation of the Differences in Goods and Services as Perceived by Organizational Buyers," *Industrial Marketing Management*, Vol. 24 (March 1995), pp. 99–108.

6  See James C. Anderson and James A. Narus, "Capturing the Value of Supplementary Services," *Harvard Business Review*, Vol. 73 (January–February 1995), pp. 75–83.

7  Gordon H. G. McDougall and Douglas W. Snetsinger, "The Intangibility of Services: Measurement and Competitive Perspectives," *Journal of Services Marketing*, Vol. 4 (Fall 1990), pp. 27–40.

8  Leonard L. Berry, A. Parasuraman, and Valarie A. Zeithaml, "Synchronizing Demand and Supply in Service Businesses," *Business*, Vol. 34 (October–December 1984), pp. 36–37; James L. Heskett, W. Earl Sasser, Jr., and Christopher W. L. Hart, *Service Breakthroughs* (New York: Free Press, 1990), pp. 135–158; and Donald J. Shemwell, Jr. and J. Joseph Cronin, Jr., "Services Marketing Strategies for Coping with Demand/Supply Imbalances," *Journal of Services Marketing*, Vol. 8 (Number 4, 1994), pp. 14–24.

9  Lawrence A. Crosby, Kenneth R. Evans, and Deborah Cowles, "Relationship Quality in Services Selling: An Interpersonal Influence Perspective," *Journal of Marketing*, Vol. 54 (July 1990), p. 68; and "Greyhound: A Plan to Hold Its Ground," *Strategy* (September 6, 1993) p. 15. See also David E. Bowen and Edward E. Lawler III, "Empowering Service Employees," *Sloan Management Review*, Vol. 36 (Summer 1995), pp. 73–84.

10  Theodore Levitt, *The Marketing Imagination* (New York: Free Press, 1983), pp. 50–71; and James S. Hensel, "Service Quality Improvement and Control: A Customer-Based Approach," *Journal of Business Research*, Vol. 20 (January 1990), pp. 43–54. See also Myron Magnet, "Good News for the Service Economy," *Fortune* (May 3, 1993), pp. 46–52.

11  "Using People to Drive Success (How One of Canada's Leading Banks Built a Successful Imaging Application)," *I.T. Magazine* (September 1993), pp. 18–22.

12  Valarie A. Zeithaml, A. Parasuraman, and Leonard L. Berry, *Delivering Quality Service* (New York: Free Press, 1990), p. 158. See also Susan J. Devlin and H. K. Dong, "Service Quality from the Customers' Perspective," *Marketing Research* (Winter 1994), pp. 5–13.

13  Zeithaml, Parasuraman, and Berry, *Delivering Quality Service*, pp. 18–22.

14  "Calgary Orchestra Hits Right Marketing Notes," *Marketing Magazine* (August 15, 1994), p. 4.

15  See Alan R. Andreasen, "Social Marketing: Its Definition and Domain," *Journal of Public Policy & Marketing*, Vol. 13 (Spring 1994), pp. 108–114; and Patricia Braus, "Selling Good Behavior," *American Demographics* (November 1995), pp. 60–64.

16  Edward T. Pound, Gary Cohen, and Penny Loeb, "Tax Exempt!" *U.S. News & World Report* (October 2, 1995), pp. 36–51; and John R. Emshwiller, "More Small Firms Complain About Tax-Exempt Rivals," *Wall Street Journal* (August 8, 1995), pp. B1–B2.

17  Statistics Canada, "Charitable Donors, 1997," *The Daily* (Thursday, December 3, 1998), www.statscan.ca/The Daily (April 28, 1999); Statistics Canada, "National Survey of Giving, Volunteering and Participating, 1997," *The Daily* (Monday, August 24, 1998), www.statscan.ca/The Daily (April 28, 1999).

18  Jim Carroll and Rick Broadhead, *1996 Canadian Internet Directory*, (Scarborough: Prentice Hall Canada), p. 252; Nan

O'Neal, "UN Taps Ad Group," *Advertising Age* (October 29, 1990), p. 12; "Dresses for Humanity Raises $140 000," *CharityVillage NewsWeek News* (November 9, 1998), www.charityvillage.com (January 9, 1999).

19  Performance 2000, "48 46 Canada Post Corp. (other)," *Canadian Business* (June 26/July 10, 1998), pp. 138–139; Canada Post Web site, www.canpost.ca.

20  Statistics Canada, "University Enrolment, Fall 1998," *The Daily* (Tuesday, November 10, 1998); Statistics Canada, "University Tuition Fees, 1997/98," *The Daily* (Monday, August 25, 1997); David North, "How to Wise Up Real Cheap," *Canadian Business* (April 10, 1998), p. 22; Chris Daniels, "Universities Go Student Shopping in the States," *Marketing Magazine* (June 22, 1998), p. 13; and Terry Bullick, "Recruitment 101," *Marketing Magazine* (March 11, 1996), p. 8.

21  Derek DeCloet, "Bloomberg for Amateurs," *Canadian Business* (April 30, 1999), pp. 47–49.

22  United Way of Canada Web site, www.uwc-cc.ca (April 29, 1999); and Keith H. Hammonds and Morton D. Sosland, "Even the United Way Is Struggling to Make Ends Meet," *Business Week* (November 5, 1990), p. 102.

**CHAPTER 9**

1  Statistics Canada, "Household Facilities and Equipment, 1997," *The Daily* (Thursday, November 27, 1997); News Line, "Clearnet Takes Aim at Home Phone," *Marketing Magazine* (March 29, 1999), p. 1; Stephanie Wittaker, "The Ant That Toted Away a Big Market Share," *Marketing Magazine* (November 16, 1998), p. 23; Jack Branswell, "Catch-up Time for Cell Phones," *Marketing Magazine* (November 2, 1998), pp. 18–19; and Lara Mills, "PCS Phones Get Dressed Up for Holidays," *Marketing Magazine* (October 19, 1998), p. 3.

2  See Roger J. Calantone, C. Anthony Di Benedetto, and Ted Haggbloom, "Principles of New Product Management: Exploring the Beliefs of Product Practitioners," *Journal of Product Innovation Management*, Vol. 12 (June 1995), pp. 235–247.

3  Sarah Smith, "New Tricks for Old Cards," *Marketing Magazine* (April 5, 1999), p. 22.

4  Peter D. Bennett (Ed.), *Dictionary of Marketing Terms*, Second Edition (Chicago: American Marketing Association, 1995), pp. 27, 201.

5  Jeffrey R. Williams, "How Sustainable Is Your Competitive Advantage?" *California Management Review*, Vol. 34 (Spring 1992), p. 29.

6  World Line, "Sony Goes 'Gonzo' with XPlod Campaign," *Marketing Magazine* (March 15, 1999), p. 6.

7  Tod Jones, "The Power of Persistence," *Price Costco Connection* (June 1995), p. 15; and "Powerbar Company Capsule," Infoseek and Hoover's Online, www.infoseek.com (May 11, 1999).

8  Alex Taylor III, "The Gentlemen at Ford Are Kicking Butt," *Fortune* (June 22, 1998), pp. 71–75.

9  Fawzia Sheikh, "Digital Camera Market Developing," *Marketing Magazine* (November 30, 1998), p. 3; and Deborah McKay-Stokes, "Old Products and New Processes," *Marketing Magazine* (April 24, 1995), p. 15.

10  Katrina Onstad, "The Midas Touch," *Canadian Business* (December 1995), p. 40.

11  Susan Ellsworth, "V-chips and Audience Numbers," *Marketing Magazine* (January 22, 1996), p. 19; and "TV Forced to Code Shows for Violence: CRTC Has Ordered Broadcasters to Establish a V-chip System by September 1 to Help Parents Control What Their Children Watch," *Vancouver Sun* (March 15, 1996), pp. A1, A10.

12  Katrina Onstad, "How Can Big Companies Keep the Entrepreneurial Spirit Alive?" *Harvard Business Review*, Vol. 73 (November-December 1995), p. 190.

13  Jo Marney, "New Product Protection," *Marketing Magazine* (October 12, 1998), p. 26; Cyndee Miller, "Survey: New Product Failure Is Top Management's Fault," *Marketing News* (February 1, 1993), p. 2; Erik Jan Hultink and Henry S.J. Robben, "Measuring New Product Success: The Difference That Time Perspective

Makes," *Journal of Product Innovation Management* (November 1995), pp. 392–405; James Dao, "From a Collector of Turkeys, A Tour of a Supermarket Zoo," *New York Times* (September 24, 1995), Section C, p. 12; and Ulrike de Brentani, "New Industrial Service Development: Scenarios for Success and Failure," *Journal of Business Research* (February 1995), pp. 93–103.

14  David Baines, "The Frying Game," *Canadian Business* (September 1994), pp. 32–36; and "Harvard Flunks Out," (editorial) *Canadian Business* (December 1994), p. 22.

15  John R. Emschwiller, "Thermalux Seeks Customers for a New Technology," *Wall Street Journal* (February 15, 1991), p. B2.

16  Federal Express Corporation reports.

17  Sandra Salmans, "RCA Defends Timing of Videodisc Canceling," *New York Times* (April 6, 1984), pp. D1, D15; Marcia Watson, Jeff Kemph, and Judith Steele, "Marketing Muscle and the Videodisc," *Business Marketing* (June 1985), pp. 130–140; Brian O'Reilly, "Pioneer's Bright Picture," *Fortune* (August 13, 1990), p. 89; and "How to Sell Yourself on a CD-Interactive Player from Philips," *Wall Street Journal* (May 1, 1992), p. A13.

18  Miller, "Survey: New Product Failure Is Top Management's Fault," p. 2; T. Erickson and L. Brenkus, *Healthcare R & D: Tools and Tactics* (Cambridge, Mass.: Arthur D. Little, October 1986), meeting notes; Laura Jereski, "Block That Innovation!" *Forbes* (January 18, 1993), p. 48; and Lara Mills, "The New Rx for Drug Marketing," *Marketing Magazine* (September 11, 1995), p. 15.

19  See Robert G. Cooper and Elko J. Kleinschmidt, "Benchmarking the Firm's Success Factors in New Product Development," *Journal of Product Innovation Management*, Vol. 12 (November 1995), pp. 374–391; and James M. Higgins, "Innovate or Evaporate," *Futurist* (September–October 1995), pp. 42–48.

20  Carol Panasiuk, "Breaking Through," *Marketing Magazine* (October 12, 1998), p. 17.

21  Teresa Riordan, "Patents," *New York Times* (June 12, 1995), p. D2; Neil Gross, "New Patent Office Pending," *Business Week* (October 23, 1995), p. 130; Masaaki Kotabe, "A Study of Japanese Patent Systems," *Journal of International Business Studies* (First Quarter 1992), pp. 147–169; World Intellectual Property Organization, "Industrial Property Statistics Publication A: Patents," World Intellectual Property Organization Web site, www.wipo.org (May, 1999); and Industry Canada, "Science and Technology Data 1998," Strategis Web site, www.strategis.ic.gc.ca (May 1999).

22  Adapted from Philip Kotler, *Marketing Management: Analysis, Planning, Implementation, and Control*, Eighth Edition (Englewood Cliffs, N.J.: Prentice-Hall, 1994), p. 331.

23  Mikala Folb, "1999 Touted as Year of DVD Takeoff," *Marketing Magazine* (December 14, 1998), p. 3.

24  Shawn Tully, "Can Boeing Reinvent Itself?" *Fortune* (March 8, 1993), p. 72. See also Alex Taylor III, "Boeing Sleepy in Seattle," *Fortune* (August 7, 1995), pp. 92–98.

25  World Line, "Campbell Testing New Supper Soups," *Marketing Magazine* (November 30, 1998), p. 6.

26  Aimee L. Stern, "Testing Goes Industrial," *Sales & Marketing Management* (March 1991), p. 30. See also Steve Blount, "It's Just a Matter of Time," *Sales & Marketing Management* (March 1992), pp. 32–43.

27  Douglas Faulkner, "The Coca-Cola Kid," *Marketing Magazine* (August 14, 1995), p. 24.

28  "Coke Quietly Tests New Diet Sweetener," *Marketing Magazine* (June 12, 1995), p. 7.

29  World Line, "Coke, Marlboro Still the World's Top Brands," *Marketing Magazine* (July 24, 1995), p. 5.

30  Editorial, "Electronic Indicators," *Marketing Magazine* (June 9, 1997), p. 23.

31  Noreen O'Leary, WPP's Brandz Quantifies Consumer Brand Loyalty," *Marketing Magazine* (October 26, 1998), p. 8.

32  Laurel Wentz, "Upstart Brands Steal Spotlight from Perennials," *Advertising Age* (September 19, 1994), pp. I-13–I-14.

33  Kevin Goldman, "U.S. Brands Lag Behind Japanese in Name Recognition by Chinese," *Wall Street Journal* (February 16, 1995), p. B8.

34 Gillette Web site, www.gillette.com (May 10, 1999).

35 Cyndee Miller, "Stay Tuned for TV Networks as Brands," *Marketing News* (October 9, 1995), pp. 1, 10; and Canadian Media Directors' Council, *23rd Annual Media Digest* (Toronto: *Marketing Magazine*, 1995), p. 8.

36 Laurence Bernstein, "The Who, What and Why of Brands," *Marketing Magazine* (May 3, 1999), p. 22.

37 Morris B. Holbrook, "Product Quality, Attributes, and Brand Names as Determinants of Price: The Case of Consumer Electronics," *Marketing Letters,* Vol. 1 (1992), p. 72.

38 Kevin Lane Keller, "Conceptualizing, Measuring, and Managing Customer-Based Brand Equity," *Journal of Marketing* (January 1993), pp. 1, 8. See also David A. Aaker, *Managing Brand Equity* (New York: Free Press, 1991); and David C. Bello and Morris B. Holbrook, "Does an Absence of Brand Equity Generalize Across Product Categories? *Journal of Business Research* (October 1995), pp. 125–131.

39 "Coke Is Still It," *Advertising Age* (July 17, 1995), p. 8.

40 Peter H. Farquhar, Julia Y. Han, and Yuji Ijiri, "Brands on the Balance Sheet," *Marketing Management*, Vol. 1 (Winter 1992), pp. 16–22.

41 Bennett, *Dictionary of Marketing Terms*, p. 28. See also Ernest Dichter, "What's in an Image," *Journal of Product & Brand Management*, Vol. 1 (Spring 1992), pp. 54–60.

42 Stephen King, WPP Group, London, as quoted in Aaker, *Managing Brand Equity*, p. 1.

43 Robert A. Mamis, "Name-Calling," *Inc.* (July 1984), pp. 67–74; and "Fortune 500," *Fortune* (April 26, 1999), pp. F1, F55.

44 Michael Davie, "Maintaining Two Solitudes," *Marketing Magazine* (March 15, 1999), pp. 12–13.

45 News Line, "Maple Leaf Spruces Up Its Logo," *Marketing Magazine* (April 5, 1999), p. 1.

46 Sean Eckford, "Corel Plans Big Marketing Relaunch for WordPerfect," *Marketing Magazine* (February 19, 1996), p. 5.

47 For a good overview of this topic, see John A. Quelch and David Harding, "Brands Versus Private Labels," *Harvard Business Review*, Vol. 74 (January–February 1996), pp. 99–109; Marcia Mogelonsky, "When Stores Become Brands," *American Demographics* (February 1995), pp. 32–38; and "Special Report: Brand Power," *Progressive Grocer* (October 1994), supplement.

48 Marketscan, "Private Label Continues Growth in U.S. Supermarkets," *Canadian Grocer* (April 1998), Maclean Hunter Bizlink, www.bizlink.com; Beverage Bulletin, "Fast Fact," *Canadian Grocer* (May 1998), Maclean Hunter Bizlink, www.bizlink.com; Laura Medcalf, "Club Monaco Cola Highlights New Trend in Private Label Pop," *Marketing Magazine* (March 18, 1996), p. 4; Chad Rubel, "Price, Quality Important for Private Label Goods," *Marketing News* (January 2, 1995), p. 24; E. S. Browning, "Europeans Witness Proliferation of Private Labels," *Wall Street Journal* (October 20, 1992), pp. B1, B5; Laurel Wentz, "Private Labels March in Europe Too," *Advertising Age* (May 9, 1994), p. 53; and Tara Parker-Pope, "U.K. Grocer Aims to Bag U.S. Customers," *Wall Street Journal* (May 16, 1995).

49 "A Quick Review of the Year 1998!" *Canadian Grocer* (December 1998), Maclean Hunter Bizlink, www.bizlink.com; Mark Stevenson, "The Hired Hand Waves Goodbye," *Canadian Business* (August 1994), pp. 12–22; Laura Medcalf, "Club Monaco Cola Highlights New Trend in Private-Label Pop," *Marketing Magazine* (March 18, 1996); p. 4; Donalee Moulton, "Sobeys Launches Premium House Brand," *Marketing Magazine* (December 11, 1995), p. 4; James Pollock, "A&P Expands No-Frills Food Basics Division," *Marketing Magazine* (November 27, 1995), p. 2.

50 Karen Welds, "Drug Use Climbing, but So Is Competition," *Pharmacy* (December 1998), Maclean Hunter Bizlink, www.bizlink.com.

51 Quelch and Harding, "Brands Versus Private Labels," pp. 99–100.

52 Edward M. Tauber, "Brand Leverage: Strategy for Growth in a Cost-Controlled World," *Journal of Advertising Research*, Vol. 28 (August–September 1988), pp. 26–30.

53 Fawzia Sheikh, "Zellers Aims for $200M in Truly Sales," *Marketing Magazine* (March 8, 1999), p. 3.

54 Carolyn Shea, "Taking License," *Promo* (June 1995), pp. 33–34; Donalee Moulton, "Green Gables Grows Greener," *Marketing Magazine* (November 6, 1995), pp. 14–16; and News Line, "Roots Buys NHL Licensing Rights," *Marketing Magazine* (December 7, 1998), p. 1.

55 Cyndee Miller, "Kiddi Just Fine in the U.K., But Here It's Binky," *Marketing News* (August 28, 1995), p. 8. See also Martin S. Roth, "The Effects of Culture and Socioeconomics on the Performance of Global Brand Image Strategies," *Journal of Marketing Research*, Vol. 32 (May 1995), pp. 163–175.

56 See Dorothy Cohen, *Legal Issues in Marketing Decision Making* (Cincinnati: South-Western, 1995), pp. 111–136.

57 Eric Swetsky, "Toblerone Topples Pretender," *Marketing Magazine* (October 26, 1998), p. 37.

58 David Chilton, "The Drive for Shelf Impact," *Marketing Magazine* (March 23, 1998), pp. 16–17; and Astrid Van Den Broek, "Message in a Bottle," *Marketing Magazine* (May 11, 1998), pp. 16–17.

59 Primo Angeli, "Thinking Out of the Box: A New Approach to Product Development," *Business Horizons*, Vol. 38 (May–June 1995), p. 18.

60 Lara Mills, "Mr. Tea," *Marketing Magazine* (May 3, 1999), pp. 17–18.

61 Sarah Smith, "Breaking Out of the Box," *Marketing Magazine* (January 4/11, 1999), p. 12.

62 News Line, "Tetley Freshens Iced-Team Look," *Marketing Magazine* (March 15, 1999), p. 3.

63 Stuart Elliott, "Advertising," *New York Times* (January 28, 1993), p. D20.

64 See Barry Berman and Joel R. Evans, *Retail Management: A Strategic Approach*, Sixth Edition (New York: Prentice Hall, 1995), pp. 232–234; and *U.P.C. Guidelines Manual* (Don Mills, Ontario: Product Code Council of Canada), pp. 1–4.

65 Everett M. Rogers, *Diffusion of Innovations*, Third Edition (New York: Free Press, 1982), pp. 164–175.

66 Ibid, pp. 246–261.

67 Fawzia Sheikh, "Digital Camera Market Developing," *Marketing Magazine* (November 30, 1998), p. 3.

68 "Gillette Readies Launch of Women's Razor," *Marketing Magazine*, (December 11, 1995), p. 5.

69 Amal Kumar Naj, "Hey, Get a Grip! Your Basic Paper Clip Is Like a Mousetrap," *Wall Street Journal* (July 24, 1995), pp. A1, A5.

70 Pat Sloan, "Lycra Stretches Fashion Appeal," *Advertising Age* (November 2, 1992), pp. 3, 36.

71 "Scott Trims White Swan Product Line," *Marketing Magazine* (September 25, 1995), p. 1.

72 Astrid Van Den Broek, "Langan Cooks Up Growth at McD's," *Marketing Magazine* (March 29, 1999), p. 2.

73 Nimisha Raja, "Branded Buildings," *Marketing Magazine* (May 27, 1966), p. 20.

## CHAPTER 10

1 Mikala Folb, "www.music.ca," *Marketing Magazine* (November 17, 1997), pp. 29–20; Debora Stokes, "Columbia Spins Two New Music Clubs," *Marketing Magazine* (September 7, 1998), pp. 19–20; Christian Allard, "Loony Tunes," *Canadian Business* (August 1995), pp. 73–74; Michael McCollough, "The Changing Sounds of Music Marketing," *Marketing Magazine* (June 19, 1995), p. 20; James Pollock, "Luckhurst Rising Fast on HMV's Charts," *Marketing Magazine* (February 5, 1996), p. 7; James Pollock, "Tower Entry Stokes Up to Record Market," *Marketing Magazine* (January 22, 1996), p. 5; Michael McCollough, "Virgin Awaits Approval for First Canadian Store," *Marketing Magazine* (February 19, 1996), p. 5; Laura Medcalf, "Music Industry Tests Way to Reach Grown-Up Consumers," *Marketing Magazine* (August 21/28, 1995), p. 3; Canadian Independent Record Production Association, "Canadian Music Industry Primer," CIRPA Web site, www.cirpa.ca; and Solutions Research Group Consultants Inc. and

Chart Communications Inc., "In the Name of Cool, Wave II," www.cartnet.com/cool.htmPress Release (April 1998).

2  Wendy Qu and Allan Staruch of Industry Canada—Service Industries and Capital Projects, "Issues-Assessment of the Competitiveness of Canadian Supply Chains," Strategis Web site, strategis.ic.gc.ca (August 14, 1996.).

3  Aimee L. Stern, "Courting Consumer Loyalty with the Feel-Good Bond," *New York Times* (January 17, 1993), Section 3, p. 10. For further information on relationship marketing, see Barry Berman, *Marketing Channels* (New York: Wiley, 1996), pp. 201–239; "Special Issue on Relationship Marketing," *Journal of the Academy of Marketing Science*, Vol. 23 (Fall 1995); Robert M. Morgan and Shelby D. Hunt, "The Commitment-Trust Theory of Relationship Marketing," *Journal of Marketing*, Vol. 58 (July 1994), pp. 20–38; Robert D. Buzzell and Gwen Ortmeyer, "Channel Partnerships Streamline Distribution," *Sloan Management Review*, Vol. 36 (Spring 1995), pp. 85–96; and Gregory T. Gundlach, Ravi S. Achrol, and John T. Mentzer, "The Structure of Commitment in Exchange," *Journal of Marketing*, Vol. 59 (January 1995), pp. 78–92.

4  Joel R. Evans and Richard L. Laskin, "The Relationship Marketing Process: A Conceptualization and Application," *Industrial Marketing Management*, Vol. 23 (December 1994), p. 451.

5  Lara Mills, "Drug Retail Rumble," *Marketing Magazine* (March 4, 1996), p. 11.

6  Mikala Folb, "Online Book Boom," *Marketing Magazine* (January 25, 1999), pp. 15–16.

7  Judy Waytiuk, "Constant Kraving," *Marketing Magazine* (March 29, 1999), p. 14.

8  Bert Rosenbloom, "Motivating Your International Channel Partners," *Business Horizons*, Vol. 33 (March–April 1990), p. 53.

9  NewsLine, "BMG Files Complaint Against Warner," *Marketing Magazine* (August 13, 1997), p. 3; Deborah Stokes, "BMG Comes Back with the Same Old Song," *Marketing Magazine* (August 3, 1998), p. 3.

10  See Kris Frieswick, "Surviving the Mass Merchant Diagnosis," *Industrial Distribution* (September 1995), pp. 28–35.

11  Maclean Hunter Bizlink, "Ban on Exclusive Distributors Stays," *Modern Purchasing* (November 1997), www.bizlink.ca.

12  Roy L. Simerly, "Should U.S. Companies Establish Keiretsus?" *Journal of Business Strategy*, Vol. 13 (November–December 1992), pp. 58–61.

13  Janet Zhang, "Asia: Opportunities Large and Small," *Chain Store Age Executive* (January 1995), Section 3, p. 7.

14  Industry Canada "Canada Business Service Centres," Strategis Web site, strategis.ic.gc.ca (March 15, 1998).

15  Saul Klein and Victor J. Roth, "Satisfaction with International Marketing Channels," *Journal of the Academy of Marketing Science*, Vol. 21 (Winter 1993), pp. 39–44.

16  Michael Jenkins, "Technology and Trade in Canada," *Logistics Today* (Winter 1997), logistx.dartgc.com.

17  Anil Kumar and Graham Sharman, "We Love Your Product, But Where Is It?" *Sloan Management Review*, Vol. 33 (Winter 1992), p. 92. See also Ronald Henkoff, "Delivering the Goods," *Fortune* (November 28, 1994), pp. 64–78.

18  Transport Canada, "Track in Operation," Transport Canada Web site, www.tc.gc.ca (May 1999); and "Performance 2000," *Canadian Business* (June 26/July 10, 1998), pp. 139–141.

19  Private Motor Truck Council of Canada, "Profile of Private Trucking in Canada 1998," Strategis Web site, strategis.ic.gc.ca; and Industry Canada, "Trucking Services," Strategis Web site.

20  Statistics Canada, "Port Activity 1997," *The Daily* (May 21, 1998).

21  Department of Foreign Affairs and International Trade, "Energy Infrastructure in Canada," Strategis Web site, strategis.ic.gc.ca (December 1996).

22  Transport Canada, "Air Cargo Carried," Transport Canada Web site, www.tc.gc.ca (May, 1999).

23  Robert Robertson, "The Hustlers," *Materials Management and Distribution* (October 1997), Maclean Hunter Bizlink, www.bizlink.com.

24  Transport Canada, "Containerized by Sector," Transport Canada Web site, www.tc.gc.ca (May, 1999).

25  See Jitendra Chhikara and Elliott N. Weiss, "JIT Savings—Myth or Reality?" *Business Horizons*, Vol. 38 (May–June 1995), pp. 73–78; Susan R. Helper and Mari Sako, "Supplier Relations in Japan and the United States: Are They Converging?" *Sloan Management Review*, Vol. 36 (Spring 1995), pp. 77–84; Lisa Phillips and Cornelia Drîge, "Quick Response: A Theoretical Framework," in David W. Stewart and Naufel J. Vilcassim (Eds.), *1995 AMA Winter Educators' Proceedings* (Chicago: American Marketing Association, 1995), pp. 295–302; Paul F. Christ and Jack Gault, "The Benefits, Costs, and Strategic Implications of Quick Response Systems," in Barbara B. Stern and George M. Zinkham (Eds.), *1995 AMA Educators' Proceedings* (Chicago: American Marketing Association, 1995), pp. 485–491; and "The Next Industrial Revolution: Canada's Manufacturers Are Hard at Work Turning Today's Factories Into Tomorrow's Success Stories," *Canadian Business* (June, 1992), pp. 96–101.

26  Marcia Berss, "Watizzit?" *Forbes* (August 28, 1995), p. 100.

27  Ron Richardson, "2000 and Beyond: View from the Top," *Modern Purchasing* (January/February 1999), Maclean Hunter Bizlink, www.bizlink.ca.

**CHAPTER 11**

1  Alan Gee, "Why Department Stores Will Fail," *Marketing Magazine* (December 7, 1998), p. 9; Sean Silcoff, "Retail That Rocks," *Canadian Business* (November 27, 1998), pp. 48–58; and Joe Chidley and Sean Silcoff, "The Job from Hell," *Canadian Business* (May 28, 1999), pp. 39–45.

2  "Retailing: Basic Analysis," Standard & Poor's Industry Surveys (June 15, 1995), p. R82; Jo Marney, "North American Shoppers," *Marketing Magazine* (April 24, 1995), p. 41; and "Canadian Council of Grocery Distributors: Supermarket Loyalty Up, Switching Down—Trends in Canada Survey," Canada NewsWire (July 18, 1995), http://www.newswire.ca:80; "Issues," *Canadian Grocer* (March 1997); "New Study Looks at Shopper's Attitudes Toward Grocery Home Delivery," *Canadian Grocer* (November 1996), www.mhbizlink.com/grocer; Issues, "Economizing Deemed Main Consumer Issue Facing Canadian Supermarkets, New Report Says," *Canadian Grocer* (March 1997), Maclean Hunter Bizlink, www.bizlink.ca; Sally Praskey, "What's Cooking," *Canadian Grocer* (December 1997), Maclean Hunter Bizlink, www.bizlink.ca; and MarketScan, "Swiping the Stripe One Billion Times," *Canadian Grocer* (January/February 1998), Maclean Hunter Bizlink, www.bizlink.ca

3  "Survey of Retail Payment Systems," *Chain Store Age* (January 1996), Section Two.

4  Sean Silcoff, "Pay Now, Buy Later," *Canadian Business* (February 12, 1999) pp. 36–37; "Performance 2000," *Canadian Business* (June 26/July 10, 1998), pp. 138–141; Fortune 500 Largest U.S. Corporations, *Fortune* (April 26, 1999), p. F1.

5  Statistics Canada, "Employment by Industry, Population 15 Years of Age and Over," *Canadian Statistics*, www.statscan.ca (May 27, 1999).

6  Paul M. Jacobson and the Retail Council of Canada, 1998 *State of the Industry Report*, www.retailcouncil.org, p. 62; *Stores*, various issues; "Progressive Grocer Annual Report," *Progressive Grocer* (April 1996); and Mary Kuntz et al., "Reinventing the Store," *Business Week* (November 27, 1995), p. 92.

7  David Berman, "Colonel Sanders," *Canadian Business* (December 12, 1997), pp. 45–46.

8  Unless otherwise indicated, the statistics in these subsections are the authors' current projections, based on data from Statistics Canada, "Retail Sales, by Trade Group, and Total Retail Sales, Canada, The Provinces And Territories," CANSIM matrix 2400 (Ottawa: Minister of Supply and Services Canada); Leonard Kubas, "Navigating the New Retail Landscape," *Marketing Magazine* (July 31/August 7, 1995) pp. 11–12; *1992 Census of Retail Trade* (Washington, D.C.: U.S. Bureau of the Census); *Stores*; *Progressive Grocer*; *Discount Store News*; *Inc.*; *Vending Times Census of the Industry* (1995); *Direct Marketing*; and Berman and Evans, *Retail Management: A Strategic Approach*.

9 Donna Jean MacKinnon, "Franchising Shrugs Off Recession," *The Toronto Star* (November 19, 1992), pp. B1, B3.

10 Canadian Franchise Association, "Franchising Has Come of Age," Advertising Supplement to *Canadian Business* (January, 1994), pp. 79–84.

11 News Line, "AT&T Connects with Radio Shack," *Marketing Magazine* (September 15, 1997), p. 3.

12 Report on Market Shares, "Department Stores," *Marketing Magazine* (May 23, 1998), p. 24.

13 "Performance 2000," *Canadian Business* (June 26/July 10, 1998), pp. 140–141.

14 Statistics Canada, "Vending Machine Operators," *The Daily* (May 1, 1997).

15 Statistics Canada, "Direct Selling, 1996 and 1997," *The Daily* (Monday, December 21, 1998).

16 Peter Verburg, "The West Edmonton Mall," *Canadian Business* (October 10, 1997), pp. 93–96.

17 See Greg Hano, "Back to Basics," *Marketing Tools* (October 1995), pp. 10–15; and Michael Hartnett, "New Technologies Simplify Retail Site Selection," *Stores* (October 1995), pp. 45–46.

18 Market Scan, "Loblaw Branches Out into Banking," *Canadian Grocer* (January/February 1998), Maclean Hunter Bizlink, www.bizlink.ca.

19 Market Scan, "Swiping the Stripe One Billion Times," *Canadian Grocer* (January/February 1998), Maclean Hunter Bizlink, www.bizlink.ca.

20 "Using Technology to Achieve Critical Success Factors," *Chain Store Age* (October 1995), Section Three, p. 8A.

21 Fanglan Du and Ira Apfel, "The Future of Retailing," *American Demographics* (September 1995), p. 28.

22 James Pollock, "Club Monaco Continues Asian Expansion," *Marketing Magazine* (November 13, 1995), p. 7; Mikala Folb, "Totally Girl," *Marketing Magazine* (January 4/11, 1999), pp. 10–12; Andrea Haman, "Chinese Market: Leon's Furniture's TV Spots," *Marketing Magazine* (November 6, 1995), p. 21; and Mark Higgins, "Price Club Opens Two Atlantic Warehouse Stores," *Marketing Magazine* (November 6, 1995), p. 15.

23 Sonja Rasula, "Beyond Clothes," *Marketing Magazine* (May 10, 1999), pp. 16–17; Mikala Folb, "All Dressed Down," *Marketing Magazine* (April 5, 1999), p. 12; and Fawzia Sheikh, "Retailers Try to Redefine Casual Days," *Marketing Magazine* (May 3, 1999), p. 4.

24 Fawzia Sheikh, "Zellers Plans to Expand Its Brands," *Marketing Magazine* (May 17, 1999), p. 3.

25 John Lorinc, "Road Warriors," *Canadian Business* (October 1995), pp. 26–43; and Mark Higgins, "Owners and Consumers," *Marketing Magazine* (November 6, 1995), pp. 14–15.

26 Fawzia Sheikh, "Grocers Get Ready for Wal-Mart Threat," *Marketing Magazine* (November 9, 1998), p. 3; Editorial, "The Wal-Mart Threat," *Marketing Magazine* (December 7, 1998), p. 35; Sean Silcoff, "Pay Now, Buy Later," *Canadian Business Canadian Economic Outlook* (February 12, 1999) pp. 36–37; Fawzia Sheikh, "Zellers Unveils Plan to Fight Wal-Mart," *Marketing Magazine* (June 8, 1998), p. 2; Fawzia Sheikh, "Martha Arrives at Zellers Stores," *Marketing Magazine* (June 8, 1998), p. 2; and Fawzia Sheikh, "Zellers Aims for $200 M in Truly Sales," *Marketing Magazine* (March 8, 1999), p. 3.

27 Paul M. Jacobson and the Retail Council of Canada, 1998 State of the Industry Report, www.retailcouncil.org, p. 76; Statistics Canada, "Labour Force Survey: Employment by Industry, Population 15 Years of Age and Over," Canadian Statistics, www.statscan.ca; and 1995 Market Research Handbook, Statistics Canada, Minister of Supply Services: Ottawa, Ontario, pp. 95–96.

28 Adapted by the authors from Walters and Bergiel, *Marketing Channels*, p. 109; and Louis W. Stern, Adel L. El-Ansary, and James R. Brown, *Management in Marketing Channels* (Englewood Cliffs, N.J.: Prentice Hall, 1989), pp. 98–99.

29 Anita Lahey, "Wholesale War," *Marketing Magazine* (April 27, 1998), pp. 18–20.

30 Robert F. Lusch, Deborah Zizzo, and James M. Kenderdine, "Strategic Renewal in Distribution," *Marketing Management*, Vol. 2 (Number 2, 1993), p. 25.

31 Jeff Cole and Susan Carey, "Boeing Co. to Get GE Job Valued at Over $3 Billion," *Wall Street Journal* (January 8, 1996), pp. A3–A4.

32 Gary Hoover, Alta Campbell, and Patrick J. Spain (Eds.), *Hoover's Handbook of American Business 1995* (Austin, Texas: Reference Press, 1994), pp. 1004–1005.

33 Fawzia Sheikh, "Drug Trading Defines Its Retail Empire," *Marketing Magazine* (March 29, 1999), p. 2; and Fawzia Sheikh, "Drugstore Chains Are Feeling No Pain," *Marketing Magazine* (May 25, 1998), p. 23.

34 "VWD Installs Canada's First Computerized Carousel System For Wholesale Drug Operations," *Canada NewsWire* (August 9, 1995), www.newswire.ca:80.

35 Thomas A. Stewart, "The Information Wars: What You Don't Know Will Hurt You," *Fortune* (June 12, 1995), pp. 120–121.

36 Heather Sterling, "Mainly Because of the Meat," *Marketing Magazine* (March 1, 1999), p. 16.

37 Finning International Inc., "Overview," Finning Limited Web site, www.finning.ca; News Release, "Finning International: Fourth Quarter and Annual 1998," *Canadian Corporate News* (February 1, 1999).

38 Holly Quan, "Going Up Against the Co-op," *Marketing Magazine* (May 24, 1999), p. 15; and "Mission Statement," Mountain Equipment Cooperative Web site, www.mec.ca.

39 Julie Cooper, "Retailing in the Year 2005 Marked by Supercenters and Consolidations," *Canadian Grocer* (December 1997), Maclean Hunter Bizlink, www.bizlink.ca.

## CHAPTER 12

1 Andrea Zoe Aster, "Gross Is Good," *Marketing Magazine* (February 1, 1999), pp. 15–16.

2 See Paula Fitzgerald Bone, "Word-of-Mouth Effects on Short-Term and Long-Term Product Judgments," *Journal of Business Research*, Vol. 32 (March 1995), pp. 213–223; and Chip Walker, "Word of Mouth," *American Demographics* (July 1995), pp. 38–44.

3 Alf Nucifora, "More Shoestring Marketing: Learn How to Work with the Press," *American City Business Journals* (July 21, 1997).

4 Advertising Age 1998, "World's Top 50 Advertising Organizations," *Advertising Age*, www.adage.com; David Chilton, "It Was a Very Good Year for All Media," *Marketing Magazine* (October 5, 1998), p. 4; Statistics Canada, "Employment According to New Classification Systems," *The Daily* (August 25, 1998), www.statcan.ca; Lara Mills, "In-Ad Promos Lift Total Coupon Distribution," *Marketing Magazine* (February 12, 1996), p. 2; and Srinath Gopalakrishna, Gary L. Lilien, Jerome D. Williams, and Ian K. Seqeira, "Do Trade Shows Pay Off?" *Journal of Marketing*, Vol. 59 (July 1995), p. 75.

5 Adapted by the authors from Peter D. Bennett (Ed.) *Dictionary of Marketing Terms*, Second Edition (Chicago: American Marketing Association, 1995), pp. 6, 206, 231, 232, and 253.

6 Astrid Ven Ben Broek, "Wayne?" *Marketing Magazine* (March 29, 1999), pp. 12–13.

7 Ayn E. Crowley and Wayne D. Hoyer, "An Integrative Framework for Understanding Two-Sided Persuasion," *Journal of Consumer Research*, Vol. 20 (March 1994), p. 561; and Advertisement for Standard Life, "We're All For Comparisons . . . But Not of Apples and Oranges," *Canadian Business* (June 1996), p. 147.

8 Michael S. LaTour and Shaker A. Zahra, "Fear Appeals as Advertising Strategy: Should They Be Used?" *Journal of Consumer Marketing*, Vol. 6 (Spring 1989), p. 67. See also Tony L. Henthorne, Michael S. LaTour, and Rajan Nataraajan, "Fear Appeals in Print Advertising: An Analysis of Arousal and Ad Response," *Journal of Advertising*, Vol. 22 (June 1993), pp. 59–69; and James B. Hunt, John F. Tanner, Jr., and David P. Eppright, "Forty Years of Fear Appeal Research: Support for the

Ordered Protection Motivation Model," in David W. Stewart and Naufel J. Vilcassim (Eds.), *1995 AMA Winter Educators' Proceedings* (Chicago: American Marketing Association, 1995), pp. 147–153.

9  See Carl L. Witte, Madhavan Parthasarathy, and James W. Gentry, "Subliminal Perception Versus Subliminal Persuasion: A Re-Examination of the Basic Issues," in Barbara B. Stern and George M. Zinkham (Eds.), *1995 AMA Educators' Proceedings* (Chicago: American Marketing Association, 1995), pp. 133–138.

10  Kristina D. Frankenberger and Ajay S. Sukhdial, "Segmenting Teens for AIDS Preventive Behaviors with Implications for Marketing Communications," *Journal of Public Policy & Marketing*, Vol. 13 (Spring 1994), p. 134.

11  Roper Starch, "The World's View of Marketers," *Advertising Age* (January 15, 1996), pp. I–10.

12  See Cyndee Miller, "Marketing Industry Report: Who's Spending What on Biz-to-Biz Marketing," *Marketing News* (January 1, 1996), pp. 1, 7.

13  Adapted by the authors from Janet Smith, "Integrated Marketing," *Marketing Tools* (November–December 1995), p. 64.

14  "Sprint Uses Local Stars in New Quebec Effort," *Marketing Magazine* (March 27, 1995), p. 3; and George Morris, "Homegrown Icons," *Marketing Magazine* (June 3, 1996), p. 14.

15  Gail Chiasson, "Quebec 13 to 24," *Marketing Magazine* (February 20, 1995), p. 13.

16  Gail E. Schares, "Colgate-Palmolive Is Really Cleaning Up in Poland," *Business Week* (March 15, 1993), p. 56.

17  Tom Duncan, "Standardized Global Marketing Communication Campaigns Are Possible, They're Just Hard to Do," in Robert P. Leone and V. Kumar (Eds.), *1992 AMA Educators' Proceedings* (Chicago: American Marketing Association, 1992), p. 355; and Dilip Subramanian, "Western Marketers Join India's Economic Boom," *Marketing Magazine* (March 11, 1996), p. 5.

18  "Data Watch," *Advertising Age* (October 26, 1992), p. I-10; and E. S. Browning, "Eastern Europe Poses Obstacles for Ads," *Wall Street Journal* (July 30, 1992), p. B6.

19  Angela Di Padova, "Moisture and Misleading Advertising," *Marketing Magazine* (March 18, 1996), p. 20.

20  Industry Canada—Competition Bureau, "Click Modelling and Talent Agency of Canada (c.o.b. as HMI International Model and Talent Agencies) and Shannon Hoehn and Misleading Advertising," *Annual Report 1997/98—Fighting Anti-competitive Activity* (January 20, 1999), Strategis Web site, strategis.ic.gc.ca.

21  Advertising Standards Canada, "Visible and Accountable," *Marketing Magazine* (February 23, 1998), pp. 10–12.

22  Cyndee Miller, "The Marketing of Advertising," *Marketing News* (December 7, 1992), p. 2.

23  Canadian Professional Sales Association, "Mandate," Strategis Web site, strategis.ic.gc.ca (May 1999).

24  Allison Lucas, "Portrait of a Salesperson," *Sales & Marketing Management* (June 1995), p. 13; and Richard T. Hise and Edward L. Reid, "Improving the Performance of the Industrial Sales Force in the 1990s," *Industrial Marketing Management*, Vol. 23 (October 1994), pp. 273–279.

25  Tom Dellecave, Jr., "Getting the Bugs Out," *Sales & Marketing Management* (December 1995), Part 2, p. 27.

26  See John J. Withey and Eric Panitz, "Face-to-Face Selling: Making It More Effective," *Industrial Marketing Management*, Vol. 24 (August 1995), pp. 239–246.

27  Barry J. Babin, James S. Boles, and William R. Darden, "Salesperson Stereotypes, Consumer Emotions, and Their Impact on Information Processing," *Journal of the Academy of Marketing Science*, Vol. 23 (Spring 1995), p. 94.

28  Canadian Professional Sales Association, "Code of Ethics," Strategis Web site, strategis.ic.gc.ca (May 1999).

29  See Kris Frieswick, "Inside Sales Takes Centre Stage," *Industrial Distribution* (October 1995), pp. 24–27.

30  Marvin A. Jolson, "The Underestimated Potential of the Canned Sales Presentation," *Journal of Marketing*, Vol. 39 (January 1975), p. 78.

31  Adapted by the authors from James E. Lukaszewski and Paul Ridgeway, "To Put Your Best Foot Forward, Start by Taking These 21 Simple Steps," *Sales & Marketing Management* (June 1990), pp. 84–86. See also Fiona Gibb, "The New Sales Basics," *Sales & Marketing Management* (April 1995), p. 81.

32  Canadian Professional Sales Association, "Four Ways to Close the Deal," Strategis Web site, strategis.ic.gc.ca (May 1999).

33  Michael Collins, "Breaking into the Big Leagues," *Marketing Tools* (January–February 1996), p. 28.

34  Adapted by the authors from William J. Stanton, Richard H. Buskirk, and Rosann L. Spiro, *Management of a Sales Force*, Ninth Edition (Homewood, Ill.: Richard D. Irwin, 1995).

35  Thomas Rollins, "How to Tell Competent Salespeople from the Other Kind," *Sales & Marketing Management* (September 1990), p. 116.

36  Geoffrey Brewer, "Caterpillar Inc.: Industrial & Farm Equipment," *Sales & Marketing Management* (September 1993), p. 61.

37  Thomas N. Ingram, Charles H. Schwepker, Jr., and Don Hutson, "Why Salespeople Fail," *Industrial Marketing Management*, Vol. 21 (August 1992), pp. 225–230; and "Pipe Down," *Sales & Marketing Management* (January 1994), p. 22. See also Goutam N. Challagalla and Tasadduq A. Shervani, "Dimensions and Types of Supervisory Control: Effects on Salesperson Performance and Satisfaction," *Journal of Marketing*, Vol. 60 (January 1996), pp. 89–105.

38  Patrick L. Schul and Brent M. Wren, "The Emerging Role of Women in Industrial Selling: A Decade of Change," *Journal of Marketing*, Vol. 56 (July 1992), p. 38.

39  Statistics Canada, *1995 Market Research Handbook* (Ottawa: Minister of Supply Services), p. 164.

40  Judy A. Siguaw and Earl D. Honeycutt, Jr., "An Examination of Gender Differences in Selling Behaviors and Job Attitudes," *Industrial Marketing Management*, Vol. 24 (January 1995), p. 51. See also Nancy Arnott, "It's a Woman's World," *Sales & Marketing Management* (March 1995), pp. 54–59.

41  John S. Hill, Richard R. Still, and Onal O. Boya, "Managing the Multinational Sales Force," *International Marketing Review*, Vol. 8 (Number 1, 1991), pp. 19–31. See also Earl D. Honeycutt and John B. Ford, "Guidelines for Managing an International Sales Force," *Industrial Marketing Management*, Vol. 24 (March 1995), pp. 135–144.

42  Canadian Professional Sales Association, "Marketing for the Next Millennium," Strategis Web site, strategis.ic.gc.ca (May 1999).

## CHAPTER 13

1  David Menzies, "So Bad It's Good," *Profit* (December/January 1999), Profit Online, www.canbus.com.

2  Ad Age Database, "Top Global Markets," Advertising Age Web site, adage.com (May 1999).

3  Computed by the authors from Schonfeld & Associates, "1995 Advertising to Sales Ratios for the 200 Largest Ad Spending Industries," *Advertising Age* (August 14, 1995), p. 26.

4  News Line, "Zurich Backs Help Line with TV Campaign," *Marketing Magazine* (February 26, 1996), p. 1.

5  Peter Kim, "Does Advertising Work: A Review of the Evidence," *Journal of Consumer Marketing*, Vol. 9 (Fall 1992), p. 5.

6  Christina Tan, "When Good Drivers Go Bad," *Marketing Magazine* (May 17, 1999), p. 26.

7  Jan Jaben, "Ad Decision Makers Favor Regional Angle," *Advertising Age* (May 15, 1995), pp. I-3, I-16.

8  Advertisement, "Certified Management Accountant," *Canadian Business* (May 28, 1999), pp. 6–7.

9  Robert J. Kent, "Competitive Clutter in Network Television Advertising: Current Levels and Advertiser Responses," *Journal of Advertising Research*, Vol. 35 (January–February 1995), pp. 49–57.

10  Michael J. McCarthy, "Mind Probe," *Wall Street Journal* (March 22, 1991), p. B3; and "Advertising Makes the Difference," *Advertising Age* (January 15, 1996), p. 30.

11 Laurel Wentz, "Major Global Study Finds Consumers Support Ads," *Advertising Age* (October 11, 1993), pp. I-1, I-21.

12 Jeffrey Casey, "How Do We Get Into This Person's Head?" *Link* (October–November 1995), pp. 37–45.

13 Michael McCullough, "Poison Threat Sinks Tout Sweet Chocolates," *Marketing Magazine* (May 6, 1996), p. 4.

14 Canadian Public Relations Society Web site, www.cprs.ca (June 1999); International Public Relations Society Web site, www.ipranet.org (June 1999); PR Report, "1999 Guide to Public Relations Services," *Marketing Magazine* (February 22, 1999), pp. 32–42.

15 Canadian Media Directors' Council, *Media Digest 1998-99*, (Toronto, Ontario: Marketing Magazine), various pages.

16 Gene Koprowski, "Extra: Smart Companies Use Public Relations Tactics to Get Good Ink," *Marketing Tools* (October 1995), p. 48.

17 Lori Rees, "Catering to the Cadres in the Land of the Lamas," *Time* (September 7, 1998) Time Web Edition, TIME.com/Asia.

18 David Kirkpatrick, "Bad Publicity? What's That?" *Fortune* (June 9, 1997), p. 136.

19 Nat B. Read, "Sears PR Debacle Shows How Not to Handle a Crisis," *Wall Street Journal* (January 11, 1993), p. A16.

20 See Gene Koprowski, "Hiring an Agency," *Marketing Tools* (October 1995), pp. 48–49.

21 H. Frazier Moore, *Public Relations: Principles, Cases, and Problems*, Eighth Ed. (Homewood, Ill.: Richard D. Irwin, 1981), pp. 163–167.

22 Christel K. Beard and H. J. Dalton, Jr., "The Power of Positive Press," *Sales & Marketing Management* (January 1991), pp. 37–43. See also Daniel P. Dern, "News That's Fit to Print," *Marketing Tools* (October 1995), pp. 52–53.

23 Lesley Daw, "Measuring PR," *Marketing Magazine* (October 12, 1998), p. 12.

24 Fraser Likely, "Performance Measurement: Can PR/Communication Contribute to the New Bottom Line," Canadian Public Relations Society, www.cprs.ca.

25 Terry Zuk, "Closing in on the Customer," *Marketing Magazine* (February 13, 1995), p. 14.

26 Don E. Shinkle, "PR Measurement Is the Answer," *Public Relations Quarterly*, Vol. 39 (Fall 1994), pp. 16–17.

27 Andrea Haman, "Causes of the Conundrum," *Marketing Magazine* (August 21/28, 1995), p. S7.

28 Lara Mills, "1995 Coupon Calendar," *Marketing Magazine* (August 21/28, 1995), p. `12; and "The 1997 Annual Report on the Promotion Industry," *Promo* (October 1998).

29 Cyndee Miller, "Marketing Industry Report: Who's Spending What on Biz-to-Biz Marketing," *Marketing News* (January 1, 1996), p. 1; and John F. Tanner, Jr. and Lawrence B. Chonko, "Trade Show Objectives," *Industrial Marketing Management* (August 1995), pp. 257–264.

30 Lara Mills, "The Biggest Fish," *Marketing Magazine* (April 8, 1996), p. 9.

31 Douglas Ajram, "Happy Kids Make Happy Moms," *Marketing Magazine* (January 25, 1999), p. 24.

32 Liz Adams, "Millennium-Size," *Marketing Magazine* (January 18, 1999), p. 18; and "The 1997 Annual Report on the Promotion Industry," *Promo* (October 1998).

33 Promo Report, "Thumbs Up and Down," *Marketing Magazine* (May 31, 1999), p. 18.

34 "Impact in the Aisles: The Marketer's Last Best Chance," *Promo* (January 1996), p. 26.

35 Jim McElgunn, "Study Says Nothing Beats Word of Mouth," *Marketing Magazine* (May 1, 1995), p. 9.

36 Lara Mills, "Cup Promo Tip of the Trinket Trend," *Marketing Magazine* (May 31, 1999), p. 2.

37 Liz Adams, "Millennium-Size," *Marketing Magazine* (January 18, 1999), p. 18

## CHAPTER 14

1 Geoffrey Colvin, "Is Content King? Not Exactly," *Fortune Magazine* (February 1, 1999), pp. 140–142; Erick Schonfeld, "The Exchange Economy," *Fortune Magazine* (February 15, 1999), pp. 67–68; and Patricia Sellers, "Inside the First E-Christmas," *Fortune Magazine* (February 1, 1999), pp. 70–73.

2 Canadian Marketing Association, "Background on CMA," Canadian Marketing Association Web site, www.cdma.org.

3 Canadian Marketing Association, "Glossary of Direct Response Marketing Terms," Canadian Marketing Association Web site, www.cdma.org.

4 Source: Statistics Canada, "Direct Selling 1996 and 1997," *The Daily* (Monday, December 21, 1998).

5 Canadian Media Directors' Council, *Media Digest 1998–99* (Toronto, Ontario: Marketing Magazine), pp. 16-18; Margaret Nearing, "A Comfy Place to Shop," *Marketing Magazine* (December 7, 1998), pp. 19–20; Lara Mills, "Foreign Cataloguers Still Puzzling Over Canada," *Marketing Magazine* (June 12, 1995), p. 8; and David Napier, "Northern Exposure: Why Competing Cataloguers Are Welcoming Spiegel's Entry into Canada," *Marketing Magazine* (April 29, 1996), pp. 12–13.

6 Philip Kotler and Ronald Turner, *Marketing Management*, Eighth Canadian Edition (Scarborough: Prentice Hall Canada), p. 632.

7 Herschell Gordon Lewis, *Direct Marketing Strategies and Tactics* (Chicago, Illinois: Dartnell, 1992), pp. 7, 12.

8 Jack Schmid and Alan Weber, *Desktop Database Marketing* (Lincolnwood, Illinois: NTC Business Books, 1998), p. 3.

9 Marilyn Stewart, *The Canadian Direct Marketing Handbook*, The Canadian Direct Marketing Association (Whitby, Ontario: McGraw-Hill Ryerson, 1992), p. 59.

10 Stephen Shaw, "Choosing Software to Manage Your Campaign," *Marketing Magazine* (October 5, 1998), p. 21.

11 Jack Schmid and Alan Weber, *Desktop Database Marketing* (Lincolnwood, Illinois: NTC Business Books, 1998), pp. 8–9.

12 Kevin Nullmeyer, "The Top 10 Reasons Why DBM Fails," *Marketing Magazine* (December 7, 1998), p. 25.

13 Chris Daniels, "CMA Amends Kid Marketing Rules," *Marketing Magazine* (March 15, 1999), p. 2.

14 Mary Lou Roberts and Paul D. Berger, *Direct Marketing Management* (Englewood Cliffs, New Jersey: Prentice-Hall, 1989), pp. 9–10; Marilyn Stewart, The Canadian Direct Marketing Handbook, The Canadian Direct Marketing Association (Whitby, Ontario: McGraw-Hill Ryerson, 1992), p. 3.

15 Mary Lou Roberts and Paul D. Berger, *Direct Marketing Management* (Englewood Cliffs, New Jersey: Prentice-Hall, 1989), pp. 67–70; and Bob Stone, Successful Direct Marketing Methods, Fifth Edition (Lincolnwood, Illinois: NTC Business Books, 1994), pp. 3–5.

16 *Info*Canada, Catalogue, Summer 1998 (Mississauga, Ontario: InfoCanada).

17 Mary Lou Roberts and Paul D. Berger, *Direct Marketing Management* (Englewood Cliffs, New Jersey: Prentice-Hall, 1989), pp. 94–97.

18 Jack Schmid and Alan Weber, *Desktop Database Marketing* (Lincolnwood, Illinois: NTC Business Books, 1998), pp. 13–14.

19 Otto Kleppner, Thomas Russell, Glen Verril, and Byron Collins, *Otto Kleppner's Advertising Procedure*, Canadian Eighth Edition (Scarborough: Prentice Hall Canada, 1984).

20 Marketing Direct, "The Shopping Channel Launches a Catalogue," *Marketing Magazine* (February 15, 1999), p. 14.

21 Margaret Nearing, "A Comfy Place to Shop," *Marketing Magazine* (December 7, 1998), pp. 19–20; and Margaret Nearing, "The Yanks Go Home," *Marketing Magazine* (December 7, 1998), p. 20.

22 James Pollock, "Eastward Ho!" *Marketing Magazine* (April 29, 1996), pp. 12–14. For an in-depth look at the global opportunities available to direct marketers, see Richard Miller, *Multinational Direct Marketing: The Methods and the Markets* (New York: McGraw-Hill, 1995).

23 Andrea Haman, "Powerful Pitches," *Marketing Magazine* (December 4, 1995), p. 14; Kim Cleland, "Infomercial Audience

Crosses Over Cultures," *Advertising Age* (January 15, 1996), p. I-8; Hershell Gordon Lewis, "Information on Infomercials," *Direct Marketing* (March 1995), pp. 30–32; and Zachary Schiller and Ron Grover, "And Now, a Show from Your Sponsor," *Business Week* (May 22, 1995), pp. 100–104.

24 Otto Kleppner, Thomas Russell, Glen Verril, and Byron Collins, *Otto Kleppner's Advertising Procedure,* Canadian Eighth Edition (Scarborough: Prentice Hall Canada, 1984) .

25 Herschell Gordon Lewis, *Direct Marketing Strategies and Tactics* (Chicago, Illinois: Dartnell, 1992), pp. 31–32.

26 Bob Stone, *Successful Direct Marketing Methods,* Fifth Edition (Lincolnwood, Illinois: NTC Business Books, 1994), pp. 362–387; and Mary Lou Roberts and Paul D. Berger, *Direct Marketing Management* (Englewood Cliffs, New Jersey: Prentice-Hall, 1989), pp. 217–237.

27 Mary Lou Roberts and Paul D. Berger, *Direct Marketing Management* (Englewood Cliffs, New Jersey: Prentice-Hall, 1989), pp. 217–237.

28 Mary Lou Roberts and Paul D. Berger, *Direct Marketing Management* (Englewood Cliffs, New Jersey: Prentice-Hall, 1989), pp. 217–237.

29 Herschell Gordon Lewis, *Direct Marketing Strategies and Tactics* (Chicago, Illinois: Dartnell, 1992), pp. 331–346.

30 Bob Stone, *Successful Direct Marketing Methods*, Fifth Edition (Lincolnwood, Illinois: NTC Business Books, 1994), pp. 323–324.

31 Raymond C. Harlan and Walter M. Woolfson, Jr., *Telemarketing That Works* (Chicago, Illinois: Probus Publishing), pp. 119–121.

32 Freeman F. Gosden, Jr., *Direct Marketing Success* (New York: John Wiley & Sons, 1985), pp. 9–10.

33 Herschell Gordon Lewis, *Direct Marketing Strategies and Tactics* (Chicago, Illinois: Dartnell, 1992), pp. 7, 12.

34 Mary Lou Roberts and Paul D. Berger, *Direct Marketing Management* (Englewood Cliffs, New Jersey: Prentice-Hall, 1989), p. 244.

35 Mary Lou Roberts and Paul D. Berger, *Direct Marketing Management* (Englewood Cliffs, New Jersey: Prentice-Hall, 1989), p. 424.

36 Mary Lou Roberts and Paul D. Berger, *Direct Marketing Management* (Englewood Cliffs, New Jersey: Prentice-Hall, 1989), p. 401.

37 Mary Lou Roberts and Paul D. Berger, *Direct Marketing Management* (Englewood Cliffs, New Jersey: Prentice-Hall, 1989), p. 346.

38 Mary Lou Roberts and Paul D. Berger, *Direct Marketing Management* (Englewood Cliffs, New Jersey: Prentice-Hall, 1989), p. 296.

39 Wayne Mouland, "The Franchise-Building Effects of FSI," *Marketing Magazine* (June 29, 1998), p. 46.

40 Otto Kleppner, Thomas Russell, Glen Verril, and Byron Collins, *Otto Kleppner's Advertising Procedure*, Canadian Eighth Edition (Scarborough: Prentice Hall Canada, 1984).

41 Bob Stone, *Successful Direct Marketing Methods*, Fifth Edition (Lincolnwood, Illinois: NTC Business Books, 1994), p. 327.

42 Freeman F. Gosden, Jr., *Direct Marketing Success* (New York: John Wiley & Sons, 1985), pp. 38–39.

43 Jack Schmid and Alan Weber, *Desktop Database Marketing*, (Lincolnwood, Illinois: NTC Business Books, 1998), pp. 13–14.

44 Press Release, "E-commerce Not a High Priority for Canadian Business," Canada NewsWire, www.newswire.ca (May 18, 1999).

45 Michael Bloch, Yves Pigneur and Arie Segev, "On the Road of Electronic Commerce—A Business Value Framework, Gaining Competitive Advantage and Some Research Issues," Strategis Web site, strategis.ic.gc.ca (May 4, 1999).

46 Erick Schonfeld, "The Exchange Economy," *Fortune* (February 15, 1999), pp. 67–68; and Patricia Sellers, "Inside the First E-Christmas," *Fortune* (February 1, 1999), pp. 70–73.

47 Fawzia Sheikh, "Custom E-flyers," *Marketing Magazine* (March 16, 1998), pp. 11–12; Press Release, "Over 150 Million Internet Users Worldwide at Year-end 1998," Computer Industry Almanac

Inc., www.c-i-a.com; Canadian Media Directors' Council, *Media Digest 1998–99* (Toronto, Ontario: Marketing Magazine), pp. 13–17; and James Careless, "E-commerce and the Feds," *Marketing Magazine* (November 16, 1998), p. 15.

48 Press Release, "Over 150 Million Internet Users Worldwide at Year-end 1998," Computer Industry Almanac Inc., www.c-i-a.com.

49 Fawzia Sheikh, "Online Outlook," *Marketing Magazine* (November 16, 1998), p. 33.

50 Patricia Sellers, "Inside the First E-Christmas," *Fortune* (February 1, 1999), p. 70.

51 Press Release, "Over 150 Million Internet Users Worldwide at Year-end 1998," Computer Industry Almanac Inc., www.c-i-a.com.

52 Press Release, "Computer Industry Almanac Says Over 364 Million PCs-in-Use Worldwide Year-End 1998," Computer Industry Almanac Inc., www.c-i-a.com.

53 Report on Market Shares, "Internet Service Providers," *Marketing Magazine* (June 7, 1999), p. 21; and Report on Market Shares, "Personal Computers," *Marketing Magazine* (June 7, 1999), p. 21.

54 Press Release, "E-commerce Not a High Priority for Canadian Business," Canada NewsWire, www.newswire.ca (May 18, 1999).

55 Alf Nucifora, "Shoestring Marketing: Despite the Hype, Internet Numbers Add Up," *American City Business Journals* (May 17, 1999).

56 John J. Dunlop, "Wired World," *Marketing Magazine* (November 16, 1998), p. 34.

57 Press Release, "E-commerce Not a High Priority for Canadian Business," Canada NewsWire, www.newswire.ca (May 18, 1999).

58 Logging On, "E-commerce Institute Planned," *Marketing Magazine* (March 15, 1999), p. 16.

59 Alf Nucifora, "Shoestring Marketing: Despite the Hype, Internet Numbers Add Up," *American City Business Journals* (May 17, 1999).

60 Bonnie Sherman, "The New Way to Shop," *Marketing Magazine* (November 16, 1998), p. 36; and Bonnie Sherman, "E-buying Takes Off," *Marketing Magazine* (May 4, 1998), p. 17.

61 James Careless, "E-commerce and the Consumer," *Marketing Magazine* (November 16, 1998), p. 31.

62 Alf Nucifora, "Shoestring Marketing: Despite the Hype, Internet Numbers Add Up," *American City Business Journals* (May 17, 1999).

63 Reports, Surveys & Trends, "Canadian Small Businesses Getting Online," *allECommerce Insider*, www.allEC.com (July 18, 1998).

64 Eryn Brown, "Selling to Businesses: Dell Computer," *Fortune* (May 24, 1999), p. 114.

65 Ann Harrington, "Customer Service: FedEx," *Fortune* (May 24, 1999), p. 124.

66 Alf Nucifora, "Shoestring Marketing: Despite the Hype, Internet Numbers Add Up," *American City Business Journals* (May 17, 1999).

67 Bonnie Sherman, "Online Ads Work," *Marketing Magazine* (March 15, 1999), p. 26.

68 HotWired, "How Not to Advertise on the Web," *Advertising Age* (December 4, 1995), p. 17.

69 Jim Carroll and Rick Broadhead, 1999 *Canadian Internet Handbook* (Scarborough: Prentice Hall Canada, 1999), p. 21.

70 Jill H. Ellsworth and Matthew V. Ellsworth, *Marketing on the Internet*, Second Edition (New York: John Wiley & Sons), pp. 63–64.

71 Alf Nucifora, "Shoestring Marketing: What to Do with a Web Site," *American City Business Journals* (November 24, 1997).

72 Jill H. Ellsworth and Matthew V. Ellsworth, *Marketing on the Internet,* Second Edition (New York: John Wiley & Sons), pp. 63–64.

73 Ernst & Young, Canada, "1997 Annual Results and Forecast," Internet Advertising Bureau of Canada, www.iabcanada.com (1998).

74 Tracey Trottenberg, "Your Online Checklist," *Marketing Magazine* (March 15, 1999), p. 25; and Shari Walczak, "Going Beyond Web Site Banner Ads," *Marketing Magazine* (March 16, 1998), p. 13.

75 Ernst & Young, Canada, "1997 Annual Results and Forecast," Internet Advertising Bureau of Canada, www.iabcanada.com (1998).

76 Fawzia Sheikh, "Custom E-flyers," *Marketing Magazine* (March 16, 1998), pp. 11–12.

77 Alf Nucifora, "Shoestring Marketing: Despite the Hype, Internet Numbers Add Up," *American City Business Journals* (May 17, 1999).

78 Jill H. Ellsworth and Matthew V. Ellsworth, *Marketing on the Internet*, Second Edition (New York: John Wiley & Sons), pp. 95–97.

79 Jim Carroll and Rick Broadhead, 1999 *Canadian Internet Handbook* (Scarborough: Prentice Hall Canada, 1999), pp. 310–311.

80 Direct Marketing Association, *Direct Marketing Industry Electronic Media Survey Results*, Direct Marketing Association Web site, www.dma.org (March 1999).

81 Direct Marketing Association, *Direct Marketing Industry Electronic Media Survey Results*, Direct Marketing Association Web site, www.dma.org (March 1999).

82 Fawzia Sheikh, "Custom E-flyers," *Marketing Magazine* (March 16, 1998), pp. 11–12.

83 Mikala Folb, "Singing from the Same Song Sheet," *Marketing Magazine* (March 16, 1998), p. 15.

84 Bob Stone, *Successful Direct Marketing Methods*, Fifth Edition (Lincolnwood, Illinois: NTC Business Books, 1994), pp. 3–5.

85 Bureau of Broadcast Measurement, "New Media: BBM Auditing Standards & Definitions," Bureau of Broadcast Measurement Web site, www.bbm.ca (June 1999); and Audit Bureau of Circulation, "Sample Web Site Advertiser Activity Audit Report," Audit Bureau of Circulation Web site, www.accessabvs.com (June 1999).

## CHAPTER 15

1 Lara Mills, "Beyond Price Wars," *Marketing Magazine* (June 7, 1999), p. 21; and Lara Mills, "The Main Front," *Marketing Magazine* (May 3, 1999), p. MD2.

2 Robert J. Dolan, "How Do You Know When the Price Is Right?" *Harvard Business Review*, Vol. 73 (September–October 1995), p. 174.

3 James K. Weekly, "Pricing in Foreign Markets: Pitfalls and Opportunities," *Industrial Marketing Management*, Vol. 21 (May 1992), pp. 173–179.

4 Newsline, "Labatt Cuts Prices for Holidays," *Marketing Magazine* (December 21/28, 1998), p. 1.

5 Catherine Lejeune-Szydwar, "Berlin Samples Shiseido Wares," *Marketing Magazine* (May 3, 1999), p. 8.

6 See N. Carroll Mohn, "Price Research for Decision Making," *Marketing Research* (Winter 1995), pp. 11–19; Stephen J. Hoch, Byung-Do Kim, Alan L. Montgomery, and Peter E. Rossi, "Determinants of Store-Level Price Elasticity," *Journal of Marketing Research*, Vol. 32 (February 1995), pp. 17–29; and Francis J. Mulhern and Robert P. Leone, "Measuring Market Response to Price Changes: A Classification Approach," *Journal of Business Research*, Vol. 33 (July 1995), pp. 197–205.

7 Ray Funkhouser, "Using Consumer Expectations as an Input to Pricing Decisions," *Journal of Product & Brand Management*, Vol. 1 (Spring 1992), p. 48. See also Richard W. Olshavsky, Andrew B. Aylesworth, and DeAnna S. Kempf, "The Price-Choice Relationship: A Contingent Processing Approach," *Industrial Marketing Management*, Vol. 33 (July 1995), pp. 207–218; and John R. Johnson, "How Valuable Is Value Added?" *Industrial Distribution* (May 1995), pp. 35–38.

8 Statistics Canada, "Labour Force Update: A New Perspective on Wages," *The Daily* (Tuesday, August 25, 1998), www.statcan.ca.

9 "Scarce Metal Hits $7000 an Ounce," *New York Times* (July 4, 1990), pp. 43, 48.

10 Chad Rubel, "Marketers Try to Ease Sting of Price Increases," *Marketing News* (October 9, 1995), pp. 5–6.

11 Technical Staff, "Policy Assessment on Climate Change," *The Energy & Environmental Research Center* (EERC) at the University of North Dakota, www.eerc.nodak.edu (1997); and James L. Williams, "Crude Oil Price History and Outlook," *WTRG Economics*, www.WTRG.com (1999).

12 Unless otherwise stated, information in this section is based on: Industry Canada—Competition Bureau, "Competition Bureau," Strategis Web site, strategis.ic.gc.ca, multiple Web pages (1999).

13 Industry Canada—Competition Bureau, "Record $30 Million Fine and Restitution by UCAR Inc. for Price Fixing Affecting the Steel Industry," Strategis Web site, strategis.ic.gc.ca (March 18, 1999).

14 Competition Bureau, Industry Canada, "Misleading Advertising and Deceptive Marketing Practices: Choice of Criminal or Civil Track," Strategis Web site, strategis.ic.gc.ca (March 27, 1998).

15 Competition Bureau, Industry Canada, "Ordinary Price Claims," Strategis Web site, strategis.ic.gc.ca (March 27, 1998).

16 Industry Canada-Competition Bureau, "Alleged Anti-Competitive Acts in the Auto Glass Industry in Canada," Strategis Web site, strategis.ic.gc.ca (May 7, 1999).

17 See Gert Assmus and Carsten Wiese, "How to Address the Gray Market Threat Using Price Coordination," *Sloan Management Review*, Vol. 36 (Spring 1995), pp. 31–41.

18 Sean Silcoff, "The Price Is (Rarely) Right," *Canadian Business* (February 1999), pp. 62–66; and Lesley Daw, "Price to Drive Kia's Launch Campaign," *Marketing Magazine* (May 3, 1999), p. 2.

19 Ralph T. King, Jr., "TPA Scores Big in Treatment of Stroke," *Wall Street Journal* (December 14, 1995), p. 8; Ron Stodghill II, "Joe Montgomery's Wild Ride," *Business Week* (April 19, 1993), pp. 50, 52; and and recommended readings, "Salt, Lemon, Platinum Card?" *Marketing Magazine* (May 10, 1999), p. 54.

20 Michael H. Morris and Roger J. Calantone, "Four Components of Effective Pricing," *Industrial Marketing Management*, Vol. 19 (November 1990), p. 327.

21 Markup can be calculated by transposing the formula above into:

$$\text{Markup per cent} = \frac{\text{Price} - \text{Product cost}}{\text{Price}} \times 100$$

22 *Industrial Outlook 1994* (Washington, D.C.: U.S. Department of Commerce, 1994), pp. 10-1–10-2.

23 See Edwin McDowell, "His Goal: No Room at the Inns," *New York Times* (November 23, 1995), pp. D1, D8.

24 "Your Check Is in the Mail," *Wall Street Journal* (December 8, 1992), p. 2.

25 Paul Hunt, "Pricing for Profit," *Marketing Magazine* (April 26, 1999), p. 38.

## CHAPTER 16

1 Betsy Morris, "Doug Is It," *Fortune* (May 25, 1998), pp. 70–84.

2 Peter D. Bennett (Ed.), *Dictionary of Marketing Terms*, Second Edition (Chicago: American Marketing Association, 1995), p. 276.

3 Alan W. H. Grant and Leonard A. Schlesinger, "Realize Your Customers' Full Profit Potential," *Harvard Business Review*, Vol. 59 (September–October 1995), p. 72.

4 Frederick E. Webster, Jr., "The Rediscovery of the Marketing Concept," *Business Horizons*, Vol. 31 (May–June 1988), pp. 37–38.

5 Frank Rose, "Now Quality Means Service Too," *Fortune* (April 22, 1991), pp. 97–108; and Earl Naumann and Patrick Shannon, "What Is Customer-Driven Marketing?" *Business Horizons*, Vol. 35 (November–December 1992), p. 44. See also John Shea and David Gobeli, "TQM: The Experience of Ten Small Businesses," *Business Horizons*, Vol. 38 (January–February 1995), pp. 71–77.

6 Toshio Nakahara and Yutaka Isono, "Strategic Planning for Canon; The Crisis and the New Vision," *Long Range Planning*, Vol. 25 (February 1992), p. 67.

7. Manab Thakur and Luis Ma. R. Calingo, "Strategic Thinking Is Hip, But Does It Make a Difference?" *Business Horizons*, Vol. 35 (September–October 1992), p. 47.

8. See Jeen-Su Lim, "Vital Cross-Functional Linkages with Marketing," *Industrial Marketing Management*, Vol. 21 (May 1992), pp. 159–165; Victoria L. Crittenden, "Close the Marketing/Manufacturing Gap," *Sloan Management Review*, Vol. 33 (Spring 1992), pp. 41–51; and Michael D. Hutt, Beth A. Walker, and Gary L. Frankwick, "Hurdle the Cross-Functional Barriers to Strategic Change," *Sloan Management Review*, Vol. 36 (Spring 1995), pp. 22–30.

9. Bennett, *Dictionary of Marketing Terms*, p. 67. See also James Krobe Jr., "Do You Really Need a Mission Statement?" *Across the Board* (July–August 1995), pp. 17–21.

10. Mountain Equipment Cooperative, "Mission Statement," Mountain Equipment Cooperative Web site, www.mec.ca.

11. Canadian Pacific Railway, "About CPR," Canadian Pacific Railway Web site, www.cpr.ca (June 1999).

12. Nina Munk, "How Levi's Trashed a Great American Brand," *Fortune* (April 12, 1999), pp. 83–90.

13. Subhash C. Jain, *Marketing Planning & Strategy*, Fourth Edition (Cincinnati: South-Western, 1993), pp. 15–19.

14. Noel M. Tichy and Stratford Sherman, *Control Your Destiny or Someone Else Will* (New York: Doubleday, 1993).

15. Canadian Pacific, "Company Profile," Canadian Pacific Web site, www.cp.ca; Dover Corporation, "Company Profile," Dover Corporation Web site, www.dovercorporation.com (June 1999); General Electric, "Overview," General Electric Web site, www.ge.com; and Johnson & Johnson, "Company Profile," Johnson & Johnson Web site, www.jnj.com (June 1999).

16. Canadian Pacific, "Company Profile," Canadian Pacific Web site, www.cp.ca.

17. Sean Eckford, "Small Brewers Play Canadian-Ownership Card," *Marketing Magazine* (August 14, 1995), p 4.

18. Tim Falconer, "Freeze Play," *Canadian Business* (September 1995), p. 100.

19. Frank Rose, "Edgar Bronfman Actually Has a Strategy—With a Twist," *Fortune* (March 1, 1999), pp. 112–124.

20. H. Igor Ansoff, "Strategies for Diversification," *Harvard Business Review*, Vol. 35 (September–October 1957), pp. 113–124.

21. Gary Hoover, Alta Campbell, and Patrick J. Spain (Eds.), *Hoover's Handbook of American Business 1995* (Austin, Texas: Reference Press, 1994), pp. 1062–1063.

22. See *Perspectives on Experience* (Boston: Boston Consulting Group, 1972); and D. Sudharshan, *Marketing Strategy: Relationships, Offerings, Timing & Resource Allocation* (Englewood Cliffs, N.J.: Prentice Hall, 1995), pp. 244–253.

23. James Pollock, "At Bat for Dylex," *Marketing Magazine* (November 13, 1995), pp. 1, 12; and "Dylex to Unload Rosen and Braemar Stakes," *Marketing Magazine* (February 19, 1996), p. 1; Leslie McNob, "Climbing Out of the Bargain Basement," *Marketing Magazine* (September 8, 1997), p. 4; Beth Mitchell, "Retailers Optimistic about Menswear Rebound," *Marketing Magazine* (September 8, 1997), p. 2; and News Line, "Dylex Ltd," *Marketing Magazine* (June 7, 1999), p. 2.

24. See Derek F. Abell and John S. Hammond, *Strategic Market Planning* (Englewood Cliffs, N.J.: Prentice-Hall, 1979), pp. 211–227; and David A. Aaker, *Strategic Market Management* (New York: Wiley, 1995), pp. 164–167.

25. *Bausch & Lomb 1992 Annual Report*; and *Bausch & Lomb 1994 Annual Report*.

26. Michael E. Porter, *Competitive Advantage: Creating and Sustaining Superior Performance* (New York: Free Press, 1985), pp. 11–26; and Michael E. Porter, *Competitive Strategy: Techniques for Analyzing Industries and Competitors* (New York: Free Press, 1980), pp. 34–46. See also Steven P. Schnaars, *Marketing Strategy: A Customer-Driven Approach* (New York: Free Press, 1991), pp. 112–131.

27. WestJet Airlines, "Corporate Profile," WestJet Airlines Web site, www.westjet.ca (June 1999); Terry Bullick, "No-Frills Airline Takes Flight in Western Canada," *Marketing Magazine* (February 19, 1996), p. 2; Cecil Foster, "Tough Guys Don't Cuss," *Canadian Business* (February 1995), pp. 23–28; Anita Lahey, "Airlines Launch Shuttle Service Ad Dogfight," *Marketing Magazine* (February 26, 1996), p. 2; and "New Air Service Destined to Dog Competition," Canada NewsWire, www.newswire.ca:80 (July 8, 1996).

28. James Pollock, "At Bat for Dylex."

29. Kerry Banks, "Blade Runner," *Canadian Business* (February 1996), p. 104.

30. Robert Frank, "Frito-Lay Devours Snack-Food Business," *New York Times* (October 27, 1995), pp. B1, B4.

31. Steven J. Heyer and Reginald Van Lee, "Rewiring the Corporation," *Business Horizons*, Vol. 35 (May–June 1992), p. 21.

32. Aaker, *Strategic Market Management*, pp. 17–18.

33. The material in this section on Labatt is based on: Mark Stevenson, "My Dear, Beer Friend," *Canadian Business* (March 1994), pp. 52–58; "Historical Report, John Labatt Ltd.," *Financial Post Datagroup* (Nov. 5, 1993), Toronto, Ont.; "The Canadian Brewing Industry: An Assessment of the Impacts of Liberalized Interprovincial Trade in Canada," *Conference Board of Canada* (June 1990), pp. 1–32; "Powell Brings New Angle to the Beer Biz," *Strategy* (July 13, 1992) pp. 1, 19; "Labatt Battles to Stay on Track," *Financial Post* (June 20/22, 1992), p. 5; "Labatt's Blues: Can the Savviest Marketer in Sudsland Revive the Flagging Fortunes of Canada's Top Brew?" *Report on Business Magazine* (June 1991), pp. 40–48; Labatt Could Cut 100 Managers, Sources Say," *Financial Post* (January 16, 1991), p. 3; Douglas Faulkner, "Powell's Big Picture," *Marketing Magazine* (November 20, 1995), pp. 12–13; Stan Sutter, "Labatt Deal Gives Interbrew a North American Beachhead," *Marketing Magazine* (June 19, 1995), p. 6; James Pollock, Labatt Stronger After Buyout by Interbrew," *Marketing Magazine* (June 19, 1995), p. 3; Labatt Breweries, *Good Things Brewing ... for 150 Years* (1998), Marketing Magazine Contract Publishing: Toronto, Ontario; Press Release, "Labatt Announces $50 Million Expansion of London Brewery," Labatt Web site, www.labatt.ca (March 4, 1999); Lara Mills, "Labatt Ties HNIC to Blue Brand," *Marketing Magazine* (October 12, 1998), p. 3; David Menzies, "Game On," *Marketing Magazine* (October 12, 1998), pp. 9–11; Lara Mills, "Kincaid's Blue Miscues," *Marketing Magazine* (February 8, 1999), p. 3; David Chilton, "Scoring with Hockey and Something Out of the Blue," *Marketing Magazine* (December 21/28, 1998), p. 13; and Peter Vamos, "Guy in a Bear Suit Launches Labatt USA's Blue Effort," *Marketing Magazine* (March 1, 1999), p. 6.

34. Brent Schlender, "Peter Drucker Takes the Long View," *Fortune* (September 28, 1998), pp. 162–173.

## CHAPTER 17

1. Darrell K. Rigby, "What's Today's Special at the Consultants' Café?" *Fortune* (September 7, 1998), pp. 162–163.

2. Shelly Reese, "The Very Model of a Modern Marketing Plan," *Marketing Tools* (January–February 1996), pp. 56–59.

3. Sam Walton and John Huey, *Made in America* (New York: Doubleday, 1992).

4. Internet Advertising Bureau of Canada, "Mission Statement," Internet Advertising Bureau of Canada Web site, www.iabcanada.ca.

5. Michael Treacy and Fred Wiersema, *The Discipline of Market Leaders* (Reading, Mass.: Addison-Wesley, 1995).

6. Peter Wright, "Competitive Strategies for Small Business," *Collegiate Forum* (Spring 1983), pp. 3–4; Steven P. Galante, "More Firms Quiz Customers for Clues about Competition," *Wall Street Journal* (March 3, 1986), p. 21; "Hot Growth Companies," *Business Week* (May 27, 1991), pp. 78–84; and Donna Fenn, "Leader of the Pack," *Inc.* (February 1996), pp. 31–38.

7. Yao-Su Hu, "The International Transferability of the Firm's Advantages," *California Management Review*, Vol. 37 (Summer 1995), p. 83.

8   IBM Advertisement, "Timbuktu," *Canadian Business Technology* (Spring 1996), p. 1; IBM Advertisement, "Connect," *Canadian Business* (August 1996), pp. 34–35; and IBM Advertisement, "Hacker," *Canadian Business Technology* (Summer 1996), p. 1.

9   William A. Band, "Customer-Accelerated Change," *Marketing Management* (Winter 1995), pp. 47–48.

10  Peter Coy and Ron Stodghill II, "Is Motorola a Bit Too Patient?" *Business Week* (February 5, 1996), pp. 150–151.

11  Oechsli Institute, "Reality Check," *Inc.* (March 1993), p. 34.

12  Reese, "The Very Model of a Modern Marketing Plan," pp. 60–61.

13  General Electric, *Annual Report 1998*, General Electric; Stephen W. Quicken, "CEO of the Year: Welch on Welch," *Financial World* (April 3, 1990), p. 62; Al Ries, "The Discipline of the Narrow Focus," *Journal of Business Strategy*, Vol. 13 (November-December 1992), p. 5; and Noel M. Tichy and Stratford P. Sherman, *Control Your Own Destiny or Someone Else Will* (New York: Doubleday, 1993).

14  Hoovers, "ABB Asea Brown Boveri Ltd.," *Hoovers Online* (1998), (www.hoovers.com); Carla Rapoport, "A Tough Swede Invades the U.S.," *Fortune* (June 29, 1992), p. 76; and Rich Karlgaard, "Perc¥ Barnevik," *Forbes ASAP* (January 2, 1995), pp. 65–68.

15  Hoovers, "Intuit Inc.," Hoovers Online, www.hoovers.com (1999); Intuit Web site, www.intuit.com (1999); Quicken Online Web site, www.quicken.com; and John Case, "Customer Service: The Last Word," *Inc.* (April 1991), pp. 88–93.

16  Justin Smallbridge, "Wrong Number," *Marketing Magazine* (May 24, 1999), p. 8, Report on Market Shares, "Communications," *Marketing Magazine* (June 7, 1999), pp. 21–22; Peter Vamos, "Ameritech Looks to Bell's Web Smarts," *Marketing Magazine* (May 3, 1999), p. 6; *Bell Canada 1995 Annual Report*; Harvey Schachter, "Ma Bell, Femme Fatale," *Canadian Business* (June 1996), pp. 121–124; and Bell Canada, "Overview," Bell Canada's Web site, www.bell.ca.

17  Beth Enslow, "The Benchmarking Bonanza," *Across the Board* (April 1992), p. 17. See also Thomas C. Powell, "Total Quality Management as Competitive Advantage: A Review and Empirical Study," *Strategic Management Journal*, Vol. 16 (January 1995), pp. 15–37; and Roland T. Rust, Anthony J. Zahorik, and Timothy L. Keiningham, "Return on Quality (ROQ): Making Service Quality Financially Accountable," *Journal of Marketing*, Vol. 59 (April 1995), pp. 58–70.

18  Tony Clayton and Bob Luchs, "Strategic Benchmarking at ICI Fibres," *Long Range Planning*, Vol. 27 (June 1994), p. 56.

19  Darrell K. Rigby, "What's Today's Special at the Consultants' Café?" *Fortune* (September 7, 1998), pp. 162–163; Jeremy Main, "How to Steal the Best Ideas Around," *Fortune* (October 1992), pp. 102–106; Cyndee Miller, "TQM's Value Criticized in New Report," *Marketing News* (November 9, 1992), pp. 1, 16; and Gilbert Fuchsberg, "'Total Quality' Is Termed Only a Partial Success," *Wall Street Journal* (October 1, 1992), pp. B1, B7.

20  Otis Port, John Carey, Kevin Kelly, and Stephanie Anderson Forest, "Quality: Small and Midsize Companies Seize the Challenge—Not a Moment Too Soon," *Business Week* (November 30, 1992), pp. 66–72.

21  Ontario Exports, "1998 Ontario Global Traders Awards," Advertising Supplement, *Canadian Business* (June 25/July 9,

1999), pp. 17–24; "1998 Entrepreneur of the Year," *Canadian Business* (December 24, 1998/January 8, 1999), pp. 83–119; Advertising Feature, "Once Again a Pair of Winners," *Canadian Business* (June 1996), p. 111; and Advertising Feature, "Celebrating Excellence in Exporting," *Canadian Business* (November 13, 1998), p. 131.

22  Thomas A. Stewart, "After All You've Done for Your Customers, Why Are They Still Not Happy?" *Fortune* (December 11, 1995), p. 179.

23  Ronald B. Lieber, "Now Are You Satisfied: The 1998 American Customer Satisfaction Index," *Fortune* (February 16, 1998), pp. 161–168.

24  John T. Mentzer, Carol C. Bienstock, and Kenneth B. Kahn, "Benchmarking Satisfaction," *Marketing Management* (Summer 1995), pp. 41–46. See also Dominique V. Turpin, "Japanese Approaches to Customer Satisfaction: Some Best Practices," *Long Range Planning*, Vol. 28 (June 1995), pp. 84–90; Abbie Griffin, Greg Gleason, Rick Preiss, and Dave Shevenaugh, "Best Practice for Customer Satisfaction in Manufacturing Firms," *Sloan Management Review*, Vol. 36 (Winter 1995), pp. 87–98; and William Keenan, Jr., "Customer Service," *Sales & Marketing Management* (January 1996), pp. 63–66.

25  See Joseph A. Ness and Thomas G. Cucuzza, "Tapping the Full Potential of ABC," *Harvard Business Review*, Vol. 73 (July–August 1995), pp. 130–138.

26  Bernard Wysocki, Jr., "Some Companies Cut Costs Too Far, Suffer 'Corporate Anorexia,'" *Wall Street Journal* (July 5, 1995), p. A1. See also Robin Cooper and W. Bruce Crew, "Control Tomorrow's Costs Through Today's Designs," *Harvard Business Review*, Vol. 74 (January–February 1996), pp. 88–97.

27  Jeff Lobb, "The Right (Pepsi) Stuff," *Marketing Magazine* (July 8, 1996), p. 15.

28  Christopher H. Lovelock and Charles A. Weinberg, *Public & Nonprofit Marketing*, Second Edition (Redwood City, Calif.: Scientific Press, 1989), pp. 47–48. See also Peter Spillard, Matthew Moriarty, and John Woodthorpe, "The Role Matrix: A Diagnostic of Marketing Health," *European Journal of Marketing*, Vol. 28 (Number 7, 1994), pp. 55–76; and Robert S. Kaplan and David P. Norton, "Using the Balanced Scorecard as a Strategic Management System," *Harvard Business Review*, Vol. 74 (January–February 1996), pp. 75–85.

29  Theodore Levitt, "The Thinking Manager," *Across the Board* (June 1992), pp. 11, 13.

30  Ronald Henkoff, "New Management Secrets from Japan: Really," *Fortune* (November 27, 1995), p. 136.

31  Thomas A. Stewart, "3M Fights Back," *Fortune* (February 5, 1996), pp. 94–99.

32  Adapted by the authors from Bernard Taylor, "The New Strategic Leadership: Driving Change, Getting Results," *Long Range Planning*, Vol. 28 (October 1995), pp. 71–81.

33  Frederick E. Webster, Jr., "The Changing Role of Marketing in the Corporation," *Journal of Marketing*, Vol. 56 (October 1992), p. 14.

34  The material in this section is based on Michael Schrage, "Brave New Work," *Fortune* (June 21, 1999), p. 196.

# Company and Name Index

# Subject Index

The page on which a key term is defined is printed in boldface.